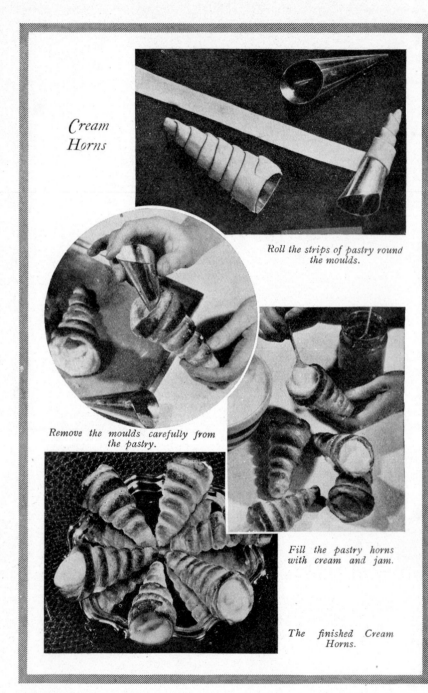

Cream
Horns

Roll the strips of pastry round
the moulds.

Remove the moulds carefully from
the pastry.

Fill the pastry horns
with cream and jam.

The finished Cream
Horns.

Modern
PRACTICAL
COOKERY

with
63 Pages of
Illustrations

ALLIED NEWSPAPERS *Ltd.*,
200 Gray's Inn Road,
London, W.C. 1.

A

CONTENTS

ILLUSTRATIONS

ILLUSTRATIONS

(Continued)

ILLUSTRATIONS

(Continued)

A COMPLETE INDEX IN
ALPHABETICAL ORDER
WILL BE FOUND AT THE
END OF THE BOOK.

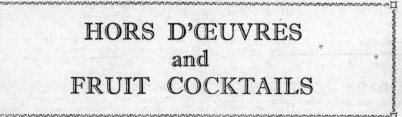

HORS D'ŒUVRES and FRUIT COCKTAILS

ALL kinds of ready prepared hors d'œuvres can be bought now from any of the big stores. They save much time and labour ; but, on the other hand, hors d'œuvres may be prepared at home if preferred quite easily.

If you wish to serve *hors d'œuvres variés*, a selection of beans in tomato sauce, sliced smoked sausage, potato salad, rice salad, sliced pimento, etc., together with a tin of sardines, is sufficient for a homely dinner party.

ANCHOVIES

FILLET them and dress with salad oil. Garnish with a little mustard and cress.

BEETROOT

PEEL and cut into dice or in small slices with a fancy cutter. Moisten with vinegar and oil and season with pepper. Sprinkle with chopped parsley. A little chopped onion may also be added, if liked.

CAULIFLOWER

BOIL it until tender, drain it well and divide the flower into small flowerets. When cold, season them and dress them with French dressing (see page 168), or mayonnaise (see this page).

CAVIARE

SERVE this as cold as possible, accompanied by fingers of toast, butter, and lemon.

A special caviare dish, which consists of a double glass dish, the under one being lined with chipped ice, is ideal for serving this delicacy.

EGGS AND MAYONNAISE

BOIL some eggs until hard (they will require fifteen minutes), then remove the shells. Cut them into quarters, then each quarter into halves again.

When cold, season with pepper and salt and then pour over some mayonnaise.

MAYONNAISE

INGREDIENTS.—1 egg yolk, ¾ to 1 gill of salad oil, 2 teaspoonfuls of white vinegar, 1 teaspoonful of malt vinegar, pepper and salt, mixed mustard.

METHOD.—Mix the yolk of egg in a small basin with a wooden spoon. Stir in the oil gradually, drop by drop. Season with pepper and salt and mixed mustard.

Stir in the vinegar last, adding it very gradually.

This sauce should be like thick cream when finished. If too thick add more vinegar ; if too thin add more oil.

GRAPE FRUIT

THIS is now a very popular hors d'œuvres. To prepare it, cut across into halves, stand it in a dish, and loosen the centre pith by cutting all round it, then remove it.

Loosen the pulp from the rind by cutting all round with a knife, then cut through each section of the pulp. When doing this be careful not to cut through the rind, otherwise the juice will escape.

Sprinkle the grape fruit with castor sugar and leave it for a few hours. If necessary cut off a thin slice of peel at the base to make it stand level.

To SERVE : Place each half on a small plate (half a grape fruit is served to each person), and, if liked, decorate the centre with a glacé cherry.

If well loosened the pulp can easily be removed with a teaspoon.

NOTE.—When either grape fruit,

prawns or oysters are served for hors d'œuvres, they are served quite alone.

MELON

Use either the ordinary melon or the cantaloup variety.

Cut it into fairly thick slices, remove the seeds, and serve it (with the rind on) as cold as possible, with ground ginger and castor sugar.

OLIVES

Just put the olives into a small dish and serve.

OYSTERS

Allow four or six for each person, and serve each in the deep shell. Garnish them with lemon and serve on a plate with chipped ice. Thin brown bread-and-butter should accompany oysters.

POTATO SALAD

Cut some cold boiled potatoes into small square pieces, season with pepper, and dress with mayonnaise (see p. 9) or other salad cream, then sprinkle with finely chopped parsley.

If the dish is first rubbed round with garlic, this will improve the flavour of the salad. Cold potatoes can, if liked, be used in the mixed vegetable salad. Some prefer them in place of the turnips.

PRAWNS

Prawns look very attractive served on lemons in individual dishes for each person.

Cut a slice off one end of each lemon to make it stand firmly. Then make a few tiny holes in the rind and stick the prawns in.

Serve brown bread-and-butter with this dish.

RADISHES

Clean and prepare the radishes in the usual way. Place them in a small dish.

RICE SALAD

Boil the rice as for curry and mix it when cold with diced ham or tongue,

add also some chopped pimento and some cold cooked peas. Season, and dress the rice with salad dressing.

SARDINES

Serve the sardines plain, in the usual way.

SMOKED SALMON

Cut the salmon in thin wafers and form each into a small roll.

Allow one or two for each person and serve them with a spoonful of scrambled egg, cold and well seasoned.

SMOKED SAUSAGE

Slices of garlic sausage or other sausages of the smoked variety, can also be served.

TOMATOES

Cut them into quarters, then again into halves, or if liked, slice them evenly. Peel and finely mince a little onion and sprinkle it over them.

Season them with pepper and salt, and pour over a plain dressing of oil and vinegar. Sprinkle with chopped parsley.

VEGETABLE SALAD

Prepare vegetables, such as turnips, carrots, peas, etc., for cooking, then cut the carrots and turnips into tiny rounds with a vegetable cutter.

Boil the vegetables separately, in the usual way, until tender ; then strain them. When cold mix them together, season with pepper, and mix with a little mayonnaise (see p. 9) or other salad cream. Sprinkle chopped parsley on the top.

Note.—If a vegetable cutter is not available, cut them into small dice.

GRAPE FRUIT COCKTAIL

Ingredients.—1 grape fruit, 1 oz. of glacé cherries, a little castor sugar, ½ teaspoonful of ground ginger.

Method.—Cool the grape fruit.

Cut it in half and scoop the pulp into a basin, removing pips and pith. Mix a little ginger with it and, if necessary, sugar, but this may often be omitted. Fill wineglasses with the fruit and place half a glacé cherry on top.

MIXED FRUIT COCKTAIL

INGREDIENTS.—2 grape fruit, 3 bananas, 2 oz of sugar, 1 orange, ½ lb. of raspberries, 1 oz. of crystallised ginger.

METHOD.—Cut the grape fruit in half with zig-zag cuts. Scoop the pulp of the orange and grape fruit into a basin. Pick the raspberries and add them, keeping back eight of the best ones. Chop the crystallised ginger and add it to the fruit with sugar to taste. Slice the bananas thinly. Scrape the loose pith from the skins of the grape fruit and wash and dry them. Fill with the fruit, arrange a circle of banana on top and put two nice raspberries in the centre.

ORANGE AND RASPBERRY COCKTAIL

INGREDIENTS.—4 oranges, ½ lb. of raspberries, sugar to taste (about 2 oz.).

METHOD.—Cut the oranges into basket shapes, leaving handles, and cut the edges a zig-zag shape.

Scoop out the pulp carefully and scrape the pith from inside the skins. Mix the pulp with half the raspberries, keeping back the best ones. Sweeten to taste. Wash the skins in cold water and dry them. Fill with the pulp and juice and put a few raspberries on top. The cocktails look very dainty served on any pretty foliage that is in season.

When fresh raspberries are not obtainable, bottled ones can be used.

OYSTER COCKTAILS

INGREDIENTS.—1 dozen oysters, a little jelly from roast veal or chicken, 1 small tin grape fruit, ½ teaspoonful of Worcester sauce.

METHOD.—Let the fishmonger remove the beards from the oysters.

If possible, keep the jelly and grape fruit on ice till it is time to make and serve the cocktails.

Put two or three oysters into cocktail glasses or small wine-glasses with a few drops of Worcester sauce.

Add a teaspoonful of jelly free from all fat and about a dessertspoonful of grape fruit pulp.

Serve in the glasses.

Sufficient for four or five persons.

PINEAPPLE CANAPES

INGREDIENTS.—6 slices of pineapple, 18 sections of orange, ¼ lb. grapes or 12 to 18 strawberries, 9 sections of grape fruit.

METHOD.—Use either tinned or fresh pineapple. If fresh, sprinkle it with sugar after it has been peeled and sliced, and leave it to stand for two hours in a cold place.

Place one slice on each serving plate. If the pineapple is tinned, drain it well before arranging it on the plates. Cut each slice five or six times across without spoiling the shape of the slice. Divide each grape fruit section across. Place three half sections of grape fruit on each pineapple slice and arrange the orange sections between. Heap slit and seeded grapes in the centre of each slice, or, if obtainable, hulled strawberries.

Serve Pineapple Canapés as a first course at either luncheon or dinner as a change from grape fruit.

Sufficient for six persons.

TOMATO HORS D'ŒUVRE

INGREDIENTS.—Tomatoes as required, cold cooked vegetables, mayonnaise (see p. 9), seasoning.

METHOD.—Cut such vegetables as carrot, turnip and potato into dice.

Cut a slice from the stalk end of each tomato and scoop out some of the pulp. Care must be taken not to break the skin. Mix the tomato pulp with the diced vegetables and moisten the mixture with mayonnaise. Season it and return it to the tomato cases and garnish the top of each one with a few cold peas.

SOUP RECIPES

STOCK

ALTHOUGH there are endless varieties of soups, the foundation of them all is stock. Stock is the liquid obtained from boiling bones in water to draw as much of the goodness out of them as possible. The bones should be chopped up and washed, then put into cold water with a little salt. About two quarts of water to two pounds of bones is an average allowance.

Bring the water *slowly* to the boil, then remove the scum and simmer gently for three or four hours, or even longer. A flavouring of carrot, onion, and turnip is usually added. These are washed and prepared and put in whole after the stock has come to the boil. One carrot, one onion, and half a turnip are sufficient for three or four quarts of stock.

VEAL bones contain more gelatinous matter than either beef or mutton, so veal bones are used for making *jellied stock*.

FISH STOCK is made from fish bones.

VEGETABLE STOCK from vegetables only.

WHITE STOCK from veal, rabbit or chicken bones.

BROWN STOCK from beef bones.

FIRST STOCK is the liquid obtained from the first boiling.

SECOND STOCK is the liquid obtained from re-boiling the bones with a second lot of water.

THE STOCK POT

A STOCK pot should always be kept "going" in every household. Odd trimmings of meat, bones, and vegetables can be added from time to time. Mushroom stalks impart a good flavour to stock.

Herbs, such as thyme and marjoram, improve the flavour of the soups, but they should be used sparingly.

At the end of each day the stock should be strained off into a basin, and the bones and other remains put into another basin. In this way it keeps more satisfactorily, and the contents can be looked over daily.

For large households an aluminium pot is best, with a tap fixture from which the stock can be drawn off as required; but for ordinary purposes a large saucepan does very well.

POT LIQUOR

THIS is the liquor in which a joint has been boiled. This does not contain as much goodness as stock, but makes a very good foundation for soup. If very greasy, leave it to get cold, and then skim off the fat before using it.

USE A HAIR SIEVE

ALL vegetable purées are much improved by rubbing through a sieve. Tomato soup should *always* be rubbed through a *hair* sieve, as it is not safe to use a wire one for anything acid.

TO REMOVE GREASE

To remove grease from a tureen of hot soup before serving, lay a piece of tissue-paper on the surface, and this will absorb the fat. Several pieces of paper may be needed.

SOUP ACCOMPANIMENTS

DICE of toast or fried bread, toast Melba, or pulled bread, can be served with soup; also dumplings.

NOTE.—Fried croûtons of bread are generally served with vegetable purées, and toast cut into small dice for meat soups.

CROUTONS

CUT slices of stale bread of about toast thickness. Cut them in fingers and then into dice.

Put them into a frying-basket and shake out the loose crumbs, stand the basket in a deep pan of hot fat, and fry the bread until it is golden. Drain on paper and serve on a doyley.

A faint smoke should rise from the centre of the fat before the bread is put into it. Afterwards, the fat should be cooled and then strained.

TOAST MELBA

Cut some stale bread very thinly in neat shapes, and toast both sides. It should be so thin that it curls in the toasting.

PULLED BREAD

PULL the crumb of new bread into rough pieces, and put them into a hot oven to crisp and brown them. Some prefer to dip the pieces first in milk. Pulled bread is suitable for serving with broths and thin soups.

DUMPLINGS TO SERVE WITH SOUP

INGREDIENTS.—¾ gill of milk, 3 oz. of flour, 1½ oz. of margarine, 1 egg, salt and pepper.

METHOD.—Put the milk and fat into a saucepan. Bring them to the boil, then stir in the flour and keep stirring quickly until the mixture boils and thickens and leaves the sides of the pan.

Draw the pan aside, cool the mixture slightly, and beat in the egg. Season to taste, make into small balls and drop into boiling soup (such as broth or other thin soup) and boil for six minutes.

ARTICHOKE SOUP

INGREDIENTS.—1½ lb. of Jerusalem artichokes, 2 pints of white stock (see p. 12), 1 oz. of butter, 1 pint of milk, lemon-juice, ¾ oz. of flour, pepper and salt.

METHOD.—Scrub the artichokes and peel them thinly. Drop them at once into a basin of cold water to which a little lemon-juice has been added.

Pour the stock into a saucepan and bring it to the boil.

Slice the artichokes thickly and add them to the stock and simmer gently till they are tender. Then rub them through a sieve.

Melt the butter in a saucepan. Add the flour to it, and when they are well blended, stir in the milk.

Bring the sauce to the boil and boil it gently for a few minutes.

Add the sieved artichokes and stock. Make the soup hot and add seasoning to taste.

A dish of freshly-made croutons (see p. 12), may be served with Artichoke Soup.

ASPARAGUS SOUP

INGREDIENTS.—Tin of asparagus, 1 oz. of butter, 1 oz. of flour, 1 dessert-spoonful of onion juice, ¾ pint of milk, ¾ pint of white stock (see p. 12), seasoning, 1 level dessertspoonful of chopped parsley.

METHOD.—Turn the asparagus out of the tin and cut off the extreme tips. Rub the remainder of the stalks through a sieve.

Melt the butter in a saucepan, add the flour, and when it is well blended, stir in the stock and the asparagus liquor. Add also the sieved asparagus and the onion juice.

Bring the soup to the boil, keeping it well stirred. Add the milk and the asparagus tips, and season the soup to taste. Cook it for two or three minutes, then stir in the chopped parsley and serve the soup.

Allow half a pint of soup for each person.

AUTUMN SOUP

INGREDIENTS.—1 small cauliflower, ½ a turnip, 2 or 3 tomatoes, 1 or 2 stalks of celery or a few celery seeds, sprig of parsley, 2 onions, seasoning, 3 carrots, 4 to 5 pints of veal and bacon liquor.

METHOD.—Prepare and clean the carrots, onions, celery, and turnip, and cut them into dice. Put them in a pan with the liquor, add some seasoning, and cook gently for an hour. Add the tomatoes peeled and cut in small pieces, with a sprig of parsley and the flower of the cauliflower. This should first be washed and divided into small branches.

Cook them all together until they are tender. Season to taste, and remove the parsley before serving the soup.

BANANA SOUP

INGREDIENTS.—6 unripe bananas, ½ lb. of green tomatoes, 2 onions, 1 turnip, ⅛ a teaspoonful of celery seeds, 1½ pints of good beef stock (see p. 12), 1 oz. of butter, 1 oz. of flour, 1 dessertspoonful of curry powder, 1 teaspoonful of Worcester sauce, 1 bunch of herbs.

METHOD.—Slice the onions, turnip and tomatoes, and fry them in the butter for ten minutes. Take out the vegetables. Put in the flour and stir till brown.

Add the curry powder, Worcester sauce, herbs, and celery seeds. Add the stock gradually and stir till it boils. Add the bananas sliced thickly and the vegetables that were fried. Simmer till the vegetables are tender. Rub through a sieve, re-heat, and season.

Vegetable extract and water could be used instead of beef stock.

Allow 1½ gills for each person.

BOUILLON

INGREDIENTS.—1 lb. of leg of beef (meat and bone), 2 pints of cold water, 1 stalk of celery, 1 small carrot, 1 small onion, ¼ of a turnip, small sprig of parsley, salt and pepper.

METHOD.—Cut up the meat, chop the bone, wash both and put them into a saucepan with the cold water. Add a level teaspoonful of salt and bring it very slowly to the boil.

Remove the scum from the broth, add the parsley, also the vegetables and celery cleaned and prepared, but not cut up.

Simmer gently for two or three hours, then strain the soup through a fine strainer.

When cold, remove the fat, re-heat the soup, and serve in cups.

This is a favourite soup to serve at a dance supper. If required for lunch, you can cut up the vegetables and serve them in the soup.

Allow a good cupful for each person.

BROWN ONION SOUP

INGREDIENTS.—2 lb. of Spanish onions, ½ head of celery, 1 quart of stock (see p. 12), 2 oz. of butter, 2 oz. of flour, 2 teaspoonfuls of meat extract, salt and pepper.

METHOD.—Peel and slice the onions, wash the celery, and cut it into one-inch pieces. Fry the vegetables in a saucepan in the butter till lightly browned. Take them out, draining all the butter from them and then fry the flour till it is a rich brown.

Add the meat extract and stock. Stir till it boils.

Chop the fried vegetables finely and add them to the soup when it boils.

Simmer for about one hour. Serve with croûtons of fried bread (see p. 12).

Sufficient for five persons.

BRUSSELS SPROUTS PUREE

INGREDIENTS.—1 lb. of Brussels sprouts, salt and soda, ½ pint of white stock (see p. 12), pepper, boiling water, ½ pint of milk.

METHOD.—Prepare and wash the sprouts in the usual way.

Cook them in boiling water, with salt and a tiny piece of soda added, until tender.

When cooked, strain them through a colander and drain them well. Rub them through a wire sieve.

Stir in the milk and strain the stock and add it. Return the purée to the pan. Season it with pepper, re-heat, and serve.

If it is too thick a little more stock may be added.

Allow a gill and a half to two gills of soup for each person.

BUTTER BEAN SOUP

INGREDIENTS.—½ pint of butter beans, ½ pint of milk, ½ lb. of onions, 1 or 2 stalks of celery, 1 carrot and turnip, salt and pepper, 2 pints of white stock or meat liquor (see p. 12), ¾ oz. of margarine.

METHOD.—Wash the beans and soak them in water for about twenty-four hours.

Peel and slice the onions.

Melt the fat in a saucepan, add the onions and the beans (well-drained), and cook them for a few minutes without browning. Then draw the pan aside.

Add the stock, the celery, the turnip

(peeled and cut up), and a little salt. The carrot should be scraped and added whole just for flavouring purposes. (Do not leave it in too long, as it is apt to discolour the soup.) Boil them gently until the beans are tender, then rub the soup through a sieve.

Return the soup to the pan, add the milk and seasoning to taste, then re-heat and serve.

Allow one and a half to two gills of soup for each person.

CABBAGE SOUP

INGREDIENTS.—3 pints of water in which the cabbage was boiled, 1 cupful of cold cabbage, 1 onion, 1 carrot, 2 oz. of butter, 2 oz. of flour, 1 dessertspoonful of chopped parsley, ½ pint of milk.

METHOD.—Boil the cabbage water till it is reduced to two pints. Chop the onion and carrot finely and add them to the boiling soup. Simmer till tender. Chop the cabbage and add it to the soup. Mix the flour to a smooth paste with the milk, thicken the soup with it, and boil for five minutes.

Season to taste and add the butter. Pour the soup on to the parsley in the tureen.

NOTE.—It is not extravagant to use 2 oz. of butter for this soup, as the rest of the ingredients are so inexpensive.

Sufficient for six or seven persons.

CARROT BROTH

INGREDIENTS.—1 lb. of carrots, 3 pints of stock (see p. 12), 1 onion, 2 oz. of fat ham, ¾ to 1 gill of chopped celery, seasoning.

METHOD.—Scrape and wash the carrots, then drain and grate them.

Wash a few stalks of celery and chop them. Peel and grate the onion. Mince the ham and put it into a saucepan and stand it over a low burner. When the fat is drawn from it, add the prepared vegetables and stir it until the fat is absorbed, being careful not to let them brown. Draw the pan aside, add the stock and seasoning to taste.

Simmer the soup gently until the vegetables are tender, then turn it into a tureen and serve it, with croûtons of fried bread (see p. 12) or boiled rice.

If any fat is on the top of the broth, skim it off before serving it.

TO PREPARE THE RICE : Cook it in slightly salted boiling water until tender. Turn it into a colander, pour cold water through it to separate the grains, then drain it and re-heat it.

Allow half a pint of soup for each person.

CARROT SOUP

INGREDIENTS.—½ lb. of carrots, 1 onion, 1 quart of stock or pot liquor (see p. 12), pepper and salt, ½ oz. of cornflour, 1 small piece of celery, 1½ oz. of bacon (raw).

METHOD.—Peel the onion and cut it into slices. Scrape the carrots, wash them, and cut them into slices. Wash and cut up the celery. Put the bacon into a saucepan, add the prepared vegetables, and stir at the side of the fire for about ten minutes, but do not brown them. Add the stock, which should be boiling to keep the carrots a good colour. Add pepper and salt. Boil the soup gently until all the vegetables are tender. Take out the bacon and rub the soup through a hair sieve. Put it back into the saucepan and thicken it with the cornflour, mixed to a smooth paste with a little water.

Boil the soup for ten minutes after the cornflour is added.

Pour into a hot tureen and serve.

CORAL CAULIFLOWER SOUP

INGREDIENTS.— 1 cauliflower, 1 large tin of tomatoes, ½ pint of white stock or more as required (see p. 12), salt, pepper, and sugar, 1 onion, butter.

METHOD.—Remove the outer leaves and trim the cauliflower. Cleanse it in cold water with salt, then drain it and put it into a saucepan of boiling water to cook, adding salt to taste. Boil it till tender, drain it in a colander, then remove the green part and press the flower through a potato ricer, leaving out one or two sprigs for garnishing.

Peel and mince the onion and cook it in a little butter without browning it, then drain off the fat.

Turn out the tomatoes from the tin and rub them through a sieve. Put them into a saucepan and add the onion and cauliflower.

Bring them to the boil, season them with salt, pepper, and sugar to taste, and simmer them for a few minutes, adding sufficient stock to make the soup of a good consistency.

Turn it into a tureen and garnish it with small sprigs of the flower.

Allow half a pint for each person.

CAULIFLOWER CREAM SOUP

INGREDIENTS.—1 large cauliflower, 1 clove of garlic, 1 oz. of flour, 1 onion, 1 oz. of margarine or butter, 2 tablespoonfuls of minced celery (when in season), 2 pints of white stock (see p. 12), 1 pint of milk, salt and pepper.

METHOD.—Trim the cauliflower and soak it in cold water with a little salt to cleanse it, then cook it in boiling water (with salt to flavour) until tender. Drain it and remove a few of the small white sprigs and rub the remainder of the white part through a sieve.

Melt the fat, stir in the celery, the onion peeled and halved, and the clove of garlic, also the cauliflower pulp.

Stir them over a low burner for a minute or two, but do not let them brown, then draw the pan aside and add the stock. Bring the soup to the boil, add seasoning and nearly all the milk, keeping back a little to mix with the flour. Add the thickening, and boil the soup for a few minutes, keeping it stirred. Remove the onion and garlic and serve the soup with a few small sprigs of the cauliflower floating in it. A little red pepper may be sprinkled on the top, if liked, to garnish.

Allow half a pint of soup for each person.

CELERY SOUP

INGREDIENTS.—1 head of celery, 2 pints of white stock (see p. 12), or milk and water, 2 onions, salt and pepper, cornflour, 2 tablespoonfuls of cream (if desired), 2 or 3 slices of bread, deep fat for frying.

METHOD.—Trim off a little from the root of the celery and cut away the green. Well wash and slice the celery, using the outer leaves as well. Peel and slice the onions. Place the celery and onions in a saucepan, add the stock and seasoning. Bring the soup to the boil and cook slowly until it is all quite tender. Then rub it all through a hair sieve. Return it to the saucepan, and if not sufficiently thick mix some cornflour to a smooth paste with a little water and stir it into the soup and boil for ten minutes.

Taste to see if well seasoned, then draw away from the fire and stir in the cream.

Pour into a hot tureen and serve with croûtons (see p. 12).

NOTE.—It is better not to use an iron saucepan for white soups. The cream can be omitted if preferred.

Allow one and a half to two gills per person.

CHESTNUT PUREE

INGREDIENTS.—1½ lb. of chestnuts, 2 large onions, 1 quart of boiling water, 2 oz. of butter, 1 bay leaf, 1 tablespoonful of chopped parsley, the rind of half a lemon, salt and pepper, 1 lump of sugar, 3 teaspoonfuls of meat extract.

METHOD.—Slit the chestnuts on the flat side and bake them for fifteen minutes in a hot oven till the shells split.

Remove the shells and peel off the inner skin.

Chop the onions.

Melt the butter in a stewpan. Fry the chestnuts and onions for five minutes.

Add the bay leaf, thinly cut lemon rind, water and meat extract.

Simmer for half an hour and then rub through a hair sieve. Return the purée to the pan, add the sugar and season to taste with salt and pepper.

Put the parsley in the tureen and pour in the hot soup.

Serve with croûtons of fried bread (see p. 12).

Sufficient for five or six persons.

CHESTNUT SOUP

INGREDIENTS.—½ lb. of chestnuts, 1 onion, 1½ pints of stock (see p. 12),

1 oz. of flour, 1 oz. of margarine, ¾ pint of milk, seasoning.

METHOD.—Put the chestnuts into cold water, bring them to the boil and boil them for two or three minutes. Strain them and remove the outer and inner skin.

Put them into a saucepan with the stock, add the onion cut in slices, and simmer them gently until tender. Then rub them through a sieve.

Melt the fat, stir in the flour, and when well blended, add the milk and the chestnut purée. Boil the soup gently for a few minutes, keeping it stirred until it comes to the boil. Add seasoning to taste and serve.

Allow half a pint of soup per head.

CELERY AND TOMATO SOUP

INGREDIENTS.—1 head of celery, small tin of tomatoes, 1 onion, salt and pepper, 2 pints of stock (see p. 12), flour or cornflour.

METHOD.—Clean and prepare the celery and cut it in slices. Some of the outer stalks can also be utilised for soup. Put it into a saucepan with the onion, peeled and sliced. Add the stock and cook gently until almost tender. Stir in the tomatoes with their liquor, and finish cooking. Rub it all through a sieve, return it to the pan, add seasoning to taste and thicken it with a little flour or cornflour, as required. A teaspoonful of sugar may also be added if liked.

Allow half a pint of soup for each person.

COCK-A-LEEKIE

INGREDIENTS.—1 boiling fowl, a bundle of leeks, 1 carrot, turnip and onion, 2 sticks of celery, 3 oz. of rice, salt and pepper, 2 quarts of cold water, 2 bay leaves.

METHOD.—Wash the leeks and peel the carrot, turnip and onion.

Cut the leeks into four and the other vegetables into dice.

Cut up the fowl and put it in a pan with the cold water and one teaspoonful of salt.

Bring very slowly to the boil and add the vegetables. Simmer very gently for two hours or till the fowl is quite tender. If it is allowed to boil it will be hard and tough. Remove the fowl and bay leaves, wash and add the rice, and simmer for twenty minutes. Water is simmering when a bubble rises now and then at the side of the pan. Cut the white meat off the fowl and put the pieces in the soup to re-heat. Season with the salt and pepper, and serve.

NOTE.—This soup is recommended to those who keep chickens, as it is a good way of disposing of an old one.

Sufficient for five or six persons.

CONSOMME JULIENNE

CLEAR soups or consommés are made from stock which has been clarified.

They are named according to whatever garnish is used.

Consommé Julienne has very fine strips of cooked vegetables served in it, such as carrot, turnip, and celery.

These should be put into the bottom of the tureen and the consommé poured over them.

Brown stock, or a mixture of brown and white, can be used for making consommé.

To Clear the Stock

First of all remove the grease, then put the stock into a saucepan with some *lean* raw minced beef (allowing five or six ounces of meat to three pints of stock) and the white of an egg lightly whisked and its shell washed and crushed, after having removed the inner skin.

Add also a small carrot, onion, half a turnip, a tiny sprig of parsley and thyme, and a few peppercorns.

Whisk the consommé well until it *almost* boils and has a good frothy head on it, then leave it at the side of the fire to simmer very gently for from twenty to thirty minutes.

Strain the liquor through a jelly bag or clean cloth, putting the frothy scum into the cloth or bag, and pouring the soup through it very slowly. If not clear enough, strain again.

The soup can then be garnished as required.

NOTE.—When re-heating consommé do not quite let it boil again, as this tends to make it cloudy.

CONSOMME

INGREDIENTS.—3 quarts of good stock (cold) (see p. 12), 1 lb. of lean, gravy beef, 1 carrot, 1 onion, a bunch of herbs, 1 bay leaf, 2 cloves, 8 peppercorns, the crushed shells and beaten whites of 2 eggs, 1 wineglassful of sherry.

METHOD.—Chop the meat finely, first removing any fat.

Slice the carrot and onion and put them into a stewpan with the meat.

Remove all traces of fat from the stock. If it is a jelly this can be done by skimming the surface and then wiping it over with a clean cloth wrung out in hot water. If the stock is a liquid, strain it through a wet cloth.

Put the stock in the pan, with all the other ingredients, and bring it *very slowly* to the boil, whisking it all the time with an egg whisk. Allow it to boil up twice; then move the pan to one side of the fire and simmer as gently as possible for thirty minutes. Strain it through a dry cloth into a clean saucepan.

Re-heat, season to taste and add the wine. The consommé is poured very gently into a hot tureen.

Allow one and a half gills of consommé for each person.

CORN SOUP

INGREDIENTS.—1 pint tin of sweet corn, 1 onion, 1½ pints of water or white stock (see p. 12), 1½ pints of milk, ¾ oz. of butter or margarine, ¾ oz. of flour, seasoning, few celery seeds.

METHOD.—Turn the sweet corn into a saucepan, add a few celery seeds tied in a piece of muslin, the onion (cut in slices) and the water or stock.

Let it simmer gently for about half an hour until the corn and onion are tender, then remove the celery seeds, and rub through a sieve all the remainder.

Melt the fat, add the flour, and when well blended stir in the milk and bring them to the boil. Add the sweet corn, season to taste, and simmer the soup gently for a few minutes before serving.

Allow half a pint of soup for each person.

CREAM OF CHEESE SOUP

INGREDIENTS.—¼ lb. of cheese, 1¼ pints of milk, ¾ pint of white stock (see p. 12), a small bay leaf, sprig of parsley, few peppercorns, salt and cayenne, 1½ oz. of butter or margarine, 1 tablespoonful of flour, 1 yolk of egg, 1 onion, small clove of garlic.

METHOD.—Peel the onion and garlic and put them into a saucepan with the milk and white stock, add also the parsley, bay leaf and a few peppercorns. Bring them slowly to the boil and leave the saucepan at the side of the fire until the milk is well flavoured, then strain it and let it cool.

Melt the butter in a saucepan, add the flour, and when well blended gradually stir in the milk and stock and bring them to the boil. Let the soup simmer for a few minutes, then draw the pan aside, let it cool a little, and stir in the finely grated cheese and beaten egg yolk.

Add seasoning to taste and cook the soup again for a few minutes, being careful not to let it boil, and keeping it well stirred.

Allow half a pint of soup for each person.

NOTE.—Use a good flavoured cheese for this soup.

CUCUMBER CREAM SOUP

INGREDIENTS.—1 cucumber, 1 cupful of shelled green peas, 12 chives, 1 carrot, ½ gill of cream, 3 pints of stock (see p. 12), 2 oz. of butter, 2 oz. of flour, salt and pepper, grated nutmeg.

METHOD.—Cut the cucumber in half, without peeling it, and scoop out the seeds. Scrape the carrot.

Cut the vegetables and cucumber into dice, or, for a high-class soup, cut them into rounds with a vegetable cutter. Mince the chives.

Boil the stock and put in the carrot and cucumber. Boil for ten minutes, and add the peas and chives.

When the vegetables are tender, pour the soup into a basin.

Melt the butter in the same saucepan, stir in the flour, and gradually add the soup.

Stir till it boils, boil for five minutes,

and season carefully with salt, pepper, and grated nutmeg.

Take the soup off the fire and add the cream.

Stir well and pour into the tureen.

Sufficient for six or eight persons.

CUCUMBER SOUP

INGREDIENTS.—2 cucumbers, 1½ pints of white stock (see p. 12), 1½ oz. of margarine, 3 dessertspoonfuls of flour, salt and pepper, ½ pint of milk.

METHOD.—Peel and remove the thin ends from the cucumbers, and cut them into thick pieces.

Put the stock into a saucepan, and bring it to the boil.

Add the cucumbers and boil them gently until tender. Rub them through a sieve and return them to the pan.

Mix the flour to a smooth paste with some of the milk. Add the remainder of the milk to the soup with the margarine. Stir in the thickening. Bring the soup to the boil, keeping it well stirred, and boil it gently for a few minutes. Season to taste and serve.

For special occasions a little cream can be added.

Allow one and a half to two gills of soup for each person.

NOTE.—If the soup is too thick, add a little more milk.

EEL SOUP

INGREDIENTS.—2 lb. of eels, 2 quarts of water, 1 carrot, 2 onions, 2 sticks of celery, 1 bunch of herbs, 4 peppercorns, 2 teaspoonfuls of salt, 1 tablespoonful of chopped parsley, 2 oz. of butter, 2 oz. of flour, 1 cupful of milk.

METHOD.—Wash the eels, cut them in pieces an inch long, and put them in a pan with the water, herbs, salt and peppercorns.

Slice the vegetables thinly, add them when the water boils, and simmer gently for an hour and a half. Mix the flour smoothly with the milk and pour it into the soup. Stir till it boils, boil for five minutes, and add the butter. Chop the parsley finely, and put it in the tureen.

Season well, pour the soup over the parsley and serve. A wineglass of sherry may be added if liked.

Allow one and a half gills for each person.

FISH SOUP

INGREDIENTS.—1 lb. of hake, 1¼ pints of fish stock or water (see p. 12), ¾ pint of milk, 2 onions, ¼ teaspoonful of powdered mace, about 1½ tablespoonfuls of flour, 1 teaspoonful of chopped parsley, a few peppercorns and 2 cloves, salt.

METHOD.—Wash the fish, and put it into a saucepan with the fish stock or water, and salt to taste.

Peel and slice the onions, and add, also the peppercorns, cloves, and mace tied in a piece of muslin.

Bring to the boil, then remove the scum and simmer for about thirty-five minutes.

Strain the soup through a colander or sieve, and put it back into the saucepan.

Remove all the skin and bones from the fish, and flake it into very small pieces.

Add the milk to the soup.

Mix the flour to a smooth paste with a little water, and thicken the soup with it.

Boil it for about six minutes, stirring all the time.

Well wash some parsley, then scald it and chop it very finely.

Add to the soup, together with the flaked fish. When thoroughly hot, pour into a hot tureen and serve.

Allow one and a half to two gills of soup per head.

GAME BROTH

INGREDIENTS.—Carcase of game, cold water to cover well, salt and pepper, 1 carrot and onion, a piece of celery, small sprig of parsley, allow ½ oz. of pearl barley to each pint of broth.

METHOD.—Break up the carcase of any game you may have left over, and put it into a saucepan, adding cold water to cover it well and a little salt. Bring it slowly to the boil, add the cleaned and prepared vegetables and parsley to flavour, and simmer them gently for two or three hours. Then strain the broth and measure it

Weigh out the pearl barley in proportion, put it into a saucepan, with cold water. Bring it to the boil and strain it.

Boil up the broth, add the scalded barley, and simmer it until tender. Season to taste and serve.

If liked, the carrot may be cut in small dice and served in the broth.

Allow half a pint of broth for each person.

GIBLET SOUP—NOT SPICED TOO MUCH !

INGREDIENTS.—The giblets from two chickens, 1 lb. of bones, 1 onion, 2 carrots, pepper and salt, a few mixed herbs, 4 cloves, 1 oz. of spaghetti, 3½ pints of brown stock (see p. 12) or water, 1½ oz. of flour, browning.

METHOD.—Cut the gall-bag from the liver ; be careful not to break it or it will give the liver a bitter taste. Cut open the gizzard, and take out the inside. Well wash all the giblets in cold water (to which a little salt has been added). Wash the bones, scald and skin the feet. Put the prepared giblets and bones into a saucepan, add the stock or water. Peel the onion, stick the cloves into it, tie the herbs in muslin, add these to the giblets, etc., season well. Bring slowly to the boil, skim it, and simmer for three hours. Scrape, wash, and slice up the carrots into small squares. Put into a saucepan of boiling water (to which a little salt has been added), and boil until tender.

They will take about one hour, so put them on after the soup has been simmering about one hour and a half to two hours. Break the spaghetti into pieces about half an inch in length, wash it, and cook it in boiling salted water for about twenty minutes. When the soup is ready, strain it into another saucepan, add a few drops of browning to colour it. Taste to see if well seasoned, skim it well, and thicken with the flour, mixed to a smooth paste with water. Bring to the boil, and simmer for about six minutes to cook the flour ; keep it well stirred after the thickening has been added. Strain off the water from the carrots and add them to the soup. Strain the water from the

spaghetti, and put the spaghetti in the bottom of a soup tureen. Pour in the soup and serve.

HADDOCK SOUP

INGREDIENTS.—¾ lb. of fillet of smoked haddock, 1 pint of milk, 1 pint of stock (see p. 12), nutmeg, ½ teaspoonful of celery seeds in muslin, pepper to taste, 2 oz. of butter, 2 oz. of flour.

METHOD.—Cut the haddock in six pieces and put it in a saucepan with some water. Bring it just to the boil ; then throw the water away and put the fish on a plate.

Melt the butter in the same saucepan, add the flour, and gradually stir in the stock and milk. Stir till it boils, then add the haddock, celery seeds, and a little grated nutmeg. Simmer gently for half an hour, remove bag of celery seeds, and serve.

This soup may be made with all milk, or a little cream may be added.

Sufficient for four or five persons.

HARICOT BEAN PUREE

INGREDIENTS.—½ pint of haricot beans, 2½ pints of white stock or liquor (see p. 12), ½ pint of milk, pepper and salt, 2 onions, a few celery seeds, 1 teaspoonful of chopped parsley.

METHOD.—Wash the beans, place in a large basin, well cover with boiling water, and soak for twenty-four hours. Strain off the water and put the beans into a saucepan with the stock and sliced onions and celery seeds and pepper and salt, cook gently until quite tender. They will take about two hours. Take out the celery seeds, and rub the soup through a sieve, return to the saucepan, add the milk, and bring to the boil. Add the chopped parsley and the soup is ready.

NOTE.—A pinch of carbonate of soda added to the water in which the beans are soaked will help to soften them. The celery seeds must be tied in a piece of muslin.

HARICOT TOMATO PUREE

INGREDIENTS.—1½ gills of haricot beans, 1½ pints of stock (see p. 12), 1 onion, a large tin of tomatoes, 1 oz. of fat bacon, a small sprig of thyme and parsley, salt and pepper, celery salt.

METHOD.—Wash the beans and soak them in cold water for about twenty-four hours. Drain them.

Peel and slice the onion. Cut up the bacon fat and put it into a saucepan to melt. Add the onion and cook it for a few minutes without browning. Add the beans, stir them until the fat is absorbed, then draw the pan aside.

Pour in the stock and boil it gently until the beans are almost tender.

Add the tomatoes with their liquor and cook all together for a few minutes until the beans are quite soft, then rub the soup through a sieve. Re-heat the purée, season and serve it. If it is too thick add more stock.

NOTE.—The thyme and parsley can be added with the stock, but they should be removed when the soup is sufficiently flavoured.

Fresh tomatoes may be used for this soup, in which case extra stock will be required.

Allow one and a half to two gills for each person.

HOLLANDAISE SOUP

INGREDIENTS.—2 oz. of flour, 2 oz. of margarine, 2½ pints of white stock (see p. 12), 2 egg yolks, ½ gill of cream, seasoning, 3 tablespoonfuls of carrot balls or dice, 3 tablespoonfuls of green peas, 3 tablespoonfuls of cucumber balls or dice, tarragon.

METHOD.—Scrape and wash the carrot and peel some cucumber. If a small, round vegetable cutter is not available, cut the vegetables into small dice.

Cook them separately (also the peas) in boiling water, with a little salt added, until tender, then strain.

Melt the margarine, add the flour and mix together until smooth, then stir in the stock and bring to the boil, keeping it stirred. Boil for a few minutes, then draw aside and cool slightly.

Beat up the egg yolks and mix with the cream and add to the soup.

Strain, then add the prepared vegetables, and stir over a very low burner for a few minutes to cook the egg, but do not let it boil.

When ready to serve, add a little chopped tarragon (about 1 small teaspoonful).

Sufficient for six persons.

HOTCH POTCH

INGREDIENTS.—1½ lb. shoulder of mutton, 2½ quarts of water, 4 spring onions, parsley, 1 level teaspoonful each of sugar and salt, pepper to taste, 1 pint of green peas, 1½ gills each of prepared turnip, carrot and cauliflower, 1 small lettuce.

METHOD.—Put the meat into a saucepan and add the cold water. Bring it to boiling point, then skim it carefully. Chop the onions, prepare and cut the carrot and turnip into dice, break the cauliflower into small sprigs and chop the lettuce. Add the prepared vegetables to the soup with the salt and sugar.

Boil it for one hour and a half, then add the bottled or tinned peas (when fresh cannot be had).

Take out the meat, cut it into small pieces and return it to the pan with the chopped parsley, and add pepper to taste. Cook for ten minutes.

LEEK SOUP

INGREDIENTS.—A bunch of leeks, about 2 pints of white stock (see p. 12), ½ pint of milk, salt and pepper, cornflour.

METHOD.—Prepare the leeks by cutting off the green tops, and the roots, and peeling off the outside layer. Wash very thoroughly.

Put the stock into a saucepan, cut the leeks into rough pieces, and add them to it. Season with salt and pepper, and boil gently until tender, then rub the leeks through a sieve.

Return the soup to the pan, add nearly all the milk, leaving out just a little to mix with the cornflour.

Mix the cornflour to a paste and stir it into the soup to thicken it. Boil it for a few minutes to cook the cornflour, and then serve.

The soup must be stirred when the thickening is added, and until it comes to the boil again.

Serve with croûtons of fried bread (see p. 12).

Allow one and a half to two gills of soup for each person.

LENTIL SOUP

INGREDIENTS.—½ pint of lentils, 1 oz. of butter, 3 pints of stock (see p. 12), 1 large carrot, 1 large onion, pepper and salt, some celery seeds or a small piece of celery.

METHOD.—Wash the lentils, prepare and cut up the carrot and onion. Melt the fat in a saucepan and stir all the vegetables in it for a few minutes without letting them brown, then draw the pan aside and add the stock, seasoning and celery.

Boil all the ingredients gently until tender and then rub the soup through a sieve. Taste it to see if it is sufficiently seasoned, and re-heat it before serving. This soup may be thickened if necessary.

LOBSTER SOUP

INGREDIENTS.—1 lobster, 3½ pints of fish stock (see p. 12), 1 carrot, 1 onion, pepper and salt, 1 small piece of celery or a few celery seeds, 1 bunch of herbs, 2½ oz. of flour, 2½ oz. of butter, 1½ teaspoonfuls of anchovy essence, ½ gill of sherry, squeeze of lemon-juice.

METHOD.—Break up the lobster and remove the flesh. Wash the shell and wipe it, and break or pound it into small pieces. Peel and slice the onion. Scrape the carrot, wash it, and cut into slices. Clean the celery and cut it up. Melt the butter in a saucepan, add the pounded shell and prepared vegetables, and fry them lightly for a few minutes. Add the flour and stir over the fire again for a few minutes. Tie up the herbs, and, if celery seeds are used, put these in muslin and add with the stock. Bring to the boil, keeping it stirred, then simmer for about ten minutes. Flake up the flesh of the lobster and either chop finely or pound it, and add to the soup. Let it simmer gently for about twenty to thirty minutes, skim it as required. Strain it through a very fine sieve. Add the seasoning, lemon-juice, sherry, and anchovy essence. Pour into a saucepan and bring almost to the boil, and it is ready.

NOTE.—If fish stock is not available use milk and water. If a cheaper soup is required, the sherry may be omitted.

LUNCHEON SOUP

INGREDIENTS.—The flower of a medium-sized cauliflower, 1½ teacupfuls of celery (sliced), 1 teacupful of carrot (cut in dice), ¾ teacupful of onion (cut in dice), ¼ teacupful potato (cut in dice), ½ teacupful of turnip (cut in dice), 1 dessertspoonful of chopped green pepper, about 3 pints of white stock (see p. 12), salt and pepper, ½ oz. of margarine, small sprig of parsley, 3 medium-sized tomatoes.

METHOD.—Clean and prepare the vegetables.

Cut them up and measure them.

Divide the flower of the cauliflower into small sprigs and wash them.

Melt the margarine, add the celery, potato, onion, carrot and turnip, and stir for a minute or two without browning.

Draw the pan aside and add the stock. Cook the vegetables in it for about three-quarters of an hour. Add the cauliflower, chopped green pepper, tomatoes (peeled and cut up), also sprig of parsley, and cook until all the vegetables are tender.

Season to taste and serve.

Allow one and a half to two gills of soup for each person.

MILK SOUP

INGREDIENTS.—1 lb. of potatoes, 1½ pints of white stock or meat liquor (see p. 12), ¾ pint of milk, a few celery seeds, ¼ oz. of margarine, salt and pepper, ¼ lb. of onion, 1 carrot and ½ turnip.

METHOD.—Peel and slice the onion. Wash and peel the potatoes, and slice them thickly.

Cook both the vegetables in the melted fat for a few minutes without letting them brown. Draw them aside.

Add the stock, the turnip (peeled thickly), some salt and a few celery seeds tied in muslin.

Boil the soup gently until the vegetables are tender, adding the carrot (whole) for flavouring purposes, but do not leave it in too long.

Rub the soup through a sieve, having first removed the celery seeds and carrot, then return it to the saucepan and add the milk.

Re-heat, season to taste, and serve. Allow one and a half to two gills of soup for each person.

MUSHROOM SOUP

INGREDIENTS.—1 pint of milk, 1 pint of stock (see p. 12), ¾ lb. of mushrooms, 2 oz. of butter, 2 oz. of flour, 1 onion, salt and pepper, 1 bay leaf.

METHOD.—Wash and peel the mushrooms, and remove the stalks.

Chop the onion and mushrooms. Cook them slowly in the butter for ten minutes.

Stir in the flour and mix well; then add the stock and a bay leaf; stir till it boils.

Pour in the milk and simmer for fifteen minutes.

Rub through a hair sieve, re-heat, season, and serve.

Sufficient for four or five persons.

MUTTON BROTH

INGREDIENTS.—2 lb. neck of mutton (scrag end), 3½ pints of cold water, 1½ oz. of pearl barley, seasoning, small piece of celery, 2 small onions, 2 small carrots.

METHOD.—Cut the neck of mutton into pieces, and wipe, or, if necessary, wash in salted water.

Put into a saucepan with the cold water and seasoning, bring slowly to the boil, then skim it. Peel the onions and cut into small pieces. Scrape the carrots, wash them, and cut into dice. Wash the celery, and cut into small dice.

Add all these prepared vegetables to the broth, together with the pearl barley, having previously well washed it. Simmer all together from one hour and a half to two hours, keeping it well skimmed.

Take out the pieces of meat, and pour the broth into a hot tureen.

NAPLES SOUP

INGREDIENTS.—½ lb. of tomatoes, 2 lb. of good beef bones, 4½ or 5 pints of cold water, slice of lean ham, a few celery seeds 1 oz. of spaghetti, 2 onions, 2 carrots, salt and pepper, grated cheese.

METHOD.—Have the bones chopped into fairly small pieces, wash them well, and put them into a saucepan with the cold water and a teaspoonful of salt. Bring them slowly to the boil and remove the scum.

Add the prepared carrots and onions, both sliced, and the celery seeds tied in a piece of muslin. If you have any celery, add one or two stalks cut up.

Mince the ham (there should be about two tablespoonfuls, or you may use any odd trimmings of ham), and add it to the pot. Let them simmer gently for three or four hours, or until the soup is reduced to about three-quarters of its bulk. Then strain it. Allow it to cool, and skim off the fat.

Return the soup to the pan, add the tomatoes, peeled and chopped finely, bring it to the boil, and add the spaghetti broken into very small pieces and washed. Season to taste and cook gently for from twenty to thirty minutes.

Serve the soup very hot accompanied with finely grated cheese.

MULLIGATAWNY SOUP

INGREDIENTS.—1½ lb of scrag of mutton, 3 pints of water (cold), about 1½ oz. of dripping, seasoning, 2 carrots, 2 onions, 2 apples (small), a few mixed herbs, a small piece of lemon, 3 dessert-spoonfuls of flour, 3 teaspoonfuls of curry powder, 2 or 3 dessertspoonfuls of rice.

METHOD.—Scrape, wash and slice the carrots. Peel and slice the onions. Peel and quarter the apples and remove the core.

Melt the dripping in a saucepan, add the carrot, onion, and apple, and fry until lightly browned.

Stir in the flour and curry powder and fry again for a few minutes, then draw aside.

Cut the mutton into small joints and add to the vegetables, with the water, herbs—tied in muslin—and seasoning to taste.

Bring all slowly to the boil, remove the scum, and simmer for about two and a half hours.

Take out the meat and herbs and rub the soup through a sieve.

Skim off any fat from the top, then re-heat the soup.

Squeeze in a little lemon-juice and serve. Have ready the boiled rice, and serve separately.

NOTE.—If necessary, add a few drops of browning to the soup just before serving.

To Prepare The Rice

WASH it well.

Put it into a saucepan of boiling water, with a little salt added, and boil until tender; it will take about fifteen minutes.

When cooked, strain it through a colander, pour cold water through it—to separate the grains—then place on a dish in a warm oven to dry, and re-heat.

Allow one and a half to two gills per person.

NORWEGIAN FRUIT SOUP
With Cinnamon Fingers

INGREDIENTS.—$\frac{1}{2}$ pint of bottled gooseberries, 3-in. stick of cinnamon, 1 quart of water, 1 oz. of cornflour, $1\frac{1}{2}$ oz. of sugar, peel of half a lemon.

METHOD.—Cut the yellow part only of the lemon rind and put it in a saucepan with the gooseberries, water and cinnamon. Simmer for one hour.

Rub through a hair sieve and remove cinnamon. Boil the soup.

Mix the sugar and cornflour with a little cold water, and pour a little of the boiling soup on to it. Pour it back into the soup, stir well, and boil for ten minutes.

CINNAMON FINGERS
To Serve With The Soup

INGREDIENTS.—1 egg, $1\frac{1}{2}$ gills of milk, 2 teaspoonfuls of castor sugar, 1 teaspoonful of ground cinnamon, deep frying fat, 2 slices of stale bread.

METHOD.—Beat the egg, and add the milk. Cut the bread into fingers and soak for ten minutes in the egg and milk. Heat the fat till it smokes. Put in the fingers and fry for three or four minutes. Take them out with a fish slice and drain on paper. Mix the cinnamon with two teaspoonfuls of castor sugar, roll the fingers in this, and serve on a lace paper.

OXTAIL SOUP

INGREDIENTS.—1 oxtail (weighing about $1\frac{1}{2}$ to 2 lb.), allow 1 quart of cold stock (see p. 12) or water to every pound of oxtail, 1 onion, 3 carrots, seasoning, 1 teaspoonful of mixed herbs, $\frac{1}{4}$ teaspoonful of powdered mace, 1 small piece of celery, dripping as required, flour.

METHOD.—Cut the tail into pieces where jointed. Wash it well in cold water with salt (use about one tablespoonful to two quarts of water), then wipe it.

Melt dripping in a saucepan and lightly fry the pieces of oxtail in it.

Pour off any dripping that is over and add the stock or water.

Add also all the other ingredients with the exception of the flour and carrots.

The mixed herbs and mace must be tied in pieces of muslin.

The celery washed and put in whole.

The onion peeled and also put in whole.

Bring the soup to the boil and skim it; then add the carrots, which should have been scraped and washed and cut into small dice.

Simmer for three or four hours.

Keep it well skimmed so that all the grease may be removed.

Take out the onion, celery, and bags of herbs and mace.

Thicken the soup with flour (as required) and boil it for six minutes, keeping it well stirred.

Pour the soup into a hot tureen and serve.

If preferred, the pieces of oxtail may be taken out before the soup is served.

NOTE.—If necessary a few drops of browning may be added.

Allow one and a half to two gills per person.

OYSTER CREAM SOUP

INGREDIENTS.—18 oysters, 2 egg yolks, $\frac{1}{2}$ gill of cream, a few peppercorns, a few celery seeds, a blade of mace (or powdered mace tied in muslin), salt and cayenne, parsley (chopped), about 1 teaspoonful, 1 tablespoonful of lemon-juice, $1\frac{1}{2}$ oz. of butter, 2 oz. of flour, $1\frac{1}{2}$ pints of fish stock (see p. 12), 1 pint of milk, 1 pint of water.

METHOD.—Melt the butter in a saucepan, add the flour, and mix until quite smooth.

Pour in the fish stock, together with the milk, water, peppercorns, mace, and seasoning.

Tie the celery seeds in muslin and add.

Stir all together until it comes to the boil, then cook slowly for about twenty to thirty minutes.

Skim it if necessary.

Strain the soup through a fine strainer, rinse out the saucepan, and pour it back into it.

Wash and scald the parsley and chop very finely.

Put the oysters into a pan with their liquor, and blanch them. Strain off the liquor and add to the soup. Remove the beards from the oysters.

Bring soup to the boil, then let it slightly cool.

Beat up the yolks of eggs and mix with the cream. Strain this into the cooled soup, and stir over the fire until the egg is cooked, being very careful not to make it too hot or it will curdle.

Taste it to see if well seasoned, add the lemon-juice and oysters. Put the chopped parsley into a soup tureen and pour in the prepared soup.

NOTE.—If there is not any fish stock, use all milk and water.

Sufficient for eight persons.

PEA SOUP

INGREDIENTS.—½ pint of split peas, 3½ pints of stock (see p. 12), seasoning, 2 or 3 onions, a piece of celery or a few celery seeds, 2 carrots, flour.

METHOD.—Wash the peas and put them to soak the previous day.

Peel and slice the onions. Scrape, wash, and slice the carrots, wash and cut up the celery—if using celery seeds, tie in muslin.

Put all the prepared vegetables into a saucepan with the stock.

Season, bring to the boil, and simmer the soup gently for two or three hours, until the peas are tender.

Rub the soup through a sieve, then return it to the saucepan and thicken with a little flour, as required.

Allow one and a half to two gills per person.

POTATO SOUP

INGREDIENTS.—10 or 12 potatoes, 2 quarts of water, 1 carrot, some roast beef bones, 2 onions, 1 large tomato, seasoning.

METHOD.—Boil the beef bones in the water for an hour. Add the onions and potatoes (chopped), grated carrot, and the tomato rubbed through a sieve. Season the soup and simmer it for an hour and a half, then serve.

PUMPKIN SOUP

INGREDIENTS.—2 lb. of pumpkin, ½ head of celery, 1 leek, 1 quart of stock (see p. 12), 2 oz. of butter, a little grated nutmeg, salt and pepper, 1 cup of milk.

METHOD.—Cut up the leek, pumpkin and celery, and put them in the boiling stock. Simmer for one hour, and rub through a hair sieve. Re-heat and add milk, salt, pepper and nutmeg to taste. Put in the butter, and serve.

Sufficient for four or five persons.

RICE AND TOMATO PUREE

INGREDIENTS.—1 large tin of tomatoes, 1 carrot and onion, 1 pint of stock (see p. 12), a few celery seeds, pepper and salt, 2 oz. of rice.

METHOD.—Peel and slice the onion. Scrape, wash, and slice the carrot. Wash the rice well. Put all these ingredients into a saucepan, add the tomatoes with their liquor, also the stock, and the celery seeds tied in a piece of muslin. Season well with pepper and salt. Bring to the boil, and cook slowly until the rice and vegetables are quite tender. Stir it occasionally to prevent the rice from sticking. Take out the celery seeds and rub the soup through a sieve. Rinse out the saucepan, pour the soup back into it and re-heat. Taste to see if well seasoned. Pour into a hot tureen.

Note.—If the soup is not a good colour, add a few drops of cochineal. If liked, this soup can be thinned down with some more stock.

Allow one and a half to two gills per person.

SCOTCH BROTH

INGREDIENTS.—1 lb. scrag of mutton, ½ turnip, 1 oz. of pearl barley, 2 to 2½ pints of water, 1 carrot and onion, salt and pepper, a few celery seeds, 1 teaspoonful of chopped parsley.

METHOD.—Wash the meat and divide it into fairly small pieces. Put it into a saucepan with cold water, add a little salt, and bring it slowly to the boil. Remove the scum and let it simmer for about an hour.

Add the vegetables, prepared and cut into dice, the celery seeds tied in muslin, and the barley scalded. Cook the soup gently until tender, season it to taste, then remove the celery seeds, add the parsley, and serve.

NOTE.—Before serving the soup take out the meat. Then remove the bones, divide the meat into smaller pieces, and return them to the broth.

SEMOLINA CREAM SOUP

INGREDIENTS.—1 quart of white stock (see p. 12), 2½ dessertspoonfuls of semolina, salt to taste, a few peppercorns, ¼ pint of cream, 1 yolk of egg.

METHOD.—Strain the stock into a saucepan and bring to the boil. Tie the peppercorns in a piece of muslin and add to the stock. When boiling, sprinkle in the semolina and cook until the latter is quite soft.

Beat up the yolk of the egg and mix with the cream.

Allow the soup to go well off boiling-point, then strain in the cream and egg and stir very carefully until the egg is cooked. Remove the peppercorns, season the soup with salt.

Pour into a hot tureen and serve.

NOTE.—This soup must be cooked very slowly after the cream and egg thickening is added, and it must not boil or the egg will curdle.

Allow one and a half to two gills per person.

SPINACH SOUP

INGREDIENTS.—½ pint of cooked spinach, 1 pint of stock (see p. 12), ½ pint of milk, ½ oz. of flour, 1 oz. of butter, seasoning.

METHOD.—Rub the spinach through a sieve. Melt the butter, stir in the

flour and when well blended add the milk and bring them to the boil. Add the spinach, then stir in the stock gradually. Simmer then gently for a few minutes, season to taste and serve.

If the soup seems too thick, add a little more stock or milk.

Allow half a pint for each person.

" TEN-MINUTES " SOUP

INGREDIENTS.—2 oz. of margarine, 2 oz. of flour, 2½ pints of milk and water, or milk and white stock (see p. 12), 3 or 4 tablespoonfuls of tomato ketchup, seasoning.

METHOD.—Melt the margarine, add the flour and mix them until well blended. Stir in the milk and water, or stock, and stir until the sauce boils and thickens. Let it boil gently for a few minutes, then add tomato ketchup and seasoning to taste.

If liked, a few drops of cochineal or carmine may be added to improve the colour of the soup.

If too thick, thin the soup down with a little more liquid. This makes an excellent emergency soup.

Allow one and a half to two gills of soup per head.

TOMATO CREAM SOUP

INGREDIENTS.—1½ lb. of tomatoes, ½ a small clove of garlic, a few celery seeds, 1 shallot (cut in halves), ⅓ level teaspoonful carbonate of soda, 1 oz. of flour, 1 oz. of margarine or butter, ¼ pint of water 1¼ pints of milk, seasoning, a sprig of parsley.

METHOD.—Stalk and slice the tomatoes and put them into a pan with about one tablespoonful of water. Add the shallot and garlic (peeled), the celery seeds tied in a piece of muslin, and a sprig of parsley. Cook them gently for a few minutes until the tomatoes are soft, and then remove shallot, garlic, celery seeds, parsley, and rub the tomatoes and the liquor from them through a sieve.

Melt the fat, stir in the flour, and when well blended add the milk and water and bring them to the boil. Boil them gently for a few minutes, then draw the pan aside.

Stir the soda into the tomato pulp,

and when dissolved mix them gradually
with the thin white sauce. Make this
hot but do not let it boil, add seasoning
to taste and serve the soup.

Allow half a pint of soup for each
person.

TOMATO SOUP

INGREDIENTS.—2 lb. of cooking
tomatoes, 3 pints of stock (see p. 12),
a few celery seeds (tied in muslin) or
a small piece of celery when in season,
1 oz. of margarine or butter, pepper
and salt, cornflour (about 1 tablespoonful), 1 or 2 carrots and 2 onions.

METHOD.—Prepare the carrot and
onion and cut them in slices. Melt
the fat in a saucepan, add the prepared
vegetables, and cook them for a few
minutes without letting them brown.
Then draw the pan aside and add the
tomatoes cut in slices, the stock,
seasoning, and celery.

Simmer all together until tender,
and then rub the soup through a hair
sieve. Return the purée to the pan,
stir in a little cornflour mixed to a
smooth paste with water. Boil the
soup for a few minutes, season it to
taste, and serve it with fried croûtons.

TURNIP PUREE

INGREDIENTS.—3 lb. of turnips,
2 pints of white stock (see p. 12),
1 pint of milk, 1 onion, clove of garlic,
salt, pepper, 1 oz. of butter.

METHOD.—Peel the turnips thickly,
cut them in quarters and cook them
in boiling water with a little salt,
until tender. Drain them and rub
them through a sieve. Melt the butter,
add the onion and garlic, halved and
peeled, also the sieved turnip. Cook
them for a few minutes without
letting them brown. Stir in the
stock and the milk. Bring to the boil
and season to taste.

Remove the onion and garlic before
serving.

VEGETABLE CREAM SOUP

INGREDIENTS.—½ lb. of carrots,
1½ pints of diced celery, 2 medium
sized onions, 2 medium sized potatoes,
3 pints of white stock (see p. 12), ¾
pint of milk, flour, a lump of butter or
margarine, celery salt, pepper and salt.

METHOD.—Clean and prepare all
the vegetables and cut them into
pieces. Cook them gently in the
stock until they are tender, then rub
them through a sieve.

Return the purée and stock to the
pan, add a small lump of butter or
margarine, and the milk.

Re-heat the soup and thicken it
with a little flour mixed to a smooth
paste with water.

Stir the soup till it boils. Cook it
gently for a few minutes, then season
it with salt, pepper, and celery salt
to taste.

VEGETARIAN TOMATO SOUP

INGREDIENTS.—2 lb. of tomatoes,
2 pints of water, 1 oz. of butter,
a few celery seeds or a small piece of
celery, 1 carrot and 2 onions, cornflour, salt and pepper, sugar, ½ clove
of garlic.

METHOD.—Prepare the carrot and
onion and cut them in slices.

Melt the butter and cook the
vegetables in it for a few minutes
without letting them brown, then
draw the pan aside and add the
tomatoes cut in slices, the water,
garlic and celery. If using celery
seeds, tie them in muslin. Cook the
vegetables until tender, then remove
the garlic and celery seeds, and rub
the soup through a sieve. Return it
to the pan, season it with salt and
pepper, and a little sugar if liked, and
thicken it with a spoonful of cornflour mixed to a smooth paste with
cold water. Boil the soup for a few
minutes and serve it with croûtons.

WHITE SOUP

INGREDIENTS.—1½ lb. of potatoes,
2½ pints of white stock or liquor (see
p. 12), 3 onions (small), seasoning,
1 small piece of celery, 1 pint of milk,
1½ oz. of rice.

METHOD.—Thinly peel the potatoes,
wash them, and cut into thick slices.
Peel and slice the onions. Wash and
cut up the celery.

Put all these vegetables into a
saucepan with the stock, and cook
gently until soft. Rub soup through a
sieve. Put it back into the saucepan,
season well, and add the milk. Wash
the rice and add to the soup and boil
the soup slowly until the rice is soft.
Pour into a hot tureen.

FISH DISHES

To many people fish either steamed or boiled suggests an invalid's diet, or at best a meal to be taken on those days when we have next to no appetite. This should not be. For, nicely cooked and served with an interesting sauce, fish can be as appetising as meat any day.

THREE KINDS OF FISH

ALL fish belong to one of three classes namely, *white, oily, or shell-fish. White* fish consists of such fish as cod, hake, sole, plaice, whiting, fresh haddock, or brill. It is more easily digested than the other kinds of fish.

The oily kinds are herrings, eels, mackerel, and salmon. There is no need to mention the names of the shell-fish for they are well known to all.

IS IT FRESH?

IT is very necessary that fish should be quite fresh, for when it is stale it becomes poisonous. When buying it from the fishmonger make sure that the eyes are not sunken, and that the flesh is firm and elastic to the touch, never flabby. Of course, it should smell sweet, too.

TO CLEAN FISH

BEFORE cooking, all fish must be thoroughly cleaned inside as well as out. The fishmonger usually attends to the inside, but the eyes must also be removed, the fins cut off, and the fish washed and wiped as is necessary with a clean cloth.

When preparing fish with scales for cooking, these must be removed. This is quite easily done if the fish is scraped with a knife.

TO FILLET AND SKIN FISH

To fillet fish, place the fish flat on the table with the tail towards you. Cut round the head, round the fins, and across the tail, then down the middle, cutting only as deep as the bone.

With a sharp, pointed knife, remove the fillet on the left side of the fish, cutting in long sharp cuts and keeping the knife as flat as possible.

Now turn the fish round so that the head is towards you, and remove the second fillet.

Turn the fish over and remove the other two fillets in the same way.

Remember that the fillet you are removing should be on the left-hand side.

To skin the fillets, place the fish skin side downwards on a board. Make a small slit at the tail end between the skin and the flesh, and then holding the tip end of the skin firmly with the left hand, work the knife along to the other end of the fillet until it is entirely separated from the skin. If the fingers are dipped in salt they are enabled to hold the skin more firmly.

HOW TO BOIL FISH

WHITE and most kinds of oily fish are suitable for boiling.

The average time to allow is six minutes to the pound and six over.

But the thickness of the fish must be considered as well as the weight. Remember that under-cooked fish is very indigestible, and if it is over-cooked it will fall to pieces when taken out of the water.

The fish should always be put into warm water to which a little salt and either lemon-juice or vinegar has been added (two teaspoonfuls of salt to a quart of water).

The salt flavours and the vinegar preserves the whiteness of the fish.

There should only be *just enough* water to cover the fish. Bring it almost to boiling point, then let it cook very gently until the flesh is tender, keeping it skimmed as required.

Salmon should be cooked rather differently. It should be put into *boiling* water to preserve its colour, and no vinegar or lemon juice should be added.

The flesh will move easily from the bone when the fish is done, and if it is of the white variety it will have a much whiter appearance than before it is cooked.

When ready lift up the fish with a slice and drain off the water, and serve it with some suitable sauce such as plain white sauce, egg, parsley, or shrimp sauce (see pp. 41 to 43). Sliced cucumber and mayonnaise (see p. 42) are correct with salmon.

A Fish Kettle

This is the most useful utensil for boiling fish, more especially when cooking a whole fish, on account of its shape. It contains a drainer on which the fish is placed while cooking so that it can be lifted out without any fear of breaking. If you have no fish kettle and have to cook a large piece of fish, tie it in a large piece of muslin and cook it in a saucepan.

STEAMING FISH

This is the lightest method of cooking fish, and very suitable for invalid diet.

The fish should be covered first with a buttered paper and then with the lid of the saucepan, in order to keep in the steam.

Steamed fish takes rather longer than boiled to cook.

It can be cooked in a steamer, or on a plate (an enamelled one for preference) over a saucepan of boiling water, covered with a basin instead of a saucepan lid.

HOW TO FRY FISH

One of the most tasty ways of cooking fish is to fry it—either in deep or shallow fat. Most kinds of fish can be fried, but, on the whole, the most popular are plaice and sole. It is not necessary to use Dover soles, unless for some special occasion. Lemon or Torbay soles are much

cheaper to buy and are quite delicately flavoured.

Frying implies cooking food in fat—either dripping, clarified fat, or special frying oil. Salad oil can be used, but it is not economical, for it is rather expensive for everyday use.

Two Ways of Frying

Fish may be cooked in a small quantity of fat—just enough well to cover the bottom of a frying-pan. This method is known as *shallow* frying. The second way is to cook the fish in a deep iron or aluminium pan with enough fat completely to cover the food. This is *deep* frying, and is a French method. The second method is rather more expensive as more fat will be necessary, but so long as it is never allowed to burn, it can be strained and used over and over again for frying fish.

To Ensure Success

Both fish and fat must be quite free from moisture, as this causes the fat to splutter. After washing the fish, roll it in a cloth and leave to dry.

Fish before frying must be coated either with dry flour, butter, or egg and breadcrumbs, and the fat must be hot before the fish is put into it. The way to test the heat is to watch for a faint bluish smoke which will rise from the centre of the fat as soon as it is hot enough for frying. (When salad oil is hot enough it turns a greenish colour.) If the fish is put in before the fat is really hot, it will become sodden, greasy, and indigestible, instead of being crisp and brown.

Do not fry more fish than will cover the bottom of the pan at one time, and remember always to re-heat the fat between frying each batch.

When it is brown on one side, the fish should be turned over and browned on the other side, and then lifted out on to white kitchen paper to drain. Serve fried fish on a dish paper which will absorb any superfluous grease.

Coating With Egg and Breadcrumbs

To coat with egg and breadcrumbs, beat up the egg on a plate, and brush the fish all over with it, using a pastry-brush. Have ready a heap of breadcrumbs on a sheet of white paper, and shake the crumbs over the fish until it is well coated. Shake off any loose crumbs before frying.

WHEN BATTER IS USED

Food coated with batter requires either deep fat for frying, or at least enough fat to float it. Fillets of fish are more suitable for this purpose than larger cutlets.

GOOD COATING BATTER

INGREDIENTS.—3 oz. of flour, pinch of salt, 1 dessertspoonful of salad oil or melted margarine, 1 gill of warm water, 1 egg white.

METHOD.—Sieve the flour with the salt. Make a well in the centre, drop in the oil, and then add the water gradually until it is all mixed to a smooth batter. Beat the mixture well and leave it to stand for about an hour.

Just before using the batter, whisk the white of egg to a stiff froth and fold it in lightly.

To coat the fish, dip each fillet in the batter separately, and when it is coated all over lift it out, drain off any superfluous batter, and put it into the hot fat. Fry till it is a light golden brown.

A batter made of flour and water can be used instead of the one given above.

THE FRYING BASKET

WHEN frying food in deep fat, it is most convenient to use a frying basket. Put enough fish into it just to cover the base, and then stand it in the pan of hot fat.

This method does not apply to batter-coated fish, which would stick to the bottom of the basket.

SOME DIFFERENT FISH TO FRY

Sprats.—Flour them and fry them in a very *small* quantity of fat.

Whitebait.—Flour and fry in deep fat, using a frying basket.

Brill.—Fillet and fry in the same way as plaice.

Cod or Hake.—Cut into slices. Flour and fry in shallow fat, or coat with egg and breadcrumbs, and fry in either deep or shallow fat.

Kippers and Bloaters.—Do not wash them, but wipe them, and use very little fat for frying. Cut the heads off bloaters and remove gut.

Fresh Herrings.—Wash and scrape off the scales, cut off the head, and remove gut. Use a very small quantity of fat.

Smelts.—Flour and fry in shallow fat, or coat with egg and breadcrumbs, and fry in deep or shallow fat.

Plaice.—Fillet, coat as desired, and fry by either method.

Sole.—Cook whole or fillet (according to size), coat with egg and breadcrumbs, and fry in either deep or shallow fat.

HOW TO COOK BLOATERS

INGREDIENTS.—Bloaters.

METHOD.—Clean and wipe two or three plump bloaters. Place them in a frying-pan, just cover them with water, and simmer them gently until they are tender. They do not taste so strong cooked in this way as when fried, and they are very tender and juicy.

Another method is to butter them and place them on a meat stand in a tin containing half a pint of boiling water.

Place them under the gas griller and broil slowly for about ten minutes, turning them two or three times.

If liked, the bloaters may be split open down the back and placed on the stand with the insides together.

A little butter is spread on the outside, and they are broiled in the same way as for whole bloaters.

Bloaters that are very hard and dry are improved by soaking in tepid water ten minutes before cooking.

BAKED BREAM, STUFFED

INGREDIENTS.—1 bream (medium size), 1 teacupful of white breadcrumbs, 2 or 3 teaspoonfuls of chopped parsley, ½ a lemon, pepper and salt, ¼ teaspoonful of mixed herbs, egg, 1½ oz. of butter or margarine, dripping for basting.

METHOD.—Thoroughly clean the bream, remove the inside, take out the eyes, etc. Then wash it and dry well.

To Make the Stuffing

Make the breadcrumbs. Wash, scald, and finely chop the parsley. Mix these together, add the herbs, pepper and salt, and grated lemon-rind. Add the butter (melted), the strained juice of the lemon, and sufficient beaten egg to mix all to a paste.

Put the stuffing inside the fish and sew it up with a trussing-needle and fine string, or skewer it securely. Put the bream into a baking-tin with a little dripping, and bake it in a moderately hot oven for about thirty to forty-five minutes, keeping it well basted with dripping. Place on a hot dish and remove the string or skewer very carefully. Serve separately a suitable sauce, such as parsley or anchovy sauce (see pp. 41 to 43).

Note.—Bream is rather a coarse fish. It requires well cooking, and needs to be exceptionally fresh.

Allow about 7 to 8 oz. for each person.

BREAM AND EGG SAUCE

Ingredients.—1 bream of about three or four pounds, tepid water to cover, 1 tablespoonful of salt, 2 tablespoonfuls of vinegar.

Method.—Wash the bream in salt water and put it into a fish-kettle containing tepid water to cover it, and salt and vinegar to flavour. Bring quickly to the boil, but do not let it go on boiling or it will break.

Simmer only till it is done (about fifteen minutes, as it is not very thick). Take it out by means of the strainer and slide it gently on to a hot dish. Keep it hot while making the sauce.

Allow half a pound of fish for each person.

Note.—A bream of three or four pounds is a small one.

When boiling a large bream or any fish weighing over four pounds, put it into a fish-kettle full of *boiling* water, and bring it just to the boil again, as it will cool the water a little. As soon as it boils *turn out the gas* and leave it to cook in the hot water, allowing ten minutes to the pound and ten minutes over.

This is an excellent way to cook large pieces of fish as they cook perfectly and never break.

To Make the Egg Sauce.

Ingredients.—1 hard-boiled egg, 1½ oz. of butter, 1½ oz. of flour, ½ pint of fish stock (see p. 12), 1 gill of milk, salt, and pepper, 1 dessertspoonful of chopped parsley to decorate.

Method.—Melt the butter, stir in the flour and milk and stock and boil up, stirring all the time.

Cut the egg in half, chop the white coarsely and add it to the sauce.

Season to taste, boil three minutes, and pour over the fish.

Rub the yolk through a coarse gravy strainer and use it to decorate the fish, together with some chopped parsley.

BREAM FILLETS

Ingredients.—1 bream, 2 level dessertspoonfuls of chopped parsley, 3 oz. of breadcrumbs, 1 oz. of ham, 1½ oz. of butter or margarine, salt and pepper, ½ rind of a lemon, ¼ teaspoonful of herbs, egg.

Method.—Choose a bream about two pounds in weight. Have it filleted, scrape off the scales, wash and dry the fillets and split each into two lengthwise.

Mince the ham and mix it with the breadcrumbs, parsley, herbs, and finely-grated lemon rind.

Season them with pepper and salt, add the butter (melted) and stir in enough egg to bind the mixture. Spread this on the four pieces of fish, keeping back just a small portion of the stuffing.

Twist the fish into rounds, and keep them in position with a short skewer, then put the rounds into a buttered dish. Cover them with a well-buttered paper or place a small piece of bacon on each, and bake them till the flesh is quite white and tender.

Serve the bream on a hot dish with either white sauce or parsley sauce (see pp. 41 to 43) poured round, and garnish each fillet with a tiny ball of the left-over stuffing, egged and crumbed and fried.

Allow one or two half fillets for each person.

BRILL AU GRATIN

INGREDIENTS.—1 small brill, 1 gill of brown sauce, 1 tablespoonful of tomato sauce (see p. 43), 1 oz. of butter or margarine, pepper and salt, a few brown breadcrumbs, squeeze of lemon-juice.

METHOD.—Thoroughly clean the fish, take out the eyes, trim the tail, remove the fins, etc.

Skin the fish, then wash it, and dry in a cloth. Put it into a greased piedish or gratin dish, sprinkle a little lemon-juice over, and put the butter on the top.

Cover with a greased paper and bake in a moderately hot oven for about twelve to fifteen minutes, or until the flesh will move easily from the bone.

Mix the two sauces together and heat in a saucepan ; add pepper and salt to taste.

Take the fish from the oven, pour the sauce over it, and sprinkle a few brown breadcrumbs over the top. Return to the oven for a few minutes to re-heat it, and serve in the dish.

FILLETS OF BRILL WITH CHEESE STUFFING

INGREDIENTS.—1 brill (about one pound), 5 dessertspoonfuls of bread-crumbs, 1 teaspoonful of chopped parsley, 1 tablespoonful of grated cheese, grated lemon-rind, pepper and salt, egg.

METHOD.—Fillet the brill, skin the fillets, then wash and dry them. Wash, scald, and chop the parsley.

Make the breadcrumbs. Mix these together, add pepper and salt, grated rind of half a lemon, and grated cheese. Beat up the egg, and add sufficient to mix to a stiff paste.

Spread this on to the skinned side of the fillets, roll each into sausage shape, and tie loosely with string. Put them on a well-buttered tin or piedish, cover with a greased paper, and bake in a moderately hot oven for about twenty minutes. Carefully untie the string and cover the fillets with white sauce (see p. 41).

FRIED BRILL

INGREDIENTS.—1 brill (about 1 lb.), egg and medium oatmeal, dripping.

METHOD.—Have the fish filleted. Wash the fillets, drain them well and roll them in a cloth to dry.

Beat up an egg, brush the fillets with some of it, and coat them with medium oatmeal in the same way as with breadcrumbs.

Heat some dripping in a frying-pan, and when a faint smoke rises, put in the fish and fry it until golden brown. Turn it over and brown the other side.

Drain the fish on paper and serve it on a dish paper.

Serve with plain white sauce (see p. 41).

Sufficient for two persons.

NOTE.—Lemon sole or plaice may be filleted and fried in the same way. Half an egg will be enough for brushing the fish, so put half aside before you begin ; it can then be utilised for some other purpose.

Medium oatmeal makes a good coating for fish, and it is useful if no stale bread is available.

DEVILLED COD

INGREDIENTS.—3 cod cutlets (large), 3 large tablespoonfuls of brown bread-crumbs, about ½ teacupful of cold water, about ½ teacupful of cold, white sauce (see p. 41), ½ teaspoonful of anchovy essence, 1 teaspoonful of mixed mustard, 1 tablespoonful of chutney, salt and cayenne, margarine (about 2 oz.).

METHOD.—Wash the cutlets and dry them in a cloth.

Make the brown breadcrumbs, or if you have any white crumbs already made, just put them on to a tin and brown them in the oven. Be careful not to make them too dark in colour.

Put the sauce into a basin and whisk it until quite smooth, then stir into it the anchovy essence, mixed mustard, and chutney. Season well with salt and cayenne.

Melt about half of the margarine, brush it over the cod cutlets, spread the sauce mixture thickly on both sides. Then coat with the brown breadcrumbs.

Place them on a greased tin, with the remainder of the margarine in small pieces on the top. Bake in a moderately hot oven for about fifteen minutes.

Filets
de
Sole
Otero

Salmon
Mould

Crimped
Skate
au
Buerre
Noir

PLATE 1

Halibut
and
Cheese Sauce

Shirred
Eggs
with
Scallops

Sole
Paprika

PLATE 2

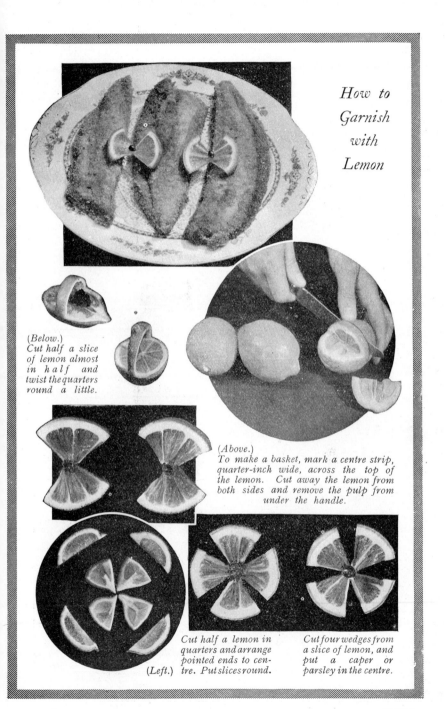

How to Garnish with Lemon

(*Below.*) Cut half a slice of lemon almost in half and twist the quarters round a little.

(*Above.*) To make a basket, mark a centre strip, quarter-inch wide, across the top of the lemon. Cut away the lemon from both sides and remove the pulp from under the handle.

(*Left.*) Cut half a lemon in quarters and arrange pointed ends to centre. Put slices round.

Cut four wedges from a slice of lemon, and put a caper or parsley in the centre.

PLATE 3

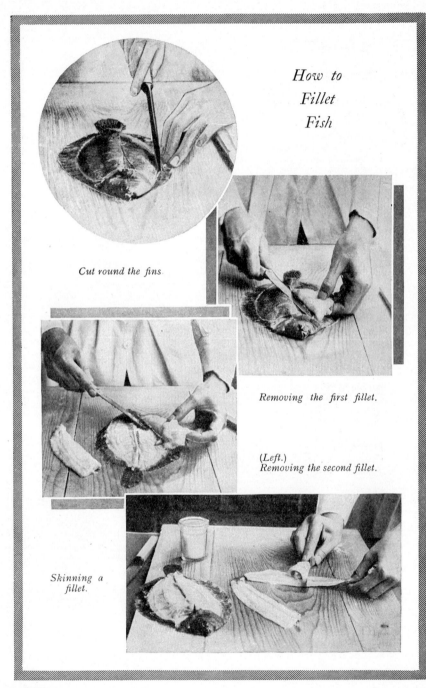

How to
Fillet
Fish

Cut round the fins.

Removing the first fillet.

(*Left.*)
Removing the second fillet.

Skinning a
fillet.

PLATE 4

Place on a dish and serve very hot.
NOTE.—When cooked, the fish will move easily from the bone.

GRILLED COD

INGREDIENTS.—1 cod steak, 2 tablespoonfuls of salad oil, 1 dessertspoonful each of chopped parsley and capers, salt and pepper, ½ gill of vinegar, lemon for garnish.

METHOD.—Wash and dry the cod. Mix the oil and vinegar with the capers and parsley, and lay the fish in it. Turn it over and leave for two hours.

Heat the oil and vinegar in a frying-pan and fry the cod for four minutes, then place it under the griller for four minutes. Fry it again for three minutes and finish under the griller, serve on a dish paper, sprinkle with salt and pepper, and garnish with lemon.

Sufficient for one or two persons.

SALT COD

STEWED IN BROWN GRAVY

INGREDIENTS.—1½ lb. of salt cod, 1 oz. of bacon fat, 1 oz. of flour, 1 large parsnip, 1 teaspoonful of chopped parsley, pepper.

METHOD.—Soak the fish for at least twenty-four hours, changing the water several times.

After soaking wash thoroughly.

Put the fish in enough cold water to cover it, and simmer for ten minutes. Throw away the water.

Peel the parsnip. Cut it into thick slices. Boil the parsnip for ten minutes, drain it and lay it on a cloth to dry.

Melt the bacon fat, and fry the pieces of parsnip a nice brown ; take them out. Then brown the flour. Add half a pint of water, and stir till it boils.

Put in the fish and parsnip and stew gently for about fifteen minutes.

Add the chopped parsley and pepper. Serve with the slices of parsnip round the dish.

Sufficient for four persons.

BAKED CRAB

INGREDIENTS.—1 large crab or two small ones, 3 tablespoonfuls of breadcrumbs, 1 dessertspoonful of mushroom ketchup, 1 teaspoonful of curry powder, 1 oz. of butter, 1 tablespoonful of thick cream, salt.

METHOD.—Take the meat from the body of the crab and the large claws. Chop it and mix it with the cream, salt, ketchup, breadcrumbs, curry powder, and half the butter. Wash and dry the shell. If there are two crabs, wash the shell of the larger one.

Put the mixture into the shell, sprinkle a few breadcrumbs over it, and put dabs of butter on top. Bake for fifteen minutes.

Sufficient for two or three persons.

DRESSED CRAB

INGREDIENTS.—1 crab (boiled), 2 to 2½ tablespoonfuls of salad oil, 1½ to 2 tablespoonfuls of vinegar (use salad oil and vinegar according to taste), pepper and salt, mixed mustard, parsley, 1 egg.

METHOD.—Boil the egg for fifteen minutes until hard, then crack the shell, and leave the egg in cold water. When buying the crab, get the fishmonger to remove the greenish hairy flesh which comes from the underneath part of the crab—this is not good to eat.

Break the claws and remove the flesh ; keep this for garnishing.

Remove all the flesh from the body of the crab, keeping the white and dark flesh separate.

Mix half the salad oil and vinegar with the dark flesh, and the remainder with the white flesh, having previously flaked the latter into small pieces ; add the seasoning to taste.

Peel the egg, cut it into halves, remove the yolk, and chop up the white ; mix this with the dark flesh.

Wash the shell and wipe it, then rub the outside with a little salad oil.

Arrange the prepared crab mixtures in separate sections in the shell.

Rub the yolk of egg through a sieve to a powder, and sprinkle a line of it between the light and dark mixtures. Next to this arrange a line of chopped parsley.

Serve on a dish paper, garnish with sprigs of parsley, and the flesh from the claws.

B

CRAB MAYONNAISE

INGREDIENTS.—1 crab, cucumber, mayonnaise (see p. 42), mustard and cress, hard-boiled egg.

METHOD.—Wash the mustard and cress and drain it thoroughly.

Remove the meat from the crab, being careful *not* to use the part which is unwholesome. The fishmonger should have removed this for you.

Flake up the crab-meat finely, and mix it with about the same quantity of cucumber, peeled and chopped. Mix it with mayonnaise.

Boil the egg hard, remove the yolk, and press it through a strainer. Chop up the white, and mix it with the crab and cucumber.

Arrange it in a dish with a border of cress, garnish with the claws, and sprinkle the powdered egg yolk in the centre.

Sufficient for three or four persons.

CRAB MAYONNAISE AND ASPARAGUS

INGREDIENTS.—1 large crab and 1 small one, ½ teaspoonful of made mustard, 1 dessertspoonful of chopped parsley, salt and pepper, ½ gill of mayonnaise (see p. 42), or salad cream, ½ bundle of cold asparagus or some nice heads of tinned asparagus.

METHOD.—Mix the crab meat with the chopped parsley, salt and pepper, and flake up the flesh unless the fishmonger has already done so. Be careful to see that there are no small pieces of shell left in.

Wash the larger of the two shells.

Add the mayonnaise and parsley to the crab mixture and fill the shell.

Cut the asparagus heads four inches long, stick them in the mayonnaise in a semi-circle.

Sufficient for two or more persons, according to size of crab.

CRAB SALAD

INGREDIENTS.—1 large crab, ½ gill of mayonnaise (see p. 42), or salad cream, ½ teaspoonful of made mustard, 1 dessertspoonful of Worcester sauce, cayenne, and salt, juice of half a lemon, 1 tablespoonful of cream, 2 oz. of rice (freshly boiled), 1 lettuce, 1 tablespoonful of vinegar.

METHOD.—Wash the rice and cook it in boiling water containing one teaspoonful of salt and the tablespoonful of vinegar. Boil fast for about fifteen minutes, not more. Strain through a colander and leave to get cold.

Take all the meat from the crab and flake it up with a fork.

Put the mustard, mayonnaise, and Worcester sauce in a basin and mix them together.

Add the crab meat, rice, and cream, and season well with lemon-juice, salt, and cayenne.

Wash the lettuce and drain the leaves on a cloth. Place a few leaves in individual dishes with a little heap of crab mixture.

Sufficient for three or four persons.

BOILED CRAYFISH

INGREDIENTS.—Required number of crayfish, boiling water to cover, 1 gill of vinegar, 1 teaspoonful of salt.

METHOD.—Crayfish are generally bought ready cooked. If uncooked they must be boiled in their shells.

Have a large saucepan of quickly-boiling water containing the vinegar and salt.

Put the crayfish into the boiling water and keep them under the water by means of a frying basket. Five minutes' boiling is enough.

Serve them on a dish paper. They can be eaten hot or cold, according to taste.

The bodies only are eaten.

Allow one to three fish for each person according to size.

BAKED EEL

INGREDIENTS.—1 nice eel weighing about 1 lb.

FOR STUFFING.—1 teacupful of breadcrumbs, grated rind of half a lemon, 1 dessertspoonful of chopped parsley, salt, pepper, and nutmeg, 1 oz. of bacon dripping, 1 small egg.

FOR THE SAUCE.—½ pint of hot water, 1 teaspoonful of Marmite, 1 tablespoonful of vinegar, 1 teaspoonful of Bisto.

FOR THE GARNISH.—Lemon and parsley, 2 crayfish.

METHOD.—Ask the fishmonger to clean the eel, but not to skin it.

Turn it on its back, and with a sharp, pointed knife cut close to the backbone, but not right through the skin. Slip the point of the knife under the backbone, and cut it out piece by piece.

There is now a cavity for the stuffing.

Wash, dry, and chop the parsley and mix it with the other stuffing ingredients. Bind with a beaten egg, make into rolls about the size of a finger, and place along the inside of the eel. Sew it up with a needle and thread. Do not put in too much stuffing as it swells in the cooking.

Curve the eel slightly, or shape it into a round, and put it in a fireproof dish or meat tin with the hot water and vinegar. Grease a paper and twist it over the edge of the dish.

Bake in a moderate oven for about forty-five minutes. Put the crayfish into the dish for the last ten minutes.

Dish up the eel with one crayfish each side of it, and put it back in the oven while making the gravy.

Put the water from the dish into a small saucepan with the Marmite and boil it up.

Mix the Bisto with a very little cold water, and pour the boiling water on it. Return it to the saucepan, stir till it boils, season to taste, and pour round the eel.

Garnish with parsley and slices of lemon.

Sufficient for two or three persons.

EEL PIE

INGREDIENTS.—2 lb. of eels, ½ pint of water, 1 teaspoonful each of flour and dried sage, salt and pepper, grated nutmeg, 1½ oz. of butter, 1 bay-leaf, ¾ lb. of flaky pastry (see p. 252).

FOR THE STUFFING.—½ lb. of bread-crumbs, 2 oz. of shredded suet, 1 table-spoonful of chopped parsley, ½ tea-spoonful of mixed herbs, 1 dessert-spoonful of Worcester sauce, salt and pepper, 2 eggs.

METHOD.—Wash the eels and cut them in pieces three inches long.

Stew them in the water with the bayleaf and a teaspoonful of salt for about twenty minutes. Remove the bones. Sprinkle the boned eels with the flour and sage and season with salt, pepper, and nutmeg.

Mix the stuffing ingredients with the well-beaten eggs.

Spread half the stuffing in a fireproof dish, put in the eels and dabs of butter, and cover with the rest of the stuffing. Roll out the pastry, cut off a narrow strip and press it on the moistened edge of the dish. Wet the strip of pastry and cover the pie, pressing the edges together and scalloping them.

Brush the top with egg and cut a star-shaped hole through the centre. Bake in a moderately hot oven for one hour.

Sufficient for four or five persons.

STEWED EELS

INGREDIENTS.—1 lb. of eels, 1 bay leaf, 2 cloves, salt, cold water, mashed potatoes.

FOR THE SAUCE.—1½ gills of stock (see p. 12), 1 oz. of flour, 1 oz. of butter, 1 dessertspoonful of chopped parsley, ½ teaspoonful of anchovy essence, ½ gill of milk, salt and pepper.

METHOD.—Wash the eels and cut off the heads and tails. Cut the eels in pieces two inches long and put them in a pan with the bayleaf, cloves, and a quarter of a teaspoonful of salt. Add a cupful of cold water, and simmer very gently for twenty minutes.

Remove the pieces of eel and take out the backbones.

Boil the stock (or the water the eels were cooked in) till it measures a gill and a half and use it to make the sauce.

FOR THE SAUCE melt the butter, mix the flour with it, and stir in the milk and stock. Stir till it boils, season to taste, and add the parsley and anchovy. Put in the eels and simmer very gently till hot. Make a border of potatoes on a hot dish, and pour in the stewed eels.

Sufficient for three persons.

STEWED EELS AND PORT WINE GRAVY

INGREDIENTS.—2 eels, flour, drip-ping, 1 onion, few mixed herbs, pepper and salt, 1 wineglassful of port wine, about 1½ pints of brown stock (see p. 12) or gravy, browning, lemon.

METHOD.—Be sure that the eels are perfectly fresh when you buy them, and have them thoroughly cleaned and skinned, the head removed, and the eels jointed.

Cut them into pieces where jointed, and dry them in flour.

Melt some dripping in a saucepan, and when hot, put in the floured eels and fry them lightly until golden-brown, then take them out of the fat and keep them warm.

Pour off the dripping and add the stock or gravy, also the onion, and a few herbs tied in a piece of muslin.

Thicken the gravy with a little flour mixed to a smooth paste with water.

Stir it until it boils, then season well, and add a few drops of browning.

Put the pieces of fried eel into this gravy and stew gently for about forty minutes, then stir in the port wine, and bring the gravy up to the boil again.

Serve on a hot dish, strain the gravy over the eel, and garnish with pieces of cut lemon. (Remove the onion and herbs.)

Allow about 6 to 8 oz. for each person.

FISH AND TOMATO PIE

INGREDIENTS.—Large tin of peeled tomatoes—quart size, large tin of salmon, 1 dessertspoonful of Worcestershire sauce, salt and pepper, 1½ oz. of breadcrumbs, 1 oz. of butter, lemon.

METHOD.—Remove the bone and skin from the salmon, and flake up the flesh. There will be about three-quarters of a pound of salmon. Season it and mix it with the Worcestershire sauce.

Turn out the tomatoes from the tin and drain off nearly all the liquor, then put a layer in the bottom of a buttered pie-dish or a Pyrex dish. Season it with pepper and salt, and add a layer of salmon. Continue in this way until the ingredients are used up, making the last layer of tomato.

Cover the top with buttered crumbs and heat the pie through in the oven.

Garnish the pie with lemon and serve it hot.

To PREPARE THE BUTTERED CRUMBS.—Melt the butter in a frying-pan, then add the breadcrumbs and stir them in it until lightly browned.

Sufficient for four or five persons.

BAKED FISH AND TOMATOES

INGREDIENTS.—4 or 5 medium-sized tomatoes, 1 oz. of margarine, salt and pepper, ½ lb. of onions, dripping, 1½ to 2 lb. of cod or hake, lemon-juice.

METHOD.—Wash the fish, drain it, and cut it into slices.

Add a sprinkle of lemon-juice. Peel and slice the onions and fry them until lightly browned and partly cooked ; then drain off the fat.

Cut the tomatoes in slices ; add a square of lemon. Butter a piedish, or fireproof dish, and arrange the fish, onion, and tomatoes in it tastefully, seasoning it well and leaving a few slices of tomato for the top.

Add the margarine cut in small dabs. Put the dish into a moderate oven to bake for about half an hour.

Serve in the dish with white sauce (see p. 41), using the liquor from the fish to mix it.

Sufficient for about six persons.

FISH CAKES

INGREDIENTS.—6 oz. of cooked fish, 4 oz. of cold potatoes, about 1 dessertspoonful of cold parsley sauce (if any left over), (see p. 41), salt and pepper, breadcrumbs, 1 egg, fat for frying.

METHOD.—Remove the bones from the fish and flake it into very small pieces. Mash the cold potatoes and mix with the flaked fish, season well with pepper and salt. Bind with the cold sauce and a small quantity of the egg previously beaten. Divide into six or eight equal portions, shape each into rounds, flatten the surface.

Brush over with the remainder of the egg, then coat with the breadcrumbs.

Put into hot fat and fry until golden brown. Drain well on paper. Serve on a dish paper and garnish with parsley.

HOT CROSS FISH CAKES

INGREDIENTS.—½ lb. mashed potatoes, ¾ lb. cooked fish, cold white sauce (see p. 41) or milk, 2 oz. of cheese, egg and breadcrumbs, seasoning, deep fat.

FOR THE SCRAMBLED EGG.—1 egg, ½ oz. of butter, 1 tablespoonful of milk, seasoning.

METHOD.—Remove the bones and skin from the fish and flake up the flesh.

Grate the cheese finely and mix it with the mashed potatoes. Stir in the prepared fish and seasoning to taste, and moisten the mixture with a little cold sauce or milk as required. Spread the mixture on a plate and, when quite cold, divide it into ten portions.

Shape each portion into a round cake with a flattened top. Coat them with egg and breadcrumbs, and fry them in hot fat till golden. Drain them, and serve them with a cross of scrambled egg on each cake.

TO PREPARE THE SCRAMBLED EGG. —Beat up the egg, add the milk and seasoning to taste. Melt the butter in a pan, stir in the egg mixture, and continue to stir until it thickens.

FISH CROQUETTES

INGREDIENTS.—¾ lb. of cooked fish, ½ lb. of cooked potatoes, 2 tablespoonfuls of cold fish sauce — anchovy, parsley, or egg sauce, etc. (see pp. 41 to 43), salt and cayenne, 1 oz. of butter, flour, fat for frying.

METHOD.—Mash the potatoes, then melt the butter and mix with them.

Remove all the bones and skin from the fish, and flake or chop the flesh finely. Mix the fish and potatoes together.

Warm the sauce and mix with them. If there is no cold sauce over, use a little milk if required, and add some anchovy essence or chopped parsley to flavour. Mix all well together and season to taste. The mixture should be quite stiff. If liked, the yolk of an egg can be added to bind.

Divide the mixture into equal portions, and make each into a fat sausage shape, then roll the croquettes in flour and coat them thinly.

Put some dripping into a frying-pan to melt, and when it smokes slightly put in some of the croquettes and fry until they are golden brown, turning them as required. When ready, drain on paper and fry the others in the same way.

Serve on a dish paper and garnish with lemon or parsley.

NOTE.—If preferred, the croquettes can be brushed over with beaten egg and coated with breadcrumbs, and fried in deep fat.

Sufficient for five persons.

CREAMED FISH

INGREDIENTS.—½ pint of milk, 1 onion, a few cloves, 1 oz. of margarine, salt and cayenne, ½ a tumblerful of breadcrumbs, 1 egg, 6 oz. of cold fish, 2 tablespoonfuls of cream, parsley.

METHOD.—Peel a small onion and stick a few cloves into it. Put it into a milk saucepan with the milk and margarine. Let it stand at the side of the fire for an hour or so, to get the milk well flavoured. Boil the egg for fifteen minutes until hard, then cut it into halves and take out the yolk. Cut the white into small pieces and press the yolk through a sieve to a powder. Remove the skin and bones from the cooked fish; any kind of white fish can be used for this. Flake the flesh into very small pieces. Bring the milk to the boil, remove the onion and cloves, and sprinkle in the breadcrumbs, add the flaked fish, white of egg, and salt and cayenne. Mix all together and stir over a very low gas until the bread is well cooked and it is all thoroughly hot. Put a few nice clean sprigs of parsley into the oven to dry, but do not let it discolour, then crumble it to a fine powder. Add the cream to the fish and re-heat again for a few minutes, then turn it all on to a hot dish, and garnish with alternate lines of powdered parsley and yolk of egg.

Sufficient for two or three persons.

CURRY OF COLD FISH

INGREDIENTS.—1 apple (small), 1 onion (medium size), 2½ oz. of butter or margarine, 3 gills of milk, milk and water, or fish stock (see p. 12), ¾ lb. of cold fish, seasoning, squeeze of lemon-juice, 3 teaspoonfuls of curry-powder, 1½ tablespoonfuls of flour, 3 or 4 oz. of rice.

METHOD.—Peel the apple, cut into quarters, and remove the core.

Either chop it or grate finely.

Peel and chop the onion.

Melt the butter in a saucepan, add the onion and apple, and fry slowly until lightly browned.

Stir in the flour and curry powder,

mix them in smoothly, then add the stock or milk, and stir it until it comes to the boil.

Now simmer this sauce for about twenty minutes.

During this time prepare the fish, then remove any bones and skin, and flake the flesh into very small pieces. (There should be ¾ lb. after the bones and skin have been removed.)

Add the fish to the sauce, also a squeeze of lemon-juice, and salt and pepper to well flavour.

Make it all thoroughly hot, and serve on a hot dish with a border of boiled rice ; or, if preferred, serve it separately.

Sufficient for about four persons.

FRICASSEE OF FISH

INGREDIENTS.—2 eggs, ¾ lb. of cooked fish (any white fish can be used), 1 teaspoonful of parsley (chopped), pepper and salt, pinch of powdered mace, ½ pint of white sauce (see p. 41).

METHOD.—Put the eggs in a saucepan, cover them with cold water, and boil them for fifteen minutes (after they have come to the boil).

Crack the shells and put the eggs in cold water.

Pick over the parsley, wash it well in cold water.

Remove all the bones from the fish, and chop or flake it up very finely.

Make the white sauce, and put the flaked fish into it, season well with pepper and salt, and add the mace.

Mix all together and make them thoroughly hot.

Scald the parsley and chop it finely and add it to the fish just before serving.

Remove the shells from the eggs, cut them into halves, take out the yolk, and make it into a powder by rubbing it through a wire sieve.

Cut the halves of the whites each into four, and stand them all round the edge of a hot dish, so as to make a border or wall.

Pour the fricassee into the centre and sprinkle the top of it with the yolk of egg.

Sufficient for three or four persons.

JELLIED FISH

INGREDIENTS.—4 slices of hake (or any other fish). ½ teaspoonful of salt, ¾ pint of water, 1 gill of vinegar, 2 teaspoonfuls of meat extract, 2 tomatoes, endive, or cress, 1 hard-boiled egg, 1 oz. of leaf gelatine.

METHOD.—Wash the fish and put it in a deep fireproof dish with the water, salt, vinegar, and meat extract. Bake for fifteen to twenty minutes. Strain the liquid into a basin and leave it to get cold.

Put in the gelatine and let it soak for five minutes.

Stir over a low gas till the gelatine dissolves.

Arrange the tomatoes round the fish in a dish, and strain the liquid over them.

When the jelly is set, decorate it with the white of egg cut in fancy shapes. Rub the yolk through a coarse wire sieve and use it also for decorating.

Garnish with a little endive or cress.

Sufficient for four persons.

FISH KROMESKIES

INGREDIENTS.—½ lb. of cooked fish—cod or hake, etc., 8 rashers of fat bacon (cut thinly), 1½ oz. of flour, 1 oz. of margarine, 1¼ gills of milk, 2 level dessertspoonfuls of chopped pimento (tinned), salt and pepper.

FOR THE BATTER.—¼ oz. of yeast, ¼ teaspoonful of castor sugar, ½ an egg, 1¼ gills of milk, deep fat, ¼ lb. of flour.

METHOD.—To make the batter, put the yeast into a small basin with a quarter of a teaspoonful of castor sugar, and mix them until they liquefy. Make the milk lukewarm and add it. Sift the flour and a pinch of salt into another basin, make a well in the centre and pour in the beaten half egg, then gradually stir in the yeast and milk and mix all to a smooth batter. Beat this well, and put it into a warm place to rise for about an hour.

Meanwhile, prepare the fish mixture.

Remove the skin and bones and flake up the fish—there should be half a pound when prepared. Put the milk and margarine into a saucepan and bring them to the boil, then add the flour and stir it quickly until the mixture is thick and smooth and leaves the side of the pan. Draw the pan aside, add the pimento, prepared fish, and seasoning to taste, and when well mixed turn it on to a plate and leave it until cold, then divide it into sixteen portions. Form each portion into a small sausage shape, using a little flour if it sticks. Remove the rind from the bacon, cut the rashers in halves, and roll a piece round each sausage. Dip each in the batter and coat it evenly. Put the kromeskies into hot fat and fry them gently until golden, then drain them and serve them hot.

Sufficient to make sixteen kromeskies.

FISH MOULD

INGREDIENTS.—½ lb. of cooked fish, 2 oz. of butter, 2 tablespoonfuls of breadcrumbs, 3 oz. of cold potatoes, anchovy essence, pepper, squeeze of lemon-juice, 1 egg, milk.

METHOD.—Remove the bones and skin from the fish and finely chop up the flesh.

Mash the potatoes and add them to the fish.

Add the breadcrumbs and mix all well together.

Add sufficient anchovy essence to flavour, season with pepper, and add a squeeze of lemon-juice.

Melt the butter and mix it in.

Beat up the egg and bind all the ingredients together, adding a little milk as required.

Put the mixture into a greased basin, cover it with a greased paper, and steam it for from one hour to one and a half hours.

When ready, turn carefully on to a hot dish, and serve with anchovy sauce (see p. 42).

FISH MOULDS

INGREDIENTS.—6 oz. of cold, cooked fish, 1 oz. of breadcrumbs, ½ to ¾ gill of milk, 1 tablespoonful of chopped capers, seasoning, 1 egg, ¾ oz. of margarine, 1 teaspoonful of Worcestershire sauce.

METHOD.—Heat the milk and margarine in a saucepan, add this to the breadcrumbs and let them soak a few minutes.

Remove the skin and bones from

the fish, and flake up the flesh. Mix this with the breadcrumbs and milk.

Beat in the yolk of the egg, and stir in the chopped capers, Worcestershire sauce, and season to taste. Then fold in the stiffly whisked egg white.

Turn the mixture into small buttered moulds and cover them with buttered papers. Steam the moulds gently till they are set, then unmould them and garnish them with a few extra capers.

Sufficient for four small moulds.

NOTE.—Fish moulds may be served either plain or with a suitable sauce.

FISH PATTIES

MADE WITH SHORT OR FLAKY PASTRY

INGREDIENTS.—¼ lb. of cooked fish (without bone), ½ gill of thick white sauce (see p. 41), 1 flat dessertspoonful of chopped parsley, pepper and salt, some flaky pastry (see p. 252).

METHOD.—The remains of cold boiled white fish makes excellent patties.

Remove the skin and bones from the fish and flake up the flesh finely. Season to taste, add the chopped parsley and sauce, and mix all together.

Roll out the pastry thinly and cut out about ten rounds. Line some patty tins, pressing the pastry a little thinner in the centre, and divide the prepared fish equally between them.

Cover with another round slightly thicker than the under one. Brush them with egg, make a hole in the centre of each, and put them into a hot oven to bake. They will take about fifteen minutes to cook.

Sufficient for about ten patties.

NOTE.—If there is no egg available, use a little milk to glaze the patties.

NORTH COUNTRY FISH PIE

INGREDIENTS.—2 to 3 lb. of halibut, 1 oz. of butter, ½ oz. of flour, ½ teaspoonful of salt, pepper, 1 teaspoonful of chopped parsley.

FOR THE FORCEMEAT.—¾ lb. of fresh breadcrumbs, 3 eggs, 3 oz. of shredded suet or butter, 1 teaspoonful of chopped thyme and marjoram, 1 tablespoonful of chopped parsley, ½ onion (chopped), salt and pepper, flaky pastry, ½ lb. (see p. 252).

METHOD.—Wash and dry the fish and cut it into nice pieces.

Mix the flour with salt, pepper and parsley, and roll the fish in it. Place the fish in a pie-dish with half a gill of hot water and put dabs of butter on top. Cover the fish with a layer of forcemeat.

To make the forcemeat, mix the breadcrumbs, suet, onion and herbs with the beaten eggs and seasoning to taste.

Smooth the forcemeat over, then roll out the pastry and cut off a strip. Wet the edge of the pie-dish and press the strip of pastry on it. Brush it with water and lay the pastry on top, pressing the edge a little.

Notch it round with the back of a knife and cut a star in the centre. Bake for one hour. Serve with boiled potatoes.

Sufficient for five or six persons.

FISH PIE

INGREDIENTS.—½ lb. of cold boiled fish (without bone), about ¼ pint of shrimps, ¾ to 1 gill of thick white sauce (see p. 41), salt and pepper, about 1 lb. of cooked potatoes, milk and margarine, parsley.

METHOD.—Remove the skin and bones from the fish and flake up the flesh.

Shell the shrimps and mix them with the fish, then add the sauce and seasoning. A little chopped parsley can also be added, if liked.

Mash the potatoes, adding a lump of margarine and some milk, as required; also pepper to taste. Line a pie-dish with potato, then add the fish and sauce, and cover them with the remainder of the mashed potato. Smooth the top over with a knife dipped in hot water, then mark lines across, both ways.

Put the pie into a good, moderately hot oven, and make it thoroughly hot. Serve garnished with a few unshelled shrimps.

Sufficient for four or five persons.

STEAMED FISH PUDDING

INGREDIENTS.—1 lb. of cod (raw), 3 oz. of breadcrumbs, 3 oz. of shredded suet, 1 tablespoonful of chopped parsley, 1 teaspoonful of chopped lemon-rind, 2 eggs, 1 gill of milk, salt and pepper.

METHOD.—Chop the fish, removing all skin and bones. Mix it with the breadcrumbs, suet, parsley, and lemon-rind.

Season with salt and pepper, and add the beaten eggs and milk.

Place the mixture in a greased cake-tin and twist greased paper over the top.

Steam for one hour, turn out carefully, and strain melted butter or anchovy sauce over the pudding.

Sufficient for three persons.

MELTED BUTTER SAUCE

INGREDIENTS.—1½ oz. of butter, 1½ oz. of flour, ½ pint of fish stock (see p. 12), 1 gill of milk, salt and pepper.

METHOD.—Melt the butter, take the pan off the fire, add the flour, and mix with a wooden spoon.

Stir in the fish stock and milk by degrees.

Place the pan on the fire and stir the sauce till it boils. Boil for five minutes and season to taste.

TO MAKE ANCHOVY SAUCE.—Add one teaspoonful of anchovy essence to the melted butter sauce. One gill of sauce is enough for three persons.

RECHAUFFE OF FISH

INGREDIENTS.—½ lb. of cold boiled or steamed white fish, 2 oz. of breadcrumbs, 1½ gills of milk, about 3 teaspoonfuls of anchovy paste, seasoning, 2 yolks and 3 whites of eggs.

METHOD.—Remove the bones and skin from the fish, then flake up the flesh and weigh it.

Heat the milk and add it to the breadcrumbs. Let them soak for a minute or two, then add them to the fish. Mix in the anchovy paste with seasoning to taste.

Beat up the egg yolks and stir them in, whisk the whites to a very stiff froth and fold them in lightly. Turn the mixture into a buttered dish, and put it into a fairly hot oven. It will take about half an hour to cook. Serve with anchovy sauce (see p. 42), parsley sauce (see p. 41), or egg sauce (see p. 41).

Sufficient for four or five persons.

COLD FISH SALAD

INGREDIENTS.—Cold boiled fish, 2 small round lettuce, 1 egg, 2 tomatoes, mustard and cress, mayonnaise or other salad cream.

METHOD.—Thoroughly wash and pick over the lettuce and cress, and leave soaking for an hour or so in cold water.

When quite clean leave it to drain and dry in a cloth.

Boil the egg for fifteen minutes until hard, then crack the shell and put it into cold water.

Take the remains of any cold, boiled white fish, remove the skin and bones, and flake the flesh into very small pieces. Season this to taste, and mix sufficient salad cream with it to moisten it well.

Break up some of the lettuce leaves and arrange the fish, piled up, on a bed of lettuce. Arrange a border of lettuce leaves round, with a few small bunches of mustard and cress. Garnish with alternate slices of hard-boiled egg and tomatoes.

FISH SANDWICH

INGREDIENTS.—6 thin slices of hake, ¼ lb. of onions (when minced), 1½ oz. of butter or margarine, 3 level dessert-spoonfuls of chopped capers, 3 oz. of breadcrumbs, salt and pepper, 1 egg, stuffed olives.

METHOD.—Peel the onions and chop them very finely. Fry them lightly in the butter, but do not brown them.

Make the breadcrumbs, mix them with the capers, add the onions and seasoning to taste, then bind all with the egg.

Wash the hake and dry it in a cloth. Place the stuffing on three of the slices and cover each with a remaining slice. Put them into a buttered dish, cover them with a buttered paper, and bake them in a moderately hot oven until the flesh is quite white and a milky liquid runs from it. The time required will be about twenty minutes.

Serve the fish garnished with slices of stuffed olives and accompanied with tartar sauce (see p. 43) or other suitable sauce.

Sufficient for three sandwiches.

FISH SAUCES

PLAIN WHITE SAUCE

INGREDIENTS.—1 oz. of flour, 1 oz. of butter or margarine, 2 gills of milk, or milk and water, or stock (see below), and milk, pepper and salt.

There are two simple methods of making a plain sauce.

METHOD 1.—Melt the fat in a saucepan. Add the flour, and mix together until smooth. Add the liquid (cold) and stir until the sauce boils. Season to taste. Simmer for six minutes.

NOTE.—If a thinner sauce is required, use ½ oz. or ¾ oz. of fat, and ½ oz. or ¾ oz. of flour to the same amount of liquid.

METHOD 2.—Mix the flour to a smooth paste with a small quantity of the liquid. Put the remainder into a saucepan with the butter and heat it.

When hot, stir it on to the mixed flour.

Return to the saucepan and bring to the boil, keeping it stirred all the time.

Season to taste. Simmer for about six minutes.

TO MAKE FISH STOCK

THIS can be made from fish bones. Put them into a saucepan, cover with cold water, add a little salt. Bring to the boil, skim it, let it simmer for about half an hour, and then strain it.

If liked, other flavouring can be added, such as onion, mace, cloves, etc. This stock makes the foundation for many excellent soups.

PARSLEY SAUCE

MAKE a white sauce as before explained. Wash, scald, and finely chop some parsley, and add to the sauce just before serving.

Use about 1 tablespoonful of chopped parsley to ½ pint of sauce.

EGG SAUCE

MAKE a white sauce as before explained.

Allow about 2 eggs to ¾ to 1 pint of sauce.

Boil them for fifteen minutes until hard.

Remove the shells, cut the eggs in halves, and take out the yolks.

Chop the whites into rough pieces and add to the sauce just before serving. Pour the sauce over the fish. Rub the yolks through a sieve to a powder and sprinkle over the top.

CHEESE SAUCE

MAKE some white sauce, and stir in grated cheese after the sauce comes to the boil.

Use about 3 or 4 oz. of cheese to ½ pint of sauce.

ANCHOVY SAUCE

MAKE some white sauce and stir in anchovy essence after the sauce comes to the boil.

Do not add any salt, as the anchovy essence is rather salt.

Use about 1 small teaspoonful to ½ pint of sauce.

SHRIMP SAUCE

INGREDIENTS.—2 gills of thick white sauce (see above), 1½ gills of shrimps, a few drops of anchovy essence, pepper.

METHOD.—Make the sauce as explained in the recipe for Plain White Sauce.

Shell the shrimps and add to the sauce.

Season with pepper and add the anchovy essence—just sufficient to flavour.

Stir all together and cook slowly for a few minutes until the shrimps are hot.

BECHAMEL SAUCE

INGREDIENTS.—½ pint of milk, 1 tablespoonful of cream, 1 oz. of butter, 1 oz. of flour, 1 shallot, 1 bayleaf, 4 peppercorns, ¾ gill of stock (see p. 12).

METHOD.—Slice the onion and cook it gently in the milk and stock, with the peppercorns and bayleaf, for fifteen minutes. Strain into a basin. Melt the butter, add the flour and mix smoothly. Add the strained liquid and stir the sauce till it boils.

Boil for five minutes, season to taste, and add the cream.

DUTCH SAUCE

INGREDIENTS.—1 onion, ¾ pint of fish stock (see p. 12), 1 bunch of herbs, 1 oz. of butter, 1 oz. of flour, 3 pepper-corns, 1 egg, juice and rind of ½ lemon, 2 anchovies.

METHOD.—Chop the onion and anchovies and put them in the stock with the herbs and peppercorns and thinly cut lemon-rind. Boil till reduced to half a pint.

Melt the butter, add the flour, and mix well. Strain on the stock, and stir the sauce till it boils.

Boil for three minutes and allow it to cool slightly.

Season to taste, add the lemon-juice and pour on to a well-beaten egg.

Stir round, strain and serve at once. This sauce is served with boiled fish.

HOLLANDAISE SAUCE

INGREDIENTS.—1½ oz. of butter, ½ oz. of flour, 1½ gills of milk, 2 yolks of eggs, 3 teaspoonfuls of lemon-juice.

METHOD.—Melt the butter in a saucepan, mix in the flour until quite smooth.

Add the milk gradually, and stir until the sauce comes to the boil.

Cook slowly for about six minutes, then draw it off the fire and cool slightly.

Whisk each yolk into the sauce separately, and cook slowly for a few minutes, but do not boil it, or the eggs will curdle.

Add the seasoning and stir in the lemon-juice and the sauce is ready.

NOTE.—The sauce should be quite thick and smooth when finished.

After the yolks are added to the sauce it is advisable to finish cooking it in a double saucepan or in a jug in a saucepan of water.

MAYONNAISE SAUCE

INGREDIENTS.—1 egg yolk, ¾ to 1 gill of salad oil, 2 teaspoonfuls of white vinegar, 1 teaspoonful of malt vinegar, pepper and salt, mixed mustard.

METHOD.—Mix the yolk of egg in a small basin with a wooden spoon. Stir in the oil gradually, drop by drop. Season with pepper and salt and mixed mustard.

Stir in the vinegar last, adding it very gradually.

This sauce should be like thick cream when finished. If too thick add more vinegar; if too thin add more oil.

TARTAR SAUCE

MAKE tartar sauce in the same way as Mayonnaise Sauce, with the addition of a few capers cut into small pieces.

HOT TOMATO SAUCE

INGREDIENTS.—½ lb. of tomatoes, ¼ gill of stock (see p. 12), ½ onion, ¼ carrot, small piece of celery, small sprig of parsley and thyme, 1 oz. of bacon, salt, pepper, and celery salt, cornflour.

METHOD.—Cut up the bacon and put it into a saucepan with the tomatoes (sliced), the onion (peeled and sliced thinly), and the carrot and celery (cleaned and prepared, but not cut up).

Cook gently for a few minutes without browning. Then draw aside, add the stock, and bring to the boil. Simmer gently until the onion and tomatoes are tender, adding a small sprig of parsley and thyme to flavour, but do not leave these in too long.

When ready, remove the carrot, rub the sauce through a sieve, then return to the pan and thicken with cornflour, mixed to a smooth paste with water.

Boil for a few minutes and season to taste. The celery may be rubbed through the sieve, if tender.

MUSTARD SAUCE

INGREDIENTS.—1 oz. of butter, 1 oz. of flour, 1 tablespoonful of vinegar, 1 gill of fish stock (see p. 12), 1 gill of milk, 2 teaspoonfuls of mustard, salt and pepper to taste.

METHOD.—Melt the butter and add the flour and mustard.

Mix well and add the milk and stock gradually.

Stir till it boils, and season to taste. Boil for three minutes and add the vinegar and season.

This sauce is good served with baked or boiled herrings.

FISH SOUFFLE

INGREDIENTS.—10 oz. of halibut, 2 oz. of flour, 1½ oz. of butter, ¼ pint of fish stock (see p. 12) or milk, 3 yolks of eggs, 4 whites of eggs, pepper and salt.

METHOD.—Remove all bones from the fish and chop it very finely; if liked, put through a mincer.

Melt the butter in a saucepan, add the flour, and mix it thoroughly with the butter.

Add the milk or fish stock, and stir well. Bring to the boil, and boil for a few minutes until it will not adhere to the sides of the saucepan, keeping it stirred all the time.

Remove from the fire and mix this thoroughly with the chopped fish.

Separate the yolks from the whites of eggs and beat each yolk one by one into the fish. Rub all this mixture through a wire sieve, season well with pepper and salt.

Well grease a round soufflé tin and tie a double piece of greased paper round the outside of the tin, so that it reaches about two inches above the top of it.

Add a pinch of salt to the whites of eggs, and whisk them to a stiff froth.

Lightly fold them into the other ingredients, pour all into the prepared soufflé tin, and steam for one hour and a half.

Turn very carefully on to a hot dish and pour thick white sauce over, which should be sufficiently thick to coat the soufflé.

NOTE.—When steaming the soufflé, stand it on a pastry-cutter or a thick fold of paper in a saucepan of boiling water, the latter not reaching more than one-third up the side of the tin.

FISH STEW

INGREDIENTS.—1 lb. of skate, 1 small fresh haddock, 6d. of picked shrimps, 1½ oz. of butter, 1½ oz. of flour, 1 tablespoonful of mushroom ketchup, salt and cayenne, ½ pint of good stock, (see p. 12), 1 gill of milk, juice and grated rind of ½ lemon.

METHOD.—When buying the haddock, have it filleted.

Wash the fish and cut it into squares.

Fry the haddock in the butter for three minutes. Put the skate into enough cold, salted water to cover it and bring it to the boil. Melt the butter in a frying-pan and add the flour, ketchup, lemon-juice and rind. Add the stock gradually and stir till it boils. Add the milk. Put in the fish and stew slowly for about ten minutes, or till it is tender.

Wash the shrimps, as they are generally salted to keep them.

Put the pieces of fish on a hot dish and keep hot in the oven.

Heat the shrimps in the sauce for three minutes.

Strain the sauce over the fish and arrange the shrimps round as a border.

Sufficient for four or five persons.

BAKED GURNARD

INGREDIENTS.—1 good-sized gurnard.

FOR THE STUFFING.—1 cupful of breadcrumbs, ½ an onion, 1 rasher of bacon, 1 dessertspoonful of chopped parsley, ½ teaspoonful of mixed herbs, grated rind of a lemon, 1 dessertspoonful of Worcester sauce, 1 egg, salt and pepper.

FOR THE STOCK AND SAUCE.—½ pint of cold water, 1 dessertspoonful of Worcester sauce, ½ an onion, a bunch of herbs, 1 oz. of butter, 1 teaspoonful of Bisto.

METHOD.—Wash the gurnard, cut off the fins, and remove the eyes. As the skin is tough, slit it along the back.

To make the stuffing, chop the onion and the bacon and parsley, and add them to the other stuffing ingredients. Bind with a beaten egg and Worcester sauce.

Put this into the body of the fish and sew it up with a needle and thread. Truss the fish into the shape of half a circle by putting the thread through the eyes and tail and tying into place.

Put the fish in a baking-tin with the cold water, Worcester sauce, and bunch of herbs.

Chop the onion, sprinkle it over the fish, and put the butter in small pieces on top.

Cover with a greased paper and bake for about twenty minutes.

While it is cooking baste it three times with the fluid in the tin, replacing the greased paper afterwards.

Dish up the fish and keep it hot.

The liquid in the pan will make a delicious sauce. To thicken, use a teaspoonful of Bisto mixed smoothly with a very little cold water. Pour into the tin, stir till it boils. Then boil for two minutes and pour round the fish.

Garnish with parsley.

Sufficient for two or three persons, according to size of fish.

Allow half a pound for each person.

HADDOCK A LA PORTUGAISE

INGREDIENTS.—1 smoked haddock, 1 lb. of tomatoes, 1 lb. of Spanish onions, 2 tablespoonfuls of salad oil, 1 tablespoonful of vinegar, ½ pint of stock (see p. 12), 1 dessertspoonful of chopped parsley, salt and pepper.

METHOD.—Slice the onions thinly and boil them for ten minutes. Cut the tomatoes in half. Place the fish in a piedish with the oil and vinegar, and sprinkle with salt and pepper. Put in the onions and tomatoes and sprinkle with parsley. Add the stock and cover with a well-greased paper. Bake in a fairly hot oven for about forty-five minutes.

NOTE.—If oil is disliked one ounce of butter can be used instead.

Sufficient for four or five persons.

HADDOCK AND TOMATOES

INGREDIENTS. — 1 dried haddock (about 1 lb.), 3 tomatoes, 1½ oz. of butter, 1 very small onion, 1 teaspoonful of chopped parsley, pepper, 3 oz. of rice.

METHOD.—Wash and wipe the haddock. Put it into a frying-pan with a little water, and cook gently until the flesh will move easily from the bone.

When cooked, take it up, remove all the bones and skin, and flake the flesh into very small pieces.

Peel and finely chop or grate the onion.

Melt the butter and cook the onion in it, but only slightly brown it.

Skin the tomatoes, cut them into slices, then into small pieces.

When the onion is almost cooked add the tomatoes, and cook gently together until quite soft.

Add the fish and season it all to taste.

Stir round until thoroughly hot.

Wash, scald, and chop the parsley finely.

Heap the haddock and tomatoes on a hot dish, garnish with lines of chopped parsley, and serve a border of boiled rice round.

Sufficient for about three persons.

CHEESE HADDOCK

INGREDIENTS.—1 fresh haddock, 2 oz. of cheese, 1½ oz. of breadcrumbs, ½ tablespoonful of lemon-juice, salt and pepper, ½ dessertspoonful of tomato ketchup, 1 egg, 1 or 2 mushrooms, brown breadcrumbs, milk, a little dripping.

METHOD.—Have the haddock cleaned and the eyes removed. Cut off the fins and trim the tail. Prepare, clean, and chop the mushrooms. Grate the cheese finely and mix it with the breadcrumbs.

Season to taste and add the lemon-juice, mushroom, and tomato ketchup.

Beat up the egg and bind the ingredients with it, leaving out just a little egg for coating the fish. Add some milk if required.

Stuff the fish and truss it into a round shape. Coat it with egg and brown breadcrumbs, stand it in a baking-tin with a little dripping and bake for about half an hour, or longer, if required.

Pour round or serve separately any suitable sauce—cheese sauce, egg sauce, or parsley sauce (see pp. 41 to 43). Some finely chopped watercress added to a white sauce makes a very good sauce.

Sufficient for three or four persons.

HADDOCK AND EGG SCALLOPS

INGREDIENTS.—¾ lb. of haddock (when cooked and prepared), 6 eggs, 1 oz. of margarine, ¾ oz. of flour, seasoning, ½ pint of milk.

METHOD.—Take a dried haddock and cook it in the oven in a little milk, until the flesh moves easily from the bones. Remove the bones and skin and flake up the flesh and weigh it.

Melt the fat, add the flour, and when well blended stir in the milk and bring it to the boil, using the milk from the haddock to make up the quantity. Let the sauce simmer gently for a few minutes, then add the haddock, make it thoroughly hot, and season it to taste.

Turn the fish into six buttered scallop dishes and serve them with a poached egg on each.

Sufficient for six persons.

DRIED HADDOCK IN MILK

INGREDIENTS.—1 dried haddock (medium size), pepper, 1 gill of milk, 2 oz. of butter or margarine.

METHOD.—Wash and wipe the haddock and trim it.

Put it into a pie-dish with the milk and butter.

Season with pepper.

Cover with a plate or greased paper.

Put it into a moderately hot oven and cook for about fifteen to twenty minutes or until the flesh will move easily from the bone. Lift on to a hot dish and pour the milk and butter round.

NOTE.—The haddock will be cooked almost as soon as the milk boils.

Pale-coloured haddocks are better than dark ones, as they are not so salt. If salt is disliked, cook the haddock in water only for five minutes, then throw away the water and cook in milk as just described.

BAKED FINNAN HADDOCK AND EGG SAUCE

INGREDIENTS.—2 small Finnan haddocks, 2 oz. of butter, pepper, ½ pint of milk, 1 egg, 2½ teaspoonfuls of flour, cold milk or water.

METHOD.—Wash and dry the haddocks, split each in half, lengthwise, and remove the fins. Place the fish in a buttered pie-dish, sprinkle them with pepper and add the milk and butter. Cover the dish, put it in the oven and bake the fish until tender and the flesh moves easily from the bone. They will take about fifteen minutes, and will be cooked almost as soon as the milk boils.

When ready, drain off the milk and turn it into a saucepan, then stir in the flour mixed to a smooth paste with a little cold milk or water. Boil this sauce for a few minutes, season it to taste, add the chopped white of a hard-boiled egg and, when hot, turn it into a sauce boat. Rub the yolk of egg through a strainer and sprinkle it on top of the sauce and serve it with the haddocks, arranged on a hot dish.

Sufficient for two or four persons.

FRESH HADDOCK A L'HORLY

INGREDIENTS.—1 fresh haddock, 3 oz. of flour, 1 egg, 4 dessertspoonfuls of salad oil, 1 dessertspoonful of tarragon vinegar, 1 dessertspoonful of malt vinegar, 1 teaspoonful of chopped onion, ½ teaspoonful of chopped parsley, 2 or 3 tablespoonfuls of warm milk and water, seasoning.

METHOD.—Fillet the haddock, wash and skin the fillets and roll them in a cloth.

To MAKE THE BATTER.—Separate the yolk from the white of egg, sieve the flour, make a hole in the centre, and put in half of the oil and the yolk of egg. Mix in some of the flour, then gradually add the warm milk and water, and work in the remainder of the flour, keeping it very smooth all the time. When well mixed beat for a few minutes and set the batter aside for about an hour. Mix together on a plate the remainder of the salad oil, the vinegar, chopped parsley, and onion and seasoning. Cut the fillets into halves and soak them in this mixture for about ten to fifteen minutes. Whisk the white to a very stiff froth and fold it into the batter lightly. Put fillets in batter, coat evenly, then place in a deep pan of hot fat and fry until golden brown.

FRIED FRESH HADDOCK

COATED WITH CHEESE BATTER

INGREDIENTS.—2 lb. of fresh haddock (1 large or 2 small), 3 oz. of flour, 1 gill of water, salt and pepper, 2 oz. of cheese, 1 egg white, deep fat for frying.

METHOD.—Have the haddock cleaned, the heads removed, and the fish cut in slices cross-wise.

Sieve the flour and mix it to a smooth batter with the water. Leave it to stand for an hour or so.

When ready to fry the fish, stir the cheese, grated finely, into the batter. Season it well, and fold in the stiffly whisked egg white.

Coat some of the fish with the cheese batter. Put it into a deep pan of hot fat and fry it until golden brown.

Drain, and fry the remainder of the fish in the same way.

Serve on a dish paper and garnish with parsley.

Sufficient for four persons.

SAVOURY BAKED HADDOCK

INGREDIENTS.—1 large fresh haddock.

FOR THE STUFFING.—½ pint of breadcrumbs, 4 spring onions, ½ teaspoonful of dried herbs and grated lemon rind, 1 tablespoonful of chopped parsley, salt and pepper, 1 rasher of fat bacon, 1 egg.

FOR THE SAUCE.—¾ oz. of butter, 2 teaspoonfuls of Bisto, ½ pint of water, 1 dessertspoonful of mushroom ketchup, 6 oysters, dripping for cooking.

METHOD.—Clean the haddock, remove the eyes, and cut off the fins with a pair of scissors.

Chop the bacon and fry it for two minutes.

Chop the onions and parsley, add them to the dry ingredients for the stuffing and bind with the egg.

Lay the haddock on its back, make the stuffing into a roll and press it into the cavity made by the fishmonger when removing the inside.

Pull the two side flaps of skin over the stuffing and sew it up with a darning needle and thread. Do not make a knot, but leave the ends free so that the thread can be pulled out when the fish is dished up.

To truss the fish pass the needle and thread through the tail and tie, next pass it through the middle of the body, and last through the eyes. Pull fairly tight till the fish is in the shape of the letter S, then tie the thread under the jaw.

Put the fish in a baking-tin, putting some small pieces of dripping on the fish.

Put in a fairly hot oven.

In ten minutes pour off the dripping and put in the water and ketchup.

Baste the fish frequently till it is done (about twenty minutes).

Good juicy oysters always have a little of their own liquor in which they lie.

This should be kept and put in the sauce, as it gives it a delicious flavour.

The fishmonger will remove the beards from the oysters.

When the fish is done the flesh is

soft enough for a skewer to be pushed into it easily.

Put the fish on a hot dish in the oven, also the oysters, which should lie in the deeper of their two shells with the flat shell on top to protect them from the heat of the oven.

To make the sauce mix the Bisto with a little cold water and pour on to it the water in the tin.

Melt the butter, pour on the water and Bisto and stir till it boils. If it is too thick through the water having boiled away, thin it a little with more water.

To serve, pour the gravy round the haddock and garnish with the oysters that have just been warmed but not cooked. Remove the flat top shells.

Allow half a pound of fish for each person.

SPAGHETTI HADDOCK

INGREDIENTS.—¾ lb. of cold, dried haddock, 3 oz. of spaghetti, 1 egg (hard-boiled), 2 oz. of butter, pepper, 1 cucumber, salad cream.

METHOD.—Remove the bones and skin from the fish, flake up the flesh and weigh it ; there should be three-quarters of a pound without the bone.

Break up and wash the spaghetti and cook it in a saucepan of boiling water to which a little salt has been added. When tender, strain it, then run cold water through it and drain well.

Melt the butter and mix it with the fish. Add the spaghetti, also the egg (chopped) and three parts of the cucumber peeled and cut in dice. Season to taste, moisten with salad cream and heap in a dish. Serve cold, garnished with the remainder of the cucumber.

Sufficient for four or five persons.

NOTE.—One or two tomatoes cut in dice may be added, if liked. These should be peeled. If dropped into boiling water for a minute the peel can easily be removed.

BOILED HAKE

WITH EGG SAUCE AND GREEN PEAS

INGREDIENTS.—1½ lb. of hake, warm water, salt and vinegar, 1½ pints of green peas (when shelled).

METHOD.—Wash and dry the hake and tie it into shape if necessary. Put it into a fish-kettle or tie it in muslin and put it in a saucepan, with warm water only just to cover, and salt added (1 small dessertspoonful to a quart of water), also a little vinegar.

Bring the water barely to boiling point, and let the fish simmer very gently until the flesh moves easily from the bones. It will take about fifteen to twenty minutes to cook according to the thickness of the fish.

When cooked, lift the fish out and drain it well. Remove the string if it was tied up, and serve it coated with egg sauce.

Serve a few boiled green peas at either end of the dish and the remainder separately. Fresh, bottled, or dried peas can be used. The dried ones need to be well soaked and well boiled.

Sufficient for four persons.

THE EGG SAUCE

INGREDIENTS.—1 oz. of margarine, 1 oz. of flour, ½ pint of milk, salt and pepper, 1 egg.

METHOD.—Melt the fat in a saucepan. Add the flour and mix them together till they are smooth. Add the liquid (cold) and stir until the sauce boils. Season it to taste, and simmer the sauce for six minutes.

Boil the egg for fifteen minutes until it is hard. Remove the shell, cut the egg in half, and take out the yolk.

Chop the white into rough pieces and add them to the sauce just before serving. Pour the sauce over the fish. Rub the yolk through a sieve to powder it and sprinkle it over the top.

HAKE CUTLETS

INGREDIENTS.—½ lb. of hake (cooked), ¾ oz. of flour, ¾ oz. of butter, ¾ gill of milk, pepper, 1 egg, bread-crumbs, fat for frying, spaghetti, anchovy essence.

METHOD.—Take all the bones from the fish, then flake it into very small pieces.

Melt the butter in a saucepan, add the flour, and mix well with it.

Add the milk, and stir over the fire until it boils, then boil for a few minutes until it leaves the sides of the saucepan.

Add to it the prepared fish, and season well with pepper and anchovy essence (about one teaspoonful). Put on to a plate until cold.

Divide evenly into about six portions, and shape into triangular pieces.

Beat up the egg and brush the cutlets with it, then coat with breadcrumbs.

Put a deep pan of fat on to heat.

Place the prepared cutlets into a frying basket, and when the fat smokes slightly place the basket in it, and fry the cutlets until they are golden brown. Drain well on paper.

Wash a few pieces of spaghetti, and break into six pieces about one inch in length. Stick a piece into the end of each cutlet.

Dish on a paper, arranging the cutlets in a circle with each one overlapping the previous one.

BAKED HAKE STEAKS

INGREDIENTS.—2 slices of hake, 2 thin rashers of bacon, a few breadcrumbs, salt and pepper, margarine.

METHOD.—Wash the slices of hake and dry them in a cloth.

Melt a small lump of margarine, brush the steaks over with it, season them, and coat them with breadcrumbs—either white or light brown crumbs can be used.

Put the fish into a buttered pie-dish or a fireproof dish with a roll of bacon on the top of each. Before rolling the bacon, remove the rind.

Put the dish into a moderately hot oven and bake the fish for about fifteen or twenty minutes, or until the flesh moves easily from the bone. If the bacon is cooked before the fish is ready, take it off and keep it warm.

If cooked in a fireproof dish, serve the fish in the dish, but if in a pie-dish, lift the hake on to another dish and pour the bacon fat round it.

NOTE.—Cod steaks may be cooked in the same way. Allow one steak for each person.

HAKE AND FRIED CUCUMBER

INGREDIENTS.—2 slices of hake, 1 cucumber, flour, 1 oz. of butter, juice of ½ lemon, 1 egg, breadcrumbs, deep frying fat.

FOR THE SAUCE.—½ gill of milk, 1 oz. of flour, 6d. of picked shrimps (may be omitted).

METHOD.—Peel the cucumber, cut it into pieces an inch and a half long, and roll them in flour. Brush them with a well-beaten egg and roll in breadcrumbs.

Heat the frying fat.

Wash the fish and place it in a steamer with a piece of butter on each piece. Steam till soft and white (about ten minutes). Keep the fish hot.

To MAKE THE SAUCE.—Mix the flour in a cup with the cold milk and pour on the liquid from the fish. If the cup is not full fill it up with water.

Put it in a saucepan and stir till it boils, season to taste and add the shrimps. Simmer gently while frying the cucumber.

When the fat smokes, put in two pieces of cucumber and fry a golden brown (about three minutes). Drain on paper. Re-heat the fat and fry the next batch.

Serve with a heap of cucumber in the middle of the dish and the hake each side. Pour the sauce round.

Sufficient for from two to four persons.

HAKE AU FROMAGE

INGREDIENTS.—2 slices of hake, each weighing ⅓ lb., 1 oz. of cheddar cheese, ½ oz. of Parmesan cheese, 1 oz. of butter, salt and pepper, squeeze of lemon-juice.

METHOD.—Wash and dry the slices of hake, season them with salt and pepper, and place them in a buttered dish.

Sprinkle them with lemon-juice, and add half the butter, cut in small dabs.

Grate the cheeses finely and mix them together, season them with cayenne and place half on each slice, then add the remainder of the butter.

Put the fish into a moderately hot oven and cook it till tender, then place it under the hot grill and brown the top.

Lift the fish on to a dish and serve it garnished with parsley.

Sufficient for two persons.

FRIED HAKE OR COD STEAK

INGREDIENTS.—Slices of hake or cod, flour, pepper and salt, fat for frying, parsley.

METHOD.—The slices should be cut at least half an inch thick.

Wash them, fold them in a dry cloth, and leave until dry.

Mix some flour, with pepper and salt to flavour it.

Put some dripping in a frying-pan to melt.

Coat the slices with the seasoned flour, then shake off the loose flour.

When a faint blue smoke rises from the fat, put in the floured slices and fry until golden-brown on one side, then turn them over and brown the other side.

Drain on paper.

Serve on a dish paper, garnish with parsley, and, if liked, serve separately some plain white sauce (see p. 41) or anchovy sauce (see p. 42).

Allow one slice for each person.

STUFFED HAKE

INGREDIENTS.—2 lb. of hake, 1 oz. of butter or margarine, 2 level dessert-spoonfuls of chopped parsley, 1 level eggspoonful of mixed herbs, grated rind of ¼ lemon, 1 egg, seasoning, few light brown breadcrumbs, dripping, 4 or 5 thin rashers of bacon, 2 oz. of breadcrumbs.

METHOD.—TO MAKE THE STUFFING. —Make the breadcrumbs and mix them with the herbs and chopped parsley. Add the finely grated rind of one-fourth of a lemon, and seasoning to taste. Stir in the butter (melted) and add about three-fourths of the egg (beaten). Rinse and dry the hake and cut off the fins, then put in the stuffing, fastening it in with skew skewers.

Brush the outside skin with the remainder of the egg, and coat it with light brown breadcrumbs. Put the fish into a baking tin with dripping and bake it till tender, keeping it basted. It will take about half an hour to cook. When cooked, serve the fish garnished with bacon rolls and accompanied by any suitable sauce (see pp. 41 to 43).

TO PREPARE THE BACON ROLLS.— Remove the rind and cut the rashers in halves. Roll up each piece and stick them on a skewer. Cook the rolls in the oven for a few minutes until the fat is semi-transparent.

SAVOURY FRIED HAKE

INGREDIENTS.—3 slices of Devonshire hake, 3 level tablespoonfuls of finely grated Parmesan cheese, 3 level tablespoonfuls of finely-grated Cheddar cheese, 4 level tablespoonfuls of breadcrumbs, about 2 oz. of dripping, seasoning, ½ oz. of margarine, 1½ level dessertspoonfuls of flour, 1¼ gills of milk, half an egg, lemon.

METHOD.—Mix the two kinds of grated cheese together. Take half of it and mix it with the breadcrumbs, and add seasoning to taste.

Wash and dry the hake, brush each piece with egg and coat it with the prepared cheese and breadcrumbs. Fry it in the hot fat, turning it over when brown.

Drain the hake on paper, and serve it garnished with lemon and accompanied with the following sauce.

TO MAKE THE SAUCE.—Melt the margarine in a saucepan, add the flour, and when it is blended, stir in the milk and bring it to the boil. Boil it gently for a few minutes, add the seasoning, and stir in the remainder of the grated cheese. When this is melted, turn the sauce into a sauce boat.

Sufficient for three persons.

HALIBUT AND CHEESE SAUCE

INGREDIENTS.—1¼ lb. of halibut, small piece of butter, lemon, salt and pepper, few stuffed olives.

FOR THE SAUCE.—2 or 3 oz. of cheese, 1 yolk of egg, 1½ gills of milk, ¾ oz. of butter or margarine, ½ oz. of flour.

METHOD.—Have the halibut cut into three pieces. Wash and dry them and put them into a buttered dish. Season them with pepper and salt, add a squeeze of lemon-juice and a few dabs of butter, cover them with a buttered paper and bake them gently until the flesh moves easily from the bone. Arrange them on a dish and garnish them with slices of stuffed olives and lemon, and serve with the cheese sauce.

To Make the Sauce.—Melt the butter or margarine in a saucepan, add the flour, and when well blended, stir in the milk and bring the sauce to the boil, add also the liquor from the fish. Simmer the sauce gently for a few minutes, draw the pan aside, add the cheese finely grated, seasoning to taste, and the egg yolk, and when the cheese is melted, pour the sauce into a tureen.

Sufficient for three persons.

Note.—Cook the sauce for a few minutes after adding the egg, but do not let it boil.

HALIBUT AND TOMATOES

Ingredients.—1 lb. of sliced halibut, 1½ lb. of tomatoes, 1 oz. of butter, salt and pepper, ½ gill of water, ¾ oz. of flour, ½ gill of milk, 1 dessertspoonful of mushroom ketchup.

Method.—Cut the tomatoes in half and put a layer of them in a buttered fireproof dish. Wash the halibut and dry it on a cloth.

Mix the flour with half a teaspoonful of salt and a little pepper.

Dip the halibut in the seasoned flour and lay it on the tomatoes.

Put bits of butter on top. Pour the water into the dish and lay the rest of the tomatoes on top of the dish.

Cover well with greased paper, and bake in a moderate oven for about twenty-five minutes.

Mix the rest of the flour in a saucepan smoothly with the milk, and stir in the liquid from the dish. Stir the sauce till it boils ; add the ketchup ; season to taste and strain into a sauce-boat.

Serve the fish in the same fireproof dish surrounded with tomatoes.

Sufficient for three persons.

Note.—Turbot or cod can be cooked in the same way.

HALIBUT BALLS

Ingredients.—1 lb. of halibut, salt and cayenne, 1 oz. of butter, flour, 1 egg (hard-boiled), deep fat for frying, 1½ oz. of flour, parsley, 1 gill of milk and water.

Method.—Wash and clean the halibut, and boil gently until quite tender.

Remove the bones and skin, and flake the flesh into tiny pieces (*there should be about half a pound of flaked fish*). Chop the egg up finely and mix with the fish.

Melt the butter in a saucepan, and stir in the flour until quite smooth.

Add the milk and water, stir until the sauce has come to the boil, and boil for a few minutes. When ready, it will easily leave the sides of the saucepan. Stir in the prepared fish and egg and season well to taste.

Leave this mixture to get quite cold and firm. Make a smooth flour-and-water paste about the consistency of a rather thick batter. Put a deep pan of fat on to get hot. Divide the prepared mixture into portions and make each into a ball-shape. Put some of them into the flour-and-water paste and coat them all over. When the fat in the pan begins to smoke, lift them carefully into it and fry until golden brown. Drain on paper, and coat and fry the others in the same way.

Sufficient for four persons.

HALIBUT CUTLETS

Ingredients.—½ lb. of cooked halibut, ½ lb. of cooked potatoes, seasoning, tomato ketchup, 1 egg, breadcrumbs, deep fat.

Method.—Remove the bones and skin from the cooked halibut and flake up the flesh. There should be half a pound of fish when prepared.

Mash up the potatoes, adding a little butter and milk, stir in the prepared fish, moisten the mixture and flavour it with tomato ketchup, and season to taste. (If you have any left-over parsley or egg sauce (see p. 41), it may be added to it, provided the mixture is not too moist.) Turn it on to a plate, spread it evenly and leave it till it is ready to fry.

Divide the paste into six or eight portions and form each one into cutlet shape. Brush it with egg and coat it with breadcrumbs, and fry the cutlets in hot, deep fat (in a frying basket) till they are golden. Drain them and serve them with a small piece of spaghetti in the end of each cutlet, and garnish them with lemon.

Sufficient for eight cutlets.

STEAMED HALIBUT

INGREDIENTS.—1 slice of halibut, ½ oz. of butter, juice of ½ a lemon, salt and pepper, lemon for garnish.

METHOD.—Wash the fish, lay it on a greased plate and sprinkle it with salt and pepper and lemon juice.

Put the butter on the top, and cover the fish with another plate.

Place these over a saucepan of boiling water for ten minutes, turning the fish over after five minutes.

Serve on a hot dish and garnish with lemon.

To Cut Lemon Butterflies for Garnishing.—Cut three rounds of lemon in half. Cut through the rind only of each half.

Separate the two quarters till they are opposite each other.

Sufficient for one or two persons.

BAKED HERRINGS

INGREDIENTS.—6 fresh herrings, vinegar, 1 or 2 bay leaves, a few peppercorns, few allspice, salt.

METHOD.—Cut the heads off the herrings, and at the same time pull out the gut. Scrape off the scales. Wash the herrings thoroughly and dry them on a cloth.

Place them in a pie-dish—three one way and three the other—so that they fit in well. Sprinkle with a little salt, add the bay leaves, peppercorns, allspice, and sufficient vinegar to cover.

Put a plate or baking-sheet over the pie-dish, and bake *slowly* for about one and a half to two hours.

Leave until cold, then lift the herrings on to a clean dish, and pour over the vinegar and garnish to suit taste.

Remove the bay leaves.

Allow one to two for each person, according to the size of the herrings.

CASSEROLE OF HERRINGS

INGREDIENTS.—6 herrings (fresh), 2 oz. of butter, pepper and salt, lemon juice.

METHOD.—Have the herrings cleaned and the heads removed. Split them open and remove also the backbone.

Scrape off the scales and rinse the fish, then put them into a casserole, adding the butter cut into small pieces, a little lemon-juice, and pepper and salt.

Put them into a moderate oven and cook them gently for about half an hour. Serve in the casserole.

Sufficient for from three to six persons.

GRILLED HERRINGS

INGREDIENTS.—Fresh herrings.

METHOD.—Cut off the heads and at the same time remove the gut.

Scrape off the scales, thoroughly wash the herrings, and dry them in a cloth.

Heat and slightly grease the bars of a gridiron.

Put the herrings on the gridiron and grill them in front of a clear fire, keeping them turned as required.

They will take about ten to fifteen minutes. Serve on a hot dish.

NOTE.—If preferred, they may be fried in a very small quantity of fat.

Bloaters and kippers may be fried or grilled in a similar way. These do not require washing, but should only be wiped. Cut the heads off the bloaters and remove the gut.

HERRINGS IN ORANGE JUICE

INGREDIENTS.—2 herrings, 2 oranges, salt and pepper.

METHOD.—Wash the herrings, scrape them from tail to head to remove the scales. Cut off the fins.

Split the fish open and take out the bones. Season them with salt and pepper and roll them up skin side outwards.

Place the rolls in a pie-dish and squeeze the orange-juice over them. Cover with greased paper and bake for about fifteen minutes.

Sufficient for two persons.

NOTE.—This is a delicious dish and at the same time nourishing, uncommon and easy to prepare.

HERRING AND POTATO STEW

INGREDIENTS.—2 or 3 herrings or kippers, 2 lb. of potatoes, ½ lb. of onions, ¼ cabbage, ½ pint of water, salt and pepper.

METHOD.—Wash the cabbage and shred it finely. Slice the onions. Boil the water with half a teaspoonful of salt and put in the onions and cabbage. Boil them for ten minutes.

Cut the potatoes in half, put them with the cabbage and simmer gently. In twenty minutes season to taste and lay the herrings on top.

Simmer till the potatoes are quite soft, and serve on a hot dish.

Sufficient for three persons.

HERRING MOULD

INGREDIENTS.—1½ lb. of fresh herrings, with soft roes, 1 dessertspoonful of vinegar, 1½ gills of water, ⅜ oz. of leaf gelatine, 1 bay leaf, few peppercorns, salt, 1 hard-boiled egg, cucumber.

METHOD.—Have the herrings cleaned and boned out. Wash and drain them thoroughly, cut off the tail, head, and fins, and cut each herring into four. Put them into a saucepan with the water, add the bay leaf, vinegar, a few peppercorns and salt to flavour, and cook them gently for a few minutes until tender. Lift them out and drain them.

Cover the bottom of a mould with slices of hard-boiled egg, then add the cooked herrings.

Dissolve the gelatine in the herring liquor and strain it into the mould. Leave it to set. When firm, dip it in warm water and unmould it. Garnish it with cucumber and serve it with a salad.

Sufficient for four persons.

HERRING ROES ON TOAST

INGREDIENTS.—Herring roes, slices of bread, butter, cheese, seasoning.

METHOD.—These roes can be bought by the pound or in boxes.

Four or five slices of bread will be sufficient for a shilling box of roes. Put the roes into a pie-dish, and put into the oven to heat through.

Toast the bread and well butter it.

Place a few of the roes on each slice of toast. Sprinkle with pepper and salt and a little grated cheese.

Put under the grill for a few minutes in order to melt the cheese.

Serve very hot.

CREAMED HUSS

INGREDIENTS.—¾ lb. of huss, juice of ½ a lemon, salt and pepper, 1½ oz. of butter, 1 oz. of flour, 1½ gills of milk, 2 tablespoonfuls of cream, 1 dessertspoonful of chopped parsley, 3 spring onions.

METHOD.—Mince the onions finely and sprinkle over a fireproof dish.

Wash the fish and place it in the dish with half oz. of butter in small pieces on top, and lemon-juice squeezed over it.

Cover with greased paper and bake in a fairly hot oven for twenty minutes.

To MAKE THE SAUCE.—Melt the butter, add the flour with the pan off the gas, and stir in the milk and any liquor that has come from the fish.

Stir till it boils, cook for three minutes, season to taste, and add the parsley and cream.

Pour over the fish and serve with boiled potatoes.

NOTE.—Huss is one of the cheapest fish, and if carefully cooked, one of the nicest. It is good to give children as there are no small bones.

Allow one lb. for three persons, as there is less waste than with other kinds of fish.

HUSS EN CASSEROLE

INGREDIENTS.—1 lb. of huss, 1 bay leaf, 2 peppercorns, 2 cloves, 1½ gills of cold water, ¼ teaspoonful of salt.

FOR THE SAUCE.—1 oz. of butter, 1 oz. of flour, ½ gill of unsweetened condensed milk, 1 hard-boiled egg, salt and pepper.

METHOD.—Wash the huss and put it in a casserole with the cold water, bay leaf, salt, cloves, and peppercorns. Put on the lid and bake the fish in a moderate oven for about twenty minutes. It is done when the flesh is soft and white.

To MAKE THE SAUCE.—Chop the white of the egg and rub the yolk through a coarse gravy strainer.

Melt the butter and mix the flour with it.

Stir in the milk and add the water in which the fish was cooked. Stir till the sauce boils, simmer for five minutes, season to taste and put in the white of egg. Place the fish on a hot dish and pour the sauce over it.

Decorate with a line of yolk of egg sprinkled along the back of the fish.

Sufficient for three persons.

Huss is an inexpensive and economical fish as there is no skin and no bones, except the backbone.

KEDGEREE

INGREDIENTS.—2 oz. of butter or margarine, 2 eggs, 10 oz. of cooked fish, 4 oz. of rice, 2 dessertspoonfuls of chopped parsley, pepper and salt, lemon-juice.

METHOD.—Take all the bones and skin from the fish, and flake or chop up the flesh. Wash the rice, and cook in a saucepan of boiling water with a little salt and lemon-juice added (about a teaspoonful of each to a quart of water).

It will take about fifteen minutes to cook. When tender, strain off the water and mix the rice with the prepared fish. Boil the eggs for fifteen minutes until hard. Remove the shells, cut the eggs into halves, take out the yolks and rub them through a sieve to a powder, and leave aside for decorating. Chop up the whites and add to the fish, etc. Melt the butter in a saucepan, put in the fish, etc., and stir all together, until thoroughly hot. Season well with salt and cayenne, add the chopped parsley—the latter must previously have been well washed and scalded.

If the mixture is too stiff, add a very small quantity of milk.

Heap the mixture on a hot dish, make it stand up well, and mark it over with a fork. Sprinkle the powdered yolks over it and serve at once.

MADRAS KEDGEREE

INGREDIENTS.—2 oz. of rice, 1½ oz. of butter, 2 level tablespoonfuls of chopped onion, 6 oz. of cooked fish, 1 teaspoonful of curry powder, salt, 2 tomatoes, 1 egg (hard-boiled).

METHOD.—Wash the rice and cook it in boiling water with salt added. Drain it in a colander and pour cold water through to separate the grains, then drain it again.

Melt the butter in a saucepan, add the onion and fry it lightly till tender, then add the tomatoes peeled and chopped, also the curry powder, and stir them for a minute or two over a low burner.

Remove the bone and skin from the fish and flake up the flesh, add this and the rice to the onion mixture, etc. Season to taste and stir till heated, then turn the kedgeree into a dish and garnish it with a hard-boiled egg cut into convenient sized pieces and a small heap of cooked rice kept back from the mixture.

Sufficient for three persons.

LOBSTER AU GRATIN

INGREDIENTS.—1 lobster (split open), 1 oz. of butter, ½ oz. of flour, juice of ½ a lemon, ¼ gill of milk, 1 egg, a little nutmeg and cayenne, salt to taste, 2 tablespoonfuls of breadcrumbs.

METHOD.—Remove the flesh from the body and claws of the lobster.

Chop it coarsely and sprinkle it with lemon-juice, salt, cayenne and nutmeg.

Melt half the butter and stir in the flour and milk. Stir till this sauce boils, then add the lobster and breadcrumbs and beaten egg.

Fill the shells with the mixture and sprinkle breadcrumbs and dabs of butter on top.

Bake for fifteen minutes.

Sufficient for two to four persons, according to the size of the lobster.

CREAMED LOBSTER

INGREDIENTS.—1 boiled lobster, 2 oz. of butter, ¾ oz. of flour, ½ pint of milk, seasoning, 2 oz. of mushrooms.

METHOD.—Have the lobster split open, remove the stomach, intestinal vein, and spongy parts which are unfit for use, then cut the lobster meat into dice, adding also the meat from the claws.

Peel and stalk the mushrooms, and cleanse them in salted water, drain them, and cut them up. Fry them in half the butter.

Melt the remainder of the butter in a saucepan, stir in the flour and when well blended add the milk and bring all to the boil. Boil this sauce gently for a few minutes, then stir in the lobster and mushrooms long enough to make them hot. Add seasoning to taste and serve the creamed lobster in the half shells.

Garnish the shell with small heaps of lobster coral, which should have been previously rinsed and drained.

NOTE.—There should be a good half-pint of diced lobster to this amount of sauce.

LOBSTER MAYONNAISE

SERVED IN THE SHELL

INGREDIENTS.—1 lobster, 1 gill of mayonnaise (see p. 42) or salad cream, 1 nice lettuce, 2 hard-boiled eggs, 1 bunch of mustard and cress, French salad dressing (see p. 168), salt, cayenne, juice of a lemon.

METHOD.—Remove the flesh from the body and claws and cut it into fairly large pieces. Lay them on a plate, sprinkle with salt, cayenne and lemon-juice, and leave for one hour. Wash the lettuce and cress and drain on a cloth. Crack and remove the shells from the eggs, putting the eggs into cold water till required. This keeps them nice and white. Mix the lobster with the mayonnaise or salad cream, and fill four shells made from the head and body.

Shred the lettuce and mix it with the cress. Mix with French dressing, slice the eggs and add them to the salad.

Put the lobster shells on top and decorate with the legs.

Sufficient for four persons if the lobster is a medium-sized one. If it is large the claws can be used as shells ; it will then serve six persons.

LOBSTER PUDDING

INGREDIENTS.—¼ lb. of lobster or tinned lobster, 2 oz. of butter and 2 oz. of margarine, ½ pint of Ideal Milk, 4 oz. of breadcrumbs, 3 eggs, salt and pepper.

METHOD.—Put the lobster through the mincer and stir in lightly the whipped Ideal Milk, breadcrumbs, seasoning, the fats (melted and warm), and the beaten yolks of eggs.

Beat the mixture till it is creamy, and lastly, add the whites of eggs, beaten to a stiff froth.

Steam the mixture for one hour in a greased basin which has been sprinkled with breadcrumbs.

Serve lobster pudding with white sauce (see p. 41) and toast.

LOBSTER SALAD

INGREDIENTS.—1 lobster, salad-lettuce, cress, hard-boiled eggs, tomatoes, beetroot, salad cream.

METHOD.—Break the claws and remove the flesh, save some of this for garnishing, and flake up the remainder. Remove the flesh from the lobster and flake it up.

Prepare and wash the salad in the usual way, then drain well. Cut up some of the salad and mix with the flaked lobster, and dress with a little salad cream. Serve in a bowl with a border of salad, and garnish with strips of beetroot and tomato, and slices of hard-boiled eggs and the flesh from the claws.

NOTE.—Do not forget to remove the part of the lobster that is not good to eat. This is usually done by the fishmonger.

LOBSTER TARTLETS

INGREDIENTS.—Some short or flaky pastry (see p. 252), small tin of lobster, 1 dessertspoonful of chopped pimento, 1 oz. of butter, 3 level dessertspoonfuls of flour, ½ pint of milk, seasoning, pimento for garnishing.

METHOD.—Roll out the pastry, stamp it into rounds and line some small tartlet tins. Prick the base of each case and line the pastry with rounds of buttered paper. Put a little rice into each case and place them in a hot oven to bake.

When the pastry is set, remove the rice and paper and finish cooking the cases.

Meanwhile make the filling. Flake the lobster meat into small pieces—there will be about four or five ounces in a small tin.

Melt the butter in a saucepan, add the flour, and when it is well blended, stir in the milk and bring it to the boil. Boil the sauce gently for a few minutes, adding seasoning to taste. Then add the lobster meat with any liquor there may be, and also the chopped pimento. Let it heat through slowly without boiling. Then fill the prepared cases and garnish each tartlet with pimento. If liked, a tablespoonful of cream may be added to the mixture.

Sufficient to fill twelve to fifteen tartlet cases.

LOBSTER SCALLOPS

INGREDIENTS.—1 large lobster, 2 hard-boiled eggs, 1 oz. of butter and flour, 1½ gills of milk, 1 tablespoonful of cream, 1 dessertspoonful of chopped parsley, juice of a lemon, cayenne and salt, a few browned breadcrumbs.

METHOD.—Choose a lobster that has large claws and ask the fishmonger to split the lobster but not to break the claws in half, only to make one slight crack on the under side.

The head, body and claws are to be used as scallop shells. The head and body make four shells and the claws two. To prepare the claws, take a tin-opener and gently cut away bits of the shell already cracked until there is a large enough opening.

Remove the flesh from the body and claws, but keep the legs for decorating. Put the flesh on a plate and sprinkle with salt, cayenne and lemon-juice. Leave it for an hour.

Melt the butter, add the flour, and gradually stir in the milk. Stir till it boils and add the parsley. Cut the lobster into fairly large chunks and put it into the sauce. Chop the eggs coarsely and add them.

Fill the shells with the mixture and sprinkle with breadcrumbs.

Put a small piece of butter in each and brown lightly in a quick oven for ten minutes.

Serve in the shells, laying one of the legs on top of each.

Enough for six persons.

FOR BREADCRUMBS.

BAKE some stale crusts of bread. Crush them with a rolling-pin and pass through a wire sieve.

GRILLED MACKEREL

INGREDIENTS.—1 mackerel, 1¼ oz. of butter, a few breadcrumbs, 1 teaspoonful of lemon-juice, 1 level teaspoonful of chopped parsley, salt and pepper.

METHOD.—Take half an ounce of butter and mash it on a plate until creamy. Gradually mix in the lemon-juice and add the chopped parsley and seasoning to taste. Form it into a block and leave it to harden, then make it into balls. Have the mackerel cleaned. Wash and dry it thoroughly. Split it open and remove the backbone.

Place the fish in the grill tin and dot it with a quarter of an ounce of butter cut in small dabs. Put the mackerel under the hot grill and grill it for a few minutes until tender.

Melt the remaining half-ounce of butter in a frying pan, add a few fresh breadcrumbs, and fry them till light golden brown.

Serve the mackerel on a hot dish, cover it with the buttered crumbs, and garnish it with the prepared balls of butter.

Allow half a pound for each person.

MACKEREL AND GOOSE-BERRY JELLIES

INGREDIENTS.—2 mackerel, ¾ gill of vinegar, ½ gill of water, 6 peppercorns, ¼ teaspoonful of salt, ¼ cucumber.

FOR THE GOOSEBERRY JELLIES.— 1 packet of aspic jelly, 1 lb. of green gooseberries, 1 oz. of Demerara sugar, ½ gill of water, salt and pepper.

METHOD.—Wash the mackerel and cut off the fins.

Put the mackerel in a baking tin with the vinegar, water, salt and peppercorns and cover well with greased paper. Bake in a slow oven for thirty minutes.

Turn the fish over and leave them in the tin till they are cold.

TO MAKE THE JELLIES.—Wash the gooseberries and top and tail them.

Put them in a saucepan with the water and sugar and stir till they are soft.

Rub the gooseberries through a hair sieve and put the purée into a cup.

Oil six small moulds with salad oil or olive oil.

Dissolve the jelly in half a pint of hot water and add the gooseberry purée. Season to taste with salt and pepper, or a little more sugar. When the jelly is cold, pour it in the small oiled moulds and leave it to set.

To serve, place the fish on a dish paper with the jellies round and garnish with slices of cucumber.

Sufficient for four persons.

FLEMISH MACKEREL

INGREDIENTS.—2 fresh mackerel, ½ gill of vinegar, 1 oz. of margarine, ½ gill of water.

FOR THE STUFFING.—½ pint of breadcrumbs, ¼ onion, a flat teaspoonful of dried herbs, 1 tablespoonful of chopped parsley, salt and pepper, 2 rashers of fat bacon, 1 egg, ¼ oz. of margarine.

METHOD.—Wash the mackerel and cut off the fins. Split them open without cutting them in half. Take out the backbone and any large bones.

TO MAKE THE STUFFING.—Chop the bacon and fry it in the margarine for three minutes. Pour the bacon and the fat that comes from it on to the breadcrumbs and add the herbs, parsley and grated onion. Season with salt and pepper and bind with a well-beaten egg.

Lay one mackerel, skin-side down, on a baking-tin and spread it with the stuffing. Lay the other mackerel on top and place pieces of margarine over it. Pour on the vinegar and water, cover the fish with a greased paper, and bake in a moderate oven for twenty minutes. Baste the fish with the water twice while it is cooking.

Sufficient for four persons.

FRIED MACKEREL

INGREDIENTS.—2 mackerel (each weighing about ¾ lb.), about ½ to ¾ gill of water, 2 or 3 tablespoonfuls of flour, fat for frying, parsley.

METHOD.—The mackerel should be filleted, and, if liked, some of the black skin removed. Wash the fillets and dry them in a cloth. They may be cut again into halves, if desired. Mix the flour to a smooth paste with water, adding enough to make a batter of coating consistency.

Melt some dripping in a frying-pan and when a faint blue smoke begins to rise, coat the fillets in the flour-and-water batter and put them into the hot fat. Fry until golden brown, then turn them over and brown the other side. When cooked drain the fillets on paper, and serve them on a dish paper, garnished with parsley.

If preferred, the mackerel may be coated with dry flour and fried, in which case less dripping will be required for cooking them.

Sufficient for three or four persons.

MACKEREL HOT-POT

INGREDIENTS.—2 mackerel, weighing about 1 lb. each, about 1 lb. of potatoes, 1 large Spanish onion, ¼ pint of vinegar and water, salt and pepper, 1½ bay leaves, a few cloves and peppercorns.

METHOD.—Peel the potatoes and parboil them, then strain off the water and cut them in slices. Peel the onion and slice it into very thin rings.

Have the mackerel filleted. Wash the fillets and drain them well. Cut them into halves or in three, and coat them lightly with flour.

Butter a pie-dish and put a layer of potato in the bottom, then add a layer of onions and one of mackerel. Continue in this way until the dish is full, leaving enough potato slices to cover the top. Season each layer well, and add the cloves, peppercorns, and bay leaves.

Pour in the vinegar and water, cover the dish with a buttered paper. Bake *slowly* for about one-and-a-half or two hours.

Sufficient for five or six persons.

SOUSED MACKEREL

INGREDIENTS.—Cold boiled mackerel, vinegar, a few peppercorns, a few allspice, bay leaves, fish liquor.

METHOD.—Take some cold boiled mackerel and remove all the bones and skin. Then put it into a dish. Do not break the fish more than you can help when removing the skin and bones.

Take equal quantities of vinegar and fish liquor (the water in which the mackerel was cooked). Add a few peppercorns and allspice and one or two bay leaves.

Boil these together for about five or ten minutes. Leave until cold, then pour it over the fish. There should be

enough to just cover. This will be
ready to eat in a few hours.

NOTE.—Mackerel must be very
fresh when cooked.

JELLIED OYSTERS

INGREDIENTS.—8 oysters, 1 gill of
fish stock (see p. 12) (or water left
after boiling fish), 1 tablespoonful of
lemon-juice, ½ tablespoonful of vinegar,
1 bay leaf, ½ teaspoonful of meat
extract, 2 strips of thinly cut lemon-
peel, cayenne, salt, ¼ oz. of leaf
gelatine.

METHOD.—The fish stock which
makes the jelly must be very nicely
flavoured. Put it in a double saucepan with the lemon-peel, bay leaf,
and the beards of the oysters, and cook
for twenty minutes. Add the vinegar,
lemon-juice, meat extract, and salt
to taste, and strain into a basin.

When cold break up the gelatine
and put it into the stock. Leave for
five minutes and dissolve slowly over
a low gas, stirring all the time. Strain
it into a basin and leave it to get cold.
Add any liquor that has come from the
oysters.

Clean four deep oyster shells and
put a little jelly in each, also two
oysters seasoned with cayenne. Let
the jelly set and pile more jelly on top.

Garnish with quarters of lemon,
as these are easier to squeeze than
slices.

Allow two oyster shells (four oysters)
for each person.

BAKED PLAICE OR SOLE

INGREDIENTS.—1 plaice or sole
(about 1 lb.), egg and breadcrumbs,
dripping, sauce.

METHOD.—Have the plaice skinned,
wash and dry it thoroughly, trim the
tail and cut off the fins.

Beat up an egg and put half aside,
brush the fish over with the remainder
and coat it with breadcrumbs, then
shake off the loose crumbs.

Melt two or three ounces of dripping
in a baking tin, and when hot put in
the fish and bake it till tender, keeping
it basted.

When cooked, lift out the fish and
drain it well. Serve it on a lace paper.

Any suitable sauce (see pp. 41 to 43)
may accompany the fish.

Sufficient for two persons.

CORNETS OF PLAICE

INGREDIENTS.—1 plaice (filleted),
6d. of picked shrimps (washed), 1 oz.
of butter, 1 oz. of flour, ½ pint of milk,
salt and pepper, 1 hard-boiled egg
(chopped), hot mashed potatoes, ½ gill
of cold water.

METHOD.—Grease four cornucopia
tins (or four carrots, scraped and
greased will do instead).

Wash the fillets and wrap them
round the tins with the skin side
inwards and starting at the pointed
end.

Lay them in a greased plate and put
a small dab of butter on each. Pour
half a gill of cold water in the plate
and twist a well-greased paper over
the top. Place the plate over a
saucepan of boiling water and steam
for fifteen minutes.

Melt the butter, mix the flour with
it and gradually stir in the milk and
any liquor from the fish. Stir till this
sauce boils and pour half of it into
another saucepan, adding salt and
pepper, the shrimps and chopped egg.

Place the fillets on a hot dish,
remove the tins (or carrots) carefully
and fill the fish cornets with the
shrimp and egg mixture.

Strain the sauce over the fish and
garnish with mashed potato.

Sufficient for four persons.

FILLETS OF PLAICE A LA PORTUGAISE

INGREDIENTS.—1 plaice (about 1 lb.),
3 or 4 tablespoonfuls of white breadcrumbs, 1 dessertspoonful of grated
cheese, 1 shallot, 1 tomato, pepper and
salt, egg, brown breadcrumbs, tomato
sauce (see p. 43).

METHOD.—Fillet the plaice and skin
the fillets, then wash and dry them.

Make the breadcrumbs, grate the
cheese, peel and chop the shallot very
finely, skin the tomato and mash it to a
pulp.

Mix all these ingredients together,
season with pepper and salt, and add
just enough of the egg to bind them.

Place the prepared fillets on the

board and spread each with some of
the mixture, then roll them up,
beginning from the wide end of the
fillet. Stand the fillets in a buttered
tin or piedish, and put any of the
mixture that is over on top of each
fillet. Cover with a buttered paper,
and bake in the oven for about fifteen
minutes. When cooked, lift on to a
dish, and pour a little hot tomato
sauce over each fillet, and sprinkle with
a few brown crumbs.

Sufficient for two persons.

FILLETS OF PLAICE AND MAITRE D'HOTEL SAUCE

INGREDIENTS.—1 plaice (about 1 lb.),
1½ oz. of butter or margarine, 1½ teaspoonfuls of flour, 1 gill of milk or
milk and water, 1 teaspoonful of
chopped parsley, squeeze of lemon-
juice, pepper and salt, brown breadcrumbs.

METHOD.—Fillet the plaice and skin
the fillets. Wash and dry them.

Take each one and roll it tightly
round your finger or thumb with the
skinned side inside.

Stand them in a greased piedish,
cover with a greased paper, and bake
in a moderately hot oven for about
ten to fifteen minutes, or until the
flesh is quite white.

When these are cooking, make the
sauce.

MAITRE D'HOTEL SAUCE

MELT half an ounce of butter in a
saucepan, stir in the flour, and mix
together until quite smooth.

Add the milk and stir until the
sauce boils, then cook slowly for about
six minutes.

Season with pepper and salt, stir
in the chopped parsley and lastly
the lemon-juice.

When the fillets are cooked, melt
the remaining ounce of butter and
brush them over with it, then coat
them with the brown breadcrumbs.
Place on a hot dish and pour the sauce
round.

Sufficient for two persons.

FRIED PLAICE IN BATTER

INGREDIENTS.—1 plaice, or more as
required, filleted, ¼ lb. of flour, 1½

dessertspoonfuls of salad oil, pinch of
salt, ⅛ pint of warm water, white of 1
egg, fat for frying, parsley, 1 tablespoonful of flour.

METHOD.—Cut each fillet across
into halves.

Wash the fish well and roll in a clean
cloth.

To MAKE THE BATTER.—Put the
flour and salt through a sieve.

Make a well in the centre of it, and
put the salad oil in the hole.

Mix this with a small quantity of
the flour until it is the consistency of a
custard.

Then slowly add the warm water
and gradually mix in the flour until
all is well mixed together.

Beat the batter for about ten
minutes, or until the surface is covered
with bubbles.

Then stand it aside for about an
hour.

Add a pinch of salt to the white of
egg and whisk it to a stiff froth ;
then lightly fold it into the batter.

Put the tablespoonful of flour on
to a plate, and pass each piece of fish
through it—this helps to dry the fish.

Put a deep pan of dripping to get
hot ; when it smokes a little, it is
sufficiently hot to put the fish into.

Cover about three or four pieces
of fish with the batter, lift them out
carefully with a skewer, and drop
lightly into the hot fat.

Fry until golden brown on both
sides, then drain well on paper.

Coat the other pieces of fish and
fry in the same way.

Serve on a dish paper and garnish
with parsley.

FILLETS OF PLAICE WITH SPINACH

INGREDIENTS.—2 plaice (each about
1 lb.), small tin of spinach, lemon-
juice, ½ pint of milk, 1 oz. of butter
or margarine, salt and pepper, 2 oz. of
butter, ¾ oz. of flour.

METHOD.—Have the plaice filleted
and the fillets skinned on both sides.
Rinse and dry them. Turn out the
spinach from the tin and drain it.
Melt the butter (two ounces) in a
saucepan, add the spinach, with
seasoning, and mix all together.

Place the fillets flat on a board,

sprinkle them with salt, pepper, and lemon-juice, and spread a thin layer of spinach on each. Roll them up and put them into a buttered fireproof dish. Cover them with a buttered paper and bake them in a moderately hot oven for from ten to fifteen minutes, or till tender.

Re-heat the remainder of the spinach and heap it in the centre of a dish. Arrange the fillets round the base of it and pour a little sauce between each fillet.

To Make the Sauce.—Melt the butter or margarine in a saucepan, add the flour, and stir it till well blended. Add the milk and bring the sauce to the boil. Add seasoning to taste and boil it gently for a few minutes.

Note.—Small tins of cooked spinach (three-quarter pint size) can be bought, which saves much time and labour in preparation.

FRICASSEE OF PLAICE

Ingredients.—2 plaice (small), 1 small onion, 3 oz. of dripping, 2 table-spoonfuls of flour, ¾ pint of stock (see p. 12), salt and cayenne, or white pepper, squeeze of lemon-juice, 1 tablespoonful of tomato sauce.

Method.—Fillet the plaice and skin the fillets. Wash and dry them. Roll each into a sausage shape, rolling from the wide to the narrow end. Tie with a piece of string (not too tightly).

Melt the dripping in a saucepan, lightly flour the rolled fillets, and fry them in the hot fat just sufficiently to brown them.

Lift on to a dish and keep warm.

Peel and grate the onion and put into the fat, and fry for a few minutes ; add the flour and fry both until golden brown, keeping them well stirred. Add the stock, and stir until the sauce comes to the boil ; it should now be thick and brown.

Season with a little salt and pepper, add the tomato sauce and a squeeze of lemon-juice.

Return the fish to this and cook all gently for about ten minutes. Arrange the rolls down the centre of a dish, remove the string, and pour the sauce over them. Garnish with small pieces of cut lemon.

PRAWNS

Prawns caught at the seaside are cooked by dropping them into boiling salted water.

They are done as soon as they turn pink (about three minutes).

CURRIED PRAWNS

Ingredients.—1 onion, 1½ oz. of butter, 2 teaspoonfuls of flour, 1 tea-spoonful of curry-powder, 1 gill of shelled prawns, 1½ gills of milk, or milk and water, or fish stock (see p. 12) and milk, squeeze of lemon-juice, 3 oz. of rice, seasoning.

Method.—Take a small onion and peel it, then grate it finely.

Melt the butter in a small saucepan, and fry the onion gently until golden brown.

Stir in the flour and curry-powder, and when well mixed add the milk, and keep stirring until it boils.

Add the seasoning and simmer this for about twenty minutes.

Shell the prawns and add these to the curry sauce, and make thoroughly hot.

Add a squeeze of lemon-juice, and serve the curry on a hot dish with a border of boiled rice, or, if preferred, serve the rice separately.

To Boil the Rice.—Wash it well, and put it into a saucepan with plenty of boiling water, add salt to flavour and a squeeze of lemon-juice.

Boil until tender, with the lid off the saucepan—it will take about twelve to fifteen minutes.

Strain through a strainer, and pour water through the rice to separate the grains. Then put it into a warm place to dry and re-heat. Use the best Patna rice.

PRAWN PATTIES

Ingredients.—For the Pastry.— 6 oz. of flour, 6 oz. of butter or mar-garine, water to mix, pinch of salt.

For the Filling.—½ oz. of flour, ½ oz. of margarine, 1 gill of milk or milk and fish stock, salt and pepper, ½ gill of shelled prawns, 4 teaspoonfuls of grated cheese.

Method.—Make some puff pastry from the ingredients given above, as in recipe (given on p. 252). After it has been rolled out six times, roll it again, to about three-eighths of an inch in thickness. Cut it into rounds and mark a small circle in the centre of each, about the size of a shilling, but do not cut right through.

Place on a baking-sheet, and brush over the top outside round with either milk or beaten egg.

Bake in a very hot oven for about fifteen minutes and until golden brown.

Place on a sieve and remove the centre-piece of pastry from each.

To Make the Filling.—Make the white sauce as explained on p. 41.

Shell the prawns, cut them into small pieces, and add these to the sauce, and make thoroughly hot. Stir in the cheese and season to taste. When the cheese has melted, fill the pastry cases with the prepared filling, and garnish the top of each with a prawn's head, if liked.

Note.—The filling can be made while the pastry is cooking.

PRAWN RAMEQUINS

Ingredients.—½ pint of prawns or shelled shrimps, 6 olives, juice of ½ a lemon, cayenne, cochineal, ¼ pint of double cream.

Method.—Chop the prawns, sprinkle them with cayenne and lemon-juice and put them on ice or in a cool place till required.

Put the cream in a basin and beat it with a fork till it is thick. Stir in a few drops of cochineal.

Mix the cream with the prawns and place them in three ramequin cases.

Place an olive at each end and the head of a prawn in the centre.

Sufficient for three persons.

PRAWN SALAD

Ingredients.—2 dozen prawns, mayonnaise (see p. 42), lettuce, 1 small tin of asparagus tips, 2 cups of chopped, boiled new potatoes, 1 hard-boiled egg.

Method.—Use fresh prawns, or tinned ones if fresh prawns are not available. Mix them with the potato and, if liked, one teaspoonful of grated onion and one teaspoonful of parsley.

Add some mayonnaise to make the mixture creamy.

Serve the salad in a dish ringed with heart of lettuce leaves. Sieve hard-boiled yolk of egg over the piled-up mixture, and plant the asparagus tips evenly round the edge. Cut the egg white into dice and make a ring of it inside the circle of lettuce leaves.

Sufficient for four or more persons.

SALMON A LA TARTAR

Ingredients.—1 slice of salmon, a small bottle of olives, gherkins and anchovies (mixed), juice of ½ a lemon, salt and pepper.

Method.—Wash and dry the salmon and sprinkle it with lemon-juice, salt, and pepper.

Wrap it in greased paper and bake it in a slow oven for thirty minutes.

When cold, place it on a lace paper and garnish with olives, gherkins, and anchovies.

Serve with Tartar Sauce.

Sufficient for two persons.

Tartar Sauce

Ingredients.—1 gill of mayonnaise dressing (see p. 42), 1 tablespoonful of capers, 1 dessertspoonful of gherkins and parsley.

Method.—Chop the capers, gherkins and parsley, and add them to the mayonnaise.

Serve cold.

SALMON FINGERS

Ingredients.—1 tin of salmon, 1 oz. of butter, 1 oz. of flour, 1 gill of milk, salt and pepper, grated nutmeg, 1 egg (beaten), ½ lb. of flaky pastry (see p. 252).

Method.—Melt the butter and add the flour.

Stir in the milk and also the liquid from the tin of salmon. Stir till it boils, add the salmon and season to taste with nutmeg, salt and pepper. Leave it to get cold. Roll out half the pastry into an oblong piece and lay it on a baking-sheet.

Spread the cold salmon mixture over it, leaving half an inch round the edge which should be moistened with water.

Roll out the other piece of pastry

the same size, lay it on top and press the edges together.

Brush the top with a well-beaten egg and mark it with a knife into a diamond pattern and then into fingers.

Leave it for twenty minutes and bake in a hot oven for about twenty minutes. Cut the pastry into fingers.

Sufficient to make ten fingers.

SALMON AU GRATIN

INGREDIENTS.—A large tin of salmon, ½ pint of thick white sauce (see p. 41). 3 oz. of cheese, seasoning.

METHOD.—Turn out the salmon, remove the bone, divide it into about eight pieces, and put into a buttered pie-dish or au gratin dish, with the liquor, piling it up well.

Make the sauce and cook it gently for a few minutes.

Grate the cheese finely, and add three-quarters of it to the sauce with seasoning to taste.

Stir until it is melted, then pour over the salmon and coat it.

Sprinkle the remainder of the cheese on the top, put into a moderately hot oven and heat through, then put under the grill for a few minutes to brown. Serve in the dish.

Sufficient for four or five persons.

SALMON AND CUCUMBER CHARLOTTE

INGREDIENTS.—1 large fresh cucumber, 1 tin of salmon, 1 packet of aspic jelly, ½ gill of cream, ½ gill of mayonnaise (see p. 42), 1 gill of thick white sauce (see p. 41), 4 sheets of gelatine, ½ gill of cold water, ¾ pint of hot water, salt and pepper.

METHOD.—Dissolve the jelly in the hot water. Oil a charlotte mould, with salad oil or olive oil, and pour in a gill of jelly.

Soak the gelatine in the cold water for ten minutes.

Put the gelatine and water into a saucepan and stir over a low gas till the gelatine is dissolved. Add to it half a pint of the dissolved aspic jelly with the salmon, and sauce, and mix well. Leave till cold, then stir in the cream and mayonnaise, and season to taste.

When the salmon mixture is almost set, line the mould with cucumber.

First cut the cucumber into pieces the height of the mould. Peel half the number of pieces and cut them lengthways into four. Stand the pieces of cucumber round the mould and put in the salmon mixture, taking care that it comes just above the top of the cucumber.

Turn out when set and garnish with sliced cucumber.

Sufficient for four or five persons.

SALMON ENVELOPES

INGREDIENTS.—6 oz. of tinned salmon, 1 egg, 3 level dessertspoonfuls of finely-minced onion, seasoning, ¾ oz. of flour, ¾ oz. of butter or margarine, 1½ gills of milk.

FOR THE PASTRY.—½ lb. of flour, 4 oz. of lard, 3 oz. of margarine, water to mix, salt, 1 egg yolk, a little milk for glaze.

METHOD.—Remove bone and skin from the salmon, and flake up the flesh.

Hard boil the egg, then shell it and chop it.

Melt the butter, add the flour, and when well blended stir in the milk and bring all to the boil. Boil this sauce gently for a few minutes, then take it off the heat and stir in the salmon, egg, onion, and seasoning to taste.

To MAKE THE PASTRY.—Sift the flour with a pinch of salt, rub in the margarine, and mix it to a stiff paste with cold water.

Press or roll out the lard into thin pieces, using a well-floured board and rolling pin. Put this aside and roll the pastry out to a square shape, turn it on to the other side, place the lard on it, fold the sides to the centre both ways, then fold it over in half again. It is then folded in eight.

To MAKE THE ENVELOPES.—Roll the pastry out to a long, oblong shape about seven by twenty-one inches, then cut it into three pieces, which will be roughly each about seven inches square. Trim them and turn them on to the other side, put a proportion of the prepared fish in the centre of each, damp the edges and fold them to resemble envelopes. Brush each with beaten yolk of egg mixed with a little milk, and put the envelopes into a hot oven to bake.

Serve hot or cold, but if cold, let out the steam with a knife.

Sufficient for three envelopes.

SALMON FISH CAKES

INGREDIENTS.—1 tin of salmon, 2 medium-sized potatoes (boiled), salt and pepper, ¼ oz. of butter, 2 dried eggs or 1 large egg, bread-crumbs, deep frying fat.

METHOD.—Mash the potatoes, which should be freshly boiled. Chop the fish finely after removing all skin and bones.

Melt the butter in a saucepan, put in the fish and potato, season to taste, and add half the eggs.

Mix and beat well with a wooden spoon.

When the mixture is smooth put it on a plate and spread it out into a smooth flat cake. Cut this, when cold, into an even number of pieces of the same size. Shape them as required, as balls, sausages, pyramids or flat cakes. Egg-and-crumb one at a time (as described on page 29) and reshape them with flat of a knife. Heat the fat, and when it is smoking, fry three or four cakes at a time, re-heating the fat before each batch.

NOTE.—Do not fry more than one or two cakes if you have not plenty of fat, as it is impossible to fry them well if the fat is cooled by having too much cool fish in it.

SALMON AND MAYONNAISE SAUCE

INGREDIENTS.—2 lb. of salmon, water to cover, salt and lemon-juice, 1 yolk of egg, 2 teaspoonfuls of white vinegar, 1 teaspoonful of malt vinegar, ¾ to 1 gill of salad oil, salt and pepper, ½ flat teaspoonful of mixed mustard, 1 small cucumber.

METHOD.—Wash the salmon and scrape off the scales.

Place in a saucepan or fish-kettle with sufficient boiling water just to cover it. Add a little salt and lemon-juice to the water before adding the fish. Cook very slowly for about fifteen minutes or until the flesh moves easily from the bone.

When cooked, carefully lift out the fish and well drain it and leave until cold.

To MAKE THE MAYONNAISE SAUCE

Mix the yolk in a small basin with a wooden spoon.

Stir in the salad oil gradually drop by drop.

Add the mustard and seasoning. Gradually stir in the vinegar. This sauce should be like thick cream when finished.

If too thick add more vinegar, if too thin add more oil.

CUCUMBER.—Do not peel this all round but cut off strips of peel, then leave an equal-sized piece not peeled, and so on alternately all round the cucumber.

Then slice it into very thin pieces.

Place the salmon on a dish, garnish the top of it with mayonnaise.

Place slices of cucumber, each one overlapping the previous one, all round the dish.

The cucumber can also be shaped into little convolvulus flowers with a small piece of beetroot in the heart of each.

SALMON MOULD

INGREDIENTS.—1 tin of salmon, 1 packet of aspic jelly, 1 hard-boiled egg, ¾ pint of hot water, ½ gill of cold water, ½ oz. of butter, ½ oz. of flour, ¾ gill of milk, ¾ gill of salad cream, 1 table-spoonful of cream, 3 sheets of gelatine, salt and pepper.

FOR THE FILLING.—A little cucumber and beetroot, 1 cupful of cold potatoes, ¾ gill of salad cream.

METHOD.—Dissolve the jelly in the hot water.

Chop the white of egg and sprinkle it into a ring mould oiled with salad oil. Pour in a gill of jelly and let it set.

Soak the gelatine in the cold water for ten minutes. Place it on a low gas and stir till the gelatine is dissolved.

Melt the butter, mix the flour with it and stir in the milk. Stir the sauce till it boils, and add the gelatine, salmon, aspic jelly, and yolk of egg.

When cold, stir in the salad dressing and cream, and season to taste.

Pour it into the mould.

To Make the Filling.—Mix the cold potatoes with the salad cream.

Turn the mould on to a dish and fill the centre with the potato salad. Decorate with cucumber and beetroot.

Sufficient for three or four persons.

SALMON PUDDING

Ingredients.—Large tin of salmon, 2 dessertspoonfuls of roughly-chopped capers, seasoning, $\frac{1}{2}$ oz. of butter, $1\frac{1}{2}$ oz. of breadcrumbs, 2 eggs and 1 extra white, 2 or 3 tablespoonfuls of milk.

For the Sauce.—$\frac{3}{4}$ oz. of flour, $1\frac{1}{4}$ oz. of butter, 1 yolk of egg, $\frac{1}{2}$ pint of milk, 1 tablespoonful of lemon-juice, seasoning.

Method.—Remove the skin and bone from the salmon and flake up the flesh. Add the capers, bread-crumbs and milk; also the butter (melted).

Beat up the two whole eggs and stir them in with seasoning to taste, and when well mixed, whisk the egg-white stiffly, and fold it in.

Turn the pudding into a well-buttered basin or plain mould, cover it securely with a buttered paper and steam it for about twenty-five minutes. Then turn it out carefully, pour the sauce over it, and garnish it with a few whole capers.

To Make the Sauce.—Melt the butter in a saucepan, add the flour, and when well blended, stir in the milk and bring the sauce to the boil. Boil it gently for a few minutes, then draw the pan aside and let it cool.

Beat up the yolk of the egg and stir it in, and cook the sauce again for a few minutes, being careful not to let it boil. Add seasoning, then take the sauce off the heat and stir in the lemon-juice gradually.

Sufficient for four persons.

COLD SALMON SALAD

Ingredients.—2 cupfuls of diced, cooked salmon, 1 hard-boiled egg, capers, chives, French dressing (see p. 168), 1 large tomato or lemon basket, lettuce or endive, 1 gherkin, mayonnaise (see p. 168).

Method.—Cut the salmon into small neat pieces suitable for a salad. Stand it in a basin and pour over it two tablespoonfuls of French dressing. Place the basin in a cool place for two hours, basting the salmon with dressing every twenty minutes. Add a few chopped capers and chives.

When ready to serve, arrange a heart of lettuce or curly endive leaves on a pretty dish and place the basted salmon on the leaves.

Cut the hard-boiled egg-white into six petals, after halving the egg length-wise and removing the yolk. To do this, cut each half into three long slices with a very sharp knife and then arrange them on the salad. Heap powdered egg-yolk in the centre.

Serve the salad with mayonnaise to which a chopped gherkin has been added.

If liked, the mayonnaise may be served in a basket made from a tomato or lemon.

SALMON STEAMED IN SALAD OIL

Ingredients.—A slice of salmon ($\frac{3}{4}$ lb.), salad oil, pepper and salt, squeeze of lemon-juice, cucumber.

Method.—Wipe the fish and season it with pepper and salt. Pour a little salad oil on to a plate, place the fish on this, pour a little oil over it, and add a squeeze of lemon-juice.

Cover the fish with a buttered paper, and then another plate, and steam it over a saucepan of boiling water for about twenty minutes.

Serve the salmon on a hot dish with the oil, and garnish it with thinly sliced cucumber.

Cucumber can be made quite attractive as a garnish, if, instead of removing all the peel, you " nick " out alternate grooves before cutting it in slices. Thinly sliced cucumber can also be formed into convolvulus flowers, with a small piece of beetroot in the centre.

Note.—The flavour of chilled salmon is much improved if cooked in this way.

SALMON TOAST

Ingredients.—1 small tin of salmon, 9 prawns, 1 oz. of butter, 1 oz. of flour, 1 gill of milk, salt and pepper, $\frac{1}{2}$ table-spoonful of mushroom ketchup, 3 pieces of hot buttered toast.

METHOD.—Melt the butter. Take the pan off the gas and stir in the flour. Add the milk gradually and stir till it boils.

Put in the salmon and ketchup, mix well and boil for three or four minutes.

Season the mixture to taste and heap it on the toast.

Decorate with the prawns.

Sufficient for three persons.

SARDINE CORSICAN SALAD

INGREDIENTS.—1 tin of sardines, 1 or 2 tablespoonfuls of mayonnaise (see p. 42), lettuce, ½ cupful of chopped cucumber, 1 tomato, minced parsley, capers or an onion.

METHOD.—Peel and chop the tomato. Mix it with the mayonnaise and cucumber. Serve the salad piled up in the centre of glass plates, which should be lined with lettuce leaves. Arrange the sardines across the top, and sprinkle the vegetable mixture with minced parsley and capers or chopped onion.

SARDINE SALAD

INGREDIENTS.—A small tin of sardines, a small piece of onion, 1 lettuce (small), two pennyworth of mustard and cress, a few slices of beetroot, 2 tomatoes, 1 hard-boiled egg, a few cold potatoes.

METHOD.—Pick over and thoroughly wash the lettuce and mustard and cress. Leave to soak for a time, then drain.

Turn out the sardines, keep some of them whole, and cut up the remainder, each in about four.

Make a bed of the lettuce in the bottom of a salad bowl, then add some of the cut sardines.

Chop up the onion and distribute evenly over them.

Add a few slices of beetroot, egg, potato, and tomato, then some more lettuce and cut-up sardines, and some mustard and cress.

Put small bunches of cress and lettuce leaves on the top, also slices of tomato, etc., and add the whole sardines, arranged tastefully. Serve with salad dressing.

NOTE.—If liked, the salad can be served in small dishes instead of in a salad bowl.

The bones of the sardines must first be removed.

Sufficient for three persons.

SCALLOPS

INGREDIENTS.—3 scallops, 1½ gills of milk, ½ oz. of flour, ¾ oz. of margarine, salt, pepper, 1½ oz. of breadcrumbs, ½ oz. of butter.

METHOD.—Have the scallops cleaned, and buy them with the shell.

Remove the fish from the shells, put them into cold water and bring them to the boil, then drain them and cut each into about six or eight pieces.

Wash and dry the shells and butter them.

Melt the margarine, add the flour, and when blended, stir in the milk and bring it to the boil. Boil it gently for a few minutes, and add seasoning to taste. Put a few buttered crumbs on each shell, add a little sauce, then the prepared scallop. Season and cover each with sauce and sprinkle buttered crumbs on top.

Put the scallops into the oven to finish cooking and serve them on the shells.

TO PREPARE THE BUTTERED CRUMBS.—Melt the butter in a frying-pan, add the breadcrumbs and stir them over a low burner until the fat is absorbed.

Allow one scallop for each person.

SHIRRED EGGS WITH SCALLOPS

INGREDIENTS.—½ pint of diced scallops, ¾ pint of white sauce (see p. 41), 6 eggs, salt and pepper, butter.

METHOD. — Choose medium-sized scallops, clean and trim them and cut them into inch cubes. Rinse them in salt water and dry them carefully. Cook them for ten minutes in white sauce.

Divide the mixture between six small buttered ramekins or shells. Break an egg on to the top of each. Sprinkle it with salt and pepper. Put a dab of butter on the top of each and bake until the eggs are firm.

Sufficient for six persons.

*Savoury
Fried
Hake*

*Shrimps
in
Ramekins*

Fillets of Sole and Horseradish Sauce

PLATE 5

Fried
Witch
Fillets

Madras
Kedgeree

Sole
and
White
Wine
Sauce

PLATE 6

Herring Mould

Bream Fillets

Haddock and Egg Scallops

PLATE 7

*How to
Fry Fish
in Batter*

Wash the fish and
leave it in a cloth
to dry.

Fold in the egg-
white before using
the batter.

Dip each fillet into the
batter and fry it.

The Fried Fillets of
Fish.

PLATE 8

SHRIMPS IN ASPIC

INGREDIENTS.—½ pint of shrimps, 1 hard-boiled egg, 1 packet of aspic jelly, ¼ pint of hot water, a little chervil or cress.

METHOD.—Pick the shrimps or, if they are bought ready picked, wash them carefully as they are always salted in order to preserve them.

Cut a little of the white of egg into crescents or diamonds. Put the jelly in a basin and pour the hot water on it, stirring till the jelly dissolves. Oil some small moulds with salad oil or olive oil and put half a tablespoonful of jelly in each and decorate with the white of egg. When set fill the moulds a little more than half full of shrimps mixed with the chopped egg.

Pour in the jelly and let it set. When firm shake the jellies on to a lace paper and decorate lightly with chervil or cress.

NOTE.—Prawns, chopped crab or lobster (either tinned or fresh) can be used for this dish instead of shrimps.

Chopped olives or champignons may be used instead of or as well as the hard-boiled egg.

Sufficient for four or five persons.

SHRIMPS IN RAMEKINS

INGREDIENTS.—1 pint of shrimps, 1¾ gills of hot stock (see p. 12), 2 egg-yolks, salt and cayenne, 1 dessert-spoonful of cream, ½ oz. of flour, ½ oz. of butter, 1 dessertspoonful of tomato ketchup, 3 dessertspoonfuls of lemon-juice, grated onion.

METHOD.—Heat the butter in a saucepan and stir in the flour. Thin the sauce down with the hot stock and add the tomato ketchup and keep stirring the sauce till it is smooth and mellow.

Draw the pan aside and cool the sauce slightly, then add the egg-yolks beaten with a little salt, cayenne, and grated onion to taste, and then the cream.

Cook the sauce gently for a few minutes, and when it is piping hot, add the shrimps. Make these thoroughly hot, remove the pan from the heat and add the lemon-juice very carefully. Put the mixture into buttered ramekins, sprinkle the tops lightly with breadcrumbs, dab each

one with tiny pats of butter and stand them under the grill for a few moments before serving them.

Sufficient for six persons.

CRIMPED SKATE AU BEURRE NOIR

INGREDIENTS.—2 pieces of skate, each about ½ lb., 1 small carrot and onion, sprig of thyme and parsley, a few cloves and peppercorns, salt, 1¼ oz. of butter, 2 dessertspoonfuls of vinegar, 2 level teaspoonfuls of chopped parsley, warm water.

METHOD.—Wash the skate and twist each piece into a circular shape.

Put them into a saucepan with enough warm water just to cover them, adding a carrot and onion, salt to taste, a few cloves and peppercorns, and a sprig of thyme and parsley.

Bring them barely to boiling point, and cook them for a few minutes until tender. Lift the fish out and drain it, and put it on a dish.

Meanwhile, melt the butter in a small frying pan and let it brown. Draw the pan aside, add the vinegar, parsley, and seasoning to taste. Boil them up and pour them over the fish.

Sufficient for two persons.

FRIED SKATE IN BATTER

INGREDIENTS.—1 lb. of skate, 1 oz. of flour, salt and pepper, deep frying fat.

FOR THE FRYING BATTER.—3 oz. of flour, salt and pepper, 1 tablespoonful of oilve oil, ¾ gill of tepid water, 1 small egg (or for a plain batter, ½ a teaspoonful of baking-powder and no egg).

METHOD.—First make the frying batter.

Put the flour, salt and pepper into a basin. Make a hollow in the centre and put in the oil, two tablespoonfuls of the tepid water, and the egg (unbeaten).

Stir in a little of the flour and gradually add the rest of the water.

Wash and dry the skate. Cut it into convenient-sized pieces. Mix the flour with pepper and salt and roll the pieces of fish in it.

Have ready a pan of deep frying fat.

When the fat smokes, put two pieces of fish in the batter. Lift them up

c

with a fork, letting some of the batter drain from them. Put them into the smoking fat, and fry for five minutes or till a golden brown.

After frying, drain on paper. Serve very hot on a lace paper.

Sufficient for four persons.

NOTE.—If fried fish is greasy, it shows that the fat is not smoking hot.

FRIED SKATE IN BREAD-CRUMBS

INGREDIENTS.—1½ lb. of skate, 1 egg, 2 teaspoonfuls of chopped parsley (if liked), white breadcrumbs, vinegar, fat for frying.

METHOD.—Thoroughly clean and skin the skate.

Cut it into convenient-sized pieces, and put it into a pie-dish with a little vinegar (*almost to cover it*).

Leave it soaking for about twenty to thirty minutes, keeping it turned occasionally, then drain it.

Make the breadcrumbs, and mix the chopped parsley with them.

Beat up the egg, and brush the skate over with it, then coat with the parsley and breadcrumbs.

Put some fat into a frying-pan to heat, and when it begins to smoke, put in the skate and fry until golden brown.

When both sides are brown, drain on paper, and serve on a dish paper. Garnish with sprigs of parsley.

NOTE.—The chopped parsley must be dried before being mixed with the breadcrumbs; or, instead of chopping the parsley, dry a few sprigs in the oven, then rub them to a powder.

Sufficient for three persons.

FRIED SMELTS

INGREDIENTS.—Smelts, flour, pepper and salt, egg, breadcrumbs.

METHOD.—Wash the fish carefully, then dry them in a cloth.

Mix some flour, pepper and salt together, and lightly flour the fish. Beat up the egg. Make the bread-crumbs. Egg the smelts, then coat them with breadcrumbs. Put them into hot fat and fry until golden brown. Drain well on paper. Serve on a dish-paper and garnish with parsley. If liked, serve plain white

sauce (see p. 41), or any other suitable sauce, separately.

NOTE.—Smelts need to be exceptionally fresh, and they should smell like a cucumber.

BAKED FILLETS OF SOLE

INGREDIENTS.—2 soles, 1½ oz. of butter, 1 oz. of flour, ½ pint of milk, 1 yolk of egg, squeeze of lemon-juice, one dessertspoonful of chopped parsley, salt and pepper, 3 spring onions.

METHOD.—Roll the fillets, skinned side inwards, and place them in a buttered pie-dish with the juice of half a lemon, and half an ounce of butter in small pieces on top. Cover with a buttered paper and bake in a fairly hot oven for about fifteen minutes.

Arrange neatly on a hot dish and pour off any juice that has come from the fish, as this should be used in making the sauce.

Chop the onions as finely as possible and fry them in the butter, without browning them, for ten minutes. Add the flour and mix well. Add half a pint of milk and stock mixed, and stir the sauce till it boils. Boil for three minutes and season to taste. Add the chopped parsley, and when the sauce has cooled slightly, add the yolk of the egg beaten in a very little water. Pour the sauce over the fish and garnish with sprigs of parsley. Serve with boiled potatoes.

FILET DE SOLE AUX CHAM-PIGNONS

INGREDIENTS.—2 lemon soles, a small bottle of button mushrooms, 2 oz. of cheese, 1 egg (hard-boiled), ½ pint of milk, 2 oz. of butter, ¾ oz. of flour, salt and pepper.

METHOD.—Have the soles filleted and skinned. Wash and dry them and make each into a roll.

Stand them in a buttered pie-dish covered with a buttered paper, and cook them in a moderate oven for about ten or fifteen minutes, or until tender.

Drain the liquor from the mush-rooms and heat them in a saucepan with about two-thirds of the butter, but do not brown them.

Make a white sauce with the milk, flour, and remainder of the butter (for method see p. 41), add the cheese, grated finely, and chopped egg-white, and seasoning to taste. Arrange the fillets in a dish, garnish each with a mushroom, pour the sauce round them and heap the remainder of the mushrooms in the centre.

Sprinkle just a little egg-yolk (rubbed to a powder) over the sauce, and serve.

Allow one or two fillets for each person.

CURRIED SOLE

INGREDIENTS.—1 sole (about 1 lb.), 3 tomatoes, 1 tablespoonful of finely-minced onion, 1 good teaspoonful of curry powder, 1 oz. of butter, 1 tea-spoonful of flour, ¾ gill of water, 3 oz. of rice, lemon-juice, salt.

METHOD.—Have the sole filleted, and the fillets skinned on both sides. Wash and dry them and cut them in halves.

Put the tomatoes into boiling water for a few seconds, then skin and chop them up.

Melt the butter, add the finely-minced onion and cook it for a few minutes, but do not let it brown. Add the flour and curry-powder, and stir all for a minute or two.

Add the tomatoes, then the water, seasoning and a few drops of lemon, and let them gently boil, for a few minutes.

Put in the fish, simmer it until tender. Turn it on to a dish and surround it with a border of rice.

To PREPARE THE RICE.—Wash it and cook it in boiling water with salt to flavour. Strain it through a colander, pour cold water through to separate the grains, then warm the rice up again.

Sufficient for two or three persons.

SOLE AND ESPAGNOLE SAUCE

INGREDIENTS.—1 lemon sole about 1 lb., 1 gill of Espagnole sauce, 1 or 2 tomatoes, 2 oz. of mushrooms, 1 tablespoonful of chopped onion, salt and pepper, a small piece of butter, hard-boiled egg-white, a slice of lemon.

METHOD.—Have the sole skinned and cut off the head, then wash it and dry it.

Peel and stalk the mushrooms, cleanse them in cold water with salt added. Drain them and chop them. Mix them with the onions and put a good half of the mixture into the bottom of a buttered fireproof dish, adding also half a tomato, cut in slices, a few dabs of butter, and seasoning.

Make four or five cuts on each side of the sole, season it and rub it over with a slice of lemon, then place it in the dish. Add the remainder of the butter, onion, and mushroom, cover it with a buttered paper and cook it in the oven for a few minutes until almost tender. Pour the Espagnole sauce over the fish, having previously heated it, and finish cooking.

Garnish the sole with tomato slices, warmed in the oven, and chopped white of egg.

Sufficient for two persons.

NOTE.—Espagnole sauce is a rich brown sauce flavoured with tomato, mushroom, bacon and cooking sherry. It can be bought ready prepared from any of the big stores (or see p. 118 for recipe).

SOLE AND HORSERADISH SAUCE

INGREDIENTS.—3 witch soles (2 lb. altogether), salt and pepper, lemon-juice, 1½ oz. of butter, 1¼ dessert-spoonfuls of flour, 1 gill of fish stock and 1 gill of milk, 4½d. of cream, 2 oz. of finely grated horseradish, 2 dessertspoonfuls of white vinegar (use half tarragon vinegar, if available), mustard.

METHOD.—Have the soles filleted, and the fillets skinned on both sides. Rinse, dry them, season them with pepper and salt and a squeeze of lemon-juice, then fold each fillet into a small circular shape. Place them in a buttered dish and put a tiny dab of butter on each, using half an ounce for all the fillets. Cover them with a buttered paper and bake them in a moderately hot oven for about ten minutes or till they are tender.

To MAKE THE SAUCE.—Blend the remaining ounce of butter with the flour, milk, and fish stock, let it boil gently for a few minutes, then take it off and stir till slightly cool. Mix the horseradish with the vinegar, then gradually add them to the lightly whipped cream. Stir in the prepared sauce by degrees, and season it with pepper, salt and mustard. Heat the sauce in a double boiler, taking care not to let it curdle, and add any liquor from the fish. Arrange the fillets on a dish, pour the sauce round and garnish with parsley. Sprinkle finely grated horseradish in the centre.

To Make the Fish Stock.—Let the fish bones simmer for from twenty to thirty minutes, adding an onion, a sprig of parsley and one or two cloves and peppercorns to flavour.

FRICASSEE OF SOLE

Ingredients.—2 lemon soles (each about 1 lb.), ¼ lb. of mushrooms, 2 or 3 oz. of butter or dripping, 1 tablespoonful of flour, salt and pepper, about ½ pint of fish stock (see p. 12).

Method.—Have the soles filleted and the fillets skinned on both sides. Wash and dry them, season them with salt and pepper and form them into rolls. Tie them with string and coat them with flour. Melt a little fat in a saucepan and fry the rolls lightly until brown. Take them out and put them on a plate. Peel and stalk the mushrooms. Cleanse them in salted water, and drain them. Chop them and fry them gently until tender, then drain off the fat into a frying-pan. Stir the remainder of the flour into this, and blend together. More or less fat may be used as required. Let the flour brown slowly, then draw the pan aside and add the fish stock. Boil it up and season it to taste and strain it over the mushrooms. If too thick, the gravy may be thinned down with more stock. Add the prepared fillets to it, and simmer them for a few minutes until hot through and tender. Untie the strings and serve the fish on a hot dish with the sauce.

To Make the Fish Stock from the fish bones, add an onion and a sprig of parsley and thyme to flavour. Cover them with water and simmer for about half an hour.

Sufficient for four persons.

FILETS DE SOLE AU GRATIN

Ingredients. — 1 sole (filleted), lemon, brown breadcrumbs, 1½ oz. of butter, ½ oz. of flour, 2 gills of milk, salt and pepper.

Method.—Well wash the fillets of sole and remove the white skin.

Roll each one into a round, twist it on the finger or a skewer.

Stand in a greased pie-dish, add half a gill of milk, some pepper and salt, and place a small piece of butter on each fillet, using about one ounce altogether.

Cover with a plate and bake in a moderately hot oven for about fifteen to twenty minutes.

Put the remainder of the milk into a saucepan with the other half an ounce of butter, and pepper and salt.

Mix the flour to a smooth paste with a little water, add the warm milk to it, pour back into the saucepan and bring to the boil, stirring all the time.

Let it simmer for about six minutes. Put the browned breadcrumbs on a piece of paper. Take the fillets from the oven and roll each one in the crumbs. Stand in a line on a dish and pour the sauce round.

Place a small piece of lemon on the top of each and serve hot.

To Make Browned Breadcrumbs. —Cut up any stale pieces of bread. Place in the oven on a baking-sheet. Bake until golden brown. Crush with a rolling-pin. Rub through a wire sieve.

Put into a jar or tin until ready for use.

These can be baked at any odd moment when the oven is being used.

They will keep for several weeks and after being used should be dried again in the oven and re-sieved, then put into a jar, and these can be used for fish again when needed.

GRILLED SOLE AND TARTAR SAUCE

Ingredients.—1 small lemon sole, salt and pepper, lemon, ½ gill of mayonnaise (see p. 42), 1 teaspoonful of chopped capers, butter.

Method.—Have the sole cleaned and the dark skin removed. Wash it and dry it, then season it with pepper and salt, and brush it with a little oiled butter.

Put it on the grill tin, place this under the grill, which should have been previously heated, and cook it for about ten minutes, or until the flesh moves easily from the bone.

Place the sole on a hot dish, garnish it with lemon, and serve it with tartar sauce.

To Make the Tartar Sauce.— Stir the capers into the mayonnaise.

Sufficient for one person.

FILETS DE SOLE OTERO

INGREDIENTS.—4 large potatoes, 1 gill of picked shrimps, salt and pepper, parsley, 4 fillets of sole, 1 oz. of butter, Cheese sauce (see p. 42), Parmesan cheese.

METHOD.—Bake the potatoes, cut off the tops and scoop out the soft potato so that only the skin remains. Chop the shrimps finely. Mash, season and enrich the potato with a little butter. Add the shrimps to the mixture and return it to the cases.

Roll up each fillet of sole and cook it in the oven, with a lump of butter and seasoning.

Put a little cheese sauce into each potato, place a cooked fillet of sole on top of each and decorate with a few shrimps. If preferred, the fish may be covered with cheese sauce and sprinkled with grated Parmesan and then browned in the oven. Decorate the finished dish with sprigs of parsley.

Sufficient for four persons.

FILLETS OF SOLE AND SHRIMP SAUCE

INGREDIENTS.—1 sole, 1 jar of shrimp paste, juice of half a lemon, 1 gill of shrimps, 1 oz. of butter, 1 oz. of flour, 1 gill of milk, salt and pepper.

METHOD.—Have the sole filleted.

Spread each fillet on the skinned side with a thin layer of paste and roll it up.

Put the rolls in a small casserole with the lemon-juice, quarter of a teaspoonful of salt, and one gill of water. Put on the lid and bake in a fairly hot oven for fifteen minutes.

Pick the shrimps, keeping back the four largest.

Dish up the rolls of fish, and keep them hot while making the sauce. Melt the butter, stir in the flour, and add the milk and water used for cooking the fish. Season to taste and add the shrimps.

Stir till it boils, boil for three minutes and pour round the rolls of fish, which should be standing upright.

Place the head of a large shrimp on each roll and decorate with slices of lemon.

Allow one fillet for each person.

FILLETS OF SOLE AND MUSHROOMS

INGREDIENTS.—1 sole (filleted), 4 large mushrooms, 1 oz. of butter, ½ gill water, ½ gill of milk, 1 teaspoonful of mushroom ketchup, a few drops of cochineal salt and pepper, ¾ oz. of flour.

METHOD.—Wash the mushrooms, peel them and remove the stalks. Place them in a steamer, under side up, with a piece of butter in each.

Wash the fillets and roll them up tightly with the skin inside. Lay the fillets in a tin plate on top of the steamer. Pour in half a gill of water, and put on the lid.

Steam till the mushrooms are tender and the fish is white and soft (about twenty minutes).

Place the mushrooms on a hot dish with a fillet of sole standing in each one. Use the liquid from the fish and mushrooms to make the sauce.

To Make the Sauce.—Mix the flour smoothly with the milk and pour the hot stock on to it, stirring well. Stir till it boils, add the ketchup and a few drops of cochineal, and season to taste. Strain the sauce round the fish.

Sufficient for four persons.

FRIED SOLE

INGREDIENTS.—1 sole, 1 egg, fresh breadcrumbs, 1 tablespoonful of flour, salt and peper, at least ½ lb. of fat for frying, 1 lemon.

METHOD.—If the dark skin on the underside of the fish has not already been removed by the fishmonger, do so as follows: Scrape off a little of the flesh from the skin at the tip of the tail, and holding the fish tightly in one hand, with the fingers dipped in salt, pull off the skin with the other hand. Put the flour on to clean white paper, add salt and pepper.

Having cut off the fins, wash and dry the fish. Dip it in the flour. Beat the egg on a plate. Put the breadcrumbs on a paper. Lay the fish in the egg, turn it over till it is well covered, or use a small brush to cover it with egg.

Lift it out and dip it in the breadcrumbs. Shake off any loose crumbs. Heat the dripping in an oval frying-pan, and when it smokes put in the fish gently. Fry for about fifteen minutes.

If there is not enough fat to cover the sole it must be carefully turned over with a fish slice when half done. To see if it is done, test with a skewer. The flesh should be soft when it is cooked.

Lift the sole out with a slice and drain it on paper. Serve on dish paper and garnish with lemon.

A sole of 6 oz. is sufficient for one person. A 1 lb. sole will be sufficient for two persons.

NOTE.—If served as a course at a dinner a 1 lb. sole will do for four persons, allowing one fillet each.

JELLIED SOLE

INGREDIENTS.—1 sole, 1 jar of lobster paste, ½ packet of aspic jelly, 6d. of picked shrimps, ½ oz. of butter, juice of ½ a lemon, salt and pepper, ½ pint of hot water.

METHOD.—Have the sole skinned and filleted by the fishmonger.

Wash the fillets, spread each of them with lobster paste, and fold in half, with the paste inside.

Put the fillets on a plate with a small piece of butter on each. Season with salt and pepper, and squeeze lemon-juice over them. Cover them with greased paper and stand the plate over a saucepan of boiling water. Steam for about ten minutes. The fillets are done when they are soft and white.

Melt the jelly in half a pint of hot water and pour it over the fillets, so that it only just covers them.

When set, lift the fillets on to a dish and neatly cut away any jelly round the edges.

Chop the rest of the jelly and mix it with the shrimps, using it to decorate the dish.

Sufficient for four persons.

NOTE.—This dish could also be made with fillets of plaice or whiting.

SOLE PAPRIKA

INGREDIENTS.—1 sole (about 1 lb.), salt and pepper, lemon-juice, 1½ oz. of cheese, 1 yolk of egg, ¾ oz. of butter, 1½ teaspoonfuls of flour, ¼ pint of milk, paprika pepper.

METHOD.—Have the sole filleted, and the fillets skinned on both sides. Wash and dry them, season them with paprika pepper, salt, and lemon-juice, and roll them into circular shapes. Place them in a buttered Pyrex dish with one third of the butter cut in four small dabs. Cover the fish with a buttered paper and cook it in a moderate oven for about ten minutes or until the flesh becomes white, and a milky fluid runs from it.

Meanwhile, melt the remainder of the butter in a saucepan, add the flour and, when blended, stir in the milk and bring all to the boil. Boil the sauce gently for a few minutes, draw the pan aside, add the finely grated cheese and seasoning to taste, also any liquid from the fish, and the beaten egg-yolk.

Stir the sauce over a low burner to melt the cheese and cook the egg, but do not let it boil. Pour it over the fillets and sprinkle them with finely grated cheese and paprika.

Sufficient for two persons.

STEAMED SOLE

INGREDIENTS.—1 sole, salt and pepper, juice of ½ a lemon, ½ oz. of butter.

METHOD.—Ask the fishmonger to fillet the sole.

Season the four fillets with salt and pepper and roll them up with the skinned side inside, and from the head to the tail end.

Butter an enamelled plate and put in the fillets with the lemon-juice squeezed over them, and on top of each a small piece of butter.

Cover with a small plate or saucepan lid, and stand the plate over a saucepan of boiling water for about ten minutes.

The fish is done when it is quite white and opaque, and when the flesh is soft.

If the fish is for an invalid, omit the butter and lemon-juice and use two tablespoonfuls of milk in its place. Add a little seasoning if allowed.

Allow one fillet for each person.

SOLE WITH MAITRE D'HOTEL BUTTER

INGREDIENTS.—1 sole, egg, few breadcrumbs, fat for frying, 1 oz. of butter, pepper and salt, ½ teaspoonful of lemon-juice, 1 flat teaspoonful of chopped parsley.

METHOD.—First of all make the maitre d'hotel, or green butter.

Press out the butter with a fork. Work the finely-chopped parsley, lemon-juice, pepper and salt into it.

Mix all together, then make it into small balls and put in a cool place to harden.

Remove the eyes from the sole, well wash it, and put in a cloth to dry.

When well dried, brush it all over with beaten egg and coat with the breadcrumbs.

Put into a pan of hot fat and fry until golden brown on both sides.

Drain on paper.

Serve on a dish paper and garnish with the balls of green butter.

NOTE.—It can be fried in either deep or shallow fat. If fried in deep fat it will not require to be turned ; but if cooked in shallow fat put the best side downwards into the pan, and when golden brown turn it over very carefully, using a fish-slice, and brown the other side. The sole can be filleted, if preferred this way.

Allow about half lb. for each person.

WITCH SOLES AND OLIVE SAUCE

INGREDIENTS.—2 witch soles (each about ¾ to 1 lb.), lemon-juice, seasoning, 1½ oz. of butter, ¾ oz. of flour, ½ pint of milk, about 24 stuffed olives.

METHOD.—Have the soles filleted and the fillets skinned on both sides. Rinse and dry them, and place them flat on a board. Sprinkle them with pepper and salt, and add a squeeze of lemon-juice.

Roll up each fillet with a stuffed olive inside it. Put the fillets into a buttered dish, dab them with half an ounce of the butter, cut into tiny pieces, cover the fish with a buttered paper, and cook it in a moderate oven till tender.

Meanwhile, make the sauce. Melt the remaining ounce of butter in a saucepan, add the flour and, when it is well blended, stir in the milk and bring it to the boil.

Let this boil gently for a few minutes, then add the liquor from the fish and the remainder of the olives (chopped), saving a few slices or halves for garnishing. Season the sauce, and if it is too thick, thin it down with a little milk.

Arrange the fillets on a dish. Garnish them with halves or slices of olive. Pour a little sauce round the fillets, and the remainder is served separately.

FRIED WITCH FILLETS

INGREDIENTS.—2 witches, egg, breadcrumbs, dripping, lemon.

METHOD.—Have the witches filleted, wash and dry them thoroughly, then cut each fillet in halves.

Brush them with egg and coat them with breadcrumbs.

Melt some dripping in a frying pan and when it smokes faintly, put in the fillets and fry them until golden brown, turning them over when brown on one side. Drain them on paper and serve them on a dish paper. Garnish the centre with a lemon basket filled with tartar sauce (see p. 43).

TO MAKE THE LEMON BASKET.—Cut the lemon *almost* in half, only leaving a piece in the centre about a quarter of an inch wide. Remove the half in two pieces, then scoop away the lemon from under the centre piece so that it forms a handle.

Now hollow out the bottom half of the lemon, and fill the basket with Tartar sauce.

Allow half a pound of fish for each person.

SOLE AND WHITE WINE SAUCE

INGREDIENTS.—2 lemon soles, tin of peas, ½ oz. of butter, salt and pepper, lemon-juice, ½ gill of white wine.

For the Sauce.—1 oz. of margarine, ¾ oz. of flour, ¼ pint of milk, ½ gill of fish stock (see p. 12).

Method.—Choose two soles, each weighing from three-quarters to one pound. Have them filleted and the fillets skinned on both sides.

Sprinkle them with a squeeze of lemon-juice, season them with pepper and salt, and fold them into shawl shapes. Put them into a buttered dish.

Pour the white wine over them and add the butter cut in small dabs. Cover them with a buttered paper and bake them in a moderate oven for from twelve to fifteen minutes, or until the flesh is quite white and a milky liquid comes from it.

When ready, arrange the fillets in a dish, garnished with small heaps of peas, previously heated, and serve them with white wine sauce.

To Make the Sauce.—Melt the margarine and stir in the flour. Blend them together, add the milk and fish stock, and bring them to the boil. Stir in the wine in which the fish was cooked, add seasoning to taste, and simmer the sauce for a few minutes. If too thick, thin it down a little.

Make the stock from the fish bones.

Sufficient for four persons.

EDDY SPRATS

Ingredients.—1 lb. of sprats, 1 lemon, cayenne, 1 tablespoonful of salt.

Method.—Ordinary fried sprats are too rich and greasy for many people. No dripping is used by this method, only salt, which absorbs the grease as it comes from the fish.

Clean the sprats by cutting them open and removing the insides. Wash and drain on a cloth. Heat a frying pan slightly, and sprinkle salt all over it.

Put in the sprats and sprinkle with lemon and cayenne.

Cook very slowly for about ten minutes, turning them over gently after three or four minutes and sprinkling with more lemon.

Serve on a dish paper on a hot dish, and garnish with lemon.

Sufficient for three or four persons.

FRIED SPRATS

Ingredients.—Sprats, flour, pepper, and salt, fat, lemon, parsley.

Method.—Thoroughly clean the fish and dry them in a cloth.

Mix some flour, pepper, and salt together, and lightly sprinkle them with it.

Put them into a frying-pan with a very small quantity of hot fat, and fry until quite lightly browned. When coloured on one side turn them over and brown the other side, then drain on paper.

Another method is to put a deep pan of hot fat on to heat, stick a skewer through the heads of as many sprats as you can get on it and when the fat begins to smoke dip them into it and fry until lightly browned. Drain well on paper.

Serve on a dish paper and garnish with cut lemon and parsley.

Note.—Sprats will require cooking about four or five minutes if fried in shallow fat, and rather less if in deep fat.

BOILED SALMON TROUT

Ingredients.—1 salmon trout (about 5 lb.), boiling water to cover, salt and vinegar, mayonnaise sauce (see p. 42), plain white sauce (see p. 41), cucumber.

Method.—The salmon-trout must be thoroughly cleaned inside; this is usually done by the fishmonger. Wash the fish, scrape off all the scales, trim the tail, cut off the fins, and remove the eyes. Lift the strainer out of the fish-kettle, place the fish on to it, then put it into the kettle, with a little salt and vinegar (one teaspoonful of each to a pint of water) and just sufficient boiling water to cover, and cook slowly for about twenty-five to thirty minutes, according to the thickness of the fish. When cooked lift out the strainer, let the fish drain for a few seconds, then serve it on a hot dish on a neatly folded table napkin. Garnish with very thin slices of cucumber. The cucumber looks very attractive if instead of peeling it all round alternate strips of peel are cut off all round it, then it is thinly sliced. Or it can be shaped into little convolvulus flowers, with a small piece of beetroot in the heart of each. Serve separately with the salmon-trout a dish of sliced cucumber, and mayonnaise sauce or plain white sauce ; or, if liked, both sauces can be served.

Allow about five or six oz. for each person.

STEWED TROUT

INGREDIENTS.—3 or 4 trout, ½ pint of water, ½ teaspoonful of meat extract, ½ an onion, 2 cloves, 4 peppercorns, ½ glass of claret, ½ a lemon, salt.

FOR THE SAUCE.—1 oz. of butter, ¾ oz. of flour, ½ pint of fish liquor.

METHOD.—Wash the trout. Put them in a stewpan with the water, onion, cloves, meat extract, salt and peppercorns. Simmer for ten minutes or more if the fish are large.

Put the fish in a dish and keep them hot. Heat the butter and fry the flour till brown, stirring well. Add the fish liquor, stir till it boils and boil for five minutes. Add the claret and lemon-juice and strain into a sauceboat.

Sufficient for three persons.

BAKED TURBOT

INGREDIENTS.—2 slices of turbot or halibut, 1 oz. of butter, ½ a lemon, salt and pepper.

METHOD.—Place the slices in a fireproof dish and season them with salt and pepper. Squeeze the lemon over them and place half the butter on each. Twist a well-greased paper over the dish and bake in a hot oven for twenty minutes.

Serve on a hot dish and use the liquid that has come from the fish for making the sauce. Serve with a gill of anchovy sauce (see p. 42), parsley sauce (see p. 41), or plain white sauce (see p. 41).

Allow half lb. for each person for a meal, or a quarter lb. for a course at dinner.

NOTE.—This recipe may be used for slices of any kind of fish, and it is as easy to cook as it is delicious.

BOILED TURBOT

INGREDIENTS.—1 turbot, warm water to cover, salt, lemon-juice.

METHOD.—The fish must be thoroughly cleansed inside and washed.

Sprinkle it with a little lemon-juice and stand it on the strainer of the fish-kettle.

Lift it into the kettle—there should be sufficient water to cover.

Add a little salt and lemon-juice. The former is to flavour the fish, and the latter to keep the flesh white. *Use about 1 tablespoonful of each to 4 or 5 pints of water.*

Bring almost to the boil, and cook slowly until the flesh will move easily from the bone.

Life up the fish on the strainer, let it drain for a few seconds, then slip it carefully on to a dish with a folded table-napkin on it. Garnish with slices of cut lemon, and serve separately any suitable fish sauce.

(See sauce recipes on pp. 41 to 43.)

NOTE.—If you have no fish-kettle, cook the turbot in a large saucepan or boiler, tied in a piece of muslin. The average time allowed for boiling fish is about five minutes to each pound of fish, then five minutes over, but remember that the thickness of the fish must also be considered. If any scum arises when fish is boiling, it must be removed. Turbot is not a very thick fish, so will probably take rather under the average time.

BOILED TURBOT AND ANCHOVY BUTTER

INGREDIENTS —1 slice of turbot weighing ½ lb. or more, 1 quart of tepid water, 1 teaspoonful of salt, 1 dessertspoonful of vinegar.

FOR THE ANCHOVY BUTTER.—½ oz. of butter, ½ teaspoonful of anchovy essence, pepper.

METHOD.—Wash the fish and tie it in a piece of muslin, leaving a long end of string for removing it from the water.

Put it in a pan containing the water, salt, and vinegar.

Bring it just to the boil and simmer as gently as possible for ten minutes.

When it is done it is perfectly white and soft enough for a fine skewer to be pushed in easily, or for a bone to be pulled out.

Lift out and undo the muslin and

with a fish slice place the fish on a hot dish.

Cream the butter on a plate with a knife and add to it the anchovy, with a shake of pepper. Put this on top of the fish and garnish with parsley and lemon.

NOTE.—Before cooking a whole turbot rub the white side with a cut lemon. When used instead of meat allow half a lb. for each person. Small portions for a course at a dinner party, quarter lb. for each person.

GRILLED TURBOT

INGREDIENTS.—3 slices of turbot, 1 oz. of butter, anchovy essence, pepper, 1 dessertspoonful of flour, $\frac{1}{2}$ oz. of margarine, $1\frac{1}{2}$ gills of milk and water.

METHOD.—Wash and dry the fish, and put it into the grill tin, with a few small dabs of butter on each slice. Heat the grill, and grill the fish for about ten minutes, or until the flesh moves easily from the bone, keeping it turned and letting it brown lightly.

Serve on a hot dish, garnished with small cubes of anchovy butter, and pour white sauce round made from the flour, margarine, milk and water. (For method of making white sauce see p. 41.)

To make the anchovy butter, beat up the remainder of the butter and work into it enough anchovy essence to colour and flavour. Season with pepper. Form it into a block and leave it in a cool place to harden, then cut in small cubes.

This should be made before the fish is cooked.

Allow one slice for each person.

FRIED WHITEBAIT

INGREDIENTS.—Whitebait, pepper and salt, flour, deep fat for frying.

METHOD.—This kind of fish is usually sold by the pint. It is considered quite a delicacy, and needs to be very carefully handled.

Wash the fish and put them in a cloth to dry.

The fat for frying needs to be very hot, so it must be put on in good time.

Before the fish are put into it, the fat must have a good smoke rising from it, but be careful not to let it burn.

Mix some flour with pepper and salt and put a few of the whitebait into it, and shake well in the flour. Then put them into a frying-basket. They must not touch each other, but should be quite separate. Shake the basket to remove the loose flour.

Stand the basket in the pan of hot fat and fry for two or three minutes, keeping the basket well shaken all the time.

Turn the whitebait on to paper and drain them well.

Now flour and fry the others in the same way, doing only a few together and re-heating the fat each time.

When all are fried and drained make the fat thoroughly hot again, put *all* the fried whitebait back into the frying basket, and stand in the very hot fat for one minute, just to crisp them. (There must be sufficient fat to cover them without any risk of it overflowing, otherwise they cannot all be put in at once.)

Drain well again.

Serve on a dish paper, garnish with slices of cut lemon, and serve brown bread-and-butter with them.

WHITING A L'ITALIENNE

INGREDIENTS.—Small tin of peeled tomatoes, $1\frac{1}{2}$ to 2 lb. of whiting, $\frac{1}{2}$ oz. of butter, seasoning, 1 dessertspoonful of flour, 3 oz. of cheese, 3 oz. of spaghetti.

METHOD.—Have the whiting cleaned and skinned, and each trussed to form a circular shape. Then wash and dry each fish and put them into a buttered casserole with the contents of a tin of peeled tomatoes. Dab them with tiny pieces of the butter and add seasoning to taste. Cover the casserole and cook it in the oven till the fish is tender.

Meanwhile, cook the spaghetti in a pan of slightly salted boiling water and, when it is tender, drain it in a colander.

Drain the liquor from the fish into a saucepan and thicken it with the flour, smoothed in a little water. Boil the sauce gently for a few minutes, then add the spaghetti and finely-grated cheese, and, when the latter is melted, season the sauce and pour over the fish.

Sufficient for six people.

FRIED FILLETS OF WHITING IN BATTER

INGREDIENTS.—3 small whiting, 4 oz. of flour, pinch of salt, ¾ gill of warm water, 1 dessertspoonful of salad oil, 1 white of egg, deep fat for frying.

METHOD.—Fillet the fish, then wash the fillets and roll them in a cloth to dry.

To MAKE THE BATTER.—Take three ounces of the flour, sieve it, and add a pinch of salt. Make a hole in the centre of it and pour in the oil, stir in some of the flour, then gradually add the warm water, and by degrees work in all the flour, keeping an even consistency all the time. When well mixed beat for a few minutes, then stand the batter aside for about one hour. Add a pinch of salt to the white of egg and whisk it to a very stiff froth, then fold it into the batter lightly after it has been standing. Dry the fillets in the remaining ounce of flour, then put them into the batter, one or two at a time, and coat them all over with it. Put the fat on to get hot in good time, and when a slight smoke rises from it, put in three or four of the coated fillets and fry until golden brown. Drain on paper. Coat and fry the others in the same way. Serve on a dish paper and garnish with parsley or lemon.

NOTE.—A deep pan of fat takes about twenty minutes to get sufficiently heated, so should be put on in good time. It should not be more than about half full, otherwise there is the danger of the fat boiling over when the fish is added. If liked, the fillet can be cut into halves before being coated with batter.

Allow about half a pound for each person.

STEAMED WHITING AND CHEESE SAUCE

INGREDIENTS.—2 whiting, lemon-juice, pepper and salt, cheese sauce.

METHOD.—Have the whiting cleaned and skinned, and the eyes removed. Truss the fish into a round.

Butter a large enamel plate, put the whiting on to it. Season it with salt and pepper, and sprinkle it with lemon-juice.

Cover the plate with a buttered paper, and a saucepan lid or basin, and stand it over a saucepan of boiling water to cook. The fish will take about fifteen minutes to steam, according to the size.

When ready, serve the fish on a hot dish and coat it with cheese sauce.

If required for an invalid, serve whiting plain or with white sauce; the lemon-juice may be omitted if desired.

CHEESE SAUCE

1½ gills of milk, ½ gill of water, 1½ dessertspoonfuls of flour, ½ oz. of butter or margarine, 2 or 3 oz. of cheese.

To make the cheese sauce, prepare a white sauce by mixing the flour to a *smooth* paste with a little milk, and adding it to the rest of the milk, heated with the butter in a saucepan. When it boils, add the cheese, grated finely. Cook for a few minutes, and season to taste.

Sufficient for two persons.

GAME and POULTRY

CAPON

THESE should have smooth legs, pliable breast bones, and white flesh. Stumps of young, undeveloped plumage will be found under the neck feathers of young birds.

Time for boiling, 1¼ to 1¾ hours.
Time for roasting, 1 to 1½ hours.
Time for braising, 1½ hours.

CHICKENS AND FOWLS

COCKERELS are the best flavoured. Breastbone and toes should be soft and pliable, legs smooth, and spurs short.

Scaly, thin legs are a sign of old age.
Time for roasting, 35 to 65 minutes, according to size.
Time for boiling, 1¼ to 1¼ hours.
Steaming an old bird, 2 to 3 hours.

DUCKS

DUCKS should have yellow, pliable bills which can be easily broken, and supple, yellow feet.

Time for roasting, about 1 hour.
Time for roasting wild duck, 25 to 30 minutes.

BLACK GAME

BLACK cock and grey hens.

These arrive frozen from Siberia. They should be cooked as soon as they are thawed. The tails of the young birds are undeveloped. A very curly large tail is a sign of age.

Time for roasting, ¾ hour to 1¼ hours, according to size.

GROUSE

GROUSE should have bright, glossy plumage and undeveloped spurs. The quill feathers of the wings are less firmly fixed in young birds than in old ones.

Time for roasting, 20 to 35 minutes.

GOOSE

THIS should have a soft, yellow bill that can be easily broken, and yellow, pliable feet.

An old goose has a reddish bill, and the legs are inclined to be hairy.

Time for roasting, 20 minutes to the pound.

Average time, 1½ hours for medium-sized goose.

PARTRIDGE

THE legs should be yellowish and the longest wing feathers sharp-pointed.

Rounded feathers and dark legs are the sign of an old bird.

The bills should be sharp-pointed and dark in colour.

Time for roasting, 20 to 25 minutes.

GUINEA FOWLS

GUINEA fowls are dry, and should always be larded.

Time for roasting, about 45 minutes.

PIGEONS

THESE are best fresh, and should not be kept for more than two days after killing.

They should be drawn as soon as killed.

If the vent is discoloured, they are stale.

The feet should be supple and pliable, and never hard and dry.

Time for roasting, 20 minutes.

PHEASANT

THE plumage should be bright and glossy and the legs smooth.

The cock bird should have short spurs; long spurs are a sign of age.

Time for roasting, 30 to 45 minutes.
Time for boiling, 1 to 1¼ hours.

PTARMIGAN

THESE are sent frozen from Siberia, and should be cooked as soon as they are thawed.

Time for roasting, about 45 minutes.

SNIPE

SHOULD not be drawn.
Time, 15 minutes.

TEAL

SHOULD have a pliable bill.
Time, 20 to 25 minutes.

TURKEY

A HEN turkey has whiter flesh and is therefore suitable for boiling. It is unprofitable to buy a very small turkey.

The breast should be plump and the flesh white, the legs smooth and black, the spurs short and the feet supple and moist. Rough, reddish legs are a sign of age and toughness.

Time for roasting, allow 15 minutes to the pound.

Average time, 2 to 2½ hours.

Time for boiling, 15 minutes to the pound.

Time for braising, about 3 hours.

WOODCOCK

Do not draw.
Time for roasting, 20 to 25 minutes.

HARE

THE cleft of the lips should be close and the claws smooth and sharp. The lower jawbone should be brittle.

Time for roasting, about 1½ hours.

Time for Jugged Hare, about 2 hours.

RABBITS

THE cleft of the lips should be close and the claws sharp.

The lower jawbone should be brittle and easily broken.

Time for roasting, 45 minutes to 1 hour.

Time for boiling, 45 minutes to 1 hour.

BAKING HINTS

GAME is ready to be cooked when the inside thigh feathers can be easily plucked.

Poultry and game can stand a hotter oven than meat.

Large birds should be cooked in a hot oven for 15 minutes, and a slower one for the rest of the time.

Small birds can have a hot oven all the time.

Frequent basting is the chief necessity to make the birds nice and brown and appetising.

HOW TO TRUSS A FOWL

To Draw a Fowl

Cut the skin down the back of the neck, open it out, and cut off the neck as close to the body as possible, being careful not to cut the top skin.

Put your fingers in at the neck end, remove the crop, and loosen the interior. Then turn the bird round, make a slit at the vent, and draw out the gut, liver, heart, gizzard, and lights.

Be very careful not to break the gall bag, which is attached to the liver, as this would give the bird a bitter flavour.

Wipe the inside with a damp cloth, cut off the feet and truss the bird into shape.

To Truss for Roasting

If the bird is to be stuffed, put the stuffing in at the neck end, fold the skin over it on to the back and tuck the tips of the wings over the skin. Put a skewer through the wing, catching in the thigh also, then through the body, and out the other side in the same way.

Keep the legs in position by tying them round the knee joint, then crossing the string over on to the back. Make a slit just above the vent and put the tail through it.

To Truss for Boiling

A fowl is trussed rather differently for boiling; the skin being loosened round the legs, then the latter pushed in and the skin drawn over them. To do this, put your fingers inside the body and work from the thick end of the leg.

The tail is usually turned inside.

As an *old* bird is more often than not used for boiling, it is advisable to draw the sinews. This should be done first. Break the leg bone just above the feet and draw out the sinews, then cut off the leg bone down to the knee joint.

THE GIBLETS

The giblets (gizzard, liver, heart and neck) should always be utilised. They can be used for gravy, soup, etc., or made into a pie or stew. The feet also contain a lot of nourishment, and can be boiled down for stock.

To CLEAN THEM.—Scald the feet, then skin them, removing the nails at the same time.

Cut open the gizzard and remove the thick inner skin and bag. Remove the gall bag from the liver, then wash the gizzard, heart, liver and neck in water, to which a little salt has been added.

USUAL ACCOMPANIMENTS TO SERVE WITH POULTRY

ROAST FOWL

Stuff with veal stuffing. Serve with boiled pork or bacon, or rolls of bacon, grilled or baked. Also bread sauce and slightly thickened brown gravy. Fried or baked sausages are also often served.

BOILED FOWL

Coat with egg or parsley sauce, and serve separately some of the liquid in which it was boiled.

ROAST DUCK

Stuff with sage and onion stuffing. Serve with apple sauce and thick brown gravy. (The stuffing for this is put in the tail end.)

ROAST TURKEY

Veal or chestnut stuffing. Stuff body of bird with sausage meat. Serve with same accompaniments as Roast Fowl.

ROAST GOOSE

Same as Duck.

CHICKEN A LA BECHAMEL

INGREDIENTS.—1 small chicken, butter, 2 to 4 oz. of mushrooms, ½ pint of stock (see p. 12).

FOR THE SAUCE.—¾ pint of milk, ¼ pint of water, 1½ oz. of margarine, 1½ oz. of flour, ½ carrot and onion, sprig of parsley, pepper and salt, small piece of celery.

METHOD.—Prepare the carrot, celery and onion, and put them whole into a saucepan, with the milk and water. Add also a sprig of parsley.

Bring them slowly to the boil, draw the pan aside and leave it until the milk is well flavoured, then strain.

Have the chicken cut into small joints. Prepare and cleanse the mushrooms.

Melt the butter in a saucepan, season the chicken, and fry it a few joints at a time, until it is pale brown, then fry the mushrooms lightly. Draw the pan aside, put back the chicken and add the stock, cover the pan, and finish cooking gently until tender.

Meanwhile, make a thick white sauce in the usual way (for method see p. 41) with the flavoured milk, margarine and flour. Boil it for a few minutes and season it to taste. When the chicken is ready, arrange it on a dish with the mushrooms, and serve with the sauce.

Sufficient for five or six persons.

CHAUDFROID OF CHICKEN

INGREDIENTS.—1 cold roast chicken, ¾ pint of chaudfroid sauce (see below), a green salad.

METHOD.—Carve the chicken into neat joints, cutting off the pinions from the wings. The drumsticks are best not used for this dainty dish. Remove all sinew and skin from the joints.

When the chaudfroid sauce is cold and beginning to thicken, coat each joint, using a tablespoon to do so. Lay them on a grid to set.

To serve, arrange them neatly round a green salad.

Sufficient for four or five persons.

THE CHAUDFROID SAUCE

INGREDIENTS.—½ pint of hot Béchamel sauce (see p. 42), 1 gill of hot water, ½ packet of aspic jelly, 1 gill of mayonnaise (see p. 42) or salad cream.

METHOD.—Melt the aspic jelly in the hot water and strain it into the

Béchamel sauce. As soon as it is cold, stir in the mayonnaise. Mix well and, when thick enough to coat the back of a wooden spoon, pour the sauce over cutlets, joints of chicken, fillets of fish or anything that it is desired to serve " in chaudfroid."

NOTE.—If liked, chaudfroid sauce may be coloured pink with cochineal or pale green with a green vegetable colouring.

CHICKEN EN CASSEROLE

INGREDIENTS.—1 chicken, butter or dripping, flour, 1 onion, 1 or 2 cloves, a few celery seeds, salt and pepper.

METHOD.—When buying the chicken, ask the poulterer to cut it into joints. Cleanse the giblets and make stock with them, adding an onion, one or two cloves, and a few celery seeds (tied in muslin) to flavour.

Dredge the joints with flour and fry them till light brown in a little hot fat, then put them into a casserole. Add thickened brown gravy. Put the chicken into the oven and simmer it gently till tender, the time depending on the age of the bird. Serve it in a casserole.

A sliced onion, lightly fried, or a few mushrooms, or some peas may be added, or forcemeat balls may be served.

FOR THE GRAVY.—Blend a little flour in the fat after frying the chicken, let this brown slowly, then draw the pan aside. Add the stock, boil it up, season and strain the gravy.

TO MAKE FORCEMEAT BALLS.— Take a good breakfastcupful of breadcrumbs and mix them with two ounces of chopped suet, add one tablespoonful of chopped parsley, half a teaspoonful of herbs, and the grated rind of half a lemon. Season them with pepper and salt, moisten with the juice of half a lemon, and a beaten egg. Form the mixture into small balls, flour, and fry them till brown in a little hot fat, then take them up and add them to the chicken, allowing them about half an hour to cook.

NOTE.—An older, less expensive, bird can be used.

CHICKEN CREAMS

INGREDIENTS.—½ lb. of cold chicken, 1 gill of milk, ½ oz. of flour, ½ oz. of butter, 2 tablespoonfuls of cream, ¾ pint of stock (see p. 12) (made from the carcase), ¾ oz. of leaf gelatine, a bunch of herbs, 1 onion, salt and pepper, 1 bayleaf, ½ lemon, 1 pint of cold water, green salad for garnish.

METHOD.—Break up the carcase and put it in a pint of cold water with any pieces of skin. Bring slowly to the boil and add the herbs, bayleaf, and onion. Simmer gently till reduced to three-quarters of a pint or a little less.

Make a gill of sauce by melting the butter and adding the flour and milk. Stir till it boils. Boil for three minutes.

Mince the cold chicken finely and mix it with the white sauce and cream, add a little lemon-juice and season to taste.

Dissolve the gelatine in the stock made from the carcase and strain it. When the stock is cold, line six small moulds or one larger one with a little of the jelly. To do this, pour in a few tablespoonfuls of stock and turn the mould round till the inside is lined with jelly.

The rest of the strained stock is added gradually to the chicken mixture and stirred till smooth. When cool, pour the mixture into the moulds and leave till set.

To serve the creams, dip the moulds for a few seconds in warm water, then slide them on to a dish. Garnish with green salad.

Sufficient for six small creams.

CHICKEN AND CUCUMBER WITH CREAM SAUCE

INGREDIENTS.—1 chicken, 1 pint of tepid water, 1 onion, 1 bunch of herbs, 1 oz. of butter, 1 oz. of flour, 2 tablespoonfuls of cream, salt and pepper, 2 sticks of celery, half a cucumber.

METHOD.—Put the chicken in a casserole with the water and half a teaspoonful of salt and a little pepper.

Peel and chop the onion and cucumber. Wash and chop the celery and add them all with the herbs to the casserole. Put on the lid and cook in a slow oven for about an hour.

When the chicken is tender, take it out, cut it into joints and pour off half the stock. Remove the herbs, cream the butter and flour on a plate and add them to the stock in the casserole.

Place the casserole over an asbestos mat, stirring the sauce till it boils. Boil for three minutes. Season to taste and put in the chicken to re-heat.

Add the cream just before serving.

Sufficient for four to six persons, according to the size of the chicken.

CURRIED CHICKEN

INGREDIENTS.—1 chicken, 2 oz. of butter, 1 onion, 1 dessertspoonful of curry powder, ¾ pint of stock (see p. 12), 1 dessertspoonful of lemon-juice, 4 oz. of rice, 1 dessertspoonful of flour, seasoning.

METHOD.—Have the chicken cut into joints, and fry it in the hot butter till lightly browned ; then put it into a casserole.

Peel and cut up the onion and fry it lightly, then add the flour and curry powder and stir them until blended, when the pan should be drawn aside from the heat. Add gradually the stock, made by boiling the giblets. Bring the curry mixture to the boil and let it boil for two or three minutes. Season it with salt and pour it over the chicken, then simmer it gently till tender.

Add the lemon-juice, and arrange the chicken on a dish with boiled rice heaped in the centre. If the gravy seems too thin, it may be thickened a little more before serving.

TO PREPARE THE RICE.—Wash it, then put it into slightly salted boiling water and boil it till tender ; then drain in a colander. Pour cold water through it to separate the grains, spread it out and warm it through again.

Sufficient for four or five persons.

DEVILLED CHICKEN LEGS

INGREDIENTS.—2 cold chicken legs, 1 teaspoonful of curry powder, ½ tea-spoonful of made mustard, 1 dessert-spoonful of Worcester sauce, 1 tea-spoonful of tomato ketchup, 1 dessert-spoonful of vinegar, 1 teaspoonful of olive oil, salt and cayenne, 1 oz. of butter.

METHOD.—Cut the chicken legs into joints and make long gashes in the flesh. Fill these with the mustard and curry powder mixed together with half the butter.

Place the chicken in a pie-dish and pour on it the rest of the ingredients. Put what is left of the butter on top and cover the pie-dish with a greased paper. Bake in a hot oven for fifteen minutes.

Sufficient for two, three, or four persons, according to size.

CHICKEN GALANTINE

INGREDIENTS.—1 boiling fowl (about 4½ lb.), ¼ lb. of ham, 1 oz. of pistachio nuts, 1 or 2 eggs, salt, pepper and ground mace, 1 lb. of sausage meat, herbs, an onion, cloves.

FOR THE WHITE CHAUDFROID SAUCE.—⅜ oz. of gelatine, ¼ pint of aspic jelly, ¼ pint of milk, onion, bay leaf, peppercorns, a sprig of parsley, celery seeds, 1 oz. of butter, 1 oz. of flour, 1 tablespoonful of cream.

METHOD.—Have the fowl boned, put the bones into cold water over the fire to make stock, flavouring it with a few herbs, an onion, and one or two cloves.

Put the ham through the mincer and mix it with the sausage meat, season the inside of the fowl and spread with the sausage and ham.

Blanch the pistachio nuts, put a line of them down the centre of the sausage and strips of hard-boiled egg on each side of this. Form it into a long roll, pressing the legs well into the side. Roll the galantine up in a pudding cloth, tie it securely, and put it into the prepared boiling stock. If there is not sufficient to cover add some boiling water.

Let the galantine simmer for about two hours, then unroll it, let out the steam and roll it in a fresh pudding cloth. Press the top slightly and leave it to get cold. Remove from cloth when cold and coat it with chaudfroid sauce. Decorate the galantine with a few pistachio nuts and some chopped aspic jelly.

TO MAKE THE CHAUDFROID SAUCE. —First of all make the savoury white sauce. Stand three-quarters of a pint of milk in a saucepan with an onion, bay leaf, a few peppercorns, a sprig of parsley, and a few celery seeds tied in muslin. Bring this slowly to the boil, and then leave aside until the milk is well flavoured. Let it cool, strain it, and use it for making a thick white sauce.

Melt just over one ounce of butter in a saucepan. Stir in a good ounce of flour, and when well blended add the flavoured milk and stir them till the sauce boils. Simmer it for a few minutes, season, and let it cool.

Dissolve the gelatine in a saucepan with the aspic jelly, then stir them very gradually into the sauce. Strain this through a fine strainer, add the cream, and leave it until the sauce coats the spoon, keeping it stirred occasionally. Pour it over the fowl, coating it evenly.

CHICKEN AND GREEN PEAS EN CASSEROLE

INGREDIENTS.—1 chicken, 1 oz. of bacon dripping, 1 onion, ½ a carrot, 1 oz. of flour, ½ pint of stock (see p. 12), ½ teaspoonful of salt, 1 bunch of herbs, pepper to taste, 1 lb. of young green peas, 1 teaspoonful of sugar.

METHOD.—Heat the dripping in a casserole placed over an asbestos mat. Put in the chicken, breast downwards, and brown it well all over. Chop the onion, and slice the carrot, and put them into the casserole to cook for five minutes. Take out the chicken and make a nice gravy, by frying the flour brown in the dripping and adding the stock. Add salt and pepper and a bunch of herbs, then put back the chicken. Put the lid on the casserole and cook the chicken in a slow oven for one hour.

Shell the peas and cook them for five minutes in boiling water containing one teaspoonful of salt and one teaspoonful of sugar. Strain them and put them in the casserole after it has been in the oven for fifteen minutes.

When the chicken is tender cut it into joints, and re-heat it in the casserole. Remove the herbs and serve the chicken and peas in the casserole.

Sufficient for five or six persons.

CHICKEN A LA MARENGO

INGREDIENTS.—1 fowl, 1 pint of brown sauce, or thick brown gravy, 1 small onion, 2 shallots, about 1 gill of salad oil, seasoning, ¼ lb. of ham, 3 or 4 tomatoes, lemon, fried sippets of bread, deep fat for frying.

METHOD.—After the fowl has been drawn, cut it into joints (about eight or ten pieces, the breast can be cut into two).

Peel and chop the onion and shallots.

Put the oil into a saucepan or frying-pan, and, when hot, put in the joints of chicken and fry until golden brown. Put on to a plate and keep warm. Fry the chopped onions and shallots in the same way, also the ham, previously cut into small pieces.

Place the fried chicken, ham and onions, etc., into a stewpan, add the brown sauce and the sliced tomato, and season well.

Bring to the boil and simmer gently for about one to one hour and a half. If old, it will take a longer time.

While it is cooking, prepare the garnish.

Cut a fairly thin slice of bread into small, triangular shapes.

Put into a frying-basket and fry in a deep pan of hot fat until golden brown.

Pile the joints in the centre of the dish, strain the sauce over them. Arrange the vegetables and ham in small piles round the dish.

Garnish the chicken with the sippets and a few small pieces of cut lemon.

NOTE.—A little sherry may be added to the sauce just before serving if desired.

Deep frying is the French method of frying, but the bread can be fried in a shallow pan with a small quantity of fat. In this case a frying-basket is not necessary.

CHICKEN MOULD

INGREDIENTS.—1 boiling fowl, 2 carrots, 2 onions, 1 bunch of herbs, rind of ½ a lemon, 1 bayleaf, ½ a teaspoonful of celery seeds, or 3 outside leaves of celery, 8 peppercorns, 1 oz. of gelatine, 2 or 3 hard-boiled eggs, 2 tomatoes, ¼ lb. of ham (salt).

METHOD.—This is a delicious dish, and is quite easy to make.

Put the fowl in a steamer over a pan of cold water. In the water put the herbs, lemon-rind, peppercorns, celery seeds, and bayleaf with a teaspoonful of salt. Put it on the gas, and when the water boils, add the onions and carrots cut in quarters.

Steam the fowl *gently* till it is tender —this will take about two hours and a half. The time varies according to the size and age of the fowl. When it is tender, put it on a plate and cut all the flesh from the bones, putting the latter into the pan with the vegetables. Boil the liquid till it is reduced to one and a half pints. Let it get cold and skim off the fat, then put in the gelatine, and allow it to dissolve.

To prepare the mould, slice the hard-boiled eggs and tomatoes. Put into a cake tin a little of the stock containing the gelatine, and when it is cold and beginning to set, run it round the tin. Line the tin with the slices of egg and tomato, and, if liked, decorate it with a few small sprigs of parsley or fine pieces of cooked onion. Pour in a little more stock to make a layer a quarter of an inch thick. When this has set, put in the chicken and ham previously cut up, and any pieces of egg or tomato that were not used for decorating.

Strain the rest of the stock into the tin and leave it to set. To turn out, dip the mould into tepid water for a minute and slip it from the hand on to a dish.

Garnish with watercress.

Sufficient for four persons.

CHICKEN PATTIES

INGREDIENTS.—½ lb. of cold chicken (chopped), 1 oz. of butter, 1¼ oz. of flour, nearly ½ pint of milk, ½ gill of cream, salt and pepper, 6 champignons (chopped), 12 patty cases (see pp. 252 and 253).

METHOD.—Melt the butter, add the flour, and stir in the milk gradually. Stir till it boils and add the champignons and chicken. Keep hot for ten minutes, season and add the cream.

If the patties are to be served hot, fill them with the hot mixture and place in the oven for five minutes.

To make twelve patties.

CHICKEN AND PEAS

INGREDIENTS.—1 chicken, 2 oz. of rice, 1 gill of cold water, 1 bayleaf, 1 tin of peas, ½ pint of hot Béchamel sauce, salt, 1 doz. champignons.

METHOD.—Put the chicken in a double saucepan with the water, half a teaspoonful of salt and a bayleaf. Cook it for two hours.

When the chicken is quite tender, cut it into joints and put these back into the saucepan with the peas and champignons.

Wash the rice and sprinkle it into a large pan of boiling water containing a dessertspoonful of salt. Boil for fifteen minutes. Strain the rice and return it to the pan to keep hot.

Make the Béchamel sauce, using the water the chicken was cooked in. Put two tablespoonfuls of the sauce with the rice and the rest with the chicken.

Serve the rice and peas in heaps round the dish with the chicken in the centre.

Sufficient for four persons.

The Bechamel Sauce

INGREDIENTS.—1 oz. of butter, 1 oz. of flour, 1 tablespoonful of cream, 4 peppercorns, 1 bayleaf, ½ onion, 1½ gills of milk, 1 gill of stock (see p. 12), pepper and salt.

METHOD.—Slice the onion and simmer it gently in the stock and milk with the peppercorns and bayleaf for fifteen minutes. Strain them into a basin.

Melt the butter, add the flour and mix them smoothly. Add the strained liquid, and stir the sauce till it boils. Boil for five minutes, add the cream, and season to taste.

CHICKEN PIE

With Ham, Sausages and Hard-Boiled Eggs

INGREDIENTS.—1 roasting fowl, ½ lb. of pork sausages, ¼ lb. of ham, 4 or 5 sheets of leaf gelatine, 2 hard-boiled eggs, an onion, cloves, egg for glaze, salt, pepper, and powdered mace, about 1½ lb. of flaky pastry (see p. 252).

METHOD.—Have the chicken drawn and then cut it into joints. It is better also to remove the skin.

Cut up the ham, hard-boil the eggs and cut them in slices. Take the sausages out of their skins and form the sausage meat into small balls.

Season all the prepared ingredients and arrange them in a pie-dish with two sheets of gelatine in the centre, then pour in about three-fourths of a gill of water. The dish should be filled level, but not packed tightly. Sausage meat may be used more or less as required.

Roll out the pastry thickly and cut an oval piece for the top of the pie, then roll the remainder rather thinly and cut a narrow strip for the rim. Damp the rim and line it with pastry, then damp the pastry rim and cover the pie. Trim and decorate the edge, then roll out the pastry trimmings thickly and cut small hearts or leaves and put them on the top. Brush the pie with egg to glaze, make a hole in the centre, and put the pie in a hot oven to bake, lessening the heat as soon as the pastry is risen and lightly browned.

It will take about an hour and a half altogether.

When cooked, fill up the pie with stock made from the giblets, feet, and skin. This requires an onion, a few cloves, salt, pepper, and mace to flavour. Just before adding it to the pie, dissolve two or three sheets of gelatine in it, and strain it. Serve the pie cold.

Sufficient for six persons.

NOTE.—The stock should jelly when cold.

BREAD SAUCE

To SERVE WITH GAME AND POULTRY

INGREDIENTS.—1 pint of milk, 1 small onion, 1 oz. of butter or margarine, ½ pint of breadcrumbs, pressed down, 2 or 3 cloves, salt and pepper, cream if liked.

METHOD.—Put the milk into a saucepan with the onion and cloves and leave it at the side of the fire for an hour or so, then bring it to the boil and add the breadcrumbs, butter, and seasoning.

Stand the pan aside for a few minutes to allow the crumbs to swell, then remove the flavourings. re-heat

the sauce, and serve it in a sauce-boat. A tablespoonful of cream may be added, if liked.

This amount of sauce is sufficient for from six to eight persons.

QUENELLES OF CHICKEN

INGREDIENTS.—10 oz. of chicken (without bone), ¼ gill of stock (white) (see p. 12), salt and pepper, ¼ oz. of butter, 1½ oz. of flour, 1 egg, a few cooked green peas.

METHOD.—Remove all skin and gristle from the chicken and put through a fine mincer, then pound it well. Melt the butter in a saucepan, add the flour, mix well together, add the stock, bring to the boil, and cook until the mixture does not adhere to the sides of the pan, keeping it well stirred. When cool, add the minced chicken to this. Season well with pepper and salt, and mix all together.

Add the egg and beat it well in.

Pound all together again, then rub through a fine wire sieve.

Well grease a frying-pan or sauté pan, and make the mixture into quenelles as explained. Place them in the pan, with boiling water or stock, and poach them for about twelve minutes, keeping them well basted.

When cooked, they will feel firm. Take them carefully from the water, drain well, and arrange down the centre of a dish.

Make some thick white sauce (see p. 41). Coat each quenelle with it, and pour the remainder round the dish.

Garnish each with one or two green peas, and place about one tablespoonful on each side of the dish. Serve at once.

To SHAPE THE QUENELLES

WELL fill a tablespoon with some of the mixture, dip a knife into hot water, and shape it up so that it forms an oval shape. Then dip another tablespoon in hot water and remove the quenelle from the first spoon into the greased pan.

CHICKEN RISSOLES

INGREDIENTS.—1 breakfastcupful of cold cooked chicken, ½ gill of thick white sauce (see p. 41), flaky pastry (see p. 252), 2 level tablespoonfuls of minced mushroom, a few grains of cayenne, egg, 1 tablespoonful of milk, salt.

METHOD.—Mince the chicken very finely. Mix it with the mushroom, seasoning and sauce. Cook it for one minute and leave the paste to cool.

Roll out the pastry very thinly and cut it into twelve four-inch rounds. Divide the paste into twelve portions and place one on each round of pastry, a little to one side of the centre. Flatten each slightly. Wet the rim of the pastry with the white of egg and fold it over.

Mix the remainder of the egg-white and yolk together and beat in one tablespoonful of milk. Brush the rissoles with the mixture very carefully. Cook the rissoles in hot fat until they are golden-brown. Drain them on paper and serve them at once.

Sufficient for twelve rissoles.

CHICKEN ROLLS

INGREDIENTS.—3 or 4 small rolls, $\frac{1}{4}$ lb. of cold chicken, 2 oz. of tongue, $\frac{1}{2}$ gill of salad cream, 1 teaspoonful of Worcester sauce, $\frac{1}{2}$ packet of aspic jelly, 1 gill of hot water, beetroot and endive or a little cress, 1 stick of celery, salt and pepper.

METHOD.—Put the aspic jelly in a small basin and pour on the hot water.

Remove any skin from the chicken.

Chop the chicken, tongue, and celery, and mix half the jelly with them. When it is cold, add the salad cream and sauce, and season to taste with salt and pepper.

Let the mixture set.

Cut off the top of the rolls and remove some of the crumb.

Fill the rolls with the chicken mixture and serve them decorated with beetroot and endive or cress, and the rest of the jelly.

Sufficient for three persons.

SPATCHCOCK OF CHICKEN

INGREDIENTS,—A very young chicken, 1 oz. of butter, salt and pepper, fresh breadcrumbs, watercress.

METHOD.—Choose only a very young tender chicken. They are very nice

from six to eight weeks old. Never make a spatchcock of fully grown birds, as they would be tough.

A poulterer will always draw the birds. If, however, they should be home killed, pluck out all the feathers and cut off the head, and then draw them as follows.

Open the vent and with the two first fingers loosen the inside from the body of the chicken When quite loose, take it in the hand and draw it out whole and clean. Cut the green gall bladder from the liver and keep the liver for grilling.

Cut off the feet and bony part of the wings.

Split the bird in half, wash it, and lay it on a chopping board. Then flatten it with a rolling pin.

Melt the butter and brush it all over the flesh with a pastry brush. Season with salt and pepper.

Put the breadcrumbs on a paper and lay the two halves of chicken in them. Press the crumbs on and gently shake off loose ones.

Brush with butter again and place on a meat stand in a baking tin.

Heat the griller till red hot, put the chicken under it and brown the outside as quickly as possible for two minutes.

Lower the gas and finish cooking very slowly, turning the chicken over every five minutes.

If it becomes dry, butter it again.

Long, slow grilling for thirty minutes is needed to keep it tender and cook it thoroughly.

Spatchcock is served with potato straws and garnished with watercress.

Dish up daintily and put a cutlet frill on each leg bone.

ROAST DUCK

WITH SAGE AND ONION STUFFING

INGREDIENTS.—1 medium-sized duck, $1\frac{1}{2}$ oz. of breadcrumbs, 1 level teaspoonful of powdered sage, $\frac{1}{4}$ lb. of minced onion, 1 oz. of butter, seasoning, dripping, flour, stock (see p. 12).

METHOD.—TO MAKE THE STUFFING : Mix the breadcrumbs with the minced onion and powdered sage. Add seasoning to taste and moisten with butter, the latter warmed sufficiently to melt it.

Have the duck drawn and trussed, then stuff it with the prepared stuffing, putting it in at the tail end.

Place it in a baking-tin with the dripping, cover the breast with a thickly greased paper and bake it till tender, keeping it well basted. It will take from one and quarter to one and a half hours.

Remove the greased paper for the last ten to fifteen minutes, dredge breast with flour, baste the duck and put it back for a final browning.

Serve it with thickened brown gravy made by browning some flour in the baking-tin after pouring off nearly all the fat. Draw the pan aside, add some stock, then boil it up, season it and strain it. Use stock made from the giblets for the foundation of the gravy.

Apple sauce should accompany this dish.

APPLE SAUCE

INGREDIENTS.—2 lb. of cooking apples, 1½ tablespoonfuls of sugar, ¾ to 1 gill of water.

METHOD.—Prepare the apples as for stewing and cook them with the sugar and water until tender. The amount of sugar and water required varies according to the kind of apples used, but the sauce should be a little tart.

When tender, mash the apples to a pulp or rub them through a sieve. Re-heat the same before serving it. A walnut of butter may be added, if liked.

DUCK AND GREEN PEAS

INGREDIENTS.—A pair of ducks, or 1 duck according to size.

FOR THE STUFFING.—3 or 4 medium-sized onions. ¼ lb. of breadcrumbs, 1 teaspoonful of powdered sage leaves, pepper and salt, 2 oz. of butter or margarine.

METHOD.—Have the ducks drawn and trussed. Cleanse the giblets and use them for making the stock, adding an onion to flavour. This will make the foundation for the gravy.

To MAKE THE STUFFING.—Peel and mince the onions and mix them with the breadcrumbs. Add the sage and

seasoning to taste, and mix the ingredients well. Then stir in the butter, warmed sufficiently to melt it. A beaten egg may also be added to this stuffing, but is not absolutely necessary. Stuff the ducks, then put them into a baking-tin with dripping, covering the breast with a greased paper. Bake them till tender, keeping them well basted. They will take about one and a half hours.

Remove the greased papers about fifteen minutes before taking them up. Dredge them lightly with flour, baste them well, and put them back for a final browning.

Serve the ducks with apple sauce (see above) and thickened brown gravy, the latter made by adding a little flour to the baking-tin after pouring off nearly all the fat. This is browned slowly, then drawn aside, some stock is added, and it is then boiled up, seasoned, and strained. Green peas are the favourite vegetable to serve with this dish.

BRAISED WILD DUCK

INGREDIENTS.—1 wild duck, 2 oz. of dripping, ¾ oz. of flour, 1 gill of water, 1 orange, 2 lemons, a small tin of cherries.

METHOD.—Spread the duck with dripping and bake it in a tin in a hot oven for fifteen minutes.

Place the duck in a casserole in a slow oven. Pour off half the dripping from the baking-tin. Add the flour and fry it brown, stirring well.

Add half a gill of lemon-juice and half a gill of cherry-juice. Pour in the water, stir the gravy till it boils, and put it with the duck.

Bake for twenty minutes.

Heat the cherries and put them inside two lemons cut to the shape of baskets.

Dish up the duck, garnished with cherries and sliced orange, and with the gravy poured round.

Sufficient for two or three persons.

ROAST WILD DUCK AND ORANGE SAUCE

HAVE the duck drawn and trussed, cover the breast with a well-buttered paper, and put it into a baking-tin with some fat. Bake it for from thirty to forty-five minutes, or till tender, keeping it well basted. Remove the paper when the duck is nearly cooked, dredge the breast with flour, baste it, and return it to the oven to finish cooking and brown.

Serve the duck on a croûton of fried bread, garnish it with water-cress and serve it with the usual game accompaniments; but make a slightly thick brown gravy flavoured with orange and lemon-juice, a little finely-minced shallot and some port wine.

Serve an orange salad with either hot or cold wild duck.

Orange Salad

Peel some oranges, removing as much of the white pith as possible, and cut them in slices. Sprinkle them with lemon-juice, and dress them with a dressing of salad oil and Tarragon vinegar, seasoned with sugar and pepper to taste.

Garnish the salad with chopped chervil. This may, if liked, be served on lettuce leaves or endive.

GAME CUTLETS

INGREDIENTS.—Scraps of left-over game, stock (see p. 12), ¾ oz. of butter or margarine, ½ oz. of flour, seasoning, 1 dessertspoonful of minced onion or onion-juice, egg, breadcrumbs, deep fat.

METHOD.—Put the scraps of left-over game through the mincer. You will require four ounces to this amount of sauce.

Melt the fat in a saucepan, add the flour, and when mixed smoothly, stir in the stock and bring it to the boil. Add the seasoning and onion, and boil the sauce gently for a few minutes, then take it off the gas and stir in the minced game. Turn the mixture on to a plate, spread it evenly and leave it to get firm, then divide into eight portions.

Shape each portion (on a lightly floured board) into a cutlet shape, then brush them with beaten egg and coat them with breadcrumbs.

Put only enough at a time into a frying-basket to cover the bottom of it, and when the fat begins to smoke

faintly, stand the basket in the pan of fat and fry the cutlets till golden.

Drain them on paper, stick a piece of spaghetti in the top of each, and serve them garnished with parsley or watercress.

SAVOURY GAME JELLY

INGREDIENTS.—1 cupful of any cold game, the juice of 3 oranges, 1 whole orange for garnish, 2 teaspoonfuls of meat extract, ¾ oz. of gelatine, 4 chives, 1 pint of water or stock, 1 hard-boiled egg, 1 onion, ½ teaspoonful of celery seeds.

METHOD.—Make some stock by breaking up the carcase of the bird and putting it in a pan with cold water to cover it (about a pint and a half). Bring it slowly to the boil and add an onion and the celery seeds. Simmer till reduced to a pint. If there is not time to make stock, use a pint of water well flavoured with meat extract.

Soak the gelatine in the orange juice for ten minutes, then dissolve it in the stock and strain the liquid into a basin.

Chop the game and mince the chives and add them both to the stock.

Season to taste, and pour half a cupful of the stock into a mould rinsed in cold water. When it has set, decorate the mould with pieces of hard-boiled egg. Pour on a little more stock, and after letting it set, fill up with the rest of the mixture.

Turn out as for other jellies, and serve with watercress.

Garnish the dish with slices of orange.

Sufficient for three or four persons.

GAME KROMESKIES

A GOOD WAY OF USING UP COLD GAME

INGREDIENTS.—¼ lb. of left-over game (minced), 1 oz. of cooked ham (minced), ½ oz. of flour, ½ oz. of butter or margarine, 1 gill of milk, seasoning, 2 medium-sized mushrooms, thin slices of fat bacon, deep fat for frying.

FOR THE BATTER.—3 oz. of flour, 1 dessertspoonful of salad oil, 1 gill of warm water, 1 or 2 egg-whites, salt.

METHOD.—Melt the butter in a saucepan, add the flour, and when well blended stir in the milk and bring it to the boil, then boil it gently for a few minutes. Peel and stalk the mushrooms, cleanse them in slightly salted water, drain them, mince them, and add them to the sauce with the prepared game and ham. Season the mixture to taste, spread it on a plate, and leave it to get thoroughly cold.

To MAKE THE BATTER.—Sift the flour with a pinch of salt, make a hole in the centre and pour in the oil, then add the warm water gradually and mix to a smooth batter. Beat it well and let it stand for a few hours. When ready to use it, fold in the stiffly-whisked egg-whites.

To FRY THE KROMESKIES.—Divide the prepared meat mixture into eight or ten portions and form each into a sausage shape, using a little flour to prevent it sticking to the fingers. Roll up each sausage in a piece of fat bacon, then dip it in batter and put them into a deep pan of hot fat to cook. Fry the sausages gently till golden, then drain and serve them.

SOUFFLE OF GAME

INGREDIENTS.—$\frac{1}{2}$ lb. of any cold game, 2 tablespoonfuls of salad cream, salt and pepper, grated rind of $\frac{1}{2}$ lemon, $\frac{1}{2}$ packet of aspic jelly, 1 pint of cold water, 1 truffle.

METHOD.—Take the skin and bones from the game and stew them in the water for one hour. Boil the water down to half a pint and strain it on to the aspic jelly. Leave it to get cold.

Cut the game into dice and mix it with the salad cream and lemon-rind, adding salt and pepper to taste. When the jelly begins to set, whisk it well with an egg-whisk till it is stiff and frothy. Stir in the seasoned game.

Tie round any dish with straight sides a double piece of paper wide enough to come two inches above the rim of the dish. Fill the dish with the jelly and game mixture, and if possible place it on ice.

To serve, remove the paper, sprinkle the chopped truffle on the top and place pieces of broken ice round.

Sufficient for two persons.

GIBLET PIE

INGREDIENTS.—2 sets of chickens' giblets, flour, pepper, and salt, 1 onion, $\frac{1}{2}$ lb. of bladebone steak, water, about 1 lb. of flaky pastry (see p. 252), yolk of egg and milk for glaze.

METHOD.—Cleanse the giblets thoroughly by soaking them in cold water with salt. Drain them well. It is important to remember to remove the gall-bag from the liver, and the inside of the gizzard, together with the inner lining. Cut up the steak. Flour both the steak and giblets, season them well, and put them into a casserole. Add the onion (minced), cover them with water, put on the lid, and simmer them gently in the oven for two or three hours until tender. Arrange the steak and giblets in a pie-dish with just a little of the gravy, and leave them to get cold. There should be sufficient meat and giblets to fill the dish.

Roll out the pastry thickly and cut a piece to fit the top of the pie-dish, then roll out the trimmings, and put a strip round the rim of the dish. Damp this and cover the pie, trim and decorate the edge and put a tassel and some leaves of pastry on the top.

Make a hole at each end to allow the steam to escape, brush the pie with beaten yolk of egg mixed with milk and put it in a hot oven to bake. It will take about half an hour to cook. Serve the pie hot with the remainder of the gravy.

Sufficient for three or four persons.

ROAST GREY HEN WITH BANANAS

INGREDIENTS.—1 grey hen (or black-cock), a rasher of fat bacon. 2 oz. of dripping, $\frac{3}{4}$ oz. of flour, $1\frac{1}{2}$ gills of hot water, juice of half an orange, salt and pepper, 2 teaspoonfuls of any jam or jelly, garnish with 3 bananas.

METHOD.—Tie the rasher of bacon over the breast and spread one ounce of dripping over the body of the bird. Put the rest of the dripping in the tin and use it for basting.

Put the bird in a hot oven and lower the heat a little after ten minutes.

Baste every ten minutes, pouring the dripping over every part.

Grey hens and blackcocks are both rather dry, and therefore need plenty of basting and a good gravy.

The time taken to cook them is about an hour, but it may be more if the bird is a large one.

When done, remove the skewer and string used by the poulterer for trussing and take off the piece of bacon.

Put the bird on a hot dish and keep it hot while making the gravy.

Pour off half the dripping, fry the flour to a rich brown in the tin in which the bird was cooked, and put in the orange-juice and jam.

Add the hot water and stir till it boils. Boil for three minutes and season to taste. Slice the bananas and heat them in the gravy for about two minutes.

Serve with the bananas and gravy round the bird.

Sufficient for about three or four persons.

ROAST GOOSE

WITH APPLE RINGS AND APPLE SAUCE

INGREDIENTS.—1 goose, apples as required.

FOR THE STUFFING.—1 lb. of onions, about 2 doz. sage leaves, 2 oz. of butter or margarine, 4 oz. of breadcrumbs, pepper and salt, egg.

METHOD.—To make the stuffing, peel and grate the onions and mix them with the breadcrumbs. Rub the sage leaves to a powder, and add them to the breadcrumbs, with seasoning to taste. Stir in the (melted) butter and moisten the stuffing with egg as required.

Have the goose trussed, and stuff it with the prepared stuffing, putting this in at the tail end. Place the goose in a baking-tin with dripping, cover the breast with a thickly greased paper. Bake the goose till tender and nicely browned, keeping it well basted—a ten-pound goose will take from two to two and a quarter hours to cook. Serve the goose with thickened brown gravy, using stock made from the giblets for the foundation, and garnish the dish with fried apple rings.

TO PREPARE THE APPLE RINGS.— Choose good-sized cooking apples,

peel and core them and slice them thickly. Fry them in hot fat (using some of the fat from the goose), turning them over when brown. These rings may be served instead of, or in addition to, apple sauce, as may be preferred.

FOR THE APPLE SAUCE.—Use sharp apples such as Wellingtons—peel, quarter, and core them, slice them and cook them till tender, adding sugar to taste and a little water as required.

Rub the apple through a sieve, return it to the pan with a walnut of butter, and re-heat the apple sauce.

GROUSE IN CASSEROLE

INGREDIENTS.—2 grouse, $\frac{1}{4}$ lb. of mushrooms, 2 tomatoes, 1 onion and carrot, seasoning, 2 oz. of butter, 1 oz. of flour, 1 pint of stock (see p. 12), fleurons of pastry (puff or flaky pastry, see p. 252).

METHOD.—Have the grouse drawn and cut into joints. Wipe the joints, season them, and sprinkle them with flour. Fry them in the hot butter for a few minutes till lightly browned, then take them up and put them into a casserole. Add the flour to the butter left in the pan, and stir it over a low burner until brown, adding a little more butter if required. Draw the pan aside, add the stock, boil it up and add seasoning to taste.

Peel and stalk the mushrooms, cleanse them in slightly salted water, drain them and cut them into quarters. Add them to the casserole with the carrot and onion (peeled and left whole). Skin and chop up the tomatoes and add them also. Strain as much of the prepared gravy over the grouse as may be required, cover the casserole and cook the grouse gently till tender.

Remove the carrot and onion, and serve the grouse garnished with fleurons of pastry.

TO PREPARE THE FLEURONS.— Roll out odd trimmings of puff or flaky pastry thinly, and stamp them into small rounds with a fluted cutter, then stamp half-way over these rounds with a plain cutter the same size. This gives you a crescent shape. Place them on a baking sheet and brush them with egg to glaze them, then bake them in a hot oven until golden.

GROUSE PIE

INGREDIENTS.—1 grouse, ½ lb. of fillet of veal, ¼ lb. of mushrooms, juice and rind of a lemon, 2 hard-boiled eggs, 1 oz. of dripping, 1 dessert-spoonful of chopped parsley, salt and pepper, ¾ pint of cold water, 1 oz. of butter, ½ oz. of flour, ½ oz. of gelatine, ½ gill of port wine.

FOR THE FORCEMEAT BALLS.—1 teacupful of breadcrumbs, ¼ onion (chopped), grated peel of ½ a lemon, 1 dessertspoonful of chopped parsley, the liver of the grouse, 1 egg, ½ oz. of suet (chopped), deep frying fat.

FOR THE CRUST.—½ gill of hot water, ¼ gill of hot milk, 6 oz. of butter, ¾ lb. of flour, ½ teaspoonful of salt.

METHOD.—The best way to prepare this dish is to cook the game and make the stock and gravy the day before.

To make the meat savoury, fry it quickly in the dripping, turning it over till nicely browned all over.

Put the grouse, veal and lemon peel in a double saucepan with the cold water and half a teaspoonful of salt, and cook for one hour. The stock thus obtained is used for making a rich brown gravy. The grouse and veal can be put aside on a plate and cut up into nice pieces after the gravy is made.

To make the gravy, melt the butter, fry the flour brown in a frying-pan, and add the lemon-juice and stock. Stir till it boils. Boil for three minutes and season.

When cool add the gelatine and dissolve it slowly.

Strain into a basin and leave till next day.

MAKING THE CRUST

The crust is a good one that can safely be eaten without fear of indigestion. To make it, melt the butter in the milk and water and add it to the flour and salt in a mixing basin.

Mix and knead well.

Put a greased game pie mould on a baking sheet and roll out a piece of pastry, the shape of the bottom (oval) and slightly larger.

Put this inside the mould flat on the baking-tin and coming about half an inch up the side.

Having lined the bottom of the mould in this way, roll out a long strip to line the sides. Press it on to the inside of the mould and make it join the piece at the bottom. Fill it up with haricot beans, rice or flour, and put on an oval piece for a lid. Glaze with a beaten egg. Bake it for about twenty-five to thirty minutes, and, when cold, empty out the beans.

MAKING THE FORCEMEAT BALLS. Chop the cooked liver, and mix it with the other forcemeat ingredients.

Shape the mixture into small balls and fry for three minutes in deep fat.

Before finishing the pie see if the gravy has set into a jelly, and if it is not firm enough, add a little more gelatine.

In any case melt it down and add the wine, but do not make it at all hot.

FILLING THE PIE

When ready to fill the pie, have ready at hand the pieces of grouse and veal, the mushrooms (peeled and chopped), the forcemeat balls, parsley, and hard-boiled eggs cut in quarters.

Put some forcemeat balls and egg at the bottom, then a layer of game and veal, sprinkle with mushrooms and parsley, and season with salt and pepper, and add another layer of game and veal. Fill up the pie in this way and put in about half the gravy. Put on the lid and bake for twenty minutes. When cold, remove the lid and fill up the pie with gravy.

Put a paper frill round the sides of the pie and decorate the top with the head and feet, the wings and some of the breast feathers, which the poulterer will prepare.

JUGGED HARE

INGREDIENTS.—1 hare, 1 carrot and onion, powdered mace, a few mixed herbs, 3 or 4 cloves, pepper and salt, 1½ lb. of bones, 4 pints of cold water, fat for frying, flour, 1 wineglassful of port wine, red currant jelly.

FOR THE FORCEMEAT BALLS.—8 tablespoonfuls of breadcrumbs, 3 oz. of suet, 1 flat tablespoonful of chopped parsley, ½ teaspoonful of mixed herbs, grated rind and juice of a lemon, 1 egg, pepper and salt.

METHOD.—Remove the inside from the hare, being careful to save the thick blood.

Skin the hare, wipe it, and cut into joints.

Wash the head, heart, and liver in some cold salted water and put into a saucepan with the blood and the bones, also previously washed.

Add the four pints of cold water and a teaspoonful of salt, and bring the stock to the boil.

Remove the scum, add the herbs tied in a piece of muslin, also the pepper and mace.

Scrape and wash the carrot, peel the onion, and stick the cloves into it, and add these to the stock, and simmer all together for three or four hours ; keep well skimmed to remove the grease.

Flour the joints of hare, melt either some butter or dripping in a pan, and fry them lightly so as to brown them slightly. Then place in a large brown jar or casserole. Mix some flour to a smooth paste with water.

When the stock is ready, strain it into another saucepan and add the thickening of flour and water, stir well and boil for a few minutes. If necessary a few drops of browning may be added.

Strain the gravy over the fried hare, leaving out about one pint of it for the forcemeat balls.

The hare should be just covered.

Place in a moderately hot oven, bring to the boil, and simmer for about two hours.

Just before serving, add to it the port wine.

FORCEMEAT BALLS

Make the breadcrumbs. Finely chop the suet. Wash, scald and chop the parsley. Mix all together with the herbs and grated lemon-rind, and pepper and salt.

Strain in the lemon-juice, beat the egg, add it, and mix well.

Divide into about twelve equal portions, and shape each into a small ball.

Roll each ball in flour, and fry in hot fat until golden brown.

Put them into a saucepan in the remainder of the hot gravy and simmer for about half an hour before the hare is ready to be served. Heap the hare into a large dish, pour some of the gravy round, the remainder serve separately. Garnish with the forcemeat balls, and serve red currant jelly with it.

NOTE.—The gravy should be quite thick.

ROAST OR BAKED HARE

INGREDIENTS.—1 hare, milk for basting (about 1½ pints), dripping for basting, 1 onion, a few cloves, a few mixed herbs, 2d. of bones, 2 pints of water, flour, seasoning, browning, red currant jelly.

FOR THE STUFFING.—2 oz. of suet, 1 breakfastcupful of breadcrumbs (well pressed down), twopennyworth of parsley, 1 teaspoonful of mixed herbs, rind and juice of 1 lemon, 1 egg, pepper and salt.

METHOD.—Skin the hare, remove the eyes. Cut it open and take out the heart, liver, etc. Wipe the hare well, inside and out.

Wash the bones, the heart, and the liver, in cold salted water.

Put them into a saucepan and add the quart of cold water, pepper and salt, and a few mixed herbs tied in a piece of muslin.

Peel the onion, stick a few cloves into it, and add.

Bring slowly to the boil, take away the scum, and simmer slowly for about three hours, then mix some flour to a smooth paste, and thicken the stock with it.

TO MAKE THE STUFFING.—Skin and finely chop the suet.

Make the breadcrumbs by rubbing stale crumb of bread through a wire sieve or on a bread-grater.

Well wash the parsley ; when quite clean, scald it, strain off the water, and chop it very finely.

Mix all these ingredients together, add the herbs, pepper and salt, and grated lemon-rind.

Squeeze the juice from the lemon and strain it into the dry ingredients.

Add the egg and mix all together into a lump.

Put the stuffing into the hare and sew it up with some string, using a trussing needle. Truss the hare into shape, skewer the head back, make it stand up well and look as much as possible the same as when alive.

If it is to be roasted, hang it inside a roasting-tin in front of a clear fire, keeping it well basted with milk. If to be baked, put it on a stand in a baking-tin with about half a pint of milk in the tin.

Put into a hot oven for the first fifteen minutes, then lessen the heat, and cook for about one hour and three-quarters to two hours altogether. Keep it well basted with milk, adding more as required ; when all has been used, put dripping into the tin to finish basting.

When cooked, stand the hare on a hot dish, pour off the fat from the baking-tin, leaving only the brown particles.

Pour the thickened stock into the tin, boil it up, add a few drops of browning.

Strain the gravy round the hare, and serve red currant jelly with it.

NOTE.—If there is any stuffing over, make it into very small balls, brush them with egg, and coat with breadcrumbs and fry until golden brown. These can be used as a garnish.

PARTRIDGE AND MUSH-ROOMS EN CASSEROLE

[INGREDIENTS.—2 partridges, ½ lb. of mushrooms, 1 cupful of hot water, ½ gill of milk, ½ onion, 1 oz. of butter, 1 oz. of flour, salt and pepper, 1 bay-leaf.

METHOD.—Chop the onion and cut the partridges in half. Put them in a casserole with the water, bayleaf, and butter, and a quarter of a teaspoonful of salt. Put the lid on and cook in a slow oven for about an hour.

Peel and wash the mushrooms, remove the stalks, and put them in the casserole to cook for the last half-hour.

To make the sauce, pour off the stock from the casserole into a sauce-pan, and keep the partridges hot in the oven.

Mix the flour and milk smoothly, and pour it into the stock. Stir till it boils. Boil for three minutes, season to taste, and then pour it over the partridges in the casserole. To make the dish look nice, place a few of the mushrooms on top. Serve in the casserole.

Sufficient for four persons.

ROAST PARTRIDGES

INGREDIENTS.—1 brace of partridges, fat bacon, dripping, flour, stock (see p. 12), seasoning, croûtons of fried bread, watercress.

METHOD.—Have the partridges drawn and trussed, and cover the breasts with fat bacon or thickly greased paper.

Place them in a baking-tin with some dripping, and cook them in the oven till tender, keeping the partridges well basted. They will take from thirty to forty-five minutes to cook.

A few minutes before taking them up, remove the bacon-fat, dredge the breasts with flour, baste them and put the partridges back for a final browning, then take up the birds, serve on croûtons of fried bread, and garnish them with watercress.

Bread sauce (see p. 83), buttered brown crumbs and brown gravy should accompany roast game, and a green or other suitable salad is usually served.

TO MAKE THE GRAVY.—Pour off the fat from the baking-tin, leaving the brown particles. Add some brown stock, then boil it up, season and strain it.

TO PREPARE THE BUTTERED BROWN CRUMBS.—Melt an ounce of butter in a frying-pan, add two ounces of breadcrumbs, and fry them gently till golden, adding a little more butter if required.

Serve the crumbs on a paper doyley.

CHAUDFROID OF PHEASANT

INGREDIENTS.—Cold pheasant, 1 lettuce, a small piece of cucumber, ½ endive, French salad dressing (see p. 168).

FOR CHAUDFROID SAUCE.—1 dessert-spoonful of Bisto, ¼ pint of water well flavoured with meat extract, 1 table-spoonful of red currant jelly, juice of half an orange, ¼ oz. of leaf gelatine.

METHOD.—To make the sauce, soak the gelatine in a gill of cold water for five minutes, then dissolve it slowly.

Mix the Bisto, meat extract, and orange-juice in a saucepan, stir till they boil, and then boil for three minutes. Add the jelly.

Strain the gelatine on to the sauce and leave till it is quite cold.

When it begins to thicken, cut the pheasant into joints and pour the sauce over them. Leave them to set.

To make the salad, wash and shred the lettuce and endive and slice the cucumber.

Mix the lettuce and endive with half the cucumber and the French dressing, and put them into a salad bowl.

Lay the pieces of pheasant on the top and decorate with cucumber.

NOTE.—This is an excellent way of using up any kind of cold game.

Sufficient for four or five persons.

COLD ENTREE OF PHEASANT

INGREDIENTS. — 1 cold roast pheasant, 1 curly lettuce, ½ an endive, 1 bunch of watercress, French salad dressing (see p. 168).

FOR THE TOMATO CREAM MOULD.— 1 gill of tomato sauce, 1 gill of cream, ½ gill of mayonnaise or salad cream (see p. 167), ½ gill of vinegar, ½ pint of meat extract, mixed with water, 1 oz. of leaf gelatine.

METHOD.—In this dish a tasty tomato cream is made in a ring mould, and pieces of pheasant are laid on it. A green salad is served in the centre.

Soak the gelatine in the tomato sauce and vinegar for five minutes ; then place it on a very low gas and stir till it is dissolved.

Strain the liquid on to the meat extract and leave it to get cold.

When quite cold, season to taste and add it to the cream and mayonnaise.

Stir from time to time till it begins to set.

Rinse a ring mould in cold water and pour in the tomato cream mixture. Leave for several hours, or till the next day.

Prepare the pheasant by cutting it into nice-looking pieces and sprinkling them with salad dressing.

Wash the lettuce, endive, and cress, and drain them well on a cloth.

Shred the lettuce and endive, and divide up the cress. Mix them with French dressing.

Turn the mould out into a round dish and arrange the pheasant on top. Put the salad in the centre.

Sufficient for five or six persons.

ROAST OR BAKED PHEASANT

INGREDIENTS.—1 pheasant, a few bones, brown stock (see p. 12) or water, 1 onion, a few cloves, a bunch of herbs, seasoning, dripping for basting and frying, 1 thick slice of bread, watercress, slice of fat bacon.

METHOD.—Pluck and draw the pheasant, singe it well. Wipe out the inside with a damp cloth. Truss it into shape. Well wash the giblets, having first removed the gall-bag from the liver, and take away the inside of the gizzard. Wash the bones and put them with the giblets in a saucepan. Well cover with stock or water. Peel an onion, stick a few cloves into it, and add. Season well, and add the herbs. Bring slowly to the boil and skim it, then simmer for three or four hours. Cover the breast of the pheasant with the fat bacon, and roast in a tin in front of a clear fire, or bake in the oven in a baking-tin with dripping. In either case it must be kept well basted. Cook for about one or one hour and a quarter, according to the age. Remove the bacon from the breast about fifteen minutes before it is cooked, so that the breast can brown. Take a slice of bread about three-quarters of an inch thick, and sufficiently large to take the pheasant. Cut out small three-corner-shaped pieces all round the edge of the slice, and then fry it in hot dripping until golden brown on both sides. Drain well, then stand on a hot dish. Take up the pheasant and stand it on the fried bread. Garnish the dish with watercress. Serve separately—brown gravy, fried breadcrumbs, and bread sauce.

TO MAKE THE BROWN GRAVY.— Pour the fat from the tin in which the pheasant was cooked, leaving only the brown particles. Strain the stock from the bones and giblets into the tin and boil it up.

If necessary add a few drops of browning.

Strain into a small tureen or sauce boat.

NOTE.—Serve about three-quarters of a pint of gravy.

FRIED BREADCRUMBS.—Make about a teacupful of breadcrumbs.

Melt about two ounces of dripping or butter in a frying-pan.

Put in the crumbs and fry very gently until golden brown.

Drain well, and serve on a lace paper.

BREAD SAUCE.

INGREDIENTS.—½ pint of milk, 1 oz. of margarine, pepper and salt, 1 onion, a few cloves, about 1 teacupful of breadcrumbs.

METHOD.—Put the milk into a saucepan, add the margarine and seasoning.

Peel the onion, stick a few cloves into it, and add to the milk.

Stand on the side of the fire for about an hour so as to well flavour the milk. Make the breadcrumbs.

Bring the milk to the boil, add the crumbs, stir well, and stand on the side of the fire for about ten minutes to soak and swell them; do not boil it again, just re-heat it.

Take out the onion and cloves and pour the bread sauce into a small tureen.

PIGEONS EN CASSEROLE

INGREDIENTS.—2 young pigeons, 1 carrot (chopped), 1 onion (chopped), 1 bayleaf, 2 oz. of dripping, 8 small potatoes, 1 lb. of young peas, ½ pint of cold water, 1 oz. of butter, ¾ oz. of flour, salt and pepper.

METHOD.—Wash and peel the potatoes, and boil them in enough water to cover them for ten minutes, adding a teaspoonful of salt.

Heat the dripping in a frying-pan and brown the pigeons all over for five minutes. Fry the carrot and onion for five minutes. Put the pigeons in a casserole with the water and bayleaf and the fried carrot and onion, without any of the dripping. Put the casserole in a slow oven in order to make the pigeons tender.

Strain the water from the potatoes, and put them into the hot fat used for frying the pigeons. Turn them over to get well browned.

Put the peas and potatoes in the casserole and bake them till the pigeons are tender (about one hour).

To MAKE THE GRAVY.—Melt the butter, stir in the flour and fry it till it is a rich brown, stirring all the time. Add the water that is in the casserole, stir well, and let it boil. Add salt and pepper to taste.

Cut the pigeons into joints and put them back into the casserole with the gravy. The peas and potatoes are left in the casserole with the pigeons.

Sufficient for four persons.

BROWN FRICASSEE OF PIGEONS

INGREDIENTS.—2 pigeons, 2 tomatoes, 1 carrot and onion, a sprig of parsley, a bayleaf, 1 tablespoonful of flour, ¾ to 1 pint of stock (see p. 12), salt and pepper, 4 fat streaky rashers, tinned or freshly boiled peas, flaky pastry (see p. 252).

METHOD.—Remove the rind from the rashers and cut the bacon into strips; then fry it lightly.

Put the strips into a casserole.

Clean the pigeons and cut them into joints. Dredge these with flour and fry them in the bacon fat (just enough to brown the outside). Add them to the bacon in the casserole.

Add the flour to the fat that remains in the pan and let it brown slowly; then draw the pan aside and add the tomatoes (peeled and chopped).

Stir in the stock, bring all to the boil, add seasoning to taste, and pour the sauce over the pigeons. Add the onion and carrot (both whole), also the parsley and bayleaf, and simmer the pigeons gently for about an hour or until tender. Before serving, remove the vegetables, bayleaf and parsley, arrange the pigeon in a dish with the gravy, and garnish it with fleurons of flaky pastry and green peas.

To MAKE FLEURONS OF FLAKY PASTRY.—Thinly rolled flaky pastry is cut into tiny half-moons or crescent shapes. These are then brushed with egg and baked till golden brown.

Sufficient for four persons.

PIGEON PIE

INGREDIENTS.—2 young pigeons, ¼ lb. of bacon, ¼ lb. of mushrooms, ½ lb. of rump steak, 1 dessertspoonful of flour, salt and pepper, $\frac{1}{2}$ pint of good stock (see p. 12).

FOR THE FORCEMEAT BALLS.—1 gill of breadcrumbs, 1 tablespoonful of bacon dripping (melted), 2 teaspoonfuls of chopped parsley, $\frac{1}{2}$ teaspoonful of mixed herbs, $\frac{1}{2}$ teaspoonful of grated lemon-peel, 1 large egg, flaky pastry made with 6 oz. of flour (see p. 252).

METHOD.—Peel and wash the mushrooms and remove the stalks. Chop the bacon and mushrooms.

Cut the steak into small chunks and the pigeons into joints. Put them on a plate and sprinkle them with flour, salt and pepper.

Make the forcemeat by mixing the breadcrumbs, parsley, herbs, and lemon-peel with the bacon fat and half the egg. Season well with salt and pepper, chop the pigeons' livers finely, and add them. Shape the mixture into balls.

Put half the chopped bacon and mushrooms into a pie-dish with some of the forcemeat balls. Then add the steak and pigeon joints and sprinkle them with chopped mushrooms and bacon. Fill up the corners with forcemeat balls. Half fill the dish with stock or cold water.

Roll out the pastry and cut off a narrow strip.

Wet the edge of the dish and press on the strip of pastry.

Wet this and cover the pie-dish with the rest of the pastry.

Trim the edge neatly and cut some of the trimmings into crescents to decorate the pie.

Brush the top with egg, put on the decorations and egg them also.

Make a hole in the centre and bake in a moderate oven for an hour and a half.

Put a couple of pigeons' feet in the centre hole, and serve hot.

Sufficient for four persons.

SALMI OF PHEASANT WITH MUSHROOMS

INGREDIENTS.—1 pheasant, 2 oz. of dripping, 1 lb. of brussels sprouts or French beans, 6 medium size mushrooms, 1 oz. of butter, $\frac{1}{2}$ oz. of flour, $1\frac{1}{2}$ gills of water, salt.

METHOD.—Spread the pheasant with dripping, place it in a hot oven and bake it for thirty-five minutes, basting it three or four times.

Peel and wash the mushrooms and remove the stalks. Place the mushrooms in a pie-dish with the water and half the butter, cover them with greased paper, and bake for twenty minutes.

Wash the sprouts and put them in a pan of boiling water with a dessertspoonful of salt. Boil them till tender, and strain them, keeping them hot in the colander placed over a pan of boiling water.

Melt half an ounce of butter, mix the flour with it and fry it brown, stirring well. Add the stock from the mushrooms, stir the gravy till it boils. Cut up the roast pheasant into neat joints and re-heat them in the gravy.

Serve the sprouts piled in the centre of a hot dish, and round them place alternately a mushroom and a joint of pheasant.

Sufficient for three or four persons.

QUAILS AND GRAPE-FRUIT

INGREDIENTS.—3 quails, 2 grape-fruit, $\frac{1}{2}$ endive or watercress, 2 oz. of butter.

FOR THE SAUCE.—$\frac{1}{2}$ oz. of flour, $\frac{1}{2}$ gill of sherry, 1 gill of good stock (see p. 12), salt and pepper.

METHOD.—Spread the quails with butter, put them in a baking-tin and bake them for fifteen minutes in a quick oven, basting them twice. Cut the grape-fruit in half and cut one-half into six slices.

Cut three halves zig-zag round the edge and scoop out some of the pulp from the centre to make room for a quail. Keep the pulp and juice for making sauce.

Put the roast quails (each in its half grape-fruit) on a dish, and keep them hot in the oven.

TO MAKE THE SAUCE.—Pour off half the butter from the tin the quails were cooked in, and stir the flour into it. Fry it a rich brown, stirring well and add the sherry, grape-fruit-juice and stock. Stir till the sauce boils and season to taste with salt and pepper.

To serve the quails, lay each one in the prepared grape-fruit, with endive or watercress in the centre of the dish. Garnish with the sliced grape-fruit.

Sufficient for three persons.

BELGIAN RABBIT

INGREDIENTS.—1 rabbit (cut up, 1 lb. of sausages, 3 onions (chopped), ¼ lb. of sultanas (washed), 1 tablespoonful of chopped parsley, ¾ pint of water, 1½ oz. of butter, 1 oz. of flour, ½ glass of burgundy, 1 teaspoonful of meat extract, pepper, ½ teaspoonful of salt.

METHOD.—Wash and dry the rabbit. Mix the flour, parsley, salt and pepper. Roll the pieces of rabbit in the seasoned flour. Heat the butter and fry the rabbit and onions gently for five minutes. Put rabbit, onions, water, sultanas and meat extract into a casserole. Put on the lid and bake them in a slow oven for one hour and a half.

Fry the rest of the flour brown in the butter used for frying the rabbit, stirring it well. Pour in the gravy from the casserole and stir till it boils.

Put the thickened gravy into the casserole with the burgundy and bake the rabbit for half an hour longer.

Fry the sausages slowly for twelve minutes, put them into the casserole and serve.

Sufficient for three persons.

BOILED RABBIT WITH PARS-LEY AND ONION SAUCE

INGREDIENTS.—1 rabbit, 3 or 4 onions, 1 carrot and turnip, 1 bunch of herbs, 1 teaspoonful of salt, water to cover, 8 small rolls of grilled bacon.

FOR THE SAUCE.—1½ oz. of butter and flour, 1 tablespoonful of chopped parsley, salt and pepper, ¾ pint of stock in which rabbit was cooked.

METHOD.—Wash and truss the rabbit and cut the vegetables in quarters. Put the rabbit in enough boiling water to cover it, with the salt, bring it to the boil again and add the herbs and all the vegetables. It must not be allowed to boil quickly, but must simmer all the time till it is tender. A young rabbit will be cooked in three-quarters of an hour, and a large one in an hour.

To make the sauce, melt the butter, add the flour and mix them together. Add three-quarters of a pint of the water in which the rabbit was cooked, and stir the sauce till it boils. Boil for three minutes.

Take the onions out from the liquor and chop them coarsely and the parsley finely, and add them to the sauce.

Dish up the rabbit and keep it hot.

One rasher of fat bacon cut in half will make two rolls for garnish. They should be rolled up tightly, put on a skewer and grilled for five or six minutes. When they are cooked, pour the sauce over the rabbit and put the bacon rolls round the dish.

NOTE.—If the onions used are large ones, they may be boiled for an hour before the rabbit is put in.

Sufficient for four persons.

CASSEROLE OF RABBIT

INGREDIENTS.—1 rabbit (medium size), ¾ lb. of onions, ¾ lb. of tomatoes, salt and pepper, ¼ pint of stock (see p. 12), flour, dripping.

METHOD.—Wipe the tomatoes and bake them until tender, then rub them through a sieve.

Have the rabbit skinned and cut into joints. Wash it, soak for a short time in slightly salted water, and dry it in a cloth.

Peel and slice the onions and fry them lightly. Drain them and put them into a casserole.

Flour the rabbit and fry it also—just enough to brown it. Add seasoning to taste.

Brown a little flour in some of the dripping, then draw the pan aside, and add the tomato pulp and some stock. Boil up, season, and strain the liquid over the rabbit. The gravy should be thick and there should be enough of it to cover the rabbit.

Simmer it gently in the oven for an hour and a quarter to an hour and a half, then serve.

Sufficient for four or five persons.

RABBIT CREAMS

INGREDIENTS.—Some cold boiled rabbit, 1 oz. of butter or margarine, ¾ oz. of flour, ½ pint of milk, salt, pepper, and ground mace, 1 table-spoonful of chopped pimento, 1 table-spoonful of cream, ¼ oz. of gelatine, ¼ gill of water.

METHOD.—Cut sufficient meat from the rabbit to make four ounces when minced.

Melt the fat in a saucepan, add the flour, and, when well blended, stir in the milk and bring all to the boil. Boil this sauce gently for a few minutes, then take it off the heat. Season it with salt, pepper, and mace, add the chopped pimento and minced rabbit. Strain in the gelatine dissolved in the water and then add the cream and mix all together lightly.

Turn the mixture into small wet moulds and leave them to set. Before serving, dip the moulds in warm water and unmould the rabbit creams.

Decorate them with pimento cut in tiny shapes.

Sufficient to fill nine small moulds.

CURRIED RABBIT

INGREDIENTS.—1 rabbit, dripping, 1½ dessertspoonfuls of flour, 3 tea-spoonfuls of curry powder, ½ an apple, 2 or 3 onions, seasoning, ¾ pint of stock (see p. 12), ¼ lb. of rice.

METHOD.—Skin the rabbit and divide it into joints. Wash it in cold water to which a little salt has been added. Let it soak for half an hour, drain it well and dry in a cloth.

Melt some dripping in a pan, fry the rabbit lightly in it, then take it out and put it into a casserole. Cut up the onions and fry them also. Stir in the flour and curry powder. If there is too much fat, pour some of it off first. There should be enough to absorb them. Cook them slowly for a few minutes, keeping them stirred. Draw them aside, add the stock, then boil it up and season to taste. Pour it over the rabbit, add the apple, peeled, cored and chopped, and simmer gently for about one to one hour and a half.

Add a squeeze of lemon-juice, and serve the rabbit with boiled rice, which can be dished separately or round the rabbit. If it is served with the rabbit, serve some of the gravy in a sauce-boat.

Sufficient for four or five persons.

To Boil Rice for a Curry
Use the best rice.

Wash it, then put into a pan of boiling water to which a little salt has been added. Boil until tender, then strain in a colander. Pour cold water through the rice grains to separate them. Then drain well. Turn on to a dish and put into the oven or in front of the fire to dry and re-heat.

BROWN FRICASSEE OF RABBIT

INGREDIENTS.—1 rabbit, 2 onions, 1 carrot (large), pepper and salt, water or stock, ¼ lb. of dripping, flour, browning, 6 rashers of streaky bacon.

METHOD.—Skin and clean the rabbit, take out the inside, cut off the head, remove eyes. Wash head, liver, and heart in cold water, and soak in cold salted water for fifteen minutes.

Put into a saucepan with an onion and enough water or stock to well cover. If liked, a few bones can be washed and added ; this will make the gravy richer. Bring to the boil, remove the scum, add the seasoning, and simmer for about two or three hours. Cut the rabbit into joints, wash them well, and dry in a cloth. Put the bacon in a saucepan and fry it gently until the fat looks transparent, then put it on to a plate. Add the dripping to the bacon fat; when hot, flour the rabbit, and put a few joints in and fry until golden brown. Take them out, and fry the others in the same way. Then put them on to a hot plate. Peel and slice and fry the onion. Add about three dessert-spoonfuls of flour to the onion and dripping, stir it round, and fry until brown. Strain off about one pint and a half of the stock, and add to the flour, bring to the boil, keeping it well stirred. Add a few drops of browning if necessary. Taste to see if well seasoned. Put back the rabbit, and cook gently for about one hour and a half to two hours. Add the bacon about fifteen minutes before serving. Pile the rabbit in the centre of the dish, with the bacon on the top of it. Pour the gravy round, and garnish with dice of cooked carrots.

Sufficient for about five or six persons.

Chicken
Rissoles

Roast
Turkey

Brown
Fricassee
of Pigeons

PLATE 9

Chicken
Galantine

Giblet
Pie

Roast
Duck
and
Green
Peas

PLATE 10

Rabbit
Creams

Roast
Partridges

Rabbit
Hot-pot

PLATE 11

Roast Goose with Apple Rings

Grouse en Casserole

Game Kromeskies

PLATE 12

RABBIT HOT-POT

INGREDIENTS.—1 young rabbit (cut into joints), 4 rashers of bacon (chopped), 1 tablespoonful of chopped parsley, grated rind of a lemon, nutmeg, salt and pepper, 1 cup of breadcrumbs, 1 cup of water, 1 oz. of flour, 1 oz. of butter.

METHOD.—Wash and dry the rabbit. Mix the flour with salt, pepper and nutmeg, and roll the rabbit in it.

Fry the pieces in the butter for five minutes.

Grease a deep fireproof dish and put in half the breadcrumbs. On this lay half the rabbit and bacon, then put more breadcrumbs and the lemon-rind. Finish with another layer of rabbit and breadcrumbs on top.

Pour over the top any butter that is left, and half fill the dish with water. Cover with greased paper and bake in a slow oven for one hour.

Sufficient for three persons.

RABBIT PIE

INGREDIENTS.—1 rabbit, ½ lb. of pickled pork, salt and pepper, 1 gill of water or stock (see p. 12), 2d. of bones (veal or pork), 1 onion, pepper and salt, water to cover, ¼ teaspoonful of powdered mace, 4 sheets of leaf gelatine, about 1 lb. of flaky pastry (see p. 252).

METHOD.—Skin and clean the rabbit, remove the inside, cut off the head. Wash the head, heart, and liver in cold salted water, and put into a saucepan with the veal bones, which should also be washed. Add the peeled onion and a little powdered mace, pepper and salt. Cover with water and bring slowly to the boil. Remove the scum and simmer for two or three hours. Cut the rabbit into joints, wash them, and dry in a cloth. Put into a pie-dish with the pickled pork, cut into slices about an inch square. Mix them together, and season with pepper, salt, and mace.

Add one gill of cold water or stock, and put two sheets of gelatine in between the joints of rabbit, etc. The pie-dish should be full or the crust will sink. Roll out the pastry until it is three-eighths of an inch in thickness. Cut a piece large enough to cover the top of the pie-dish, and put aside. Roll the remaining pieces of pastry until thinner, and cut a narrow strip for the edge of the pie-dish. Damp the edge, and place the strip of pastry on it. Damp the strip, and put the top crust on. Press the edges together, and trim off the rough edges. Decorate the edge with a fork or knife. Make four leaves and a tassel from the remaining pieces of pastry. Make a hole in the centre of the pie, put in the tassel, arrange the leaves from it. Then make a hole at either end of the piecrust. Brush over the pastry with milk or beaten egg. Place in a hot oven for about the first twenty-five minutes until the pastry is cooked and golden brown. Then remove the browning-shelf and lessen the heat, and cook for about another hour and a quarter. Remove from the oven, take out the centre tassel, open the holes so that the steam can escape. Add two sheets of gelatine to the stock. When dissolved, strain it, and remove the fat. Fill the pie up with the stock. Serve hot or cold, preferably the latter.

NOTE.—Replace tassel before serving.

BOILED TURKEY AND EGG SAUCE

INGREDIENTS.—1 turkey (medium size), 2 lb. of sausages, 1 onion, 1 carrot, 1 turnip, a few cloves, a few mixed herbs, water to cover.

METHOD.—Pluck, draw, and singe the turkey. To draw it, cut off the head, slip down the skin round the neck, and cut off the neck. Remove the crop. Turn the bird round, and from the other end take out all the inside, being careful not to break the gall-bag. Cut off the feet and part of the leg to the first joint, draw the sinews. Wipe out the inside of the turkey.

Loosen the skin round the legs, and draw the legs under it, press them well in so as to push up the breast, skewer them in position. Fold the loose skin from the neck over the back, and turn the wings and skewer them so that they keep this skin in position. Turn the turkey on to its breast, and tie the bird securely with strings, as for roasting.

Put some thin slices of lemon over

D

the breast, then a greased paper over it, and tie the bird in a piece of muslin. Then put it into a large saucepan of boiling water or stock.

Tie the herbs in muslin and add them, but do not leave them in more than about half an hour, or they will discolour the stock.

Peel the onion, and stick a few cloves into it. Scrape the carrot. Peel the turnip thickly. Wash these, and add to the turkey. Simmer gently for about two and a half to three hours, keeping it skimmed. Add the sausages about forty minutes before serving.

When nearly cooked, prepare the sauce.

EGG SAUCE

INGREDIENTS.—3 oz. of butter, 3 eggs, 3 oz. of flour, pepper and salt, 1 pint of milk, ½ pint of water.

Put the eggs into a saucepan of cold water, bring to the boil, and cook for fifteen minutes. Crack them well, and then put them into cold water. Put the milk, butter, and seasoning into a saucepan to get hot.

Mix the flour to a smooth paste with some of the water, and add the rest to the milk. Pour the hot milk, etc., on to the mixed flour, pour back into the saucepan, and bring to the boil, keeping it well stirred all the time. Cook slowly for about six minutes. The sauce should be thick enough to coat the spoon well.

Remove the shells from the eggs, cut in half, take out the yolks, and cut the whites into small square pieces, and add to the sauce.

Press the yolks through a wire sieve. Place the turkey on a large dish, put the sausages round, and pour over the egg sauce, coating it all over. Sprinkle the yolks over the sauce, and serve a tureen of the liquor separately.

ROAST TURKEY WITH CHESTNUT STUFFING

INGREDIENTS.—Turkey, 1 lb. of sausage meat, bread sauce (see p. 83), buttered brown crumbs (see p. 91), boiled bacon or rolls of bacon (see p. 155).

FOR THE STUFFING.—¾ lb. of chestnuts, 3 oz. of breadcrumbs, 1 good-sized onion, 1 tablespoonful of chopped parsley, 1½ oz. of butter, salt, pepper, 1 egg, milk, stock (see p. 12) or water.

FOR THE GRAVY.—The giblets, an onion, cloves, peppercorns, a sprig of parsley, a small blade of mace, salt, a little flour, cold water.

METHOD.—Choose a nice plump bird, one weighing from ten to twelve pounds being a good medium size. Have it drawn and trussed, then stuff it. Put the sausage meat in the body of the bird. Put the chestnut stuffing into the neck end and draw the flap of skin over on to the back and fasten it securely. This will keep the stuffing in position.

Put the turkey into a baking-tin with plenty of dripping, and bake it for about two hours and a half, keeping it well basted. It is advisable to cover the breast with either a thin piece of caul or else a thickly greased paper, to keep it moist.

When ready, dish up the turkey and serve it with brown gravy, bread sauce and buttered brown crumbs, and either boiled bacon or rolls of bacon.

TO MAKE THE STUFFING.—Put the chestnuts in water and boil, and remove the outer and inner skin. Put them into a saucepan with either stock or water, and boil them until tender. Strain off the stock, rub the chestnuts through a sieve and mix them with the breadcrumbs, parsley, and onion peeled and minced finely. Stir in the butter (melted), add seasoning to taste, and bind the stuffing with egg and moisten it with milk.

TO MAKE THE GRAVY.—The foundation for the gravy is made from the giblets. Clean them, then put them in a saucepan with an onion, a few cloves, and peppercorns, a sprig of parsley, and a small blade of mace. Cover them with cold water, add a little salt, then bring the gravy to the boil and simmer it gently for two or three hours. Strain it and boil it up in the baking-tin after browning a little flour in a spoonful of the turkey dripping, kept back after pouring off the bulk of it.

ROAST TURKEY AND CRANBERRY SAUCE

INGREDIENTS.—A turkey of from 10 to 12 lb., flour, salt and pepper, about 3 oz. of dripping.

FOR THE VEAL STUFFING FOR THE CROP.—1 breakfastcupful of bread-crumbs, 3 oz. of shredded and chopped suet, 2 oz. of bacon, 1 tablespoonful of chopped parsley, 1 level teaspoonful of mixed herbs, grated rind of ½ a lemon, 1 large egg.

FOR THE CHESTNUT STUFFING FOR THE BODY.—60 chestnuts, 2 pork sausages, 1½ oz. of butter, 1 teacupful of breadcrumbs, a flat teaspoonful of mixed herbs, salt and pepper.

FOR THE GRAVY.—1 oz. of dripping, 1 oz. of flour, ¾ pint of hot stock (made by stewing the giblets), nutmeg, salt and pepper.

FOR THE GARNISH.—2 bunches of watercress, 1 lb. of small sausages. Served with the turkey : hot boiled ham (see p. 117) and cranberry sauce (see below) or bread sauce (see p. 83).

METHOD.—The poulterer will have drawn and trussed the turkey and will have sent the giblets wrapped up in greaseproof paper.

First wash the giblets (neck, gizzard, heart, and liver). Keep back the liver and put the other giblets in a saucepan with a pint of cold water and half a teaspoonful of salt, to simmer gently for stock all the time the turkey is cooking.

Add half an onion and carrot to the stock when it boils.

To make the veal stuffing, chop the bacon and fry it gently for five minutes. Mix all the other dry ingredients in a basin. Add the bacon and the fat that has come from it, and bind all together with a beaten egg. Fill the crop with this and keep it in place by pulling over it the loose skin of the neck, which can either be skewered or tucked under the ends of the wings.

To make the chestnut stuffing, slit the chestnuts on the flat side and put them on a tin in a hot oven for fifteen minutes, till the shells split open. Scrape off the inner skins and boil the chestnuts for twenty minutes in enough stock (or water) to cover them. Strain them and put them through a mincer. Mix all the chestnut-stuffing ingredients together and put them inside the body of the turkey.

Season the bird with salt and pepper, spread it all over with dripping, and dredge it lightly with flour. Put more dripping in the tin and place the bird in a hot oven for the first fifteen minutes.

Baste it by pouring the dripping over it with an iron spoon. Lower the gas and finish cooking in a moderate oven.

To make the bird nice and brown, it *must* be basted about every twenty minutes. It is not a hot oven that browns it so much as plenty of basting. Time allowed is fifteen minutes to the pound.

A turkey of from ten to twelve pounds will be cooked in two hours. A turkey of from twelve to sixteen pounds will take from two and a half to two and three-quarter hours. Put the liver in the tin for the last fifteen minutes.

The best way to cook the sausages is to put a string of them in a warm frying-pan, prick them to prevent bursting, and fry slowly for about fifteen minutes, keeping them turned so that they brown evenly. To make the gravy and dish up, put the turkey on a hot dish in the oven, after removing all strings and skewers.

Pour off nearly all the dripping into a basin, leaving in the baking-tin about one tablespoonful of dripping, any brown particles, and the liver.

Add to the dripping enough flour to make a soft paste (about an ounce), and fry it to a nice rich brown, remembering that it will not brown any more after the stock is added.

Put the liver on a chopping board and mince and chop it as finely as possible. Put it back in the tin with the hot gravy and stir till it boils. Season to taste and serve in a tureen.

Garnish the turkey with water-cress and hang the fried sausages round it.

CRANBERRY SAUCE.

INGREDIENTS.—1 lb. of cranberries, 1 cup of sugar, ½ pint of water, 1 small dessertspoonful of cornflour.

METHOD.—Wash the cranberries and put them in a saucepan with the water. Boil for about five minutes or until soft. Rub them through a sieve, add the sugar, and then reheat them.

Mix the cornflour smoothly with half a gill of cold water, and pour the hot purée on to it.

Return it to the pan and stir till it boils.

MEAT DISHES

ROASTING AND BAKING MEAT

OFTEN the family stand-bys might taste fresher and be more interesting if someone had spent a little more effort and time in their preparation.

You will find people who will be surprised that there is anything to learn, for instance, about roasting meat.

But what a difference when anything even so simple is prepared by professional cooks!

IT IS MOSTLY BAKED

A VERY small percentage of people actually roast meat these days; although they term it "roast," it is more often baked.

To roast meat is to cook it *in front of the fire*. For this, the meat is hung in a Dutch oven or roasting jack.

To bake meat is to cook it in the oven, and that is how most of us must manage it.

If cooked in a gas oven the meat can be hung on a hook or placed on one of the racks. In both cases, as the meat cooks the fat drips into the tin at the bottom of the oven.

If cooked in a fire oven the meat should be placed on a meat stand in a baking-tin containing some dripping. It can be cooked in this way in a gas oven if you find the method more convenient.

Remember to wipe the meat before cooking it.

EXPOSE MEAT TO A GOOD HEAT FIRST

WHEN roasting or baking, the meat should be exposed to a good heat for about the first ten minutes so as to harden the outside albumen and keep in the goodness. But it should be lessened afterwards, otherwise the meat becomes overcooked outside before it is cooked in the middle of the joint.

The oven, therefore, should always be looked to beforehand, so that it is hot when required. A good clear fire is required for roasting.

TO KEEP MEAT BASTED

THE joint should be well basted to prevent it getting dry on the outside. This is very important. The "outside" is a favourite cut with many if the joint has not been allowed to get dry.

If the meat is placed on a rack or hung in the oven it is a good plan to place a piece of thick caul or some other fat on the rack above—this keeps it continually basted.

And remember meat should be turned during the cooking.

IS IT COOKED?

THE average times to allow are:

FOR BEEF.—Fifteen minutes to the pound and fifteen minutes over.

MUTTON AND LAMB.—Fifteen to twenty minutes to the pound and twenty minutes over.

VEAL AND PORK.—Twenty to twenty-five minutes to the pound and twenty-five minutes over.

But do not forget that the thickness of the joint must be considered as well as the weight and also that a small joint will take longer in comparison than a large one.

A THIN BROWN GRAVY.

To make gravy, pour off the dripping from the pan, leaving just the brown pieces. Add some stock and boil it up. Season to taste and add a little browning as required, then strain.

A thin brown gravy (as given above) should be served with roast or baked meat, beef or mutton, unless the latter is stuffed. A thickened gravy is served with veal and pork and all stuffed meat.

A THICK GRAVY

AFTER pouring off nearly all the dripping, add a little flour and stir it until it is evenly browned. Draw the pan aside for a minute and gradually pour in some stock. Bring it to the boil, season to taste, and strain. If the flour is browned sufficiently, the addition of other browning should not be required.

Another method of making thick gravy is to thicken the stock with flour mixed to a smooth paste with water, pouring it into the baking-tin after pouring off the dripping.

Boil it for a few minutes, season to taste, add a little browning as required, then strain.

One small dessertspoonful of flour is enough to thicken half a pint of stock.

ECONOMICAL JOINTS

FOR ROASTING

Topside of beef—3 lb.

Top rib of beef—2½ lb. to 3 lb.

Back rib of beef—3 lb.

Ribs of beef (boned and rolled)— 4 lb. to 5 lb.

Half shoulder of mutton (blade end)—3 to 3½ lb.

Sheep's heart.

Breast of mutton or lamb (stuffed and rolled).

Thin flank (rolled and with the gristle removed)—3 lb.

Thick flank (braised or baked)— 2½ lb.

FOR LARGE FAMILIES

Half a pig's head roasted is very good, besides being economical and new to many people.

Ox heart (steamed for two hours, then roasted).

Aitchbone of beef is an excellent joint, weighing about 11 lb.

The butcher will saw it in two and salt half for use later in the week.

The other half is very good baked.

SUITABLE ACCOMPANIMENTS

BEEF. — Baked potatoes. Cauliflower and white sauce or almost any kind of green vegetable. Batter pudding. Grated horseradish or horseradish sauce.

MUTTON.—Boiled potatoes. Mashed turnips or a green vegetable, or tomatoes, the latter baked whole. With leg, serve red-currant jelly. With shoulder, serve onion sauce.

LAMB.—New potatoes. Spring greens. Mint sauce.

PORK.—Boiled potatoes. Sprouts or other suitable green vegetable. Apple sauce. If the pork is stuffed, sage and onion stuffing.

VEAL (this should be stuffed with veal stuffing). — Boiled potatoes. Sprouts or other suitable green vegetables. Bread sauce. Boiled bacon, or a few rashers. They are usually made into rolls and a skewer run through them. If liked, a few sausages can be served.

A FEW HINTS

MEAT should always be wiped with a cloth before it is cooked.

If it should be at all stale or discoloured on the outside, wash it in cold water to which a little salt or vinegar has been added. Then dry it in a cloth.

Stale meat is better baked, rather than boiled or stewed, and it requires a very sharp oven for cooking.

BOILED MEAT

BOILED MEAT! It sounds so uninteresting—and yet it need not be so. Properly prepared and served in an appetising manner, it should be just as much favoured as the popular " roast."

It is quite a mistaken idea to think— as so many housewives do—that a boiled dinner can be put on to cook and then left to its own resources. It requires careful attention to make sure that it remains at the right temperature, for if it goes much off the boil it will not be cooked to time, and if it should boil too fast, the meat will become hard.

FRESH OR SALT MEAT

EITHER fresh or salt meat can be used for boiling. It should be cooked as a whole joint, and not cut up.

FRESH MEAT should always be put into boiling water to which a little salt has been added. Let it come to the boil, and remove the scum. Then boil it for three or four minutes (just to harden the outside albumen and keep in the goodness), and afterwards let it simmer gently until tender. There should only be sufficient water to cover the meat.

SALT MEAT should be put into *warm* water so as to draw out some of the salt.

THE TIME TO ALLOW

THE average time to allow for mutton is twenty minutes to the pound and twenty minutes over, but the thickness of the joint must be considered as well as the weight. Also, a small joint takes longer to cook in comparison than a large one.

Salt meat needs a longer time for cooking than fresh—on an average, about twenty-five to thirty minutes to the pound.

MEAT LIQUOR

THE water in which a piece of meat has been boiled is known as meat liquor. Some of this should be served with the meat. The remainder should be allowed to get cold, the fat removed and clarified, and the liquor (if not too salt) saved and used for a foundation for soups and gravies.

SUITABLE PARTS AND ACCOMPANIMENTS

MUTTON.—Scrag and middle neck, breast (this is better served cold), knuckle, half leg, or whole leg. Serve with onions and turnips (the latter can be mashed or served whole) and caper or parsley sauce (see pp. 132 and 163).

SALT PORK.—Leg or hand and spring. Serve with parsnips or turnip tops, the latter cooked separately, and pease pudding (see p. 139), if liked.

SALT BEEF.—Silverside, flank or brisket. The two latter are better pressed and served cold. Serve hot salt beef with carrots and onions.

BACON.—Almost any part—a forehock or a piece of collar is the most economical. Serve with broad beans and parsley sauce (see p. 163).

VEAL.—Knuckle (cut full), neck, or breast can be used. Boiled veal and bacon cooked together make a good dish. Serve with parsley sauce (see p. 163) and carrots and onions.

THE BEST WAY TO BRAISE MEAT

SUITABLE PARTS

MUTTON.—Leg, 3 hours; saddle, 3 hours; neck, 2 hours; mutton cutlets, 1½ hours; sheep's tongues, 1 hour.

BEEF.—Rump or fillet, 1½ to 2 hours; rib, 2½ hours; ox cheek, 2½ hours.

VEAL.—Breast, 1½ hours; neck or loin, 2 hours; liver, 1 hour.

PORK.—Ham, from 4½ hours.

How to Braise

BRAISING is a delicious and quite easy way of cooking that deserves to be better known. The joint is first browned and then stewed.

A large carrot and onion are sliced, and a stick of celery cut in short pieces. These vegetables, with a bunch of herbs, two cloves, and four peppercorns, are put in a casserole with three or four rashers of fat bacon or some dripping. The vegetables are browned in the casserole standing on an asbestos mat.

When the vegetables are slightly browned the joint is put in and browned also. A little stock or water —about one pint, unless the joint is large—is then poured in, and the casserole, with the lid on, is placed in a moderate oven to stew gently.

The meat should be well basted with the liquor in the pan.

STEWS—WHITE AND BROWN

STEWING is one of the most economical methods of cooking meat ; it is not as popular as it should be, probably owing to the fact that so many people do not make their stews sufficiently appetising.

As a method of cookery it has many advantages, the chief one being that very little preparation is required. Only a very small quantity of fuel is used, and last, but by no means least, the cheaper and less prime parts of meat can be used, as the long, slow cooking makes it tender.

Beef, mutton and veal are all suitable for stewing.

When using mutton, the scrag and middle neck are the most suitable parts, the breast is rather too fat for this purpose.

There are various parts of beef that can be used, some requiring longer cooking than others—bladebone or chuck steak, silverside steak, neck or leg of beef ; the last two require the most time.

COMMON FAULTS

THE most common faults in cooking stews are, firstly, that they are often allowed to cook too quickly, when the meat becomes hard and indigestible. Remember that a "stew boiled is a stew spoiled." It should be brought to the boil quickly, and then should simmer very gently indeed.

Secondly, they are often served with too much grease on top of the gravy, which makes them most unappetising. This fat should always be skimmed off before the stew is sent to table.

VARIETIES OF STEWS

THERE are two kinds of stew—a white stew, such as Irish stew, which has a thin white gravy, or a brown stew, which has a thick brown gravy—but the same principles apply to both.

A brown stew can be cooked on top of the stove or in the oven, whichever place is most convenient. Casseroles are used largely for this purpose.

TO FRY MEAT

ONLY the best parts of meat are suitable for frying.

It is impossible to fry the parts of meat intended for stewing as they would be made tough and uneatable.

The object is the same as for baking, the outside is to be browned and the albumen hardened by very quick cooking, and as soon as this is done the inside is to be kept tender by very slow cooking.

The cooking cannot be too quick at first and can hardly be too slow to finish.

SUITABLE PARTS

ONLY small parts of meats are suitable for *frying*—such as veal cutlet, sweetbread, liver, sausages, chops, and steak.

Before frying, the meat is usually coated with either flour or egg and breadcrumbs (according to the kind of meat used), but this is not required for sausages or mutton chops.

About half an ounce of dripping should be made smoking hot in a frying-pan over a high gas, the meat is put in and browned very quickly for not more than two minutes. It is then turned over without sticking a fork into the lean and the other side is browned in the same way.

Having now sealed the outside so as to keep in all the juices, the gas should be turned as low as possible and the meat should cook very slowly and should be turned over two or three times.

Frying is not so extravagant as is sometimes supposed; even though the best parts of meat are used. Steaks, fillets and veal cutlets go farther than scrag or neck, because there is no bone, and so less meat is needed.

FILLET of chilled beef makes the most tender and delicious steaks.

When buying it for frying it is a good plan to ask the butcher to cut a small joint of fillet for *roasting*, so as to get a piece without a lot of thin, straggly end.

This will weigh a little over one pound, and can be cut at home into four or six nice little steaks.

THE BEST FAT

CLARIFIED fat, or dripping, is the best fat to use for frying meat. Dripping from a joint must have all the gravy removed from the bottom, before melting it down.

When the fat is heated enough for frying, a faint blue smoke will rise from it. It is important to remember that the fat must be heated before the meat is put into it, in order to seal the outside and keep in the goodness. Also, both the fat, and food to be fried, must be free from moisture, which causes the fat to splutter. The meat must be turned frequently, and care should be taken to prevent overcooking, or it will be hard and indigestible.

GRILLING MEAT

GRILLING is a quick method of cooking meat, but again an expensive one, as only the best parts of meat can be used. It makes meat more easily digested than if it is fried.

The grill should be lighted a few minutes before the meat is to be cooked so that it will be hot when the meat is put under it. This heat will seal the outside and keep in the goodness. For the same season, the bars of the grill tin should be previously heated.

Only small pieces of meat can be grilled, and they require frequent turning while cooking.

BOILED BACON AND BUTTER BEANS

INGREDIENTS. — 1½ lb. of collar bacon (in one piece), ½ lb. of butter beans, 1 oz. of flour, 1 oz. of butter, 1 tablespoonful of chopped parsley, ½ pint of milk-and-water, salt and pepper.

METHOD.—Soak the beans for twenty-four hours in cold water.

Strain them, put them into a saucepan of cold water with a dessert-spoonful of salt, heat them slowly, and simmer gently for about two hours.

Fit a steamer on top of the saucepan, and put into it a basin containing the bacon. Let this steam while the beans are cooking.

Make a sauce by melting the butter, stirring in the flour and adding the milk-and-water by degrees. Stir till it boils. Boil for three minutes, add the parsley, and season to taste.

Strain the beans when they are tender and put them into the sauce.

Cut off the bacon rind, and put the bacon and beans on a hot dish.

Sufficient for four or five persons.

NOTE.—If liked, after removing the bacon rind, sprinkle the fat with browned breadcrumbs, made of stale bread baked in the oven, crushed with a rolling pin and put through a sieve.

BACON AND EGGS

MILD bacon is pale in colour ; salt bacon is dark red. To make salt bacon less salt, put the slices in a frying-pan, cover them with cold water and bring them to the boil. Throw away the water, which now contains much of the salt, and fry the bacon as usual.

To fry bacon, warm the frying-pan by putting it on the gas a few minutes. Cut the rind off the bacon and put it in the pan. Turn it frequently while it is frying and cook it for four or five minutes, till it is lightly browned and crisp, but not at all hard or dry. If the frying-pan is a large one, push the bacon to one side while frying the eggs ; otherwise, dish up the bacon and keep it hot.

The most general mistake in frying eggs is to have the fat too hot. It should not be hot enough to make the white splutter and form bubbles. If it is hot as this the white will become very hard and perhaps browned. When it is like this it is most indigestible.

Before frying the eggs, tip the pan up slightly, and having broken the eggs into a cup, gently slide them into the fat. Heat gradually, and do not touch the eggs till the white is nearly set. To make yolks white on top, pour some of the hot fat carefully over them. Take the eggs out of the pan with a fish slice when they are fried, which will take four or five minutes.

GRILLED BACON

BACON is much improved if it is grilled instead of fried.

Remove the bars from the grill-tin and heat the tin and the grill. Meanwhile, cut the rind from the rashers, and cut strips of bread about toast thickness, and rather smaller than the rashers.

Put the rashers together with the bread in the heated grill-tin and grill for a few minutes until the fat is semi-transparent, keeping the rashers turned. The bread should be turned over when brown. Serve each rasher on a finger of the prepared bread, and garnish with a heap of scrambled eggs at each end of the dish. Pour the bacon fat round.

BOILED BACON AND BROAD BEANS

INGREDIENTS.—About 4 lb. of bacon, water to cover.

METHOD.—Put the bacon into a saucepan with sufficient water to cover. Bring to the boil, remove the scum, and simmer gently for about two hours, according to the thickness.

Serve with broad beans and parsley sauce (see p. 163).

NOTE.—When broad beans are not in season, haricot beans can be used instead. These need to be soaked for about twenty-four hours, and require about two hours or more to boil.

GRILLED BACON AND PEAS

INGREDIENTS.—1 pint of shelled cooked peas, 8 rashers of bacon.

METHOD.—Remove the rind from

the rashers and cook them under the grill for a few minutes until the fat is semi-transparent. Keep them turned about as required.

Use either freshly cooked or tinned peas. When they are well drained season them with pepper and arrange them on a dish in layers with the rashers, pouring the fat from the bacon over them.

Serve with boiled new potatoes.

Sufficient for four persons.

BACON AND SAUSAGE PIE

INGREDIENTS.—1½ lb. of pork sausages or sausage meat, 1 lb. collar of bacon, 2 eggs (hard-boiled), salt and pepper, 1 onion, 1 level teaspoonful of powdered sage leaves, 2 or 3 leaves of gelatine, ½ to ¾ gill of water, about 1¼ lb. of flaky pastry (see p. 252).

METHOD.—Remove the rind from the bacon and put the bacon through a mincer.

If using sausages, take them out of the skins.

Put the sausage and bacon into a pie-dish in layers, adding the sliced eggs and minced onion, seasoning each layer with salt, pepper, and sage.

When half full, add the gelatine, then fill up the pie-dish with the remainder of the ingredients, and pour in just enough water to cook with it.

Roll out the pastry *thickly* and cut out a piece for the top of the pie. Put a thin strip of pastry on the rim of the dish, then cover the pie, dampening the rim to make the pastry adhere

Trim and decorate the edge, make a *hole* in the centre, and decorate the top of the pie with leaves, half moons, or other small shapes of pastry.

Brush the top with egg to glaze it and put the pie into a hot oven to bake, lessening the heat when the pastry has risen, and browned lightly. It will take about forty-five minutes to cook. Fill up the pie with stock that will jelly, and serve it cold.

Sufficient for from six to eight persons.

GAMMON RASHER AND ASPARAGUS

INGREDIENTS.—A gammon rasher, about ¾ to 1 lb. 4 small thin, fat, streaky, or back rashers, a slice of bread, a tin of asparagus, 1 tomato.

METHOD.—Heat the grill and the grill-tin, remove the bars from the latter, and put in the gammon rasher. Grill it gently for from ten to fifteen minutes, keeping it turned frequently. Put it on a dish and keep it warm.

Cut a slice of bread of toast thickness, a little smaller than the gammon rasher. Put it into the grill-tin with the bacon fat, and brown it under the grill, turning it over when brown on one side.

Remove the rind from the rashers, roll them up and stick them on a skewer. Cook them with the bread until the fat is semi-transparent.

Serve the gammon rasher on the bread, pour the bacon fat round, and garnish the dish with rolls of bacon, and asparagus, which should have been previously heated, and formed into bundles with a ring made from a slice of tomato round each.

Sufficient for four persons.

BEEHIVE PUDDING

INGREDIENTS.—3 oz. of macaroni, 1 cup of breadcrumbs, 1 cup of cold meat (chopped), 1 tomato (sliced), 1 egg (beaten), salt and pepper, ½ oz. of flour, 1 oz. of butter, ½ gill of milk, tomato sauce.

METHOD.—Put the macaroni and salt in a large pan of boiling water. Boil it for thirty minutes and strain it. Let the macaroni cool.

Grease a basin and sprinkle breadcrumbs over the inside. Line the basin round and round with long pieces of macaroni, pressing it against the basin and adding a few breadcrumbs to make it keep in place.

Fry the tomato in the butter for five minutes, and stir in the flour and chopped meat. Season to taste and add the rest of the breadcrumbs and macaroni.

Bind with the egg and milk and fill the basin with the mixture. Cover with greased paper and steam for one hour.

Leave for five minutes, turn out carefully and serve with tomato sauce (see overleaf).

Sufficient for three persons.

TOMATO SAUCE

INGREDIENTS.—1 lb. or small tin of tomatoes, ½ onion, 1 bayleaf, 6 peppercorns, 1 oz. of butter, 1 oz. of flour, ¾ gill of water, salt.

METHOD.—Peel and chop the onion and slice the tomatoes. Melt the butter, put in the onion, bayleaf, peppercorn and tomatoes, and simmer very gently for twenty minutes. Rub the sauce through a sieve.

Mix the flour smoothly with the water. Put it with the tomatoes in a saucepan and stir till boiling. Boil for five minutes and season.

BENGAL MINCE

INGREDIENTS.—4 oz. of rice, 2½ oz. of butter, ½ lb. of onions, 10 oz. of cold meat, seasoning, 2½ gills of stock (see p. 12) or gravy, 3 teaspoonfuls of curry powder, 1¼ oz. of flour.

METHOD.—Wash the rice and cook it in boiling water, with a little salt added, until tender, then drain it in a colander. Pour cold water through to separate the grains, and drain it again.

Peel and mince the onions and fry them till lightly browned in the butter. Lift out half of them, and put them into a saucepan. Stir two teaspoonfuls of curry powder into the remaining onions and butter and, when blended, add the rice and make it hot. If necessary, another dab of butter may be added.

Add a teaspoonful of curry powder to the onions in the saucepan, cook them a minute, then add the stock, and stir in the flour smoothed in a little water. Boil them for a few minutes, then mince the meat and add it. Season the mince and make it hot; if not brown enough, add a few drops of browning.

Heap the prepared rice in the centre of a dish, pour the mince round it, and garnish it with sippets of toast.

If the mince seems too thick, thin it down with a little more stock.

Sufficient for four persons.

BOILED CALF'S HEAD

WITH PARSLEY AND BRAIN SAUCE
INGREDIENTS.—½ calf's head, water to cover, salt, 1 onion, 1 carrot, a few mixed herbs, lemon.

FOR THE PARSLEY AND BRAIN SAUCE.—1 egg (boiled hard), brains, seasoning, 2½ oz. of flour, 2½ oz. of margarine, or butter, 1 pint of milk, 1 tablespoonful of chopped parsley, 1 gill of water.

METHOD.—Remove the brains from the head and chop off the nose. Skin the brains.

Soak the head and brains in warm water for about half an hour (with a little salt added).

Tie the head in a piece of muslin and put into a large saucepan with a little salt and a few herbs tied in a piece of muslin.

Peel an onion, scrape and wash the carrot, add these, and well cover with water.

Bring to the boil, skim it, and simmer from two and a half to three hours.

Tie the brains in muslin and add about twenty minutes before the head is cooked.

TO MAKE THE SAUCE.—Melt the butter in a saucepan, mix in the flour to a smooth paste.

Add the milk and water gradually. Bring to the boil, keeping it well stirred.

Simmer for about six minutes and season well.

Put half a pint of this sauce into another saucepan.

Take out the brains, chop them up, and add to the half-pint of sauce, also the hard-boiled egg, cut into small square pieces or chopped.

To the larger portion of sauce add the chopped parsley.

Place the head on a large dish, pour over it the parsley sauce, garnish with pieces of cut lemon.

Serve the extra brain sauce separately, also a little of the liquor, strained.

NOTE.—The sauce should be sufficiently thick to coat the head.

The parsley must be well washed and scalded before being chopped.

The herbs should not be left in the liquor for more than about half an hour, or they will discolour it.

CALF'S HEAD VINAIGRETTE
A FRENCH DISH

INGREDIENTS.—Half a calf's head (boned by the butcher), 6 small tomatoes, 6 bread fingers, 2 oz. of dripping 1 teaspoonful of salt, 6 peppercorns, 1 bayleaf.

FOR THE SAUCE.—3 tablespoonfuls of vinegar, ¾ gill of salad oil, 1½ tablespoonfuls of chopped parsley, 1 tablespoonful of grated onion, salt and pepper, 1 teaspoonful of mustard.

METHOD.—Wash the head, roll it up neatly, skin side out, and tie it with tape. Lay it in a pan of cold water, bring it just to the boil and throw away the water.

Put it back into the pan with the salt, six peppercorns and a bayleaf, and enough cold water to cover it. Simmer gently for three hours.

In two hours put the tomatoes in a steamer and cook them above the head for one hour. Strain the water from the calf's head, and keep it for making soup.

To MAKE THE SAUCE.—Put the mustard in a basin, stir in the oil gradually, and add the vinegar, parsley and onion with salt and pepper to taste. Pour the sauce over the calf's head and heat it for five minutes.

Heat the dripping till it smokes, and fry the fingers of bread for two minutes. Drain them on paper. Dish up the head with the sauce poured over it and the tomatoes and fried bread placed round.

Sufficient for four or five persons.

BEEF AND BEETROOT STEAKS

INGREDIENTS.—1 lb. of minced steak, 1 lb. of cooked beetroot, 2 eggs, 4 oz. of breadcrumbs, salt, sugar, and pepper, 2 oz. of butter, about 1 gill of water, brussels sprouts.

METHOD.—Mince the beetroot, mix it with the steak, and put it through a mincer two or three times. Add the eggs, breadcrumbs, salt, pepper and sugar, and mix well.

Shape the mixture into round flat cakes of equal size, about half an inch thick, using two knives and a little flour. Fry them in butter. Add a little water and cover the pan with an enamel plate, and allow the cakes to simmer for about half an hour.

Lift out the steaks, season and thicken the sauce. Serve them garnished with brussels sprouts.

NOTE.—These steaks may be flavoured with a little minced onion, if liked.

Sufficient to make nine steaks.

PRESSED BRISKET OF BEEF

THIS is a delightful and very economical cold meat dish. It is also suitable for special occasions, such as parties, or wedding breakfasts, in which case it should be glazed and decorated to make it look attractive.

INGREDIENTS.—About 6 to 8 lb. of salt brisket, water to cover, glaze and butter (for decoration).

METHOD.—Have the meat boned out, put it into a pan with enough warm water to cover it, and bring it to the boil. Remove the scum, and let the meat simmer gently for about four hours, if it is a middle cut, and five if it is the end cut. When cooked, turn out the gas and leave the meat in the water for two or three hours.

TO PRESS THE BRISKET

Lift it up with a slice and put it into a pie-dish or oblong-shaped tin (it should be a very tight fit), placing the best side downwards.

Lay a piece of greaseproof paper on the top, then a baking sheet, and press them with heavy weights. When the meat is thoroughly cold and firm, turn it out and serve.

GLAZING

For special occasions. To glaze the galantine, brush the top and sides evenly with glaze, using a pastry brush. (The glaze can be bought ready prepared in bottles, from any big stores.) It should first be warmed slightly to make it liquify.

When set, decorate with butter forced through an icing bag with a loose tube fixed in the end of it. The butter must first be beaten to a soft consistency.

SALT BRISKET OF BEEF

THIS *dish requires a long time to cook*. Most people do not cook it nearly enough.

First have the meat boned out, and then put it into warm water, bring it to the boil, remove the scum and simmer it gently until tender.

A piece of brisket weighing about six to eight pounds will require probably four hours to cook if it is a middle cut; if it is an end cut, it will take five hours. When cooked, turn out the gas and leave the meat in the water for two or three hours.

To Press the Brisket.—Lift it into an oblong-shaped tin or pie-dish, putting the better side downwards. It must fit very tightly into the dish, or it will not press well. Lay a sheet of greaseproof paper on the top, then a baking sheet, and press them with heavy weights. Leave the meat until it is quite cold before turning it out.

It is advisable to stand it in another tin when pressing it, to catch the fat and liquor that is pressed out of the meat.

Flank of Beef

To press a joint of flank of beef, have it boned out and *rolled*, and cook it until it is tender. Leave it in the water for an hour or two, then press it in a round cake tin.

A considerable amount of fat forms on the .liquor in which a piece of brisket has been cooked. If this is clarified, it can be used for making cakes. To do this, leave the liquor to get quite cold, and then skim off the fat with a fish slice and put it into a good-sized saucepan. Cover it with cold water and boil it until the water has evaporated. Strain it into a basin.

Suet Dumplings

Dumplings are delicious served with boiled meat. To make them, use half as much suet as flour. Chop the suet finely and mix it with the flour. Add enough cold water to make a stiff paste. Some cooks add a little baking powder to the flour. Divide it into small portions and form each into a smooth ball. Cook them in with the meat, allowing about an hour.

BOILED SALT BEEF AND SUET DUMPLINGS

INGREDIENTS.—3 or 4 lb. of silver-side of beef, tepid water, carrots, suet dumplings, 4 oz. of flour, 2 oz. of beef suet, water to mix.

METHOD.—Wash and wipe the meat, and tie it into shape, so that it cuts into round slices when cold. Put it in a pan of tepid water and bring it

slowly to the boil. As soon as the water boils, put in the carrots, scraped and cut in quarters, and lower the gas. The meat must only simmer till it is done.

This is important for any kind of boiled meat, but especially for salt meat, which is inclined to be hard. For boiling, allow twenty-five minutes to each pound and twenty-five minutes over. A joint of four pounds will need cooking for at least two hours and five minutes.

The Dumplings

The dumplings should be put in half an hour before the meat is done. To make them, remove the skin from the suet and chop the latter finely, first covering it with a little flour till it is of the same consistency as bread-crumbs. Add the rest of the flour, mix to a rather stiff dough with a little cold water, and shape into smooth little balls.

To dish up, place the meat in the centre of a large hot dish and arrange the carrots and dumplings round it.

NOTE.—Boiled salt beef is extremely good served with bread sauce (see p. 83).

BRAISED FLANK OF BEEF

INGREDIENTS.—2 lb. of thick flank beef, $\frac{1}{2}$ oz. of flour, 1 oz. of dripping, $\frac{3}{4}$ pint of water, 4 large onions (sliced), salt and pepper, 1 dessertspoonful of Worcester sauce, 1 Oxo cube.

METHOD.—Spread the meat with dripping and lay it on the onions in a baking-tin.

Pour in the water and bake the meat in a slow oven for one and a half hours, basting the meat frequently.

Put meat and onions on a hot dish. Pour the flour mixed smoothly with the sauce and half a gill of cold water into the gravy. Add the Oxo cube.

Stir till boiling, season to taste, and boil for three minutes.

Strain round the meat.

Sufficient for three persons.

BRAISED FILLET OF BEEF

INGREDIENTS.—$3\frac{1}{2}$ to 4 lb. of fillet of beef, some dripping or butter, about $\frac{1}{2}$ pint of stock (see p. 12), or more as required, a sprig of parsley, thyme and marjoram, 2 onions and

2 or 3 carrots, ½ a turnip, flour for thickening, seasoning, grated horse-radish.

METHOD.—Prepare the vegetables and cut them in quarters or in very thick chunky pieces.

Melt some butter or dripping in a saucepan or braising pan, and steam the vegetables in it for a few minutes, and then put them on a plate.

Put the meat into the pan and brown it lightly on all sides, then take it out, pour off the fat, put the vegetables back into the pan, arranging them to form a bed, and then place the meat on top of them.

Add the herbs and the stock, which should be boiling and should not reach quite as far as the meat.

Cover them with a buttered paper, then close the pan and put the beef into a moderately hot oven to cook. It will take about an hour and a half.

Serve the meat on a hot dish garnished with grated horseradish and slices of cooked carrot. Thicken and brown the liquor, season it and strain it and serve it with the beef.

BEEF FILLETS AND BUTTON ONIONS

INGREDIENTS.—3 slices of fillet of beef, butter or dripping, 1 teaspoonful of flour, ¼ pint of stock (see p. 12), seasoning, about 2 dozen button onions.

METHOD.—Peel the onions and put them into a saucepan with cold water to cover them well. Bring them to the boil and let them boil for two minutes, then pour off the water and leave the onions to drain. Melt some butter or dripping in a pan, add the onions and toss them in the fat until lightly brown and tender.

Have the steak cut thickly and trim it into neat fillets. Heat some butter in another frying-pan, season the fillets and fry them gently for a few minutes until tender, keeping them turned as required.

Serve them on a hot dish, garnish each fillet with onions, pour thick gravy round and place a small heap of onions on each side of the dish.

If liked, the fillets may be served on small rounds of bread fried lightly in butter.

To MAKE THE GRAVY.—Add the flour to the butter, after frying the fillets. Stir it over a low burner till brown, draw the pan aside and add the stock. Boil it up, add season-ing to taste, and strain the gravy. If too thick, more stock may be added.

Sufficient for three fillets.

NOTE.—The trimmings from the fillets can be minced and used for making Vienna Steaks (see p. 165).

FILLETS OF BEEF WITH FRIED BANANAS

INGREDIENTS.—1½ lb. of fillet of beef, 3 bananas, parsley butter, mashed potatoes, ½ oz. of dripping.

METHOD.—The fillets should be about three-quarters of an inch thick and trimmed into neat rounds. Heat the dripping, and when it begins to smoke, fry the fillets as quickly as possible for two minutes, to brown the outside. Then turn them over and brown the other side. Finish cooking *very slowly* for ten minutes, or less if liked underdone.

The bananas are cut in half and fried at one side of the pan. They will only take a few minutes to cook.

Dish up the fillets on a roll of mashed potato and place the bananas round the dish. Keep the meat hot while making the gravy. The fat should be poured off, and any brown pieces which have collected on the sides of the pan should be scraped together. A gill and a half of good stock should be added, boiled up, seasoned, and poured round the meat.

A little parsley butter should be placed on each fillet just before serving.

Sufficient for six persons.

PARSLEY BUTTER

INGREDIENTS.—1 oz. of butter, 1 heaped teaspoonful of chopped parsley, 1 teaspoonful of lemon-juice, salt and pepper.

METHOD.—Put the butter in a saucer and cream it with a knife till it is soft. Work in the lemon-juice, seasoning and parsley. Shape it into rounds and keep in a cool place till required for serving on grilled steak or fish.

FILLETS OF BEEF AND HORSERADISH

INGREDIENTS.—1 lb. of fillet of beef, tomato, finely-grated horseradish, seasoning, stock (see p. 12), flour, some French or runner beans.

METHOD.—Cut the fillet of beef into neat round fillets, and trim off the fat. They should be three-quarters of an inch thick.

Season both sides, and heat the grill, then put the fillets on the rack in the grill-tin, and grill them for about eight minutes, keeping them turned.

When cooked (and remember not to overcook them, as they should be quite red in the centre), place each fillet on half a large tomato, the latter cut crosswise, seasoned, and baked gently in the oven.

Heap a teaspoonful of finely-grated horseradish in the centre of each fillet, and serve the fillets with a few cooked French beans on the other side.

Pour some slightly thickened gravy round the dish.

TO MAKE THE GRAVY.—Brown a little flour in the grill-tin after grilling the fillets, draw this aside and cool it for a minute, then add a gill of stock ; then boil it up, season it and strain it.

NOTE.—The trimmings of steak left over from this dish can be added to and made into Steak Rolls (see p. 150).

FILLETS OF BEEF AND MUSHROOMS

INGREDIENTS.—1 lb. of fillet steak (cut thickly), 1½ gills of brown stock (see p. 12), seasoning, ¼ lb. of mushrooms, dripping, flour.

METHOD.—Cut the fat away from the steak and cut three round fillets from it.

Make them even by beating them out with a cutlet bat or large knife, then cut off any uneven pieces. The fillets should be about three-quarters of an inch in thickness.

Cut three rounds of fat, not quite as large as the fillets, and about half an inch in thickness.

Skin the mushrooms and remove the stalks.

Melt some dripping in a frying-pan and fry the mushrooms rather slowly for about twenty minutes.

While these are frying, grill the fillets of steak for about ten minutes, keeping them frequently turned. At the same time, grill the rounds of fat.

Place the fillets on a hot dish, with a round of fat on each, and a mushroom on the fat.

Keep this hot together with the remainder of the mushrooms.

Pour off some of the dripping in which the mushrooms were cooked, leaving only about one tablespoonful in the pan.

To this add a sprinkling of flour and brown slowly. Then add stock and bring to the boil.

Pour off the fat from the grill tin, leaving the brown particles in the bottom of the tin.

Pour the gravy on to these, boil up again, and season.

If necessary, add a few drops of browning.

Strain round the fillets and heap the remainder of the mushrooms on either side of the dish.

FILLETS OF BEEF AND TOMATOES

INGREDIENTS.—1½ lb. of fillet of beef, hot mashed potatoes, 4 tomatoes, a jar of glaze (this can be bought ready prepared from any big stores), parsley butter, ½ oz. of dripping, 1 gill of water.

METHOD.—Cut the fillet into neat rounds, three quarters of an inch thick.

Halve the tomatoes and put them cut side up in a meat tin with a gill of water. Bake them for twenty minutes.

Heat the dripping till it smokes, put in the fillets and fry them quickly, a minute for each side.

Finish cooking slowly (ten minutes in all).

Melt the glaze by standing the jar in hot water.

Dish up the fillets on the mashed potato and brush them over with glaze. Lay the tomatoes round the potato.

Add a teaspoonful of glaze to the water used for cooking the tomatoes, and strain it round the fillets. Put a little parsley butter on each fillet.

Sufficient for four persons.

PARSLEY BUTTER

INGREDIENTS.—1 oz. of butter, 1 dessertspoonful of chopped parsley, 1 teaspoonful of lemon-juice, salt and pepper.

METHOD.—Cream the butter till soft with a knife and work in the lemon-juice, parsley and seasoning.

Put the butter on a saucer and shape into a smooth, flat pat.

Keep it in a cool place till required.

Cut it into small squares or rounds, and serve on steak or fillets.

GALANTINE OF BEEF

INGREDIENTS.—1¼ lb. of buttock or thick flank steak, 3 eggs (1 hard-boiled), ¼ lb. of breadcrumbs, ¼ lb. of bacon, about ½ gill of stock (see p. 12), salt, pepper, powdered mace, glaze and butter for decoration.

METHOD.—Put the steak and bacon through the mincer, first removing the fat from the steak and the rind from the bacon.

Add the breadcrumbs and chopped hard-boiled egg and season to taste. Bind the mixture with the remaining two eggs well beaten, and the stock.

Form the galantine into a fat roll, roll it up tightly in a scalded pudding cloth and tie it securely at either end, as for a roly-poly pudding. Put the roll into a pan of boiling water or stock (the pan must be wide enough to take the roll without bending it) and simmer it gently for about two hours.

When cooked, take out the meat, unroll it carefully, and let out the steam. Then roll it up tightly in a dry cloth and tie as before.

Place it with the best side uppermost and put a dish and a few weights on the top of it—*just enough slightly to flatten the top.* Leave the galantine like this until cold, then remove the cloth and brush it with glaze. (This can be bought, ready prepared, in bottles, from any big stores.)

Decorate with butter forced through an icing bag with a plain icing tube fixed on the end of it, and put chopped aspic jelly round.

BEEF OLIVES

INGREDIENTS.—1 lb. of buttock steak (cut thinly), 1¼ pints of brown stock (see p. 12), more if required, flour, ¼ lb. of dripping, salt and pepper, 6 tablespoonfuls of breadcrumbs, 1½ oz. of suet, 2 teaspoonfuls of chopped parsley, ¼ teaspoonful of mixed herbs, rind and juice of ½ a lemon, 1 egg, mashed potato.

METHOD.—Cut the beef into pieces about four or five inches long and two or three inches wide. Beat each piece out with a cutlet bat or large knife.

To MAKE THE STUFFING.—Make the breadcrumbs. Chop the suet finely. Well wash and scald the parsley and chop it very finely. Grate the lemon-rind. Mix all these ingredients together, add also the herbs and seasoning. Strain in the lemon-juice.

Beat up the egg and add about half of it to the stuffing, and bind all together.

Spread each piece of steak with some of the stuffing, and then roll it into a round shape. Tie with string, and roll in flour.

If any stuffing is over, make it into small balls and brush them over with the remainder of the egg; coat with breadcrumbs.

Melt the dripping in a frying-pan, and, when hot, put in the olives and fry until just light brown.

Put the stock into a saucepan, season it well, brown it, and thicken it with the flour previously mixed to a smooth paste with a little water.

When boiling, put the fried olives into it and simmer for about one hour. There should be sufficient gravy just to cover.

Fry the small forcemeat balls in hot fat.

Serve the olives on mashed potato and garnish with the forcemeat balls. Strain the gravy round the dish.

BEEF RECHAUFFE

INGREDIENTS.—½ lb. of cold beef, a small tin of peeled tomatoes, 2 onions, 1 teaspoonful of flour, seasoning, 1½ lb. of potatoes, milk, margarine, 1 or 2 fresh tomatoes.

METHOD.—Peel and mince the onions, put them into a saucepan with a little fat, and cook them until tender and just lightly coloured. Draw the pan aside and drain off the fat.

Add the contents of a small tin of peeled tomatoes and thicken the mixture with the flour smoothed in a spoonful of water. Boil it for a few minutes, keeping it stirred, then take it off the gas and let it cool.

Boil the potatoes in the usual way and mash them up. Season them with pepper, add a lump of margarine, and moisten them with a little milk.

Put a thin layer of the mashed potato in the bottom of the buttered Pyrex or pie-dish.

Mince the beef and mix it with the tomato and onion, season it, and turn it into the dish, then heap the remainder of the potatoes on top to form a border.

Put the réchauffé into the oven and make it hot. Garnish the centre with quarters of lightly baked fresh tomato.

Sufficient for four persons.

RIB OF BEEF

A LONG rib of beef is far more easily carved if the bone is removed, and it is rolled into a round shape.

It can be served either hot or cold, but cold is preferable, as it becomes a rather ragged joint when carved hot.

It is most appetising when accompanied by horseradish sauce and served with a tomato salad. It is also quite a suitable joint to take when going for a picnic.

To MAKE HORSERADISH SAUCE.— Scrub a stick of horseradish, peel it thinly, and grate it finely. Weigh off one and a half ounces of this, and mix it with two dessertspoonfuls of white vinegar, and season it with pepper, salt and mixed mustard.

Whisk half a gill of cream until thick, and stir in the prepared horseradish.

To PREPARE THE TOMATO SALAD.— Cut firm tomatoes into quarters or eighths, dress them with French dressing (see p. 168) and sprinkle them with finely-chopped parsley, and, if liked, just a little minced onion.

The tomatoes may be skinned if preferred. To do this, drop them into boiling water for a few seconds, when the skins will peel off quite easily.

ROAST BEEF AND YORK-SHIRE PUDDING

COOKED IN A CASSEROLE OR IRON POT ON THE SMALLEST GAS BURNER.

INGREDIENTS.—3 lb. of top rib of beef, 2 oz. of dripping, flour, clear gravy (see below), $\frac{1}{2}$ pint of boiling water, salt and pepper.

METHOD.—Wash the meat quickly, wipe it and dredge it with a little flour.

Put the casserole on an asbestos mat and place in it the dripping.

Heat it until it begins to smoke and put in the meat. Brown it quickly all over, turning it as soon as one side is brown. Do not stick a fork into the lean part as this would let out the juices.

After about ten minutes' browning, put on the lid and turn the gas *very* low. The meat must now be cooked as slowly as possible to make it tender.

Turn it over and baste it every twenty minutes. If there is not room for the casserole on top of the stove, it can be placed in a slow oven. Allow twenty minutes to each pound and twenty minutes over.

Top rib of beef is a cheap joint suitable for a small family.

NOTE.—Other joints that can be cooked in the same way are small sirloins, rolled ribs, fillet of beef, or any small joint of lamb, mutton or veal.

A casserole must be " seasoned " before use.

The French way to season a casserole is to fill it with cold water and tie a string round it.

Next stand it on an asbestos mat over the gas and bring it slowly to the boil. Let the water get cold in the casserole.

It will then stand moderate cooking heat for several years, but it will, of course, break easily if knocked against anything hard.

Never put cold water in a hot casserole.

YORKSHIRE PUDDING

INGREDIENTS.—$\frac{1}{2}$ pint of milk, fresh or sour, 1 large egg, 4 oz. of flour, $\frac{1}{2}$ tablespoonful of dripping, $\frac{1}{4}$ teaspoonful of salt.

METHOD.—Sift the flour and salt into a basin, make a hollow in the centre, and put in the egg, unbeaten.

Add two tablespoonfuls of milk and begin stirring in the flour with a wooden spoon. Do not stir in enough flour to make the centre dry, but keep it a smooth batter.

Stir until half the milk has been gradually added, and then beat the batter for five minutes, and let it stand for fifteen minutes or longer. While the batter is standing, put the dripping in a pie-dish and heat it in a quick oven. Make sure that the dish is well greased all round the sides.

Add the rest of the milk to the batter and pour it into the pie-dish, which should be very hot.

The success of the pudding depends on having a hot dish. Bake in a hot oven for thirty minutes.

NOTE.—Sour milk makes very good Yorkshire puddings.

If liked, the pudding may be made with a gill and a half of milk and half a gill of water.

The batter may be poured into the meat tin and cooked under a joint of beef. In this case three-quarters to one pint of batter should be made. When it is cooked it should be cut into squares.

Sufficient for four or five persons.

CLEAR GRAVY

AFTER the baking of a joint the tin contains dripping and savoury brown particles. In making the gravy, care must be taken to retain all these particles because of their delicious flavour. Pour off all the dripping very carefully so as not to disturb the sediment, and hold back any pieces with an iron spoon.

Scrape off any brown particles adhering to the sides of the tin, and pour on half a pint of boiling water. Stir the gravy till it boils, season to taste and serve in a gravy-boat.

BEEF ROLYS

INGREDIENTS.—3 oz. of cold beef, 6 oz. of cold potato, 1 dessertspoonful of minced onion, 2 or 3 dessertspoonfuls of thick tomato sauce (see p. 43), pepper and salt, ¾ lb. of short or flaky pastry (see p. 252).

METHOD.—Put the meat and potato through the mincer and mix them with the onion. Season to taste and moisten the mixture with tomato sauce. Divide it into eight portions and form each into a sausage shape.

Roll out the pastry fairly thinly, and cut oblong-shaped pieces the same width as the rolls and long enough to reach round them. Roll them, the sausage shapes, in these, and damp the edge where the pastry joins.

Brush the rolys with beaten egg-yolk mixed with a little milk. Stand them on a baking sheet, and put them into a hot oven to bake. They will take about fifteen or twenty minutes.

Serve beef rolys with or without thick gravy).

Sufficient for eight rolys.

BAKED SIRLOIN OF BEEF

THE average time to allow for baking a sirloin is fifteen minutes to the pound and fifteen over, but remember always to consider the thickness of the joint as well as the weight. A small joint will take longer in comparison than a large one. A piece of sirloin weighing from five to six pounds will require about one hour and a half. Meat (especially the lean kind) needs to be kept well basted.

TO MAKE THE GRAVY

Pour off the dripping (leaving only the brown particles), add to the latter some good stock, previously browned and seasoned, boil up and then strain.

Horseradish sauce (see p. 112) is the usual accompaniment to this dish.

NOTE.—Two hot dishes can be made from this joint, if liked. Remove the undercut and use for tournedos (see p. 114), then bake or roast the remainder of the joint.

TWO HOT DISHES FROM ONE SIRLOIN

HAVE a joint of sirloin weighing about five pounds. The top part of this, which is less tender, can be cut off and braised, and the remainder of the joint roasted.

TOP OF SIRLOIN (BRAISED)

INGREDIENTS.—Top of sirloin, about 1½ lb., flour, pepper and salt, stock (see p. 12), a small sprig of thyme and parsley, dripping, 1 large carrot, 1 large onion.

METHOD.—Prepare the vegetables and cut them in quarters or in thick chunky pieces. Melt some dripping in a saucepan and cook them in it for a few minutes without letting them brown. Put them on a plate. Flour the meat lightly and brown it on both sides. Pour off the dripping.

Arrange the vegetables in the bottom of the pan or in a casserole, place the meat on top of them, and pour in sufficient boiling stock almost to cover the vegetables.

Add the thyme and parsley, cover the meat with a greased paper and cook it gently for about an hour and a half or until tender, the first half of the time on top of the stove, and the remainder in the oven.

Thicken and season the gravy and serve it with the meat. Garnish the dish with the vegetables cut into neat pieces.

Sufficient for four persons.

ROAST SIRLOIN AND BAKED POTATOES

Put the meat into a hot oven, and when the outside is sealed, lessen the heat as required. This joint, which weighs three and a half pounds, without the top, will take about an hour and a quarter to cook. It should be basted occasionally.

Serve the sirloin with thin brown gravy. Make this by boiling up stock (see p. 12) in the baking-tin after pouring off the dripping. Add seasoning to taste and a few drops of browning, if required, then strain the gravy.

To prepare the baked potatoes, peel and wash them, then dry them thoroughly. Put them into a baking-tin with hot dripping, sprinkle them with salt and bake them till brown and tender, turning them over as required. They will take about an hour to cook, according to the size.

TIMBALE OF BEEF

I n g r e d i e n t s.—1 teacupful of chopped cooked beef, 2 oz. of chopped cooked ham, a few chopped mushrooms, 1 teacupful of crumbs, salt and pepper, a little nutmeg, 2 eggs, 1 gill of milk or stock (see p. 12), 1 tablespoonful of cream, 6 oz. of thick straight macaroni.

Method.—Boil the macaroni for about ten minutes (it should not be quite cooked), drain it, and cut it into pieces about one-third of an inch in length. Butter a plain mould, begin at the centre of the mould and line the base and the sides with macaroni, putting the cut side to the tin. Use a skewer or hatpin to do this.

Mix all the other ingredients together, pack them carefully into the mould. Cover it with a buttered paper and steam it slowly for one hour. Turn out the Timbale of Beef and serve it with a good white sauce (see p. 41).

Sufficient for five or six persons.

BEEF TOURNEDOS

Ingredients.—Fillet of beef (undercut taken from sirloin), tomatoes (allow half a tomato to each fillet), croûtes of fried bread (allow one for each fillet), dripping, seasoning, stock (see p. 12).

Method.—Cut the tomatoes into halves, in a little dripping, until tender.

Cut the fillet of beef into thick slices, trim off the fat, and make each into a neat round shape. Heat the grill, put the fillets under, and grill for about ten minutes. If liked, some of the fat can be cut into even-sized pieces and grilled.

When cooked, dish up each fillet on a round of fried bread (about the same size as the fillet) and place half a tomato on each, skin side uppermost. Serve with gravy, the latter made from stock boiled up in the grill-tin and slightly thickened and browned.

Allow one fillet for each person.

BEEF AND VEAL CASSEROLE

Ingredients.—1 lb. of fresh silverside of steak, 1 tablespoonful of flour, salt and paprika pepper, 1 pint of stock (see p. 12), 2 onions, ¼ pint of butter beans, ¾ lb. of stewing veal, 2 tomatoes, 2 carrots.

Method.—Wash the beans and soak them overnight then put them on to cook and boil them till tender. They will probably take two hours to cook. Cut the steak into five or six pieces, mix it with the flour and season it with salt and paprika. Put it into a casserole and stir in the stock. Put it in the oven, bring it to the boil, and let it simmer for two or three hours.

Cut the veal into four or five pieces, dredge it with flour and fry it lightly in a little dripping just to brown it, then put it on a plate, add the onions, peeled and sliced, and fry them till light brown.

Prepare and cut up the carrots and add them to the stew when it comes to the boil, add also the onions and veal, allowing these an hour and a half or two hours to cook. Stew all together until tender, then serve them on a dish, or in the casserole.

The beans should be strained off when tender and cooked in with the meat for the last half an hour. At the same time add the tomatoes, peeled, and sliced.

Sufficient for six persons.

VENETIAN MINCED BEEF

INGREDIENTS.—2 onions, butter or dripping, ½ pint of stock (see p. 12)— add more if required—seasoning, ¾ oz. of flour, a small tin of peeled tomatoes. ¼ lb. of spaghetti, cold beef (about 10 oz.).

METHOD. — Peel and mince the onions, and fry them gently till golden in a little hot fat. Then pour off the fat that remains.

Add the stock, and stir in the flour smoothed in either a little water or stock. Bring it to the boil and boil it for two or three minutes, adding a little browning as required.

Meanwhile, cook the spaghetti in a pan of slightly salted boiling water ; when it is tender, drain it, and return it to the pan, with the liquor drained from the tin of tomatoes. Simmer them gently for a few minutes.

Add the drained tomatoes to the gravy. Mince the meat and add it, together with seasoning to taste. Make the mixture thoroughly hot, turn it on to a dish and serve it with a border of the prepared spaghetti.

Sufficient for five or six persons.

WING RIB AND HORSERADISH SAUCE

INGREDIENTS.—A wing rib of beef weighing about 6 lb.

FOR THE HORSERADISH SAUCE.—

A stick of horseradish, 3 dessert-spoonfuls of white vinegar, pepper, salt, mustard, about ¼ pint of cream.

METHOD.—Put the meat into a hot oven at first and lessen the heat later as required. It will take about one hour and a half to cook.

Serve the meat with brown gravy, the latter made from the brown particles left in the baking-tin after pouring off the dripping. This requires a little good brown stock (see p. 12) added to it. Then it should be boiled up, seasoned and strained.

To MAKE THE HORSERADISH SAUCE. —Scrub a stick of horseradish, then peel it thinly and grate it finely.

Weigh off two ounces and a half of the grated horseradish. Mix it with the white vinegar and season it with pepper, salt and a little mixed mustard.

Take the cream and whisk it till it is thick. Then gradually stir it into the prepared horseradish.

A COOL, TEMPTING BRAWN

INGREDIENTS.—½ pig's head, 2 lb. of knuckle of veal, water to well cover, ½ a nutmeg, ½ teaspoonful of powdered mace, ½ flat teaspoonful of pepper, salt if required.

METHOD.—Buy half a pig's head that has been in salt for not more than two days. (Remove the brains ; these are not used for this dish.) Wash it and put it into a boiler with the knuckle of veal. Wash the latter and chop it into five or six pieces.

Add the water, pepper, mace and grated nutmeg.

Bring it to the boil and skim it. Then simmer for about three hours. Taste to see if sufficiently salt, and if necessary add some.

Lift the head and veal on to a large dish.

Skin the tongue, and remove every piece of bone and gristle from the meat.

Put the bones, etc., back into the boiler with the liquor, and boil until it jellies. This takes about two hours.

Set aside the veal and head to cool. When cold, cut up (fat and lean) into small squares, and half fill some wet moulds, or one large mould, with them. Strain the stock and pour into the moulds.

Leave until quite set.

Scrape off the fat from the top, shake the brawn well, and turn on to a dish.

NOTE.—Test the liquor to see if sufficiently boiled; put a small quantity on to a saucer. When cold, it should form a jelly.

ITALIAN CASSEROLE

INGREDIENTS.—1 lb. of stewing steak, a small tin of peeled tomatoes, 1 carrot and onion, 1 tablespoonful of flour, seasoning, 2 oz. of spaghetti.

METHOD.—Wipe the steak and cut it into pieces. Mix it with the flour, adding pepper and salt to taste, and put it into a casserole.

Strain the liquor from the tomatoes and add it to the steak. Cover the casserole. Bring the meat to the boil, then let it simmer until it is tender. Add the diced carrot and onion.

Cook the spaghetti in slightly salted boiling water, strain it and add it to the stew, with the drained tomatoes, about half an hour before it is ready to be served.

Sufficient for four persons.

CORNISH PASTIES

INGREDIENTS.—About 10 or 12 oz. of short or slightly flaky pastry (see p. 252), ½ onion (uncooked) 3 oz. of potatoes (uncooked), 3 oz. of beef steak (uncooked), salt and pepper, stock (see p. 12) or water.

METHOD.—Peel the onion and chop finely. Peel the potato and cut into small pieces. Put the meat through the mincer.

Mix all together, season well and moisten with just a little cold stock or water.

Roll out the pastry and cut into three large rounds (use a saucepan lid to do this). Turn them over on to the other side and put some of the prepared meat and vegetables in the centre.

Damp the edges and draw the opposite sides together, forming a half-circle over the meat.

Flute the edge with your finger and thumb, brush over with milk, put on to a baking-sheet and bake in a hot oven for about three-quarters of an hour. The heat should be lessened as soon as the pastry is cooked.

Make a hole so that the steam can escape.

Allow one or two for each person.

NOTE.—Delicious meat pasties can also be made with cooked meat flavoured with a little fried onion. These will require less time to cook.

CROQUETTES

(See p. 126.)

MEAT, SOUP AND COW-HEEL BRAWN

ALL MADE FROM ONE COW-HEEL!

INGREDIENTS.—1 large cow-heel, 2 pickled sheeps' tongues, 1 tin of tomatoes, 2 hard-boiled eggs, 4 oz. of fat bacon (in one piece), 4 peppercorns, 2 cloves, 4 onions, 4 carrots, ½ oz. of sago, 4 pints of cold water, 1 lb. of veal bones (chopped), 1½ teaspoonfuls of salt, 2 sheets of gelatine.

METHOD.—Put the cow-heel and tongues into a pan of cold water, bring them slowly to the boil and pour away the water.

Add the veal bones and four pints of cold water with the salt, cloves and peppercorns, and heat them slowly till boiling.

Simmer very gently for four hours.

Peel the onions and scrape the carrots, and, if large, cut them into quarters.

In two hours and a half take out the tongues and put in the vegetables and tomatoes. Lay the tongues in a basin of cold water and peel off the skin.

When the stew is cooked, put the tongues back into it and boil the liquid down till it measures two pints and a half.

FOR THE MEAT DISH AND THE SOUP

Put half the cow-heel and one tongue into a double saucepan with the vegetables and keep them hot.

Wash the sago.

Add a gill of water to one pint and a half of the liquid stock. Bring it to the boil, sprinkle in the sago and simmer it till it is transparent (fifteen minutes).

Put a gill of the soup with the cow-heel and vegetables and serve them on a hot dish.

FOR THE SOUP

HEAT up the rest of the thickened stock with any vegetables that remain.

FOR THE BRAWN

WET a basin and put into it a tongue and the hard-boiled eggs, cut in half.

Soak the gelatine in half a gill of cold water.

Cut up half the cow-heel and chop the bacon.

Boil them in a pint of the stock till it is reduced to three-quarters of a pint.

Stir in the gelatine and, when it is dissolved, pour it into the basin containing the tongue and eggs.

When cold, turn it out of the basin and serve it with salad.

Sufficient for two or three persons.

MIXED GRILL

THIS is a somewhat expensive method of cooking, as it is only suitable for tender parts of meat, such as chops, steaks, etc., but it has its advantage in that it is a quick method.

It is important to remember to heat the grill before putting the food under it, so that the outside of the meat may be sealed at once, and thus all the goodness kept in it. For the same reason, the grill-tin should also be previously heated.

Chops require from fifteen to twenty minutes to cook ; steak about twelve minutes ; cutlets about ten minutes ; and kidneys about ten minutes.

Frequent turning is required during the cooking.

A MIXED GRILL FOR ONE

A MIXED grill usually consists of a sausage, kidney, tomato, cutlet, and rasher of bacon.

Remove the rind from the rasher, cut the tomato in halves or leave it whole as preferred, skin the kidney, split it open, and remove the core.

Put all the prepared ingredients, together with a sausage and a mutton cutlet, on the bars of the grill-tin, put the tin under the hot grill and grill for about ten minutes or longer as required, keeping everything turned frequently, and dishing up each piece as it is cooked.

The bacon will only take a few minutes, and is better if cooked in the bottom of the grill-tin. It is ready as soon as the fat is semi-transparent.

Serve all on a hot plate, with slightly thickened gravy.

BOILED HAM

INGREDIENTS.—1 ham (weighing 10 lb.), water to cover, browned crumbs.

METHOD.—Soak the ham for about twelve hours in cold water. Put into a large boiler, cover with water, bring to the boil, and remove the scum. Simmer gently from three to three hours and a half. Put on a large dish and carefully take off the rind. Sprinkle with brown crumbs. Place on another clean dish and serve.

To make the brown crumbs, break up some stale pieces of bread—crust and crumb can be used. Put them on a baking-sheet, and bake in the oven till golden brown. Crush with a rolling-pin, then rub through a sieve.

HAM, WITH CIDER SAUCE

INGREDIENTS.—1 lb. of cold cabbage, 1 slice of gammon.

FOR THE SAUCE.—1 oz. of butter, 1 oz. of flour, ¼ bottle of cider, ½ teaspoonful of made mustard, pepper, 1 gill of water.

METHOD.—Heat the cabbage in a double saucepan. Put the gammon and enough cold water to cover it into a fireproof dish. Bake in a slow oven for twenty minutes with the lid on.

Pour off the water as it will be rather salt.

Melt the butter and mix the flour with it. Fry it till it is a rich brown, stirring all the time.

Add the mustard, pepper, cider and one gill of water, stir till it boils and pour it over the gammon.

Bake for thirty minutes.

Put the cabbage in the casserole with the gammon on top of it, and serve in the same dish.

Sufficient for three or four persons.

HAM MOUSSE

INGREDIENTS.—6 oz. of lean ham (cooked), 1½ gills of espagnole sauce (see overleaf), 1½ gills of savoury calf's-foot jelly, ½ oz. of French leaf gelatine (very light weight), 1 gill of cream, ½ gill of water, seasoning, a pinch of powdered mace, black truffle. cochineal

METHOD.—Put the ham through a very fine mincer, then mix with the espagnole sauce, season well with pepper, and add a pinch of mace and salt if required.

Rub this all through a fine wire sieve.

Take a china soufflé case and tie a band of foolscap round it, to stand just above the top.

Melt the gelatine in half a gill of water, but do not boil it.

Whisk the cream until quite thick. Melt half of the jelly, and when cold whisk it until it becomes frothy.

Stir the cream and the frothed jelly lightly into the ham mixture. Lastly, strain in the dissolved gelatine. If you wish to improve its colour, add a few drops of cochineal.

Mix all lightly together. Place in the prepared soufflé case and leave it to set. Cut the truffle into fancy shapes.

Melt the remainder of the calf's-foot jelly, dip the pieces of truffle into a little of it, then use them to decorate the top of the soufflé.

When set, carefully pour over a thin layer of the jelly. Leave until quite firm, take off the foolscap band, and stand the soufflé case on a lace paper.

NOTE.—The gelatine must be only warm when added to the cream mixture.

Sufficient for about five or six persons.

The Espagnole Sauce

INGREDIENTS.—2 oz. of flour, 2 oz. of butter, ¼ lb. of tomatoes, 1 stalk of celery (cut up), 1 carrot and onion (sliced), 1 oz. of mushrooms (chopped roughly), 1½ oz. of bacon, 1 pint of brown stock (see p. 12), seasoning, and salt, pepper and paprika, a small sprig of parsley and thyme.

METHOD.—First melt the butter in a saucepan.

Then cut up the bacon and add it with the celery, mushroom, carrot, and onion to the melted butter.

Stir until beginning to brown, then add the flour and continue stirring till brown.

It must brown *slowly* or the flavour of the sauce will be spoiled.

Draw the pan aside, add the tomatoes (which should have been sliced), the stock, and a small sprig of parsley and thyme.

Stir the sauce until it boils, then cook it very gently for about half an hour, adding seasoning to taste.

Strain it through a sieve and add a little sherry just before using it.

If too thick the sauce may be thinned down a little.

NOTE.—A plainer brown sauce can be made by omitting the sherry and mushrooms, and using margarine instead of butter.

HOT-POT

INGREDIENTS.—¾ lb. of beef steak, 1 dessertspoonful of flour, salt and pepper, 1 or 2 onions, 1¼ lb. of potatoes, stock.

METHOD.—Cut the steak into pieces and mix it with the flour, pepper and salt.

Peel the onions and slice them thinly, then put them into a casserole with the steak and add sufficient stock just to cover.

Peel and wash the potatoes, put them into a saucepan with cold water, and salt to flavour. Bring them to the boil, strain off the water, and cut the potatoes into thick chunks.

Meanwhile, put the casserole into the oven and bring the contents to the boil, then add the potatoes. Cover the top with a well-greased paper and put the hot-pot back into the oven and cook it gently for about one hour and a half.

Sufficient for three persons.

IRISH STEW WITH BUTTER BEANS

INGREDIENTS.—About 1½ to 2 lb. of scrag and middle neck of mutton, ½ lb. of onions, some white stock (see p. 12), or bean water, ¼ pint of butter beans, salt and pepper, 2 lb. of potatoes.

METHOD.—Wash the beans and soak them for about twenty-four hours, then boil them until almost tender and strain them.

Peel and slice the onions. Divide the mate into portions, where chopped.

Put both into a large saucepan, add the butter beans and about one pint of stock, or enough almost to cover. Season with salt and pepper. Bring the stock to the boil and remove the scum, then simmer it gently from one and a half to two hours.

Peel and wash the potatoes, split them into halves, sprinkle them with salt, and add them when the stew is about half cooked.

Before serving, skim off the fat, place the meat, beans and onions in the centre of the dish and arrange the potatoes to form a border. Pour round some of the gravy.

Sufficient for four or five persons.

DEVILLED KIDNEYS

INGREDIENTS.—4 sheep's kidneys, 2 squares of hot buttered toast, 1 teaspoonful each of curry powder, made-mustard, flour, and tomato ketchup, 1 dessertspoonful of lemon-juice and Worcester sauce, 1½ oz. of butter, pinch of salt.

METHOD.—Wash the kidneys and split them open, but do not separate the two halves. Pull off the skin.

Mix the flour, salt and curry powder, and roll the kidneys in it. Open them out flat and stick a skewer through so as to keep them open. If they are not skewered they will curl up.

Heat the Worcester sauce, mustard, ketchup and lemon-juice in a small pan.

Heat half the butter and, when it smokes, put in the kidneys cut side down. Brown them quickly (one minute for each side). Cook them slowly for three more minutes. Make the hot buttered toast.

Pour off the butter and any gravy from the kidneys on to the hot buttered toast. Lay two kidneys on each piece cut side up. Put a small piece of butter in each, and pour the hot mixture over. Serve at once.

Sufficient for two persons.

SMALL KIDNEY PIES

INGREDIENTS.—½ lb. of ox kidney, pepper and salt, 3 oz. of lard, 3 oz. of margarine, 9 oz. of flour, 1 flat tea-spoonful of baking powder, water to mix, milk or egg to glaze pastry.

METHOD.—Mince the kidney very finely, flour it well and add the seasoning.

Make a good short or flaky pastry with the rest of the ingredients (for method see p. 252), omitting the baking powder for the flaky kind.

Roll it out to almost a quarter of an inch thick and cut out about eight small rounds.

Roll out the remainder of the pastry rather more thinly, and cut out the same number of rounds. Line patty pans with these, then put in the prepared kidney.

Damp the edges and cover the pies with the thicker rounds of pastry.

Make a hole in the centre of each, and decorate the pies with tiny leaves of pastry.

Brush them over with milk or egg, stand them on a baking-sheet and put them into a hot oven to bake. They will take from twenty to thirty minutes to cook.

Sufficient to make about eight small pies.

KIDNEY STEW

INGREDIENTS.—1 lb. of ox kidney, ½ pint of cooked peas (fresh or tinned), ¼ lb. of mushrooms, 1 onion, flour, pepper and salt, stock (see p. 12).

METHOD.—Wash the kidney, dry it well and cut it into pieces, then coat them with seasoned flour. Peel and stalk the mushrooms, cleanse them in salted water, then drain them and cut them into quarters. The stalks can also be trimmed, washed and used in the stew.

Peel and mince the onion.

Put the prepared kidney and vegetables into a Pyrex dish, cover them with stock, mix them together and put on the lid.

Cook the stew in the oven, allowing it to simmer gently for from three-quarters to an hour, or until tender. After it comes to the boil add the peas later, giving them only enough time to get hot through.

Serve the stew all together in the dish in which it is cooked, arranging a few pieces of kidney in the centre and a circle of peas round.

If the gravy seems too thin, thicken it with a little flour mixed to a smooth paste with water. The stew must be cooked again for a few minutes after this is added.

Sufficient for four persons.

BAKED LEG OF LAMB

INGREDIENTS.—1 leg (about 4½ lb.), 2 oz. of dripping, ¾ oz. of flour, salt and pepper, ¾ pint of hot water.

METHOD.—Lamb and mutton need more care in cooking than beef or veal, because if the oven is *too* hot the meat will be tough.

Wash and wipe the meat and spread it with dripping.

Lay it on a trivet in a baking-tin, or if the tin is too small, lay the meat on the oven shelf under the browning sheet and remove the lower shelves.

The oven must be very hot for the first ten minutes, and afterwards reduced, to make the meat tender.

Baste every fifteen minutes. Allow fifteen minutes to each pound and fifteen minutes over.

When it is cooked, put the meat on a hot dish and keep it hot.

To make the gravy, pour off nearly all the dripping, leaving half a table-spoonful. Scrape all the brown particles together that have come from the meat and add the flour, frying it a rich brown and stirring well to prevent burning.

Add the water and boil up.

Boil for three minutes, season to taste, and pour a very little round the meat. Put the rest into a gravy-boat.

Serve mint sauce (see p. 121) with lamb.

BLANQUETTE OF LAMB

INGREDIENTS.—2 breasts of lamb, ½ pint of cold water, 2 onions, 1 bay-leaf, 2 cloves, 1 oz. of butter, 1 oz. of flour, ½ head of celery, ½ gill of milk, 2 slices of bread, 2 oz. of dripping, salt and pepper.

METHOD.—Slice the onions, chop the celery and cut the meat into neat pieces.

Put the meat into a pan with the cold water, bayleaf and cloves and bring it slowly to the boil. Add the onions and celery, with a half a tea-spoonful of salt.

Simmer very gently for one hour.

Place the meat on a dish.

Blend the butter and flour on a plate with a knife and add them to the stock, with the milk.

Stir the sauce till it boils, and season it with salt and pepper.

Heat the meat in the sauce.

Cut the bread into small triangles.

Heat the dripping till it smokes, and fry the bread in it for about two minutes. Drain it on paper.

Serve the blanquette on a dish with the sippets of bread round.

Sufficient for four or five persons.

BOILED LEG OF LAMB WITH PARSLEY SAUCE

INGREDIENTS.—A 5 lb. leg of lamb, carrots, turnips, cauliflower, pepper and salt, 1 pint of white sauce (see p. 41), 2 small level tablespoonfuls of chopped parsley.

METHOD.—Boil the lamb slowly for one hour and three-quarters. When tender dish it up and garnish it with slices of boiled carrots and turnips and sprigs of cauliflower tossed in butter and seasoned.

Season the white sauce and add the chopped parsley. Pour half the sauce over the leg of lamb. Serve the remainder of it in a sauce-boat. Put a frill on the bone and serve the leg of lamb with baked potatoes.

CROWN ROAST OF LAMB

INGREDIENTS.—2 necks of lamb (the best end), some odd pieces of fat bacon, cutlet frills, forcemeat balls (see p. 79), or mashed turnips.

METHOD.—Have the chine bone removed from the two necks and scrape the meat from the ends of the bones to a depth of about one inch. Form each piece of lamb into a half-circle, and arrange the two pieces together to form a crown—the bones should be outside and the fat part inside. Sew them here and there to keep them in position, using a trussing needle and fine string, then wrap pieces of bacon fat round the top of the bones to keep them from burning.

Bake this crown for about an hour and a quarter or an hour and a half, then replace the bacon fat with a cutlet frill. Heap forcemeat balls in the centre, or mashed turnips, and serve the crown accompanied with slightly thickened gravy.

Veal or chestnut stuffing can be made for the forcemeat balls. Divide it in small portions, form them into balls, egg and crumb them and fry them gently until golden brown.

Sufficient for six persons.

LAMB CUTLETS

INGREDIENTS.—1½ lb. of best end neck of lamb, 1 egg, breadcrumbs, 2 oz. of margarine (melted), ½ oz. of flour, 1½ gills of stock (see p. 12), hot mashed potatoes, 1 oz. of butter, salt and pepper, 1 dessertspoonful of mushroom ketchup.

METHOD.—Let the butcher saw off the chine bone and the ends of the ribs. This is more economical than buying the cutlets ready trimmed. Cut the meat into neat cutlets. Brush these with egg. Dip them in breadcrumbs, then in melted margarine and lastly in breadcrumbs. Press them flat and shake off any loose crumbs.

Heat the margarine and fry the cutlets quickly for a minute on each side. Finish cooking them slowly (eight minutes in all), in order to make them tender.

Heap the mashed potatoes on a dish with the cutlets round them and keep them hot.

Fry the flour in the butter, stirring it well, and when it is brown add the ketchup and stock. Boil up, season with salt and pepper, and strain round the cutlets.

Sufficient for four or five persons.

LAMB CUTLETS MILANNAISE

INGREDIENTS.—6 bones of best neck of lamb, egg and breadcrumbs, butter or dripping.

FOR THE SAUCE.—2 or 3 small mushrooms, 1 oz. of spaghetti, 1 to 1½ oz. of cooked ham, 1½ gills of milk, ¾ oz. of flour, 1 oz. of margarine, 1 teaspoonful of onion-juice, seasoning.

METHOD.—Have the chine bone removed from the best neck of lamb, then cut it into cutlets, shaping the meat to a point at the end of each bone. Brush them with egg and coat them with breadcrumbs and fry them gently in a little heated butter or dripping, turning them over when brown on one side.

Serve them on a hot dish, placing a cutlet frill on the end of each and arranging them with the bone to the left, pour thick gravy round the cutlets, and heap the white sauce mixed with the spaghetti, mushrooms and ham on one side. Make the white sauce in the usual way, season it and flavour it with onion-juice. Add the spaghetti, ham, and mushrooms, all cooked and cut in strips, and make them hot.

Allow two cutlets for each person.

LAMB CUTLETS AND PEAS

INGREDIENTS.—4 bones of best neck of lamb, 1 egg, white breadcrumbs, 1½ gills of brown sauce or thick gravy, seasoning, butter or dripping for frying, 4 tablespoonfuls of green peas (freshly cooked or bottled).

METHOD.—Prepare the cutlets. Beat up the egg and brush them over with it. Coat each with breadcrumbs. Melt the dripping in a pan, and when hot put in the cutlets and fry them a golden brown on both sides.

Place on a hot dish with the bone to the left.

Melt about two ounces of butter in a sauté pan or frying-pan, and sauté the peas in it. Heat the brown sauce or gravy and strain round the cutlets. Heap the peas on each side of the cutlets. Put on the cutlet frills and serve.

DRIED GREEN PEAS can be used if liked, but these must be soaked the previous day. They also require well boiling to make them tender.

TINNED PEAS.—Some brands require to be boiled before being sautéd in butter. In any case, the peas should first be strained from the water in which they have been tinned and well rinsed before using them.

CUTLET FRILLS can be bought from any good stationery store.

ROAST LOIN OF LAMB

INGREDIENTS.—Loin of lamb (about 4 lb.).

FOR THE MINT SAUCE. — 2 level tablespoonfuls of finely-chopped mint, 3 level tablespoonfuls of sugar, 2 tablespoonfuls of boiling water, ¼ pint of vinegar.

METHOD.—A loin of lamb is a good

roasting joint and is a change from a leg or shoulder. It is more economical to have the chine bone removed, as it can then be carved into smaller chops.

Put the loin into a hot oven to bake, and cook it for about an hour and a half, lessening the heat as required. Serve it with thin brown gravy, made by boiling up stock in the baking-tin after pouring off the dripping. Add seasoning, also a little browning if required, then strain the gravy.

To Make the Mint Sauce.—Pick the mint from the stalks, wash, drain and chop it finely. Put it into a sauce tureen with the sugar. Add the boiling water, and when dissolved stir in the vinegar.

If boiling greens, use two table-spoonfuls of the greens water to dissolve the sugar.

MOULD OF LAMB

Ingredients.—Cold lamb, 1 level teaspoonful of salt, 1 cupful of finely shredded cabbage, 1 tablespoonful of lemon-juice, 1 hard-boiled egg, ½ oz. of gelatine, ½ pint of water, 2 to 2½ dessertspoonfuls of castor sugar, ¼ gill of vinegar, 1½ pimentoes tinned, 1 tablespoonful of cooked peas.

Method.—Dissolve the gelatine in hot water and add the lemon-juice to it with the sugar, salt and vinegar. Strain it and leave it to cool.

When it is beginning to stiffen, add the chopped pimentoes, cabbage, peas and slices of egg. Turn it into a wet mould and allow it to set.

Turn the jelly out on to a dish lined with lettuce leaves, ringed with over-lapping slices of lamb and more lettuce leaves.

This makes a good Sunday night supper dish, and served with hard-boiled eggs or tomatoes and mayonnaise.

Sufficient for six persons.

GRILLED LAMB NOISETTES

Ingredients.—6 noisettes of lamb, 6 slices of tinned pineapple, salt and pepper, paprika, parsley.

Method.—Have a loin of lamb boned and rolled. Cut it into thick slices and keep it in shape, while it is cooking, with tiny skewers. Grill the noisettes and season them with pepper, salt and paprika.

Drain the pineapple slices well, then simmer them in a very little butter in the frying-pan till they are a delicate brown. Place the pineapple slices on a hot dish and arrange a noisette on top of each. Garnish them with parsley. Serve the dish with mashed potatoes and spinach.

STUFFED LEG OF LAMB

Ingredients.—Leg of Canterbury lamb, ¼ lb. of breadcrumbs, 2 oz. of suet or margarine, seasoning, ⅓ tea-spoonful of mixed herbs, 1 small onion (minced), some finely chopped parsley, egg or milk.

Method.—Have the leg boned, or if preferred it can be partly boned, as shown, removing two bones but leaving the knuckle bone.

Make the stuffing by mixing the dry ingredients together, and moistening them with egg or milk. If suet is used, chop it finely, but if margarine is preferred, melt it and add it to the other ingredients.

Stuff the leg, and either skewer or sew it up securely, then place in a baking-tin with some dripping and cover it with a piece of thin caul fat. Bake it till it is tender, allowing about one and a half or two hours, according to the size.

Serve stuffed leg of lamb with slightly thickened brown gravy (for method see p. 100), using stock made from the bones for a foundation.

LIVER AND BACON

Ingredients.—½ lb. of streaky rashers, ¾ lb. of calve's liver, 1 table-spoonful of flour, salt and pepper, ½ pint of stock (see p. 12), 3 oz. of dripping.

Method.—Wash the liver in warm water with a little salt added. Dry it thoroughly, and cut it into slices about one-fourth of an inch thick. Dip them in the flour, mixed with pepper and salt.

Melt the dripping in a frying-pan, and when hot put in the liver and fry it gently for about ten minutes, keeping it turned as required.

Remove the rind from the bacon, and cut each rasher in half. Roll up eight halves into small rolls, and stick them on a skewer. Leave the remainder not rolled. Put all together into the grill-tin, and cook them under the hot grill for a few minutes until the fat is semi-transparent.

Serve the liver on a hot dish, arrange the bacon rolls on the top, and the half-rashers on each side. Pour the bacon fat and some thick gravy over the meat.

To MAKE THE GRAVY.—Pour off some of the dripping in which the liver was cooked, then add the remainder of the flour to the fat in the pan and let it brown slowly. Draw the pan aside, add the stock, then boil it up, season and strain it.

Sufficient for four persons.

LIVER AND ONION HOT-POT

INGREDIENTS.—½ lb. of ox liver, 4 onions, 8 potatoes, ½ oz. of flour, salt and pepper, ½ pint of water, 1 teaspoonful of powdered sage.

METHOD.—Chop the liver.

Peel and chop the onions and wash, peel and slice the potatoes.

Mix the liver and onions with the flour and half the potatoes. Season with salt, pepper and sage. Place them in a pie-dish with the water.

Arrange the rest of the potatoes on the top.

Cover with greased paper and bake for one hour and a half.

Sufficient for four persons.

MARROW BONE AND APPLES

INGREDIENTS.—¼ lb. of dried apple-rings or 1 lb. of cooking apples, 2 lb. of freshly boiled potatoes, 1 oz. of bacon dripping, 1 marrow bone, salt and pepper, ¼ cupful of milk, ½ lemon, 6 oz. of flour, ½ oz. of butter.

METHOD.—Wash the apple-rings in warm water. Pour boiling water on them and let them soak all night.

Mix the flour stiffly with cold water and use it to cover up the two ends of the marrow bone.

Bake the bone for one hour, or tie it in a cloth, and boil it for one hour and a half.

Bring the apples just to the boil in the water in which they were soaked. Strain them and fry them in the bacon fat till tender.

Mash the potatoes with a fork over a low gas, adding the butter and milk. Season to taste with salt and pepper.

Arrange the apples round a hollowed heap of mashed potatoes and squeeze lemon-juice over them. Scoop out the marrow from the bone and put it in the middle of the potatoes.

Sufficient for four persons.

NOTE.—Baking a marrow bone is more convenient than boiling.

STUFFED MARROW

INGREDIENTS.—1 marrow, ½ lb. of cooked meat, 2 tomatoes, egg, dripping, 2 oz. of breadcrumbs, 1½ dessert-spoonfuls of chopped parsley, salt and pepper, thick brown gravy, flour.

METHOD.—To make the stuffing, put the meat through a mincer.

Make the breadcrumbs. Wash, scald, and finely chop the parsley.

Skin the tomatoes and mash to a pulp. Mix all these ingredients together and season with salt and pepper.

Beat up the egg and add.

Peel the marrow thinly and split it into halves lengthways, and remove all the seeds. Put the prepared stuffing into the marrow and place the two halves together again, and tie round with string in two or three places.

Dredge it with flour and put into a baking-tin with some dripping.

Bake in a moderately hot oven until tender, keeping it well basted with the fat.

When cooked, lift it carefully on to a hot dish, remove the string, and serve thick gravy over and round it.

Sufficient for four or five persons.

MEAT LOAF AND BANANAS

INGREDIENTS.—1½ lb. of minced steak, 1 well-beaten egg, salt and pepper, 5 bananas, ½ onion (grated), 2½ oz. of fresh breadcrumbs, 2½ oz. of chopped salt pork.

METHOD.—Mix the meat with the onion, salt, pepper, breadcrumbs, pork and egg. Shape the mixture into a loaf with lightly floured hands and press it into a buttered bread pan.

Cook the meat loaf in a moderately hot oven until it is tender, and then turn it out.

Peel and halve the bananas and

then cut them crosswise. If they are small, only halve them. Sprinkle them with salt and pepper and bake or grill them until they are delicately browned.

Sufficient for six or more persons.

MEAT AND BREAD PATTIES

INGREDIENTS.—Stale loaf to use as required, 1 egg, ¾ to 1 gill of milk, 1 small onion, 3 oz. of cold meat, ¾ gill of stock (see p. 12), 1½ teaspoonfuls of flour, seasoning, deep fat.

METHOD.—Peel and mince the onion and fry it till tender in a little hot dripping, then draw the pan aside and pour off the fat.

Add the stock, stir in the flour, smoothed in a little water and bring it to the boil. Add seasoning and a few drops of browning if required. Stir in the meat minced, and make it hot.

Cut the bread into slices about one and a half to one and three-quarter inches thick and stamp it into rounds two and three-quarter inches in diameter. Then, with a smaller cutter, stamp out a piece about half way through and remove the centre.

Beat up the egg and mix it with the milk, season them, and use them for soaking the prepared bread cases in. Drain the cases well, fry them in deep fat till golden brown. Drain them, fill them with the prepared meat mixture, and serve them hot.

Sufficient filling for about four cases.

MEAT CAKES

INGREDIENTS.—6 oz. of cold meat, 2 oz. of breadcrumbs, 1½ teaspoonfuls of chopped parsley, pepper and salt, ¼ teaspoonful of mixed herbs, 1 egg, breadcrumbs (for coating), dripping (for frying), stock (see p. 12) or gravy.

METHOD.—Make the breadcrumbs. When doing these, make sufficient for the coating at the same time. Put the meat through a mincer or chop it finely. Wash, scald, and finely chop the parsley. Mix all these ingredients together, add the herbs, and season well, and moisten with just a little stock or gravy. Beat up the egg, and add as much as required to mix it all to a stiff paste. Divide

into about six or eight portions, and make each into a small round shape. Brush them over with the remainder of the egg, and coat each with breadcrumbs. Melt about a quarter of a pound of dripping in a frying-pan, and when it is hot put in the cakes and fry until golden brown. Drain on paper, serve on a dish-paper, garnish with parsley.

Serve separately thick brown gravy.

FOR THE GRAVY.—Make stock (see p. 12) from the bones. Brown, season, thicken, and strain it.

NOTE.—These are very tasty if made with the remains of cold veal and bacon. If not enough egg to coat the cakes, just flour them.

Sufficient for three persons.

DEVILLED COLD MEAT

INGREDIENTS. — ½ lb. of any cold meat cut in rather thick slices. 1 teaspoonful of curry powder, ½ teaspoonful of made mustard, 1 dessertspoonful of Worcester sauce, 1 teaspoonful of tomato ketchup 1 dessertspoonful of vinegar, 1 teaspoonful of olive oil, salt and cayenne, 1 oz. of butter.

METHOD.—Add all the liquid ingredients to the curry powder, season with salt and cayenne. Dip the slices of meat in the mixture, coating both sides, and lay them in a pie-dish or on a tin plate.

Pour the rest of the mixture over them, and place the butter in small pieces on top. Cover with a greased paper or another plate, and bake in a hot oven till heated through, about fifteen minutes.

Underdone meat is best for this dish.

Serve with dry toast.

Sufficient for three persons.

GATEAU OF COLD MEAT

INGREDIENTS.—1 breakfastcupful of cold minced meat, 1 breakfastcupful of breadcrumbs, 1 onion, 1 dessertspoonful of Worcester sauce, 1 teaspoonful of chopped parsley, 2, tomatoes, 1 large egg, salt and pepper, ¾ gill of stock (see p. 12), 1 oz. of good dripping or butter, parsley to decorate.

METHOD.—Chop the onion and fry it in the dripping. Heat the stock and pour it on the breadcrumbs.

Add to this, well-chopped, the onion, a tomato, the parsley, and the Worcester sauce, with the minced meat.

Mix with a well-beaten egg. Grease a small round cake-tin or pie-dish and line it with slices of tomato. Fill with the meat mixture and bake in a moderate oven for forty minutes or till set. Turn out on to a hot dish and decorate with parsley.

Sufficient for three persons.

"LEFT-OVER" MEAT DISHES

" LEFT-OVER " meat dishes are often very dull, but when a little extra care is taken, cold meat can be transformed into the most delectable of dishes.

There are four important details to remember about food that has been already cooked once :

1. That it only needs to be heated through the second time, and not to be cooked again. If it is twice *cooked* it will lose most of its nourishment.

2. It will require extra seasonings, such as onions or herbs, or it will be lacking in flavour. If gravy is to be served with it, use a good stock for its foundation.

3. Cooked and uncooked foods should not be mixed together unless it is certain the latter will cook while the former is heating.

4. If the meat is to be re-heated in the oven or fried, it should be protected in some way by the addition of potatoes, batter, egg and breadcrumbs, or pastry. These will help to make the meat more tasty.

MEAT SALAD

REMOVE all skin and gristle from the meat ; then mince it and season it to taste. A *tiny* piece of garlic put through the mincer with the meat will improve the flavour, but only a *soupçon* is required.

Moisten the prepared meat with salad cream, serve it on a bed of lettuce leaves, and garnish it with small bunches of mustard and cress, slices of hard egg, tomato, beetroot, and cucumber when in season—or else make a floral design with the hard-boiled egg for garnishing.

MINCE

INGREDIENTS.—1 lb. of cooked meat, ¾ lb. of onions, salt and pepper, 2 tablespoonfuls of flour, 1¼ pints of stock (see p. 12) or gravy, dripping.

METHOD.—A favourite way of re-heating meat is to make a mince.

Peel and slice the onions. Put them into a saucepan with a little dripping and fry them until tender and golden. Draw the pan aside and drain off the fat.

Put the meat through the mincer, removing all skin and gristle, then season it well.

Mix the flour to a smooth paste with some of the stock, add the remainder to the onions, then stir in the thickening and continue to stir until the gravy boils, when it should be thick. Season to taste, add some browning as required, let it boil for a few minutes, then add the meat and make it hot.

Serve the mince with mashed potatoes. They may be served separately or round the mince, in which case the gravy must be made a little thicker.

RISSOLES

INGREDIENTS.—6 oz. of cold meat, some stock (see p. 12) or gravy, salt, pepper, celery salt, 2 or 3 mushrooms, dripping, 10 oz. of flour, 5 oz. of fat (margarine), ½ teaspoonful of baking powder, water to mix, egg and breadcrumbs, hot fat.

METHOD.—Peel the mushrooms and remove the stalks. Cleanse the mushrooms and chop them up roughly and fry them in a little dripping, and then drain off the fat.

Mince the meat, season it to taste, add the mushrooms and moisten them with some stock or gravy, barely half a gill are required.

Sieve the flour and baking powder, rub in the fat, then mix to a stiff paste with cold water. Roll the paste out and cut it into small rounds. Turn them on to the other side and put some of the prepared meat on one half. Damp the edge and fold the other half over, making the edges secure.

Brush the rissoles with beaten egg and coat them with breadcrumbs, then fry them in hot fat till golden brown. Drain them and serve them.

Sufficient for five persons.

CROQUETTES

INGREDIENTS.—½ gill of good stock (see p. 12) or thin brown gravy, ¾ oz. of flour, ½ oz. of margarine, 2 oz. of cold beef, 2 oz. of cooked ham, salt, pepper, celery salt, powdered mace, egg and breadcrumbs, fat for frying.

METHOD.—Make a thick sauce with the stock, flour and margarine (for method see p. 41).

Boil it for a minute or two, keeping it stirred, then draw it aside and stir in the beef and ham (both minced). Season the mixture to taste—if liked, a little fried onion can be added to flavour—turn the mixture on to a plate and leave it until cold and firm.

Divide the paste into small portions, form them into sausage shapes. Brush them over with egg and coat them with breadcrumbs, then fry them until brown. Drain them on paper and serve the croquettes on a dish-paper.

Sufficient for five persons.

MEAT MOULD

INGREDIENTS.—10 oz. of cold meat, 1½ oz. of breadcrumbs, half or 1 small onion, 2 eggs (one hard-boiled), salt and pepper, stock (see p. 12) if required.

METHOD.—Peel and finely chop the onion and fry for a few minutes, then strain off the fat.

Boil one egg for about fifteen minutes until hard, then remove the shell and chop up the egg finely.

Mince the meat and mix with the onion and chopped egg.

Make the breadcrumbs and add, season well to taste, and mix all together.

Beat up the egg and bind the prepared ingredients. If any more moisture is required, a little stock may be added, but the mixture should be quite stiff.

Put into a well-greased mould or pie-dish, pressing it down firmly. Cover with a greased paper, and bake in a moderately hot oven for about forty minutes.

Turn out carefully and serve cold. Sufficient for four persons.

NOTE.—If the meat is all lean, add a little melted butter to the mixture, in which case no stock would be required.

This is an excellent method of using up cold meat, more especially if the latter is rather underdone. Slices of the meat mould put between bread-and-butter will make tasty sandwiches.

ITALIAN MEAT PIE

INGREDIENTS.—½ lb. of short pastry (see p. 252) made with lard, ½ lb. of cold meat, 2 oz. of macaroni (cooked), 2 oz. of ham, 1 shallot, 1 tablespoonful of grated cheese, 1 tablespoonful of Worcester sauce, 1 oz. of butter, 1 oz. of flour, 1½ gills of milk, dripping and browned breadcrumbs.

METHOD.—Line a pie-dish or meat-tin with the pastry. Cut up the macaroni and spread it at the bottom of the dish. (Cold macaroni cheese may be used for this.)

Pass the cold meat, shallot and ham through a mincer, season it with salt and pepper, the Worcester sauce and grated cheese.

To make a sauce, melt the butter, stir in the flour and add the milk gradually. Stir the sauce till it boils and put the minced meat in it. Mix well together and pour into the dish.

Sprinkle a few browned breadcrumbs over the pie and put pieces of dripping on top.

Bake in a fairly hot oven for thirty minutes.

Sufficient for three or four persons.

MEAT PLATE PASTIE

INGREDIENTS.—9 oz. of flour, 4 oz. of margarine, 5 oz. of lard, pinch of salt, water to mix, 7 oz. of cold beef, about ½ gill of thick gravy, 1 small onion, salt and pepper.

METHOD.—Put the meat and onion through the mincer. Season them well and moisten the mince with gravy.

Sieve the flour with a pinch of salt, and rub in the margarine. Mix it to a stiff paste with cold water.

Put the lard on a well-floured board and press out with a rolling pin into thin pieces. Roll out the pastry, turn it on to the other side, spread the lard all over it, then fold the sides to the centre both ways, then over again in half. The pastry is then folded into eight.

Divide the pastry into two. Roll out one piece fairly thinly, cut out a round, and line an enamel plate.

Fill this with the prepared meat, then roll out the other piece of pastry rather thickly, cut a round and cover the pastie.

Trim the edge, decorate it with rings of pastry and make a hole in the centre. Brush the top with egg. Put the pastie in a hot oven to bake. It will take about twenty minutes to cook. Serve it hot or cold.

Sufficient for from four to six persons.

NOTE.—If liked, a layer of sliced tomatoes may be put in the centre of the meat.

MEAT PUDDING

INGREDIENTS.—¾ lb. of ox cheek, ½ lb. of ox kidney, 1 oz. of flour, salt and pepper, ½ cup of water, 6 oz. of flour, 2 oz. of breadcrumbs, 4 oz. of shredded suet, ¼ teaspoonful of salt.

METHOD.—Put the water on to boil, grease a basin and dip into boiling water and wring out the middle of a pudding cloth. Then flour it lightly.

Cut the meat and kidney into small square pieces, and dip them into the flour, which has been seasoned with salt and pepper.

If everything is prepared the pastry is more likely to be light than if it is kept waiting after it is mixed. The skin should be removed from the suet, and then it should be covered with flour and finely shredded and chopped. When it is of the same consistency as fine breadcrumbs, put it into a mixing-basin with the rest of the flour. Suet pastry should be mixed with enough water to make a soft but not sticky dough. It should be moister than short pastry. Cut off two-thirds of the dough and roll it out one and a half times the width of the top of the basin. Line the basin smoothly with it, pressing out any folds. Then put in the mixture of meat and seasoned flour, and add cold water to half fill the basin. The flour and water will make a thick gravy. Roll out the smaller piece of dough, wet the edges, and cover the pudding with it. Tie the cloth very tight over the top. This pudding does not need room to rise. Place it in plenty of boiling water, bring it quickly to the boil again, and let it cook for three hours if

stewing steak or ox cheek has been used, or two hours and a half if made with buttock steak.

NOTE.—Kidney suet is very good for meat puddings. Very good puddings may be made from stewing steak or buttock steak. Meat puddings are not turned out, but served with a folded napkin fastened round the basin.

Sufficient for four persons.

SAVOURY MEAT PIES

INGREDIENTS.—Some flaky pastry (see p. 252), 1 large lean chump chop, 2 dessertspoonfuls of minced onion, flour, pepper and salt, stock (see p. 12), butter or dripping.

METHOD.—Remove the bone from the chop and cut the meat into very small pieces, or put it through the mincer.

Melt a small lump of butter in a pan, add the onion and fry it gently until it begins to colour. Add the meat, and cook it for a minute or two to seal the outside, then lift it on to a plate.

Add a little flour to the fat in the pan, and brown it slowly, and add barely half a gill of stock. Boil it up, and season the gravy. Mix it with the meat and onion, then leave it to cool.

Meanwhile make the pastry and roll it out to quarter of an inch thick. Stamp it into rounds. Put these aside, and roll the remainder of the pastry out again till it is fairly thin, and cut it into the same number of rounds.

Line some small patty tins with the thin rounds, and fill the cases with the prepared meat and gravy. Damp the edges, and cover each case with a thick round of pastry. Brush it with milk, make a hole in the centre of each pie. Put the pies into a hot oven to bake. They will take from twenty to thirty minutes to cook. Garnish them with parsley, and serve them either hot or cold.

Sufficient for eight or ten small pies.

SAVOURY MEAT ROLL

INGREDIENTS.—½ lb. of self-raising flour, a pinch of salt, ¼ lb. of suet, a pinch of mixed herbs, 1 level teaspoonful of chopped parsley, water to mix, $\frac{3}{4}$ lb. of buttock steak, 1 onion, 1 egg-white, salt and pepper.

METHOD.—Sift the flour and salt, chop the suet finely and add it with the herbs and parsley. Mix all to a pliable dough with cold water.

Put the steak and onion through the mincer, mix them together and add seasoning to taste.

Roll the suet crust to an oblong shape, brush it with slightly beaten egg-white and cover it with the prepared meat, leaving a small margin on all sides. Roll it up.

Roll the savoury roll in a floured pudding cloth, tie this securely at each end and put it into a pan of boiling water. Boil it gently for from an hour and a half to two hours.

Serve savoury meat roll with thick brown gravy (see p. 100).

Sufficient for four persons.

MEAT ROLY-POLY

INGREDIENTS.—$\frac{1}{2}$ lb. of flour, 4 oz. of shredded suet, $\frac{1}{2}$ teaspoonful of salt, 1 onion, $\frac{1}{2}$ lb. of liver or cold meat, 1 gill of water, 1 gill of thick gravy (see p. 100).

METHOD.—Dip one end of a pudding cloth into a pan of boiling water. Press the saucepan lid against it on drawing it out, and sprinkle it with flour. Chop the onion and meat.

Mix flour, suet, meat, salt, and onion with the water, and shape into a roll. Lay the roll on the wet cloth and roll it up. Tie the ends tightly, place the roly-poly in boiling water, and boil for two hours.

Remove the cloth, and serve the pudding with hot gravy.

Sufficient for three persons.

MINCE AND MASHED POTATOES

INGREDIENTS.—$\frac{1}{2}$ lb. of cooked meat, 1 or 2 onions, $\frac{1}{2}$ pint of stock (see p. 12), 1 oz. of margarine, milk, seasoning, browning, dripping, 1 tablespoonful of flour, $1\frac{1}{2}$ lb. of potatoes.

METHOD.—Peel and slice the onions and fry in a little dripping until brown, then draw aside and pour off the remainder of the dripping.

Add the stock, mix the flour to a smooth paste with water and add.

Bring to the boil, keeping it stirred, then boil gently for a few minutes.

Mince the meat and add, stir in some gravy browning, and season to taste, then make thoroughly hot. Boil the potatoes, then mash up with a little milk and margarine. Arrange a border of mashed potatoes round a dish and turn the mince into the centre.

Sufficient for four persons.

MOCK GOOSE

INGREDIENTS.—2 lb. of pig's fry, 2 medium-sized onions, 12 to 15 sage leaves, pepper and salt, boiling water, 3 medium-sized potatoes.

METHOD.—Wash and dry the pig's fry and cut it into slices, leaving the thin caul fat uncut, which should be kept whole for covering the top of the fry.

Peel and grate or chop the onions. Dry the sage leaves and rub them to a powder—these can be dried in a cool oven or some other warm place, until crisp.

Put the fry into a pie-dish or fire-proof dish in layers, sprinkling each layer with pepper, salt, sage and onions.

Peel, wash and slice the potatoes, and put them round the edge of the dish, then cover the fry with the thin caul, and pour in enough boiling water to fill the dish half or three parts full.

Put the dish into a moderately hot oven, and bake it gently for about one hour and a half.

Serve hot or cold—if hot, with extra potatoes, cooked separately.

Sufficient for six or eight persons.

PAIN DE VIANDE

INGREDIENTS.—1 lb. of cold meat (minced), $\frac{1}{2}$ lb. of sausage meat, $\frac{1}{2}$ lb. of breadcrumbs, 1 egg, 3 oz. of flour, pepper and salt, mixed herbs or tomato sauce, melted margarine or lard, brown breadcrumbs.

FOR THE SAUCE.—$1\frac{1}{2}$ gills of milk, 1 oz. of flour, $\frac{1}{2}$ gill of water, 1 oz. of margarine.

METHOD.—Remove any gristle from the meat, and if very fat remove some of it. Put the meat through a fine mincer, and mix with it the sausage meat.

Steak and Kidney Pie

Roll each piece of kidney in a piece of steak.

Cut an oval of pastry for the top of the pie.

The Finished Pie

PLATE 13

Loin of
Pork

Steak
Maitre
d'Hotel

A
Roast
of
Veal

PLATE 14

Make the white crumbs, using a grater or a wire sieve. Add these, together with three ounces of flour, to the meat, and mix.

To Make the Sauce

Mix the flour to a smooth paste with half a gill of water. Put the milk in a saucepan with the ounce of margarine, and when hot pour it on to the mixed flour. Pour back into the saucepan and bring to the boil. Cook slowly for a few minutes, keeping it well stirred. This sauce should be quite thick when finished.

Add the sauce to the meat, etc. Season with pepper and salt, and flavour either with a few mixed herbs or a little tomato sauce. Mix thoroughly, then beat the egg and mix it in. Leave it to cool. If after cooling it is not stiff enough, add more flour.

Put it on a slightly floured board, and roll it into a large fat sausage. Leave until quite cold and firm. Then brush it over with the melted margarine or lard, and coat it well with brown breadcrumbs. Place on a well-greased baking-tin and bake in a moderately hot oven for about three-quarters of an hour. Place on a dish. Serve either hot or cold ; if hot, serve thick gravy (see p. 100) with it.

To Make Brown Breadcrumbs

Break up some stale crusts of bread, put them into the oven, and bake until crisp and golden brown. Crush with a rolling pin, then rub through a sieve. When cold, put them into a tin or jar. They will keep for several weeks.

Sufficient for about seven or eight.

FRIED PELOTES

(" Pelote " is the French for a little pincushion.)

INGREDIENTS.—6 oz. of cold meat, pepper and salt, gravy.

FOR THE PASTRY.—$\frac{1}{2}$ lb. of flour, 3 oz. of margarine, 1 teaspoonful of baking-powder, water to mix, deep fat for frying.

METHOD.—Remove any gristle from the meat and mince it finely, using fat and lean together. Moisten it with a little thick gravy and make it into a damp paste.

To make the pastry, mix the flour

and baking-powder together. Rub the margarine into the flour until it resembles fine breadcrumbs.

Add sufficient water to mix it all to a stiff paste. It must not be too wet, but just pliable. Roll out this paste to the thickness of about an eighth of an inch, and cut it into rounds with a tumbler.

On one round put a good heaped-up pile of meat, cover it with another round, and press the edges well together, damping if necessary. Prepare all the others in the same way.

Put on to heat a deep pan half full of dripping. When it slightly smokes, put in two or three of the pelotes, and fry until a golden brown.

Sufficient to make about six pelotes.

PICNIC MOULDS

INGREDIENTS.—$\frac{1}{4}$ lb. of lean veal, $\frac{1}{4}$ lb. of lean beef, 3 oz. of stale crumb of bread, $\frac{1}{2}$ lb. of gammon of bacon or long back (not too fat), 1 egg, 1 small clove of garlic, salt, pepper and paprika, $\frac{1}{4}$ pint of stock (see p. 12), brown breadcrumbs.

METHOD.—Remove the bacon rind and mince the veal, bacon, and beef.

Heat the stock and add it to the bread, let it soak for a minute or two, and then break it up with a fork, and add it to the prepared meat.

Stir in the finely chopped garlic, add seasoning to taste, and bind the mixture with the beaten egg.

Turn it into small greased moulds pressing the mixture down firmly.

Cover them with a greased paper and steam them for about one hour and a half.

When cooked, turn out the moulds and serve them cold, coated with brown breadcrumbs.

Sufficient for seven moulds.

BREAST OF MUTTON

(STUFFED AND ROLLED)

INGREDIENTS.—A breast of mutton (about 2$\frac{1}{2}$ lb.), 1$\frac{1}{2}$ oz. of suet, 2 oz. of breadcrumbs, $\frac{1}{2}$ dessertspoonful of mixed herbs, 1 tablespoonful of chopped parsley, salt and pepper, $\frac{1}{2}$ lemon, 1 egg, dripping.

METHOD.—Choose a breast of mutton cut rather wider than usual, and have it boned.

E

Make the stuffing and spread it over the meat, then roll it up and tie it securely.

Put it into a baking-tin with some dripping and bake it for about one hour and a half, keeping it well basted.

Serve with thick brown gravy and baked potatoes.

THE STUFFING

To make the stuffing, chop the suet finely and mix it with the bread-crumbs, herbs, parsley, and grated lemon-rind. Season well and bind it with the egg. Add some lemon-juice to taste as required.

Sufficient for six persons.

CASSEROLE OF MUTTON

(WITH TOMATOES AND SPAGHETTI)

INGREDIENTS.—2 lb. of middle neck of mutton, 1 lb. of tomatoes, about 1 pint of stock (see p. 12) or water, 2 onions, salt and pepper, celery salt, flour, 2 oz. spaghetti.

METHOD.—Divide the meat into chops and put it into a casserole with the onions, peeled and sliced, and tomatoes, skinned and cut up. Add a little salt, also stock or water to just cover.

Bring the stock to the boil, skim it, and simmer gently for about an hour and a half or two hours.

Break up and wash the spaghetti, put it into slightly salted boiling water, and boil it until partly tender. Strain and finish cooking it in the casserole. Before serving, skim off the grease and thicken the gravy with flour mixed to a smooth paste with water. Cook this for a few minutes, add browning and seasoning to taste. Serve in the casserole.

Sufficient for six persons.

CHAUDFROID OF MUTTON CUTLETS

INGREDIENTS.—2 lb. of best end of neck of lamb or small mutton, jar of potted ham, ¾ pint of chaudfroid sauce.

METHOD.—When buying the meat have the chine bone sawn off and the ribs cut as for cutlets. Steam the meat till it is tender, or allow it to simmer gently for an hour. When cold, cut it into joints, trim off pieces of fat or gristle, and scrape the ends of the bones. Spread one side of each neatly trimmed cutlet with the potted ham. When the chaudfroid sauce is cold and begins to thicken, coat each cutlet, using a tablespoon to do so.

Lay them on a grid to set, and serve them in a dish with a dainty green salad in the centre.

Sufficient for six or eight persons.

CHAUDFROID SAUCE

INGREDIENTS.—½ pint of hot Béchamel sauce (see p. 42), 1 gill of aspic jelly, 1 gill of mayonnaise, ¾ oz. of leaf gelatine.

METHOD.—Melt the aspic jelly, which may be obtained ready made in packets or bottles for about a shilling, and dissolve the gelatine in it.

Strain the jelly into the Béchamel sauce, and when cold, but before it begins to set, stir in the mayonnaise. Mix thoroughly, and use when it is thick enough to coat the back of a spoon.

When there is no mayonnaise or aspic jelly to be had, a very plain chaudfroid sauce may be made by dissolving three-quarters of an ounce of gelatine in three-quarters of a gill of stock, and straining it into three-quarters of a pint of hot Béchamel sauce or any white sauce. When cold, this looks similar to the ordinary chaudfroid sauce. It does not, however, taste so good.

Chaudfroid sauce may, if liked, be coloured with a few drops of cochineal or spinach-green colouring.

GRILLED MUTTON CHOPS AND ASPARAGUS TIPS

INGREDIENTS.—4 loin chops, a tin of asparagus tips, salt and pepper, stock (see p. 12).

METHOD.—Heat the grill-tin and the grill. Season the chops with pepper and salt, and put them on to the bars of the grill-tin. Put them under the hot grill and cook them for about fifteen or twenty minutes, keeping them turned frequently. Serve them on a hot dish, and garnish them with bundles of asparagus tips, which should have been previously heated in a saucepan.

Serve also thin brown gravy and tomato sauce (see next page).

The bundles of asparagus tips are

held in position with rings cut from slices of tomato.

To MAKE THE GRAVY.—After pouring off the fat from the grill-tin, add some stock and two or three drops of browning. Season to taste, boil up the gravy, and strain it.

Sufficient for four persons.

TOMATO SAUCE

INGREDIENTS.—A small onion, ½ lb. of sliced tomatoes, ½ oz. of margarine, ½ gill of water, a sprig of parsley and thyme, cornflour, pepper and salt.

To MAKE THE TOMATO SAUCE.—Peel and mince a small onion and steam it in half an ounce of margarine for a few minutes. Add half a pound of sliced tomatoes, half a gill of water, and a sprig of parsley and thyme. Simmer them till tender and remove the herbs. Rub the sauce through a sieve, then return it to the pan. Thicken it with cornflour and add seasoning to taste.

GRILLED CHOPS WITH POTATO STRAWS

INGREDIENTS.—2 thick loin chops, 1 oz. of dripping or butter, salt and pepper, Worcester sauce, 2 potatoes, a pan of deep frying fat, 2 pats of mint butter.

METHOD.—Trim a little fat off the chops and spread a very little dripping on them. Season with salt and pepper. Put the rest of the dripping inside a piece of muslin and use it to brush the chops over while they are grilling.

While the deep fat is heating, wash and peel the potatoes and cut them first into thin slices and then into straws. Roll them in a cloth to dry. Put the potatoes in a frying-basket, and when a bluish vapour rises from the deep fat lower the basket gently into it. Fry for about ten minutes till the straws are a golden brown. While they are frying, cook the chops. Heat the gas griller till it is red hot. Put the chops underneath close to the gas for two minutes till brown, then turn them over and brown the other side as quickly as possible. Lower the gas and put the chops farther away so that they may finish cooking slowly.

Turn them over two or three times

without sticking a fork into the lean part. Each time they are turned over rub them lightly with the dripping tied in muslin.

Cook for about ten to twelve minutes in all.

To MAKE MINT BUTTER FOR TWO CHOPS

Cream ¾ oz. of butter and chop 1 dessertspoonful of mint.

Work the mint into the butter with a knife and add salt and pepper and one teaspoonful of vinegar.

Put a diamond-shaped piece of mint butter on each chop before serving.

The potato straws will be done at about the same time as the chops. Turn them out on to soft paper to drain. Sprinkle with salt and serve at once with the chops.

NOTE.—Mint butter is served with fried or grilled chops just in the same way as parsley butter is served with steak.

MINT BUTTER (GENERAL RECIPE).—1½ oz. of butter, 1 tablespoonful of chopped mint, salt and pepper, 1 dessertspoonful of vinegar.

To make the mint butter, cream the butter on a saucer till it is soft, add the seasoning and mint and gradually work in the vinegar.

FRIED CUTLETS AND ONION SAUCE

INGREDIENTS. — 2 medium-sized onions, ½ gill of milk, 1 teaspoonful of arrowroot, ¼ oz. of butter, pepper and salt, 1 lb. of best neck of mutton, dripping, egg and breadcrumbs.

METHOD.—Have the chine bone removed, and divide the mutton into cutlets. Trim them and shape the meat to a point at the end of the bone, so as to allow a cutlet frill to slip on easily.

Brush the cutlets with egg, and coat with breadcrumbs.

Melt some dripping in a frying-pan. When hot, put in the cutlets. Fry gently until golden brown, then turn them over and brown the other side.

When cooked, arrange them on a dish with the bone of each cutlet to the left, and put on the cutlet frills. Pour thick brown gravy (see p. 100) round, and heap the onion sauce in the centre.

The Onion Sauce

Peel the onions and cook them in water until tender. Then strain them, drain them well, and chop finely.

Mix the arrowroot to a smooth paste with some of the milk, add the remainder to the onions and return to the saucepan. Add the butter, stir in the arrowroot, boil for a few minutes, and season to taste. The sauce should be rather stiff.

Allow one or two cutlets for each person.

GRILLED LEG OF MUTTON CUTLET

(Two Hot Dishes From One Joint)

The knuckle end of a half-leg of mutton will provide two hot dinners.

Cut off a steak or leg cutlet and serve it grilled, then boil the remainder of the joint the next day.

Ingredients.—1 leg cutlet cut from half a leg knuckle, 6 tomatoes, dripping, seasoning, gravy.

Method.—Wipe and stalk the tomatoes and bake them in a tin with a little dripping until tender. They will take about half an hour to cook.

Grill the cutlet for about ten or fifteen minutes, keeping it turned frequently.

The grill must be heated before the cutlet is put under it.

Serve the cutlet on a hot dish with the tomatoes and thin, brown gravy.

To make the gravy, pour some good stock (see p. 12) or gravy into the grill-tin. Season it and boil it up. Add a few drops of browning if required, then strain.

Sufficient for two or three persons.

BOILED HALF-LEG OF MUTTON

Ingredients.—Knuckle half-leg (3 lb. after removing cutlet), boiling water to cover, 1½ to 2 lb. of onions, salt.

For the Caper Sauce.—1½ oz. of flour, 1½ oz. of butter or margarine, ¾ pint of milk, one 4½d. bottle of capers.

Method.—Put the joint into boiling water with just a little salt added. Boil it up, remove the scum, let it boil for three or four minutes to harden

the outside albumen, and so keep in the goodness, then simmer it gently for about an hour and a half.

Peel the onions, tie them in muslin, and cook them with the mutton, allowing them about an hour, according to their size. When seasonable, a few turnips can be boiled in with the meat.

To serve boiled mutton, place it on a hot dish with a few of the vegetables and some liquor, then pour a little of the sauce over it. Serve the rest of the vegetables separately.

If preferred, the turnips may be mashed.

The Caper Sauce

To make the caper sauce, melt the fat in a saucepan. Add the flour, and mix together until smooth. Add the liquor (cold) and stir until the sauce boils. Then stir in the capers, which can be chopped coarsely or cut in halves. Pour off the vinegar before adding the capers or the sauce will curdle.

Some people prefer this sauce to be made with water or with meal liquor instead of milk, in which case a spoonful of the vinegar from the bottle of capers may be added.

Sufficient for six persons.

MUTTON CUTLETS AND TOMATOES

Ingredients.—4 bones of best neck of mutton, ¾ lb. of tomatoes, dripping, 1½ gills of brown gravy (see p. 100), seasoning.

Method.—Remove the chine bone from the neck of mutton. Cut it into four cutlets, with a bone in the centre of each. Trim each cutlet and cut off the meat about one inch from the top, so that, when cooked, a cutlet frill can be slipped on. Wipe the tomato and cut into halves. Melt the dripping in a pan and fry the tomatoes, being careful not to break them. Grill the cutlets, keeping them frequently turned; they will take about twelve minutes. Place them on a hot dish with the bone of each cutlet to the left. Pour off the fat from the grill-tin, pour the gravy round the tin, boil it, and season well. Strain round the cutlets. Take up the tomatoes, drain off the fat, and heap them on both sides of the cutlets. Place a cutlet frill on each, serve at once.

MUTTON DUCK

INGREDIENTS.—Shoulder of mutton (boned), 2 oz. of dripping.

FOR THE SAGE AND ONION STUFFING. —2 Spanish onions (medium sized), 1 breakfastcupful of breadcrumbs, 1 tablespoonful of crushed dried sage. 1½ oz. of bacon dripping, 1 egg (beaten), salt and pepper.

FOR THE GRAVY.—1 tablespoonful of flour, ¾ pint of hot water or stock (see p. 12).

METHOD.—The butcher will bone the meat and saw off the knuckle bone, which represents the duck's head.

TO MAKE THE STUFFING.—Peel the onions and boil them for thirty minutes. Chop them, add the dripping, sage, breadcrumbs, salt and pepper and bind the mixture with the egg.

Put the stuffing inside the meat, and tie it round firmly. Stand the knuckle up at one end and use a skewer to keep it in place. Put the meat in a baking-tin with the dripping spread on top, and place it in a hot oven for ten minutes. Baste well, and lower the gas, in order to keep the meat tender.

Allow twenty minutes for each pound of meat and twenty minutes over.

Place the joint on a hot dish and remove string and skewer.

Serve with thick gravy.

Sufficient for from four to six persons.

THICK GRAVY

POUR off nearly all the dripping, leaving one tablespoonful in the tin.

Add one tablespoonful of flour and mix well.

Stir over the gas until the flour is fried a rich brown. Add three-quarters of a pint of hot water or stock. Stir the gravy till it boils.

Season to taste, and strain.

HARICOT MUTTON

INGREDIENTS.—1½ lb. of middle neck of mutton, ¾ gill of haricot beans, ½ gill of turnip cubes, 1½ gills of carrot cubes, 1 or 2 onions (cut in small pieces), 1½ pints of stock (see p. 12), 2 tablespoonfuls of flour, 2 oz. of dripping, seasoning.

METHOD.—Wash the beans and soak them overnight, then cook them in boiling water with salt to flavour until almost tender. Strain them and add them to the mutton with the other vegetables.

Cut the meat into chops, dip them in the flour, and season them with salt and pepper.

Melt the dripping, and when hot, add the meat and fry it for a minute or two until lightly browned, then put it on a plate.

Add the remainder of the flour to the fat in the pan and stir it over a low burner until brown. Draw the pan aside and add the stock gradually. Boil it up and add seasoning to taste.

Put the meat into a saucepan or casserole, pour the prepared gravy over it and add the vegetables. Stew them all together until tender. More gravy may be added if required.

Sufficient for four persons.

BRAISED NECK OF MUTTON

BRAISING is a combined method of baking and stewing, and meat cooked by this method is most appetising.

A braising pan consists of a strong pan with a well-fitting lid, with a small handle on each side, but if one is not available, you can use an ordinary strong saucepan, provided you can get it in the oven.

The meat is placed on a bed of vegetables, and only sufficient stock added barely to cover the *vegetables*. It is cooked on top of the stove for the first part of the time, and in the oven for the latter part.

INGREDIENTS.—2½ to 3 lb. of best end of the neck of lamb or mutton, 1 or 2 onions, 2 or 3 carrots, 1 turnip, a sprig of parsley and thyme, dripping or bacon fat, stock (see p. 12).

FOR THE STUFFING.—3 oz. of breadcrumbs, 1 level tablespoonful of chopped onion, 1 level tablespoonful of finely chopped parsley, ¼ teaspoonful of mixed herbs, 1½ oz. of margarine or butter, seasoning, milk.

METHOD.—To make the stuffing, mix the breadcrumbs with the onion, parsley and herbs, add seasoning to taste, then stir in the butter (melted), and moisten them with milk.

Have the meat boned out, and make stock from the bones.

Season the meat, spread it with the stuffing. Roll it up, and sew it securely, using a trussing needle and string.

Prepare the vegetables and cut them in halves or quarters or thick chunky pieces.

Melt a little fat in the pan, add the vegetables, and let them just colour slightly, then put them on a plate and brown the meat lightly on all sides.

Pour off the fat, arrange the vegetables to form a bed, and place the meat on top of them. Pour in sufficient boiling stock barely to cover the vegetables. Add a sprig of parsley and a small piece of thyme. Cover the meat with a buttered paper, close the pan tightly, and cook the meat gently, first on top of the stove, and then in the oven, allowing twenty to twenty-five minutes to the pound, and twenty-five minutes over.

When cooked, place the meat on a hot dish and garnish it with vegetables. Serve the gravy in a sauce-boat.

To PREPARE THE GRAVY.—Slightly thicken the stock left in the braising-pan, add a few drops of browning or a little glaze. Season and strain it.

The vegetables used for the garnish consist of large diced carrots and turnips, and some peas and beans. These are all cooked separately, and then mixed together and re-heated in a little butter.

NOTE.—If liked, the meat may be brushed with hot glaze before it is served.

NOISETTES OF MUTTON

INGREDIENTS.—1½ lb. of best end neck of mutton or lamb, 6 or 8 mushrooms (of even size), 3 or 4 tomatoes, pepper and salt, flour, browning.

METHOD.—Have the mutton boned out, the outside skin removed, and the meat rolled and tied securely.

Prepare and cleanse the mushrooms. Cut the meat into slices about half an inch thick and tie them with string to keep them a good shape.

Heat the grill, put the noisettes on to the rack of the grill-tin, and the mushrooms in the bottom of the tin, so that the fat from the meat drips on to them. Grill the noisettes, keeping them turned, then keep them warm while the mushrooms finish cooking.

To serve, stand a thick slice of tomato, grilled or fried lightly, on each piece of meat, put a mushroom on the top, and pour thick, brown gravy round.

The gravy should be made first by preparing a stock from the mutton bones, adding the trimmings of tomato and mushroom to flavour it. Some of this stock is added to the brown particles in the grill-tin, it is thickened, browned and seasoned to taste, then strained.

NOTE.—If preferred, the mushrooms may be fried.

This amount of meat will cut into six or eight slices.

MUTTON PATTIES

INGREDIENTS.—½ lb. of cold mutton, 2 oz. of ham, 1 teaspoonful of flour, 1 teaspoonful of chopped capers, ½ teaspoonful of dried herbs, 1 teacupful of thick gravy (see p. 100), salt and pepper, ½ lb. of flaky pastry (see p. 252), 1 egg.

METHOD.—Chop the mutton and ham and mix with the flour, capers and herbs. Season well.

Roll out the pastry, cut out six rounds for the lids and six very small rounds for centre ornaments. Roll out the remains of the pastry again, cutting six more rounds. Use these to line six good-sized patty pans, and moisten the edges.

Fill them with the mixture, putting a tablespoonful of gravy in each. Cover with pastry lids, make a hole in the centre and cover with centre ornament. Press the edges lightly and scallop them.

Brush the top with egg, but not the sides as it would prevent the patties rising. Bake in a moderately hot oven for about twenty minutes.

Heat the gravy, and when the patties are done, remove the small centre decorations and pour the gravy into them slowly, using a funnel to do so.

To make six patties.

RAGOUT OF MUTTON

INGREDIENTS.—1½ lb. of middle neck of mutton, 2 oz. of dripping, 2 oz. of flour, 2 small carrots, 2 small onions, about 1½ pints of stock (see p. 12) or water (more if required), seasoning.

METHOD.—Scrape the carrots, cut them into small dice, and stand in cold water. Melt the fat in a saucepan. Wipe the meat and make into cutlets and flour them. Place them in the hot fat and fry gently until golden brown on both sides. Do not fry them sufficiently to cook them, but just to brown. Put on a plate and keep warm.

Peel and slice the onions, and fry in the remainder of the fat. Then add the rest of the flour and stir together. Add a little more dripping if necessary. Stir over the fire until the flour becomes brown, but do not let it burn. This is known as a " brown roux " and is the foundation for the gravy.

When ready, add the stock. Stir until it comes to the boil. Season well.

Put the fried cutlets into the gravy, add the strained carrots. Cook all slowly for about one hour and a half.

Before serving, skim off the fat. Heap the cutlets in the centre of a dish, strain the gravy and pour round. Place the vegetables at either end. Serve very hot.

NOTE.—The gravy should be thick and brown, if necessary a few drops of browning may be added. There should be just sufficient gravy to cover the meat.

MUTTON RISSOLES MITH VERMICELLI

INGREDIENTS.—½ lb. of cooked mutton, gravy or stock (see p. 12), 1 onion, pepper and salt, 2 oz. of vermicelli, 1 egg, fat for frying, 6 oz. of flour, 3 oz. of margarine, salt, water to mix.

METHOD.—Remove the bone and gristle from the mutton also some of the fat.

Put the meat through a mincing machine ; there should be about six ounces when minced.

Peel and chop the onion and fry in a small quantity of dripping.

Add the fried onion to the minced meat, season well with pepper and salt, and slightly moisten with a little gravy or stock.

Sieve the flour and salt together.

Rub the margarine into the flour until it resembles fine breadcrumbs.

Add sufficient cold water to make a stiff paste.

It must be just pliable, without being sticky.

Roll out the pastry to the thickness of about one-eighth of an inch.

Cut it into rounds with a plain cutter, about three inches in diameter.

Turn them over on the other side and put about a dessertspoonful of the minced meat, etc., in the centre of each round of pastry.

Damp round the edge of each, and seal together over the centre of the rissole.

Flute the edge with the finger and thumb.

Beat up the egg and brush over each rissole with it, then coat on the vermicelli, the latter broken into small pieces.

Put into a deep pan of hot fat and fry until golden brown.

Drain well on paper.

Serve on a dish paper and garnish with parsley.

NOTE.—If liked, thick brown sauce or gravy may be served separately.

BAKED SHOULDER OF MUTTON

EXPOSE meat to a good heat for the first ten or fifteen minutes, so as to seal the outside and keep in the goodness, then lessen the heat as required, so that the meat does not get scorched outside before it is cooked through.

The average time to allow for mutton or lamb is about fifteen or twenty minutes to the pound and fifteen over. But remember that a small joint will take longer in comparison than a large one, and that the thickness must be considered as well as the weight. A shoulder weighing about five pounds will require about one and a half to one and three-quarter hours.

Meat (especially lean kind) needs to be kept well basted.

Serve thin brown gravy, with roast

or baked meat, unless stuffed, in which case serve thick gravy.

To Carve a Leg of Mutton

Cut thick slices down towards the bone in the thick part of the leg, and also slice in the same direction from the knuckle end—the latter is better if eaten hot.

Things to Remember

In nearly every joint you will find that some cuts are more prime than others, and these should be served out equally so that each person has a fair share of both, and then also the joint is not left with all the less prime cuts and none of the better. In almost every case when carving meat, the joint should be cut the way of the grain. Two exceptions to this are the undercut of sirloin and a saddle of mutton.

Remember that a shallow dish is easier to carve in than a deep one, and you must see that your knife is sharp.

To Carve a Saddle of Mutton

Cut slices down the centre of the two loins from one end to the other. Cut also slices parallel with these from the fatter part at the sides.

OX-BRAIN FRITTERS

Ingredients.—1 ox brain, 1 egg, breadcrumbs, a little salt and pepper, deep fat for frying, 1 oz. of flour.

Method.—Soak the brain, in cold salt water for an hour and remove the membrane. Stew the brain, in enough water to cover it, for ten minutes, then strain it.

When cold, slice it thickly and dip it into flour seasoned with salt and pepper.

Brush the slices with egg and coat them with breadcrumbs.

Fry them for three minutes in smoking hot fat, and drain them on paper.

Serve the fritters on lace papers. Sufficient for two persons.

OX LIVER AND PARSNIPS

Ingredients.—1 lb. of ox liver, 2 rashers of bacon (chopped), 1½ lb. of parsnips, 1 oz. of flour, ½ teaspoonful of salt and pepper, 1 cupful of water, 1 teaspoonful of Worcester sauce, a little dripping if necessary.

Method.—Wash and peel the parsnips. Boil them for ten minutes, then slice them thickly.

Wash, dry, and slice the liver, and roll it in the flour. Season it with salt and pepper.

Fry the bacon for five minutes, and put it on a hot dish.

Fry the liver and parsnips *slowly* together for about fifteen minutes, keeping them well turned.

Put them on the dish. Fry the flour brown in the fat from the bacon, stirring it well and adding a little dripping if too dry.

Pour in the water and sauce and stir it till it boils. Boil for three minutes and strain over the liver.

Sufficient for four persons.

Note.—Ox liver is very economical and quite good if bought when fresh and cooked as slowly as possible to make it tender and digestible.

Liver when fresh is firm and of a good colour. If soft and watery it is not good.

OX TAIL EN CASSEROLE

Ingredients.—1 ox tail, 1½ pints of stock (see p. 12) (or sufficient to just cover), 1 carrot and onion, a few celery seeds, seasoning, 2 oz. of dripping, butter, or salad oil, 2 oz. of flour, 3 oz. of cooked ham, 1 tablespoonful of chutney or mixed pickle, gravy browning, ½ gill of Marsala (if liked).

Method.—Cut the ox tail into pieces where jointed, and wash it well in cold salted water. Then wipe thoroughly. Prepare the vegetables and cut them into small squares.

Cut the ham into slices. Melt the dripping in a saucepan, flour the ox tail and fry it lightly, just sufficiently to brown it. Put it into a casserole. Fry the prepared vegetables and ham until light brown, and add to the ox tail.

Pour over the stock, season well, and add the pickles and celery seeds (the latter tied in muslin). Cover the casserole and put it into the oven, or on top of the stove on an asbestos mat. Bring to the boil, and simmer gently for about two hours and a half.

Skim all the fat from the top. Mix the remainder of the flour to a

mooth paste with a little water,
tir into the casserole.

Put it back into the oven for a few
minutes to cook the flour ; remove the
celery seeds. Serve in the casserole.

NOTE.—If the Marsala is used, stir
t in just before serving.

OX TONGUE

(BOILED AND PRESSED)

INGREDIENTS.—1 ox tongue
slightly salted), water to cover.

METHOD.—Well wash the tongue,
put it into a large saucepan or boiler,
cover with warm water, and bring to
he boil.

Remove the scum, and simmer
gently for about three and a half to
our hours for a small tongue. If
large, allow a little longer.

When cooked put on to a dish, skin
he blade of the tongue, and take out
he three or four small bones which
re in the root.

Twist into a round shape, and put
nto a cake-tin. (It should be a
very tight fit.)

Place a piece of greaseproof paper
n the top, then a tin or plate with
ome very heavy weights.

Leave until quite cold and firm ; it
vill take about twelve hours.

Turn out on to a dish and garnish
vith parsley.

NOTE.—It is advisable to stand the
ake-tin in a large baking-tin, so that
he moisture pressed out of it can run
nto the tin.

The liquor (this is the water in
vhich the tongue is cooked) should be
eft to stand until the next day, then
he fat can be skimmed off and
larified.

The liquor itself can be used as a
oundation for soup.

If it is rather salt, it can be diluted
nd a few fresh bones cooked in it.

When buying a tongue, choose one
vith a good blade and not too much
oot.

GLAZING A TONGUE OR PRESSED BEEF

A PLAIN glaze may be made for small
ouseholds by dissolving an ounce of
elatine in a pint of strong Bovril.
n a large household, however, where
stockpot is always ready, *real*
glaze may be used. It is not difficult
to prepare, but it is expensive and
takes a long time to cook.

REAL MEAT GLAZE

INGREDIENTS.—$\frac{3}{4}$ lb. of shin beef,
$\frac{3}{4}$ lb. of knuckle of veal, 1 lb. of veal
bones, 1 calf's foot, 1 carrot, 1 onion,
1 bayleaf, 2 sticks of celery, 2 oz. of
dripping.

METHOD.—Heat the dripping and
fry the sliced vegetables in it till they
are nicely browned.

Put the vegetables in a large saucepan, heat the fat again and quickly
brown the meat and bones. Add
these to the vegetables without any
of the dripping. Cover the meat and
vegetables with cold water and bring
them very slowly to the boil. Simmer
gently for six hours. The veal will
be cooked long before this, and it can
be removed and used for making a
ragoût. After this cooking, the stock
should be strained through a clean
teacloth and put into a smaller pan
than the one used originally for all
the meat and bones. The strained
stock should be boiled till it is reduced
to one-third ; it should then continue
boiling, but should be stirred all the
time till it is ready to be used. When
it is reduced to about a pint it will be
a very rich brown and will feel slightly
sticky. It should be allowed to cool
to see if it is thick enough to use for
glazing.

If it is still too thin it can be boiled
down a little more. The glaze should
be put on the tongue with a pastry
brush. When one layer is set another
can be put on. When the glaze is
thick enough the tongue can be
finished by pouring glaze quickly over
it and using a brush to spread it where
necessary. Care must be taken not
to pour it over if the glaze is too cold,
or it will set in lumps. The glaze that
falls on to the dish and sets hard can
be put back in the pan, melted, and
used again.

To decorate the tongue use aspic
jelly that has been poured into a plate
and allowed to cool. This can be
cut into diamonds or other fancy
shapes. The diamonds of jelly are
placed on the tongue, which can be
further decorated with creamed butter
in a rose forcer. A tongue frill should
be placed round the root.

OX TONGUE

(How to Prepare it for Glazing)

Soak a pickled ox-tingue in cold water for three hours. Wash it well and truss it into shape with two skewers, one under, but not through, the tip of the tongue, and the other through the root. Form the tongue into an arch by tying the skewers together with string.

Put it in a large pan of cold water with a good bunch of herbs, and bring slowly to the boil. On no account allow it to go on boiling, but lower the gas so that it only simmers. Cook slowly and continuously for three hours, or longer for a large one. When tender, plunge it in cold water for one minute to loosen the skin, which can then be peeled off by passing the finger under it. If it is cooked long enough it will peel very easily. Peel quickly while the tongue is still hot, and do not leave it in the cold water. As soon as it is peeled, put it back in the hot water in which it was cooked, replace the lid, and leave it there till nearly cold.

Before pressing, remove the small bones in the root of the tongue. Lay the tongue sideways on a large dish and place a pastry board on it. On top of this put very heavy weights, especially at the root end, and leave till next day.

Before glazing the tongue, the root should be trimmed and cut neat and square.

ROAST PIG'S HEAD

Ingredients.—Half a pig's head (fresh), 2 lb. of large cooking apples, 1 lb. of onions, 1 pint of water.

For the Gravy.— 1 oz. of dripping, 1 oz. of flour, ¾ pint of water used for cooking the head, salt and pepper.

Method. — Peel and slice the onions and place them in a baking-tin.

Wash the head and score the skin with a sharp knife.

Lay the head on the onions, pour the water over them and bake them in a moderate oven for two hours, basting the head with the liquid every fifteen minutes.

Wipe the apples and take out the cores with a small knife

Stand the apples round the mea for the last half-hour it is baking.

Place the head and onion surrounded with apples, in a hot dis and put this in the oven to keep ho Pour off the liquid.

Melt the dripping, stir in the flou and fry it till brown, stirring all th time. Add three-quarters of a pir of the liquid and stir till it boil Boil for three minutes, and serve in sauce-boat.

Sufficient for six persons.

COLD ENTRÉE OF PORK

Ingredients.—4 small pork chop 2 oz. of sugar, 1½ lb. of cooking apple ½ gill of water, 1 packet of aspic jell salt and pepper, apple and chico salad (see p. 169), a pot of red currra jelly, ½ pint of hot water.

Method.—Cut the fat off th chops and fry it for five minute Put in the chops and fry them quick for a minute on each side. Turn th gas low and fry the chops slowly fc fifteen or twenty minutes, turnin them several times.

Peel the apples and stew them to mash in the water previously seasone with salt and pepper. To half a pi of apple purée add the sugar and th aspic jelly dissolved in half a pint hot water, and leave it till cold.

When the apple jelly begins t thicken, pour it over the cold chop The apple left over is poured int small oiled moulds and allowed to se

To serve, arrange the chops again a bed of salad, turn out the sma moulds and place them in the dis Decorate with red currant jelly.

Sufficient for four persons.

Note.—Cold duck or goose is ve good served in the same way.

STUFFED BLADEBONE O PORK

Ingredients.—A small bladebo of pork (about 2 lb.), 2 oz. of brea crumbs, 1 oz. of margarine, 1 or medium-sized onions, salt and peppe 10 or 12 sage leaves.

Method.—Make the stuffing firs Dry the sage leaves and crumb them up finely ; there should be abo a level teaspoonful.

Peel and chop the onions and m

them with the breadcrumbs and sage. Mix them all together, add the seasoning, then stir in the margarine (melted).

Remove the bladebone from the pork, insert the stuffing, and put a skewer through the meat to keep it in position.

Place the pork in a baking-tin with some dripping, and bake it for about one hour and a half, keeping it well basted.

Serve with apple sauce (see below), and slightly thickened brown gravy (see p. 100).

Sufficient for about five persons.

NOTE.—This is one of the less expensive parts of pork suitable for roasting.

BOILED PORK AND PEASE PUDDING

INGREDIENTS.—2 lb. of pickled pork, 2 lb. of parsnips, water to cover.

FOR THE PUDDING.—½ pint of split peas, ¼ pint of haricot beans, 1 egg, 1 oz. of margarine, salt and pepper.

METHOD.—Wash the peas and beans and soak them for about twenty-four hours. Then tie them loosely in a pudding-cloth, put them into a saucepan with cold water, and boil them for about three hours until quite soft.

Put the pork into a pan with warm water to cover it well. When it boils, remove the scum, and simmer it gently for about one hour and three-quarters.

Wash the parsnips, peel them thinly, and split them into four lengthwise if they are large ones. Add these to the pork, allowing them about one hour to cook.

When the peas and beans are soft, lift them out and drain them, rub them through a wire sieve.

Add the margarine, the egg (beaten) and seasoning to taste. If required, a little stock may be added, but be careful not to make the pudding too moist.

Mix well together, turn the pudding into a greased tin or basin, cover it with a greased paper, and steam it for about an hour or an hour and a half. When cooked, turn it out and serve it with the pork and parsnips.

Sufficient for from six to eight persons.

NOTE.—If a larger joint is required it would be more economical to buy a salt hand of pork. One weighing four pounds would require about two hours and a half to cook.

GRILLED PORK CHOPS AND APPLE RINGS

INGREDIENTS.—3 pork chops, 3 good-sized apples, seasoning, stock (see p. 12), flour.

METHOD.—Heat the grill, then season the chops and put them under it, placing them on the rack inside the grill-tin.

Cook them until well-browned, keeping them turned frequently. Meanwhile, peel and core the apples, cut them in slices crosswise and fry them lightly until golden brown, using some of the dripping from the chops, which can be poured off when they are partly cooked.

Arrange the chops and apple rings on a dish, and serve them with thick gravy.

TO MAKE THE GRAVY.—Pour the fat from the grill-tin, leaving about a tablespoonful in the tin. Add a little flour and brown it slowly over a low burner, keeping it stirred. Draw the pan aside and add half a pint of stock. Boil the gravy for a few minutes, add the seasoning and a few drops of browning if not brown enough, then strain it.

Sufficient for three persons.

NOTE.—The apples should be sliced thickly.

LOIN OF PORK AND APPLE SAUCE

INGREDIENTS.—Loin of pork.

FOR THE SAUCE.—2 lb. of apples, ¾ gill of water—add more if required—1½ tablespoonfuls of sugar, ½ oz. of butter.

METHOD.—Loin of pork can be bought with or without the kidney as preferred, and with or without crackling.

Put the pork into a baking-tin with some dripping, and bake it till tender, basting it frequently. A piece weighing about five pounds will take about two hours to cook, but the time varies according to the thickness of the joint.

Serve the pork with apple sauce and thickened brown gravy, made by browning some flour in the baking-tin after pouring off nearly all the fat. It is then drawn aside, some stock is added gradually, and it is then boiled up, seasoned and strained.

To Make the Apple Sauce.—Peel, quarter and core the apples. Cut them into slices, and then stew them till tender, adding water and sugar to taste. Mash them up or rub them through a sieve. Return them to the pan with the butter and re-heat.

The amount of sugar and water required varies according to the kind of apples used, but the sauce should be a little sharp. Bramleys or Wellingtons are the best kind of apple to use.

PORK PIE

Ingredients.—1 lb. of sparerib pork, 1 teaspoonful of chopped sage, salt and pepper, ½ packet of aspic jelly.

For the Raised Crust.—¾ lb. of flour, ¼ teaspoonful of salt, 4 oz. of lard, ¾ gill of water, 1 egg for glazing.

Method.—Cut the meat into small pieces and season it with sage, salt and pepper. Put the flour and salt in a basin, and the lard and water into a saucepan. Boil the water and lard, let it cool slightly for two minutes, stir it gradually into the flour, mixing it to a stiff paste.

Cut off a little less than a quarter of the paste and keep it for the lid. Make the remainder flat and round like a scone.

An easy way to start shaping the paste into a pie is to lay it on a small cake tin turned upside down, and press it down round the sides for about two inches. Lift it off the tin carefully and fill the bottom with pork, pressing it in so that it will help to keep the pie a good shape. Work up the edges gradually until they are about four inches high, then put in the rest of the meat and one tablespoonful and a half of water.

Moisten the edges and roll out the small pieces of paste to fit the top. Cover the pie, press the edges together, and notch them slightly.

Make a hole in the centre, and glaze the pie by brushing it all over with a beaten egg. Bake it for one hour, having a hot oven for the first fifteen minutes to cook the pastry. Finish in a moderate oven in order to keep the meat tender and not to over-cook the pastry.

Stew any meat bones or skin for an hour in one pint of water, adding a quarter of a teaspoonful of salt. Simmer till it measures barely half a pint, then pour it on the aspic jelly and stir till it is dissolved.

Remove the pie from the oven, and when it is nearly cold put a funnel in the hole in the top and gradually pour in the jelly.

Sufficient for three persons.

Note.—Five sheets of gelatine can be used instead of the aspic jelly.

RAISED PORK PIE

Ingredients.—10 oz. of flour, ¾ gill of milk and water, 3 oz. of lard, 1 lb. of pork (neck), pepper, salt, and mace, 1 egg, 2 or 3 sheets of leaf gelatine, a few pork or veal bones, 1 onion.

Method.—Remove any gristle and bone from the meat, and cut the pork into small square pieces. Wash the bones and put them into a saucepan and well cover them with water. Add seasoning and onion. Bring to the boil, remove the scum, and simmer slowly for two or three hours.

Sieve the flour into a basin, put the lard and milk and water in a saucepan and bring to the boil. When well boiling pour into the centre of the flour and mix together to a stiff paste ; if necessary, add more boiling milk. Put on to a slightly-floured pastry-board and knead it for a few minutes, until smooth. Cut off about quarter of the paste and keep it warm. Work the large piece into the shape of a bowl, make the sides stand up well, and be sure it is free from cracks.

Trim round the top with a pair of scissors.

Fill it with the pork, which should be well-seasoned and slightly moistened with water.

Roll out the other piece of pastry to fit the top of the pie. Damp round the edge and fix on the top, decorate the edge with a fork.

Roll out the remaining trimmings

of pastry to an oblong shape, rather thick. Cut four diamond - shaped pieces to represent leaves, and mark veins on them with the back of the knife. Make a small tassel from any small pieces of pastry that still remain.

Just roll them out very thinly to an oblong shape, make cuts down the side of it, then roll it up.

Make a hole in the centre of the pie. Then put the end of the tassel (not cut) into it. Arrange the cut end to look like a tassel.

Place the four leaves round the tassel. Make two small holes on either side of the leaves.

Beat up an egg and glacé the top pie-crust.

Place on a greased baking-sheet and bake in a hot oven for the first twenty minutes, then lower the gas and cook for about one hour and a half to two hours altogether. When the pie is sufficiently browned, the browning-sheet can be removed.

When cooked, take out the tassel.

Add two or three sheets of gelatine to the stock, when dissolved, and strain into a jug.

Fill up the pie with the stock. Serve quite cold and set.

NOTE.—Keep the holes on the top of the pie open, so that the steam can escape when cooking.

STUFFED LEG OF PORK

INGREDIENTS.—Leg of pork (about 6 lb.), dripping (for basting), 2d. of bones, water to well cover, flour (for thickening), 1 onion, pepper and salt.

FOR THE STUFFING.—1 lb. of onions, 3 teaspoonfuls of powdered sage, ¼ lb. of breadcrumbs, 1 oz. of margarine, 2 oz. of suet, seasoning, 1 egg.

METHOD.—To make the Stuffing: Peel the onions and chop them finely, make the breadcrumbs, chop the suet, add these to the onions with the sage and seasoning. Mix together, add the margarine (melted), and bind with the egg.

Make an incision at the knuckle end and at the fillet, and put some of the stuffing into each; push it well in.

Stand the leg on a meat-stand in a baking-tin, with plenty of dripping.

Bake in a hot oven for the first fifteen minutes, then lower the gas.

Cook for about two hours altogether, keeping it well basted.

Wash the bones, and put into a saucepan with the water, seasoning, and onion.

Bring to the boil, remove the scum, and simmer for two or three hours. (These should be put on before the stuffing is made.)

When the pork is nearly cooked, slightly thicken the stock with a little flour and water, and add some browning.

Skim it well, to remove all the grease.

Place the pork on a large dish, and keep warm in the oven.

Pour off the dripping from the baking-tin, leaving only the brown particles.

Add to these the prepared stock, bring to the boil, and strain a small quantity round the pork.

Serve the rest separately.

NOTE.—Apple sauce should be served with this dish.

APPLE SAUCE

INGREDIENTS.—2 lb. of apples, 2 oz. of demerara sugar, ¾ gill of water.

METHOD.—Choose sharp apples— Wellingtons are the best. Peel and slice them, and remove the cores. Put into a saucepan with the water. Cook gently until almost tender.

Add the sugar, and leave until quite cooked.

Mash well with a fork, or rub through a wire sieve.

NOTE.—If rubbed through a sieve, they must be re-heated again before serving.

POTATO BRIDIES

INGREDIENTS.—4 oz. of scraps of cooked meat, chopped finely, salt and pepper, ¼ gill of stock (see p. 12) or gravy, 1 level teaspoonful of flour.

METHOD.—Mix the flour, seasoning and stock, bring them to the boil and add the meat. Re-heat the mixture and turn it out to cool.

Make a potato paste in the following proportions, by kneading one level tablespoonful of flour with a little salt into each heaped tablespoonful of finely mashed potato, and when smooth roll it out thinly.

Cut the paste into rounds about the

diameter of a breakfast cup. Put a little of the meat mixture into each, damp the edges, fold over the paste and fix the edges securely together. If liked, the Potato Bridies can be made into rolls or three-cornered shapes. Fry them in deep fat.

Allow two or more for each person.

RICE AND TOMATO PIE

INGREDIENTS.—¾ lb. of cold meat, ¼ lb. of rice, 1 lb. of tomatoes, gravy, pepper and salt, ½ oz. of margarine.

METHOD.—Wash the rice, put it into a saucepan of boiling water with a little salt added, and boil until tender. Then strain and cool it. Put the meat through a mincer, season it and *moisten well* with gravy.

Place about half the meat in the bottom of a pie-dish, then add a layer of sliced tomatoes and one of rice, both well seasoned.

Add another layer of tomatoes, then one of meat and one of rice. Decorate the top with sliced tomatoes, and put the margarine (cut in small pieces) here and there.

Make thoroughly hot in the oven, and serve with some extra gravy, thickened slightly.

Sufficient for six to eight persons.

RISSOLES

(See p. 125.)

SAUSAGE AND EGG PIE

INGREDIENTS.—2 lb. of pork sausages, 2 eggs, ¾ gill of water or stock (see p. 12), 4 sheets of leaf gelatine, ½ lb. of flour, ½ lb. of margarine, a pinch of salt, water to mix.

FOR THE STOCK.—Salt, pepper, mace, 1 lb. of veal or pork bones, water to cover, 1 onion, a few cloves, a few mixed herbs.

METHOD.—Wash the bones, then put them into a saucepan, cover with water, add a little salt, and bring slowly to the boil. Peel the onion and stick a few cloves in it, and tie the herbs in muslin. Skim the stock, add the onion and herbs, and simmer for about two or three hours. Take the herbs out after the first half an hour or they will discolour the stock.

Boil the eggs for fifteen minutes, and cut them in slices.

Skin the sausages. If you put them in cold water for a few minutes, and then split them down the side, the sausage will easily come out of the skin.

Put a layer of sausage in a pie-dish and one of egg alternately, until the dish is full. The top layer should be of sausage.

Sprinkle a little salt and pepper on the egg, but the sausage will not require any extra seasoning.

When the dish is about half full, put in two sheets of gelatine and three-quarters of a gill of stock.

TO MAKE THE PASTRY.—Add a pinch of salt to the flour and sieve it.

Add cold water gradually, and mix to a stiff paste.

Put it on to a pastry-board, and knead it lightly for a few minutes until smooth.

Roll it out to a thick oblong shape.

Turn it over on to the other side.

Put the margarine on the board, and with a well-floured rolling-pin press it nearly one-half the size of the pastry.

Put it on one-half of it, fold the pastry over, press the edges together, turn it round, and roll out.

Fold into three, and roll out again as before.

Do this three times; the fourth time the pastry should be rolled to a thickness of almost three-eighths of an inch.

Cut out a piece large enough to cover the top of the pie-dish.

Roll out the trimmings, and cut strips of pastry and place on the edge of the pie-dish, having previously damped it.

Damp the edge of pastry, and place on the top crust, press the edges together lightly, and trim off all rough pieces.

Make a hole in the centre of the crust and also one at each end.

Decorate the edge with a knife or fork.

Now make a pastry tassel. To do this take a small oblong piece of pastry and cut one side of it into tiny strips.

Then roll it up and put the end not cut in the centre hole of the pie, and arrange the cut ends to look like a tassel.

Roll out the other pieces of pastry

to about three-eighths of an inch in thickness, and cut four small diamond-shaped pieces to represent leaves. Mark veins on them.

Arrange them round the tassel.

Brush over the pie and decorations with beaten egg or milk.

Place in a hot oven and bake for about three-quarters of an hour.

When the pastry is cooked, and golden brown, slightly lessen the heat, and remove the browning shelf.

Put two sheets of gelatine into the stock; when dissolved, strain it and skim off the fat. When the pie is cooked, take out the tassel and fill the pie up with stock. Open the holes so that the steam can escape. When quite cold, replace the tassel and serve the pie.

SAUSAGES AND TOMATO FRITTERS

INGREDIENTS. — 1 small tin of tomatoes, ¾ lb. of small Paris sausages, 3 eggs, 1 breakfastcupful of bread-crumbs, 1 dessertspoonful of chopped parsley, salt and pepper, 1 oz. of dripping.

METHOD.—Rub the tomatoes through a hair sieve into a basin and add the breadcrumbs, which should make a soft but not very wet paste. Season the mixture with salt and pepper and leave to soak overnight. Next morning heat the dripping in a frying-pan, and prick the sausages with a fork to keep them from bursting. Cook the sausages rather slowly in the pan and keep them well turned. In ten minutes, when they should be nicely browned, put them on a hot dish, and keep them hot in the oven with the door ajar. Wash, dry, and chop the parsley and beat the eggs. Add the eggs and parsley to the tomato mixture. Pour off the drip-ping from the pan, leaving only one tablespoonful. Pour in the tomato and egg mixture, and stir it well until it thickens (about five minutes). Heap spoonfuls in the centre of the dish with the sausages round.

Sufficient for five or six persons.

GRILLED SAUSAGES AND TOMATO SAUCE

INGREDIENTS.—1 lb. of pork sausages, ½ lb. of tomatoes, ¼ gill of water, ½ clove of garlic, a small sprig of thyme and parsley, 1 small onion, 1 teaspoonful of cornflour, pepper and salt, ½ oz. of margarine, a level tea-spoonful of castor sugar.

METHOD.—Heat the grill, put the sausages in the grill-tin and cook them for about fifteen to twenty minutes, when they should be well browned on all sides. They must be turned frequently.

Serve them on mounds of mashed potatoes accompanied by tomato sauce. Thick gravy can also be served with them. Grilled sausages do not burst so easily as when they are fried.

To MAKE THE TOMATO SAUCE.—Melt the margarine, add the onion, peeled and minced, and cook them for a few minutes, without browning, then add the tomatoes (sliced), the garlic, herbs, and water. Cook the sauce until tender, then remove the garlic and herbs and rub the sauce through a sieve. Return it to the pan, thicken it with the cornflour, smoothed in a little water, and season it with salt, pepper, and sugar.

Sufficient for three persons.

SAUSAGE AND RICE MOULD

INGREDIENTS.—1 lb. of pork sausages, ¼ lb. of rice, 2 or 3 dessert-spoonfuls of tomato ketchup, 1 egg (hard-boiled), salt, pepper, and powdered mace, some veal stock (see p. 12), 3 or 4 sheets of leaf gelatine.

METHOD.—Wash the rice, put it into slightly salted boiling water, and boil it until almost tender—about ten minutes. Strain it and cool it. Skin the sausages and cut the egg in slices.

Take a plain mould or cake-tin, put a layer of rice in the bottom, using one-third of it. Add a little tomato ketchup, then half the sausage meat and a few slices of egg, with seasoning to taste.

Add another layer of rice, then the remainder of the tomato ketchup, sausage, and egg, and seasoning. Cover this with rice, then pour in half a gill of good veal stock, put a buttered paper over the top and cook it in a moderately hot oven for about three-quarters of an hour.

When cooked, fill up the tin with stock, leave it until cold and set, then unmould.

Garnish with a little chopped parsley, and serve with a few lettuce leaves round.

NOTE.—Remember to season stock well. If it is a firm jelly no gelatine need be added, but if gelatine is necessary, dissolve it in the stock then strain into the mould.

Sufficient for six persons.

SAUSAGE PUDDING

INGREDIENTS.—1 lb. of pork sausages, 2 medium-sized onions, a few sage leaves, stock (see p. 12), ½ lb. of flour, ¼ lb. of suet, water to mix.

METHOD.—Peel, and grate or chop the onions. Dry about twelve sage leaves and rub them to a powder.

Skin the sausages and mix them with the prepared sage and onion.

Chop the suet finely and add it to the flour. Stir in some cold water and mix to a stiff paste. Cut off one-third of this paste and put it aside. Turn the larger piece on to a floured board and roll it out to a round shape about one and a half times the size of the top of the pudding basin.

Grease the basin and line it with crust.

Put in the sausage meat, and add a little stock. Roll out the remaining piece of crust and put it on top of the pudding, damping the edge to make it adhere.

Cover the pudding with a greased paper and a floured pudding cloth, and boil it for about two hours.

Serve with thick brown gravy (see p. 100).

Sufficient for four or five persons.

SAUSAGE ROLLS

INGREDIENTS.—1 lb. of sausages, about 1½ lb. of flaky pastry, egg-yolk and milk to glaze pastry.

METHOD.—Use either pork sausages or sausage meat. To remove the skins from the sausages, place them in cold water for a few seconds, then split down the skin, when the sausage can be removed cleanly.

One pound of sausages will make about fifteen rolls, so divide the sausages into the number of portions required, and form each piece into a roll.

Roll out the pastry fairly thinly, cut it into wide strips, then cut each strip into pieces not quite square. Turn them over and place a piece of sausage on each piece. Damp the edge and fold the paste over, mark two lines (with the back of a knife) on top of the rolls and along the other three sides. Trim up the edges, place the rolls on a baking-sheet, and brush them with beaten yolk of egg mixed with a little milk. Put the rolls in a hot oven to bake. They will take about twenty minutes to cook.

FLAKY PASTRY

INGREDIENTS.—½ lb. of flour, a pinch of salt, 3 oz. of margarine or butter, water to mix, 4 oz. of lard.

METHOD.—To make the pastry, sieve the flour and salt into a basin, rub in the margarine, and mix them to a stiff paste with cold water.

Put the lard on to a well-floured board and press it out with a rolling-pin into thin pieces. Put this aside and roll out the pastry fairly thinly and to a squarish shape. Turn it over on the other side, place the lard all over it, then fold the sides to the centre both ways, and then fold it over in half.

The pastry is now folded in eight and ready to be rolled out as required.

SAUSAGE TOAD - IN - THE - HOLE

INGREDIENTS.—½ lb. of sausages, tomato ketchup, ¼ lb. of flour, salt and pepper, ½ level teaspoonful of powdered sage, 1 egg, ½ pint of milk, dripping—about ½ oz.

METHOD.—Sift the flour into a basin, pour the egg into the centre of it, and mix it with a little of the flour. Then take half the milk and add it gradually until the whole is mixed to a smooth batter. Beat this well, stir in the remainder of the milk, and leave the batter to stand for an hour, or more.

Remove the skins from the sausages, cut them in halves, and form them into smaller rolls. Dip each in a little tomato ketchup.

Melt a lump of dripping in a pie-dish

and put in the sausages. Season the batter, mixing in the sage, and pour it over them. Put the toad-in-the-hole into a good, moderately hot oven to bake. It will take about three-quarters of an hour.

Sufficient for three persons.

A MIXED SAUTE

INGREDIENTS.—3 slices of liver (ox, sheep's or calves'), ½ lb. of sausages, 3 rashers of bacon, ¼ lb. of ox kidney, flour, pepper, and salt, dripping, stock (about ½ pint) (see p. 12).

METHOD.—Melt some dripping in a frying-pan, put in the sausages and fry them gently for about twenty minutes.

Flour the liver, cut the kidney into three chunky pieces, and flour them also. Add these to the pan when the sausages have been cooking for about ten minutes, and fry them all gently until tender.

They should all be turned frequently during the cooking.

Meanwhile, remove the rind from the rashers and grill them until the fat looks semi-transparent. They will take about five minutes, according to their thickness. If preferred, they may be fried before the sausages and liver are cooked, and then kept hot. No fat is required for frying bacon; just put it into a warm pan.

When cooked, arrange the liver, kidney, and sausages on a dish with the bacon on top, pour the bacon fat over the meat and thick brown gravy all round.

Sufficient for three persons.

NOTE.—Stew the ox kidney for about half an hour in a little stock, then drain it well before frying it.

SAVOURY SEA-PIE

INGREDIENTS.—½ lb. of flour (self-raising), ¼ lb. of suet, 1½ lb. of stewing steak, 1½ tablespoonfuls of plain flour, ¾ pint of water, salt and pepper, a few carrots and onions, cold water.

METHOD.—Cut the steak into chunky pieces, season them well and mix them with one tablespoonful and a half of flour. Put them in a casserole and add the water.

Stand the casserole on an asbestos mat over the gas-jet and bring the

water to the boil, then let it simmer for about three hours, keeping it stirred and skimmed occasionally.

Prepare the vegetables and cut them into dice. Add these to the meat, allowing them an hour and a half or two hours to cook.

Chop the suet finely and mix it with the self-raising flour, add cold water and mix them to a soft dough. Roll this out to the shape of the casserole but just a shade smaller. Place it on top of the meat and vegetables, put on the lid and finish cooking the sea-pie.

Allow the suet crust about the same time as the vegetables for cooking, but let the latter boil up before adding the crust.

Serve sea-pie on a hot dish with the crust divided into four or six pieces and placed on the top.

Sufficient for five or six persons.

SHEEP'S HEAD AND BARLEY BROTH

INGREDIENTS.—1 sheep's head and trotters, 1 lb. of scrag of mutton, 1 lb. each of carrots, turnips and onions (cut in quarters), ¼ lb. of pearl barley (washed), 8 pints of cold water, ½ oz. of salt, pepper to taste, 1½ table-spoonfuls of chopped parsley.

METHOD.—Wash the head and trotters. Put them into cold water and bring slowly to the boil. Throw away the water.

Put the head, trotters and the scrag of mutton into a pan with the salt and cold water and heat them slowly. When they are boiling, skim the stock and lower the gas. Add the vegetables and barley.

Simmer the meat gently for three hours, taking out the scrag and trotters in two hours' time.

Cut the meat from the scrag.

When the stew is done, put back the meat and trotters. Add the parsley and seasoning to taste.

In five minutes serve the head, trotters and vegetables in a dish and pour the broth into a casserole or tureen.

Sufficient for four to six persons, with soup for next day.

NOTE.—A stew is simmering when bubbles rise now and again at the side of the pan.

STUFFED SHEEP'S HEARTS

INGREDIENTS. — 3 small sheep's hearts, ¼ lb. of onions, 2 oz. of breadcrumbs, 1 level teaspoonful of powdered sage leaves, 1 oz. of suet, ½ egg, seasoning, dripping, stock (for gravy), flour (for gravy).

METHOD.—Wash the hearts thoroughly in warm water, to which a little salt has been added, so as to cleanse them and draw out the blood. Dry them in a cloth. Cut off the ear-shaped pieces which are at the top on either side of the hearts. Make also a cut through the inside division of the hearts so as to have a good space for the stuffing.

To make the stuffing, chop the suet finely and mix it with the breadcrumbs and sage leaves, which should have been dried in a cool oven or some other warm place and, when crisp, rubbed to a powder. If preferred, packet sage, which is ready for use, may be used.

Peel, and either grate or chop the onions and add them to the suet. Season with salt and pepper and bind with the egg.

Stuff the hearts, put them into a baking-tin containing some dripping, and bake them gently for about three-quarters of an hour, keeping them well basted. When ready, dish them up and serve with thick brown gravy.

Sufficient for from four to six persons.

BRAISED SHEEP'S TONGUES

INGREDIENTS.—4 sheep's tongues (pickled), 1 small tin of tomatoes, a bayleaf, 1 oz. of butter, 1 oz of flour, 3 rashers of bacon, 1 tin of peas. some hot mashed potatoes, 4 peppercorns.

METHOD.—Soak the tongues in cold water for one hour. Put them into a pan with cold water to cover them, and simmer them gently for one hour and a half.

Plunge them in cold water, remove the skins and cut off the windpipes.

If the skins do not come off easily it shows that the tongues have not been boiled long enough.

Melt the butter and fry the flour brown in it, stirring well.

Add the tomatoes and stir them till boiling.

Put the sauce into a double saucepan with the tongues, peas, bayleaf and peppercorns, and simmer them while cooking the potatoes.

Cut the rashers in half, roll them up and stick them on a skewer. Place the skewer across a meat-tin and grill the rashers for six minutes, turning them over twice.

To dish up, arrange the potatoes in a ring with the peas in the centre. Lay the tongues on the potato. Strain the sauce round, and garnish with the rolls of bacon.

Sufficient for four persons.

NOTE.—If fresh tongues are bought they can easily be pickled by rubbing ordinary cooking salt into them. Afterwards lay them in a plate and pile salt over them. Leave for two days, then wash them.

SOMERSET FAGGOTS

INGREDIENTS.—½ lb. of lights, ½ lb. of liver, ½ lb. of melt, 6 oz. of breadcrumbs, ¼ lb. of onions, salt and pepper, ½ lb. of caul.

METHOD.—Put the meat and onions through a mincer. Mix them with the breadcrumbs and season with salt and pepper. Shape the mixture into lumps the size of a small teacup.

Wrap them each in a piece of caul, tucking the ends underneath.

Place them in a tin or pie-dish, half fill it with water and bake them for one hour.

As the water boils away it leaves a nice gravy.

Sufficient for four persons.

SQUAB PIE

INGREDIENTS.—2 pork chops, 1 lb. of apples, 2 onions, 3 medium-sized potatoes, 1 gill of water, salt and pepper, 1 teaspoonful of dried sage, 1 oz. of sultanas.

METHOD.—Peel the apples, onions and potatoes, and slice them thinly. Wash the sultanas and pick off the stalks.

Lay half the onions in the pie-dish with some slices of apple and a little potato over them, and sprinkle the vegetables with sage, salt, pepper, and a few sultanas. Put in the chops and the rest of the sage and sultanas, also the onions and apples. Fill the pie-dish half full of cold water, arrange the slices of potato neatly on top, and twist a piece of greased paper over the edge of the dish.

Bake in a moderate oven for an hour and three-quarters.

NOTE.—This is an old recipe, and there are many variations of it.

Sufficient for two persons.

OLD DEVONSHIRE SQUAB PIE

INGREDIENTS.—½ lb. of veal, ½ lb. of neck of mutton, ½ lb. of steak, 1 teaspoonful of dried herbs, the peel of 1 lemon, a pinch of nutmeg, 2 eggs, 6 onions, 6 apples, 6 potatoes, pepper and salt.

METHOD.—Cut the meat up into small pieces and sprinkle them with the herbs, grated lemon-peel, nutmeg, pepper and salt.

Add the eggs, hard-boiled and sliced, and mix with the meat the onions and apples, thinly sliced. Grease a pie-dish, put in the meat and vege-tables, cover the pie with sliced potatoes and greased paper, and bake it in a moderate oven for two hours.

STEAK A LA MAITRE D'HOTEL

INGREDIENTS.—1 lb. of steak, ¾ oz. of butter, seasoning, a squeeze of lemon-juice, 1 teaspoonful of finely chopped parsley, a little stock (see p. 12).

METHOD.—Soften the butter on a plate by mashing it with a fork, then stir in the parsley, seasoning and lemon-juice to taste. Form the butter into a lump and leave it to harden, then roll it into little balls.

Grill the steak for about ten minutes, keeping it turned.

Serve on a dish and garnish it with balls of green butter. Pour just a little stock into the fat, and brown particles left in the grill-tin, boil it up, season it and serve it in a sauce-boat.

Either rump steak, or a porter-house steak can be used—the latter is a slice cut from a sirloin of beef (with undercut).

Sufficient for three or four persons.

STEAK BALLS

INGREDIENTS.—1 lb. of rump steak, 1 onion, 2 small parsnips, salt and pepper, a pinch of dried mixed herbs, 1 oz. of dripping, 1 oz. of flour, 1 dessertspoonful of Worcester sauce, ½ pint of water.

METHOD.—Mince the steak and mix it with the finely chopped onion. Season, and form the mixture into three or four flat cakes. Peel and slice the parsnips and boil them for ten minutes. Put them in a baking-tin with an ounce of dripping. Make this hot in the oven, put in the meat and return the tin to the oven. Bake for thirty minutes in a fairly hot oven, turning the meat over when half done. Dish up the meat and parsnips and keep them hot. Then make a thick brown gravy in the same tin by frying the flour brown in the dripping and adding the sauce and water.

Strain the gravy round the meat.

Allow a pound of steak for four persons.

GRILLED STEAK A LA FRANCAISE

INGREDIENTS.—1 lb. of fillet steak (cut very thickly), pepper and salt, ½ tablespoonful of salad oil, 2 tea-spoonfuls of vinegar, 2 oz. of butter, 2 teaspoonfuls of chutney, 1½ tea-spoonfuls of chopped parsley, 1 carrot, 1 gill of stock (if required).

METHOD.—First prepare and cook the carrot for the garnish as explained later. Split the steak into two or three slices according to the thickness. Each fillet should be about three-quarters of an inch in thickness. Make each into a neat round and trim off the fat. To make them even, beat with a cutlet bat or a large knife.

Place on a dish, sprinkle with pepper and salt, and pour over them the oil and vinegar. Allow them to soak in this for about fifteen minutes. Turn them occasionally. Press half the butter on to a plate and work into it the chopped parsley and chutney. Then make it into small dice and leave in a cool place. Grill the fillets for about ten minutes, keeping them turned fre-quently. At the same time grill some of the fat that was trimmed off; this can be first cut into small rounds.

Place the fillets down the centre of a dish with some fat between each.

Garnish the dish with small heaps of cooked carrot. Put a few dice of prepared butter on each fillet and serve at once.

TO PREPARE THE GARNISH OF CARROTS.—Scrape and wash the carrot, and cut into small squares. Put into a saucepan of boiling water to which a little salt has been added, and cook until tender. Strain off the water, melt the other ounce of butter in a saucepan, and toss the carrots in it, but do not fry them.

NOTE.—If desired, serve gravy with the fillets, pour off a little of the fat left in the grill-tin, then add to the remainder one gill of good stock. Boil it up, season well, and add a few drops of browning. Strain round the dish or serve separately.

GRILLED POINT STEAK AND MUSHROOMS

INGREDIENTS.—¾ lb. of point end of rump, 6 oz. of mushrooms, butter, stock (see p. 12), seasoning, a little flour.

METHOD.—Wipe the steak and season it with pepper and salt.

Peel the mushrooms, remove the stalks and trim them. Put both mushrooms and stalks in cold water, sprinkle them with salt and soak them for a few minutes to clean them. Drain them and fry them till tender in a little butter.

Heat the grill and grill-tin, put the steak on the bars of the grill-tin and cook it under the hot grill for about ten minutes, keeping it turned frequently. Lift it on to a hot dish and pour over it the fat from the steak. Place the mushrooms round the steak, garnish it with the stalks, and serve it with gravy.

TO MAKE THE GRAVY.—Dredge a little flour into the mushroom butter, brown it slowly and draw the pan aside. Boil up a little stock in the grill-tin and add it to the mushroom butter. Season, boil up, and strain the gravy.

Sufficient for two or three persons.

MINCED STEAK

INGREDIENTS.—¾ lb. of buttock steak, 2 or 3 tomatoes, 2 dessert-spoonfuls of chopped onion, ½ oz. of flour, ½ oz. of butter or dripping, seasoning, ½ pint of stock (see p. 12), toast.

METHOD.—Put the steak through the mincer and mix it with the onion.

Melt the fat in a saucepan, add the flour and stir it over a low burner until brown. Draw the pan aside, add the stock gradually, bring it to the boil and then add the prepared meat, onion, and seasoning to taste. Simmer the steak gently for about three-quarters of an hour, then turn it on to a hot dish and garnish it with half slices of tomato, which should have been heated in the oven, and small triangles of toast.

Sufficient for three persons.

SIMPLE BEEF STEAK PIE

INGREDIENTS.—2 lb. of round steak, 1½ level teaspoonfuls of salt, water, fat, 1 tablespoonful of flour, ½ level teaspoonful of pepper, 2 slices of minced onion, puff pastry (see below).

METHOD.—Cut the meat into thin slices. Mix the flour, salt and pepper on a plate, and roll each slice of meat in the mixture. Put a small piece of fat on each.

Roll up each piece of meat and place it in a deep dish with the onions, and add a little water.

Roll out some rough puff pastry and cut a piece to fit the top of the dish. Cut bands about half an inch wide. Moisten the rim of the dish with water. Lay the bands of pastry round the edge, moisten them and cover the dish with the piece of pastry for the top. Trim the edges and cut a hole in the centre of the top. Brush the top only with some egg, and decorate it with leaves of pastry.

Bake the pie in a quick oven at first, then reduce the temperature and finish cooking.

Sufficient for six or eight persons.

STEAK AND KIDNEY PIE

INGREDIENTS.—Rough puff pastry (see below), 1½ lb. of buttock steak, ½ lb. of ox kidney, flour, pepper and salt, water.

METHOD. — Cut up the steak and kidney and flour it well, seasoning it at the same time.

You can either cut it up in chunky pieces or else in thin, oblong slices.

Put a small piece of kidney on each oblong of steak, and roll it up neatly.

Arrange the meat in the pie-dish, remembering that the dish must be full or the crust will sink. Pour in a little water—about three-quarters of a gill is sufficient.

If using a less expensive steak, it is advisable to cook it first, putting it into a casserole after it has been cut up, floured, and seasoned. Cover it with water and let it simmer for three hours after it comes to the boil.

Let the steak get cold, then put it in a pie-dish, adding gravy as required.

Now roll out the pastry thickly to an oval shape, rather larger than the top of the pie-dish, and cut a cover for the pie. Roll out the remainder of the pastry thinly, and cut strips for the rim of the dish.

Put the trimmings together, roll them out thickly and cut off small hearts or other suitable shapes to decorate the pie.

Damp the rim of the dish and line it with pastry, then damp the pastry and cover the top of the dish. Trim the edge with a sharp knife dipped in flour, holding the pie in the left hand and slanting the handle of the knife towards the side of the pie-dish. Cut up the edge, then flute it.

Brush the top of the pie (not the edge) with beaten egg to glaze it, and decorate it with hearts of pastry, also glazed. Make a hole in the centre of the pie and put it in a hot oven to bake.

The pie will take about one hour and a half to cook if the steak is not cooked first. The heat should be lessened as soon as the pastry has risen and is lightly browned. If the meat has been cooked first, bake the pie for about half an hour or a little longer.

ROUGH PUFF PASTRY
(For Steak and Kidney Pie.)

INGREDIENTS.—¾ lb. of flour, ½ lb. of fresh butter, 1 oz. of lard, lemon-juice, a good pinch of salt, cold water to mix.

METHOD.—Put the butter in a lightly floured pudding-cloth and squeeze out the moisture, then shape it into a squarish shape, and leave it in a cool place to harden.

Sift the flour with the salt, put the lard in the centre (in a lump), add a good squeeze of lemon-juice, and sufficient cold water to make a pliable paste. Turn the mixture on to a pastry board, and knead it lightly until it is smooth, then roll it out to an oblong shape.

Turn the pastry over on to the other side, place the butter on one half, leaving a good margin all round it; then fold over the other half of pastry so as to cover the butter completely. Press the edges together securely.

Leave the pastry in a cool place for from fifteen to twenty minutes. When ready to roll it out, place the pastry on the board with the fold to the left and roll it to an oblong shape about half as long again as before. Then turn it over and fold it into three.

Repeat this process three times, leaving the pastry in a cool place for from fifteen to twenty minutes between each or every other roll; then roll it to the shape and thickness required.

Another method of making this kind of pastry is to sift the flour and salt on to the board in a heap, and roughly chop up all the fat into it. Then add the lemon-juice and sufficient water to mix the flour to a paste.

Roll the pastry to an oblong shape, turn it over, and fold it into three.

Repeat this process three times, placing the fold to the left each time, and leaving the pastry in a cool place between each or every other roll, as before. The fourth time roll out the pastry and use it as required.

THE PASTRY DECORATIONS
HOW TO MAKE THEM

THESE are made from the trimmings of pastry.

To make the leaves, roll out pastry till a quarter of an inch thick, cut strips three-quarters to an inch wide, trim off a piece from the top of each strip, cutting in a slanting direction, then cut pieces parallel with the top at equal distances apart, making diamond-shaped leaves. Mark veins on them with the back of your knife.

To make a tassel, roll out some pastry quite thinly, and cut a strip four and a half inches long by an inch and a half wide.

Cut along one side of it, little parallel cuts like a fringe, then roll it up, stand the uncut end in the centre of your pie, and arrange the cut ends, which form the tassel, in position.

STEAK AND KIDNEY PUDDING

INGREDIENTS.—1½ lb. of bladebone steak, ⅓ lb. of ox kidney, flour (for coating the meat), pepper and salt, bones (about 1 lb.), ¾ lb. of flour, stock (see p. 12) or water, 6 oz. of suet, a pinch of salt, water to mix.

METHOD.—Wash the bones, put into a saucepan, cover with cold water, and bring slowly to the boil.

Skim it, season it, and simmer for about three hours.

Well wipe the steak and kidney with a damp cloth, and cut the steak into small square pieces; the pieces of kidney should be slightly larger.

Coat them with plenty of flour, and season with pepper and salt; leave aside until the crust is made.

Take a large pudding-basin and well grease it.

Put a saucepan half full of water on to boil.

Add the salt to the flour and sieve it into a basin. Skin and finely chop or grate the suet, mix it well into the flour. Add cold water gradually, and mix to a stiff paste.

Cut off not quite one-third of the pastry, and put aside for the lid.

Roll out the larger piece to a round shape, about one and a half times the size of the top of the basin.

Line the greased basin with the crust, press it to the basin and make it quite even, cut off the rough pieces from the top. Fill the basin with the floured steak and kidney, and almost fill it up with cold water or stock. Roll out the smaller piece of pastry to fit the top of the basin exactly.

Damp round the top edge of pastry, fix to the lid, and press the edges well together, but do not tuck them underneath the rim of the basin.

Cover with a greased paper and floured pudding-cloth, which should be tied tightly with string. Tie the ends of the cloth over the top.

Put into a saucepan of boiling water and boil for three and a half to four hours.

There should be sufficient water to cover, and as it boils away more boiling water must be added.

When cooked, remove the pudding from the saucepan, take off the cloth and paper.

Wipe the basin round with a damp cloth; fold a table-napkin and pin round the basin.

Stand on a hot dish and serve at once.

Add a few drops of browning to the stock, skim it well and strain it off, and serve separately.

STEAK AND ONIONS

INGREDIENTS.—¾ lb to 1 lb. of rump steak, 2 lb. of Spanish onions, salt, 1 oz. of butter, Worcester sauce.

METHOD.—Spanish onions are best. Slice them thinly and put them into a pan of boiling water with a teaspoonful of salt. After boiling them for twenty minutes, strain and put them in a frying-pan with an ounce of butter or good beef dripping.

Cook them gently till they are done, stirring now and again. When the onions are done, make the gas griller as red-hot as possible. Brush the steak all over with butter and place it under the red-hot griller for two minutes to brown the outside. When one side is browned, turn it over *without sticking a fork into it,* and brown the other side, the quicker the better.

Lower the gas as much as possible and finish cooking quite slowly to make it tender. Turn it over two or three times. It will take from fifteen to twenty minutes, according to its thickness. Before dishing up, it should be seasoned and placed on a hot dish, with the onions round.

Serve with Worcester sauce.

Enough for three or four persons.

STEAK ROLLS

INGREDIENTS.—1 lb. of minced steak, 2 oz. of breadcrumbs, 1 tablespoonful of horseradish cream ; or to taste, 3 tablespoonfuls of stock (see p. 12), seasoning, 1 egg, flour, breadcrumbs for coating, dripping.

METHOD.—Mix the minced steak and breadcrumbs together, add the horseradish cream and seasoning to taste. Stir in half the beaten egg and moisten with the stock.

Turn on to a board, divide into nine portions, and shape, using a little flour as required, then brush with the remainder of the egg, and coat with breadcrumbs.

Fry gently in a little hot dripping and serve with green peas and thickened brown gravy (see p. 100).

Sufficient to make nine.

STEWS

STEWS are not very popular in this country—probably because as a rule they are made so badly.

And yet a stew is such an easy dish to prepare.

The most frequent cause of failure is that they do not receive the slow cooking which is absolutely essential. If a stew is cooked quickly the meat becomes hard.

There are two distinct kinds of stew—white and brown. Brown stews are the most popular and very convenient, as they can be cooked on top of the stove or in the oven. Either a saucepan or casserole can be used, but it should have a well-fitting lid. This method of cooking has the great advantage that the inferior parts of the meat can be used, the *long*, *slow* cooking making them tender.

TWO IMPORTANT POINTS

Do not let your stew boil. Remember that a stew boiled is a stew spoiled. It should be *brought to boiling point*, then allowed only to simmer. At boiling point the liquid bubbles, but when simmering it should only just move slowly. Do not forget to skim off the grease before serving the stew.

THE MEAT TO USE

IF mutton, buy the scrag or middle neck of mutton, as the breast is often too fat.

If beef, either the neck, leg, bladebone, chuck or silverside steak is suitable. The two former require the longest time.

If veal, either the neck or breast of veal is most suitable for stewing.

IRISH STEW
(A WHITE STEW)

INGREDIENTS.—1½ lb. of scrag and middle neck of mutton, ½ lb. of onions, salt and pepper, white stock or water, ½ lb. of potatoes.

METHOD. — Wipe the meat and divide it into portions where chopped.

Peel and slice the onions. Put them into a large saucepan with the meat, add a little salt and pepper, and sufficient stock or water just to cover it. Bring it to the boil, remove the scum from the top, then leave the stew to simmer gently for from one and a half to two hours, keeping it skimmed as required.

Scrub the potatoes, peel them thinly, wash and split them into halves, and cut them across again if they are very large.

Place these on top of the stew (when the latter is about half cooked) and sprinkle them with salt. When the meat is ready, the potatoes should be tender.

To serve the stew, place the meat and onions in the middle of the dish and the potatoes round the edge to form a border. Pour some gravy round, making quite sure first that it is free from grease.

STEWED STEAK AND DUMPLINGS
(A BROWN STEW)

INGREDIENTS.—2 lb. of stewing steak, flour, pepper and salt, stock (see p. 12), or water.

FOR THE DUMPLINGS.—½ lb. of flour, ¼ lb. of suet, 1 flat teaspoonful of baking powder, water to mix.

METHOD.—Wipe the steak and cut it into about six or eight pieces.

Flour them well and season them with pepper and salt, then put them into a casserole and cover them with stock or water.

Put the casserole into the oven, bring it to the boil, skim it if required, then let it simmer gently for about three hours.

TO MAKE THE DUMPLINGS.—Chop the suet finely, and mix it with the flour (to which the baking powder has been added). Add cold water, and mix to a stiff paste, then divide it into portions and make it into dumplings.

Add these to the stew when it is about half cooked, allowing them about one hour and a half. Serve the stew in the casserole or on a hot dish.

STEWED STEAK AND TOMATOES

INGREDIENTS.—1 lb. of buttock steak (cut thick), 2 onions, 1 lb. of tomatoes, 1 oz. of rice, 1 bunch of herbs, ½ pint of cold water, 1 tablespoonful of Bisto, pepper to taste, 1 oz. of dripping.

METHOD.—Wipe the meat with a damp cloth and cut it into four or five pieces. Chop the onions.

Cut a little fat off the steak and make it very hot in a frying-pan.

Put in the pieces of steak and fry them quickly for two minutes to brown the outside.

Put the browned steak on a plate and fry the onions slowly for ten minutes, adding a little dripping if necessary.

Put the meat in a double saucepan with cold water to cover it and cook it slowly. In twenty minutes (or when the steak is hot), add rice, onions, and herbs. Simmer for two hours, making sure that the saucepan lid fits very closely.

When the meat is cooked, thicken the stock in which it was cooked with Bisto.

Cut the tomatoes in half and fry them in the dripping and serve them round the meat.

NOTE.—If cheaper parts of meat are used, longer time must be allowed for cooking. Meat cooked according to these directions will be beautifully tender.

BRAISED SWEETBREADS AND CUCUMBER

INGREDIENTS.—One pair of sweetbreads, 1 carrot and onion and 2 strips of celery, 2 rashers of fat bacon, ½ pint of stock (see p. 12), 2 cucumbers, veal stuffing (see p. 155), 1 oz. of butter or dripping, ¾ pint of brown sauce or good gravy.

METHOD.—Soak the sweetbreads in cold water for two hours. Put them in a pan with enough cold water to cover them. Bring them just to the boil and then plunge them into cold water. After this, trim them and remove the fat. Press them between two dishes till they are cold. When cold, the sweetbreads are generally larded.

To braise them, put a sliced carrot and onion in a casserole with a bunch of herbs and the celery cut in short pieces. Lay the sweetbreads on this, and cover each with a rasher of bacon. Pour in the stock, cover the casserole, and put it in a fairly hot oven till the stock boils. Baste the sweetbreads and return them to the oven, cooking them rather quickly for twenty minutes or half an hour. They can be served in the casserole or else dished up on croûtons of fried bread surrounded with the stuffed cucumbers and the brown sauce in which they were cooked. The cucumbers are stuffed with veal stuffing (see p. 155) after the centres have been removed and the two halves are tied together with string. They are fried brown, the fat is poured off, and they then simmer in brown gravy for an hour, either in the oven or in a frying-pan.

SWEETBREADS AND FRENCH BEANS

INGREDIENTS.—2 calves' sweetbreads, 1 jar of glaze, 2 oz. of freshly boiled rice.

FOR THE GARNISH.— 1 lb. of French beans, ½ gill of double cream, salt and pepper.

FOR THE SAUCE.—¾ oz. of butter, ¾ oz. of flour, 1 gill of stock (see p. 12), 1 gill of milk, 1 bayleaf, 4 peppercorns, ½ teaspoonful of salt, 1 tablespoonful of cream.

METHOD.—Soak the sweetbreads in cold water for one hour. Put them in a pan with cold water to cover, bring them just to the boil, and throw away the water. Remove all skin and gristle.

Put the sweetbreads in a double saucepan with the stock, salt, bayleaf, and peppercorns, and simmer for one hour. Boil and strain the beans and mix them with half a gill of cream and a little salt and pepper. Melt the glaze by standing the jar in a pan of hot water.

Melt the butter, mix it with the flour and stir in the stock and milk. Stir till boiling, keep half the sauce for pouring round the sweetbreads, put half of it in another pan with the boiled rice. Lay the sweetbreads on the rice.

Brush them with glaze and pour the sauce round. Garnish with beans in heaps.

Sufficient for two persons.

NOTE.—It is not necessary to press the sweetbreads after par-boiling them as is often done. They can quite well be cooked at once.

SPANISH STEW AND SAVOURY ROLLS

INGREDIENTS.—1 lb. stewing beef, 1 lb. of tomatoes, 1 carrot, onion and turnip, 1 pint of stock (see p. 12), 1½ tablespoonfuls of flour, salt and pepper.

FOR THE SAVOURY ROLLS.— 1 level teaspoonful of baking powder, 6 oz. of flour, 3 oz. of suet, 1 dessertspoonful of minced onion, ¼ teaspoonful of salt, ¼ teaspoonful of mixed herbs, 1 level teaspoonful of chopped parsley, water to mix.

METHOD.—Cut the meat into convenient-sized pieces. Mix it with the flour (one and a half tablespoonfuls) and season it well. Put it into a casserole and stir in the stock. Put it in the oven, bring it to the boil and simmer it gently for about three hours.

Prepare the carrot, turnip and onion. Cut them into dice and add them to the stew when this is half cooked.

Take half the tomatoes, skin them, cut them into small pieces and add them with the other vegetables to the casserole. Halve the remainder of the tomatoes crosswise, and bake them lightly on a tin. Use them to put round the dish. They will take about fifteen minutes to cook.

TO MAKE THE SAVOURY ROLLS.— Chop the suet finely and add it to the flour, sifted with the salt and baking powder.

Stir in the onion, parsley and herbs, and mix all to a pliable dough with cold water.

Divide the dough into small portions,

make them into rolls, and add them to the stew, allowing them an hour or an hour and a half to cook.

Sufficient for four or five persons.

CREAMED TONGUE

INGREDIENTS.—½ lb. of cold tongue, 1¼ oz. of butter, 1 oz. of flour, ¾ pint milk, 1 teaspoonful of onion juice, 1 level dessertspoonful of chopped parsley, green peas, seasoning.

METHOD.—Melt the butter in a saucepan, add the flour and, when well blended, stir in the milk and bring it to the boil.

Boil the sauce gently for a few minutes, then add the onion-juice and seasoning to taste.

Cut the tongue into small dice and add to the sauce. Make it hot and stir in the parsley, serve the Creamed Tongue in a dish surrounded with a border of hot green peas.

Sufficient for four persons.

TRIPE OLIVES

INGREDIENTS.—1 lb. of tripe, 2 Spanish onions, 1 teaspoonful of made mustard, 1 dessertspoonful of chopped parsley, ½ pint of hot water, ½ gill of milk, 1½ oz. of butter, 1½ oz. of flour, salt and pepper.

FOR THE STUFFING.—1 cupful of breadcrumbs, 1 egg, 1 tablespoonful of chopped parsley, grated rind of ½ a lemon, 1 rasher of bacon, salt and pepper.

METHOD.—Put the tripe in a pan of cold water and bring it just to the boil.

Throw away the water and scrape any fat from the tripe.

Cut the tripe into strips about two inches wide and three or four inches long.

Wash, dry, and chop the parsley, and mix it with the other stuffing ingredients. Spread stuffing on the smooth side of each strip, roll it up and tie it with string. Slice the onions thinly and put them in a double saucepan with half a pint of hot water. Cook them for fifteen minutes with boiling water in the lower pan. Add half a teaspoonful of salt and the tripe olives, and cook them steadily for two hours. Tripe cooked like this cannot possibly stick and burn.

When the tripe is tender, take it out,

remove the strings, put the rolls on a hot dish with the onions, and keep them hot.

Blend the flour, butter, and mustard, add them to the water in which the tripe was cooked, and stir till it boils. Add the milk and parsley, and boil for three minutes. Pour over the tripe.

Sufficient for four persons.

BOILED VEAL ROLL AND BACON

INGREDIENTS.—2 lb. of middle neck veal, ½ lb. of pork sausages, a small joint of bacon (about 1 lb.), 2 lb. of onions, 1½ lb. of carrots.

FOR THE PARSLEY SAUCE.—2 oz. of flour, 2 oz. of margarine, ¾ pint of milk, ¼ pint of water, or liquor from the meat, 1 tablespoonful of chopped parsley.

METHOD.—Have the veal boned, then place it flat on a board. Skin the sausages and place them on the veal. Roll it up neatly and tie it with string.

Put the veal into a saucepan with boiling water to cover it. Bring it to the boil, remove the scum, and boil it for two or three minutes, then let it simmer gently for about one hour and a half.

Cook the vegetables and bacon in with the veal. The bacon will require about one hour and a quarter to cook. The carrots should be scraped and split in halves or quarters ; these will take as long as the veal. Peel the onions and cook them whole, allowing them about one hour, according to their size.

To serve, coat the veal with some of the parsley sauce, and arrange a few vegetables round it. Serve the remainder separately.

Sufficient for six to eight persons.

PARSLEY SAUCE

To make the sauce, melt the fat in a saucepan. Add the flour, and mix together until smooth. Add the liquid (cold) and stir it until the sauce boils. Season to taste. Simmer for six minutes.

Wash, scald, and finely chop the parsley, and add it to the sauce just before serving.

BRAISED BREAST OF VEAL

INGREDIENTS.—1 breast of veal (2½ lb.), 1 bunch of young onions,

1 lb. of carrots, 3 turnips, 1 bunch of herbs, 1 oz. of dripping, 1 oz. of flour, ¾ pint of stock (see p. 12), 1 oz. of rice, salt and pepper, ½ gill of cold milk.

FOR THE STUFFING.—½ pint of breadcrumbs, 3 oz. of suet, 1 rasher of bacon, 1 tablespoonful of chopped parsley, 1 level teaspoonful of mixed herbs, grated peel of ½ a lemon, 1 large egg, pepper and salt.

METHOD.—Choose a rather wide breast of veal. Lay it on a board, skin side down, and cut away the bones. Make stock with the bones by putting them in a pan with the herbs, one teaspoonful of salt, and one quart of cold water, and cook them slowly for two hours.

Peel the vegetables, leaving them whole if they are young and slicing them if they are old. Add the vegetables to the stock when it boils, and then simmer for about fifteen minutes while making the stuffing and browning the meat.

To stuff the meat, chop the suet finely, chop and fry the bacon, add all the other ingredients, and mix with a beaten egg.

Spread the stuffing on the meat, roll it up, and tie it round with string.

Heat the dripping in a casserole over an asbestos mat, put in the meat, and brown it all over quickly for ten minutes, keeping it turned all the time.

Pour off *all* the dripping.

Put the vegetables that have been boiling in the casserole with the meat, one pint of stock, and the rice.

Make sure that the lid fits closely, turn the gas down very low, and cook the veal slowly for an hour and three-quarters, or till tender.

Dish up the meat and remove the string.

Put the vegetables round the meat and keep hot while thickening the gravy.

Mix the flour to a smooth liquid with the milk, pour it into the gravy in the casserole, and stir till it boils. Boil for three minutes.

Serve some of the gravy round the dish, and put the rest in a sauce-boat.

BRAISED VEAL CUTLETS

INGREDIENTS.—2 thin slices of leg of veal (about 1¼ to 2 lb.), 2 carrots,

1 or 2 onions, $\frac{1}{2}$ a small turnip, 1 stalk of celery, spring of parsley, thyme and marjoram, $\frac{1}{2}$ pint of stock (see p. 12), seasoning, $1\frac{1}{2}$ oz. of butter, 2 oz. of fat bacon, tin of peas, or some freshly boiled peas.

METHOD.—Cut as many oval-shaped fillets as possible from the veal and beat them well with a cutlet bat, or failing this a wooden rolling-pin. Trim them so that they are as evenly shaped as possible.

Prepare the vegetables, cut them into quarters or thick chunky pieces, and steam them in the butter for a few minutes. Arrange them in a saucepan to make a bed on which to place the fillets. Fry the latter in the butter just enough to seal the outside and lightly brown them, then put them on to the bed of vegetables and pour in the stock (boiling)—this should not quite reach to the fillets. Add the seasoning and the herbs.

Cover the top with a buttered paper, put the lid on the pan and simmer the cutlets gently for about half an hour (fifteen minutes on top and fifteen in the oven), or until tender.

To serve the braised cutlets, arrange the fillets on a dish, thicken and brown the gravy, and strain it round them. Garnish each cutlet with a spoonful of bacon, chopped and fried until crisp, and heap cooked peas (previously heated, if tinned ones) on each side.

Allow one or two fillets (according to size) for each person.

BRAISED VEAL OLIVES

INGREDIENTS.—2 lb. of veal cutlets, 2 or 3 carrots and onions, $\frac{1}{2}$ small turnip, small sprig of parsley and thyme, seasoning, stock (see p. 12), 6 thin streaky rashers.

FOR THE STUFFING.—3 oz. of breadcrumbs, $1\frac{1}{2}$ oz. of butter, rind of half a lemon, 2 level dessertspoonfuls of chopped parsley, 2 teaspoonfuls of finely-chopped onion, $\frac{1}{2}$ teaspoonful of mixed herbs, egg or milk, seasoning.

METHOD.—Have the veal cut *very thinly*, beat it out with a cutlet bat, or if this is not available use the back of a large wooden spoon (dipping it in cold water).

Then cut the veal into oblong-shaped pieces, removing the skin.

Spread each with stuffing, roll it up and fasten with string or a tiny skewer. Flour the rolls, and let them brown in a saucepan with a little hot dripping, and put them on a plate.

To MAKE THE STUFFING.—Mix the breadcrumbs with the chopped onion and parsley, adding also the grated lemon-rind, mixed herbs and seasoning, then stir in the butter (melted), and moisten with egg or milk.

Prepare the vegetables and cut them into thick chunky pieces. There should be enough to form a bed in the bottom of the pan.

Steam these for a few minutes in the fat left in the pan, letting them colour only very slightly. Pour off the fat and arrange the veal on top of the vegetables.

Pour in sufficient boiling stock to reach almost to the top of the *vegetables*, add a small sprig of thyme and parsley. Cover them with a buttered paper, put the lid on the pan and cook gently for about half an hour or till all are tender. (Fifteen minutes on top and fifteen in the oven.)

Remove the string or skewers, arrange the olives on a dish, garnish them with bacon rolls and serve them with *slightly* thickened gravy, using the stock from the pan.

To PREPARE THE BACON ROLLS.— Remove the rind from the rashers, cut each in half, crosswise, roll them up and stick them on a skewer. Cook them under the grill or in the oven.

Trimmings of veal left over from this dish can be minced, mixed with a few breadcrumbs, seasoned and flavoured to taste, moistened with a spoonful of stock, then formed into cakes, floured and fried.

VEAL BRAWN

INGREDIENTS.—$\frac{3}{4}$ lb. of lean veal, salt and pepper, ground mace, about $\frac{1}{4}$ pint of stock (see p. 12), 6 oz. of collar of bacon, 1 saltspoonful of mixed herbs, 1 or 2 eggs, 1 onion, watercress.

METHOD.—Remove the bone from the veal and make a little stock, using the veal bone and adding an onion to flavour, and salt, pepper, and mace to taste.

Cut the rind from the bacon and

cut both the bacon and veal into dice, and season them with the herbs, salt, pepper, and mace to taste.

Hard-boil the egg, chop up the white and put it aside, and then chop the yolk. Put the veal and bacon into a tin, sprinkling it in layers with the chopped yolk of egg. Pour in sufficient stock to fill the tin about three parts full, then cover it with a well-greased paper and cook it gently in the oven for about an hour and a quarter, or longer if required. Fill up the tin with stock and leave it to set.

Turn it out, garnish it with chopped white of egg and watercress, and serve it with a salad.

Sufficient for four or five persons.

NOTE.—The stock should jelly when cold; if necessary, a little gelatine should be dissolved in it before it is added to the veal.

VEAL CAKES

INGREDIENTS.—¼ lb. of lean veal (trimmings from the veal rolls can be used), 1 oz. of breadcrumbs, 1 level teaspoonful of chopped parsley, pepper, salt, powdered mace, pinch of mixed herbs, egg and breadcrumbs for coating, lemon, gravy.

METHOD.—Put the veal through the mincer. There should be four ounces when minced.

Add the breadcrumbs, a little grated lemon-rind, parsley and herbs, and season them with salt, pepper and mace to taste. Add just a small part of a beaten egg to bind the mixture.

Divide the mixture into two portions, and form them into round cakes, flat at the top. Brush them with egg and coat them with breadcrumbs, and fry them gently in a little hot dripping until nicely browned, turning them over when brown on one side.

Serve the cakes on a hot dish with slightly thickened gravy, and garnish them with lemon.

TO MAKE THE GRAVY.— Pour off nearly all the dripping, leaving just enough to mix with the flour. Add a level teaspoonful of flour and stir it over a low burner until brown. Draw the pan aside and add about half a gill of stock. Boil this up, season and strain it.

Sufficient for one person.

CREAMED VEAL

INGREDIENTS.—Veal trimmings, ¼ pint of milk, ¼ pint of stock (white) see p. 12), ¾ oz. of flour, ¾ oz. of margarine, 1 dessertspoonful of onion-juice, salt and pepper, 6 mushrooms, butter.

METHOD.—Remove the skin from the veal and put the meat through the mincer. For this amount of sauce you will need quite half a pound of veal when minced.

Melt the margarine, add the flour, and when well blended stir in the milk and stock and bring all to the boil. Add the onion-juice, and seasoning to taste, then mix in the veal, and one mushroom prepared, cleansed, and chopped. Turn the mixture into a small casserole (if it seems too thick, thin it down slightly), and simmer it gently for from three-quarters of an hour to an hour, or until tender.

Serve the creamed veal on a hot dish and garnish it with the remainder of the mushrooms, which should have been peeled, washed, then halved and cooked in butter.

Sufficient for three persons.

CURRIED VEAL

INGREDIENTS.—1½ lb. of middle neck of veal, 2 onions, a few cloves, water, pepper and salt, 2 or 3 oz. dripping (for frying), 1½ oz. of desiccated coconut, ¾ gill of milk, lemon-juice, ½ oz. of flour, 3 oz. of rice, 1½ tablespoonfuls of curry powder.

METHOD.—Cut all the bones and gristle from the veal. Wash the bones and place in a saucepan, with an onion (peeled) and a few cloves stuck in it. Cover with water, season well, and bring slowly to the boil. Remove the scum, and simmer gently for about two or three hours.

Put the coconut and milk in a small pan, bring to the boil, and leave it soaking in the milk for about thirty minutes. This improves the flavour.

Cut the veal into square-shaped pieces, and peel and slice the other onion.

Melt the dripping in a saucepan, add the onion, and fry gently until very pale biscuit colour.

Take it out, and put in the meat. Fry lightly in the same way, and put aside.

To the remaining dripping add the curry powder and flour, and stir well until smooth (do not fry it). Then sprinkle in a little lemon-juice.

Strain off about three-quarters of a pint of the prepared stock, which should be free from grease.

Add this gradually to the curry powder, etc., and bring to the boil, keeping it well stirrred. Then add the strained milk from the coconut, and bring to the boil again.

Put in the meat and onion, and simmer gently for about one hour and a half.

Heap the veal and onion in the centre of a dish.

Pour round a little of the white gravy. Serve the rest separately.

Garnish with rice.

NOTE.—Wash the rice and put into a saucepan of boiling water with a little salt, and add the lemon-juice. Boil until tender. Strain, pour cold water through to separate the grains, and then re-heat and dry.

CURRIED VEAL AND PINE-APPLE

INGREDIENTS.—1 lb. of fillet of veal, 1 oz. of dripping, 1 heaped dessert-spoonful of curry powder, 1 onion, juice of ½ a lemon, 1 dessertspoonful of desiccated coconut, 1 dessert-spoonful of flour, a pinch of ground ginger and cinnamon, ½ cupful each of stock (see p. 12) and pineapple-juice, salt to taste, 1 tin of pineapple-slices, 4 rashers of bacon, 4 oz. of boiled rice.

METHOD.—Cut the meat into square chunks and chop the onion.

Cook the meat rather quickly in the dripping in a saucepan till it is light brown. Cook the onion for ten minutes ; then stir in the curry powder, flour, spice, and lemon-juice, and add gradually the stock and fruit-juice. Bring it to the boil and simmer for five minutes.

Add the meat and cook very gently at the side of the fire for thirty minutes.

Put in the coconut and simmer for ten minutes more.

Make the rashers of bacon into neat rolls, stick them on skewers, and grill them for five minutes.

Allow a slice of pineapple for each person, and place them on the dish in the oven to heat through.

Place a spoonful of curry on each slice, with a roll of bacon between.

To serve, pile the rice in the centre of the slices of pineapple.

Sufficient for six persons.

VEAL CUTLETS

INGREDIENTS.—1 lb. of veal cutlet, salt and pepper, 1 egg (beaten), breadcrumbs, 2 oz. of butter, 1 gill of thick gravy (see p. 100), ½ a lemon, 3 rashers of bacon, 1 small tin of asparagus.

METHOD.—Cut the cutlet into four or five neat rounds and season them with salt and pepper. Brush them over with egg and roll them in bread-crumbs.

Melt the butter, dip the cutlets in it and roll them in breadcrumbs again.

Heat the rest of the butter and fry the cutlets in it slowly for fifteen to twenty minutes, turning them several times.

Remove the rind from the bacon, cut the rashers in half, roll them up and put them on a skewer. Grill them for six minutes.

Heat the asparagus for five minutes in a baking-tin of hot water and heat the gravy. Place the cutlets round the asparagus and pour the gravy round them. Garnish with bacon and slices of lemon.

Sufficient for three or four persons.

VEAL CUTLET AND BACON

INGREDIENTS.—1 lb. of veal cutlet (from the leg of veal), 1 egg, white breadcrumbs, 4 or 5 rashers of bacon (medium thickness), stock (see p. 12), flour, browning, lemon, dripping.

METHOD.—The cutlet should not be cut very thick. Take out the small bone from the centre, and cut the cutlet into four or five even pieces.

Beat up the egg and brush them over with it, then coat with white breadcrumbs. Put a little dripping into a frying-pan, and when hot put in the prepared cutlets, and fry gently until golden brown on one side, then turn them over.

They will take about fifteen or twenty minutes altogether.

While the cutlets are cooking, the rashers of bacon can be grilled. Just remove the rind and grill them for about four or five minutes.

When both are ready, dish the veal cutlets on a hot dish with a rasher of bacon on each. Pour round the bacon fat, and keep warm whilst the gravy is made.

Pour off some of the dripping in which the veal was cooked, leaving only a small quantity in the bottom of the pan.

Dredge in a little flour, and stir slowly over the fire until brown. Be careful not to burn it.

Draw the pan off the fire and pour in some stock ; boil it up and season it. The gravy should now be brown and thick. Strain it round the veal and bacon, and garnish with slices of cut lemon.

Sufficient for four persons.

VEAL CUTLET AU FROMAGE

INGREDIENTS.—1 lb. of veal cutlet, 2 oz. of dripping or butter, 1 level dessertspoonful of flour, ½ pint of stock (see p. 12), seasoning, 1 oz. of margarine or butter, ¾ oz. of flour, 1 oz. of strips of cooked ham, 1 oz. of spaghetti, 1½ oz. of Parmesan cheese (finely grated), 1½ oz. of Cheddar cheese (finely grated), 1 egg, ½ pint of milk, 2½ tablespoonfuls of breadcrumbs.

METHOD.—Beat out the cutlet and divide it into about four pieces as evenly shaped as possible. Mix the breadcrumbs with one tablespoonful of each of the grated cheeses, and season it with pepper and salt.

Separate the egg, beat the white slightly and brush the veal with it. Coat the cutlet with the breadcrumbs and cheese.

Heat the dripping in a frying-pan and fry the cutlet gently till tender, turning it over when brown. Serve it accompanied by thickened brown gravy, and surrounded with some of the following sauce, the remainder of which may be served in a separate dish.

TO MAKE THE SAUCE.—Cook the spaghetti in boiling water with salt to flavour, and when tender, drain it.

Make a sauce with the margarine, flour and milk, let it boil for two or three minutes, then add the spaghetti, ham and remainder of the cheeses, and stir till the latter is dissolved. Take the pan off the heat and cool

the sauce slightly, add seasoning to taste and stir in the beaten yolk of egg. Cook it again for a minute or two without letting it boil.

TO MAKE THE GRAVY.—Pour off nearly all the dripping after frying the cutlets, add the flour (one level dessertspoonful) and stir it over a low burner till brown. Draw the pan aside and let the gravy cool for a minute. Add the stock, then boil it up. Add the seasoning and strain this gravy.

Sufficient for four persons.

BAKED VEAL CUTLET

INGREDIENTS.—2 lb. of veal cutlet (a thick slice of fillet or a slice from the shoulder), 2 onions, 1 lb. of tomatoes, 1 oz. of butter, 1 oz. of flour, ½ a lemon, salt and pepper, ½ pint of stock (see p. 12).

METHOD.—Mix the flour, salt and pepper, and dip the veal in it, so that it is well coated. Heat the butter in a baking-tin, and when it is very hot put in the veal and brown the outside as quickly as possible—two minutes for each side. Chop the onions. Put the meat on a plate and fry the onions. Cut the tomatoes in half and put them in the tin, with the meat in the centre lying on the onions. Bake in a moderate oven for thirty or forty minutes. Dish up with the tomatoes round the meat, and make a brown gravy by frying the flour and adding half a pint of stock. Boil the gravy and season well, flavouring it with lemon-juice. Strain round the meat.

Enough for four or five persons.

VEAL CUTLETS ITALIENNE

INGREDIENTS.—1¼ lb. of best end of neck of veal, 1 egg, 1 oz. of vermicelli, dripping, 1 oz. of breadcrumbs.

FOR THE SAUCE.—½ oz. of butter or margarine, ½ pint of peeled tomatoes (tinned), 1 tablespoonful of minced onion, ½ gill of stock (see p. 12), a small sprig of parsley and thyme, seasoning, 1½ dessertspoonfuls of flour, 1 oz. vermicelli.

METHOD.—Have the chine bone removed from the best end of the neck of veal and cut it into cutlets, scraping the meat from the end of the bones and trimming the cutlets into shape.

Season them and brush them with beaten egg, then coat them with a mixture of breadcrumbs and one ounce of vermicelli, crushed as finely as possible. Fry the cutlets in hot dripping and serve them on a dish, arranging them as shown, and with the sauce poured at one side.

Thickened brown gravy may also be served in a sauce boat.

To MAKE THE SAUCE.—Melt the fat in a saucepan and cook the onion in it for a few minutes without browning it. Draw the pan aside and add the tomatoes with the liquor, also the sprig of parsley and thyme, and the stock.

Cook them gently till tender, then rub them through a sieve.. Thicken the sauce with the flour smoothed in a little water, boil it for a few minutes, season it and add the remaining ounce of vermicelli. The latter should have been previously cooked in slightly salted boiling water until tender.

Sufficient for four cutlets.

FRICASSEE OF VEAL

INGREDIENTS.—½ lb. of cold veal, ¼ lb. of mushrooms, 3 new-laid eggs, 2 rashers of bacon, salt and pepper, ½ oz. of butter, ½ oz. of flour, ½ gill of stock (see p. 12), ½ gill of milk, 1 tablespoonful of lemon-juice.

METHOD.—Cut the bacon in strips and fry it. Peel, remove the stalks and chop the mushrooms and fry them gently for five minutes in the bacon fat. Pour off the fat and put in the butter. Stir in the flour, stock and milk and bring it to the boil.

Add the veal, cut in neat square pieces, and bring it just to the boil. Simmer *very gently* to heat the meat through; it should not be allowed to go on boiling or it will be tough. Season to taste and pour into a hot dish.

Serve the fricassee with three poached eggs on the top.

To POACH THE EGGS.

Have ready a small pan of boiling water containing a teaspoonful of salt and a dessertspoonful of vinegar. The eggs should be new-laid. Stale eggs will never poach properly. Break the eggs into a cup and slide them gently into the water. The vinegar helps the white to set. Cook them for three minutes and place on top of the veal.

One of the best ways of heating the fricassee is to put it in a double saucepan for about twenty minutes.

Sufficient for three persons.

GALANTINE OF VEAL

A GALANTINE makes a very attractive luncheon dish and is also suitable for parties or wedding breakfasts. This simple recipe takes only a short time to prepare, and is most delicious.

INGREDIENTS.—1¼ lb. of veal (when minced), ½ lb. of bacon, 4 hard-boiled eggs, 2 raw eggs, 4 oz. of breadcrumbs, 2 teaspoonfuls of chopped parsley, powdered mace, pepper and salt, ¼ pint of stock (see p. 12), meat glaze, butter, 1 carrot and 2 small onions.

METHOD.—For galantine you will need a piece of the middle of the shoulder, or the meaty end of the knuckle of veal.

Do not get it too near the knuckle or it will be gristly.

If you buy from one and a half to one and three-quarter pounds of veal, this will allow for the bone; or you can use veal cutlet, which is more expensive, but has less bone.

Remove the bone, skin the veal, and put it through the mincer.

Then make some stock with the bone—if any—adding an onion and a little mace to flavour.

Remove the rind and then mince the bacon. Mix it with the veal, adding the breadcrumbs, parsley, salt, pepper, and mace to taste. Beat up the eggs and stir them in with the stock.

Have the four eggs ready hard-boiled. Remove the shells and let them cool. They will take from twelve to fifteen minutes to boil.

Arrange the prepared veal mixture on the pastry board to form a fat roll about the desired length of the galantine. Make a hollow down the centre of it and press the eggs into it.

Next draw the veal mixture over them, so as to cover them completely, and form a roll again.

Roll it tightly in a scalded pudding-cloth, and tie it securely at each end like a roly-poly.

Put the roll into a pan with sufficient boiling stock or water to cover it, adding the veal bone and prepared carrot and onion to flavour. Let the roll simmer gently for about an hour and a half.

Lift out the roll carefully and drain it. Unroll the cloth and let out the steam. Then roll the galantine in a clean, dry cloth, and tie it as before.

Place a board or dish and two two-pound weights on top of it, just to press the top slightly. Leave the galantine till it is quite cold.

To Glaze and Decorate the Galantine.—Remove the pudding-cloth and put the roll on a rack, placed on a meat dish.

Open the glaze, stand the container in a saucepan with a little water and heat it until it liquefies, then brush the galantine roll quickly over with it.

Leave the glaze to set, then decorate the galantine with butter, beaten until creamy and forced through an icing-pump.

Trim off a slice from each end of the galantine and serve salad with it.

The glaze can be obtained from almost any grocery store in small jars.

GATEAU OF COLD VEAL

INGREDIENTS.—½ lb. of cold veal, 1 oz. of butter or good veal fat, 2 eggs, 1 gill of fresh breadcrumbs, dry bread-crumbs for frying, ½ gill of hot milk, 4 rashers of bacon, salt and pepper, grated peel of a lemon.

METHOD.—Soak the fresh bread-crumbs in the hot milk and squeeze them dry. Mince the meat and fat and add them to the breadcrumbs, with the grated lemon-peel and season-ing. Beat the eggs and add them to the mixture, keeping back a little to brush over the gateau. Shape the mixture into a flat cake, brush it over with the rest of the egg, and roll it in dry breadcrumbs and place it in a baking-tin.

Place a few small pieces of dripping on the top and bake the gateau in a hot oven till nicely browned.

Remove the rind from the bacon and cut the rashers in half. Roll them up, run a skewer through them and bake them in the same tin as the meat

for about ten minutes, or grill them under the gas griller.

Serve the gateau on a hot dish, garnished with the rolls of bacon and surrounded with tomato or piquante sauce.

Sufficient for three or four persons.

VEAL, HAM AND EGG MOULD

INGREDIENTS.—1½ lb. of middle neck of veal, 1 onion, water to cover the veal bones, 2 eggs, pepper, salt, and mace, 4 sheets of leaf gelatine, a few cloves and mixed herbs, 6 oz. of bacon or ham, ¾ to 1 gill of water or stock (see p. 12).

METHOD.—Bone the veal. Wash the bones and put them into a sauce-pan. Cover them with water, add a little salt, and bring slowly to the boil.

Peel the onion and stick a few cloves into it, tie the herbs in muslin.

Skim the stock, and add the onion, herbs, pepper, and mace to flavour, simmer for about two or three hours.

Boil the eggs for fifteen minutes until hard.

Peel them and cut into slices.

Wash the veal and dry in a cloth.

Cut the bacon and veal into small pieces.

Take a small basin or pie-dish and line the bottom of it with slices of egg.

Chop up the remainder of the egg and mix with the veal and bacon, season well with pepper, salt, and powdered mace.

Put in about half the veal, etc., then two sheets of gelatine, three-quarters to a gill of water or stock, then the remainder of the veal, etc.

Cover with a greased paper, and bake in a moderately hot oven for about one hour and a half, being careful not to brown it.

Add two sheets of gelatine to the stock; when dissolved, strain it and skim off the fat.

When the mould is cooked, pour in sufficient stock to cover the meat well.

Leave until quite set, then turn on to a dish.

Garnish with parsley.

NOTE.—Take out the herbs after the first half an hour or they will discolour the stock.

*Galantine
of
Veal*

Press the eggs
into the
centre.

Decorate the
galantine
with creamed
butter.

*The Finished
Galantine*

PLATE 15

Fried Mutton Cutlets and Green Peas

Brush the cutlets with egg and coat them with bread-crumbs.

Fry them gently, turning them over when brown on one side.

The Finished Dish

PLATE 16

VEAL AND HAM PIE

INGREDIENTS.—2 lb. of scrap and middle neck of veal or best end of knuckle, 1 lb. of pork sausages, ¾ lb. of bacon, 2 eggs, 4 sheets of leaf gelatine, salt, pepper, powdered mace, 1 onion, ½ teaspoonful of mixed herbs.

FOR THE PASTRY.—¾ lb. of flour, a pinch of salt, water to mix, 6 oz. of lard, 5 oz. of margarine.

METHOD.—To make a good flaky pastry, first sieve the flour with the salt, and rub in the margarine. Add a little cold water, and mix the flour with it to make a stiff paste.

Place the lard on a well-floured board, and roll it out into thin pieces. Put them on one side.

Now roll out the pastry fairly thinly to a square shape, turn it on to the other side and place the lard all over it, pressing it down lightly. Fold the sides to the middle each way, then fold the pastry in half again. (The paste should now be folded into eight.)

If the pastry is made a day before it is to be baked, it will be improved. It should be kept in a cool place, covered with a piece of buttered paper to prevent it from getting dry on the outside.

PREPARING THE MEAT

HAVE the veal boned out. Put the bones into a saucepan with a peeled onion, a little salt, and enough water to cover well. Bring them to the boil slowly, remove the scum, and let the stock simmer gently for two or three hours, adding pepper and mace to season it, and a few herbs tied in muslin to flavour. (The herbs should be removed after about half an hour's cooking, as if they are left in longer they will discolour the stock.)

Cut the veal into chunky pieces.

Boil the eggs for fifteen minutes until hard, shell them, and cut them into slices.

Cut up the bacon after first removing the rind, then skin the sausages. This will be quite easy to do if they are placed in cold water for a minute and then cut down the length of the skin.

Put about one-third of the veal in the bottom of the pie-dish (two-pint size), season it well, add a layer of bacon, some slices of egg, and some sausage meat, using half only of each. Continue in this way until the dish is full, leaving enough veal for the top. Each layer must be well seasoned with mace, salt and pepper, and two sheets of leaf gelatine placed in about the centre of the layers. Pour in a little water (three-quarters of a gill), just enough to keep the meat moist while it is cooking. It is then ready for the pastry cover.

COVERING THE PIE

ROLL out the pastry thickly—about three-eighths of an inch thick—and cut a piece to fit the top of the dish. Put this aside, and roll out some of the pastry trimmings to make them thinner. Cut a strip for the edge of the pie-dish, damp the edge of the dish, and cover it with pastry. Next damp the pastry edge and put the cover on. Trim the edge and make a hole in the centre of the lid.

Roll out the remaining pastry and cut four leaves and make a tassel for the top of the pie (as described later). Brush the pastry with egg or milk, place the tassel in the centre, and arrange the leaves on the pie. About one inch from each edge make a slit, and put the pie into a hot oven to bake.

When the pastry has risen well and browned lightly, turn the gas quite low and finish cooking the pie. It should take about an hour and a half.

The pie may be covered with a sheet of paper to prevent further browning.

When cooked, remove the centre tassel, and be *sure to see that the holes are well opened so that the steam may escape.*

Now fill up the pie with veal stock (made from the bones), pouring it through a funnel. Replace the tassel before serving the pie cold. It should cut firmly, the stock having formed a jelly.

When the stock has simmered for a few hours, add to it two sheets of leaf gelatine. When this is dissolved, strain the liquor and skim off any fat that may be on top. The stock is now ready for the pie

THE LEAVES AND TASSEL

To make the leaves, roll out the pastry to a quarter-inch thickness.

F

Cut a strip three-quarters of an inch wide, then cut four diamond-shaped pieces of pastry by first trimming a piece from the top, cutting in a slanting direction, and then making four parallel cuts three-quarters of an inch apart. On these diamond-shaped pieces, mark lines with a knife.

For the tassel the pastry should be rolled out to an eighth-of-an-inch thickness, and cut into a piece two and a quarter inches by four and a half inches. Cut along one side of this, making a fringe, then roll it up and place the uncut edge in the centre of the pie, arranging the cut ends on the top.

RAISED VEAL PIE

INGREDIENTS.—1 lb. of stewing veal (after bone is removed), 1 hard-boiled egg, 6 oz. of bacon, salt and pepper, powdered mace, 1 lb. of flour, 1 onion, 6 oz. of lard, 1½ gills of milk, gelatine if required.

METHOD.—Remove the bone from the veal and put the meat through the mincer.

Cut the rind from the bacon and mince it also.

Chop up the hard-boiled egg and mix it with the veal and bacon, and add seasoning to taste.

Sift the flour with a pinch of salt, heat the milk and lard in a saucepan, and when the latter is melted and the mixture boiling, stir it on to the flour and mix it to a pliable dough.

Cut off one-third of the dough, put this aside, and keep it warm. Meanwhile, turn the remainder on to a board, work it until free from cracks, and roll it out. Cut a round and line a buttered raised pie-tin, pressing the pastry to the shape of the tin. Moisten the prepared meat with just a very little stock, and put it into the lined tin, which should be full.

Now roll out the remainder of the paste and cut a round exactly to fit the top. Damp the edge of the lining and cover the pie, pressing the edges together.

Trim and decorate the edge, *make a hole* in the centre, and put a few leaves of pastry on the top.

Brush the top with egg and put the pie into a hot oven at first, then lessen the heat later as required.

It will take about two hours to cook.

Cool the pie a little, then fill up with warm stock made from the veal bones and flavoured with onion and mace.

Serve the raised veal pie cold.

Sufficient for from six to eight persons.

NOTE.—The stock should form a jelly when cold, so, if necessary, dissolve two or three leaves of gelatine in it before adding it to the pie. The centre of the pie can be decorated with a tassel of pastry, but it must be removed directly the pie is taken from the oven, to allow the steam to escape. When cold, it may be replaced.

RICH VEAL PIE

INGREDIENTS.—1 lb. fillet of veal, ¼ lb. of bacon (chopped), ¾ packet of aspic jelly, 2 hard-boiled eggs (sliced), ¾ lb. of flaky pastry (see p. 252), 1 egg (beaten).

FOR THE FORCEMEAT.—½ cupful of breadcrumbs, 1 oz. of shredded suet, 1 egg, 1 tablespoonful of chopped parsley, ½ teaspoonful of mixed herbs, salt and pepper, grated rind of a lemon.

METHOD.—Mix the dry forcemeat ingredients and bind with the beaten egg.

Cut the veal in strips three inches long, spread them with forcemeat, and roll them up.

Put the veal rolls, bacon and hard-boiled eggs in a pie-dish with half a gill of water.

Roll out the pastry, cut off a strip and press it on the edge of the dish which should be moistened. Brush the strip of pastry with water and cover the pie.

Press the edges lightly and scallop them with a knife. Decorate the pie with leaves made from diamond-shaped pieces of pastry.

Brush the top of the pie with a beaten egg and bake for one hour and a half, having a hot oven for the first fifteen minutes and a slow one to finish.

Dissolve the jelly in half a pint of hot water, pour it slowly through the hole in the pie and leave it to set.

Sufficient for four or five persons.

VEAL AND HAM RISSOLES

INGREDIENTS.—About ½ lb. of flaky pastry (see p. 252), 3 oz. of cold veal and ham, ½ gill of thick white sauce (see p. 41), salt, pepper, and powdered mace, egg and breadcrumbs, deep fat for frying.

METHOD.—Mince the meat and season it well. Make the white sauce, stir in the prepared meat, and leave until cold. Roll out the pastry fairly thinly and cut into small rounds—about three inches in diameter.

Put some of the meat and sauce on one half of each round of pastry, damp the edge, fold the other half over, and press the edges together. Brush with egg, coat with breadcrumbs, and fry in a deep pan of hot fat until golden brown.

Drain on paper and serve on a dish paper.

Sufficient to make about a dozen small rissoles.

VEAL AND HAM SHORTCAKE

INGREDIENTS.—FOR THE FILLING : 9 oz. of veal (cooked), 3 oz. of ham (cooked), ¾ pint of milk, 1½ oz. of margarine, 1¼ oz. of flour, 1 dessert-spoonful of finely minced onion, salt and pepper, ½ teaspoonful of finely grated lemon-rind, pinch of herbs, 1 teaspoonful of finely chopped parsley.

FOR THE SHORTCAKE.—¾ lb. of flour, 3 oz. of margarine, 3 teaspoonfuls of baking powder, ¼ teaspoonful of salt, milk or milk-and-water to mix.

METHOD.—To make the shortcake, sift the flour with the salt and baking powder, rub in the margarine, then mix them to a soft dough with milk-and-water.

Divide the dough into two portions. Roll each out to a round the size of your sandwich tin, which should be buttered, and put one piece of dough in the bottom of the tin. Brush the top of it with melted butter, and place the other round of dough on top.

Put it in a fairly hot oven to bake. It will take about half an hour.

Remove the top round, heap the filling on the under one and cover it with the top round.

Serve the shortcake on a hot dish and garnish it with parsley.

To PREPARE THE FILLING.—Cut the veal and ham into small dice, removing skin and gristle, and mix it with the onion, lemon-rind, herbs, parsley, and seasoning.

Melt the margarine, stir in the flour, and when well blended, add the milk and bring it to the boil.

Season, and let it simmer for a minute or two, then add the prepared meat and make it hot.

Sufficient for six persons.

BOILED KNUCKLE OF VEAL

INGREDIENTS.—Knuckle of veal, 2 or 3 onions, outside leaves of a head of celery or ½ teaspoonful of celery seeds, 2 carrots and turnips, peel of ½ a lemon, 1 teaspoonful of salt, 1 bunch of herbs.

FOR THE SAUCE.—1½ oz. of butter and flour, ½ pint of water in which the veal is cooked, ¼ pint of milk, 1 table-spoonful of chopped parsley, salt and pepper.

METHOD.—Put the veal in a pan with enough warm water just to cover it, add the salt, and bring it to the boil. Put in the vegetables, peeled and cut in quarters, the celery seeds tied in muslin, and the herbs.

Put on the lid and simmer very gently till tender (about two hours). Skim when necessary. Serve the veal with the parsley sauce poured over and the vegetables put round as a garnish.

NOTE.—Knuckle of veal may be either a knuckle cut from the leg or from the shoulder. The shoulder knuckle is smaller. The butcher should chop it into three or four pieces.

It is economical because it furnishes soup, meat, and vegetables in the one dish.

Enough for four persons.

PARSLEY SAUCE

PICK the stalks off the parsley, wash the leaves, and squeeze them dry in a cloth. Chop finely.

Melt the butter in a saucepan and add the flour.

Take the pan off the gas and stir in the flour. Add the hot stock (the water in which the veal was cooked).

Stir till it boils and boil for three minutes ; add the milk and heat for a few minutes.

Add the parsley and season to taste

VEAL KROMESKIES

INGREDIENTS.—¼ lb. of cooked veal, 2 oz. of cooked ham, pepper and salt, and mace, 2 teaspoonfuls of chopped onion (cooked), 3 tablespoonfuls of thick white sauce (see. p. 41), 6 or 8 slices of thin fat bacon (raw).

FOR THE BATTER.—3 oz. of flour, 1 egg, 1 dessertspoonful of salad oil, ¾ gill of warm water, a pinch of salt, fat for frying.

METHOD.—Sieve together the flour and salt, and make a hole in the centre.

Separate the yolk from the white of egg, put the yolk in the hole in the flour with the oil and mix with a small quantity of flour until like a thick custard. Then gradually add the water and slowly mix in the flour.

Beat well until the surface is covered in bubbles, then stand it aside for about one hour.

Mince the cooked veal and ham.

Heat the white sauce, add the minced meat and chopped onion, and season well with pepper, salt and powdered mace.

Leave until cool, then divide into about six equal portions.

Make each into the shape of a sausage.

Roll a piece of fat bacon round the outside.

Whisk the white of eggs to a stiff froth and fold into the batter.

Put three or four kromeskies into the batter and well coat them, then put into a deep pan of hot fat and fry until golden brown; they will take about ten minutes to cook. Then drain well on paper.

Coat and fry the others in the same way.

Serve on paper, garnish with parsley.

VEAL MINCE

INGREDIENTS.—¾ lb. of veal cutlet, or 1¼ lb. of knuckle veal (the meaty end), ¼ lb. of bacon (6 thin rashers), 1 onoin, ½ pint of thick brown gravy (see p. 100), salt, pepper and powdered mace.

METHOD.—Remove any bone or gristle from the veal, and put the meat through the mincer.

Peel and grate the onion and put it into a saucepan with some dripping. Fry it gently until brown, then draw it aside, pour off the fat, and add the gravy. Bring it to the boil, and

season it well. Add the veal and cook the mince gently for about three-quarters of an hour.

Remove the rind from the rashers, roll them, and stick them on to an iron skewer. Cook them in the oven or under the grill for a few minutes—any fat that comes from them can be added to the mince. To serve, turn the gravy and veal on to a hot dish and garnish it with the rolls of bacon.

Sufficient for four persons.

MINCE OF FRESH VEAL

INGREDIENTS.—1 lb. of fillet of veal, 4 oz. of ham, 1 apple, 1 onion, 1 potato, 1 oz. of butter, 1 oz. of flour, 1½ gills of stock (see p. 12), salt and pepper, juice of ½ a lemon, fried croûtons (see p. 12).

METHOD.—Mince the veal and ham. Chop the apple, onion and potato.

Heat the butter in a baking-tin and fry the vegetables for five minutes. When they are soft, add the minced veal, mix well together and season.

Place the mixture in a hot oven for eight minutes (not longer). If left too long in a hot oven the meat will be tough.

Mix the flour smoothly with the stock and lemon-juice, and stir this gradually into the mince. Place it in a *very slow* oven for half an hour.

Stir the mince well several times while it is cooking so that no lumps may be formed.

Serve in a hot dish, surrounded with fried croûtons of bread.

Sufficient for four of five persons.

NOTE.—A mince can be made of any kind of fresh meat (steak or mutton cutlet would be suitable). Fresh meat makes a more tasty mince than cold meat re-heated.

A ROAST OF VEAL

(WITH STUFFING, SAUSAGES AND BACON ROLLS)

INGREDIENTS.—Chump end of loin of veal, dripping, 1 lb. of sausages, 6 streaky rashers.

FOR THE STUFFING.—4 oz. of bread-crumbs, 2 oz. of chopped suet, 2 level tablespoonfuls of chopped parsley, ½ lemon (rind and juice), 1 level tea-spoonful of mixed herbs, 1 egg, seasoning.

METHOD.—Choose a chump of veal

about four or four and a half pounds,
and have the cup-bone removed.
Stuff it with veal stuffing made from
the rest of the ingredients and make
it secure with a skewer.

Put it into a baking-tin with
dripping, cover it with a thickly
greased paper or a piece of thin caul
and bake it for about an hour and
three-quarters, basting it occasionally.

The sausages can be cooked in the
tin with the veal, allowing them about
half an hour.

Serve the veal with slightly thickened gravy, and garnish it with the
sausages and bacon rolls. If preferred,
a piece of boiled bacon can be served.
Bread sauce is also a suitable
accompaniment (see p. 83).

To Prepare the Bacon Rolls.—
Remove the rind from rashers, cut
them in halves and form them into rolls.
Stick them on a skewer and cook them
in the oven or under the grill.

VEAL ROLLS

Ingredients.—About 1 lb. of veal
cutlet (cut thinly), 1 oz. of butter,
1 dessertspoonful of finely-minced
onion, salt, pepper, and ground mace,
3 oz. of breadcrumbs, egg, parsley,
dripping.

Method.—Cut the veal into about
three pieces, measuring roughly about
five inches by three, or a little smaller,
and beat out so as to flatten them as
much as possible.

Mix the onion with the breadcrumbs,
and season them with salt, pepper,
and mace. Add the butter (melted)
and sufficient egg to bind.

Season the veal and spread the
prepared stuffing over it ; then roll
the meat up and sew it with string
to keep the rolls in shape.

Put them into a baking tin, with
dripping, and bake them for about
thirty-five minutes, or until tender,
keeping them well basted. Dish up
the rolls, remove the string, and stand
them on end. Garnish them with parsley, and serve with slightly thickened
gravy poured round the dish.

Allow one or two rolls for each
person.

VIENNA STEAKS

Ingredients.—1 lb. of lean buttock
steak, 1 large Spanish onion, flour,

1 egg, 1½ oz. of breadcrumbs, salt and
pepper, 6 slices of tomato a little stock
(see p. 12), if required, dripping.

Method.—Peel the onion and slice
it thinly, then remove some of the
outer rings, being careful to keep
them whole.

Put the remainder of the onion
through the mincer with the steak.
Add the breadcrumbs and seasoning
to taste, and moisten them with the
yolk of the egg, and a spoonful of stock
if required.

Divide the mixture into six portions,
and form them into round, flat cakes.
Dredge them with flour, and fry them
gently, turning them over when
brown.

Serve a slice of tomato, lightly
baked in the oven, on each steak.
Garnish the dish with fried onion
rings, and serve it with thick gravy.

To Prepare the Onion Rings.—
Dip them in lightly beaten white of
egg and in flour, then fry them until
golden brown in dripping.

Sufficient for six steaks.

WESTERN EGGS

Ingredients.—2 eggs, 2 tablespoonfuls of milk, salt and pepper,
1 oz. of butter, 2 oz. of cold meat,
2 oz. of onion, 1 teaspoonful of flour,
½ gill of stock (see p. 12), 4 slices of
tomato, 4 rounds of fried bread.

Method.—Peel and mince the onion
and fry it in a little dripping until
golden brown. Draw the pan aside
and drain off some of the fat, if there
is too much. Add the flour, and when
well blended, stir in the stock and boil
it up.

Add browning as required, and
seasoning to taste, also the meat,
previously put through the mincer,
and make them hot.

Serve the mince on rounds of fried
bread, then add a slice of tomato
lightly baked in the oven, and top it
with scrambled egg.

To prepare the eggs, beat them up,
add the milk and seasoning to taste.
Melt the butter in a saucepan, stir
in the eggs, and continue to stir them
over a low burner until they begin to
thicken and set.

Sufficient for two persons.

SALADS

SALADS, both sweet and savoury, are becoming more and more popular.

They may be served with hot or cold meat or poultry ; or they may make a course of their own, served in dainty individual dishes.

The most popular salad is made from a mixture of green plants— lettuce, mustard and cress, endive, batavia, and watercress. Batavia and endive are slightly bitter, and they should be used with discretion.

DRAINING THE PLANTS

ALL these plants should be picked over carefully and thoroughly washed in cold water. Then leave them to soak for a short time in a bowl of clean cold water. Later they should be lifted out into a colander to drain. Toss them lightly in the colander or in a cloth, and you will get rid of most of the water.

TO SERVE SALAD

IF you like the flavour of onion, the bowl in which the salad is to be served should be rubbed with a piece of garlic. This imparts that delicate oniony flavour which is such an improvement. Spring onions, too, can be peeled and cut up with the other green plants, or they can be added whole.

Chicory is often used in this kind of salad, but it is rather bitter, so it should be used sparingly. Wash it and trim it and cut into small pieces.

Some people like their salads dressed in a plain French dressing. If you prefer it so, you should just toss the salad plants in the dressing a minute or two before you are ready to serve the salad. If you do this too long beforehand the leaves will lose their crispness and their fresh colour.

Many would rather serve a salad cream, and this can be made at home or bought ready-made at any grocers.

TO KEEP LETTUCE CRISP

LETTUCES keep best when they are turned upside down and laid in a cool, shady place. If kept too long in water, they soon decay.

A lettuce with a good heart feels firm inside when pressed.

A green salad should be mixed just before it is required in order to be crisp. If kept waiting, it becomes limp.

When making up a Green Salad, remember to break up the leaves instead of cutting them with a knife.

Salads can be made attractive by garnishing them in various ways, such as with sliced hard-boiled eggs, powdered egg-yolk, or whites cut into petal shapes with a centre of powdered yolk, radishes cut to give a floral effect, beetroot cut in fancy shapes, or cucumber cones.

TO HARD-BOIL AN EGG.—Put it into boiling water and boil it for fifteen minutes.

When cooked, crack the shell and put the egg into cold water for a few minutes—this prevents the dark lines which sometimes form between the yolk and the white.

TO PEEL TOMATOES.—Drop them into boiling water for a second or two, when the peel can be easily removed.

PICKLED EGGS FOR SALADS

BOIL the eggs for ten minutes, dip them in cold water and remove the shells. Put the eggs in a glass jar and pour on enough cold vinegar to cover them.

NOTE.—If the eggs are kept well covered with vinegar they will keep for a long time and are ready to use as required.

CHEESE BALLS

INGREDIENTS.—2 hard-boiled eggs, 1 cream cheese, 2 tablespoonfuls of grated cheese, $\frac{1}{2}$ tablespoonful of mayonnaise (see p. 168), cayenne.

METHOD.—Mince the eggs as finely as possible, and put them in a basin with the cream cheese. Add the other ingredients and blend all together with a wooden spoon. Shape into small balls and use them to decorate a salad.

CARROT AND CHEESE BALLS

INGREDIENTS.—2 carrots, $\frac{1}{4}$ onion, 1 cream cheese, the yolks of 2 hard-boiled eggs, cayenne.

METHOD.—Scrape the carrots and grate them on a bread grater. Chop the onion finely.

Mash the yolks, mix them with the other ingredients and form them into balls.

HOME-MADE SALAD CREAM

INGREDIENTS.—2 oz. of flour, 2 oz. of margarine, $\frac{1}{2}$ pint of milk and water, $\frac{3}{4}$ gill of salad oil, 1 teaspoonful of castor sugar, 3 teaspoonfuls of mustard, 1 teaspoonful of salt, pepper, $1\frac{1}{2}$ gills of vinegar.

METHOD.—Melt the fat in a saucepan, stir in the flour and, when it is mixed smoothly, add the milk and water.

Bring the liquid to the boil and let it go on boiling for a few minutes, keeping it well stirred. Then turn it into a basin and cover it with cold water.

When cold, pour off the water and whisk up the sauce. Next, whisk in the salad oil and vinegar alternately, adding only a very small quantity of each at one time.

Mix the mustard with some vinegar (extra to that given in the list of ingredients), and add it with the sugar, salt and pepper to the cream.

Thoroughly whisk and blend all the ingredients. Then bottle the cream and keep it to use as required.

If the cream should become a little too thick, whisk in some more vinegar; if too thin, add more oil. You will find the cream keeps a good white colour if you use half or all *white* vinegar.

CREAM SALAD DRESSING

INGREDIENTS.—3 tablespoonfuls of double cream, 1 teaspoonful of lemon-juice, 1 teaspoonful of grated onion, 1 teaspoonful of tomato ketchup, 1 dessertspoonful of vinegar, salt, pepper.

METHOD.—Beat the cream till thick with a fork.

Mix it gradually with the other ingredients and season to taste with salt and pepper.

To make one gill of dressing.

ANOTHER CREAM DRESSING

INGREDIENTS.—2 tablespoonfuls of thick cream, $\frac{1}{2}$ a teaspoonful of Worcester sauce, a pinch of castor sugar, salt and pepper, lemon-juice to suit taste (about one dessertspoonful).

METHOD.—Mix the cream gradually with the Worcester sauce, sugar, salt and pepper, and stir in the lemon-juice by degrees.

CORNFLOUR SALAD DRESSING

INGREDIENTS.—1 egg, $1\frac{1}{2}$ teaspoonfuls of cornflour, $\frac{3}{4}$ pint of milk, 1 gill of white vinegar, 3 teaspoonfuls of mustard, 2 dessertspoonfuls of salad oil, salt and pepper, 2 dessertspoonfuls of castor sugar.

METHOD.—Whisk up the egg, then pour the milk on to it.

Put the mustard and cornflour into a basin and mix them to a paste with the oil, add the sugar and vinegar, stirring the latter in *gradually*.

Add these ingredients to the egg and milk *by degrees*, season with pepper and salt and strain into a saucepan.

Boil for a few minutes, keeping it well stirred. Bottle when cool, and when cold cork securely.

CONDENSED MILK SALAD DRESSING

INGREDIENTS.—2 hard-boiled yolks, 1 teaspoonful made mustard, 1 tin of unsweetened condensed milk, $\frac{3}{4}$ gill of vinegar, $\frac{1}{2}$ oz. of sugar, pepper, salt.

METHOD.—Mix yolks and mustard smoothly. Add sugar and milk by degrees. Stir in vinegar, season to taste. To make two gills of dressing.

ECONOMICAL SALAD DRESSING
(WITHOUT OIL)

INGREDIENTS.—1 oz. of butter, $\frac{1}{2}$ pint of milk, 1 oz. of flour, 2 teaspoonfuls of made mustard, 1 raw yolk,

1 teaspoonful of sugar, salt and cayenne to taste, ¾ gill of vinegar.

METHOD.—Melt the butter, add the flour and mustard, and stir in the milk. Stir till it boils, and add salt and cayenne to taste.

Mix the yolk and sugar together and pour them on the hot sauce.

Add the vinegar by degrees.

To make three gills of salad dressing.

FRENCH SALAD DRESSING

INGREDIENTS.—3 tablespoonfuls of olive oil, ¾ saltspoonful of salt, ¾ saltspoonful of mixed mustard, pinch of white pepper, 1½ tablespoonfuls of vinegar.

METHOD.—Put the oil into a large basin, stir in the salt, mustard, and pepper.

Mix all together thoroughly with a wooden spoon.

Add drop by drop the vinegar, keeping it well stirred all the time.

Toss the prepared salad into the dressing just before sending to table. If the green salad is allowed to lie in the vinegar for any length of time it will turn limp and black.

ITALIAN SALAD DRESSING

INGREDIENTS.—1 teaspoonful of grated onion, ½ teaspoonful of salt, a shake of pepper, 1 hard-boiled egg, 4 tablespoonfuls of olive oil, 2 tablespoonfuls of vinegar.

METHOD.—Mix the yolk smoothly with the oil, onion, salt and a little pepper. Stir in the vinegar.

To make one gill dressing.

OIL MAYONNAISE

INGREDIENTS.—1 yolk of egg, 1 gill of salad oil, 1 or 2 teaspoonfuls of Tarragon vinegar, salt and pepper, mixed mustard, 1 teaspoonful of plain vinegar.

METHOD.—Put the yolk of egg in a small basin and break it up with a wooden spoon. Season it with salt, pepper and mustard, and stir in the oil drop by drop. As the sauce thickens, gradually stir in a little of the vinegar. Continue mixing slowly until all the ingredients are used, then taste the mayonnaise to see if it is sufficiently seasoned.

The sauce should be like thick cream when it is finished. The oil thickens it and the vinegar thins it, so, if necessary, add a little more of either ingredient until a thick, well-blended sauce is obtained. *It is most important to add the oil very slowly,* otherwise the sauce will curdle.

This salad dressing can be flavoured with a little onion-juice, if liked.

MINT SALAD DRESSING

INGREDIENTS.—1 tablespoonful of mint sauce (see p. 121), 2 chives (minced), ¼ teaspoonful of mustard, 3 tablespoonfuls of olive oil, salt and pepper.

METHOD.—Put the mustard and chives in a basin and add the oil gradually, stirring all the time.

Stir in the mint sauce and add salt and pepper to taste.

This dressing is suitable for lamb, mutton, peas, and other salads.

APPLE, BANANA AND GINGER SALAD

INGREDIENTS.—4 bananas, 2 eating apples, 1 tablespoonful of preserved ginger and syrup, 1 lettuce, ½ head of celery, juice of ½ lemon, bottled salad cream.

METHOD.—Peel and core the apples and cut each into three thick rounds, laying them in lemon-juice to preserve the colour.

Slice the bananas and chop the celery and ginger, mixing them with the ginger, syrup, lemon-juice, and salad cream.

Wash and shred the outside leaves of the lettuce, lay the slices of apple on them, and heap them with the banana mixture.

Decorate with small lettuce leaves.

Sufficient for three persons.

APPLE AND CHEESE SALAD

INGREDIENTS.—2 eating apples, 8 small spring onions, 1 cream cheese, cayenne, 4 squares of brown bread and butter.

METHOD.—Peel, core and chop the apples and mince the onions. Mix the apples and onions with the cheese and season with cayenne. Serve heaped on squares of brown bread and butter. Hand celery and cheese biscuits.

APPLE AND CHICORY SALAD

INGREDIENTS.—2 eating apples, $\frac{1}{2}$ lb. of chicory, 1 beetroot, $\frac{1}{4}$ onion (grated), bottled salad cream, salt and pepper, juice of $\frac{1}{2}$ a lemon, 1 tablespoonful of vinegar.

METHOD.—Peel and core the apples, cut them into strips, and moisten them in lemon-juice and salad cream.

Cut the beetroot into strips and sprinkle it with salt and pepper, vinegar and grated onion. Wash the chicory and cut it into shreds.

Arrange the salad on a plate with a heap of apple in the centre. Surround these with a narrow circle of beetroot and put a row of chicory on the outside.

Sufficient for three or four persons.

ASPARAGUS MAYONNAISE

INGREDIENTS.—1 tin of asparagus or 1 bundle of cold cooked asparagus, 1 hard-boiled egg, 1 gill of peas (cooked), 1 gill of mayonnaise (see p. 168), 2 tablespoonfuls of vinegar, salt and pepper.

METHOD.—Season the asparagus and peas by sprinkling them with vinegar, salt and pepper. Lay the asparagus on a dish and coat the centre of it with mayonnaise.

Garnish with the peas and a few slices of hard-boiled egg.

BANANA AND CELERY SALAD

INGREDIENTS.—4 bananas, 1 round lettuce, 2 cups of celery.

METHOD.—Clean and prepare the celery in the usual way and cut into small pieces.

Wash the lettuce thoroughly, then drain well.

Peel and slice the bananas.

Mix the celery and bananas together and serve on lettuce leaves.

Salad cream should accompany this salad.

NOTE.—Do not prepare the bananas until ready to use them, as they soon discolour.

BEEF AND TOMATO SALAD

INGREDIENTS.—$\frac{1}{4}$ lb. of cold beef, $\frac{1}{2}$ packet of aspic jelly, $\frac{1}{2}$ gill of tomato ketchup, 2 lettuces, $\frac{1}{2}$ lb. of tomatoes, mustard and cress, bottled salad cream, salt and pepper.

METHOD.—Remove fat and skin from the beef and cut the meat into small slices. Lay it on a dish and season with salt and pepper.

Dissolve the jelly in one and a half gills of hot water and add the ketchup. Pour it over the beef and let it set.

Shred and wash the lettuce and cress and slice the tomatoes. Mix them with salad cream and place the jellied beef on top.

Sufficient for four persons.

BEETROOT AND RICE SALAD

INGREDIENTS.—3 carrots (raw), $\frac{1}{4}$ lb. of shelled Brazil nuts, 1 beetroot (uncooked), 1 onion (raw), 1 lettuce, juice of $\frac{1}{2}$ a lemon, 2 tablespoonfuls of salad oil, salt and pepper to taste, 2 tablespoonfuls of grated cheese.

METHOD.—Peel the carrots, beetroot and onion, and grate them into a basin with a bread grater. Wash and shred the lettuce and chop the nuts.

Mix the cheese, nuts, and lettuce with the grated vegetables in a salad bowl, and season them with the lemon-juice, salad oil, and salt and pepper. Decorate with some small lettuce leaves.

Sufficient for four persons.

BIRD'S NEST SALAD

INGREDIENTS.—Lettuce leaves, French dressing (see p. 168), cream cheese.

METHOD.—Divide the cheese into tiny portions and shape them into egg shapes.

Cleanse the lettuce leaves, drain them well and shake off the loose moisture. Dress them with French dressing and arrange a few eggs on each leaf.

The eggs look more attractive if smeared with a little colouring.

CARROT SALAD

INGREDIENTS.—3 or 4 medium-sized cold carrots, 1 dessertspoonful of chopped parsley, 1 dessertspoonful of capers, French dressing (see p. 168).

METHOD.—Slice the carrots thinly, add the capers to them, and mix all with French dressing. Sprinkle with finely chopped parsley.

Sufficient for three or four persons.

RAW CARROTS AND NUT SALAD

INGREDIENTS.—3 oz. of rice, 1 tablespoonful of capers and caper vinegar, ¾ gill of bottled salad cream, 2 hard-boiled eggs, 1 tablespoonful of chopped parsley, 4 tablespoonfuls of pickled beetroot (chopped), 2 shallots, salt.

METHOD.—Wash the rice and sprinkle it into a large pan of boiling water containing a dessertspoonful of salt. Boil it for fifteen minutes, strain into a colander, and leave it to get cold. Chop the capers and shallots and one of the eggs, and stir them into the rice with the vinegar and salad dressing. Do not mash the rice.

Place slices of egg round the salad and decorate with parsley and beetroot.

Sufficient for three or four persons.

CAULIFLOWER MAYONNAISE

INGREDIENTS.—1 cauliflower, strips of pimento, lettuce leaves, hard-boiled egg, a few capers, oil mayonnaise (see p. 168).

METHOD.—Choose a cauliflower with a large, firm flower. Remove the outer leaves and trim the stump, leaving just enough green round the flower to keep it together. Cleanse it in salted water and boil it in the usual way until it is tender, being careful not to overcook it or it will break. Take it up, and let it drain well, and, when cold, serve it in a dish with a border of lettuce leaves and sliced hard-boiled egg. Pour a little oil mayonnaise over the flower and garnish it with capers and rings of pimento.

Serve the Cauliflower Mayonnaise with oil mayonnaise.

CAULIFLOWER AND PRAWN MAYONNAISE

INGREDIENTS. — 1 cauliflower, 1 lettuce (round), a few prawns, hard-boiled egg slices, 1 tomato, a small piece of beetroot, some mayonnaise or other salad cream (see pp. 167 and 168).

METHOD.—Choose a medium-sized cauliflower with a firm flower. Remove the outside leaves and some of the stump, leaving only about one layer of green leaves round the cauliflower to keep it together. Wash thoroughly in salted water, and boil in the usual way until tender, being careful not to overcook it. Lift it out and drain it well then leave it until cold. If the flower is inclined to break, squeeze it together in a pudding cloth.

Serve with a border of lettuce leaves well washed and drained. Pour some mayonnaise over the flower, and garnish it with slices of beetroot and hard boiled egg, quarters of tomato, and a few shelled prawns. Sufficient for five or six persons.

CAULIFLOWER SALAD

INGREDIENTS.—Cold cauliflower, 1 dessertspoonful of chopped parsley, French dressing (see p. 168).

METHOD.—Divide up the cauliflower and mix well with the dressing. Serve sprinkled with finely chopped parsley.

SMALL CAULIFLOWER SALADS

INGREDIENTS. — Cold cauliflower, salt and pepper, 1 dessertspoonful of Worcester sauce, 1 tablespoonful of chopped parsley, French salad dressing (see p. 168).

METHOD.—Put the cauliflower on a plate, season with salt and pepper, and sprinkle with a little French salad dressing. Leave it for an hour or two to become well flavoured.

Wash the parsley, squeeze it dry in the corner of a cloth, and chop finely. Mix the Worcester sauce with three tablespoonfuls of salad dressing.

Put the cauliflower daintily on small individual dishes, and sprinkle well with the mixture of sauce and dressing.

Decorate with a little chopped parsley. One medium cauliflower will be sufficient for five or six salads.

CELERY SALADS

INGREDIENTS.—1 head of celery, 1 apple, cut in strips, 1 teaspoonful of Parmesan cheese, 1 teaspoonful of Worcester sauce, French dressing (see p. 168), cheese balls (see p. 176).

METHOD.—Wash the celery well, cut it in strips and lay on a cloth to dry. Put it in a bowl with the apple, and mix thoroughly with French dressing and the Worcester sauce.

Sprinkle lightly with Parmesan cheese. Garnish with cheese balls.

CELERY AND NUT SALAD

INGREDIENTS.—1 head of celery, ¼ lb. of shelled walnuts, 1 cream cheese, ½ teaspoonful of made mustard, 2 tablespoonfuls of salad cream or mayonnaise (see p. 168).

METHOD.—Wash the celery and cut the stalks into fingers.

Chop the walnuts and mix them in a basin with the cheese, mustard, and mayonnaise.

Fill each finger of celery with the mixture and arrange daintily.

CELERY AND TOMATO SALAD

INGREDIENTS.—½ head of celery, ½ cup of shelled walnuts, 1 cream cheese, ½ lb. of small tomatoes, 1 dessertspoonful of mayonnaise or salad cream (see pp. 167 and 168), cayenne.

METHOD.—Wash and chop the celery and chop the walnuts. Put the cheese and mayonnaise in a basin, and add celery and walnuts.

Mix well, and season with cayenne.

Cut the tomatoes in half and arrange them round a dish with the celery mixture piled in the centre.

CHEESE SALAD

GRATE some cheese finely and serve on a bed of lettuce—the latter well washed and drained.

Garnish with slices of apple and quarters of tomato, and serve with salad cream (see page 168).

This is a very appetising salad, and very dainty in appearance.

CHEESE AND TOMATO SALAD

INGREDIENTS.—3 oz. of cheese, 2 medium sized tomatoes, seasoning, salad cream, lettuce leaves.

METHOD.—Grate the cheese finely. Then skin and chop up the tomatoes and mix them to a paste with the cheese, adding seasoning to taste.

Serve the mixture on individual plates, heaping it in the centre of the plates and surrounding it with lettuce leaves.

Sprinkle the salads with a little finely-grated cheese and decorate them with small pieces of tomato — extra to that given in the recipe.

Serve them with salad cream. Sufficient for three persons.

CHERRY SALAD

INGREDIENTS.—1 lb. of large cherries or 1 tin of cherries, 1 curly lettuce, 5 fancy cups made of grape fruit or orange skins, French dressing (see p. 168).

METHOD.—Stone the cherries and put them in a basin with the pulp that has been scooped out of the grape fruit skin. (If cooking cherries are used, they must be cooked before being made into the salad.) Season to taste with French dressing, and fill the fancy cups. Serve each cup on a lettuce leaf.

Enough for four large or six smaller salads.

CHICKEN SALAD

INGREDIENTS.—⅓ lb. of cold chicken, ½ head of celery, 1 lettuce, 2 hard-boiled eggs, ½ cup of mayonnaise dressing (see p. 168) or salad cream.

METHOD.—Cut the chicken into fair-sized dice. Cut the celery into coarse strips. Line the bowl with some nice lettuce leaves and shred the rest. Cut the eggs in half and then in quarters. Mix chicken, celery and shredded lettuce with mayonnaise and put in centre of bowl. Decorate with quarters of egg.

CUCUMBER BASKETS
(WITH SALMON FILLING)

INGREDIENTS.—3 large cucumbers, a small tin of salmon, mayonnaise.

METHOD.—Trim off the stalk end of the cucumber, cut off a slice from the opposite end, then cut each cucumber into about three pieces.

To shape the baskets, split along the centre half of each piece, cutting from each end *not* quite to the centre, leaving about one-fourth of an inch not cut, then cut down on each side and remove the two pieces. Then trim away the cucumber from under the centre piece so as to form a handle. Peel off the skin—if liked, it may be left on the handle—and scoop out some of the cucumber so as to form a hollow for the basket. Remove the bone from the salmon, flake up the flesh, mix it with the chopped, scooped-out cucumber, and moisten it with mayonnaise, then fill the prepared baskets. Sometimes a few chopped capers may be added to the salmon to give variety.

Sufficient for about nine baskets.

CUCUMBER AND CAVIARE SALAD

INGREDIENTS.—4 pieces of cucumber 1½ inches long, 2 tablespoonfuls of caviare, 2 shallots (minced), 2 teaspoonfuls of lemon-juice, cayenne, 1 lemon, 1 tablespoonful of mayonnaise (see p. 168), watercress sandwiches of new brown bread and butter.

METHOD.—Mix the caviare with the mayonnasie, lemon-juice, cayenne and shallots. Cut the cucumber with a fluted cutter and scoop out the seeds. Put caviare and cucumber on ice till required. Cut about one dozen thin watercress sandwiches and remove the crusts. To serve, fill the cucumber with caviare and arrange round the sandwiches. Garnish with quarters of lemon.

Sufficient for four persons.

CUCUMBER CUPS

INGREDIENTS.—2 medium-sized cucumbers, salad cream, pepper and salt, some cold cooked vegetables, peas, carrot, potato, etc.

METHOD.—Cut the cucumbers into pieces about one and a half inches in depth. There should be four or five pieces from each. Peel them and scoop out some of the centre part.

Cut the vegetables into small dice and mix them with a few peas, season to taste and dress with a little salad cream, then heap them in the cucumber cups.

Sufficient for about eight or ten cups.

CUCUMBER JELLY SALAD

INGREDIENTS.—1 cucumber, ½ packet of aspic jelly, 1 tin of salmon, 1 lettuce, ¼ onion (minced), 2 hard-boiled eggs, salad cream or mayonnaise (see p. 167), 1 gill of hot water.

METHOD.—Slice an inch of the cucumber and grate the rest.

Dissolve the aspic jelly in one gill of hot water and mix it with the grated

cucumber, making nearly half a pint in all.

Oil some small moulds, put in a little chopped white of egg and a teaspoonful of jelly to keep it in place. Let this set and fill up with cold jelly.

Wash and shred the lettuce and mix it with the onion. Lay the salmon on this, coat it with mayonnaise dressing and decorate it with slices of cucumber.

Turn out the jellies and place them round the dish.

Sufficient for three or four persons.

DANISH SALAD

INGREDIENTS.—2 oz. of macaroni, ½ head of celery, 1 beetroot, 1 dessertspoonful of chopped capers, salt and pepper, bottled salad cream, 1 hard-boiled egg.

METHOD.—Break up the macaroni and cook it for thirty minutes in plenty of fast-boiling water containing half an ounce of salt. Strain it and leave it to cool.

Peel the beetroot and cut it in diamonds, cut the celery in strips and cut the macaroni into pieces one inch long. Mix all together with capers and salad dressing, and season to taste with salt and pepper.

Decorate with beetroot and hard-boiled egg.

Sufficient for two persons.

NOTE.—Cold macaroni cheese makes a nice salad instead of freshly boiled macaroni.

DUCK SALAD

INGREDIENTS. — Remains of cold duck, 1 nice lettuce, 2 oranges, 1 gill of tinned cherries, French dressing, (see p. 168), juice of ½ a lemon.

METHOD.—Remove skin and bones from the duck and sprinkle the pieces with lemon-juice.

Wash and dry the lettuce, peel and slice the oranges, and stone the cherries.

Line a shallow bowl with half the lettuce leaves, shred the rest and put it in the centre.

Sprinkle with dressing and lay the pieces of duck on top.

Arrange the oranges round in a circle and decorate with the cherries.

To serve two or three persons.

EGG SALAD

INGREDIENTS.—3 eggs, 1 oz. of butter, salt and pepper, mayonnaise (see p. 168), 3 level teaspoonfuls of minced spring onion, endive and lettuce, parsley.

METHOD.—Put the eggs into boiling water and boil them gently for fifteen minutes. Shell them, cut them in halves crosswise, and remove the yolks, being careful not to break the whites.

Put the yolks into a basin, with the butter and mix them until smooth, moisten them with mayonnaise, add seasoning to taste, and stir in the minced onion, then heap in the half-whites. Garnish the top of each with a sprig of parsley or cress, and serve the salad surrounded with endive and lettuce, well washed and drained.

Sufficient for two persons.

NOTE.—Cut a small piece from the base of each half-white so that they stand firmly. This can be put into the white cups before the yolk mixture is added.

EGG AND BEETROOT SALAD

INGREDIENTS.—1 lettuce, 1 medium beetroot, 2 hard-boiled eggs, 2 or 3 spring onions, French salad dressing (see p. 168).

METHOD.—Shred the lettuce. Slice the eggs and the beetroot thinly, and cut the latter in half across. Chop the onions. Mix all the ingredients with French salad dressing, and decorate with a few slices of egg, diamond-shaped pieces of beetroot, and some small pieces of lettuce heart.

EGG AND GREEN PEA SALAD

INGREDIENTS.—6 hard-boiled eggs, 1 round lettuce, plain French dressing (see p. 168), 1 teaspoonful of minced chives or spring onions, 12 dessert-spoonfuls of cold cooked green peas.

METHOD.—Pull the lettuce leaves apart, wash them thoroughly and drain them well.

Hard-boil the eggs and split them in halves lengthwise. Scoop out the yolks and fill each halved white with about one dessertspoonful of cold peas, the latter previously mixed with the chives and a little French dressing.

Arrange the eggs on individual plates, allowing three halved whites to each person.

Surround the eggs with a border of lettuce leaves dressed with French dressing, and sprinkle the salad with powdered egg-yolk.

Sufficient for four persons.

EGG AND RICE SALAD

INGREDIENTS.—4 oz. of rice, 1 onion (grated), 1 bunch of radishes, 1 gill of bottled salad cream, 3 hard-boiled eggs, 1 beetroot, ½ cucumber, 1 lettuce, salt and pepper.

METHOD.—Boil the rice for fifteen minutes in plenty of water. Strain it but do not mash it.

Chop the whites of egg and rub the yolk through a gravy strainer with a teaspoon.

When the rice is cold, add the onion, chopped whites, and nearly all the salad cream, and season to taste with salt and pepper.

Decorate with yolk of egg.

Surround the rice with beetroot, radishes, cucumber and shredded lettuce sprinkled with a little salad dressing.

Sufficient for four persons.

EGG AND TOMATO SALAD

INGREDIENTS.—3 hard-boiled eggs, 2 large English tomatoes, a little endive or 1 punnet of mustard and cress, 2 spring onions, a little mayonnaise (see p. 168), French dressing (see p. 168).

METHOD.—Hard-boil the eggs, cut them in half and carefully remove the yolks. Rub the yolks through a strainer, and mix them with a teaspoonful of mayonnaise and the onion, very finely chopped. Slice the tomatoes. Stand half an egg on each slice and fill with the yolk mixture. Sprinkle with salad dressing, and decorate with cress or endive.

Sufficient for six small salads.

FIG SALAD

INGREDIENTS.—½ lb. of best dried figs, 1 gill of vinegar, 2 oz. of preserved ginger and syrup, small piece of cucumber, ½ head of celery, bottled salad cream, salt and pepper, a little cress, 2 oz. of boiled rice.

METHOD.—Soak the figs overnight in the vinegar, and cut them into quarters. Chop the celery and ginger.

Mix together the figs, rice, celery and ginger, and season them with salad cream, salt and pepper, and any vinegar not soaked up. Put them into a dish and decorate with cress and sliced cucumber.

Sufficient for three persons.

NOTE.—This salad can also be made with fresh figs.

FISH SALAD

INGREDIENTS. — The remains of some cold boiled or steamed fish, a little salad cream, 1 lettuce, tomatoes, radishes, cucumber, 1 hard-boiled egg.

METHOD.—Remove all the bones and skin from the fish, and flake up the flesh very finely.

Then season it and mix with a little salad cream.

Serve on a bed of lettuce leaves or endive with slices of tomato, cucumber or radishes, and hard-boiled egg.

FISH AND POTATO SALAD

INGREDIENTS:—Any cold fish, 1 cupful of cold potatoes, ½ cup of cold peas, ¾ gill of bottled salad cream, 1 teaspoonful of Worcester sauce, 1 dessertspoonful of chopped parsley, salt and pepper, 1 lettuce.

METHOD.—Wash and shred the lettuce.

Cut the fish in nice pieces free from skin and bone, and sprinkle with Worcester sauce.

Mix the fish carefully with the potatoes, half the salad cream, and the shredded leaves of the lettuce.

Season with salt and pepper. Mix the peas with a little of the salad cream and lay them on top with some of the fish.

Decorate with chopped parsley.

Sufficient for three or four persons.

INDIVIDUAL FISH SALAD

INGREDIENTS.—1 slice of hake, 1 dessertspoonful of chopped pimento, mayonnaise (see p. 168), pepper and salt, mustard and cress, few lettuce leaves.

METHOD.—Wash the hake and put it into warm water barely to cover it, adding a little salt, and cook it for a few minutes until the flesh moves easily from the bone. Take it up, remove the skin and bones and flake the flesh into small pieces.

Season it, add the chopped pimento and moisten it with mayonnaise. Line a grapefruit glass with some of the small leaves of a lettuce, put in the prepared fish and garnish it with a little mustard and cress. The cress and lettuce must be thoroughly washed and drained before they are used. Pimentoes can be bought from any store, and are sold in tins.

Sufficient for one person.

PLAIN FRENCH SALAD AND DRESSING

TAKE two nice heads of lettuce, remove outside leaves. Wash well in cold water and soak for about an hour. Drain well in a colander.

Tear the heart into fine strips and shake well. Then toss in the plain French dressing (see p. 168). Serve at once.

NOTE.—This salad is generally served in France with various kinds of roasts, especially chicken.

FRENCH BEAN SALAD

INGREDIENTS.—1 cup of cold French beans, 1 cold cauliflower, salad dressing (see p. 167), salt and pepper, 1 dessertspoonful of chopped capers.

METHOD.—Cut the French beans across into squares and season with salt, pepper, capers, and half the salad dressing.

Put them on a plate inside a ring of cauliflower sprinkled with the rest of the salad dressing.

Sufficient for three persons.

FRUIT MAYONNAISE

INGREDIENTS.—4 bananas, 2 eating apples, 2 oranges, juice of ½ a lemon, 1 lettuce, 2 oz. of shelled walnuts, ½ gill of mayonnaise (see p. 168).

METHOD.—Slice the bananas and peel, core, and slice the apples. Lay them on a plate and squeeze lemon-juice over them to keep them a good colour.

Peel the oranges, removing all pith and pips, and cut the sections in half.

Wash and shred the lettuce and chop the walnuts. Mix the fruit and nuts with mayonnaise and place it on a bed of shredded lettuce.

Sufficient for four or five persons.

GREEN PEA SALAD

INGREDIENTS.—1 cupful of cold green peas, 1 curly lettuce, mint dressing (see p. 168), cucumber for garnish.

METHOD.—Line a salad bowl with small lettuce leaves and shred the rest. Mix the peas and shredded lettuce with mint dressing and put them in the centre of the leaves.

Cut the cucumber into thin slices, and use it for decorating the salad.

To serve two or three persons.

ITALIAN SALAD

INGREDIENTS.—2 cupfuls of cold, cooked macaroni, ½ cup of grated raw carrot, ½ cup of cooked French beans, 2 level tablespoonfuls of chopped spring onions, French dressing and mayonnaise (see pp. 167 and 168), lettuce leaves.

METHOD.—Add the macaroni to the vegetables and mix them all together. Moisten them with French dressing.

Leave the salad to stand for one hour.

Serve the salad on a dish lined with lettuce leaves. Decorate it with mayonnaise and with mustard and cress, if liked.

JAPANESE SALAD

INGREDIENTS.—2 curly lettuces, 1 apple, 1 large sweet orange, 3 or 4 radishes, ½ small tin of sliced pineapple, ¼ lb. of ripe English tomatoes, some cream salad dressing (see p. 167).

METHOD.—Wash the lettuce and arrange the leaves in a circle in a salad bowl. Cut the orange sections in half and cut up the pineapple. Peel and slice the tomatoes and apples, and slice the radishes.

Mix the fruit with cream dressing, and heap in the centre of bowl.

LETTUCE AND CHEESE SALAD

INGREDIENTS.—1 lettuce, 1 bunch of watercress, 1 bunch each of mustard and cress, 2 hard-boiled eggs, ¼ lb. of cheese, 1 onion (grated), French dressing (see p. 168), carrot and cheese balls (see p. 167).

METHOD.—Wash and shred the lettuce. Wash the cress. Cut the eggs in quarters and slice the cheese thinly.

Mix them with salad dressing and a grated onion and decorate with the eggs placed round the salad.

Serve carrot and cheese balls and some slices of cheese on the top, and eat with cheese biscuits.

Sufficient for two or three persons.

LOBSTER MAYONNAISE

INGREDIENTS.—1 tin of lobster or a fresh lobster, 2 hard-boiled eggs, 1 tablespoonful of capers, 1 beetroot, ¾ pint of hot water, 1 packet of aspic jelly, 6d. of picked shrimps (these can be omitted), ½ cup each of cold peas or beans, cauliflowers and potatoes, ¾ gill of mayonnaise (see p. 168).

METHOD.—Dissolve the jelly in three-quarters of a pint of hot water, and when cold pour three-quarters of a gill into an oiled border mould.

When set, wash the shrimps and sprinkle them in the mould with the capers, adding one gill of jelly. Put the mould in a cool place to set. Cut the eggs in quarters and the lobster into nice pieces.

When the jelly is set put in alternate pieces of egg and lobster with two tablespoonfuls of jelly to keep them in place.

When firm fill up the mould with jelly and pieces of beetroot and egg.

While the jelly is setting chop all the vegetables coarsely and mix them with the mayonnaise.

To serve, shake the mould on to a cold dish and heap the mayonnaise in the centre.

Sufficient for four persons.

LOBSTER SALAD

INGREDIENTS. — 1 medium - sized lobster, 2 lettuces with good hearts, 2 hard-boiled eggs (sliced), 2 bunches of watercress, ½ endive, a little mustard and cress, 1 gill of mayonnaise dressing (see p. 168), a small piece of cucumber.

METHOD.—Take out all the meat from body and claws of the lobster and cut it into nice-sized pieces.

Cut and shred the lettuce and divide up the watercress. Wash the mustard and cress.

Mix lettuce, cress, lobster and egg with the mayonnaise and put them in a salad bowl.

Decorate with a little endive and sliced cucumber and the claws of the lobster.

Sufficient for four persons.

LOGANBERRY SALAD

INGREDIENTS.—½ lb. or 1 tin of loganberries, 3 bananas, 2 oz. of shelled walnuts, mayonnaise (see p. 168), or cream salad dressing, 1 curly lettuce.

METHOD.—Slice the bananas and mix them with the loganberries. Place in small heaps on separate lettuce leaves, and place a dessert-spoonful of dressing on each with a walnut on top.

Sufficient for three or four persons.

MARGUERITE SALAD

INGREDIENTS.—1 beetroot, ½ gill of vinegar, ¾ lb. of cold potatoes, 1 onion (grated), 2 hard-boiled eggs, 4 table-spoonfuls of bottled salad cream, salt and pepper, cheese balls.

METHOD.—Peel and slice the beet-root, sprinkle it with salt and lay it in the vinegar for an hour or two. Mix the potatoes with the grated onion, salad cream, and salt and pepper, and if possible leave it for an hour or two to get nicely flavoured. Put the potatoes in a salad bowl and cover them smoothly with slices of beetroot.

Decorate the salad with strips of white of egg arranged to form a marguerite, putting a cheese ball in the centre.

Serve with cheese balls and biscuits on a separate dish.

Sufficient for three persons.

THE CHEESE BALLS

INGREDIENTS.—2 yolks of eggs (hard-boiled), 1½ oz. of butter, 6 oz. of grated cheese, cayenne, ¼ teaspoonful of made mustard, 1 dessertspoonful of vinegar.

METHOD.—Mix the mustard and vinegar in a cup, put in the yolks and butter, and mash them with a fork till smooth.

Season with cayenne.

Gradually work in the cheese and form the mixture into balls.

NOTE.—One cream cheese may be used instead of grated cheese.

MAYONNAISE OF COLD FISH

INGREDIENTS.—Remains of any cold fish, 1 lemon, 2 curly lettuce, 1 gill of mayonnaise (see p. 168) or salad cream French dressing (see p. 168).

METHOD.—Cut the cold fish into neat fillets and sprinkle with lemon-juice, salt and pepper. Leave till ready to serve. Wash and shred the lettuce and mix with French dressing. Lay the pieces of fish on top of the salad, and coat each of them carefully with mayonnaise.

MEAT SALAD
(MADE WITH COLD MEAT)

INGREDIENTS.—The remains of a cold joint, salt and pepper, a little salad cream, mustard and cress, 1 lettuce, watercress, cucumber, toma-toes, 1 hard-boiled egg, beetroot.

METHOD.—Remove all the skin and gristle from the meat and cut the flesh into small cubes, or, if preferred, put it through the mincing machine. Season it to taste.

Dress the meat with a little of the cream or with French dressing, and serve with a border of cress, lettuce, sliced cucumber, tomato, egg and beetroot.

THE PLAIN FRENCH DRESSING

INGREDIENTS.—2 tablespoonfuls of oil to each 1 of vinegar, salt, pepper, mixed mustard.

METHOD.—All the ingredients must be thoroughly well mixed together. The vinegar should be added very gradually.

MIXED SALAD WITH CELERY

INGREDIENTS. — Small head of celery, 1 round lettuce, mustard and cress, endive, cucumber or beetroot, 2 or 3 tomatoes, garlic.

METHOD.—Trim and clean the celery in the usual way and cut it in short lengths. Pick over and wash the salad plants—lettuce, cress and endive —then drain them well. Peel and halve a clove of garlic and rub the salad bowl with it, to give a delicate flavour of onion to the salad. Break up the salad and put it into the bowl with the celery. Add also some sliced cucumber or beetroot, sliced tomato, and if liked a hard-boiled egg.

Either serve the salad with mayonnaise dressing (see p. 168) or else dress the green salad with a plain French dressing (see p. 168) just before serving.

MUTTON SALAD

INGREDIENTS.—½ lb. or more of cold mutton or lamb, 1 tablespoonful of mint sauce, 1 gill of cooked peas, 2 tablespoonfuls of mayonnaise (see page 168) or salad cream, 1 lettuce, 1 hard-boiled egg.

METHOD.—Cut the meat into neat strips and lay them on a plate in the mint sauce. Boil the egg for ten minutes. Put it in cold water for a minute, and remove the shell. If the egg is not wanted at once it can, after shelling, be put in cold water. This will keep it white.

Shred half the lettuce, mix it with the peas and mayonnaise and put in the middle of a salad-bowl.

Arrange a few leaves round the bowl and lay the slices of meat on top of the shredded lettuce and peas.

Decorate with slices of hard-boiled egg. Cold potatoes or any other cold vegetables could be used instead of peas.

Sufficient for four persons.

MAYONNAISE OF PEAS AND RICE

INGREDIENTS.—1 cupful of cold peas, 2 oz. of rice, ½ gill of mayonnaise (see p. 168), or salad cream, 1 tablespoonful of vinegar, salt and pepper, 1 dessertspoonful of chopped parsley, a clove of garlic.

METHOD.—Wash the rice and put it in fast boiling water with a teaspoonful of salt.

Boil for fifteen minutes. Strain and put in a cold place. Mix the peas with the vinegar and salt and pepper.

When the rice is cold, mix it with the mayonnaise.

Bruise the garlic and rub the salad bowl with it.

Mix the peas with a tablespoonful of the rice and put them in the bowl

with a heap of rice at each end Decorate with chopped parsley.

Sufficient for three or four persons.

ORANGE AND LETTUCE SALAD

INGREDIENTS.—3 seedless oranges, ½ lb. of plums, 1 good lettuce, ½ endive, French salad dressing (see p. 168).

METHOD.—Divide the oranges into sections and remove all pith. Cut each section in half. Peel and stone the plums and cut them in half.

Wash and shred the lettuce and mix it with the fruit and salad dressing. Heap them in a bowl and surround them with sprigs of endive.

This salad is very delicious served with hot roast meat.

Sufficient for three or four persons.

NOTE.—For a specially good salad use tinned grape-fruit instead of orange, straining off the juice first.

PINEAPPLE SALAD

INGREDIENTS.—1 tin of sliced pineapple, 1 lettuce, ¼ of an onion, 1 bunch of mustard and cress, French salad dressing (see p. 168), 1 small tin of cherries.

METHOD.—Wash and shred the lettuce and cress and grate the onion on a bread grater. Line individual compôte dishes with small lettuce leaves sprinkled with dressing.

Mix lettuce, cress and onion with salad dressing and place it in the lined dishes with two or three stoned cherries.

Lay a slice of pineapple on top with a cherry in the centre and pour on a little dressing.

Sufficient for four persons.

PINEAPPLE AND CELERY SALAD

INGREDIENTS.—½ tin of sliced pineapple, ½ head of celery, 1 curly lettuce, French salad dressing (see p. 168), a little endive.

METHOD.—Remove any coarse stalks from the celery. Wash the white stalks, cut them into dice, and soak them in a small basin with the salad dressing. Wash the lettuce and endive. Place a slice of pineapple on each lettuce leaf and sprinkle with the pieces of celery and the rest of the dressing. Decorate with endive.

Sufficient for four persons.

PINEAPPLE AND STRAW-BERRY SALAD

INGREDIENTS.—2 slices of tinned pineapple, ½ lb. of strawberries, 1 curly lettuce, ½ gill of mayonnaise or cream dressing (see p. 168), 1 tablespoonful of lemon-juice or vinegar.

METHOD.—Lay each slice of pineapple on two or three nicely washed fresh lettuce leaves, and sprinkle with lemon-juice.

Pick the strawberries and arrange a small heap on each slice of pineapple. Pour a spoonful of dressing over and serve.

PRAWN TOMATOES

INGREDIENTS. — 3 tomatoes, 18 prawns, seasoning, mayonnaise (see p. 168).

METHOD.—Turn the tomatoes upside down and cut off a slice, using a sharp knife. Scoop out some of the pulp and season the inside of the tomatoes with salt and pepper.

Shell the prawns, saving three of the heads, mix the prawns with mayonnaise and heap them in the tomatoes, then garnish each with a prawn's head. If preferred, the prawns may be broken into small pieces before being mixed with the mayonnaise.

Sufficient for three tomatoes.

RUSSIAN SALAD

INGREDIENTS.—½ lb. of beans French or scarlet runners, 1 lb. of peas, ½ lb. of potatoes, small cauliflower, ½ lb. of carrots, 3 or 4 dessertspoonfuls of mayonnaise (see p. 168), seasoning, garlic.

METHOD.—String the beans and cut them *across* in thick slices, divide the flower of the cauliflower into small branches. Shell the peas, peel the potatoes and scrape the carrots.

Cook all these prepared vegetables in separate pans of slightly salted water, and, when tender, drain and leave them until cold. Cut the carrots into dice and the potatoes into rounds or dice, and leave a few of these aside for garnishing, the remainder mix

with the other vegetables, adding the mayonnaise and seasoning to taste.

Rub the dish in which the salad is to be served with garlic, heap the prepared vegetables in it and garnish with lines of carrots and potatoes.

Serve with some mayonnaise—extra to that given in the recipe.

Sufficient for six persons.

SALAD JELLIES

INGREDIENTS.—½ pint of aspic jelly, 1 gill of diced cucumber, 1 gill of cold cooked peas, 1 hard-boiled egg, a few slices of cucumber, lettuce leaves.

METHOD.—Melt the aspic jelly and pour a thin layer in the bottom of seven small moulds. Leave it to set, then add a slice of cucumber dipped in jelly, and when set cover it with jelly and let it set again.

Shell the egg, cut it in halves crosswise, remove the yolk and press this through a strainer, then chop up the white. Fill the moulds with alternate layers of peas, chopped egg white, cucumber cut in dice, and powdered egg yolk, covering each layer with jelly, and leaving it to set before adding the next.

When the moulds are full, leave the jelly till quite firm, then dip the moulds in warm water and turn out the jelly. Serve them on a dish surrounded with lettuce leaves.

Sufficient for seven small moulds.

ASPIC JELLY

INGREDIENTS. — 1½ pints of stock (see p. 12), 2 shells and whites of eggs, sprig of parsley and thyme, few peppercorns, few celery seeds, salt, if required, ¾ oz. of leaf gelatine, 1 tablespoonful of Tarragon vinegar, 1 tablespoonful of malt vinegar, 2 tablespoonfuls of cooking sherry.

METHOD.—The stock must be freed from every particle of grease. Put it into a saucepan with all the given ingredients. The celery seeds must be tied in a piece of muslin, the eggshells washed, the inner skin removed, and the shells crushed.

Stir the stock until the gelatine is dissolved, then whisk it until it *almost* boils and has a good head of scum on the top, then stop whisking and let it boil up.

Simmer it gently for a few minutes, then strain it through a scalded jelly bag.

SARDINE SALAD

INGREDIENTS.—1 tin of sardines, ½ lb. of tomatoes, 1 lettuce, 1 bunch of radishes, 2 hard-boiled eggs, 1 onion (grated), ½ endive, French dressing (see p. 168).

METHOD.—Wash and shred the lettuce and mix it with the sliced eggs and tomatoes, chopped radishes and grated onion. Decorate with endive.

Drain the oil from the sardines and lay them on top of the salad.

Sufficient for two or three persons.

SAVOURY FRUIT SALAD

INGREDIENTS.—Apples, bananas, the juice of 1 lemon, salad cream (see p. 167), 1 lettuce, shelled and skinned nuts (if liked).

METHOD.—Peel, core, and slice some apples and mix the pieces with slices of banana.

Sprinkle them with lemon-juice and then dress them with salad cream.

Serve the fruit on lettuce leaves.

Some shelled and skinned nuts may be added if liked.

SMOKED SALMON AND POTATO MAYONNAISE

INGREDIENTS.—¼ lb. of Canadian smoked salmon, ½ onion (grated), 1 dessertspoonful of chopped parsley, 1½ lb. of cold potatoes, 1 gill of mayonnaise dressing (see p. 168), salt, pepper.

METHOD.—New potatoes look best for this dish, as they do not break easily. Slice them thickly and season with grated onion, salt and pepper.

Mix them with the mayonnaise at least two hours before the salad will be required, lay strips of smoked salmon on top and sprinkle with parsley.

Sufficient for two persons.

NOTE.—Canadian smoked salmon is very good and much cheaper than the Norwegian salmon. It is not really expensive as a little goes a long way.

SPINACH SALAD

INGREDIENTS.—½ pint of cooked spinach, 1 tablespoonful of oil mayonnaise—or more if required (see p. 168),

seasoning, 1 hard-boiled egg, mustard and cress.

METHOD.—You can use any left-over cooked spinach, or the tinned kind. Drain it well and measure it, then season it and mix it with the mayonnaise. Arrange it in a mound in the centre of a dish, decorate it with petals of egg white, with powdered yolk in the centre, and serve the spinach salad with a border of mustard and cress.

To hard-boil eggs, boil them for fifteen minutes, then crack the shells and cool the egg for a few minutes in cold water.

To cut petals, cut a hard-boiled egg in halves lengthwise, remove the yolk, and cut each half-white into four pieces lengthwise. The yolk is powdered by pressing it through a wire sieve or strainer.

TRI-COLOUR SALAD

INGREDIENTS.—1 lb. of cold butter beans, 5 tomatoes, 1 onion, 4 hard-boiled eggs, bottled salad cream.

METHOD.—Mix the beans in a bowl with grated onion and salad cream, and cover with sliced tomatoes.

Decorate with the whites of eggs and sprinkle with the yolks rubbed through a gravy strainer.

Sufficient for four persons.

TOMATO CUPS

INGREDIENTS. — 6 medium-sized tomatoes, 1 tablespoonful of cooked green peas, 1 tablespoonful of diced cooked carrot, 1 tablespoonful of diced cooked potato, about 1 dessertspoonful of mayonnaise (see p. 168), seasoning, watercress.

METHOD.—Choose firm tomatoes, wipe them, remove the stalks, and cut a small slice from the opposite end of each. Scoop out some of the soft pulp and season the inside of the tomatoes with pepper and salt.

Mix the cold, cooked vegetables together, add the mayonnaise and about two tablespoonfuls of the tomato pulp. Season them well and divide the vegetables between the tomatoes.

Garnish the top with a few extra peas and diced vegetables, and serve the tomato cups in a dish with sprigs of watercress.

Sufficient for six persons.

TOMATO AND CUCUMBER SALAD

INGREDIENTS.—1 lb. of large English tomatoes, ½ a cucumber, 3 small spring onions, 4 tablespoonfuls of mayonnaise (see p. 168), 1 curly lettuce.

METHOD.—Cut the tomatoes in half across and scoop out the centre. Chop the cucumber and drain the moisture from it. Chop the onions finely. Mix the chopped cucumber and onions with the tomato pulp and fill the half tomatoes with the mixture. Heap a dessertspoonful of mayonnaise on top of each and serve each one on a lettuce leaf.

Makes four or five individual salads.

TOMATO AND PINEAPPLE SALAD

INGREDIENTS.—½ lb. of tomatoes, ½ tin of sliced pineapple, 1 large curly lettuce, a little endive, French salad dressing, (see p. 168), cheese balls (see p. 166).

METHOD.—Wash and dry the lettuce and endive and slice the tomatoes.

Roll the cheese into small balls. Cut half the pineapple into small pieces, keeping back a few slices to decorate the top.

Shred the lettuce into a salad bowl and mix it with the cut up pineapple and half the sliced tomatoes.

Flavour with French dressing.

To decorate, cover with slices of pineapple and on each one put a piece of tomato and a cheese ball.

TOMATO EGG CUPS

INGREDIENTS.—4 tomatoes, 4 small eggs, mayonnaise (see p. 168), 1 pimento, lettuce leaves, seasoning.

METHOD.—Turn the tomatoes upside down and cut off a slice from the opposite end to the stalk, then scoop out some of the pulp and season the inside of the tomatoes with salt and pepper.

Hard boil the eggs, then shell them and leave them to get cold. Pour over them a thin coating of mayonnaise.

Stand an egg in each tomato cup, decorate the top with tiny half moons of pimento and put a strip of pimento round the centre.

Arrange the cups in a dish, with lettuce leaves.

Allow one or two for each person.

STUFFED TOMATOES

INGREDIENTS.—4 even-sized tomatoes, 1 level teaspoonful of finely-minced onion, 3 dessertspoonfuls of finely-grated cheese, 2 or 3 tablespoonfuls of chopped cucumber, seasoning, endive, French dressing.

METHOD.—Stalk and skin the tomatoes. Cut a slice from the stalk end of each and put them aside. Scoop out the pulp from the tomato and season the inside of the cup with pepper and salt.

Mix the cucumber with the cheese, onion and tomato pulp, and stir in one tablespoonful of French dressing. If the mixture is too moist, do not add all the tomato pulp.

Fill the tomato cups with the mixture. Cover each cup with a top slice and replace the stalk. Serve the tomato cups on slices of cucumber and surround them with endive dressed with French dressing.

To SKIN TOMATOES.—Drop them into boiling water for a few seconds when the skin will peel off quite easily.

THE FRENCH DRESSING

INGREDIENTS.—2 or 3 tablespoonfuls of salad oil, 1 dessertspoonful of plain vinegar, 1 dessertspoonful of Tarragon vinegar, salt and pepper, mixed mustard.

METHOD.—Put the salad oil on a plate, add the vinegars and a seasoning of salt, pepper and mixed mustard, and stir them till thoroughly mixed.

Remember to use only the best vinegar and oil for making salad dressings. If Tarragon vinegar is not to hand, you can use two dessertspoonfuls of plain vinegar, but the former improves the flavour of the dressing.

TONGUE MAYONNAISE

INGREDIENTS.—1 lb. of cold tongue mayonnaise (see p. 168), ½ a cup of diced beetroot, 3 or 4 hard-boiled eggs, watercress, ½ a cup of minced celery.

METHOD.—Chop the tongue into dice. Mix it with the minced celery, diced beetroot, and mayonnaise to taste.

Heap the salad in the centre of a glass dish fringed with watercress. Quarter the eggs and arrange them in a ring inside the circle of watercress.

Decorate the salad with the sieved yolk of one quarter of an egg and the chopped white. If liked this salad may be sprinkled with chopped chives.

Sufficient for six or eight persons.

TOMATO, ONION AND CUCUMBER SALAD

INGREDIENTS.—1½ lb. of tomatoes, ½ a cucumber, 1 Spanish onion, 3 tablespoonfuls of thick cream, 1 tablespoonful of vinegar, salt and pepper.

METHOD.—Dip the tomatoes in boiling water, and peel and chop them. Chop the cucumber and mince the onion. Mix them with the tomatoes and cream and season with salt and pepper.

Add the vinegar last.

Sufficient for four persons.

MAYONNAISE OF TURBOT

INGREDIENTS.—Cold turbot, ½ a tin of prawns or ½ doz. of fresh prawns, 1 small jar of calf's foot jelly (wine flavoured), or jelly from a roast joint, French dressing (see p. 168), mayonnaise (see p. 168) or salad cream, 2 lettuces.

METHOD.—Sprinkle the pieces of turbot with a little French dressing and salt and pepper. Leave it for an hour or two. Wash and shred the lettuce and mix with French dressing. Place the pieces of turbot on top and coat carefully with half a pint of thick mayonnaise. Chop the jelly or cut it in fancy shapes and surround the salad with it.

Decorate with the prawns.

NOTE.—Tinned salmon may also be done in this way. Calf's foot jelly is used for the sake of convenience, but the jelly from a roast joint could be used instead.

The jelly and prawns may be omitted altogether for a more simple dish.

MIXED VEGETABLE SALAD

INGREDIENTS.—1 bunch of radishes, 1 bunch of young carrots, 3 gherkins, 1 small piece of cucumber, 1 small beetroot, 1 lb. of cold potatoes, 1 gill of mayonnaise dressing (see p. 168) or salad cream (bottled), salt, pepper, juice of ½ a lemon, 6 shallots.

METHOD.—Mince the shallots and mix them with the potatoes sliced in a salad bowl, adding lemon-juice, salt and pepper and the mayonnaise, and, if possible, leave it for an hour or two to get nicely flavoured.

Cut radishes, carrots, gherkins and cucumber into thin slices, keeping each kind separate.

Cut the beetroot into small pieces.

Mix the beetroot and any odd scraps or uneven pieces of the vegetables with the potatoes.

To finish the salad heap the potatoes up, smooth them over and cover them neatly with circles of each kind of vegetable, cucumber outside, then carrots, radishes and gherkins till all are used.

Sufficient for four persons.

NOTE.—This is an unusual and pretty salad and a useful one for using up any cold vegetables.

Other vegetables that could be used in this salad are cauliflowers, scarlet runners, broad beans or peas.

WINTER SALAD

INGREDIENTS.—1 cooked beetroot (small), 3 or 4 cooked potatoes (medium size), 2 tomatoes, 2 eggs (hard-boiled), salad dressing.

METHOD.—Put the eggs into a saucepan, cover with cold water, bring to the boil, and boil for about twelve to fifteen minutes. Then crack the shells well, and put into cold water until ready for use.

Peel the beetroot thinly and cut it into very thin slices.

Thickly slice (rather thicker than beetroot) the potatoes and tomatoes.

Remove the shells from the eggs, cut one of them into slices, yolk and white together.

Take the yolk from the other egg and crumble it, or rub through a sieve, and put aside for the dressing.

Cut the white into rings.

Arrange the slices of beetroot and potato and tomato alternately in a shallow bowl, garnish with the slices of eggs, and serve with the following dressing.

The Salad Dressing

INGREDIENTS.—The powdered yoke of egg (from above recipe) 2 tablespoonfuls of vinegar, salt and pepper, $\frac{1}{4}$ teaspoonful of castor sugar, $\frac{1}{4}$ teaspoonful of mixed mustard, 2 tablespoonfuls of salad oil.

METHOD.—Put the powdered yolk into a small basin, add the mustard, and mix well. Then add the oil drop by drop, stirring it all the time. Use a wooden spoon.

Add the salt, pepper and sugar, and lastly the vinegar, very gradually.

YULETIDE SALAD

INGREDIENTS.—1 pint of cranberries, 6 oz. of sugar, $\frac{1}{2}$ cup of chopped apple, $\frac{1}{2}$ pint of water, $\frac{1}{2}$ oz. of gelatine, $\frac{1}{2}$ cup of diced celery, $\frac{1}{4}$ cup of ground walnuts, lettuce, mayonnaise (see p. 168).

METHOD.—Pick and wash the berries. Boil them with the water and sugar until they are soft, and then rub them through a sieve.

Dissolve the gelatine in a little water and stir it into the cranberry purée and leave it to cool. When it is beginning to set, add the prepared apple and celery and nuts.

Turn the mixture into wet individual moulds. When the jellies are quite set serve them arranged on a glass dish lined with lettuce leaves.

Garnish each jelly with a spoonful of mayonnaise. Serve the jellies with cold turkey or chicken.

Sufficient for six or eight persons.

VEGETABLES

The secret of cooking green vegetables is to keep them "green." Greens served with a bad colour are most unappetising.

To prepare *greens*, remove the outside leaves and stump and pull the leaves well apart.

Cabbages and savoys should be cut into quarters.

Marrow should be cut lengthwise and across. Peel and remove the seeds then cut into convenient-sized pieces.

Brussels sprouts.—Remove outside leaves and trim the stalk.

String Beans.—Pare off the stringy part round the sides, and then cut them in thin slices.

Cauliflower.—Remove outside leaves cut off bottom of stump, then cut stump across each way.

Greens need well washing to remove dirt and insects. If soaked for a time in salted water this greatly helps to cleanse them. Before cooking, lift them from the water, leaving any grit in the bottom of the bowl, and drain them in a colander before putting them into the saucepan.

COOKING GREEN VEGETABLES

Put them into *boiling water* to which salt and soda has just been added (one tablespoonful of salt, and enough soda to cover a threepenny piece to about two quarts of water). Use a large saucepan and plenty of water.

Bring them to the boil quickly, then remove the saucepan lid and boil the vegetables until tender, skimming them when necessary.

Drain them in a colander, press out the water (if greens or cabbages, etc.), and serve them in a vegetable dish with a flat strainer or upturned saucer in the bottom of it.

Average Times to Allow After
They Come to the Boil

Spring Greens and Spring Cabbages.—Twenty minutes.

White-heart Cabbage.—Thirty minutes.

Peas.—Twenty to thirty minutes, according to age. Do not add soda, but add a little sugar and a sprig of mint.

Runner Beans.—Twenty minutes.

Broad Beans.—Twenty to thirty minutes, according to age. Soda not required. Serve with parsley sauce.

Marrow.—Ten to fifteen minutes. Soda not required. Serve with white sauce.

Savoys.—Twenty to thirty minutes.

Turnip Tops.—About twenty-five minutes.

Brussels Sprouts.— Twenty minutes.

Cauliflower.—Thirty to forty-five minutes. Serve with white sauce.

To Prepare and Cook Spinach

Remove the discoloured leaves, and take away the centre stalk that runs up each leaf.

Spinach needs to be washed in three or four waters as it is always very gritty.

It contains a lot of water itself, and as it cooks, this moisture is drawn from it, so only enough water should be allowed to cover the bottom of the pan. Let it boil, then add the salt ($\frac{1}{2}$ to $\frac{3}{4}$ dessertspoonful to 2 or 3 lb. of spinach) with the spinach. Stir occasionally at first, and boil for about twenty or twenty-five minutes. When tender, drain the spinach well and press out the water. Turn it on to a board and chop finely, then return it to the pan with a lump of butter season with pepper and re-heat.

BOILING POTATOES AND ROOT VEGETABLES

Potatoes should be cooked in slightly salted water.

If prepared before they are ready to be cooked, stand them in cold water or they will discolour.

OLD POTATOES.—Peel thinly and cook in just sufficient water to cover. When tender, drain off the water, and leave for a few minutes to dry. Boil about thirty minutes.

NEW POTATOES.—Scrape and put into boiling water. Add a sprig of mint, but do not leave in too long or it will discolour them. Serve with finely chopped parsley sprinkled on the top.

CARROTS.—Scrape. If large, cut in quarters lengthwise. Cook in boiling water to well cover.

Allow about one to one hour and a half.

YOUNG CARROTS.—Are usually cooked whole. Allow about thirty-five minutes.

TURNIPS.—Peel thickly. If large, cut in quarters or halves. Cook in boiling water to well cover, and allow about one hour.

PARSNIPS.—Peel thinly. Cook in the same way as carrots.

JERUSALEM ARTICHOKES.—Peel, and drop at once into cold water, to which a little lemon-juice has been added. Put into boiling water to cook, with salt and lemon-juice (about one dessertspoonful to two quarts of water). They will take from twenty to twenty-five minutes. Serve with white sauce (see p. 41).

BOILED ARTICHOKES AND WHITE SAUCE

INGREDIENTS.—1½ lb. of Jerusalem artichokes, boiling water, salt, lemon-juice (about 1 tablespoonful to 2 quarts of water).

THE SAUCE.—1 oz. of flour, 1 oz. of margarine, 1½ gills of milk, ½ gill of water, pepper and salt.

METHOD.—Scrub the artichokes, then peel them rather thickly. As they are very irregular in shape, they will require to be peeled very carefully. Artichokes very quickly discolour, therefore when they are being peeled it is necessary to frequently dip them in cold water. As each one is finished it should be immediately put into a basin of cold water to which a little lemon-juice has been added, and left until ready to be cooked. Put on to boil a large saucepan with plenty of water.

When boiling add the salt and lemon-juice, and put in the artichokes. Boil for about twenty-five minutes, until quite tender.

Keep the lid off the saucepan, and do not boil them too quickly or they will break. When cooked pour into a colander and drain well. Stand in a vegetable dish, and coat with thick, white sauce. The sauce can be made while the artichokes are cooking.

NOTE.—Do not use an iron saucepan for cooking the artichokes.

THE WHITE SAUCE

PUT the milk, margarine, and seasoning into a saucepan to heat. Mix the flour to a smooth paste with the water, pour the hot milk on to the flour, return to the saucepan, and bring to the boil, keeping it well stirred all the time. Simmer for six minutes, and pour over the artichokes.

ARTICHOKE CRISPS

INGREDIENTS.—Artichokes, as required, deep fat for frying, salt.

METHOD.—Peel the artichokes and drop them at once into cold water. Slice them as *thinly* as possible, and drop them again into cold water.

Let the slices soak for a time, then drain them well, and dry them in a cloth.

Meanwhile, heat some deep fat and when a faint smoke rises from it, add the prepared artichokes and fry them till golden, frying only a few at a time, and using a frying basket.

Drain the artichoke crisps on paper and sprinkle them with salt. Crisp them in the oven before serving them.

ASPARAGUS

INGREDIENTS. — A bunch of asparagus, boiling water, salt, slice of toast, butter.

METHOD.—Scrape the white part of the asparagus stalks, scraping downwards.

Cut a piece off the end of each, then put into cold water, and leave in soak for a short time to clean it.

Tie into small bundles, placing the heads all the same way.

Put into a saucepan of boiling water with a pinch of salt, bring quickly to the boil, remove the lid of the pan, and boil gently for about twenty-five minutes or until tender.

Put a slice of toast in the bottom of the vegetable dish, lift the bundles of asparagus on to it (putting the heads all one way), and remove the string.

Serve separately oiled butter. Just melt some butter in a pan, remove the scum, and serve in a sauce-boat.

If preferred, white sauce (see p. 41), may be served instead of the oiled butter.

FRIED AUBERGINES OR EGG PLANT

INGREDIENTS.—3 egg plants, deep frying fat.

METHOD.—Peel the egg plants and cut them in half. Cut each into slices half an inch thick, and fry in deep fat as for potato chips. They will take three or four minutes.

GRILLED AUBERGINES OR EGG PLANT

INGREDIENTS.—3 egg plants, ½ oz. of butter.

METHOD.—Peel the egg plants or aubergines and cut them in slices a quarter of an inch thick.

Melt the butter in a frying-pan and put in the slices. Grill them under the gas griller for ten minutes. These may be served with bacon for breakfast, sprinkled with chopped parsley.

BAKED BANANAS

INGREDIENTS.—6 bananas, 1 oz. of flour, 1 teaspoonful of curry powder, 1 egg, breadcrumbs, 1 oz. of margarine, salt and pepper.

METHOD.—Mix the flour and curry powder with salt and pepper to taste. Peel the bananas and dip them in the flour. Brush them with egg and roll them in the breadcrumbs.

Melt the margarine in a baking-tin. Lay the bananas in it and turn them over. Bake for fifteen minutes and serve with roast meat.

Sufficient for six persons.

NOTE.—If preferred the bananas can be fried in deep fat.

CREAMED BEETROOT

INGREDIENTS.—2 beetroots (raw), 1 oz. of butter 1 oz. of flour, ½ onion (grated), 1 hard-boiled egg, salt and pepper, ½ pint of milk.

METHOD.—Wash the beetroots and take care not to break the roots. Cook them in boiling water with a dessertspoonful of salt till tender (about one hour).

Melt the butter, add the flour, and stir in the milk.

Stir till it boils, season with salt and pepper and add the grated onion and the egg coarsely chopped.

Skin the beetroots and cut them into large dice. Place in a hot dish and pour the sauce over them.

Sufficient for four persons.

BROAD BEANS AND PARSLEY SAUCE

IT is essential that broad beans should be young, otherwise they are very tough.

To prepare them, shell and then wash the beans.

Put into a saucepan of boiling water with salt, and boil until tender—the time taken depends on their age, but they will require from about twenty to thirty minutes.

When cooked, strain off the water and drain well.

Serve in a vegetable dish and coat with parsley sauce.

FOR THE SAUCE

MAKE some thick white sauce, and stir in some finely chopped parsley just before serving.

Allow about half a peck of beans for three or four persons.

FRENCH BEANS IN CREAM

INGREDIENTS.—1 lb. of young French beans, salt, pepper and nutmeg, ½ gill of double cream.

METHOD.—Wash the beans and cut them along the side to remove the strings.

Cut them into thin strips about an inch long.

Boil them fast with the lid off till tender (about twenty minutes) adding a teaspoonful of salt to the water.

Strain the beans and put them back in the saucepan over a low gas. Stir in the cream and add salt and pepper and a grating of nutmeg.

Sufficient for three or four persons.

FRENCH BEANS IN GRAVY

INGREDIENTS.—1 lb. of young French beans, ½ oz. of butter, ½ oz. of flour

½ teaspoonful of meat extract, ½ finely minced onion, salt and pepper.

METHOD.—Choose young French beans or scarlet runners. The very large ones are tough. Cut the beans along their sides to remove the strings, then wash them, and cut them across into diamond shapes.

Get ready a large pan of boiling water, and add to it a dessertspoonful of salt and enough soda to lie on a threepenny bit. Put in the beans and boil them fast with the lid off till tender (about twenty minutes). Strain them through a colander.

Melt the butter in a saucepan, fry the minced onion in it for six minutes, then add the flour and brown it in the fat. Add the meat extract, and a gill of the water in which the beans were cooked.

Put in the beans and re-heat them for ten minutes. Serve them in a hot dish.

NOTE.—A pound of French beans will be sufficient for three or four people. If served for two persons there should be enough left for a salad next day.

FRENCH BEANS AND WHITE SAUCE

INGREDIENTS.—1½ lb. of French beans, boiling water, salt and soda, ½ pint of milk, ¾ oz. of flour, 1 oz. of margarine, seasoning.

METHOD.—String the beans, wash them well, and put them whole into a saucepan of boiling water with salt added to flavour and a tiny piece of soda. Bring them to the boil quickly, remove the lid and boil the beans till tender. They will take about fifteen minutes to cook. Drain them through a colander, then arrange them in a vegetable dish and serve them with white sauce.

TO MAKE THE WHITE SAUCE.—Melt the fat in a saucepan, add the flour, and when well blended stir in the milk and bring the sauce to the boil. Add seasoning to taste and boil it gently for a few minutes before turning it into a sauce-boat.

Sufficient for four persons.

BRUSSELS SPROUTS

TRIM the stalks and remove the outside leaves if necessary. Wash and soak in cold salted water, then drain. Put into a pan with plenty of boiling water, and salt and soda added (1 tablespoonful of salt to about 2 quarts of water and sufficient soda to cover a threepenny piece).

Put the lid on the pan and bring quickly to the boil, then remove the lid and boil the sprouts (not too quickly) until tender, removing the scum as it rises. They will take about twenty minutes after they come to the boil. Strain and drain well, and serve.

One pound of sprouts is sufficient for about three persons.

BRUSSELS SPROUTS AND CHEESE SAUCE

INGREDIENTS.—1½ lb. of Brussels sprouts, boiling water, ½ pint of milk, 3½ oz. of cheese, 1 oz. of margarine, ¾ oz. of flour, salt and pepper, soda.

METHOD.—Prepare the sprouts in the usual way, removing the outer leaves and the base of the stalk. Wash them thoroughly in cold water with salt and cook them in boiling water, adding salt and a tiny piece of soda. They will take about twenty minutes to cook. When tender, pour them through a colander and when well drained, turn them into a dish and coat them with cheese sauce.

TO MAKE THE SAUCE.—Melt the fat, add the flour, and when blended stir in the milk and bring it to the boil. Simmer the sauce for a few minutes, add three ounces of the finely-grated cheese and seasoning to taste, and when the cheese is melted pour it over the sprouts.

Sprinkle the remainder of the cheese on the top and brown it lightly in the oven or under the grill.

Sufficient for four persons.

BRUSSELS SPROUTS FRITTERS

INGREDIENTS.—1 lb. of Brussels sprouts, 3½ oz. of flour, pinch of salt, 1 dessertspoonful of salad oil, ¼ pint of warm water, 1 egg white, deep fat for frying.

METHOD.—Sift the flour and salt into the basin and make a well in the centre. Pour in the oil, and add the warm water gradually, mixing it all to a smooth batter. Beat the batter well, then let it stand for an hour or more.

Prepare the sprouts in the usual way, soak them in cold salted water to cleanse them, and put them into boiling water to cook, adding salt to flavour. Boil the sprouts gently for about fifteen minutes until they are *lightly* cooked, then drain them well and let them cool.

Whisk the egg white stiffly and fold it into the batter. Then dip each sprout in separately and coat it with batter. Fry the sprouts in hot deep fat till they are golden, then drain them and serve them.

Sufficient for four persons.

BRUSSELS SPROUTS IN GRAVY

INGREDIENTS.—1 lb. of sprouts, 1 pint of gravy or beef tea.

METHOD.—Wash the sprouts well, removing any decayed leaves and cutting the stalks of the largest ones across into four.

Put the sprouts into a casserole and pour over them a pint of strong made gravy or beef-tea, which should be *boiling*.

Put on the lid closely and bake the sprouts in a moderate oven for about an hour. Turn them over in the gravy twice while they are cooking.

FRENCH CABBAGE

INGREDIENTS.—1 cabbage (medium size), 1 lb. of potatoes, pepper and salt, grated nutmeg, 2 oz. of margarine, milk.

METHOD. — Remove the outside leaves from the cabbage, cut it into four and wash well in two or three waters. Then soak for at least an hour in cold salted water.

The latter frees the vegetable from insects.

Peel the potatoes and boil until tender.

Put the cabbage into a saucepan of boiling water. Add a little salt and soda (about one tablespoonful of salt to two quarts of water, and a very tiny piece of soda), and boil for about fifteen minutes or until tender. Remove the lid from the saucepan when the cabbage comes up to the boil.

Then strain through a colander and drain well.

Chop it up very finely or put it through a fine mincer.

Strain the potatoes when they are cooked and mash up well with a fork. Then add half the margarine and a little drop of milk.

Mix the minced cabbage and the mashed potato. Season well, and add a little grated nutmeg.

Melt the other ounce of margarine in a saucepan, add the cabbage, etc., and re-heat, but do not fry.

Heap in a vegetable dish and serve very hot.

SPRING CABBAGE

INGREDIENTS. — Spring cabbages, boiling water, salt, soda.

METHOD.—Remove the stump and outside leaves, divide the cabbages into quarters, and pull well apart. Wash well in plenty of salt water, and leave in soak for a time.

Lift into a colander and drain well.

Put into a large saucepan with *plenty* of boiling water, and a little salt and soda—one tablespoonful of salt to about two quarts of water, and sufficient soda to cover a threepenny piece.

Bring quickly to the boil, remove the saucepan lid, and boil until tender, removing the scum as it rises.

When cooked, strain through a colander, squeeze out the water, and serve.

CABBAGE AND CHEESE SAUCE

INGREDIENTS. — 1 medium sized cabbage, salt, soda, 1 oz. of margarine or butter, 1 oz. of flour, ¾ pint of milk, seasoning, 3 oz. of cheese.

METHOD.—Boil the cabbage till tender, then strain it through a colander.

Melt the fat in a saucepan, add the flour, and when they are well blended, stir in the milk and bring the sauce to the boil. Boil it gently for a few minutes, then draw it aside.

Grate the cheese finely and add it to the sauce. Season it with salt and pepper, and stir it over a low burner until the cheese is melted.

Butter a dish, and fill it with

alternate layers of sauce and cabbage, making the last layer of sauce. Sprinkle a little cheese on top, and put the dish into the oven for a few minutes to make it thoroughly hot.

Sufficient for five or six persons.

CARROT CROQUETTES

INGREDIENTS.—1 lb. of carrots, ½ oz. of flour, 1 oz. of margarine, ½ gill of milk, 1 teaspoonful of chopped parsley, 1 oz. of breadcrumbs, 1 teaspoonful of lemon-juice, grating of nutmeg, salt and pepper, egg, breadcrumbs, deep fat.

METHOD.—Scrape and wash the carrots, split them in halves or quarters and put them into slightly salted boiling water to cook.

Boil the carrots till tender, then drain them well in a colander. Mash up the carrots with a fork, or rub them through a wire sieve.

Melt the fat in a saucepan, stir in the flour, and when they are well blended add the milk and bring the sauce to the boil. Boil it for a minute or two, keeping it stirred, then draw the pan aside and stir in the mashed carrots, breadcrumbs, lemon-juice, parsley and add seasoning to taste. Mix the ingredients well, then spread the paste on a plate and leave it till it is firm.

Divide it into eight or nine portions and form each one into a roll, using a little flour to prevent the carrot mixture from sticking. Brush each roll with beaten egg and coat it with breadcrumbs. Then place the rolls in a frying-basket and fry them in hot deep fat until they are golden. Drain them on paper and serve them.

Sufficient to make nine croquettes.

FRENCH CARROTS

INGREDIENTS.—1 bunch of carrots, 1 gill of hot milk or water, ½ oz. of butter, 1 dessertspoonful of chopped parsley, ½ oz. of flour, pepper and salt, cold water.

METHOD.—Wash and scrape the carrots.

Put them in a double saucepan with the milk, quarter of a teaspoonful of salt, and butter,

Put boiling water in the lower pan and keep it boiling for one hour.

Mix the flour smoothly with a little cold water, and pour it on to the carrots.

Put the inner pan on the gas and stir till it boils.

Boil for three minutes, and add parsley, salt, and pepper.

Sufficient for three persons.

SWEET CARROTS

INGREDIENTS.—¾ lb. of carrots, 2 oz. of butter, 2 oz. of castor sugar, salt, boiling water, pepper, parsley or mint.

METHOD.—Scrape and wash the carrots and cut them into thin slices. Put them into a saucepan of boiling water with a little salt added and boil them for about fifteen minutes until almost tender. Strain off the water through a colander.

Melt the butter in a saucepan, add the sugar, stir them over a low burner until dissolved. Add the carrots and toss them frequently until they are quite tender. Season and serve them. Sometimes some chopped parsley may be sprinkled over them, or else add a little chopped mint to the butter and sugar when adding the carrots.

Sufficient for three persons.

YOUNG CARROTS

INGREDIENTS.—A bunch of young carrots, stock (see p. 12), 1 oz. of butter or margarine, chopped parsley, boiling water, salt.

METHOD.—Scrape and wash the carrots.

Put them into a saucepan of boiling water to which a pinch of salt has been added, and boil for about ten minutes.

Strain off the water, put the carrots into cold water, and scrape again.

Put about two teacupfuls of stock (strained) into a saucepan, and season with pepper and salt.

Add the butter, and bring to the boil.

Add the carrots, and boil gently until tender.

Strain off the stock, place the carrots in a hot vegetable dish, and keep warm.

Return the stock to the pan, and boil fast until reduced, then pour over the carrots.

Garnish with chopped parsley and serve.

BOILED CAULIFLOWER

CUT a piece off the stalk and remove the outside leaves of the cauliflower. Then scoop a piece out from the base of the stalk or split it across.

Put it into a bowl of salted water and leave in soak to draw out any insects. Then drain.

Put into a pan of boiling water with salt added, also a tiny piece of soda. Place the lid on the pan, bring quickly up to the boil, then remove the lid and boil gently until tender, keeping it skimmed as required.

The time depends on the size of the cauliflower. The cauliflower should be placed flower side down in the pan so that the scum does not discolour it. When cooked, lift up with a slice, drain well, and serve with thick white sauce (see p. 41).

CREAMED CAULIFLOWER

INGREDIENTS.—1 small cauliflower, 1 oz. of butter, 1 gill of milk, ½ oz. of flour, salt and pepper.

METHOD.—Cut the cauliflower into quarters, and wash it well.

Put it in a double pan with the butter and milk, cover and cook till tender, from forty to fifty minutes.

Strain off the liquid and dish up the cauliflower, keeping it hot while making the sauce.

Mix the flour smoothly with a little cold milk, and add this to the liquid. Stir till it boils, boil for three minutes and season to taste. Pour over the cauliflower and serve.

A medium-sized cauliflower is sufficient for two persons.

CAULIFLOWER SUPREME

INGREDIENTS.—1 cauliflower, 1 gill of hot water, 1 oz. of butter, 1 egg, salt and pepper.

METHOD.—Cut the cauliflower into quarters and wash it well.

Cook the pieces in a double pan with a gill of water and the butter for forty or fifty minutes or till tender.

Dish up the cauliflower and return the liquid to the saucepan. Beat an egg till quite frothy and add this to the hot—but not boiling—liquid in the pan.

Season to taste and pour over the cauliflower.

A medium-sized cauliflower is sufficient for two persons.

CELERY FRITTERS

INGREDIENTS.—1 head of celery, 3 oz. of flour, pinch of salt, 1 dessertspoonful of salad oil, 2 egg whites, deep fat for frying, 1 gill of warm water, seasoning.

METHOD.—Sift the flour with the salt, make a well in the centre, and pour in the oil, then add the warm water gradually and mix a smooth batter. Beat it well and leave it to stand for an hour or more.

Clean and prepare the celery. Put it into boiling water with a little salt and boil it for about fifteen minutes, then drain it and let it cool. Cut it into convenient sized pieces, and season it.

When ready to fry, whisk the whites of eggs stiffly and fold them into the batter, put in some of the celery, and coat it, then lift it into the hot fat and fry it until golden. Coat and fry the remainder, drain it on paper, and serve the fritters with a dish of finely grated cheese, or sprinkle some cheese over it.

Sufficient for four or five persons.

BOILED CELERIAC

INGREDIENTS.—Celeriac as required, boiling water, salt, allow 3 oz. of butter to 3 pints of diced celeriac, pepper, parsley.

METHOD.—Peel the celeriac, wash it well and cut it into large dice, then measure it.

Cook it in boiling water with salt to flavour, until it is tender, then drain it well.

Melt the butter in a large saucepan, add the celeriac and toss it in the butter for a few minutes, then season it with pepper, turn it into a dish and garnish it with finely minced parsley.

If liked, the butter may be omitted, and the celeriac served with a plain white sauce.

STEWED CHESTNUTS

INGREDIENTS.—1 lb. of chestnuts, stock (see p. 12), seasoning, flour.

METHOD.—Put the chestnuts into cold water, bring them to the boil and boil them for a few minutes. Then remove the outer shell and the inner skin, and put the prepared chestnuts into a casserole.

Add about half a pint of stock or sufficient almost to cover the chestnuts. If liked the liquor in which celery has been cooked may be used, as this gives the chestnuts an excellent flavour. Put the lid on the casserole and cook the chestnuts in a moderate oven until they are tender.

When the chestnuts are ready, pour off the remaining stock and thicken it slightly with flour, then return it to the casserole. Season and re-heat the chestnuts before serving, then this dish is suitable to serve with roast chicken or turkey.

Sufficient for three or four persons.

BOILED CHICORY

INGREDIENTS.—1 lb. of chicory, salt, 1½ oz. of butter, 1½ oz. of flour, 1 gill of milk, 1 tablespoonful of grated cheese, salt and pepper, 1 tablespoonful of vinegar.

METHOD.—Remove any discoloured leaves and wash the chicory well in salt and water.

Boil one quart of water in a wide stewpan, and add a dessertspoonful of salt and the vinegar.

Lay the chicory in the water with the leaves all lying the same way, and stew it with the lid on for fifteen minutes. Then drain the chicory and serve it in a hot dish.

Melt the butter in a saucepan, stir in the flour, milk, and half a gill of the water in which the chicory was cooked, and boil it up, stirring all the time. Add cheese and seasoning, and boil for three minutes. Then pour the sauce over the chicory.

BOILED CUCUMBER

INGREDIENTS.—Cucumbers, as required, boiling water, salt.

METHOD.—Peel the cucumbers, split them into halves lengthwise, then cut them across and remove the seeds.

Cook them in boiling water, to which a little salt has been added, for about twenty minutes, or until tender. Lift them out and drain them well and serve them with white sauce (see p. 41) or oiled butter.

BUTTERED CUCUMBER

INGREDIENTS.—3 small cucumbers, 2 oz. of butter, seasoning.

METHOD.—Peel the cucumbers and split them in quarters lengthwise; remove the stalk end and cut the cucumbers into thick pieces.

Put the butter into a saucepan, add the prepared cucumber and cook it gently until tender, keeping it well tossed about and stirred occasionally. Season well, and serve with the butter.

It will take about forty-five minutes to cook.

Sufficient for three persons.

BOILED LEEKS AND WHITE SAUCE

INGREDIENTS.—Leeks, as required, boiling water, salt, slice of bread, white sauce (see p. 41).

METHOD.—To prepare the leeks, cut off the roots and some of the green tops, and peel off the outside layer, then wash them thoroughly as they are usually very gritty. To ensure cleanliness they may be split down a little way along one side.

Put them into a saucepan of boiling water, to which a little salt has been added, and boil them gently until tender. They will take from thirty-five to forty-five minutes, according to the size. Some prefer to tie them in bundles before cooking. Have the bread ready toasted and put it in the bottom of the vegetable dish, drain the leeks and serve them on the toast, arranging the heads all one way. Serve leeks with white sauce, or, if preferred, oiled butter. Make the sauce in the usual way (see p. 41), allowing ¾ oz. of flour and ¾ oz. of margarine to half a pint of milk or milk and water.

A bunch of leeks is sufficient for three or four persons.

BAKED MARROW

INGREDIENTS.—1 small to medium-sized marrow, seasoning, 2 oz. of butter, finely chopped parsley.

METHOD.—Peel and quarter the marrow and remove the seeds and soft part, then cut the quarters into smaller pieces—about half as large as you would for boiling.

Wash and drain them thoroughly,

and put them into a buttered Pyrex dish with dabs of butter and seasoning of pepper and salt on each layer. Cover the dish and bake the marrow in a moderate oven until tender, keeping it well basted. It will take about an hour to cook.

Sprinkle the marrow with finely chopped parsley, and serve it in the dish.

Sufficient for three or four persons.

MARROW EN CASSEROLE

INGREDIENTS. — 1 medium-sized marrow, 2 oz. of butter, pepper and salt, milk, parsley, 1½ dessertspoonfuls of flour.

METHOD.—Peel and quarter the marrow, remove the seeds. Wash it, and cut each quarter into four.

Put the marrow into a buttered casserole with the butter cut into small dabs. Season it and cover it.

Cook the marrow gently in the oven until it is tender, basting it occasionally with the butter.

When it is cooked, drain off the liquid and make it up to half a pint with milk. Then pour it into a saucepan and thicken it with the flour, smoothed in a little milk.

Bring the sauce to the boil and boil it for a few minutes, keeping it stirred. Season the sauce and pour it over the marrow, and sprinkle it with finely minced parsley.

Sufficient for three or four persons.

FRIED VEGETABLE MARROW

INGREDIENTS.—1 vegetable marrow, egg and breadcrumbs, dripping or butter.

METHOD.—Peel the marrow and cut it crosswise into slices about half an inch thick, remove the seeds from the centre, leaving a thick ring of marrow.

Beat up the egg, brush the marrow over with it and coat it with breadcrumbs.

Heat some fat in a frying-pan and when hot, fry the marrow rings, a few at a time, until tender, turning them over when brown.

Drain them, and serve on a paper.

MUSHROOMS

MUSHROOMS can be cooked in various ways—grilled, stewed and fried ; their addition to a meat pie, pudding or casserole is a great improvement. Whichever way they are to be used they must first be prepared. To do this, peel them and remove the stalks, then put them into cold water (to which a little salt has been added) for a few minutes, to cleanse them, then drain them well.

To FRY MUSHROOMS.—Melt some butter or dripping in a frying-pan, put in the mushrooms and fry them gently until tender. They will take about ten or fifteen minutes.

To STEW THEM.—Put into a saucepan with a little stock and butter, season with pepper and salt, and cook gently. Thicken the liquor in which they are cooked before serving.

To GRILL THEM.—Cook in the bottom of the grill-tin with a lump of butter. If cooked with a steak or chop, let the fat from the meat drip on to them when cooking.

Or, some prefer to cook them in the oven with a lump of butter.

NOTE.—Mushroom trimmings can be used for flavouring stocks and gravies.

MUSHROOMS IN GRAVY

INGREDIENTS.—1 gill of water, 1 teaspoonful of Bisto, ½ teaspoonful of Bovril, 1 dessertspoonful of chopped parsley, 1 oz. of butter, ½ lb. of small mushrooms.

METHOD.—Peel the mushrooms and remove the stalks. Put the mushrooms into a double pan with a small piece of butter in each. Add the Bovril and water, cover and cook them for about forty minutes. Strain off the juice and thicken it with the Bisto mixed to a smooth paste. Dish up the mushrooms.

Stir the gravy till it boils, add the parsley, and pour it round the mushrooms.

MUSHROOMS IN MILK

INGREDIENTS.—½ lb. of small mushrooms, 1 oz. of butter, 1 gill of milk, salt and pepper, 2 slices of bread, 2 oz. of dripping.

METHOD.—Wash and peel the mushrooms and remove the stalks. Place mushrooms cup side up in a pie-dish with the butter and milk, and season them with salt and pepper. Cover with greased paper and bake in a quick oven for twenty minutes. To make the sippets of fried bread cut the slices into strips an inch wide and cut these across into squares. Cut each square in half from corner to corner. Heat the dripping till it smokes, put in the bread and fry for a minute on each side (or less if the fat is very hot). Drain the sippets on paper and place them round the inside of the pie-dish when serving.

Sufficient for two persons.

ONIONS IN BATTER

INGREDIENTS.—2 small Spanish onions, 1 oz. of dripping, 1 egg, 4 oz. of flour, salt, ½ pint of milk.

METHOD.—Peel the onions, put them in boiling water with a tea-spoonful of salt. Boil them for one hour, and then strain them. Put the onions and dripping into a fireproof dish, and bake them for half an hour.

Put the flour and a quarter of a teaspoonful of salt into a basin with the egg in the centre. Gradually stir in half the milk. Beat well and add the rest of the milk.

Pour the batter round the onions and bake them for forty minutes.

Sufficient for from two to four persons.

BRAISED ONIONS

INGREDIENTS.—4 large Spanish onions, 2 oz. of butter, 1 pint of water used for boiling the onions, 1 dessert-spoonful of salt.

METHOD.—Put a large saucepanful of water on to boil with the salt in it. Peel the onions and boil them for one hour.

Take the onions out of the water and put them in a baking-tin, with the butter and one pint of the water that the onions were boiled in.

Bake for one and a half to two hours in a moderate oven, turning the onions over now and again.

Place the onions in a dish and pour the savoury sauce over them.

Sufficient for four persons.

SAVOURY SAUCE

INGREDIENTS.—¾ oz. of butter, ¾ oz. of flour, 1 teaspoonful of glaze or meat extract, 1 teaspoonful of

Worcester sauce, salt and pepper, ½ pint of water in which onions were baked (or stock).

METHOD.—Add the glaze to the water in which the onions were baked, and boil it down until it measures half a pint. Melt the butter and fry the flour a rich brown, stirring well. Add the onion water and Worcester sauce and stir till it boils. Boil for a minute, season to taste, and pour over the onions.

ONION FRITTERS

INGREDIENTS.—1 lb. of very small onions, deep frying fat, salt and pepper.

FOR THE BATTER.—3 oz. of flour, ½ tablespoonful of salad oil, ¾ gill of tepid water, 1 egg (beaten).

METHOD.—Peel the onions and boil them for ten minutes.

Drain them and sprinkle with salt and pepper.

To make the batter, mix the flour smoothly with the oil, egg and water. Put in the onions.

Heat the fat and when it begins to smoke put in three onions coated with batter.

Fry them for three minutes and drain on paper. Re-heat the fat before frying the next batch.

Serve on lace paper.

Sufficient for four or five persons.

STEWED SPANISH ONIONS

INGREDIENTS.—1 Spanish onion, 1 oz. of butter, 1 gill of milk, ½ oz. of flour, salt and pepper.

METHOD.—Slice the onion thinly, and put it in a double pan with the milk and butter.

Close tightly, and cook for an hour or till tender.

Put the onion in a hot vegetable dish, straining off the juice.

Add sufficient extra milk to the juice to make a gill.

Mix a dessertspoonful of flour smoothly with the juice, put it in the pan and stir till it boils. Season to taste and pour over the onions.

Sufficient for two persons.

FRIED PARSNIPS

INGREDIENTS.—2 parsnips, 1 oz. of dripping, salt and pepper.

METHOD.—Wash and peel the

Rice
Potatoes

French
Beans

Sweet
Carrots

PLATE 17

New Potatoes
with
Maitre
d'Hotel
Butter

Buttered
Cucumber

Artichoke
Crisps

PLATE 18

Baked
Bananas

Baked
Marrow

Braised
Onions

PLATE 19

Brown
Potato
Balls

Spinach
Mould

Mace-
doine
of Peas
and
Carrots

PLATE 20

parsnips and cut them in thick slices. Boil for ten minutes till half cooked, and then strain off all the water. Heat an ounce of good beef or pork dripping in a frying-pan, and put in the slices of parsnips. Cook them gently till they are tender and slightly browned, and turn them over when half done. They will take from ten to fifteen minutes. Sprinkle with salt and pepper.

Sufficient for two to four persons, according to size of parsnips.

MASHED PARSNIPS

INGREDIENTS.—2 or 3 parsnips, 1 oz. of butter, salt and pepper.

METHOD.—Wash and peel the parsnips and cut them into quarters. Boil them till tender (about half an hour). Strain off the water and rub the parsnips through a wire sieve, or else mash them with the back of a fork. Add the butter and salt and pepper, and heat the parsnips over a very low gas for five minutes, stirring them carefully to prevent burning.

NOTE.—Parsnips vary in weight a good deal. A large one weighing 1 lb. or more is sufficient for two persons.

MACEDOINE OF PEAS AND CARROTS

TAKE equal quantities of shelled peas and carrots cut into dice.

To prepare the carrots, scrape and wash them, and cut them into thick slices, then into small dice.

When fresh peas are not in season, use tinned ones.

Cook the vegetables in separate pans of boiling water with salt added to flavour, and when cooked, pour them into a colander and drain off the water. Mix these together and put them into a saucepan with a lump of butter, and toss the vegetables in it for a few minutes. Season with pepper, add a pinch of sugar, and serve in a hot vegetable dish.

SAVOURY PEAS

INGREDIENTS.—1 pint of young shelled peas, 1 lettuce, ½ onion (chopped), 1 oz. of butter, ½ oz. of flour, 1 gill of boiling water, salt and pepper,

1 teaspoonful of sugar, mint, ½ gill of cold water.

METHOD.—Wash and shred the lettuce. Put peas, lettuce, onion and mint in a double saucepan, with the butter and hot water.

Put boiling water in the lower pan. Boil for forty minutes or till tender. Mix the flour smoothly with the cold water and pour it in with the vegetables.

Stir until it boils, standing the inner pan on the gas. Season with salt, pepper and sugar.

Sufficient for two or three persons.

STEWED PUMPKIN

INGREDIENTS.—A 2 lb. slice of pumpkin, ½ pint of hot water, ½ teaspoonful of salt, ½ oz. of butter and flour, pepper, ½ gill of cold milk, ¼ teaspoonful of cinnamon.

METHOD.—Cut off the rind and remove the seeds, and cut the slice of pumpkin across into one-inch trips.

Place in a double saucepan with the water, salt and butter, put the lid on, and cook till tender (about forty-five minutes).

Put the pieces of pumpkin in a hot vegetable dish, and drain off any water that comes from them.

Mix the flour smoothly with the milk, and pour on to it the hot water in which the pumpkin was stewed.

Return to the pan, and stir till it boils.

Season to taste with pepper and cinnamon, and pour over the pumpkin.

To make mashed pumpkin stew the pumpkin till tender, as explained above, then mash it with a wooden spoon, and carefully drain off all water.

Melt an ounce of butter in the pan, add half an ounce of flour, and the mashed pumpkin.

Stir till it boils, and boil for three minutes. Season with pepper, salt and cinnamon.

Two pounds of pumpkin will serve two or three persons, not more, as it goes to a mash like marrow.

POTATOES BAKED IN THEIR SKINS

INGREDIENTS.—Large, old potatoes of even size.

METHOD.—Scrub some large, old

G

potatoes of even size, and dry them. Prick them all over with a fork in order to allow the steam to escape from them, and to make them dry and floury. Bake them in the top of a moderate oven, and turn them over once or twice. They will take from one to one and a half hours, unless very large.

To tell if they are done, press them between the finger and thumb. If they are soft inside they are done. Serve with butter.

BOILED POTATOES

INGREDIENTS.—Potatoes of the same size, and cold water to cover, salt.

METHOD.—Wash the potatoes and peel them as thinly as possible. Put them in cold water till you are ready to cook them.

Then put them in a saucepan with enough cold water just to cover them. If there is too much water they are likely to break when cooked.

Bring them quickly to the boil, and finish cooking them slowly. If boiled quickly all the time they will be broken and watery.

They will take from twenty to thirty minutes or longer to cook if they are very large potatoes.

To see if they are tender, stick a fine skewer into them. Drain off all the water and replace the saucepan on a very low gas, keeping the lid partly off. Leave them to dry for ten minutes. When dry and floury, place them in a vegetable dish with a spoon in order not to break them.

BROWNED POTATOES

BOIL the required number of potatoes for ten minutes, strain off the water, and cut them in quarters. Put two ounces of dripping in a baking-tin and heat it in the oven. Put in the potatoes, and bake for thirty minutes in a moderate oven, turning them two or three times while they are cooking.

BROWN POTATO BALLS

INGREDIENTS.—2 lb. of potatoes, 2 eggs, salt and pepper, 1 dessertspoonful of chopped onion, lump of margarine or butter, breadcrumbs, deep fat.

METHOD.—Peel the potatoes and boil them with some salt added until tender. Drain them and rub them through a sieve.

Separate the eggs, beat up the yolks and add them to the potato with the butter, finely-minced onion and seasoning to taste. Mix them well, leave the mixture to cool, then divide it into small portions and shape them into balls. Brush them with the slightly beaten egg whites, coat them with breadcrumbs, put them in a frying-basket and fry them in deep fat until golden brown. Drain the balls and serve them immediately.

Sufficient for six persons.

POTATO CHIPS

WASH, peel and dry some old potatoes. Cut them into slices a quarter of an inch thick, and cut each slice into strips of the same thickness. Lay them in a cloth, and heat some deep frying fat. It should be heated till a distinct bluish smoke rises from it. Put in half the potatoes, using a frying-basket if possible. If too many potatoes are put in at once the fat will be cooled, and the potatoes will be soft and greasy.

Fry the chips quickly for about ten minutes till a golden brown. Turn them on to a tin, covered with soft paper to absorb the grease, and keep them hot while frying the second batch. Sprinkle with salt.

CREAMED POTATOES

INGREDIENTS.—2 lb. of potatoes, ½ pint of milk, 1 good dessertspoonful of flour, 1 oz. of margarine, salt and pepper, some chopped parsley.

METHOD.—Peel the potatoes thinly and boil them gently in slightly salted water until tender. Drain them. Cut them into fairly thick slices, and put them into a vegetable dish. Pour white sauce over them and sprinkle them with a little very finely chopped parsley.

To make the sauce, melt the margarine in a saucepan, add the flour and mix them until smooth. Add the milk and stir until the sauce boils. Let it boil gently for a few minutes, and add seasoning to taste.

Sufficient for four or five persons.

POTATO CROQUETTES

INGREDIENTS.—1 lb. of cold potato, pepper, celery salt, few drops of onion-juice, 1 level teaspoonful of finely chopped parsley, ½ oz. of butter, salt, few grains of cayenne, 1 egg yolk, breadcrumbs.

METHOD.—The ingredients should be mixed together and heated thoroughly.

Spread the paste on a plate to cool. Cut it into suitable pieces and shape each piece into a roll, handling it as carefully as possible.

Brush each croquette with egg and then coat it with crumbs.

Fry the croquettes quickly in deep fat, using a frying-basket and drain them on brown paper.

Potato croquettes can be made into different shapes. If preferred, the paste may be rolled into a ball and then flattened slightly to form a cake. Small balls of this potato paste coated with egg could also be made.

Sufficient for twelve croquettes.

DUCHESSE POTATOES

INGREDIENTS.—1 lb. of potatoes, 1 oz. of butter, salt and pepper, 1 egg, 2 tablespoonfuls of milk, 1 oz. of flour.

METHOD.—Wash, peel, and boil the potatoes and drain them.

Add the butter and milk and mash the potatoes with a fork.

Beat the egg and mix nearly all of it with the potatoes. Season with salt and pepper.

Turn the potatoes on to a floured board and shape into five or six squares. Put in a tin and brush the tops with the remainder of the egg.

Bake in a quick oven for ten to fifteen minutes.

Sufficient for four persons.

POTATO FRITTERS

INGREDIENTS.—1 lb. of freshly-boiled potatoes (dry and floury), 1 oz. of butter, 1 large egg, salt and pepper, deep frying fat.

METHOD.—Mash the potatoes with a fork while they are still hot. Add the butter, salt and pepper, and a well-beaten egg. Mix well, and leave till cold.

Heat the fat till it smokes *slightly* and drop in three teaspoonfuls of the mixture, turning up the gas a little so as to keep the fat at the same heat.

Fry for about three minutes till a pale golden colour, take them out with a fish slice and drain on paper.

If the fat smokes too much, it is too hot and will cause the fritters to burst open.

Those who are not used to deep frying should test the heat of the fat by dropping in a tiny ball of the potato mixture. If it fries nicely, then begin frying the batch, never doing more than three at a time, and heating the fat before frying the next.

This quantity will make about sixteen fritters.

TO FRY POTATOES

POTATOES should be fried in plenty of fat, the deep method is the best for this purpose. *They can be cut into various shapes*—balls, strips, chips, and ribbons. For the balls a vegetable cutter will be necessary.

The strips should be cut very finely.

To cut the chips, cut round a potato first, then cut it across into very thin slices.

To cut ribbon potatoes, choose nice round potatoes and peel them evenly so that you have a smooth surface, then cut round and round into ribbons.

The potatoes should then be soaked for a time in cold water, then *drained well*, and *dried* in a cloth.

To fry them wait until a faint smoke rises from the fat, then put the potatoes into a frying-basket, stand it in the deep pan of fat, and fry them until golden brown.

Drain on paper and serve.

If fried in batches, put them in again altogether at the last for just a few seconds, to crisp them, then drain and serve.

Be very careful when deep-frying not to fill the pan too full so that the fat overflows.

MASHED POTATOES

INGREDIENTS.—1 lb. of potatoes, ½ oz. of butter, ½ gill of milk, salt and pepper.

METHOD.—After washing and peeling the potatoes, boil them carefully in enough water just to cover them and a teaspoonful of salt. Dry them over the gas to make them floury, break them up with a fork, and be careful to remove *all* lumps. Add butter, milk, salt and pepper, and beat till perfectly smooth and creamy. The longer they are beaten the better they will be. Serve very hot.

MASHED POTATOES AND APPLE SAUCE

INGREDIENTS.—1½ lb. of potatoes, salt and pepper, 1½ lb. of apples, 2 oz. of butter, 2 oz. of sugar, ½ gill of milk.

METHOD.—This is a simple but very nice dish. Wash and peel the potatoes, and put them into a saucepan with water enough just to cover them, and a teaspoonful of salt. Boil them gently till they are tender, strain off the water and dry them over a low gas. Mash them with a fork and add an ounce of butter and the milk. Season with salt and pepper. Peel, core, and quarter the apples, and stew them till they go to dry mash. Add the sugar and an ounce of butter. Make a border of the potatoes, and mark it with a fork. Pour in the apples and serve.

Sufficient for four or five persons.

MASHED POTATOES AND CHEESE

INGREDIENTS.—1½ lb. of potatoes, 1 egg, 2 oz. of butter, ½ gill of cream or milk, salt and pepper, 2 table-spoonfuls each of fresh breadcrumbs and grated cheese.

METHOD.—Boil and dry off the potatoes.

Mash them carefully with the back of a fork, and add the butter, milk or cream, and seasoning. Beat the egg, and add it to the potatoes.

Put the mashed potato into a buttered pie-dish and place small pieces of butter over the surface. Sprinkle lightly with cheese and breadcrumbs, and bake in a hot oven for fifteen minutes, or till brown.

Sufficient for four or five persons.

NEW POTATOES

WASH and scrape the potatoes, then drop into cold water. Put into a saucepan of boiling water—there should be just enough to cover them—add a little salt and a small piece of mint and boil gently until tender. Strain off the water, leave at the side for a few seconds to dry, then add a lump of butter or margarine, and when melted shake the potatoes gently in it. Serve with finely chopped parsley sprinkled over them.

NOTE.—Do not leave the mint in too long or it will discolour the potatoes.

NEW POTATOES

WITH MAITRE D'HOTEL BUTTER

INGREDIENTS.—2 lb. of new potatoes, boiling water, salt, a small sprig of mint, 1 oz. of butter, salt and pepper, ½ teaspoonful of lemon-juice, 1 level teaspoonful of chopped parsley.

METHOD.—Put the butter on a plate and work it until soft and creamy, then gradually mix in the lemon-juice, and add the finely chopped parsley and seasoning to taste. Form the butter into a block and leave it to harden.

Scrape and wash the potatoes and put them into boiling water to cook with salt to flavour and a small sprig of mint. Do not leave this in too long as it is apt to discolour the potatoes.

When tender, drain off the water, add half the butter and toss the potatoes in it, then turn them into a vegetable dish and garnish them with the remainder of the butter made into small balls.

Sufficient for six persons.

RICED POTATOES

BOIL the potatoes in the usual way, drain them and let them dry. Put them through a potato ricer into the dish in which they are to be served. The potatoes should be left just as they fall from the ricer, otherwise they lose their " riced " appearance.

This is only suitable for floury potatoes, and is a good way of serving them when they become very broken during the cooking.

After putting them through the ricer, return the dish to the oven for a minute or two to be sure the potatoes are quite hot before serving them.

SCALLOPED POTATOES

INGREDIENTS.—2 lb. of potatoes, 3 to 4 oz. of cheese, $1\frac{1}{2}$ oz. of butter, $2\frac{1}{2}$ gills of milk, salt and pepper, $1\frac{1}{4}$ oz. of flour.

METHOD.—Peel the potatoes, wash them and cut them into thin slices.

Put them into a buttered pie-dish or Pyrex dish in layers, sprinkling each layer with flour, pepper and salt, finely grated cheese and dabs of butter.

Pour in the milk, sprinkle cheese on top, cover the dish with a buttered paper, and bake the potatoes in a moderately hot oven for about one hour and a half, until the potatoes are tender.

Sufficient for six persons.

BOILED RADISHES

RADISHES are excellent when cooked and served as a vegetable.

Stalk and wash them and put them into boiling water to cook with salt to flavour. Boil them till tender. They will take about half an hour to cook. Strain them and serve them with white sauce.

Choose good-sized radishes, and allow a small bunch for each person.

TO MAKE THE SAUCE.—Melt one ounce of butter or margarine in a saucepan, add three-quarters of an ounce of flour, and when blended stir in half a pint of milk and bring the sauce to the boil. Boil it gently for a few minutes, and add seasoning to taste.

CREAMED SCARLET RUN-NERS

INGREDIENTS.—1 lb. of small scarlet runners, $\frac{1}{2}$ oz. of butter, $\frac{1}{2}$ oz. of flour, $\frac{1}{2}$ gill of milk, $\frac{1}{2}$ gill of water in which the beans have been cooked, 1 teaspoonful of lemon-juice, a little grated nutmeg.

METHOD.—Put on a large pan of water to boil, adding one dessert-spoonful of salt and a piece of soda as large as a pea.

String and wash the beans, and cut them across into diamond-shaped pieces.

Boil them quickly in the water with the lid off for twenty minutes, and strain them.

Melt the butter in a saucepan, add the flour, and stir in the milk and the water in which the beans were cooked, with the pan off the gas. Add the lemon-juice and season to taste with nutmeg, salt and pepper.

Pour the sauce over the beans, and serve.

SEAKALE AND HOLLANDAISE SAUCE

INGREDIENTS.—1 lb. of seakale, boiling water, salt and lemon-juice (1 tablespoonful to 2 quarts of water), 1 slice of bread, 1 teaspoonful of dried parsley.

FOR THE SAUCE.—$\frac{1}{2}$ oz. of flour, $1\frac{1}{2}$ oz. of margarine or butter, $1\frac{1}{2}$ gills of milk, 2 egg yolks, seasoning, 2 or 3 teaspoonfuls of lemon-juice.

METHOD.—Trim the bottom of the stalks to a point; if very big the sea-kale can be split into halves or quarters lengthways.

Wash it well in plenty of cold water, and leave soaking for at least half an hour. Then tie in bundles.

Put into a saucepan of boiling water (to which a little salt and lemon-juice has been added), and boil gently until tender; it will take about twenty-five minutes.

Toast the bread and place in the bottom of the vegetable dish.

Lift the seakale into a colander with a fish slice, remove the string, drain the seakale, and place on the toast.

Coat with the Hollandaise sauce, and sprinkle with the dried parsley.

TO DRY THE PARSLEY.—Put a sprig of parsley into a warm oven and leave until dry. Rub it between the fingers into a fine powder.

TO MAKE THE SAUCE.—Melt the margarine in a saucepan, mix in the flour until quite smooth.

Add the milk and stir until it comes to the boil, simmer for about six minutes, season well, draw away from the fire, and cool slightly.

Whisk the yolks separately into the sauce, put over the fire and simmer slowly until the eggs are cooked, but do not boil it, or they will curdle. Add the lemon-juice; then it is ready for serving.

NOTE.—After the yolks are added

to the sauce, it is advisable to finish cooking it in a double saucepan, or in a jug in a saucepan of water. The sauce should be quite thick and smooth when finished.

SPINACH

PICK over the spinach and pull off the stalk that runs through each leaf. Wash it well in several waters (with salt added), and leave to soak for a while.

Spinach is usually very gritty, so it needs to be thoroughly washed. Put it into a saucepan with about a cupful of boiling water and a little salt. Cover the pan and boil gently until tender—it will take from twenty-five to thirty minutes.

Strain through a colander and press out all the water, then turn the spinach on to a board and chop it up.

Return it to the pan, add a lump of butter or margarine, season with pepper, make thoroughly hot, and serve.

Allow three-quarters to one lb. for each person.

SPINACH MOULD

INGREDIENTS.—1½ lb. of spinach, 2 oz. of butter, 1½ oz. of flour, 2 raw eggs, salt and pepper, 2 hard-boiled eggs.

METHOD.—Wash the spinach four or five times and remove the largest stalks. Put the spinach in a saucepan with a teaspoonful of salt and cook it with the lid on for thirty minutes, stirring now and again.

Pour the spinach on a wire sieve and keep the juice that runs through.

Rub the spinach through the sieve and measure half a pint of the purée, if necessary adding some spinach juice to make up the quantity. Melt the butter, stir in the flour and spinach purée.

Season to taste and stir till it boils. Beat the eggs and add them. Pour the mixture into a greased pie-dish or small mould. Cover with greased paper and bake for one hour in a moderate oven. Leave for five minutes, turn out gently and decorate with quarters of hard-boiled egg.

Sufficient for four persons.

STEWED SPINACH

WITH SIPPETS OF FRIED BREAD

INGREDIENTS.—1 lb. of spinach, 1 oz. of butter, 1 oz. of flour, salt and pepper.

FOR THE SIPPETS OF FRIED BREAD. —2 slices of bread, ¼ in. thick, 2 oz. of dripping.

METHOD.—Wash the spinach four times and pick off the largest stalks.

Put the wet spinach into a saucepan with a teaspoonful of salt.

Put on the lid and cook till tender (about thirty minutes). Turn the spinach on to a sieve and let the water run through.

Melt one ounce of butter, stir in the flour and a cupful of the spinach water.

Stir till it boils, chop and add the spinach and simmer for five minutes. Season with salt and pepper. Garnish with sippets of fried bread.

TO MAKE THE SIPPETS OF FRIED BREAD

CUT the bread into small squares, then into triangles.

Heat the dripping till it smokes, put in the bread and fry it for one minute, turning it over when one side is brown. Drain on paper.

Sufficient for four persons.

BAKED TOMATOES

INGREDIENTS.—4 large English tomatoes, 1 oz. of butter, ½ pint of stock (see p. 12).

METHOD.—Cut the tomatoes in half and stand them in a tin, cut side up. Pour the stock round them, and place a piece of butter in the centre of each. Bake in a moderate oven for about twenty minutes until tender. Serve on croûtons of fried bread (see p. 12).

MASHED TURNIPS

PEEL the turnips thickly (down to the dark line) and cut into quarters.

Put into boiling water with a little salt added and boil gently until tender —they will take about an hour and a half, according to the size. When ready, strain through a colander and drain well. Then mash up with a fork. Return to the saucepan, add a lump of butter or margarine, season with pepper, then make thoroughly hot and serve.

HOT PUDDINGS

BOILING AND STEAMING PUDDINGS

STEAMED puddings have more taste and are always lighter than boiled ones, as there is no weight of water on top to prevent their rising.

If there is no steamer, place the pudding in a large pan containing enough boiling water to come half-way up the pudding basin. The water must be quite boiling when the pudding is put in, and it must be kept boiling evenly and steadily all the time. When it boils away, fresh boiling water must be added from time to time, pouring it in gently at the side of the pan so that none gets into the pudding.

Always prepare the water and grease the basin before mixing the pudding. A steamed pudding is covered with a piece of well-greased paper, twisted over the edge of the basin. A boiled pudding is covered with a scalded and floured cloth, which should be tied tightly in place.

If the string is tied in a bow it will be quite easy to undo when the pudding is to be dished up.

To scald a cloth, dip the middle of it in a pan of boiling water and press it tightly with the saucepan lid on the edge of the pan. Sprinkle lightly with flour, to make it waterproof, and it is ready for the pudding. After boiling, leave a pudding for five minutes so that in cooling it may shrink slightly from the sides of the basin, and be more easily turned out.

There is no need always to cook a pudding in a plain pudding basin. A cake tin or jelly mould will look nicer.

If a suet pudding does not fill the basin, crusts of bread can be put on top.

This is especially suitable for puddings that have to cook a long time, such as fig or Christmas pudding.

ALEXANDRA PUDDING

INGREDIENTS.—6 oz. of bread (crumbs only), 2 eggs, ¾ pint of milk, 1 lemon (grated rind), 3 oz. of sugar, 2 oz. of currants, 2 oz. of sultanas, 2 oz. of candied peel, gravy browning.

METHOD.—Beat the eggs and mix with the milk. Cut the bread into small cubes, and put into eggs and milk.

Wash and dry and remove stalks from currants and sultanas. Cut peel into small pieces. Add grated lemon-rind, sugar, peel, and fruit to the eggs and milk, etc. Colour with a few drops of browning as used for browning gravy.

Put into a greased basin, cover with greased paper. Put into a saucepan of boiling water, and steam for an hour and a half. Turn on to a hot dish and serve.

ALMOND PUDDING

INGREDIENTS.—2 oz. of sweet Valencia almonds, 4 oz. of castor sugar, 3 oz. of flour, 4 oz. of margarine, 2 eggs, 1 level teaspoonful of baking powder, 1½ oz. of ground rice, milk, almond flavouring essence, apricot jam, short pastry (see p. 252).

METHOD.—Roll out the pastry. Line the rim and half-way down the sides of a pie-dish with it, damping the dish to make the paste adhere, and trim the edge.

Now cut small rounds of pastry and place them on the rim of pastry, damping the latter to make them adhere.

Butter the lower part of the dish and put a layer of jam in the bottom. Blanch and skin the almonds and split each into three pieces. Cream the fat and sugar, add each egg separately, stirring it in quickly and beating it well.

When both have been added, stir in the flour sifted with the ground rice and baking-powder, add a little milk as required and just a few drops of almond flavouring essence, and half the prepared almonds.

Mix all together lightly, and brush the pastry edge with milk before turning the pudding into the prepared dish. Sprinkle castor sugar and the remainder of the almonds on the top of the pudding, bake it in a hot oven at first to set the pastry, then reduce the heat and finish cooking.

GROUND ALMONDS PUDDING

INGREDIENTS.—¼ lb. of ground almonds, 2 eggs, 1 oz. of castor sugar, 1 oz. of butter, 2 tablespoonfuls of cream, 1½ oz. of cakecrumbs.

METHOD.—Grease a fire-proof dish. Cream the butter and sugar and beat in the yolks of the eggs.

Add the cream, cake-crumbs, ground almonds and mix well.

Add the stiffly beaten whites, pour into the greased dish and bake for twenty-five minutes in a moderately hot oven.

ALMOND SOUFFLE

INGREDIENTS.—2 dessertspoonfuls of flour, 1 oz. of butter or margarine, ¼ pint of milk, 2 eggs and 1 extra white, 1 oz. of almonds, almond flavouring, 1 oz. of sugar.

METHOD.—Blanch and cut up the almonds.

Sieve the flour. Then melt the fat in a saucepan and stir it in.

When smoothly mixed add the milk, and stir until the mixture boils and thickens and then leaves the sides of the pan.

Draw aside and cool slightly. Add the sugar, almonds and flavouring to taste, and beat in each egg yolk separately.

Whisk the egg whites to a very stiff froth and fold in lightly, then turn into a prepared soufflé tin, cover with a buttered paper and steam for about three-quarters of an hour.

Before turning out the soufflé, remove the band of paper very carefully. Serve with apricot jam sauce. Sufficient for five persons.

APRICOT JAM SAUCE

Put one and a half tablespoonfuls of apricot jam into a saucepan with a

quarter pint of water. Boil for a minute or two, and pour round the soufflé. A squeeze of lemon-juice or a spoonful of sherry may be added if liked.

APPLE AMBER

INGREDIENTS.—4 oz. of short pastry (see p. 252), 1½ lb. of apples, 4 oz. of Demerara sugar, 2 oz. of butter, 2 eggs, ½ cup of water, 1 oz. of castor sugar.

METHOD.—Peel, core, and cut up the apples and stew them till soft, with the sugar and water. Mash the apples well with a wooden spoon and add the butter.

Separate the whites of eggs from the yolks. Break up the yolks and stir them into the hot fruit mixture. Line the top of a pie-dish with a strip of pastry and pinch up the edges.

Pour the fruit into the dish and beat up the whites as stiffly as possible. When beaten mix in one ounce of castor sugar, and pile it up on top of the fruit.

Bake for twenty minutes in a hot oven, lowering the heat a little after the first ten minutes.

Sufficient for four or five persons.

BAKED ALMOND APPLES

INGREDIENTS.—4 large apples, 2 oz. of almonds, flour, 1½ oz. of breadcrumbs, 1 egg, 4 oz. of sugar, 2 oz. of butter.

METHOD.—Peel and core the apples.

Blanch and chop the almonds and mix them with half the sugar. Beat the egg and the rest of the sugar together and stir in one ounce of the breadcrumbs.

Coat the apples with flour.

Melt the butter in a fireproof dish in the oven, put in the apples, fill the centre hole with almonds and sugar and mix the remainder with the breadcrumbs and egg and pour it over the apples.

Sprinkle the remaining half ounce of breadcrumbs on top and bake the apples in a moderate oven till they are tender and brown.

Sufficient for four persons.

BAKED APPLE MOULD

INGREDIENTS.—1 lb. of cooking apples (weighed after peeling), ½ gill of water, 1 oz. of butter, 2 oz. of sugar, 2 eggs, 2 oz. of breadcrumbs.

METHOD.—Peel, core and slice the apples and stew them in the water till soft. Mash them with a wooden spoon and add the butter, sugar and half the breadcrumbs. Beat the eggs and stir them in.

Grease a pie-dish or cake-tin, pour in the apples and spread the rest of the breadcrumbs over them.

Cover the pudding with greased paper and bake it in a slow oven for one hour.

Leave it for five minutes and turn out carefully.

Sufficient for two persons.

NOTE.—This is equally good served hot or cold.

BAKED APPLES WITH SHERRY

CORE some large cooking apples and place them in a baking-tin with just a little water in the base of it.

Put a piece of thinly peeled lemon-rind or some finely grated rind in the centre of each apple and also a teaspoonful of sugar.

Bake the apples till they are tender, and then place them on a serving dish and put a lump of butter in each one.

Dredge the apples with sugar and serve them with sherry.

CASSEROLE APPLES

INGREDIENTS.—$1\frac{1}{2}$ to 2 lb. of large cooking apples, 2 oz. of loaf sugar, juice and rind of $\frac{1}{2}$ a lemon, 4 cloves, 1 oz. of sultanas (picked and washed).

METHOD.—Wash the apples and remove the core with a small sharp knife. Cut round the side of the apple without cutting it in half. If this is done the skin will be loose when baked, and can be removed easily.

Put the apples in a casserole; put one or two pieces of sugar in each, with a clove, and fill up with sultanas. Peel the lemon-rind thinly and put it in the casserole with the water and the rest of the sugar.

Put on the lid and place the casserole on an asbestos mat over a low gas. In five minutes turn the apples over.

Cook gently for about fifteen minutes or till the apples are tender.

Pour off the syrup and boil it for ten minutes. Let it cool slightly to thicken.

Place the apples in a dish and pour the syrup over. Four large apples will weigh about two pounds.

APPLE CHARLOTTE

INGREDIENTS.—$\frac{1}{2}$ lb. of breadcrumbs, $\frac{1}{4}$ lb. of suet, 2 lb. of apples, 6 oz. of Demerara sugar, 1 lemon (grated rind).

METHOD.—Make the breadcrumbs—use stale crumb of bread, and either rub it on a grater or through a sieve. If neither is available, rub two pieces of stale bread together.

First remove the skin from the suet, then shred the suet and chop it finely. Grease a pie-dish, then coat the sides and bottom of it with a few of the breadcrumbs. These will adhere to the grease if put into the dish before the grease has hardened. Mix the remainder of the breadcrumbs with the suet and grated lemon-rind. Peel, core, and slice the apples. Put a layer of breadcrumbs and suet, then a layer of apples, with some of the sugar sprinkled over them. Continue this until all the ingredients are used, leaving sufficient breadcrumbs and suet to cover the top of the pudding. Bake in a moderately hot oven for one hour and a half. Turn out or serve in the dish.

Sufficient for about five or six persons.

FRENCH APPLE CHARLOTTE

INGREDIENTS.—$1\frac{1}{2}$ lb. of cooking apples, $\frac{1}{2}$ gill of water, 3 oz. of butter, 3 oz. of sugar, $\frac{1}{2}$ a small stale loaf, 2 cloves.

METHOD.—Peel and core the apples and cut them in quarters. Stew them in the water with the cloves till mashed. They should not be at all watery. Add the sugar and half an ounce of butter. Butter a charlotte mould or pie-dish, and melt the rest of the butter in a frying-pan.

Cut the bread in neat strips the height of the tin and dip them in the butter. Line the bottom of the tin with the pieces of bread, and press pieces neatly together round the sides of the mould. Pour in the apples and cover them with bread dipped in butter. Twist a greased paper over the top and bake in a moderate oven for fifty minutes, removing the paper after the first half hour.

Sufficient for four persons.

SPICED APPLE CHARLOTTE

INGREDIENTS.—2 lb. of cooking apples, 4 tablespoonfuls of Barbados sugar, 9 oz. of breadcrumbs, ¼ lb. of chopped or shredded suet, 1 teaspoonful of ground cinnamon, a few cloves, 1 oz. of butter.

METHOD.—Peel and quarter the apples, remove the core, and cut the fruit in slices of moderate thickness.

Butter a pie-dish and coat it with one ounce of the breadcrumbs ; then shake out the loose crumbs.

Mix the rest of the breadcrumbs (there should be half a pound) with the cinnamon and shredded suet, and put a layer of about one-third of the mixture in the bottom of the prepared dish.

Add half the apples, sprinkle them with half of the sugar, and add a few cloves. Then add another layer of crumbs and suet.

Fill up the dish with the remainder of the apples and sugar, and add a few more cloves ; then cover the apples with a top layer of suet and breadcrumbs, pressing it down firmly.

Dab small pieces of butter on top of the dish, and bake the charlotte in a moderately hot oven for from one to one and a half hours. The apples should then be tender and the charlotte nicely browned.

APPLE DUMPLINGS

INGREDIENTS.—6 good-sized cooking apples, castor sugar and ground cinnamon, ¾ lb. of flour, salt, ½ lb. of margarine, 1½ oz. of castor sugar, milk, water to mix, angelica.

METHOD.—Peel the apples thinly, and remove the core with an apple corer.

Sift the flour with a pinch of salt, rub in the fat and add the sugar, then mix them to a stiff paste with cold water.

Divide this into six portions, form each piece into a smooth, round shape and roll out to a round large enough to cover the apple.

Place an apple in the centre of each piece, and fill up the centre hole with castor sugar and ground cinnamo allowing one level teaspoonful of grou cinnamon to two level tablespoonfu of castor sugar.

Damp the edge and mould th pastry round each apple until it completely covered, pinching th pastry together at the top.

When quite smooth, turn th dumpling over, shape it evenly, mal a slight depression in the centr then place it on a baking-sheet. Brus the pastry with milk to glaze it, ar bake the dumpling about half an hou or until the apples are tender. Th oven should be hot at first to cook th pastry, but can be moderated later.

Serve the dumplings hot or col sprinkle them with sugar and decora each with a stalk and leaves of angelic

Sufficient for six dumplings.

APPLE GINGER PUDDING

INGREDIENTS.—1 lb. of cookin apples, sugar and water, 3 oz. of sel raising flour, ½ level teaspoonful ground ginger, ¼ lb. of golden syru 1 oz. of margarine, 1 egg.

METHOD.—Peel and quarter th apples and remove the cores ; the cut the fruit in slices. Stew it ti tender, adding sugar to taste and little water to moisten the frui Mash it to a pulp, then let it cool an turn it into a buttered pie-dish.

Warm the golden syrup and mel the margarine in a saucepan. Ad these to the beaten egg, then stir th mixture into the flour, the latte sifted into a basin with the ginger.

Mix the ingredients and beat ther well ; then pour the mixture over th apple pulp and bake the pudding in very moderate oven.

A few almonds may be sprinkle on top of the pudding before baking.

APPLES IN RICE

INGREDIENTS.—4 apples (to weig 1 lb.), ½ lb. of rice, 4 teaspoonfuls o castor sugar, 4 cloves.

FOR THE SAUCE.—1 gill of water 2 tablespoonfuls of apricot jam.

METHOD.—Wash the rice well, plac in a saucepan of boiling water with little salt and boil for about te minutes, then strain it.

Grease four tiny basins (holdin about 1 gill).

Divide the partly-cooked rice into six portions, and put one portion into each of the four greased basins, and press it to the sides and bottom, so that it completely coats them.

Peel and core the apples and place one apple into each basin, together with a teaspoonful of castor sugar and a clove ; press in carefully on to the rice.

Take the other two remaining portions of rice, divide each again into half, and cover each basin with a portion of rice, press it well down, and well cover the apple.

Cover each basin with a greased paper. Place in a steamer over boiling water, and steam for about one hour, or until the apples are soft, and the rice quite tender.

When cooked, turn carefully on to a hot dish and serve with apricot sauce.

To MAKE THE SAUCE.—Boil the jam and water together for six minutes and pour round the dish, or serve separately.

A HINT

SHOULD you have no apple corer, scoop out as much as possible from each end without breaking the apple.

If the apples are carefully washed the peelings can be boiled with a little water and coloured with cochineal and used instead of jam sauce.

APPLE MERINGUE

INGREDIENTS.—2 lb. of cooking apples, ½ gill of water, 1 oz. of butter, 3 oz. of sugar, 2 large eggs, a little castor sugar, 1 oz. of glacé cherries.

METHOD.—Peel and core the apples and cut them in quarters. Stew them in the water till they mash. Add the butter and sugar.

Separate the whites of the eggs from the yolks, beating the whites stiffly and adding the yolks to the slightly cooled apple mixture.

Pour the apples into a pie-dish and place the beaten whites on top in rocky heaps. Dredge well with castor sugar and bake in a hot oven for a few minutes, just enough to colour the meringue lightly.

Decorate with the cherries and serve hot.

APPLE MERINGUE PIE

INGREDIENTS.—Short pastry (see p. 252), 1¼ lb. of cooking apples, ¼ lb. of Barbados sugar, 1½ gills of water, 1 dessertspoonful of flour, ½ oz. of butter, 2 yolks of eggs, 2 whites, 2 tablespoonfuls of castor sugar, ¼ level teaspoonful of ground cinnamon, glacé cherries and angelica.

METHOD.—Roll out the pastry thinly, cut a round from it and line a Pyrex plate. Fold the pastry over at the edge, towards the sides of the plate, to make a thick edge, and flute it with thumb and finger. Prick the base. Line the pastry with a round of buttered paper, scatter rice over it, and put it in a hot oven to bake. When the pastry is set, remove the paper and rice, and finish cooking the case. Then cool it.

Prepare the apples as for stewing, and cook them till they are tender, adding the Barbados sugar and one and a quarter gills of the water. Then rub them through a sieve and return them to the saucepan.

Smooth the flour in the remainder of the water and stir it into the apple pulp. Boil the mixture for a few minutes, then take it off the gas and add the butter, and when it is a little cooler, add the beaten egg yolks.

Cook it again for a few minutes without letting it boil. Then cool the apple mixture and turn it into the prepared pastry case.

Whisk the egg whites stiffly, and fold in the castor sugar mixed with the cinnamon. Heap this on top of the apple, dredge it with castor sugar and put the pie into a cool oven to set the meringue.

Serve the pie hot or cold, decorated with glacé cherries and with rings of angelica.

Sufficient for six persons.

APPLE OMELET SOUFFLE

INGREDIENTS.—1 gill of apple pulp, 2 eggs, ½ lemon (rind only), about 2 dessertspoonfuls of castor sugar.

METHOD.—To obtain the apple pulp prepare some apples and stew until tender, adding only just sufficient water to keep them from burning. When cooked, rub through a sieve. Separate the eggs. Beat up the yolks.

Whisk the whites to a very stiff froth.

Add the sugar and finely-grated lemon-rind to the apple pulp, and stir in the yolks of eggs. When well mixed, fold in the whisked whites.

Turn into a buttered pie-dish and bake in a moderately-hot oven for about twenty minutes and until lightly browned. Serve in the dish.

Sufficient for two persons.

APPLE ROLL

INGREDIENTS.—About ¾ lb. of short pastry (see p. 252), 4 oz. of apple purée, 2 oz. of raisins, 2 oz. of almonds, 3 oz. of breadcrumbs, 2 oz. of sugar, ½ grated lemon-rind, 1 egg.

METHOD.—Roll out the pastry to an oblong shape. Cover it with the apple purée mixed with the raisins, peeled and chopped almonds, breadcrumbs, lemon-rind, sugar, and the beaten egg.

Roll it up like a Swiss roll, turn it on to a baking-sheet and brush it with a little beaten egg kept back from the mixture.

Bake the Apple Roll and serve it hot with or without custard.

APPLE SNOWBALLS

INGREDIENTS.—5 apples, 9 oz. of rice, a few stoned raisins, and a few cloves, 5 teaspoonfuls of brown sugar, some finely-grated lemon-rind.

METHOD.—Wash the rice and put it into a pan of slightly salted boiling water. Boil it for twelve minutes, then strain it through a colander and drain it well.

Meanwhile, peel the apples thinly and remove the cores.

Take five small basins and butter them well. Divide the rice into five portions.

Take about three-fourths of each portion of rice, and put it into the buttered basins, line them evenly with the rice and then press an apple into the centre of each dish.

Put a little grated lemon-rind, a clove, one or two stoned raisins and the sugar into the centre hole of the apples, then cover them with the remainder of the rice, and press it down firmly.

Cover each basin with a buttered paper and steam the Apple Snowballs

for about forty-five minutes, until both the apple and rice are tender. Then turn them out carefully, and garnish them with one or two cloves.

Serve them with hot golden syrup, sharpened with a little lemon-juice.

If small basins are not available, the rice can be put into pudding-cloths. It should be shaped round the apples, and then they should be tied up and boiled till the apples are tender.

APPLE SOUFFLE PIE

INGREDIENTS.—½ lb. of apples, 1½ dessertspoonfuls of granulated sugar, 1 tablespoonful of water, grated rind of ½ lemon, 3 egg yolks and 4 whites, 1 oz. of butter, 1 oz. of flour, ¼ pint of milk, 1 tablespoonful of castor sugar, some short pastry (see p. 252.).

METHOD.—Prepare the apples and stew them till they are tender with the granulated sugar and water. Then mash them up finely or rub them through a sieve, and let them cool.

Roll out the pastry and line the rim and half-way down the pie-dish with it.

Trim the edge and decorate the rim with small circles of pastry, damping the latter to make them adhere. Melt the butter in a saucepan, add the flour, and when they are well blended stir in the milk and bring the sauce to the boil.

Cook the mixture until it leaves the sides of the pan, keeping it well stirred. Then draw it aside and cool it slightly.

Add the grated lemon-rind and castor sugar. Beat in the egg yolks one at a time, then add one gill of the apple pulp before folding in the stiffly-whisked egg whites.

Butter the unlined part of the pie-dish, and glaze the pastry by brushing it with milk. Turn in the mixture, and bake it in a hot oven at first, lessening the heat as soon as the pastry is set.

Sufficient for six persons.

APRICOT OMELET SOUFFLE

INGREDIENTS.—2 yolks of eggs, 3 whites, 1 tablespoonful of castor sugar, 1 dessertspoonful of water, 1 tea-spoonful of flour, a few drops of apricot essence, apricot jam.

METHOD.—Whisk the yolks of egg

with the sugar until thick and creamy and free from dark streaks. Stir in the water, a few drops of apricot essence and the sifted flour.

Whisk the whites of egg stiffly, and fold them in.

Turn the mixture into a greased and lined omelet pan, and cook it in a hot oven for about nine to twelve minutes, until spongy.

Turn the omelet out at once on to a sugared paper, spread some apricot jam, previously warmed, on one half, fold the other half over it, and serve at once.

TO PREPARE THE OMELET PAN.— Cut a round of paper of double thickness, large enough to line the pan, and stand above the top of it. In the centre mark a circle the exact size of the base of the pan, then make eight cuts (leaving an equal space between each) from the edge of the paper to the edge of the circle.

Butter the pan and paper, and fit it into the pan, letting the cut edges overlap.

Sufficient for one or two persons.

APRICOT PUDDING

INGREDIENTS.—2 eggs, their weight in margarine, 5 oz. of flour, 2½ oz. of castor sugar, ¼ flat teaspoonful of carbonate of soda, 2 tablespoonfuls of apricot jam, rind of ½ lemon, milk.

METHOD.—Beat the sugar and fat to a cream, and stir in the grated lemon-rind.

Separate the eggs, and sift the flour with the carbonate of soda. Beat the yolks into the creamed fat and sugar, then stir in the jam, and add the flour and soda, and just a little milk, if required. Fold in the stiffly-whisked whites of eggs.

Turn the ingredients into a buttered mould, cover it with a buttered paper, and steam the pudding for about one hour and a half.

Serve it with a hot custard (see p. 217) or with apricot-jam sauce (see p. 200). To make the latter, mix two tablespoonfuls of apricot-jam with one gill of water, sharpen it with lemon-juice, and boil it for a few minutes.

ARROWROOT PUDDING

INGREDIENTS.—1¼ oz. of arrowroot (2½ dessertspoonfuls), ½ oz. of butter or margarine, 1 pint of milk, 2 dessertspoonfuls of sugar, flavouring, 1 egg.

METHOD.—Mix the arrowroot to a smooth paste with some of the milk. Put the remainder into a saucepan with the sugar, and butter, and when hot, add to the arrowroot. Return to the pan, and bring to the boil, keeping it well stirred.

Boil for a few minutes, then cool slightly and beat in the egg. Add flavouring to taste. Turn into a pie-dish, and bake gently for about half an hour, without boiling. Serve hot or cold.

Cornflour, or ground rice, may be used in the same way.

Sufficient for three or four persons.

ARUNDEL PUDDING

INGREDIENTS.—2 eggs, 1 pint of milk, 3 slices of stale bread-and-butter, 1½ oz. of sugar, 2 oz. of currants, grated nutmeg, 1 tin of loganberries or any stewed fruit.

METHOD.—Pick, wash, and dry the currants, and put half of them in a greased pie-dish. Put in the slices of bread-and-butter with currants and sugar between. Use rather more bread than for an ordinary bread-and-butter pudding, as it is turned out when cold.

Beat the eggs and milk, pour them over the bread and grate a little nutmeg on the top. Let it stand for fifteen minutes. Bake in a slow oven for about forty minutes or till set.

This may be served cold; turn it out into a glass dish, and pour tinned or stewed fruit round.

Sufficient for four persons.

AUTUMN PUDDING

INGREDIENTS.—3 dessertspoonfuls of blackcurrant jam, 2 oz. of Barbados sugar, 4 oz. of margarine, 2 eggs, ¼ lb. of flour, 1 level teaspoonful of baking-powder, milk, boiled custard (see p. 217).

METHOD.—Beat the sugar and fat to a cream, then add each egg separately, stirring it in quickly and beating it well.

When both eggs are added, mix in the jam, and stir in the flour, sifted with the baking-powder, and add some milk if required.

Mix all together lightly, then turn

the mixture into a buttered mould. Cover it with a buttered paper and steam it for about one hour and a half.

Unmould the Autumn Pudding, and serve it with hot boiled custard.

Sufficient for five persons.

BAKEWELL PUDDING

INGREDIENTS.—1 egg, 3 tablespoonfuls of breadcrumbs, 2 tablespoonfuls of ground almonds, 3 oz. of castor sugar, 2½ oz. of margarine, apricot jam, vanilla or almond flavouring, about 6 or 8 oz. of short or flaky pastry (see p. 252), about a tablespoonful of milk.

METHOD.—Roll out the pastry, and line a small pie-dish. Be careful not to stretch the pastry when doing this, or it will shrink from the rim and fall into the dish when cooked. Damp the pastry round the rim, and place a strip of pastry on it so as to make a double rim. Trim and decorate the edge. Beat the sugar and fat to a cream. Separate the egg.

Add the yolk to the creamed fat and sugar, and beat it in well.

Stir in the ground almonds and breadcrumbs, also a few drops of flavouring and about a tablespoonful of milk.

Whisk the egg-white to a very stiff froth, and stir in lightly.

Put a little jam in the bottom of the pastry, then add the prepared mixture.

Place in a hot oven and bake for about twenty-five or thirty minutes, lessening the heat as required.

Serve hot or cold.

Sufficient for four or five persons.

BALMORAL PUDDING

INGREDIENTS.—¼ lb. of margarine, 3 oz. of small seedless raisins, 2 eggs, ¼ lb. of castor sugar, 5 oz. of flour, ¼ flat teaspoonful of carbonate of soda, ½ pint of custard (see p. 217), 1 lemon.

METHOD.—Wash, pick over, and dry the fruit. Sieve the flour with the carbonate of soda.

Grate the lemon-rind finely. Beat the sugar and fat to a cream. Add each egg separately. Stir in quickly, and beat well before adding the second.

When both are well beaten in, stir in the flour, lemon-rind and raisins,

and a spoonful of milk and water, as required. Mix together lightly, turn into a greased basin or mould, cover securely with a well-greased paper, and steam for two hours.

Just before you are ready to dish up the pudding, make half a pint of custard (with custard powder).

Turn the pudding on to a hot dish, and pour the custard round it.

Sufficient for about six or seven persons.

BANANA CUSTARD

INGREDIENTS.—2 bananas, 3 thin slices of stale bread-and-butter, 1 large egg, ½ pint of milk, grated rind of a lemon, 1 oz. of sugar, nutmeg.

METHOD.—Slice the bananas.

Put a slice of bread-and-butter in a greased pie-dish, and cover it with slices of banana and grated lemon-rind.

Put in another slice of bread, and some more of the bananas, and finish with a slice of bread sprinkled with sliced banana.

Beat the egg and sugar, add the milk, and pour it over the bread. Grate nutmeg over the pudding, and bake it in a moderate oven for about forty-five minutes.

Sufficient for two or three persons.

BANANA MERINGUE

INGREDIENTS.—3 bananas, 1 tablespoonful of jam, ½ cup of breadcrumbs, 1 cupful of milk, 2 oz. of sugar, ½ oz. of butter, 2 eggs, grated rind of ½ a lemon, 1 oz. of castor sugar.

METHOD.—Mash two bananas with the jam and put them in a greased pie-dish. Boil together the milk, sugar, butter, breadcrumbs and lemon-rind.

Let them cool for a minute or two, and then stir in the slightly-beaten egg-yolks. Pour the mixture over the bananas, and bake for thirty minutes.

Beat the whites stiffly, and stir in the castor sugar.

Heap the meringue on the pudding, and brown it in the oven. Decorate with sliced banana.

Sufficient for three persons.

MAKING BATTERS

A batter, as the word implies, has to be well beaten. The beating introduces air, which expands when heated, and so makes the batter rise. All batters should be allowed to stand for at least an hour after being mixed, before they are cooked.

The egg is a very important ingredient in a batter-pudding. Do not economise too much in the amount of eggs you allow. It is better to use half milk and half *water*, than too little egg.

If you find it necessary to use less egg, make your batter slightly thicker.

There is no need to whisk the egg before adding it to the flour, as it gets well beaten afterwards.

THE MIXING.

THE mixing of a batter is also important.

An even consistency—similar to that of a thick sauce—should be kept during the whole process of mixing. Do not let the batter get very stiff or too thin, or it will be lumpy instead of smooth.

A thin batter, such as the recipe given, should be beaten when only half the liquid has been added, as when finished it is too thin to get much air beaten into it.

BATTER PUDDING

INGREDIENTS.—1 egg, ¼ lb. of flour, a pinch of salt, ½ pint of milk, dripping.

METHOD.—Sieve the flour and salt, put into a basin and make a well in the centre.

Break the egg into a cup, pour it into the well and mix with a small quantity of the flour until a smooth paste is formed. Then take half the milk, and add it gradually, mixing in the flour by degrees. When it is all mixed and free from lumps, before adding the other half of the milk, beat the batter for a few minutes. Then stir in the remainder of the milk and leave the batter to stand for about an hour, or longer if time will allow.

Melt about an ounce of dripping in a small baking-tin or pie-dish, and when hot, pour in the batter. Put into a fairly-hot oven to bake. It will take about forty-five minutes. Serve at once.

FOR A YORKSHIRE PUDDING.

WHEN the batter has risen it should be put underneath the joint while the latter is baking, so that the goodness from the meat can drip into the pudding.

BLACKCAP BATTER

INGREDIENTS.—1 oz. of currants, 4 oz. of flour, 2 eggs, ½ pint of milk, 1 oz. of sugar, pinch of salt.

METHOD.—Grease a mould or basin. Pick and wash the currants, and put them in the mould. Put flour and salt in a basin, and hollow out the centre. Put in the eggs unbeaten, and about two tablespoonfuls of milk. Stir *in the centre* only, till there is a stiff batter, and then gradually add half the milk. Beat till smooth, and add rest of milk. Allow the batter to stand for one hour. Pour into the mould, and cover with greased paper. Steam steadily for one hour.

Leave it for two or three minutes, then turn out gently on to a hot dish.

Sufficient for four or five persons.

BLACKCURRANT PUDDINGS

INGREDIENTS.—3 oz. of flour, 1 level teaspoonful of baking-powder, 1 egg, 3 oz. of margarine, 3 oz. of castor sugar, milk, ½ lb. of blackcurrants, 1½ tablespoonfuls of sugar, or to taste, water.

METHOD.—Beat the castor sugar and fat to a cream, then add the egg, stirring it in quickly and beating it well.

Sift the flour and baking-powder together, and mix it in, adding a little milk as required. Turn the mixture into four buttered moulds, filling them only two-thirds full. Cover them with buttered papers, and steam them for from thirty-five to forty-five minutes.

Meanwhile, string and wash the blackcurrants, and stew them till tender with a little water and sugar to taste.

When the puddings are ready, turn them out, and serve the puddings with the hot stewed currants.

NOTE.—When fresh fruit is not in season, hot blackcurrant jam may be served.

Sufficient for four puddings.

BLACKCURRANT SUET PUDDING

INGREDIENTS.—10 oz. of flour, 5 oz. of suet, water to mix, 1½ lb. of blackcurrants, 2 or 3 tablespoonfuls of Demerara sugar, water.

METHOD.—Stalk and wash the blackcurrants.

Skin, shred, and chop the suet

finely, and mix it well into the flour.

Add sufficient cold water to make a stiff paste—not hard, but pliable.

Slightly flour a pastry-board and rolling-pin, cut off about one-third of the suet crust, and put aside for the top of the pudding.

Roll out the large piece to a round shape, about one and a half times the size of the top of the pudding-basin.

Grease the basin and line it with this crust, making it very even by pressing it lightly against the sides and bottom of basin.

Put in a few blackcurrants, then the sugar, and the remainder of the fruit on to the top. Add sufficient water to make the syrup, about one to one gill and a half.

Roll out the small piece of suet crust to the exact size of the top of the basin, and press it on to the top of the crust that lines the basin, using a little water to make it adhere.

Cover with a greased paper.

Tie a floured pudding-cloth tightly round it, place in a saucepan of boiling water, and boil for about two hours and a half.

Turn out very carefully and serve with cream.

NOTE.—The basin must be full of fruit or the water will get into the pudding.

Sufficient for about six or eight persons.

BRAMLEY PUDDINGS

INGREDIENTS.—1½ lb. of Bramley apples, rind of ½ lemon, 2 or 3 dessert-spoonfuls of sugar, ½ gill of water, 1 egg, 1 tablespoonful of castor sugar, ¼ lb. of flour, ¼ pint of milk, ½ flat tea-spoonful of ground cinnamon, 1 flat teaspoonful of baking-powder, 3 oz. of margarine, a few glacé cherries.

METHOD.—Peel and quarter the apples, remove the cores, and cut them in slices. Stew them until tender, adding the finely grated lemon-rind, a little water as required, and sugar to taste. Mash them roughly.

Sift the flour with the baking-powder and cinnamon, rub in the fat and add the castor sugar. Whisk the egg, stir it in, and add the milk.

Divide the prepared apples between six small buttered pie-dishes, or Pyrex

dishes. Pour a little of the cake-mixture over each. Dredge them with castor sugar, and put them in a good moderately-hot oven to bake. They will take about twenty to thirty minutes.

Serve with a glacé cherry in the centre of each.

Sufficient for six persons.

BRAZIL PUDDING

INGREDIENTS.—9 oz. of flour, 3 oz. of shelled Brazil nuts, 5 oz. of margarine, 1 teaspoonful of baking-powder, ¼ lb. of sugar, ¾ lb. of apricot or marrow jam, 1 egg, milk.

METHOD.—Grind two-thirds of the nuts to a powder, and mix with the jam.

Rub the margarine well into the flour.

Cut the remainder of the nuts into small pieces, and add to the flour with the sugar and baking-powder, and mix all together.

Beat up the egg and add, with some milk as required, and mix well.

Grease a pie-dish, and put half the mixture in it. Then add the jam and ground nuts, and spread over evenly. Now put the remainder of the pudding-mixture on the top.

Bake in a moderately-hot oven for about one hour and a half, lessening the heat as required.

Sufficient for about six or eight persons.

BREAD-AND-BUTTER PUD-DING

INGREDIENTS.—2 eggs, 4 small slices of thin bread-and-butter, 1 pint of milk, nutmeg, 1½ oz. of sugar, flavouring—lemon or ratafia, 2 oz. of sultanas.

METHOD.—Grease a pie-dish and place two of the slices of bread-and-butter in it. Beat the eggs, add the milk and flavouring to the beaten eggs.

Prepare the sultanas, wash and remove the stalks. Sprinkle the sugar and sultanas on the bread-and-butter in the bottom of the pie-dish. Pour over half the eggs and milk. Place the remainder of the bread-and-butter in the dish. Pour over the remainder of the eggs and milk. Grate some nutmeg on to the top of the pudding.

Stand aside for one hour to soak the bread-and-butter.

Bake in a moderately-warm oven for forty minutes, or until set.

Do not allow the pudding to boil, or the eggs will curdle. When the pudding is set, if it is not sufficiently brown, put it under the grill for a few minutes.

Place the pie-dish on a dish and serve hot.

BROWN BREAD - AND - BUTTER PUDDING

INGREDIENTS.—Slices of brown bread-and-butter (about 3 to 4 oz.), a little mincemeat, 2 eggs, 1 pint of milk, ratafia flavouring, 1 to 1½ tablespoonfuls of sugar.

METHOD.—Stale bread-and-butter, left over, can be used, or freshly cut. Spread each slice with mincemeat, and cut into two or three pieces—this, of course, depends upon the size of the slices. Put half of them into a pie-dish and sprinkle with sugar.

Beat up the eggs, mix with the milk, and add a few drops of flavouring. Pour some over the bread-and-butter in the dish, then add the remainder of the slices and the egg and milk. Leave to soak for an hour or so, then bake in a moderately-warm oven until set, being careful not to let the pudding boil

BREAD-AND-JAM PUDDING

INGREDIENTS.—½ lb. of stale bread, 3 oz. of shredded suet, 1 oz. of sugar, grated nutmeg, 2 tablespoonfuls of jam.

METHOD.—Lay a clean cloth in a basin, and put the bread in it.

Pour on enough boiling water to cover the bread and let it soak till soft. Then twist the ends of the cloth in opposite directions until *all* the water is squeezed out and the bread is dry.

Turn the bread out of the cloth and mash it with a fork. Add the suet, sugar and nutmeg.

Put the jam in a greased pie-dish with the bread on the top.

Bake in a moderate oven for one hour.

Sufficient for three persons.

BROWN BETTY

INGREDIENTS.—1½ lb. of cooking apples, 2 oz. of sultanas, 1 oz. of margarine, ½ cup of golden syrup, ¼ teaspoonful of mixed spice, 2 breakfastcupfuls of breadcrumbs, 2 oz. of sugar, the juice of a large lemon.

METHOD.—Peel, core, and slice the apples. Wash and pick the sultanas. Grease a pie-dish, and fill it with alternate layers of apples, sultanas, and breadcrumbs sprinkled with sugar and spice. Warm the syrup and lemon-juice, and pour them over the pudding. Sprinkle with breadcrumbs, and put small dabs of margarine over the top. Bake for one hour.

Serve sprinkled with castor sugar.

Sufficient for four persons.

BROWN BREAD PUDDING

INGREDIENTS.—½ lb. of stale brown bread, 2 oz. of flour, 6 oz. of suet, ¼ lb. of glacé cherries, ½ lb. of raisins, 2 oz. of candied peel, 1 lemon, ¼ lb. of sugar, some grated nutmeg, 1 egg.

METHOD.—Put the bread into a basin, cover with water, and leave to soak until soft. Then strain off the water, and squeeze all the moisture out of the bread.

Turn the soaked bread into a dry basin, and break it up with a fork.

Wash, stone, and chop the raisins.

Cut up the peel and cherries.

Chop the suet finely.

Add the flour and suet to the bread, also some grated nutmeg, lemon-rind, sugar, and prepared fruit.

Mix all well together, then whisk the egg and stir in.

Put into a greased pie-dish, and bake in a moderately-hot oven for about one hour and a half, lessening the heat as required.

NOTE.—Milk is not usually required, but a very little may be added if needed.

Sufficient for about six or eight persons.

STALE BREAD FRITTERS

INGREDIENTS.—½ lb. of stale bread, ¼ lb. of flour, a pinch of salt, 1 egg, ½ pint of milk, deep fat for frying.

METHOD.—Pour boiling water over the bread, and let it soak; then drain it in a colander and squeeze it dry. Break it up with a fork.

Sift the flour with a pinch of salt, pour the egg in the centre, and mix it with a small quantity of the flour;

then take half the milk and add it gradually and mix it to a smooth batter.

Beat this well, stir in the remainder of the milk and leave it to stand for about an hour or more.

When ready to fry, stir the bread into the batter, then drop it into a deep pan of hot fat in small spoonfuls, and fry them gently until brown. Drain, and fry the remainder in the same way.

These fritters should be eaten directly they are cooked, as they so soon become soft.

Serve bread fritters with jam. If liked, a little sugar may be added to the mixture.

Served plainly, these fritters may be eaten with fried bacon.

This quantity makes about thirty fritters.

CABINET PUDDING

INGREDIENTS.—1 egg, ½ pint of milk, 1 oz. of sultanas, 1 oz. of candied peel, 1 oz. of sugar, grated rind of 1 lemon, ½ cup of cakecrumbs or a slice of stale cake.

METHOD.—Beat the egg and sugar, and add the milk. Grate the lemon-peel thinly. Pour the egg and milk on to the cakecrumbs, and add the grated lemon-peel. Leave soaking while decorating the basin. Cut the candied peel in strips, and pick and wash the sultanas. Grease a pudding-basin or mould, and press the sultanas against the sides, in any pattern desired, with a few strips of peel.

Any sultanas or peel not used for decorating should be put into the pudding. Pour the custard mixture in gently, and twist a well-greased paper over the top of the basin. Steam *slowly* till set (about one hour).

Sufficient for two persons.

CANARY PUDDING

INGREDIENTS.—2 eggs and their weight in butter, sugar and flour, ½ teaspoonful of baking-powder, vanilla essence.

METHOD.—Grease a mould or basin, and a piece of paper to go over the top, and put some water on to boil. Cream the butter and sugar till soft. Beat in the eggs, one at a time, and lightly stir in the flour. Add a few drops of

vanilla essence and the baking-powder.

Put at once into the mould, and steam for an hour and a quarter, either in a steamer or else in a saucepan, with enough boiling water to come half-way up the mould.

Serve with jam sauce (see p. 241).

Sufficient for three or four persons.

CANTON APPLES

INGREDIENTS.—¾ lb. of apples, ½ to ¾ gill of water, about 2 dessertspoonfuls of sugar, 1 egg, 4 oz. of golden syrup, 1 oz. of margarine, 3 oz. of flour, ⅛ flat teaspoonful of carbonate of soda, ¼ flat teaspoonful of ground ginger, ¼ flat teaspoonful of ground cloves, a few almonds, if liked.

METHOD.—Peel and quarter the apples, remove the cores and slice them thickly. Stew them until tender, adding sugar to taste, and water as required. Mash them up finely or rub them through a sieve and leave them to cool.

Melt the margarine and golden syrup in a saucepan, then add them to the well-beaten egg.

Sieve the flour with the soda and spices, stir in the wet ingredients and beat all together. Turn the apple pulp into a buttered Pyrex dish. Cover it with the ginger cake mixture, and put it in a moderate oven to bake. It will take about half an hour to cook.

If adding almonds, blanch, skin, and chop them, and mix them with the flour.

Sufficient for four persons.

CARAMEL CUSTARD

INGREDIENTS :

FOR THE CUSTARD.—2 gills of milk, 2 eggs, 1½ dessertspoonfuls of castor sugar, flavouring as desired.

FOR THE CARAMEL.—3 oz. of lump sugar, ¾ gill of cold water.

METHOD.—Take a small charlotte tin, and put into the oven to warm.

To make the caramel, put the sugar and water into a small saucepan, let the sugar dissolve, then boil together until the syrup becomes a *pale* brown colour.

Pour it quickly into the warm tin, and *coat all round* the sides and bottom of the tin with it, then leave until cool and set.

Make the custard. Beat up the eggs.

Put the sugar and milk into a saucepan. Bring to the boil, then let it cool slightly. Pour on to the eggs, mix together, and add desired flavouring.

Strain this into the prepared mould, and cover with a greased paper.

Stand it in a saucepan of boiling water on a pad of paper, or on a pastry-cutter without a handle, just so that it does not touch the bottom of the saucepan.

The water must not reach more than half-way up the tin. Steam *slowly* for about thirty to forty-five minutes, until the custard is set. The water round the tin should only just simmer, otherwise the custard is liable to curdle.

When cooked, lift it out, leave for a few seconds, then turn *very carefully* on to a dish.

Serve either hot or cold.

NOTE.—If by any chance any part of the tin does not get coated with the caramel when the latter has set, the uncoated parts must be buttered, otherwise the pudding will stick.

CARAMEL FRUIT PUDDINGS

INGREDIENTS.—4 oz. of castor sugar, 3 dessertspoonfuls of hot water, 2 oz. of mincemeat, 1½ oz. of almonds, 2½ gills of milk, 4 oz. of bread, 2 oz. of glacé cherries, 2 eggs, 1 oz. of citron peel.

METHOD.—Use bread one day old. Remove the crust and cut the crumb into quarter-inch slices, then into small dice, and weigh them.

Shred the peel, cut the cherries into small pieces, blanch, skin, and chop the almonds. Put a few aside for garnishing. Add the prepared ingredients to the bread, together with the mincemeat, and half the sugar, and mix well.

Put the remainder of the sugar into a small strong saucepan with the hot water, dissolve it slowly, then bring this syrup to the boil, and boil till deep golden-brown. Leave it to get cold. Add the milk and dissolve the caramel very slowly, but do not let it boil. Stir it on to the beaten eggs, then strain it over the dry ingredients.

Allow the mixture to soak for half an hour. Turn it into small buttered moulds, cover them with a buttered paper, and steam them gently for about half an hour. Serve them with cream, and garnish each pudding with half an almond.

Sufficient for six persons.

CARROT PUDDING

INGREDIENTS.—¼ lb. of flour, 1 teacupful of breadcrumbs, 1 teacupful of grated carrots, ¼ lb. of sultanas, ¼ lb. of shredded suet, ¾ teaspoonful of baking-powder, 3 oz. of sugar, 1 gill of milk, 1 egg, grated nutmeg.

METHOD.—Wash and peel two or three large carrots and grate them on a bread grater. Wash and pick the sultanas, and beat the egg.

Mix all the ingredients together, put them into a greased mould, and cover them with greased paper.

Steam steadily for four hours, adding more boiling water as it boils away.

Let the pudding stand for five minutes before turning it out. Serve sprinkled with castor sugar.

Sufficient for four persons.

CASTLE PUDDINGS

INGREDIENTS.—1 oz. of butter, 1 oz. of sugar, 1 oz. of flour, ½ teaspoonful of baking-powder, 1 egg, a little milk.

METHOD.—Grease six small castle moulds. Cream the butter and sugar, add the egg and beat well.

Add the flour and a little milk. Fill the small moulds three-parts full and bake them in a moderately-hot oven for twenty minutes.

This quantity makes five or six small castle puddings, or four medium ones.

CHERRIES IN BATTER

INGREDIENTS.—1 pint of milk, 2 large eggs, ½ lb. of flour (light weight), ½ oz. of butter, ½ lb. of cherries, 1 oz. of sugar.

METHOD.—Put the flour in a basin, and make a hollow in the centre ; put in the eggs and a little milk, and make a batter in the centre of the flour. Beat well, after adding half the milk. Add the rest of the milk, and let the batter stand for an hour. The pudding can be baked in a pie-dish or meat-tin, but looks best if baked in small cup moulds ; a little butter should be put in each mould, and they should be well heated in the oven till too hot to touch. Put the cherries in the hot moulds, and pour on the batter. Bake in a moderately-hot oven for thirty-five minutes.

NOTE.—It is better to sift sugar over afterwards, instead of cooking it in the batter, as it burns so easily.

When cherries are out of season, a small tin of preserved cherries can be used instead. Sultanas may be used instead of cherries, or the batter may be baked plain and served with butter and lemon-juice. This quantity makes a large batter, enough for about six persons.

CHESHIRE PUDDING

INGREDIENTS.—½ lb. of flour, ¼ lb. of breadcrumbs, ¼ flat teaspoonful of carbonate of soda, 6 oz. of margarine, about 3 tablespoonfuls of marrow jam, 6 oz. of sugar, milk, 1 egg.

METHOD.—Sieve the flour and soda. Make the breadcrumbs, and mix with the flour.

Add the sugar and mix all together.

Grease a basin, and put the jam in the bottom.

Melt the margarine.

Beat up the egg, and mix in with the dry ingredients.

Add the melted margarine and milk as required. Mix all together.

Put into the prepared basin.

Cover securely with a thick, well-greased paper.

Steam for about two to two and a half hours.

Turn carefully on to a hot dish and serve ; the jam will run over the top of the pudding and coat it.

CHESTNUT PUDDING

INGREDIENTS.—30 chestnuts, 4 oz. of butter, 3 oz. of granulated sugar, 4 eggs, 1 gill of milk, 1 oz. of glacé cherries, rind of a lemon (grated), 1 gill of whipped cream.

METHOD.—Slit the chestnuts on the flat side with a pointed knife.

Put them on a tin and bake them in a hot oven until the skins split (about ten minutes).

Peel off the shells and the inner skin, and put the chestnuts in a saucepan with boiling water to cover them.

Simmer till they are very soft (thirty minutes).

Strain and mash the chestnuts or rub them through a wire sieve.

Cream the butter and sugar till soft and white, and beat in the eggs, one at a time. Beat for ten minutes. Add the chestnut purée, milk, and grated lemon-rind.

Cut the cherries in half, and press them against the inside of a greased ring-mould.

Put in the mixture and cover it with greased paper. Steam for two hours. Let the pudding stand for five minutes, then turn it out gently and fill the centre with whipped cream.

Decorate with cherries.

Sufficient for three persons.

CHOCOLATE AND BANANA PUDDING

INGREDIENTS.—6 oz. of flour, 3 oz. of margarine, 3 bananas, 4 oz. of sugar, 1½ oz. of cocoa, 1 teaspoonful of baking-powder, 1 egg, milk.

METHOD.—Rub the margarine into the flour. Add the sugar, cocoa, and baking-powder, and mix together. Peel and slice the bananas, and mix with the dry ingredients. Beat up the egg and add, with the milk as required, and mix all together.

Put into a small, greased pie-dish, and bake in a moderately-hot oven for about three-quarters of an hour. Lift on to a hot dish, and serve with hot custard (see p. 217).

Sufficient for about six persons.

BAKED CHOCOLATE PUDDINGS

INGREDIENTS.—1 oz. of butter, 1 oz. of sugar, 1 oz. of flour, 1 oz. of cocoa, 1 egg, ½ teaspoonful of baking-powder.

METHOD.—Grease six small, plain moulds.

The butter and sugar are creamed till light, and the egg is added and beaten well into the mixture.

The flour and cocoa are sifted together, and stirred lightly in with the baking-powder.

The small, greased moulds are filled three-quarters full, and the puddings baked for twenty minutes.

Note.—They are very good served with marshmallow sauce. Quarter of a pound of marshmallow dissolved in one gill of water.

CHOCOLATE CASTLE PUDDINGS

Ingredients.—2 oz. of cocoa, ½ lb. of breadcrumbs, 3 oz. of margarine, 6 oz. of castor sugar, 2 eggs, milk to mix, vanilla flavouring.

Method.—Make the breadcrumbs and mix with the cocoa and castor sugar. Beat up the eggs.

Warm the margarine sufficiently to melt it. Add the eggs and melted margarine to the dry ingredients, together with some milk, as required, and mix well.

Add flavouring to taste.

Put into small greased castle moulds, cover with greased papers and steam for about three-quarters of an hour.

Turn on to a dish and serve with hot custard.

Sufficient for about six persons.

CHOCOLATE CHERRY PUDDING

Ingredients.—3 oz. of castor sugar, 1½ oz. of butter or margarine, 2 dessert-spoonfuls of cocoa, 1 oz. of glacé cherries, ¼ pint of milk, 2 eggs, vanilla, 4 oz. of breadcrumbs.

Method.—Cut the cherries into small pieces. Beat the sugar and fat to a cream. Make the breadcrumbs and mix with the cocoa. Separate the yolks from the whites of the eggs.

Beat up the yolks and add to the creamed fat and sugar, stirring quickly, then beat well for a few minutes.

Whisk the whites to a very stiff froth.

Stir the breadcrumbs and cherries into the creamed fat and sugar, alternately with the milk, and mix all together.

Add the whisked whites and stir in very lightly.

Put into a greased mould, cover securely with a well-greased paper, and steam for about one hour and a half. Turn out carefully and serve with custard.

Sufficient for about four persons.

CHOCOLATE GINGER SOUFFLE

Ingredients.—1 oz. of cocoa, 2½ oz. of butter or margarine, ½ pint of milk, 3 oz. of flour, 3 eggs, 2 tablespoonfuls of sugar (castor), 3 oz. of preserved ginger (sold in jars in syrup), 2 tablespoonfuls of ginger syrup.

Method.—Sieve the flour.

Put the milk and butter in a saucepan and leave until the butter has melted and the milk is boiling well.

Add the flour, stir it in quickly, and beat until smooth, and continue to stir over a low gas until the mixture leaves the sides of the pan ; then draw to the side and cool slightly. Separate the yolks from the whites of eggs. Add the yolks separately to the mixture in the saucepan, beating each one in thoroughly before adding the next.

When all are added, stir in the cocoa, sugar and ginger, cut into small pieces, also the ginger syrup.

Whisk the whites to a very stiff froth, then fold in lightly. Put the mixture into a prepared soufflé tin, cover with a greased paper and steam gently for about one hour, then turn out very carefully on to a hot dish.

To Prepare The Souffle Tin

This should be done before the soufflé is made. Well grease it, and tie a band of greased paper round the outside of the tin, so that it stands two or three inches above the top.

If a soufflé-tin is not available, a small, round cake-tin can be used.

Note.—Hot soufflés must be dished up directly they are cooked, otherwise they sink.

Sufficient for about five or six persons.

CHOCOLATE PUDDING

Ingredients.—3 oz. of breadcrumbs, 2 oz. of castor sugar, 1 egg and 1 yolk, 2 tablespoonfuls of grated chocolate, 1 pint of milk, ¼ teaspoonful of powdered cinnamon, vanilla flavouring, a few ratafias.

Method.—Boil three-quarters of a pint of the milk, add it to the breadcrumbs. Soak them for about fifteen to twenty minutes.

Mix the chocolate with the sugar

and cinnamon in a saucepan, add the remainder of the milk and stir until dissolved. Add this to the bread-crumbs, then whisk the eggs and stir them in with vanilla flavouring to taste. More sugar may be added if required.

Turn the pudding into a pie-dish or Pyrex dish, put a few ratafia biscuits on the top, and bake it gently until set, being careful not to let it boil. Serve chocolate pudding hot or cold with cream.

Sufficient for four persons.

CHOCOLATE COTTAGE PUD-DING

INGREDIENTS.—1½ oz. of cocoa, 4½ oz. of flour, 3 oz. of margarine, 3 oz. of sugar, milk to mix, vanilla flavouring, ½ teaspoonful of baking-powder.

METHOD.—Mix the flour and cocoa together.

Rub in the margarine.

Add the sugar and baking-powder, and mix well.

Add a few drops of vanilla and sufficient milk to mix all to about the consistency of a cake. Put into a small greased pie-dish, and bake for about thirty minutes in a moderately-hot oven.

STEAMED CHOCOLATE PUD-DING

INGREDIENTS.—3 oz. of stale sponge cakes, 1 oz. of cocoa, 1 oz. of butter, 1 oz. of flour, 1 egg, 1½ oz. of sugar, 1 gill of milk, ½ teaspoonful of baking-powder, vanilla flavouring.

METHOD.—Crumble the sponge cakes and mix with the cocoa. Boil the milk and pour over it, and leave to soak. Beat the sugar and fat to a cream. Add the egg, stir it in quickly, and beat well for a few minutes. Mix the flour and baking-powder and stir in, add also the soaked sponge cake and milk gradually.

Mix all together and flavour with vanilla. Put into a greased basin, cover securely with a greased paper, and steam gently for one hour and a half. Turn out carefully and serve with marshmallow sauce.

MARSHMALLOW SAUCE.

MELT quarter of a pound of marsh-mallows in a gill of water.

Sufficient for about four persons.

CHOCOLATE SUFFOLK PUD-DING

INGREDIENTS.—¼ lb. of sugar, ¼ lb. of margarine or butter, ¼ lb. of self-raising flour, 1 oz. of cocoa, pinch of salt, 2 eggs, ½ teaspoonful of vanilla flavouring, a few almonds.

METHOD.—Blanch and skin the almonds. Well grease a mould and decorate with the almonds. Sieve the flour, cocoa, and salt together. Beat the sugar and fat to a cream. Add each egg separately and stir in quickly, and beat well for a few minutes before adding the next.

When both are well beaten in, stir in the flour and cocoa and mix all together lightly, adding about a table-spoonful of milk if required.

Stir in the vanilla flavouring, then put the mixture into the prepared mould, cover with a well-greased paper and steam for about two hours. Turn out carefully and serve with hot custard.

NOTE.—If preferred, the mixture can be put into small moulds, in which case they will require about thirty minutes to steam, or about twenty minutes to bake.

CHRISTMAS PUDDING

INGREDIENTS.—½ lb. of suet, ½ lb. of raisins, ¼ lb. of flour, ¼ lb. of currants, ¼ lb. of peel, ¼ lb. of sultanas, 1 oz. of almonds, rind of ½ a lemon (grated), 2 tablespoonfuls of golden syrup, 2 eggs, ½ gill of milk, ¼ of a nutmeg (grated).

METHOD.—Prepare the fruits. Chop the suet. Mix the flour and suet together. Add the lemon-rind and nutmeg and prepared fruit. Cut the peel into small pieces, blanch the almonds and cut into pieces. Add these to the other ingredients and mix well.

Whisk up the eggs, add the golden syrup, and whisk together. Add to the dry ingredients with the milk, and mix all together. Put into a greased basin, cover with greased paper and floured pudding-cloth. Put into a saucepan of boiling water, and steam for eight hours. Turn on to a hot dish and serve.

CHRISTMAS PUDDING
(MADE WITH FIGS AND DATES.)

INGREDIENTS.—1½ lb. of dates (when stoned), 1 lb. of figs, ½ lb. of mixed peel, 1½ lb. of seeded raisins, 2 lb. of suet, ½ lb. of breadcrumbs, ¾ lb. of flour, ½ lb. of sugar, 2 oz. of ground almonds, 1 large carrot, ¼ lb. of shelled walnuts, 1 orange and 1 lemon (rind and juice), 1 nutmeg, 1 large saltspoonful of ground ginger, 8 eggs, 1 lb. of black treacle, 1½ gills of milk, ¾ gill of rum, a little ratafia flavouring.

METHOD.—Wash the figs, dry them thoroughly, then remove the stalks and cut the fruit into small pieces, or put it through a mincer. Cut up the peel and separate the raisins. Stone and cut up the dates.

Chop the suet finely and mix well with the flour and breadcrumbs ; add also the ginger, grated nutmeg, ground almonds, and sugar, and mix together.

Scrape the carrot, then grate it finely, and add to the dry ingredients with the grated orange and lemon-rind, prepared fruit, and the walnuts (chopped up roughly).

When well mixed, stir in the beaten eggs, mixed with the treacle (this may be warmed slightly). Add also the milk.

Beat all together, then stir in the rum and ratafia flavouring.

Put into well-buttered basins, cover with buttered papers and floured pudding-cloths, and cook in boiling water for about six hours.

Sufficient to make three large puddings or four medium-sized ones.

NOTE.—The puddings may be served plain or stuck with baked almonds.

To PREPARE THE ALMONDS.—Blanch them and put them on a baking-sheet lined with a sheet of white paper, and bake slowly in the oven until golden-brown.

INDIVIDUAL CHRISTMAS PUDDINGS

INGREDIENTS.—4 oz. of suet, ½ lb. of raisins, ¼ lb. of currants, 2 oz. of sultanas, 2 oz. of candied peel, 1 oz. of shelled walnuts, 4 oz. of sugar, 3 oz. of breadcrumbs, 1½ oz. of flour, grating of nutmeg, ¼ flat teaspoonful of ground cinnamon, ¼ flat teaspoonful of ground cloves, 2 eggs, ½ gill of noyau or rum.

METHOD.—Wash, pick over, and dry the fruits, and stone the raisins.

Shred the candied peel and chop up the walnuts.

Sieve the flour with the spices, add the finely-chopped suet and the breadcrumbs, then stir in the sugar, prepared fruits and nuts and mix all together.

Whisk the eggs and add them. Moisten the mixture with the rum and some milk as required. Beat it well and leave it to stand overnight, adding more moisture after that time, if necessary. Turn the mixture into six buttered moulds. Cover them securely with buttered papers and steam them for about an hour and a half or two hours. Unmould the puddings and serve them with half a shelled walnut on each.

Sufficient for six persons.

CINNAMON PUDDING

INGREDIENTS.—9 oz. of flour, ¼ flat teaspoonful of carbonate of soda, 4 oz. of margarine, ½ dessertspoonful of powdered cinnamon, 4 oz. of sugar, 2 tablespoonfuls of golden syrup, 1 egg, milk.

FOR THE SAUCE.—4 tablespoonfuls of golden syrup, 1 tablespoonful of water, 1 tablespoonful of lemon-juice.

METHOD.—Sieve the flour and cinnamon. Beat up the eggs.

Put the sugar, margarine and golden syrup into a saucepan, and dissolve, but do not boil. Let it cool slightly, then add to the egg. Pour into the dry ingredients, mix all together and beat well.

Stir in the soda mixed with a little milk.

Put into small greased castle moulds and cover securely with greased paper.

Steam for about three-quarters of an hour, then serve with the sauce.

To MAKE THE SAUCE

PUT the golden syrup, water, and lemon-juice in a saucepan and boil together for a few minutes.

Sufficient for about six or seven persons.

CINNAMON FRUIT PUDDING

INGREDIENTS.—3 oz. of flour, 3 oz. of breadcrumbs, 3 oz. of suet, 3 oz. of Barbados sugar, 6 oz. of sultanas, 1 level teaspoonful of ground cinnamon, 1 egg, castor sugar, milk.

METHOD.—Wash, pick over and dry the fruit. Sift the flour and cinnamon, add the breadcrumbs and finely-chopped suet, and mix them well. Then stir in the sugar and prepared fruit.

Moisten the ingredients with the beaten egg and some milk, as required, beat the mixture well and turn it into a greased basin or a plain mould. Cover the basin with a greased paper, and steam the pudding for from two to two and a half hours.

Serve the pudding sprinkled with castor sugar mixed with a little ground cinnamon.

Sufficient for five persons.

BAKED COCONUT CUSTARD

INGREDIENTS.—2 eggs, 1 pint of milk, 1½ tablespoonfuls of sugar, flavouring, 3 or 4 tablespoonfuls of desiccated coconut.

METHOD.—Beat up the eggs. Put the milk and sugar in a saucepan and make them hot, then add them to the eggs.

Strain into a pie-dish, add the coconut, and flavouring to taste, then bake in a moderately-warm oven until set, being careful not to let it boil. It will take from about thirty to forty-five minutes. Serve hot or cold, with some coconut sprinkled on the top.

COCONUT FRUIT DUFF

INGREDIENTS.—¼ lb. of desiccated coconut, 2 oz. of candied peel, 6 oz. of raisins, 1 lemon (rind only), ¼ lb. of flour, 6 oz. of breadcrumbs, 5 oz. of sugar, 5 oz. of suet, 1 egg, milk and water to mix.

METHOD.—Wash the raisins, stone them and cut them in halves. Cut up the peel. Chop the suet finely and mix with the flour. Add the breadcrumbs, coconut, grated lemon-rind, sugar, and prepared fruit, and mix together.

Beat up the egg and add with some milk and water as required. Turn into a greased basin or mould, cover securely with a well-greased paper and steam for about two and a half to three hours, when turn on to a hot dish and serve.

Sufficient for eight or ten persons.

COCONUT PUDDING

INGREDIENTS.—½ lb. of flour, ¼ lb. of margarine, 1 teaspoonful of baking-powder, 3 oz. of castor sugar, 2 oz. of desiccated coconut, 1 egg, milk to mix, ¼ lb. of apricot jam.

METHOD.—Grease a pie-dish and put the jam in the bottom of it.

Rub the margarine into the flour, then add the sugar and coconut. Whisk up the egg and add to the dry ingredients with some milk as required. Beat well, then stir in the baking-powder mixed with a spoonful of flour.

Turn into the prepared dish, dredge on some castor sugar and desiccated coconut (extra to that given in the recipe), and bake in a moderate oven. It will take about three-quarters of an hour.

Serve in the dish, with some more apricot jam (heated).

Sufficient for five or six persons.

COCONUT AND TAPIOCA CREAM

INGREDIENTS.—3 oz. of tapioca, water to cover (about 1 pint), 3 oz. of sugar, 2 pints of milk, 3 tablespoonfuls of desiccated coconut, 1 gill of cream.

METHOD.—Wash the tapioca, then place in a pie-dish and cover with cold water and leave to soak for a few hours.

During this time the tapioca will absorb the water, but should there be any not absorbed this can be poured off.

Then mix the sugar and two tablespoonfuls of the coconut with the tapioca and add the milk.

Bake in a moderately-warm oven, bring the pudding to the boil, then cook it very slowly for about one hour.

When cold, slightly whip the cream and shake on to the top of the pudding.

Sprinkle the remainder of coconut on to the cream.

Serve plain, or with apricot jam.

NOTE.—The cream may be omitted, if wished.

Sufficient for about seven or eight persons.

COCONUT TREACLE PUDDING

INGREDIENTS.—2 oz. of desiccated coconut, 1 gill of milk, 2 eggs, 6 oz. of flour, 1 teaspoonful of baking-powder, 4 oz. of castor sugar, 4 oz. of margarine, ½ lb. of golden syrup.

METHOD.—Soak the coconut in the milk for a few minutes.

Grease a pudding-basin and pour the golden syrup into the bottom of it. Beat the sugar and fat to a cream, and then stir in the eggs, one at a time, and beat well. Sift the flour and baking-powder and add them with the milk and coconut.

Mix all together lightly, adding a little more milk if required.

Turn the mixture into the prepared basin, cover it with a greased paper, and steam it for from one hour and a half to two hours. Turn it out carefully on to a hot dish. The golden syrup will form a sauce round the pudding.

Sufficient for six persons.

COTTAGE PUDDING

INGREDIENTS.—1 teacupful of flour, 3 oz. of lard or margarine, ¼ teacup of sugar, rind of a lemon, 1 teaspoonful of baking-powder, milk to mix.

METHOD.—Grease a pie-dish and grate the lemon-rind thinly.

Rub the margarine into the flour, add the sugar, baking-powder, and grated lemon-rind. Mix quickly with milk to a rather stiff paste. Bake at once in a greased pie-dish in a moderately-hot oven for forty-five minutes.

BAKED EGG CUSTARDS

THESE custards can be served hot or cold. They need careful cooking, and must not be allowed to boil or they will become watery.

Use two eggs to one pint of milk.

If less egg is used the custard will not set.

Either hot or cold milk can be added to the eggs, but a custard will set more quickly if the milk is hot.

Do not add boiling milk.

In hot weather, it is a good plan to boil the milk, and then let it go off the boil. This enables it to keep better.

Small biscuits are sometimes put on top of a custard to give variety. These are added before the custard is cooked.

BAKED CUSTARD

INGREDIENTS.—2 eggs, 1 pint of milk, nutmeg, 1 oz. of sugar.

METHOD.—Beat the eggs with the sugar and pour the milk on them. Put the custard in a buttered pie-dish, or individual fireproof dishes, grate nutmeg over them and bake them in a very moderate oven till set (about forty-five minutes).

Custard must never be baked quickly or it will be watery and full of holes.

NOTE.—A bread-and-butter pudding is made with custard, as above, but before baking, three slices of thin bread-and-butter should be put in the dish and two ounces of sultanas, most at the bottom of the dish and a few on top. Sufficient for four petsons.

RICH BOILED CUSTARD

INGREDIENTS.—2 eggs, ¾ pint of milk, a strip of lemon-rind, sugar to taste (about 1 oz.).

METHOD.—Put the milk, sugar, and lemon-rind in a double saucepan and heat slowly to extract the flavour of the lemon. Beat the eggs well, let the milk cool for a few minutes and pour it on the eggs. Stir well and return to the pan. Stir over a low gas till the custard is thick enough to coat the back of the spoon. If cooked too long or made too hot the eggs will harden and form lumps. When the custard is cooked, do not leave it standing in the double saucepan, but stand it in a basin containing a little cold water, so that it cannot go on cooking. When cool strain to remove the lemon.

NOTE.—Custard that has curdled slightly can be restored by whisking it with an egg whisk.

CUSTARD PUDDING

INGREDIENTS.—¼ lb. of jam, 1 tumblerful of breadcrumbs, flavouring.

FOR THE CUSTARD.—1 pint of milk, 1½ oz. of sugar, custard-powder.

METHOD.—Put the jam into the bottom of the pie-dish. Make the breadcrumbs and sprinkle on top of the jam. Make the custard according to instructions given on the outside of packet. Pour it over the breadcrumbs, and mix well, being careful not to mix with the jam at the bottom of the dish. Bake in a moderately-hot oven for twenty to thirty minutes. Serve hot.

DAMSON PUDDING

INGREDIENTS.—10 oz. of self-raising flour, 5 oz. of suet, water to mix, 1½ lb. of damsons, or sufficient to fill the basin, 3 to 4 tablespoonfuls of sugar, water.

METHOD.—Stalk, pick over, and wash the damsons. Sift the flour into a basin, add the shredded suet, and mix them well together before adding the water.

Stir in sufficient water to make a soft, rollable dough. Cut off a small piece and put this aside for the top of the pudding.

Roll out the large piece to a round about one and a half times the size of the top of the basin. Grease the basin (you will require one holding about one and three-quarter pints) and line it with the suet crust, smoothing it with the fingers and making it as even as possible.

Fill it with damsons, sprinkling each layer with sugar, but making the last layer of damsons without sugar. Pour in enough water to fill the basin about half-full. Now roll the remaining piece of suet crust to a round the same size as the top of the basin, damp the edge of crust and fix the round on to it.

Finally, cover the pudding with a greased paper and a floured pudding-cloth, and tie it securely. Knot the ends of the cloth over the top, and stand the pudding in a pan of boiling water. Boil it for from two to two and a half hours.

Take out the pudding, remove the cloth and paper and let it stand a few seconds before turning it on to a dish.

Serve damson pudding with cream or custard.

NOTE.—Plain flour and baking-powder may be used instead of self-raising flour, if preferred, using one level teaspoonful of baking-powder to the ten ounces of flour.

SMALL DAMSON PUDDINGS

INGREDIENTS.—Damsons, sugar.

FOR THE SUET CRUST.—10 oz. of flour, cold water, 1 level teaspoonful of

baking-powder, 6 oz. of suet, a pinch of salt.

METHOD.—To make the suet crust, sift the flour, salt, and baking-powder into a basin. Add the suet shredded finely, and the water, and mix to a soft and pliable paste.

Divide the suet crust into equal portions for each pudding and cut off a piece from each sufficient for a "lid." Roll the larger piece into a round for lining the basin, and mould it firmly to the side of the buttered basin.

Fill up each pudding with damsons, add the sugar, and pack the fruit tightly into the basin. Turn in an edge of the pastry and moisten it with water.

Roll out the crust for the lid so that it fits inside the rim of the basin, and put it on. Cover the puddings with a buttered paper and steam them for from one and a half to two hours.

Sufficient for from four to six persons.

DATE AND FIG PUDDING

INGREDIENTS.—½ lb. of flour, grated rind of 1 orange, 3 oz. of castor sugar, ¼ lb. of chopped figs, ¼ lb. of chopped dates, ¼ lb. of finely-chopped beef suet, a pinch of salt, 2 level teaspoonfuls of baking-powder, milk.

METHOD.—First sift together the flour, salt, and baking-powder into a basin.

Add the suet, sugar, figs, dates, and the orange-rind, finely grated.

Moisten the ingredients with milk and turn them into a buttered mould. Cover the mould closely and steam the pudding for two and a half hours. Then unmould it, and serve.

Sufficient for six persons.

DATE RICE PUDDING

INGREDIENTS.—¼ lb. of dates, 1½ oz. of sugar, 2 oz. of shredded suet, 1 egg, 4 tablespoonfuls of rice, 1 pint of milk.

METHOD.—Wash the rice in hot water.

Boil the milk and sprinkle in the rice. Simmer them gently till the rice is quite soft and the milk is absorbed (about twenty-five minutes). Stir now and again as the mixture thickens. Add the suet and sugar.

Remove the stones from the dates and chop them. Beat the egg.

Mix all the ingredients together and put them in a well-greased basin.

Cover with a greased paper and steam for two hours.

Sufficient for three persons.

DATE SANDWICH FRITTERS

INGREDIENTS.—¼ lb. of dates, slices of bread-and-butter, 2 dessertspoonfuls of castor sugar, ¼ gill of water, fritter batter (see p. 222), deep fat for frying.

METHOD.—Stone and mince the dates, and put them in a saucepan with the sugar and water. Stir over a low burner until mixed to a paste, and boiled for a minute or two. When cool, it should be a good consistency for spreading.

Take slices of bread-and-butter and spread them evenly with the mixture. Make them into sandwiches, pressing them firmly together.

Cut into small shapes, as desired—round, square, or three-sided, etc. Coat with batter and fry in hot fat until golden-brown.

Drain on paper and serve as hot as possible.

Allow three or four fritters for each person.

DUCHESS PUDDING

INGREDIENTS.—½ lb. of flour, 2 eggs, ¼ lb. of margarine, 1 teaspoonful of baking-powder, 3 oz. of castor sugar, 2 oz. of glacé cherries, milk.

METHOD.—Well grease a pudding-basin and decorate the bottom of it with a few cherries cut into halves. If you find it difficult to make them adhere to the bottom of the basin, just dip them in melted butter. Sieve the flour and baking-powder. Beat the margarine and sugar to a cream. Cut the remainder of the cherries into small pieces. Separate the yolks from the whites of the eggs. Whisk the whites to a stiff froth. Add each yolk separately to the creamed sugar and fat, stir it in quickly and beat well before adding the next.

When both are added, fold in the flour, baking-powder, and cherries, together with about a tablespoonful of milk.

Lastly add the whites of the eggs,

stir them in lightly, and when thoroughly mixed put the mixture into the prepared basin, and cover with a thick piece of greased paper and twist the latter underneath the rim of the basin.

Steam for about two hours, then turn carefully on to a hot dish and serve.

DUPTON PUDDING

INGREDIENTS.—4 oz. of bread-crumbs, 1 gill of apricot syrup, 2 eggs, 1 gill of milk, tinned apricots, 1 oz. of almonds, 1 oz. of castor sugar.

METHOD.—Butter pie-dish well. Break the eggs into a basin, and beat them well. Add the sugar and milk and the apricot syrup.

Put a layer of breadcrumbs in the bottom of the pie-dish, then a good layer of apricots cut into thin slices, then more crumbs, then fruit, and lastly a layer of crumbs on top.

Pour the prepared mixture over this, and allow it to stand for half an hour before baking.

Blanch the almonds, skin them and cut them into shreds. Sprinkle them over the top of the pudding.

Bake the pudding in a moderate oven till it is firm and brown. It will take about thirty minutes.

Serve Dupton Pudding at once with whipped cream.

Sufficient for six persons.

EMPRESS PEACHES

INGREDIENTS.—4 oz. of Carolina rice, 4 fresh peaches, 2 oz. of castor sugar, 4 spoonfuls of red current jelly, 1½ pints of milk, vanilla flavouring.

METHOD.—Cook the rice in the milk in a double boiler, adding the sugar, till the rice is soft and the milk has been absorbed ; then add flavouring to taste.

Peel and halve the peaches, remove the stones and place the fruit on a baking-tin. Cook them for two minutes in the oven.

Heap the rice on a hot dish and arrange the cooked peaches on top.

Put the jelly in the baking-tin, and when it is dissolved, pour it over the peaches.

This sweet can be served either hot or cold.

Sufficient for four persons.

FAMILY PUDDING

INGREDIENTS.—5 oz. of flour, 3 oz. of breadcrumbs, 5 oz. of sugar, ¼ lb. of suet 1 level teaspoonful of mixed spice, 1½ oz. of desiccated coconut, ½ lb. of seeded raisins, 2 oz. of candied peel, milk.

METHOD.—Chop the suet finely and mix it with the flour, spice, and breadcrumbs.

Cut up the raisins and shred the peel, add these to the flour, etc., with the sugar and coconut. Mix the ingredients well and moisten them with milk as required.

Turn the mixture into a greased basin.

Cover it with a buttered paper and floured pudding-cloth, stand it in a pan of boiling water, and steam it for from two and a half to three hours.

FIG AND RAISIN PUDDING

INGREDIENTS.—6 oz. of breadcrumbs 6 oz. of flour, 6 oz. of sugar, ½ lb. of suet, ½ lb. of figs, ½ lb. of raisins, 2 oz. of peel, 1 lemon, milk and water to mix, 2 eggs.

METHOD.—Well wash and stone the raisins.

Wash and dry the figs, remove stalks, and cut them into small pieces.

Make the breadcrumbs by rubbing some bread on a grater or through a wire sieve.

Skin, shred, and chop the suet very finely.

Mix the suet into the flour, and add the breadcrumbs and grated lemon-rind and sugar.

Cut the peel into small pieces, and add, together with the figs.

Mix all well together.

Beat the eggs and add to the dry ingredients, with some milk and water as required, and mix all together.

Put into a greased mould, cover with a greased paper, then a floured pudding-cloth.

Tie tightly and put into a saucepan of boiling water, and boil for three hours and a half.

Turn on to a hot dish.

Sufficient for about ten or twelve persons.

STEAMED FIG PUDDING

INGREDIENTS.—½ lb. of figs, 1 oz. of citron peel, 7 oz. of breadcrumbs, ½ teaspoonful of ground ginger, ¼ teaspoonful of mixed spice, 5 oz. of margarine, 6 oz. of castor sugar, 2 eggs, milk.

METHOD.—Make the breadcrumbs and mix with the ground ginger and mixed spice.

Wash and stalk the figs, dry them and cut into fairly small pieces. Cut up the peel. Beat the sugar and fat to a cream, then gradually add the breadcrumbs and prepared fruit, alternately with the well-breaten eggs and some milk, as required.

Beat together well, turn into a greased basin or mould, and cover securely with a well-greased paper. Steam for about two hours and when cooked turn on to a hot dish, and, if liked, serve hot custard with it.

Sufficient for about six persons.

FLAKED RICE PUDDING

INGREDIENTS.—2 teacupfuls of flaked rice, 1½ pints of milk, 1 egg, 3 dessert-spoonfuls of sugar, flavouring (as desired).

METHOD.—Put the flaked rice into a pie-dish with the sugar. Beat up the egg, and mix with the milk.

Add these to the rice, and mix together.

Stir in a few drops of flavouring.

Put the pudding into a moderately-warm oven and bake for about forty-five minutes. Be very careful not to let it boil, or the egg will curdle.

Just before serving, put under the grill and brown it lightly.

Serve hot or cold.

FLEMISH RICE PUDDING

INGREDIENTS.—1½ tablespoonfuls of rice, 2 dessertspoonfuls of white sugar, 1 pint of milk, 1 teaspoonful of powdered cinnamon, 2 oz. of margarine or butter.

METHOD.—Well wash the rice and put it into a pie-dish. Mix with it the sugar, cinnamon, and margarine.

Add the milk and stir thoroughly.

Place in a moderately-hot oven and bring to the boil. Then cook slowly for one hour and a half to two hours.

Sufficient for about three persons.

FRUIT BATTER PUDDING

INGREDIENTS.—¾ lb. of damsons, 2 tablespoonfuls of sugar, 6 oz. of flour, a pinch of salt, 1 egg and 1 extra yolk, 2 gills of milk.

METHOD.—Add the salt to the flour and make a well in the centre of it.

Pour in the whole egg and yolk and mix with a small quantity of the flour.

Then take about half of the milk and add gradually, mixing all to a smooth batter.

When well mixed beat for a few minutes.

Stir in the remainder of the milk and leave the batter to stand for about an hour. Pick over and wash the damsons.

Well grease a pudding-basin and put in half of the damsons, putting the sugar (one tablespoonful) in between them.

Pour over the batter; the basin should not be more than three parts full.

Cover securely with a well-greased paper and steam for about two hours.

Turn out carefully, dredge with castor sugar, and serve with the remainder of the damsons and sugar stewed separately.

Sufficient for about five persons.

HOT FRUIT SPONGE

INGREDIENTS.—1 sponge ring, a tin of fruit salad (small), 1od. of cream, sugar and vanilla, 1 or 2 tablespoonfuls of cooking sherry.

METHOD.—Put the sponge ring into a Pyrex or other fireproof dish and warm it through in the oven. Meanwhile turn the fruit salad into a saucepan and heat it. Flavour the syrup with sherry and when the sponge is ready, pour it over it and heap the fruit in the centre.

Whisk the cream until it thickens, sweeten it and flavour to taste, and then cover the top of the pudding. Decorate this with a few cherries and serve it hot.

Sufficient for four persons.

FRENCH PANCAKES

INGREDIENTS.—3 eggs, 4 oz. of flour, ½ pint of milk, 1 level teaspoonful of baking powder, 2 oz. of margarine or butter, 3 oz. of castor sugar, grated rind of ½ lemon, grated rind of 1 small orange.

METHOD.—Beat the sugar and fat to a cream and add the finely grated rind of the orange and lemon.

Sift the flour with the baking-powder and stir them in gradually, adding the well-whisked eggs and then the milk.

Butter some old strong saucers and pour some of the mixture into each. Bake it in a fairly hot oven for about twenty minutes, and serve the pancakes as soon as possible after baking, heaped on a dish and sprinkled with castor sugar.

Sufficient for about nine pancakes.

FRENCH PUDDING

INGREDIENTS.—1¼ oz. of butter, 1½ oz. of castor sugar, 1½ oz. of flour, 1 egg, ½ gill of cream or milk, rind of ½ a lemon, a few glacé cherries, 3 tablespoonfuls of jam, lemon butter sauce.

METHOD.—Butter three saucers and light the gas in the oven.

Put the butter and sugar in a basin and cream them with a wooden spoon till they are soft and white. Add the lemon-rind, egg, and cream to the creamed butter and sugar, and beat them for five minutes.

Stir in the flour lightly, and divide the mixture between the three saucers.

Bake in a hot oven for about ten minutes. The puddings are done when the centre feels elastic on being pressed.

Have ready the jam (heated).

Dish the puddings up one on top of the other with jam spread between. Decorate with cherries. Pour lemon butter sauce over, and serve at once.

Sufficient for three persons.

LEMON BUTTER SAUCE

INGREDIENTS.—1½ oz. of butter, 1½ oz. of sugar, 4 tablespoonfuls of lemon-juice.

METHOD.—Melt the sugar and butter in the lemon-juice. Boil for four minutes, and pour the sauce over the pudding.

FRITTERS

FRITTERS consist of small portions of food coated with batter and fried in hot fat. They may be made of fruit, fish, meat or vegetables. The success of fritters depends firstly on the lightness of the batter and, secondly, on the care taken in frying them.

The batter should be made first, as it is improved if it stands for a while before being used.

There are various recipes for making Fritter Batters, but this is usually the favourite. Fritters are more crisp if water is used in mixing the batter, but milk may be used if preferred. Whichever batter is made, it should be of a coating consistency when finished.

A Fritter Batter

INGREDIENTS.—3 oz. of flour, a pinch of salt, 1 gill of warm water, 1½ dessertspoonfuls of salad oil, 2 egg whites.

METHOD.—Sift the flour with a pinch of salt into a basin. Make a well in the centre and pour in the oil, then stir in the warm water gradually and mix to a smooth batter.

Beat well and then leave the batter to stand for about an hour or more.

Just before you are ready to fry the fritters, add a pinch of salt to the egg whites and whisk them to a stiff froth, then fold them lightly into the batter.

NOTE.—If a milk batter is preferred, omit the salad oil and drop the yolks of eggs into the centre of the flour and mix to a smooth batter with cold milk. Add the whisked whites when ready to fry the fritters.

Preparing Food for the Fritters

APPLES.—Remove the core and peel the apples, then cut them in slices crosswise.

Put them on to a dish, sprinkle them with a little lemon-juice and dredge with castor sugar. Cover them and leave them for about twenty to thirty minutes, then drain well.

BANANAS.—Peel and split the bananas lengthwise, then cut each half into two or three pieces, cutting crosswise.

Sprinkle them with lemon-juice and castor sugar and let them stand for a short time, then drain.

POTATOES.—Peel and wash the potatoes, cut them in *very thin* slices and dry them in a cloth. Season and coat each in batter, then fry.

CAULIFLOWER.—Boil the cauliflower in the usual way until almost tender. Take it up and drain and leave it to get cool. Take the flower and divide it into small branches. Season before coating with the batter.

CELERY.—Wash and prepare the celery in the usual way, and boil until barely tender. Drain it and let it cool, then cut it into convenient lengths.

TINNED FRUITS.—Drain the fruit very thoroughly.

ORANGES.—Peel and divide the oranges into quarters, removing as much white pith as possible.

DRIED FIGS.—Stalk and wash the figs, soak them for a few hours, then stew them until tender in the water in which they have been soaked, adding sugar to taste and a flavouring of lemon-rind. Leave them until cold, then drain them thoroughly.

CHEESE.—Remove the rind and cut the cheese in thin slices of convenient size.

Frying the Fritters

DEEP frying is required for fritters, so use a strong, deep pan about half full of fat, or at least sufficient to float the fritters. The fat may consist of either lard or clarified dripping.

A Few Special Hints

BE sure the food is well drained, and do not coat it with batter until it is ready to be put into the fat.

A faint blue smoke must rise from the centre of the fat before the coated food is put into it.

Do not fry too many fritters at one time, as this would cool the fat down too much.

When the fritters are golden on both sides, drain them on paper and fry the remainder in the same way.

Remember to re-heat the fat between frying each batch.

Serve at once, as they so soon lose their crispness.

NOTE.—The fat should be allowed to cool when finished with. It may then be strained and used again.

To Make Sandwich Fritters

CUT thin slices of bread as for sandwiches, spread them with butter, then with jam, marmalade or mince-meat, or some other suitable filling.

Cover each slice with another slice of bread-and-butter and make them into sandwiches, then cut into small shapes, dip in batter and fry.

APPLE FRITTERS

INGREDIENTS.—¼ lb. of flour, 1 egg white, 1 lb. of apples, deep fat for frying, ¼ pint of water.

METHOD.—To make the batter, sieve the flour with a pinch of salt and mix to a smooth batter with the water.

Whisk the egg-white until slightly frothy and stir in. Beat well, then leave the batter to stand for a few hours.

Peel and core the apples, and slice, but do not cut them in halves and quarters. The slices should be about a quarter-inch in thickness. Put the fat on the fire to get hot. For this a deep iron pan is required about half full of fat. Put about six slices of apple into the batter and coat them all over with it. When the fat is hot, put these coated apple slices into it and fry until they are golden brown and cooked inside. The best method of putting them into the fat is with an iron skewer. Proceed in this method until all the apple slices have been fried. Drain the fritters on paper. Sprinkle with castor sugar and place on a lace paper on a dish and serve hot at once.

Sufficient for about six persons.

To Test the Heat of Fat

NOTE.—To test the heat of fat for frying—a slight smoke rises from it when sufficiently hot. An excess of smoke signifies that the fat is burning. The same fat can be used again for frying if it is strained, provided it has not been overheated and burnt.

BANANA FRITTERS

INGREDIENTS.—3 or 4 bananas, juice of $\frac{1}{2}$ a lemon, castor sugar, deep frying fat.

FOR THE FRYING BATTER.—2 oz. of flour, $\frac{1}{2}$ tablespoonful of salad oil, $\frac{1}{2}$ gill of water, white of an egg.

METHOD.—Cut the bananas in half lengthways, and sprinkle them with lemon-juice. Make a smooth batter with the flour, oil and water and let it stand for an hour if possible. Add the stiffly beaten white of the egg just before frying. Coat each banana by dipping it in the batter. Put it carefully into smoking hot fat and fry a golden brown, turning it over when brown on one side. Fry only three halves at a time. After frying the fritters for about three minutes drain them on paper. Sprinkle with castor sugar and serve very hot on a lace paper.

NOTE.—For apple fritters, core and peel the apples and cut them in rings. For orange fritters remove all the white pith and separate the oranges into sections.

Each banana makes two fritters.

FRUIT SALAD FRITTERS

INGREDIENTS.—1 small tin of fruit salad in syrup, $\frac{1}{4}$ lb. of flour, 1 dessert-spoonful of salad oil, a pinch of salt, 1 gill of warm water, 1 egg, deep fat for frying.

METHOD.—Take the fruit salad out of the syrup and put into a colander to drain.

Mix the flour and salt together and put through a sieve.

Separate the yolk from the white of egg.

Make a hole in the centre of the flour, put into it the yolk of egg and salad oil, and mix with a little of the flour.

Gradually add the warm water and gradually mix in the flour, so that the same consistency is maintained all the time—it should be like a thick custard.

When well mixed beat the batter for about ten minutes, or until the surface is covered with bubbles.

Then stand the batter aside for about one hour.

Put a deep iron pan half full of fat on the fire to get hot.

Add a pinch of salt to the white of egg, and whisk to a stiff froth, and fold lightly into the batter.

Put four or five pieces of the fruit salad into the batter and well coat them.

When the fat in the pan is slightly smoking lift the coated fruit out of the batter and put into the hot fat. (Use an iron skewer for this.)

Fry until a golden-brown, then drain them on kitchen paper.

Fry the remainder in the same way, but the fat must be re-heated before each lot is put into it.

When well drained serve at once on a lace paper, and sprinkle well with castor sugar.

NOTE.—Use either dripping, or a mixture of dripping and lard, for frying.

ORANGE FRITTERS

MAKE a fritter batter as given on p. 222. Peel and slice some oranges crosswise, removing as much pith as possible, also the pips. Sprinkle with castor sugar and a little lemon-juice.

Put a deep pan of fat on to get hot, and when a faint blue smoke begins to rise, coat some of the orange slices with batter, then lift into the fat and fry until golden brown. Do not fry too many at a time, or you will cool the fat too much.

Drain on paper, and serve as soon as possible, with castor sugar sprinkled over them.

Allow three or four fritters for each person.

PINEAPPLE FRITTERS

INGREDIENTS.—1 tin of sliced pine-apple, castor sugar.

FOR THE FRYING BATTER.—2 oz. of self-raising flour, white of an egg, ¼ tablespoonful of salad oil, ½ gill of tepid water, deep frying fat.

METHOD.—Cut the pineapple slices into four. Mix the flour smoothly with the oil and water and stir in the stiffly beaten white of egg.

Put three pieces of pineapple into the batter.

Lift out one with a skewer and place it in the *smoking* fat. Fry it a golden brown (about three minutes). *Do not fry more than three fritters at a time.*

Drain them on paper and sprinkle with castor sugar.

Serve hot on lace paper.

Sufficient for three or four persons.

GENOESE PUDDING

INGREDIENTS.—Marmalade, 3 eggs, 4 oz. of castor sugar, 3 oz. of margarine, 6 oz. of flour.

METHOD.—Separate two of the eggs.

Put two yolks and one whole egg into a basin with the sugar, and then whisk well until thick and creamy and free from dark streaks of egg. It will probably take about ten or fifteen minutes to whisk.

Warm the margarine just sufficiently to melt it.

Sieve the flour.

Grease a pie-dish and put some marmalade in the bottom of it.

Whisk the egg-whites to a very stiff froth.

Stir the flour and melted margarine into the sugar and eggs, adding just a little milk if required.

Last of all add the whisked whites, stirring them in lightly.

Put into the prepared dish and bake in a moderately hot oven for about an hour, lessening the heat as required.

Serve in the dish.

Sufficient for about five persons.

GINGER PUDDING

INGREDIENTS.—½ lb. of flour, ½ lb. of breadcrumbs, ¼ lb. of suet, 2 tea-spoonfuls of ground ginger, 2 oz. of candied peel, ¼ lb. of Demerara sugar, 2 tablespoonfuls of golden syrup, milk and water to mix, ¼ teaspoonful of carbonate of soda.

METHOD.—Put a saucepan of water on to boil. Mix the ginger with the flour and soda. Chop the suet and add to the flour. Make the bread-crumbs. Cut the peel into small pieces.

Mix all the dry ingredients together. Slightly warm the golden syrup and put into the middle of the dry ingredients.

Add the milk and water and mix to a wet consistency; beat well. Put into a greased basin, and cover with a greased paper. Stand in a saucepan of boiling water and steam for two hours and a half to three hours.

Turn on to a hot dish and serve with hot custard.

BAKED GINGER PUDDING
(WITH APPLE SAUCE)

INGREDIENTS.—3 oz. of butter or margarine, 1 level teaspoonful of grated orange-rind, 1 well-beaten egg, ¾ lb. of treacle, ¾ lb. of flour, 1 level teaspoonful of baking soda, salt, 1½ level tea-spoonfuls of ginger, ¼ level teaspoonful of nutmeg, 1 level teaspoonful of cinnamon.

METHOD.—Cream the butter.

Add the warm treacle, well-beaten egg and the grated orange-rind.

Sift together the flour, soda, salt, ginger, cinnamon and nutmeg. Com-bine both the mixtures and beat thoroughly.

Turn the mixture into a buttered pan and bake it in a very moderate oven.

Cool the ginger pudding for a minute, cut it in half crosswise, then cut it into squares.

Almond
Pudding

Family
Pudding

Date
and Fig
Pudding

PLATE 21

*Apple
Fritters*

Peel and core
the apples and
slice them.

There should be
enough *f a t t o*
float the fritters.

*The Finished
Dish*

PLATE 22

Black
Currant
Puddings

Chocolate
Pudding

Rhubarb
Ginger
Pudding

PLATE 23

Pancakes

Cook Baked
Spiced Pancakes
in old saucers.

Spread Batter
Soufflé Pancakes
with filling and
fold them in half.

Thin Pancakes are rolled ; thick,
crisp ones are served flat.

PLATE 24

Serve the ginger pudding with hot apple sauce—stewed sweet apples put through a sieve.

Sufficient for eight persons.

GINGER FIG PUDDING

INGREDIENTS.—½ lb. of flour, ¼ lb. of suet, ½ level teaspoonful of carbonate of soda, 1 teaspoonful of ground ginger, ½ pint of water, ¼ lb. of golden syrup, 1 egg, butter, ¼ lb. of Barbados sugar, ¼ lb. of cooking figs.

METHOD.—Wash the figs and soak them in the cold water overnight. Drain, and remove the stalks and cut up the figs.

Butter a plain mould and decorate the base with a few slices of figs dipped in a little melted butter, and when set add the golden syrup.

Sift the flour with the soda and ginger, chop the suet finely and add it with the sugar. Mix them well, stir in the figs, and moisten the mixture with the well-beaten egg and the water in which the figs were soaked.

Turn the mixture into the prepared tin, cover it securely with a well-greased paper, and steam it for about three hours. Unmould it and serve it on a hot dish.

Sufficient for six persons.

GINGER AND LEMON PUDDING

INGREDIENTS.—About ¾ to 1 lb. of flaky pastry (see p. 252), 7 oz. of breadcrumbs, 2 eggs, 6 oz. of margarine, 1 teaspoonful of ground ginger, 1 lemon, about ½ gill of milk, 6 oz. of sugar.

METHOD.—Roll out the pastry and line a pie-dish, putting a double layer of pastry round the rim of the dish.

Make the breadcrumbs and mix with the ginger.

Put the margarine and milk (half a gill) into a saucepan, dissolve slowly, then draw aside and add the sugar and breadcrumbs. Whisk up the eggs and stir them in, then add the finely grated lemon-rind and strained juice, and mix all together.

Turn into the prepared dish and put into a hot oven to bake. It will take about half an hour.

Sufficient for six to eight persons.

PRESERVED GINGER PUDDING

INGREDIENTS.—5 oz. of sugar, 6 oz. of margarine, ½ lb. of flour, 1 teaspoonful of baking powder, 2 eggs, milk, 3 oz. of glacé ginger or preserved ginger (sold in jars in syrup).

METHOD.—Cut the ginger into small pieces.

Sieve the flour and baking-powder.

Beat the sugar and fat to a cream.

Add each egg separately and stir in quickly, and beat well before adding the next.

When both are well beaten in, stir in the flour, etc., and ginger lightly, and mix all together, adding a little milk as required.

Put into a greased pie-dish and bake in a moderately hot oven for from one to one hour and a half, or put into a greased mould. Cover securely with a well-greased paper and steam for two hours.

NOTE.—If using the preserved ginger in syrup, some of the latter can be heated and served with the pudding.

Sufficient for about six or eight persons.

GINGER SPONGE PUDDING

INGREDIENTS.—3 oz. of flour, 1½ oz. of butter or margarine, 2 oz. of granulated sugar, 1 egg, ½ teaspoonful of baking powder, ½ gill of milk, ½ teaspoonful of ground ginger, rind of a lemon (grated), a little grated nutmeg, ginger sauce.

METHOD.—Cream the butter and sugar till soft and white, add the egg and beat well for ten minutes.

Grate the lemon-rind thinly, using the yellow part only, as the white pith is bitter.

Add the rest of the ingredients and mix in the milk.

Pour the pudding mixture into a greased mould, and twist greased paper over the top. Steam steadily for three hours, adding more boiling water after one hour. Leave the pudding for five minutes to cool slightly, then turn it out carefully. Pour ginger sauce round.

Sufficient for three persons.

GINGER SAUCE

INGREDIENTS.—1 oz. of butter, ¾ oz. of flour, 1 oz. of preserved ginger,

H

1 tablespoonful of ginger syrup, ½ pint of milk.

METHOD.—Melt the butter and stir in the flour.

Add the milk gradually and stir till it boils. Chop the ginger and add it to the sauce with the syrup.

Boil for three minutes and pour round the pudding.

GOLDEN PUDDING

INGREDIENTS.—6 oz. of flour, 6 oz. of suet, ¼ lb. of sultanas, ½ flat tea-spoonful of carbonate of soda, 6 oz. of breadcrumbs, 6 oz. of golden syrup, a little grated nutmeg, 1 egg, milk and water to mix (about 1½ to 2 gills).

METHOD.—Wash the sultanas, rub in a cloth, remove the stalks, dry them well. Mix the soda with the flour, and sieve through into a basin. Make the breadcrumbs. Skin and finely chop the suet. Add these, together with the sultanas and grated nutmeg, to the flour ; mix well.

Beat up the egg, add the golden syrup, and whisk together. Then add to the dry ingredients with sufficient milk and water to make a rather wet mixture ; it should be about the same consistency as a cake.

Put into a greased basin, cover with a greased paper and floured pudding-cloth, and steam for two and a half to three hours.

Turn on to a hot dish and serve with golden sauce round it.

NOTE.—The water must be kept boiling all the time.

GOLDEN SAUCE

INGREDIENTS.—1 gill of golden syrup, ½ gill of water, 1 tablespoonful of lemon-juice.

METHOD.—Boil together for five minutes and pour round the pudding.

BAKED GOLDEN PUDDING

INGREDIENTS.—10 oz. of self-raising flour, ¾ lb. of golden syrup, 6 oz. of breadcrumbs, 2 oz. of candied peel, ½ lb. of suet, about 1¼ gills milk and water, 1 flat teaspoonful of ground ginger.

METHOD.—Chop the suet finely and mix well into the flour.

Make the breadcrumbs and add with the ginger and the peel—cut into small pieces.

Mix all the dry ingredients and make a hole in the centre, then pour in the golden syrup (warmed *slightly* to make it thinner) and beat all together, adding some milk and water as required.

Turn into a greased pie-dish and put into a moderately hot oven to bake. It will take about one hour and a half. It can be turned out or served in the dish.

Sufficient for about eight persons.

NOTE.—To weigh golden syrup, weigh a small saucepan, to this weight add the weight of syrup required, then pour in sufficient syrup to balance.

GOOSEBERRY AMBER

INGREDIENTS.—1½ lb. of goose-berries, 2 oz. of margarine or butter, 2 eggs, 4 oz. of Demerara sugar, ½ gill of water, 1 oz. of castor sugar, ½ oz. of glacé cherries, 6 oz. of short pastry (see p. 252).

METHOD.—Pick and wash the goose-berries and stew them with the water and Demerara sugar until they are very soft. Stir in the margarine. Mash the fruit thoroughly with a wooden spoon. To make it really smooth and particularly good, rub it through a hair sieve.

Roll out the pastry into a long strip two inches wide, and lay it against the sides and on the rim of a greased pie-dish.

Decorate the edge of the pastry with the back of a knife.

Stir the yolks of the eggs into the fruit, pour the mixture into the pie-dish, and bake it for twenty minutes.

Beat the egg-white stiffly, add the castor sugar, and heap the meringue mixture on the top.

Brown the gooseberry amber slightly in the oven for five minutes, and decorate it with the cherries cut in half.

Sufficient for four persons.

GOOSEBERRY CHARLOTTES

INGREDIENTS.—¾ lb. of gooseberries, ¼ lb. of breadcrumbs, 2 oz. of suet, grated rind of ½ orange, 3 oz. of sugar, ½ oz. of butter.

METHOD.—Top and tail the goose-berries, then wash and drain them.

Grate the orange-rind finely and mix it with the sugar.

Butter four small basins and coat them with a few of the breadcrumbs.

Shred the suet very finely and mix it with the remainder of the crumbs.

Put a layer of crumbs and suet in each basin, and add a layer of gooseberries sprinkled with sugar and orange-rind.

Repeat this, and finally cover the gooseberries with the remainder of the crumbs and suet, and add the butter, cut into tiny dabs.

Place the basins on a baking-sheet, and cover them with a buttered paper. Bake them in a moderate oven for about forty-five minutes.

Sufficient for four charlottes.

HAWAIIAN SPONGE PUDDING

INGREDIENTS.—4 penny sponge-cakes, a large tin of pineapple, 2 oz. of desiccated coconut, 2 oz. of almonds, 2 dessertspoonfuls of castor sugar, ½ pint of milk, 2 eggs.

METHOD.—Drain the syrup from the pineapple and heat it. Crumble the sponge-cakes and stir the hot fruit syrup on to them and let them soak.

Cut the pineapple into small pieces and place them in a buttered pie-dish. Blanch and split the almonds.

Beat the eggs and stir them into the sponge-cake mixture. Add also the milk, sugar and coconut.

When they are all well mixed, pour them over the pineapple in the pie-dish.

Scatter the almonds on the top. Bake the pudding in a moderate oven from about thirty to forty-five minutes until it is set, being careful not to let it boil.

HONEY PUDDING

INGREDIENTS.—2 or 3 tablespoonfuls of honey, 3 oz. of breadcrumbs, 3 oz. of flour, ¼ lb. of margarine, 5 oz. of castor sugar, barely ¼ flat teaspoonful of carbonate of soda, 2 eggs, milk.

METHOD.—Grease a basin and put the honey in the bottom of it.

Sieve the flour with the carbonate of soda, then mix with the breadcrumbs. Cream the fat and sugar. Separate the eggs. Beat the yolks into the creamed fat and sugar, then stir in the flour and breadcrumbs with some milk as required.

Whisk the egg whites to a stiff froth and fold in lightly.

Turn into the prepared basin, cover securely with a well-greased paper and steam for about one hour and a half.

Sufficient for six or eight persons.

BAKED JAM PUDDING

INGREDIENTS.—1 lb. of flour, ½ lb. of lard, water to mix, 1 lb. of black-currant jam.

METHOD.—Put the flour into a basin. Rub the lard into the flour until it is like fine breadcrumbs. Add the water and mix to a dry paste. Flour a board slightly and roll the paste until it is about a quarter of an inch in thickness. Grease a pie-dish and stand it on the rolled-out pastry, and cut a piece large enough to line the bottom and sides of the pie-dish.

Line the pie-dish with this pastry. Put layers of jam and pastry alternately until the dish is full.

Place a piece of pastry on the top and fold the top of the lining from the four sides of the pie-dish to the centre ; press well together.

Brush over with milk. Bake in a moderately hot oven for about one hour.

Turn on to a hot dish and serve.

JAM RISSOLES

INGREDIENTS.—½ teacup of margarine, about 2 teacupfuls of flour, ¼ teacup of water, jam, fat for frying.

METHOD.—Melt the margarine in a saucepan. Then add the water and bring to the boil. Set aside until warm.

Work in the flour and mix thoroughly to rather a soft paste. If necessary, add more flour or water, but be careful not to make too moist.

Place on a floured board and knead until smooth. Roll it out to the thickness of a quarter of an inch. Cut into rounds with a tumbler.

Put in the centre of one round a half teaspoonful of thick jam, damp the edge all round, and lay another piece over this. Pinch the edges well together. Do all in the same way.

Have ready a deep pan half full of hot fat. When the latter slightly smokes, put in the rissoles and fry them until golden brown. Only fry three or four at a time. The fat must be re-heated before the next batch are put in.

Drain them well on paper. Roll in castor sugar and serve at once.

NOTE.—Use lard or dripping for frying.

Allow one or two for each person, according to the size.

JERSEY PUDDING

INGREDIENTS.—2 lb. of apples, about 1 gill of water, 2 tablespoonfuls of granulated sugar, 2 eggs, their weight in castor sugar and margarine, 5 oz. of flour, 1 flat teaspoonful of baking powder, milk.

METHOD.—Peel and quarter the apples, remove the cores, and cut in slices. Cook in a saucepan with the water and granulated sugar, and when tender mash to a pulp. More or less water may be required according to the kind of apples used. Beat the castor sugar and fat to a cream. Add each egg separately, stir in quickly and beat well before adding the second.

When both are added, sieve the flour and baking powder and stir in. Mix together lightly, adding a little milk as required.

Grease a pie-dish or Pyrex dish, put the apple pulp in the bottom of it, and turn the prepared mixture on top of the apples. Put into a moderately hot oven to bake. It will take about one hour and a quarter.

Sufficient for six to eight persons.

JORDAN PUDDINGS

INGREDIENTS.—6 oz. of flour, 3 oz. of margarine, 2 oz. of Jordan almonds, 2 eggs (separated), 1 teaspoonful of baking powder, 4 oz. of castor sugar, ½ flat teaspoonful of ground ginger, ½ flat teaspoonful of ground cinnamon, milk.

METHOD.—Blanch and skin the almonds and bake them in the oven until golden brown. Chop them or put them through the mincer.

Sieve the flour with the baking powder and spices. Separate the eggs. Beat the sugar and fat to a cream, stir in the yolks of the eggs, then add the flour mixture with some milk as required. Last of all, fold in the stiffly whisked egg-whites.

Turn the pudding into buttered moulds, cover them with buttered papers, and steam them for about forty-five minutes.

Serve Jordan Puddings with a hot custard flavoured with almond essence.

Sufficient for six persons.

KING EDWARD PUDDING

INGREDIENTS.—2 eggs, their weight in flour, sugar and margarine, vanilla flavouring, 1 tablespoonful of milk, ¼ lb. of jam or golden syrup, 1 flat teaspoonful of baking powder.

METHOD.—Beat the margarine and sugar together until it resembles thick cream. Separate the whites from the yolks of the eggs. Whisk the whites to a stiff froth. Beat the yolks and add to the sugar and margarine—beat these all thoroughly for a few minutes. Add the flour, baking powder, vanilla flavouring and milk. Last of all, very lightly mix in the whites of the eggs. Put the mixture into a greased pie-dish and bake in a moderately hot oven for one hour.

Turn on to a hot dish. Serve with hot jam or golden syrup.

LEMON DUMPLINGS

INGREDIENTS.—½ lb. of flour, 5 oz. of suet, 1 good-sized lemon (rind and juice), ¼ lb. of sugar, 1 egg, milk and water to mix, lemon cheese (if liked).

METHOD.—Chop the suet very finely and mix well into the flour.

Grate the lemon-rind finely and add with the sugar.

Add the strained lemon-juice and mix in.

Then add the beaten egg and sufficient milk and water to make a stiff paste.

Divide into about six portions, and make each into a smooth round shape. Put into floured pudding-cloths and tie securely, then boil for about an hour and a half. These may, if liked, be served with some hot lemon-cheese.

NOTE.—If a cheaper dumpling is required, omit the egg.

Sufficient for about six persons.

LEMON SUET PUDDING

INGREDIENTS.—½ lb. of suet, 1 lb. of flour, 2 teaspoonfuls of baking powder, 2 lemons (grated rind and juice), ½ lb.

of granulated sugar, water to mix (about ½ pint).

METHOD.—Chop the suet finely and mix with the flour and baking powder.

Add the sugar and grated lemon-rind, and mix all these dry ingredients together.

Make a hole in the centre.

Squeeze the juice from the lemons and pour it into the hole.

Add the water and mix all together to rather a sticky consistency.

Put into a greased pie-dish and bake in a moderately hot oven for one hour and a half.

Serve on a hot dish.

LEMON PUDDING

INGREDIENTS.—3 oz. of castor sugar, 2 eggs, 1 lemon, 2½ gills of milk, 3 tablespoonfuls of flour (3 oz.), 2 oz. of margarine.

METHOD.—Whisk the eggs and sugar together until thick and creamy and free from dark streaks.

Grate the lemon-rind finely and stir in with the flour.

Warm the margarine just sufficiently to melt it, and add.

Stir in the milk gradually and mix all together.

Turn the mixture into a well-greased pie-dish and bake in a moderately hot oven, lessening the heat as required. It will take about three-quarters to one hour.

Dredge with castor sugar and serve in the dish.

Sufficient for three or four persons.

BAKED LEMON SPONGE PUD-DING

INGREDIENTS.—3 sponge-cakes or 1 cupful of stale cakecrumbs, juice and rind of 2 lemons, ½ oz. of flour, 1 gill of milk, 3 oz. of castor sugar, 2 eggs, 1 oz. of butter, 1 oz. of glacé cherries, a little angelica for decorating.

METHOD.—Mix the flour smoothly with the milk. Put them in a saucepan and stir till boiling. Leave to get cold.

Cream the butter, sugar and yolks of eggs together with a wooden spoon, and when soft and white beat well for ten minutes.

Grate the lemon-rind thinly. Squeeze the juice from the lemons and remove the pips. Add the grated rind, the juice and crumbled sponge-cakes to the butter and sugar.

Stir in the cold flour-and-milk and mix well together.

Beat the whites of the eggs stiffly and fold them carefully into the mixture.

Place it in a greased pie-dish and put the cherries on top.

Bake the pudding in a moderate over for about forty minutes.

To serve, sprinkle a little castor sugar over the top and decorate with strips of angelica.

Sufficient for three persons.

SMALL LEMON PUDDINGS

INGREDIENTS.—1 egg, 1½ oz. of butter, sugar and flour, grated rind of a lemon.

FOR THE SYRUP.—2 lemons, 6 lumps of sugar, cochineal.

METHOD.—Grease five or six small castle moulds. Grate the lemon-rind, yellow part only, as the white pith is bitter. Cream the butter and sugar well. Add the egg and beat till light and creamy.

Add lemon-rind, and half fill the moulds with the mixture. Bake for twenty minutes in a hot oven. Serve with lemon-syrup. Sufficient for five or six small puddings.

THE LEMON SYRUP

Boil the sugar in the lemon-juice for about ten minutes or until it makes a thin syrup. Add six drops of cochineal and pour into a small jug or sauce-boat.

LEMON TOFFEE SPONGE

INGREDIENTS.—7 small sponge-cakes, 7 small slices of tinned pineapple, 1 tablespoonful of desiccated coconut, 4 glacé cherries, 1 lemon.

FOR THE TOFFEE MIXTURE.—¼ lb. of margarine, ½ lb. of golden syrup, ½ lb. of Demerara sugar.

METHOD.—Lay each sponge-cake on a slice of pineapple and soak it with pineapple and lemon-juice (about a tablespoonful of each). Dissolve the margarine in the golden syrup, add the sugar and boil it slowly for fifteen minutes. To test if it has boiled enough, drop a very little into a cup of cold water, and if it sets into a soft ball when rubbed between finger and thumb, it is done. Stir till it is as thick as treacle. Pour a spoonful over each cake. Decorate with a line of coconut, and put a cherry in the middle. Children will like this dish.

This quantity will make seven or eight sponges.

LOGANBERRY PUDDING

INGREDIENTS.—I tin of loganberries, I egg, its weight in castor sugar, margarine and flour, ⅛ flat teaspoonful of carbonate of soda, 2 tablespoonfuls of loganberry syrup.

METHOD.—Turn out the loganberries and drain off the syrup.

Beat the sugar and fat to a cream, then beat in the yolk of the egg.

Sift the flour with the soda and stir it in with the loganberry syrup. Beat them well, then stir in the white of egg, whisked to a stiff froth.

Turn the drained loganberries into a buttered pie-dish or Pyrex dish, cover them with the prepared mixture and bake them in a moderately hot oven. The pudding will take about half an hour. Serve it hot.

Sufficient for four persons.

MACARONI SOUFFLE PUDDING

INGREDIENTS.—2 eggs, 1½ pints of milk, 2½ oz. of macaroni, flavouring, 2 dessertspoonfuls of white sugar.

METHOD.—Break the macaroni into small pieces and wash it well.

Put it into a saucepan with the milk, bring to the boil, and cook gently until the macaroni is quite soft ; then draw off the fire and cool slightly.

The macaroni will take about twenty to thirty minutes to cook.

Separate the yolks from the whites of the eggs.

Beat up the yolks.

Add a pinch of salt to the whites and whisk them to a stiff froth.

Fold the yolks and whites together lightly.

Add the sugar and flavouring to the macaroni and lightly stir in the eggs.

Mix all together, then put into a pie-dish, and bake slowly for about forty minutes, until the pudding is just set and lightly browned.

Be careful not to let it boil.

Serve hot.

MADEIRA PUDDING

INGREDIENTS.—3 oz. of Madeira cake, 2 eggs, 2 dessertspoonfuls of marmalade, 1½ dessertspoonfuls of castor sugar, ¾ pint of milk, vanilla.

METHOD.—Grease a pudding-basin with some butter or margarine and put the marmalade in the bottom of it.

Crumble the cake finely (*stale cake can be used.*)

Beat the eggs, add the milk, cake-crumbs, and sugar, and a few drops of vanilla.

Mix all together, pour into the prepared basin, cover securely with a well-buttered paper, and steam the pudding gently for about one hour and a quarter to one hour and a half.

Turn carefully on to a hot dish and serve.

NOTE.—This pudding must not be steamed too quickly or it will curdle.

Sufficient for about five persons.

MARGUERITE PUDDING

INGREDIENTS.—¾ lb. of flour, 6 oz. of margarine, 5 oz. of sugar (granulated) 1½ teaspoonfuls of baking powder, 1½ gills of milk, I egg, 4 tablespoonfuls of golden syrup.

METHOD.—Put a saucepan of water on to boil. Grease a pudding-basin and put the golden syrup into the bottom of it. Place the flour and baking powder into a basin. Rub the margarine into the flour. Add the sugar and mix well with the other dry ingredients. Beat the egg in another basin, add the milk to it.

Add the egg and milk to the dry ingredients, and beat well for three minutes. Put this mixture into the pudding-basin ; do not mix it with the golden syrup, but let it remain on the top of it. Cover with a greased paper.

Put into the saucepan of boiling water and steam for two hours. Turn on to a hot dish and serve.

MARMALADE PIE

INGREDIENTS.—6 oz. of suet, 6 oz. of flour, 4 oz. of breadcrumbs, 3 oz. of castor sugar, water to mix, about ½ lb. of marmalade.

METHOD.—Chop the suet finely and mix with the flour. Add the breadcrumbs and sugar, then stir in sufficient water to make a soft dough.

Roll it out. Cut out a round and line a greased pie-tin. Add half the marmalade, then a round of the prepared crust, then the remainder of the marmalade.

Roll out the remainder of the crust to fit the top, damp the edge and fix it on. Brush with milk, put in a moderately hot oven, and bake for about one to one hour and a half.

Dredge with castor sugar, and serve hot.

Sufficient for six or eight persons.

BAKED MARMALADE PUDDING

INGREDIENTS.—½ lb. of breadcrumbs, ¼ lb. of flour, 2 teaspoonfuls of baking powder, 6 oz. of suet, 3 tablespoonfuls of marmalade, ¼ teaspoonful of ground ginger, 5 dessertspoonfuls of sugar, 1 egg, milk to mix.

METHOD.—Sieve the flour, ginger and baking powder. Chop the suet finely and add with the breadcrumbs and sugar. When well mixed, put the marmalade in the centre.

Beat up the egg and add with some milk as required and mix all together.

Put into a greased pie-dish and bake in a moderately hot oven for about one hour and a half.

Sufficient for eight persons.

STEAMED MARMALADE PUDDING

INGREDIENTS.—6 oz. of breadcrumbs, 4 oz. of shredded suet, 2 oz. of flour, 4 oz. of lemon marmalade, 1 large egg, ½ teaspoonful of baking powder.

METHOD.—Grease a mould or basin and a round of paper. Put a pan of water on to boil. Beat the egg. Mix breadcrumbs, flour, and baking powder and add the marmalade and egg. Pour into the greased mould so as to fill it three-quarters full.

Twist greased paper over the top and put the mould into the pan with enough boiling water to come halfway up outside.

Steam steadily for two hours. Leave the pudding for five minutes before turning out, so that it may not break. Turn out carefully and pour sauce round.

Sufficient for four persons.

SCOTCH MARMALADE PUDDING

INGREDIENTS.—4 oz. of breadcrumbs, 4 oz. of suet, 2 oz. of flour, 1 level teaspoonful of baking powder, 1½ oz of desiccated coconut, 2 oz. of sugar, ½ lb. of marmalade, juice of ½ orange, 1 egg.

METHOD.—Shred the suet and chop it finely, or else grate it on a suet grater. Sift the flour and baking powder and mix them with the breadcrumbs and suet, then add the sugar and coconut.

Whisk up the egg, stir in the marmalade, and whisk both together. Add this to the dry ingredients and mix them together well, adding also the orange-juice.

If any more moisture is required, a little milk may be added.

Turn the mixture into a buttered mould, cover it with a buttered paper. Steam the pudding for about two hours and a half.

MARMALADE SPONGE PUDDING

INGREDIENTS.—2 tablespoonfuls of marmalade, 9 oz. of flour, 1 teaspoonful of cream of tartar, ¼ flat teaspoonful of carbonate of soda, 2 eggs, 5 oz. of castor sugar, 3 oz. of margarine, milk—as required.

METHOD.—Sieve the flour, cream of tartar, and carbonate of soda.

Whisk the eggs and sugar until thick and creamy and free from dark streaks of eggs.

Put the margarine into a saucepan, and warm it sufficiently to melt it, but do not make it hot.

Gradually stir the flour into the eggs and sugar, together with the melted margarine, and some milk as required.

When well mixed, put into a greased mould or basin, make a hole in the centre, and put in the marmalade, then cover it with some of the mixture.

Cover the basin securely with a well-greased paper and steam for two hours.

Turn on to a hot dish and serve with marmalade sauce, or pile some hot marmalade on top of the pudding (extra to that given in the recipe).

MARMALADE SAUCE

INGREDIENTS.—2 tablespoonfuls of marmalade, 3 tablespoonfuls of cold water, a squeeze of lemon-juice.

METHOD.—Put the marmalade and water into the saucepan and mix together. Bring to the boil and boil for two or three minutes, then add the lemon-juice. If necessary, strain it and serve round the pudding.

MILK PUDDINGS

A GOOD milk pudding should be creamy. There are many varieties, and they can usually be made with or without eggs. If made with eggs, they must not be allowed to boil after the eggs are added. Sometimes a lump of butter or margarine is added to enrich them. Nutmeg, or any other suitable flavouring—ratafia, vanilla, or lemon-rind etc., can be used.

Although such easy, quick puddings to make, the results are often very poor. There are two very common faults. The first is, that too much cereal is often used. A good general proportion for such grains as rice, sago, semolina or powders such as cornflour and arrowroot, or pastes such as spaghetti and macaroni, is :

One ounce and a half to one pint of milk.

The second frequent mistake is, that they are cooked too quickly.

Either of these faults will result in a stodgy pudding.

If, for instance, a rice pudding is cooked quickly, the milk boils away before the rice has time to soften and swell, and absorb it. Therefore, if you wish to make a creamy rice pudding you must cook it slowly, and give it plenty of time.

RICE PUDDING

INGREDIENTS.—3 oz. of rice (weigh the rice very accurately), 2 pints of milk, 2 oz. of sugar, nutmeg.

METHOD.—Wash the rice and put it into a pie-dish with the sugar. Stir in the milk and mix them together.

Grate a little nutmeg on the top and put the pudding into a warm oven.

Bring it slowly to the boil, and cook it gently for from one and a half to two hours.

NOTE.—If scales are not available, remember that four dessertspoonfuls of rice are equal to three ounces.

CARAMEL RICE PUDDING

INGREDIENTS.—$\frac{1}{2}$ gill of water, 3 dessertspoonfuls of sugar (caramel), $1\frac{1}{2}$ oz. of rice (2 dessertspoonfuls), $\frac{1}{2}$ tablespoonful of sugar, 1 pint of milk.

METHOD.—Put the sugar (three dessertspoonfuls) in a small strong saucepan with the water. Let it dissolve slowly, then boil until a rich golden brown. Draw aside and leave until cold. Add the milk, stand it over a *low* gas burner until the caramel has dissolved, then strain, and leave again until cold.

Wash the rice and put it in a pie-dish with the sugar (half a tablespoonful). Add the caramel milk and mix together, then put into a warm oven and bake slowly. It will take about one and a half to two hours after it comes to the boil.

MONDAY PUDDING

INGREDIENTS.—2 oz. of stale bread, 1 egg, $\frac{1}{2}$ pint of milk, 1 oz. of almonds, 2 dessertspoonfuls of castor sugar, orange flavouring essence, grated nutmeg, $\frac{1}{4}$ lb. of seeded raisins.

METHOD.—Break up the bread into small pieces, pour the milk over it and let it soak for a few hours. Stir in the raisins cut into small pieces, the almonds blanched and chopped, and a little grated nutmeg.

Whisk the egg and sugar together till thick and creamy, mix in the bread mixture lightly, and flavour it with orange essence.

Turn the mixture into a buttered pie-dish or Pyrex dish, and bake it in a moderately hot oven. It will take from twenty to thirty minutes.

NOTE.—The bread should be stale, but not hard.

Sufficient for four persons.

MOUSSE A LA RUSSE

INGREDIENTS.—Whites of 4 eggs, $\frac{1}{2}$ lb. of apricot jam, 1 tablespoonful of water, castor sugar.

METHOD.—Put the jam into a saucepan, mix with the water, slightly warm it. Then rub it through a fine sieve to get rid of any pieces of skin.

Whisk the whites of eggs to a very stiff froth.

Fold the jam lightly into the whisked whites.

Pile it all on the dish in which it is to be served and sprinkle with castor sugar.

Place into a cool oven to set, but avoid browning it. Serve hot or cold.

Sufficient for about four persons.

MUSCATEL PUDDING

INGREDIENTS.—1 lb. of self-raising flour, $\frac{3}{4}$ lb. of muscatel raisins, $\frac{1}{4}$ lb. of candied peel, $\frac{1}{2}$ lb. of suet, $\frac{1}{4}$ lb. of sugar, grated nutmeg, 1 egg, about $\frac{1}{2}$ pint of milk and water.

METHOD.—Wash and dry the muscatels and remove stones. Chop the suet finely and mix well with the flour. Add to this the sugar, grated nutmeg, stoned raisins, and candied peel—the latter cut into small pieces. Mix all these ingredients together. Beat the egg and mix with the milk and water. Add the egg and milk to the dry ingredients and beat well. Pour into a greased pie-dish and bake in a moderately hot oven for an hour and a half. Turn on to a hot dish and serve.

NURSERY PUDDING

INGREDIENTS.—2 oz. of minute tapioca, $\frac{1}{2}$ lb. of seedless raisins, $\frac{1}{4}$ lb. of breadcrumbs, 6 oz. of Demerara sugar, 2 oz. of suet, grated nutmeg, 1 tablespoonful of treacle, 1 egg, about $1\frac{1}{2}$ gills of milk.

METHOD.—Chop the suet finely and mix it with the breadcrumbs. Add the sugar, raisins, tapioca and a little grated nutmeg.

Whisk the egg, warm the treacle and add it to the egg, then whisk them together and stir them into the dry ingredients, adding milk as required.

Beat the mixture well, turn it into a buttered mould, cover it securely with a buttered paper, and steam it for about three hours.

Unmould it and serve it sprinkled with castor sugar.

Sufficient for six persons.

NUT FRUIT BATTER

INGREDIENTS.—4 oz. of seedless raisins, 1 oz. of almonds, 2 eggs, $\frac{1}{2}$ lb. of flour, 1 pint of milk, pinch of salt.

METHOD.—Sieve the flour and salt into a basin, make a well in the centre and pour in the eggs. Mix these with some of the flour, then take half the milk and add gradually and mix to a smooth batter. Beat well, then stir in the remainder of the milk and leave the batter to stand for an hour or so. When ready to bake, stir in the raisins and the almonds, which must be blanched and cut up previously. Turn into a greased pie-dish or Pyrex dish and bake for about an hour.

Serve with castor sugar.

Sufficient for six or eight persons.

ORANGE FRUIT SOUFFLES

INGREDIENTS.—Oranges as required, $1\frac{1}{2}$ oz. of flour, 2 oz. of sugar or to taste, $1\frac{1}{2}$ oz. of butter, 3 eggs.

METHOD.—Cut a circular slice off the top of each orange. Scoop out the pulp, but do not break the skins. Rub sufficient pulp through a sieve to give half a pint.

Melt the butter in a stew-pan. Add the flour and, when well blended, stir in the orange pulp and boil it until it is thick.

Remove it from the heat and cool it.

Add the sugar and three yolks, one at a time. Whisk the whites very stiffly, and stir them lightly into the mixture.

Fill the orange cases with the preparation and set them on a baking sheet in a moderate oven for twenty minutes. Serve them quickly.

NOTE.—Any left over mixture may be baked in a buttered soufflé dish.

Sufficient for six persons.

ORANGE GINGER PUDDING

INGREDIENTS.—Flaky pastry as required (see page 252), 3 oz. of breadcrumbs, 1 level teaspoonful of ground ginger, 1 orange, $\frac{1}{2}$ level teaspoonful of ground cinnamon, rind of $\frac{1}{2}$ lemon, 3 oz. of margarine, 2 oz. of sugar, about 1 or 2 tablespoonfuls of milk, as required, 1 egg, orange marmalade.

METHOD.—Make the breadcrumbs and mix them with the ground ginger and cinnamon. Add also the finely-grated orange and lemon-rind, and the sugar.

Warm the margarine sufficiently to melt it and stir in, adding the orange-juice and beaten egg, and some milk as required.

Roll out the pastry and line a small pie-dish, put an extra rim of pastry round the dish and trim and decorate the edge, then put some marmalade in the bottom. Turn the prepared mixture into the pie-dish and bake it in a hot oven. It will take from twenty minutes to half an hour to cook. Serve hot.

ORANGE PUDDING

INGREDIENTS.—Grated rind of 2 oranges, ¼ lb. of breadcrumbs, 1 oz. of flour, 3 tablespoonfuls of sugar, 2 oz. of butter or margarine. 2 eggs, ¼ pint of milk, 6 oz. of short pastry (see p. 252) 1 oz of castor sugar.

METHOD.—Roll out the pastry into a long strip about two inches wide, and line the sides of a pie-dish with it.

Wet the edge and decorate it with pieces of pastry cut into small rounds or diamonds.

Put milk, butter and sugar into a saucepan and heat them till the butter is dissolved.

Pour the milk over the breadcrumbs and leave them to soak while grating the orange-rind as thinly as possible.

Mix the egg yolks with the flour and a tablespoonful of the milk, and add them to the other pudding ingredients, with the thinly-grated orange-rind and a tablespoonful of orange-juice.

Pour the mixture into the dish and bake it for thirty-five minutes.

Beat the egg-whites stiffly, stir in the castor sugar, and heap the mer-ingue mixture on top of the pudding.

Brown in the oven for a few minutes. Sufficient for four persons.

NOTE.—The orange-rind should be grated quite thinly as the white pith is bitter.

QUEEN PUDDING

INGREDIENTS.—3 oz. of bread-crumbs, 2 eggs, 1 pint of milk, 1½ oz. of sugar, flavouring—lemon or vanilla, 2 tablespoonfuls of jam.

METHOD.—Make the breadcrumbs and put them into the bottom of a pie-dish.

Put the milk on to heat with the sugar. Separate the yolks from the whites of the eggs. Beat the yolks of eggs and mix with the hot milk and sugar. Add this mixture to the bread-crumbs and stir well together.

Place in a moderately warm oven and cook until the custard has set; it will take about thirty minutes. When this has cooked and been allowed to cool, spread the jam over the surface of the custard.

Whisk the whites of eggs to a stiff froth. Place this on to the top of the jam and dredge well with castor sugar. Put the pudding into the oven again until the white of egg is set and light brown on the top.

Sufficient for four or five persons.

BATTER PANCAKES

INGREDIENTS.—¼ lb. of flour, pinch of salt, 1 egg, ½ pint of milk, lard, lemon-juice, castor sugar.

METHOD.—Sift the flour and salt into a basin, pour the egg in the centre and mix with a little of the flour; then take half the milk and add it gradually, until all are mixed to a smooth batter. Beat it well for a few minutes then stir in the remainder of the milk. Let the batter stand for an hour or two.

To FRY THE PANCAKES. — Melt a small piece of lard (half an ounce) in a frying-pan, and when a faint smoke rises from it pour in sufficient batter to coat the bottom of the pan thinly— for a small frying-pan half a gill of batter is enough for each pancake.

Fry each pancake gently till golden brown, turn or toss it on to the other side and brown it. *It is important to remember when turning a pancake to use a knife with a rounded blade*, a pointed blade is so liable to cut into the pancake. When cooked on both sides, turn it on to a baking-sheet lined with kitchen paper, and allow it to drain. Squeeze lemon-juice and sprinkle castor sugar over each pan-cake, and roll it up.

Fry the remainder in the same way. Serve the pancakes at once, as they so soon become tough.

For those who prefer a crisp pan-cake, make them a little thicker, and use more fat for frying them, when they will become quite crisp. These should not be rolled, but be served flat, heaped one on top of the other.

The foundation batter can be varied by adding a little spice; this should be sifted with the flour, or a few currants can be added to each lot of batter as it is poured into the pan.

To vary the filling, jam and whipped cream may be used as in Soufflé Pancakes. The following filling is sometimes preferred:

Take one ounce of castor sugar and half an ounce of butter and beat them to a cream. Add the finely-grated rind of half an orange and about a teaspoonful of rum or sherry.

BATTER SOUFFLE PANCAKES

INGREDIENTS. — ¼ lb. of flour, 1½ gills of milk, pinch of salt, lard, castor sugar, 1 whole egg and 1 white, cream, raspberry jam.

METHOD.—Sift the flour and salt into a basin, separate the egg and pour the yolk into the centre of the flour, then take one gill of milk and add this gradually until all is mixed to a smooth batter. Beat it well, then stir in the remainder of the milk and let the batter stand, as before.

When ready to fry the pancakes, whisk the two whites of eggs to a stiff froth and fold them lightly into the batter; then fry them as in the recipe for Batter Pancakes, only using rather more lard than before. Owing to the texture of the mixture these will be somewhat thicker pancakes.

Turn each pancake out when cooked and spread it with filling, then fold it lightly in half, dredge it with castor sugar. Serve as quickly as possible.

To PREPARE THE FILLING.—Whisk the cream until it hangs from the whisk, then stir in an equal amount of raspberry jam.

BAKED SPICED PANCAKES

INGREDIENTS.—4 oz. of castor sugar, 4 eggs, 6 oz. of flour, 3 gills of milk, ½ teaspoonful of ground cinnamon, 3 oz. of butter or margarine, 1 teaspoonful of baking powder.

METHOD.—Sift the flour with the baking powder and cinnamon, and whisk the eggs. Cream the fat and

sugar, stir in the flour and eggs alternately, add the milk gradually.

Butter some old strong saucers, pour a little of the mixture into each and put them in a fairly hot oven to bake. They will take about twenty minutes.

Lift them out when cooked, and serve the pancakes dredged with sugar.

RICE PANCAKES

INGREDIENTS.—3 oz. of rice, 2 eggs, 2 oz. of flour, ½ oz. of butter or margarine, 1½ pints of milk, sugar to taste, lard.

METHOD.—Bring the milk to the boil, then wash the rice and add it to the milk. Cook it gently until it is tender and until the mixture is quite thick, keeping it stirred occasionally. It is better to use a double boiler for this purpose.

Leave the mixture until it is cold, add the butter (melted) and sugar, then stir in the beaten yolks of the eggs and the flour.

Whisk the whites stiffly and fold them into the mixture.

Fry the pancakes in hot fat, using about a dessertspoonful of the mixture for each, and making them into as neat rounds as possible. They are very soft, so require to be carefully turned.

Drain the pancakes well and serve as soon as possible after they are fried.

Maple syrup is an excellent accompaniment for these pancakes or lemon flavouring can be used for the mixture.

Sufficient for about twenty-four pancakes.

STOCKHOLM PANCAKES

INGREDIENTS.—4 oz. of flour, ½ teaspoonful of ground cinnamon, 1 large egg, ½ pint of milk, 1 lemon, castor sugar, ¼ lb. of lard.

METHOD.—Sift the flour and cinnamon into a basin. Make a hollow in the flour and put in the unbeaten egg and a little milk.

Stir slightly, in the centre only, with a wooden spoon so as to make a smooth batter. Add half the milk by degrees, stirring all the time.

Beat well, add the rest of the milk, and if possible let the batter stand for one hour. Heat a piece of lard as small as a cherry and put in a good tablespoonful of batter with the pan off the gas.

Cook quickly and turn over with a knife when lightly browned. The other side will only take a few seconds. Turn on to sugared paper but do not roll up.

Keep the pancakes hot as they are done, piling them flat one on top of the other on a plate over a saucepan of boiling water.

To serve, cut the pile into wedges as if you were cutting a slice of cake and hand lemon and sugar.

Half a pint of batter will make six or eight pancakes, according to their thickness and the size of the pan.

PATTISDALE PUDDING

INGREDIENTS.—4 oz. of butter or margarine, 6 oz. of flour, 4 oz. of sugar, 2 eggs, 1 teaspoonful of baking-powder, about ½ gill of milk.

METHOD.—Grease a pie-dish.

Rub the butter into the flour. Add the sugar and baking-powder.

Mix to a rather stiff paste (the consistency of moist scones), using the two eggs (well beaten) and a little milk.

Put in the pie-dish and bake for forty-five minutes in a moderately hot oven.

PEAR CHARLOTTE

INGREDIENTS.—2 lb. of stewing pears, 1 lemon, 1 oz. of crystallised ginger, 9 oz. of breadcrumbs, 4 oz. of suet, 4 tablespoonfuls of sugar, ½ oz. of margarine.

METHOD.—Skin the suet, then grate or chop it finely. Make the breadcrumbs. Grease a pie-dish and coat with some of them, then shake out the loose ones. Mix the remainder with the suet.

Peel and core the pears, and grate them on the suet grater.

Grate the lemon-rind finely and mix with the grated pear. Add the ginger cut into small pieces. Put about a third of the breadcrumbs and suet in the bottom of the dish, then add half the grated pear sprinkled with half the sugar.

Add another third of the crumbs, then the remainder of the pears and sugar. Cover with the remaining portion of crumbs and press down firmly.

Place two or three dabs of margarine on the top. Put in a moderately hot oven to bake. It will take about one and a half hours.

Sufficient for six persons.

STEAMED PINEAPPLE PUDDING

INGREDIENTS.—3 oz. of stale sponge cake, small tin of pineapple, 3 dessert-spoonfuls of sugar, 2 eggs, 1½ gills of milk.

METHOD.—Drain the pineapple. Put it through a mincer and then make it up to half a pint with some of the syrup. Crumble the sponge cake finely and mix with the prepared pineapple.

Separate the eggs. Beat up the yolks, add the milk, then stir into the pineapple, etc., with the sugar.

Whisk the egg whites to a very stiff froth and fold in lightly.

Turn the mixture into a well-buttered mould, cover securely with a buttered paper, and steam for about one and a half hours. The water should simmer, not boil fast, and should not reach more than half-way up the mould.

When cooked, turn out carefully and serve hot or cold.

If liked, the remainder of the syrup can be heated and coloured with a few drops of cochineal, and poured round the pudding.

Sufficient for about four or five persons.

PINEAPPLE SUET PUDDING

INGREDIENTS.—Large tin of pineapple, ¼ lb. of flour, ¼ lb. of breadcrumbs, ¼ lb. of suet, ¼ lb. of granulated sugar, some Demerara sugar.

METHOD.—Drain the syrup from the pineapple and put the fruit through a mincer. Chop the suet finely.

Make the breadcrumbs and mix with the flour and suet, add the granulated sugar and minced pineapple, and mix all together.

Grease a pudding basin and coat it with Demerara sugar, turn the prepared mixture into it, cover with a greased paper, and steam for two and a half to three hours.

Sufficient for six or eight persons.

DELICIOUS PLUM PUDDING

INGREDIENTS.—5 tablespoonfuls of plum jam (stoneless), ½ lb. of breadcrumbs, 1 lemon, ¼ lb. of suet, 1 egg, milk to mix.

METHOD.—Make the breadcrumbs.

Grate the lemon-rind and add.

Chop the suet finely and mix it with the breadcrumbs.

Beat up the egg.

Squeeze the lemon and strain the juice.

Put the jam in the centre of the dry ingredients add the lemon-juice and mix with some of the breadcrumbs, etc.

Add the egg with some milk as required and mix all together.

Put into a greased pudding-basin, cover securely with a greased paper, and steam for about two hours to two hours and a half.

Turn on to a hot dish, dredge with castor sugar, and serve.

Sufficient for about five persons.

POMMES DE LUXE

INGREDIENTS.—6 oz. of flaky pastry (see p. 252), 2 lb. of good cooking apples, 2 tablespoonfuls of jam, ½ gill of water, 3 oz. of butter, 3 oz. of sugar, 3 oz. of cake crumbs, 1 oz. of ground almonds, 1 large egg, juice of a lemon.

METHOD.—Line the sides of a pie-dish with flaky pastry and decorate the edges. Bake in a hot oven for twenty minutes. Stew the apples in the water till soft, mash them with a wooden spoon, and add the jam and one ounce of butter. Pour into the pie-dish. Cream the rest of the butter and the sugar till soft, add the yolk of the egg, the almonds, cake crumbs and lemon-juice. Beat the egg-white to a stiff froth, and stir it into the mixture. Bake in a moderate oven for about twenty minutes.

NOTE.—For a plainer pudding use short pastry (see p. 252) instead of flaky, and substitute desiccated coconut for the ground almonds. Sufficient for four or five persons.

PRUNE PUDDING

INGREDIENTS.—½ lb. of prunes, 1 lb. of flour, 2 oz. of mixed peel, 1 egg, ¼ flat teaspoonful of carbonate of soda, ½ lb. of currants, ½ lb. of suet, 4 oz. of granulated sugar, ¼ teaspoonful of mixed spice, milk.

METHOD.—Wash the prunes well in warm water and dry them. Stone and chop up roughly. Wash and dry the currants, pick them over. Mix together the flour, soda, and spice, and sieve them. Chop the suet very finely and mix with the flour.

Cut the peel into small pieces and add to the flour, together with the sugar, currants, and prunes. Then mix well.

Beat up the egg and add together with the milk.

Mix all to rather a sticky consistency and beat well for a few minutes.

Put into a well-greased pudding-basin, cover with a greased paper, then a floured pudding-cloth, tie round tightly, and tie the ends of the cloth over the top of the pudding.

Put into the saucepan of boiling water and boil for three hours.

Turn on to a hot dish and sprinkle the top with castor sugar.

Sufficient for ten or twelve persons.

PORCUPINE PIPPINS

INGREDIENTS.—¼ lb. of dried apples, 2 oz. of almonds, rind and juice of ½ a lemon, 2 cloves, 4 oz. of sugar, apricot jam.

METHOD.—Pour on the apples enough boiling water to cover them, and let them soak for at least twelve hours.

Cook the apples slowly in the water, adding the cloves, thinly-cut lemon-rind and sugar. When tender, put the apples carefully in a dish and let the water continue boiling till reduced to about one gill.

Blanch the almonds by pouring boiling water on them. Slip off the skins and put the almonds in cold water. Drain them on a cloth and cut into strips.

To dish up, fill the centre of each apple with jam, and pour a spoonful of the boiled-down syrup over each. Stick almonds all over the apples and serve them with cream, handed separately.

About five dried apples weigh a quarter of a pound and cost fourpence. Allow one to each person.

STEAMED RAISIN BATTER

INGREDIENTS.—½ lb. of flour, 2 eggs, ¾ pint of milk, 3 oz. raisins, 3 oz. granulated sugar, 1 teaspoonful of baking-powder.

METHOD.—Put the flour into a basin and make a hole in the centre of it. Break the eggs into a cup and put into the hole in the flour ; it is not necessary to beat them first, as they will be well beaten in the batter. With a wooden spoon stir a small quantity of the flour with the eggs until they are about the consistency of a thick custard. This consistency is to be maintained until all the flour is mixed, therefore, as a little more flour is put to the eggs so a little milk must be added, until all flour from the side of the basin is mixed with the eggs, etc.

When all the flour has been added, and only half of the milk, the batter must be beaten.

Beat well for about ten minutes—this introduces air, and so makes the the pudding rise when cooked. Mix in the remainder of the milk and stand the batter aside for about an hour.

Prepare the raisins ; these must be washed and stoned.

Grease a pudding-basin and decorate the bottom and sides with some of the raisins ; these will adhere to the grease if put in before the latter gets hard. Add the sugar and the remainder of the raisins to the batter. Add the baking-powder.

Pour into the prepared basin, cover with greased paper and floured pudding-cloth. Put into a saucepan of boiling water and steam for two hours. Turn on to a hot dish and serve.

RASPBERRY PUDDING AND SWEET SAUCE

INGREDIENTS.—3 oz. of butter or margarine, 1 or 2 eggs, ¼ flat teaspoonful of carbonate of soda, 1½ oz. of castor sugar, 6 oz. of flour, milk, 3 tablespoonfuls of raspberry jam.

METHOD.—Sieve the flour and soda. Beat the sugar and fat to a cream. Add each egg separately, stir it in quickly, and beat well before adding the next.

When both are added, mix in the flour and soda.

Stir in the jam and milk as required.

Mix all together and put into a greased basin, cover securely with a

well-greased paper, and steam for about two hours.

Turn carefully on to a hot dish and pour sweet sauce round. (See recipe below.)

Dredge the top of the pudding with castor sugar.

SWEET SAUCE.

INGREDIENTS.—1½ teaspoonfuls of cornflour, 1½ teaspoonfuls of castor sugar, ½ pint of milk, flavouring as desired.

METHOD.—Mix the cornflour to a smooth paste with some of the milk.

Heat the remainder and stir on to it.

Return to the saucepan, bring to the boil, and simmer for a few minutes, keeping it well stirred all the time.

Add the sugar and flavouring, and pour the sauce round the pudding.

STEAMED RASPBERRY PUDDING

INGREDIENTS.—3 oz. of flour, ¼ lb. of raspberry jam, 1½ oz. of butter, 2 eggs, ½ teaspoonful of bicarbonate of soda. 1 oz. of breadcrumbs, 1½ oz. of sugar.

METHOD.—Grease a one-pint fancy mould or basin and put on some water to boil.

Cream the butter and sugar till soft.

Add the eggs and beat them well in. Add jam and breadcrumbs.

Sift flour and soda together, and mix into the pudding. Pour into the greased mould or basin, which should not be more than three-quarters full. twist a greased paper tightly over the top. Stand in fast-boiling water that comes half-way up the mould. Put the lid on the pan and steam steadily for one hour. Add more boiling water after half an hour.

The pudding will rise a good deal and should feel spongy when done. Leave for five minutes before turning out. This will allow it to shrink slightly from the sides of the tin, and it will be less likely to break. Serve with jam sauce (see p. 241). This quantity makes a pudding large enough for four persons.

RHUBARB BETTY

INGREDIENTS.—1 pint of rhubarb, 1 lemon, 1 orange, 7 oz. of sugar, 2 tablespoonfuls of desiccated coconut, 5 oz. of breadcrumbs, 2 oz. of butter

METHOD.—Wipe some rhubarb and cut it in small pieces, then measure it. Melt the butter and mix it with the breadcrumbs.

Grate the rinds of the orange and lemon and squeeze out the juice, then mix it with the coconut.

Place about one-third of the breadcrumbs in a buttered dish, add half the rhubarb and sprinkle it with half the sugar.

Add half the coconut with the fruit rind and juice. Add another portion of breadcrumbs, and remainder of fruit, sugar and coconut, then cover it with the remainder of the crumbs. Cover the pudding with a buttered paper and bake it in a moderately hot oven until the rhubarb is soft, then decorate it with pieces of lightly cooked rhubarb.

Sufficient for four persons.

RHUBARB GINGER PUDDING

INGREDIENTS.—$\frac{1}{2}$ lb. of self-raising flour, 2 level teaspoonfuls of ground ginger, 4 oz. of suet, water to mix, $\frac{1}{2}$ bundle of rhubarb—or sufficient to fill the basin, 2 tablespoonfuls of Barbados sugar, 1 level teaspoonful of ground ginger, water.

METHOD.—Wipe the rhubarb sticks, remove the green leaves and tips, and cut the rhubarb into short lengths.

Sift the flour with two level teaspoonfuls of ginger. Chop the suet finely and add it, then mix all to a pliable dough with cold water.

Put barely one-third of this dough aside for the top of the pudding, the remainder roll to a round shape about one and a half times as large as the top of the pudding-basin. Grease this and line it with crust. Put in half the rhubarb then add the sugar mixed with one level teaspoonful of ginger. Fill up with rhubarb and add a little water.

Roll out the remaining piece of crust and cover the pudding, damping the edge to make it adhere. Cover it with a greased paper and floured pudding-cloth. Put it into a pan of boiling water and boil it for about two hours or two hours and a half.

Sufficient for six persons.

RICE BALLS

INGREDIENTS.—$3\frac{1}{2}$ oz. of rice, 1 pint of milk, sugar (about $1\frac{1}{2}$ dessert-spoonfuls), 1 lemon, 1 egg, breadcrumbs, deep fat for frying, jam, marmalade, or golden syrup.

METHOD.—Wash the rice, put it into a saucepan with the milk and finely-grated lemon-rind, and bring to the boil. Then cook gently until the rice is tender and the mixture quite stiff, keeping it stirred occasionally. Add the sugar and let it cool slightly, then beat up the egg and stir in not quite half of it, and cook slowly again for several minutes. Do not boil.

Spread the mixture on a plate and leave until thoroughly cold and firm, then divide into small portions and shape into balls. Brush them over with the remainder of the egg and coat with breadcrumbs.

Have a deep pan of hot fat ready. When it begins to smoke slightly, put in some of the balls and fry until golden brown, then drain on paper.

Fry the remainder in the same way. Serve with either hot jam, marmalade, or golden syrup.

Sufficient for about four of five persons.

RICE CUSTARD

INGREDIENTS.—$\frac{1}{4}$ lb. of rice, 1 or 2 eggs, $1\frac{1}{2}$ pints of milk, flavouring, $\frac{1}{2}$ oz. of butter, nutmeg, 3 dessert-spoonfuls of sugar.

METHOD.—Wash the rice and put it into boiling water to cook with a little salt added. Let it boil gently until tender, then strain off the water.

Put the cooked rice into a pie-dish and add the butter and sugar. Beat the eggs and mix them with the milk, stir them into the rice and add some flavouring essence as desired. Grate nutmeg on top and bake the custard in a moderate oven for about forty minutes, being careful not to let it boil.

Serve rice custard hot or cold, with preserved ginger.

Sufficient for six persons.

RICE PUDDING
(For Recipe see p. 232.)

STEAMED RICE PUDDING

INGREDIENTS.—$\frac{1}{2}$ lb. of cooking figs, $1\frac{1}{2}$ pint of milk, 3 oz. of Barbados sugar, $\frac{1}{4}$ lb. of rice, 2 eggs, $\frac{1}{4}$ lb. of suet, grated nutmeg.

METHOD.—Bring the milk to the boil in the top of a double boiler. Wash the rice and add it to the milk.

Stand it in a pan of boiling water and cook it till the rice is tender and the mixture very thick, stirring it occasionally. Then take it off and turn it into a mixing basin to cool slightly.

Stalk and wash the figs, cut them into small pieces. Add them to the rice mixture with the sugar and grated nutmeg to taste. Then stir in the well beaten eggs and finely chopped suet.

Turn the mixture into small, well-buttered basins, cover them with buttered papers, and steam them for about two and a half hours.

RICE AND FIG PUDDING

INGREDIENTS.—6 oz. of cooking figs, 3 oz. of rice, $1\frac{1}{2}$ oz. of sugar, $1\frac{1}{2}$ oz. of mutton suet, $1\frac{1}{2}$ pints of milk, nutmeg.

METHOD.—Stalk, wash and cut up the figs. Wash the rice and put it in a pie-dish with the sugar and figs. Mix together and stir in the milk. Grate the suet finely and mix in. Then grate a little nutmeg on top of the pudding.

Leave to soak for two or three hours, then put into a warm oven to cook, letting it simmer gently. It will take about one and a half hours after it comes to the boil.

Serve hot or cold. If cold, sprinkle with desiccated coconut.

NOTE.—Raisins (stoned) may be used in the place of figs, if preferred. So many children will not eat a plain milk pudding, but the addition of fruit gives it an extra touch which they will enjoy.

Sufficient for about six persons.

ROLY POLY PUDDING

(WITH A SPECIAL NUT FILLING)

INGREDIENTS.—$\frac{1}{2}$ lb. of flour, $\frac{1}{4}$ lb. of suet, 1 flat teaspoonful of baking-powder, water to mix, 2 tablespoonfuls of golden syrup, 2 oz. of breadcrumbs, $\frac{1}{2}$ flat teaspoonful of ground ginger, $1\frac{1}{2}$ oz. of shelled Brazil nuts.

METHOD.—To make the filling, warm the golden syrup in a saucepan, then stir in the breadcrumbs mixed with the ground ginger, also the Brazils (previously put through a mincer). Mix all together, then leave to cool.

Chop the suet finely and mix with the flour and baking-powder, add water gradually, and mix to a dough. It must not be at all sticky.

Turn on to a floured board and roll to an oblong shape (not too thin). Then turn on to the other side and spread over the prepared filling, leaving a good margin all round.

Damp the edges and roll up, pinching it well together at either end; then roll in a scalded and floured pudding-cloth and tie securely.

Put into boiling water and boil for about one and a half to two hours.

Sufficient for about six persons.

NOTE.—Some prefer to roll a roly poly in a greased paper, in which case place the latter on the pudding-cloth (floured but not scalded) and roll the pudding in both *at the same time*. In this way the paper and cloth will unroll together.

RUM OMELET

INGREDIENTS.—2 eggs, 1 oz. of castor sugar, rum, $\frac{1}{2}$ oz. of butter.

METHOD.—Separate the eggs.

Beat the yolks and sugar together until thick and creamy.

Stir in a few drops of rum or sufficient to flavour; whisk the egg-whites to a very stiff froth and fold in lightly.

Melt the butter in an omelet-pan, and, when hot, pour in the egg mixture and stir lightly to prevent it from sticking.

When it begins to set round the edge, fold the edges over and draw the omelet towards the handle of the pan, keeping the latter tilted that way.

Leave for a few seconds to brown underneath, then put under the hot grill for a few seconds and brown the top.

Turn on to a hot dish, pour round some rum, set it alight, and serve at once.

Sufficient for one person.

PUDDING SAUCES

APRICOT JAM SAUCE

Put one and a half tablespoonfuls of apricot jam into a saucepan with quarter of a pint of water. Boil it for a minute or two and serve it. A squeeze of lemon-juice or a spoonful of sherry may be added if liked.

BRANDY CUSTARD SAUCE

Make a boiled egg custard, using two eggs to one pint of milk. Heat the milk and pour it on to the beaten eggs; add one tablespoonful of sugar. Turn the mixture into the top of a double boiler and stir it until it thickens. Care must be taken not to let it curdle. Take it off the heat and stir in *gradually* sufficient brandy to flavour the Custard Sauce.

CHOCOLATE SAUCE

(To Serve with Plain, Baked or Steamed Puddings.)

Ingredients.—1½ teaspoonfuls of cornflour, 1 dessertspoonful of cocoa, ½ pint of milk, sugar and vanilla.

Method.—Mix the cornflour and the cocoa to a smooth paste with a little of the milk. Heat the remainder and stir on to it.

Return it to the pan and bring it to the boil.

Add sugar to taste and boil gently for a few minutes to cook the sauce, keeping it well stirred.

Add vanilla and serve.

CUSTARD SAUCE

Ingredients. — 2 eggs, ¾ pint of milk, a strip of lemon-rind, sugar to taste (about 1 oz.).

Method.—Put the milk, sugar, and lemon-rind in a double saucepan and heat slowly to extract the flavour of the lemon. Beat the eggs well, let the milk cool for a few minutes, and pour it on the eggs. Stir well and return to the pan. Stir over a low gas till the custard is thick enough to coat the back of the spoon.

GINGER SAUCE

Ingredients.—1 oz. of butter, ¾ oz. of flour, 1 oz. of preserved ginger, 1 tablespoonful of ginger syrup, ½ pint of milk.

Method.—Melt the butter and stir in the flour.

Add the milk gradually and stir till it boils. Chop the ginger and add it to the sauce with the syrup.

Boil for three minutes and pour it round the pudding.

GOLDEN SAUCE

Ingredients.—1 gill of golden syrup, ½ gill of water, 1 tablespoonful of lemon-juice.

Method.—Boil the ingredients together for five minutes and pour the sauce round the pudding.

HARD SAUCE

Ingredients.—½ lb. of icing sugar, ¼ lb. of butter, flavouring, brandy, rum or vanilla.

Method.—Rub the icing sugar through a fine sieve. Beat the butter with half the sugar to a cream, then add the remainder, and beat it again. Flavour it with vanilla, or a little rum or brandy.

JAM SAUCE

Ingredients.—½ cup of raspberry jam, juice of a lemon, ½ pint of water, a little cochineal, 1 tablespoonful of sugar, ½ dessertspoonful of cornflour.

Method.—Put the jam, lemon-juice and sugar in a small pan, add half the water and boil up.

Mix the cornflour to a smooth paste with the rest of the cold water and pour the boiling sauce on it, stirring well.

Return it to the pan and stir till it boils. Add a little cochineal. Simmer for ten minutes and strain.

LEMON SAUCE

Ingredients.—2 tablespoonfuls of lemon marmalade, 1 dessertspoonful of lemon-juice, ¼ pint of water.

Method.—To make the sauce, mix the marmalade with the water and lemon-juice, and boil them for a few minutes.

MARMALADE SAUCE

Ingredients.—Rind and juice of a nice lemon, 1 tablespoonful of marmalade, ½ oz. of cornflour, ½ pint of water, 1 dessertspoonful of sugar.

Method.—Cut the lemon-rind as thinly as possible, and put it in a small pan with the marmalade and water.

Boil for about five minutes, to extract the flavour of the lemon.

Mix the sugar and cornflour with the lemon-juice to a thin paste and pour the hot water and marmalade on to it.

Stir and return to the pan. Stir till it boils, simmer for ten minutes, and strain.

MARSHMALLOW SAUCE

Melt a quarter of a pound of marshmallows in a gill of water.

ORANGE SAUCE

INGREDIENTS.—1 large juicy orange, 2 oz. of sugar, 6 drops of cochineal.

METHOD.—Squeeze the orange juice on to the sugar.

Dissolve the sugar slowly and boil it for eight minutes. Add the cochineal.

SWEET SAUCE

INGREDIENTS.—1½ teaspoonfuls of cornflour, 1½ teaspoonfuls of castor sugar, ½ pint of milk, flavouring as desired.

METHOD.—Mix the cornflour to a smooth paste with some of the milk.

Heat the remainder and stir it on to it. Return it to the saucepan, bring it to the boil and simmer it for a few minutes, keeping it well stirred all the time.

Add the sugar and flavouring and pour the sauce round the pudding.

TOFFEE SAUCE

INGREDIENTS.—¼ lb. of margarine or butter, ½ lb. of golden syrup, ½ lb. of Demerara sugar.

METHOD.—Melt the butter and add the sugar and syrup, and stir till it boils. Boil it for fifteen minutes. Stir till it begins to thicken and pour it quickly over the pudding.

SAGO PUDDING

INGREDIENTS.—1½ oz. of sago, 1 pint of milk, 1 egg, flavouring, 2 dessertspoonfuls of sugar.

METHOD.—Boil the milk, sprinkle in the sago and cook gently until it is clear, and the mixture a little thick and creamy, keeping it stirred occasionally.

Draw aside and cool slightly, then add the beaten egg, sugar and flavouring to taste. Turn into a pie-dish, and bake gently for about half an hour. *Do not let it boil.*

A few stoned dates or raisins may be added to give variety. A semolina, or *crushed* tapioca pudding may be made in the same way.

Sufficient for four persons.

NOTE.—If using lemon-rind to flavour, peel it very thinly, and add to the milk before it is brought to the boil; then remove when the mixture is turned into the pie-dish.

SAGO PLUM PUDDING

INGREDIENTS.—3 tablespoonfuls of sago. 1½ gills of hot milk, ½ cup of breadcrumbs, ¾ cup of sultanas (washed), ½ cup of sugar, 2 oz. of butter, 1 egg, ½ teaspoonful of bicarbonate of soda, toffee sauce (see opposite column).

METHOD.—Wash sago, and strain it.

Pour the hot milk on the sago and let it stand for three hours.

Add the sultanas to the sago with the breadcrumbs, sugar and butter.

Put the mixture in a saucepan and heat it till the butter is melted. Beat the egg with the soda and stir it in.

Pour it into a small greased cake tin, and twist a greased paper over the top, or else cover with a lid.

Steam for two hours, adding more boiling water in one hour. Leave the pudding for three minutes before turning out. Pour toffee sauce round.

Sufficient for three persons.

SEMOLINA PUDDING

INGREDIENTS.—2 oz. of semolina, 1 egg, 1 oz. of margarine, 1½ pints of milk, nutmeg, 2 dessertspoonfuls of sugar.

METHOD.—Put the milk into a saucepan and bring to the boil, then sprinkle in the semolina and cook slowly for a few minutes until thick and creamy, keeping it well stirred.

Draw to the side and cool slightly, then beat up the egg and stir in.

Add the sugar and margarine and some grated nutmeg, and mix all together. Then turn into a pie-dish.

Bake slowly for half an hour, being careful not to let the pudding boil.

Sufficient for four persons.

SILVER SHRED PUDDING

INGREDIENTS.—½ lb. of self-raising flour, ½ level teaspoonful of ground cloves, ¼ lb. of margarine, ¼ lb. of castor sugar, 1 whole egg and 1 extra white, ¾ lb. of lemon marmalade, milk.

METHOD.—Beat the sugar and fat to a cream, then add the whole egg. Stir it in quickly and beat well. Sift the flour with the ground cloves, and mix them in lightly, adding a little milk as required. Whisk the egg-white to a stiff froth and fold it in.

Grease a pie-dish, put the marmalade in the bottom, then turn in the prepared mixture and put the pudding into a moderately hot oven to bake.

It will take about three quarters to an hour.

Turn it out carefully and serve it on a hot dish.

Sufficient for six persons.

SNOWDON PUDDING

INGREDIENTS.— 5 oz. of bread-crumbs, 1 tablespoonful of ground rice, ¼ lb. of suet, 1 lemon, 2 oz. of candied peel, 4 tablespoonfuls of marmalade, 3 oz. of castor sugar, 2 eggs, milk to mix (about ½ teacup).

METHOD.—Grease a pudding-basin and put half the marmalade in the bottom of it. Cut up the peel.

Grate the lemon-rind.

Make the breadcrumbs.

Chop the suet finely and add to the prepared crumbs.

Add also the ground rice and lemon-rind, sugar, and peel.

Mix all together, make a hole in the centre and put in the remainder of the marmalade.

Beat up the eggs and add, together with some milk as required.

Mix together well and beat for a few minutes.

Put into a pudding-basin, cover securely with a greased paper and steam for about two hours.

Turn on to a hot dish and serve.

Sufficient for about six persons.

SODA PUDDINGS

INGREDIENTS.—2 eggs, their weight in flour, 2 oz. of castor sugar, 3 oz. of margarine, ½ flat teaspoonful of ground ginger, ¼ flat teaspoonful of carbonate of soda, 3 dessertspoonfuls of lemon marmalade, 3 or 4 almonds.

FOR THE SAUCE.—2 tablespoonfuls of lemon marmalade, 1 dessertspoonful of lemon-juice, ¼ pint of water.

METHOD.—Cream the fat and sugar, add each egg separately, stirring it in quickly and beating well.

Sift the flour with the soda and ginger and stir it into the egg mixture, then add the lemon marmalade and mix all together.

Grease five moulds and decorate them with blanched and halved almonds. Two-thirds fill them with the pudding mixture, then cover them with a buttered paper and steam them for about forty-five minutes.

Turn out the puddings and serve them with the sauce.

TO MAKE THE SAUCE.—Mix the marmalade with the water and lemon-juice, and boil them for a few minutes.

Sufficient for five persons.

HOT SOUFFLES

SOUFFLES consist of a very light, fluffy mixture, either sweet or savoury. These have usually a panada for a foundation, which is a mixture of flour, butter, and milk, all blended together, and it is very important when making this to cook it sufficiently without overcooking it, as the success of a soufflé depends largely on the cooking of the panada. When sufficiently cooked the mixture leaves the sides of the pan quite freely, and does not stick to the finger when touched lightly, but if overcooked it becomes oily.

Remember that the eggs must be very fresh, and for this purpose they are always separated, the whites being whisked to a stiff froth and added last.

TO COOK SOUFFLES.—They may be baked or steamed, the latter being the lighter method. But whichever way is chosen, they must be cooked directly they are mixed.

If baked, cook the soufflé in a buttered fireproof soufflé dish, or Pyrex, or pie-dish, filling it to only two-thirds of its capacity.

If steamed, cook it in a soufflé case; or, if this is not available, in a plain round cake tin.

TO STEAM A SOUFFLE.—Put it into a saucepan of water, boiling slowly. The water should reach only one-third up the sides of the tin. Steam the soufflé very gently.

It is advisable to stand the tin on a round pastry cutter, as this prevents it from touching the bottom of the pan.

Soufflés must be taken up directly they are cooked.

Steamed Cherry Souffle

Ingredients.—Small tin of cherries, 1½ oz. of flour, 1½ oz. of butter, 1½ gills of milk, 3 yolks and 4 whites of eggs, 2½ dessertspoonfuls of castor sugar.

Method.—Butter a soufflé tin (holding about a pint and a half) and tie a treble band of buttered paper round the outside of it, so that it stands well above the top. This will hold up the soufflé when it rises.

Drain the syrup from the cherries and weigh off two ounces. Stone these and cut them into small pieces.

Sift the flour and weigh it very accurately. Separate the eggs.

Melt the butter in a saucepan, add the flour and, when blended, stir in the milk. Bring the panada to the boil and cook it until the mixture leaves the sides of the pan, keeping it well stirred, then remove it and cool it for a minute.

Add the sugar and beat in the yolks of the eggs one at a time, and when all are added stir in the prepared cherries.

Lastly, add the stiffly-whisked whites of eggs, folding them in lightly with a metal spoon so as to preserve their lightness.

Turn the mixture into the prepared tin, cover it with a buttered paper, and steam it gently for about fifty minutes, then take it up and carefully remove the paper before turning it on to a hot dish.

Serve the soufflé immediately, with the remainder of the cherries heaped at each end of the dish. The syrup should be reduced a little to thicken it and, if liked, may be coloured with cochineal and flavoured with sherry.

A Plain Souffle

Ingredients.—1 oz. of butter, 1 oz. of castor sugar, 1 oz. of flour, 2 egg yolks and 3 whites, ¼ pint of milk, flavouring essence to taste.

Method.—Prepare the soufflé in the same way as the Cherry Soufflé, omitting the cherries and adding flavouring essence.

Steam it for about forty minutes and serve it with Jam Sauce.

A still fluffier soufflé can be made by adding another yolk and white.

To Make Jam Sauce.—Put one tablespoonful and a half of jam into a saucepan with a quarter of a pint of water. Mix them together and boil them for a minute or two, then pour the sauce round the soufflé.

A squeeze of lemon-juice may be added and, if necessary, the sauce may be strained. This depends on the kind of jam used.

Baked Chocolate Souffle

Ingredients.—1 oz. of chocolate, ¼ level teaspoonful of powdered cinnamon, 1½ dessertspoonfuls of castor sugar, 1 oz. of flour, 1 oz. of butter, 1 gill of milk, vanilla flavouring, 2 egg yolks and 4 whites.

Method.—Grate the chocolate and dissolve it in a small quantity of the milk, then take it off the gas and add the remainder of the milk.

Melt the butter in a saucepan, stir in the flour sifted with the cinnamon, and when well blended add the chocolate milk and bring them to the boil. Cook this panada until the mixture leaves the sides of the pan, keeping it well stirred, then draw the pan aside. Add the sugar and flavour the soufflé with vanilla essence, then beat in the yolks of eggs, one at a time.

Lastly, fold in the stiffly-whisked whites of eggs, and turn the mixture into a buttered soufflé dish (only two-thirds filling it). Bake it till well risen and nicely browned.

Serve the soufflé in the dish immediately it is cooked. It may be accompanied by a vanilla custard. This can be made with the two remaining yolks of eggs and barely half a pint of milk, adding sugar and vanilla essence.

BAKED SOUFFLE PIE

Ingredients.—About ½ lb. of short pastry (see page 252), orange marmalade or jam, 1 oz. of butter, 2 dessertspoonfuls of flour, 2 eggs and 2 extra whites, ¼ pint of milk or milk and water, grated rind of 1 lemon and 1 orange, 3 dessertspoonfuls of castor sugar, orange essence.

Method.—Roll out the pastry, then line the rim and half-way down the sides of a buttered pie-dish. Cut leaves of pastry and place them round the pastry-lined edge, damping it to make them adhere. Put some orange ginger in the bottom of the dish.

Make the soufflé as directed for Almond Soufflé (p. 200). Flavour it with finely grated orange and lemon-rind, and a few drops of orange essence.

Turn into the prepared dish, brush the pastry with milk, and put in a hot oven to bake. It will take about half an hour. Serve at once.

Sufficient for four persons.

SPAGHETTI PUDDING

INGREDIENTS.—1½ oz. of spaghetti, 1 egg, 1 pint of milk, 2 dessertspoon-fuls of sugar, flavouring.

METHOD.—Break the spaghetti into short lengths, and wash it.

Put the milk into a saucepan (top of double boiler) and bring to the boil, then add the spaghetti and cook gently until tender, stirring occasionally. Draw aside and cool slightly, then beat up the egg and add with the sugar and flavouring to taste.

Turn into a pie-dish and bake gently for about half an hour or until set, being careful not to let it boil. Serve hot or cold.

A macaroni or vermicelli pudding may be made in the same way.

Sufficient for three or four persons.

SPANISH PUDDING

INGREDIENTS.—3 oz. of rice, 1 pint of milk, 2 oz. of suet, 3 oz. of sugar, 6 oz. of sultanas, 1 egg, grated lemon-rind.

METHOD.—Wash the rice and put into a saucepan with the milk, and cook this slowly until the rice has absorbed the milk (it will take about forty minutes). Wash and prepare the sultanas. Chop the suet finely. Add the sugar, grated lemon-rind, suet and sultanas to the rice and milk and mix thoroughly together ; add the beaten egg. Put into a greased basin, cover with a greased paper. Stand the pudding in a saucepan of boiling water and steam for two hours and a half. Turn on to a dish and serve.

SPICE BOX PUDDING

INGREDIENTS.—9 oz. of flour, 6 oz. of treacle, 6 oz. of golden syrup, ¼ lb. of margarine, 1 egg, ¾ flat teaspoonful of carbonate of soda, ¼ flat teaspoonful of ground mace, ½ flat teaspoonful of ground cloves, 1 flat teaspoonful of ground ginger, 1 flat teaspoonful of ground cinnamon.

METHOD.—Sift the flour into a basin with the spices. Beat up the egg. Put the margarine, golden syrup and treacle into a saucepan and warm them sufficiently to melt, then add them to the egg and whisk all together. Turn them into the flour, mix and beat well. Add the soda mixed with a little milk.

Put the mixture into a well-buttered mould, cover it with a buttered paper, and steam it for about one hour and a half.

Serve Spice Box Pudding with a hot custard.

Sufficient for five or six persons.

NOTE.—The mould should be only about two-thirds full when put on to cook.

SPIFF CHOCOLATE PUDDING

INGREDIENTS.—½ lb. of flour, 5 oz. of suet, 1 oz. of cocoa, few stoned raisins, ¾ pint of milk, 1 flat teaspoonful of carbonate of soda, 6 oz. of moist sugar.

METHOD.—Well grease a basin and decorate the bottom of it with stoned raisins to form a " cap." Sieve the flour and cocoa together. Add the suet, chopped finely, and mix well with the flour, then mix in the sugar. Boil the milk, then draw to the side and stir in the soda.

Add this at once to the dry ingredients and mix all together.

Put into the prepared basin ; the latter should only be about two-thirds full. Cover securely with a paper well greased on both sides, and steam for about four or five hours.

Turn on to a dish and, if liked, serve with chocolate sauce.

Sufficient for seven or eight persons.

SPONGE PUDDINGS

INGREDIENTS.—2 oz. of raisins (stoned and chopped), 1 oz. of butter, 1 oz. of flour, 1 oz. of sugar, grated rind of an orange, 1 egg.

METHOD.—Grease some small moulds.

Cream the butter and sugar, add the egg and beat them well.

Add the flour, raisins, and orange-rind to the mixture and fill the moulds three parts full.

Bake in a hot oven for twenty minutes, turn out, and pour orange sauce round.

Sufficient for two or three persons.

ORANGE SAUCE.

INGREDIENTS.—1 large juicy orange, 2 oz. of sugar, 6 drops of cochineal.

METHOD.—Squeeze the orange-juice on to the sugar.

Dissolve the sugar slowly and boil it for eight minutes. Add the cochineal.

STRAWBERRY OMELET

INGREDIENTS.—1 dessertspoonful of flour, 1½ dessertspoonfuls of castor sugar, 2 eggs, flavouring, strawberry jam.

METHOD.—Butter a small frying or omelet pan and line with buttered paper to stand well above the sides. Separate the yolks from the whites of the eggs.

Add the sugar to the yolks and whisk together for about eight minutes until the mixture becomes thick and creamy and free from dark streaks of egg.

Stir in the flour lightly and add a few drops of vanilla or other flavouring.

Add a pinch of salt to the whites of eggs and whisk them to a very stiff froth and fold lightly into the other ingredients and mix together. Pour into the prepared pan, and bake in a hot oven for about eight to ten minutes. Warm some strawberry jam, and when the omelet is cooked turn it over on to a sugared paper, remove the greased paper and lightly spread one half of the omelet with jam. Fold the other half over and serve immediately on to a hot dish with a lace paper.

STRAWBERRY PUDDING

INGREDIENTS.—1 cupful of flour, 2 oz. of shredded suet, ½ cup of jam, 2 eggs, ½ gill of milk, ½ teaspoonful of bicarbonate of soda, 1 oz. of sugar.

METHOD.—Mix the flour, suet and sugar. Stir in the jam and the well-beaten egg.

Dissolve the soda in the milk and add it last.

Fill a greased cake-tin or basin about three parts full with the mixture and cover it with a greased paper.

Steam steadily for two hours and a half.

Let the pudding cool for about five minutes before turning it out carefully on to a hot dish.

Sprinkle with castor sugar before serving.

Sufficient for four persons.

SUET PUDDINGS

WHEN boiling and steaming puddings remember that they must be put into *boiling* water to cook. (Steamed puddings can, if preferred, be cooked in a steamer over boiling water.) The water must also be kept *boiling* all the time, and the pan replenished with boiling water as it boils away. If these precautions are not taken the puddings will be heavy.

When boiling a pudding, the water should cover the rim of the basin, but *the basin must be full*, and the pudding well protected with a greased paper and floured pudding-cloth. This should be tied securely round the rim and the ends of the cloth then tied on the top.

When steaming a pudding, the water should reach only half-way up the side of the basin, which, in this case, should not be full, and a greased paper is sufficient to cover it. But the greased paper must be tucked securely under the rim.

It is a good plan when steaming a pudding to stand it on a pastry cutter. This allows for more depth of water in the pan, and thus lessens the risk of of boiling dry.

A steamed pudding will take longer to cook then a boiled one, but is a lighter method of cooking

THE PROPORTIONS TO USE

SUET puddings, although simple, are often very imperfectly made. They are sometimes dry and leathery, and sometimes heavy. A plain suet pudding is the basis of many puddings—meat, fruit, jam, etc.

The average proportion to use is half as much suet as flour.

Or you may use part flour and part breadcrumbs. Either beef or mutton suet can be used, the latter makes a lighter pudding, although not quite so rich as beef. Whichever you use must be chopped finely.

If you remove the skin first, then shred the suet, it can be chopped easily. Should it stick to the board, sprinkle a little flour over it (from your pudding —not extra flour).

The mixing is very important.— So many make a suet crust too dry. It should be mixed to a pliable dough, not dry, but not too moist so that it is difficult to roll out. A suet pudding that has *not* to be rolled out, and is going to be cooked in a basin, can be made a good deal moister.

Puddings containing breadcrumbs require more liquid to mix them than those made with all flour.

PLAIN SUET PUDDING

INGREDIENTS.—$\frac{1}{2}$ lb. of flour, 1 flat teaspoonful of baking-powder, $\frac{1}{4}$ lb. of suet, water to mix.

METHOD.—Sieve the flour with the baking-powder, chop the suet finely and add, then mix with water.

SURPRISE FRUIT PUDDING

INGREDIENTS.—$\frac{3}{4}$ to 1 lb. of mixed f r u i t — redcurrants, blackcurrants, cherries and loganberries, 2 to 3 tablespoonfuls of sugar, 2 or 3 tablespoonfuls of water, $\frac{1}{4}$ lb. of breadcrumbs, $\frac{1}{4}$ lb. of suet, $\frac{1}{4}$ lb. of flour, water to mix.

METHOD.—Pick over and wash the fruit, and drain it. Chop the suet finely and mix it with the flour and breadcrumbs, and mix them to a soft dough with water.

Roll out the dough and line a greased pudding-basin with it. Fill it up with the prepared fruit, adding the sugar when it is only half filled. Pour in the water, cover with the remainder of the dough, rolled out and cut to fit the top, damping the edges to make them adhere.

Cover the pudding with a greased paper and a floured pudding-cloth, and boil it for two hours.

Turn out the pudding, sprinkle it with castor sugar and serve with cream. Sufficient for five persons.

SWISS PUDDING

INGREDIENTS.—2 eggs, their weight in sugar, margarine and flour, 1 lemon (rind), 1 teaspoonful of baking-powder, $\frac{1}{2}$ gill of milk, 2 tablespoonfuls of apricot jam.

METHOD.—Put a saucepan of water on to boil. Cream the sugar and margarine until they resemble thick cream. Beat the eggs, one at a time, into the sugar and margarine. Beat these three ingredients together for ten minutes. Grate the lemon-rind and add to the flour with the baking-powder.

Grease a basin and put the apricot jam into the bottom of it. Fold the flour, etc., lightly into the mixture of sugar, fat and eggs. Add the milk. Put into the greased basin on top of the jam but do not mix with the jam.

Cover with a greased paper. Place in a saucepan of boiling water and steam for two hours.

Turn on to a hot dish and serve with apricot sauce.

APRICOT SAUCE.—1 tablespoonful of apricot jam, 1 gill of water, 1 teaspoonful of lemon-juice. Boil together for five minutes.

SWEDISH VANILLA SPONGE

INGREDIENTS.—3 large eggs, 4 oz. of castor sugar (exact weight), $2\frac{1}{2}$ oz. of potato flour or cornflour, vanilla essence.

METHOD.—Grease a pint and a half jelly mould or eight sponge-cake tins. Mix a teaspoonful of flour and castor sugar, put it in the tin and shake it round till the sides are coated. Beat the egg yolks and sugar for half an hour with a wooden spoon.

Be sure that the oven is hot before adding the potato flour. Sift the potato flour and sprinkle it in gradually. Whisk the whites to a very stiff froth and fold them in lightly with a few drops of vanilla essence. Pour into the tin, which should be large enough to allow for rising.

Bake in a moderate oven for forty minutes.

If baked in sponge-cake tins put in a quick oven for twenty minutes. Leave a few minutes before turning out.

DUTCH SYLLABUB

INGREDIENTS.—$\frac{1}{2}$ pint of hock, the juice of 3 lemons and the rind of one, 3 eggs, 2 oz. of sugar.

METHOD.—Cut the rind thinly, put it in a saucepan with the hock and lemon-juice and heat them. Beat the eggs and sugar till light and frothy and pour them on the hot wine, stirring well.

Pour them into a double saucepan and stir till the custard coats the back of the spoon.

Taste the syllabub, and if it is not sweet enough, add a little more sugar. Strain it into a jug, then pour into custard glasses.

Serve with sponge fingers.

Sufficient for two or three persons.

TAPIOCA AND PRUNE PUD-DING

INGREDIENTS.—2½ oz. of tapioca, 1½ pints of milk, 1 to 1½ tablespoonfuls of sugar, nutmeg or other flavouring, ½ oz. of margarine or butter, 6 oz. of prunes, sugar, ½ pint of water.

METHOD.—Wash the prunes and soak them in about half a pint of water. Then stew until tender, adding sugar to taste, and leave to get cold. Strain off the syrup, wash the tapioca and soak it in the prune syrup (about a gill) for a few hours, or until the latter is absorbed.

Put the prunes in a pie-dish, add the sugar and tapioca and stir in the milk.

Grate some nutmeg on the top, add the butter cut in small pieces and bake gently, allowing it about one hour after it comes to the boil.

Serve hot or cold.

If making a plain tapioca pudding, omit the prunes and soak the tapioca in one gill of water.

TOFFEE PUDDING

INGREDIENTS.—½ lb. of flour, ¼ lb. of margarine, ¼ flat teaspoonful of carbonate of soda, 4 or 5 oz. of golden syrup, 1 good tablespoonful of coffee essence, ¼ lb. of soft brown sugar, 1 egg, a few almonds.

METHOD.—Grease a basin and decorate it with a few blanched almonds.

Put the margarine, golden syrup, sugar and coffee essence in a saucepan to melt, but do not let them boil. When dissolved, cool a little.

Whisk the egg, then add the toffee mixture and whisk together. Pour into the centre of the flour and beat

well. Lastly, stir in the soda mixed in a spoonful of milk. Put into the prepared basin, cover securely with a well-greased paper and steam for about two hours.

Serve with hot custard.

Sufficient for eight persons.

TORRIJAS

INGREDIENTS.—8 fingers of stale bread (crusts removed), ½ pint of milk, 1 egg, 3 oz. of butter or margarine, a small jar of honey.

METHOD.—Soak the bread in the milk for five minutes in a pie-dish.

If the bread is very stale soak it for ten minutes.

Heat the butter till it smokes, and fry the slices of bread for two minutes on each side.

Drain them on soft white paper.

Beat the egg and put it in a plate. Dip the fried slices in the egg and fry them again for a minute on each side.

Place the jar of honey in a saucepan of hot water for about ten minutes to make it liquid.

Dip the torrijas in the honey and serve them on a hot dish.

A nice variation of this dish is to fry the slices as described, and instead of dipping them in honey to roll them in a mixture of one tablespoonful of castor sugar and two teaspoonfuls of cinnamon.

Sufficient for four persons.

NOTE.—If fresh bread is used for this dish it will only require soaking for about two minutes. It should be moist, but not wet enough to break when it is placed in the frying pan.

TREACLE PUDDING

INGREDIENTS.—¼ lb. of self-raising flour, ¼ lb. of breadcrumbs, ¼ lb. of chopped or shredded suet, grated rind of 1 lemon, ½ lb. of golden syrup, 1 egg, milk.

METHOD.—Sift the flour and mix it with the shredded suet, stir in the breadcrumbs and finely grated lemon-rind.

Whisk up the egg, warm the golden syrup, then whisk them together and stir them into the dry ingredients. Mix well, adding a little milk as required. Turn the mixture into a greased pudding-basin, cover it with a greased paper and steam for about two hours.

Turn the pudding out and serve it with some more golden syrup, the latter heated and served in a sauce-boat.

TRI-COLOUR PUDDING

INGREDIENTS.—¼ lb. of flour, 1 oz. of currants (washed), 2 oz. of margarine, 2 tablespoonfuls of sugar, cochineal, ½ oz. of cocoa, 1 dessertspoonful of sugar extra, 1 egg, vanilla essence, ½ teaspoonful of baking-powder, ½ cup of milk, jam sauce (see next column).

METHOD.—Grease a basin and put the currants at the bottom.

Put some water on to boil.

Cream the margarine and sugar till soft, and beat in the egg. Add the flour, milk and baking-powder.

Leave one-third of the mixture in the bowl used for mixing, and do not colour it.

Put one-third of the mixture into another bowl, and stir into it the cocoa mixed with the dessertspoonful of extra sugar. Add a few drops of vanilla. Put one-third of the mixture into a basin and colour it red with cochineal. Take dessertspoonfuls of the red, white and brown mixtures alternately, and put them in the greased basin, which should be a little more than half full.

Cover the mixture with greased paper, and stand it in a saucepan containing enough boiling water to come half-way up the basin. Steam steadily for one hour.

Pour jam sauce round, and if desired decorate with cream.

Sufficient for three persons.

UPSTAIRS PUDDING

INGREDIENTS.—¾ lb. of flour, 6 oz. of suet, water to mix, ¾ lb. of jam.

METHOD.—Grease a pudding-basin. Chop the suet finely and mix with the flour. Add the water and mix to a stiff paste. Divide this crust into two pieces. Flour a board, and roll out one piece to a round shape, about one and a half times the size of the top of the basin. Line the prepared basin with this.

Divide the other half of the crust into half again. Roll out one of these pieces to the size of the top of the basin and put aside for the top of the pudding.

Roll out the remaining piece and cut into four. Then put in layers of jam and crust alternately until the basin is full. Damp the top edge of the pudding and fix the top crust on to it. Cover with a greased paper. Put into a saucepan of boiling water and steam for about two and a half to three hours.

Turn on to a hot dish and serve.

NOTE.—The water should reach about half-way up the side of the basin.

VANILLA PUDDINGS

INGREDIENTS.—1 egg and its weight in butter, sugar and flour, ½ teaspoonful of vanilla essence, jam sauce.

METHOD.—Grease six small moulds. Cream the butter and sugar, add the egg, and beat them well together. Stir in the flour and vanilla, and fill the moulds half full. Bake for twenty minutes.

Turn out and pour jam sauce round the puddings.

Sufficient for three persons.

JAM SAUCE

INGREDIENTS.—½ cup of raspberry jam, 1 oz. of sugar, ½ lemon, 1 teaspoonful of cornflour, ½ pint of water.

METHOD.—Mix the cornflour, sugar, and lemon-juice. Boil the water and jam and pour it on the cornflour, stirring well. Simmer for ten minutes.

VICTORIA PUDDING

INGREDIENTS.—2 eggs, 1 table-spoonful of castor sugar, ¼ lb. of raisins, 3½ gills of milk, almond flavouring, 4 penny sponge-cakes, butter for greasing.

METHOD.—Wash and stone the raisins.

Well grease a basin with butter, dip the raisins in a little butter (melted), and decorate the bottom of the basin with them.

Crumble the sponge-cakes into a powder, and mix with the remainder of the raisins.

Beat up the eggs, pour in milk and mix together with the sponge-cake crumbs, etc. Add the sugar and flavouring and mix well in.

Pour carefully into the greased basin, without moving the raisins in the bottom.

Cover with a greased paper, twist it well under the rim of the basin. Steam gently for about one to one and a half hours, or until firm.

Turn on to a hot dish and serve.

NOTE.—The water round the basin should only just simmer, and not reach more than one-third up the side of it.

If cooked too quickly the custard will curdle.

WHOLEMEAL PUDDING

INGREDIENTS.—¼ lb. of wholemeal, ¼ lb. of flour, ¼ lb. of suet, ¼ flat teaspoonful of carbonate of soda, 1 teaspoonful of ground ginger, 1 flat teaspoonful of ground cinnamon, 3 oz. of sugar, 1½ oz. of candied peel, 1 egg, milk and water to mix, 4 tablespoonfuls of golden syrup.

METHOD.—Grease a mould or basin and put the golden syrup in the bottom of it. Sieve the flour with the wholemeal, carbonate of soda, ground ginger and cinnamon. Chop the suet finely, and mix with these sieved ingredients.

Cut up the peel and add with the sugar.

Whisk the egg and stir in with some milk and water as required. Beat well, turn into the prepared mould, cover securely with a well-greased paper and steam for about two and a half to three hours.

The syrup will form a sauce round the pudding.

Sufficient for eight or ten persons.

YEAST APPLE CAKE

INGREDIENTS.—1 lb. of cooking apples—use as required, 4 level dessert-spoonfuls of castor sugar, 1 level teaspoonful of ground cinnamon, ¼ level teaspoonful of ground cloves, ¼ level teaspoonful of ground ginger, ½ lb. of flour, a pinch of salt, ½ oz. of yeast, ½ teaspoonful of castor sugar, 1½ oz. of margarine, 1 gill of milk, 1 egg.

METHOD.—Sift the flour and salt into a basin. Melt the fat in a saucepan, add the milk and make it lukewarm. Put the yeast and sugar (half a teaspoonful) into a small basin, and mix them until they liquefy. Then stir in the warm milk and fat.

Add this mixture to the beaten egg. Strain them into the flour and mix them together. Beat the mixture well, cover it and put it to rise in a warm place for about an hour and a half or till it has risen to double the size.

Peel and quarter the apples, remove the core and cut each section in half or into three according to its size.

When the yeast mixture is ready, turn it on to a floured board. Knead it lightly and roll it to the shape and size of a medium-sized baking-tin. Butter the tin and fit the dough into the base of it. Let it stand in a warm place for a few minutes till it begins to rise. Then arrange the slices of apple on it, letting them overlap and completely cover the dough.

Sprinkle the castor sugar mixed with the spices on top, and bake in a moderately hot oven for about half an hour, or a little longer if required.

If preferred, the dough may be slightly sweetened and flavoured with spice.

Sufficient for six persons.

YULETIDE PUDDING

INGREDIENTS.—4 eggs, 1¼ lb. of mincemeat, 5 oz. of flour, milk.

METHOD.—Separate the eggs. Whisk the whites to a stiff froth, and beat up the yolks. Sift the flour and add it to the mincemeat gradually with a little milk as required, then fold in the stiffly whisked egg whites.

Turn the mixture into a buttered mould, cover it securely with a buttered paper and steam it for about three hours. Turn it out and serve at once.

The mould should be only about two-thirds full.

Sufficient for five persons.

PASTRY

THE three golden rules for making perfect pastry are : Handle it lightly ; keep it cool ; bake it in a hot oven.

Every good housewife wishes to turn out light pastry, but many fail, although they may excel in all other branches of cookery. You will, however, have every reason to be successful if you try to remember these few important details.

There are various kinds of pastry, but the main rules apply to the preparation of all of them. First of all we will deal particularly with short crust, which is the easiest of all to make.

It is used chiefly for flans, tarts, and fruit and meat pies.

FLOUR AND BAKING POWDER

ALWAYS use the best flour and, after measuring it, pass it through a sieve. This helps to aerate it. The more air we introduce into the pastry the lighter it will be, as the air expands when the pastry is put into the hot oven.

A little baking-powder is usually added to plain short pastry (one *flat* teaspoonful is sufficient for half a pound of flour), and it should be sieved with the flour into the mixing basin so that it becomes well mixed.

It is not necessary to use baking-powder in a rich short crust, but you can do so if you prefer it.

MARGARINE, LARD, OR BUTTER

PASTRY made with margarine is very good, but it is even better made with half margarine and half lard, and of, course, for special occasions, pastry made entirely with butter is best of all.

It is inadvisable to economise too much in the amount of fat you use. So many cooks spoil their pastry by doing this. For a plain short crust you should use half as much fat as flour, and for a richer crust about two-thirds or three-quarters as much. Whatever kind of fat you use must be rubbed into the flour lightly with the tips of the fingers until it resembles fine breadcrumbs.

If you shake the basin occasionally when doing this, the lumps will rise to the top.

You will find that a small quantity of fat is more easily rubbed into the flour than a large one.

MIXING

MIXING the pastry is a very important part of the preparation. The flour and fat should be mixed with cold water to a stiff paste which is neither dry nor sticky but just pliable.

If the dough is mixed too wet extra flour will have to be added, but the pastry is likely to become hard, as the extra flour contains no fat. On the other hand, if the dough is too dry, so much pressure will be needed to roll it out that the pastry will very likely be heavy.

The average quantity of water to be added to each half-pound of flour and quarter-pound of fat is about half a gill. If you have used more fat, or if it is very soft, less water will be required.

The water should always be added gradually to the centre of the flour, which should be mixed in with it by degrees until quite a stiff paste is formed. The best method is to start mixing with a knife and to finish with the hand, so that you can feel the consistency.

ROLLING THE PASTRY

ALL rolling should be done evenly in a forward direction, neither too heavily nor over the edges, and roll only on one side of the crust.

Flour the board slightly before you begin, but not more than necessary, as you do not want to work more flour into the pastry.

PASTRY BAKING

PASTRY must always be put into a

hot oven so as to burst the starch grains in the flour when they will absorb the fat. If the oven is not hot enough when the pastry is first put in, the fat will not be absorbed, and it will be hard.

The richer the pastry the hotter the oven should be.

Here are some good recipes for short pastry:

PLAIN SHORT PASTRY

INGREDIENTS.—½ lb. of flour, a pinch of salt, 1 level teaspoonful of baking-powder, ¼ lb. of fat, cold water to mix.

METHOD.—Sieve the flour with the salt and baking-powder.

Rub in the fat.

Add cold water gradually and mix the ingredients to a stiff paste. Then roll out the dough and use it as required.

RICH SHORT CRUST

INGREDIENTS.—½ lb. of flour, pinch of salt, 1 flat teaspoonful of baking-powder (if liked), 6 oz. of fat, cold water to mix.

METHOD.—Prepare this in the same way as plain short pastry.

The yolk of an egg mixed with a little water is sometimes used for mixing a rich short crust.

FLAKY PASTRY

INGREDIENTS.—¾ lb. of flour, a pinch of salt, water to mix, 6 oz. of lard, 5 oz. of margarine.

METHOD.—To make a good flaky pastry, first sieve the flour with the salt, and rub in the margarine.

Add a little cold water, and mix the flour with it to make a stiff paste.

Place the lard on a well-floured board, and roll it out into thin pieces. Put them on one side.

Now roll out the pastry fairly thinly to a square shape, turn it on to the other side and place the lard all over it, pressing it down lightly. Fold the sides to the middle each way, then fold the pastry in half again. (The paste should now be folded into eight.)

If the pastry is made a day before it is to be baked it will be improved. It should be kept in a cool place,

covered with a piece of buttered paper to prevent it from getting dry.

PUFF PASTRY

INGREDIENTS.—½ lb. of flour, pinch of salt, a squeeze of lemon-juice, water to mix, ½ lb. of fresh butter.

METHOD.—Squeeze the butter in a floured cloth to remove the moisture. Form it into a squarish shape and leave it in a cool place until ready to use. Sieve the flour with the salt. Make a well in the centre, and add a squeeze of lemon-juice and enough water to make a pliable paste of about the same consistency as the butter.

Turn the paste on to a lightly floured board and knead it light to make it smooth. Roll it out to an oblong shape about three-eighths of an inch thick.

Turn it over on to the other side, put the butter on one half (it should not quite reach to the edge) and fold the other half over it, pressing the edges well together.

Leave it in a cool place for about fifteen or twenty minutes. *Place the lump of pastry on the board so that fold is at the left-hand side and roll it to a long oblong shape. Turn it over on to the other side and fold it in three.*

Continue in this way, putting the pastry into a cool place for fifteen minutes between each or every other roll until it has been rolled out and folded in three, six times. The seventh time roll it out and use it as required.

To bake puff pastry, put it into a very hot oven. A good bottom heat is required for this.

"HALF PUFF" PASTRY

INGREDIENTS.—9 oz. of flour, 6 oz. of butter, a pinch of salt, water to mix, squeeze of lemon-juice.

METHOD.—Sieve the flour and salt. Add a squeeze of lemon-juice and sufficient water to mix the flour to a pliable paste.

Put the butter into a cloth and squeeze out the moisture, then stand it in a cold place until ready to use it.

Put the paste on to a slightly-floured board, and knead it for a few minutes until quite smooth.

Roll it out to an oblong shape, about half an inch thick. Turn it over on to the other side. Press the butter to almost half the size of the rolled-out pastry.

Put on one-half of it. It must not quite reach to the edges of the pastry. Fold the pastry over it, and press the edges of paste well together. Leave it in a cool place for about fifteen to twenty minutes, then roll it (keeping the fold to the right) to an oblong shape; it should now be about three times as long as it is wide; turn it on to the other side, and fold into three. Repeat this until the pastry has been rolled four times, then make it up as required.

NOTE.—The pastry should be put into a cool place between each or every other roll, after it is folded into three. It must also be turned round, so that there is a fold on either side, and cut edges at top and bottom, and rolled out in this direction each time.

USEFUL PASTRY HINTS
GLAZING PASTRY

To glaze pastry, it can be brushed with milk, egg, or yolk of egg beaten with a little milk. This must be done before the pastry is cooked.

Egg or egg-and-milk glaze are suitable for meat-pies, sausage rolls, etc., and the milk glaze for a fruit-pie or mince-pies.

Pastry may also be glazed after it is cooked, in the following manner: Brush it with slightly frothed white of egg, dredge with castor sugar, and return the pastry to the oven for a minute or two.

PUFF PASTE PATTY CASES

ROLL out half a pound of puff paste six times, wet the surface, then fold in three and roll out a quarter of an inch in thickness.

For cutting out use two cutters, the larger one about two and a half inches across and the smaller one, one and a half inches.

Dip the cutters in boiling water before cutting out each patty.

Cut a small circle in the centre of each patty, but only cut half-way through the pastry. Place them on a baking-tin and brush the top with egg.

Leave them on the tin for twenty minutes to keep them a good shape, then bake them in a quick oven for twenty minutes.

Remove the tops and pick out the centre of each patty. Fill the patties and replace the tops.

To make twelve patty cases.

ALMOND PIE

INGREDIENTS.—2 oz. of ground almonds, 1 oz. of almonds (blanched), 2 oz. of butter, 3 oz. of sugar, 2 oz. of cake crumbs, 1 oz. of flour, 2 small eggs, almond essence, $\frac{1}{2}$ lb. of rich short pastry (see p. 252).

METHOD.—Roll out the pastry and line a sandwich tin.

Cream the butter and sugar till soft.

Separate the eggs, add the yolks to the butter and sugar and beat well.

Stir in the cake crumbs, ground almonds, flour and almonds cut in strips, adding a few drops of almond essence.

Add the stiffly-beaten whites lightly and pour the mixture into the pastry case.

Lay twisted strips of pastry across the top and bake for thirty minutes.

ALMOND PIE CAKE

INGREDIENTS.—2 oz. of ground almonds, 4 oz. of flour, 2 oz. of margarine or butter, $3\frac{1}{2}$ oz. of castor sugar, a small level saltspoonful of carbonate of soda, 1 egg, almond flavouring, milk, some short pastry (see p. 252), jam.

METHOD.—Roll out some short pastry, line a deep sandwich-tin or pie-tin and put in a thin layer of jam in the bottom.

Beat the sugar and fat to a cream, add the egg, stir it in quickly and beat it well. Add the ground almonds, the flour and soda, sifted together, and mix all lightly, adding a little milk as required.

Flavour the mixture with a few drops of almond essence and turn it into the prepared tin. Put a lattice of pastry strips across, brush the top over with white of egg, just broken up, but not frothed, and dredge it with castor sugar. Place the cake in a hot oven to bake.

Sufficient for five or six persons.

ALMOND SHORTCAKE

INGREDIENTS.—3 oz. of ground almonds, 1 oz. of margarine or butter, 1 egg, 2 oz. of castor sugar, almond flavouring, about 6 oz. of short pastry (see p. 252), 1 oz. of glacé cherries.

FOR THE ICING.—¼ lb. of icing sugar, almond flavouring, 2 tablespoonfuls of cold water.

METHOD.—Roll out the pastry to a round shape about one-eighth of an inch thick and line a deep, round sandwich-tin with it.

Trim and decorate the top edge.

Cut the cherries into small pieces and place in the bottom of the pastry.

TO MAKE THE FILLING.—Beat the sugar and fat to a cream.

Stir in the egg quickly, and beat well for a few minutes. Add the ground almonds and a few drops of flavouring.

Mix all well together, put into the prepared tin, and spread over evenly.

Bake in a hot oven for about fifteen to twenty minutes, then put on to a sieve and leave until cold.

TO MAKE THE ICING.—Rub the icing sugar through a fine sieve.

Put it into a saucepan, and mix to a smooth paste with the cold water.

Add a few drops of flavouring.

Put over a low gas, and stir until the base of the saucepan feels just warm.

Ice the top of the cake only with the prepared icing. Just pour it on, and let it run to the edge of the pastry.

AMERICAN PEACH PIE

INGREDIENTS.—6 oz. of self-raising flour, 4½ oz. of margarine, 2 dessert-spoonfuls of castor sugar, ½ an egg to mix, a pinch of salt.

FOR THE FILLING.—Large tin of peaches, 2 oz. of flour, 1 tablespoonful of castor sugar, or to taste, ½ oz. of butter, juice of ½ an orange, ½ an egg, 1 tablespoonful of lemon-juice, cream for decorating.

METHOD.—First make the pastry by sifting the flour into a basin with a pinch of salt, rub in the margarine and add the sugar. Then beat up the egg and mix the pastry to a stiff paste with half of it (reserving the other half for the filling), if necessary add a little cold water.

Butter the pie plate. Then roll out the pastry thinly and cut a round,

allowing rather more than sufficient to line the plate.

Fit it evenly into the plate and turn in the small margin of pastry that stands above the edge.

Now snip the double edge with scissors, cutting it at equal distances apart. Turn down every alternate cut piece. Or it may be fluted with thumb and finger.

The next step is to prick the paste in the bottom of the plate with a fork, and line it with a round of buttered paper.

Scatter rice on the paper and put the pie into a hot oven to bake. When the pastry is set, remove the paper and rice, and finish cooking the case, then let it cool.

The pastry can be varied slightly by mixing it with water instead of egg, or by omitting the sugar.

TO MAKE THE FILLING.—Turn out the peaches and drain off the syrup. Reserve three or four half peaches for decorating the pie and mash up the remainder roughly on a plate.

Mix the flour and sugar together to a smooth paste with the peach syrup. Add the mashed peaches and turn the mixture into a saucepan.

Stir it well and bring it to the boil. Add lemon and orange-juice, and boil it again gently for a few minutes. Take the mixture off the heat, add the butter and cool it for a minute.

Stir in the remaining half an egg and cook the filling again for a few minutes without letting it boil. When it is quite cool, turn it into the prepared case of pastry.

Before serving this pie decorate the centre with half a peach placed cup-side uppermost. Fill it with whipped cream sweetened and flavoured to taste, and arrange eighths or quarters of peach round, with cream between them.

If preferred the filling may be topped with meringue and the cream omitted. In this case use one yolk and a little water to mix the pastry, and one or two yolks for the filling in the place of the half-egg.

The whites can then be reserved for the meringue.

To prepare the meringue, add a pinch of salt to the whites and whisk them to a stiff froth. Fold in the sugar, allowing one tablespoonful to each egg-white.

Heap the meringue on top of the filling. Sprinkle it with castor sugar and return it to a cool oven to set and brown lightly. When it is cold, decorate it with slices of peaches.

Varieties of this pie, which are named according to the filling, can be made by using different fruits.

APPLE FLAN

INGREDIENTS.—1 lb. of cooking apples, 1 oz. of glacé cherries, ¾ gill of water, 6 oz. of loaf sugar, 2 cloves, 8 oz. of short pastry (see p. 252).

METHOD.—Cover a sandwich-tin neatly with the pastry. Bake for twenty minutes. Remove the tin.

Boil the sugar, water, and cloves for five minutes. Peel and core the apples and cut them in triangular slices.

Put the apples in the syrup and stew them till they are soft, but not broken.

Arrange the apple in the flan-case, boil the juice till it is a thick syrup and pour it over the apple. Decorate with cherries.

APPLE PIE

INGREDIENTS.—½ lb. of flour, ¼ lb. of margarine, ¼ lb. of lard, water to mix (about 1 gill), 3 lb. of apples, 5 oz. of sugar, 1 gill of water, cloves, lemon-rind.

METHOD.—Peel the apples, remove the cores, and cut into slices.

Rub the margarine into the flour until it is as fine as breadcrumbs. Mix to a stiff paste with cold water —add this gradually.

Put on to a floured board and roll it out until it is about one-eighth of an inch thick, then turn it over on to the other side.

Either spread the lard in small pieces all over the pastry, or flour the board and rolling-pin well and roll the lard out until it is quite thin, and place on the rolled-out pastry.

Fold up the pastry and roll it out again.

Cut a piece from the outside of the pastry, about half an inch in width, and place it on the edge of the pie-dish —having previously damped the pie-dish.

Place a small cup or egg-cup upside down in the centre of the pie-dish.

Put half the apples in the dish, then the sugar and flavouring, then the remainder of the apples on the top—add the water.

Damp the edge of pastry round the dish, and place the cover on to the pie, pressing the edges together.

Cut off any rough edges and decorate the edge of the pie with a fork or knife.

Make a small cut in the middle of the top of the pie.

Brush the pie over with milk.

Bake in a very hot oven for thirty minutes—when cooked the pastry should be light brown and the apples soft.

Sprinkle the top of pie with castor sugar, and serve either hot or cold. If the pastry is sufficiently browned before the apples are cooked, remove the browning shelf from the oven.

NOTE.—For special occasions, to improve the flavour of an apple pie, add a little sherry with the apples. This gives a delicious flavour. The pie-dish must be full of fruit or the crust will sink.

Apples cook best when they are cut in thick slices.

When putting the pastry over the top, be careful not to stretch it, or it will shrink from the edges of the pie-dish when cooked.

APPLE AND RAISIN TART

INGREDIENTS.—½ lb. of apples, ¼ lb. of seedless raisins, 1 lemon (rind only), 2½ gills of cold water, 2 teaspoonfuls of cornflour, 2 dessertspoonfuls of granulated sugar, 1 oz. of almonds, about ¾ to 1 lb. of flaky pastry (see p. 252).

METHOD.—Wash the raisins and soak them in two gills of the water for about an hour. Then turn them into a saucepan, add the sugar, and stew them gently until soft. Draw the pan aside from the flame.

Mix the cornflour to a smooth paste with the half gill of cold water. Stir the syrup from the raisins on to the cornflour. Turn it into a pan and boil for a few minutes, keeping it stirred.

Draw the pan aside, add the raisins, grated lemon-rind, chopped almonds, and apples (peeled, cored, and either grated or chopped, but not cooked). Mix all well together and leave until cold.

Roll out the pastry into two rounds, one rather thinner than the other. Line a sandwich-tin with the thinner piece, put in the prepared mixture, then damp the edge and cover the fruit with a thicker round of pastry.

Mark straight lines across the top (both ways), brush it with milk, and put into a hot oven to bake.

It will take about twenty minutes. Sufficient for six persons.

APPLE AND SULTANA PIE

INGREDIENTS.—1½ lb. of cooking apples, 3 oz. of sugar, 3 cloves, 2 oz. of sultanas (washed), ½ gill of water, ¾ lb. of short pastry (see p. 252), castor sugar for dredging.

METHOD.—Roll out half the pastry into a round and line a sandwich-tin with it.

Peel, core, and slice the apples and heap them in the lined tin, mixing them with the sultanas, sugar, and cloves. Sprinkle the water over. Moisten the edge of the pastry.

Roll out the rest of the pastry and cover the pie, pressing the edges together neatly. Brush the top with water, and dredge it thickly with castor sugar.

Bake the pie in a moderate hot oven for about thirty minutes.

NOTE.—To tell if the fruit is soft, insert a skewer between the two layers of pastry.

APRICOT CHEESE CAKES

INGREDIENTS.—Some flaky pastry —as required (see p. 252), 2 oz. of crystallised apricots, 1 egg, 2 oz. of margarine or butter, 3 dessertspoonfuls of castor sugar, 3 dessertspoonfuls of ground rice, 1 dessertspoonful of cornflour, apricot essence, and apricot jam.

METHOD.—Roll out some flaky pastry thinly, cut it into rounds and line about eighteen patty pans or small cake-tins. Put a little jam in each.

Beat the sugar and fat together until creamy. Add the egg, stir it in quickly and beat well. Sieve the cornflour and ground rice and mix

them in lightly with the apricot cut into small pieces and a few drops of apricot essence.

Put some of the mixture into each tin—covering the jam—dredge the tops with castor sugar, place the tartlets on a baking-sheet and bake them in a quick oven for fifteen minutes.

Decorate with crystallised fruit.

APRICOT FLAN

INGREDIENTS.—7 oz. of flour, 4 oz. margarine, pinch of salt, 1 flat tea spoonful of baking-powder, water 1 yolk of egg, tin of apricots (small) ¼ pint of packet apricot or lemon jelly (to 1 gill of apricot syrup), or about 2 dessertspoonfuls of sugar (to 1 gill of apricot syrup).

METHOD.—Grease a flan-ring and stand it on a greased baking-sheet.

Sieve the flour with the salt and baking-powder.

Rub in the margarine. Break up the yolk of egg, and mix it with just a spoonful of water, and add it to the dry ingredients.

Mix them to a stiff paste, adding little more water if required, *but be careful not to make it too moist.*

Form it into a smooth lump, then turn it on to a slightly floured board and roll it out to almost a quarter of an inch thick and cut out a round. Put this inside the flan-ring and line it, pressing the pastry a little thinner in the base.

Trim the edge, then line the flan case with a round of buttered paper and shake in some uncooked rice.

Bake it for from twenty-five to thirty minutes or until lightly browned. The oven should be hot at first to set the pastry, then lessened as required.

When cooked, lift up the flan-ring remove the paper and rice, and leave the pastry on a sieve until cold. If liked, the rice and paper can be removed after about fifteen or twenty minutes, and the flan returned to the oven to finish cooking.

Turn out the apricots, and leave them to drain thoroughly. Then add sugar to the syrup, and when dissolved boil it until it will jelly when cold, or else heat the syrup and dissolve the jelly in it.

Cheese Cakes

Apricot Flan

Apple Meringue Vol au Vent

PLATE 25

Lemon
Meringue
Pie

Cut a round of pastry.

Flute the edge with
thumb and finger.

Heap the meringue
on top of the
filling.

The Finished Pie.

PLATE 26

In either case, when it is on the point of "jellying," arrange the apricots in the pastry-case with the cup-side downwards and pour the prepared syrup over the fruit.

NOTE.—The rice is added to keep the flan-case flat, and can be used over and over again.

The syrupy part of jam is sometimes used to pour over the fruit, but it must be warmed first, then rubbed through a sieve.

There are various little details which may cause a flan to be sodden. If you do not make your pastry sufficiently short, if it is mixed too moist, or if the oven is not hot enough at first, it may become sodden. But more often than not it is caused by not draining the fruit thoroughly before putting it into the flan-case, or by putting it in before the pastry is cold.

Another point, the syrup must be on the point of "jellying" before it is poured over, so that it sets without having time to soak into the pastry.

To make the syrup jelly, it can either be boiled with some more sugar, or else part of a table jelly can be dissolved in it.

APRICOT AND CHERRY FLAN

INGREDIENTS.—6 oz. of short pastry (see p. 252), 1 tin of apricots, 1 small tin of cherries, $\frac{1}{2}$ a lemon, 2 oz. of sugar, $1\frac{1}{2}$ teaspoonfuls of cornflour.

METHOD.—Cover the outside of a sandwich-tin neatly with the pastry and bake it for twenty minutes.

Add enough apricot syrup to the cherry-juice to make one and a half gills.

Mix half a gill of the syrup smoothly with the cornflour.

Boil the rest with the sugar and lemon-juice, and pour it on the cornflour, stirring well. Boil for eight minutes.

Arrange the apricots and cherries in the flan-case, and pour the *cool* syrup over.

APPLE MERINGUE VOL-AU-VENT

INGREDIENTS.—Vol - au - vent case (see p. 288), 1 lb. of apples, water, sugar to taste, $\frac{1}{2}$ lemon (rind only), $\frac{1}{2}$ oz. of butter, 1 egg, 1 tablespoonful of castor sugar.

METHOD.—Prepare the apples as for stewing and cook them till tender, adding sugar to taste, and sufficient water to keep them from burning. Then rub them through a sieve.

Return them to the saucepan, add the butter and finely-grated lemon-rind, and beat in the yolk of the egg. Cook this for a minute or two without letting it boil, then cool it a little before turning the mixture into the vol-au-vent case.

Whisk the egg-white to a stiff froth and fold in the castor sugar. Heap this on top of the apple and put the vol-au-vent into a cool oven to set and lightly brown the meringue.

Serve it decorated with pieces of crystallised rose-leaves.

Vol-au-vent cases can be bought ready prepared, or you can buy puff pastry and shape and bake your own.

Sufficient for four persons.

APRICOT PATTIES

INGREDIENTS.—$\frac{1}{2}$ tin of apricots, cream, essence of vanilla, 3 oz. of castor sugar, apricot liquor, puff or flaky pastry (see p. 252).

METHOD.—Line some patty pans with the pastry. Line the pastry with buttered papers, and put a little rice in the bottom of each to prevent the pastry rising in the middle. When the patties are set remove the paper and rice.

Boil the sugar and liquor until they are quite thick. Put in the apricots and simmer them for a few minutes.

When cold, place half an apricot in each piece of pastry and ornament it with whipped cream, sweetened and flavoured with vanilla.

Sufficient to make nine patties.

APRICOT PIE

INGREDIENTS.—Large tin of Californian apricots, 2 yolks and 3 egg-whites, 4 tablespoonfuls of castor sugar, juice of $\frac{1}{2}$ lemon, 3 dessertspoonfuls of cornflour, $\frac{1}{2}$ oz. of butter, about 10 oz. of short pastry (see p. 252), crystallised rose petals.

METHOD.—Roll out the pastry thinly and cut a round a little larger than a Pyrex plate. Line this, then fold the

I

top edge of pastry in towards the rim of the plate and flute it with finger and thumb.

Prick the base, line it with a round of buttered paper and sprinkle rice over it. Put it into a hot oven to bake, removing the paper and rice about five minutes before the pastry is ready to take out of the oven.

Drain the syrup from the apricots and rub the fruit through a sieve, measure the pulp, then make it up to a pint with some of the syrup.

Turn it into a saucepan, stir in the cornflour mixed to a smooth paste with the lemon-juice and a little extra syrup if required. Bring them to the boil and continue boiling for a few minutes, keeping the mixture stirred.

Draw the pan aside, add the butter, about one tablespoonful of sugar, or to taste, and the beaten egg-yolks.

Cook the mixture for a few minutes, but do not let it boil. Allow it to cool, then turn it into the prepared pastry case.

Whisk the egg-whites to a stiff froth and fold in the castor sugar (three tablespoonfuls). Cover the pie-filling with some of this, and spread it evenly, then force the remainder through an icing pump. Dredge it with castor sugar and put it in a cool oven to set the meringue, and brown it lightly.

Serve the pie cold, and sprinkle it with crushed rose petals just before-hand.

Sufficient for from six to eight persons.

DRIED APRICOT PIE

INGREDIENTS.—1 lb. of dried apricots, ½ lb. of flour, ½ teaspoonful of baking-powder, cold water, about 3 or 4 tablespoonfuls of Demerara sugar, 6 oz. of margarine, water to mix, 1 egg.

METHOD.—Wash the apricots in two or three waters, place in a basin, well cover with cold water, and soak for twenty-four hours.

Strain the water from the apricots and put them into a pie-dish with the sugar.

Add about one gill of the water in which the apricots were soaked.

Put the flour and baking-powder through a sieve.

Rub the fat into the flour until it is like fine breadcrumbs.

Separate the yolk from the white of egg.

Mix the yolk of egg with about a tablespoonful of water, add to the flour, and mix to a stiff paste, adding more water if required.

Roll out the pastry, and cut out a piece large enough to cover the top of the pie-dish.

Roll out the pieces that are over, cut strips of pastry, damp the edges of the pie-dish, and place them on to it.

Damp the edge again and lightly press the top pastry on to it ; decorate the edge by drawing it up with a fork or knife.

Place the pie in a hot oven and bake for about thirty minutes, or until the pie is light brown and the fruit tender.

Take the pie from the oven, slightly beat the white of egg and brush over the pie, then dredge with castor sugar and put back into the oven for about five minutes.

Serve either hot or cold.

NOTE.—The pie must be full of fruit or the crust will sink inside the pie-dish.

If liked, the remainder of the apricot water can be boiled with sugar and served with the pie.

Sufficient for about six or eight persons.

ASPARAGUS HORNS

INGREDIENTS.—Flaky pastry made from 4 oz. of flour (see p. 252), 1 egg, 1 bundle of cooked asparagus (cold), 1 cup of cold chicken, salt and pepper, 1 gill of mayonnaise (see p. 42) or salad cream.

METHOD.—Roll out the pastry as thinly as possible, and cut it into long strips three-quarters of an inch wide.

Wind each of these round a cornucopia tin, beginning at the bottom and taking care not to pull the pastry.

Brush with egg and lay on a baking-sheet, but let them stand for twenty minutes before baking so as to give the pastry time to lose its elasticity and thus make the cornets a good shape.

Bake for fifteen minutes in a moderate oven.

Chop the chicken and mix it with the mayonnaise. Add salt and pepper.

Just before serving, remove the horns from the tins and put some mayonnaise mixture in each.

Stick in two or three heads of asparagus, and serve at once.

Tinned asparagus can be used instead of fresh.

This quantity of pastry will make about eight horns.

BALMORAL TARTLETS

INGREDIENTS.—1 oz. of cake crumbs, 2 teaspoonfuls of flour, 1 oz. of butter, 1 oz. of sugar, ½ oz. of candied peel (chopped), ½ oz. of glacé cherries (chopped) 1 egg, ½ lb. of flaky pastry (see page 252).

METHOD.—Line eight to twelve patty-pans with rounds of pastry. Cream the butter and sugar and the yolk of the egg. Stir in the flour, cherries, peel, and cake crumbs. Beat the white of egg stiffly and add it lightly.

Put some of the mixture into each tart with two narrow strips of pastry crosswise on top. Bake for twenty minutes in a fairly hot oven.

BANANA FLAN

INGREDIENTS.—4 bananas, the juice of 1 orange, 6 oz. of granulated sugar, ¾ gill of water, 3 or 4 glacé cherries, a little whipped cream. 6 oz. of short pastry (see p. 252).

METHOD.—Roll out the pastry and lay it in a flan-ring placed on a baking-sheet. Press it against the sides and fill it with a smaller sized tin. Bake it for about twenty minutes and remove the tin.

Stir the orange-juice, sugar, and water till it boils. Boil for ten minutes.

Arrange sliced rounds of banana in the flan-case and pour the cool syrup over. When cold decorate with cream and cherries.

BANBURY TARTS

INGREDIENTS.— 6 oz. of flour, 6 oz. of margarine, pinch of salt, water to mix, mincemeat, 1 white of egg, castor sugar.

METHOD.—Add a pinch of salt to the flour, and sieve it into the basin.

Pour in the cold water gradually and mix to a stiff, but pliable paste.

Put it on to a slightly floured board and knead it lightly until quite smooth.

Roll it out to an oblong shape, about half an inch thick, and turn it on to the other side.

Press out the margarine until not quite half the size of the rolled-out pastry. Put it on one half and fold over the other. Press the edges well together.

Now roll it out and fold it in three. Repeat this twice again. Then roll out the pastry rather thinly.

Turn it over and cut out oval-shaped pieces. Place mincemeat in the centre of each and spread lightly.

Damp round the edges. Then put the edges to the centre and press together. Turn over on to the other side, and shape them so that they taper at either end.

Make one or two light cuts in the centres. Place on a baking-sheet and bake in a very hot oven for about fifteen minutes.

Beat egg-white until it slightly froths.

When cooked, glaze over the tarts with the white, and dust with castor sugar. Return to the oven for two or three minutes.

BUTTER CREAM TARTS

INGREDIENTS.—Some short or flaky pastry (see p. 252), 2 oz. of butter, crystallised fruit, 4 oz. of icing sugar, 2 oz. of ground almonds, ½ lemon.

METHOD.—Roll out the pastry, stamp it into rounds and line some patty-tins with it. Line these with rounds of buttered paper and put some rice in the bottom of each.

Place the tarts in a hot oven to bake, and when the pastry is set, remove the rice and paper and finish cooking the cases. Then cool them.

Sift the icing sugar.

Beat the butter to a cream with half the sugar, then add the remainder and beat it until it is creamy. Stir in the ground almonds and grated lemon-rind, and moisten the mixture with the lemon-juice.

Put a spoonful of the mixture into each pastry-case and decorate with a piece of crystallised fruit.

Sufficient filling for from fifteen to eighteen small tarts.

BUTTERSCOTCH TARTS

INGREDIENTS.—1 oz. of lump sugar, $\frac{1}{4}$ gill of water, 3 oz. of Barbados sugar, $1\frac{1}{2}$ gills of water, 1 oz. of cornflour, 1 oz. of butter, 1 yolk of egg, about $\frac{3}{4}$ lb. of flaky pastry (see p. 252), a few almonds.

METHOD.—Put the lump sugar into a small, strong saucepan with a quarter of a gill of water. Dissolve it slowly, and then bring the syrup to the boil, and boil till deep golden brown. Draw the pan aside and let the syrup cool.

Mix the cornflour to a smooth paste with some of the one and a half gills of water, and add the remainder to the caramel, add also the Barbados sugar and let all dissolve, then stir this on to the cornflour.

Return the mixture to the pan, add the butter, and stir it till it boils and thickens. Cook the mixture gently for a few minutes, then draw the pan aside and let it cool slightly.

Add the yolk of egg and stir the mixture over a low burner for three or four minutes, but do not let it boil.

Cool it a little before turning it into small pastry-cases, and stand a blanched almond in the centre of each. If liked, the mixture can be forced through an icing pump.

TO PREPARE THE PASTRY-CASES.—Roll out the pastry fairly thinly, stamp it into rounds, and line about twelve small cake-tins. Line each with a round of buttered paper, sprinkle a little rice in the bottom and bake them in a hot oven. When the pastry is set, remove the paper and rice, and finish cooking the cases, then let them cool. These should be baked before the filling is made.

Sufficient for about twelve tarts.

CAKE CRUMB TART

INGREDIENTS.—5 oz. of cake crumbs, 1 oz. of castor sugar, $1\frac{1}{2}$ oz. of margarine or butter, 1 egg, jam, short pastry (see p. 252).

METHOD.—Rub the stale cake through a wire sieve and make it into fine crumbs—madeira or other suitable stale cake can be used.

Beat the sugar and fat to a cream, add the egg, stirring it in quickly and beating well, then add the cake crumbs and mix all together.

Roll out some short pastry and line a sandwich-tin, put some jam in the bottom, then add the prepared mixture.

Cut strips of pastry, brush them with milk and lay them across the tart. Put it into a hot oven to bake.

Sufficient for from four to six persons.

CALIFORNIAN APPLE PIE

INGREDIENTS.—1 lb. of apples (when prepared), 2 oz. of Barbados sugar, 2 oz. of castor sugar, $\frac{1}{4}$ lb. of seedless raisins, $\frac{1}{2}$ teaspoonful of ground ginger, $1\frac{1}{2}$ flat teaspoonfuls of ground cinnamon, 1 orange (rind and juice), $\frac{1}{2}$ lemon (rind and juice), $\frac{1}{2}$ lb. of flour, 1 egg, 3 oz. of margarine, $\frac{1}{2}$ teaspoonful of baking-powder, water.

METHOD.—Peel and core the apples and chop them up roughly, add the finely grated orange and lemon-rind, the sugar, raisins, and spices.

Mix these together and add the orange and lemon-juice.

Sift the flour and baking-powder into a basin, rub in the margarine, then add the beaten egg-yolk mixed with a little water, and mix all to a stiff paste.

Put one-third of this mixture aside. Roll out the larger portion, and line a buttered pie-dish. Fill this with the prepared apples, and cover them with the remaining piece of paste, rolled out to the size of the dish.

Bake the pie in a fairly hot oven at first, then reduce the heat. It will take from three-quarters to an hour to cook.

Brush the top, when cooked, with slightly frothed egg-white, dredge it with castor sugar, and return the pie to the oven to brown a little. Serve the pie hot or cold.

Sufficient for six persons.

CHEESE PASTRIES

INGREDIENTS.—$\frac{1}{2}$ lb. of flaky pastry (see p. 252), $\frac{1}{2}$ gill of cream, 4 oz. of grated cheese, 1 hardboiled egg, cayenne, 1 egg (beaten).

METHOD.—Roll out the pastry and cut out six small rounds and twelve larger ones with fluted cutters dipped in hot water.

Place six large rounds on a baking-sheet and brush them with egg.

Sprinkle a teaspoonful of cheese on each round. Cover with a round of pastry the same size and brush it with egg.

With the small cutter, press the centre of each pastry, cutting about half-way through. The small pieces of pastry are used for lids. These also are brushed with egg and placed on the tin. Before baking leave the pastries for at least twenty minutes, to make them keep a good shape.

Bake for fifteen to twenty minutes in a hot oven. Chop the egg and beat the cream till it is thick. Mix cheese, cream, and egg, and season with cayenne. When the pastries are cold scoop out a little of the centre, fill them with the mixture and cover with the lids.

To make twelve cheese pastries.

CHERRY FLAN

INGREDIENTS.—1 lb. of cherries, 1 cup of loaf sugar, 1 gill of water, juice of ½ lemon, 6 oz. of short pastry (see p. 252), cochineal.

METHOD.—Line a small flan-ring with the pastry, and fill it with a smaller-sized tin.

Bake for about twenty minutes, and remove the tin.

Boil the sugar and water.

Pick and wash the cherries, and put them in the syrup with the lemon-juice.

Simmer *gently* for seven minutes.

Remove the cherries and stone them. Boil the syrup for ten minutes, colour it with cochineal, and put in the cherries.

Pour the cool fruit and syrup into the cold flan.

CHERRY TARTLETS

INGREDIENTS.—4 oz. of short pastry (see p. 252), 1 small tin of Cirio cherries, 1 lemon, 2 tablespoonfuls of sugar, a few pennyworths of double cream.

METHOD.—Roll out the pastry to the thickness of a quarter of an inch. Flour a plain cutter and cut out rounds.

Place in patty-pans and prick the bottom of the pastry to prevent it rising in the centre. Flake the edges,

and bake in the top of a hot oven for about twelve minutes.

While baking put the cherry syrup in a pan with the sugar and finely-grated lemon-rind, pour in the strained juice of the lemon, and boil for about ten or twelve minutes, or till there is a thick syrup.

Remove the tarts from the oven, and if they are slightly coloured underneath, they are done. Place them on a sieve to cool. When quite cold, place four or five cherries in each tart, and cover with half a tablespoonful of thick syrup.

Whip the cream and sweeten it to taste with a little castor sugar. Decorate round the edge of the tarts with the cream.

Sufficient for about six tartlets.

CHERRY AND LEMON TARTLETS

INGREDIENTS.—About ½ lb. of short pastry (see p. 252), ½ lemon (rind and juice), 1 yolk of egg, ¼ oz. of butter, 1 oz. of glacé cherries, 1 oz. of flour, 3 oz. of castor sugar, 1 gill of water.

METHOD.—Roll out the pastry thinly, cut it in rounds, and line twelve tartlet tins. Line these each with a round of buttered paper, and put a little rice in the bottom; then bake them in a hot oven. When cooked, remove the rice and paper, and leave the cases to cool.

Mix the flour and sugar together, stir in the water gradually, and mix all to a smooth paste; add also the finely-grated lemon-rind, the lemon-juice, and butter.

Turn the mixture into a saucepan, bring it to the boil, and let it boil gently for a few minutes, keeping it stirred; then draw the pan aside, stir in the cherries cut in small pieces, and the beaten egg-yolk.

Cook the mixture again for a minute or two, but do not let it boil. Cool it slightly, then heap it in the prepared pastry-cases and decorate each with a quarter of glacé cherry.

Sufficient for about twelve tartlets.

CHOCOLATE CREAM PIE

INGREDIENTS.—3 gills of milk, ¾ oz. of butter, 3 oz. of flour, 3½ dessert-spoonfuls of castor sugar, 2 oz. of chocolate, ½ level teaspoonful of powdered cinnamon, 3 yolks of eggs, 1 oz. of almonds, 10d. of cream, vanilla, some short pastry (see p. 252), glacé cherries, sugar to sweeten the cream.

METHOD.—Line a Pyrex pie-plate with a round of thinly-rolled short pastry, allowing sufficient for a double edge.

Turn this edge in towards the rim of the plate, and flute it with the thumb and finger, then line the pastry with a round of buttered paper and put a little rice in the bottom.

Place the pastry in a hot oven to bake, and when set remove the paper and rice, finish cooking, and then let it cool.

Grate the chocolate finely and dissolve it in a small quantity of the milk.

Put the flour, cinnamon, and sugar together and mix them to a smooth paste with the remainder of the milk.

Turn it into a saucepan, add the dissolved chocolate, and bring it to the boil, keeping it well stirred.

Boil it gently for a few minutes, then draw the pan aside, add the butter and cool the paste slightly ; then beat in the egg-yolks one at a time.

Cook the mixture again for a few minutes, but do not let it boil.

Stir in the blanched and chopped almonds, turn the mixture into the pastry-case, and leave it till cold.

Whisk the cream until thick, add sugar and vanilla to taste, and decorate the pie with this, forcing it through an icing pump.

Top the cream with glacé cherries. Sufficient for eight persons.

CHOCOLATE PIE

INGREDIENTS.—1 oz. of butter, 1½ oz. of flour, 1 oz. of cocoa, 4 oz. of Demerara sugar, 2 large eggs, ½ pint of milk, ¼ teaspoonful of cinnamon, 2 oz. of castor sugar, a baked pastry-case (as described in the previous recipe).

METHOD.—Melt the butter in a saucepan and stir in the flour, cinnamon, cocoa, and Demerara sugar. Mix well, and add the milk gradually.

Stir the mixture till it boils, and simmer for three minutes. Separate the eggs and pour the mixture on to the slightly-beaten yolks.

Spread the mixture in the pastry-case and cover with the stiffly-beaten whites mixed with the castor sugar.

Brown in the oven.

CHOCOLATE TARTLETS

INGREDIENTS.—About ½ lb. of flaky pastry (see p. 252), 2 teaspoonfuls of cocoa, 2½ oz. of castor sugar, 1 oz. of margarine, 3 oz. of ground almonds, vanilla flavouring, 1 egg, jam.

METHOD.—Roll out the pastry thinly, cut into rounds, and line some patty-tins. Put a little jam in the bottom of each. Beat the sugar and fat to a cream. Add the egg, stir it in quickly, and beat the mixture for a few minutes.

Mix the cocoa and ground almonds together, and stir in with a few drops of vanilla. Put a little of the mixture into each tin.

Place on a baking-sheet and bake in a hot oven for about fifteen minutes.

Leave on a sieve until cold, then dust with sieved castor sugar.

Sufficient to make about twelve or fifteen tartlets.

ICED CHOCOLATE TARTLETS

INGREDIENTS.—1 dessertspoonful of chocolate powder or cocoa, 1½ oz. of margarine or butter, 1 egg, 2 oz. of castor sugar, 1 oz. of ground rice, 1 oz. of flour, 1 oz. of almonds, vanilla flavouring, apricot jam, about ½ lb. of short or flaky pastry (see p. 252).

THE ICING.—5 oz. of icing-sugar, 1 tablespoonful of chocolate powder, ¼ gill of cold water, vanilla, a few almonds.

METHOD.—Roll the pastry out rather thinly. Cut it into rounds, and line some small fluted tartlet-tins.

TO MAKE THE FILLING.—Sieve together the flour, ground rice, and chocolate powder.

Blanch, skin, and chop the almonds.

Beat the sugar and fat to a cream.

Stir in the egg quickly, and beat for a few minutes.

Add the ground rice, flour, chocolate powder, and almonds, and a few drops of vanilla, and mix all together.

Put a little apricot jam in the bottom of each tartlet, then put in sufficient of the prepared mixture to three-parts fill the tins.

Place on a baking-sheet, and bake in a hot oven for about fifteen to twenty minutes, then put on to a sieve and leave until cold.

To MAKE THE ICING.—Rub the icing sugar through a sieve. Put the chocolate powder into a small pan, and mix to a smooth paste with the water.

Cook slowly for a few minutes, keeping it stirred.

Leave until quite cool, then add the icing sugar and a few drops of vanilla. Mix all to a smooth paste and beat for a few minutes.

Stir over a low burner until the base of the saucepan feels just warm. If necessary, a little more cold water may be added, but the icing should be sufficiently thick to coat the back of a spoon.

Pour a little of the icing on each tartlet, and let it run to the edge of the pastry. Have ready a few almonds (blanched and skinned), and place one or two small pieces on each.

COCONUT FLAKES

INGREDIENTS.—6 oz. of puff or flaky pastry (see p. 252), castor sugar, egg-white, desiccated coconut.

METHOD.—Roll out the pastry thinly and stamp it into rounds with a fluted cutter.

Place these on a baking-sheet and bake them in a quick oven till well risen and golden.

Then take them out and brush them with frothed egg-white.

Sprinkle them freely with castor sugar and desiccated coconut, and return them to a cool oven for a few minutes to set the meringue. This is a good way of using up scraps of left-over pastry.

Sufficient for eighteen little pastry cakes.

COCONUT PASTRIES

INGREDIENTS.—Flaky pastry (see p. 252), jam, desiccated coconut, white of egg, sugar (castor).

METHOD.—Roll out the pastry rather thinly and cut into small square-shaped pieces.

Turn them over on to the other side and spread with jam.

Use rather stiff jam, and do not spread it too near to the edges. Now sprinkle freely with desiccated coconut, and spread over a little more jam.

Damp round the outside edge of pastry and roll each up.

Press the ends together lightly.

Place the rolls on a baking-sheet and bake in a hot oven for about fifteen minutes.

Beat the white of an egg until slightly frothy, and brush the rolls over with it, then sprinkle with castor sugar and coconut.

Return to the oven for two or three minutes until lightly browned, then place on a sieve to cool.

NOTE.—This is an excellent method of using up trimmings of pastry left over from fruit pies, etc.

COCONUT TARTLETS

INGREDIENTS.—½ lb. of short pastry (see p. 252), 1 tablespoonful of jam, 3 oz. of stale cake, 2 tablespoonfuls of desiccated coconut, 3 oz. of sugar, 2 oz. of butter, 1 egg, juice of ½ a lemon.

METHOD.—Grease ten patty-pans. Roll out the pastry, cut it into rounds, line the tins, and put a small dab of jam in each.

To make the filling, cream the butter and sugar, beat in the egg, and add the coconut, crumbled cake, and lemon-juice. Beat till smooth and half-fill each tart.

Bake for twenty minutes.

This quantity will make ten or twelve small tartlets or eight large ones.

COFFEE AND FRUIT CHEESE-CAKES

INGREDIENTS.—1 egg, its weight in margarine and castor sugar, 1 oz. of sultanas, 1½ oz. of flour, 1 oz. of ground rice, coffee essence, short or flaky pastry (see p. 252), jam.

FOR THE BUTTER ICING.—2 oz. of butter, 4 oz. of icing sugar, coffee essence or vanilla, as desired.

METHOD.—Roll out the pastry and line some small cake-tins, either oblong or round. Put a little jam in the bottom.

Wash, pick over and dry the sultanas.

Beat the sugar and fat to a cream, add the egg, stir it in quickly and beat well, then stir in the flour and ground rice, sieved together, also the sultanas and a little coffee essence.

Turn the mixture into the prepared tins, filling them about two-thirds full. Put them into a hot oven to bake. They will take about fifteen minutes to cook.

When cold, decorate the cheesecakes with butter icing and a few sultanas, extra to those given in the recipe.

To make the icing, rub the sugar through a hair sieve, beat the butter to a cream with half the sugar, then add the remainder and beat it until creamy. Add flavouring as desired.

Sufficient for from twelve to fifteen cheesecakes.

COFFEE TARTLETS

INGREDIENTS.—About ½ lb. of short pastry (see p. 252), apricot jam, 1 oz. of shelled walnuts, 1 or 2 teaspoonfuls of coffee essence, 1 oz. of ground rice, 1 oz. of flour, 2 dessertspoonfuls of castor sugar, 1½ oz. of margarine, 1 egg-yolk, a little milk.

METHOD.—Roll out the pastry, cut it into rounds, and line twelve tartlet tins.

Chop up the walnuts (leaving out a few for the top of the tartlets) and mix them with some apricot jam, then put a little of the jam in the bottom of each tin.

Cream the fat and sugar. Add the yolk of egg, stirring it in quickly, and beat well. Add the ground rice and flour (sieved together), also enough coffee essence to flavour, and just a little milk if required.

Cover the jam in the tins with this mixture. Stick a piece of walnut on the top and put the tartlets into a fairly hot oven to bake.

They will take about twenty minutes.

Sufficient to make about twelve tartlets.

COMPOTE OF FRUIT PIE

INGREDIENTS.—½ lb. of flour, 5 oz. of margarine, 1 oz. of castor sugar, water

to mix, ½ lb. of red currants, ½ lb. of black currants, ½ lb. of raspberries, ¼ lb. of cherries, milk, about 4 table-spoonfuls of granulated sugar, ½ gill of water.

METHOD.—Prepare all the fruits and put them into a pie-dish, sprinkling each layer with sugar, but leaving the top layer free from sugar.

Then pour in the water.

A pie-funnel placed in the centre of the dish will help to keep the juice from boiling over, this should be put in the pie-dish before the fruit and sugar.

Sift the flour and rub in the fat, then add the castor sugar and mix a stiff paste with cold water.

Roll out the pastry, and cut an oval to fit the top of the dish, put this aside and cut a strip of pastry for the rim.

Damp the rim, line it with the pastry, then damp it again and cover the pie.

Trim and decorate the edge, brush it with milk and put it into a hot oven to bake.

It will take about half an hour.

NOTE.—The dish must be filled with fruit, otherwise the crust will sink.

Sufficient for six persons.

CREAM HORNS

To make the horns, you will require some small cone-shaped moulds which can be obtained from any large store. They cost from 1s. 6d. a dozen, and they are known as cornucopia moulds.

INGREDIENTS.—Puff pastry (see p. 252), jam, flavouring, cream, or other filling as suggested.

METHOD.—Roll out the pastry very thinly and cut it into long strips about three-quarters of an inch wide.

Take one strip for each mould and roll it round, beginning at the apex and letting each layer overlap the previous one until the whole is covered.

Trim off any pastry that remains, and damp the end to make it adhere. Then place the mould on a baking-sheet.

Cover the other moulds in the same way.

Leave them for twenty minutes to allow the pastry to settle.

To glaze the pastry, brush it with

lightly-beaten egg-white, or water, and dredge it with castor sugar. Or it may be just brushed with milk and not sugared. But in either case the pastry should be glazed just before it is baked.

Bake the puffs in a hot oven at first, then reduce the heat when they begin to brown. They will take about ten minutes.

After the puffs are baked, let them rest a minute ; then very carefully remove the moulds.

To fill the puffs put a spoonful of jam into each, then fill them up with whipped cream sweetened and flavoured to taste. Little or much cream can be used as preferred. Some people only fill the wide end.

If a less expensive filling is required, a whisked egg-white may be added to the whipped cream. But this should be done only just before the puffs are required.

Here are three alternative fillings for those who prefer a change.

JELLY AND CREAM FILLING

For this filling dissolve a packet of jelly in the usual way, and when it is set chop it up and mix it with a little lightly whipped cream.

MOCK CREAM AND COCONUT FILLING

INGREDIENTS.—2 level dessertspoon-fuls of desiccated coconut, 2 oz. of butter, 1¼ gills of milk, 1 oz. of castor sugar, 1 oz. of flour, flavouring essence.

METHOD.—Smooth the flour in a small quantity of the milk.

Heat the remainder of the milk with half the butter and add them to the flour mixture.

Return them to the pan and bring the mixture to the boil, keeping it well stirred.

Boil it gently for a few minutes, then take it off the heat and continue to stir until the mixture is almost cold.

Have the remainder of the butter ready beaten to a cream with the sugar, then beat them gradually into the flour mixture until it is creamy. Then add the coconut and flavouring to taste.

CUSTARD FILLING

INGREDIENTS.—¼ oz. of butter, ½ oz. of flour, 1 gill of milk, 1 or 2 yolks of egg, flavouring essence, 2 dessert-spoonfuls of castor sugar.

METHOD.—Mix the sugar and flour together and smooth them in a small quantity of the milk.

Heat the remainder of the milk in the top of a double boiler and add it to the sugar and flour. Return the mixture to the pan and bring it to the boil, keeping it well stirred.

Boil it gently for a few minutes, then draw it aside and cool it slightly.

Add the butter and beaten egg yolks and stand the pan in another pan of hot water.

Cook the custard for a few minutes, keeping it stirred, being careful not to let it curdle.

Take the custard off the heat and add the flavouring essence. When the filling is cold, it is ready for use.

A little chopped preserved ginger, or a little finely grated chocolate, may be added to give variety.

CREAM SLICES

INGREDIENTS.—½ lb. of flaky or puff pastry (see p. 252), 1 gill of cream, sugar to taste, a few crystallised cherries and leaves cut out of peel or angelica or a tablespoonful of chopped walnuts, 6 oz. of icing sugar, 1½ table-spoonfuls of water, essence of lemon.

METHOD.—Roll out the pastry into a large oblong piece the size of a Swiss-roll tin. Lay it on the tin and cut it into long strips three and a half inches wide, using a knife dipped in hot water.

Allow it to lie on the tin for twenty minutes before baking, so that the pastry may lose its elasticity and keep a good shape.

Bake in the top of a hot oven for about fifteen minutes. When cold, cut each strip into oblongs from one and a half to two inches wide.

Each slice consists of two of these oblongs placed on top of each other with a layer of jam and whipped cream on the lower one.

Ice the top only with a spoonful of water icing.

To make the icing rub the icing sugar through a hair sieve and put it in a small saucepan.

Mix with the water and a few drops of essence of lemon. Stir over the fire for about ten seconds or till it softens and dissolves. The icing must not be made hot.

Pour a spoonful over each slice and sprinkle the chopped nuts at each end.

This quantity makes about six or eight slices.

CUSTARD PIE

A CUSTARD PIE is not difficult to make, but it needs a little special care.

INGREDIENTS.—$\frac{1}{4}$ lb. of flour, 2 oz. of margarine, $\frac{1}{2}$ level teaspoonful of baking-powder, 1 oz. of castor sugar, egg to mix.

FOR THE CUSTARD.—$\frac{3}{4}$ pint of milk, 2 eggs, $1\frac{1}{2}$ dessertspoonfuls of castor sugar, a few drops of flavouring essence, grated nutmeg.

METHOD.—To prepare the pastry, sift the flour and baking-powder into a basin. Rub in the fat and mix in the sugar. Then beat up the egg and add sufficient of it to mix the dry ingredients to a stiff paste.

The left-over egg can be added to the custard to enrich it.

Roll out the pastry, cut a round and line the lightly buttered pie-tin with it. Then decorate the edge.

To MAKE THE CUSTARD.—Beat up the two eggs, adding to them any of the egg left over after mixing the pastry. Add the sugar and milk (cold) and stir till the sugar is dissolved, then add a few drops of flavouring essence.

Strain the mixture into the pastry-lined tin, grate a little nutmeg on the top of the custard mixture. Put it into a hot oven to bake at first, and when the pastry is set, reduce the heat and cook until the custard is set, being careful *not to let it boil*.

It will take from thirty to forty-five minutes to bake.

Let the custard pie get cold before taking it out of the tin.

NOTE.—A pie-tin is a round tin with sloping sides. It is better to use one of these, if possible, when making a custard pie, as it will be more easily turned out than if made in a tin with straight sides.

If liked the custard may be baked in small tartlet tins lined with pastry.

SMALL CUSTARD TARTS

INGREDIENTS.—$\frac{1}{2}$ lb. of short pastry (see p. 252), 1 small tablespoonful of custard-powder, $1\frac{1}{2}$ cups of milk, grated peel of $\frac{1}{2}$ lemon, a little jam, 1 tablespoonful of grated chocolate.

METHOD.—Line some deep patty-pans with rounds of short pastry, about a quarter of an inch thick.

Boil a cupful of milk with the grated lemon-peel and mix the rest of the milk very smoothly with the custard-powder.

Pour the boiling milk on to the mixed custard-powder and stir well.

Return to the saucepan and stir till it boils.

Sweeten to taste, and use when cold.

If the patty-pans are very deep it is better to put a piece of paper, filled with rice, in each before baking.

If they are not deep it is enough to prick the bottom of the tarts.

Fill the tarts when cold and sprinkle with grated chocolate.

A teaspoonful of jam may be placed at the bottom of each tart.

Sufficient for about eight tarts.

DAMSON VOL-AU-VENT

INGREDIENTS.—$\frac{1}{2}$ lb. of flour, $\frac{1}{2}$ lb. of butter, pinch of salt, water to mix, 1 lb. of damsons, 3 dessertspoonfuls of Demerara sugar, $\frac{3}{4}$ gill of water, 1 gill of cream, vanilla flavouring, castor sugar.

METHOD.—Put the Demerara sugar and water in a saucepan to boil for about five minutes, until a thick syrup is formed.

Wash the damsons, and add to the syrup, and cook very gently until tender, being very careful to keep them quite whole. Then leave until cold.

If the butter is very moist, put it into a cloth and squeeze out the water, then put it in a cool place.

Put the flour and salt through a wire sieve, make a well in the centre of the flour, and add sufficient water to make a stiff paste. It should be pliable but not sticky.

Slightly flour the pastry-board and lightly knead the paste for a few minutes to make it smooth.

Roll it out to an oblong shape, about half an inch in thickness.

Take the butter and press it with the floured rolling-pin until it is almost the same width as the rolled-out pastry, and nearly one half of the length.

Turn the pastry over, so that the floured side is uppermost, place the butter on one half and fold the other half of the pastry over it and press the edges together to keep the butter in.

Flour the board and pin, and roll out again to an oblong shape ; turn the pastry over, and fold into three again.

This must be repeated six times altogether. If the butter comes through slightly just lightly dust with flour. If it becomes very sticky, place the pastry in a cool place for about twenty minutes between each rolling.

After the sixth time roll the pastry to a round shape, about one inch in thickness.

Cut out a round as evenly as possible with a saucepan lid or plate, place on a baking-sheet, then make a smaller round, about one inch and a half from the edge.

Cut this not quite half-way through, then it can be taken out when the pastry is cooked. Brush the outer circle with milk.

Place the pastry in a very hot oven and bake until a light brown.

It should rise considerably.

When cooked place on a sieve to cool—away from a draught.

Take out the inner circle of pastry, and when the case is cold fill it with the damsons, leaving out a few for decoration, and pour over some of the syrup.

Place on a lace paper on a plate.

Mix a few drops of vanilla and a sprinkling of castor sugar with the cream and whisk until it thickens.

Shake on to the fruit, and garnish with one or two damsons.

NOTE.—If liked, a teaspoonful of lemon-juice can be added to the flour when it is mixed with water ; this counteracts the richness of the pastry.

DATE PATTIES

INGREDIENTS.—About 1 lb. of puff pastry (when mixed) (see p. 252), 3 oz. of dates, 1 tablespoonful of desiccated coconut, 1 dessertspoonful of sugar, about a tablespoonful of water.

METHOD.—Roll out the pastry to about three-eighths of an inch thick, and with a fancy cutter cut it into rounds about two inches in diameter. Mark out a small round in the centre of each, but only cut half through the pastry.

Stand the patties on a baking-sheet and put them in a very hot oven to bake.

When cooked, remove the centre pieces of pastry and return the pastry-cases to the oven for a minute. Leave them on a sieve until cold.

Meanwhile, stone the dates and put them through the mincer. Turn them into a saucepan with the water and sugar, and bring them to the boil. Add the coconut and mix all together.

Leave the mixture until cold, then fill the patty-cases and sprinkle some coconut on the top.

Sufficient for from eight to ten patties.

DATE TRIANGLES

INGREDIENTS.—6 oz. of short pastry (see p. 252), 3 oz. of dates (when stoned), 1 oz. of shelled walnuts, lemon cheese, water, castor sugar.

METHOD.—Stone the dates and weigh them after they are stoned, then put them through the mincer with the walnuts.

Roll out the pastry to an oblong shape, turn it on to the other side and spread it sparingly with lemon cheese.

On half of this put the dates and walnuts, fold the other half over, and press it lightly, then cut it into triangular shapes.

Brush them with water and dredge them with castor sugar.

Place them on a baking-sheet and put them into a hot oven to bake. They will take from ten to fifteen minutes.

This quantity makes about twelve triangles.

EGG PIE

INGREDIENTS.—About $\frac{3}{4}$ lb. of flaky pastry—when mixed (see p. 252), 3 eggs, 1 oz. of cheese, salt and pepper.

METHOD.—Roll out the pastry and cut a fairly thick round large enough to fit the top of a small sandwich-tin.

Roll the remainder of the pastry rather thinner. Cut a larger round and line the tin. Grate the cheese finely. Break the eggs each into a cup, then pour them whole into the pastry-lined tin. Sprinkle them with the cheese, and season with pepper and salt.

Damp the edge of the pastry and cover it with the thicker round, pressing the edges well together.

Brush the top with milk or egg to glaze the pastry and put the pie into a hot oven to bake. It will take about twenty minutes to cook. Serve cold.

NOTE.—If liked, some powdered, hard-boiled egg-yolk can be sprinkled over it afterwards.

Sufficient for four persons.

TO MAKE FLANS

FLAN-RINGS (either fluted or plain) are sold in small, medium, and large sizes. They are useful because with them it is possible to make high-class looking flans with perfectly straight sides and a fancy edge.

Plain flans can, however, be made with an ordinary sandwich-tin.

HOW TO USE A FLAN-RING.—Place the ring on a greased baking-sheet and lay in it a round of pastry that has been rolled slightly larger than the ring. The pastry should be one-third of an inch thick. Six ounces of pastry will make the smallest sized flan. With the hand, press the pastry flat against the tin and round the sides, making it fit the ring neatly and smoothly. Notch the top edge very slightly with a knife when using a plain ring.

The best way to keep the flan a good shape and prevent the bottom rising is to stand a smaller tin inside filled with rice. Another way is to fill it with flour or uncooked rice placed on grease-proof paper.

Bake in a moderately hot oven for twenty minutes, remove the tin, or paper of flour, and bake for ten minutes more, to cook the pastry that was covered with the flour.

MAKING FLANS WITHOUT A FLAN-RING.—An easy way to make a flan is to place a sandwich-tin upside down on a baking-sheet, grease the outside, and cover it neatly with a round of pastry, pressing it firmly on the bottom and against the sides. Use about half a pound of short pastry and have it fairly thick.

Prick it all over with a fork to keep it flat, and bake it in a moderately hot oven for twenty minutes.

To prevent it breaking let it cool for about ten minutes, then lift the pastry case off the tin and turn it upside down.

Quite a good flan can be made in this way, the only drawback is that the edges cannot be ornamented.

Flans are generally served cold when the empty case is filled with stewed or tinned fruit and a thick syrup.

In order to save labour and gas it is a good plan to bake several flan-cases at the same time, and keep in a tin lined with grease-proof paper any that are not wanted at once. They keep well if the tin is airtight and will then be ready for any emergency when they can be filled as desired with fruit and syrup or jelly.

Sometimes flans are spoiled through the fruit syrup sinking into the pastry. To prevent this it is best, after removing the inner tin, to brush the inside of the flan-case over with a lightly beaten white of egg before returning it to the oven to finish baking.

This makes a smooth crisp surface and prevents the pastry becoming sodden.

THE FILLING.—The fruit must be well drained from the syrup before it is put into the case. Remember, also, that the fruit must be whole, or the appearance of the flan will be spoiled.

(In the case of strawberries or raspberries the fruit should be stood in a pan at the back of the range with a little castor sugar sprinkled over it, The warmth of the stove will draw out the juice and form a syrup.)

Arrange the fruit tastefully in the case, then boil up the syrup with extra sugar added until it will form a jelly when cold. When the jelly is on the point of setting, pour some over the fruit. Another method of thickening the syrup is to dissolve part of a table jelly in it, and leave it until it is beginning to set before pouring it into the flan-case. It is possible, also, to use the syrupy part of jam, melted down.

A FLAN OF FIGS

INGREDIENTS.—About ½ lb. of short pastry (when mixed) (see p. 252), ½ lb. of stewing figs, 1 tablespoonful of sugar, ¼ pint of packet lemon jelly, 1 dessertspoonful of sherry.

METHOD.—Wash the figs, cover them with cold water and soak them overnight.

Next day, cut off the stalks, and stew the figs in the water in which they have soaked, adding the sugar to sweeten them.

When tender, strain off all the syrup and dissolve the jelly in rather less than a gill of it, then stir in the sherry.

Roll out the short pastry, and cut out a round. Place the flan-ring on a baking-sheet, put the pastry inside it and line the ring and the part of the baking-sheet that is encircled.

Trim the edge neatly, then line the pastry with a round of buttered paper and put some uncooked rice in the bottom. This will prevent the pastry from rising up in the centre, and will also help it to keep its shape.

Put the pastry into a hot oven to bake. It will take about twenty minutes. When nearly cooked, remove the paper and rice and finish cooking without it, and then lift up the flan-ring and cool the case on a sieve.

Drain the figs well and arrange them in the flan as evenly as possible—perhaps it will not take quite all of them—and when the jelly is beginning to set, pour it over the figs.

When quite set the flan is ready for use.

NOTE.—If a flan-ring is not available a sandwich-tin can be used.

Sufficient for four or five persons.

HOT FRUIT FLAN

INGREDIENTS.—FOR THE PASTRY : ¼ lb. of flour, pinch of salt, 2½ oz. of butter or margarine, 1 oz. of castor sugar, 1 yolk of egg, water to mix.

FOR THE FILLING.—½ lb. of red currants, 3 oz. of sugar, 1 whole yolk and an extra white, 1½ oz. of butter, 1½ oz. of flour, 1 oz. of ground almonds, shredded almonds for the top.

METHOD.—String and wash the currants, and cook them gently with two ounces of the sugar until tender. Leave them to get cold.

To make the crust, sift the flour with a pinch of salt, rub in the fat and add the sugar. Stir in the egg yolk beaten up with barely a dessertspoonful of water and mix all to a stiff paste, adding more water if required.

Butter a flan-ring and place it on a buttered baking-sheet, then line it with rolled-out pastry.

To MAKE THE FILLING.—Melt the butter in a saucepan, add the flour, and when well blended, stir in the prepared fruit, ground almonds, and remainder of the sugar, also one beaten yolk of egg.

Mix them well, then fold in the stiffly-whisked egg-whites.

Turn the mixture into the prepared pastry, sprinkle shredded almonds on top and put the flan in a hot oven to bake.

Serve it at once with cream.

If liked, the egg-yolk may be omitted from the pastry, and an extra one added to the filling.

Sufficient for from four to six persons.

FRENCH FRUIT TART

INGREDIENTS.—FOR THE PASTRY : 8 oz. of flour, 2 oz. of margarine, 4 oz. of lard, water to mix.

FOR THE FILLING.—1 lb. of apples, 2 oz. of Demerara sugar, 2 tablespoonfuls of water, 1 egg, large pinch powdered cinnamon.

METHOD.—Peel the apples, core and cut into quarters and into slices. Add them to a mixture of the sugar and two tablespoonfuls of water in a saucepan, and cook until they are quite soft.

Take care they do not burn, as they are rather liable to with only a small quantity of water. When cooked mash them to a pulp.

If preferred they can be rubbed through a sieve.

Separate the yolk from the white of egg, beat the yolk into the apple pulp, adding the cinnamon.

This mixture should be quite thick, like jam. Make some flaky pastry as explained on p. 252.

Roll it out to nearly a quarter of an inch in thickness, cut out a large round to fit the top of a jam-sandwich tin.

Put this on one side, and press the remaining pieces together, and roll out thinly. Cut out a round sufficiently large to line the tin.

When lined, fill it with the apple mixture.

Damp the edge of the pastry, and fix on the top round. Make two sharp cuts in the form of a cross on the top of the tart, so that when cooked some of the filling will be seen.

Place in a hot oven, and bake until light brown : it will take about twenty minutes.

While it is cooking, whisk the white of egg to a froth.

Take the tart from the oven, brush it over with the frothed white, and sprinkle well with castor sugar.

Put it back into the oven for a few minutes just to lightly brown the top.

Serve the tart either hot or cold.

Sufficient to serve about six persons.

FRUIT PIE

INGREDIENTS.—7 oz. of flour, 4 oz. of margarine, 1 flat teaspoonful baking-powder, fruit (just over a pound). sugar to taste, water.

METHOD.—Prepare the fruit and put it into a pie-dish with a little water and sugar to taste.

The sugar should be added when the dish is only about half full, so that it does not touch the crust. A pie funnel or upturned egg-cup placed in the centre will help to keep the juice in the pie.

Sieve the flour with the baking-powder.

Rub in the fat, then add sufficient water to mix it to a stiff paste.

Roll it out and cover the pie as explained above.

Brush the pie with milk and place in a hot oven to bake.

NOTE.—Remember to make a small outlet for the steam.

FRUIT SALAD PIES

INGREDIENTS.—1 large tin of fruit salad, 2 apples, 2 oranges, ½ lb. of flour, ¼ lb. of butter or margarine, 2 oz. of castor sugar, 1 egg, water, a pinch of salt, 1 level teaspoonful of baking-powder.

METHOD.—Turn out the fruit salad and drain off the syrup.

Peel and quarter the apples, remove the cores, and cut the fruit in slices.

Peel and slice or quarter the oranges and remove the pips.

Cut the fruit salad into convenient sized pieces and mix them with the raw fruit. Fill three small pie-dishes, then pour about a spoonful of syrup into each.

Sift the flour with the salt and baking-powder, rub in the fat and add the sugar. Break up the yolk of egg and mix it with a little water and add it to the flour. Mix all to a stiff paste, adding more water as required.

Divide the paste into three portions and roll out each until a little larger than the top of the pie-dish. Cut off a piece from the edge and place it on the rim of the dish, which should have been damped, then damp the pastry rim and cover the pie.

Trim and decorate the edge, brush the top with white of egg, broken up but not frothed, and dredge it with castor sugar.

Put the pies in a hot oven to bake.

They will take about fifteen minutes to cook.

Serve them cold with cream.

Sufficient to make three small pies.

FRUIT TARTLETS

INGREDIENTS.—About ½ lb. of short pastry (see p. 252), some stewed fruit, as required, chopped almonds.

METHOD.—Such fruit as black currants, red currants, gooseberries, cherries, or loganberries can be used.

Drain the syrup from the fruit.

You will need a good half a pint of cooked fruit, without syrup, for about one dozen small tartlets, and the fruit should be cooked carefully so as to keep it whole.

Put the syrup into a saucepan with a little more sugar, adding about one and a half or two dessertspoonfuls to one gill of syrup.

Let this dissolve, then boil it until it will jelly when cold. A little colouring may be added if necessary.

Roll out the pastry, cut it into rounds and line some small cake tins.

Line these each with a round of buttered paper and put a little rice in the bottom before baking the pastry in a hot oven.

When the pastry is set, remove the paper and rice, and finish cooking the cases. Let them cool.

Heap the fruit in the prepared cases and when the syrup is almost a jelly, pour a little into each.

Sprinkle the tops with chopped almonds or small pieces of angelica, and put a dab of whipped cream, sweetened and flavoured to taste.

GINGER CHEESECAKES

INGREDIENTS.—About $\frac{1}{2}$ to $\frac{3}{4}$ lb. of flaky pastry (see p. 252), 1 oz. glacé ginger, 1 egg and its weight in flour, margarine and castor sugar, $\frac{1}{4}$ flat teaspoonful ground ginger, marmalade.

METHOD.—Roll out the pastry fairly thinly. Cut it into rounds and line about sixteen or eighteen greased patty-pans.

Put just a little marmalade in the bottom of each patty-pan.

Beat the sugar and fat to a cream. Add the egg, stir it in quickly and beat well together.

Stir in the flour and ground ginger, sieved together, also the glacé ginger, minced finely.

Mix all the ingredients lightly. Put about a teaspoonful of the mixture into each patty-pan.

Stand the cakes on a baking-sheet and put them into a hot oven to bake.

They will take about fifteen to twenty minutes to cook. Cool them on a sieve and dredge finally with castor sugar.

Sufficient for sixteen or eighteen cheesecakes.

GOOSEBERRY FLAN

INGREDIENTS.—$1\frac{1}{2}$ pints of gooseberries, 1 cupful of loaf sugar, $1\frac{1}{2}$ gills of water, rind of $\frac{1}{2}$ a lemon, $\frac{1}{2}$ lb. of short pastry (see p. 252), cream for decoration.

METHOD.—Place a flan-ring on a baking-sheet and line it with pastry.

Fill it with a smaller tin, and bake for twenty minutes.

Remove the tin.

Top and tail the gooseberries, and stew them gently in the water

with the sugar and lemon-rind, without breaking the skins.

Put the gooseberries in a basin.

Boil the syrup for ten minutes.

Put the fruit in the syrup, and when cool arrange it in the flan-case.

Decorate with cream.

GINGER PIE

INGREDIENTS.—$\frac{3}{4}$ pint pot of preserved ginger, 1 oz. of butter, $2\frac{1}{2}$ oz. of cornflour, 2 yolks and 3 whites of eggs, 2 oz. of castor sugar, 3 tablespoonfuls of icing sugar, $\frac{1}{2}$ lb. of short pastry (see p. 252), water.

METHOD.—Roll out the pastry *thinly* and line a shallow round fireproof-dish with it.

Cut the round of pastry a little larger than the dish, then fold under the piece that is over and flute the edge. This will make a thicker edge. Prick the pastry in the bottom of the dish and put it into a very hot oven to bake. It will take about fifteen minutes to cook. Leave it until cold.

Take the ginger and put it through the mincer. Mix it with the syrup and make it up to three and a half gills with water—used for rinsing out the jar.

Mix the cornflour to a smooth paste with another half gill of water. Heat the ginger and syrup and stir it on to the cornflour. Return the mixture to the pan and bring it to the boil. Boil gently for a few minutes, keeping it stirred. Then draw it aside, add the butter and castor sugar and cool slightly.

Beat up the egg-yolks and stir them in, and cook the mixture over a low gas *again* for a few minutes, but do not let it boil. When cool, turn the filling into the pastry.

Rub the icing sugar through a hair sieve. Whisk the egg-whites to a stiff froth and fold in the icing sugar.

Heap the meringue on top of the pie and put it into a cool oven until set and lightly tipped to a golden brown.

Sufficient for six or eight persons.

GROUND RICE CHEESECAKES

INGREDIENTS.—Short or flaky pastry (see p. 252), 2 oz. of castor sugar,

1½ oz. of ground rice, ½ oz. of flour, 2 oz. of margarine, vanilla flavouring, jam, 1 egg.

METHOD.—Roll out the pastry thinly. Either stamp it into rounds and line small round tart-tins, or else cut shapes and line boat-shaped tins.

Beat the sugar and fat to a cream.

Add the egg, stirring it in quickly and beating well. Stir in the flour and ground rice, which should have been sifted, and mix all lightly together, adding a few drops of vanilla to flavour.

Put a little jam in the bottom of each pastry-lined tin, cover this with the prepared ground rice mixture, but do not fill the tins more than half or two-thirds full.

Bake the cheesecakes in a quick oven. They will take about fifteen minutes.

GINGER LAYER TART

INGREDIENTS.—About ½ to ¾ of lb. of flaky pastry (see p. 252), 6 oz. of icing sugar, 3 oz. of butter, 2 oz. of glacé or crystallised ginger.

METHOD.—Divide the pastry into three portions and roll each piece out fairly thinly to a round shape.

Cut three rounds all the same size—about six or seven inches in diameter, according to the size of the bottom of the sandwich-tin to be used.

Place one round in the bottom of the tin, then the other two very lightly on top of it. Stand the tin on a baking-sheet and put it into a *hot* oven to bake it. It will take about fifteen to twenty minutes to cook. The centre layer may require a little longer cooking ; if so, carefully remove the top round with a slice, lift the centre one on to the baking-sheet and put it back in the oven for a few minutes.

When cooked and cold, spread each layer with the filling. Put them together and sprinkle the top with icing sugar.

THE GINGER FILLING.

To make the filling, rub the sugar through a hair sieve. Put the ginger through the mincer.

Beat the butter and sugar to a cream, and stir in the ginger.

Sufficient for five or six persons.

HAM PATTIES

INGREDIENTS.—6 patty cases (see p. 253), 2 oz. of mushrooms, 3 oz. of ham, 1½ gills of milk, ¾ oz. of flour, 1 egg-yolk, ¾ oz. of butter or margarine, salt and pepper.

METHOD.—You can make the patty-cases at home or buy them ready prepared, whichever you prefer.

Peel and stalk the mushrooms and wash them in cold water with a little salt added, then drain, chop them and fry them in butter—extra to that given in the ingredients.

Put the ham through the mincer.

Melt the three-quarters of an ounce of butter in a saucepan, add the flour and when nicely blended add the milk and stir until the sauce boils.

Let it cook gently for a few minutes, then draw the pan aside, and add the ham, mushrooms, and egg-yolk.

Season the mixture and make it hot, but do not let it boil.

Heap it in the patty-cases, which should be hot, and top each with the small round of pastry cut from the centre of the cases.

Sufficient for six cases.

HONEY TART

INGREDIENTS.—¼ lb. of flour, 1½ oz. of lard, pinch of salt, 3 tablespoonfuls of honey, 3 or 4 tablespoonfuls of breadcrumbs, 1½ oz. of margarine, water to mix, 1 lemon.

METHOD.—Sieve the flour and salt.

Rub in the margarine.

Add a little cold water and mix to a stiff paste.

Well flour the board and rolling-pin, and press out the lard into thin pieces.

Roll the pastry to an oblong shape, about one-eighth of an inch thick, turn it over on to the other side, and place the lard over it evenly.

Fold into three, press the edges well together, and roll out the pastry.

Cut out a round and line a sandwich-tin with it, trim and decorate the top edge.

Warm the honey in a saucepan, add the breadcrumbs, and mix together.

Remove from the fire, add the grated

lemon-rind and just a squeeze of lemon-juice.

When well mixed let it cool, then put into the prepared tin and spread over evenly.

Use up the trimmings of pastry by putting strips across the tart.

Bake in a hot oven for about fifteen to twenty minutes.

Sufficient for four persons.

ICED APPLE FLAN

INGREDIENTS.—9 oz. of flour, pinch of salt, 1 level teaspoonful of baking-powder, ¾ level teaspoonful of powdered cinnamon, 3 dessert-spoonfuls of castor sugar, 1 egg-yolk, 6 oz. of margarine, milk and water to mix, 1 lb. of apples, 2 to 3 dessert-spoonfuls of granulated sugar, ½ lb. of icing sugar, water, colouring and flavouring to taste, crystallised rose leaves.

METHOD.—Sift the flour with the salt, baking-powder, and cinnamon, rub in the margarine, and add the castor sugar. Mix them to a stiff paste with egg-yolk mixed with some milk and water.

Butter a flan-ring and place it on a buttered baking-sheet.

Roll out rather more than half the paste to a round shape, put it inside the ring and line it, then fill it up with the apples, peeled, quartered, and sliced, and mixed with the granulated sugar.

Roll out the remainder of the pastry, cut out a round and cover the flan so that the top exactly fits on to the lining.

Put the flan in a hot oven to bake. It will take about half an hour to cook. When cool, lift up the flan-ring and ice the top of the crust with soft icing, then decorate it with crystallised rose leaves.

To MAKE THE ICING.—Sift the icing sugar and mix it to a smooth paste with warm water, adding a few drops of colouring and flavouring to taste.

Sufficient for five persons.

NOTE.—This flan can be made in a sandwich-tin.

ICED CHOCOLATE TART

INGREDIENTS.—About 6 or 8 oz. of short or flaky pastry (see p. 252), 1 dessertspoonful of cocoa, 1½ oz. of margarine, 1¼ oz. of castor sugar, 2 sponge cakes (stale), 1 egg, almond flavouring, jam.

FOR THE WHITE ICING.—¼ lb. of icing sugar, about 1 tablespoonful of cold water, almond flavouring, glacé cherry and angelica (for decoration).

METHOD.—Roll out the pastry rather thinly, cut out a round, and line a sandwich-tin.

Trim and decorate the edge neatly.

Cream the fat and sugar.

Rub the sponge cakes through a wire sieve and mix with the cocoa.

Separate the egg, then whisk the white to a very stiff froth. Add the yolk of egg to the creamed fat and sugar, stir it in quickly and beat well, then add the sponge-cake crumbs and cocoa and a few drops of flavouring.

Lastly, add the white of egg and fold it in lightly.

Spread a thin layer of jam in the bottom of the prepared tin and cover with the above mixture.

Place in a hot oven and bake for about fifteen to twenty minutes.

When cold, ice the top with white icing, stick a cherry in the centre with stalks of angelica round it.

To MAKE THE ICING.—Roll the lumps out of the sugar, then rub it through a fine sieve.

Put it into a saucepan, and mix to a smooth paste with the water.

Add flavouring to taste.

Stand it over a very low burner, and stir until the bottom of the pan feels just warm.

Sufficient to cut into eight portions.

JAM PUFFS

ODD trimmings of puff pastry can be utilised for making jam puffs.

Roll it out quite thinly and stamp it into rounds five inches in diameter.

Turn them on to the other side. Put a spoonful of jam in the centre of each, and damp round the edge with water.

Take the sides and draw them to the centre, pinching the edges together securely and forming a three-cornered shape. Then turn them over.

Brush the puffs with water. Dredge them thickly with castor sugar, and put them in a hot oven to bake.

JAM TURNOVERS

INGREDIENTS.—3 oz. of lard, water to mix (about ½ gill), 6 oz. of flour, pinch of salt, 3 oz. of margarine, jam.

METHOD.—Sieve the flour (to which has been added a pinch of salt). Rub the margarine in until like fine bread-crumbs. Add cold water and mix to a stiff paste.

Roll out the pastry to an oblong shape. Turn it over on to the other side.

Divide the lard into three equal portions. Take one portion and spread it over the surface of the pastry in small dabs.

Fold into three and roll out again. Turn it over, and spread on it another portion of lard.

Fold into three and repeat the rolling. Repeat the process and the last time roll out the pastry rather thinly. Cut into rounds.

Turn on to the other side, place a teaspoonful of jam on one half. Damp round the edge of the pastry, then fold over the other half.

Press the edges together. Brush over with milk.

Bake in a hot oven for about fifteen minutes.

JELLY PIE

INGREDIENTS.—About ¾ lb. of short pastry (see p. 252) (when mixed), 1½ pint packet of cherry jelly, rather less than 1½ pints of hot water, cream, sugar, vanilla.

METHOD.—Roll out the pastry and cover an inverted (buttered) pie-tin. Stand it on a baking-sheet, prick the pastry with a fork, and put it into a hot oven to bake.

When the pastry is nearly cooked, remove the tin very carefully and finish cooking the pastry-case on the baking-sheet, placing it the right way up.

Dissolve the jelly in the hot water and leave it until it begins to set. Then turn it into the pastry-case, which should be quite cold.

Leave the jelly until firmly set, then decorate it with whipped cream, sweetened and flavoured.

The cream can be either heaped up roughly in the centre, or put through an icing-bag and used for decoration according to taste.

Sufficient for from six to eight persons.

NOTE.—When lining an inverted tin, the pastry must not overlap the edge of the tin or the case will break when the tin is removed.

LEMON MERINGUE PIE

INGREDIENTS.—FOR THE PASTRY: 7 oz. of flour, pinch of salt, 4 oz. of margarine or butter, water to mix.

FOR THE FILLING.—1½ lemons, 9 oz. of castor sugar, 3 oz. of flour, ¾ pint of water, 1 oz. of butter, 3 egg-yolks.

FOR THE MERINGUE.—3 egg-whites, 3 tablespoonfuls of castor sugar, pinch of salt.

METHOD.—To Make the Pastry: Sift the flour with a pinch of salt, rub in the fat, and then mix to a stiff paste with cold water. Roll out the pastry *thinly*, then put the pie-plate in the centre and cut out a round, allowing sufficient for a double rim. (This makes a thicker edge.)

Line the plate with pastry, then fold the edge in towards the rim and flute it with your finger and thumb. Prick the pastry and line it with a round of buttered paper, sprinkle with rice (uncooked), and put it into a hot oven to bake. When the pastry is set remove the paper and rice very carefully and finish cooking the pastry. It will take from fifteen to twenty minutes to cook, and should then be allowed to cool.

To MAKE THE FILLING.—Grate the rinds of the lemons finely and squeeze out the juice.

Mix the nine ounces of castor sugar with the flour, add the water gradually, and mix the ingredients to a smooth paste ; then turn it into a saucepan with the rind and juice of the lemons. Stir it until it boils and thickens, and let it boil gently for a few minutes. Then draw the pan aside, add the butter to the mixture and cool it very slightly.

Beat up the yolks of the eggs and stir them in gradually. Cook the mixture again for a few minutes, but do not let it boil. Let it cool, and then turn it into the prepared pastry-lined plate and leave it until cold.

To MAKE THE MERINGUE.—Add a pinch of salt to the whites of eggs and whisk them to a stiff froth, then lightly fold in the three tablespoonfuls of castor sugar. Heap the meringue on top of the filling, dredge with castor sugar, and put the pie into quite a cool oven to set the meringue. Serve cold.

If more meringue is preferred, four whites of eggs and four tablespoonfuls of castor sugar may be used. If a still more sugary meringue is liked, *whisk* the castor sugar gradually into the whisked whites of eggs (instead of folding it in), and continue to whisk until the mixture is quite stiff. This kind of meringue can be forced through an icing-pump.

A soft, fluffy meringue can be made by folding in sieved *icing* sugar instead. Whipped cream can be used in place of the meringue. The cream should be whisked until it hangs from the whisk, then sprinkled with sugar and flavoured to taste.

Pineapple Filling

INGREDIENTS.—1 tin of grated pineapple, 2 oz. of cornflour, 1 gill of water, 1 oz. of butter, 2 or 3 egg-yolks, 1 tablespoonful of castor sugar.

METHOD.—Mix the cornflour to a smooth paste with the water. Turn the contents of the tin of pineapple into a saucepan, stir in the cornflour, and bring the mixture to the boil.

Boil the mixture gently for a few minutes, keeping it well stirred ; then draw it aside, add the butter and sugar, cool it a little, then stir in the beaten yolks of eggs. Cook it again for a few minutes, but do not let it boil, then leave the filling to cool before turning it into the pastry.

LEMON PIE

INGREDIENTS.—Rind and juice of 2 lemons, 1½ tablespoonfuls of cornflour, 1¼ cupfuls of boiling water, 1 cupful of sugar, 1 oz. of butter, 2 eggs, a ready-baked flan-case (see p. 268), 2 oz. of castor sugar (for the meringue).

METHOD.—Boil the water with the sugar, butter, lemon-rind and juice.

Mix the cornflour smoothly with a little cold water and pour on the boiling water, stirring well.

Boil for ten minutes.

Let it cool, separate the eggs, stir in the yolks, and pour the mixture into the pastry-case.

Beat the whites stiffly and add the castor sugar.

Heap the whites on top, dredge with sugar, and brown in the oven.

LEMON NUT PIE

INGREDIENTS.—Rind and juice of 1½ lemons, 9 oz. of castor sugar, 3 oz. of flour, 1 oz. of butter, 3 eggs, 1½ oz. of almonds, 3 gills of water, about ½ to ¾ lb. of short pastry (see p. 252), angelica, 3 tablespoonfuls of icing sugar.

METHOD.—Roll out the pastry very thinly, cut a round, and line a Pyrex tart-plate.

The round should be cut rather larger than the plate so as to allow the edge to be turned in ; this makes it thicker.

Flute the edge with finger and thumb, line the pastry with a round of buttered paper and put some rice in the bottom.

Bake this in a hot oven for about fifteen to twenty minutes, removing the paper and rice just before the pastry is quite cooked.

TO MAKE THE FILLING.—Mix the flour with the castor sugar, stir in the water gradually, and mix them together until smooth. Turn the filling into a saucepan, and add the finely grated lemon-rind and juice. Bring it to the boil and boil it for a few minutes, keeping it stirred. Let it cool very slightly, then add the beaten egg-yolks and butter, also the almonds (blanched and chopped roughly). Cook the filling again for a minute or two, but do not let it boil, cool, then turn into the prepared pastry.

Whisk the whites of the eggs to a stiff froth, then gradually whisk in the icing sugar (previously sieved), cover the pie roughly with this, and put it in a cool oven to set and brown lightly.

Serve lemon pie cold, decorated with rings of angelica.

Sufficient for from six to eight portions.

LOGANBERRY PIE

INGREDIENTS.—2 tins of loganberries, about ½ lb. of short or flaky pastry (see p. 252).

METHOD.—Strain the syrup from

two tins of loganberries. Take a small pie-dish, put an egg-cup turned upside down in the centre, and then fill up the dish with loganberries. Add about two tablespoonfuls of the syrup.

Roll out the pastry, cut out a piece to fit the top of the dish, then cut a narrow strip off the edge.

Damp the pie-dish edge and cover with a strip of pastry then damp this and fix on the top. Trim and decorate the edge, brush the pastry with milk, and bake in a hot oven for about fifteen or twenty minutes.

Dredge with castor sugar and serve.

A delicious jelly can be made with juice left over from the loganberries used in place of water, and an ordinary packet jelly.

Sufficient for about five or six persons.

LOBSTER PATTIES

INGREDIENTS.—1 tin of lobster, 1 oz. of butter, ¾ oz. of flour, ½ pint of milk, salt and pepper, 2 oz. of mushrooms, patty - cases (see p. 253), butter for frying.

METHOD.—Make a sauce with the flour, butter, and milk. Season it well and boil it for a few minutes. Then add lobster cut in dice, also the mushrooms, previously peeled and cleansed and fried in butter and cut into convenient sized pieces.

Make the mixture hot, and heap it into the hot patty-cases.

NOTE.—There should be a good half-pint of diced lobster for this amount of sauce.

MACAROON TARTS

INGREDIENTS.—About ¾ lb. of flaky pastry (see p. 252).

FOR THE FILLING.—Strawberry jam, 7 oz. of castor sugar, 4 oz. of ground almonds, 1 tablespoonful of ground rice, vanilla, 2 whites of egg, water.

METHOD.—Roll out the pastry rather thinly.

Take some patty-pans and cut the pastry into rounds to fit them.

Line the tins with the pastry rounds.

To MAKE THE FILLING.—Mix together the ground rice, almonds, and castor sugar.

Whisk the whites to a stiff froth.

Fold it into the dry ingredients, together with the vanilla flavouring and a little cold water as required. Mix to a soft paste.

Put about a quarter of a teaspoonful of jam in the bottom of each tart.

Cover it with the macaroon mixture.

Brush over the tops of the macaroons with cold water.

Make some small, thin rolls of pastry from the trimmings, and place two across each tart.

Stand on a baking-sheet and bake in a hot oven for about fifteen or twenty minutes until the tarts are lightly browned and the macaroon crisp. Place on a sieve until cold. Serve on a lace paper.

MACAROON FRUIT TARTS

INGREDIENTS.—Some flaky pastry—as required (see p 252), 6 oz. of castor sugar, 3 oz. of ground almonds, 3 dessertspoonfuls of ground rice, 2 slices of tinned pineapple, about 1½ egg-whites.

METHOD.—Drain the pineapple and cut it into small pieces.

Roll out the pastry and line some patty-tins, putting just a little of the pineapple into each.

Mix the ground rice, sugar, and ground almonds together and add the remainder of the pineapple to them.

Whisk the whites of egg to a very stiff froth, stir them in lightly and mix the ingredients to a soft paste.

Turn the mixture into the prepared tins and put strips of pastry across each way. Dredge with castor sugar and bake in a quick oven.

MAIDS OF HONOUR

INGREDIENTS.—2 oz. of butter, 2 oz. of sugar, 1 egg, 2 tablespoonfuls of desiccated coconut, 1 teaspoonful of flour, 1 tablespoonful of cooked sago (cold), ½ lb. of flaky pastry (see p. 252), rind and juice of ½ a lemon.

METHOD.—Wash an ounce of sago, sprinkle it in a little boiling water and boil it for fifteen minutes or till the grains are transparent. Strain it and leave it till quite cold.

Cream the butter and sugar together until they are soft and white and beat in the egg and thinly grated lemon-rind.

Mix the flour smoothly with the lemon-juice and stir it into the mixture, adding the coconut and sago and mixing all well together.

Line some patty-pans with pastry and fill them half full.

Bake in a fairly hot oven for twenty-five minutes.

Sufficient for ten or twelve small tartlets.

NOTE.—Two ounces of ground or finely chopped almonds may be used instead of the coconut.

MAPLE TART

INGREDIENTS.—6 oz. of flour, 3 oz. of lard, 2 oz. of margarine, pinch of salt, water to mix, $1\frac{1}{2}$ gills of maple syrup, 3 oz. of breadcrumbs, $\frac{1}{4}$ flat teaspoonful of ground cinnamon, grated rind of $\frac{1}{2}$ lemon.

METHOD.—Make the breadcrumbs and mix them with the ground cinnamon and finely-grated lemon-rind.

Heat the maple syrup in a saucepan, add the breadcrumbs and leave them to cool.

Sieve the flour and salt, rub in the margarine, and mix them to a stiff paste with water.

Flour the lard and press it with a rolling-pin into thin pieces. Put these aside.

Roll out the pastry, turn it on to the other side and place the lard all over it, then fold sides to centre both ways, then over in half.

Now roll it out, cut a round, and line a sandwich-tin.

Trim and decorate the edge and fill this case with the maple syrup and breadcrumbs.

Ornament the top with small pieces of pastry cut with a fancy cutter.

Put the tart in a hot oven and bake it for about twenty minutes.

Sufficient for from four to six persons.

MARROW AND GINGER TART

INGREDIENTS.—$\frac{1}{4}$ lb. of flour, 2 oz. of lard, 2 oz. of margarine, pinch of salt, water to mix, 2 or 3 tablespoonfuls of marrow and ginger preserve.

METHOD.—Make a flaky crust and roll it to almost an eighth of an inch in thickness.

Take a jam sandwich-tin and cut

about a round of pastry large enough to line it.

Put into the tin and press it lightly into shape, and cut off the rough edges.

Decorate the edge with a fork.

Spread the preserve over the pastry.

Cut narrow strips from the pastry trimmings, twist them, and place across the jam.

Place in a hot oven and bake for fifteen to twenty minutes, and until the pastry is light brown.

Remove from the tin and cool on a sieve.

Serve on a lace paper.

Sufficient for four persons.

MERINGUE TARTLETS

INGREDIENTS.—About $\frac{1}{2}$ lb. of flaky pastry (see p. 252), apricot jam, white of 1 egg, 1 tablespoonful of castor sugar.

METHOD.—Roll out the pastry, cut into rounds, and line some patty-pans.

Place a small lump of bread in the centre of each, then put the tarts on a baking-sheet and bake in a hot oven for about twelve to fifteen minutes.

When cooked, remove the bread and cool the pastry on a sieve.

Whisk the egg-white to a very stiff froth, then fold in the castor sugar lightly.

Put a little jam in the centre of each tart, then cover it with about a teaspoonful of the meringue, shaping it to a smooth, round shape.

Return to a *cool* oven for about fifteen to twenty minutes—until the outside of the meringue is just set.

Heat and sieve some of the thick syrup part of the apricot jam, and pour a small teaspoonful over the meringue.

Sufficient to make about eight or twelve tartlets.

A LARGE MINCE PIE

INGREDIENTS.—About 1 lb. of flaky pastry (see p. 252), mincemeat as required.

METHOD.—Roll out the pastry to almost a quarter of an inch thick.

Take a sandwich-tin and cut a round large enough to cover the top. Again roll the remainder of the pastry thinly and cut out a round large enough to line the tin.

Press it into shape and fill with mincemeat. Damp round the top edge of the pastry, and fix the lid on to it. Press the edges together.

Decorate the edge with a fork.

Brush over with milk.

Bake in a hot oven for about twenty to thirty minutes, and until golden brown.

Serve hot or cold.

Sufficient for about six persons.

MINCE PIES

INGREDIENTS.—½ lb. of flour, ¼ lb. of lard, ¼ lb. of margarine, pinch of salt, water to mix, mincemeat.

METHOD.—Add a pinch of salt to the flour and sieve it. Rub in the margarine until quite fine.

Gradually add cold water and mix to a stiff paste. It should be just pliable.

Well flour the pastry-board and rolling-pin, and press out the lard into thin pieces.

Roll out the pastry to an oblong shape, then turn it over.

Divide the lard into three equal portions.

Spread one portion over the surface of the rolled-out pastry.

Fold into three, and roll out again the same way as before.

Turn it over and spread on it another portion of lard, fold into three. Repeat this once again, when all the lard will be used.

Cut off a third of the pastry and roll it out quite thinly. Shape into rounds to fit the patty-tins; about ten or twelve will be sufficient.

Line the tins with the rounds of pastry, and put about a dessertspoonful of mincemeat into each.

Now roll out the large piece of pastry thickly. Cut into rounds and place one on each tin, and slightly press the edges together.

Stand on a baking-sheet and glaze the tops with milk.

Place in a hot oven and bake for about twenty minutes.

When cooked, they should be well risen and golden brown. Place on a sieve until cool.

Dredge well with castor sugar and serve.

MINCEMEAT CHEESECAKES

INGREDIENTS.—1 egg, 2 oz. of margarine, 2 oz. of Barbados sugar, 1 oz. of flour, 1 oz. of ground rice, 1 oz. of ground almonds, ¼ level teaspoonful of ground cinnamon, short or flaky pastry (see p. 252 for either), mincemeat.

METHOD.—Roll out the pastry, stamp it into rounds, and line some small cake-tins.

Beat the sugar and fat to a cream, add the egg, stirring it in quickly and beating it well; then add the flour, sifted with the ground rice and cinnamon. Stir in the ground almonds and mix all together.

Put a little mincemeat in the bottom of each pastry-lined tin, cover it with the prepared filling. Bake the cheesecakes for about fifteen minutes. When cold, decorate them with icing and stick a tiny red ball of almond paste in the centre.

FOR THE ICING.—Mix sifted icing-sugar to a soft paste with lightly-beaten egg-white and water, and add flavouring to taste.

Sufficient for about eighteen small cakes.

MINT PIE

INGREDIENTS.—½ lb. of flaky pastry for lining tin (see p. 252), ½ cup of chopped mint (pressed down), 2 oz. each of raisins (stoned), currants, suet and sugar, 2 apples, 1 oz. of candied peel, juice of ½ a lemon.

METHOD.—Peel and chop the apples. Chop the suet and peel.

Mix all the ingredients for the filling.

Roll out half the pastry and line a tin or plate with it.

Put in the mixture.

Wet the edges of the pastry and cover with the rest of the pastry.

Brush the top with water and dredge with castor sugar.

Bake in a hot oven for twenty-five minutes.

NEW YEAR PASTRIES

INGREDIENTS.—¾ lb. of flaky pastry (see p. 252), 1 oz. of butter, 2 oz. of castor sugar, 2 oz. of shelled walnuts, 2 oz. of raisins, 2 oz. of ground almonds, 1 egg, 1 tablespoonful of desiccated coconut.

METHOD.—Roll out the pastry thinly and line a small baking-sheet.

Put the walnuts and raisins through the mincer and mix them with the coconut.

Beat the sugar and fat to a cream, then stir in the egg quickly and beat well.

Add the ground almonds and prepared fruit and nuts and mix them all together.

Cover the pastry with this mixture and bake in a quick oven. When cooked, brush over the top with frothed egg-white, dredge with castor sugar and coconut.

Return the pastry to the oven to dry and brown lightly.

As soon as it is cold, cut it into slices.

ORANGE CHEESECAKES

INGREDIENTS.—Short or flaky pastry (see p. 252), its weight in castor sugar, margarine, flour, ½ orange, 1 egg, orange marmalade.

METHOD.—Roll out the pastry and line some small tins as described before.

Grate the rind of the orange finely, and squeeze out the juice.

Beat the sugar and fat to a cream, add the orange-rind, and beat in the egg ; then stir in the sifted flour and a spoonful of orange-juice.

Put a little marmalade in the bottom of each pastry-lined tin, cover it with the cake mixture, and bake the cheesecakes.

ORANGE CURD TARTLETS

INGREDIENTS.—½ lb of flaky or puff pastry (see p. 252), 1 egg.

FOR THE ORANGE CURD FILLING.—2 oz. of butter, ½ lb. of castor sugar, 3 eggs, juice of 2 oranges and the rind of one.

METHOD.—Roll out the pastry on a floured board until it is about a third of an inch thick.

Cut out rounds with a cutter dipped in hot water, and place them carefully on a baking-sheet, so as not to spoil their shape.

Cut the centre half-way through with a small cutter dipped in hot water.

Leave for twenty minutes.

Glaze the top only with a beaten egg, and bake in a hot oven for about fifteen minutes. Scoop out the centre.

Sufficient for about twelve tartlets.

TO MAKE THE ORANGE FILLING.—Melt the butter in a double pan and stir in the sugar. Beat the eggs and grate the orange-rind thinly.

Add eggs, rind, and juice to the mixture, and stir with a wooden spoon until it thickens.

The curd must not boil. It is thick enough when it will coat the back of the spoon.

When cold, fill the tarts with the mixture.

ORANGE SLICES

INGREDIENTS.—Rind of 1 orange, juice of 1½ oranges, juice of ½ lemon, 4 oz. of granulated sugar, 2 oz. of flour, ½ oz. of butter, cold water, 2 eggs, 2 oz. of icing sugar, some short pastry (see p. 252.)

METHOD.—Roll out the pastry thinly, cut an oblong-shaped piece, and line the bottom of a small baking-tin ; then split it down the centre so that it can be separated into two strips when cooked.

Cover it with a buttered paper, and sprinkle rice over it ; then put it into a hot oven to bake.

When the pastry is set, remove the paper and rice, and finish cooking the pastry, then cool it on a sieve.

Grate the orange-rind finely, and mix it with the orange and lemon-juice.

Make it up to half a pint with cold water.

Mix the flour with the granulated sugar, gradually stir in the water and fruit-juice, and then turn them into a saucepan with the butter, and bring it to the boil, keeping it stirred.

Boil it gently for a few minutes, draw the pan aside to let it cool a little, and beat in the yolks of egg one at a time.

If the mixture seems too moist, omit the second yolk.

Cook it again for a few minutes, but do not let it boil ; then cool it and spread it thickly over the two strips of pastry.

Whisk the egg-whites to a stiff froth, then gradually whisk in the sifted icing sugar.

Put it into an icing pump and force

it on to the orange mixture in lines, across, both ways.

Put it into a cool oven to set, and brown a little.

Serve the pastry cold—cut in slices.

PASTRY CAKE

INGREDIENTS.—About ½ lb. of short pastry (see p. 252), 4 oz. of flour, 2 oz. of margarine, 2 oz. of sugar, 4 oz. of currants, 2 oz. of candied peel, ½ flat teaspoonful of ground ginger, ½ flat teaspoonful of ground cinnamon, ⅛ flat teaspoonful of carbonate of soda, 1 egg, milk.

METHOD.—Lightly grease a small round cake-tin. Roll out the pastry thinly and line the cake-tin evenly. Trim and decorate the edge.

Wash, pick over, and dry the fruit. Cut up the peel.

Sieve the flour with the carbonate of soda, ground ginger, and cinnamon. Rub in the fat and add the sugar and fruit.

Mix all these dry ingredients together.

Whisk the egg, add it to the dry ingredients, and mix together to a fairly-stiff cake consistency, adding only a very small quantity of milk.

Beat well. Turn the filling into the pastry-lined tin and bake it for about one and a half hours.

The oven must be rather hotter than usual at first on account of the pastry, but the heat should be lessened afterwards.

PEACH FLAN

INGREDIENTS.—1 tin of peaches, 1 small bottle of maraschino cherries, 6 oz. of sugar, 6d. of whipped cream, ½ lb. of short pastry (see p. 252).

METHOD.—Place a medium-sized flan-ring on a baking-sheet.

Roll out the pastry, lay it in the ring, and press it neatly against the sides. Fill it with a smaller tin, and bake for about twenty minutes. Remove the tin.

Boil the sugar in three-quarters of a gill of peach syrup and maraschino (mixed) for ten minutes, and let it cool slightly. Put the peaches in the flan and pour the syrup over. Decorate with whipped cream and the cherries.

PASTRY CUSHIONS

INGREDIENTS.—About ¾ lb. of flaky or puff pastry (see p. 252), jam or mincemeat, 1 egg-white, castor sugar.

METHOD.—Roll out the pastry fairly thinly and cut it into oblong-shaped pieces, about two inches by four.

Turn them over and put a little mincemeat or jam in the centre of one half. If using jam, a stiff kind is the best.

Damp the edges and fold each piece over into half, pressing the two halves together round the edge. Twist or pinch each corner to a point. Place the Pastry Cushions on a baking-sheet and put it into a hot oven to bake. They will take about fifteen minutes to bake.

When cooked, brush the cushions with frothed white of egg, and dredge them with castor sugar. Return them to a cooler oven to brown lightly.

Cool on a sieve.

Sufficient to make about fifteen pastry cushions.

PICNIC PIES

INGREDIENTS.—½ lb. of pork sausages, ½ lb. veal cutlet, ¼ lb. of bacon, 2 hard-boiled eggs, salt and pepper, ground mace.

FOR THE PASTRY.—¾ lb. of flour, 6 oz. of margarine, 6 oz. lard, water to mix, egg and milk for glaze.

METHOD.—To prepare the meat remove the rind from the bacon, and any skin there may be from the veal cutlet. Put both the veal and bacon through the mincer.

Take the sausages out of their skins and mix the sausage-meat with the minced veal.

Season them with pepper, salt, and mace, and moisten the mixture with about a quarter of a gill of water.

TO MAKE THE PASTRY.—Sift the flour into a basin, rub in the margarine and mix them to a stiff paste with water.

Put the lard on to a well-floured board and press or roll it into thin pieces, then put these aside.

Roll out the pastry fairly thinly and to a squarish shape, turn it on to the other side, then cover it with the prepared lard, pressing it on lightly. Now fold the pastry, sides to the centre, both ways, then over in half again. It will then be folded into eight.

To Make up the Pies.—Roll the pastry to barely one-fourth of an inch in thickness, and stamp it into rounds. Put these aside for the lids.

Put the remainder of the pastry together and roll it out again (thinly this time), and stamp out the same number of rounds as before.

Line some patty-tins with the thinner rounds of pastry, put a little of the prepared meat into each, then add a slice of egg and cover it with some more meat, pressing it down evenly.

Damp the edge of the pastry, and put on the lids ; make a hole in the centre and decorate each pie with a few tiny leaves of pastry.

Brush the pies with beaten egg-yolk, mixed with a little milk, to glaze them, and put them into a hot oven to bake, lessening the heat when the pastry has risen and browned lightly. They will take about three-quarters of an hour to cook.

When cooked, re-open the centre holes (if these have closed up during the cooking), so that the steam may escape.

This quantity will make about one dozen little pies.

PINEAPPLE CHEESECAKES

Ingredients.—$\frac{3}{4}$ to 1 lb. of flaky pastry (see p. 252), 1 gill of minced (tinned) pineapple (well drained), $\frac{1}{4}$ lb. of flour, $\frac{1}{8}$ flat teaspoonful of carbonate of soda, 1 flat teaspoonful cream of tartar, 3 oz. of castor sugar, 1 egg, 1 oz. of margarine, pineapple syrup.

For the Soft Icing.—$\frac{1}{2}$ lb. of icing sugar, about 1 to $1\frac{1}{2}$ tablespoonfuls of pineapple syrup, colouring if desired.

Method.—Roll out some flaky pastry fairly thinly, and line eighteen or twenty patty-pans or small cake-tins. Sieve the flour with the carbonate of soda and cream of tartar. Warm the margarine just enough to melt it.

Whisk the castor sugar and egg together until they are thick and creamy and free from dark streaks then stir in the flour lightly, also the melted margarine (when cool) and some pineapple syrup as required.

Put some minced pineapple in the bottom of each pastry-lined tin, and cover it with the prepared mixture. Bake in a hot oven. The cheesecakes will take about fifteen to twenty minutes to cook. When cold, pour a little thick soft icing in the centre to coat the tops only.

Sufficient to make eighteen to twenty cakes.

Soft Icing

To make the icing, rub the icing sugar through a hair sieve. If very lumpy, crush it first under the rolling pin.

Put it into a saucepan and mix to a thick, smooth paste with pineapple syrup.

Add a few drops of colouring, if desired, then stir the sugar over a low burner until the base of the pan feels warm.

If of the correct consistency, it should coat the spoon thickly. If by chance you make it too thin, stir in some more sieved icing-sugar.

PINEAPPLE FLAN

Ingredients.—1 tin of sliced pineapple, 1 oz. of glacé cherries, $1\frac{1}{2}$ gills of pineapple syrup, 4 oz. of sugar, $1\frac{1}{2}$ teaspoonfuls of cornflour, $\frac{1}{2}$ lb. of short pastry (see p. 252).

Method.—Cover the outside of a sandwich-tin neatly with short pastry, and bake it for twenty minutes. Remove the tin.

Boil one gill of the syrup with the sugar. Mix half a gill of the syrup smoothly with the cornflour. Pour it into the boiling syrup and stir well till it boils. Simmer for eight minutes and let it cool a little.

Arrange the pineapple and cherries in the cold flan-case, and pour the syrup over.

PINEAPPLE COCONUT FLAN

Ingredients.—Some short pastry (see p. 252), 1 tin of pineapple, 2 oz. of desiccated coconut, 1 tablespoonful of sugar.

Method.—Butter a flan-ring and place it on a buttered baking-sheet.

Roll out the pastry, cut out a round and line the flan-ring. Trim and decorate the edge, then line the pastry with a round of buttered paper and sprinkle some rice in the bottom. Put the case into a hot oven to bake, and when nearly cooked, remove paper and rice and finish cooking. Cool the pastry on a sieve.

Add a gill of pineapple syrup to the coconut. Bring them to the boil and boil them for a minute or two, then leave them to soak till the liquid is nearly all absorbed.

Make a foundation of this coconut mixture in the pastry flan-ring and arrange small rings of pineapple on top of it.

Put another gill of pineapple syrup into a saucepan with one tablespoonful of sugar, boil them to a thick syrup, and when cool and nearly jellied, pour the syrup over the pineapple.

Sufficient for five persons.

SMALL PINEAPPLE PIES

INGREDIENTS.—1 large tin pineapple, ½ oz. of butter, ¾ lb. of short pastry (see p. 252), 2 good dessertspoonfuls of cornflour, 1½ gills of milk or pineapple syrup, 3 or 4 tablespoonfuls of castor sugar, 2 yolks and 2 or 3 whites of egg.

METHOD.—Roll out the pastry fairly thinly, cut it into rounds and line some small tartlet tins. Press the pastry lightly into the bottom of the tins to make it a little thinner there than at the sides.

Line each pie with a round of buttered paper, and put in it about a teaspoonful of uncooked rice.

Stand the pies on a baking-sheet and put them into a hot oven to bake. When nearly cooked, remove the paper and rice and finish cooking without them.

Stand the pastry-cases on a sieve to cool.

To make large-sized pies—if there are no suitable tins available—turn the tins upside down and line the outside of them. Be careful when doing so not to let the pastry overlap the edge of the tin, or you will have difficulty in removing it when cooked.

THE PINEAPPLE FILLING.—Drain the syrup from the pineapple and put it through the mincer.

Mix the cornflour to a smooth paste with a small quantity of the milk.

Heat the remainder with the butter and add it to the cornflour. Return the cornflour to the pan and boil it for a few minutes, keeping it stirred. Then cool it very slightly and beat in the egg-yolks separately.

Gradually add the minced pineapple (drained again if necessary), also about one tablespoonful of sugar. Turn the filling into the prepared cases.

THE MERINGUE.—Whisk the egg-whites to a stiff froth, then fold in the castor sugar, allowing one tablespoonful to each white.

Heap the egg-froth on top of the pies and put them into the oven to set and lightly colour the meringue. Serve cold.

Sufficient for from ten to sixteen pies according to size.

PINEAPPLE PUFFS

INGREDIENTS.—FOR THE PASTRY: ½ lb. of flour, ½ lb. of margarine, pinch of salt, water to mix.

FOR THE FILLING.—3 oz. of lump sugar, 1 small tin pineapple.

METHOD.—Make the pastry as explained in Banbury Tarts on p. 259 but roll it six times instead of three. Roll it again until nearly half an inch thick.

Cut it into oblong shapes about two inches and a half wide and three inches and a half long.

Mark out lightly another small oblong in the centre of each piece, but do not quite cut it through to the bottom. Place on a baking-sheet.

Glaze the top surface with milk. Bake in a very hot oven for about fifteen minutes.

When cooked they should have risen considerably, and be lightly browned. Place on a sieve to cool. Remove the centre piece of pastry from each.

Strain the syrup from the pineapple. Pour it into a saucepan with the sugar.

Bring to the boil, and boil for about ten minutes, until the syrup is quite thick, then cool slightly Cut the pineapple into small pieces, and place some into each puff. Pour a small quantity of the thick syrup over the pineapple.

PRINCESS TARTS

INGREDIENTS.—Flaky pastry—as required (see p. 252), 1 oz. of ground almonds, 1 oz. of icing-sugar, 1½ teaspoonfuls of flour, ¾ gill of milk, 1 oz. of castor sugar, 2 dessertspoonfuls of desiccated coconut, 1 yolk of egg, vanilla, cochineal.

METHOD.—Mix the flour and castor sugar together and mix them to a smooth paste with some of the milk.

Heat the remainder and add it to the mixture, then return to the pan and bring to the boil, keeping it well stirred. Boil the mixture gently for a few minutes, then draw the pan aside and let it cool slightly.

Beat in the yolk of the egg and cook it again for a few minutes, being careful not to let the mixture boil. Remove the pan, add flavouring, and leave it to get cold.

Mix the ground almonds and icing-sugar together and stir them into the prepared mixture with the coconut. A little egg-white may be added to moisten if required.

Roll out the pastry, cut it into rounds and line some patty-tins or small cake-tins. Line these with rounds of buttered paper and put a little rice into them. Bake the tarts in a hot oven, and when the pastry is set remove the paper and rice and finish cooking the cases. Cool them on a sieve.

Colour the mixture with cochineal, turn it into the pastry-cases, and sprinkle coconut on the top.

Sufficient for six or more tarts, according to the size.

PUFF SQUARES

INGREDIENTS.—FOR THE PASTRY: ½ lb. of flour, ½ lb. of margarine, pinch of salt, water to mix, white-icing (see p. 273).

FOR THE FILLING.—2 whites of eggs, 2 tablespoonfuls of castor sugar, ½ gill cream, vanilla.

METHOD.—Make the pastry (as explained in Banbury Tarts on p. 259), only roll it six times instead of three. Then roll it again until half an inch thick.

Cut into squares of two inches and a half.

Place on a baking-sheet. Bake in a very hot oven for about fifteen minutes.

Then place on a sieve (away from a draught) until cold.

TO MAKE THE FILLING.—Whisk the whites to a very stiff froth, then fold in the castor sugar.

Beat up the cream until thick and add to the whites.

Mix lightly together and flavour with vanilla.

Split the squares into halves, spread on the cream mixture, then fit together again.

Make some white-icing (as explained in Iced Chocolate Tart on p. 273), and pour over the top of each.

Leave until set.

NOTE.—If the fat comes through the pastry when rolling it, stand in a cool place for about half an hour between each rolling, or every other rolling.

PUMPKIN PIE

INGREDIENTS.—½ lb. of short pastry (see p. 252), 2 lb. of pumpkin, 1 oz. of butter, 4 oz. of sugar, 2 eggs, ½ teaspoonful of ground ginger, a pinch of cinnamon, 1 cupful of milk.

METHOD.—Line the sides of a pie-dish or baking-tin with short pastry and decorate the edges.

Peel the pumpkin and remove the seeds.

Cut it in slices across, put in boiling water; boil for about ten minutes till tender. Strain away the water and rub the pumpkin through a sieve, or mash it with a wooden spoon.

Add to it the butter, sugar, and ginger.

Beat the eggs and milk, and add them to the mixture. Pour into the dish and bake in a fairly hot oven for about an hour, or till set.

QUEEN TART

INGREDIENTS.—About ¾ lb. of short pastry (see p. 252), 3 gills of breadcrumbs (not pressed down), 1 tablespoonful of custard-powder, ¾ pint of milk, almond flavouring, 1 heaped tablespoonful of sugar, 3 tablespoonfuls of jam, few glacé cherries.

METHOD.—Roll out the pastry and line a case large enough to hold about a pint and a half when cooked, or if preferred make two smaller cases. Two sandwich-tins may be lined or an inverted pie-tin may be covered, whichever is most convenient.

Put the cases in a very hot oven to bake. They will take about fifteen minutes. Let them cool on a sieve.

Make a thick custard with the milk and custard-powder, adding sugar and flavouring to taste.

Put the jam in the bottom of the pastry, then the breadcrumbs. Add some of the custard and mix it with the crumbs, pouring the remainder on the top.

Put the tart into a warm oven for about fifteen minutes till the crumbs are soaked.

When cold, decorate the top with halved glacé cherries.

Sufficient for from six to eight persons.

RASPBERRY AND CURRANT TARTLETS

INGREDIENTS.—¾ lb. of short pastry (see p. 252), 1 lb. of raspberries, ½ lb. of currants, 1 lb. of sugar, ½ gill of water, 1 gill of cream, if liked.

METHOD.—Pick the fruit and put it in a pan with the sugar and water ; stew gently for five or ten minutes. Strain the fruit and put it in a basin, return the syrup to the pan, and boil it till it becomes a thick syrup. It should be reduced to about half the original quantity.

Line fifteen deep patty-pans with short pastry, and put a piece of grease-proof paper filled with rice in each.

Bake for fifteen minutes in a hot oven. Remove the rice and paper, and, when cold, put a little of the stewed fruit in each tartlet and pour a spoonful of syrup over it.

If the tartlets are for some special occasion, decorate them with cream.

Put some double cream in a cup and beat with a fork or teaspoon till it thickens ; then sweeten to taste. Put dabs of cream on each tart, or force it through an icing pump, using a rose tube.

This quantity makes fifteen tarts.

RATAFIA CHEESECAKES

INGREDIENTS.—2 oz. of margarine, 1 oz. of ground almonds, 1½ oz. of castor sugar, 1 oz. of ratafia crumbs, 1 oz. of sponge-cake crumbs, 2 egg-whites, ratafia flavouring, apricot jam, 12 ratafia biscuits for top of cakes, some short or flaky pastry (see p. 252 for either).

FOR THE ICING.—6 oz. of icing sugar, warm water, colouring as desired, ratafia flavouring.

METHOD.—Roll out the pastry thinly and line twelve boat-shaped tins, putting a spot of jam in the bottom of each.

Beat the castor sugar and fat to a cream, add the ground almonds, and ratafia and sponge-cake crumbs. Mix them together, adding a spoonful of milk if required, then fold in the stiffly-whisked egg-whites and a few drops of ratafia flavouring. Turn the mixture into the pastry in the prepared tins and bake them in a hot oven. They will take about fifteen minutes to cook.

When cooked and cold put a little icing on each and top it with a ratafia biscuit.

To MAKE THE ICING.—Rub the icing sugar through a hair sieve and mix it to a smooth, thick paste with a spoonful of warm water. Stir in a few drops of flavouring and colouring as desired.

Sufficient for twelve cheesecakes.

RATAFIA PIE

INGREDIENTS.—2 oz. of ratafias, 2 oz. of shelled walnuts (chopped), 2 eggs, 2 oz. of castor sugar, 2 oz. of flour, 1½ oz. of butter (melted), apricot jam, ½ lb. of short pastry (see p. 252).

METHOD.—Line a large sandwich-tin neatly with short pastry and spread it with jam.

Whisk the eggs and sugar till they are thick and creamy.

Stir in the flour, butter, and walnuts. Pour the mixture into the pastry, and place it in a hot oven.

After ten minutes lower the gas and bake for thirty minutes in all.

Decorate with ratafias stuck in place with a little jam.

RICE FLAN

INGREDIENTS.—$\frac{1}{2}$ lb. of flour, $\frac{1}{4}$ level teaspoonful of powdered cinnamon, $\frac{1}{4}$ lb. of margarine, 4 dessertspoonfuls of castor sugar, 3 dessertspoonfuls of rice, $\frac{3}{4}$ pint of milk, 1 egg, orange essence, mincemeat, $\frac{1}{4}$ oz. of butter.

METHOD.—Bring the milk to the boil. Wash the rice and add it to the milk and cook it in the top of a double boiler until tender, and the mixture is thick and creamy, keeping it stirred occasionally.

Draw the pan aside and let it cool a little, then beat up the egg, stir in half of it, also half the sugar, the butter, and a few drops of orange essence.

Sift the flour with the cinnamon, rub in the margarine, and add the remainder of the sugar. Mix all to a stiff paste with the half-egg and some water, as required.

Butter a flan-ring and stand it on a buttered baking-sheet, then roll out the pastry, cut a round, and line it.

Trim the edge and put a layer of mincemeat in the bottom, then fill up with the prepared rice. Put the flan into a hot oven to bake, and serve it hot or cold.

Sufficient for four or five persons.

ROYAL TARTLETS

INGREDIENTS.—About $\frac{1}{2}$ lb. of flaky pastry (see p. 252), 2 penny stale sponge-cakes, $1\frac{1}{2}$ oz. of margarine or butter, 1 tablespoonful of castor sugar, 1 egg, vanilla, raspberry jam, few glacé cherries.

METHOD.—Roll out the pastry rather thinly, cut it into rounds, and line some tart-tins.

To MAKE THE FILLING.—Rub the sponge-cakes through a wire sieve. Beat the sugar and butter to a cream. Separate the yolk from the white of egg. Add the yolk to the creamed butter and sugar, stir it in quickly, and beat for a few minutes.

Add a few drops of vanilla and the sponge-cake crumbs and mix together.

Whisk the white to a stiff froth and fold it in lightly. Put a little jam in the bottom of each tart-tin, then cover up with the prepared mixture.

Stand on a baking-sheet and bake in a hot oven for about fifteen to twenty minutes, and until lightly browned.

When about half-cooked, carefully place a piece of cherry in the centre of each.

Stand on a sieve when cooked and leave until cold. Dredge with castor sugar before serving.

SAGO FLAN

To MAKE THE FLAN CASE—Roll out some short pastry to about a quarter of an inch thick, and cut out a round large enough to line a flan-ring.

Lightly butter the ring and stand it on a buttered baking-sheet. Lift the round of pastry into the ring, and line it evenly. Trim the edges and prick the bottom.

Now line the case with a round of buttered paper and sprinkle rice in the base. This will prevent the pastry from rising in the centre. Put the pastry into a hot oven to bake. It will take about twenty minutes. Just before it is quite cooked, remove the paper and rice, and finish cooking the case without it. When it is cooked, lift up the flan-ring carefully and cool the case on a sieve. It should be quite cold before it is filled.

To MAKE THE SAGO FILLING.— Take one and a half ounces of sago and sprinkle it into three-quarters of a pint of boiling milk. Let the mixture cook gently until it is creamy, stirring occasionally. Add a lump of butter and sugar to taste, also a few drops of orange flavouring essence.

When the flan-case is cold, cover the bottom with marrow and ginger preserve, or plain preserved ginger, put through a mincer, and mixed with a little of the syrup.

Cover this with a layer of chopped walnuts and pour the sago cream on the top when it is cool. Decorate with a meringue mixture, forcing it through an icing-bag. Return the flan to a cool oven to set and lightly brown the meringue. Decorate it to taste and serve cold.

To MAKE MERINGUE

WHISK the white of an egg to a stiff froth, then gradually whisk in a tablespoonful of castor sugar. When it is quite stiff, fold in lightly another quarter of a tablespoonful of sugar, and use the meringue as required.

SANDRINGHAM TARTLETS

INGREDIENTS.—FOR THE FLAKY PASTRY : 6 oz. of flour, 3 oz. of butter or margarine, 3 oz. of lard, water to mix.

FOR THE FILLING.—1 egg, its weight in butter, castor sugar, and ground rice, raspberry jam, vanilla or almond flavouring.

METHOD.—Make the pastry (see p. 252). Roll it out until about one-eighth of an inch in thickness.

Cut into small rounds with a fancy cutter. Line some small tart-tins with the pastry.

Cream the sugar and butter together.

Beat in the egg, mix well, and add the ground rice.

Add the flavouring and mix all lightly together.

Place half a teaspoonful of raspberry jam in the bottom of each of the prepared tart-tins.

Place one dessertspoonful of the prepared mixture over the jam, but do not mix with the jam.

Proceed until all the mixture is utilised.

Bake in a hot oven for about fifteen to twenty minutes.

When cooked the mixture in the tarts should be just firm and light-brown in colour.

Serve cold.

SAUSAGE ROLLS

INGREDIENTS.—1 lb. of pork sausages, ½ lb. of flour, ¼ lb. of lard, ¼ lb. of margarine, pinch of salt, water to mix, 1 egg or a little milk.

METHOD.—Skin the sausages—put them into cold water for a few minutes. Split the skin down one side, and the sausage will easily come out of the skin. Divide each into three portions and put on one side.

To MAKE THE PASTRY.—Add the salt to the flour. Sieve the flour into a basin. Rub in the margarine until it resembles fine breadcrumbs. Add cold water gradually, and mix to a stiff paste, so that it is just pliable, but not too soft.

Well flour the pastry-board and rolling-pin, and press or roll out the lard into very thin pieces, then put aside. Roll the pastry to an oblong shape.

Turn it over on to the other side.

Divide the lard into three equal portions, and put one portion of it all over the surface of the rolled-out pastry. Fold into three and roll it out again as before.

Repeat this until all the lard is in, then roll the pastry to nearly an eighth of an inch thick, and cut it into pieces about four inches square.

Turn them over on to the other side.

Roll the pieces of sausage into thinner rolls, not quite as long as the pieces of pastry.

Place a roll on each piece—not quite in the centre—damp round the edges of the pastry, and fold it over in half.

Press the edges together, trim off any rough pieces, and with the back of a knife mark two lines on top of the roll and just inside the three cut edges.

Brush the rolls over with beaten egg or with milk. Put on to a baking-sheet and bake in a hot oven for about thirty to forty minutes. When the pastry is cooked and golden brown, the heat can be slightly lessened, and, if necessary, the browning-shelf removed. When cooked, place on a sieve until cold. Serve on a dish paper. Garnish with parsley.

SEVILLE CHEESECAKE

INGREDIENTS.—1½ oz. of butter or margarine, 2 oz. of sponge-cake crumbs, 2 oz. of ground almonds, 1 egg, 1½ oz. castor sugar, orange marmalade, orange essence, about ¼ lb. of flaky pastry (see p. 252).

METHOD.—Roll out the pastry, cut out a round, and line a sandwich-tin. Trim and decorate the edge and spread a thin layer of marmalade in the bottom.

Beat the sugar and fat to a cream, add the egg, stir in quickly, and beat it well. Then mix in the sponge-cake crumbs and ground almonds.

Flavour the mixture with a few

drops of orange-essence, and add a little milk if required.

Turn it into the pastry-lined tin, lay three narrow strips of pastry across each way, and put it into a hot oven to bake.

It will take about fifteen or twenty minutes to cook.

Serve Seville cheesecake cold.

Sufficient for four or six persons.

SPICED CHEESECAKES

INGREDIENTS.—Flaky pastry, as required (see p. 252), lemon cheese, 3 oz. of ground rice, 1 level teaspoonful of ground cinnamon, 2 oz. of castor sugar, 2 oz. of margarine, 1 egg, milk if required.

METHOD.—Roll out the pastry thinly, stamp it into rounds and line about one dozen small deep cake-tins. Put a little lemon cheese in the bottom of each.

Beat the sugar and fat to a cream. Add the egg, stirring it in quickly and beating well. Then stir in the ground rice, sifted with the cinnamon and mix all together lightly, adding a little milk if required.

Turn the mixture into the prepared tins, dredge sugar on the top and put the cheesecakes into a hot oven to bake.

They will take from fifteen to twenty minutes to cook.

SPONGE CHEESECAKES

INGREDIENTS.—Short or flaky pastry (see p. 252), 1½ oz. of butter, 1 egg (separated), 2 sponge-cakes, 1½ dessert-spoonfuls of castor sugar, almond or ratafia flavouring, damson jelly.

METHOD.—Crumble the sponge-cakes finely by rubbing them through a wire sieve.

Cream the butter and sugar, separate the egg and beat in the yolk ; then stir in the crumbled sponge-cakes and a few drops of flavouring essence. Lastly fold in the stiffly-whisked white of egg.

Turn the mixture into pastry-lined tins with just a spot of damson jelly in the bottom, and bake the cakes.

SUGAR AND FRUIT FLAKY CAKES

INGREDIENTS.—6 oz. of flour, 3 oz. of lard, 3 oz. of margarine or butter, water to mix, castor sugar, 3 oz. of sultanas or currants (washed and dried).

METHOD.—Sieve the flour.

Rub the margarine into the flour until it is like fine breadcrumbs. Add the water and mix to a dry paste.

Well flour the pastry-board and rolling-pin and either press out or roll out the lard until it is quite a thin layer.

Put the lard aside and roll out the pastry until it is about one-eighth of an inch in thickness.

Turn this on to the other side and place the rolled-out lard all over the surface of the pastry.

Fold the sides of the pastry to the middle, then fold in three.

Roll out the pastry to an oblong shape, turn it over, fold into three and roll out again until rather thin.

Turn the pastry on to the other side, sprinkle all over the surface with castor sugar and the prepared fruit.

Damp all round the edge with cold water, using a small pastry brush.

Fold into three, press the edges together.

Cut into oblong-shaped pieces (about three inches by two inches).

Mark parallel lines across the surface of each—use the back of a knife for this—from corner to corner.

Brush the cakes over with milk. Bake in a hot oven for fifteen minutes.

Place on a sieve to cool.

Sprinkle with castor sugar and serve cold.

SUGAR SHORT CAKES

METHOD.—Roll out some short pastry (see p. 252) to an oblong shape —a good eighth of an inch thick—turn it on to the other side and then sprinkle it freely with castor sugar. Add a few currants and a dash of water to make them adhere to the paste.

Fold up the oblong evenly until it is quite thick, then roll it out to about half an inch in thickness and cut it into small rounds, oblong or square shapes.

Put them on to a baking-sheet, brush them with milk (to glaze the pastry), and bake them in a hot oven. They will take about fifteen minutes to cook.

TOFFEE PIE

INGREDIENTS.—2 oz. of cornflour, ½ pint of water, ¼ lb. of Demerara sugar, 1 egg-yolk, 2 oz. of butter or margarine, 2 tablespoonfuls of castor sugar, about ¼ lb. of short pastry (see p. 252).

FOR THE MERINGUE.—3 egg-whites, 3 tablespoonfuls of castor sugar, a pinch of salt.

METHOD.—To make the pastry-case, roll out the pastry, cut out a round and line a fairly deep sandwich-tin. Line this with a round of buttered paper and put some uncooked rice in the bottom.

(This is to keep the case's shape.)

Trim and decorate the edge and put it into a hot oven to bake. It should only be lightly browned.

When the pastry is set, remove the paper and rice very carefully and put the case back in the oven for a few minutes to finish cooking.

When cooked, leave it on a sieve until cold.

THE TOFFEE FILLING.—To make the filling, put two tablespoonfuls of castor sugar into a small, strong saucepan with about two dessertspoonfuls of water, and let it dissolve slowly. Then boil it until brown. When ready draw aside and cool slightly.

Mix the cornflour to a smooth paste with a little water, add the half pint of water to the caramel, with the Demerara sugar.

Dissolve both slowly.

Stir the toffee mixture on to the cornflour and return it to the pan.

Add the butter and bring the mixture to the boil.

Boil gently for about six minutes, keeping it stirred.

Draw the pan aside, beat up the yolk of egg and add it to the toffee mixture, stirring it over a *low* burner for a few minutes to cook the egg.

When cool turn into the prepared pastry-case.

THE MERINGUE

Add a pinch of salt to the egg-whites and whisk them to a very stiff froth. Fold in the castor sugar. Heap this on top of the filling and put it into a cool oven to set, and brown the tips very lightly.

Serve cold.

If less meringue is preferred, use two egg-whites and two tablespoonfuls of castor sugar.

Sufficient for six or eight persons.

A TREACLE TART

INGREDIENTS.—About ¼ lb. of short pastry (see p. 252), ½ lb. golden syrup, 3 oz. of breadcrumbs, ½ flat teaspoonful of ground ginger.

METHOD.—Roll out the pastry to rather more than an eighth of an inch in thickness. Cut out a round and line a sandwich-tin or Pyrex plate. Be careful not to stretch the pastry as you do this or it will shrink when it is cooked. Remember also to cut the round large enough to line the sides as well as the base of the tin.

When the pastry is in the tin it should be pressed a little thinner in the centre. Trim and decorate the edge.

Warm the golden syrup in a saucepan, stir in the breadcrumbs and ginger, and then turn them into the already lined tin.

Cut six strips of pastry about a quarter of an inch wide from the trimmings, twist them, and put them across the tart—three each way.

Stand the tart on a baking-sheet and put into a good hot oven to bake. It should take about twenty minutes. When it is cooked, remove it from the tin and cool it on a sieve away from any draughts.

VOL-AU-VENT

A VOL-AU-VENT is a large case of puff pastry (see p. 252), round or oval, which may be filled with a fruit or savoury filling.

To make it, roll some puff pastry to half an inch thick, and another piece to a quarter of an inch thick.

Cut a large round or oval shape from each piece of pastry, with a cutter. Then from the *thick* oval, stamp out the centre, leaving an inch margin.

The diameter of the small cutter should be two inches smaller than the large one. Now take the pastry ring

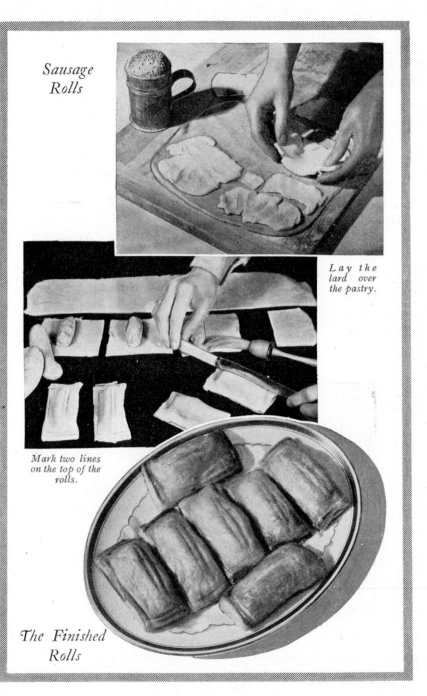

Sausage Rolls

Lay the lard over the pastry.

Mark two lines on the top of the rolls.

The Finished Rolls

PLATE 27

Custard Pie

Butter
Cream
Tarts

Compote of Fruit Pie

PLATE 28

and place it on the large thin oval of pastry, damping the edge to make the two pieces adhere.

Place the case on a baking-sheet, and brush the top with milk to glaze it. Bake it in a hot oven until well risen and lightly browned. It will take about twenty to thirty minutes. Care must be taken not to let the case brown too quickly, or it will not rise sufficiently.

If the vol-au-vent is to be served hot, fill it at once with a savoury filling; otherwise, leave it to get cold.

If it is made in advance, the case can always be re-heated before being filled.

The remaining small oval of pastry can be glazed and baked, and is sometimes used as a cover when a savoury filling is added.

To Make a Fruit Salad Filling.— Take a tin of fruit salad (three-quarters to one pint size) and drain off the syrup. Pour the syrup into a saucepan, adding a tablespoonful of sugar to one gill of the syrup.

Let it dissolve slowly, then boil it till it is well reduced and quite thick like jam. Leave it to cool.

Fill the case of pastry with the fruit, and pour over the thick syrup. Serve the sweet with cream.

Damson or other stewed fruit may be used in the same way.

To Make a Savoury Filling.—Use a foundation of white sauce with the addition of either shelled shrimps or prawns, diced cold chicken, lobster or crab meat, or cold salmon.

About one gill and a half of meat or fish is sufficient for half a pint of sauce. Any suitable flavourings may be added, such as chopped pimento, or onion-juice with chicken, chopped capers with salmon, and a little lemon-juice and a few drops of anchovy essence with shrimps or prawns.

For the sauce, use one ounce of butter and three quarters of an ounce of flour to half a pint of milk.

After boiling the sauce for a few minutes, let it cool a little, then add the beaten yolk of an egg. Or, if preferred, a tablespoonful of cream may be added to the filling, but this should be added last of all. Either of these fillings are suitable for patty cases or vol-au-vent.

VOL-AU-VENT OF SWEET-BREADS

INGREDIENTS.—2 sweetbreads, 1 set of calf's brains, 12 button-mushrooms, 2 truffles, ½ pint of Bechamel sauce (see p. 42), 1 onion, 8 peppercorns, salt and pepper, puff pastry (see p. 252).

METHOD.—Soak the sweetbreads in cold water for an hour. Put them in a pan of cold water, bring them to the boil and plunge them in cold water.

Trim them and press between two plates till cold. Skin and wash the brains and slice the onion.

Put the sweetbreads in a pan and add enough water to cover them, also the sliced onion and peppercorns.

Simmer for thirty minutes, putting in the brains for the last fifteen minutes.

Use the stock to make half a pint of Bechamel sauce; this will be greatly improved by the addition of cream in the place of half a gill of milk. Add to the sauce the mushrooms and the truffles cut into dice.

Slice the sweetbreads and brains and heat them in the sauce for about fifteen minutes. Season to taste and pour into a large hot pastry-case (see previous recipe) just before serving.

The pastry lid should be placed on top.

WEST INDIAN TARTLETS

INGREDIENTS.—Plain or puff pastry (see p. 252), bananas sliced, raspberry jam, blanched almonds, currant-jelly.

METHOD.—Line some small boat-shaped pans with pastry.

Line the pastry with buttered papers and put a little rice in the bottom of each. Bake the pastry in a hot oven until delicately browned, removing the rice and paper as soon as the pastry is set.

When the pastry cases are cool, half fill them with jam. Cover this with overlapping slices of banana, dipped in melted currant-jelly and sprinkled with blanched almonds, which should have been browned in the oven and finely chopped.

If preferred, the tartlets can be decorated with halved baked almonds.

K

COLD SWEETS

ALMOND JELLIES

INGREDIENTS.—¾ pint of Ideal Milk (unsweetened), 3 oz. of almonds, vanilla flavouring, 2 oz. of sugar, ½ oz. of leaf gelatine, ½ gill of water, chocolate.

METHOD.—Peel and chop the almonds and whip the Ideal Milk. Mix these together.

Add the sugar and vanilla and strain in the gelatine, which should be melted in hot water. Leave the mixture till it begins to thicken.

Pour it into individual moulds which have been rinsed out with cold water, and put it on the ice to set.

Unmould the jellies and sprinkle them with grated chocolate.

Sufficient for eight small moulds.

ALMOND JUNKETS

INGREDIENTS.—½ lb. of ratafias, almond essence, 1 teaspoonful of rennet, 1 pint of fresh milk, 6d. of double cream, nutmeg.

METHOD.—Put a few ratafias in four individual dishes, keeping back twelve for decoration.

Sprinkle the ratafias with a very few drops of essence of almonds.

Warm the milk till just tepid, add the rennet, stir quickly, and pour at once over the biscuits.

Leave till set and cold.

Whip the cream, sweeten it to taste, and put a spoonful on each junket with three ratafias on top.

NOTE.—Junket will not set if the milk is made too hot, or if the dish is moved before it has time to set.

ALMOND AND RAISIN SPONGE

INGREDIENTS.—1 sixpenny sponge-cake ring, 6 oz. of raisins, 2 or 3 oz. of almonds, 1 tablespoonful of brandy or sherry, 3 eggs, 1½ pints of milk, 1 tablespoonful of sugar, almond flavouring.

METHOD.—Wash and stone the raisins, and blanch the almonds. Leave out a few of each for decorating, then put the remainder through the mincer.

Split the sponge cake into halves and spread with the minced raisins and almonds (moistened with the brandy), then put together again.

Beat up the eggs.

Boil the milk and when just off the boil add to them.

Stir in the sugar, add a few drops of flavouring, then strain.

Put the sponge ring in a pie-dish or Pyrex dish, pour in the custard and decorate with the remainder of the almonds and raisins.

Bake in a moderately warm oven for about forty minutes or until set, and serve cold.

Do not let it boil.

Sufficient for about nine persons.

AMBER SHAPE

INGREDIENTS.—1 pint packet of pineapple jelly, 1 pint of hot water, 2 eggs, 2 dessertspoonfuls of sugar, 2 oranges, 1 oz. of almonds, cream.

METHOD.—Dissolve the jelly in hot water, then stir it on to the beaten eggs. Add the grated rind and juice of one orange and the sugar, then turn the mixture into a saucepan and cook it for a few minutes, keeping it stirred.

Take it off the gas and add the almonds, blanched and chopped, and more sugar if required. Turn it into a wet mould and when set dip it in warm water and unmould it.

Garnish with slices of orange and heap whipped cream in the centre.

Sufficient for five persons.

APPLE BORDER

INGREDIENTS.—1 pint of apple pulp, 1 gill of cream, 1 oz. of crystallised ginger, ⅝ oz. of leaf gelatine, ½ gill of water or apple syrup, sugar, glacé cherries.

METHOD.—Rinse a border mould and decorate the bottom of it with a few glacé cherries, halved and dipped in jelly. When set, cover with jelly and set again. For this use a quarter of a packet of lemon jelly dissolved in water. Let it get cold, then use as required. To obtain the apple pulp stew some apples in the usual way, adding sugar to taste, and only a small quantity of water.

When cooked, rub through a sieve and leave until cold.

Cut the ginger into small pieces and add.

Whisk the cream until it stiffens and stir in lightly.

Put the gelatine into a saucepan with the water or apple syrup and dissolve slowly, but do not boil, then strain into the other ingredients and mix all together.

Add castor sugar as required. Turn into the mould, which must be wet, and leave until set, then turn on to a dish.

Sufficient for five or six persons.

APPLE CUSTARD

INGREDIENTS.—2 lb. of apples, about 2 tablespoonfuls of Demerara sugar, a few cloves, a few strips of lemon-rind, 1½ gills of water, 1 pint of milk, 1 tablespoonful of custard powder 1 oz. of white sugar, vanilla or lemon flavouring, 1 gill of cream, a large pinch of castor sugar, crushed crystallised violets.

METHOD.—Put the Demerara sugar and water into a saucepan and boil together for about five minutes.

Peel the apples, cut into quarters, remove the core, and slice them.

Add them to the syrup, together with the cloves, and thinly cut lemon-rind.

Cook until quite soft.

Remove the flavourings, and rub the stewed apples through a sieve.

Mix the custard powder with a little milk, put the remainder in a saucepan with the white sugar. When boiling, pour it on to the custard powder, stirring well all the time.

Add the flavouring.

Put the apples into a glass dish, pour over the custard slowly, but avoid mixing them.

Set aside until cold.

Add the sugar and vanilla to the cream, whisk until thick.

Shake on to the custard and sprinkle with the crushed violets.

Sufficient for about six or eight persons.

APPLE FANCIES

INGREDIENTS.—2 lb. of cooking apples, 1 gill of hot water, ¾ lb. of sugar, juice of a lemon, 2 tablespoonfuls of sherry, ½ gill of water, 1 oz. of gelatine, cochineal, 6d. of cream, 6 long thin strips of angelica (if liked), 6 slices of Swiss roll, whipped cream.

METHOD.—Soak the gelatine with half a gill of water and the lemon-juice for one hour. Turn it over now and again, so that all of it is well moistened.

Peel, core, and slice the apples and stew them in hot water till they go to a mash.

Rub the apples through a sieve on to the sugar.

Place in a saucepan and stir over a low gas till it boils.

Add the sherry and the soft gelatine and let it dissolve. Colour with a little cochineal. Pour one inch thick into an oiled tin. When firm, cut into rounds with a fluted cutter dipped in hot water.

Place each apple round on a slice of Swiss roll and, if liked, stick in a handle made of a thin strip of angelica.

Decorate with whipped cream.

Sufficient for six apple fancies.

NOTE.—To make the angelica pliable dip it in hot water.

APPLE MERINGUE PUDDING

INGREDIENTS.—2 lb. of apples, 2 eggs, 2 tablespoonfuls of Demerara sugar, ¾ gill of water, 1 lemon (grated rind), a few glacé cherries.

METHOD.—Peel and core the apples and cut into slices. Put them into a saucepan with the sugar and water and cook until soft. Either mash the apples or rub them through a sieve with the juice.

Separate the yolks from the whites of eggs. Beat the yolks and mix in with the apples. Add the grated lemon-rind.

Put into a greased pie-dish and bake

in a moderately warm oven for about twenty minutes, being careful not to brown the pudding. Whisk the whites to a stiff froth, fold in the castor sugar, and place on the top of the pudding.

Put the pudding back into a cool oven to set the white of egg and until it is light brown. Decorate with a few glacé cherries. Serve cold.

Sufficient for about six persons.

APPLE SNOWBALLS

INGREDIENTS.—4 apples, 4 cloves, whites of 2 eggs, 1½ to 2 tablespoonfuls of castor sugar, angelica.

METHOD.—Peel the apples, and with an apple corer remove the core from the centre of each, being careful not to break them.

If a corer is not available, scoop out as much of the core as possible from each end of the apple.

Place them in a pie-dish, and put a clove into the centre of each apple.

Pour in a little water and bake the apples until they are soft, but not broken ; they will take about thirty minutes.

Remove them carefully into a shallow dish and arrange them at equal distances apart.

Whisk the whites to a stiff froth and lightly fold the castor sugar into them. Cover each apple all over with the white of an egg and return to a cooler oven until the meringue is set. Garnish with stalks of angelica.

Serve cold.

Sufficient for four persons.

STUFFED APPLES

INGREDIENTS.—3 large apples, 15 dates, desiccated coconut, water, jam or jelly.

METHOD.—Peel the apples and remove the cores. Put them into a fireproof dish with a little water. Stone the dates, keeping six of them whole ; put these aside, then cut up the remaining nine and stuff them inside the apples.

Bake the apples until almost tender, brush them with melted jam or jelly, and sprinkle them with desiccated coconut. Return them to the oven to finish cooking, and brown the coconut lightly. Serve stuffed apples hot or cold, decorated with the whole dates.

Sufficient for three persons.

APRICOT BASKETS

INGREDIENTS.—1 tin of apricots, 6 round cornflour cakes, 6 long thin strips of angelica, 6d. of cream 1 tablespoonful of jam, castor sugar, 1 oz. of desiccated coconut.

METHOD.—Dip the cakes into the apricot syrup and roll in coconut. Cut a hole in the top of each cake and put in a small teaspoonful of jam.

Put the cakes in a glass dish with half an apricot, cut side down, on each.

Dip the angelica in boiling water and stick it in the cakes to form handles.

Beat the cream till thick, add a teaspoonful of sugar.

Decorate the baskets with cream.

Sufficient for six baskets.

APRICOT CREAM

INGREDIENTS.—¼ lb. of dried apricots, 1½ pints of water, 4 oz. of sugar, 1 gill of cream, 1 oz. of leaf gelatine, almond essence, juice of a lemon and rind thinly cut.

METHOD.—Pour one pint of boiling water on the apricots and leave them soaking overnight. Add the sugar, lemon-rind and juice, and stew the apricots gently in the water in which they were soaked.

Rub them through a hair sieve.

Soak the gelatine for five minutes in half a pint of cold water and dissolve it over a low gas, stirring well with a wooden spoon.

Strain the gelatine on to the apricot purée and mix well. Stir frequently till it is cold. Add the cream and almond essence, and when it begins to thicken pour into a mould that has been rinsed in cold water.

To turn it out when set, dip the mould for one minute in a basin of tepid water, shake it out on to the hand, and let it slide gently on to the dish.

APRICOT GATEAU

INGREDIENTS.—1 small tin of apricots in syrup, 2 eggs, 1 pint of milk, vanilla flavouring, cochineal, 4 sponge cakes (small), 1 dessertspoonful of sugar.

METHOD.—Take a border mould and grease it well with margarine or butter. Beat the egg. Heat the milk in a saucepan with the sugar and add to the egg. Crumble the sponge cakes and mix with the egg and milk. Add also vanilla and a few drops of cochineal—just sufficient of the latter to make the custard look deep yellow in colour, but not to make it pink. Pour this into the greased mould and cover with a greased paper. Now put into a saucepan of hot water. Stand the mould on a saucer turned upside down in the bottom of the saucepan. The water in the saucepan must not reach to more than halfway up the side of mould, and must not boil, but simmer, otherwise the custard will curdle. Steam this custard until set ; it will take from thirty to forty minutes. When cooked, remove from saucepan and turn carefully on to a dish and leave until cold.

Arrange the apricots round the top of the gâteau, so that each apricot overlaps the previous one, the cut side downwards.

Pour the apricot syrup all round the gâteau, and serve.

NOTE.—If liked, the custard may be baked instead of steamed.

Sufficient for about six persons.

APRICOT JUNKET

INGREDIENTS.—Small tin of apricots, 1 pint of milk, 1 good dessertspoonful of castor sugar, 1 good teaspoonful of essence of rennet, vanilla flavouring.

METHOD.—Dissolve the sugar in the milk and make just lukewarm. Add a few drops of vanilla. Pour into a dish, stir in the rennet, and leave until set.

Strain the syrup from the apricots and arrange some of them on top of the junket with the cut side downward.

Put the syrup into a sauce-boat and serve with the junket, if liked.

Sufficient for about five persons.

APRICOT LAYER CREAM

INGREDIENTS.—A large tin of apricots (use as required), ½ pint packet apricot jelly, rather less than

½ pint of hot water, ½ oz. of leaf gelatine, 2 oz. of castor sugar, 9d. of cream (about ¾ gill).

METHOD.—Dissolve the jelly in the hot water, and when cold set a thin layer in the bottom of a plain mould, previously rinsed in cold water. Drain the syrup from the apricots and put sufficient through a sieve to make half a pint of pulp. Cut the remainder into slices, dip some of them in jelly and decorate the bottom of the mould. When set, cover with jelly and set again. Whisk the cream until it thickens, then gradually stir in the apricot pulp and sugar.

Dissolve the gelatine in a saucepan with half a gill of the apricot syrup, strain into the cream, etc., and mix together lightly.

Turn a good layer of the prepared cream into the mould and when set add some more apricot slices dipped in jelly. Cover these with jelly and set again, then fill up the mould with the creamy mixture. When ready, dip in warm water and unmould.

Sufficient for six persons.

APRICOT MACAROONS

INGREDIENTS.—A small tin of apricots in syrup, 1 dozen macaroon biscuits, vanilla flavouring, ¼ teaspoonful of castor sugar, 1 gill of cream.

METHOD.—Place the macaroon biscuits in a dish and soak with the apricot syrup. Put an apricot on each macaroon.

Whisk the cream until it thickens—be careful not to over-whisk, as this will curdle the cream.

Add the vanilla and sugar.

Decorate round each macaroon and the top of each apricot with the cream.

APRICOTS AND PISTACHIOS

INGREDIENTS.—1 large tin of apricots, 3 flat tablespoonfuls of ground rice, 1 pint of milk, 3 oz. of castor sugar, 1 yolk of egg, ½ lemon, 1 oz. of pistachio nuts, lemon flavouring.

METHOD.—Rub the apricots through a sieve (but leave out a large one ; you will want it later).

Squeeze and strain the juice from the lemon and add the apricot pulp, together with half of the sugar.

Mix together, and pour into a glass dish.

Mix the ground rice to a smooth paste with half a gill of apricot syrup.

Heat the milk, pour it on to the rice, return to the saucepan, and bring to the boil, keeping it well stirred.

Add the sugar, and simmer for about six minutes.

Draw away from the fire and cool slightly, add the flavouring and egg-yolk, and cook very slowly for a few minutes.

Pour slowly over the apricot pulp, but do not mix together.

Leave until quite cold.

Blanch the pistachio nuts and chop up finely.

Put the whole apricot in the centre of the rice and sprinkle the nuts all round.

NOTE.—Put the nuts in cold water and bring to the boil, the skins can then be easily removed.

If the nuts are very moist when chopped, dry them in a warm place for a few minutes, but be careful not to spoil their fresh green colour.

Sufficient for about eight persons.

APRICOT PUDDINGS

INGREDIENTS.—½ pint of stewed apricots (fresh or tinned), 3 tea-spoonfuls of desiccated coconut, 1 level teaspoonful of powdered gelatine, stale bread.

METHOD.—Cut some stale crumb of bread into slices a quarter of an inch thick. Stamp out rounds and place these in the bottom of three small basins, then line the sides with bread.

Dissolve the gelatine in a little of the fruit juice, add the stewed fruit, mash it up and make it hot. Stir in the coconut, and pour sufficient of the mixture into each basin to fill it.

Cover the top of each with another round of bread and press this down, leaving it pressed until cold, then turn out the puddings.

Decorate the top of each with half an apricot, and pour stewed apricots (cut up small) round the puddings. These stewed apricots should be extra to those given in the recipe, as the half pint is required for the inside of the puddings. If using fresh apricots, they must be stoned.

Sufficient for three puddings.

APRICOT AND TAPIOCA PUDDING

INGREDIENTS. — 1 small tin of apricots, 1½ pints of milk, 3 oz. of sugar, 3 oz. of tapioca, lemon flavouring.

METHOD.—Well wash the tapioca, cover with cold water, and soak for a few hours (all night, if possible). The next morning strain off the water (if any). Place the tapioca in a sauce-pan with the milk and sugar and simmer carefully until it is quite soft, and the milk is absorbed.

Flavour with a few drops of lemon essence.

Take two or three apricots from the syrup, and cut each into seven or eight pieces, and stir into the tapioca.

Pour this into a wet mould and leave until quite set.

Turn on to a dish carefully ; just ease the tapioca from the sides of the mould and shake gently, and it will easily turn out. Heap two or three apricots on the top of the pudding ; the remainder arrange in heaps at either end of the dish.

Pour the apricot syrup round the pudding and serve.

CARAMEL BANANAS

INGREDIENTS.—2 eggs, 1 pint of milk, 1 dessertspoonful of castor sugar, 2 oz. of lump sugar, ½ gill of water, 3 or 4 bananas, cream flavouring.

METHOD.—Put the lump sugar into a saucepan with the water and dissolve it slowly. Then bring it to the boil and boil it until golden brown. Draw the pan aside and leave the syrup until cold. Add the milk and stand it over a low burner to dissolve the caramel.

Beat up the eggs and add the caramel milk to them, then turn them into the top of a double boiler and stir until the custard thickens.

Remove it at once from the hot water, add the castor sugar and leave them until cold. Turn the mixture into six custard glasses, filling them about half or two-thirds full. Fill the glasses up with sliced bananas and heap whipped cream (sweetened and flavoured to taste) on top with a slice of banana in the centre.

Sufficient for six custard cups.

NOTE.—Use a small, strong pan for making the caramel.

BANANA CREAM

INGREDIENTS.—½ pint of banana pulp, barely ¾ oz. of gelatine, ¼ lb. of icing sugar, 1 gill of whipped cream, ½ pint of milk, Fairy Sauce.

METHOD.—Dissolve the gelatine in a little hot water, and then remove it from the heat.

Stir in the sugar and mix it with the milk. Gradually add this to the banana pulp and mix it with the whipped cream, and when it is beginning to thicken pour it into a wet mould.

When it is set, turn it out and decorate it with sliced banana, and serve it with Fairy Sauce.

FAIRY SAUCE

INGREDIENTS.—¾ gill of milk, 1 egg, 2 oz. of castor sugar, 1 teaspoonful of vanilla, ¾ gill of whipped cream.

METHOD.—Beat the sugar and egg together for five minutes.

Bring the milk to the boil in a double boiler.

Add the sugar and egg mixture, and allow it to cool.

Stir in the vanilla and the whipped cream.

Sufficient for six persons.

BANANA FINGERS

INGREDIENTS.—4 sponge fingers, 2 bananas, 1 gill of ginger wine, ¼ packet of raspberry jelly, 1 egg, ½ pint of milk, ½ oz. of sugar, 1 gill of hot water.

METHOD.—Divide the sponge fingers and lay half a banana (cut lengthwise) inside the two pieces.

Pour the wine over slowly.

Beat the egg and sugar and pour on the hot milk.

Put in a double saucepan and stir till thick.

Strain round the sponge fingers.

Dissolve the jelly in the water and when set use it to decorate the dish.

Sufficient for two or three persons.

BANANA FOOL

INGREDIENTS.—10 bananas, 1 lemon, 1 pint of milk, 3 tablespoonfuls of castor sugar, 1 tablespoonful of custard powder, 1 oz. of white sugar, 2 whites of eggs, vanilla flavouring, glacé cherries.

METHOD.—Peel the bananas, then mash them up with a fork.

Then add the strained lemon-juice, together with two tablespoonfuls of castor sugar.

Mix thoroughly.

Make the custard—mix the custard powder with a little milk. Put the remainder in a saucepan with the white sugar.

Bring to the boil, pour on to the custard powder, keeping it well stirred. Flavour with vanilla.

Cool slightly, and add to the banana mixture.

Stir thoroughly.

Leave until quite cold.

Whisk the whites of eggs to a very stiff froth, fold into them the remainder of the castor sugar.

Add half of this meringue mixture to the banana etc., and mix lightly together.

Put into custard glasses and shake some of the meringue mixture on to the top of each, and decorate with small pieces of glacé cherries.

BANANA AND LEMON JELLY

INGREDIENTS.—6 lemons, 4 or 5 bananas, 2 oz. of leaf gelatine, 2 egg-whites, 2 egg shells, 6 oz. of sugar, 1½ pints of water, a few cloves.

METHOD.—Choose good juicy lemons. Peel two of them *thinly*, and put the peel into a large saucepan with the juice of all of them well squeezed out. Add the water and sugar. Remove the inner skin from the egg shells, then wash them and break them up, and add them with the egg-whites, cloves, and gelatine.

Whisk them over a fairly low burner until the gelatine and sugar are dissolved, and there is a good head of frothy scum on the top, but remember to stop whisking just before the mixture boils.

Bring it up to the boil, leave it at the side of the fire for a few minutes, then strain it through a scalded jelly bag, putting the froth first into the bag and pouring the jelly slowly through it.

Take a plain mould and set a thin layer of jelly in the bottom, then decorate this with slices of banana dipped in jelly. When set, cover them with jelly and set this again. Continue in this way until the mould is full, and when firm unmould the jelly and serve it with cream.

Sufficient for six persons.

BANANA AND PINEAPPLE ROYAL

INGREDIENTS.—7 bananas, ¼ pint of milk, a small tin of pineapple, ½ oz. of leaf gelatine.

METHOD.—Peel six of the bananas and mash them to a pulp. Drain the syrup from the pineapple and put the fruit through a mincer.

Dissolve the gelatine in a saucepan with half a gill of the pineapple syrup, add the remainder to the banana pulp. Stir in also the minced pineapple, leaving out a little for decoration.

Strain in the dissolved gelatine, then add the milk, and some castor sugar if required. Turn into a dish and leave to set.

Just before you are ready to serve it, heap some minced pineapple in the centre and add the remaining banana cut in slices.

Serve with cream.

Sufficient for about six persons.

COLD BANANA PUDDING

INGREDIENTS.—6 bananas, rind and juice of ½ lemon, 1½ tablespoonfuls of castor sugar, 1 tablespoonful of cornflour, 1 pint of milk, 1 large tablespoonful of apricot jam, crystallised violets.

METHOD.—Mix the cornflour with half a gill of the milk.

Put the remainder of the milk on to heat, with one tablespoonful of sugar and the grated rind of half a lemon. When hot, pour it on to the mixed cornflour, stirring well.

Pour all back into the saucepan and boil slowly for six minutes, again stirring well to prevent it from getting lumpy.

Peel the bananas, mash them with a fork, and put them into the bottom of a china or glass dish.

Sprinkle the lemon-juice and remainder of the castor sugar over the bananas, add the apricot jam, and mix all well together. When the cornflour has slightly cooled, pour it carefully over the top of the bananas, etc., but do not allow it to mix with them. Sprinkle the top with crystallised violets.

BANANA AND RHUBARB MOULD

INGREDIENTS.—1 pint packet of orange jelly, ½ pint of rhubarb-juice, 3 bananas, hot water, cream, chopped pistachio nuts.

METHOD.—Dissolve the jelly in half a pint of hot water and when cool make it up to a pint with rhubarb syrup from stewed rhubarb.

When the jelly begins to thicken, peel the bananas, mash them up and stir them into the jelly. Turn it into a wet mould. Leave it to set, then unmould it and top it with whipped cream, sweetened and flavoured to taste, and sprinkle it with chopped blanched pistachio nuts. Serve with some sliced banana round the base of the mould.

Sufficient for five persons.

BANANA SPONGE

INGREDIENTS.—6 bananas, 2 oz. of sugar, 2 large lemons, ¾ oz. of gelatine, ½ pint of cold water, 2 whites of eggs, a few glacé cherries.

METHOD.—Rub three bananas through a sieve and add sugar and lemon-juice. Soak the gelatine in the water for five minutes, then heat, stirring till the gelatine is dissolved. Strain and, when cold, add it to the bananas.

Beat the whites till stiff, stir them in and whisk with an egg whisk till frothy and solid. Oil a mould, one and a half pint size, and pour in the mixture.

Decorate with cherries and half bananas.

Sufficient for three or four persons.

BANANA TRIFLE

INGREDIENTS.—6 bananas, a bought Savoy cake, apricot jam, 2 lemons, 2 eggs, ¾ pint of milk, 2 oz. of sugar, 1 gill of cream, 1½ wineglassfuls of sherry, 1 oz. of ratafias, 1 oz. of glacé cherries, 1 oz. of Jordan almonds, ½ gill of hot water.

METHOD.—Cut the cake across into three pieces, scooping a little out of the top one.

Melt half a pot of jam in half a gill of water. Mix the bananas and jam, while hot, and spread on each layer of the cake, putting a spoonful into the hole in the top one.

Fit the three pieces of cake together again.

Sprinkle with the sherry and lemon-juice.

Put the eggs and sugar in a double pan, beat with an egg whisk, add the milk and stir till it is thick enough to coat the back of the spoon. When cold, strain over the cake and, if possible, leave it till next day.

Pour boiling water on the almonds, and slip off the skins.

Put the almonds in cold water, then cut them in strips.

Stick almonds and ratafias all over the cake, and decorate with cream and cherries.

Sufficient for four persons.

BAVAROISE AU CAFE

INGREDIENTS.—1 pint of milk, castor sugar, 2 or 3 tablespoonfuls of coffee essence, 2 eggs (large), 1 oz. of French leaf gelatine (light weight), $\frac{1}{2}$ gill of cold water, $1\frac{1}{2}$ gills of cream.

METHOD.—Put the milk, castor sugar, and coffee essence in a saucepan, stir and bring to the boil. Beat up the eggs, and when the milk, etc., has slightly cooled add it to the eggs.

Mix well and pour into a jug, stand in a saucepan of water, and stir over the fire until the custard thickens. Be careful not to get it too hot or it will curdle.

Pour the custard into a basin and leave until cold.

Dissolve the gelatine in three-quarters to one gill of cold water. Do not boil it or it will not dissolve readily.

Whisk the cream until quite thick, then fold it into the cold custard. Add a little sugar, as required.

Lastly, strain in the gelatine and mix very lightly.

Stir thoroughly (if possible over a piece of ice) until the mixture begins to thicken.

Pour into a wet mould and allow it to set.

Turn on to a dish and serve.

If liked, decorate with cream.

Sufficient for about eight persons.

BISCUIT CREAM

INGREDIENTS.—$\frac{1}{2}$ pint packet of lemon jelly, $\frac{1}{2}$ pint of hot water, 3 oz. of petit beurre biscuits, 1 pint of milk, 1 tablespoonful of custard powder, vanilla or almond flavouring, 2 dessertspoonfuls of castor sugar, 2 tablespoonfuls of thick cream, $\frac{3}{8}$ oz. of leaf gelatine, $\frac{1}{2}$ gill of water, 1 oz. of angelica, a cherry.

METHOD.—Make the jelly—dissolve it in hot water and leave until cold, but not set.

Take a plain mould (charlotte tin), rinse it with cold water, then mask the sides with a little jelly, and set a thin layer in the bottom. (*How to mask a mould is explained below.*)

Cut small leaves of angelica and dip in jelly.

Decorate the bottom of the mould with these, and a cherry in the centre of them.

When set, pour in sufficient jelly to just cover, and set again.

Roll out the biscuits with a rolling-pin and crush them to a powder.

Cut the remainder of the angelica into small pieces.

TO MAKE THE CUSTARD.—Mix the custard powder to a paste with some of the milk.

Put the remainder into a saucepan with the sugar and bring to the boil, then pour it on to the custard powder.

Add the biscuit powder and angelica, stir all together, and leave until quite cool.

Dissolve the gelatine slowly in a saucepan with the water (half a gill) ; do not boil it. Add the flavouring to the custard and stir in the cream.

Lastly, strain in the gelatine, mix all together lightly.

Put into the prepared mould and leave until set.

Dip into warm water, turn on to a dish.

Chop the remainder of the jelly and serve round.

NOTE.—If you have any biscuit

crumbs, use these instead of crushing whole ones.

To "Mask" A Mould

To mask a mould with jelly, pour a little cold jelly into it and turn it round—*on a piece of ice, if possible*—until a thin layer begins to set all round the tin, then tip out any that is not required. This method gives a delicate coating of jelly to the outside of "creams."

Sufficient for about six persons.

BLACKBERRY AND APPLE FLUMMERY

INGREDIENTS.—1 lb. of blackberries, 1 lb. of apples, 1 pint of water, sugar to taste, 2 oz. of flour, ½ teaspoonful of mixed spice.

METHOD.—Pick the blackberries and peel and core the apples. Stew the fruit in the water, sweeten it to taste, and rub through a hair sieve. Mix the flour and spice to a perfectly smooth liquid with a little cold water. Boil the fruit purée and pour it on the flour, stirring well. Return the mixture to the pan, stir till it boils. Boil for five minutes, and when cool enough pour it into a glass dish. Serve cold with milk, custard, or cream.

Any kind of fruit can be used, but sharp-tasting fruits are best.

To serve five or six persons.

BLACKBERRY FOOL

INGREDIENTS.—A tin of blackberries, ½ pint of custard, 6d. of cream, sugar, vanilla flavouring, cochineal.

METHOD.—Strain the syrup from the blackberries, then rub them through a sieve or colander, or mash to a pulp.

Make half a pint of custard, and when cold stir it into the fruit pulp; add also half a gill of the syrup. Colour with a few drops of cochineal if required, and mix all together. Serve in small custard glasses, with a little whipped cream piled in the centre.

To WHIP CREAM, whisk it until it stiffens, then sweeten and flavour to taste.

Sufficient for five persons.

BLANCMANGE DAINTIES

(FOR THE CHILDREN'S PARTY)

INGREDIENTS.—½ oz. of packet gelatine, 1 pint of milk, 2 dessertspoonfuls of sugar, flavouring, cochineal, a few almonds, glacé cherries and angelica.

METHOD.—Put the gelatine into one cup of the milk and leave to soak for about a couple of hours, after which time boil the remainder of the milk in a saucepan with the sugar. Then mix with the soaked gelatine and milk and stir until dissolved. Strain, add flavouring to taste, then turn half of it into small tartlet-tins (previously rinsed with cold water).

Add a few drops of cochineal to the remainder, and when evenly coloured to a pale pink colour, pour into some more wet tins.

When set, turn out and decorate some of them with a blanched almond, and the others with a small piece of glacé cherry and leaves of angelica.

Sufficient to make twelve dainties.

BREAD JELLY MOULD

INGREDIENTS.—3 oz. of stale bread, 1 pint packet of cherry jelly, ½ pint of hot water, ½ pint of left-over fruit syrup, 2 tablespoonfuls of desiccated coconut.

FOR THE CUSTARD.—1 yolk and 1 whole egg, ¾ pint of milk, 1½ dessertspoonfuls of sugar, vanilla.

METHOD.—Dissolve the jelly in hot water, boil the syrup and add it to the jelly.

Put the stale bread in a basin, pour over the hot jelly, cover them, and leave them until the bread is thoroughly softened, then break it up with a fork.

Stir in the coconut and some sugar if required, and turn the mixture into a wet mould to set. Dip it in warm water, unmould, and serve the jelly mould surrounded by a custard.

More or less fruit syrup may be used, with a proportionate amount of hot water.

To MAKE THE CUSTARD, bring the milk almost to the boil and add it to the beaten eggs. Turn them into the top of a double boiler, add the sugar, and stir the custard over hot water until it thickens.

Remove it from the hot water, let it cool, and add vanilla to taste.

Sufficient for five or six persons.

BUTTERSCOTCH CREAMS

INGREDIENTS.—2 oz. of butterscotch, ½ gill of cream, 1 egg, ¾ pint of milk, ¾ oz. of flour, ⅜ oz. of gelatine, ½ gill of water, 2 oz. of butter, ¼ lb. of Barbados sugar.

METHOD.—Mix the flour to a smooth paste with just a little of the milk. Heat the remainder of the milk and stir it into the paste. Return this to the saucepan and bring it to the boil. Boil it for two or three minutes, then take it off the heat and cool it slightly.

Beat up the egg and stir it in gradually and cook the mixture over the hot water until it thickens, then let it cool.

Melt the butter and heat half the water in a saucepan, add the sugar and when it is dissolved bring it to the boil and boil it for two or three minutes until it thickens. Take it off the heat, and when it is quite cool add it by degrees to the cooled custard, stirring it in till it is dissolved.

Leave it till it is quite cold, then add the lightly whipped cream. Strain in the gelatine, dissolved in the remainder of the water, and add the crushed butterscotch.

Turn the prepared cream into small wet moulds, and when these are set unmould them and decorate them with a little whipped cream (extra to that given), and top each cream with a silver ball.

CABINET CARAMEL MOULD

INGREDIENTS.—2 oz. of lump sugar, 1 gill of water, ½ oz. of gelatine, 3 sponge cakes, 2 eggs, ¾ pint of milk, 2 tablespoonfuls of cream, a few silver balls, some angelica.

METHOD.—Put the lump sugar into a small strong saucepan with half the water, let it dissolve slowly, then boil it until golden brown. Leave it until cold. Add the milk, and dissolve the caramel over a low burner.

Beat up one whole egg and one yolk and mix them with the caramel milk, then strain this into the top of a double boiler and cook it over hot water until the custard thickens, keeping it stirred, then take it off the gas and cool.

Crumble the sponge cakes and add them to the custard, strain in the gelatine dissolved in the remainder of the water, and when the mixture is thoroughly cold stir in the cream, adding a little sugar as required. Lastly, fold in the stiffly whisked egg-white.

Turn the mixture into a wet mould, and when set, unmould it and decorate it with silver balls and angelica.

Sufficient for five persons.

CALIFORNIAN MOULD

INGREDIENTS.—½ lb. of prunes, water to cover, 2 oz. of sugar, 1 lemon (rind and juice), angelica, ½ oz. of gelatine, ½ gill of water, 1 pint packet of lemon jelly, ¾ pint of hot water.

METHOD.—Wash the prunes in two or three warm waters, and soak in cold water for at least twelve hours. Dissolve the jelly in the hot water; less water than usual is used for this jelly, as it is required to be firmer.

After the prunes have been soaked, place them in a saucepan with the water in which they have been soaking, add the sugar, and stew until tender. Use a fancy mould, if possible a border mould (one with a hole in the middle). Scald the mould, then rinse in cold water. Mask the mould with some of the jelly; the latter should be cold but not set. To do this, put about one tablespoonful of the jelly into the mould, put the mould on its side, and turn it about on a small piece of ice (if available) until the jelly forms a thin coating all round the sides of the mould. Then stand the mould straight, and let a coating form at the bottom of the mould.

When this is set, decorate the bottom of mould with pieces of angelica and prunes alternately all round.

Dip each piece of decoration in jelly before putting it into the mould, and use a decorating needle or new hat-pin. Leave this decoration until set. Cover it with more of the jelly and leave again until set. Now finish making the sweet.

Remove the stones from the prunes and add to the prunes the grated lemon-rind and juice. Dissolve the gelatine in half a gill of water, then strain it into the prunes, etc. Stir all together and pour into the prepared mould. Leave until set. Turn on to a dish. Chop the remainder of the jelly and serve with it round the dish. If liked, whipped cream may also be served with it, in the hollow of the mould.

CARAMEL CREAM CUSTARD

INGREDIENTS.—12 to 15 lumps of sugar, 2 eggs, 1½ dessertspoonfuls of castor sugar, ½ pint of milk, 3 to 4 tablespoonfuls of hot water, ½ gill of cream.

METHOD.—TO MAKE THE CARAMEL : Put the lump sugar into a small, strong saucepan with the hot water.

Let it dissolve slowly, and then bring it to the boil. Boil the syrup gently till it is deep golden.

Meanwhile, warm some small moulds, and, directly the caramel is ready, pour a little into the bottom of each one and let it set. Then butter the sides of the moulds.

TO MAKE THE CUSTARD.—Heat the milk and castor sugar and pour it on to the beaten eggs, then strain it into the prepared moulds.

Cover each securely with a buttered paper, and steam them *very gently* for about half an hour, or until they are set, being careful not to let them boil.

Take up the moulds and leave them for a few minutes before turning them out. Then unmould them and, when they are cold, decorate each one with a little cream, the latter whipped and sweetened and flavoured to taste.

Sufficient for four small moulds.

CARAMEL FRUIT FOOL

INGREDIENTS.—A large tin of pears, 1 egg, 1½ gills of milk, 1 oz. of ground Brazil nuts, 2 dessertspoonfuls of sugar, 1½ dessertspoonfuls of water.

METHOD.—Drain the syrup from the pears, then rub the fruit through a sieve.

Put the sugar in a small, strong saucepan with the water. Let it dissolve slowly, then boil until a rich golden brown. Draw aside and leave until cold. Add the milk and dissolve the caramel over a *low* burner.

Beat the egg, add the caramel milk, strain into a jug and cook in a saucepan of water until it thickens.

When cold, mix this with the pear pulp, add about three parts of the ground nuts and a little sugar if required. Two or three tablespoonfuls of pear syrup may be added if liked, but take care not to make the mixture too thin.

Serve in custard glasses with the remainder of the ground nuts sprinkled on the top.

Sufficient for six glasses.

CARAMEL SHAPE

INGREDIENTS.—2 oz. of lump sugar, 1 tablespoonful of water, ½ oz. of margarine, 1 egg, 5 flat tablespoonfuls of ground rice, 1 lemon, about 2 dessertspoonfuls of sugar, 1½ pints of milk.

METHOD.—Put the lump sugar and water into a small saucepan and dissolve slowly, then boil until brown.

Have ready a small plain tin mould previously warmed. Pour the caramel into it and coat the sides and bottom, then leave until set. Mix the ground rice to a smooth paste with some of the milk. Heat the remainder and stir on to it, then return to the pan and bring to the boil, keeping it well stirred.

Add the sugar, margarine, and finely-grated lemon-rind and boil gently for about eight minutes, then cool slightly.

Beat up the egg, stir in, and cook slowly for a few minutes, but do not let it boil.

Pour into the prepared mould and leave until set, then turn on to a dish— the caramel will coat the shape and form a sauce round it.

Sufficient for about five persons.

CARAMEL TRIFLE

INGREDIENTS.—2 sixpenny sponge rings, 1 pint of milk, 2 oz. of lump sugar, ½ gill of water, 2 eggs, 1 dessertspoonful of castor sugar, cooking sherry, vanilla, 5d. of cream, or more as liked, a few almonds, apricot jam.

METHOD.—Put the lump sugar into a saucepan with the water and dissolve it slowly. Then bring it to the boil and boil it until golden brown. Draw the pan aside and leave the syrup till cold.

Add the milk and stand it over a very low burner to dissolve the caramel.

Beat up the eggs, add the caramel milk, and strain into the top of a double boiler, stirring until the custard thickens. Remove the pan *at once* when ready. Add the castor sugar and leave the custard to cool.

Split the sponge rings in half and use three halves for the trifle ; the other half can be utilised for some other purpose. Spread the slices with jam and arrange them in a dish, soaking them with milk, sherry, or fruit-juice, then pour the custard round the sponge.

Whisk the cream until it thickens and add sugar and vanilla to taste. Put this cream on top of the ring and decorate it with a few baked almonds.

Sufficient for from six to eight persons.

CHARLOTTE AU CAFE

INGREDIENTS.—½ packet of plain jelly, 6 oz. of oblong biscuits, ¾ oz. of gelatine, 2 tablespoonfuls of coffee essence, ¼ pint of cold water, ½ gill of cream, 1 pint of milk, 2 eggs, 2 oz. of sugar, ½ pint of hot water.

METHOD.—Oil a small cake-tin. Dissolve the jelly in half a pint of hot water, and when cold pour into the tin. When set, arrange the biscuits close together round the tin right side out.

Put the gelatine in a saucepan with the water and coffee essence, and dissolve it over a very low gas, stirring all the time.

Beat the eggs with the sugar ; heat the milk, but do not boil it, and pour it on the eggs. Stir in a double saucepan till thick enough to coat the back of the spoon. Add the gelatine and strain. When cold add the cream. Leave till it is nearly set, then pour into the lined tin. If the mixture is poured in when too thin, it will make the biscuits soft.

When set, place a dish on top, turn it over and shake gently.

Decorate with cream.

Sufficient for two or three persons.

CHARLOTTE RUSSE

CHARLOTTE RUSSE consists chiefly of a cream filling set in a charlotte-tin, which has been first decorated with jelly and the sides lined with finger biscuits.

The cream filling is set lightly with gelatine, and care must be taken not to make it too stiff, otherwise the Charlotte Russe entirely loses its delicacy. In very hot weather it may be necessary to add just a little more gelatine than the quantity given in the recipe.

INGREDIENTS.—½ pint packet of lemon jelly, 1½ gills of hot water, a few glacé cherries and pieces of angelica, 2 oz. of Savoy biscuits, 1½ gills of cream, ½ gill of milk, ¼ gill of water, ¼ oz. of gelatine, 1 white of egg, 3 level dessertspoonfuls of castor sugar, ½ teaspoonful of vanilla flavouring.

METHOD.—Dissolve the jelly in the hot water, and when cold pour about one tablespoonful of it into the bottom of a charlotte-tin, or sufficient just to coat the bottom of the tin. The latter should be first rinsed with cold water, and for this quantity of ingredients you will need a charlotte-tin to hold about a pint and a quarter. A charlotte-tin is just a plain tin with slightly sloping sides.

When the jelly in the tin is set, halve some glacé cherries and dip them in a little of the remaining jelly, then arrange them in the bottom of the tin to form a decoration. A few leaves, cut from a piece of angelica and dipped in jelly, may be used with them. Let the decoration get firm, then cover it with jelly and leave it to set again.

Meanwhile you can prepare the biscuits. First split them in halves. As they are usually very brittle, this must be done carefully, then straighten the sides of each half and cut a piece off one end, so that they may stand firmly on the jelly, and be about the same height as the tin.

Now arrange them round the tin, filling up any cracks with a paste made from biscuit-crumbs and jelly, so as to prevent the cream mixture from oozing through the cracks.

To Prepare the Cream Mixture.—Whisk the cream until it hangs from the whisk, stir in the castor sugar and vanilla, and gradually add the milk.

Dissolve the gelatine in a saucepan with the water, and strain it in, when of a moderate heat, keeping the mixture stirred lightly.

Lastly, whisk the egg-white to a stiff froth and fold it in. Leave till the mixture begins to thicken, then turn it into the prepared tin and let it set.

To Unmould.—Dip the bottom of the mould in warm water, then turn it over and shake it sharply, keeping one hand firmly on each end of the mould. When you can feel it is loosened, slip the Charlotte Russe carefully on to a dish.

Chop up the remainder of the jelly on a piece of wet paper and serve a little of it round the base of the charlotte.

The filling can be varied in numerous ways, and sometimes when making this sweet half a pint of cream may be used and the white of egg omitted.

To Make a Chocolate Filling.—Dissolve a little grated chocolate in the milk and add it.

To Make a Coffee Filling.—Flavour the cream with coffee essence and omit the vanilla.

Sufficient for six persons.

AN APRICOT CHARLOTTE RUSSE

Ingredients.—A tin of apricots, ¼ pint of cream, ½ gill of apricot syrup, ¼ oz. of gelatine, castor sugar, 2 oz. of Savoy biscuits, ½ pint packet of lemon jelly, 1½ gills of hot water, glacé cherries, 1 dessertspoonful of lemon-juice.

Method.—Decorate a charlotte-tin with jelly and cherries as explained in the previous recipe, or substitute quarters of apricots for the cherries. Arrange the biscuits round the tin.

Rub sufficient apricots through a sieve to give a quarter of a pint of pulp, then stir the lemon-juice into it.

Whisk up the cream, and add the apricot pulp with sugar to taste, then stir in the gelatine dissolved in the apricot syrup. Leave the mixture till it is beginning to thicken, then

mould it. When set, turn out the charlotte and decorate it with chopped jelly. Place an apricot in the centre.

Sufficient for six persons.

CHERRY APPLES

Ingredients.—1 lb. of cooking apples, ½ gill of water, 2 oz. of sugar—or to taste, 2 oz. of glacé cherries, rind of ½ lemon, 1 egg, 1 oz. of butter, barely ¼ oz. of gelatine, 2 tablespoonfuls of water.

Method.—Peel, quarter and core the apples, and slice them thickly. Cook them with the half a gill of water and the sugar until tender, then rub them through a sieve.

Return the pulp to the saucepan, and add the butter, beaten egg, and grated lemon-rind.

Stir the purée over a low burner for a few minutes to cook the egg, being careful not to let it boil, then take it off the heat and cool it.

Cut up one ounce of the cherries and add them to the apple mixture. Then dissolve the gelatine in a saucepan with two tablespoonfuls of water and strain it into the apple mixture.

Turn it into custard cups, and when it is set decorate each cup with the remainder of the cherries cut into pieces and arranged in the form of a cross.

Serve cherry apples with cream.

Note.—A few cloves may be added to the apples, but they should be removed before the fruit is sieved, or the mixture may be flavoured with a little sherry, if preferred.

Sufficient for four persons.

CHERRY BLANCMANGE

Ingredients.—5 oz. of flaked rice, ¾ pint tin of red cherries, 1½ pints of milk, 3 oz. of castor sugar, or more if required, 1 oz. of butter, flavouring, cochineal.

Method.—Turn out the cherries and strain off the syrup. Stone and halve about two-thirds of them, and leave the remainder whole.

Put the milk and fruit syrup into a saucepan, add the flaked rice, and cook it till the mixture is quite thick and the rice cooked, keeping it well stirred.

Add the sugar and butter, and stir them till they are dissolved. Then add flavouring to taste, and also the stoned and halved cherries.

Colour the mixture to a pink shade with cochineal.

Turn the mixture into a wet mould to set, and, when it is firm, unmould it and decorate it with the remainder of the cherries.

Sufficient for eight persons.

CHERRY CREAM

INGREDIENTS. — Some stewed cherries (about 1 pint), 1 gill of cream, 1 pint of packet cherry jelly, ¼ pint of hot water.

METHOD.—Prepare some stewing cherries and cook them till tender, adding a little water and sugar to taste, then drain them and remove the stones. Rub the fruit through a coarse sieve, or put it through a mincer, being careful to save the syrup.

Dissolve the jelly in a quarter of a pint of hot water plus the same amount of hot cherry syrup. Leave it to get cold, then add a quarter of a pint of the cherry pulp or minced cherries.

When the jelly is beginning to thicken, whisk the cream until thick ; then gradually stir the cherry jelly mixture into it, and mix all together lightly.

Turn the mixture into a wet mould, and when set, unmould and decorate the centre with a cherry.

CHERRY SHAPES

INGREDIENTS.—1 lb. of cooking cherries, 1 gill of water, 3 oz. of sugar, 1 yolk of egg, ¼ pint of milk, 1 white of egg, ¾ gill of cream, ½ oz. of gelatine, angelica.

METHOD.—Stalk and wash the cherries, then stone them. Cook them with the water and sugar until tender, then rub them through a sieve and leave them to get cold.

Heat the milk and add it to the beaten egg-yolk and cook them in the top of a double boiler till the custard thickens, keeping it stirred. Remove it from the gas and let it cool.

Dissolve the gelatine in a little cherry syrup—which should have been kept back before rubbing the fruit

through a sieve, and strain it into the cherry purée. Stir in also the custard, whipped cream, and stiffly-whisked egg-white, and more sugar if required.

Mix them lightly, and turn the mixture into small moulds. When set, unmould the cherry shapes and decorate them with angelica.

Sufficient to fill six small moulds.

CHERRY SNOW CAP

INGREDIENTS.—1 lb. of cherries (when stoned), 1 gill of water, 4 dessert-spoonfuls of granulated sugar, a round flat sponge cake, 2 pairs of meringue cases, cream (as required), sugar and vanilla, 2 oz. of icing sugar, 1 oz. of butter.

METHOD.—Stalk and stone the cherries. Put the water and sugar into a saucepan, dissolve, then boil for two or three minutes. Add the cherries and stew until tender, then leave to cool. The syrup should be fairly thick. If necessary boil it again for a few minutes after taking up the fruit.

Either make or buy a round sponge such as you would use for a jam sandwich. Split it in halves and cover one half with some of the stewed cherries.

Spread the other half with a thin layer of vanilla butter icing (made by beating the icing sugar and butter to a cream and flavouring with vanilla) and sandwich together. Put the remainder of the fruit and syrup on the top. Whip some cream, sweeten and flavour it to taste and put into the meringues. Arrange these on the fruit and heap a little cream in the centre.

Sufficient for six persons.

CHERRY SPONGE

INGREDIENTS.—1 small tin of red cherries in syrup, ½ gill of sherry, 1 pint of hot water, 1 sponge-cake ring, 1 pint packet of cherry jelly, 1 gill of cream, sugar and vanilla.

METHOD.—Dissolve the jelly in hot water and leave until cold, but not set.

Place the sponge-ring in a glass dish.

Heat the syrup from the cherries

and well soak the sponge with this and the sherry.

When the jelly is just beginning to set, stir it up well and mask the top and sides of the sponge with some of it, taking about a tablespoonful at a time and gently pouring it over.

Now place a line of cherries closely together, all round the top of the sponge, on the jelly.

Put the remainder of the jelly round in the bottom of the dish, and arrange the remainder of the cherries on this jelly, just leaving one out for decoration

Leave until the jelly is quite set, then sweeten and flavour the cream, and whisk it until it stiffens.

Heap it up in the centre hole of the sponge-ring and put a cherry on the top.

CHERRY WHIRL

INGREDIENTS.—$\frac{1}{2}$ small tin of cherries, 1 pint packet of raspberry jelly, $\frac{3}{4}$ pint of hot water, 2 eggs, $\frac{1}{2}$ pint of milk, $1\frac{1}{2}$ dessertspoonfuls of castor sugar, vanilla flavouring.

METHOD.—Dissolve the jelly in the hot water, then stir in half a gill of cherry syrup. When the jelly is half set stir it up, then whisk the whites of the eggs to a very stiff froth, and stir three parts of them into the jelly. When well (but lightly) mixed in, turn into a wet pie-tin and leave to set.

To serve, turn out, arrange the cherries on the top, and decorate with the remainder of the egg-white, whisked up again, and one dessertspoonful of the castor sugar folded into it.

Make an egg custard with the egg-yolks and milk, sweeten and flavour it to taste and serve with it.

Sufficient for six persons.

CHOCOLATE AND BANANA MOULD

INGREDIENTS.—$\frac{1}{2}$ packet of vanilla jelly, 4 bananas, 1 tablespoonful of cocoa, 2 oz. of sugar, 2 eggs, 1 pint of milk, 1 gill of cream, 1 oz. of gelatine.

METHOD.—Dissolve the jelly in half a pint of hot water.

Rinse a mould in cold water, pour in a little jelly and decorate to taste with pieces of banana. Let it set and

pour in more jelly. When firm do the sides in the same way.

Break up the gelatine and soak it in a basin with a gill of cold milk.

Mix sugar and cocoa with half a gill of milk, boil the rest and pour it on the cocoa. Return it to the pan and boil slowly for two minutes.

Beat the eggs and put them in a double saucepan. Pour on the hot, but *not boiling*, cocoa and stir till it coats the back of the spoon. Let the custard cool.

Dissolve the gelatine over a low gas, and when it is cool strain it into the custard and stir.

When cool, strain the custard into another basin and add the cream.

Stir from time to time, and when it begins to thicken turn it into the mould.

To serve, dip the mould in hot water, shake it on to the hand and slide into a glass dish.

Sufficient for four or five persons.

CHOCOLATE BLANCMANGE

INGREDIENTS.—3 level tablespoonfuls of cornflour, 3 oz. of sugar, 2 oz. of best cocoa, $1\frac{1}{2}$ pints of milk, $\frac{1}{2}$ oz. of butter.

METHOD.—Put the cornflour, sugar, and cocoa in a basin. Add gradually about half a cup of cold milk and mix to a smooth liquid. Boil the rest of the milk, and pour it on the mixed cornflour and cocoa, stirring hard all the time. Return it to the saucepan, add the butter, and stir till it boils. Place over an asbestos mat and boil gently for ten minutes. Pour into a mould that has been rinsed in cold water. Turn out when cold and decorate with a little cream, or, if preferred, leave it plain.

NOTE.—The cocoa and cornflour can be mixed more quickly and easily if sugar is first added to them.

CHOCOLATE CREAM

INGREDIENTS.—3 eggs, 1 pint of milk, 3 dessertspoonfuls of chocolate powder, 3 or 4 dessertspoonfuls of castor sugar, vanilla flavouring, $1\frac{1}{2}$ gills of cream, angelica, $\frac{1}{2}$ gill of water, 1 oz. of leaf gelatine.

METHOD.—Take two of the eggs, and separate the yolks from the whites. Then beat up the remaining egg together with the two yolks. Mix the chocolate powder to a smooth paste with a little milk. Put the remainder on to boil, and pour on to the powder. Stir well.

When slightly cool, add this to the beaten eggs, mix together, and strain into a jug.

Add the sugar, and stand the jug in a saucepan of warm water and stir over the fire until the custard thickens. Be careful not to overheat it or it will curdle.

When cooked, add the vanilla flavouring and pour into a basin, leave until cold.

Dissolve the gelatine in the water, but be sure to remember not to boil it.

Whisk the whites to a stiff froth, and whip up the cream until quite thick.

Fold half the cream and both the whisked whites into the chocolate custard, and mix.

Lastly, strain in the gelatine, and stir lightly until the mixture begins to thicken.

Pour into a wet border mould and leave until set.

Turn on to a dish. Put the remainder of the cream in the centre hole of the mould, decorate with a few stalks of angelica.

NOTE.—If preferred, put the cream into an icing-bag, and force it into the hole in the centre.

Sufficient for about eight persons.

CHOCOLATE CUPS

INGREDIENTS. — Sponge fingers, about ½ pint of chocolate custard, ¼ packet of vanilla jelly, ½ pint of hot water, 6 dessertspoonfuls of ground Barcelona nuts, whipped cream (for decoration), glacé cherries (for decoration).

METHOD.—Crumble up as many sponge fingers as will be required to two-thirds fill six custard glasses. Dissolve the jelly in the hot water. Add a spoonful of the ground nuts to each glass and mix with the sponge crumbs. Soak them with vanilla jelly.

Make some chocolate custard (as described in the following recipe), leave it until cold, then pour over the sponge crumbs, etc., and fill up the custard glasses.

Decorate the top of each with some whipped cream and stick half a glacé cherry in the centre.

Stale Madeira cake could be used in place of the sponge fingers, if preferred, in this recipe.

Sufficient for six persons.

CHOCOLATE CUSTARD

INGREDIENTS.—1 oz. of cocoa, 1½ oz. of sugar, 1 pint of milk, 2 eggs, vanilla essence, 2½d. of cream, 6 walnuts or ratafias.

METHOD.—The cocoa and sugar are mixed gradually with the milk and put in a double saucepan with the well-beaten eggs.

The custard should be stirred all the time till it is thick enough to coat the back of the spoon. When cold, it should be strained and served in custard glasses with a dab of cream and a walnut or ratafia placed on top.

CHOCOLATE CUSTARD JELLY

INGREDIENTS.—½ pint of milk, ½ tablespoonful of custard powder, 1 dessertspoonful of chocolate powder, 1 dessertspoonful of castor sugar, vanilla flavouring, 1 pint packet of vanilla jelly, ½ pint of hot water, glacé cherries.

METHOD.—Dissolve the jelly in hot water, then set aside to cool.

Mix the custard and chocolate powders together, and stir into a smooth paste with about half a gill of milk.

Pour the remainder of the milk into a saucepan, together with the sugar, and bring to the boil, add to the custard powder, etc., and stir well.

Flavour with a few drops of vanilla and leave until cold, keeping it stirred occasionally.

Rinse a mould with cold water and set a little jelly in the bottom.

Take a few cherries, dip them in jelly, and use them to decorate the bottom of the mould.

When set, just cover with jelly and once more leave to set.

Stir the remainder of the jelly into the custard.

Pour into the prepared mould and leave until firm.

Stand the bottom of the mould in warm water and turn on to a dish.

Sufficient for about five persons.

CHOCOLATE GINGER TRIFLE

INGREDIENTS.—2 oz. of chocolate, 1 whole egg and 1 yolk, ¾ pint of milk, 1 dessertspoonful of sugar, 3 oz. of preserved ginger, ½ gill of ginger syrup, 1 sponge-ring (sixpenny size), jam—marrow or apricot, ½ gill of cream, vanilla, angelica, ½ pint packet of lemon jelly.

METHOD.—Dissolve the jelly in hot water, making it up to half a pint, and leave it to set. Split the sponge-ring in half and spread each with jam. Put them in a dish, pour over the ginger syrup and a little of the melted jelly to soak it.

Grate the chocolate and dissolve it in a small quantity of the milk, add the remainder and bring it almost to the boil, then add it to the beaten eggs.

Pour this custard into the top of a double boiler, add the sugar and stir until the custard thickens, then remove it from the gas and let it cool. Add vanilla flavouring.

Cut a few pieces of ginger and place them on top of the ring. Chop up remainder and add it to the custard then pour the latter round the ring.

Chop up the jelly, put it in the centre, and top it with whipped cream (sweetened and flavoured to taste), and stalks of angelica.

Sufficient for five persons.

CHOCOLATE JELLY FISH

INGREDIENTS.—1 pint packet of lemon jelly, ½ pint packet of chocolate jelly cream, 1½ gills of boiling milk.

METHOD.—Dissolve the jelly in hot water, making it up to one pint. Let it cool, and then pour three parts of it into a shallow dish and leave it to set. Pour the boiling milk on to the contents of the packet of chocolate jelly cream, and stir till dissolved. Turn this into three fish moulds previously rinsed with cold water. Leave the jelly to set in the fish moulds, then turn them out on to the bed of jelly and put tiny pieces of glacé cherry to resemble the eyes of the fish.

Chop the remainder of the jelly roughly, mix it with a spot of cream, and heap it at one end of the dish. This makes a pretty party dish for children. It is easily prepared and quite inexpensive.

Sufficient for three persons.

CHOCOLATE MACAROON PUDDING

INGREDIENTS.—¼ lb of small macaroon biscuits (use as required), 2 dessertspoonfuls of cocoa, about 2½ tablespoonfuls of sugar, 3 eggs, 1½ pints of milk, 4 dessertspoonfuls of desiccated coconut, vanilla flavouring.

METHOD.—Mix the cocoa to a smooth paste with a small quantity of the milk. Boil the remainder and stir on to it, return to the pan and boil for one minute, then cool slightly.

Whisk up the eggs, put them in a pie-dish, and stir in the hot milk and cocoa.

Add the sugar and coconut and a few drops of vanilla and mix all together. Place the small macaroon biscuits all over the top, cover the pudding with a plate, and bake in a moderately warm oven for from thirty to forty-five minutes, or until set being careful not to let it boil.

Serve cold.

Sufficient for about six persons.

CHOCOLATE MERINGUE

INGREDIENTS.—3 bought meringue cases, 1 oz. of cocoa, 2 oz. of sugar, 1 pint of milk, 2 eggs, vanilla essence, ½ gill of water, ¼ oz. of gelatine, 2 bananas, 6d. of whipped cream.

METHOD.—Soak the gelatine in the water. Mix the milk gradually with the cocoa and sugar. Stir till it boil and add the gelatine. Cool slightly and add the beaten eggs. Stir in a double saucepan till it thickens. Add the vanilla and strain into three compôte dishes.

When set, put sliced bananas round the edge and a meringue case decorated with cream in the centre of each.

Sufficient for three persons.

CHOCOLATE MOULD

INGREDIENTS.—2½ oz. of cornflour, 2½ oz. of sugar, 2 pints of milk, vanilla flavouring, 2 dessertspoonfuls of chocolate powder or cocoa.

METHOD.—Mix the chocolate powder and cornflour together and then mix

to a smooth paste with about half a
gill of the milk.

Heat the remainder of the milk with
the sugar.

Add this to the mixed cornflour, etc.

Pour back into the saucepan and
boil for six minutes slowly, stirring all
the time.

Pour into a wet mould.

If liked, plain chocolate can be
bought and used instead of the cocoa
or chocolate powder. This must be
grated before it is mixed with the
cornflour.

CHOCOLATE RICE CREAM

INGREDIENTS. — 1 good dessertspoonful of cocoa, 4½ gills of milk,
3 flat tablespoonfuls of ground rice,
2 or 3 dessertspoonfuls of sugar,
vanilla flavouring, apricot jam, 1 oz.
of almonds, 1 egg.

METHOD.—Mix the ground rice and
cocoa together, and mix to a smooth
paste with some of the milk. Heat the
remainder and stir on to it, return to
the saucepan, add the sugar and stir
until it boils. Simmer gently for
about six minutes, keeping it stirred,
then draw to the side and cool slightly.

Beat up the egg and add, and stir
over a low gas for a few minutes to
cook it, but do not let it boil. Add
flavouring to taste.

Put some jam in the bottom of a
dish, pour the prepared mixture over
it, and leave until cold. Blanch, skin
and chop the almonds and sprinkle on
the top.

Sufficient for about four persons.

CHOCOLATE SHAPE

INGREDIENTS.—1 pint of milk, 1 good
dessertspoonful of cocoa, ¾ oz. of leaf
gelatine, ½ gill of water, about 2 dessertspoonfuls of sugar, vanilla flavouring.

METHOD.—Put the cocoa into a
basin and mix to a smooth paste with
some of the milk. Boil the remainder
and stir on to it. Return to the
saucepan, add the sugar and boil for
one minute, then leave to cool.

Put the gelatine into another saucepan with the water, and dissolve
slowly but do not boil. Strain this
into the cocoa and milk and mix
together. Add vanilla flavouring to
taste.

Stir occasionally until it begins to
set, then pour into a wet mould.

When quite firm turn out carefully.

Sufficient for about five persons.

CHOCOLATE SPONGE CUS-TARD

INGREDIENTS.—1 toast-rack shaped
sponge, 2 oz. of shelled walnuts, 1 whole
egg and 1 yolk, ¾ pint of milk, 1½
dessertspoonfuls of castor sugar, vanilla
flavouring, 2½ oz. of butter, 5 oz. of
icing sugar, 1½ oz. of grated chocolate.

METHOD.—Rub the icing sugar
through a hair sieve. Beat the butter
to a cream. Add the icing sugar
to it and beat them till they are
creamy.

Put the chocolate into a saucepan
with about a spoonful of water. Stir
it till it is dissolved, and when it is
cool add it to the butter cream.
Flavour it with vanilla and stir in half
the walnuts previously chopped. Beat
the whole egg and yoke together.
Heat the milk and add it to them.
Turn the custard mixture into the top
of a double boiler and stir it over hot
water until it thickens. Then take it
off and add castor sugar and vanilla
to taste.

Slice the sponge cake and spread
the pieces thickly with the chocolate
butter.

Stick the slices together again to
form a whole sponge. Then place it
in a dish and pour the custard over it
and decorate it with walnuts.

CHOCOLATE TAPIOCA

INGREDIENTS.—4 oz. of small tapioca,
1 pint of milk, 1 pint of water, 2 tablespoonfuls of cocoa, 3 oz. of sugar, ¼ teaspoonful of mixed spice, vanilla essence,
4d. of whipped cream.

METHOD.—Soak the tapioca in the
water overnight.

Mix the cocoa, sugar, and spice
smoothly with the milk and stir till it
boils. Put in the soaked tapioca and
simmer till clear and thick, stirring well
all the time (about fifteen to twenty
minutes).

Add the essence and pour into a wet
mould. When set turn out and decorate with cream.

Sufficient for five persons.

CHOCOLATE SPONGE

INGREDIENTS.—1 oz. of cocoa (good weight), 1 pint of milk, 2 oz. of sugar, 1 oz. of thin leaf gelatine, vanilla essence.

METHOD.—Mix the cocoa and sugar and add gradually a gill of milk. Boil half a pint of milk, pour it on to the cocoa mixture and return to the saucepan. Simmer for three minutes and leave it to cool.

Pour a gill of cold milk into a basin, break up the gelatine and soak it in the milk.

Dissolve slowly over a low gas, keeping it well stirred.

Strain into the chocolate when both are cool and stir now and again. Add the essence.

When quite cold whisk with an egg whisk till light and frothy.

Rinse a pint mould in cold water and turn the sponge into it.

When required dip the mould in hot water for a moment, shake on to the hand and slide on to a glass dish.

Serve with sponge fingers.

Enough for four or five persons.

CHOCOLATE TRIFLE

INGREDIENTS.—½ lb. of chocolate roll, 1½ pints of milk, 2 eggs, 1 good dessertspoonful of cocoa, about 2 or 3 dessertspoonfuls of sugar, 1 oz. of almonds, vanilla flavouring, cream, glacé cherries.

METHOD.—Boil half a pint of the milk. Put the roll into an oval glass dish and soak with as much of the hot milk as required. Prick the roll with a fork so as to get it well soaked.

With the other pint of milk make the custard. Mix the cocoa to a smooth paste with a little milk, boil the remainder and stir on it. Return to the pan and boil for one minute, then cool slightly.

Beat up the eggs, stir the hot milk and cocoa on to them, then pour into a jug and add the sugar.

Stand the jug in a saucepan of hot water and cook until the custard thickens, being careful not to curdle it. It must be stirred occasionally. When cooked, remove from the hot water, add vanilla essence, and leave to cool. Blanch, skin, and split the almonds and stick into the roll. Pour the custard over and leave until thoroughly cold. Decorate the top of the roll with whipped cream and a few glacé cherries.

Sufficient for about six or eight persons.

COCONUT FRUIT JELLY

INGREDIENTS.—1 oz. of desiccated coconut, tin of loganberries, ½ pint of hot water, 1 pint packet of plain jelly, 2 egg-whites, rings of angelica.

METHOD.—Dissolve the jelly in the hot water, then drain the syrup from the loganberries and add it to the jelly. Make the liquid up to one pint with water if there is not sufficient syrup.

Add the coconut and the drained loganberries and leave the mixture to get cold. Then whisk the egg-whites to a stiff froth and add them to the mixture.

Whisk it for a minute until the jelly is evenly frothed, then turn it into a dish. When it is set, decorate it with rings of angelica and small heaps of coconut — the latter extra to the amount given in the ingredients.

Sufficient for from six to eight persons.

COFFEE CREAM

INGREDIENTS.—2 tablespoonfuls of coffee essence, 1 pint of water, 1 pint of milk, 2 oz. of sugar, 3 oz. of cornflour, a few sponge fingers, 1 oz. of butter, whipped cream.

METHOD.—Boil the water and butter. Mix the cornflour and sugar together and gradually stir in the cold milk so that there are no lumps.

Pour the mixed cornflour and milk quickly into the boiling water and stir hard till it boils.

Simmer gently for ten minutes, stirring now and again to prevent burning. Add the coffee essence and cream, taste, and if it is sweet enough pour into a wet mould.

Turn out and place sponge fingers round.

Sufficient for four persons.

WHIPPED CREAM

INGREDIENTS.—1 gill of double cream, sugar to taste, about 1 or 2 teaspoonfuls.

METHOD.—Put the cream in a cold basin or cup and beat it with a fork till it thickens. Good thick cream only takes a few minutes.

When quite thick but smooth-looking, stir in the sugar. If the sugar is put in before beating it is likely to make the cream oily especially in hot weather.

COFFEE CREAM SPONGE
(No Cooking Required)

INGREDIENTS.—4 oblong and 1 round sponge cakes, ¼ lb. of butter, 2 oz. of castor sugar, about 3 dessertspoonfuls of coffee essence, 2 eggs.

METHOD.—Split the sponge cakes in halves and use them to line the sides of a plain mould (one pint size). Then fit one half of the round sponge cake in the bottom of the mould.

Cream the fat and sugar. Add the egg yolks, stir in quickly, and beat well. When both are added, stir in sufficient coffee essence to flavour and colour, then fold in the whisked egg-whites. Turn into the mould, put the other half of the round sponge cake on the top, cover with a saucer and leave pressed for an hour or so in a cool place, then turn out.

Decorate with some whipped cream.

If liked, a little rum may be poured over the sponge when turned out.

Sufficient for about five or six persons.

COFFEE HONEYCOMB

INGREDIENTS. — 3 dessertspoonfuls of coffee essence, ¾ oz. packet of gelatine, 1 pint of milk, 3 or 4 dessertspoonfuls of sugar, 2 eggs and 1 extra white.

METHOD.—Put the gelatine to soak in half the milk for about two hours or a little more. Then boil the other half and pour on to it. Stir until dissolved, then strain and put into a saucepan.

Add the coffee essence and sugar. Beat up the yolks of the eggs and add, and stir until the mixture thickens lightly. Then draw aside.

Whisk the egg-whites to a very stiff froth and fold in lightly. Turn into a wet mould to set, then turn on to a dish.

Sufficient for six to eight persons.

COFFEE SOUFFLES

INGREDIENTS.—2 yolks and 3 egg-whites, 2 or 3 dessertspoonfuls of coffee essence, 1 oz. of almonds, ½ oz. of leaf gelatine, ½ gill of water, 3 dessertspoonfuls of castor sugar.

METHOD.—Put the yolks of eggs and castor sugar in a basin and whisk together, then stir in the coffee essence, and whisk over a saucepan of hot water until thick and creamy. Remove from the hot water and add the almonds — blanched and chopped finely. Dissolve the gelatine in a saucepan with the water and strain in.

When beginning to set, whisk the egg-whites to a very stiff froth and fold in lightly. Add a little more sugar if required.

Turn into small soufflé cases, and when quite set put a dab of whipped cream in the centre of each.

Sufficient to fill ten or twelve small soufflé cases.

COFFEE TRIFLE

INGREDIENTS.—1 sponge ring and a half (the 6d. size), 3 dessertspoonfuls of coffee essence, 2 to 2½ tablespoonfuls of castor sugar, 2 eggs and 1 extra white, 1 pint of milk, ½ gill of sherry, apricot jam, 1 oz. of angelica, 1½ oz. of shelled Brazil nuts.

METHOD.—Split the sponge ring into halves and spread the three halves with jam, then sprinkle with ground Brazil nuts (put through mincer). Arrange them in a dish, one on top of the other, and soak each with sherry and a little milk (extra to that given).

Put the milk (one pint) into a saucepan with the coffee essence and bring to the boil. Then cool slightly and add the two eggs (beaten). Stand the coffee-custard in a saucepan of hot water and cook until it thickens, sweeten to taste, and when cool pour over the sponge ring.

Decorate the top of the ring with halved Brazils and chopped angelica. Whisk the white of egg to a stiff froth, fold in one tablespoonful of castor sugar, and heap in the centre of the ring.

Sufficient for eight persons.

COFFEE WALNUT CHARLOTTE

INGREDIENTS.—$\frac{1}{4}$ lb of Savoy biscuits, $1\frac{1}{2}$ pint packets of coffee jelly cream, $1\frac{1}{4}$ pints of milk, $\frac{1}{2}$ pint packet of orange or lemon jelly, $1\frac{1}{2}$ gills of hot water, $1\frac{1}{2}$ oz. of shelled walnuts, some crystallised rose leaves.

METHOD.—Dissolve the jelly in the hot water, pour a thin layer in the bottom of a charlotte tin and leave it to set, then line the sides of the tin with Savoy biscuits, having first split them in half and straightened the sides.

Dissolve the one and a half packets of jelly cream in the milk, pouring boiling milk on to the contents, and stirring till dissolved, as directed on the packet. When beginning to set, chop up the walnuts and mix them in, saving a few whole ones for decorating, then turn the coffee mixture into the prepared mould and leave it to set.

To unmould the charlotte dip the base of the tin into warm water, turn the charlotte out on to a dish and decorate it with the remainder of the jelly (chopped up roughly), walnuts, and crystallised rose leaves.

Sufficient for five or six persons.

CORNFLOUR JELLY

INGREDIENTS.—1 pint packet of raspberry jelly, $1\frac{1}{2}$ pints of hot water, 1 dessertspoonful of sugar, $2\frac{1}{2}$ teaspoonfuls of cornflour.

METHOD.—Dissolve the jelly in the hot water, then leave until cold.

Mix the cornflour to a smooth paste with some of the cold jelly, then stir in the remainder. Turn it all into a saucepan and bring to boil, keeping it well stirred. Add the sugar, then cook slowly for about six or eight minutes. Pour into a wet mould and, when set, turn on to a dish.

Sufficient for about six persons.

CORNFLOUR COCONUT CREAM

INGREDIENTS.—1 oz. of cornflour, 2 oz. of coconut, $\frac{3}{4}$ pint of milk, $\frac{1}{2}$ oz. of butter, 2 oz. of castor sugar, $\frac{1}{4}$ oz. of gelatine, 1 tablespoonful of water, cochineal, orange flavouring essence, 2 egg-whites.

METHOD.—Mix the cornflour to a smooth paste with a small quantity of the milk, heat the remainder, and add it also to the cornflour. Return this to the pan and bring it to the boil, keeping it well stirred. Boil it gently for a few minutes, take it off the gas, and add the coconut, butter, and sugar. Dissolve the gelatine in the water and add it with flavouring to taste and sufficient cochineal to pink the mixture.

Let the mixture cool, then fold in the stiffly whisked egg-whites. Turn the cream into a wet mould, and when set unmould it and serve it with some coconut sprinkled on top.

Sufficient for five persons.

CORNFLOUR PINEAPPLE CUBES

INGREDIENTS.—Small tin of pineapple cubes, cornflour, cochineal, sugar (if required).

METHOD.—Strain the syrup from the fruit.

Mix the cornflour to a smooth paste with some of the syrup, heat the remainder and stir on to it.

Now return to the saucepan, bring to the boil, and boil very gently for about six minutes, keeping it well stirred.

Colour with a few drops of cochineal add a little sugar if required, and stir in the pine chunks.

Turn it all into a dish and serve when cold.

NOTE.—Allow one teaspoonful of cornflour to every gill of syrup.

CRANBERRY CREAMS

INGREDIENTS.—1 lb. of cranberries, $\frac{3}{4}$ to 1 gill of water, sugar to taste, 1 gill of cream, 1 level teaspoonful of powdered cinnamon, 1 egg, $\frac{1}{4}$ pint of milk, $\frac{1}{2}$ oz. of gelatine, $\frac{1}{2}$ gill of water.

METHOD.—Put the cranberries into a saucepan with the water and sugar to taste, and stew them until tender. Rub them through a sieve.

Separate the egg, beat the yolk and mix it with the milk (heated) and cook this custard in the top of a double boiler until it thickens, keeping it stirred.

Whisk the cream until thick, stir in the custard, and a good half pint of cranberry purée, when cold, and the strain in the gelatine, dissolved in half a gill of water.

Add the cinnamon and sugar to taste, and fold in the stiffly whisked egg-white. Turn the mixture into small moulds rinsed out with cold water and when set turn them out carefully.

Sufficient for six small moulds.

CRANBERRY FOOL

INGREDIENTS.—½ lb. of cranberries, about 3 dessertspoonfuls of granulated sugar, ½ gill of water, a good pinch of ground cinnamon, ½ pint of milk, 1 egg, 1 dessertspoonful of castor sugar, vanilla or orange flavouring essence, ½ gill of cream.

METHOD.—Pick over and wash the cranberries, and cook them with the sugar and water until tender. Rub them through a sieve and stir in the ground cinnamon.

Make a boiled egg custard with the egg and milk, adding one dessertspoonful of castor sugar and flavouring essence to taste.

Leave both the custard and cranberry purée to get cold. Mix them together and stir in the lightly whipped cream, and add more sugar if required. Chill the mixture, and serve it in custard cups, decorated with a cross of whipped cream forced through an icing tube.

CRANBERRY FOLLY

INGREDIENTS.—1 lb. of cranberries, 6 sponge cakes, ½ gill of sherry, 1 lb. of apples, water (about 1½ to 2 gills), 2 eggs, 1 pint of milk, flavouring, 3 or 4 tablespoonfuls of sugar.

METHOD.—Peel, core and slice the apples, wash and stalk the cranberries. Stew these together until tender, adding a little water and about two or three tablespoonfuls of sugar, or sufficient to sweeten them.

When cooked, rub through a sieve, then crumble the sponge cakes and add. Mix all together and, when cool, stir in the sherry.

Beat up the eggs. Heat the milk and add to them. Then strain into a jug or double boiler. Add the sugar (one good tablespoonful) and cook in a saucepan of water until the custard

thickens, keeping it stirred occasionally and being careful not to let it curdle. Add flavouring to taste and leave until cold.

Turn the cranberry mixture into a dish, pour the custard on top, and just before serving decorate with a few cranberries (stewed whole).

Sufficient for about eight persons.

CRANBERRY TRIFLE

INGREDIENTS.—½ lb. of cranberries, 2½ tablespoonfuls of sugar, 1 gill of water, ½ level teaspoonful of powdered cinnamon, 1 oz. of almonds, ½ pint of lemon jelly, hot water, 3 oblong sponge cakes, 1 round sponge cake, 1 egg, ½ pint of milk, 1 dessertspoonful of sugar, flavouring essence, 2 tablespoonfuls of cooking sherry (this may be omitted if desired), few stalks of angelica, cream.

METHOD.—Wash and pick over the cranberries and stew them with the water and sugar until they are tender. Rub them through a sieve. Stir in the cinnamon and half the almonds, blanched and chopped roughly.

Cut up the jelly and dissolve it in hot water, making it up to a quarter of a pint. Then stir it into the above mixture and leave it until it begins to set.

Use sponge cakes not more than one day old. Split them in half, and use five of the oblong pieces for lining the sides of a plain pint-sized mould.

Place the round sponge cake in the base of the mould. In each case the cut side should be towards the centre of the mould.

When the cranberry mixture is ready, turn it gently into the prepared mould and leave it to set.

Meanwhile, make the custard.

Beat up the egg, heat the milk and add it to the egg, then strain them in to the top of a double boiler. Add the sugar, and stir the custard over hot water until it thickens. Be careful not to let it curdle. Take it off the heat, cool it and add flavouring to taste.

If a double boiler is not available, cook the custard in a jug in a saucepan of hot water. It will take a little longer to cook in this way.

To serve the trifle, turn the cranberry and sponge mould on to a dish. A spoonful or two of sherry may be poured over it.

Decorate the top of the trifle with whipped cream, flavoured and sweetened to taste, and a few stalks of angelica.

Blanch and split the remainder of the almonds and stick them between the sponge cakes and pour the custard round.

Sufficient for six persons.

HOW TO DECORATE WITH CREAM

A simple decoration with whipped cream gives a touch of luxury to the most every-day sweet, and it is quite easy to accomplish.

A gill of cream, a sprinkling of castor sugar, a flavouring of vanilla (just one or two drops), and a square of grease-proof paper.

This is all you need.

Sprinkle the sugar into the cream, add the flavouring, and then whisk it well with an egg whisk.

When sufficiently whisked you should be able to mark the cream with the end of the whisk and leave an impression. If, however, the cream flows back again and no trace is left—it means that you must do some more whisking.

With a bag of greaseproof paper you can make all sorts of attractive decorations.

To make the bag, cut a square of paper in half diagonally (so that you have two triangles) and then roll one of the triangles to a cone shape, like a sugar bag.

For ordinary use—that is, for a plain piping of cream—just cut the tip of the bag to the required size.

Keep the shape of the greaseproof paper bag as narrow as possible, as this makes the point of the bag stiffer.

Put some of the whipped cream into the bag and twist the end of it.

With a little practice you will find you can make all sorts of pretty shapes. One hand squeezes the bag—lightly if a narrow stream of cream is desired, and more heavily for a wider stream.

The second hand is used for steadying and guiding purposes.

The most realistic stars, cone shapes, or leaves can be made this way.

A fairly heavy squeeze of the bag makes the beginning, or wide part of a leaf. The movement should be jerky, and as the cream comes out the bag should be pushed forward (this makes a little ridge).

The next squeeze must be lighter, and again the bag is pushed forward. Perhaps one more squeeze will be required, and then the final one to make the point of the leaf. By a deft movement this point can be left suspended in the air. (It looks much better than having the whole leaf flat.)

Once you begin decorating you will find you can evolve all sorts of pretty decorations.

CREAMS AND SPONGES

Rich creams are made with equal quantities of fruit purée and whipped cream, and plain creams are made with custard, a little cream, and any flavouring or colouring required.

The cream or custard mixture is stiffened with gelatine, which must be dissolved. To do this, break it up and soak it in a basin with a gill of cold fruit-juice or water. After soaking it for five minutes, heat it over a low gas and stir till dissolved. Never try to dissolve gelatine in boiling water as it simply becomes a soft, gluey mass. It should be stirred while dissolving, and an asbestos mat may be placed underneath, as it burns easily.

The gelatine is added to the fruit and cream mixture when both are cold, but before they begin to set. In order to make them nice and smooth a cream should be frequently stirred while cooling. When it begins to thicken and set it should be poured into a mould that has been rinsed in cold water.

Moulds for jellies and creams may be decorated before the mixture is poured into them.

Savoury creams and jellies are more often decorated than sweet ones. To decorate a mould use clear aspic or lemon jelly, according to whether it is for a sweet or savoury. When the jelly is nearly set, pour it into the mould—just enough to cover the bottom—if possible, standing the mould in a basin of broken ice. Cut the decorations to the desired shape, using truffles, pistachio nuts, or white of egg. Make the desired pattern on the thin layer of jelly and pour in very carefully a very little jelly. Just enough to set the decorations and keep them in place, but not enough to make them float. When the jelly has set, pour in the prepared cream.

To turn out a jelly, dip it right into a basin of tepid water for one minute. Place the hand under it and shake.

Let it slide from the hand on to a dish. Do not have the unmoulding water too hot or leave the cream in it too long.

The thin leaf gelatine, weighing ten sheets to an ounce, dissolves very easily and is convenient to use.

It is sold by the ounce. In summer an ounce of leaf gelatine to a pint of jelly is the usual proportion.

In winter, three-quarters of an ounce to a pint is enough.

Thick creams need slightly less gelatine than thin jellies.

A very large jelly needs a little extra gelatine in order to hold it together.

It is a good plan to oil moulds for creams as they can be turned out easily by gentle shaking. This saves dipping the mould in warm water which takes longer and is sometimes inclined to melt the cream too much.

CREAM COCONUT MOULDS

INGREDIENTS.—1 tablespoonful of desiccated coconut, 10d. of cream, 1 egg, $\frac{1}{4}$ pint of milk, $1\frac{1}{2}$ to 2 dessert-spoonfuls of castor sugar, $\frac{1}{4}$ oz. of gelatine, $\frac{1}{4}$ gill of water, vanilla flavouring, angelica.

METHOD.—Separate the egg, and make a boiled custard with the milk and the yolk of egg, and when it is sufficiently thickened, add the sugar and leave it to cool.

Whisk the cream until it thickens, stir in the custard gradually, add the desiccated coconut, and strain in the gelatine dissolved in a saucepan with the water.

Flavour the mixture with vanilla and fold in the stiffly whisked egg-white.

Turn it into four small moulds rinsed with cold water, and leave it to set. Unmould the coconut cream moulds, and decorate each one with a leaf of angelica.

NOTE.—More custard, and less cream, may be used for these, if preferred.

Sufficient for four small moulds.

RED CURRANTS AND COCONUT

INGREDIENTS.—$\frac{1}{2}$ lb. of red currants, $\frac{3}{4}$ gill of water, cream, 3 oz. of castor sugar, $\frac{1}{2}$ oz. of flour, 2 yolks of eggs, 2 tablespoonfuls of desiccated coconut.

METHOD.—Sift the flour with the castor sugar and mix it smoothly with the water.

String and wash the currants and, when drained, turn them into a basin and mash them up roughly; then add them to the flour, sugar, and water.

Turn the mixture into a saucepan, dissolve it slowly, and bring it to the boil, keeping it stirred. Take the pan off the heat and add half the coconut and, when the mixture has cooled a little, stir in the beaten egg-yolks.

Turn the mixture into a buttered pie-dish or Pyrex dish, and bake it gently for from twenty to thirty minutes, without letting it boil.

Serve red currants and coconut cold, with the remainder of the coconut sprinkled round the edge. Decorate the dish with a few whole currants and serve it with cream.

Sufficient for three persons.

CUSTARD CREAMS

INGREDIENTS.—1 egg and 1 yolk, $2\frac{1}{2}$ gills of milk, $\frac{1}{2}$ gill of cream, $\frac{1}{2}$ gill of water, $\frac{3}{8}$ oz. of leaf gelatine, orange essence, slices of pineapple, about 2 dessertspoonfuls of castor sugar.

METHOD.—Beat up the eggs. Bring the milk almost to boiling-point, let it cool for a minute, and then add the beaten egg. Strain it into a jug and stand it in a saucepan of hot water. Cook the mixture gently until the custard thickens, keeping it stirred occasionally. The water round it should simmer and not boil fast. When ready, turn the custard into a basin and leave it till cold.

Whisk the cream until it begins to

stiffen, gradually stir in the custard, also the sugar and orange essence to taste.

Dissolve the gelatine in a saucepan with the water and strain it into the custard. Mix them together lightly, and when the mixture begins to thicken turn it into small, wet moulds to set. Unmould the custard creams and serve each one on a slice of pineapple.

Sufficient for four or five small moulds.

CUSTARD BREAD PUDDING

INGREDIENTS.—2 oz. of stale bread, 2½ gills of milk, 2 yolks or 1 whole egg, 1 small tablespoonful of sugar, 1 oz. of butter, few sultanas or seeded raisins.

METHOD.—Break up the bread and put it into a basin, bring the milk to the boil and pour it over. Cover the bread and leave it to soak.

Mash the soaked bread with a fork, and add the sugar, a few cleaned sultanas or raisins, also the butter (melted) and then stir in the beaten yolks or whole egg. Turn the mixture into a buttered dish, grate nutmeg on the top and bake it gently until set. Do not let it boil.

Serve hot or cold, and decorate with a circle of sultanas or raisins.

Sufficient for two persons.

CUSTARD CREAM

INGREDIENTS.—¾ pint of milk, 2 eggs, ½ oz. of gelatine, ½ gill of water, vanilla or orange flavouring essence, 4 oz. of castor sugar, ¾ gill of cream, ½ pint packet of cherry jelly.

METHOD.—Separate one of the eggs. Beat the whole egg and yolk together, bring the milk almost to the boil, and add it to them, then turn them into the top of a double boiler with the sugar. Stir them over hot water until the custard thickens, then turn this into a basin and leave it to get cold.

Dissolve the gelatine in the water and strain it into the custard. Whisk the cream until it hangs from the whisk, then gradually stir in the custard mixture. Add flavouring to taste, and when beginning to set fold in the stiffly-whisked egg-white.

Turn the mixture into a wet mould, and when set dip it into warm water and unmould. Decorate with chopped jelly.

Dissolve the jelly in one and a half gills of hot water and put it to set before making the cream. When ready to use, turn it on to a sheet of wet, greaseproof paper, and chop it roughly.

Sufficient for five persons.

CUSTARD JELLY

INGREDIENTS.—1 pint packet of jelly, hot water, ½ pint of milk, 1 egg, 1 dessertspoonful of sugar, flavouring essence as desired.

METHOD.—Dissolve the jelly in half a pint of hot water and leave it to get cold.

Beat up the egg. Scald the milk, and when it is off the boil add it to the egg; then turn the custard into the top of a double boiler and add the sugar.

Cook the custard over a pan of hot water until it thickens, keeping it stirred and being careful not to let it curdle. Strain it into a basin, and add flavouring essence as desired, according to the flavour of jelly you are using.

Let the custard get cold, and then mix it with the cold jelly and turn it into a wet mould.

NOTE.—A powder custard may be used in place of the egg custard, if desired.

DAMSON FOOL

INGREDIENTS.—1½ lb. of damsons, about 3 tablespoonfuls of sugar, 2 eggs, 1 pint of milk, sugar and vanilla, cream, 2 or 3 marshmallows, a few glacé cherries.

METHOD.—Stalk, pick over and wash the damsons and stew them gently with the sugar and a very little water. Rub them through a sieve.

Beat the eggs, bring the milk almost to boiling point and add it to them. Turn it into the top of a double boiler or a jug, stand it in a saucepan of hot water and cook the custard until it thickens, keeping it stirred frequently. Remove it from the hot water, add sugar and vanilla to taste and leave it until cold, then mix with the damson purée.

Stand the damson fool in a cool place for a few hours before turning it into glasses. Decorate it with pieces of marshmallow and glacé cherries and serve with cream.

If you want to enrich this sweet, stir in a gill of thick cream just before turning it into the glasses.

Sufficient for six persons.

DAMSON SOLIDS

INGREDIENTS.—½ oz. of gelatine, 1¼ gill of water, 1 lb. of damsons, ¼ lb. of sugar, ½ pint of custard (as described in the previous recipe), cream.

METHOD.—Stalk and wash the damsons and stew them till very soft with the sugar and three-quarters of a gill of water. Then rub them through a sieve.

Dissolve the gelatine in half a gill of water and strain it into the damson purée, and taste it to see if it is sweet enough. Then turn it into wet moulds.

When set, turn the solids on to a dish and decorate them with a little whipped cream, which should have been sweetened and flavoured to taste. Serve the damson solids with a boiled custard, made with either egg or custard powder.

Sufficient to fill three moulds.

DATE TRIFLE

INGREDIENTS.—1 toast-rack sponge cake and half of another, 6 oz. of stoned dates, 1 oz. of shelled walnuts, 3 tablespoonfuls of rum, apricot jam, 2 eggs, 1 pint of milk, 1 tablespoonful of sugar, vanilla, 3 dessertspoonfuls of desiccated coconut, cream, angelica.

METHOD.—Split the whole sponge cake in half, and spread the three pieces very sparingly with apricot jam.

Keep some whole dates for decorating and put the rest of the dates and walnuts through the mincer and moisten them with about half the rum.

Spread the date mixture on the sponge halves and sandwich the three pieces together, soaking each with a little rum and some milk—the latter extra to that given.

Make a custard with the two eggs and a pint of milk. Sweeten and flavour it to taste and add the coconut. When cool, pour the custard round the sponge cake.

Decorate the trifle when cold with whipped cream, sweetened and flavoured to taste, also stalks of angelica, and a few extra stoned dates.

Sufficient for from six to eight persons.

DURBAN PUDDING

INGREDIENTS.—8 sponge cakes, ½ lb. of red currants, 1½ tablespoonfuls of Demerara sugar, ½ gill of water, 1 pint packet of red currant jelly, 1 pint of hot water.

METHOD.—Put the sugar and half a gill of water into a saucepan and boil for five minutes. This makes the syrup.

Prepare the red currants—remove the stalks and wash them.

Put into a saucepan with the syrup and cook slowly until tender. This will take about twenty minutes.

Dissolve the packet of jelly in the pint of hot water.

Line a pie-dish with sponge cakes—split the cakes in halves and place the top halves to the bottom and sides of the dish, so that they will be on the top when the pudding is turned out.

Mix the stewed fruit with the jelly and cover the sponge cakes with this mixture until the dish is full.

Then place the other halves of the sponge cakes on the top, with the cut side inside.

Press these well down so that the fruit and jelly soak into them. Cover the top with a dish and press with a heavy weight, and leave until cold and set. Turn on to a dish and serve.

NOTE.—Any kind of stewed fruit may be used for this, also stale bread can be substituted for the sponge cakes.

Sufficient for about six persons.

EASTERN CUPS

INGREDIENTS.—½ lb. of dessert figs, box of dates, ½ pint of water—or more if required, 1½ oz. of shelled walnuts, 2 oz. of glacé ginger, 1 dessertspoonful of ginger syrup, ½ gill of cooking sherry or rum, 1 white of egg, sugar and vanilla, 1od. of cream.

METHOD.—Stalk and cut up the figs and stone and cut the dates into small pieces. Put both into a saucepan with the water and stew them until " mushy," then leave them to get cold.

Cut up the ginger and add it to the prepared fruit with the ginger syrup, add also the sherry or rum and the walnuts, chopped roughly, keeping back a few to put on top of the cream.

Mix all together and turn the mixture into custard cups or stemmed glasses.

Whisk the egg-white to a stiff froth, and whisk the cream until it thickens, combine the two and add sugar and flavouring to taste. Heap this on the fruit and sprinkle chopped walnuts on top.

Sufficient for six persons.

EGG MOULD

INGREDIENTS.—3 eggs, ½ oz. of leaf gelatine, 1 lemon, 6 oz. of sugar, 2½ gills of water.

METHOD.—Separate one of the eggs.

Beat the yolk and the two whole eggs together. Grate the lemon-rind finely, squeeze out the juice and strain it. Put these prepared ingredients into a saucepan with the sugar and half a pint of the water, and stir over a low burner until the eggs are cooked and the mixture slightly thickened. Then draw aside.

Dissolve the gelatine in another saucepan with the other half gill of water, and strain in. Leave until cold and beginning to set.

Then whisk the remaining egg-white to a stiff froth and fold in lightly.

Turn into a wet mould, and, when quite set, unmould.

FAIRY DELIGHT

INGREDIENTS.—¼ lb. of blanched almonds, 12 maraschino cherries, 1 pint packet of cherry jelly, 1 gill of whipped cream, 12 marshmallows, ¾ pint of hot water, 1½ oz. of castor sugar, 6 macaroons.

METHOD.—Chop the almonds, marshmallows, cherries, and macaroons.

Add boiling water to the jelly and dissolve it. Let it cool and then whip it till it is light and creamy.

Fold in the whipped cream, marshmallow mixture, and the sugar. Turn the mixture into a wet mould and allow it to set. Then turn it out into a dish and decorate it with maraschino cherries and angelica. (These are extra to those given in the ingredients.)

Sufficient for six persons.

FIG TRIFLE

INGREDIENTS.—8 sponge cakes, 2 eggs, 1 pint of milk, 1 tablespoonful of sugar, vanilla flavouring, a little rum and some milk (for soaking sponge cake), small box of dessert figs, 1 oz. of shelled walnuts, angelica.

METHOD.—Put the figs through a mincer, leaving out a few whole ones for decoration.

Mince the walnuts and mix with the minced figs, then moisten with a little rum. Split the sponge cakes into halves and spread with this mixture, then arrange them in a dish, and soak with a little hot milk and some rum.

Beat up the eggs, heat the pint of milk and add to them. Strain into a jug, add sugar to taste, then stand in a saucepan of hot water and cook until the custard thickens, keeping it stirred occasionally and being careful not to let it curdle.

When ready, remove from the hot water, add some flavouring, and when sufficiently cool, pour over the sponge cakes.

Before serving, decorate with some whole figs and leaves of angelica.

Sufficient for eight persons.

FRUIT COMPOTE

INGREDIENTS.—½ lb. of black currants, ½ lb. of red currants, ½ lb. of strawberries, ¼ lb. of raspberries, 1 pint of gooseberries, ¼ lb. of cherries, about 5 tablespoonfuls of Demerara sugar, about 2 gills of cold water.

METHOD.—Put the sugar and water into a saucepan and dissolve, then boil for a few minutes until a syrup is formed.

String the currants, top and tail the gooseberries, and pick over the cherries, strawberries, and raspberries.

Wash the fruit.

Add the cherries and currants to the syrup, and when they have cooked slowly for a few minutes add the rest of the fruit, and cook all slowly until tender. Do not get the fruit broken.

When cool, pour into a china or glass bowl and serve with thick cream.

Sufficient for about ten or twelve persons.

FRUIT CREAM CHARLOTTES

INGREDIENTS.—6 oz. of Casino biscuits, ½ pint packet of pineapple jelly, 2 thick slices of tinned pineapple, ½ gill of cream, 1 dessertspoonful of sugar, 1¾ gills of hot water, angelica.

METHOD.—The small tub carton cases used for these can be bought from any large store in the stationery department. Cut the biscuits the same length as the tubs and line the sides, then cover the bottom with some of the trimmings. Dissolve the jelly in the hot water, and, when cold, stir in the pineapple either minced or cut up small. When beginning to set, whisk the cream until thick and stir in lightly with the sugar. Heap in the prepared tubs when on the point of setting, and serve decorated with angelica and a dab of cream. If preferred, Savoy biscuits may be used. These should first be split lengthwise to separate them.

Sufficient to fill three tubs.

FRUIT GATEAU

INGREDIENTS.—1 tin of fruit salad, bought sponge or Madeira cake, packet of pineapple jelly, 4d. of cream.

METHOD.—Cut a slice off the top of the cake and scoop out some of the centre to make room for the fruit.

Put the fruit, syrup, and jelly in a saucepan and stir till the jelly is dissolved.

Pour the fruit into a colander placed over a basin.

Heap the fruit into the hole in the cake. Pour the hot syrup very slowly over the cake.

Put on the lid and decorate with cream.

Sufficient for five persons.

RICH FRUIT GATEAU

INGREDIENTS.—1 small tin of fruit salad in syrup, 1 sponge cake ring, apricot jam, ½ gill of sherry, 3 eggs, ½ pint of milk, 3 tablespoonfuls of castor sugar, vanilla flavouring, ½ oz. of pistachio nuts.

METHOD.—Split the sponge cake ring into halves, spread it with apricot jam.

Place the bottom half in a dish.

Strain the syrup from the fruit salad. Heat it, and soak the half of the sponge with some of the hot syrup, then put on the top half of the sponge and soak with the remainder of the syrup. Pour the sherry over also.

Take two of the eggs and separate the whites from the yolks.

Beat together the one whole egg and the two yolks, add to them the milk and one tablespoonful of sugar.

Pour into a jug, stand in a saucepan of water, and stir over the fire until the custard thickens, being very careful not to make it too hot or it will curdle.

Add the vanilla flavouring.

When the custard is cool, pour it round the outside of the sponge ring until it is not quite level with the top of the ring; leave until cold. Heap the fruit in the centre of the ring. Add a pinch of salt to the whites of eggs and whisk them to a stiff froth.

Fold into them two tablespoonfuls of castor sugar.

Shake all round the top of the ring, leaving some of the fruit showing in the centre.

Sprinkle with chopped pistachio nuts.

NOTE.—The nuts must be scalded and blanched before being chopped, and, if very moist, slightly dried, or they cannot be sprinkled easily.

Sufficient for about eight or ten persons.

FRUIT JUNKET

INGREDIENTS.—1 pint of milk, 1 dessertspoonful of coffee essence, 5 slices of tinned pineapple, 5 glacé cherries, 1 teaspoonful of rennet.

METHOD.—Warm the milk till it is tepid. Add the coffee essence and rennet, stir, and pour quickly into a glass dish.

When set, arrange the fruit on top.

DRIED FRUIT PUDDING

INGREDIENTS.—2 oz. of dried apple rings, 2 oz. of dried pears, 2 oz. of dried peaches, 3 oz. of raisins, 3 oz. of Demerara sugar, 4 oz. of semolina, 2 pints of milk, grated rind of 1 small lemon, 1 gill of cream, 2 whites of eggs, 2 dessertspoonfuls of granulated sugar, angelica.

METHOD.—Thoroughly wash all the dried fruits, including the raisins.

Cut the peaches and pears into three or four pieces. Put all the fruit into a basin and well cover with cold water, and soak for twenty-four hours. Put them into a saucepan with the water in which they have been soaking, add the Demerara sugar, and cook well until they are quite soft. Take out the fruit and put into a dish, and boil the syrup fast for about five minutes to thicken it.

When cold pour over the fruit.

Put the milk on to boil, sprinkle in the semolina, add the grated rind and granulated sugar, and cook until quite soft and creamy. Stir it well to keep it from burning.

When slightly cool, pour over the fruit, but do not mix together.

Whisk together to a stiff froth the cream and white of egg ; fold into it about a teaspoonful of castor sugar. Shake on to the top of the semolina, and decorate with strips of angelica.

NOTE.—If a plain pudding is required, this may be served without the addition of the cream and white of egg.

FRUIT SALAD

INGREDIENTS.—2 oranges, 2 apples, 3 bananas, a few black and white grapes, a small piece of melon, a few strawberries, raspberries, and white heart cherries, castor sugar, 4 gills of water, 8 oz. of granulated sugar, 3 tablespoonfuls of sherry, cochineal, 1½ gills of cream.

METHOD.—Prepare all the fruit. Peel and quarter the oranges, removing pith and pips. Peel, core, quarter, and slice the apples, then cut across.

Peel and slice the bananas.

Cut the melon into small squares, having removed the skin and seeds.

Wash and pick over the other fruits. Mix them all together, sprinkle well with castor sugar, and leave them to soak for about an hour. (Leave out a few black grapes for decoration.)

Boil the granulated sugar and water together until a thick syrup is formed. Skim it well.

When cold, add three tablespoonfuls of sherry and sufficient cochineal to make a pale pink syrup.

Heap the raw fruit in fancy custard glasses ; add a little syrup to each glass, but not sufficient to cover the

fruit. Whisk the cream until it thickens. Shake a little on to each and garnish with black grapes.

DRIED FRUIT SALAD

INGREDIENTS.—Equal quantities of prunes, raisins, and figs, few almonds, 1 or 2 eating apples.

METHOD.—Prepare and wash the fruit and soak for a few hours. Then stew until tender, adding sugar to taste and grated lemon-rind to flavour Turn into a dish when cold.

Blanch the almonds and add with the apples—the latter peeled, cored and quartered, and cut into slices Serve with cream.

INDIVIDUAL FRUIT SALADS

INGREDIENTS.—Tinned fruits such as pears, pineapple, apricots, peaches etc., glacé cherries, almonds, cochineal angelica, bananas, and oranges.

METHOD.—Drain the syrup from any of the tinned fruits you may be using and mix together. Then strain and colour with a few drops of cochineal If the syrup is thin it can be boiled for a few minutes with a little extra sugar to thicken it.

Blanch a few almonds, peel and thinly slice one or two bananas, and divide some oranges into quarters.

Arrange a pear on a slice of pine apple with a stalk of angelica, or peach on a slice of pineapple with cherries and almonds round, or some apricots, orange quarters, and banana slices in rings.

There are, of course, various other ways of arranging the different fruits Grapes and apples can also be introduced.

Pour a little syrup round each plate of salad, and serve with cream.

FRUIT SALAD JELLY CREAM

INGREDIENTS.—Half tin of fruit salad, 1 pint packet of lemon jelly, hot water, sugar, 5d. of cream, ¼ pint of milk, 1 yolk of egg, rings of angelica.

METHOD.—Drain the syrup from the fruit, remove any stones, and put the fruit through the mincer. Then drain it again.

Make a boiled custard with the yolk of egg and milk and let it cool.

Cut up the jelly and dissolve it in

the hot syrup, making it up to barely half a pint with hot water and jelly. Let this get cold. Then stir in the minced fruit, custard, and cream, the latter whisked until it is thick.

Add sugar to taste, and when the mixture is beginning to thicken, turn it into a wet mould and leave it to set. Then dip the mould into warm water and turn the jelly cream on to a dish.

Decorate the base with rings of angelica, and heap a little extra whipped cream in the centre, if liked. Sufficient for five or six persons.

KENTISH FRUIT SALAD

INGREDIENTS.—6 slices of pineapple, ¾ to 1 pint of raspberries or loganberries, fruit salad dressing, 2 bananas, 1 tablespoonful of chopped walnuts, grenadine syrup, 2 fresh pears.

METHOD.—Cut the pineapple, pears, and bananas into suitable pieces. Mix them with the berries.

Add one tablespoonful of grenadine syrup and enough pineapple-juice to moisten them. Serve the salad in tall glasses covered with the fruit salad dressing.

Decorate the dish with berries and nuts.

FRUIT SALAD DRESSING

INGREDIENTS.—½ pint of orange-juice, 1 tablespoonful of grape fruit-juice, 3 oz. of sugar, ¾ gill of cream, ¼ gill of pineapple-juice, 2 tablespoonfuls of lemon-juice, 2 eggs.

METHOD.—Heat all the fruit juices together in the top of a double boiler. Beat the eggs with the sugar until they are light. Then stir them into the hot fruit juice.

Cook them together until the mixture coats the spoon like a boiled custard. Then stand it in a basin of cold water and stir it till it is cool.

Fold in the whipped cream and serve very cold.

FRUIT SALAD WHIP

INGREDIENTS.—Large tin of fruit salad, 2 egg-whites, about 1 tablespoonful of castor sugar, ¼ pint of milk, 1 teaspoonful of custard powder, ¾ oz. of leaf gelatine.

METHOD.—Make a quarter of a pint of custard with the milk and custard powder, and leave to cool.

Drain the syrup from the fruit salad. Put a few slices aside for decoration. Then put the rest of the fruit through a mincer, having first removed any stones.

Put the gelatine (take light weight) into a saucepan with about half a teacupful of the fruit syrup, and let it dissolve.

Turn the minced fruit into a basin with the remainder of the syrup, stir in the custard and sugar to taste, then strain in the gelatine. Leave until beginning to set. Then whisk the egg-whites stiffly and fold in.

Serve in glasses, and arrange a small piece of fruit in the centre of each.

Sufficient to fill about seven glasses.

FRUIT SEMOLINA

INGREDIENTS.—1½ pints of stewed fruit (red currants and raspberries), semolina, cream, sugar.

METHOD.—When stewing fruit for this dish, add more water than usual so that you have a good proportion of syrup. Strain the syrup from the cooked fruit, measure it, and pour it into a saucepan. Bring it to the boil and sprinkle in the semolina, allowing one dessertspoonful to half a pint of syrup. Cook it gently till the semolina is tender, keeping it well stirred, then add the fruit and cook them together for two or three minutes. Add more sugar if required, and let the semolina cool before turning it into a dish. Decorate, when cold, with whipped cream, flavoured and sweetened to taste, and top the dish with red currants, or whatever fruit is used.

Sufficient for five persons.

FRUIT SPONGE CUSTARD

INGREDIENTS.—5 sponge cakes, 1 whole egg and 2 whites, ½ pint of hot milk, 1 dessertspoonful of castor sugar, vanilla flavouring, 1 tin of raspberries, angelica, cream.

METHOD.—Beat up the whole egg and mix it with the hot milk. Turn them into a double boiler, add the sugar, and stir the custard over hot water until it thickens, then take it off and leave it to cool.

Drain the syrup from the fruit, rub the fruit through a sieve, then mix about half a gill of the syrup with the fruit purée.

Whisk the egg-whites to a stiff froth and add them to the purée, then whisk them together lightly.

Split the sponge cakes in half. Dip each half in the custard and arrange them in a dish. Pour in the remainder of the custard, and heap the raspberry mixture in the centre. Decorate the sponge custard with whipped cream and angelica.

Sufficient for six or more persons.

STEWED DRIED FRUIT

INGREDIENTS.—½ lb. of dried apricots, 1½ pints of boiling water, rind of a lemon, 4 to 6 oz. of sugar, 3 oz. of cold boiled rice, 2½d. of cream, 2 oz. of castor sugar.

METHOD.—All kinds of dried fruit should be soaked, and the best way to do this is to pour boiling water on it, adding the thinly cut lemon - rind. Cover the fruit, and leave it for twenty-four hours. The fruit will swell and soak up a good deal of the water.

Before cooking the fruit, make a syrup by boiling the sugar in the water that has not been soaked up. This should be boiled for about ten minutes ; add the fruit ; cook gently for fifteen or twenty minutes till it is soft, but not broken.

Mix the rice with the cream and sugar, and heap in the centre of a glass dish with the fruit round.

Cold rice pudding would be nice used up in this way.

GINGER CUSTARD

INGREDIENTS.—¼ lb. of glacé stem ginger, 2 eggs, 1 pint of milk, 2 or 3 dessertspoonfuls of castor sugar, vanilla flavouring, ⅝ oz. of leaf gelatine, ½ gill of water, angelica, cream or whisked egg-white.

METHOD.—Beat up the eggs. Heat the milk and add to them. Strain into a jug and stand in a saucepan of hot water. Cook until the custard thickens, keeping it stirred occasionally and being careful not to let it curdle. When ready, turn into a basin and leave until cold.

Cut some slices of ginger for decoration and put aside, then cut up the remainder into small pieces and add to the custard, with flavouring and sugar to taste.

Dissolve the gelatine in a saucepan with the water, and when of a moderate temperature strain into the custard. Leave until beginning to set, then turn into a wet mould.

When quite set, unmould and decorate with slices of ginger and leaves of angelica.

Just before serving, heap some whisked egg-white or cream in the centre.

Sufficient for about five persons.

CREAM GINGER SNAPS

INGREDIENTS.—4 oz. of honey, 4 oz. of flour, 2 oz. of butter, 4 oz. of Demerara sugar, 1 teaspoonful of ground ginger, 1s. of cream, 1 oz. of crystallised ginger, 1 oz. of castor sugar.

METHOD.—Melt the butter and honey in a saucepan, but do not make it hot. Stir in the sugar. Add the flour and ground ginger, mix well and stir till it boils. Place over an asbestos mat and boil for three minutes stirring all the time.

Pour into a pie-dish. When cold cut off small pieces and roll into balls the size of a walnut.

Roll out the balls on a floured board to the size of a small plate. Place four at a time on a baking-sheet, and bake for ten minutes in a moderate oven.

Leave them for one minute to cool then lay a small bottle on the side of each snap and roll it up quickly round the bottle. If left too long to cool they will not roll up.

Whip the cream, and stir in the castor sugar and chopped crystallised ginger. Fill the ginger snaps and if liked decorate with cream.

To make from eight to twelve ginger snaps.

GINGER SOUFFLE

INGREDIENTS.—Preserved ginger in syrup, use 3 oz. of ginger and ½ gill of the syrup, 1½ gills of cream, 2 eggs, 1½ gills of milk, 2 dessertspoonfuls of castor sugar, ½ oz. of leaf gelatine, angelica.

METHOD.—Separate the yolks from the whites of eggs, beat up the yolks and mix with the milk. Pour into a jug, and stand in a saucepan of boiling water and cook gently.

Rhubarb Cups

Golden Peach Ring

Tangerine Baskets

PLATE 29

Charlotte Russe

Split the biscuits in half.

Dip half-cherries in jelly and decorate the tin.

Arrange the biscuits round the tin.

The Finished Dish

Plate 30

Leave a small lump of ginger out for decoration, the remainder cut into small dice.

Dissolve the gelatine in half a gill of the syrup, if very thick add a dessert-spoonful of water to it.

Whisk the cream until thick, and put half of it aside for decoration.

The other half add to the custard when the latter is cold, and mix lightly together. Add also the sugar and cut ginger.

Whisk the whites to a stiff froth, and fold into the other ingredients.

Lastly, strain in the dissolved gelatine, and mix all together. Stir over ice until it begins to thicken.

Pour into a soufflé case, and leave until set.

Decorate the soufflé with the remainder of the whipped cream.

Place a small lump of ginger in the centre, and a few pieces of angelica round the ginger.

Serve in the soufflé case.

GINGER TRIFLE

INGREDIENTS. —8 sponge cakes, ginger marmalade, 2 oz. of glacé ginger (or preserved ginger in syrup, sold in jars, can be used), milk, 1½ oz. of almonds, 1 gill of cream, 1 pint of custard sugar, vanilla flavouring.

METHOD.—Split open the sponge cakes and spread with ginger marmalade. Arrange them in a dish and soak with milk. Cut the ginger into small pieces and add, leaving out one larger piece for decoration. If using the preserved ginger in syrup, some of the latter can be poured over the sponge cakes.

Make the custard, either a powder or an egg custard will do (see p. 217). Sweeten and flavour it to taste and leave to cool.

Blanch the almonds and split into pieces, then stick into the sponge cakes.

Pour the custard over and leave until thoroughly cold. Whisk the cream until it stiffens, add sugar and vanilla to taste. Heap this on top of the trifle and place a piece of ginger in the centre.

Sufficient for about six or eight persons

GOLDEN PEACH RING

INGREDIENTS. — A large tin of peaches, 1 oz. of shelled walnuts, ½ oz. of gelatine, 3 dessertspoonfuls of sugar—or to taste, 1½ gills of milk, 1 egg, lemon-juice.

METHOD.—Drain the syrup from the peaches and rub enough of them through a sieve to give half a pint of pulp.

Make a boiled custard with the egg and milk, and leave it to cool.

Add the lemon-juice from half a small lemon and sugar to the peach pulp, and stir in the finely chopped walnuts, and the custard.

Dissolve the gelatine in a saucepan with one gill of the peach syrup, and strain it into the mixture. Add more sugar if required.

Leave the mixture till it begins to thicken, then turn it into a border mould, and when it is set, unmould it and serve it with the remainder of the peaches.

Sufficient for five or six persons.

GOOSEBERRY CUSTARD

INGREDIENTS.—1½ pints of gooseberries, ½ pint of custard, 1 gill of cream, vanilla flavouring, 4 oz. of Demerara sugar, or to taste, 3 sponge cakes, ½ oz. of "hundreds and thousands," castor sugar.

METHOD.—Place the fruit and sugar in a jar and put it on the top of a stove or in the oven till the fruit is soft. No water is necessary.

Arrange the cakes in a glass dish and put the pulp on top. Leave it till it is set and cold, and then pour the custard over it.

Whip the cream gently till it will hang on the whisk.

Flavour the cream with castor sugar and vanilla, and heap it roughly on top of the sweet. Lastly, shake the "hundreds and thousands" over in the cream.

NOTE.—Save a few whole cooked berries for decoration.

Sufficient for six persons.

GOOSEBERRY FOOL

INGREDIENTS.—1½ lb. of gooseberries, ½ cup of water, 4 to 6 oz. of sugar (according to taste), 2 eggs, ¾ pint of milk.

L

METHOD.—Pick and wash the goose-berries and stew them in the water with the sugar. Stew gently, and when soft rub through a hair sieve. Beat the eggs, add the milk and put it in a double saucepan. Stir the custard till it is thick enough to coat the back of the spoon, and when cold add it to the fruit purée.

A richer gooseberry fool may be made by omitting the custard and adding to the fruit purée an equal quantity of cream.

GOOSEBERRY FUDGE

INGREDIENTS.—6 sponge cakes, 3 oz. of macaroon biscuits, 3 pints of goose-berries, ¾ pint of water, 4 or 5 table-spoonfuls of sugar, or to taste, 2 yolks of eggs, 1 oz. of flour, 2 oz. of butter.

METHOD.—Top, tail and wash the gooseberries. Stew them with the water and sugar until tender, then strain off the syrup.

Split the sponge cakes and arrange half of them in a dish with half the macaroons broken in pieces. Cover them with half the gooseberries, then add the remainder of the sponge cakes and macaroons, and the remainder of the fruit. If the cakes and macaroons are stale, use some of the syrup to soak them in.

Melt the butter in a saucepan, add the flour, and when well blended gradually stir in one pint of gooseberry syrup. If not sufficient, make this up with water. Bring the sauce to the boil and boil it gently for a few minutes, then draw the pan aside and let it cool slightly.

Beat up the egg-yolks, stir them in, and cook the sauce again for a few minutes, but do not let it boil. Add more sugar, if required, then pour the sauce over the fruit and sponge cake.

Serve gooseberry fudge cold, decor-ated with a few whole cooked goose-berries, and whipped cream, sweetened and flavoured to taste.

In place of the cream, you can whisk a white of egg until stiff, then fold in one tablespoonful of castor sugar, and heap this on top.

Sufficient for from six to eight persons.

GOOSEBERRY SNOW

INGREDIENTS.—4 desertspoonfuls of granulated or Demerara sugar, ⅜ gill of water, 1 oz. of butter, 2 pints of goose-berries, 2 eggs, 3 dessertspoonfuls of castor sugar, angelica.

METHOD.—Top and tail and wash the gooseberries. Put them into a saucepan with the water and granulated sugar, and stew together until they are quite soft, then rub them through a fine sieve with the juice.

Separate the yolks from the whites of eggs.

Beat up the yolks and add to the gooseberry pulp when it has slightly cooled, stir quickly and mix together, adding the butter at the same time.

Pour the mixture into a pie-dish and cook in a moderately warm oven until just set; it will take about twenty minutes. Be careful not to let it boil or the eggs will curdle.

Remove from the oven when ready and let it cool a little.

Add a pinch of salt to the whites of eggs and whisk to a very stiff froth, then fold the castor sugar lightly into them.

Cover the top of the pudding with this, and put into a *cool* oven for about twenty minutes to set the meringue.

Decorate the centre with a few leaves of angelica.

Serve cold.

GOOSEBERRY SPONGE CUS-TARD

INGREDIENTS.—1 small sponge ring, 2 lb. of gooseberries, ½ pint of water, 4 tablespoonfuls of sugar, 2 eggs.

METHOD.—Top, tail and wash the gooseberries and stew them with the sugar and water until tender. Strain off the syrup and measure it.

Split the sponge ring in half and place one half in a Pyrex dish. Cover it with the cooked gooseberries and press the other half of the ring on top. If the sponge is stale, pour some of the gooseberry-juice over it.

Beat up the eggs and mix with the remaining gooseberry syrup. There should be three-quarters of a pint, so if there is not sufficient add a little water to it.

Add more sugar if required, then turn the sponge custard into the dish with the gooseberries, etc., and bake it gently for about half an hour.

Decorate the centre of the ring with a few gooseberries, cooked whole, and serve it cold with cream.

Sufficient for six persons.

GRAPE FRUIT MOUSSE

INGREDIENTS.—2 grape fruit, 1 egg, ½ gill of milk, ½ oz. of leaf gelatine (take light weight), ½ gill of water, 5 dessertspoonfuls of castor sugar, a few crystallised violets or rose leaves.

METHOD.—Cut the grape fruit into halves crosswise, then remove the pulp and rub it through a sieve.

The best way to loosen the pulp is first to remove the centre pith and pips, then cut round the side of the pulp to loosen it from the rind, and again through each section.

Separate the egg. Beat up the yolk and mix with the milk, and cook in a double boiler until it thickens. When cold, add it to the grape fruit pulp with the sugar.

Dissolve the gelatine in a saucepan with the water and strain in. Mix together, then leave until beginning to set. Then fold in the egg-white (whisked to a stiff froth).

Turn into the grape fruit rinds and, just before serving, decorate with some crushed, crystallised violets or rose leaves.

Allow half a grape fruit for each person.

GRAPE FRUIT SALAD

INGREDIENTS.—1 tin of grape fruit, 1½ apples, 1 oz. of almonds, a few glacé cherries, cochineal, sugar (about 1 oz.), 1½ oranges, 2 bananas, a few black grapes.

METHOD.—Peel and quarter the oranges and remove as much white pith and as many pips as possible.

Peel the apples, divide into quarters and remove the cores, then slice. Peel and slice the bananas.

Blanch the almonds.

Strain the syrup from the grape fruit into a saucepan, add the sugar and a few drops of cochineal to colour, and boil for a few minutes, then cool.

Mix all the prepared fruit and a few almonds and grapes with some of the grape fruit (the latter can be cut into smaller pieces if liked, but a few large pieces should be left for the top), and put into a bowl.

Decorate with glacé cherries, black grapes, almonds, and grape fruit, and when the syrup is cold pour it over, but do not add sufficient to cover the fruit. Serve with cream.

Sufficient for about six persons.

HAZEL PEAR COMPOTE

INGREDIENTS.—Hazel pears (as required), to each pound, when prepared, allow ½ lb. of sugar, ½ gill of water, 1 lemon (rind and juice), ½ oz. of lump ginger.

METHOD.—Peel the pears, cut in quarters and remove the cores. Then weigh them. Put into a pan with the sugar and water, also the finely-grated lemon-rind and strained lemon-juice, and the ginger (bruised and tied in muslin).

Cook slowly until the sugar is dissolved, then boil gently until the pears are tender and the syrup quite thick.

Serve with cream.

HARLEQUIN RICE

INGREDIENTS.—1½ pints of milk, 3 oz. of rice, 2 dessertspoonfuls of castor sugar, 6 oz. of crystallised fruits, 2 egg-yolks, ½ oz. of butter, ¼ oz. of gelatine, ¼ gill of water, ½ gill of thick cream, 1 tablespoonful of rum, or other flavouring as desired.

METHOD.—Bring the milk to the boil in the top of a double boiler, wash the rice, add it, and cook them over hot water, stirring occasionally until the rice is soft and the mixture quite thick.

Draw the pan aside, add the butter and sugar and cool the mixture slightly, then beat in the yolks of the eggs.

Stand the pan over hot water again and stir it for a few minutes to cook the egg, then take it off the gas and let it cool.

Dissolve the gelatine in the water and strain it in.

Add the fruit cut in small pieces, and the rum, and when quite cold stir in the cream. If this is thin, whisk it first.

Turn the harlequin rice into a wet

mould and when set dip it in warm water, unmould it, and serve it surrounded with crystallised fruits—extra to those given in the recipe.

Sufficient for five or six persons.

ITALIAN CREAM

INGREDIENTS.—¾ oz. of leaf gelatine, 2 eggs, ½ gill of water, 2½ gills of milk, 2 oz. of castor sugar, vanilla flavouring.

METHOD.—Dissolve the gelatine in a saucepan with the water, then add the milk and make hot.

Separate the yolks from the whites of the eggs.

Beat up the yolks, stir the hot milk, etc., on to them, then strain and return to the pan and cook slowly for a few minutes until the custard begins to thicken. Do not let it boil.

When ready, draw aside and add the sugar and vanilla flavouring to taste.

Whisk the egg-whites to a very stiff froth and fold in, then turn into a wet mould.

When set, unmould carefully and serve very cold.

Sufficient for about five persons.

MAKING JELLIES

LEAF GELATINE is used mainly in these recipes. This does not require soaking. The thin leaves are the best.

The average proportion to use when making creams, etc., is :

Half an ounce of leaf gelatine to a pint mould.

The gelatine must always be weighed very accurately.

If a mould is too stiff, it loses its creamy texture. On the other hand, it must be sufficient set to turn out whole.

Packet gelatine can also be obtained and sometimes it is the more convenient to use.

HELPFUL HINTS

Do not dissolve leaf gelatine in milk, or it will curdle it. If required to set milk or creamy mixtures, dissolve the gelatine in a little water, and then add it.

Do not let gelatine boil, or it will not dissolve readily. Always add it at a moderate temperature and *strain* it in.

If added too cool it is liable to

" rope " which means that the gelatine sets again in small lumps before it gets mixed into the ingredients, in which case the mould will not set.

If added too hot, it is liable to curdle milk or creamy mixtures.

UNMOULDING SECRETS

To enable jellies, creams, blancmanges, etc., to be turned out easily, always put them into wet moulds to set.

When ready to unmould, dip the mould in warm water. Then with one hand on either end of the mould give it a sharp shake in a downward direction, when it should be sufficiently loosened.

The water will be required a little warmer for china than for tin or aluminium moulds.

Cornflour and other similar blancmanges will unmould without being dipped in water.

JELLIED FRUITS

INGREDIENTS.—1 pint packet of vanilla or lemon jelly, stewed or tinned fruit, cream, crystallised rose petals.

METHOD.—The fruit may be cooked specially for this purpose, or left-over stewed fruit can be used.

Use about a pint of stewed fruit to a packet of jelly.

Dissolve the jelly in the syrup (strained from the fruit and heated), making it up to a pint with hot water.

Arrange the fruit in individual custard cups, and when the jelly is cold, pour it over the fruit and let it set.

Decorate the jellied fruits with whipped cream, sweetened and flavoured to taste, and sprinkle each cup with crushed crystallised rose petals.

Sufficient for six custard cups.

JELLY FINGERS

INGREDIENTS.—6 sponge fingers, 1 oz. of almonds, 1 pint packet of raspberry jelly, 1 pint of hot water.

METHOD.—Scald the almonds, skin them, and split each into three or four pieces.

Dissolve the jelly in the hot water, and cool slightly.

Then pour a thin coating into a rather shallow dish.

When it has set, arrange the sponge fingers in the dish, leaving about one inch of space between each.

Soak them with a small quantity of jelly, and stick the almonds into them so that they well cover the top, then leave until set.

Pour over the remainder of the jelly, being careful to keep the biscuits in position.

Leave until quite firm.

Cut out each jelly finger, using a sharp knife.

Arrange tastefully on a dish.

Sufficient for six persons.

When you have a little jelly left over after making a sweet, place it on a piece of wet grease-proof paper and chop it up with a knife. It can then be used for decorative purposes.

JELLY-MANGE

INGREDIENTS.—1 pint packet of jelly, hot water, 6d. of cream.

METHOD.—Put the jelly into the hot water (using less than usual to allow for the cream) and stir it occasionally until dissolved, then leave until cold, but not set.

Stir the cream into the cold jelly and whip them together for ten minutes or longer.

Pour into a wet border mould.

Leave until set.

Turn on to a dish and serve.

JELLY MEDLEYS

INGREDIENTS. — 1 pint packet of vanilla or lemon jelly, hot water, 1 good-sized ripe pear, 1 orange, ½ grape fruit, 2 oz. of stoned raisins, 1 oz. of almonds, ½ oz. of shelled walnuts, cream, glacé cherries.

METHOD.—Dissolve the jelly in hot water, making it up to one pint, then leave it until it begins to thicken and set.

Meanwhile, prepare the other ingredients. Blanch and skin the almonds and chop them roughly with the walnuts. Prepare the grape fruit in the usual way, then remove the pulp in small pieces. Peel the orange, slice it crosswise, and remove the pips, then cut the slices in small pieces.

Peel and quarter the pear, remove the core, and cut the fruit into dice. Chop the raisins roughly.

Mix the prepared fruits and nuts together, and stir them into the jelly when it is beginning to set. Turn this into small wet moulds, and, when set, unmould and heap whipped cream (sweetened and flavoured to taste) in the centre.

Decorate each with half a glacé cherry.

Sufficient for eight small moulds.

JELLIED PEACHES

INGREDIENTS. — 1 tin of sliced peaches, 1 pint packet of lemon or cherry jelly, hot water.

METHOD.—Dissolve the jelly in half a pint of hot water.

Drain the syrup from the peaches, measure it and make it up to half a pint with water. Add it to the dissolved jelly.

Arrange the sliced peaches in a dish, pour the jelly over them, and, when set, serve the jellied peaches with cream or custard.

JELLY RING

INGREDIENTS.—Half a sponge ring, 1 pint packet of orange jelly, 1 pint of hot water, 6d. cream, a few glacé cherries, angelica, sugar and vanilla or orange flavouring.

METHOD.—Dissolve the jelly in hot water and leave it to cool.

Put the half of a sponge ring (cut side uppermost) into a dish, and pour the jelly over it slowly. Leave this to set, then decorate it with halved glacé cherries and stalks of angelica. Whisk the cream until it stiffens, sweeten it and flavour it to taste and heap it in the centre.

Sufficient for four persons.

LEMON CREAM

INGREDIENTS.—3 lemons (rind of two and juice of three), water, 6 oz. of castor sugar, 1½ dessertspoonfuls of custard powder, 1 oz. of butter, ½ gill of cream, crystallised lemon slices and glacé cherry (for decoration), ½ oz. of leaf gelatine.

METHOD.—Wipe the lemons and grate the rinds finely.

Squeeze out the juice and strain it, then make up to three-quarters of a pint with water.

Mix the custard powder to a smooth

paste with some of it. Put the remainder into a saucepan with the grated rind, sugar, and butter, and when boiling stir on to it, then leave until cold, stirring occasionally. Whisk the cream until it stiffens and stir in. If thick, it need not be whisked.

Dissolve the gelatine in a saucepan with half a gill of water (extra to that given in the recipe) and strain it, mixing all together lightly.

Turn into a wet mould or basin, and when set turn out and decorate with crystallised lemon slices. If these are not available, use slices of fresh lemon.

Sufficient for five persons.

LEMON JELLY

INGREDIENTS. 6 lemons, 2 egg-whites, 2 egg-shells, 2 oz. of leaf gelatine, a few cloves, $1\frac{1}{2}$ pints of water, $\frac{3}{4}$ to 1 breakfastcupful of sugar, or to taste.

METHOD.—Put the water and gelatine into a large saucepan and let it soak while preparing the other ingredients. Peel the rind of one lemon very thinly and half of another, and squeeze the juice from all of them. There should be two gills of juice, but if not, add the juice of another lemon.

Turn the rind and juice into the pan with the gelatine and water; add also the cloves, sugar, egg-whites, and shells—the latter washed and crushed after removing the inner skin.

Whisk all together with a wire whisk until the mixture *almost* boils and a good head of frothy scum forms on top.

Be very careful not to let it burn at the base of the pan—this sometimes happens if any undissolved gelatine remains at the bottom.

Let it boil up, then leave the saucepan at the side of the fire for a few minutes while getting the jelly bag ready. To do this—fix the bag on to the four legs of an upturned chair, standing this chair on top of another.

Put a basin under the bag and pour boiling water through the bag to scald it. When this has drained through, remove the basin of boiling water and put an empty one in its place.

Now lift the scum from the top of the pan into the bag and pour the jelly slowly through, and it should be clear. If not, pour it slowly through once again, then turn it into a wet mould to set.

To unmould the jelly, dip it in warm water, give one sharp shake downwards to loosen it, keeping one hand firmly at either end of the mould, then turn it on to dish.

If a jelly bag is not available, tie a clean cloth over the four legs of an upturned chair, letting it sag slightly in the centre, then scald, and strain the jelly as explained before.

Sufficient for six persons.

SOME POINTS TO REMEMBER :

1. Great care must be taken to see that all utensils are perfectly clean.
2. Whites and shells of eggs are used to clarify the jelly; but it is necessary to separate the eggs very carefully, as a small trace of yolk will probably cloud the jelly. The shells must be washed and the inner skin removed.
3. Whisking the jelly brings a good head of scum to the top of the mixture, but it should be stopped just before the jelly boils. The jelly is poured through the scum, which acts as a filter. A jelly bag, made of felt, is required for straining the jelly. If there is not one available, a clean linen cloth can be used.

LEMON RICE

INGREDIENTS.—8 oz of rice, 8 oz. of sugar, water, 2 lemons.

METHOD.—Boil the rice and drain it. Pour cold water over it till the water is clear.

Boil barely one gill of water with the sugar, lemon-juice, and the grated rind of the lemons until this syrup is quite thick (letting the sugar dissolve before it comes to the boil). Mix this with the rice.

Simmer them in a double saucepan for an hour. Remove it from the heat, let the rice cool. Then turn it out on to a crystal dish and garnish it with lemon and plainly boiled rice and serve it with stewed fruit.

LEMON SNOW

INGREDIENTS.—1 pint of water, 2 lemons, $1\frac{1}{4}$ pints of breadcrumbs (not pressed down), 3 eggs, 3 table-spoonfuls of castor sugar, 4 table-spoonfuls of granulated sugar—add more if required.

METHOD.—Grate the lemon-rinds finely and mix with the breadcrumbs, then turn into a pie-dish or Pyrex dish.

Separate the eggs.

Beat up the yolks, stir the water on to them, then add to the bread-crumbs. Stir in the granulated sugar and the strained juice of the lemons.

Then put into a warm oven and bake until set. Leave to cool. Whisk the egg whites to a very stiff froth, and fold in the castor sugar.

Heap this on top of the pudding, dredge with castor sugar and return to a cool oven to set the meringue. Serve cold.

Sufficient for about six or eight persons.

LEMON SOUFFLE

INGREDIENTS.—1 lemon, 2 yolks of eggs, 3 whites of eggs, ½ gill of cream, ¼ oz. of gelatine, ⅓ gill of water, 4 oz. of castor sugar, angelica.

METHOD.—Grate the lemon-rind finely and put it into the top of a double boiler with the juice of the lemon, the castor sugar, and yolks of eggs. Stand it over a pan of hot water and whisk it until thick and creamy, being careful not to let it curdle. Remove the custard from the hot water and cool it a little.

Dissolve the gelatine in the water and strain it into the custard. Whisk the cream until it thickens and stir this in lightly. Finally, fold in the stiffly whisked egg-whites and when the mixture begins to set turn it into prepared soufflé cases.

Before serving decorate the soufflés with whipped cream (extra to that given) and leaves of angelica.

To prepare the soufflé cases, pin a band of foolscap paper round each so that it stands a little above the top. Remove the paper carefully before decorating the soufflés.

This quantity will fill about six cases.

LEMON SPONGE

INGREDIENTS.—1¾ oz. of leaf gelatine, 1¾ pints of water, ¾ lb. of castor sugar, juice of 5 lemons, rind of 3 lemons, whites of 3 or 4 eggs.

METHOD.—Place the gelatine in a saucepan with the water and dissolve it slowly.

Strain this when dissolved into another saucepan. Add to it the sugar, the grated lemon-rind, and the strained lemon-juice.

Simmer from ten to fifteen minutes, then pour into a basin and stand aside until it has cooled.

Add a pinch of salt to the whites of eggs and whisk them to a very stiff froth.

Add these to the gelatine, etc., and stir all together and whisk it all until it forms a stiff froth.

Pour into a wet mould and leave until set.

Turn carefully on to a dish and serve.

NOTE.—If preferred, instead of setting the sponge in a mould, it may be piled roughly on a dish and served. In this case garnish with stalks of angelica and crushed violets.

LIQUEUR CREAM

INGREDIENTS.—2 eggs, 1 pint of milk, 1½ dessertspoonfuls of castor sugar, 1 pint packet of strawberry jelly, ½ pint of hot water, 1 wine-glassful of maraschino.

METHOD.—Dissolve the jelly in the hot water and leave until cold, but not set.

Make the custard, beat up the eggs, add the milk to them.

Pour this into a jug and add the sugar.

Stand in a saucepan of cold water and cook over the fire until the custard thickens.

Be very careful not to overheat it, or it will curdle, and keep it frequently stirred.

When ready, remove from the saucepan, and leave until quite cool, giving it an occasional stir.

Rinse a mould with cold water, and when the jelly is cold pour a little into the bottom of it and leave until set.

Stir the maraschino into the custard, then gradually stir in the remainder of the jelly. Mix together and pour into the prepared mould and leave until firm.

Dip the bottom of the mould into warm water, give it a sharp shake and turn carefully on to a dish.

NOTE.—Set only about three or four tablespoonfuls of jelly in the bottom of the mould.

LOGANBERRY MOULD

INGREDIENTS.—1 tin of loganberries, 2 oz. of sugar, 1 large, sweet orange, 1 egg, ½ pint of milk, 1 oz. of gelatine, cochineal, 1 juicy lemon, 5d. double cream.

METHOD.—Rub half the loganberries through a hair sieve. Grate the orange-peel. Squeeze the orange and lemon and add the juice to the fruit purée and syrup with the grated rind. Measure and, if necessary, add water to make three-quarters of a pint. Soak the gelatine in this, dissolve slowly over a low gas and strain.

Put the egg and sugar in a double pan, and whisk with an egg whisk. Add the milk and stir till the custard thickens. When cold, strain the purée on to it and mix. Stir now and again till it thickens. Pour into a wetted mould. Dip in warm water, shake and slide on to a dish. Decorate with dabs of cream and half the loganberries.

Sufficient for four persons.

LOGANBERRY SPONGE

INGREDIENTS. — 1 tower - shaped sponge cake, 1 oz. of almonds, ¼ pint of loganberry purée, some loganberry syrup, 1 egg-yolk, ¾ gill of milk, 9d. of cream, sugar, vanilla.

METHOD.—Cut a slice from the top of the sponge cake, then cut the remainder into three. Stamp out the centre part from these three pieces with a round cutter, but do not cut right through the bottom piece but leave a base to it.

Arrange the three rings in a dish, building them into a tower-shape and soaking each piece with loganberry syrup.

Make a boiled custard with the milk and yolk of the egg, adding sugar and flavouring to taste, and when cold, mix this with the loganberry purée.

Whisk the cream till thick and add it to this mixture, keeping back a little for the top.

Rub some of the sponge cake, taken from the centre of the shape, through a sieve, and add about two tablespoonfuls of these crumbs to the loganberry and cream mixture ; then turn it all into the centre of the sponge cake.

Replace the top and soak it with a little syrup. Decorate the sponge with almonds and whipped cream, topped with a loganberry.

Use a new sponge cake for this dish.

To obtain the loganberry purée, prepare some loganberries and stew them till tender, adding sugar to taste, then drain off the syrup and rub the fruit through a fine sieve.

Sufficient for six persons.

MACAROON FRUIT JELLY

INGREDIENTS.—1 pint packet of red jelly, 9 macaroon biscuits (medium size), a few white grapes, 1 gill of cream, 1 pint of hot water, 1 banana, 1 white of egg, 1 dessertspoonful of castor sugar, a few pistachio nuts.

METHOD.—Dissolve the jelly in the hot water.

Peel the banana, split into halves, cut each half into three pieces.

Arrange eight macaroon biscuits in the bottom of a glass or silver dish, with grapes and banana between them. Slowly pour over the hot jelly, the latter will soak the macaroons. Leave until firm. Whisk the white of egg to a stiff froth. Whisk the cream until thick, lightly mix both together and fold in one dessertspoonful of castor sugar. Shake on to the top of the jelly.

Scald and blanch one or two pistachio nuts and cut into strips.

Decorate the top with one macaroon in the middle, and a few pieces of pistachio nut round.

MACAROON PUDDING

INGREDIENTS.—¼ lb. of macaroon biscuits, 1 dessertspoonful of cornflour, 3½ gills of milk, 2 eggs, ½ pint of apple pulp, 2 tablespoonfuls of jam, 1 tablespoonful of castor sugar.

METHOD.—Crumble up the biscuits, leaving out one whole one.

Mix the cornflour to a smooth paste with a small quantity of the milk, heat the remainder in a saucepan with some of the macaroon crumbs (all but a dessertspoonful) then add to the cornflour. Return to the pan and bring to the boil, keeping it well stirred. Boil for a few minutes, then cool slightly.

Separate the eggs. Beat up the yolks and add to the macaroon mixture. Turn into a pie-dish and bake in the oven until set, being careful not to let it boil.

When nearly cold, cover with the jam and apple pulp mixed together.

Whisk the egg-whites to a stiff froth, fold in the castor sugar and dessertspoonfuls of macaroon crumbs. Spread this over the jam and apple pulp, and, if liked, sprinkle a few more crumbs on the top. Return to a cool oven to brown lightly, and serve cold with a macaroon biscuit in the centre.

To make the apple pulp, stew some apples, adding sugar to taste, then mash them to a pulp.

Sufficient for about six persons.

MACAROON TRIFLE

INGREDIENTS.—½ lb. of macaroon biscuits, 7 sponge cakes, lemon cheese, a few almonds, 2 eggs, 1 pint of milk, almond flavouring, about 1 tablespoonful of castor sugar.

METHOD.—Split the sponge cakes into halves and spread with lemon cheese. Then arrange them in a dish with some of the macaroons and soak with milk (extra to that given) or fruit juice.

Make an egg custard, sweeten to taste, and when cooked flavour with almond flavouring. Leave this to cool. Then pour it over the trifle. Arrange the remainder of the macaroon on the top.

Blanch and split the almonds and stick them round the edge of the dish, and put a few stalks of angelica in the centre.

To make the custard, boil the milk, and when well off the boil add to the eggs (beaten). Sweeten to taste, and cook in a double boiler or in a jug in a saucepan of hot water until it thickens, keeping it stirred occasionally.

Sufficient for eight persons.

MARASCHINO CREAM

INGREDIENTS.—½ pint packet of lemon jelly, 1¾ gills of hot water,

2 tablespoonfuls of maraschino (or sufficient to flavour), ½ oz. of leaf gelatine, ½ gill of cold water, 1½ gills of cream, 1 egg, 1½ gills of milk, sugar, angelica.

METHOD.—Dissolve the jelly in the hot water and leave until cold.

Rinse a mould and decorate the bottom of it with angelica dipped in jelly. When set, cover with some more jelly and set again. Beat up the egg and add the milk to it—the latter should be hot but not boiling.

Turn into a jug and add the sugar.

Stand it in a saucepan of hot water and cook until the custard thickens, being careful not to let it curdle.

When ready, remove from the hot water and leave until cold.

Put the gelatine into a saucepan with the cold water and dissolve slowly.

Whisk the cream until it stiffens, then stir in the custard, maraschino, and sugar to taste. Lastly, strain in the gelatine and mix all together lightly.

Pour into the prepared mould and leave until set, then turn out carefully.

Chop up the remainder of the jelly roughly and serve round it.

Sufficient for about five persons.

MARASCHINO SPONGE

INGREDIENTS.—1 small bottle of maraschino cherries, 1 large juicy lemon, whites of 2 eggs, 2 oz. of sugar, ½ pint of water, ¾ oz. of leaf gelatine.

METHOD.—Break up the gelatine and soak it in the water for five minutes.

Squeeze the juice from the lemon.

Put lemon-juice and sugar with the gelatine, dissolve slowly over a low gas, strain and leave till cold.

Whisk the egg-whites stiffly and add the liquid to them, also the maraschino from the cherries. Whisk with an egg beater till stiff and frothy.

Put the cherries into two or three sundae or custard glasses, and pile the sponge mixture on top.

Decorate each with a cherry.

Sufficient for two or three persons.

MARROW CREAM

INGREDIENTS.—4 flat tablespoonfuls of ground rice, 1½ pints of milk, 2

dessertspoonfuls of sugar, 1 tablespoonful of cream, lemon flavouring, ½ lb.
of marrow jam, ½ oz. of pistachio
nuts.

METHOD.—Mix the ground rice with
about half a gill of the milk. Put the
remainder of the milk in a saucepan
to heat with the sugar.

Pour this on to the ground rice and
stir well.

Return to the saucepan and boil
slowly for eight minutes—stirring
all the time.

Add the flavouring and the cream.

Put about half of the jam into the
bottom of a glass or china bowl.

Pour the ground rice mixture over
this and leave until set.

Then spread the remainder of the
jam on the top of the ground rice, etc.
Decorate with chopped pistachio nuts
sprinkled on the jam.

MARSHMALLOW SUNDAES

INGREDIENTS.—2 ice-cream bricks,
¾ gill of boiling water, ½ lb. of marshmallows, ½ lb. of icing sugar, minced
walnuts, cherries and angelica, whipped
cream.

METHOD.—Cut the marshmallows
into four and melt them in the top of
a double boiler. Add the sugar
dissolved in water and stir it till it is
smooth.

Pour this over portions of ice-cream
arranged in sundae glasses.

Top this with a spoonful of whipped
cream and sprinkle minced walnuts
over the cream.

Decorate each glass with a cherry
and put spikes of angelica in the
centre of each sundae.

MIXED MEDLEY

INGREDIENTS.—7 sponge cakes, 4
sponge fingers, 1½ pints of milk, ½ a
gill of sherry, jam, custard powder, 1½
dessertspoonfuls of sugar, 1½ oz. of
almonds, vanilla flavouring, any odd-
ments of tinned fruits, ½ pint packet of
cherry jelly, ½ pint of hot water.

METHOD.—Dissolve the jelly in the
hot water and leave until set. Split
the sponge cakes and fingers and
spread with jam.

Arrange the bottom halves in
rather a large shallow glass dish, with
with sponge cakes in the centre and

fingers round. Boil the half a pint o
milk, and well soak the sponge piece
with some of it.

Place on the top halves, and soa
again with more milk. Pour over th
sherry.

Blanch the almonds, put them in a
saucepan with cold water to cover
bring to the boil and remove th
skins.

Cut each almond into two or thre
long strips. Stick these into the soake
sponge cakes and fingers. Put a fev
pieces of the fruit at intervals on to
of the sponge fingers.

Mix the custard powder with a smal
quantity of the pint of milk, put th
remainder in a saucepan with the sugar
Bring to the boil, pour on to the mixe
custard powder, stirring all the time
Flavour with vanilla.

When slightly cool, pour over th
sponge cakes and fruit, etc. Leave unti
cold.

Chop the jelly, and garnish all roun
the top of the trifle.

NOTE.—Use the custard powder i
proportion to quantity given o
packet.

Sufficient for about eight or te
persons.

MERINGUE CHARLOTTE

INGREDIENTS.—1 packet of pine
apple jelly, 6 oz. of fancy finger-shape
meringue biscuits, 2 eggs, 1 pint of ho
milk, 3 oz. of sugar, ½ pint of cream
1 oz. of gelatine, 2 oz. of crystallise
pineapple (chopped), ½ gill of col
water.

METHOD.—Dissolve the jelly in on
pint of hot water, pour half into
tin and let it set. Soak the gelatine i
the cold water for five minutes, an
dissolve it in the remainder of th
liquid jelly.

Beat the eggs and sugar ; stir in th
hot milk.

Pour the custard into a doubl
saucepan and stir until it is thic
enough to coat the back of a spoon
When cold, strain in the gelatine.

Whip the cream, and add it to th
mixture with the pineapple, stirrin
it often as it begins to thicken. Plac
the biscuits round the tin (right sid
out and close together).

When the cream mixture is almos

solid put it into the lined tin ; it should come just above the top of the biscuits. To serve, shake gently out on to a dish.

Sufficient for four persons.

MERINGUE GATEAU

INGREDIENTS.—1 sponge cake ring, 1 small tin of red cherries in syrup, 2 whites of eggs (large), 4 dessert-spoonfuls of castor sugar, angelica, ½ gill of sherry, cream.

METHOD.—Strain the syrup from the cherries. Soak the sponge ring with sherry and some of the syrup.

Add a pinch of salt to the whites of eggs, and whisk them to a very stiff froth.

Fold the castor sugar into them very lightly.

Coat the sponge ring with the meringue mixture, spreading it on evenly.

Put into a warm oven for about twenty minutes to dry the meringue, but see that it does not brown.

Leave until cold, then fill the centre hole with the cherries. Heap them high.

Decorate with some leaves of angelica and serve with cream.

Sufficient for about six to eight persons.

This gâteau can be varied by using other kinds of fruit such as loganberries, pineapple cubes, apricots, etc.

When making trifles and gâteaux it is important to get the sponge cake soaked sufficiently without getting it too soft. Special attention must be given to this when making a meringue gâteau, as if the sponge cake is soaked too much it is difficult to coat with meringue. The sherry can be omitted, although the flavour of it improves the gâteau.

TO MAKE LEAVES OF ANGELICA.—Cut a narrow strip of angelica (about three-eighths of an inch wide), cut a slice from the top, in a slanting direction, then cut pieces parallel with this, about the same width as the strip. When cut, they are diamond shaped.

MERINGUE JELLY

INGREDIENTS.—1 pint packet of jelly, hot water, 2 whites of egg.

METHOD.—Dissolve the jelly in the hot water, making it up to a pint with the jelly. Then turn it into a fairly large basin and leave it till it begins to set.

You can use any flavoured jelly, and sometimes can utilise left-over fruit juice for this purpose instead of using so much water. You can also flavour the jelly with a little sherry or rum if you wish.

When the jelly begins to thicken, add a pinch of salt to the whites of the eggs and whisk them to a stiff froth. Then add them to the jelly, and whisk them all together before turning the meringue jelly into a glass dish.

Let the jelly set, and then decorate it tastefully and serve it with cream.

Meringue jelly looks just as attractive served in individual glasses.

MERINGUE RICE

INGREDIENTS.—Lemon rice, (see p. 326), 2 whites of egg, 4 oz. of icing sugar, 2 oz. of almonds, 2 oz. of chocolate, cream.

METHOD.—Heap the lemon rice in a fireproof-dish. Beat the whites of egg and add the sugar gradually, and also the chopped almonds.

Cover the rice with the mixture. Put into a cool oven to brown the meringue slightly.

Melt the chocolate and add a little water. Pour it over the rice so that it runs down in streaks.

Serve meringue rice with whipped cream.

NOTE.—A thicker covering of meringue may be made, if liked.

Sufficient for four persons

MERINGUE RICE PUDDING

INGREDIENTS.—3 dessertspoonfuls of rice, 1¼ dessertspoonfuls of granulated sugar, 1¼ pints of milk, 1½ oz. of glacé cherries, 2 egg-whites, 2 tablespoonfuls of castor sugar, ½ lemon.

METHOD.—Wash the rice and put it into a dish with the granulated sugar, add the finely grated lemon-rind, and stir in the milk. Cook them gently in the oven for about an hour and a half or two hours or until the rice is tender, and the mixture of a creamy consistency, keeping it stirred occasionally to prevent a skin forming. When ready, remove the dish from the oven and let the rice cool a little. Cover it with a layer of glacé cherries cut in small pieces. Whisk the whites to a stiff froth, fold in the castor sugar, and then the lemon-juice. Heap this on top of the pudding and put it in a cool oven to set, and brown the meringue lightly.

Serve cold.

Sufficient for four or five persons.

MERINGUE TRIFLE

INGREDIENTS.—6 pairs of meringue cases, 3 or 4 sponge cakes, about 2 tablespoonfuls of rum, milk, 1 or 1½ gills of cream, glacé cherries, angelica, sugar and vanilla flavouring.

METHOD.—Arrange the meringue cases in a dish in pairs to form a border. Whisk the cream until it stiffens, and sweeten and flavour it to taste.

Split open the sponge cakes and then use them to fill up the centre of the ring, soaking each layer with a little milk and rum, and putting whipped cream between. Heap the remainder of the cream on the top, and decorate with two or three glacé cherries and leaves of angelica.

Sufficient for about six or eight persons.

MILK JELLY

INGREDIENTS.—1 pint packet of jelly, ½ pint of hot water, cold milk.

METHOD.—Dissolve the jelly in the hot water and leave it to get cold ; then stir in sufficient cold milk to make it up to a pint. Turn the jelly into a wet mould to set.

NOTE.—Let the jelly get quite cold before mixing it with the milk, otherwise the mixture will curdle.

MOCK CREAM

INGREDIENTS.—2 oz. of butter, 1 oz. of castor sugar, 1 oz. of flour, 1¼ gills of milk, vanilla flavouring.

METHOD.—Beat the butter and sugar to a cream. Mix the flour to a smooth paste with a spoonful or two of the milk, heat the remainder and add it to the flour. Return all to the pan and bring it to the boil. Boil it gently for a few minutes, keeping it stirred. Take it off the gas and continue to stir until almost cold, then beat in the creamed fat and sugar *very gradually*. Beat until the mixture

is creaming, then add vanilla flavouring to taste.

Serve with stewed fruit, jellies, and fruit pies.

MOTTLED JELLIES

INGREDIENTS.—1 pint of cherry jelly, ¼ pint of milk, ¾ pint of hot water.

METHOD.—Dissolve the jelly in the hot water and leave until cold and partly set, then beat it up with a fork and stir in the milk. This will give it a mottled appearance.

Pour into small, wet moulds, and when set turn out in the usual way.

Sufficient for four or five persons.

NUT GATEAU

INGREDIENTS.—2 eggs, 1 pint of milk, 2 dessertspoonfuls of sugar, 2 oz. of shelled walnuts, 6 oz. of icing sugar, 3 oz. of butter, vanilla flavouring, 1 sponge ring, jam, a small tin of pineapple slices or cubes, sherry or rum, about 2 tablespoonfuls (if liked).

METHOD.—Roll the lumps out of the icing sugar and rub it through a fine sieve.

Add the butter, and beat both to a cream.

Flavour with vanilla

Beat up the eggs, heat the milk and stir on to them.

Pour into a jug and add the sugar (two dessertspoonfuls). Stand it in a saucepan of hot water and cook until the custard thickens, being careful not to let it curdle.

When cooked, remove from the hot water ; leave until cool. Flavour with vanilla. Split open the sponge ring and spread with jam.

Put it into a dish and soak lightly with pineapple syrup, and either rum or sherry (if liked). Leave two or three walnuts whole, and chop up the remainder into rough pieces.

Spread some of the butter icing on the top of the ring and a little way down the sides, then coat with walnuts If there are any over, put them in the bottom of the dish.

Place some of the pineapple in the centre of the ring and the remainder round the base. If using pineapple slices, cut them into smaller pieces

Pour the custard round, but do not cover the top of the ring.

Heap the remainder of the butter icing over the pineapple and stick a walnut on the top.

NOTE.—If preferred, the butter icing can be put into an icing-bag and forced out as when icing a cake.

Sufficient for eight persons.

ORANGE BLANCMANGE

INGREDIENTS.—4 oranges (grated rind and juice), $1\frac{3}{4}$ pints of milk, $2\frac{1}{2}$ oz. of cornflour, $\frac{1}{4}$ lb. of castor sugar, cochineal.

METHOD.—Very lightly grate the rinds of the oranges. Squeeze the juice from them, and strain it and measure it. Mix the cornflour to a smooth paste with orange-juice.

If there is not as much as a quarter of a pint of orange-juice from the oranges, a little extra milk must be added to make up, but it must not be added to the orange-juice until it has been mixed with the cornflour, or it will curdle.

Put the milk and sugar into a saucepan and heat it.

Pour the hot milk on to the mixed cornflour, then return it all to the saucepan and bring to the boil, and boil for eight to ten minutes.

Add a few drops of cochineal, sparingly.

Pour into a wet mould and leave until set. Turn carefully on to a dish and serve.

ORANGE CHARLOTTE RUSSE

INGREDIENTS.—6 oz. of sponge fingers, $\frac{1}{2}$ packet of lemon jelly, 1 orange.

FOR THE FILLING.—2 oranges, 1 oz. of gelatine, 2 eggs, $\frac{3}{4}$ pint of milk, 2 oz. of sugar, 1 gill of cream.

METHOD.—Peel one orange, divide it into sections and remove the pith.

Dissolve the jelly in half a pint of hot water.

Rinse a cake-tin in cold water and pour in enough jelly to cover the bottom. Let it set, and lay on it a circle of orange sections with three in the middle. Pour on a few spoonfuls of jelly to keep the orange in place and let it set, then pour on the rest of the jelly.

Cut the sides of the biscuits straight and make them all the same length. When the jelly is firm arrange the biscuits standing in it side by side all round the tin.

To make the filling, grate the rind of one orange and put it in a double saucepan with the eggs and sugar. Whisk with an egg-beater and add the milk. Stir the custard till it is thick enough to coat the back of the spoon. Let the custard stand where it will keep warm.

Squeeze the juice from the oranges on to the gelatine and add half a gill of cold water.

Dissolve the gelatine slowly over a low gas, stirring all the time and when cool strain it into the custard.

Whip the cream and add it to the mixture when quite cold.

Stir as it cools, and when it thickens (but not before) pour it into the prepared tin.

When set, dip for a moment into hot water to loosen the jelly from the tin.

Place a dish on top, turn upside down, and shake very gently.

Enough for five persons.

ORANGE CREAMS

INGREDIENTS.—3 dessertspoonfuls of castor sugar, 2 oranges, 1 gill of cream, 1 white of egg, angelica, $\frac{1}{2}$ gill of water, $\frac{1}{4}$ oz. of leaf gelatine.

METHOD.—Cut the oranges into halves, and remove the pulp without splitting the rinds. If you draw the skin of the orange away from the rind and slip your finger in between the two, it is possible to remove the inside without spoiling the shape of the case in any way.

Take out the pips.

Rub the pulp through a fine sieve and mix well with the castor sugar.

Whip the cream until it thickens, and add half of it to the orange pulp, etc.

Whisk the white to a stiff froth and fold in lightly.

Dissolve the gelatine in the water, but do not bring it to the boil.

Strain it into the other ingredients and mix all thoroughly.

Wipe the orange rinds, stand them on a plate, and fill each half with the mixture.

Leave until set, then decorate the top of them with the remainder of the cream and a few stalks of angelica.

Stand on a lace paper and serve in the orange cases.

ORANGE CUPS

INGREDIENTS.—Oranges as required, about ½ pint of orange-juice, or rather more, 1 egg, 1 pint packet of orange jelly, 1 egg, ½ pint of milk, 1 dessertspoonful of castor sugar, orange flavouring essence, crystallised cherries, some almonds.

METHOD.—Cut the oranges in halves crosswise, squeeze out the juice and scrape out the pulp, leaving the shells as clean as possible. Care should be taken not to break them or spoil their shape.

Strain the juice and pulp through a coarse strainer, and heat it. Cut up the jelly and dissolve it in the hot juice, making it up to barely three-quarters of a pint with the jelly. Leave it to cool.

Heat the milk and add it to the beaten egg. Cook it in the top of a double boiler until it thickens, keeping it stirred. Then take it off the heat and add the sugar and flavouring essence. Leave it also to cool before mixing it with the cold jelly.

When it begins to thicken, fill up the orange cups with the mixture, and leave them to set. Decorate each with the cherries and the almond spikes.

NOTE.—If the oranges are small, cut a good slice off the top, instead of halving them.

ORANGE FLUFF

INGREDIENTS.—3 yolks and 2 whites of eggs, ½ pint of milk, 2 or 3 dessert-spoonfuls of castor sugar, ¾ oz. of leaf gelatine, ½ gill of water, orange essence, angelica and orange peel for decoration.

METHOD.—Beat up the yolks and add the milk—hot but not boiling—then strain into a jug and stand in a saucepan of hot water. Cook gently until the custard thickens, keeping it stirred occasionally. Turn into a basin. Put the gelatine in a saucepan with the water, dissolve slowly, then strain in. Add sugar and orange essence to taste.

Leave until beginning to set, then whisk the egg-whites to a stiff froth and fold in lightly.

Turn into soufflé cases, and when quite set decorate with stalks of angelica and small rounds of orange-peel cut very thinly.

Sufficient for six persons.

ORANGE MOULD

INGREDIENTS.—1½ level tablespoonfuls of cornflour, 3 large sweet oranges, ½ pint of water, 1 oz. of sugar.

METHOD.—Squeeze all the juice from two of the oranges, and peel the other, dividing it into sections and removing the pith.

Mix cornflour and sugar smoothly with the orange-juice. Boil the water and pour it on the mixed cornflour, stirring well. Pour back into the pan and boil for ten minutes, stirring all the time. Rinse a half-pint mould or basin in cold water, and pour in the mixture. When cold and set, turn out carefully and decorate with orange sections.

Sufficient for two persons.

ORANGE PUDDING

INGREDIENTS.—4 sponge cakes, 1 pint of milk, 3 eggs, 1 orange, some orange marmalade (3 tablespoonfuls), 3 or 4 dessertspoonfuls of sugar.

METHOD.—Separate two of the eggs, and beat the third whole egg and the two yolks together.

Crumble the sponge cakes finely and add to the eggs with the finely-grated orange-rind and strained juice. Stir in the marmalade and sugar and mix all together, then turn into a Pyrex dish or pie-dish and gradually stir in the milk.

Whisk the egg-whites to a stiff froth and fold in lightly.

Bake gently until set, being careful not to let it boil.

Serve cold, decorated with a few quarters of orange extra to that given in the recipe.

Sufficient for six persons.

ORANGE SALADS

INGREDIENTS.—2 large oranges, a few almonds, a few glacé cherries, 1 large ripe pear.

METHOD.—Cut the oranges in halves across the sections, and prepare as you would a grape fruit. Then remove the pulp and cut the peel round the edges.

Peel and quarter the pear and remove the core. Cut the fruit into pieces, then mix with the orange.

Blanch and split the almonds. Cut the cherries in quarters. Arrange the pear and orange in the orange cups, and decorate with almonds and cherries. Serve with cream.

NOTE.—When fresh pears are not in season use tinned ones.

Sufficient for four persons.

ORANGE SOUFFLE

INGREDIENTS.—¼ lb. of castor sugar, 2 eggs, 2 oranges (small), ⅜ oz. of gelatine, ½ gill of water, 1 gill of cream.

FOR DECORATION.—½ oz. of crystallised rose-leaves or violets, ½ gill of cream.

METHOD.—For this soufflé small paper soufflé cases are needed ; these can be obtained from a stationer's store. Procure about six of these cases and pin round each one a piece of foolscap paper, so that it reaches about one inch above the top of the case. Separate the whites from the yolks of the eggs. Squeeze the juice from the oranges and grate the rinds. Put the yolks of eggs, sugar, and grated rind and juice of oranges into a saucepan and whisk over the fire until it thickens, being very careful not to overheat it. Pour into a basin to cool.

Whip the cream and add to this mixture when it has cooled. Whisk the whites of eggs to a stiff froth and add. Melt the gelatine in the water and strain into the other ingredients. Mix these all lightly together and pour the mixture into each soufflé-case so that it comes nearly to the top of the paper.

Leave until set. Remove foolscap paper very carefully from each case. Decorate the top of each soufflé with whipped cream and crushed violets or rose leaves. Serve on a dish.

ORANGE SPONGE

INGREDIENTS.—3 juicy oranges, whites of 2 large eggs, ½ pint of cold water, 2 oz. of castor sugar, ¾ oz. of leaf gelatine.

METHOD.—Peel one orange and divide it into sections, and squeeze the juice from the others.

Soak the gelatine in the water for five minutes, and dissolve it slowly over a low gas. Strain it on to the sugar and orange-juice, and leave it to get quite cold.

Whisk the whites stiffly and add the liquid to them.

Whisk with an egg-beater till stiff and frothy.

Pile in a glass dish or pour into a wetted mould.

Place quarters of orange round and serve.

Sufficient for two or three persons.

ORANGE TRIFLE

INGREDIENTS.—6 sponge cakes, 1¼ pints of milk, 2 oranges (large) ½ gill of orange wine, 1 oz. of pistachio nuts, 3 eggs, orange marmalade, crystallised violets, 3½ dessertspoonfuls of castor sugar.

METHOD.—Split the sponge cakes and spread them with marmalade. Arrange the lower halves in a glass dish.

Boil one gill of the milk, and soak them with some of the hot milk. Then pour over half of the wine.

Wipe the oranges, grate the rind of one of them, squeeze, and strain the juice.

Sprinkle the grated rind on to the soaked portions. Fit on the top halves and soak with the remainder of the hot milk and wine. Sprinkle the orange-juice over the sponge cakes.

Thinly peel the remaining oranges, and cut some of them into fancy shapes. This is used later for decorations.

Scrape off the pith, divide the orange into quarters. Remove the pips and arrange the quarters between the sponge cakes.

Take two eggs and separate the yolks from the whites. Then beat up the remaining egg with the other two yolks. Add the pint of milk, together with one and a half dessertspoonfuls of sugar, and flavour with a few pieces of orange-rind.

Pour into a jug, stand in a saucepan of cold water, stir over the fire until it thickens. Be careful not to make it too hot, or it will curdle.

When cooked lift from saucepan, remove the rind and leave the custard until cool.

Blanch and split the pistachio nuts, then stick them into the sponge cakes.

When cold pour the custard over the sponge cakes, etc.

Whisk the whites to a stiff froth, fold in the castor sugar (two dessert-spoonfuls), and cover trifle with it.

Decorate with violets and orange-peel.

PEACH BLANCMANGE

INGREDIENTS.—1 large tin of peaches and syrup, ½ lemon, ¼ lb. of castor sugar, ½ pint of milk, ½ oz. of leaf gelatine.

METHOD.—Take about half of the peaches and rub them through a sieve.

Add the strained lemon-juice to the pulp.

Dissolve the gelatine in about half a gill of the peach syrup. It must not boil, or it will not dissolve.

Add the castor sugar and milk to the peach pulp, and mix thoroughly.

Lastly strain in the dissolved gelatine.

Stir lightly until the mixture begins to thicken.

Pour into a wet border mould and leave until set.

Turn out into a glass dish.

Pile the remainder of the peaches in the centre of the mould, and pour round the rest of the syrup (previously strained).

PEACH CREAM

INGREDIENTS.—A tin of peaches in syrup (small), 1 gill of cream, 2 oz. of castor sugar, 1 pint packet of lemon jelly, ¾ pint of hot water, ½ oz. of pistachio nuts, ½ oz. of gelatine.

METHOD.—Make the lemon jelly and leave until quite cold.

Scald a mould and rinse in cold water, then mask it with jelly.

Decorate the bottom of the mould with pieces of peach and chopped pistachio nuts dipped in jelly, and leave to set.

The pistachio nuts should be scalded and blanched before being chopped.

Cover the decoration with jelly and leave to set again.

Take the peaches from the syrup and rub through a wire sieve.

Whip the cream slightly and add to the peach pulp with the sugar. Mix lightly together.

Dissolve the gelatine in about three-quarters of a gill of the peach syrup and strain this into the other ingredient.

Mix together lightly and pour this into the prepared mould.

Leave until set.

Turn on to a dish.

Serve with chopped jelly round the cream.

Sufficient for about five persons.

PEACH CUPS

INGREDIENTS.—1 large tin of peaches, 1 gill of cream, a few crystallised violets, angelica, castor sugar, vanilla.

METHOD.—Open the tin of peaches, take them out of the syrup and let them drain well.

Then arrange them in a rather shallow dish with the cut side uppermost.

Sweeten and flavour the cream with a little vanilla and castor sugar.

Whisk it until it is thick.

Heap some of the cream in the centre of each peach. Place a violet in the middle, and cut small leaves of angelica and arrange them round it. Strain the peach syrup round and serve.

PEACH GATEAU

INGREDIENTS.—A border ring of sponge cake, 1 large tin of peaches, 2 oz. of almonds, ¾ gill of sherry, ½ pint of cream, vanilla and castor sugar, crystallised violets.

METHOD.—Place the sponge cake ring on a glass or silver dish and soak it well with the sherry and some of the peach syrup.

Put the almonds into water, bring them to the boil, then strain off the water and skin them.

Cut each almond into four pieces lengthways and stick them all round the sponge cake ring.

Cut two or three peaches into quarters and place all round the base of the ring.

Pile the remaining peaches and syrup in the centre of the ring.

Mix the cream with a sprinkling of castor sugar and a few drops of vanilla and whisk until quite thick.

Shake the cream roughly on to the peaches in the centre of the ring and garnish with a few violets.

NOTE.—If liked, the sponge cake ring can be made at home ; just make an ordinary sponge mixture and bake in a border mould.

If the peach syrup is very thick and will not soak into the sponge dilute with half a gill of water and bring to the boil, and soak the ring with the hot syrup.

PEACH JELLY

INGREDIENTS.—1 tin of peaches, 1 packet of lemon jelly, 1 gill of cream, 1 cup of broken cake, 1 small bottle of maraschino cherries.

METHOD.—Add enough water to the peach and cherry syrup to make it up to one pint. Heat this and use it to dissolve the jelly.

Put three tablespoonfuls of cake into custard or sundae glasses.

Fill half full with jelly.

When set, cover with a little cream and lay on it a peach with a cherry in the hollow. Decorate the edges of the peaches with cream.

Sufficient for four persons.

PEACH MERINGUES

INGREDIENTS.—A small tin of peaches some shortbread biscuits (allow one for each peach), 1 egg - white, 1 table-spoonful of castor sugar, jam.

METHOD.—Drain the peaches from the syrup and place one on each biscuit—cup side downwards.

Whisk the egg-white to a stiff froth and then fold in the castor sugar. Turn the meringue into an icing-bag, with a rose or shell tube fixed in the bottom of it, and force it out to form a border all round each peach.

Put in a cool oven to set and lightly brown the meringue, and when cold serve with a little jam on top of peach.

Allow one for each person.

NOTE.—For these use the round shortbread biscuits (with or without currants). They can be obtained from almost any baker, and the cost is about seven for sixpence.

PEACH MILK MOULD

INGREDIENTS.—A large tin of sliced peaches, 2 oz. of castor sugar, juice of $\frac{1}{2}$ lemon, $\frac{3}{4}$ oz. of gelatine, $\frac{3}{4}$ gill of water, $\frac{1}{2}$ pint of milk, cream.

METHOD.—Turn the peaches and syrup into a basin, keeping back a few slices for decorating. Then add the castor sugar and strained lemon-juice and stir till the sugar is dissolved.

Dissolve the gelatine in a saucepan with the water, and strain it into the peaches. Stir in the milk.

Leave the mixture till it begins to thicken, then turn it into a mould, previously rinsed with cold water.

Unmould the Peach Milk Mould when it is set. Decorate it with whipped cream, sweetened and fla-voured to taste, and a few sliced peaches.

Sufficient for eight persons.

SMALL PEACH MOULDS

INGREDIENTS.—1 pint packet of lemon jelly, $\frac{3}{4}$ pint of hot water, a few pistachio nuts, 1 gill of thick custard, 2 oz. of castor sugar, 1 small tin of peaches, 1 gill of cream, $\frac{3}{4}$ oz. of French leaf gelatine.

METHOD.—Dissolve the jelly in hot water and stand aside to cool. Scald and blanch the pistachio nuts and cut across into thin slices.

Prepare some very small fluted moulds.

Scald them, and rinse them with cold water.

Mask each mould with some of the jelly, turning them slowly on ice until a thin coating sets all round the sides and bottom.

Cut tiny pieces of the outside part of one of the peaches, and dip in jelly and set in the bottom of each mould, together with a few pieces of pistachio nuts, making a pretty design.

When quite set, cover with jelly and leave until set again.

Make a gill of custard from custard powder, according to directions given on the packet, and leave until cold.

Strain the peaches from the syrup, and rub through a wire or hair sieve.

Add the sugar to the peach purée, also the custard. Put the gelatine into a saucepan to dissolve with half a gill of peach syrup, but do not boil it.

Whisk the cream until thick; lightly mix into it the peach purée, etc.

Strain in the dissolved gelatine, mix all together and pour into the prepared moulds. When set turn on to a silver dish and serve with chopped jelly round.

PECHES AU RHUM

INGREDIENTS.—1 sponge cake ring, 1 wineglassful of rum, strawberry jam, 1 large tin of peaches in syrup, 3 eggs, 1½ pints of milk, 2 dessertspoonfuls of castor sugar, vanilla, 1 gill of cream (more, if liked), angelica, 1 oz. of almonds.

METHOD.—Blanch and chop the almonds. Drain off all the syrup from the peaches and heat it.

Split the sponge ring in two, and spread each half with jam. Put the lower half into a glass dish. Soak it with some of the hot syrup and some of the rum, then put the chopped almonds over the jam. Place on the top half of the sponge and soak with the remainder of the syrup and rum. Put some of the peaches into the centre hole and pile them up well. Cut the remainder into quarters and place in the bottom of the dish.

To make the custard, beat up the eggs, add the milk, and mix together. Pour into a jug and add the castor sugar. Stand it in a saucepan of cold water and cook over the fire until the custard thickens. Be very careful not to overheat it, or it will curdle. Keep the custard frequently stirred, and do not let the water quite boil round the saucepan. When cooked remove at once, add flavouring to taste, and keep it stirred for a few minutes.

When slightly cool pour it round the outside of the sponge ring. Do not let any of it run into the centre hole with the peaches.

Leave until quite cold, then sweeten and flavour the cream to taste and whisk it until it stiffens. Cover all round the top of the sponge ring with the cream, and decorate the cream with rings of angelica.

PEACH SPONGE RING

INGREDIENTS.—1 sponge ring, a large tin of sliced peaches, 1 egg-white, 1 tablespoonful of castor sugar, 1 dessertspoonful of lemon-juice.

METHOD.—Put the sponge ring into a fireproof dish and warm it through in the oven. Turn the peaches and syrup into a saucepan to heat. When the sponge ring is warm, pour the hot syrup over it gently, arranging the fruit round the base and keeping back a few slices for decorating.

Whisk the egg-white to a stiff froth, fold in the castor sugar and lemon-juice. Place the meringue in small heaps on top of the sponge ring, sprinkle it with sugar, and return it to a cool oven to set the meringue. Then decorate the sweet with the remaining slices of peaches, and serve it either hot or cold.

PEAR COMPOTE

INGREDIENTS.—1½ lb. of winter pears, juice of a lemon and half the peel, 4 cloves (or more if strong clove flavour is liked), 1½ gills of water, 4 oz. of sugar, cochineal.

METHOD.—Peel the lemon thinly and put the peel in a small saucepan with the water and sugar. Boil for ten minutes. Peel the pears, cut them in half and remove the cores. Put them in a casserole or stewpan with the cloves and pour the syrup over, and add the juice of a lemon.

If a casserole is used, bake the pears in a slow oven till tender; some kinds take three or four hours. If liked they can be stewed *slowly* on the gas.

When tender take them out with a spoon and place them in a glass dish, sticking one or two cloves in each pear.

Colour the syrup with cochineal and pour it round the pears. With a pastry brush, paint the centre of each pear with a line of cochineal.

Allow at least one pear for each person.

PEAR CUSTARD

INGREDIENTS.—A small tin of pears (pint size), 2 oz. of butter, 1½ oz. of flour, milk, 2 dessertspoonfuls of castor sugar, 2 yolks of eggs.

METHOD.—Drain the syrup from the pears and make it up to one pint with milk.

Save a few pears for the top, and cut the remainder each into four or five portions.

Melt the butter, add the flour and, when well blended, stir in the milk and pear-juice and bring them to the boil. Boil them gently for a few minutes, draw the pan aside, and let the mixture cool slightly, then add the sugar and beaten yolks of eggs.

Turn the cut pears into a buttered Pyrex dish, pour the custard over them, and bake them gently for about twenty minutes, being careful not to let them boil. Serve the pear custard cold with the remainder of the pears arranged tastefully.

Sufficient for four persons.

NOTE.—A pretty effect is obtained by colouring the custard with cochineal.

PEAR GATEAU

INGREDIENTS.—1 small tin of pears, 1 oz. of almonds, 6 glacé cherries, ½ gill of cream, 2 oz. of rice, ½ pint of milk, essence of almonds, ½ lemon jelly, ½ pint of hot water, 3 oz. of sugar, ½ oz. of butter, 1 sponge ring.

METHOD.—Dissolve the jelly in the hot water and pour slowly all over the sponge ring and leave till next day. Wash the rice, put it in a pan of boiling water and boil for just five minutes. Strain off all the water and put in the milk and butter with one ounce of sugar.

Simmer very gently till it turns to a mash, and then leave it to get cold. Drop the almonds in boiling water, slip off the skins and put the almonds in cold water. Cut them into strips and stick them into the cake.

Flavour the rice with almond essence, mix it with half the cream and fill the centre of the mould with it.

Put half a pint of the pear syrup in a small pan with the rest of the sugar and boil till reduced to half. Let it cool and pour over the gâteau. Decorate with a dab of sweetened and whipped cream and six glacé cherries.

PEAR JELLY

INGREDIENTS.—1½ lb. of stewing pears 3 oz. of sugar, ¾ pint of water, lemon-rind and cloves for flavouring, 1 pint packet of lemon jelly, ½ pint of hot water.

METHOD.—Peel the pears, split in halves and remove cores. Put into a saucepan with the sugar, water, and flavouring, and cook until tender. Very hard pears will take about two hours to cook. Mix the packet of jelly with the half-pint of hot water and stir until it is dissolved. Strain the juice from the stewed pears and add to the half-pint jelly, making it up to one pint. Arrange the pears in a glass dish. Pour the jelly over them and leave until set. Serve in the dish. Instead of stewing the pears, a tin of pears can be used if desired.

Sufficient for about six or eight persons.

PEAR MACAROONS

INGREDIENTS.—A tin of Bartlett pears (use as required), large macaroon biscuits (one for each pear), red jam and apricot jam, desiccated coconut, angelica, cream.

METHOD.—Put the macaroons into a shallow dish and soak with the pear syrup, having previously heated it. Warm the jams and spread some of the pears with red jam and the others with apricot jam, then coat with desiccated coconut.

Put stalks of angelica into the pears, place one on each macaroon, and serve with cream.

Allow one for each person.

PEAR PUFF

INGREDIENTS.—1 small tin of pears, 2 whites of eggs, ½ dessertspoonful of custard powder, 1½ dessertspoonfuls of castor sugar, ¼ pint of milk, vanilla flavouring, ¾ oz. of leaf gelatine (light weight), ¾ gill of pear syrup.

METHOD.—Mix the custard powder to a smooth paste with a small quantity of the milk.

Boil the remainder and add to the powder, keeping it well stirred all the time.

Flavour with vanilla, and leave until cool.

Rub the pears through a sieve. Then add the sugar and pear pulp to the custard mixture. Dissolve the gelatine in the pear syrup, but do not boil it.

Whisk the whites to a very stiff froth, fold them lightly into the pear pulp, etc.

Lastly strain in the gelatine and mix all together.

Pour into a border mould and leave until set.

Turn on to a dish and serve.

Sufficient for about six persons.

PEAR AND RICE MOULD

INGREDIENTS.—3 oz. of rice, 2 oz. of sugar, 1 pint of milk, 1 oz. of butter, 3 strips of lemon-rind, 1 tin of pears, cochineal, 6 cloves, 1 cherry, 3 oz. of loaf sugar.

METHOD.—Wash the rice, put it in a pan of boiling water, and boil for five minutes (not more) then strain. Put the rice in a saucepan with the milk, lemon-rind, butter, and sugar, and cook as gently as possible till the rice goes to a mash. When it begins to get thick put an asbestos mat underneath and stir to prevent burning. Rinse a border mould in cold water, and pour in the rice, removing the lemon-rind. Turn out when set, and fill the centre with pears, putting a clove in each of the top ones to represent a stalk. Boil half a pint of the pear syrup with the sugar till it is reduced to half the quantity, then cool slightly. Brush the centre of the top five or six pears with cochineal, and pour the syrup over them.

PEAR SPONGE CROUTES

INGREDIENTS.—6 tinned pears, 6 sponge cakes, 3 oz. of fresh butter, damson jelly, 1 oz. of chopped walnuts, 1od. cream, sugar and vanilla flavouring, angelica.

METHOD.—Use one-day-old sponge cakes and cut them roughly to the shape of the pears. Make the butter hot in a frying-pan, and fry the cakes until golden, turning them over so that all sides may brown a little.

When ready, spread them with damson jelly and sprinkle them with the chopped nuts. Place a pear on each—the jelly may be warmed slightly to make it spread more easily. Whisk the cream until it thickens, and flavour it with sugar and vanilla to taste.

Arrange the pear croûtes on a dish, heap whipped cream in the centre and decorate this with stalks of angelica.

Sufficient for six persons.

PINEAPPLE AND CHOCOLATE MOULD

INGREDIENTS.—1 small tin of pineapple, 2 gills of milk (½ pint), 1 dessertspoonful of chocolate powder, 1 egg, 3 dessertspoonfuls of castor sugar, ⅝ oz. of leaf gelatine, ½ gill of pineapple syrup.

FOR DECORATION.—1 gill of cream, vanilla.

METHOD.—Mix the chocolate to a smooth paste with some of the milk, then boil the remainder and stir on to it and cool slightly.

Beat up the egg and add the hot milk and chocolate to it.

Strain into a jug, stand in a saucepan of cold water and cook until the custard thickens.

Keep it well stirred and be careful not to let it curdle.

When cooked, remove from the saucepan, add the sugar and leave until cold.

Rub the pineapple through a sieve to a pulp, then mix with the cold chocolate custard.

Put the gelatine in a saucepan with the pineapple syrup and dissolve it slowly; do not let it boil.

Strain this into the pineapple and chocolate, etc., and mix together.

Pour into a wet border mould and leave until set.

Whisk the cream until it stiffens, sweeten and flavour it to taste, pile in the centre hole of the mould and serve.

Sufficient for about five or six persons.

PINEAPPLE CREAM

INGREDIENTS.—1 large tin of pineapple cubes, 1 gill of cream, 2 oz. of castor sugar, 1 pint packet of lemon jelly, ¾ pint of hot water, ½ oz. of pistachio nuts, ¾ oz. of French leaf gelatine (light weight).

METHOD.—Dissolve the jelly in the hot water and leave until cold, but not set. Scald and blanch the pistachio nuts and chop them finely. Take a border mould, scald it, and then rinse with cold water. Mask the mould with lemon jelly. Leave this until quite set, then decorate the bottom of the mould alternately with pieces of pineapple and chopped pistachio nuts, having previously dipped each piece of decoration in some of the melted lemon jelly. Leave this until quite set, then cover the decoration very carefully with more of the jelly, then leave until set again. Take about two cubes of pineapple and cut into small squares, and put on one side. The remainder of the pineapple remove from the syrup and rub it through a hair sieve. Put half a gill of syrup into a saucepan, add the gelatine and dissolve it slowly, but do not let it boil. Add the castor sugar and pineapple squares to the sieved pineapple. Whisk the cream until it begins to stiffen, then very lightly add the pineapple, etc. Lastly, strain in the melted gelatine and stir all very lightly together. Pour this mixture into the prepared mould and leave until set. Turn very carefully on to a dish, and garnish with chopped lemon jelly round the cream.

NOTE.—To turn out the cream just dip it quickly in warm water, wipe the surface of the cream lightly, and shake it carefully on to the dish. The jelly is easily chopped on a piece of wet paper. Be careful not to chop it too much or it will look cloudy. The gelatine must be of a moderate temperature when added to the cream.

Sufficient for about six or seven persons.

PINEAPPLE CREAM SLICES

INGREDIENTS.—Small tin of pineapple slices, few glacé cherries, cream, castor sugar, and vanilla.

METHOD.—Put the slices of pineapple each on a small plate. Whisk the cream until it stiffens, then sweeten and flavour it to taste.

Put it into an icing-bag with a rose tube fixed in the end, and force some cream round each slice of pineapple and a little in the centre. Stick a cherry in the centre and serve, with the syrup in a sauce-boat.

Allow one slice for each person.

PINEAPPLE DELIGHT

INGREDIENTS.—A large tin of pineapple slices, ½ oz. of shelled walnuts, 3 dessertspoonfuls of cornflour, castor sugar, ½ oz. of butter.

METHOD.—Drain the syrup from the pineapple, put one slice aside for decoration and the rest through a mincer. Mix the cornflour to a smooth paste with a small quantity of the syrup. Put the remainder of the syrup into a saucepan with the butter and minced pineapple. There should be about one pint and a quarter altogether. If necessary, make up with a little water. Heat this, then stir on to the cornflour. Return to the pan and bring to the boil, keeping it stirred.

Chop up the walnuts and add, with sugar to taste, and boil gently for a few minutes to cook the cornflour. Turn into a wet mould.

When set, turn out and serve with half a slice of pineapple on each side.

NOTE.—The amount of sugar required depends entirely on the sweetness of the pineapple. Usually about one tablespoonful is sufficient.

PINEAPPLE JELLY MOULD

INGREDIENTS.—1 large tin of pineapple, 1 pint packet of pineapple jelly, ¾ gill of cream.

METHOD.—Drain the pineapple and put it through the mincer. Heat the pineapple syrup and dissolve the jelly in it, and when cold, stir in the minced pineapple.

Whisk the cream until it thickens, and when the jelly and pineapple is beginning to thicken, stir in the cream lightly and turn the mixture into a wet mould.

PINEAPPLE MEDLEY

INGREDIENTS.—A large tin of sliced pineapple, 2 bananas, 1½ oz. of almonds, 2 oz. of glacé cherries, 3 dessertspoonfuls of orange-juice, 1 tablespoonful of rum (this may be omitted), ½ oz. of gelatine, cream.

METHOD.—Drain the pineapple and put it through the mincer, keeping back three slices for decoration.

Blanch and chop the almonds, cut up the cherries, and peel the bananas and cut them into small dice.

Dissolve the gelatine in a saucepan with half a gill of the pineapple-juice, warmed, then strain it into the remainder of the juice, and add the rum and orange-juice.

Stir in the minced pineapple and other prepared fruits and almonds, then turn them into a mould which has been rinsed out in cold water. When quite set, unmould the medley and decorate it with whipped cream and the remainder of the pineapple.

Sufficient for six persons.

PINEAPPLE MERINGUE

INGREDIENTS.—A large tin of pineapple slices, 1 large egg, 2 teaspoonfuls of cornflour, a small lump of butter ($\frac{1}{4}$ to $\frac{1}{2}$ oz.), $4\frac{1}{2}$ dessertspoonfuls of castor sugar.

METHOD.—Drain the syrup from the pineapple slices and put the latter through the mincer. Take a quarter of a pint of the syrup and heat in a saucepan with the butter. Mix the cornflour to a smooth paste with a little cold syrup, stir the hot on to it, then return to the pan and bring to the boil, keeping it stirred. Boil gently for a few minutes, then draw aside and cool slightly.

Separate the egg. Beat up the yolk and stir in, then gradually mix in the grated pineapple. Add two dessertspoonfuls of sugar, or more if required, then turn it all into a pie-dish and put in a moderately warm oven for about twenty minutes, until set slightly.

Whisk the egg-white to a stiff froth, fold in the remainder of the castor sugar (two dessertspoonfuls and a half) and cover the top of the pudding with it.

Return to a cool oven, to set and lightly colour the meringue, and serve cold.

Sufficient for four or five persons.

NOTE.—If preferred, the meringue mixture may be forced through an icing-bag.

PINEAPPLE MERINGUES

INGREDIENTS.—A tin of grated pineapple, 4 pairs of meringue shells, 10d. of cream, sugar and vanilla, 4 Jordan almonds, a few pistachio nuts.

METHOD.—Blanch the almonds and pistachio nuts and remove the skins. Split the almonds in half and bake them till light brown, and chop the pistachio nuts finely.

Arrange meringue shells on a dish with the round side at the base, then drain the syrup from the pineapple and heap grated pineapple on each shell.

Whisk the cream until it thickens, sweeten and flavour it to taste and heap it on top of the fruit. Put half a baked almond on each meringue and sprinkle the cream with pistachio nuts.

Allow one or two meringues for each person.

PINEAPPLE AND ORANGE SALAD

INGREDIENTS.—A tin of pineapple slices, 2 or 3 oranges.

METHOD.—Cut the pineapple into chunky pieces and put into a dish with the oranges—the latter peeled and quartered. Boil the pineapple syrup for a few minutes with a little sugar to thicken it, and when cold pour it over.

If liked, the pineapple slices can be arranged on individual plates with quarters of orange placed on them and a glacé cherry in the centre. Serve with cream.

PINEAPPLE SAGO

INGREDIENTS.—1 tin of grated pineapple, $\frac{1}{2}$ packet of pineapple jelly, 1 small tin of cherries, 3 oz. of sago, 1 lemon, 2 oz. of sugar, $1\frac{1}{2}$ gills of hot water.

METHOD.—Put the jelly in a basin. Pour on the hot water and stir till the jelly is dissolved. Pour it into a wet mould and let it set. Wash the sago and pour off the water.

Mix the syrup from the tin of pineapple with the lemon-juice and half the cherry syrup, and add enough hot water to make it up to one pint and a half. Boil it and sprinkle in the sago, stirring all the time.

Simmer until the grains of sago are soft and transparent (about twenty-five minutes). Stir frequently as the mixture thickens in order to prevent it burning. Let it cool.

Add the sugar and grated pineapple and pour into the mould on top of the jelly. When set, shake carefully on to a dish and surround the mould with cherries.

Sufficient for four persons.

NOTE.—This shape can also be made with tapioca.

PINEAPPLE SOUFFLE

INGREDIENTS.—1 large sliced pineapple, $1\frac{1}{2}$ gills of milk, 4 oz. of castor sugar, 2 eggs and 1 extra white, ¾ oz. of French leaf gelatine, a sprinkling of crystallised roses.

METHOD.—Separate the yolks from the whites of eggs. Beat the yolks and add to them the milk. Pour this into a jug, stand the jug in a saucepan of cold water, and stir the custard over the fire until it thickens, being careful not to let it get too hot or it will curdle. When cooked stand aside to cool.

Rub the pineapple slices through a hair or wire sieve, then mix with the custard and castor sugar. Dissolve the gelatine in about half a gill of the pineapple syrup, but do not boil it. Add a pinch of salt to the whites of eggs and whisk them to a stiff froth, then lightly fold them into the pineapple, etc. Lastly, strain in the dissolved gelatine and stir it all together.

Rinse a fancy mould with cold water. Pour this mixture into it, and leave in a cold place until set.

PINEAPPLE SPONGIES

INGREDIENTS.—1 egg, its weight in castor sugar and flour, grated rind of ½ lemon, water or pineapple syrup, cooking sherry, sliced pineapple, cream.

METHOD.—Whisk the egg and sugar together until thick and creamy and free from dark streaks, then stir in the flour (sifted), the finely grated lemon-rind, about a spoonful of pineapple syrup.

Butter eight small rim twin cake shell pans, drop about a dessert-spoonful of the mixture into each, then bake it till spongy. Turn out the spongies and let them cool.

Pour a teaspoonful of sherry over each, and place two *small* slices of pineapple in the centre. Decorate the spongies with whipped cream, sweetened and flavoured to taste. The *small* slices of pineapple are found in the South African brands.

Sufficient for eight spongies.

NOTE.—If rim twin cake shell pans are not available, bake the sponge mixture in a sandwich tin, and then stamp it into rounds. Cooked in this way it will not cut into so many spongies.

PINEAPPLE TAPIOCA

INGREDIENTS.—Small tin of pineapple slices, 1 yolk of egg, ½ oz. of butter, 1 tablespoonful of lemon-juice, 1 tablespoonful of castor sugar, 1 oz. of crushed tapioca, water, few glacé cherries.

METHOD.—Drain the syrup from the pineapple and make it up to three-quarters of a pint with water. Put this into a saucepan with the lemon-juice, bring it to the boil, then sprinkle in the tapioca and stir it till clear, letting it cook gently. Draw the pan aside, add the sugar and butter and, when dissolved, stir in the beaten yolk of egg. Cook the mixture again for a few minutes, being careful not to let it boil.

Keep back four slices of pineapple, cut the remainder into small pieces, and add them to the tapioca ; then turn this into a serving - dish and arrange the whole slices on the top.

Decorate the pineapple tapioca with glacé cherries, and serve with cream if liked.

Sufficient for three or four persons.

NOTE.—It is better, if possible, to cook the tapioca in a double boiler. It will take longer, but need not be stirred continuously.

PINEAPPLE TRIFLE

INGREDIENTS.—A sponge cake (toast-rack shape), tin of pineapple chunks, 1 pint of custard, 1 or 2 tablespoonfuls of rum, jam, 1 oz. of almonds.

METHOD.—Make the custard and leave to cool.

Strain the syrup from the pineapple and heat it.

Split open the sponge and spread with jam.

Put it into a dish and soak with the pineapple syrup and rum.

Arrange some of the chunks on top of the sponge and the remainder in the bottom of the dish.

Blanch and skin the almonds and put with the pineapple.

Pour the custard round and serve with cream if liked.

PINK AND WHITE

INGREDIENTS.—1 pint of milk, 1 oz. of cornflour, 1 oz. of sugar, 1 oz. of butter, vanilla flavouring, cochineal.

METHOD.—Mix the cornflour to a smooth paste with some of the milk.

Put the remainder in a saucepan and add the sugar and butter.

When hot, pour on to the cornflour, return to the saucepan and bring to the boil, keeping it well stirred.

Simmer for six minutes, add the vanilla flavouring.

Take about six small moulds and rinse them with cold water.

Fill three of them with the prepared cornflour, etc., and colour the remainder with a few drops of cochineal.

Pour this into the other moulds.

Leave until set, turn out, and arrange alternately on a silver dish.

NOTE.—Empty potted meat or paste jars can be used instead of small moulds. These look quite attractive when turned out.

PLUM FOOL

INGREDIENTS.—¾ pint of plum purée ½ pint of thick custard (see below), cream, sugar, and vanilla.

METHOD.—To make the plum purée, stalk and wash the plums. Stew them till they are tender, adding sufficient sugar to sweeten them and enough water to keep them from sticking to the pan. Being a very soft fruit, the plums make a good quantity of juice as they cook.

Any kind of plums may be used, but Victorias are usually considered the best.

When the fruit is cooked, remove the stones and rub the plums through a sieve. Leave the purée to get cold.

TO MAKE THE CUSTARD.—Allow either one whole egg or two yolks to half a pint of milk.

Bring the milk to boiling point, then let it go off the boil before adding it to the beaten egg. Return the mixture to the top of a double boiler. Add one dessertspoonful of sugar, and cook the custard over hot water until it thickens, keeping it well stirred and being careful not to let it curdle. When it is ready, strain it at once into a basin.

Flavour it with vanilla and leave it to get cold before mixing it with the fruit purée.

Turn the fool into individual glasses and serve it as cold as possible, decorated with whipped cream sweetened and flavoured to taste.

NOTE.—Half a pint of powder custard may be substituted for the egg custard if preferred.

A Plum Mould can be made with the same ingredients as the Plum Fool.

For this, after mixing the cold fruit purée with the cold custard, strain in half to five-eighths of an ounce of gelatine dissolved in half a gill of water or plum-juice, then turn it into a wet mould and leave it to set.

PLUM MOUSSE

INGREDIENTS.—About 1 doz. large Victoria plums, sugar and water, ¼ oz. of gelatine, 1 yolk and 2 whites of egg, ¼ pint of milk, ½ gill of cream, cochineal, 1½ dessertspoonfuls of castor sugar.

METHOD.—Prepare and stew the plums, adding sugar to taste and very little water, and when tender, drain them ; then stone the plums and rub the fruit through a sieve. There should be sufficient to make half a pint of pulp.

Make a boiled custard with the yolk of egg and the milk and, when cold, add it to the plum pulp with castor sugar.

Whisk the cream until thick and stir it in lightly. Dissolve the gelatine in two tablespoonfuls of the plum syrup and strain it in, mixing it in thoroughly and colouring the mixture with a few drops of cochineal.

Taste the mixture to see if it is sufficiently sweetened, and leave it till it is beginning to thicken, and then fold in the stiffly-whisked egg-whites and turn the mousse into a soufflé dish to set. Decorate Plum Mousse with whipped cream (extra to that given in the recipe) and sprinkle it with hundreds and thousands.

COLD PLUM PUDDING

INGREDIENTS.—1½ lb. of red plums, 2 tablespoonfuls of Demerara sugar, ½ to ¾ lb. of stale bread, 1 pint of custard, 1 gill of water.

METHOD.—Boil the sugar and water together for about five minutes. Stalk and wash the plums, add them to the syrup, and cook until quite soft. Then remove the stones.

Take a pudding basin and neatly

line it with slices of stale bread, using only the crumb.

Place a small round also in the bottom of the basin.

Carefully soak this lining with some of the juice from the stewed fruit, then put in a layer of plums and a layer of bread until the basin is full.

Place a large round slice over the top of the basin, put a saucer or plate over it and press with a heavy weight.

Leave until quite cold, then turn on to a dish.

Make a thick custard from custard powder according to directions given on packet, and when cold pour it over pudding.

NOTE.—Small pieces of stale crust may be used inside the pudding.

PRUNES WITH APPLE FLUM-MERY

INGREDIENTS.—½ lb. of prunes, 1 lb. of cooking apples, 2 cloves, juice and rind of ½ a lemon, 1 pint of boiling water, 1 oz. of cornflour, 4 oz. of sugar, 4 macaroons, 3d. of cream,

METHOD.—Wash the prunes and put them in a basin. Pour on the boiling water and let them soak overnight.

Put the water from the prunes in a saucepan with the sugar and lemon-juice and thinly cut lemon-rind and boil for ten minutes.

Put in the prunes and stew gently for about ten minutes till they are tender but not too soft. Peel the apples, cut them in quarters and core them. Stew them with the cloves and two ounces of sugar and a cup of water.

When the apples are soft mash them up with a spoon and remove the cloves.

Mix the cornflour smoothly with a little cold water and pour on the hot apple purée.

Stir quickly, return to the saucepan, and stir till it boils. Boil for ten minutes over a low gas.

Put the prunes in a glass dish, and when the flummery is cool enough strain it over. When cold, decorate with macaroons and a dab of whipped and sweetened cream in the centre.

Serve cold.

Sufficient for four or five persons.

PRUNE CREAM JELLY

INGREDIENTS.—½ lb. of prunes, ½ pint of water, ½ pint of Ideal Milk, 4 oz. of sugar, ¼ oz. of gelatine, ¼ gill of water.

METHOD.—Wash and boil the prunes. When they are tender, remove the stones and chop them quite finely, mixing in the juice in which they were cooked, and also the sugar.

Melt the gelatine in hot water and add it to the prunes.

Stir in also the whipped Ideal Milk, and pour the jelly into a crystal dish.

Decorate the Prune Jelly with a few extra prunes and serve it cold.

Sufficient for six persons.

PRUNE AND DAMSON BOR-DER

INGREDIENTS.—1 lb. of prunes, ½ lb. of damsons, 5 oz. of sugar, juice of 2 lemons, rind of 1 lemon, 1½ pints of boiling water, 2 oz. of almonds, (blanched), 1 oz. of gelatine, cold rice pudding, 3d. of cream, 1 small pot of red currant jelly.

METHOD.—Pour the boiling water over the prunes and damsons and the thinly-cut rind of one lemon, and let it soak overnight. Add the jelly, sugar, and lemon-juice and stew till the fruit is soft.

Pour on to a wire sieve, and remove the stones. If there is time, crack them, and take out the kernels.

Rub the fruit through the sieve, and measure it; there should be just over one pint and a half. Soak the gelatine in the purée for ten minutes, and stir over a low gas till the gelatine is dissolved. As the mixture is thick stir well to prevent burning. Add the kernels, and pour in an oiled mould.

When set, shake on to a dish. Cut the almonds in strips and stick them over the shape.

Fill the centre with cold rice pudding mixed with cream.

Sufficient for four or five persons.

PRUNE MOULD

INGREDIENTS.—1 lb. of prunes, 1½ pints of water, ¾ oz. of leaf gelatine, juice and rind of a lemon, 4 oz. of sugar.

METHOD.—Soak the prunes over-night in one pint and a quarter of boiling water, putting the thinly cut lemon-rind with them.

Stew the prunes till soft in the water in which they were soaked, adding the sugar and lemon-juice.

Remove the stones from the prunes, and put the pulp through a mincer. For special occasions it is better to rub the pulp through a wire sieve.

Soak the gelatine in one gill of cold water for five minutes, and dissolve it slowly over a low gas. When cold, strain it on to the pulp. Stir several times till it begins to set, and pour into a border mould that has been rinsed in cold water. When set, dip in hot water, and turn out as for other jellies. Fill the centre with cold boiled rice, mixed with cream or custard, or, if preferred, with whipped and sweetened cream only. To make a change, the mould is sometimes stuck all over with blanched almonds or prune kernels cut in strips.

Sufficient for four persons.

PRUNE AND RICE MOULD

INGREDIENTS.—$\frac{1}{4}$ lb. of prunes, 1 dessertspoonful of Demerara sugar, 1 oz. of candied peel, $1\frac{1}{2}$ pints of milk, 3 oz. of rice, 2 dessertspoonfuls of granulated sugar.

METHOD.—Wash the prunes well, put them into a basin, cover with cold water and soak for about twelve hours.

When soaked, put them into a saucepan with the water in which they have been soaking. Add the Demerara sugar and the peel cut into small pieces, and cook until quite soft.

Take the prunes out and remove the stones, and boil the syrup fast for five minutes to thicken it.

Wash the rice well, put it into the saucepan with the milk and granulated sugar and cook slowly until the rice is quite soft and the milk absorbed. Stir it occasionally.

Stir the prunes into the rice (do this very carefully, so as not to break them too much).

Pour into a wet mould, and leave until set.

Turn on to a dish and pour the prune syrup round.

NOTE.—The candied peel is added to improve the flavour of the prunes. It can be served in the syrup if liked.

RAINBOW JELLY

INGREDIENTS.—$\frac{1}{2}$ pint packet of pineapple jelly, a small tin of sliced pineapple, $\frac{1}{2}$ packet of raspberry jelly, $\frac{1}{2}$ pint packet of lemon jelly, hot water, angelica, cream.

METHOD.—Drain the pineapple and put it through the mincer, then drain it again.

Heat the pineapple syrup and dissolve the pineapple jelly in it, making it up to half a pint (with the jelly).

Dissolve also the lemon and raspberry jellies separately in the same way, using hot water in place of the pineapple syrup.

Leave the three jellies to get cold, and when the lemon jelly begins to stiffen whisk it until frothy ; then turn it into a wet mould and let it set.

Mix the drained, minced pineapple with the pineapple jelly, and when it is on the point of setting, pour it into the mould gently. When this is firm fill up the mould with the raspberry jelly, which should be whisked till frothy in the same way as the lemon jelly.

When the Rainbow Jelly is set, dip it in warm water and unmould it. Decorate it with rings of angelica and serve it with cream.

RAISIN JELLIES

INGREDIENTS.—$\frac{1}{4}$ lb. of raisins, 1 pint packet of pineapple jelly, $3\frac{1}{2}$ gills of hot water.

METHOD.—Wash the raisins, then stone them and cut them into halves.

Dissolve the jelly in the hot water and when cold, set a thin layer in the bottom of six small moulds (previously rinsed in cold water). Decorate the bottom of each with half a raisin dipped in jelly, and when set cover with a little more jelly and set again.

When the remainder of the jelly is beginning to set, stir in the raisins and fill up the moulds. Dip in warm water before turning out.

Sufficient for four to six persons.

RASPBERRY AND BANANA TRIFLE

INGREDIENTS.—6 small sponge cakes, raspberry jam, 3 bananas.

½ lb. of raspberries (fresh fruit), 1½ oz. of castor sugar, ½ gill of sherry, 1 gill of hot milk, 1 gill of cream, vanilla and castor sugar, pistachio nuts.

FOR THE CUSTARD.—1 pint of milk, 2 eggs, 1 oz. of sugar, vanilla.

METHOD.—Leave out a few raspberries for decoration ; the remainder spread on a large dish and sprinkle with castor sugar, and leave for about half an hour. Mash the bananas and mix with the raspberries.

Split the sponge cakes and spread with jam, arrange tastefully in a glass dish, and soak with hot milk first and then sherry.

Make the custard, beat the eggs, mix with the milk, add the sugar, and stand in a jug in a saucepan of cold water and stir over the fire until it thickens, but do not let it boil.

Remove the jug from the fire, add the vanilla flavouring to the custard, and leave until cool.

When the sugar has well soaked into the raspberries and bananas, place them in small heaps on the soaked sponge cakes.

Carefully pour over the custard and stand the trifle in a cool place.

Scald, blanch and chop a few pistachio nuts. If very moist, just put them in a warm place to dry for a few minutes.

Whisk the cream together with a sprinkling of sugar and a few drops of vanilla flavouring.

Shake the whipped cream on to the top of the trifle and garnish with chopped pistachio nuts and one or two raspberries.

RASPBERRY CREAM

INGREDIENTS.—½ lb. of Osborne biscuits, 1 wineglassful of sherry, 1 lb. of raspberry jam, 1 oz. of almonds, 1 oz. of cherries, 1 gill of cream, 1 pint of boiled custard (see p. 217), (vanilla flavouring).

METHOD.—Crush the biscuits into a powder. Add the jam and sherry to the crushed biscuits, and mix well together. Put into a glass dish. Make the custard. Pour this over the biscuits, etc. Leave until cold.

Whip the cream and shake on to the top of the custard. Blanch the almonds and chop them finely. Decorate the top of the pudding with the chopped almonds and glacé cherries.

RASPBERRY FLUFF

INGREDIENTS.—1 lb. of raspberries, whites of 2 large eggs, 1½ gills of cold water, 1 lemon, 2 oz. of castor sugar, ¾ oz. of leaf gelatine, ½ pint of cream custard or unsweetened condensed milk, cochineal, ¼ lb. of meringue finger biscuits.

METHOD.—Pick the raspberries and rub three quarters of a pound of them through a hair sieve.

Mix the raspberry purée with the lemon-juice.

Soak the gelatine in the cold water for five minutes, put it in a saucepan and stir over a low gas till the gelatine is dissolved. Add the fruit-juice and sugar, colour with a few drops of cochineal and strain into a basin. Leave it to get cold. When it is just beginning to thicken beat the egg-whites stiffly and stir the cold liquid into them gradually. Whisk well with an egg beater till stiff and frothy.

Heap in fancy dishes and pour over the mixture a little cream, custard or unsweetened condensed milk. Put a few raspberries on top and one or two finger biscuits at the side.

Sufficient for five persons.

RASPBERRY FOOL

INGREDIENTS.—1 lb. of ripe raspberries, 2 oz. of sugar, ¾ pint of milk, 2 large eggs, cochineal.

METHOD.—Beat the eggs with the sugar and add the milk. Put the custard mixture in a double saucepan and stir till it is thick enough to coat the back of a spoon. Do not let it boil or cook too long. Rub the raspberries through a hair sieve without cooking them first. Strain the *cold* custard on to them and mix well. Colour pink with a few drops of cochineal.

A richer dish may be made by using a gill of cream and only half a pint of custard.

Strawberry Fool is made in exactly the same way.

RASPBERRY MARSHMALLOW

INGREDIENTS.—1½ lb. of raspberries, 2 egg-whites, about 2 tablespoonfuls of icing sugar.

METHOD.—Pick over the raspberries and arrange them on individual plates.

Add a pinch of salt to the egg-whites, whisk them to a froth, then stir in the icing sugar and whisk until of a rather stiff consistency.

Heap this in the centre of the raspberries and serve. This will take the place of cream and is much less expensive.

The icing sugar must be rubbed through a hair sieve before it is added to the egg-whites.

Sufficient for five or six persons.

RASPBERRY MOULD

INGREDIENTS.—1 lb. of raspberries, 4 oz. of sugar, ¾ pint of water, juice of 2 lemons, 3d. of cream, cochineal, ¼ packet of lemon jelly, ¾ oz. of leaf gelatine.

METHOD.—Pick the fruit and stew it in one gill of water with the sugar and lemon-juice.

Keep back twelve nice raspberries, and pour the rest on to a hair sieve.

Melt the jelly in one gill of water and pour half of it into a mould rinsed in cold water. When set, put in the twelve raspberries, and then the rest of the jelly.

Rub the fruit through a sieve.

Soak the gelatine for five minutes in half a pint of cold water and dissolve slowly.

Strain it into the fruit purée and leave till cold.

Add the cream and cochineal to colour, and stir now and again till it begins to set.

Pour into the mould.

When firm, dip in warm water, shake and slide on to the dish.

Sufficient for three or four persons.

RASPBERRY SANDWICH

INGREDIENTS.—1 bought jam sandwich, 1 lb. of raspberries, 1 packet of pineapple jelly, ½ pint of cream or custard, sugar to taste.

METHOD.—Dissolve the jelly in one pint of hot water. Lay the two halves of the sandwich on soup plates with the inside uppermost and pour half the hot jelly slowly over each.

Keep a few raspberries for decorating, and mash the rest, pouring the juice on to the cake.

Beat the cream till stiff and mix half of it with the fruit, sweeten to taste and spread between the two pieces of cake.

Decorate with cream and fruit.

Sufficient for from four to six persons.

RASPBERRY SNOW

INGREDIENTS.—1 lb. of raspberries, 1½ gills of milk, 2 yolks of eggs, 3 whisked whites of eggs, 1 gill of whipped cream, ¼ lb. of castor sugar, cochineal or carmine, angelica.

METHOD.—Rub the raspberries through a hair sieve, leaving out about half a dozen for decoration. Make a custard with the yolks of eggs and milk as described for Pineapple Soufflé (see p. 342). Add the castor sugar to the raspberry purée, also the custard when cool. Whisk the whites to a very stiff froth and lightly fold into the raspberries, etc. Colour a delicate pink with either cochineal or carmine.

Fill some small fancy custard glasses with this mixture.

Whisk the cream together with a little vanilla flavouring and half a teaspoonful of castor sugar.

Garnish the top of each glass with whipped cream and a raspberry, and a few pieces of angelica. Serve cold.

RATAFIA CROQUANTE

INGREDIENTS.—½ lb. of ratafias, 1 breakfastcupful of granulated sugar, 1 gill of water, 6 meringue cases (crushed), 3 oz. of shelled walnuts (chopped), ½ pint of double cream.

METHOD.—Put the sugar and water in the inner pan of a double saucepan. Lift the pan out of the saucepan, place it on the gas and stir the sugar and water till it boils.

Boil fast for five minutes, but do not let it get brown. Put the saucepan back into the lower pan containing boiling water.

Oil a cake-tin with a movable base.

Stick a skewer in the ratafias one at a time, and dip quickly in the syrup. Place them close together flat side down in the tin till the base is covered. Place the rest against the side of the tin right side out. When set firm, push up the bottom of the tin, take out the croquante shape and put it on a fancy dish. Whip the cream, mix with walnuts and meringues and fill the case.

If the case is difficult to remove, heat the tin a very little and it will come out easily.

Sufficient for four persons.

RATAFIA TRIFLE

INGREDIENTS.—6 sponge cakes, 1 wineglassful of sherry, 2 eggs, ¾ pint of milk, ¼ oz. of gelatine, 2 oz. of sugar, juice of a lemon, ½ pot of apricot jam, cream, 1 oz. of ratafias, 1 oz. of glacé cherries.

METHOD.—Heat the jam in a saucepan.

Split the cakes in half, spread them with hot jam, place in a glass dish and moisten with the sherry and lemon-juice.

Heat the milk in a double saucepan, beat the eggs and sugar, pour on the hot milk and return to the saucepan. Stir the custard till thick enough to coat the back of the spoon. Soak the gelatine in three-quarters of a gill of cold water, and dissolve it over a low gas.

Strain it into the custard.

Let the custard cool and strain slowly over the sponge cakes.

Leave till next day or longer, and cover with ratafias. Beat the cream till thick and sweeten to taste. Decorate with dabs of cream and cherries.

Sufficient for four or five persons.

NOTE.—If the custard becomes a little curdled through over-cooking, it can be made smooth again by beating quickly with an egg whisk.

RHUBARB CREAM

INGREDIENTS.—1¼ pint packets of lemon jelly, 2 oz. of almonds, ¾ gill of water, 2 pints sliced rhubarb, 6 oz. of granulated sugar, 1 gill of cream.

METHOD.—Steam the rhubarb with the sugar and drain off the juice. Blanch and skin the almonds. Dissolve the quarter of a pint packet of jelly in three-fourths of a gill of water, and when cold set a thin layer in the bottom of a plain mould. Decorate it with almonds, halved and dipped in jelly, and when these are

set cover them with jelly and set this again.

Dissolve the pint packet of jelly in the hot rhubarb-juice and let it cool, then rub the rhubarb through a sieve and mix it with the jelly.

Leave them until the jelly is beginning to thicken, then stir in the whipped cream and chopped almonds, saving a few halved ones. Turn the mixture into the prepared mould and, when set, dip it in warm water and unmould it.

Decorate the Rhubarb Cream with the remainder of the almonds and serve it cold.

To steam rhubarb, prepare it in the usual way by wiping the sticks and trimming off the green part. Slice it and measure it, and to each pint of sliced rhubarb allow three ounces of sugar.

Put the rhubarb into the top of a double boiler, sprinkling each layer with sugar, then cover the boiler and cook the rhubarb over hot water till tender.

Sufficient for six persons.

RHUBARB CUPS

INGREDIENTS.—1¼ pints of sliced rhubarb, 4 oz. of granulated sugar, 1 whole egg or two yolks, barely ½ pint of milk, cream, 1 dessertspoonful of castor sugar, 2 tablespoonfuls of desiccated coconut, vanilla flavouring, hundreds and thousands.

METHOD.—Cook the rhubarb with the granulated sugar, drain off the juice, save one or two pieces for decoration and rub the fruit through a sieve.

Beat up the egg or egg-yolks, heat the milk and add it to them, stir in the castor sugar, and cook this custard over hot water till it is thick, keeping it stirred.

Add the coconut and flavouring to taste, let it get cold, then mix it with the rhubarb pulp. Stir in as much of the rhubarb syrup as may be required, but be careful not to make the mixture too thin.

Serve the rhubarb mixture in custard glasses, and decorate with whipped cream (sweetened and flavoured to taste) and hundreds and thousands, and a few whole pieces of cooked rhubarb.

Sufficient for six persons.

RHUBARB FINGERS

INGREDIENTS.—Rhubarb (as required), 2 large sponge fingers, sugar and water, 1 pint packet of cherry jelly, hot water, cream.

METHOD.—Split the sponge fingers in half, then cut each piece into four, cutting them lengthwise, then across, making sixteen pieces altogether.

Wipe some rhubarb and cut it into lengths rather longer than the pieces of sponge. Put it into a pie-dish with a generous amount of water, and sugar to taste, and cook it in the oven until tender, being very careful to keep the rhubarb whole.

Lift out the rhubarb when cooked and put it on a plate.

Dissolve the jelly in half a pint of hot water, and make it up to one pint with the rhubarb water, adding more sugar if required.

Arrange some of the pieces of sponge in a dish and pour a little jelly over them. When nearly set, place a piece of rhubarb on each and add some more jelly. Let this get firm, then arrange the other pieces of sponge and rhubarb and add jelly as before.

Leave the fingers to set before decorating them with dots of whipped cream.

Sufficient for five persons.

RHUBARB MARSHMALLOW PIE

INGREDIENTS.—About ½ lb. of short pastry (see p. 252), 1 pint of sliced rhubarb, 3 oz. of granulated sugar, grated rind of ½ a lemon, 1½ oz. of flour, 1 dessertspoonful of castor sugar, water, ½ oz. of butter, 1 yolk of egg, ¼ lb. of marshmallows, desiccated coconut.

METHOD.—Roll out the pastry thinly and line a Pyrex pie-plate, folding the edge over (towards the rim) so as to make it a little thicker, then flute it to give a decorative finish.

Line the pastry with a round of buttered paper and put some rice in the bottom, Bake the pastry in a hot oven, and when it is set remove the

paper and rice and finish cooking, then let it cool.

Steam the rhubarb with the granulated sugar and, when tender, mash it up roughly. Mix the castor sugar with the flour and mix them to a smooth paste with half to three-quarters of a gill of water. Add this paste to the rhubarb with the finely-grated lemon-rind.

Bring the mixture to the boil, keeping it well stirred, and boil it gently for a few minutes ; then take it off the gas and let it cool slightly.

Add the butter and stir in the beaten egg yolk, and cook the mixture again for a minute or two, without boiling it. Let it cool before turning it into the pastry-lined plate.

Put the marshmallows in the top of a double boiler and stand them over a pan of boiling water till dissolved, stirring occasionally. Turn them on to the rhubarb mixture. Sprinkle the top with coconut and place the pie under the hot grill till light brown.

Serve Rhubarb Marshmallow Pie cold, decorated with a few whole pieces of cooked rhubarb.

Sufficient for six persons.

RHUBARB MERINGUE PIE

INGREDIENTS.—1½ lb. of rhubarb (weighed after it is sliced), 1½ dessertspoonfuls of cornflour, barely ½ lb. of granulated sugar, ½ oz. of butter, rind of ½ a lemon, rind of 1 orange, 2 eggs, 2 tablespoonfuls of castor sugar.

METHOD.—Wipe the rhubarb sticks with a damp cloth and remove the green leaves. Then cut up and weigh the rhubarb. Put it into the top of a double boiler, sprinkling each layer with sugar. Put the lid on well, and cook the rhubarb over hot water until it is tender. Then turn it into a strainer and drain off the juice. Save a few whole pieces of rhubarb for decoration.

Smooth the cornflour in a small quantity of the rhubarb-juice. Stir in the remainder of the juice and add the cooked rhubarb, mashed to a smooth pulp, and the finely-grated lemon and orange-rind.

Return the rhubarb mixture to the saucepan and bring it to the boil, keeping it well stirred. Boil it gently for a few minutes, then take it off the heat and add the butter.

Separate the eggs. Beat up the yolks and stir them into the rhubarb mixture. Turn it into a pie-dish, bake it gently for from fifteen to twenty minutes. Then let it cool a little. Whisk the egg-whites to a stiff froth and fold in the castor sugar. Heap them on top of the pudding.

Dredge it with sugar and return it to a cool oven to set, and lightly colour the meringue.

Serve the Rhubarb Meringue Pie cold, decorated with a few whole pieces of cooked rhubarb.

RHUBARB RIBBON MERINGUE

INGREDIENTS.—2 pints of sliced rhubarb, 6 oz. of granulated sugar, 3 sponge cakes, 3 yolks of eggs, 1 white of egg, 1 oz. of icing sugar.

METHOD.—Steam the rhubarb with the sugar and, when tender, rub it through a sieve, or mash it up finely with the juice.

Crumble the sponge cakes and add them, and stir in the beaten egg-yolks. Turn the mixture into a buttered dish and bake it till set, being careful not to let it boil. Leave it to get cold.

Whisk the egg-white to a stiff froth, sift the icing sugar and whisk it in gradually. Force it on to the rhubarb mixture in straight lines across each way, using an icing pump with a ribbon tube affixed.

Put the Rhubarb Ribbon Meringue into a cool oven till light brown, and serve it cold.

NOTE.—If you prefer not to use the icing pump, just heap the meringue mixture roughly over the top.

Sufficient for six persons.

RHUBARB WHIP

INGREDIENTS.—Some stewed rhubarb, 1 yolk and 2 egg-whites, 1od. of cream, 1 gill of milk, ¼ oz. of gelatine, sugar, cochineal.

Method.—Drain the syrup from the rhubarb, and rub sufficient fruit through a sieve to make half a pint of pulp.

When stewing the rhubarb, cook it without water, either in a casserole in the oven, or in a double boiler.

Make a boiled custard with the yolk of egg and milk, and when cold add it to the rhubarb pulp.

Whisk the cream until it is thick. Add half of it to the rhubarb and keep back the remainder for decorating purposes.

Dissolve the gelatine in half a gill of rhubarb syrup and strain it into the rhubarb purée, mixing it lightly and adding sugar to taste and a few drops of cochineal.

When the mixture begins to thicken, whisk the whites of the eggs stiffly and fold them into the mixture. Turn it into custard cups or stemmed glasses and leave it to set. Then decorate each glass with the remainder of the cream.

Sufficient for five persons.

RIBBON JELLY

INGREDIENTS.—1 tin of raspberries, 2 juicy lemons, ¾ oz. of gelatine, 2 oz. of sugar, cochineal, 4d. of cream.

METHOD.—Mix the lemon-juice and raspberry syrup and add water to make three-quarters of a pint.

Add the gelatine and stir it over a low gas till dissolved. Add sugar and a little cochineal and strain.

When cold, pour one-third into a saucepan and one-third into an oiled mould, letting it set. Whisk the remainder with an egg whisk till frothy, then pour into the mould.

When set, melt the rest of the jelly and pour it on.

Shake out the mould and put raspberries and cream round.

Sufficient for two or three persons.

RICE FRUIT CUPS

INGREDIENTS.—3 oz. of rice, 1½ pints of milk, ½ oz. of butter, 1½ lb. of plums, 1½ tablespoonfuls of water, sugar to taste, to ¾ pint of plum pulp allow ⅜ oz. of leaf gelatine dissolved in ½ gill of water, a few almonds.

METHOD.—Bring the milk to the boil. Wash the rice, add it and cook gently until tender and the mixture thick and creamy, keeping it stirred occasionally. Add the butter and sugar to taste. Then leave until cold.

Stew the plums with the water and sufficient sugar to sweeten them. Then remove the stones and rub the fruit and syrup through a sieve.

Measure the pulp, strain in the dissolved gelatine, in the given proportions, and leave to set.

Arrange the prepared rice in glasses, heap the plum mixture in the centre and stick with a few almonds.

NOTE.—Flavour the rice with almond essence or other suitable flavouring.

Sufficient for six persons.

RICE JELLY

INGREDIENTS.—3 oz. of rice, 1 pint of milk, 1 good tablespoonful of sugar, nutmeg, 1 pint packet of raspberry jelly, 3 gills of hot water.

METHOD.—Wash the rice and put it in a saucepan with the milk. Let it simmer gently until tender and the mixture thick and creamy. Then add the sugar and a little grated nutmeg, and leave to cool. It must be stirred occasionally while cooking. If preferred, cook it in a double boiler.

Dissolve the jelly in the hot water, and when cold pour about half a gill of it into the bottom of mould (previously rinsed in cold water), and leave to set.

Stir the remainder of the jelly into the rice, and when beginning to set turn into the prepared mould.

When firm, dip the bottom in warm water and unmould carefully.

If preferred, the top of the rice jelly can be decorated with chopped jelly instead of first setting some in the bottom of the mould.

Sufficient for about seven or eight persons.

RICE SOUFFLE

INGREDIENTS.—1½ pints of milk, 2 eggs, 2 tablespoonfuls of ground rice, 4 tablespoonfuls of strawberry jam, ¾ oz. of leaf gelatine, ½ gill of water, a few drops of cochineal.

METHOD.—Mix the ground rice to a smooth paste with a small quantity of the milk. Heat the remainder in a saucepan and stir on to the ground rice.

Return to the saucepan and bring to the boil, keeping it well stirred.

Simmer for about five minutes, then draw to the side and cool slightly.

Separate the yolks from the whites of eggs.

Beat up the yolks and add to the rice.

Stir over a very low gas for a few minutes to cook the eggs, but do not let it boil or it will curdle, then draw to the side again and cool a little.

Put the gelatine in a saucepan with the water and dissolve it slowly, but do not boil it.

Add a small pinch of salt to the whites of eggs and whisk them to a very stiff froth.

Mix the strawberry jam into the ground rice, lightly fold in the whites of eggs, and, lastly, strain in the gelatine.

Mix all together lightly and pour into a wet mould.

Leave until set, then turn out carefully.

NOTE.—Add a few drops of cochineal to the mixture before moulding it.

Sufficient for about eight persons.

SAGO JELLY

INGREDIENTS.—¾ lb. of red currant and raspberry jam, 3 oz. of sago, 1 pint of water, 1 oz. of almonds, 1 dessertspoonful of sugar—or to taste, 1 tablespoonful of lemon-juice.

METHOD.—Turn the jam into the top of a double boiler, stir in the water, and bring it to the boil, then wash the sago and add it.

Stand the pan in another pan of boiling water and cook the sago and jam till the sago is clear and the mixture thick, keeping it stirred occasionally. Take it off the gas, add the lemon-juice, and sugar to taste.

Blanch and skin the almonds, split them in four, and stir them into the sago before turning it into a wet mould.

When set, unmould the sago jelly and serve it with custard or cream.

Sufficient for four or five persons.

SAGO MOULD

INGREDIENTS.—3 oz. of sago, 1 pint of milk, lemon-rind, 1 egg, 1½ dessertspoonfuls of sugar, 1 oz. of butter.

METHOD.—Put the milk into a saucepan with a few pieces of very thinly-cut lemon-rind, and bring it to the boil.

Well wash the sago and sprinkle it into the milk, and simmer gently until the sago is cooked, and the mixture is thick, keeping it frequently

Gooseberry
Fudge

Tangerine
Trifle

Pear
Sponge
Croutes

PLATE 31

Meringue Jelly

Add the whisked egg-whites to the jelly.

Whisk the egg-whites and jelly well together.

The Finished Jelly

PLATE 32

stirred. Then draw to the side and cool it slightly.

Beat up the egg.

Remove the lemon rind from the sago, add the butter, sugar, and egg.

Mix together and stir over a very low gas for a few minutes to cook the egg. Do not boil it, or it will curdle.

When ready pour into a wet mould and leave until set.

Turn on to a dish and serve either jam or stewed fruit with it.

SALLY LUNN PUDDING

INGREDIENTS.—Sally Lunn—as required, ½ lb. of red currants, ½ lb. of raspberries, 3 tablespoonfuls of sugar, water, cream, angelica.

METHOD.—String the currants and stew them with the raspberries, adding the sugar and a little water.

Take a plain mould or basin holding about a pint and a quarter and line the base and sides with sliced Sally Lunn. Drain off a little syrup from the fruit, and pour the hot stewed fruit with the remainder of the syrup into the prepared mould. Cover it with a round slice of Sally Lunn, put a saucer on top and press it with weights until cold. Turn it out and serve it with the syrup—previously drained off from the fruit.

Decorate the top with whipped cream, sweetened and flavoured to taste, and stalks of angelica.

Sufficient for four persons.

SAND CASTLES

INGREDIENTS.—1½ pints of milk, 3 oz. of rice, 3 oz. of desiccated coconut, 4 oz. of sugar, 1½ oz. of butter, 1 yolk of egg, pineapple essence, ½ pint packet of pineapple jelly, ½ pint of hot water, 2 slices of tinned pineapple.

METHOD.—Bring the milk to the boil, wash the rice and add. Cook in a double boiler until tender and the mixture very thick, keeping it stirred occasionally. Then draw aside. Add the coconut, sugar, and butter, then beat in the egg-yolk.

Stir over a low burner for a minute or two, being careful not to let it boil. Add a few drops of pineapple essence, turn into a shallow dish and leave until cold. Dissolve the jelly in the

hot water, or if there is any pineapple syrup use this instead. Mince the pineapple or cut it in small pieces, and stir into the jelly and when beginning to thicken turn into small castle moulds.

Leave to set, unmould, and arrange on the rice.

Sufficient for six persons.

SEMOLINA BLANCMANGE AND CHERRIES

INGREDIENTS.—1 small tin of cherries in syrup, ¼ lb. of semolina, 3 dessertspoonfuls of castor sugar, 2 pints of milk, 1 lemon (grated rind) or essence of vanilla, cream.

METHOD.—Put the milk in a saucepan to boil.

When boiling sprinkle in the semolina and stir well until the latter is cooked and the mixture is quite creamy.

Add the grated lemon-rind or vanilla flavouring, also the sugar.

Rinse a mould with cold water, and when the sugar is dissolved, pour the semolina, etc., into the mould, and leave until set. Turn on to a dish, heap the cherries at each end of the dish, pour the syrup round.

Serve cream separately.

SEMOLINA CUSTARD

INGREDIENTS.—2 oz. of semolina, 1½ pints of milk, 1 tablespoonful of sugar, 2 tablespoonfuls of desiccated coconut, 1 egg, flavouring, nutmeg.

METHOD.—Put the milk into a saucepan and bring it to the boil, sprinkle in the semolina and cook it gently until it is clear, keeping it well stirred. Take it off the gas and let it cool slightly.

Beat up the egg and mix it in with the sugar and coconut and a few drops of flavouring as desired. Turn it into a buttered pie-dish, sprinkle grated nutmeg on the top and bake it slowly for about half an hour, or until set, being careful not to let it boil.

Serve hot or cold.

Sufficient for four or five persons.

SEMOLINA JELLY CREAMS

INGREDIENTS.—1 pint of cherry jelly, ½ pint of hot water, 2 tablespoonfuls of semolina, ¾ pint of milk,

M

1 oz. of glacé cherries, 1 oz. of shelled walnuts, 3 dessertspoonfuls of desiccated coconut.

METHOD.—Dissolve the packet of jelly in the hot water. Bring the milk to the boil, sprinkle in the semolina, and cook gently until tender, and the mixture thick and creamy. Then leave until almost cold.

Now stir it up and gradually stir in the jelly (also cold).

Add the coconut, also the cherries and walnuts (cut up), saving a few of the latter for decoration.

When beginning to set, turn into small, wet moulds, and, when firm, turn out and place a shelled walnut on top of each.

Sufficient to fill eight or nine small moulds.

SHERRY JELLY

INGREDIENTS.—1 pint packet of lemon jelly, ½ gill of sherry, 3½ gills of hot water.

METHOD.—Scald a mould and rinse with cold water. Dissolve the packet of lemon jelly in the hot water. When cool, add the sherry and mix well with the jelly. Pour into the wet mould. Leave until set. Turn on to a dish and serve.

SMYRNA MOULD

INGREDIENTS.—½ lb. of stewing figs, 3½ gills of water, 1 lemon (rind only), 1 tablespoonful of rum, 2 oz. of sugar, ½ oz. of leaf gelatine, 1 oz. of almonds.

METHOD.—Stalk, wash and cut up the figs. Put them into a basin with three gills of the water and soak all night. Then stew until tender in the water in which they have been soaking, adding the grated lemon-rind and sugar. Leave to cool.

Dissolve the gelatine in a saucepan with the other half gill of water and strain it. Add the rum, and some more sugar, if required, also the almonds, blanched and cut up. When beginning to set, turn into a wet mould, and leave until firm. Unmould, and serve with cream or custard.

Sufficient for five or six persons.

SNOWFLAKE JELLY

INGREDIENTS.—1 pint packet of red jelly, 1 pint of hot water, 3 or 4 dessert-spoonfuls of desiccated coconut.

METHOD.—Dissolve the jelly in the hot water and leave until cold, and just beginning to set. Then stir in the coconut. Pour into a wet mould and leave until set. Dip the mould into warm water, give it one sharp shake and turn carefully on to a dish.

NOTE.—It is not necessary to cut up the jelly ; it will dissolve quite easily without. The water should be just below boiling point.

SPANISH CREAM

INGREDIENTS.—6 sponge cakes, 1 oz. of almonds (blanched), 1 oz. of glacé cherries, 1 oz. of cornflour, 1 oz. of sugar, strawberry jam, 1 pint of milk, juice of a lemon, 1 egg (beaten).

METHOD.—Split the sponge cakes, spread them with hot jam and squeeze lemon-juice over them.

Boil half a pint of milk. Mix the sugar and cornflour smoothly with half a pint of cold milk, and pour it into the hot milk, stirring till it boils. Boil for ten minutes. Stir in the egg and pour the custard over the sponge cakes.

Cut the almonds into strips and stick them into the cakes. Decorate with cherries.

Sufficient for six persons.

SPONGE BANANA MOULD

INGREDIENTS.—3 oz. of sponge cake crumbs, 1 pint packet of cherry jelly, ¾ pint of hot water or fruit-juice, a small tin of Ideal Milk, 3 bananas.

METHOD.—Dissolve the jelly in the hot water or fruit-juice and leave it to get cold.

Add the sponge cake crumbs and leave the jelly again until it is beginning to thicken. Then add two of the bananas, finely mashed. Add also the Ideal Milk, which should be whisked until it is thick just before it is added.

Mix all the ingredients together and turn them into a wet mould. When the mixture is set, unmould it and decorate the sweet with the remaining banana, cut in slices.

The syrup left over from tinned or bottled plums is ideal for dissolving the jelly, and gives it a delightful flavour.

SPONGE CAKE AND FRUIT MOULD

INGREDIENTS. — About 6 sponge cakes, 1 lb. of apples, 1 lemon, sugar and water, ½ oz. of leaf gelatine.

METHOD.—Split the sponge cakes into halves.

Now butter a small pudding-basin and line the bottom and sides with the sponge cakes, filling up any small cracks with pieces of sponge.

Prepare the apples for stewing and cook in the usual way, adding sugar to taste and a little water.

Dissolve the gelatine in about two or three tablespoonfuls of apple syrup. If there is not sufficient of the latter, use water. When the apples are ready rub them through a sieve, then strain the dissolved gelatine into them.

Turn into the prepared basin and place the remainder of the sponge cakes on the top. Cover with a saucer and put a weight on it.

When cold and set, turn on to a dish and serve with custard or cream.

A little chopped jelly can be used as decoration, if liked.

Sufficient for about five persons.

SPONGE CAKE MOULD

INGREDIENTS.—4 sponge cakes, ¾ pint of milk, custard powder, vanilla flavouring, 2 oz. of castor sugar, 2 whites of eggs, ½ to ¾ oz. of French leaf gelatine, ½ gill of water, 1 pint packet of cherry jelly, ¾ pint of hot water, a few glacé cherries, angelica.

METHOD.—Dissolve the jelly in the hot water and leave until cold but not set.

Rinse a mould with cold water, put about one tablespoonful of jelly in it, put the mould on its side and turn it about on a piece of ice (if available) until the jelly forms a thin coating all round the mould.

Decorate all round the bottom of the mould alternately with cherries and pieces of angelica, first dipping each in jelly. When set, cover with jelly and set again. Mix the custard powder with a small quantity of the milk.

Boil the remainder and add to the mixed powder, stirring well to prevent it from being lumpy.

Crumble the sponge cakes and add to the custard, together with the sugar and vanilla, and leave to soak until quite cool.

Dissolve the gelatine in half a gill of water, but do not boil it.

Whisk the whites to a stiff froth and fold into the custard, etc.

Lastly, strain in the dissolved gelatine. Mix all together, pour into the prepared mould and leave until set.

Dip in warm water and turn on to a dish.

Chop the remainder of the jelly and serve round it, if liked.

STRAWBERRY BORDER

INGREDIENTS.—1 lb. of strawberries, 1½ gills of milk, 2 or 3 tablespoonfuls of cream and a little extra for the decoration, 2 oz. of castor sugar, ½ oz. of gelatine, ½ gill of cold water, ½ gill of boiling water, cochineal.

METHOD.—Put the gelatine to soak for a few hours in the cold water.

Remove the hulls from the strawberries and rub half the fruit through a sieve. Add the sugar, stir in the milk, and then the two or three tablespoonfuls of cream.

Add the boiling water to the soaked gelatine, and when dissolved strain into the strawberry mixture.

Colour with a few drops of cochineal, and when beginning to thicken turn into a wet border mould. When set, turn out and decorate with whole strawberries and whipped cream. Whipped white of egg mixed with castor sugar may be used in place of the cream for decorating.

Sufficient for five persons.

STRAWBERRY CREAM

INGREDIENTS.—1 lb. of strawberries, ¾ oz. of gelatine, 1 gill of cream, ⅓ gill of water, 3 oz. of castor sugar, ½ packet of lemon jelly, hot water.

METHOD.—Wash, drain and hull the strawberries. Dissolve the jelly in the hot water, making it up to half a pint.

Pour two tablespoonfuls of the melted jelly into the base of a mould. Let this set, then decorate it with strawberries dipped in jelly. When these, too, are set, cover them with jelly and set it again.

Rub the remainder of the strawberries through a fine sieve, leaving out about four or five good shaped ones for a final decoration.

Whisk the cream until it thickens. Add the sugar to the strawberry pulp and stir it lightly into the cream. Strain the gelatine dissolved in the water into the mixture.

When it is beginning to thicken, turn it into the prepared mould to set. Unmould it and surround it with chopped jelly.

Decorate the sweet with a few whole strawberries.

STRAWBERRY FOOL

INGREDIENTS.—1 lb. of strawberries, 1 teaspoonful of lemon-juice, about 2 tablespoonfuls of castor sugar, 1½ gills of milk, 1 egg, cochineal, 1 gill of cream, vanilla flavouring.

METHOD. — Wash the strawberries very carefully and remove the stalks. Save three or four medium-sized ones for decoration, and rub the remainder through a hair sieve, then add to this purée the castor sugar and lemon-juice. Beat the egg and mix with the milk (previously heated). Pour the egg and milk into a jug, stand the jug in a saucepan of hot water, and stir the custard over the fire until it thickens, being very careful not to let it curdle. When cooked, remove the jug from the saucepan and leave the custard to get cold. Mix the strawberry purée, etc., with the custard, whisk the cream until it stiffens, sweeten and flavour it to taste, and stir in half of it. Colour to a pale pink shade with a few drops of cochineal, pour into a dish, and garnish with the remainder of the cream and a few strawberries.

Sufficient for about six persons.

STRAWBERRY DELIGHT

INGREDIENTS.—1 tin of strawberries (medium size), 1 tablespoonful of lemon-juice, 1 gill of cream, 1 egg-white, ⅝ oz. of gelatine.

METHOD.—Drain the syrup from the strawberries and rub the fruit

through a sieve, keeping back a few whole berries.

Dissolve the gelatine in a saucepan with one gill of the syrup, stir the remainder into the strawberry pulp and add the lemon-juice.

Whisk the cream until thick, then gradually mix in the strawberry pulp and strain in the gelatine. Leave the strawberry delight till beginning to thicken, then fold in the stiffly-whisked egg-white.

Turn the delight into a wet mould. When set, dip this in warm water, unmould it and serve it with a few whole berries round the dish.

Sufficient for five persons.

STRAWBERRY SPONGE DELIGHT

INGREDIENTS.—1 lb. of strawberries, 3 to 4 oz. of castor sugar, 6 new sponge fingers, 1 yolk and 2 whites of egg, ¼ pint of milk, ½ gill of cream, 1 or 2 tablespoonfuls of water, vanilla, ¼ oz. of gelatine.

METHOD.—Wash, drain and hull the strawberries. Then rub them through a fine sieve, leaving two or three whole for decoration.

Make a custard with the milk and yolk of egg. Sweeten it with a teaspoonful of sugar and flavour it with vanilla. Leave it to cool.

Split the sponge fingers in halves. Dip them in custard and arrange them round the sides of a dish. Put the remaining two or three pieces in the base.

Add the castor sugar to the strawberry pulp. When it is dissolved, stir in the lightly whipped cream and stiffly whisked egg-whites.

Whisk them all together lightly, then strain in the gelatine, dissolved in a saucepan with the water.

Taste the mixture to see if it is sufficiently sweetened before turning it into the prepared dish. When the delight is ready to serve, decorate it with whipped cream, extra to that given in the ingredients, and a few halved strawberries.

STRAWBERRY JELLY

INGREDIENTS.—1 tin of strawberries in syrup, 1 pint packet of strawberry jelly, ¾ pint of hot water, a few pieces of angelica.

METHOD.—Dissolve the jelly in hot water. Strain the syrup from the strawberries and add one gill of it to the dissolved jelly. Rinse a mould with cold water, and set a little of the jelly in the bottom of it, then decorate the bottom with a few pieces of angelica dipped in jelly. When set, cover with jelly and set again.

Put in a layer of strawberries, cover with jelly and, when firm, add another layer.

Proceed in this way until all the fruit and jelly are used. The top layer should be jelly. When all is set, dip the mould in warm water, and turn on to a dish.

STRAWBERRY MERINGUE PIE

INGREDIENTS.—1 lb. of strawberries, 1 yolk of egg, ¼ lb. of castor sugar, ½ oz. of butter, 1½ oz. of flour, 2 egg-whites, ¾ gill of water, 2 tablespoonfuls of castor sugar, some short pastry (see p. 252).

METHOD.—Wash, drain and hull the strawberries. Keep one or two aside for decoration.

Put the remainder in the top of a double boiler and sprinkle them with the quarter of a pound of sugar.

Leave the boiler at the side of the fire or place it over a very low burner for a few minutes until the juice runs and the sugar is dissolved. Then take the pan away from the heat. Let the fruit stand for a few hours till more juice is extracted.

Meanwhile, roll out some short pastry thinly. Cut a round of it and line a Pyrex plate with it.

Fold in the edge of the pastry towards the plate to make a thicker edge. Then flute it with your thumb and finger. Line the pastry with a round of buttered paper. Sprinkle rice in the base of it, and put the pastry in a hot oven to bake.

When the pastry is set, remove the paper and rice and finish cooking the case. Then put it aside to cool. Mix the flour to a smooth paste with water. Add the mixture to the strawberries. Bring them to the boil and boil them for a few minutes,

keeping them well stirred. Then cool the fruit slightly.

Add the beaten egg-yolk and butter, and cook the mixture again for a few minutes without letting the mixture boil.

Then let it cool before turning it into the prepared pastry.

Whisk the whites of eggs to a stiff froth and fold in the two tablespoonfuls of castor sugar. Heap the meringue on top of the strawberry mixture.

Dust it with sugar and put it into a cool oven to set and be lightly coloured.

STRAWBERRY SEMOLINA

INGREDIENTS.—2 oz. of semolina, 1 tablespoonful of sugar, ¾ to 1 lb. of strawberries, 3 to 4 oz. of castor sugar, 1 pint of milk, ½ oz. of butter, cream, cochineal.

METHOD.—Wash, drain and hull the fruit and put it into a saucepan.

Sprinkle the fruit with the castor sugar. Leave the pan at the side of the fire, or stand it over a very low burner for a minute or two, until the juice runs and the sugar is dissolved.

Put the milk into a saucepan. Bring it to the boil and sprinkle in the semolina. Cook it till the mixture is thick and the semolina tender. Be sure to keep it well stirred.

Add one tablespoonful of sugar and the butter. Stir in half a gill of the juice from the strawberries—this will give it a slightly curdled appearance. Cook the semolina mixture again for a few minutes, and colour it with a few drops of cochineal. Turn it into a plain wet mould and leave it to set.

Unmould the sweet and decorate it with whipped cream. Surround it with a few of the prepared strawberries, and serve the remainder separately.

STRAWBERRY SHORTCAKE

INGREDIENTS.—6 oz. of flour, a pinch of salt, 2 teaspoonfuls of baking-powder, ½ oz. of cornflour, 1½ oz. of butter or margarine, 1½ oz. of castor sugar, about ¾ gill of milk.

FOR THE FILLING.—1 lb. of strawberries, ¼ pint of cream, 3 to 4 oz. of castor sugar.

METHOD.—Sift the flour with the salt, baking-powder, and cornflour. Rub in the fat and add the sugar. Mix them to a soft dough with milk.

Turn the dough on to a lightly-floured board and roll it out to a thick round the size of your sandwich-tin. Butter the tin and put in the rolled-out dough. Place it in a fairly hot oven to bake. It will take from twenty to thirty minutes. Remove the pastry from the tin, split it in half and let the steam escape.

Meanwhile prepare the filling. Put a few of the best strawberries aside for decorating.

Stalk the remainder, wash and drain them well, then halve them, partially mash them, and mix them with the sugar.

Cover the cake with some of the prepared strawberries with their juice. Sandwich the two pieces together and put the remainder on the top.

Whisk the cream, sweeten and flavour it to taste and heap it in the centre. Decorate the shortcake with a few whole berries.

Sufficient for six persons.

SUMMER DELIGHT

INGREDIENTS.—$\frac{1}{4}$ lb. of raspberries, $\frac{1}{2}$ lb. of cherry plums, 3 dessertspoonfuls of sugar, $\frac{3}{4}$ gill of water, 1 oz. of sponge cake, 1 yolk of egg, $\frac{1}{4}$ pint of milk, sugar, cream, vanilla.

METHOD.—Stalk the plums and cook them with the water and two dessert-spoonfuls of the sugar until tender. Then remove the stones and mash the fruit to a pulp to rub it through a sieve.

Mash up the raspberries, add the remainder of the sugar and mix the raspberry purée with the plum pulp.

Add the crumbled sponge cake.

Make a boiled egg custard with the yolk of egg and milk, adding sugar and flavouring essence to taste, and when cold stir this into the fruit mixture.

Serve the Summer Delight in stemmed glasses, heap whipped cream, sweetened and flavoured to taste, in the centre, and decorate each glass with a few extra raspberries and pieces of angelica.

Sufficient for three persons.

SUMMER JELLIES

INGREDIENTS.—1 pint packet of lemon jelly, fruit syrup, 2 oz. of macaroon biscuits, 2 whites of eggs, leaves of angelica, cream, 1 or 2 gills (drained) of stewed red currants and raspberries.

METHOD.—Heat the syrup, drained from the red currants and raspberries, and dissolve the jelly in it, making it up to a pint with other left-over syrup that will blend with it nicely ; or, if this is not available, make it up with hot water.

Break up the macaroons into small pieces and add them to the jelly with the fruit, then leave the mixture to get cold.

Whisk the whites of eggs to a stiff froth and add them, and whisk all together until an even froth is obtained all over the jelly. Turn the frothed jelly into individual cups and leave it to set.

Decorate the jellies with clusters of red currants and leaves of angelica, and serve them with cream.

SUMMER PUDDING

INGREDIENTS.—$1\frac{1}{2}$ lb. of black currants, 4 to 6 oz. of sugar, according to taste, half a stale loaf, $\frac{1}{2}$ pint of custard (see p. 217) or cream.

METHOD.—This is a delicious pudding and quite easy to make.

Pick the fruit and stew it with the sugar and about a gill of water.

Cut the bread in thick slices (about one-third of an inch) and line a pudding-basin with them. Pour in the boiling fruit and cover the top with a round of bread.

Stand the pudding in a soup plate and put on top of it a small plate and a heavy weight to press it into shape.

Leave it till the next day, or for twenty-four hours, if possible.

Turn it out carefully and pour over it half a pint of custard or thick cream, or, if preferred, it may be coated with custard and served with cream handed round.

Any sharp-tasting fruit, such as damsons or raspberries and currants, may be served in this way.

SUNFLOWER SWEET

INGREDIENTS.—7 sponge cakes, $1\frac{1}{4}$ pints of hot water, 2 bananas, 1 small tin of peaches, $1\frac{1}{2}$ pint packets of lemon jelly, sugar, 1 gill of cream, 1 lemon, jam.

METHOD.—Peel and mash the bananas.

Split open the sponge cakes and spread with a little jam, then with some of the banana, and sandwich them together again.

Arrange them in a large glass dish in the form of a star, leaving a small circle in the centre for the cream.

Dissolve the jelly in hot water, then make it up to one pint and a half with peach syrup ; if not sufficient, use a little more water.

Soak the sponge cakes with the jelly, then pour the remainder round, being careful to keep the cakes in position, and not to break them.

Leave until almost set, then cut pieces of peach to resemble the petals of a sunflower and arrange one on each sponge cake and leave until the jelly is quite set.

Sweeten the cream and whisk it until it thickens, then put in the centre of circle.

Grate the lemon-rind and sprinkle it thickly over the cream.

SURPRISE JELLY

INGREDIENTS.—1 packet of lemon jelly, $\frac{1}{2}$ oz. of gelatine, 1 small bottle of maraschino cherries, $\frac{1}{2}$ gill of cream, 1 pint of hot water.

METHOD.—Soak the gelatine for five minutes in one gill of cherry syrup, and stir over a low gas till dissolved.

Dissolve the packet of jelly in a little less than a pint of hot water, and add to it one tablespoonful of the dissolved gelatine. Let it cool.

Oil a mould, put in six cherries and pour in enough jelly to cover them.

Let it set firm, then stand on it a glass of water, well oiled on the outside. Pour the cold jelly round to fill the space between the glass and the mould.

Let it set firm. Remove stones from the other cherries. Whisk the cherry syrup containing the dissolved gelatine. When light and frothy, stir in the cream and cherries.

When the jelly is quite solid and firm, take out the glass carefully, and fill the hole in the jelly with the cream mixture.

To turn out, shake gently on to a dish, and decorate with whipped cream.

Sufficient for three persons.

TANGERINE BASKETS

INGREDIENTS.—5 tangerines, $\frac{1}{2}$ pint packet of orange jelly, 2 tablespoonfuls of cream, $\frac{1}{4}$ pint of hot water, angelica, 6 pistachio nuts, a few silver balls.

METHOD.—Cut the rinds of the tangerines not quite in half crosswise, leaving the larger half to form the basket. Remove the fruit from the rinds, being careful not to split the latter, and press the juice out of the fruit by rubbing it through a sieve.

Cut up the orange jelly and dissolve it in the hot water. Let it get cold, then stir in the tangerine-juice (there should be about a quarter of a pint), also the cream. When beginning to thicken, turn the jelly into the tangerine cases and leave it till set. Decorate the tops with silver balls and shamrocks.

Cut strips of angelica, dip them in hot water to soften them, then bend them round to form handles, and fix one on each half tangerine.

To make the shamrocks, blanch the pistachio nuts. Cut one in fine strips lengthwise, for the stalks, the remainder cut crosswise in slices ; these will make the leaves of the shamrock.

Sufficient for four or five baskets.

TANGERINE CREAMS

INGREDIENTS.—Tangerines—as required, 1 yolk of egg, $\frac{1}{4}$ pint of milk, 1 tablespoonful of castor sugar, $\frac{1}{2}$ gill of cream, gelatine (barely $\frac{1}{2}$ oz.), $\frac{1}{3}$ gill of water, a little lemon jelly.

METHOD.—Squeeze the juice from enough tangerines to give half a pint of juice, putting aside three slices for decorating the moulds.

Beat the egg-yolk, mix it with the milk, and cook them in a double boiler until the custard thickens, keeping it stirred, then take it off the gas and leave it till cold.

Mix the tangerine-juice with the cold

custard, stir in sugar to taste and the lightly-whisked cream.

Finally strain in the gelatine, dissolved in the water. Leave it until beginning to thicken, and then turn it into decorated moulds. When set unmould the creams.

The moulds should be decorated before making the cream mixture. To do this, pour a thin layer of jelly in the mould, and when set add a slice of tangerine dipped in jelly. Cover this with jelly and leave it to set before pouring in the cream, etc.

Sufficient to fill five or six small moulds.

TANGERINE JELLY

INGREDIENTS.—1 pint packet of orange jelly, 1 pint of hot water, 4 tangerines, 1 gill of cream, vanilla, castor sugar.

METHOD.—Dissolve the packet of orange jelly in one pint of hot water. Peel the tangerines, remove all the white pith and pips, and divide them into quarters.

Take a rather shallow silver or glass dish. Just cover the bottom with the orange jelly, and, when set, dip the quarters of tangerines in some of the remaining jelly and arrange them all round the edge of the set jelly so that each quarter overlaps the previous one.

Leave until set, then cover with jelly and set again.

Continue in this way until all the jelly and tangerines are used, remembering that the last layer must be jelly.

Whisk the cream until it stiffens, then sweeten and flavour it to taste. Serve the jelly in the dish and pile the whipped cream in the centre of the jelly. Garnish with a few pieces of thinly-cut tangerine-rind cut in fancy shapes.

Sufficient for about five or six persons.

TEA JELLY

INGREDIENTS.—½ pint of Ideal Milk (unsweetened), 2 yolks of eggs, 6 oz. of sugar, ¾ oz. of gelatine, about ½ gill of water, ½ pint of strong cold tea.

METHOD.—Whisk the egg-yolks and the sugar. Gradually add half of the Ideal Milk and the tea, and turn the mixture into the top of a double boiler.

Whisk it over hot water until it thickens.

Remove it from the hot water, turn it into a basin, and strain in the gelatine, dissolved in the water. When the mixture is beginning to thicken, stir in the remainder of the Ideal Milk (previously whipped).

Pour the mixture into a rinsed-out mould and put it on ice to cool. When set, unmould it and serve.

Sufficient for six persons.

TIPSY CAKE

INGREDIENTS.—1 bought Savoy cake (1s. 6d.), 2 eggs, ¾ pint of milk, almond essence, 2 oz. of sugar, raspberry jam, 1 gill of cream, juice of ½ lemon, 1 oz. of glacé cherries, 2 oz. of Jordan almonds, 1 wineglassful of sherry, ½ wineglassful of port or brandy.

METHOD.—Scoop out a little from the top of the cake, squeeze in the lemon-juice, and put in two tablespoonfuls of jam.

Cut the cake in three pieces and spread thickly with jam. Replace the three pieces and soak the cake all over with wine, leaving it till next day to get thoroughly soaked and flavoured.

To make the custard, put the eggs and sugar in a double saucepan and whisk well with an egg whisk.

Add the milk and two or three drops of almond essence, and stir till the custard is thick enough to coat the back of the spoon. Leave till cold, and strain slowly over the cake.

Pour boiling water on the almonds, slip off the skins and put the almonds in cold water. Cut them in fine strips and stick all over the cake.

Whip the cream and place it on the top and at the sides of the cake. More cream can, of course, be used if desired.

Decorate with cherries just before serving.

To serve about six persons.

NOTE.—Jordan almonds are more suitable for Tipsy Cake, as they are longer than other kinds.

TOFFEE SOUFFLES

INGREDIENTS.—$\frac{1}{4}$ lb. of Barbados sugar, 1 tablespoonful of hot water, 1 oz. of butter, $\frac{3}{4}$ oz. of flour, $\frac{1}{2}$ pint of milk, 1 oz. of almonds, 1 yolk of egg, 2 whites, $\frac{1}{4}$ oz. of gelatine.

METHOD.—Blanch the almonds, chop them and then bake them gently till golden.

Melt two ounces of the butter in a saucepan, add the hot water and the sugar. Dissolve slowly and boil the syrup for a few minutes, then leave it to cool.

Melt the remaining ounce of butter in another saucepan, stir in the flour and, when it is well blended, add the milk and bring it to the boil. Boil the sauce gently for a few minutes, then draw the pan aside and let the sauce cool for a minute. Stir in the beaten egg-yolk. Cook it again without letting it boil, then take it off the heat and stir in the toffee mixture by degrees.

Dissolve the gelatine in one or two tablespoonfuls of water. Strain it into the mixture and add half of the baked almonds.

When it is beginning to set, fold in the stiffly-whisked egg - whites, then turn it into soufflé cases.

Serve Toffee Soufflés with the remainder of the nuts sprinkled on the top.

Sufficient to fill six soufflé cases.

TRIFLES

THE amount of liquid required for soaking the sponge cakes depends entirely on the degree of their staleness. Be careful not to add too much. So many spoil their trifles by making them too moist. Milk, wine, or fruit juice can be used for this purpose.

Some make egg custards and some powder custards, but the former are preferable.

A very good egg custard can be made using *two eggs to the pint*. Add the milk when just off the boil, then cook the custard in a jug in a saucepan of hot water, being careful not to let it curdle.

If a custard shows signs of curdling, remove it at once from the hot water, strain into a cold jug and keep it well stirred for a few minutes. Allow about eight sponge cakes to a pint of custard.

INDIVIDUAL TRIFLES
GINGER FLAVOUR

INGREDIENTS.—5 or 6 oz. of Casino biscuits, $\frac{1}{3}$ to $\frac{1}{2}$ small jar of preserved ginger, $\frac{3}{4}$ pint of milk, 1 egg and 1 yolk, sugar, cream—for decorating.

METHOD.—Take some of the syrup from the ginger, thin it down with a little water and bring to the boil.

Cut the ginger into small pieces, leaving a few larger slices aside for decorating. Arrange the biscuits tastefully in glasses, cutting them as required. Add the ginger and soak the biscuits with the warm syrup.

Beat up the whole egg and yolk. Heat the milk and add, then cook in a double boiler until it thickens, adding sugar to taste. When a little cool, pour some custard into each glass. Before serving, decorate with whipped cream, sweetened and flavoured to taste, and the ginger slices. If preferred, loose ginger, glacé or crystallised, can be used ; a quarter of a pound will be sufficient. In which case some ginger wine can be used in place of the ginger syrup for soaking the biscuits.

Sufficient to fill four good-sized glasses.

JELLY TRIFLE

INGREDIENTS.—$\frac{1}{2}$ a sponge ring, 1 pint packet of jelly, hot water, 1 oz. of almonds, cream.

METHOD.—Split the sponge ring in half (you must, of course, buy a whole one), and place one half in a glass dish. The other piece can be utilised for some other purpose.

Dissolve the jelly in one pint of hot water (if liked, it may be flavoured with a spoonful or two of sherry), then pour it very slowly over the sponge ring and leave it to set.

Blanch and split the almonds and stick them round the edge of the ring. Heap whipped cream in the centre.

TANGERINE TRIFLE

INGREDIENTS. — 1 sponge ring, orange or tangerine marmalade, $\frac{3}{4}$ to 1 gill of tangerine-juice, a few slices of tangerine, some crystallised cherries, 1 whole egg and 1 yolk, $\frac{3}{4}$ pint of hot milk, 1½ dessertspoonfuls of sugar, orange flavouring essence.

METHOD.—Beat up the whole egg and the yolk together, add the hot milk and sugar, and turn them into the top of a double boiler. Stir this over hot water until the custard thickens. Remove it from the heat and cool it, adding a few drops of orange essence to flavour it.

Split the sponge ring in halves and spread them with the marmalade. Put the lower half into a glass dish and soak it with the tangerine-juice, cover it with the top half and soak this also. Pour the custard over it.

Serve the Tangerine Trifle decorated with crosswise slices of tangerine and crystallised cherries.

PLAIN TRIFLE

INGREDIENTS.—6 small sponge cakes, strawberry jam, 1½ pints of milk, 1 oz. of white sugar, 1 tablespoonful of custard powder, 1½ oz. of glacé cherries, vanilla flavouring.

METHOD.—Split the sponge cakes open, and spread them with jam.

Arrange the lower halves in a dish with the cut side uppermost.

Boil half a pint of milk, and soak the cakes with some of it.

Put on the top halves, and soak with the remainder of the hot milk.

To make the custard—mix the custard powder to a smooth paste with a little of the milk.

Boil the remainder with the sugar, pour on to the mixed powder, keeping it well stirred. Add vanilla flavouring to taste.

When half cold, pour the custard over the sponge cakes, and set aside until quite cold.

Decorate with glacé cherries.

RICH TRIFLE

INGREDIENTS.—1 large sponge cake (tower-shaped), apricot jam, ¾ gill of sherry, 1½ pints of milk, 3 eggs, 2 dessertspoonfuls of white sugar, ¼ teaspoonful of castor sugar, vanilla flavouring, 2 oz. of almonds, angelica, 1½ gills of cream.

METHOD.—Split the sponge cake into three portions, spread each with jam, and soak with hot milk, then with sherry. (Use about one gill of the milk.)

When well soaked, build it up into its original shape.

Beat up the eggs and stir in one pint and a quarter of milk, together with the white sugar.

Pour into a jug, stand in a saucepan of water, and stir until the custard thickens.

When cooked, lift it out of the saucepan, add the flavouring, and set aside to cool.

Blanch the almonds, and split each into three or four pieces.

Stick them all over the sponge cake, but especially on the top.

Pour over the custard, then leave until cold.

Sweeten and flavour the cream, whisk it until it thickens.

Decorate the trifle with the whipped cream and a few stalks of angelica.

NOTE.—The custard should be thick enough to coat the sponge.

VALENTINE TRIFLE

INGREDIENTS. — 1 heart - shaped sponge cake, ½ pint packet of vanilla jelly, ½ pint of hot water, raspberry jam, 2 oz. of almonds, 1 egg, cream, ½ pint of milk, 1 dessertspoonful of sugar, vanilla flavouring.

METHOD.—Dissolve the jelly in the hot water. If liked a little less water may be added, and when the jelly is cool a little sherry may be added to make up the quantity.

Make a boiled custard with the egg-and-milk (adding sugar and flavouring to taste), and let it get cold.

Split the sponge cake in half, and spread each piece with jam. Sandwich these together, then put them into a dish and pour the jelly over the sponge gently.

Let this set, then add the custard, pouring it round the sides, and scatter spikes of blanched almonds over it.

Garnish the centre of the heart-shaped sponge with a glacé cherry, and serve the trifle with cream.

Sufficient for six persons.

VANILLA CREAM

INGREDIENTS.—1½ gills of cream, 2 whites of eggs, ¾ oz. of leaf gelatine, few pistachio nuts, 2 oz. of castor sugar, vanilla flavouring, ½ gill of water, ½ pint packet of lemon jelly, ½ pint of hot water.

METHOD.—Dissolve the jelly in the hot water and leave until set. Whisk the cream until it stiffens.

Add a tiny pinch of salt to the whites of eggs and whisk to a very stiff froth.

Put the gelatine into a saucepan with the water and let it dissolve slowly, but do not boil it.

Fold the whites of eggs lightly into the cream, sweeten with castor sugar, and add sufficient vanilla to flavour.

When the gelatine has cooled slightly, strain it into the cream, and stir all together.

Pour into a wet mould, and leave until set, then turn on to a dish, sprinkle with chopped pistachio nuts and serve chopped jelly round.

VERMICELLI SOUFFLE

INGREDIENTS.—2 oz. of vermicelli, 1 pint of milk, 2 oz. of castor sugar, vanilla, ¾ oz. of leaf gelatine, ¾ gill of water, 2 eggs.

METHOD.—Break the vermicelli into short lengths, and wash it. Bring the milk to the boil, add the vermicelli and cook gently until it is tender, keeping it stirred occasionally. Add the sugar and cool slightly. Separate the eggs. Beat up the yolks and add and stir over a lower burner for a few minutes, being careful not to let it boil. Leave until cold.

Put the gelatine into a saucepan with the water, dissolve slowly, then strain into the vermicelli. Add vanilla flavouring to taste, and when beginning to set fold in the stiffly whisked egg-whites. Turn into a wet mould and when set unmould and surround with stewed fruit.

Sufficient for six persons.

WALNUT BLANCMANGE

INGREDIENTS.—1 pint of milk, 2½ dessertspoonfuls of cornflour, 1 tablespoonful of sugar, ½ oz. of butter, 3 dessertspoonfuls of sherry, 1½ oz. of shelled walnuts.

METHOD.—Mix the cornflour to a smooth paste with a small quantity of the milk. Heat the remainder in a saucepan with the sugar, and stir it on to the cornflour. Return the mixture to the pan and bring it to the boil, keeping it well stirred.

Add the butter, and boil it gently for a few minutes, then take it off the heat and add the walnuts (chopped). Gradually stir in the sherry.

Turn the mixture into a wet mould, and when it is set, unmould it and serve it decorated with a few extra walnuts.

Sufficient for four persons.

WINE FLUFF

INGREDIENTS.—½ gill of port wine or sherry, 1 egg and 1 extra white, 3 oz. of sugar, 1 lemon, 1 oz. of almonds, ½ pint of water, ¾ oz. of leaf gelatine, crystallised violets.

METHOD.—Blanch and finely chop the almonds. Put the gelatine into a saucepan with the water and dissolve slowly, then strain into another pan. Grate the lemon-rind finely, and add with the sugar and strained lemon-juice and the beaten yolk of the egg, and stir for a few minutes over a low burner to cook it.

Stir in the almonds and, when cool, add the sherry, then leave until thoroughly cold.

Whisk the egg-whites to a very stiff froth and add, and whisk together for a few minutes, then turn into a dish and leave to set; or, if liked, set in a mould, then turn out.

Decorate with crushed crystallised violets.

Sufficient for about five or six persons.

SAUCES

SAUCE-MAKING plays an important part in cookery, the success of many dishes depending almost entirely on the way the sauce is prepared. A little more time and care given to the sauce will make all the difference.

The three most general faults in sauces are that they are lumpy, not well seasoned, or else not cooked sufficiently.

A White Sauce

This is the foundation of many other sauces, and it may be thin, medium, or thick.

The Proportions to Use

FOR A THIN SAUCE.—½ oz. of butter, and ½ oz. of flour to ½ pint of milk.

FOR A MEDIUM SAUCE.—¾ oz. of butter and ¾ oz. of flour to ½ pint of milk.

FOR A THICK SAUCE (FOR COATING).—1 oz. of butter and 1 oz. of flour to ½ pint of milk.

If you require a cheaper sauce, use margarine instead of butter, and three parts milk and one part water instead of all milk.

One Method

The first method of making the sauce is to melt the butter in a saucepan, stir in the flour and mix together until well blended. Then add the milk (if adding *hot* milk, add it gradually) and stir until the sauce boils and thickens. Season to taste and let the sauce boil gently for at least five or six minutes.

Another Way

The second method is to mix the flour to a smooth paste with some of the milk. Heat the remainder in a saucepan with the butter and stir on to it. Then return to the pan and bring to the boil, keeping it well stirred. Season to taste and let the sauce boil gently for five or six minutes.

It is better to make your sauce by this method if using a less proportion of fat than that given.

NOTE.—When making sauces to serve with meat or fish, a little meat or fish stock may, if liked, be used with the milk (instead of all milk) to give additional flavour.

Hints

When making a fish sauce, first melt the butter, mix the flour smoothly with it, *take the pan off the fire* and add the stock or milk gradually.

The sauce is easier to mix smoothly if the pan is off the fire. After adding the liquid, stir all the time till it boils. If the sauce is not well stirred it is certain to be lumpy.

A sauce is of the right consistency when it will coat the back of a wooden spoon. Two tablespoonfuls (or two ounces) of flour will thicken one pint of liquid.

One gill of sauce is enough for three or four persons.

Anchovy Sauce

Add sufficient anchovy essence to flavour the sauce. Probably about one teaspoonful to half a pint white sauce. As the essence is salt, do not add salt to this sauce.

Caper Sauce

A small bottle of capers will be sufficient for half to three-quarter pint of sauce. They may be chopped coarsely or cut in halves. This sauce is sometimes made with meat liquor instead of milk, in which case a little vinegar from the capers may be added.

Cheese Sauce

Add three or four oz. of finely grated cheese to half pint of white sauce, and stir until melted.

Egg Sauce

Allow one hard-boiled egg to half a pint of white sauce. Chop up the white and mix into the sauce. The yolk rub through a strainer (this is usually sprinkled on top of the sauce).

Hollandaise Sauce

Make half a pint of white sauce (medium thickness), adding a little extra butter. When the sauce has boiled sufficiently, cool it a little and beat in the yolks of two eggs. Cook for a few minutes without boiling, and add a squeeze of lemon-juice before serving it.

Maitre d'Hotel Sauce

Make half a pint of white sauce (medium thickness), and just before serving add two flat teaspoonfuls chopped parsley and a squeeze of lemon-juice. For special purposes a little cream may be added.

Parsley Sauce

Add one flat tablespoonful of finely chopped parsley to half a pint of white sauce.

Shrimp Sauce

Add a few picked shrimps and a little anchovy essence to white sauce.

ANCHOVY SAUCE
(See p. 364)

APPLE SAUCE

Peel and core the apples and cut them into slices. Cook them with a little water and sugar to taste.

The amount of sugar and water depends entirely on the kind of apples used, but do not make the sauce too sweet.

If liked, a lump of butter may be added to them and less water. When tender, mash to a pulp or rub through a sieve, re-heat and serve.

ASPARAGUS SAUCE

INGREDIENTS.—2 oz. of butter, 2 tablespoonfuls of vinegar.

METHOD.—This is a delicious, piquant sauce that should be served very hot.

Put the vinegar and butter in a small pan and boil till the butter is melted. Stir quickly and serve in a very hot sauce-boat.

BECHAMEL SAUCE
(A Savoury White Sauce)

INGREDIENTS.—1½ oz. of flour, 1½ oz. of butter, 1 pint of milk, milk and water, or milk and white stock (see p. 12), small piece of celery (cut up), ½ a carrot (sliced thickly), 1 small onion (whole), a bayleaf and a small sprig of parsley, seasoning.

METHOD.—Put the milk (milk and water or milk and stock) into a saucepan with the cleaned and prepared vegetables, the bayleaf, and parsley. Bring slowly to the boil, then leave at the side of the fire until the milk is well flavoured. (If the stock is already flavoured, you may require less vegetables and herbs.)

Melt the butter, stir in the flour and mix until well blended. Then strain the milk and add it gradually, keeping the sauce well stirred until it boils.

Boil gently for a few minutes and add seasoning to taste.

A little cream may be added if liked.

BRAIN SAUCE

INGREDIENTS.—1 egg (hard-boiled), brains, seasoning, half a pint of white sauce.

METHOD.—Make the white sauce in the usual way. Take out the brains, chop them up and add them to the sauce and add also the hard-boiled egg cut into small square pieces or chopped.

BREAD SAUCE

INGREDIENTS.—1 pint of milk, 1 onion, 1 oz. of butter or margarine, few cloves, seasoning, 1 tumblerful of breadcrumbs (pressed down).

METHOD.—Peel the onion and stick a few cloves in the sides of it, then put it into a saucepan with the milk and butter.

Bring slowly to the boil, then leave at the side of the fire until the milk is well flavoured. Now bring again to the boil and stir in the breadcrumbs.

Stand the pan at the side of the fire, or in a double boiler, to allow the crumbs to swell.

Remove the onion, season the sauce and make thoroughly hot before serving. A little cream may be added if liked.

CAPER SAUCE
(See p. 364)

CHAUDFROID SAUCE

INGREDIENTS.—½ pint of hot Béchamel sauce (see p. 365), 1 gill of hot water, ½ packet of aspic jelly, 1 gill of mayonnaise (see p. 367), or salad cream.

METHOD.—Melt the aspic jelly in the hot water and strain it into the Béchamel sauce. As soon as it is cold, stir in the mayonnaise. Mix well. The sauce should be thick enough to coat the back of a wooden spoon.

CHEESE SAUCE
(See p. 364)

CHOCOLATE SAUCE

INGREDIENTS.—1½ teaspoonfuls of cornflour, 1 dessertspoonful of cocoa, ½ pint of milk, sugar and vanilla.

METHOD.—Mix the cornflour and cocoa to a smooth paste with a small quantity of the milk. Heat the remainder and stir on to it.

Return to the pan and bring to the boil.

Add sugar to taste, and boil gently for a few minutes to cook the sauce, keeping it well stirred.

Add vanilla and serve.

CRANBERRY SAUCE

INGREDIENTS.—½ lb. of cranberries, 1 teacupful of sugar, 1 gill of water, 1 teaspoonful of cornflour, pinch of cinnamon.

METHOD.—Boil the cranberries and water for five minutes, rub them through a hair sieve and re-heat them with the sugar.

Mix the cornflour and the cinnamon with two tablespoonfuls of cold water and pour them on the hot purée. Return it to the saucepan and stir till it boils.

Boil for five minutes.

DUTCH SAUCE

INGREDIENTS.—1 onion, ¾ pint of fish stock (see p. 12), 1 bunch of herbs.

1 oz. of butter, 1 oz. of flour, 3 peppercorns, 1 egg, juice and rind of ½ lemon, 2 anchovies.

METHOD.—Chop the onion and anchovies and put them in the stock with the herbs and peppercorns and thinly cut lemon-rind. Boil till reduced to half a pint.

Melt the butter, add the flour and mix well. Strain on the stock, and stir the sauce till it boils.

Boil for three minutes and allow it to cool slightly.

Season to taste, add the lemon-juice and pour on to a well-beaten egg.

Stir round, strain and serve at once.

This sauce is served with boiled fish.

EGG SAUCE
(See p. 365)

ESPAGNOL SAUCE

INGREDIENTS.—2 oz. of flour, 2 oz. of butter, ¼ lb. of tomatoes, 1 stalk of celery (cut up), 1 carrot and onion (sliced), 1 oz. of mushrooms (chopped roughly), 1½ oz. of bacon, 1 pint of brown stock (see p. 12), seasoning and salt, pepper, paprika, small sprig of thyme and parsley.

METHOD.—Melt the butter in a saucepan, cut up the bacon and add it with the celery, mushrooms, carrot, and onion. Stir until beginning to brown, then add the flour and stir until brown. It must brown *slowly* or the flavour of the sauce will be spoiled.

Draw aside, add the tomatoes (sliced), the stock, and a small sprig of thyme and parsley. Stir until it boils, then cook very gently for about half an hour, adding seasoning to taste. Strain through a sieve. Add a little sherry just before using it.

If too thick, the sauce may be thinned down.

NOTE.—A plainer brown sauce can be made by omitting the sherry and mushrooms, and using margarine instead of butter.

HARD SAUCE
(A CHRISTMAS PUDDING SAUCE)

INGREDIENTS.—6 oz. of icing sugar, 3 oz. of butter, vanilla essence or rum.

METHOD.—Sieve the sugar first; then beat the butter and sugar to a cream and add vanilla essence or rum to taste.

HOLLANDAISE SAUCE
(See p. 365)

HORSERADISH SAUCE

INGREDIENTS.—2 oz. of horseradish (grated finely), salt, pepper and mixed mustard, 2 dessertspoonfuls of white vinegar, ¾ gill of cream.

METHOD.—Mix the horseradish with the vinegar, and add seasoning to taste. Whisk the cream until quite thick and mix in gradually.

MAITRE D'HOTEL SAUCE

INGREDIENTS.—½ oz. of butter or margarine, 1½ teaspoonfuls of flour, 1 gill of milk or milk and water, 1 teaspoonful of chopped parsley, squeeze of lemon-juice, pepper and salt.

METHOD.—Melt half an ounce of butter in a saucepan, stir in the flour and mix together until they are quite smooth.

Add the milk and stir until the sauce boils, then cook it slowly for about six minutes.

Season it with pepper and salt, stir in the chopped parsley and lastly the lemon-juice.

MAYONNAISE

INGREDIENTS.—1 yolk of egg, 1 gill of salad oil, 1 or 2 teaspoonfuls of Tarragon vinegar, salt and pepper, mixed mustard, 1 teaspoonful of plain vinegar.

METHOD.—Put the yolk of egg in a small basin and break it up with a wooden spoon. Season it with salt, pepper and mixed mustard, and stir in the oil drop by drop. As the sauce thickens, gradually stir in a little of the vinegar. Continue mixing slowly until all the ingredients are used, then taste the mayonnaise to see if it is sufficiently seasoned.

The sauce should be like thick cream when it is finished. The oil thickens it and the vinegar thins it, so, if necessary, add a little more of either ingredient until a thick, well-blended sauce is obtained. *It is most important*

to add the oil very slowly, otherwise the sauce will curdle.

This salad dressing can be flavoured with a little onion-juice if liked.

MELTED BUTTER SAUCE

INGREDIENTS.—1½ oz. of butter, 1½ oz. of flour, ½ pint of fish stock (see p. 12), 1 gill of milk, salt and pepper.

METHOD.—Melt the butter, take the pan off the fire, and add the flour, mix well with a wooden spoon till smooth.

Add the fish stock by degrees, stirring well. Add the milk and seasoning, place the pan on the fire again and stir well till the sauce boils. Boil for five minutes.

NOTE.—All fish stock may be used instead of part milk. The quantity of stock and milk may vary according to taste and convenience, so long as the proportions are two ounces of flour and butter to one pint of liquid.

MINT SAUCE

PICK the mint from the stalks, wash, drain, and chop it finely.

To two flat tablespoonfuls of chopped mint allow one tablespoonful and a half of sugar and a quarter of a pint of vinegar.

Put the mint in a sauce-boat with the sugar, add about two tablespoonfuls of boiling water. If cooking greens use some of this water, and when the sugar is dissolved, stir in the vinegar.

MUSTARD SAUCE

INGREDIENTS.—2 or 3 chillies, ½ pint of water, a small piece of lump ginger (bruised), 2 teaspoonfuls of flour, a few peppercorns and allspice, 2 teaspoonfuls of mustard, 1 gill of vinegar, a lump of butter or margarine (about ½ oz.), salt and pepper.

METHOD.—Mix the flour and mustard together, and mix to a smooth paste with some of the water.

Heat the remainder with the butter and stir on to it. Return to the pan and boil for a few minutes, keeping it stirred, then stir in the vinegar (flavoured with the spices).

NOTE.—Boil the vinegar with the spices for a few minutes, leave until well flavoured, then strain and stir into the sauce.

ONION SAUCE

INGREDIENTS.—1 lb. of onions, ¾ oz. of butter or margarine, salt and pepper, 2 teaspoonfuls of cornflour, ½ gill of milk and ½ gill of onion liquor, or 1 gill of milk.

METHOD.—Peel the onions, boil until tender, then drain and chop finely.

Return to the pan, add the milk, onion liquor, and butter. Mix the cornflour to a smooth paste with a spoonful of milk, and stir it in. Bring it to the boil, keeping it stirred. Let it cook gently for a few minutes, then season and serve.

PARSLEY SAUCE
(See p. 365)

SHRIMP SAUCE
(See p. 365)

TARTAR SAUCE

INGREDIENTS.—2 egg-yolks, ½ pint of salad oil, about a tablespoonful of vinegar, 1 teaspoonful of onion-juice, a few capers, seasoning.

METHOD.—Mix the yolks of the eggs in a basin, using a wooden spoon, then stir in the oil drop by drop, adding the seasoning to taste and also the onion-juice.

As the sauce thickens, stir in a little vinegar. When ready to use it should be a thick, creamy consistency. The oil has a thickening effect, while the vinegar thins it, so add more vinegar as required. A little Tarragon vinegar improves the flavour of this sauce.

Finally, stir in a few chopped capers, and serve the sauce in a separate dish. It is essential to add the oil very gradually, or the sauce will curdle.

TOMATO SAUCE

INGREDIENTS.—1½ lb. of tomatoes, 1 medium-sized onion, ½ pint of vinegar, 4 oz. of sugar, a few cloves, 2 or 3 teaspoonfuls of salt, 1 oz. of allspice, 2 teaspoonfuls of peppercorns, cornflour.

METHOD.—Wipe the tomatoes, and cut them into slices. Peel and slice the onion. Put these into a pan and add the vinegar, sugar, and salt. Tie the spices in muslin, and add.

Bring to the boil, and cook gently for about one hour and a half to two hours, then remove the spices, and rub the sauce through a sieve.

Return to the pan, and thicken with cornflour mixed to a smooth paste with a little vinegar. (*To one gill and a half of sauce allow about one flat teaspoonful of cornflour.*)

Boil for a few minutes to cook the cornflour and when cold, bottle.

HOT TOMATO SAUCE

INGREDIENTS.—½ lb. of tomatoes, ¾ gill of stock (see p. 12), ½ onion, ½ carrot, a small piece of celery, a small sprig of parsley and thyme, 1 oz. of bacon, salt, pepper, and celery salt, cornflour.

METHOD.—Cut up the bacon and put into a saucepan with the tomatoes (sliced) the onion (peeled and sliced thinly), and the carrot and celery (cleaned and prepared, but not cut up).

Cook gently for a few minutes without browning. Then draw aside, add the stock and bring to the boil. Simmer gently until the onion and tomatoes are tender, adding a small sprig of parsley and thyme to flavour, but do not leave these in too long.

When ready, remove the carrot, rub the sauce through a sieve, then return to the pan and thicken with cornflour, mixed to a smooth paste with water.

Boil for a few minutes and season to taste. The celery may be rubbed through the sieve, if tender.

WHITE SAUCE
(See p. 364)

WHITE WINE SAUCE

INGREDIENTS.—1 oz. of margarine, ¾ oz. of flour, ¼ pint of milk, ½ gill fish stock (see p. 12), ½ gill of white wine.

METHOD.—Melt the margarine and stir in the flour. Blend them together, add the milk and the fish stock and bring them to the boil. Stir in the wine, add seasoning to taste, and simmer the sauce for a few minutes. If the sauce is too thick, thin it down a little.

SAVOURIES AND SUPPER DISHES

AFTER-DINNER SAVOURIES

INGREDIENTS.—1 teaspoonful of Taragon vinegar, ¼ oz. of butter, 2 egg-yolks, 1 teaspoonful of malt vinegar, seasoning, six small oblongs of fried bread, parsley.

METHOD.—Cut tiny oblongs of bread (toast thickness) and fry them lightly in butter—extra to that given in the ingredients.

Break up the egg-yolks and put them into a saucepan with the butter (quarter of an ounce) and vinegar. Season them with salt and pepper and a dash of mustard. Stir the mixture till it thickens, being careful not to let it curdle. Then serve it on the prepared fried bread and garnish it with parsley.

Sufficient for about six small oblongs of toast.

ALMOND SAVOURIES

INGREDIENTS.—6 small rounds of buttered toast, 1 oz. of salted almonds (chopped), 1 tomato, 1 dessertspoonful of minced onion, 1 oz. of butter, 1 teaspoonful of flour, 1 teaspoonful of Yorkshire Relish, pepper, 6 extra salted almonds.

METHOD.—Melt the butter in a frying-pan and cook the minced onion in it until it begins to colour. Add the skinned and chopped tomato and cook it for a few minutes. Draw the pan aside, stir in the flour and cook it for a minute or two, then add the chopped, salted almonds and the Yorkshire Relish.

Make the mixture hot, add seasoning to taste and serve it on rounds of buttered toast and top each one with a salted almond.

Sufficient for two or three persons.

AMERICAN GOLDEN BUCK TOAST

INGREDIENTS.—½ lb. of Cheddar cheese, 1 oz. of butter, 1 teaspoonful of made mustard, 1 teaspoonful of Worcester sauce, salt and pepper, ¾ gill of beer or cider, 2 new laid eggs, 1 pint of boiling water, salt and 1 dessertspoonful of vinegar, 2 squares of hot buttered toast.

METHOD.—Boil the water in a small pan, and put in it the vinegar and half a teaspoonful of salt. Break the eggs into a cup and slide them gently into the water.

Cook for four minutes, but not too quickly. While they are cooking make the hot buttered toast and keep it hot. Slice the cheese thinly and melt it slowly in the butter. Stir in the other ingredients and pour the liquid over the toast.

Lift the eggs out with a fish slice, drain away the water, and serve one egg on each piece of toast.

Sufficient for two persons.

ANCHOVY EGGS

INGREDIENTS.—4 hard-boiled eggs, 4 tomatoes, 1 oz. of butter, anchovy essence, Worcester sauce, ½ teaspoonful of lemon-juice, salt and cayenne to taste, mayonnaise (see p. 367).

METHOD.—Halve the eggs. Scoop out the yolks into a basin and beat them to a paste with the butter.

Season the paste with anchovy essence, a little Worcester sauce, cayenne, lemon-juice, and salt to taste.

Fill the eggs with the mixture and serve each half egg standing on half a tomato which should first be spread with mayonnaise.

Garnish the eggs with cress.

Sufficient for four persons.

ANCHOVY TOAST

INGREDIENTS.—6 anchovies (boneless), 6 or 8 small oblongs of buttered toast or fried bread (fried in butter), 2 eggs, 1 oz. of butter, pepper.

METHOD.—Put the eggs into boiling water and boil them for from twelve to fifteen minutes until hard. Remove the shells, halve the eggs and take out the yolks. Mash up the anchovies and mix them with the butter and yolks, then rub them through a sieve and season with pepper.

Put this on to the prepared toast, and garnish it with finely-chopped white of egg.

Serve hot or cold.

Sufficient for six or eight pieces of toast.

NOTE.—If preferred, the mixture may be flavoured with anchovy paste instead of the mashed anchovies.

ANGELS ON HORSEBACK

INGREDIENTS.—Slices of bread, 6 small slices of bacon, 6 oysters, pepper, squeeze of lemon-juice, chopped parsley, fat for frying.

METHOD.—Cut six small oval-shaped pieces of bread about three-eighths of an inch thick, and fry them in hot fat until golden brown, then drain them and keep warm. Remove the beards from the oysters. Cut the rind from the bacon, the latter should be very thinly sliced. Place an oyster on each piece of bacon. Sprinkle with a little pepper, lemon-juice, and chopped parsley. Roll up the bacon with the oyster inside it. Fry very gently until the bacon is cooked and the oyster hot. Stand a roll on each piece of fried bread and serve on a hot dish garnished with parsley.

NOTE.—Use rather fat bacon.

APPLE AND CHEESE SAVOURY

INGREDIENTS.—1 large apple (good cooker), 1 oz. of butter, 4 squares of cheese, 4 pieces of hot buttered toast.

METHOD.—Peel and core the apple and cut it into four nice rounds. Fry the apple in the butter for about ten minutes, or till soft. Make the hot buttered toast. Put a round of apple on each piece of toast. Lay a piece of cheese on top of each apple-round and place them under the gas-griller till the cheese melts.

CREAMED ASPARAGUS

INGREDIENTS.—A tin of asparagus tips, 2 oz. of butter or margarine, 1¾ oz. of flour, 1 pint of milk, 3 oz. of cheese, salt and pepper, 2 egg-yolks, 1 dessertspoonful of onion-juice.

METHOD.—Turn out the asparagus and drain it well. Melt the butter, add the flour, and when well blended stir in the milk and bring the sauce to the boil. Boil it gently for a few minutes then draw the pan aside. Add the cheese, finely grated, the onion-juice, also beaten egg-yolks and seasoning to taste. Stir it over a low burner to cook the egg and melt the cheese, being careful not to let it boil.

Turn the mixture into a buttered fireproof dish, putting alternate layers of sauce and asparagus. Put sauce on the top and leave out a few asparagus tips for garnishing.

Cover the dish, and heat the creamed asparagus through in the oven, then arrange a few tips (heated separately) on the top.

Sufficient for four persons.

ASPARAGUS SCALLOPS

INGREDIENTS.—1½ oz. of butter, 1¼ oz. of flour, ¾ pint of milk, 2 oz. of cheese, seasoning, 1 hard-boiled egg, small tin of asparagus tips, 1 tablespoonful of breadcrumbs.

METHOD.—Melt the fat in a saucepan, add the flour, and when well blended stir in the milk and bring them to the boil.

Boil the mixture gently for a few minutes, then stir in the finely-grated cheese, keeping back one tablespoonful. Add seasoning to taste and keep stirring till the cheese is melted.

Drain the liquor from the asparagus and cut it into fairly small pieces, and chop up the egg-white and yolk together.

Butter some fireproof scallop dishes, pour a little sauce into each and add a portion of asparagus and chopped egg. Season this and cover it with sauce.

Mix the remainder of the cheese with the breadcrumbs, sprinkle it on top, heat it through in the oven, and put it under the grill to brown.

Serve each scallop garnished with an asparagus tip.

Sufficient for four persons.

ASPARAGUS SCRAMBLE

INGREDIENTS.—$1\frac{1}{2}$ gills of chopped asparagus tips, 1 pimento, 2 eggs, 1 oz. of butter, salt and pepper, 8 pieces of buttered toast.

METHOD.—Cut eight heads from the tips and put them aside for garnishing, drain the tips and chop them up. Drain them again and measure.

Chop up the pimento and add it to them with salt and pepper to taste. Beat up the eggs and mix them in.

Melt the butter in a saucepan, stir in the asparagus and egg mixture, and continue to stir until it thickens. Have eight pieces of hot buttered toast ready prepared, heap the asparagus scramble on them and garnish each with a head of asparagus.

Sufficient for eight pieces of toast.

ASPARAGUS SQUARES

INGREDIENTS.—1 small tin of asparagus tips, squares of fried bread, 4 level teaspoonfuls of flour, $\frac{3}{4}$ oz. of butter, $\frac{1}{2}$ gill of milk, $\frac{1}{2}$ gill of asparagus liquor, seasoning, 1 oz. of cheese.

METHOD.—Turn the asparagus into a pie-dish with the liquor. Save a few of the best tips for garnishing, and drain, and chop up the remainder.

Melt the butter in a saucepan. Add the flour, and when they are well blended, stir in the milk and asparagus liquor and bring the sauce to the boil. Boil it gently for a few minutes. Add the chopped asparagus, grated cheese, and seasoning to taste, and when they are hot, serve the sauce on squares of fried bread.

Garnish the squares with the few remaining tips, heated through in the remainder of the liquor.

STUFFED BAKED AUBERGINE

INGREDIENTS.—1 aubergine, 2 oz. of mushrooms, 2 tablespoonfuls of minced onion, $1\frac{1}{2}$ oz. of breadcrumbs, salt and pepper, $1\frac{1}{2}$ oz. of butter, some grated cheese.

METHOD.—Parboil the aubergine for about fifteen or twenty minutes, adding a little salt to the water, then lift it out carefully. Split it in half lengthwise, scrape out the inside and rub it through a sieve, or else chop it finely.

Peel and stalk the mushrooms, wash them in slightly salted water, then drain and chop them and fry them in the butter for a few minutes. Then take them out and fry the onion lightly. Mix these with the sieved aubergine, add the breadcrumbs and seasoning to taste. Return the mixture to the two halves and bake it about twenty minutes.

Sprinkle it lightly with finely-grated dry cheese, or buttered crumbs, before serving.

Sufficient for two persons.

BACON AND CHEESE PIE

INGREDIENTS.—About $\frac{3}{4}$ lb. of flaky pastry (see p. 252), $\frac{1}{4}$ lb. of streaky bacon, 3 oz. of cheese, 1 egg, hard-boiled, 1 raw egg, seasoning—pepper, salt and mixed mustard, a few breadcrumbs.

METHOD.—Remove the rind from the rashers and cut the bacon into dice. Mix it with the finely grated cheese and the chopped hard-boiled egg. Then season it to taste and mix the ingredients to a stiff paste with the beaten raw egg.

Roll out the pastry and cut a round for the top of the pie, roll out the remainder of the pastry and cut a round for the lining—this should be thinner than the top.

Line an enamel plate with the thinner pastry, and sprinkle about a spoonful of breadcrumbs in the base. Add the bacon and cheese mixture and spread it over as evenly as possible. Sprinkle a few more crumbs on the top, and cover the filling with pastry. Damp the rim to make the two edges adhere. Trim and decorate the edge, and make a hole in the top of the pie. If there is any pastry over make a few leaves for decorating the pie.

Brush the pie with milk and place it in a hot oven to bake. It will take from twenty to thirty minutes to cook. Serve the pie hot or cold.

Sufficient for six persons.

BACON OMELET

INGREDIENTS.—2 small rashers of streaky bacon, 2 eggs, 1 level teaspoonful of minced parsley, salt and pepper, $\frac{1}{2}$ oz. of butter, cold water.

METHOD.—Remove the rind from the rashers and cut the bacon into dice then put it into an omelet pan and fry it gently till the fat is semi-transparent.

Separate the eggs and beat up the yolks, season them with pepper and salt, add the parsley and a dessert-spoonful of cold water. Now whisk the egg-whites to a stiff froth, and combine them with the yolks, folding them together lightly.

Add the butter to the bacon in the omelet pan (if the bacon is fat you may not require quite so much butter), and when it is hot, turn the egg mixture into the pan.

Cook the omelet till the underpart is golden, drawing it towards the handle of the pan. Then place the pan under the hot grill for a few seconds to brown the top of the omelet.

Serve it at once on a hot plate.

Sufficient for one person.

BACON AND PRUNE SAVOURY

INGREDIENTS.—6 prunes, 6 thin rashers of bacon, salt and pepper, 6 almonds, 6 small slices of bread.

METHOD.—Wash the prunes and soak them overnight, then stew them gently until tender. Remember that you must not add any sugar.

When cooked, drain off the water, split each prune down one side, remove the stone and season the inside with salt and pepper. Then insert a blanched almond and close it up again.

Cut the rind from the rashers and roll up a prune inside each rasher. Put them into a baking-tin and cook them gently in the oven until the bacon fat is semi-transparent.

Meanwhile, cut slices of bread the same size as the rolls and fry or grill them in some bacon fat until they are golden brown.

Serve a roll on each piece of bread, arrange on a hot plate covered with a lace paper, and garnish with parsley.

Allow one or two for each person.

GRILLED BACON AND SCRAMBLED EGGS

INGREDIENTS.—4 streaky rashers, 4 slices of bread, 2 eggs, 1 oz. of butter, salt, pepper, 2 tablespoonfuls of milk.

METHOD.—Remove the rind from the rashers and cut four strips of bread about toast thickness, and rather smaller than the rashers.

Put both the rashers and the bread in the bottom of the grill-tin, having removed the rack from the tin, then put the tin under the hot grill and cook them for a few minutes until the fat is semi-transparent, keeping them turned. The bread should be turned over when brown.

Serve a rasher on each finger of bread, pour the bacon fat round, and arrange the scrambled eggs in alternate lines with the bacon.

TO SCRAMBLE THE EGGS.—Beat them up and mix them with the milk, add seasoning to taste. Melt the butter, add the egg mixture, and stir them over a low burner until thick and creamy. A little chopped parsley may be added to this, if liked.

Sufficient for two persons.

BACON AND TOMATO TOAST

INGREDIENTS.—4 rounds of bread, 4 slices of tomato, 4 rashers of bacon, butter, seasoning, parsley for decorating.

METHOD.—Toast the bread only on one side and butter the untoasted side.

Remove the rind from the bacon. Put the rashers through the mincer and fry them until they are tender. Heap the minced bacon on the French toast. Place a lightly cooked slice of tomato (seasoning with salt and pepper) on top, and garnish the savoury with a small sprig of parsley.

BACON, TOMATO AND SAUSAGE

INGREDIENTS.—½ lb. of sausages, 3 streaky rashers, 3 tomatoes, ½ an egg, breadcrumbs, dripping, seasoning.

METHOD.—Skin the sausages and divide the whole into six portions. Shape these into round cakes with flattened tops. Brush them with egg and coat them with breadcrumbs and fry them gently in the dripping until brown.

Meanwhile halve the tomatoes crosswise, sprinkle them with salt and pepper and bake them lightly, being careful to prevent them breaking. Place half a tomato on each round of sausage and top it with a roll of bacon.

To prepare the bacon rolls, remove the rind, halve the rashers crosswise and roll up each piece. Stick them on a skewer and cook them in the oven or under the grill until the fat is semi-transparent.

Allow two for each person.

BANANA AND CHEESE SAVOURY

INGREDIENTS.—3 bananas, 1 tablespoonful of capers, ¼ lb. of cheese, 6 fingers of brown bread-and-butter, anchovy paste.

METHOD.—Spread the fingers of brown bread-and-butter with anchovy paste.

Cut the cheese into thin fingers, and place one on each finger of bread.

Skin the bananas and cut them in half lengthways.

Put a banana flat side down on each piece of cheese, and decorate it down the centre with a row of capers.

Sufficient for six persons.

BATTER TIMBALES
(WITH MEAT FILLING)

INGREDIENTS.—½ lb. of cold meat, 1 pimento, 2 teaspoonfuls of onion-juice, ¼ teaspoonful of chopped parsley, salt and pepper, 1 oz. of margarine, ¾ oz. of flour, ½ pint of milk, deep hot lard for frying.

FOR THE BATTER.—¼ lb. of flour, a pinch of salt, 1 egg, 1 gill of milk.

METHOD.—Sift the flour and salt, whisk the egg, and stir it in gradually with the milk, and mix to a smooth batter. Beat it well, and let it stand for about an hour or so.

When ready to fry, heat some lard in a saucepan, and when hot put in the timbale iron (sometimes known as a fairy mould) and make it warm, then put it into the prepared batter and coat it thinly, being careful not to let it come over the top. If the batter is too thick, thin it down, if too thin, add a little more flour. Return the coated iron to the hot fat and fry for a minute until golden, then lift off the case and drain the timbale on paper.

Fry the remainder of the batter in the same way, then put a meat filling in the centre of each timbale, and serve them hot.

To PREPARE THE FILLING.—Cut the meat in small dice and mix it with the chopped pimento and finely-chopped parsley. Melt the margarine and three-quarters of an ounce of flour, and when well blended stir in the milk and bring it to the boil. Let it simmer for a minute or two, add the onion-juice, prepared meat, and seasoning to taste, and make this filling hot.

Sufficient to make about fifteen timbales.

BLOATER SAVOURY

INGREDIENTS.—1 large cold bloater, 2 oz. of butter, ½ jar of bloater paste, 5 or 6 fingers of toast.

METHOD.—Make the toast and let it get cold. Cut the flesh from the bloater, keeping the pieces as whole as possible, and removing all skin and bones.

Spread the fingers of toast with a little butter and paste, and lay a nice piece of bloater on each.

Cream the rest of the butter and put it in an icing pump with a rose tube screwed on at the end.

Decorate the fingers by forcing on butter roses, or, if preferred, sprinkle with a little chopped white of egg and parsley.

One large bloater makes about five fingers.

BOBOTJES
(AN INDIAN RECIPE)

INGREDIENTS.—1 large onion, 1 cup of cold meat, 1 cup of bread-crumbs, juice of ½ lemon, 1 egg, ¼ pint of stock (see p. 12) or water, ½ oz. of curry-powder, 1 oz. of flour, 1 oz. of margarine, ¼ teaspoonful of salt, parsley for garnishing, ½ gill of water.

METHOD.—Put the meat through a mincer. Chop the onion and fry it in the margarine for six minutes.

Stir in the flour, curry-powder, and lemon-juice, add the stock, and stir the sauce till it boils.

Put the meat, breadcrumbs, and half the sauce into a saucepan and mix them over a low gas.

Add the beaten egg, season to taste with salt and put the mixture into greased cups.

Cover with greased paper and bake for thirty minutes.

Heat the remainder of the sauce with half a gill of water. Turn out the bobotjes into a hot dish and pour the sauce round them. Garnish with parsley.

NOTE.—This dish can also be made with fish.

BREAKFAST TOASTS

INGREDIENTS.—½ lb. of fat streaky rashers, 2 medium - sized cooking apples, oblongs of bread.

METHOD.—Remove the rind from the rashers and put the bacon through the mincer.

Peel and core the apples and cut them into thick slices.

Fry the bacon till it is crisp, then drain off the fat into another pan. Make it hot again and fry the apple rings till they are golden-brown and tender. Take them up and put them on a plate.

Fry the oblongs of bread till golden, adding some butter to the fat, if there is not sufficient left after frying the apple rings.

To serve the Breakfast Toasts, cover the fried bread with the minced bacon, place an apple ring on each piece and heap a little minced bacon in the centre of it.

Sufficient for four pieces of bread.

BUCK RAREBIT

INGREDIENTS.—6 eggs, 6 slices of buttered toast, 2 oz. of butter, 8 oz. of cheese, salt and pepper, 2 flat teaspoonfuls of mixed mustard, 2 or 3 tablespoonfuls of milk.

METHOD.—Prepare six slices of buttered toast. Remove the rind and grate the cheese on a bread-grater. Melt the butter in a saucepan, stir in the grated cheese, add the milk, and stir all together at the side of the fire until creamy. Be careful not to overheat it, or it will become oily. Season well and add the mustard.

Spread evenly on the slices of buttered toast and keep warm while the eggs are poached.

To POACH AN EGG.—Put about one pint of water into a frying-pan, add a flat teaspoonful of salt.

Bring the water to the boil. Very carefully break the egg into a cup, then put into the frying-pan and simmer slowly until the white is firm. Cut away any rough edges. Lift out with a fish-slice and place on to the prepared toast and serve.

SAVOURY CABBAGE

INGREDIENTS.—1 cabbage, 1 onion (grated), 2 sausages, salt and pepper.

METHOD.—Cut the cabbage in four and remove the coarse stalk.

After washing the cabbage, place it in a large pan of boiling water with a dessertspoonful of salt and boil it quickly with the lid off till tender.

Fry the sausages slowly for ten minutes and then cut them up small.

Pour the cabbage on to a sieve. Press out the water and chop it small.

Put the cabbage back in the saucepan with the sausages and onion. Season with salt and pepper, stir well, and serve hot.

Sufficient for two or three persons.

STUFFED CABBAGE EN CAS-SEROLE

INGREDIENTS.—1 young cabbage, ½ lb. of sausage meat, 1 onion, 1 dessertspoonful of chopped parsley, 2 oz. of butter, 2 oz. of flour, 1 pint of boiling water, 1 dessertspoonful of Bisto, salt and pepper, ¼ teaspoonful of Marmite.

METHOD.—Separate the leaves of the cabbage, remove some of the coarse stalk and wash well.

Pour boiling water on eight nice leaves and soak them for fifteen minutes. Chop the onion and parsley, and mix them with the sausage meat.

Lay some of the sausage mixture on each leaf, and roll it up.

Place the rolls in a casserole with the butter, and cook for fifteen minutes. Add the boiling water, replace the lid and cook slowly till tender—about an hour.

Place the rolls in a vegetable dish, and put them to keep warm.

Put the Marmite into the water in the casserole.

Mix the Bisto to a smooth liquid with a little cold water, pour it into the casserole and stir till it boils. Boil for two minutes and pour over the cabbage rolls.

NOTE.—Stuffed cabbage will cook equally well in a wide, shallow stew-pan on the gas instead of in the oven.

Cabbage cooked in this way is far more nourishing than if boiled with soda in the old-fashioned way. Soda destroys the vitamines.

Enough for four or five persons.

YOUNG CARROTS AND CHEESE SAUCE

INGREDIENTS.—½ bunch of young carrots, slices of bread, as required, butter.

FOR THE SAUCE.—1 oz. of flour. 1 oz. of margarine, ½ pint of milk or milk and water, 3 oz. of grated cheese, salt and pepper.

METHOD.—Scrape the carrots and cook in boiling water with a little salt added. Drain and split into halves. Cut as many oblong pieces of bread as you have carrots, toast and butter them, then arrange two halves of carrot on each piece.

Make a thick white sauce and, when it boils, stir in the cheese, grated finely. Season to taste and cook for a few minutes. Then coat the carrots and toast with the cheese sauce, and serve them with some finely-grated cheese sprinkled over.

Allow one or two for each person.

CAULIFLOWER FRITTERS

INGREDIENTS.—¼ lb. of flour, pinch of salt, 1 egg-white, ¼ pint of water, 1 cauliflower, seasoning, vinegar, deep fat for frying.

METHOD.—Sieve the flour and salt and mix to a smooth batter with the water. Whisk the egg-white until slightly frothy and stir in.

Beat well for a few minutes, then leave the batter to stand for at least an hour.

Take the cauliflower—use only the white.

Break it into small, neat branches and soak them well in cold salted water.

Then put into boiling water to which a little salt has been added (use about one tablespoonful to two quarts of water), and cook gently

until tender, but take care it does not break.

Drain them well, then sprinkle with pepper and salt and a few drops of vinegar.

Take a deep pan about half full of dripping and put on to heat ; it will be sufficiently hot when a faint blue smoke rises from it.

Dip each piece of prepared cauliflower in the batter, coat them well, then lift them into the hot fat and fry until golden brown. Then drain well on paper.

Only fry four or five pieces at a time.

Remember to lift them into the fat with an iron skewer.

Re-heat the fat before frying the next batch.

When all are cooked, serve on a dish-paper at once and sprinkle with salt.

CHEESE CAULIFLOWER

INGREDIENTS.—1 cauliflower (medium size), boiling water, salt and soda, 2 oz. of butter or margarine, 3 oz. of cheese, 1½ oz. of flour, 2 gills of milk, 1 gill of water, pepper and salt, a few browned crumbs.

METHOD.—Choose a nice firm cauliflower, take away the stump and outside leaves, just leaving sufficient green round to keep the cauliflower together.

Wash it well and leave it to soak for about an hour in plenty of cold water with a little salt added.

Then put it into a saucepan of boiling water with a tiny piece of soda and about a tablespoonful of salt to half a gallon of water.

Boil gently until tender, keeping the flower downwards. It will take about thirty minutes.

TO MAKE THE SAUCE.—Melt the margarine in a saucepan, stir in the flour until quite smooth.

Add the milk and water gradually, keeping it well stirred until it comes to the boil.

Season with pepper and salt, and let the sauce simmer for about six minutes.

Grate the cheese finely, add about half of it to the sauce, and stir it round. The sauce should be sufficiently thick to coat the cauliflower.

Keep it hot, and dish up the cauliflower.

Lift this carefully out of the water with a fish-slice, and put it into a colander to drain.

Place in an *au gratin* or earthenware dish, pour over it the prepared sauce.

Sprinkle the remainder of the cheese on the top, also a teaspoonful of browned crumbs.

Put under the grill for a few minutes until golden brown on the top. Serve hot.

CAULIFLOWER AND TOMATO SOUFFLE

INGREDIENTS.—1 cold cauliflower, 1 lb. of tomatoes, 1½ oz. of butter, 1 oz. of flour, 3½ oz. of grated cheese, 2 eggs, 1½ gills of milk, salt and pepper, 1 tablespoonful of breadcrumbs.

METHOD.—Slice the tomatoes and divide the cauliflower into sprigs.

Put the tomato and cauliflower into a fireproof dish and season them with salt and pepper and two ounces of the cheese.

Melt one ounce of the butter, stir in the flour and add the milk gradually. Stir till it boils.

Take the pan off the gas and add one ounce of cheese and the beaten yolks of eggs.

Stir in the stiffly-beaten whites and pour over the cauliflower.

Sprinkle with breadcrumbs and the rest of the cheese and place the rest of the butter in small dabs on top.

Bake in a moderate oven for forty-five minutes. Serve in the same dish.

CELERY AND CHEESE SAUCE

INGREDIENTS.—1 large head of celery, salt, boiling water, ½ pint of milk or milk-and-water, 1 oz. of margarine, 1 oz. of flour, pepper and salt, 5 oz. of cheese.

METHOD.—Remove the outside stalks, etc., and prepare the celery in the usual way, dividing it into about six or eight pieces lengthwise.

Wash thoroughly. Then cook in boiling water with a little salt until tender. It will take about thirty minutes.

When cooked, drain well, cut into short lengths, and put into a fireproof dish.

Melt the fat in a saucepan, stir in the flour, and when mixed smoothly add the milk and stir until the sauce boils.

Add about three parts of the cheese (grated finely) and cook for a few minutes until melted and the sauce cooked. Season well with salt and pepper, then pour over the celery and sprinkle the remainder of cheese on the top.

Put under the hot grill to brown and serve hot, garnished with a little uncooked celery.

Sufficient for four persons.

CELERY IN GRAVY

INGREDIENTS.—2 young heads of celery, 1 oz. of butter, 1 teaspoonful of meat extract, ½ oz. of flour, 1 teaspoonful of Bisto, ½ pint of hot stock (see p. 12), or meat gravy, 2 or 3 slices of fried bread, 2 or 3 rashers of bacon (according to whether the heads of celery are large or small), 2 oz. of dripping.

METHOD.—Remove the leaves and some of the coarse outer stalks from the celery, and use these for soup.

Wash the celery and cut it into strips an inch long. Put it in a double pan with the butter and hot stock, and see that the water in the lower pan is boiling.

Cook for fifty minutes with the lid on.

Strain off the liquid.

Mix the flour and Bisto with half a gill of cold water, and pour the hot liquid on to them.

Return this liquid to the pan, stir till it boils. Boil for three minutes.

Season to taste and keep hot while frying the rashers of bacon and bread. Cut the rind off the bacon, put the rashers in a warm pan and fry them for about six minutes, till they are transparent. Turn frequently.

Fry the bread in the dripping, made smoking hot. Turn it over when one side is done. Put the fried bread in a hot dish, pour the celery over it and serve the bacon on top.

Sufficient for two or three persons.

STUFFED CELERY

INGREDIENTS.—1 head of celery, 3 oz. of cream cheese, 1 oz. of shelled walnuts, pepper and salt, mixed mustard.

METHOD.—Remove all the outside leaves and trim the celery in the usual way. Divide into four lengthwise, wash it thoroughly and drain well.

Separate the stalks and stuff the groove of each with the cheese and walnut stuffing.

To prepare the stuffing, beat the cheese until soft and creamy, chop the walnuts and mix with it, adding seasoning to taste.

Sufficient for four persons.

CHEESE AIGRETTES

INGREDIENTS.—2 oz. of cheese, $\frac{3}{4}$ oz. of butter or margarine, 1 gill of water, 2 oz. of flour, pepper and salt, 1 egg, deep fat for frying.

METHOD.—Grate the cheese very finely. Use either Cheddar or Parmesan.

Put the water and butter in a saucepan and bring to the boil.

Sieve the flour ; the latter must be very accurately weighed.

When the water is boiling add the flour, and stir quickly over the fire until the mixture will easily leave the sides of the saucepan, then draw to the side of the fire and let it cool slightly. Add the egg and stir it in quickly.

Add three-quarters of the grated cheese and season well with salt and pepper.

When thoroughly mixed, spread on a plate and leave until cool.

Put a deep pan of fat on to get hot, and leave until a faint blue smoke rises from it.

Take a teaspoon and dip in the fat, then fill it with the cheese mixture and drop gently into the hot fat with the aid of another teaspoon (also dipped in fat).

Continue in this way until the pan is sufficiently full, leaving room for them to swell.

Fry until golden brown—they will take about twenty minutes. Drain on paper.

Serve at once on a lace paper, and sprinkle the remainder of the cheese over them.

NOTE.—Use stale, hard cheese for this dish.

FLUFFY CHEESE BALLS

INGREDIENTS.—3 whites of eggs, $\frac{1}{4}$ lb. Cheddar cheese, cayenne pepper, deep fat for frying.

METHOD.—Heat the pan containing the fat.

Grate up the cheese very finely, having first removed the rind.

Then whisk up the eggs into a stiff froth. A pinch of salt should be added before beating up the whites. Fold the grated cheese into the whisked whites and flavour with cayenne.

Mix all lightly together.

When the fat in the pan commences to smoke slightly, drop in a teaspoonful of the mixture. In a few seconds the little white lump puffs up into a large ball, turns golden brown and floats.

Take it out with a fish-slice, and drain it on paper.

Re-heat the fat and fry the others in the same way. Three or four can be cooked at a time.

Heap them on a dish paper and serve at once.

These should be served as a savoury.

CHEESE FRITTERS

INGREDIENTS.—$\frac{1}{4}$ lb. of flour, $\frac{1}{2}$ teaspoonful of baking-powder, 2 tablespoonfuls of beer, $\frac{3}{4}$ lb. of cheese, pinch of salt, 2 teaspoonfuls of salad oil, $\frac{3}{4}$ to 1 gill of water, deep fat for frying.

METHOD.—Mix the flour and salt together and pass through a sieve.

Make a hole in the centre of it and pour in the oil, mixing it with a little flour. Then add the beer and more flour. Gradually add the water, and by degrees the remainder of the flour.

Keep an even consistency all the time. When well mixed, beat for about ten minutes, until the surface is full of bubbles.

Set aside for at least an hour.

Remove the cheese rind. Then cut the cheese into pieces about two or three inches long and one inch wide, and a quarter of an inch thick.

Put the pan of fat on the fire and heat it until a faint smoke arises from it.

Mix the baking-powder into the

batter, then put four or five pieces of cheese into it and well coat them.

Lift them into the hot fat and fry until well browned. The cheese will then be thoroughly cooked.

Drain well on paper, re-heat the fat, and fry the others in the same way.

When all are cooked, place on a dish-paper, garnish with parsley and serve at once.

NOTE.—The pan must be not more than half full of fat.

The batter must be thick enough to coat the cheese.

Sufficient for six or eight persons.

CHEESE CREAM

INGREDIENTS.—1 lettuce, 1 cream cheese, 1 egg, ½ gill of salad oil, 2 tablespoonfuls of vinegar, 2 teaspoonfuls of meat extract, 1 teaspoonful of made mustard, ¾ pint of cold water, 1 oz. of leaf gelatine, cayenne, salt, 3d. of cream.

METHOD.—Break up the gelatine and soak it in the cold water for five minutes. Dissolve it on a low gas, stirring well, and then strain.

Put the yolk of the egg in a basin and add the oil gradually, stirring all the time. Add the vinegar.

Cream the cheese with a wooden spoon and work into it the mayonnaise just made with yolk, oil, and vinegar. Add also the meat extract, mustard, and cream.

To this soft cream mixture stir in little by little the dissolved gelatine and whisk with an egg whisk to make the cream nice and smooth.

Season to taste with salt and cayenne and leave it till it begins to set. Whisk well again.

Rinse a pint mould or basin in cold water and pour in the mixture. When set, dip the mould in warm water, shake on to the hand and slide on to a dish lined with well-washed lettuce leaves.

NOTE.—This is a delicious savoury to eat with salad. Sufficient for four persons.

CHEESE CREAMS

INGREDIENTS.—Aspic jelly or savoury calf's foot jelly about ½ pint, 1 gill of cream, 2 oz. of cheese, seasoning, black truffle.

METHOD.—Melt about half of the aspic jelly. Take four or five small plain moulds and rinse with cold water, then pour in sufficient jelly just to cover the bottom of each. Cut some truffle into small half-moon shapes, dip them in jelly, and set in the bottom of the moulds.

When quite firm, cover with some more jelly and set again.

Grate the cheese very finely; all Cheddar cheese can be used, but a mixture of Parmesan and Gruyère cheese gives the creams a better flavour.

Whisk the cream until it stiffens, and stir in the grated cheese.

Season with cayenne and salt to taste, and a little mixed mustard.

Take three-quarters of a gill of melted aspic jelly and stir into the cream lightly; the jelly must not be hot when added.

Stir until it begins to thicken, then pour quickly into the prepared moulds and leave until quite set.

Dip each into warm water and turn carefully on to a dish.

Chop the remainder of the aspic jelly, and serve round.

CHEESE CROQUETTES

INGREDIENTS.—2½ oz. of fine breadcrumbs, salt and cayenne, 1 egg, deep hot fat, 5 or 6 oz. of grated cheese.

METHOD.—Mix the dry ingredients well together and moisten them with the egg.

Form the mixture into small balls and dip each one into some beaten egg.

Coat it with the fine breadcrumbs and fry the croquettes in boiling fat.

Cheese croquettes may be served with any green salad.

CHEESE EGGS

INGREDIENTS.—4 eggs, 1½ oz. of butter, 1 teaspoonful of chopped parsley, 4 dessertspoonfuls of grated cheese, salt and pepper, hot buttered toast.

METHOD.—Make four pieces of hot buttered toast and keep them warm. Beat up the eggs. Grate the cheese finely and add to them. Wash, scald, and chop the parsley finely and add this also.

Mix together and season with pepper and salt. Melt the butter in a small saucepan, add the eggs, etc.

Stir over a very low gas until the cheese melts and the eggs thicken and set. Heap on the toast and serve at once.

Sufficient for four persons.

CHEESE EGGS ON TURNIP TOPS

INGREDIENTS.—3 lb. of turnip tops, 4 eggs, 4 dessertspoonfuls of grated cheese, 1 oz. of margarine, salt and pepper.

METHOD.—Remove the outer leaves and stalks from the turnip tops, wash them in cold water with salt added, and leave them soaking for a time, to cleanse them. When ready to cook, lift them from the water into a colander to drain. Put them into plenty of boiling water with salt and soda (one tablespoonful of salt, and enough soda to cover a threepenny-piece to about every two quarts of water). Bring them to the boil quickly, remove the lid, and boil the greens until tender, keeping them skimmed as required. They will take about twenty minutes to cook.

Strain and drain them well and squeeze out as much water as possible. Chop them up on a board. Return them to the saucepan with the margarine. Season and make them quite hot again, then put them into a dish and arrange the cheese eggs on the top. A few sippets of toast or fried bread may also be added.

To prepare the eggs, poach them in the usual way, lift them on to a plate and sprinkle a dessertspoonful of cheese over each yolk. Put them under the grill to melt the cheese, being careful not to make the eggs hard.

Sufficient for four persons.

CHEESE FLAKES

INGREDIENTS.—2 oz. of cheese, salt and cayenne, ¼ lb. of flaky pastry (see p. 252), white of egg.

METHOD.—Grate the cheese finely. Take a good flaky crust and roll it out very thinly, then turn it on to the other side.

Beat up the white of egg until slightly frothy.

Cut the pastry into small squares. Take one-third of the squares and brush them over with some of the white of egg.

Sprinkle grated cheese over, then season with salt and cayenne.

Place another square on the top of each, press it down lightly, brush over with white of egg, and sprinkle with cheese as before, then cover with another square and again press lightly.

Brush the tops with white of egg. Place on a baking-sheet.

Bake in a hot oven for from ten to fifteen minutes.

CHEESE FLAN

INGREDIENTS.—4 oz. of cheese, 1 yolk of egg, 1 tablespoonful of chopped pimento, strips of pimento for top of flan, 2 oz. of butter or margarine, 1½ oz. of flour, ¾ pint of milk, salt and cayenne.

FOR THE PASTRY.—6 oz. of flour, ½ teaspoonful of baking-powder, 4 oz. of margarine, water to mix, a pinch of salt.

METHOD.—TO MAKE THE FLAN CASE : Sift the flour with baking-powder and a pinch of salt. Rub in the margarine and mix to a stiff paste with cold water. Grease a flan-ring, and place it on a greased baking-sheet, roll out the pastry, cut a round and line the flan-ring and centre of the baking-sheet. Trim the edge, line the pastry with a round of buttered paper and sprinkle rice in the bottom. Put the case in a hot oven to bake and when the pastry is set remove the paper and rice, and finish cooking the pastry, then lift up the flan-ring.

Meanwhile, prepare the filling. Melt the butter in a saucepan, add the flour and when well blended stir in the milk and bring it to the boil. Boil it gently for a few minutes, then draw the pan aside, add the finely-grated cheese, chopped pimento, seasoning to taste, and the beaten egg-yolk. Stir the filling over a low burner to melt the cheese, and cook the egg, but do not let it boil, then turn it into the prepared pastry case, and garnish it with strips of pimento. Serve Cheese Flan hot.

Sufficient for four persons.

CHEESE AND MACARONI PUDDING

INGREDIENTS.—2 oz. of macaroni, ¼ lb. of cheese, 2 oz. of soft brown breadcrumbs, 1 oz. of white breadcrumbs, ½ pint of milk, 2 eggs, 1½ pimentos, salt and pepper.

METHOD.—Put the macaroni into a pan of slightly salted boiling water and boil it till it is tender, then drain it and chop it into small pieces.

Make the brown and white breadcrumbs, heat the milk and pour it over the breadcrumbs, and let them soak.

Meanwhile, grate the cheese finely, chop up the pimentos and beat the eggs.

Add these prepared ingredients to the soaked crumbs and mix them all together.

Add also the chopped macaroni and seasoning to taste. Then turn the mixture into a buttered basin, cover it securely with a buttered paper and steam it for from one and a half to two hours.

Unmould the pudding, and serve it plain, or with white sauce (see p. 364).

CHEESE AND POTATO BALLS

INGREDIENTS.—1½ lb. of potatoes, ½ oz. of butter of margarine, 2 oz. of cheese (grated), pepper and salt, 1 egg and 1 extra yolk, breadcrumbs, deep fat for frying.

METHOD.—Peel the potatoes and put them on to boil with sufficient water to cover them, and a little salt. Cook gently until tender, strain off the water and dry them in the steam for a few minutes.

Well mash them with a fork, or rub them through a wire sieve.

Put them back into the saucepan, add the yolk of egg, grated cheese, and butter.

Season well and stir at the side of the fire for a few minutes until the egg is cooked and the cheese melted.

Put on to a plate and leave until cold.

Divide into equal portions and make into balls ; slightly flour if necessary. Brush over with egg. Coat with the white breadcrumbs.

Place in a frying-basket in a deep pan of hot fat and fry until golden brown.

Drain well on paper.

Serve on a dish paper, garnish with fried parsley.

CHEESE AND POTATO PIE

INGREDIENTS.—2 lb. of freshly boiled potatoes, ¼ cup of milk, ¼ lb. of cheese, 1 thick slice of bread, 1 oz. of bacon fat, salt and pepper.

METHOD.—Mash the potatoes with a fork and stir in the milk and half the bacon fat. Add salt and pepper to taste.

Crumble the bread, chop the cheese and mix them together.

Put layers of potato and bread and cheese into a greased pie-dish.

Put dabs of bacon fat on top and bake for twenty minutes.

Sufficient for three persons.

CHEESE PUFF

INGREDIENTS.—2½ oz. of finely-grated cheese, 2 yolks and 3 whites of eggs, 1 oz. of butter or margarine, 1 oz. of flour, ¼ pint of milk, seasoning.

METHOD.—Melt the butter in a saucepan, stir in the flour and when well blended add the milk and bring them to the boil. Boil for a minute or two, keeping the sauce stirred, when draw aside. Add the finely-grated cheese, then the beaten egg-yolks and seasoning to taste. Whisk the whites to a stiff froth and fold them in lightly. Turn the mixture into buttered ramequins and bake it in a fairly hot oven until well puffed up and golden brown. Serve at once with finely grated cheese sprinkled over.

Sufficient for six puffs.

CHEESE PUDDING

INGREDIENTS.—3 thin slices of bread-and-butter, 2 oz. of cheese (grated), 1 egg, ½ teaspoonful of made mustard, ½ pint of milk, pepper and salt.

METHOD.—Spread the bread-and-butter with a little mustard.

Put alternate layers of bread-and-butter and grated cheese seasoned with salt and pepper into a fireproof dish. Beat the eggs and stir in the milk.

Pour the egg and milk over the

bread and bake the pudding in a slow oven for about forty-five minutes or till set.

NOTE.—If this pudding is baked too quickly it will be watery.

CHEESE SAUSAGES

INGREDIENTS.—1 oz. of Parmesan cheese, 2 oz. of Cheddar cheese, 1 whole egg and 1 yolk, 1 oz. of margarine ¼ pint of milk, 2 oz. of flour, salt and cayenne, egg and breadcrumbs, deep fat for frying.

METHOD.—Melt the margarine in a saucepan, add the milk, and bring it to the boil, then stir in the flour (sifted) and continue stirring until the mixture becomes thick and smooth and leaves the sides of the pan, then draw the pan aside and cool the mixture a little.

Add the egg-yolk, and when well mixed in, add the whole egg, and beat it well for a few minutes. Stir in the finely grated cheese, add seasoning to taste, then turn the mixture on to a plate and leave it till firm.

Divide the firm mixture into twelve portions. Form them into sausage shapes, brush them with egg and coat them with breadcrumbs, then put them into a frying-basket and fry them in hot, deep fat until golden brown.

Drain the cheese sausages and serve them garnished with parsley.

Sufficient to make twelve sausages.

CHEESE SOUFFLE

INGREDIENTS. — 1 tumblerful of breadcrumbs, pressed down (4 oz.), 1½ pints of milk, 1 onion, 5 oz. of grated cheese, 2 eggs, salt, pepper, mustard, 1 oz. of butter.

METHOD.—Peel the onion and put it into the saucepan with the milk and let it stand for about an hour at the side of the fire, then bring it to the boil.

Add the butter. Make the breadcrumbs and stir into the milk, and leave it to stand again at the side of the fire until the crumbs are well soaked.

Remove the onion. Grate the cheese and mix it into the breadcrumbs and milk. Stir over a low gas for a few minutes.

Season well with salt, pepper, and

mixed mustard, then let it cool slightly.

Separate the whites from the yolks of eggs.

Beat up the yolks and add gradually to the breadcrumbs and stir quickly for a few minutes.

Add a pinch of salt to the whites of eggs and whisk them to a stiff froth, then fold them into the other ingredients very lightly.

Put into a greased pie-dish and bake in a moderately hot oven for about thirty minutes.

SMALL CHEESE SOUFFLES

INGREDIENTS.—2 oz. of cheese, 1 yolk and 2 whites of eggs, salt, pepper and mixed mustard, 1 gill of milk, ½ gill of water, 4 sheets of leaf gelatine.

METHOD.—Beat up the yolk of the egg, heat the milk and add to it and cook in a double boiler until it thickens, keeping it stirred occasionally. Remove from the pan and leave until cold.

Grate the cheese very finely (use a hard, well-flavoured cheese) and add to the custard. Season with salt, pepper and mixed mustard.

Dissolve the gelatine in a saucepan with the water and strain into the cheese mixture. Leave until beginning to set. Whisk the egg-whites to a very stiff froth and fold in lightly. Put in small soufflé cases, and, when quite set, sprinkle a little finely-grated cheese on the top of each.

Sufficient to fill ten small soufflé cases.

BAKED CHEESE SOUFFLES

INGREDIENTS.—1½ oz. dry Cheddar cheese, 1½ oz. of Parmesan cheese, 1 oz. of butter, 3 level dessertspoonfuls of flour, 1 gill of milk, salt and cayenne pepper, 2 yolks of eggs, 3 whites of eggs.

METHOD.—Melt the butter in a saucepan, add the flour and when well blended stir in the milk and bring them to the boil. Cook the mixture for a minute or two, still stirring, then draw the pan aside and allow it to cool slightly. Beat in the egg-yolks one at a time, then add the finely-grated cheese, keeping out a little for decoration. Season the mixture and fold in the stiffly-whisked egg-whites.

Turn the soufflé into small buttered soufflé dishes, filling them about half or two-thirds full, and bake them in a moderately hot oven until well risen and golden. They will take about fifteen minutes to cook. Serve soufflés immediately, with a little finely-grated cheese sprinkled on the top.

Sufficient for six persons.

CHEESE STICKS

INGREDIENTS.—10 oz. of flaky pastry (see p. 252), 3 oz. of Parmesan cheese, salt and cayenne, egg.

METHOD.—Grate the cheese finely and divide it into four portions.

Roll out the pastry quite thinly to an oblong shape, turn it on to the other side, damp one-half of it slightly and sprinkle it with one portion of the cheese. Season this with salt and cayenne, then fold the other half over it and press the edges firmly together.

Roll the pastry out again to an oblong shape and repeat this process three times more, until all the cheese is used, being careful to fold and roll evenly. Roll out the pastry to barely one-fourth of an inch thick and cut it into strips half an inch wide and about five and a half inches long. Place these on a baking-sheet, brush the tops with egg, and bake them in a hot oven for about ten minutes.

Sufficient to make about thirty sticks.

CHEESE STRAWS

INGREDIENTS.—2½ oz. of cheese, 2½ oz. of flour, 2 oz. of butter or margarine, seasoning, 1 yolk of egg.

METHOD.—Sieve the flour. Grate the cheese very finely and add it. Use a piece of stale Cheddar or Parmesan cheese. Chop the fat finely into the flour. Season with salt and pepper and mix all the dry ingredients together.

Beat up the yolk of egg and mix two or three teaspoonfuls of water with it. Add this to the flour and mix to a stiff paste, adding more water if required. Put it on to a slightly-floured board and roll out to one-eighth of an inch thick. Cut it into strips about three inches and a half in length, and place on a baking-sheet,

lined with paper, very slightly buttered. Put the trimmings together and roll out again as before.

Cut into rings about one-eighth of an inch in width and about an inch in diameter.

Put these also on to the baking-sheet and bake in a moderately hot oven for about ten to fifteen minutes, or until crisp and a pale biscuit colour.

Place on a sieve to cool, then serve on a lace paper, arranging the strips in the rings.

CREAMED CHEESE TOAST

INGREDIENTS.—¾ oz. of butter, salt, 1 egg, 1½ oz. of grated cheese, ¾ oz. of flour, 1¼ gills of milk, hot buttered toast.

METHOD.—Melt the butter in a saucepan and stir in the flour and salt. When it is smooth, add the milk slowly and stir the mixture constantly until it boils.

Boil it gently for a few minutes, then place the mixture over hot water. Add the cheese and cook it till it melts, stirring all the time.

Add the beaten egg and slowly cook the mixture till it thickens again. Serve the creamed cheese on rounds of hot buttered toast.

Sufficient for four persons.

PUFFED CHEESE TOAST

INGREDIENTS.—2 squares of bread, 2 oz. of cheese (finely grated), 2 egg-whites, ¼ level teaspoonful of chopped chives, seasoning, butter.

METHOD.—Cut the bread toast thickness, toast it on one side, remove the crusts and butter the untoasted side.

Whisk the egg-whites to a stiff froth, then lightly stir in the finely-grated cheese, chopped chives and seasoning to taste.

Cover the two slices of prepared toast with this mixture and bake them till golden. Serve the Puffed Cheese Toasts garnished with parsley.

CHEESE AND TOMATO ROLL

INGREDIENTS.—6 oz. of wholemeal, 6 oz. of flour, 6 oz. of margarine, 1 flat teaspoonful of baking-powder, water to mix, ¾ lb. of tomatoes, 4 oz. of breadcrumbs, 3 oz. of cheese, pepper and salt, 1 egg.

METHOD—Bake the tomatoes until tender, then rub them through a sieve. Grate the cheese finely and add it with the breadcrumbs, then season to taste. Beat up the egg and add it also, and mix all well together.

Sieve the flour, wholemeal, and baking-powder. Rub in the margarine, then add cold water and mix them to a stiff paste. Divide it into two portions and roll each out to an oblong shape. Spread each oblong with the tomato mixture, damp the edges and roll up neatly.

Brush the rolls with milk and put them into a fairly hot oven at first. They will take about half an hour to bake.

Sufficient to make two rolls.

CHESTNUT SAVOURY

INGREDIENTS.—1 lb. of chestnuts, 1 egg, 2 oz. of butter, 1 oz. of flour, $\frac{1}{4}$ teaspoonful of dried herbs, $\frac{1}{4}$ teaspoonful of mustard, 2 oz. of grated cheese, cayenne, salt, 1 gill of milk.

METHOD.—Slit the chestnuts on the flat side and put them on a tin in a hot oven for fifteen minutes. When the shells begin to split open, remove them and peel off the inner skins.

Boil the chestnuts till tender (about twenty minutes) and strain off the water.

Mash the chestnuts and put them in a pan with an ounce and a half of the butter and the mustard and herbs. Add the flour and mix well; add the milk and stir till it boils. Season with salt and cayenne, and add nearly all the cheese and a beaten egg.

Put into a fireproof dish and sprinkle with the rest of the cheese. Put bits of butter on top and bake for ten minutes in a hot oven. This savoury is good either hot or cold.

Sufficient for four persons.

CHICKEN LIVER OMELET

INGREDIENTS.—3 eggs, 1 tablespoonful of milk, 1 oz. of butter, salt and pepper, $\frac{1}{4}$ of an onion (grated).

FOR THE GARNISH: 2 or 3 chicken livers, $\frac{1}{2}$ oz. of butter, $\frac{1}{4}$ oz. of flour, $\frac{3}{4}$ gill of stock (see p. 12), 1 teaspoonful of mushroom ketchup.

METHOD.—Wash and slice the livers and fry them slowly in the butter for five minutes.

Put the liver on a plate and brown the flour in the butter, stirring well.

Add the stock and ketchup and stir till it boils. Put in the liver and keep it hot.

Mix the onion in a cup with the yolks, milk, salt and pepper.

Heat the butter in an oval frying-pan.

Beat the egg-whites stiffly, fold in the yolks lightly, and pour the egg at once into the hot butter. Do not stir it.

Lower the gas and cook the omelet slowly for four minutes, moving the pan about so that the omelet cooks evenly all over.

Place the pan under the red hot griller to set the top (about four minutes). Pour the garnish on to the omelet, fold it in half and turn it on to a hot dish.

NOTE.—The whites of the eggs are beaten separately to make the omelet larger and lighter.

CHICKEN LIVERS ON TOAST

INGREDIENTS.—2 or 3 chicken livers, $\frac{3}{4}$ gill of gravy or stock (see p. 12), 2 rashers of bacon, 1 teaspoonful of flour, a few drops of lemon-juice, 2 pieces of hot buttered toast, 1 teaspoonful of sauce for flavouring, salt and pepper.

METHOD.—Fry the bacon and keep it hot. Wash and slice the livers and dip them in the flour.

Fry them gently in the bacon dripping for five minutes. Remove the livers and pour off nearly all the dripping. Brown the rest of the flour in the pan, add lemon-juice and add a teaspoonful of sauce to flavour.

Add the stock and boil up.

Season the gravy and heat the livers in it for a minute or two.

Pour the liver and gravy over the hot buttered toast and serve the bacon on top.

CORN FRITTERS

INGREDIENTS.—1 tin of corn, 3 oz. of flour, 1 teaspoonful of baking-powder, seasoning, 2 level dessertspoonfuls of chopped parsley, 2 eggs, deep fat for frying.

METHOD.—Turn the corn into a strainer and drain it well.

Separate the eggs and whisk the whites to a stiff froth. Beat the yolks of eggs and add them to the corn.

Stir in the flour and baking-powder. Add also the parsley and seasoning to taste, then fold in the stiffly-whisked egg-whites.

Drop the mixture in small heaps into deep hot fat and fry them until golden.

Drain them on paper and fry the remainder in the same way. Serve at once, whilst crisp.

Sufficient to make from twenty to twenty-four fritters.

SWEET CORN AU GRATIN

INGREDIENTS.—1 pint tin of sweet corn, ¼ pint of milk, 2½ oz. of breadcrumbs, seasoning, 1 egg, ¾ oz. of butter, 3 oz. of cheese, 1 teaspoonful of chopped parsley.

METHOD.—Turn the corn into a basin and stir in the beaten egg, milk, and one and a half ounces of the breadcrumbs.

Grate the cheese finely, add half of it to the corn mixture with seasoning to taste and the chopped parsley. Then turn it into a buttered pie-dish.

Mix the remainder of the cheese and breadcrumbs together and sprinkle them thickly on top of the corn. Put small dabs of butter on top and bake the corn for about half an hour in a moderately hot oven. Brown it under the grill before serving it.

Sufficient for five persons.

HOT CORN MOULD

INGREDIENTS.—1 tin of corn-on-the-cob, 7 tablespoonfuls of sago, 2 oz. of flour, salt and pepper, 1 tin of tomatoes, 2 oz. butter, 1 cupful of breadcrumbs, ½ gill of cream.

METHOD.—Wash the sago.

Rub the tomatoes through a hair sieve. Boil one pint of the purée. If there is less than one pint add a little water. Pour it on the sago, letting it stand for three hours.

Melt the butter and stir in the flour, sago, and tomato.

Stir till it boils, add two cobs of corn broken up, and season with salt

and pepper. Stir in the breadcrumbs and cream and pour into a greased mould.

Cover with greased paper and steam for two hours. Heat the rest of the corn in boiling water. Turn out the mould and place the corn round. Serve with piquante butter sauce.

Sufficient for five persons.

NOTE.—Ordinary tinned sweet corn can be used instead of the corn-on-the-cob.

PIQUANTE BUTTER SAUCE

INGREDIENTS.—2 oz. of salt butter, juice of a lemon, 1 onion (grated).

METHOD. — Boil the butter and lemon-juice together. Add the grated onion and serve in a hot sauce-boat.

SWEET CORN SAVOURY

INGREDIENTS.—½ pint of sweet corn, ¼ lb. of cheese, 1½ gills of milk, 1 egg, seasoning, ¼ oz. of butter or margarine, ½ oz. of flour, triangles of buttered toast.

METHOD.—Melt the fat, add the flour, and when well blended stir in the milk and bring it to the boil.

Add the corn (if too wet this may be drained first). Boil them gently for a few minutes, then draw the pan aside.

Stir in the finely-grated cheese and well-beaten egg, and cook the mixture again for a few minutes, but do not let it boil.

Add seasoning to taste, turn it into a dish, and garnish with triangles of buttered toast.

Sufficient for four persons.

CRACKNEL SAVOURIES

INGREDIENTS.—¼ lb. of toy cracknel biscuits, a small tin of sardines, watercress, salad cream, salt.

METHOD.—Turn out the sardines and mash them up with a fork, removing the tails and any bones as you do so. Then mix with a little salad cream.

Pick over and wash the watercress, then drain and chop.

Heap the sardine mixture on the cracknel biscuits and sprinkle with chopped watercress, the latter seasoned with salt.

Allow two for each person.

Cheese
Sausages

Stuffed
Aubergine

Creamed Asparagus

PLATE 33

Tomatoes
au
Gratin

Mushroom
Omelet

Asparagus
Squares

PLATE 34

Egg and Onion Triangles

Bacon and Cheese Pie

Spinach Savouries

PLATE 35

Ham Patties

Scotch Eggs

Cheese
Sticks

PLATE 36

FRIED CUCUMBERS

INGREDIENTS.—1 large cucumber, 1 egg, breadcrumbs, flour, 5 small onions, ½ oz. of butter, 1 oz. of flour, ¾ gill of milk or stock (see p. 12), salt and pepper, 5 thick slices of tomato, 1 oz. of margarine, deep fat for frying.

METHOD.—Peel the onions. Peel the cucumber and cut it across into five pieces.

Boil the cucumber and onions for ten minutes.

Fry the tomato slowly in the margarine. Melt the butter, stir in half an ounce of flour and milk. Stir till the sauce boils and then put in the onions. Season with salt and pepper, and simmer gently while frying the cucumber.

Scoop out the seeds and roll the pieces of cucumber in flour.

Egg and breadcrumb each piece.

Heat the fat and when it smokes fry two pieces at a time for three minutes and drain them on paper. Keep them hot and re-heat the fat before frying each batch.

Put an onion and a little sauce in each cucumber, and stand each of them on a slice of tomato.

Sufficient for four or five persons.

NOTE.—If preferred the onions and tomato can be omitted and the cucumber can be served plain, simply egged, crumbed, and fried.

STUFFED CUCUMBERS

INGREDIENTS.—2 good-sized cucumbers, 2 oz. of good dripping, 1 onion, 2 oz. of ham or bacon, 1 cup of breadcrumbs, 1 tomato, 1 teaspoonful of Worcester sauce, 1 egg, salt and pepper, 1 dessertspoonful of chopped parsley, 1 oz. of flour, ¾ pint of stock (see p. 12).

METHOD.—Peel the cucumbers, cut them in half lengthways and remove the seeds.

Chop the onion and bacon and fry them gently for five minutes ; add the tomato sliced, and fry a few more minutes.

Add the breadcrumbs, Worcester sauce, egg, parsley, and seasoning, and stuff the cucumbers with the mixture.

Put the halves together face to face, and tie them in place with two or three pieces of string.

Heat the dripping in a large frying-pan and when a blue vapour begins to rise, put in the cucumbers and brown them all over. Take them out of the pan.

Pour off half the dripping and make a brown gravy by frying the flour and adding the stock.

Season with salt and pepper and a little Worcester sauce and boil for three minutes.

Place the browned cucumbers in the gravy, cover the pan with a saucepan-lid or dish, and allow them to stew gently till tender (for about an hour).

Sufficient for four persons.

CURRIED BANANAS

INGREDIENTS.—3 oz. of rice, 4 bananas, ½ oz. of margarine, ½ oz. of flour, ½ apple, ½ onion, 1 teaspoonful of salt, 1 dessertspoonful of curry-powder, 1½ gills of water, juice of ½ lemon, 2 hard-boiled eggs.

METHOD.—Wash the rice and boil it for fifteen minutes with the salt in plenty of fast-boiling water.

Boil the eggs for ten minutes, put them in cold water, and remove the shells.

To make the curry sauce, peel and chop the apple and onion, and fry them in the margarine for five minutes. Stir in the flour, curry-powder, lemon-juice, and a pinch of salt, and add the water gradually.

Stir the sauce till it boils, lay the skinned bananas in the sauce and heat them for about five minutes. Add a little more water, if necessary. Strain the rice into a colander and grate the onion on to it. Do not mash the rice. If it is boiled for exactly the right time each grain will be separate.

Heap the rice on a hot dish with the bananas and sauce round and garnish with quarters of hard-boiled egg.

CURRIED EGGS

INGREDIENTS.—4 eggs, 1½ oz. of butter, 3 teaspoonfuls of flour, 1 teaspoonful of curry-powder, 1½ gills of milk and water, seasoning, 1 very small onion, half a small apple, 3 oz. of rice.

METHOD.—Melt the butter in a

N

saucepan, peel and chop the onion, and fry in it.

Mix the flour and curry-powder together and stir into the fried onion.

Peel, core, and finely chop the apple, and cook with the onion, etc., for a few minutes.

Add the milk and water, stir well, and bring to the boil and cook slowly for about twelve minutes ; season to taste.

Put the eggs into boiling water and boil for fifteen minutes, remove the shells and cut the eggs across into halves, then cut each half into four.

Arrange as many of these pieces as required closely together round a dish. Chop up the remainder and add to the curry.

Well wash the rice, put into a saucepan of boiling water with a teaspoonful of salt and lemon-juice and boil for twelve minutes or until tender, then strain it.

This can be boiled while the curry is cooking.

Pour the curry into the centre of the arranged pieces of egg.

Put a border of cooked rice round the outside and serve. If preferred, the eggs can go inside the rice, and the curry can be poured round.

CURRIED LENTILS

INGREDIENTS.—½ pint of split lentils, 2 oz. of rice, ½ oz. of flour, 2 onions, 1 oz. of sultanas, ½ oz. of curry-powder, ½ gill of vinegar, 1 gill of water used for boiling the lentils, salt to taste, 1 oz. of bacon fat.

METHOD.—Wash the lentils.

Put them into a saucepan with one pint of cold water and a quarter of a teaspoonful of salt and simmer them till they are soft (about thirty minutes).

Wash the rice and sprinkle it into a large pan of boiling water containing a dessertspoonful of salt. Boil it fast for fifteen minutes. Strain it into a colander, and keep it hot over a pan of water. Be careful not to mash the rice.

Mix the curry-powder, flour, and vinegar with a gill of water from that used for cooking the lentils. Add the sultanas and bacon fat and stir the sauce till it boils, and boil it for three minutes.

Strain the lentils and put them into a saucepan with the sauce.

Mix well and add the onion grated on a bread grater. Dish up the curry surrounded with neat heaps of rice.

Sufficient for four persons.

CURRIED MUSHROOMS

INGREDIENTS.—½ lb. of small mushrooms, 1 hard-boiled egg, 1 dessertspoonful of curry-powder, ½ oz. of flour, 1 oz. of butter, juice of ½ lemon, 1 gill of milk, ½ onion, salt, 3 oz. of rice.

METHOD.—Peel and wash the mushrooms and remove the stalks. Chop the onion and egg. Fry the onion and mushrooms gently in the butter for five minutes. Put the mushrooms on a plate. Mix the curry-powder and flour with the butter and fried onion, and add the milk gradually. Stir till it boils, and add the egg, salt, and lemon-juice.

Place the mushrooms in a double saucepan and pour the sauce on to them, leaving them for thirty minutes, or till tender.

Wash the rice and boil it for fifteen minutes in plenty of fast-boiling water.

To serve, heap the rice in the middle of a hot dish with the mushrooms round it.

Sufficient for three persons.

CURRIED SARDINES

INGREDIENTS.—1 tin of sardines, 2 cooking apples, ½ lemon, 1 oz. of flour, ½ oz. of curry-powder, ¼ teaspoonful of salt, 1½ gills of water, 1 oz of margarine, ½ onion (minced), 2 oz. of boiled rice.

METHOD.—Peel, core and slice the apples, and fry them slowly in the margarine.

Fry the onion for five minutes in the sardine oil, add the rice, half the sardines (chopped) and the flour, currypowder, salt, lemon-juice, and water.

Stir the mixture till it boils, and boil for three minutes.

Place the apples round the rice and a few whole sardines on top.

CURRY SQUARES

INGREDIENTS.—3 tablespoonfuls of boiled rice, 1 teaspoonful of currypowder, 1 onion, 2 tomatoes, 1 oz. of butter, seasoning, buttered toast.

METHOD.—The rice should be prepared as for a curry. After boiling it, strain it in a colander, then pour cold water through to separate the grains, and drain it well.

Peel and mince the onion, and fry it lightly in the butter, add the curry-powder, and stir till well blended.

Skin the tomatoes, chop up and add them to the curry and cook them for a minute or two. Add the rice and seasoning to taste and stir until hot.

Meanwhile make six squares of buttered toast, remove the corners and heap the prepared curry on each square.

Sufficient for six squares.

CURRIED VEGETABLE PAT-TIES

INGREDIENTS.—1 cup of any cold vegetables, 1 oz. of sultanas (washed), 1 onion, ½ oz. of flour, ½ gill of vinegar, ½ oz. of curry-powder, 1 gill of water, ¼ teaspoonful of salt, deep frying fat, parsley, three or four slices of stale bread, about 2 in. thick, ¾ oz. of butter.

METHOD.—Mince the onion and fry it in the butter for five minutes. Stir in the flour, curry-powder, and vinegar.

Add the water and sultanas, and stir till boiling. Season to taste. Chop the cold vegetables and add them to the sauce. Keep them hot on a very low gas while making the fried bread cases.

To make the cases, cut the bread into rounds and scoop out the centre. Fry one at a time in smoking hot fat for about three minutes, turning them over when one side is done. They should be a golden brown.

Drain them on paper and fill with the hot vegetable mixture.

Serve on lace paper, and garnish with parsley.

Sufficient for four persons.

NOTE.—For a change vegetable patties can be made with tomato or béchamel sauce (see pp. 365 and 368) instead of a curry-sauce.

Cold meat or fish can also be chopped and added to the vegetable.

DEVILLED BLOATER PASTE CROUTES

INGREDIENTS.—½ jar of bloater paste, 1 dessertspoonful of curry-powder, 1 oz. of butter, 1 lemon, 1 large slice of bread.

METHOD.—Mix the bloater paste with the curry-powder.

Toast the bread, cut it into six or eight rounds with a small, fluted cutter, and spread with butter.

Spread thickly with the bloater paste and squeeze lemon over ; then put them in a hot oven for five minutes.

Dish up on lace paper, and squeeze more lemon over just before serving.

This quantity makes about six or eight croûtes.

DEVILLED MACARONI

INGREDIENTS.—3 oz. of macaroni, 1½ oz. of butter, 2 oz. of flour, 1 tablespoonful of curry-powder, 2 onions, 1 apple, 2 tablespoonfuls of desiccated coconut, juice of ½ lemon, ½ pint of milk, ½ pint of stock (see p. 12), 1 oz. of grated cheese, ½ teaspoonful of made mustard.

METHOD.—Break the macaroni into pieces an inch long. Boil it in plenty of salt fast-boiling water till tender, and strain through a colander. Chop the onions and apple. Fry the onions till lightly browned. Add the apple, flour, curry-powder, mustard, coconut, and lemon-juice and mix well. Pour in the stock and stir till it boils. Add the milk, cheese, and macaroni. Simmer gently for twenty minutes. Serve surrounded with sippets of toast, or if preferred, serve on small individual dishes with fingers of toast.

Sufficient for four persons.

DEVILLED MUSHROOMS

INGREDIENTS.—4 medium mushrooms, 1 oz. of butter, or a little more if the mushrooms are very large, 1 teaspoonful of curry-powder, ½ teaspoonful of made mustard, 1 dessertspoonful of Worcester sauce, salt and cayenne, juice of ½ lemon, 1 teaspoonful of tomato ketchup, 4 squares of hot buttered toast, 1 oz. of rice, ½ gill of vinegar, ½ gill of water.

METHOD.—Peel and wash the mushrooms, after removing the stalks, place them, cup side up, on a baking-tin, and pour the vinegar and water round them.

Cream the butter and add to it the

curry-powder, made mustard, and a little salt and cayenne. Put a quarter of the mixture into each mushroom and bake in a fairly hot oven for fifteen or twenty minutes.

Wash the rice and boil it for fifteen minutes.

Mix the Worcester sauce, ketchup, and lemon-juice with the rice, and make the hot buttered toast.

Place a mushroom on each piece of toast and put some of the devilled rice mixture of sauce and lemon-juice on each.

Pour over them the juice left in the tin, return to the oven for two minutes, and serve piping hot.

EGG CAKES

INGREDIENTS.—4 eggs, 1 gill of milk, ½ gill of water, anchovy essence, 1 oz. of margarine or butter, 1½ oz. of flour, pepper, breadcrumbs for coating, fat for frying.

METHOD.—Boil three of the eggs for fifteen minutes until hard.

Crack the shells and leave the eggs in cold water until ready for use, then shell them, and chop or grate them finely.

Mix the flour to a smooth paste with the water.

Put the milk and butter into a saucepan to heat.

When hot, stir it on to the flour, return to the saucepan and bring to the boil, and cook for a few minutes, keeping it well stirred.

Add the chopped eggs and sufficient anchovy essence to flavour.

Season with pepper and mix all well together, then spread on a plate and leave until quite cold and firm.

Divide the mixture into small equal portions and shape each into round shapes with flattened tops.

Beat up the remaining egg and brush the cakes over with it, then coat them in white breadcrumbs.

Put them into hot fat and fry them until golden brown.

Drain on paper and serve on a lace paper.

EGG AND CHEESE SAVOURY

INGREDIENTS.—4 hard-boiled eggs, 2 oz. of rice, ½ pint of milk, 1 oz. of butter, 1 oz. of flour, 2 oz. of grated cheese, ½ teaspoonful of made mustard, cayenne, salt.

METHOD.—Wash the rice. Boil it for fifteen minutes in plenty of fast-boiling water, and strain.

Melt the butter. Add the flour and mustard, and gradually stir in the milk. Stir till it boils, then add the cheese and season to taste. Add the rice and simmer for five minutes.

Cut the eggs in half and each half into four, and arrange the pieces round a dish and put them in the oven to get hot for a few minutes.

Pour the savoury into the border of eggs, and serve with sippets of fried bread.

Sufficient for four or five persons.

EGGS WITH CORN SAUCE

INGREDIENTS.—½ tin of corn, ½ oz. of butter, 1 to 1½ teaspoonfuls of flour (according to consistency of corn), 2 teaspoonfuls of onion-juice, seasoning, 3 or 4 eggs, squares of hot buttered toast, a few cooked green peas.

METHOD.—Turn the corn into a saucepan and heat it. If it seems tough, cook it for a few minutes, then rub it through a wire sieve. Melt the butter, add the flour and, when blended, stir in the sieved corn and onion-juice and bring this sauce to the boil. Boil it gently for a few minutes and add seasoning to taste. If the sauce is too thick, thin it down with a little milk, but it should be of a coating consistency.

Poach three or four eggs and put them on squares of buttered toast. Pour the sauce round the white part of the egg and garnish it with a few cooked green peas, previously heated in a little butter.

Sufficient for three or four eggs.

EGG FRITTERS

INGREDIENTS.—8 eggs, ¼ lb. of fat streaky rashers, seasoning, 3 oz. of flour, a pinch of salt, ¼ pint of warm water, 1 dessertspoonful of salad oil, 1 white of egg, deep fat for frying.

METHOD.—Sift the flour and salt into a basin, make a hole in the centre and drop in the oil. Then add the warm water gradually and mix the ingredients to a smooth batter. Beat it well and let it stand a few hours.

Put the eggs into boiling water and boil them gently for from twelve to fifteen minutes. Shell them and cut them in half crosswise. Remove the yolks, without breaking the halved whites.

Cut the rind from the rashers put the bacon through the mincer and fry it till tender.

Mash up the egg-yolks, and stir into them the fried bacon, adding also the bacon fat and seasoning to taste. Mix all together, refill the halved whites, then put them together again, making whole eggs.

When the eggs are ready to fry, whisk the white of egg stiffly and fold it into the batter.

Flour the eggs and coat them with the prepared batter. Fry them till they are golden in deep hot fat, then drain them and serve them at once.

Sufficient for eight persons.

EGG NEST

INGREDIENTS.—1 new-laid egg, 1 tablespoonful of cold mince or fricassee, 1 teaspoonful of tomato ketchup, salt and pepper, ¼ oz. of butter.

METHOD.—Butter a rather deep fireproof dish.

Put in the mince and season with ketchup and salt and pepper.

Separate the white of the egg from the yolk.

Beat the white to a very stiff froth and put it in the dish, making a hollow in the centre.

Put in the yolk and butter and bake in a moderate oven till the white is set (seven minutes). The white must not be browned.

EGG AND ONION TRIANGLES

INGREDIENTS.—¼ lb. of onion, 2 hard-boiled eggs, triangles of buttered toast, ¾ oz. of butter, ½ oz. of flour, ½ gill of milk, ½ gill of onion liquor, seasoning.

METHOD.—Peel the onions. Put them in cold water and bring them to the boil. Then drain them and slice them thinly.

Cover the onions with fresh cold water and boil them gently till they are tender. Drain them again and save the liquor.

Hard-boil the eggs, and save a few slices for decorating, and chop the remainder finely.

Make a thick sauce with the butter, flour, milk, and onion liquor. Boil it gently for a few minutes and add seasoning to taste. Stir in the chopped egg and cooked onions. Make the sauce hot and serve it on the triangles of hot buttered toast, garnishing each with a slice of egg.

EGGS AU PARMESAN

INGREDIENTS.—4 eggs, salt and pepper, 1½ gills of milk, ½ oz. of flour, ½ oz. of margarine, 2 oz. of cheese (Parmesan), a few capers and one pimento.

METHOD.—Melt the fat in a saucepan, add the flour and when well blended stir in the milk and bring it to the boil. Simmer it for a few minutes, add seasoning to taste, and the finely-grated cheese, and stir until melted. Pour a spoonful of the sauce into four buttered fireproof " cocotte " dishes, break an egg into each, then cover them with sauce. Garnish with a ring of pimento and a few capers and put the " cocottes " into the oven until the egg is set.

Sufficient for four persons.

STUFFED EGG PLANTS

INGREDIENTS.—3 egg plants, 1 oz. of butter, 1 small tomato, 3 or 4 mushrooms, ½ cup of breadcrumbs, 1 egg, salt and pepper, 1 small onion, 1 gill of stock (see p. 12), ½ oz. of butter.

METHOD.—Put the egg plants in boiling water and boil for ten minutes. Cut them in half and remove a little of the centre. Peel and chop the mushrooms and onion, and fry them in the butter for five minutes. Add the tomato sliced and cook for a few minutes. Mix the breadcrumbs with the mushrooms, onion, and tomato, season, and bind with a beaten egg. Pile this mixture on to the egg plants and place them in a baking-tin or fireproof dish with the stock and a small piece of butter. Bake in a moderate oven for an hour, basting them with the liquor in the tin.

RIVIERA EGGS

INGREDIENTS.—2 lb. of potatoes, 4 eggs, ½ pint of thick white sauce (see p. 364), 4 heaped tablespoonfuls of grated cheese, pepper and salt, 2 oz. of margarine, milk.

METHOD.—Wash the potatoes and peel them thinly. Put them in a saucepan and cover with water containing a little salt. Cook until tender.

Make the white sauce.

Put the eggs into a saucepan of cold water and boil for fifteen minutes, crack them well, and put in cold water.

Remove the shells and chop up the eggs roughly. Mix them into the sauce, season well, and keep hot.

Strain the potatoes when cooked. Mash them up well with a fork, then add half the margarine and a little milk.

Mix all together and season with pepper.

Take an au gratin dish stand a wall of mashed potato all round the edge of it ; make it look even. Then mark it with a fork.

Pour the sauce and egg mixture into the centre of the dish. Sprinkle the grated cheese over the top of the sauce.

Put the remainder of the margarine in small pieces on the top of the potato wall.

Place in a hot oven until the top has lightly browned.

Sufficient for eight persons.

STEAMED EGGS ON KIPPER TOAST

INGREDIENTS.—3 slices of bread, butter, 3 eggs, kipper fish paste.

METHOD.—Toast the bread and butter it. When the latter is melted, spread the toast with kipper paste, or any other suitable fish paste, and keep it warm.

Poach the eggs carefully in a steam egg poacher, and place one egg on each piece of prepared toast.

If you have not a steam poacher, poach the eggs in the usual way.

A steam poacher will enable you to poach an egg perfectly with the least amount of trouble.

Put some water in the bottom of the poacher, and when it is hot, put a tiny dab of butter in each egg container and butter it freely.

Then break an egg into each one.

Put the lid on the poacher and cook the eggs gently for a few minutes until the white is set.

STEAMED EGGS WITH TOMATO SAUCE

INGREDIENTS.—6 eggs, $\frac{1}{2}$ onion, seasoning, $\frac{1}{4}$ small level teaspoonful of salt, barely $\frac{1}{2}$ oz. of flour, $\frac{1}{2}$ pint of stewed or tinned tomatoes, $\frac{1}{2}$ small level teaspoonful of sugar, $\frac{1}{2}$ oz. of butter, bayleaf and one clove.

METHOD.—Cook the tomatoes with the sliced onion, sugar, salt, a tiny piece of bayleaf, and one clove, for ten minutes. Rub the purée through a sieve. Melt the butter in a saucepan, stir in the flour till it is well blended, and mix it with the tomato, stirring all the time. Cook the sauce till it is thick and season it to taste.

Steam the eggs in an egg steamer, or, if liked, they can be poached. Arrange them on a dish or, if preferred, each egg may be placed on a round of fried bread. Pour the sauce round them.

EGG SAUSAGES

INGREDIENTS.—$\frac{1}{2}$ oz. of margarine, $\frac{1}{2}$ gill of milk, $1\frac{1}{2}$ dessertspoonfuls of flour, 2 hard-boiled eggs, salt and pepper, 1 teaspoonful of chopped parsley, 1 oz. of cheese, egg and breadcrumbs, frying fat.

METHOD.—Shell the eggs and put them through the mincer.

Melt the fat in a saucepan, stir in the flour and mix together, then add the milk.

Continue stirring until the mixture boils and thickens and leaves the sides of the pan, then draw the pan aside. Stir in the chopped parsley, minced eggs, and cheese grated finely, season to taste, and when well mixed turn on to a plate and leave to get cold and firm.

Divide the mixture into eight or nine portions, form them into sausage shapes, brush them with beaten egg (half an egg will be sufficient) and coat them with breadcrumbs.

Fry the sausages in hot fat until golden brown. Then drain them and serve on a dish paper.

Sufficient for three persons.

EGG AND TOMATO SAVOURY

INGREDIENTS.—4 eggs, 1 oz. of butter or margarine, 1 oz. of cooked ham, 6 tomatoes (medium size), 2 teaspoonfuls of chopped parsley, ½ an onion, seasoning.

METHOD.—Peel and finely chop the onion. Cut up the ham. Slice the tomatoes. Well wash the parsley. Then scald it, drain well, and chop very finely. Keep it in a piece of damp paper until ready to use it, otherwise it will lose its colour.

Melt the butter in a pan, add the onion and fry until golden-brown.

Add the sliced tomatoes and cook rather quickly until tender, keeping them well stirred all the time. Season with pepper and salt.

Rub the cooked onion and tomatoes through a sieve, return to the pan and then thicken with just a little cornflour.

Well grease a pie-dish or au gratin dish and pour this into it.

Make four little holes in the pulp and carefully break an egg into each hole.

Sprinkle with a little chopped ham and garnish each with parsley.

Put into a moderately warm oven and bake until the eggs are just set.

Serve at once.

NOTE.—Remember to break each egg first into a cup, as if not fresh it would spoil the whole dish.

Sufficient for four persons.

FISH IN ASPIC

INGREDIENTS.—A slice of cold fish or some tinned salmon, 1 tablespoonful of capers and caper vinegar, ½ a packet of aspic jelly, 1 hard-boiled egg, some slices of cucumber, salt, pepper.

METHOD.—Put the fish in a fairly deep dish after removing the skin and bone.

Chop the white of egg and capers and mix them with the fish, leaving a little of the chopped egg for decorating. Sprinkle them with salt, pepper, and caper vinegar.

Pour half a pint of hot water on the jelly crystals, stir well and let it cool. Pour the jelly over the fish, and when set decorate it with cucumber and chopped egg.

FISH RAREBIT

INGREDIENTS.—3 oz. of cold fish, 6 oz. of cheese, 1½ oz. of butter, 1 teaspoonful of made mustard, pepper, ½ gill of milk, ½ gill of water, 1 teaspoonful of flour, 2 squares of hot buttered toast spread with a little anchovy essence.

METHOD.—Chop the fish, removing all skin and bones. Slice the cheese. Melt the butter, put in the cheese, fish, and milk, and place the pan over a very low gas.

Mix the flour, mustard, pepper, and water smoothly, add it to the cheese and stir till it boils.

Boil for three minutes.

Make the toast and pour the mixture over it.

FISH SCALLOPS

INGREDIENTS.—1 cupful of cold fish, 2 medium potatoes, 1 oz. of margarine, 1 dessertspoonful of anchovy sauce, pepper, ¼ tablespoonful of chopped parsley, ½ gill of milk.

METHOD.—Wash, peel and boil the potatoes. Chop the fish, first removing the skin and bones.

When the potatoes are tender, drain off the water and put the pan over a low gas.

Mash the potatoes with a fork and stir in the fish, anchovy, milk, pepper, and half the margarine.

Beat this mixture till smooth, put it into greased scallop shells with dabs of margarine on top.

Brown the scallops under the griller and sprinkle with parsley.

FRENCH SAVOURY PIE

INGREDIENTS.—¼ lb. of rice, 1 pint of water, 1 pint of milk, 1 oz. of butter, pepper and salt, 3 oz. of cheese.

METHOD.—Well wash the rice and put it into a saucepan with the water. Bring to the boil and simmer gently until the water is absorbed. Be careful not to let it burn.

Pour in the milk and simmer again until the milk is absorbed and the rice cooked.

Stir in the butter and season well.

Grate the cheese and stir about half of it into the rice.

Turn it all into an au gratin dish

and sprinkle the top thickly with the remainder of the cheese.

Place in a hot oven or under the grill until thoroughly heated and brown on the top.

GNIOCHHI A LA ROMANA

INGREDIENTS.—2 oz. of semolina, ½ pint of milk, 1 oz. of butter, 2 oz. of grated cheese, 1 teaspoonful of anchovy sauce, pepper, ½ cup of breadcrumbs, croûtons of bread.

METHOD.—Boil the milk with the anchovy sauce and sprinkle in the semolina and breadcrumbs, stirring well all the time. Simmer till thick (about fifteen minutes), stirring occasionally.

Stir in half the butter and half the cheese and add pepper to taste. Spread the mixture fairly thickly on a soup-plate and, when cold, cut it into round cakes with a pastry cutter.

Melt the remainder of the butter in a frying-pan, dip in each round cake and roll them in grated cheese. Place them in a baking-tin and brown them in a very hot oven for ten minutes.

Cut the croûtons of bread a trifle larger than the cakes and fry them for one minute in smoking-hot fat.

Serve each cake on a croûton of fried bread and sprinkle them with grated cheese.

NOTE.—If preferred, sago can be used instead of semolina in making this dish. The method is exactly the same.

HADDOCK PASTIES

INGREDIENTS.—½ cup of cold haddock, 1 oz. of grated cheese, 1 dessertspoonful of chopped parsley, ¼ oz. of butter, ¼ oz. of flour, ½ gill of milk and water, pepper, 1 egg, breadcrumbs, 6 oz. of flaky pastry (see p. 252).

METHOD.—Melt the butter and stir in the flour. Add the milk by degrees with the pan off the gas, and still till it boils.

Add the cheese, parsley, and haddock and season to taste.

Boil the mixture for a minute, turn it on to a plate and set it aside to cool.

Roll out the pastry and cut it into rounds. Put some of the cold mixture in the centre of each round and brush the pastry half-way round with a little water.

Fold each round over into half and press the edges together to form a crescent shape.

Brush the crescents with a well-beaten egg and toss them in a paper full of breadcrumbs.

Shake off any loose crumbs and bake the pasties in a hot oven for fifteen minutes.

NOTE.—Any kind of cold or tinned fish can be used for making pasties.

HADDOCK SAVOURY

INGREDIENTS.—1 small smoked haddock, 3 eggs, 1 oz. of butter, ½ pint of milk, salt and pepper to taste, 2 or 3 pieces of hot buttered toast.

METHOD.—Place the haddock in a baking-tin with the milk, and put the small pieces of butter on top. Bake in a moderate oven for twenty minutes. Take out the haddock and remove all the skin and bones. Flake the flesh and return it to the pan containing the milk. Add salt and pepper and the three eggs well-beaten. Stir the mixture over a slow fire till it thickens, and pour over hot buttered toast.

Sufficient for two or three persons.

HADDOCK AND RICE SAVOURY

INGREDIENTS.—1 smoked haddock, ¾ pint of milk, 1 oz. of butter, ½ oz. of flour, 2 oz. of best rice, salt and pepper, 1 dessertspoonful of chopped parsley.

METHOD.—Cook the haddock for twenty minutes in a baking-tin or fireproof dish with the milk, putting the butter in small pieces on the top.

Boil the rice for fifteen minutes.

Remove the skin and bones from the haddock and flake the flesh.

Strain the rice.

Put haddock and rice on a plate while thickening the liquor in the dish.

Mix the flour with a little cold milk or water, pour into the dish, place on an asbestos mat, and stir till it boils.

Add the haddock and boiled rice, season to taste, and re-heat.

Decorate with a little chopped parsley.

Enough for four persons.

HAM CAKES

INGREDIENTS.—5 oz. of cooked ham, ½ small onion, salt and pepper,

½ lb. of cold potatoes, 3 eggs, ½ level teaspoonful of chopped parsley.

METHOD.—Peel the onion and put it through the mincer with the ham and the potatoes, then mix them together and add the parsley and seasoning to taste. Divide the mixture into three portions, and make each into a flat round cake. Fry these very carefully in a little heated dripping or bacon fat, then serve them on a hot dish and top each cake with a fried egg.

Sufficient for three cakes.

HAM CORNETS

INGREDIENTS.—2 large slices of boiled ham, 1 breakfastcupful of mixed cold vegetables (potatoes and carrots or cauliflower), ½ packet of aspic jelly, 3 tablespoonfuls of salad cream, ½ oz. of butter, ½ oz. of flour, ¾ gill of milk, 1 cup of cooked or tinned peas, ½ teaspoonful of made mustard, salt and pepper.

METHOD.—Spread the peas on a small flat dish.

Dissolve the jelly in half a pint of hot water and pour it over the peas, keeping back three tablespoonfuls of jelly.

Melt the butter, stir in the flour and mustard, and add in the milk gradually with the pan off the gas. Stir it till it boils, season with pepper and salt to taste, and add the rest of the jelly and the vegetables.

Let the mixture cool, and add the salad-cream. When it is beginning to set fold the ham into cornet shapes.

Fill the cornets with some of the vegetable mixture and lay them on the jellied peas.

Garnish with the rest of the vegetables.

DRIED HADDOCK AND EGGS

INGREDIENTS.—1 dried haddock, (medium size), 1½ oz. of butter or margarine, ½ gill of milk, pepper, 3 oz. of cheese, 3 or 4 eggs.

METHOD.—Wash and dry the haddock. Put it into a pie-dish with the milk and butter. Cover with a plate and bake in a moderately hot oven until the flesh will move easily from the bone.

When cooked, put it on to a dish,

remove all the bones and skin and flake the flesh into small pieces.

Grate the cheese finely and mix with the flaked fish ; mix in also the butter and milk in which the fish was cooked. Season well with pepper and put into a pie-dish or au gratin dish. Put into the oven until the cheese has melted and it is all thoroughly hot.

While this is heating, poach the eggs. Arrange them on the haddock and serve at once.

Sufficient for three or four persons.

HAM EGGS

INGREDIENTS.—3 eggs, salt, pepper, mixed mustard, 3 dessertspoonfuls of chopped ham, 1 oz. of butter, 1 flat teaspoonful of chopped tarragon or parsley.

METHOD.—Boil the eggs for fifteen minutes until hard, then crack the shells and leave the eggs in cold water until cool.

Chop the ham very finely, or put it through a mincer.

Remove the shells from the eggs, cut them into halves and carefully remove the yolks. Beat these with the butter until creamy, then mix well with the ham.

Season with salt, pepper, and mixed mustard.

Cut a small piece from the end of each half white of egg, so that they stand firmly. These pieces can be chopped up and put into them. Now fill them up with the prepared mixture, heaping it up well.

Sprinkle a little chopped tarragon or parsley on the top of each, and serve on a lace paper ; garnish the dish with a few sprigs of parsley.

Serve separately a plain salad made from lettuce leaves and tomato.

Sufficient for three persons.

HAM AND EGGS IN ASPIC

INGREDIENTS.—¼ lb. of ham, 2 or 3 hard-boiled eggs, ½ packet of aspic jelly, 1 tablespoonful of grated onion, a few slices of tomato.

METHOD.—Put the onion and some slices of tomato in two small dishes. Cut the eggs in quarters lengthwise, and stand them on the tomato.

Arrange slices of ham like a wall round the eggs.

Dissolve the jelly in half a pint of hot water and when it is cool pour it into each dish. There should be enough jelly just to fill the dishes.

This recipe is particularly nice when served with lettuce salad.

HAM KEDGEREE

INGREDIENTS.—½ cup of rice, 2 oz. of ham (chopped), 3 sprigs of parsley, 1 raw onion (grated), salt and pepper, 2 hard-boiled eggs (sliced), 1 oz. of butter.

METHOD.—Wash the rice and boil it for fifteen minutes in a large pan of salted water and strain.

Melt the butter and add the rice, eggs, ham, grated onion, and salt and pepper. Mix together carefully without mashing the rice.

Wash the parsley, squeeze it dry in a cloth and chop it finely.

Heap the rice on a hot plate and decorate with parsley.

Serve at once.

HAM SCRAMBLE

INGREDIENTS.—6 squares of buttered French toast, ½ oz. of butter, ¼ lb. of ham, 1 egg, 1 tablespoonful of milk, salt, pepper, and made mustard, hard-boiled egg-yolk or chopped parsley.

METHOD.—Toast the bread on one side and butter the untoasted side, and keep it warm.

Mince the ham and mix it with the beaten egg.

Melt the butter in a saucepan, stir in the ham and egg, also the milk, and add seasoning to taste.

Continue to stir over a low burner till it thickens.

Then serve it on the prepared toast and sprinkle it either with minced parsley or powdered egg-yolk.

This is obtained by rubbing a hard-boiled yolk of egg through a strainer.

Sufficient for six squares of toast.

HERRING ROES AND BACON

INGREDIENTS.—½ lb. of fresh soft roes, 2 small rashers of bacon, juice of 1 lemon, cayenne.

METHOD.—Fresh roes are best for this delicious savoury, but those sold in wooden boxes are very good. Wash the roes well, especially if tinned ones are used, as they are salted.

Cut off the bacon-rind and lay one or two roes on each rasher. Sprinkle with lemon-juice and cayenne, roll up neatly and run a skewer through them. Broil the rolls under the gas griller, keeping them turned. They will take five or six minutes. Serve on hot buttered toast, and squeeze more lemon-juice over them just before serving.

If large rashers of bacon are used they can be cut in half.

Sufficient for three or four persons.

ITALIAN CELERY

INGREDIENTS.—¾ pint of diced celery, ¼ lb. of spaghetti, 1 lb. of tomatoes, ¼ to ½ pint of water or stock (see p. 12), clove of garlic, 1 onion, a sprig of parsley and thyme, salt and pepper, ½ oz. of flour, 3 oz. of cheese.

METHOD.—Clean and prepare the celery and cut it into small pieces. Put it into boiling water with a little salt and boil it gently until tender, then drain it.

Wash the spaghetti and cook it in another pan of boiling water with salt, and drain it when tender. Slice the tomatoes and put them into a pan with the onion, also sliced, add the stock or water, seasoning, herbs, and garlic.

Simmer them until soft and then remove herbs and garlic and rub the sauce through a sieve.

Return this to the pan and thicken it with the flour mixed to a smooth paste with water. If the sauce seems too thick add a little more stock.

Stir in the cooked celery and spaghetti, also the finely-grated cheese, and make all thoroughly hot.

Season to taste, turn the Italian Celery into a dish and garnish it with a small quantity of finely-chopped celery.

Sufficient for from four to six persons.

ITALIAN RISOTTO

INGREDIENTS.—3 oz. of rice, ½ lb. of tomatoes, 1 to 1½ oz. of butter or margarine, about 1 gill of stock (see p. 12), 2 or 3 tablespoonfuls of cheese, 1 tablespoonful of minced ham, 1 small onion, 2 level teaspoonfuls of chopped parsley, salt and pepper, squeeze of lemon-juice.

METHOD.—Cook the tomatoes until they are tender, then rub them through a sieve.

Wash and drain the rice.

Melt the fat and fry the rice slowly in it until it begins to turn golden.

Add the onion, minced, and fry it until both are golden brown.

Draw the pan aside and pour off any fat that remains.

Add the stock and tomato pulp. Cook them gently, until the rice is tender and the liquid absorbed.

Stir in the grated cheese, ham, and parsley. Season to taste, make thoroughly hot and add a squeeze of lemon-juice. Turn the risotto into a dish, sprinkle it with cheese and garnish it with pieces of tomato (extra to that given in the recipe) baked very lightly.

Sufficient for three or four persons.

KIDNEYS IN ONIONS

INGREDIENTS. — 5 large Spanish onions, 5 small kidneys, salt and pepper, 5 oz. of butter.

METHOD.—Skin the kidneys.

Peel the onions, put them into a saucepan with cold water to cover, and salt to flavour. Bring to the boil ; then strain off the water.

Stand them in a baking-tin with the butter, and cook in a moderately hot oven for about one hour and a quarter, or until almost cooked, keeping them well basted. Remove from the oven.

Cut off a slice from the top of each, and scoop out a piece from the centre sufficiently large to take a kidney. Season the inside of the onions with pepper and salt, put in the kidneys, and season again. One end of the kidney should stand above the top of the onion.

Return to the oven and bake until the onions and kidneys are quite cooked, basting them frequently. Serve on a hot dish ; strain the butter round.

KIDNEY TOAST

INGREDIENTS.—4 kidneys, 4 oblong or squares of bread, seasoning, butter.

METHOD.—Skin the kidneys. Split them open and remove the core. Then season them with pepper and salt.

Toast the bread on one side and butter the untoasted side.

Place the toast in the bottom of the grill-tin, butter side uppermost. Arrange the kidneys on the rack of the tin, just above the toast, and grill them till they are tender, keeping them turned.

Any goodness that oozes from them will thus drop into the prepared toast.

When the kidneys are ready, serve them on the toast.

JELLIED LAMB

INGREDIENTS.—1 packet of aspic jelly, 1 gill of mint sauce, 1 cup of peas, 1 cup of cold lamb (chopped), salt and pepper.

METHOD.—Dissolve the jelly in half a pint of hot water and add the mint sauce.

Chop the meat and season with salt and pepper. Oil a mould and strain into it three-quarters of a gill of jelly. When this has set, put in a row of peas with two tablespoonfuls of jelly.

Let this set and put in the meat and more peas. Keep some peas for garnishing. Fill up with jelly. When set, shake the mould on to a dish and decorate with heaps of peas.

RED LENTIL CAKES

INGREDIENTS.—1½ gills of red lentils, 3 thin fat back rashers, 1 oz. of butter, 1 oz. of flour, small piece of a ham-bone, 1 tablespoonful of minced onion, seasoning, egg and breadcrumbs, deep fat.

METHOD.—Wash the lentils and put them on to cook with water well to cover and some hambone to flavour. Boil them till tender, then remove the hambone and turn the lentils into a colander and leave them to drain thoroughly. Melt the butter in a saucepan, add the finely minced onion and cook it for a few minutes without browning, then add the flour. Another small dab of butter may be added if required.

Stir in the lentils and seasoning to taste and continue stirring for a few minutes over a low burner. Then turn the mixture on to a plate and leave it till cold and firm.

Divide it into six portions and form

it into oval-shaped cakes with flattened tops, using a little flour to prevent sticking. Brush them with beaten egg, coat them with breadcrumbs, put them in a frying-basket and fry them in deep fat until golden, then drain them.

Remove the rind from the rashers, cut each in half and roll it up. Stick them on a skewer, place them on a tin and cook them either in the oven or under the grill until the fat is semitransparent, then cut off the lean part and chop it up. Stick a roll of fat bacon in the centre of each cake and top it with the chopped lean bacon.

Sufficient for six cakes.

NOTE.—If a hambone is not available, add a little minced ham to the cooked lentils.

LENTIL MOULD

INGREDIENTS.—½ pint of red split lentils, 1½ oz. of butter, salt and pepper, 1 tablespoonful of cornflour, 1 onion, ½ cup of milk, 2 eggs.

FOR THE CROUTONS.—2 slices of bread, 2 oz. of dripping.

METHOD.—Pour boiling water on the lentils, and let them soak overnight.

Wash the lentils, peel the onion and cut it in quarters and put both in a saucepan with boiling water to cover (about three-quarters of a pint).

Add an eggspoonful of salt and simmer for half an hour or till very soft. Pour on to a wire sieve. Keep the water for soup and rub the lentils through the sieve.

Melt the butter and add the lentil purée.

Mix the cornflour smoothly with the milk and beat the eggs.

Pour the milk and cornflour on to the eggs and add gradually to the purée. Season to taste.

Grease a mould or pie-dish, pour in the mixture and bake for about thirty minutes till set and firm.

Remove from oven and leave while frying the croûtons.

Cut the bread into dice, heat the fat and fry for two minutes or till golden brown. Drain on paper.

Turn the mould out gently and serve with croûtons.

Sufficient for four to six persons.

LOBSTER CANAPES

INGREDIENTS.—1 oz. of butter, 2 level tablespoonfuls of chopped cress, 1 small level teaspoonful of curry, 2 small level teaspoonfuls of flour, 2 level teaspoonfuls of chopped onions, 2½ oz. of lobster, fried canapés (slices of fried bread), pimento.

METHOD.—Melt the butter in an omelet pan, add the onion and the cress and cook them for a few moments without browning them.

Mix the flour with the curry and add it to the onion and cress.

When it is well blended stir in the flaked lobster and make it hot. Spread canapés of fried bread or buttered toast, about one and a half inches wide and three and a half inches long, with the mixture.

Decorate the top with a curled strip of pimento.

Sufficient for two or three persons.

LOBSTER CREAMS

INGREDIENTS.—1 tin of lobster, ¾ gill of cream, 2 tablespoonfuls of salad cream, ¼ packet of aspic jelly, salt and cayenne, ¼ teaspoonful of made mustard, a few drops of cochineal, 1 gill of béchamel sauce (see p. 365), a little cress for garnishing.

METHOD.—Put the mustard and aspic jelly into the béchamel sauce and heat it till the jelly is dissolved. Chop the lobster and add it to the sauce with salt and cayenne to taste.

When cold stir in the salad cream and a few drops of cochineal. Whip the cream and add it just before serving.

Place in ramekin cases and garnish with cress.

LYONNAISE POTATOES

INGREDIENTS.—6 potatoes (about 2 lb.), ¼ lb. of cheese, about 1 teacupful of tomato sauce, 2 tablespoonfuls of breadcrumbs, seasoning.

METHOD.—Scrub the potatoes and cook them slowly in their skins until quite tender, but not broken. They may be either boiled or baked.

For boiling allow about half an hour and about twice as long for baking.

When cooked, peel them and cut them into slices of medium thickness.

Well grease a pie-dish and put in a layer of potatoes.

Remove the rind from the cheese and grate it finely.

Make the breadcrumbs, using a grater or a sieve. These ingredients can be prepared while the potatoes are cooking.

Sprinkle the layer of potatoes in the pie-dish with some of the grated cheese. Season each layer with pepper and salt and repeat until all the potatoes are used.

Then pour over a cupful of home-made tomato sauce.

Mix the remainder of the cheese with the crumbs and sprinkle well over the top. Put into a hot oven until it browns lightly on top. Serve at once.

NOTE.—The tomato sauce can be made with either fresh or tinned tomatoes.

Sufficient for about six persons.

MACARONI CHEESE

INGREDIENTS.—3 oz. of macaroni, 1½ oz. of flour, 5 oz. of cheese, 1 pint of milk, 1½ oz. of butter, salt and pepper, 1 slice of bread.

METHOD.—Break up the macaroni into small pieces and wash it. Put into a saucepan of boiling water with a little salt and boil until tender and strain it.

Remove the rind from the cheese and grate it.

Mix the flour to a smooth paste with a small quantity of the milk. Put the remainder of the milk in a saucepan to heat with the butter.

When hot pour on to the flour, then return to the saucepan and bring to the boil and boil slowly for six minutes, keeping it well stirred all the time, then draw to the side of the fire. Season well, add the macaroni.

Add about half of the cheese to the macaroni, etc., stir it well, then pour into a greased pie-dish. Sprinkle the remainder of the cheese on the top.

Put under the grill and brown it. Serve with sippets of toast round.

MACARONI EGGS

INGREDIENTS.—2 eggs, 1 onion, ½ lb. of tomatoes, ½ oz. of margarine, ⅛ gill of water, a small sprig of parsley and thyme, seasoning, ½ clove garlic,

1 teaspoonful of cornflour, 2 oz. of macaroni.

METHOD.—Peel and mince the onion and cook it for a few minutes in the margarine, but do not let it brown. Add the sliced tomatoes, also the water, herbs, and garlic, and cook them gently till tender. When ready, remove the herbs and garlic and rub the sauce through a sieve, then thicken it with the cornflour smoothed in a little water, and add seasoning to taste.

Meanwhile, break up the macaroni, leaving two long pieces. Wash it and cook it in boiling water with salt, drain it when tender, and mix it with half the tomato sauce. Turn this into a fireproof dish, make two hollows and break an egg into each, season them well, pour the remainder of the sauce over them, and put them in the oven long enough to cook the eggs.

Garnish the dish with the two long pieces of macaroni.

Sufficient for two persons.

MACARONI AND TOMATO

INGREDIENTS.—3 oz. of macaroni, 2 oz. of cheese (chopped), 1 onion, salt and pepper, 1 teaspoonful of made mustard, 2 oz. of margarine, 1½ oz. of flour, 1 gill of water, 1 tea-cupful of milk, ⅓ gill of tomato sauce, 1 oz. of breadcrumbs.

METHOD.—Break the macaroni into pieces an inch long and boil it fast for thirty minutes in a large pan of boiling water containing a dessertspoonful of salt.

Strain off the water and put the macaroni into a fireproof dish with the tomato sauce. Peel an onion and grate it over the macaroni, using an ordinary bread-grater. Melt the margarine, stir in the flour, and add the milk and water gradually, with the saucepan off the gas. Add the cheese, stir till it melts, and season with salt, pepper, and mustard.

Boil the sauce for three minutes and pour it over the macaroni, sprinkle with breadcrumbs and a little grated cheese, and place dabs of margarine on top. Brown under the griller for a few minutes or bake for ten minutes in hot oven.

MARROW AU FROMAGE

INGREDIENTS.—Half a medium-sized marrow, 6 dessertspoonfuls of grated cheese, 1½ dessertspoonfuls of bread-crumbs, seasoning, ½ oz. of butter, parsley.

METHOD.—Peel half a medium-sized marrow, cut it into two pieces, remove the seeds and then put it into boiling water with a little salt added. Boil it gently for about ten minutes until it is lightly cooked, then drain it thoroughly and place it in a fireproof dish.

Season each piece and sprinkle them thickly with the grated cheese, keeping back one dessertspoonful and a half of the cheese.

Mix this with the breadcrumbs and sprinkle it on the top of the marrow, then dot it with small dabs of butter. Put it under the grill to melt the cheese and brown the top of the marrow.

Serve the marrow garnished with parsley.

Sufficient for two persons.

MEAT PANCAKES

INGREDIENTS.—1 egg, ¼ lb. of flour, a pinch of salt, 1½ gills of milk, 3 oz. of cold meat, salt and pepper, 1 dessert-spoonful of chopped pimento, or a pinch of herbs and ½ teaspoonful of chopped parsley, lard.

METHOD.—Sift the flour and salt, make a well in the centre and pour in the egg, then take one gill of the milk and add it gradually and mix a smooth batter. Beat it well, stir in the remainder of the milk and leave it to stand for an hour or so.

Meanwhile, cut the meat in very small pieces or put it through the mincer, and when ready to fry the pancakes add it to the batter with pepper and salt to taste, and flavouring of pimento or parsley as desired—or a little minced onion may be added, if preferred.

Melt a small piece of lard in a frying-pan and when it begins to smoke faintly pour in sufficient batter to cover the bottom of the pan well. Fry it gently until golden, then turn it over and brown it. Turn it out on to a baking-sheet lined with paper, to drain. Fold it in half and keep it warm. Fry the remainder in the same way and serve it at once.

Sufficient for four or five pancakes.

MUSHROOMS AU GRATIN

INGREDIENTS. — 6 medium - sized mushrooms, 1 small onion, 1 tea-spoonful of Bovril, 1 tomato, 1 tea-spoonful of flour, 1 tablespoonful of brown stock (see p. 12), 2 tablespoon-fuls of minced ham, 1 oz. of butter—or more if required, seasoning, finely-grated cheese and rounds of fried bread.

METHOD.—Peel and stalk the mush-rooms, then cleanse them in salted water and drain them. Trim and wash the stalks also. Fry both lightly in the butter till tender, and put them on a plate. Add the finely-minced onion to the mushroom butter and when tender and lightly browned, add the tomato peeled and chopped up and cook them for a few minutes.

Mix the flour to a smooth paste with the stock and stir it in with the minced ham, Bovril, and seasoning to taste. Cook the mixture for three or four minutes, stirring it frequently and heap it in the centre of the mushrooms. Sprinkle a little finely-grated cheese on the top and brown it under the grill. Stick the stalks of the mushrooms in the centre of each and serve them on rounds of fried bread.

Sufficient for six mushrooms.

GRILLED MUSHROOMS AND OYSTERS

INGREDIENTS.—6 medium mush-rooms, 1 oz. of butter, 6 oysters, cayenne and salt, juice of ½ lemon, 3 nice rashers of bacon.

METHOD.—Peel the mushrooms, wash them and remove the stalks. Melt the butter and dip the mushrooms in it. Season them with salt and cayenne and place them on a greased grid-iron. Grill the mushrooms under the gas, turning them constantly; they take about eight minutes.

After five minutes, place an oyster and some lemon-juice in each mush-room. Cover with a rasher of bacon and finish grilling.

Serve the mushrooms on the bacon.

MUSHROOM OMELET

INGREDIENTS.—2 eggs, 2 dessert-spoonfuls of water, salt and pepper, ¾ oz. of butter, 2 oz. of mushrooms, ½ teaspoonful of onion-juice.

METHOD.—Peel and stalk the mushrooms, cleanse them in cold water with salt added, then drain them and fry them gently until tender in a little butter, extra to that given in the ingredients.

Separate the eggs, beat the yolks and mix them with the water, onion-juice and seasoning. Whisk the whites to a stiff froth and fold them in lightly.

Melt the butter in an omelet pan and, when hot, turn the prepared egg-mixture into it. Cook it for a few seconds until lightly set and pale brown underneath, then place it under the hot grill and colour the top. Turn the omelet on to a hot dish, cut up some of the mushrooms and put them on one half and fold the other half over them.

Serve mushroom omelet at once, garnished with the remainder of the mushrooms.

Sufficient for one person.

MUSHROOMS AND OYSTERS

INGREDIENTS.—½ lb. of small mushrooms, 1 oz. of butter, 1½ gills of milk, 1 oz. of flour, 8 oysters, juice of ½ a lemon, cayenne, salt, ½ gill of water, 4 squares of bread, 2 oz. of dripping.

METHOD.—Peel the mushrooms, wash them and remove the stalks.

Place them in a pie-dish (cup-side up) with the milk and water, a seasoning of salt and very little cayenne, and put the butter in small pieces on top.

Cover the pie-dish with greased paper and bake the mushrooms in a hot oven for about twenty minutes or till tender. While they are cooking fry the bread in a frying-pan in smoking hot fat till it is golden-brown. Turn it over when half done. It should take about two minutes to fry. Lift it out of the fat, keep hot till required.

Remove the beards from the oysters.

Put the flour in a cup and mix smoothly with the lemon-juice.

Place the mushrooms on the fried bread and put them in the oven while making the sauce. Pour the liquor

from the pie-dish into the cup of flour and lemon-juice and then add the oyster liquor.

If it is less than half a pint add a little water. Put into a saucepan, stir till it boils and boil for three minutes. Cut the oysters in quarters and put them in the sauce. Pour the oyster sauce over the toast and lay the mushrooms on top. Garnish with lemon.

Sufficient for four persons if served as one course in a meal.

BAKED SAVOURY MUSH-ROOMS

INGREDIENTS.—5 or 6 mushrooms, slices of bread, fat for frying, 2 or 3 tomatoes, 3 tablespoonfuls of bread-crumbs, 1 small piece of onion, 2 flat teaspoonfuls of chopped parsley, 3 teaspoonfuls of grated cheese, 4 oz. of butter, pepper and salt, 1 egg.

METHOD. — Choose medium-sized mushrooms.

Peel them and remove the stalks and put them in cold water to soak with a little salt and leave for about an hour ; this will cleanse them.

Then take them out and dry in a cloth. Chop the onion very finely, melt about a quarter of the butter in a pan and fry the onion in it.

Make the breadcrumbs, add the parsley, grated cheese, and fried onion. Season well with pepper and salt and mix together.

Beat up the egg and add sufficient to mix all to a stiff paste. Heap the stuffing in the centre of the mushrooms where the stalk was removed.

Stand them in a baking-tin with the remainder of the butter and bake in a moderately hot oven for about twenty minutes.

Cut as many thick slices of tomatoes as there are mushrooms and cook these gently in the oven in a greased tin until tender.

Cut rounds of bread about three-eighths of an inch thick, sufficiently large to take the mushrooms and tomato slices. Fry them in hot fat until golden brown, then drain on paper. Stand a slice of tomato on each crout of fried bread and a mushroom on the tomato and serve on a hot dish.

Pour the butter in which the

mushrooms were cooked in a small gravy-boat and serve separately.

STUFFED MUSHROOMS

INGREDIENTS.—4 large mushrooms, 2 oz. of ham or bacon, 1 dessertspoonful of chopped parsley, 1 tomato, ½ cup of breadcrumbs, 1 egg, 1 oz. of butter, ½ pint of water, ½ oz. of Bisto, 1 dessertspoonful of vinegar.

METHOD.—Cut the bacon into dice and fry it, add it to the breadcrumbs, with the bacon dripping. Chop and add the tomato and parsley, and season to taste and mix with a beaten egg. Peel and wash the mushrooms and remove the stalks. Place them upside down in a baking-tin and fill each with the stuffing.

Put half a pint of water in the tin, place a piece of butter on top of each mushroom, and bake in a rather hot oven for fifteen or twenty minutes. Place the mushrooms on a hot dish.

To make the sauce, mix the Bisto and vinegar and pour into the water in the tin. Boil up and pour round the mushrooms.

Sufficient for two to four persons, according to whether the mushrooms are large or medium size.

MUSHROOM TOAST

INGREDIENTS.—1 tin of French mushrooms, 8 small squares of buttered toast, ½ oz. of flour, ¾ oz. of butter or margarine, ¼ pint of milk, 1 teaspoonful of onion-juice, salt and pepper.

METHOD.—Drain the liquor from the mushrooms and roughly chop sufficient to make a quarter of a pint.

Melt the fat, stir in the flour, and when well blended add the milk and stir the sauce till it boils. Add the onion-juice, season the sauce with salt and pepper and add the chopped mushrooms.

Simmer it for a few minutes, turn it on to squares of hot buttered toast and decorate them with halved mushrooms, previously heated in a little butter, extra to that given.

Sufficient for eight squares of toast.

OMELETS

OMELETS are made almost entirely of eggs with a savoury addition. Or they may be made sweet.

They can be prepared without separating the eggs, but a much lighter omelet is obtained if they are separated, and each is whisked apart and then folded together lightly.

An omelet pan is used for cooking them. This is similar to a small frying-pan, and should be kept only for this purpose.

Omelets must be served as soon as they are cooked, as they quickly lose their lightness.

CHEESE OMELET

INGREDIENTS.—½ oz. of butter, 2 eggs, 2 dessertspoonfuls of grated cheese, pepper and salt.

METHOD.—Separate the eggs.

Beat up the yolks, then stir in the grated cheese, and pepper and salt. Use dry cheese, grated very finely.

Add a pinch of salt to the egg-whites and whisk them to a very stiff froth, then fold them into the yolks. Melt the butter in an omelet pan and when hot turn in the egg mixture. Shake the pan occasionally to prevent sticking, and when it begins to set round the edges, draw it towards the handle of the pan, keeping the latter tilted that way.

Continue to cook for a few seconds, then put under the hot grill and lightly brown the top.

Turn on to a hot dish and serve at once.

Sufficient for one person.

A dessertspoonful of milk is sometimes mixed with the yolks after beating them.

If a plain omelet is required, omit the cheese and season only with pepper and salt.

For a Sweet Omelet, whisk some castor sugar with the yolks.

To make variety, finely-chopped parsley or minced ham may be used in place of the cheese.

ANOTHER METHOD
(EGGS NOT SEPARATED)

WHISK the eggs and add seasoning and cheese.

Melt the butter in an omelet pan and when hot pour in the eggs, etc. Stir at first to prevent them from sticking (use a spoon for this), and as the omelet begins to set round the edges fold the latter over, drawing the omelet towards the handle of the pan, keeping the pan tilted that way.

When cooked, turn on to a hot dish and serve at once.

FRENCH SAVOURY OMELET

INGREDIENTS.—3 eggs, 1 oz. of butter, 1 tablespoonful of milk, ¼ onion, 1 dessertspoonful of chopped parsley.

METHOD.—Mince the onion very finely and fry it in the butter for five minutes. Beat the eggs well with the milk and add seasoning and parsley. Pour the beaten eggs into the pan and stir over a fairly high gas till it begins to set. Push it to one side of the pan, and when it is slightly browned fold it in half and turn out on to a hot dish.

A SWEDISH OMELET

INGREDIENTS.—4 eggs, 8 table-spoonfuls of cream, 1 teaspoonful of potato flour, a pinch of salt, ½ oz. of butter.

FOR THE GARNISH.—½ oz. of butter and flour, ¾ gill of milk, 1 tablespoonful of cream, 4d. of picked shrimps, cayenne, squeeze of lemon-juice.

METHOD.—Mix the yolks of the eggs smoothly with the potato flour, and add the salt and cream. Whisk the whites very stiffly and add them lightly to the mixture. Heat the butter and pour in the eggs without stirring. Cook for about four minutes over a rather low gas, and finish under the griller. Fold in half and turn on to a hot dish.

TO MAKE THE GARNISH.—Melt the butter, stir in the flour, and add the milk gradually. Stir till it boils, and boil three minutes. Wash the shrimps and heat them five minutes in the sauce. Add cream, cayenne, and a squeeze of lemon. Serve dainty heaps of the garnish round the omelet.

NOTE.—In Sweden the garnish is not put inside the omelet, but the omelet is served plain, folded in half, with the garnish in small heaps round as a border.

Anything tasty such as chicken, sweetbreads, mushrooms, etc., could be heated in the sauce and served as a garnish instead of shrimps.

Sufficient for two or three persons.

SCALLOPED ONIONS

INGREDIENTS.—1 lb. of onions, 1 oz. of margarine or butter, ¾ oz. of flour, 1 gill of milk, 1 gill of onion liquor, 1 oz. of breadcrumbs, ½ oz. of butter, seasoning.

METHOD.—Peel the onions, cover them with cold water and bring them to the boil. Then drain them. Cover the onions again with fresh water, and cook them gently till they are tender.

Drain the onions, saving some of the liquor. Cut them up and season them with salt and pepper.

Melt the margarine in a saucepan, add the flour, and when they are well blended, stir in the milk and onion liquor. Bring the sauce to the boil. Boil it gently for a few minutes and add seasoning to taste.

Butter four scallop dishes, put a little sauce into each, heap the prepared onions on this and cover them with sauce. Then sprinkle buttered crumbs on the top, and heat the Scalloped Onions through in the oven.

To prepare the buttered crumbs, melt the half an ounce of butter in a frying-pan, and when it is hot, add the fresh breadcrumbs and fry them till golden, keeping them stirred.

Sufficient for four persons.

ONION SOUFFLE

INGREDIENTS.—1½ lb. of onions, 3 eggs, 1½ oz. of butter, 1½ oz. of flour, salt and pepper, boiling water.

METHOD.—Peel the onions, cook them till soft in a pan of boiling water containing a teaspoonful of salt. Put the onions on a sieve and press out *all* the water as they must be as dry as possible.

Chop the onions and measure them. There should be about half a pint after they are cooked.

Melt the butter, stir in the flour, and add the cooked onions. No water is necessary.

Stir till the mixture boils, season well with salt and pepper and boil for three minutes.

Beat the eggs and stir them in gradually with the pan off the fire. Beat the mixture well and bake it in a well-greased fireproof dish in a fairly hot oven for thirty minutes. Serve as quickly as possible.

Sufficient for four persons.

NOTE.—Other vegetable soufflés, such as spinach or tomato, can be made from this recipe, using half a pint of the desired purée instead of using onions.

STUFFED ONIONS

INGREDIENTS.—4 large Spanish onions, stuffing, 2 teaspoonfuls of chopped parsley, 2 oz. of cooked ham, 1½ oz. of cheese, 1 oz. of margarine (melted), pepper and salt, 4 tablespoonfuls of breadcrumbs, ½ an egg, butter (about ¼ lb.).

METHOD.—Peel the onions, cut off a small slice from the top of each, hollow out a piece from the centre of the onions.

Make the breadcrumbs, chop up the ham, grate the cheese, wash, scald, and finely chop the parsley.

Mix all these ingredients together, chop up the slices of onion that were cut off, and add to the stuffing.

Season well, moisten with the melted margarine, bind with the egg, and mix all into a lump ; if necessary, a tablespoonful of milk can be added. Put a little stuffing into each onion and pile it well up on the top, and sprinkle a little cheese on the stuffing. Put into a baking-tin or pie-dish with the butter.

Bake in a moderately hot oven for about one to one hour and a half, or until tender ; keep them well basted. Stand on a dish, garnish with a sprig of parsley on each onion, and pour round the butter.

NOTE.—Care must be taken to keep the onions whole.

Keep a little of the grated cheese for sprinkling on the top.

Allow one for each person.

STUFFED SPANISH ONIONS

INGREDIENTS.—3 Spanish onions, 2 oz. of breadcrumbs, ¼ lb. of sausage-meat, ½ oz. of butter, 1 small egg, 2 oz. of dripping.

METHOD.—Cook the Spanish onions in a large pan of boiling water. It is not necessary to peel them before cooking.

Boil for an hour, then strain off the water and peel the onions.

Scoop out the centres of each one, chop them and put them in a small basin with the breadcrumbs, sausage meat, butter, and an egg to bind. Stuff the onions with the mixture, and put them into a fireproof dish or baking-tin with the dripping.

Cover the tin with greased paper and bake in a moderate oven for an hour or till tender. Baste the onions with the dripping two or three times.

OYSTERS WITH MACARONI

INGREDIENTS.—2 oz. of macaroni, ½ oz. of butter, ½ oz. of flour, 1 gill of milk, 1 dozen oysters, juice of ½ lemon, salt and cayenne.

METHOD.—Break the macaroni into pieces an inch long and put it into fast boiling water with a teaspoonful of salt. Boil till tender (about twenty minutes) and strain. Melt the butter in a saucepan, add the flour and mix well. Stir in the milk with the pan off the gas. Replace over the gas and stir till it boils. Season with lemon-juice, salt, and cayenne. Remove the beards from the oysters and put the oyster liquor into the sauce with the macaroni. Cut six of the oysters in half and add them to the macaroni. Pour into a fireproof dish and lightly brown in a hot oven for five minutes. Put six whole oysters on the top and serve.

Sufficient for three persons.

PARSNIP PIE

INGREDIENTS.—2 lb. of parsnips, ½ oz. of margarine, ½ oz. of flour, salt and pepper, ¼ lb. of cheese (chopped), 1 gill of water used for boiling the parsnips.

METHOD.—Wash and peel the parsnips. Boil them till tender, strain and mash them with a fork.

Melt the margarine, stir in the flour, and, when smooth, add the water.

Stir till it boils, add the parsnips and half the cheese, and season to taste.

Put the rest of the cheese on the top, and brown the pie in the oven for about ten minutes.

Sufficient for three persons.

NOTE.—If preferred, milk or milk

and water may be used instead of water.

SCALLOPED PEAS

INGREDIENTS.—¾ pint of cooked peas (hot or cold), ½ pint of milk, 1 oz. of butter or margarine, ¾ oz. of flour, seasoning, 3 oz. of cheese, 2 dessertspoonfuls of breadcrumbs.

METHOD.—Melt the fat in a saucepan add the flour and when it is well blended stir in the milk and bring it to the boil.

Boil the sauce gently for a few minutes, then add the finely-grated cheese, keeping back about one tablespoonful. Stir the sauce till the cheese is melted and add seasoning to taste.

Butter four scallop dishes, put a little sauce in each one and heap some peas on top and season them.

Cover the peas with the remainder of the sauce, and sprinkle the breadcrumbs mixed with the remainder of the cheese on top.

Heat the scalloped peas through in the oven, and brown them under the grill.

NOTE.—If the peas are hot, only browning will be required.

Sufficient for four persons.

SUFFOLK PEAS

INGREDIENTS.—1 packet of dried green peas, 2 oz. of bacon, 1 tablespoonful of chopped pimento, pepper, salt.

METHOD.—Cook the peas according to the directions on the packet, and when they are cooked, drain them.

Cook the chopped bacon, stir in the chopped pimento, and then lightly toss the peas in the mixture.

If liked, add a lump of butter as well. Season the peas with salt and pepper and serve them.

TOASTED PEARS

INGREDIENTS.—4 tinned pears, 1 egg, ½ oz. of butter, 3 oz. of grated cheese, 1 teaspoonful of curry-powder, 1 tablespoonful of breadcrumbs, 6 oz. of flaky pastry (see p. 252).

METHOD.—Roll out the pastry and cut it into eight diamond-shaped pieces. Sprinkle four pieces with water and a teaspoonful of cheese. Cover each piece with another piece of pastry, and brush them over with a little beaten egg. Bake in a hot oven for ten minutes.

Mix the butter, breadcrumbs, cheese, and curry-powder. Put the filling on the pears, standing them cut side up on each pastry diamond. Bake for six minutes.

PEASE PUDDING AND DUMP-LINGS

INGREDIENTS.—1 packet of peas, 1 egg (beaten), 2 oz. of bacon fat, 1 teaspoonful of dried mint, salt and pepper.

FOR THE DUMPLINGS.—3 oz. of self-raising flour, 1½ oz. of shredded suet, ¼ teaspoonful of salt.

METHOD.—Soak and boil the peas as directed on the packet. Rub them through a wire sieve. Stir in the egg, bacon fat, and mint and season with salt and pepper.

Put the mixture into a greased basin and tie a cloth over it. Boil for one hour.

To make the dumplings, mix the flour, suet and salt stiffly with water, and shape it into six balls. Drop these into the boiling water and simmer them for thirty minutes.

Sufficient for from four to six persons.

STUFFED PEPPERS

INGREDIENTS.—6 large sweet peppers, 1 onion, ¾ lb. of sausage meat, 1 egg, ½ oz. of butter, 2 oz. of breadcrumbs, ½ pint of stock (see p. 12) or water.

METHOD.—Chop the onion and fry it in the butter for five minutes. Cut the peppers in half lengthways and remove the seeds.

Mix the fried onion with the sausage meat and breadcrumbs and bind with a beaten egg. Stuff the peppers with the mixture and bake in a moderate oven for forty-five minutes, putting the stock or water into the baking-tin to keep them from becoming dry.

One sweet pepper, cut in half, is sufficient for two persons.

PIMENTO RAREBIT

INGREDIENTS.—2 level teaspoonfuls of chopped pimento, 4 oz. of cheese, 1½ oz. of butter, ¼ level teaspoonful of chopped chives, milk, seasoning, buttered toast.

METHOD.—Use dry cheese and grate it finely. Melt the butter in a saucepan, add the cheese, pimento, and chives and stir the mixture over a very low burner until the cheese is melted, stirring in sufficient milk to make it a creamy mass. Add seasoning to taste and serve the mixture on hot buttered toast garnished with small pieces of pimento.

Sufficient for four pieces of toast.

POTATO FRITTERS

INGREDIENTS.—Potatoes (as required), 4 oz. of flour, 1 white of egg, 2 teaspoonfuls of salad oil, warm water (1 gill), pinch of salt, lard or salad oil for frying (if preferred, substitute dripping).

METHOD.—Mix the flour and salt and pass through a sieve into a basin. Make a well in the centre, pour in the oil and mix with a small quantity of the flour. Gradually add the water and mix in the flour by degrees, keeping an even consistency all the time. When all the flour is well mixed beat the batter for about ten minutes or until the surface is full of bubbles. Set aside for at least an hour.

Wash and thinly peel the potatoes and cut them into *very thin* slices, then dry them in a cloth. Whisk the white of egg to a stiff froth and lightly fold into the batter. Put some lard or oil in a pan to heat. Use sufficient to float the fritters. Coat a few of the potato slices in the batter, put them into the hot fat or oil and fry until golden brown Then drain them on paper.

Reheat the fat and fry the others in the same way. Serve at once on a dish-paper ; sprinkle with salt.

NOTE.—Use a fairly deep pan.

POTATO ROLL

INGREDIENTS.—1 lb. of potatoes (freshly boiled), 1 oz. of boiled rice (dry), 1 oz. of butter, salt and pepper, 1 egg, 1 tablespoonful of milk, parsley, a jar glaze or meat extract, a little flour.

METHOD.—The potatoes should be quite dry. While they are still hot mash them in the saucepan with a fork.

Add the rice, butter, and milk, season with salt and pepper and mix well.

Beat the egg and stir it in.

Form the mixture into a roll.

Scald a pudding-cloth by dipping half of it in a pan of boiling water. Press a saucepan lid against it when taking it out and flour lightly.

Lay the potato mixture on the end of the wet cloth, roll it up and tie each end firmly.

Place it in fast boiling water and boil for an hour and a half.

Melt the glaze by standing the jar in a pan of boiling water.

Turn the roll out carefully after letting it stand for five minutes and remove the cloth. Brush the top of the roll with glaze and decorate with parsley.

Sufficient for three persons.

NOTE.—Hot potatoes are much easier to mash than cold ones.

POTATO AND SHRIMP SAVOURIES

INGREDIENTS.—2 lb. of potatoes, salt and pepper, ¾ oz. of flour, 4 oz. of cheese (grated), ¼ lb. of butter or margarine, 1½ gills of milk, 2 yolks of eggs, 3 gills of picked shrimps, browned crumbs.

METHOD.—Peel and wash the potatoes. Boil them with just sufficient water to cover and salt to flavour. When cooked strain them and leave in the saucepan to dry for a few minutes.

Mash them very finely, or rub them through a sieve. Return to the saucepan and stir in one half of the cheese and a quarter of the butter.

Stir over a low gas until the cheese melts, then draw to the side and cool slightly. Beat up the yolks of eggs and add.

Mix well together and season with pepper and salt. Turn on to a slightly-floured board, divide into small equal portions and mould each into a basin shape. Smooth the outside and tops of them with a knife, then melt about two ounces of butter and brush them over with it and coat with the brown crumbs.

Stand them on a greased baking-sheet and make thoroughly hot in the oven. Melt the remaining ounce of butter in a pan, stir in the flour and when well mixed add the milk.

Stir until the sauce boils, then cook slowly for a few minutes. Wash the shrimps, cut them up and add to the sauce with the remainder of the grated cheese. Stir until the latter has melted and all is thoroughly hot.

Season with salt and pepper, then fill the potato cases with the prepared mixture. Stick a sprig of parsley in each. Stand on a lace paper and serve.

POTATO SOUFFLE

INGREDIENTS.—1 lb. of potatoes, 1½ oz. of butter, 1 egg, 1 gill of milk, 1 oz. of grated cheese, salt and pepper.

METHOD.—Wash, peel and boil the potatoes and dry them over a low gas.

Mash carefully, adding the butter, milk, salt and pepper and the yolk of the egg. Beat the white to a stiff froth and stir it into the mixture. Put it into a fireproof dish and sprinkle with the cheese. Bake in a hot oven for ten or fifteen minutes.

PRAWN SAVOURIES

INGREDIENTS.—½ gill of shelled prawns, some mayonnaise (see p. 168), about ¼ lb. of flaky pastry (see p. 252), seasoning.

METHOD.—Divide the prawns into small pieces and mix with a little mayonnaise and seasoning to taste.

Roll out the pastry thinly to an oblong or square shape. Turn it over on to the other side, spread the prawns lightly over one half, then damp the edge and fold the other half over them.

Press down lightly and, with a sharp knife, cut into narrow strips. Prick the tops, put them on a baking-sheet, brush with milk and bake in a hot oven. They will take about ten minutes.

Serve on a dish garnished with a few whole prawns.

Sufficient to make about one dozen.

STUFFED PRUNES

INGREDIENTS.—6 large stewed prunes, 1 tablespoonful of chutney, 3 rashers of bacon, juice of ½ lemon, 1 cup of cold potatoes, 1 oz. of dripping,

METHOD.—Remove the stones from the prunes carefully, and fill the cavity with chutney.

Cut off the bacon-rind and wrap half a rasher round each prune separately. Stick a skewer right through and place them in a tin or fireproof dish.

Squeeze lemon-juice over them and bake them for about ten minutes.

Heat the dripping, slice and fry the potatoes slowly, stirring well. Serve the potatoes surrounded with the stuffed prunes.

RAINBOW EGGS

INGREDIENTS.—½ pint of milk, 1 oz. of butter or margarine, ¾ oz. of flour, ½ a pimento, 5 eggs, 1 dessertspoonful of onion-juice, seasoning, 1 gill of cooked green peas.

METHOD.—Put the eggs into boiling water and boil them gently from twelve to fifteen minutes. Remove the shells and chop up four eggs, leaving one for garnishing.

Melt the butter, add the flour and when well blended stir in the milk and bring it to the boil. Boil this sauce gently for a few minutes, add the onion-juice, chopped eggs, peas, and chopped pimento. Make the mixture hot and add seasoning to taste. Turn it into a dish and garnish it with the remaining egg. Serve hot.

Sufficient for two or four persons.

RICE CAKES AND BACON

INGREDIENTS.—¾ lb. of cooked rice, 2 oz. of flour, rashers of fat Wiltshire bacon, 2 tablespoonfuls of milk, ½ level teaspoonful of baking-powder, 1 beaten egg, ½ small level teaspoonful of salt.

METHOD.—Sift the flour, salt, and baking-powder into a basin.

Stir in the egg mixed with the milk, and then the rice.

Fry the bacon and arrange it in a circle on a round dish.

Drop the rice batter in tablespoonfuls into the fat remaining from the bacon and fry the cakes on both sides till they are brown. They should only be turned once.

Heap up the rice cakes in the centre of the bacon.

NOTE.—If there is not sufficient bacon fat a little lard may be added.

Sufficient for four persons.

RICE TOMATOES

INGREDIENTS.—5 tomatoes, ¼ lb. of rice, salt and pepper, 2½ oz. of cheese, 2½ tablespoonfuls of breadcrumbs.

METHOD.—Wash the rice, put it into a saucepan of boiling water (slightly salted), boil it until tender and then strain it and drain it well. Take about two-thirds of the rice, divide it into five portions. Make each portion into a flat round cake on which to stand a tomato.

Wipe and stalk the tomatoes, cut off a slice from the other end and scoop out some of the pulp. Remove the skin from the slices you cut off, and mix these pieces of tomato with the pulp.

Add the remainder of the cooked rice, also the cheese, grated finely, and the breadcrumbs.

Mix all together, season well and heap the mixture in the tomatoes. Stand one on each cake of rice, put into a lightly greased baking-tin and bake gently until tender.

Allow one tomato for each person.

SARDINE BISCUITS

INGREDIENTS.—1 cream cheese (4 oz.) a tin of sardines (in olive oil), oatmeal or breakfast biscuits, watercress (small bunch), 2 hard-boiled yolks of eggs, cayenne pepper.

METHOD.—Pick over and wash the watercress. When quite clean, drain it.

Remove the bones and flake up the sardines, and mix with the yolks of eggs and cream cheese.

Pound all together well and season with cayenne.

Pile the mixture on either oatmeal or breakfast biscuits. Place on a dish and garnish with watercress.

NOTE.—If liked, the mixture can be forced through an icing-bag on to the biscuits.

SARDINE BOUCHEES

INGREDIENTS.—1 tin of sardines, ¾ cup of breadcrumbs, ½ onion, 1 dessertspoonful of capers, pepper, ½ oz. of flour, ½ gill of vinegar, 1 egg (hard-boiled and chopped), 6 oz. of short pastry (see p. 252).

METHOD.—Chop the sardines, keeping back a few whole ones for decorating.

Grease four large patty-pans. Cut the pastry into four, roll it out and line the tins.

Chop the onion, fry it in the sardine oil for five minutes, stir in the sardines, flour, capers, the egg, pepper and vinegar and the breadcrumbs to make a stiff mixture. Fill each tart and bake them for about twenty minutes in a hot oven.

SARDINE FINGERS

INGREDIENTS.—5 large sardines, 5 fingers of bread, tomato ketchup, about 1 tablespoonful of grated cheese, butter, seasoning.

METHOD.—Cut oblongs of bread about toast thickness, and the same size as the sardines. Toast them on one side and butter the untoasted side, then spread them with tomato ketchup, sprinkle them with cheese and season with pepper and salt, and put them under the grill to melt the cheese.

Meanwhile, split open the sardines and remove the backbones, close them up again and warm them through in the oven. Serve them on the fingers of prepared toast.

SARDINES AU GRATIN

INGREDIENTS.—1 tin of sardines, 1 lb. of tomatoes, 2 oz. of breadcrumbs, 1 oz. of margarine, ½ an onion, salt and pepper, 1 tablespoonful of chopped parsley, 1 oz. of cheese.

METHOD.—Mince the onion finely and cut the tomatoes in half.

Wash, dry and chop the parsley and grate the cheese.

Grease a pie-dish and cover the bottom with tomatoes.

Lay half the sardines on top and sprinkle with onion, parsley, breadcrumbs, cheese, and salt and pepper.

Put another layer of tomatoes and sardines and sprinkle the rest of the breadcrumbs on top.

Pour the oil in the tin over the breadcrumbs and put small pieces of margarine on top.

Cover with greased paper and bake for twenty minutes in a hot oven, taking off the paper after fifteen minutes to let it brown.

Decorate with chopped parsley.

Sufficient for four persons.

SARDINES ON TOAST

INGREDIENTS.—6 sardines, 6 slices of buttered toast, 1 oz. of butter, 1 oz. of flour, 1 gill of milk, pepper and salt, ¾ gill of salad oil, ½ gill of vinegar, 1 flat teaspoonful of mixed mustard, 1 flat teaspoonful of castor sugar, 1 teaspoonful of chopped tarragon.

METHOD.—Open the sardines, remove the backbone, close them up again and place on a baking-sheet and heat them in the oven for about ten minutes.

Prepare six slices of buttered toast, each piece about the same shape and size as the sardines.

Place a sardine on each piece of toast and keep hot while the sauce is made.

Melt the butter in a saucepan, mix in the flour, add the milk, and bring to the boil and simmer for about five minutes, keeping it well stirred all the time. Pour into a basin, cover the sauce with cold water and leave to cool. Pour off the water, stand the basin over a saucepan of hot water, and whisk in alternately the salad oil and vinegar, being careful not to let the sauce get too hot or it will curdle.

Add the sugar, mustard, pepper and salt.

When finished the sauce should be sufficiently thick to coat the savoury. Place the sardines on toast on a rack and stand the rack on a dish.

Take a tablespoonful of the sauce at a time and coat each sardine and toast with it.

When all are coated lift carefully on to a dish with a lace paper and sprinkle a little chopped tarragon on each. Serve hot.

SARDINE TOMATOES

INGREDIENTS. — 6 medium-sized tomatoes, small tin of sardines, salt and pepper, some mayonnaise (see p. 168), a few shelled walnuts, 1 round lettuce.

METHOD.—Wipe the tomatoes, remove the stalks and cut off a slice from the opposite end. Scrape out some of the pulp—this can be used for some purpose. Remove the backbone from the sardines, flake the fish into small pieces and mix it with two or three teaspoonfuls of mayonnaise.

Season the inside of the tomatoes with pepper and salt, then heap the sardines in them. Garnish with a dab of mayonnaise and some pieces of shelled walnut and serve on lettuce leaves.

Allow one for each person.

SARDINES AND TOMATOES ON TOAST

INGREDIENTS.—3 or 4 sardines, 3 or 4 slices of bread, butter, tomato ketchup, 1 whole egg and 1 yolk, 1½ dessertspoonfuls of vinegar, mustard, salt and pepper, 1 teaspoonful of cold water (if required), parsley.

METHOD.—Open the sardines, take out the backbone and put them together again. Cut the slices of bread oblong shape, the same size as the sardines. Toast and butter them and spread with just a little tomato ketchup, then place one sardine on each. Put in the oven and make hot.

Put the eggs and vinegar into a saucepan, add a small lump of butter, and season with salt, pepper, and mixed mustard. Whisk all together over a low gas until quite thick, being careful not to let it boil ; a teaspoonful of cold water can be added if too thick.

Take the sardines and toast from the oven, stand them on a rack over a dish and coat with the prepared sauce.

Sprinkle a line of dried parsley on each and serve hot.

NOTE.—To dry parsley, wash and wipe a few sprigs and put into the oven to dry, but be careful not to let them brown. Then rub the parsley to a powder.

Allow one piece of toast for each person.

SAUSAGE FRITTERS

INGREDIENTS.—1 lb. of sausages, 3 oz. of flour, 1 dessertspoonful of salad oil, 1 gill of warm water, a pinch of salt, 2 whites of eggs, deep fat for frying, tomato ketchup.

METHOD.—Parboil the sausages for five minutes, take them out of the water and leave them to get cold, then skin and cut them in slices crosswise.

Sift the flour with salt, make a hole in the centre and pour in the oil, then add the warm water gradually and mix to a smooth batter. Beat it well and leave it to stand for an hour or more, then fold in the stiffly whisked egg-whites.

Dab the sliced sausages with tomato ketchup, then dip some in the batter, fry them in hot fat until golden and drain them on paper. Coat and fry the remainder in the same way and serve the fritters as quickly as possible, as they so soon lose their crispness.

Sufficient for six persons.

SAUSAGE SAVOURY

INGREDIENTS.—$\frac{1}{2}$ lb. of small sausages, 2 medium-sized mushrooms, 2 or 3 rashers of streaky bacon, seasoning, butter, 5 oblongs of bread.

METHOD.—Peel and stalk the mushrooms, wash them in cold water with a little salt added, then drain and chop them. Remove the rind from the rashers and put the bacon through the mincer.

Fry the mushrooms and bacon in a little butter and at the same time fry the sausages in another pan.

Cut bread to toast thickness, toast it on one side and butter the untoasted side, put a little mushroom and bacon on each piece, season to taste and arrange two sausages on top of it.

Sufficient for five persons.

SAUSAGE TARTLETS

INGREDIENTS.—1 lb. of flaky pastry (see p. 252), $\frac{1}{2}$ lb. of pork sausages or sausage meat, 1 hard-boiled egg, 1 raw yolk of egg, $\frac{1}{4}$ level teaspoonful of powdered sage.

METHOD.—Roll out the pastry a quarter of an inch thick, and cut out ten rounds. Put these aside. Roll out the remainder of the pastry thinly and cut out the same number of rounds. Line ten patty-pans with the latter.

Remove the skin from the sausages, mix the latter with the sage (if not already flavoured with sage), add also the hard-boiled egg (chopped finely), and mix in the beaten egg-yolk.

Divide this between the ten lined patty-pans, and cover them with the thick rounds of pastry.

Make two cuts in the centre of each, brush them with egg and put them into a hot oven to bake. They will take about twenty minutes to cook.

Serve sausage tartlets hot or cold.

Sufficient to make ten tartlets.

SAVOURY BAKED PUDDING

INGREDIENTS.—$\frac{3}{4}$ lb. of stale bread, 1 lb. of onions (chopped), $\frac{1}{2}$ lb. of shredded suet, $\frac{1}{4}$ lb. of fine oatmeal, 2 teaspoonfuls of powdered sage, 1 egg, $\frac{1}{2}$ gill of milk, salt and pepper.

METHOD.—Put the bread in a cloth, lay it in a bowl and pour boiling water on to it. When the crusts are soft, squeeze out *all* the water.

Break up the bread finely and mix it with the onions, suet, sage and oatmeal. Season with salt and pepper and bind with milk and a beaten egg.

Put the pudding into a greased pie-dish, and bake it for one hour and a quarter.

Sufficient for three persons.

SAVOURY CHARLOTTE

INGREDIENTS.—6 oz. of tomatoes, 6 oz. of onions, 3 oz. of breadcrumbs, $1\frac{1}{2}$ oz. of suet, $1\frac{1}{2}$ oz. of cheese, salt and pepper, $\frac{1}{2}$ oz. of margarine.

METHOD.—Grease a pie-dish and coat it with a few of the breadcrumbs.

Chop the suet finely and mix it with the remainder of the bread-crumbs, and season with salt and pepper. Peel and slice the onions, and grate the cheese finely. Cut the tomatoes into slices.

Put about half the crumbs and suet in the bottom of the dish. Then add a layer of tomato and onion slices and a little grated cheese.

Continue in this way until all the ingredients are used, leaving sufficient tomato and onion for the top layer. Add a few pieces of margarine, and remember to season each layer. Put in a moderately hot oven to bake It will take about one hour.

Sufficient for four or five persons.

SAVOURY CORNETS

INGREDIENTS.—Small corner wafers (the kind used for ice-cream), 1 tin of sardines, 1 tablespoonful of capers and caper vinegar, salt and pepper, ½ cup of breadcrumbs, 2 slices of bread, 2 oz. of dripping, parsley for garnishing.

METHOD.—Chop half the sardines and mix them with the capers, caper vinegar and breadcrumbs, making a stiff paste.

Season to taste with salt and pepper and fill the cornets.

Lay them in a tin and cover them with paper, or put them in a paper bag and lay it in a tin. Bake for ten minutes in a hot oven.

Heat the sardine oil and dripping in a frying-pan until it smokes.

Cut the crust off the bread and cut each slice into three fingers.

Put them into the smoking fat and fry them for one minute on each side. Drain them on paper.

Serve a sardine on each finger and place a cornet on top.

Garnish with parsley.

NOTE.—If ice-cream cornets cannot be obtained the mixture can be made into sandwiches by using ordinary oblong ice-cream wafers.

SAVOURY EGGS

INGREDIENTS.—6 eggs, 1 oz. of butter, salt, pepper, ¾ oz. of flour, ½ lemon, 3 medium onions, ½ pint of onion water, 2 tablespoonfuls of thick cream, nutmeg.

METHOD.—Boil the eggs till they are hard. Remove the shells and cut the eggs crosswise into thick slices.

Peel and slice the onions and place them in a saucepan. Cover them with boiling water. Boil them quickly for twenty minutes. Drain them and cover them again with fresh water. Boil them for about twenty minutes, till they are tender. Drain them again, saving the water.

Melt the butter in a saucepan, stir in the flour and when frothy gradually add the water. Stir it till it boils and continue boiling for a few minutes. Add the salt and pepper and the juice of lemon and a grating of nutmeg. Stir in the cream.

When the sauce is piping hot, add the egg and onion slices very carefully, but do not let it boil in case the cream curdles. Toss them lightly till they are quite hot. Serve the Savoury

Eggs on a hot dish garnished with triangles of toast and slices of egg.

Sufficient for five or six persons.

SAVOURY EGG JELLIES

INGREDIENTS.—1½ pints of aspic or calf's foot jelly, 4 eggs, salt, mayonnaise (see p. 168), grated cheese.

METHOD.—Boil the eggs for fifteen minutes, until hard, then crack the shells and leave them in cold water.

Remove the shells, halve the eggs, and carefully remove the yolks.

Chop up the white, and rub the yolks through a sieve to a powder ; season both with salt.

Rinse some small moulds with cold water.

Melt about one pint of the jelly and set a thin layer in the bottom of each mould.

Decorate the bottom of each with about half a teaspoonful of the powdered yolks, sprinkled in evenly, then cover the decoration with a thin layer of jelly and leave until set.

Now fill up the moulds with alternate layers of white of egg and jelly, and yolk of egg and jelly, leaving each layer to set before adding the next.

The last layer should be of the jelly. When all are set, dip each into warm water and turn on to a dish.

Chop the remainder of the jelly and serve round ; sprinkle a little grated cheese over the chopped jelly. Serve mayonnaise sauce separately.

SAVOURY EGG TOAST

INGREDIENTS.—2 eggs, salt and pepper, buttered toast, anchovy paste, 2 tablespoonfuls of milk, 1 oz. of butter.

METHOD.—Prepare the buttered toast in the usual way, and spread it thickly with anchovy paste, and keep it warm.

Beat up the eggs and mix them with the milk, adding seasoning to taste. Melt the butter in a saucepan, add the eggs and stir these till they thicken and begin to set. Then turn the egg mixture on to the prepared toast and serve.

Sufficient for one person.

SAVOURY LENTILS

INGREDIENTS.—1 lb. of onions, ½ lb. of split lentils (washed), 1 oz. of butter,

1 oz. of flour, salt and pepper, 1 teaspoonful of dried mint.

METHOD.—Peel the onions and boil them till soft. Put them on a covered plate.

Simmer the lentils in the onion water for thirty minutes, standing the plate of onions on top of the saucepan. Strain the lentils. Melt the butter and stir in the flour, lentils, mint, and a gill of the onion water.

Boil for three minutes. Season to taste. Dish up with the onions round the lentils.

Sufficient for three persons.

SAVOURY MEAT TOAST

INGREDIENTS.—2 rounds of buttered toast, ½ gill of thick white sauce (see p. 364), 2 oz. of cooked ham, 2 eggs, seasoning.

METHOD.—Make the white sauce, then mince the ham and add to it.

Season with pepper and powdered mace and make thoroughly hot.

Toast and butter two rounds of bread, cover with the prepared ham mixture, and poach an egg and serve on each.

Allow one for each person.

SAVOURY MOULDS

INGREDIENTS.—1½ to 2 dessertspoonfuls of semolina, ½ pint of water, ¼ lb. of cheese, salt, pepper and mustard, 2 or 3 tablespoonfuls of cooked peas, 2 teaspoonfuls of gelatine, 3 tablespoonfuls of water.

METHOD.—Put the gelatine to soak for an hour or so in one tablespoonful and a half of cold water. Bring the half a pint of water to the boil in a saucepan, then sprinkle in the semolina, and cook for a few minutes until tender and the mixture thick and creamy, keeping it stirred occasionally. Add the cheese (grated finely) and stir until melted, then draw aside. Season with pepper, salt and mixed mustard and add the peas. Pour one tablespoonful and a half of boiling water on to the soaked gelatine and when dissolved strain into the semolina and cheese.

When beginning to set put in small wet moulds.

When firm turn out and sprinkle a little grated cheese on the top of each.

Sufficient to fill six small moulds.

SAVOURY PANCAKES

INGREDIENTS.—1 egg, 4 oz. of flour, ½ pint of milk and water, ¼ teaspoonful of salt, 2 oz. lard.

FOR THE FILLING.—1 cup of cold meat (minced), ½ an onion (grated), 1 tablespoonful of chopped parsley, ¾ gill of thick gravy.

METHOD.—Heat the meat, onion, and parsley in the gravy. Hollow out the centre of the flour and put in the egg (unbeaten), the salt and two tablespoonfuls of milk.

Stir a little to mix the centre only.

Gradually stir in half the milk. Beat well and add the rest of the milk and water.

To fry the pancakes, heat a piece of lard the size of a cherry. Pour in one large tablespoonful of batter with the pan off the gas.

Place the pan over a high gas for one minute. When slightly browned turn the pancake over with a knife and brown the other side.

Turn the pancake on to a paper, put in a dessertspoonful of filling and fold it in half. Cook as many pancakes as you have enough batter in the same way.

Cover the filled pancakes with a tin and heat for ten minutes in the oven.

Serve very hot on a lace paper.

SAVOURY SARDINES

INGREDIENTS.—1 large tin of sardines, 2 oz. of butter or margarine, 1¾ oz. of flour, 1 pint of white stock or milk, salt and cayenne, 4 teaspoonfuls of tomato ketchup, 1 teacupful of breadcrumbs, a sprinkle of lemon-juice, a few browned crumbs.

METHOD.—Melt the butter in a saucepan, add the flour and mix it well in, add the stock or milk gradually, stir all the time until it comes to the boil, then cook slowly for a few minutes.

Cut the tails from the sardines, open them and remove all the bones.

Flake the flesh into small pieces.

Make the breadcrumbs and add to the sauce with the flaked sardines. Add the tomato ketchup, lemon-juice, and seasoning. Mix all well together.

Put into a pie-dish, sprinkle the top with brown crumbs and make thoroughly hot in the oven.

Serve in the same dish.

Sufficient for about eight persons.

SAVOURY SPAGHETTI

INGREDIENTS.—¼ lb. of spaghetti, ¼ lb. of cheese, 1 lb. of tomatoes, ½ pint of stock (see p. 12), ½ oz. of cornflour, ¼ teaspoonful of mixed herbs, 1 onion, pepper and salt, 1 oz. of butter.

METHOD.—Wipe the tomatoes and cut into slices, peel and slice the onion.

Melt the butter in a saucepan, add the tomatoes and onions, and cook in the fat for a few minutes.

Add the stock and the herbs tied in muslin.

Bring to the boil, season well and simmer until all the vegetables are tender.

Break the spaghetti into small pieces, wash it well, put into boiling water with a little salt and cook until tender.

Strain off the water.

Take the rind from the cheese and grate or chop the cheese finely.

Remove the herbs from the tomato sauce and rub the sauce through a sieve.

Return it to the saucepan and thicken it with the cornflour, previously mixed with a little water.

Boil for a few minutes, keeping it well stirred.

Add the spaghetti and mix together.

Grease a pie-dish and put half of the grated cheese in the bottom of it.

Pour the tomato sauce and spaghetti over this.

Sprinkle the remainder of the cheese on the top.

Put into the oven to get thoroughly hot and then under the grill to brown lightly.

SAVOURY TARTLETS

INGREDIENTS.—3 oz. of flour, 1 yolk of egg, ¼ pint of milk, ½ gill of water, salt and pepper, 3 oz. of cheese.

METHOD.—Sieve the flour, pour the egg-yolk into the centre, then add the milk gradually and mix it all to a smooth batter. Beat well, stir in the water and leave to stand for about an hour or so.

Meanwhile, grate the cheese finely and, when ready to bake the batters, stir it in and add seasoning to taste.

Turn into well-greased tartlet-tins and put into a fairly hot oven to bake. They will take about fifteen to twenty minutes.

Serve hot, sprinkled with a little finely-grated cheese.

Sufficient for twelve small tartlets.

SAVOURY TOMATO OMELET

INGREDIENTS.—2 eggs, 1¼ oz. of butter, 1 teaspoonful of grated cheese, 1 teaspoonful of chopped onion or shallot, 1 tomato, pepper and salt.

METHOD.—Melt the butter in a small omelet or frying-pan. Skin the tomato—to do this, put it into boiling water for a minute ; the skin can then easily be removed. Cut it into small pieces, put it into the pan with the onion and fry gently until tender.

Separate the yolks from the whites of eggs. Beat up the yolks, add salt and pepper and the grated cheese.

Add a pinch of salt to the egg-whites and whisk to a stiff froth, then fold them lightly into the yolks.

Add this to the tomato, etc.

When the mixture begins to set round the edge, fold the edges over and draw the omelet towards the handle of the pan, keeping the latter tilted that way. Continue to cook for a few seconds, then put under the hot grill and lightly brown the top.

Turn on to a hot dish and serve at once.

Sufficient for one person.

SCOTCH EGGS

WITH HAM AND SAUSAGE MEAT

INGREDIENTS.—½ lb. of pork sausages or sausage meat, 6 eggs, 3 oz. of ham, 1 oz. of breadcrumbs, seasoning, 1 level teaspoonful of finely-minced onion, 2 tablespoonfuls of hot milk, deep fat for frying, breadcrumbs for coating.

METHOD.—Boil five of the eggs gently until hard. They will take about twelve minutes to cook. Remove the shells.

If using sausages, take them out of the skins and mix them with the ham, minced finely.

Soak the breadcrumbs in the milk, and add them to the onion and seasoning to taste and beaten egg-yolk. Mix well and divide the mixture into five portions. Wrap a portion evenly round each hard-boiled egg, so as to cover it completely. Brush the Scotch Eggs with the remaining white of egg, beaten slightly, coat them with breadcrumbs, and fry them in deep hot fat until golden, then drain them.

Cut each egg in half, and serve them on a mound of mashed potato.

Allow one or two for each person.

SCOTCH WOODCOCK

INGREDIENTS.—Anchovy paste, 1 gill of milk, 1 oz. of butter or margarine, 1 flat teaspoonful of chopped parsley, hot buttered toast, 1½ teaspoonfuls of flour, 2 yolks of egg, salt and cayenne.

METHOD.—Make some hot buttered toast and cut it into small squares or rounds. Spread each well with anchovy paste and keep warm.

Mix the flour to a smooth paste with about a tablespoonful of the milk. Put the remainder into a saucepan to heat with the butter.

When hot, stir it on to the flour, mix together, return to the saucepan and bring to the boil. Simmer for a few minutes, keeping it well stirred ; then draw to the side and cool slightly.

Add the yolks separately ; stir each one in thoroughly before adding the next.

Stir over a very low gas for a few minutes to cook the eggs, being careful not to let it boil.

Season well with salt and cayenne, add the parsley and mix together. The sauce should be thick and creamy when finished. Spread neatly on the prepared squares of hot toast. Serve very hot on a lace paper.

SHRIMP AND CHEESE SAVOURY

INGREDIENTS.—½ pint of shelled shrimps or 12 prawns, 1 cream cheese, 4 pieces of hot buttered toast.

METHOD.—Spread the toast with cream cheese and sprinkle thickly with shrimps, or put four prawns on each piece of toast.

Sufficient for three persons.

SHRIMP TOASTS

INGREDIENTS.—1½ gills of picked shrimps, ½ pint of milk, ½ teaspoonful of salt, 1 oz. of butter, barely ½ oz. of flour, cayenne, nutmeg, hot buttered toast.

METHOD.—Pour the milk into a saucepan.

Add the shrimps (if these are too salt, soak them in water for thirty minutes), and cook them for fifteen minutes. Season them to taste with salt, cayenne, and grated nutmeg.

Knead the butter and flour together on a plate.

Mix this into the milk and shrimps a little at a time and cook the mixture for three minutes longer.

Serve the mixture on squares of hot, lightly-buttered toast for lunch or supper, or as a savoury.

Sufficient for four persons.

SEAKALE FLAN

INGREDIENTS.—1 lb. of seakale, 1½ gills of milk, ¾ oz. of margarine, ¾ oz. of flour, salt and pepper, 3 oz. of cheese, short pastry (as required) (see p. 252).

METHOD.—Prepare the seakale. Split each piece into halves or quarters, trim the stump to a point, cutting it away as far as the dark line. Wash it well, then cook it in boiling salted water until tender.

Roll out some short pastry and line a flan-ring or deep sandwich or pie-tin. Trim the edge neatly, then line the pastry with a round of buttered paper and put some uncooked rice in the bottom. Put it into a hot oven to bake. It will take about twenty minutes, and when nearly cooked, remove the paper and rice and finish cooking the flan-case.

Make a thick white sauce with the flour, margarine, and milk, then stir in three-quarters of the cheese (grated finely), add seasoning to taste and stir until the cheese is melted.

When the seakale is cooked, lift it out and leave it to drain thoroughly. Then cut it up and put it into the pastry.

Cover with the cheese-sauce, sprinkle the remainder of the cheese on the top and brown under the grill. Serve hot.

Sufficient for six persons.

SPAGHETTI SAUSAGES

INGREDIENTS.—1 teaspoonful of flour, ½ gill of milk, 2 oz. of cheese, salt and cayenne, 4 oz. of spaghetti, 1 whole egg and 1 yolk, breadcrumbs, fat for frying.

METHOD.—Break the spaghetti into small pieces and wash it. Put it into a saucepan of boiling water with a little salt added, and boil until tender, then strain off the water and chop up the spaghetti. Grate the cheese finely.

Mix the flour to a smooth paste with some of the milk, mix in the remainder of it, then pour into a saucepan and stir until it boils and thickens.

Add the grated cheese and spaghetti and mix all well together, then draw to the side and cool slightly.

Break up the yolk of egg and stir into the mixture and season well with salt and cayenne, then spread on a plate and leave until thoroughly cold and firm. Put a deep pan of fat on to get hot. Divide the mixture into small equal portions and make each into a sausage shape.

Beat up the egg and brush them over with it, then coat with breadcrumbs.

Put them into the fat when it begins to smoke and fry until golden brown.

Drain on paper. Serve at once on a dish paper.

SPANISH SAVOURY

INGREDIENTS.—6 rounds of bread, ½ an onion, 6 rashers of bacon (cut very thinly), 1½ oz. of butter, ½ lb. of tomatoes, 2 eggs, salt and pepper, fat for frying.

METHOD.—Peel the onion and grate or chop it finely.

Melt the butter in a pan and fry the the onion in it until soft and golden brown. Skin the tomatoes. To do this, put them into boiling water for a minute ; the skins can then be easily removed.

Mash the potatoes to a pulp and add to the onion, mix together and cook until tender. Cut the rind from the rashers, roll each into a sausage shape and stick them all on an iron skewer. Place in a baking-tin in a moderately hot oven until the bacon is cooked. Cut six small pieces of bread about

three-eighths of an inch thick and fry in hot fat until golden brown, then drain on paper and keep warm.

When the tomatoes are cooked draw to the side and cool them slightly.

Beat up the eggs and stir into them, then cook over a very low gas until the mixture thickens. Keep it well stirred and do not let it boil. Season well with pepper and salt. Pile the prepared mixture on the croûtons of fried bread. Arrange on a hot dish, with a roll of bacon between each, and pour the bacon fat round. Serve very hot.

SPINACH EGGS

INGREDIENTS.—1 large tin of spinach, 3 oz. of butter, seasoning, 6 or 8 eggs, sippets of fried bread.

METHOD.—Turn out the spinach and rub it through a sieve.

Melt the butter in a saucepan, then add the spinach and stir until hot, then add seasoning to taste. Turn it on to a dish and keep it warm, then poach the eggs and arrange them on top of it. Garnish with sippets of fried bread.

To prepare the sippets, cut slices of bread about one-fourth of an inch thick, remove the crust and cut the bread into one-inch squares, then cut each across cornerwise and fry them till light brown in a little butter.

Sufficient for six persons.

SPINACH AU GRATIN

INGREDIENTS.—¾ pint tin of spinach or an equal amount of home-cooked spinach, 2 oz. of butter, 1¼ oz. of flour, ¾ of a pint of milk, 4 oz. of cheese, seasoning, 1 tablespoonful of breadcrumbs, 1 lemon.

METHOD.—Turn out the spinach and drain off the moisture.

Melt one and a half ounces of the butter in a saucepan, add the flour, and when it is well blended stir in the milk and bring the sauce to the boil.

Boil it gently for a few minutes, then draw the pan aside and add three-parts of the finely-grated cheese and seasoning to taste.

Butter a fireproof dish and add a layer of sauce, then a layer of spinach. Season the latter with pepper and salt and add a few dabs of butter, then add more sauce and spinach and continue in this way.

Cover the top layer of spinach with the remainder of the sauce and sprinkle it with the remainder of the cheese mixed with the breadcrumbs.

Heat it through in the oven, then brown the top under the grill. Serve Spinach au Gratin decorated with quarters of lemon and tiny heaps of spinach—the latter kept back and warmed separately.

Sufficient for four persons.

SPINACH SAVOURIES

INGREDIENTS.—½ oz. of butter, 1½ teaspoonfuls of flour, ½ pint of milk, ¼ pint of cooked spinach, pastry cases (see p. 253), soft roes.

METHOD.—Spinach pastries are made by filling small pastry cases with delicious creamed spinach. Either tinned or freshly-cooked spinach may be used.

Melt half an ounce of butter in a saucepan, add the flour, and when this is well blended stir in the milk. Boil the sauce gently for a few minutes and remove it from the heat. Mix in a quarter of a pint of cooked spinach gradually, re-heat the mixture and season it to taste.

Fill the prepared pastry cases with the creamed spinach and top them with a curl of soft roe. The latter should be lightly fried in butter, extra to that given in the ingredients.

FRIED SUET PUDDING AND BEANS

INGREDIENTS.—1 tin of baked beans and tomato, 6 oz. of self-raising flour, 3 oz. of shredded suet, ½ teaspoonful of salt, 1 gill of water, 2 oz. of bread-crumbs, 2 oz. of dripping.

METHOD.—Have ready a large pan of boiling water.

Dip the end of a pudding-cloth in the water and sprinkle it with flour.

Put the flour, breadcrumbs, suet, and salt into a basin.

Mix them to a soft dough with the water.

Roll this up in the floured cloth, tie the ends tightly and boil it for two hours.

Remove the cloth and cut the pudding into thick slices.

Fry the slices brown in the dripping.

Put the unopened tin of beans in the boiling water and boil it for ten minutes.

Empty the tin on to a dish with the slices of pudding round it.

Sufficient for four persons.

NOTE.—Fried suet pudding is also good served with roast leg of mutton and makes the joint go farther. The slices of pudding should be fried rather slowly to prevent them becoming hard.

TOAST AND CHEESE

INGREDIENTS.—6 oz. of cheese, 2 oz. of margarine, pepper, 2 teaspoonfuls of made mustard, 2 eggs, 1 teaspoonful of Worcester sauce, 2 pieces of hot buttered toast.

METHOD.—Melt the margarine, but do not make it hot.

Grate the cheese and stir it into the margarine with the mustard, pepper and sauce.

Beat the eggs well, and add them.

Make the hot buttered toast and spread the mixture on it. Place the slices under a red-hot griller till the cheese melts and begins to brown.

Serve at once on hot plates.

NOTE.—Any kind of sharp sauce will do for this recipe.

TOAST SNACK

INGREDIENTS.—1 large square of buttered toast, 1 egg, salt and pepper, 1 slice of tomato, 2 oz. of bacon, 2 oz. of mushroom, grated cheese, 1 oz. of butter.

METHOD.—Peel and stalk the mushrooms, cleanse them in salted water, then drain and chop them. Melt the butter and fry the mushrooms for a minute or two, add the chopped bacon and fry it gently until both are cooked, then draw the pan aside.

Beat up the egg and stir it in with seasoning to taste, and stir the mixture over a low burner until it thickens, then turn it on to a square of hot toast.

Place a slice of tomato in the centre, sprinkle a little grated cheese on top, and put the toast under the grill for a minute or two before serving.

Sufficient for one person.

TOMATOES AND CHEESE SAUCE

INGREDIENTS.—¾ lb. of tomatoes, salt and pepper, 1 oz. of butter, ¾ oz. of flour, ½ pint of milk, 3 oz. of cheese, 1 yolk of egg, a pinch of castor sugar.

METHOD.—Stalk and wipe the tomatoes, cut one in slices and the remainder in half crosswise. Sprinkle them with pepper and salt and add a pinch of castor sugar.

Melt the butter in a saucepan, add the flour and when blended stir in the milk and bring them to the boil. Boil this sauce gently for a few minutes, draw the pan aside, and add three parts of the cheese finely grated, also seasoning to taste, and the beaten egg-yolk.

Pour a little of the sauce into a buttered fireproof dish, add the halved tomatoes, and cover them with sauce, then sprinkle the remainder of the cheese on top. Bake them gently till the tomatoes are tender, but do not let the sauce boil, then put the dish under the grill and brown the top.

Garnish it with four slices of tomato, baked lightly.

Sufficient for three persons.

TOMATO CHARLOTTE

INGREDIENTS.—1½ lb. of tomatoes, 2 teaspoonfuls of meat extract, ⅛ gill of cream, ½ gill of mayonnaise (see p. 168) 1 cream cheese, pepper to taste, 1 oz. of leaf gelatine, ¾ pint of water, 6 oz. of dinner roll finger biscuits.

METHOD.—Soak the gelatine in the water and add the meat extract. Dissolve the gelatine slowly over the fire and pour about three-quarters of a gill of the liquid into a small cake-tin, rinsed in cold water. When it is nearly set, run a little of it all round the inside of the tin and, when quite firm, line the tin with biscuits, standing upright on the jelly and close together.

Cut half an inch off each end of the biscuits and trim the sides quite level.

To make the tomato cream filling, pour boiling water on the tomatoes, leave them for three minutes, then throw the water away, and rub the tomatoes through a hair sieve.

Add the remainder of the jelly to the tomato pulp.

Cream the cheese with a wooden spoon and gradually mix in first the mayonnaise and cream, and then the tomato pulp.

When all is mixed, season to taste, and beat with an egg-whisk till perfectly smooth.

Leave it till it begins to thicken, stirring it occasionally.

Just before it sets pour it into the lined mould, taking care that the mixture reaches the top of the biscuits. If it does not quite do so, cut the biscuits level with the cream.

NOTE.—Be sure that the tomato cream filling is almost set before putting it in. If put in when liquid the biscuits will not be crisp.

Sufficient for six or seven persons.

TOMATO AND CHEESE SAVOURY

INGREDIENTS.—¾ packet of aspic jelly, 1 small cream cheese, 2 tablespoonfuls of salad cream, ½ teaspoonful of made mustard, cayenne, 2 large tomatoes, cress.

METHOD.—Put the jelly into a saucepan and dissolve it with one gill of hot water. Leave it till cold.

Put the cheese, cayenne, mustard, and salad-cream into a basin and mix them together till smooth. If there is less than half a pint of the mixture, add a little more water.

Stir in nearly all the jelly by degrees, leaving about a teaspoonful to use later.

When the soufflé mixture begins to set beat it with an egg-whisk till it is frothy and smooth.

Oil four cups with salad oil and pour the mixture into them. Each cup should be half full. Melt the remainder of the jelly, cut the tomatoes in half, and dip the cut side into the jelly.

Press half a tomato on to the cheese mixture in each cup, and pour in any jelly that is over. When set, shake the savouries on to a dish and garnish them with cress.

TOMATO CREAMS

INGREDIENTS.—1 tin of tomatoes, 3d. of double cream, salt and pepper, mustard and cress, 3 level table-spoonfuls of cornflour (measured exactly).

METHOD. — Rub the tomatoes through a hair sieve with a wooden spoon, measure the purée and make it up to a pint with water.

Put the cornflour in a basin and mix smoothly with half a gill of cold water.

Boil the tomato purée and pour on to the mixed cornflour, stirring all the time.

Return to the saucepan, place it on an asbestos mat over a low gas and stir for ten minutes to cook the cornflour.

Season to taste and add the cream.

Rinse four fancy pudding moulds in cold water and pour in the tomato mixture.

When quite cold, shake on to the hand and place on a dish.

Garnish with cress.

NOTE.—Sufficient for four persons. It is very good served with cold meat.

TOMATO AND EGG SAVOURY

INGREDIENTS.—2 new laid eggs, 1 gill of tomato ketchup, ½ oz. of butter, salt and pepper, ½ gill of gravy.

METHOD.—Place a spoonful of sauce and gravy and a small piece of butter in two ramekin cases.

Put an egg in each and cover with tomato sauce and the rest of the butter.

Bake for seven or eight minutes, or till set, in a fairly hot oven.

TOMATO EGGS

INGREDIENTS.—5 tomatoes (large), 5 eggs (small), pepper and salt, 2½ teaspoonfuls of grated cheese, 5 croûtons of fried bread.

METHOD.—Wipe the tomatoes, remove the stalks, cut off a slice from the top of each and scoop out some of the tomato pulp.

Season the inside of the tomato with pepper and salt, and sprinkle in half a teaspoonful of grated cheese.

Stand them on a greased baking-tin and bake in a moderately hot oven until the tomatoes are almost cooked, being very careful not to let them break. Remove from the oven and cool slightly.

Break each egg into a cup, then pour one into each tomato.

Return to the oven and leave until the eggs are just set.

Cut five rounds of crumb of bread, about three-eighths of an inch thick, and sufficiently large to take the tomatoes.

Fry them in hot fat until golden brown on both sides, then drain on paper.

Lift each tomato very carefully on to a croûton of fried bread.

Arrange on a lace paper and serve hot.

TOMATO FRITTERS

INGREDIENTS.—Tomatoes (as required), flour, seasoning, egg, bread-crumbs, deep fat for frying.

METHOD.—Choose firm tomatoes. Stalk and wipe them and cut them in half crosswise, then season them and dip them in flour.

Brush the tomatoes with beaten egg and coat them with breadcrumbs. Then place in a frying-basket enough of the tomatoes to cover the bottom of it.

Put the basket into a deep pan of hot fat and fry the tomato fritters till they are golden. Then lift them out carefully, drain them, and serve them on a dish lined with a paper doyley.

TOMATOES AU GRATIN

INGREDIENTS.—2 good-sized tomatoes, 4 dessertspoonfuls of finely-grated cheese, 2 dessertspoonfuls of breadcrumbs, salt, pepper.

METHOD.—Wipe and stalk the tomatoes; cut them in half cross-wise, and then sprinkle them with salt and pepper.

Mix the cheese and breadcrumbs together, season the mixture and heap a portion on each half tomato. Place the tomatoes on a buttered baking-sheet and bake them in a moderate oven for about ten to fifteen minutes till tender. Then place the tomatoes under the hot grill for a minute to brown the tops. Serve them on rounds of hot buttered toast.

NOTE.—If the tomatoes are too small to halve, cut a good thick slice from the top of each, then scoop out some of the pulp from the centre of each tomato before heaping the cheese and breadcrumbs on them.

Sufficient for four persons.

Macaroni Eggs

Sausage Savoury

Cheese Puff

PLATE 37

Spinach
Eggs

Creamed
Cheese
Toast

Baked
Stuffed
Tomatoes

PLATE 38

Cheese
Eggs

Almond
Savouries

Cheese and Macaroni Pudding

PLATE 39

Egg
Fritters

Vegetable
Shortcakes

Vegetable
Curry

Plate 40

JELLIED TOMATOES

INGREDIENTS.—1 lb. of ripe English tomatoes, 1 cream cheese, 2 tablespoonfuls of thick salad dressing or mayonnaise (see p. 168), ½ pint of aspic jelly, or jelly from roast veal.

METHOD —Cut the tomatoes nearly through into four, and put them in shallow dishes with a little melted aspic or some jelly from roast veal. Mix the cream cheese with the mayonnaise and season with cayenne. Put a spoonful of the cream cheese mixture in the centre of each tomato.

Sufficient for four persons.

TOMATO MOULDS

INGREDIENTS.—1 small tin of tomatoes, 1 cup of breadcrumbs, 1½ oz. of butter (melted), 2 eggs (beaten), 1 oz. of grated cheese, salt, pepper, 1 cold cauliflower, ½ pint of mustard sauce (see p. 367).

METHOD.—Rub the tomatoes through a hair sieve and mix them with the breadcrumbs, butter, cheese, eggs, salt and pepper, and half the sauce.

Fill some greased moulds and cover them with greased paper.

Put the cauliflower and the rest of the sauce in a basin and cover it with a plate.

Steam the moulds and cauliflower together for forty minutes.

Turn out the moulds gently on a hot dish, with the cauliflower in the centre.

TOMATOES AND MUSH-ROOMS

INGREDIENTS.—1 lb. of tomatoes, ½ lb. of mushrooms, 2 oz. of grated cheese, 1 oz. of butter, 1 oz. of flour, ½ pint of milk, salt and pepper.

METHOD.—Peel and wash the mushrooms, remove the stalks and slice the tomatoes. Arrange the mushrooms and tomatoes alternately in a fireproof dish. Melt the butter, mix in the flour and add the milk gradually. Stir till it boils ; add nearly all the cheese and season. Pour the sauce into the dish, and put some slices of tomato and grated cheese on top. Bake in a fairly hot oven for twenty minutes.

Sufficient for four persons.

TOMATO RAREBIT

INGREDIENTS.—¼ lb. of tomatoes, ¼ lb. of cheese, 1 oz. of butter, salt, pepper, mustard, 1 teaspoonful of flour, 2 yolks of eggs, triangles of buttered toast.

METHOD.—Peel the tomatoes and cut them in small pieces. Melt the butter, add the tomato, and cook it for a minute or two, then stir in the flour smoothed in a little water, and boil them for a few minutes.

Draw the pan aside, add the finely-grated cheese, and beaten egg-yolks, stir over a low burner until creamy, but do not let it boil. Season well with salt, pepper, and mixed mustard, and serve the rarebit on triangles of buttered toast.

Grated cheese may be sprinkled on the top.

Sufficient for eighteen triangles.

TOMATO AND RICE SAV-OURY

INGREDIENTS.—1 teacupful of rice, 1 onion, 2 tomatoes, 2 gills of tomato purée, 3 oz. of cooked ham, salt and pepper, 2 oz. of butter or margarine, chopped parsley, dripping.

METHOD.—Wipe the tomatoes and cut into slices. Put them into a baking-tin with a little dripping and cook in the oven until tender, being careful to keep the slices whole. Wash the rice and boil it until soft in a saucepan of boiling water with a little salt added —it will take about fifteen minutes— and then strain it. Chop the ham. Peel and chop or grate the onion. Melt the butter in a saucepan and fry the onion in it until tender. Stir in the rice and ham.

Season with pepper and salt and mix together.

Stir in the tomato purée and make all thoroughly hot, then put into a pie-dish, place the slices of tomato on the top and sprinkle over chopped parsley.

Serve very hot.

Sufficient for about eight persons.

TOMATO SLICES AU GRATIN

INGREDIENTS.—6 slices of tomato, 3 tablespoonfuls of finely-grated cheese, 3 streaky rashers, 6 rounds of French toast, salt and pepper, parsley.

METHOD.—Cut six thick slices of

O

tomato and warm them through in the oven.

To make the French toast, cut rounds of bread the same size as the tomatoes, toast them on one side and butter the untoasted side.

Cut the rind from the rashers, fry the bacon until crisp, then chop it into small pieces.

Put a slice of tomato on each round of toast, season them with pepper and salt, cover each with chopped bacon, and heap grated cheese on top.

Place the tomato slices under the hot grill until the cheese is melted and becomes brown. Serve them garnished with parsley.

Sufficient for six slices.

STUFFED TOMATOES

INGREDIENTS.—5 large tomatoes, 5 dessertspoonfuls of breadcrumbs, 1 teaspoonful of chopped parsley, a pinch of mixed herbs, pepper and salt, 1 truffle, 1 small onion, 1 oz. of butter, ½ egg, 3 teaspoonfuls of grated cheese.

METHOD.—Remove the stalks from the tomatoes and scoop out a small round piece from the top of each, being careful not to break them when doing this.

Make the breadcrumbs and mix with the herbs, pepper and salt, and half the grated cheese.

Scrape out a little of the inside from each of the tomatoes and add this also.

Wash, scald and finely chop the parsley.

Chop the truffle; peel, chop and fry the onion.

Add these also to the breadcrumbs, etc.

Melt the butter and add, together with the egg; mix all well together.

Stuff each tomato with this mixture, heaping it well up on the top.

Place on a greased baking-sheet and bake in a moderately hot oven until the tomatoes are tender, being very careful not to break them.

Sprinkle the top of the stuffing of each with the remainder of the grated cheese.

Put under the grill and brown slightly.

Remove carefully to a hot dish and serve.

STUFFED TOMATOES AND CUCUMBER

INGREDIENTS.—3 or 4 large tomatoes, ½ lb. of sausage meat, ½ a cucumber, 1 oz. of butter, 1 oz. of flour, 1½ gills of milk, 1 tablespoonful of grated cheese, salt and pepper, 2 tablespoonfuls of breadcrumbs.

METHOD.—Remove the core from the tomatoes with a pointed knife and fill them with a mixture of sausage meat and breadcrumbs.

Cut half the cucumber into dice and the remainder into four long pieces. Put cucumber and tomatoes in a tin with one gill of hot water, cover them with greased paper and bake them in a hot oven for about twenty minutes until the cucumber is tender.

The water keeps the vegetables from getting hard and dry.

Melt the butter, add the flour and stir in the milk with the pan off the gas.

Add the cheese and the cucumber dice and season the mixture to taste with salt and pepper. To dish up, have three or four heaps of the mixture with a tomato on each and garnish them with the large pieces of cucumber.

BAKED STUFFED TOMATOES

INGREDIENTS.—4 tomatoes, lemon-juice, 1 small onion, 3 medium mushrooms, ½ oz. of butter, ½ oz. of dry breadcrumbs, ¼ lb. of chicken livers, ½ level teaspoonful of chopped parsley, salt and pepper to taste.

METHOD.—Remove a thick slice from the top of each tomato and scoop out the pulp. Invert the case to allow it to drain.

Heat the butter (or, if preferred, the bacon fat).

Stir in the chopped onion, brown it slightly and add the chopped stewed livers.

Stir in the crumbs, chopped mushrooms, lemon-juice, seasoning, and enough of the pulp of the tomatoes to moisten the mixture slightly. Stuff the tomato cases with this. Cover them with the slices taken from the top and bake them. Serve the tomatoes on rounds of buttered toast garnished with parsley. If liked, the toast may be spread with minced fried bacon before placing the tomatoes on top.

Sufficient for four persons.

TOMATO RISSOLES

INGREDIENTS.—¾ lb. of flour, 1½ level teaspoonfuls of baking-powder, ¼ lb. of margarine, water to mix, 2 tomatoes (about 6 oz.), 1 small onion, about 2 oz. of breadcrumbs, seasoning, ⅓ gill of thick white sauce (see p. 364), 2 hard-boiled eggs, 1 raw egg, deep fat.

METHOD.—Skin and chop up the tomatoes, peel and mince the onion and mince the hard-boiled eggs. Mix these together with the sauce and stir in the breadcrumbs and seasoning to taste. If the mixture seems too moist a few more crumbs may be added.

Sift the flour with the baking-powder, rub in the margarine, then mix the ingredients to a stiff paste with water.

Roll the pastry out thinly and stamp it into rounds about two and three-quarters to three inches in diameter. Put a small heap of the prepared mixture in the centre of half of these rounds, damp the edge and cover them with the remainder of the rounds, pressing the edges together securely.

Brush the rissoles with egg and fry them in deep fat till golden, frying only a few at a time. Then drain them and serve them.

Sufficient for about twenty-two rissoles.

TOMATO TARTLETS

INGREDIENTS.—1 large tomato, 1 sausage, ½ cup of breadcrumbs, salt and pepper, ½ oz. of dripping, 1 teaspoonful of tomato ketchup, 4 oz. of short pastry (see p. 252).

METHOD.—Line four patty-pans with pastry. Skin the sausage and fry it in the dripping for ten minutes. Pour boiling water on the tomato and leave it for two minutes. Skin and slice the tomato and fry it with the sausage for ten minutes. Pour off the fat and stir in the ketchup, breadcrumbs and salt and pepper. Fill the tarts and bake them for fifteen minutes in a hot oven.

TOMATO TOAST

INGREDIENTS. — 3 tomatoes, 4 streaky rashers, 1 egg, seasoning, 1 level teaspoonful of finely-minced onion, 4 oblongs of buttered toast, parsley.

METHOD.—Cut four slices of tomato and put them aside, skin the remainder and mash them to a pulp.

Remove the rind from the bacon. Cut two of the rashers in half crosswise and form each piece into a roll. Put the remaining two rashers through the mincer.

Cook the minced bacon in a frying-pan for a minute. Add the tomato pulp and onion and cook the mixture for another minute or two, then draw the pan aside and stir in the beaten egg.

Season the mixture well and stir it over a low burner until it thickens.

Serve the mixture on oblongs of hot buttered toast and sprinkle it with a little finely-chopped parsley. Place a slice of tomato topped with a roll of bacon in the centre of each.

The slices of tomato should be lightly baked and the rolls of bacon cooked on a skewer, either in the oven or under the grill.

Sufficient for four persons.

TONGUE SAUTE

INGREDIENTS.—3 oz. of cold tongue, 3 oz. of cold potato crumbs, 1 dessert-spoonful of minced onion, 1 tomato, seasoning, 1 oz. of butter, 1 teaspoonful of grated cheese.

METHOD.—Chop the tongue into small pieces or mince it coarsely. Mix it with the chopped-up potato.

Melt half the butter in a frying-pan and cook the onion in it until it begins to colour, then add the peeled and chopped tomato and stir in the potatoes and tongue. Cook the mixture for a few minutes, keeping it stirred, and add seasoning to taste. Then draw the mixture to one half of the pan and shape it.

Add the remainder of the butter to the pan and let the tongue mixture brown slowly, then turn it over and shape it again and let it brown.

When it is ready turn it on to a plate, sprinkle the cheese on top of it and put it under the grill for a minute before serving the Tongue Sauté. Garnish it with parsley.

Sufficient for one person.

TUNNY FISH SAVOURY

INGREDIENTS.—1 tin of tunny fish, ¼ packet of aspic jelly, 1 hard-boiled egg (chopped), salt and pepper, ¼ pint of hot water, parsley for garnish.

FOR THE ANCHOVY BUTTER.—2 OZ. of fresh butter, 1 dessertspoonful of anchovy essence.

METHOD.—Melt the jelly in the water, put in the egg and let it set.

Put pieces of tunny fish into some ramekin cases, season it with salt and pepper and cover it with pieces of jelly.

To make the anchovy butter, cream the butter with a wooden spoon and stir in the anchovy.

Put the butter into an icing-pump fitted with a rose forcer, and use it for decorating.

Garnish with parsley.

STEAMED TURKEY CREAM

(A GOOD WAY OF USING UP COLD TURKEY)

INGREDIENTS.—½ lb. of cold turkey, 2 oz. of ham, 1 oz. of butter, 1 large egg, 1 teacupful of breadcrumbs, salt and pepper, 1 oz. of cold stuffing, sippets of fried bread, cranberry sauce.

METHOD.—Chop the turkey, removing all sinew and skin. Chop the ham.

Melt the butter and stir in the turkey, ham, breadcrumbs, and stuffing.

Season with salt and pepper and bind with a well-beaten egg.

Pour the mixture into a greased mould and cover with greased paper.

Steam for forty-five minutes.

Let the cream stand for a few minutes so that it will turn out easily. Turn it on to a hot dish, coat it with cranberry sauce and place sippets of bread round.

CRANBERRY SAUCE

INGREDIENTS.—½ lb. of cranberries, 1 teacupful of sugar, 1 gill of water, 1 teaspoonful of cornflour, a pinch of cinnamon.

METHOD.—Boil the cranberries and water for five minutes, rub them through a hair-sieve and re-heat them with the sugar.

Mix the cornflour and cinnamon with two tablespoonfuls of cold water and pour them on the hot purée. Return it to the saucepan and stir till it boils.

Boil for five minutes.

VEAL TOAST

INGREDIENTS.—1½ oz. of cold veal, a few drops of onion-juice, 1 dessertspoonful of chopped pimento, 2 whole eggs and 2 yolks, 3 tablespoonfuls of milk, 1 oz. of butter, seasoning, parsley, 6 triangles of buttered toast.

METHOD.—Beat up the whole eggs and yolks together.

Stir in the milk, chopped pimento, and the onion-juice.

Put the veal through the mincer and add it to the egg mixture with seasoning to taste.

Melt the butter in the saucepan. Add the prepared mixture. Stir it over a gentle heat until it thickens, then serve it on triangles of hot buttered toast and garnish the triangles with parsley.

Sufficient for six triangles.

VEGETABLE CHARLOTTE

INGREDIENTS.—1 lb. of peas (cooked), 1 lb. of broad beans (cooked), 1 onion (grated), ½ oz. of cornflour, ½ pint of thick white sauce (hot) (see p. 364), bread, fat for frying, ½ gill of cold water, salt and pepper, rolls of bacon (if liked) for garnish, 1 tablespoonful of chopped parsley.

METHOD.—Stir the peas, beans, parsley, and grated onion into the hot sauce. Add the cornflour after mixing it smoothly with half a gill of cold water. Stir the mixture till it boils and season to taste.

Cut two or three slices of bread to fit the top of a cake-tin and enough fingers to line the inside.

Fry the bread a few pieces at a time in smoking hot fat. It will take about a minute for each side.

Lay large pieces of the fried bread in the greased tin, and fit the fingers round the sides.

Put the hot vegetables in and lay

fried bread on top. Cover with greased paper and bake for twenty-five minutes.

Turn the charlotte out carefully and, if liked, garnish with the rolls of bacon.

Sufficient for four or five persons.

NOTE.—When fresh peas and broad beans are out of season a very good charlotte can be made with a tin of baked beans and tomato.

PLAIN VEGETABLE MOULD

INGREDIENTS.—1 to 1½ pints of savoury calf's foot or aspic jelly, 1 gill of turnip balls or new potatoes, 1 gill of green peas, 1 gill of carrot balls.

METHOD.—Scrape and wash the carrots, peel the turnips thickly and cut them into small balls, as near as possible to the size of the peas. To do this you will need a special vegetable cutter—they are quite inexpensive to buy—failing this, cut the vegetables into dice, but remember that the balls make the mould look more attractive. Cook these and the peas, all in separate pans of boiling water with a little salt added, until tender, being very careful not to let them break. Then strain off the water and leave the vegetables until cold.

If you have already any cold vegetables, these can be cut up and utilised, instead of boiling fresh ones.

Rinse a mould with cold water.

Melt the jelly and set a very thin layer in the bottom of the mould.

Decorate the bottom with a few of the peas dipped in some of the melted jelly, and when the decoration is set cover it with a little more jelly and set again.

Now mix the remainder of the peas with the carrots and turnips, and put a layer of mixed vegetables in the mould; cover with more jelly and set again.

Continue in this way until the mould is full and all the vegetables and jelly are used, letting each layer set before adding the next.

When the mould is quite firm dip it into warm water, give it one sharp shake, and turn it out carefully on to a dish, and serve separately some salad cream.

NOTE.—The jelly can be bought ready prepared. If preferred, tiny cubes of cold new potatoes can be used instead of the turnips.

Sufficient for eight persons.

MIXED VEGETABLE MOULD

INGREDIENTS.—1 gill of shredded cabbage (raw), 1 gill of minced carrot (raw), 1 gill of finely diced celery (raw), 1 gill of green peas, ½ oz. of gelatine, ½ pint of water, salt, 2 dessertspoonfuls of castor sugar, ¼ gill of lemon-juice, ¼ gill of tomato-juice, ⅛ gill of vinegar, 1 or 2 tomatoes.

METHOD.—Dissolve the gelatine in the water, then strain it into a basin, add the sugar and leave it to cool.

Clean and prepare all the vegetables, draining them well before cutting them up—the carrots can be put through the mincer. Use either cold cooked peas or tinned ones.

Add the tomato-juice, lemon-juice and vinegar to the cooled gelatine water. Season it with salt, and when it is beginning to thicken stir in the prepared vegetables.

Mix all the ingredients together well. Turn the mixture into a wet mould, and when it is set unmould it. Garnish it with tomatoes, and serve it with salad cream. If liked, the Vegetable Mould may be served on a bed of lettuce leaves.

Sufficient for six persons.

FRIED VEGETABLE PATTIES

INGREDIENTS.—1 cupful of any cold vegetables.

FOR THE CURRY SAUCE.—1 oz. of butter, ½ oz. of curry-powder, ¾ oz. of flour, 1 gill of stock (see p. 12), 1 tea-spoonful of Worcester sauce, the juice of ½ lemon, salt, ½ onion, ½ apple, deep frying fat, ½ stale loaf.

METHOD.—Chop the onion and fry it slowly for ten minutes in the butter.

Chop and add the apple, the curry-powder, and lemon-juice, and cook for five minutes.

Stir in the flour, Worcester sauce, and stock, and boil up.

Chop the cold vegetables, add them to the sauce and keep it hot in a double boiler.

Cut the bread into oblongs about

three inches long, and cut a triangular piece out of the centre of each piece.

Fry them in very hot, deep fat for about three minutes till they are golden brown all over.

Drain on paper. Fill the cases with the hot vegetable mixture, using the triangular pieces as lids.

Serve on a dish-paper.

Sufficient for four persons.

VEGETABLE SHORT CAKES

INGREDIENTS.—$\frac{1}{2}$ lb. of flour, a pinch of salt, 3 teaspoonfuls of baking-powder, 2 oz. of margarine, melted butter, milk and water.

FOR THE FILLING.—$\frac{1}{4}$ lb. of mushrooms, 1 pimento (canned), $\frac{1}{4}$ pint of cooked carrot (cut in small dice), 2 tablespoonfuls of cooked green peas, $\frac{1}{2}$ pint of milk, 1 oz. of margarine, $\frac{3}{4}$ oz. of flour, salt and pepper.

METHOD.—Sift the flour into a basin with the salt and baking-powder, rub in the fat, and then mix them to a soft dough with milk and water. Divide the dough into twelve portions, shape them lightly into rounds and put six into buttered patty-tins. Brush the top of these with melted butter and place the remaining six on top of them. Put them into a moderately hot oven to bake—they will take about fifteen or twenty minutes to cook. Remove the top pieces, heap filling on the under ones, then replace top pieces and serve the short cakes, garnished with parsley.

To make the filling, peel and stalk mushrooms, wash, drain, chop and fry them in a little butter.

Melt the margarine, add the flour, and when well blended stir in the milk and bring it to the boil. Boil it gently for a few minutes, add seasoning, also prepared vegetables and pimento (chopped) and make them hot.

Serve any filling that is over in a separate tureen.

Sufficient for six short cakes.

VEGETABLE TARTLETS

INGREDIENTS.—$\frac{1}{2}$ lb. of flaky or puff pastry (see p. 252), 1 tin of macedoine of vegetables, $\frac{3}{4}$ oz. of flour, 1 oz. of butter or margarine, $1\frac{1}{2}$ to 2 gills of milk, 2 oz. of cheese, 1 teaspoonful of onion-juice, seasoning.

METHOD.—Roll out the pastry thinly, stamp it into rounds, and line some tartlet-tins. Line these with rounds of buttered paper, and put a spoonful of uncooked rice into each tin. Put them into a hot oven to bake, and when the pastry is set, remove the paper and rice and finish cooking the cases.

Meanwhile, drain the liquor from the vegetables.

Melt the butter in a saucepan, add the flour, and when it is well blended stir in the milk and bring the sauce to the boil. Boil it gently for a few minutes, then add the cheese, and when it is melted, stir in half a pint of the drained vegetables, add also the onion-juice and seasoning to taste.

Make the mixture thoroughly hot before filling the prepared cases of pastry, and serve them garnished with a few of the vegetables.

Sufficient for twelve tartlets.

WORCESTER EGGS

INGREDIENTS.—3 hard-boiled eggs, 1 oz. of butter, 1 teaspoonful of Worcester sauce, 1 teaspoonful of made mustard, 1 oz. of cream cheese, 6 small sandwiches of brown bread and anchovy paste, 2 tomatoes (cut in 6 slices) and cress to garnish.

METHOD.—Cut the eggs in half and cut a small piece off the end of each. Remove the yolks. Cream the butter till soft.

Add the yolks, cheese, Worcester sauce, and mustard. Work into the butter till smooth, add pepper and salt to taste.

Lay a slice of tomato on each sandwich. Put one teaspoonful of the egg mixture into each of the whites or force it through a forcing-bag.

Place the eggs on the sandwiches and garnish with a little cress.

Sufficient for six persons.

CAKES

The veriest beginner may make a success of cake-making if she remembers certain rules and has a " light hand " when mixing her ingredients.

THE FOUR METHODS OF CAKE-MAKING

THERE are four methods of cake-making.

THE FIRST WAY is to *rub the fat into the flour*. This method is used for everyday cakes, and should be done with the tips of the fingers until the flour is of the same consistency as fine breadcrumbs.

THE SECOND WAY is to *cream the fat and sugar*. This method is employed for better cakes. If the fat becomes oily, or the two ingredients are not creamed sufficiently, the cake is likely to become heavy. In very cold weather the fat may be warmed *slightly* to make it soft enough to work, but it must be watched most carefully to make sure that it does not oil.

Creaming consists of beating the fat and sugar together until the mixture becomes much paler in colour, and has a creamy texture. Always use a wooden spoon for this purpose. When the mixture drops easily from the spoon, you may know it is sufficiently creamed.

Add the eggs next. They need not be beaten first, but should be dropped in one at a time, and stirred *very quickly*, beating the mixture well before the next egg is added. Unless the mixture is stirred quickly, it is liable to become curdled. If this should happen, stir in a little of the flour.

An alternative method is to whisk the eggs first in a separate basin and then add them alternately with the flour to the creamed fat and sugar, mixing them in lightly.

THE THIRD METHOD is to *whisk the eggs with the sugar*—as used for making sponge cakes. The whisking should be stopped when no dark streaks of egg can be detected.

THE FOURTH METHOD is to *melt the fat with the sugar and the golden syrup*. This method is used when mixing gingerbread. The sugar must be all dissolved, but the mixture should not boil.

A very light cake mixture can be made by separating the yolks from the whites of the eggs. Then the whites should be added at the last, whisked to a stiff froth, and folded in lightly.

THE RAISING PROPERTY

Baking-powder may be used for raising cakes, or carbonate of soda and cream of tartar. If soda is used alone it darkens the mixture and is, therefore, not very suitable for light, fluffy cakes—with the exception of coffee or chocolate cakes. If baking-powder is used, the cake must be baked directly it is mixed.

HINTS FOR CAKE MAKING

Look to your oven first.

Then prepare your cake-tin— grease it and line it with greased paper.

Have all ingredients ready weighed before beginning to mix them.

Bake large cakes in a moderate oven and small cakes in a quick oven.

The time for large cakes to cook depends on the depth of the mixture in the tin. Always test them with a warm iron skewer before taking them up from the oven.

All fruit which is to be used in cake making must be thoroughly washed and dried beforehand, as damp fruit is liable to make a cake heavy.

The mixture for cakes containing fruit must not be made too moist, or the fruit will sink to the bottom of the tin.

Keep an even consistency when mixing cakes. This can be managed quite easily if the dry ingredients are added gradually and alternately with the liquid.

If cakes brown too quickly, cover them with a sheet of paper—*not* greased.

BREAKING EGGS

It is always advisable to break each egg separately into a small basin, or one bad egg might spoil other good ones. Remember that the object of beating is to introduce air to cause lightness, but all mixtures must be well beaten *before* baking-powder is added. After the latter is mixed into the cake, the sooner the cake is in the oven the better will be the result.

AFTERNOON TEA CAKES

INGREDIENTS.—6 oz. of flour, 2 oz. of cornflour, 1 teaspoonful of baking-powder, ¼ lb. of castor sugar, ¼ lb. of margarine or butter, 1 egg, 3 oz. of glacé cherries, milk.

METHOD.—Sieve the flour, corn-flour, and baking-powder. Cut the cherries into small pieces. Beat the sugar and fat to a cream. Separate the yolk from the white of egg.

Add a pinch of salt to the white, and whisk it to a stiff froth.

Add the yolk to the creamed fat and sugar, and beat it in thoroughly.

Gradually add the flour, etc., and cherries, together with a little milk, and mix lightly.

Lastly, fold in the white of egg.

Put into small greased tins and bake in a hot oven for about fifteen to twenty minutes.

AFTERNOON TEA FANCIES

THESE can be made from the trimmings left over from the Lemon Baskets (see p. 497).

Cut them into tiny shapes as most convenient. Place on a rack over a dish, and coat them with soft icing, coloured to any desired shade.

When coating them, take a spoonful of the icing at a time, and coat each one separately. Decorate with a dab of cream, and leaves of angelica, and serve in tiny paper cases.

SOFT ICING

To make the icing, sieve the icing sugar and put it into a saucepan. Mix it to a smooth paste with water. Add colouring and flavouring to taste, and stir over a very low burner until the base of the pan feels warm. Then use as required.

The icing should just be thick enough to coat the back of the spoon.

ALMOND BALLS

INGREDIENTS.—3 eggs, 8 oz. of sugar, 4 oz. of almonds, 8 oz. of flour.

METHOD.—Beat the eggs and sugar very well and add the chopped almonds and flour.

Allow the mixture to stand for a few hours.

Make the mixture into small balls and roll them in granulated sugar.

Bake the Almond Balls in a good oven.

Sufficient to make about twenty balls.

ALMOND BISCUITS

INGREDIENTS.—1 oz. of almonds, 1 egg, 2 oz. of margarine, 2½ oz. of castor sugar, 4 oz. of flour, almond essence, a little egg-yolk and milk for glaze.

METHOD.—Beat the sugar and fat to a cream, add the egg, stir it in quickly and beat well. Stir in the flour and a drop or two of almond essence, and mix to a soft paste.

If the mixture is too soft to roll, put it aside for a time, when it will harden slightly.

Roll it out and stamp it into rounds, place them on a lightly buttered baking-sheet, brush the tops with beaten egg-yolk mixed with a little milk, and place half a blanched almond on each.

Bake the biscuits for about ten minutes in a moderate oven.

Sufficient for fifteen biscuits.

ALMOND CAKE

INGREDIENTS.—6 oz. of margarine or butter, 2 thin slices of citron peel, 6 oz. of castor sugar, 1 teaspoonful of baking-powder, 10 oz. of best white flour, 3 eggs (large), or 4 small ones. ½ gill of milk (if required), 1 teaspoonful of almond flavouring.

METHOD.—Grease and prepare a round cake-tin and line it with greased paper. Beat the sugar and butter to a cream.

Sieve the flour and baking-powder together.

Beat each egg separately into the creamed sugar and fat.

Beat well for a few minutes.

Lightly fold the flour, etc., into the sugar, fat, and eggs.

Add the almond flavouring and a little milk if required.

Put into the prepared cake-tin.

Bake in a moderately hot oven for about three-quarters to one hour.

Turn carefully on to a sieve and leave until cold.

NOTE.—Very lightly place the peel on the cake when it is about half cooked.

RICH ALMOND CAKE

INGREDIENTS.—¾ lb. of flour (self-raising), 6 oz. of mixed peel, ¾ lb. of margarine, 5 eggs, ½ lb. of brown sugar, 1½ teaspoonfuls of mixed spice, ¾ lb. of sultanas, ½ gill of sherry, ¾ lb. of currants, 2 oz. of almonds, milk (if required).

ALMOND PASTE ICING

INGREDIENTS.—1¾ lb. of icing sugar, whites of about 5 eggs, 1¾ lb. of ground almonds, vanilla flavouring, green colouring, 2 yards of holly ribbon, 2¼ lb. of sweet Valencia almonds (for decoration).

METHOD.—Wash, pick, and dry the fruit.

Cut the peel into small pieces.

Blanch two ounces of almonds and chop up roughly.

Well grease a strong, round cake-tin, and line it with two or three layers of greased paper.

Sieve the flour and spice together.

Beat the butter and sugar to a cream.

Stir in each egg quickly and beat well for five minutes before adding the next.

Add the flour, almonds, and fruit gradually together with the sherry.

Beat thoroughly for about ten minutes.

Place in the cake-tin and bake in a moderately hot oven for the first twenty minutes, then lessen the heat.

Cook altogether for about three or four hours.

Put on a sieve until cold. Then wrap in grease-proof paper and store in an airtight tin for at least two or three weeks.

Ice it three or four days before you wish to serve it.

NOTE.—Thoroughly beat in each egg separately, otherwise the mixture is liable to curdle. If this should happen, mix in a little of the flour immediately. If time will not allow to store the cake before icing it, do not make the mixture quite so rich.

The top of the cake is to be covered with baked almonds, which should be prepared before making the almond paste.

Put them into a saucepan, cover with water, and bring to the boil, then remove the skins.

Spread them over two or three baking-sheets and put in a warm oven until they are pale biscuit colour.

When baked on one side turn them over.

Now make the almond paste.

Sieve the icing sugar and mix with the ground almonds. Beat the whites of eggs slightly and add sufficient with a few drops of vanilla to make a stiff paste.

Put the almond paste on to a board, dusted with icing sugar, and knead it for a few minutes until smooth, then roll it out to about half an inch in thickness.

If necessary, straighten the cake at the top and cut away any portions that may be too baked.

Cover the sides with almond paste making them very even. Put nearly all the remaining pieces together and roll to a round shape, the size of the top. Fit on and make perfectly even. Then stand the cake on a large dish turned upside down.

NOTE.—Leave out a small piece of almond paste for the top decoration.

Stick the baked almonds all over the top and in the sides of the cake.

Begin from the centre of the top and work in circles to the outside edge, letting each almond overlap the previous one. Similarly cover the sides.

Then stand in a *cool* oven for about an hour to set and dry the almond paste.

Leave for a day, then decorate the

top with a few sprigs of imitation mistletoe.

This is made from the almond paste. Make a few small balls to represent the berries.

Colour the remainder a light green colour.

Mark out and vein a few mistletoe leaves. This gives them a natural look. Mould some stems and make up a few sprays. Decorate the top of the cake.

Remove very carefully on to a cake-board. Tie the cake with a band of holly ribbon, and finish with a large bow.

ALMOND FINGERS

INGREDIENTS.—3 eggs, 4 oz. of flour, 4 oz. of castor sugar, 2 oz. of butter.

FOR THE ALMOND MIXTURE.—½ lb. of cooking almonds (blanched), 3 oz. of castor sugar, the white of one of the eggs.

METHOD.—Separate the whites of the eggs from the yolks and put aside one of the whites.

To make the cake-mixture, line a small swiss-roll tin neatly with greased paper, letting the paper come an inch above the sides of the tin.

Cream together the yolks of the eggs and the sugar and stir in the butter, which should be melted but not hot.

Beat them well for fifteen minutes.

Whisk two whites of eggs to a stiff froth and stir them into the mixture alternately with the flour.

Pour the mixture into the lined tin and bake it in a moderately hot oven for about fifteen minutes.

When it has baked for about ten minutes, beat the one white of egg to a stiff froth and stir in the almonds and sugar.

Spread this almond mixture quickly over the cake.

Let it bake till the almonds are slightly browned.

When cold cut the cake into fingers.

ALMOND GATEAU

INGREDIENTS.—1 teacupful of castor sugar, 4 oz. of butter or margarine, ½ lb. of flour, 1 teaspoonful of cream of tartar, ¼ flat teaspoonful of carbonate

of soda, 2 oz. of almonds, 3 eggs, almond flavouring, milk (if required).

FOR THE FILLING.—2 oz. of ground almonds, 2 tablespoonfuls of plum jam (stoneless).

FOR THE ICING.—1 teacupful of cold water, 1 lb. of lump sugar, a pinch of cream of tartar, 2 whites of egg, a few almonds (for decoration).

METHOD.—Grease a cake-tin and line with greased paper, to stand above the top.

Sieve the flour, soda, and cream of tartar.

Blanch, skin, and chop up the almonds roughly.

Beat the sugar and fat to a cream.

Separate the yolks from the whites of eggs and whisk the whites to a stiff froth.

Beat up the yolks and add gradually to the creamed fat and sugar, keeping the mixture stirred quickly. Beat for a few minutes, then stir in the flour and the whisked whites.

Mix all together lightly, add a few drops of almond flavouring, and a little milk if required.

Put into the prepared tin and bake in a moderately hot oven for about three-quarters of an hour. When cooked, turn carefully on to a sieve and leave until quite cold.

To PREPARE THE FILLING.—Warm the jam slightly and rub it through a sieve, then mix with the ground almonds and leave until quite cold. Split open the cake, spread with the prepared filling, then put together again, and stand on a rack over a dish ready for the icing.

To PREPARE THE ICING AND DECORATION.—Blanch and skin a few almonds. Place on a sheet of paper on a baking-sheet, and put into a warm oven until lightly browned. Put the sugar and water into a saucepan and dissolve slowly.

Add a good pinch of cream of tartar, bring to the boil, and keep boiling until a small quantity of the syrup, when dropped into cold water and left for about a second or so, can be lifted out and rolled into a soft ball between your finger and thumb.

(If you have a saccharometer, the syrup, when ready should register 238° to 240°.)

Have ready the whites of eggs whisked slightly, stir the prepared syrup on to them, and keep stirring quickly until the icing begins to thicken and set, then pour it over the cake and coat it evenly.

Decorate the top tastefully with the baked almonds.

COFFEE ALMOND GATEAU

INGREDIENTS.—6 oz. of flour, 4 oz. of butter or margarine, 4 oz. of castor sugar, 3 eggs, ½ teaspoonful of baking-powder, 1 tablespoonful of water, 2 oz. of almonds.

FOR THE ICING.—6 oz. of icing sugar, 3 oz. of butter, 2 oz. of almonds, 1 tablespoonful of coffee essence.

METHOD.—Grease an oblong tin. Cream the butter and sugar till soft and white. Add the yolks of the eggs and beat the mixture for five minutes.

Pour boiling water on the almonds and slip off the skins.

Chop the almonds and stir half of them into the cake.

Sift the flour and baking-powder, and add them to the cake. Add the water. The stiffly beaten whites should be stirred in last of all as lightly as possible.

Pour the mixture into the tin and bake it for about twenty-five minutes in a moderate oven.

When the cake is cold, cut it in half.

TO ICE THE CAKE.—Beat the butter and icing sugar to a cream and stir in the coffee essence.

Spread one half of the cake with icing and sprinkle it with chopped almonds. Fit the two halves of the cake together and decorate the top with icing and almonds.

GROUND ALMOND CAKE

INGREDIENTS.—6 oz. of flour, 1 teaspoonful of baking-powder, 3 oz. of ground almonds, 4 oz. of margarine, 6 oz. of castor sugar, 2 eggs, almond flavouring, milk.

METHOD.—Sieve the flour and baking-powder.

Beat the sugar and fat to a cream.

Stir in the eggs quickly, adding each one separately, and beating the mixture

for a few minutes between each addition.

Mix in the ground almonds, and gradually stir in the flour with some milk, if required.

Mix all together lightly and add half a teaspoonful of almond flavouring.

Turn the mixture into a prepared cake-tin, dredge the top with castor sugar, and put it into a moderately hot oven to bake. It will take about one hour and a quarter to cook.

ALMOND MADEIRA CAKE

INGREDIENTS.—5 oz. of flour, 1½ oz. of ground almonds, 3 oz. of margarine, 3 oz. of castor sugar, 1 teaspoonful of baking-powder, 2 eggs and 1 extra white, few drops of almond flavouring, milk, castor sugar.

METHOD.—Beat the margarine and sugar to a cream. Add each of the whole eggs separately, stir them in quickly and beat each well before adding the next.

When both are well beaten in, stir in the ground almonds, also the flour and baking-powder, which should previously have been sifted.

Mix them all lightly, adding a little milk as required. Flavour with almond essence and fold in the remaining egg-white whisked up stiffly.

Put a baking case in a cake-tin, turn the mixture into it, but only two-thirds fill it.

Dredge the top with castor sugar and bake the cake in a moderate oven.

NOTE.—The large baking cases can be bought together with a tin to fit them. No greasing is required. If these are not available, bake in the usual way in a greased cake-tin.

ALMOND PASTE SANDWICH

INGREDIENTS.—2 oz. of flour, ¼ teaspoonful of baking-powder, 1 yolk and 2 whites of eggs, 2 oz. of castor sugar, 1 oz. of butter or margarine, about ½ to ¾ lb. of almond paste (see next page), cream, or butter icing (see p. 487), jam.

METHOD.—Put the eggs and sugar into a basin and whisk them over hot water until thick and creamy and free from dark streaks. Take them off the hot water.

Warm the butter enough to melt it,

and sift the flour with the baking-powder.

Stir the flour and butter alternately into the whisked eggs and sugar and mix all together lightly. Turn the mixture into a buttered sandwich-tin and bake it in a hot oven until spongy.

When cold, split it in halves and spread the smallest possible amount of jam on each half—just sufficient to make the paste adhere. Put a layer of almond paste on one piece, and sandwich the two together.

Decorate the top of the sandwich with leaves of almond paste using a little jam to make them adhere, and add finally a few blobs of whipped cream, sweetened and flavoured to taste, or butter icing.

To Make the Almond Paste.—Use either equal quantities of ground almonds and icing sugar, or else one part almonds to two parts sugar. Mix them to a stiff paste with white of egg, and add colouring and flavouring as desired.

Form the paste into a smooth lump, roll it out and cut a round the same size as the sandwich, the remainder make into leaves. To do this, cut the paste into strips, then into diamond shapes, and mark veins on each leaf, using the back of a knife.

ALMOND AND RAISIN CAKE

INGREDIENTS.—1 lb. of flour, 1 lb. of raisins, $\frac{1}{4}$ lb. of almonds, $\frac{3}{4}$ lb. of margarine, $\frac{1}{2}$ lb. of sugar, 1 lemon, 2 teaspoonfuls of cream of tartar, $\frac{1}{4}$ teaspoonful of carbonate of soda, 3 or 4 eggs, milk.

METHOD.—Grease a cake-tin and line with greased paper. Wash and dry the raisins, then stone and cut into halves.

Blanch the almonds, leave a few whole, and cut up the remainder. Grate the lemon-rind.

Sieve the flour, cream of tartar, and carbonate of soda. Whisk up the eggs. Cream the fat and sugar.

Gradually stir in the flour, raisins, lemon-rind, and almonds alternately with the eggs and some milk as required. Do not make the mixture too moist or the fruit will sink.

Mix all together and beat well. Put into the prepared cake-tin, place the whole almonds on the top, and bake in a moderately hot oven for about two and a half hours, lessening the heat as required.

WHEN BUYING ALMONDS

Valencia almonds should be used for cooking purposes. These are less expensive than Jordan almonds. Remember to ask for sweet ones, as bitter can also be obtained.

ALMOND RINGS

INGREDIENTS.—$\frac{1}{2}$ teacupful of castor sugar, 1 egg, $\frac{1}{4}$ lb. of flour, 1 flat teaspoonful of baking-powder, $1\frac{1}{2}$ oz. of margarine, milk, almond flavouring, red and yellow jam.

FOR THE ALMOND PASTE.—$\frac{1}{4}$ lb. of icing sugar, 2 oz. of ground almonds, egg (as required), almond flavouring.

METHOD.—Sieve the flour with the baking-powder. Warm the margarine just enough to melt it.

Whisk the castor sugar and egg together until they are thick and creamy and free from dark streaks.

Stir in the flour lightly, also the margarine (melted, but not hot), some almond flavouring, and a little milk as required.

Turn the mixture into a greased sandwich-tin, and bake it in a quick oven for about ten or fifteen minutes, until it feels spongy. Then leave it on a sieve to cool.

THE ALMOND PASTE

Rub the icing sugar through a hair sieve, and mix it with the ground almonds.

Beat up the egg and add enough of it, with a few drops of almond flavouring, to make a stiff paste.

Work the paste until smooth. Roll it out and cut it into rounds about two inches in diameter. Then cut a small round from the centre of each.

To Cut the Rings.—Split the sponge cake into thin layers.

Then cut it into rounds the same size as the almond paste rings.

Spread each sponge ring with jam (some yellow and some red), place an almond ring on each, and drop a little more jam in the centre where the hole comes in the almond paste.

This quantity makes about twelve cakes.

ALMOND ROLL

INGREDIENTS.—2½ oz. of butter or margarine, 4 oz. of castor sugar, 2 eggs and 1 yolk, ¼ lb. flour, 1 level teaspoonful of baking-powder, milk, damson jelly.

FOR THE ALMOND PASTE.—2 lb. of icing sugar, ¼ lb. of ground almonds, 1 egg-white, vanilla, royal icing (see p. 486).

METHOD.—Beat the sugar and fat to a cream.

Stir in the yolk of egg, then add each whole egg separately, stir each in quickly and beat well.

Sift the flour and baking-powder, and stir them in lightly with a little milk as required.

Turn the mixture into a buttered baking-sheet lined with buttered paper to stand above the sides. Spread the mixture evenly, and bake it in a quick oven until it feels spongy.

When cooked, turn it on to a sugared paper, cut off the outside rim and spread the sponge with warm damson jelly, then roll it up and let it cool on a sieve.

TO MAKE THE ALMOND PASTE.— Sift the sugar and mix it with the ground almonds. Add the white of egg, beaten slightly, and a few drops of vanilla. Mix to a stiff paste, adding a little water if required.

Form the paste into a smooth roll, the length of the sponge roll, then, with a rolling pin, roll it until it is wide enough to wrap round it.

To cover the sponge roll, brush it with a little melted damson jelly, then mould the paste round it evenly.

Decorate with dots of royal icing, tinted to any desired shade, and then forced through an icing pump with a piping tube affixed.

NOTE.—When moulding the paste round the roll, stand the latter on the paste, and roll up, then trim off any pieces that overlap.

ALMOND SANDWICH

INGREDIENTS.—5 eggs and their weight in flour and white sugar, 1 teaspoonful of baking-powder, 1 oz. of sweet almonds, jam, 4 oz. of ground almonds, 4 oz. of icing sugar, 2 tablespoonfuls of lemon-juice.

METHOD.—Grease two sandwich-tins.

Whisk four eggs and the white sugar till light and creamy.

Sift the flour and the baking-powder and add them lightly to the eggs. Pour the mixture into the tins and bake for ten minutes in a quick oven.

To MAKE THE FILLING.—Rub the icing sugar through a hair sieve and mix it with the ground almonds, the yolk of an egg and lemon-juice. Roll the paste out and put it between the two cakes. Trim the edges and use the trimmings to make rolls to decorate the top. Put a dab of jam in the centre. Blanch the almonds and use them for decoration, sticking them on with jam.

ALMOND SHORTBREAD

INGREDIENTS.—¾ lb. plain flour, ¼ lb. of margarine, ¼ lb. of butter, ¼ lb. of castor sugar.

FOR THE ALMOND MIXTURE.—2 oz. of butter, 2 oz. of castor sugar, 2 oz. of cooking almonds (blanched), 3 oz. of ground almonds, 2 oz. of flour.

METHOD.—To make the shortbread mixture, cream the butter and margarine till soft and gradually work in the sugar and flour.

Knead them slightly to make a smooth dough.

Prepare the almond mixture by creaming the butter and sugar with a wooden spoon till they are very soft, and gradually working in the ground almonds and flour.

Split the blanched almonds into thin slices.

Roll out the shortbread into a narrow strip about one-third of an inch thick and press the sides, making them thicker than the centre.

Lay the shortbread on a greased tin and spread the almond mixture in the centre. Sprinkle almonds on top and cut the strip of shortbread across into fingers.

Bake in a rather slow oven for about twenty minutes. The cakes should not be browned, but coloured only a pale yellow.

ALMOND SLICES

INGREDIENTS.—3 oz. of ground almonds, 2 oz. of cake-crumbs, 3 oz.

of castor sugar, 1 egg, juice of ½ a lemon, jam.

FOR THE ICING.—4 oz. of icing sugar, 1 tablespoonful of lemon-juice.

METHOD.—Mix the almonds, cake-crumbs, and sugar to a fairly stiff dough with the egg, and knead till smooth.

Roll out into a strip five inches wide and cut it in two equal lengths.

Spread one piece with jam and lay the other on top. Place in a moderate oven till dry and firm.

When the slices are cold rub the icing sugar through a hair sieve and put it in a thin saucepan with the lemon-juice. Mix to a smooth paste and stir over the gas till it softens and dissolves—about twelve seconds.

Pour over the cake, spreading with a knife if necessary. When set and dry cut into fingers.

ALMOND SPONGE

INGREDIENTS.—3 eggs, 4 oz. of granulated sugar (good weight), 3 oz. of flour (light weight), 1 oz. of cornflour, 1 oz. of sweet almonds (blanched), ½ oz. of bitter almonds (blanched), 1 tablespoonful of water, ½ teaspoonful of baking-powder, 1 teaspoonful of castor sugar.

FOR THE ICING.—4 oz. of icing sugar, 1 tablespoonful of tepid water, a few drops of almond essence.

METHOD.—Grease a fluted ring mould (or any other shape if desired). Put in it a teaspoonful each of castor sugar and flour and shake the mould until the inside is coated.

Chop the almonds and sift the flour, cornflour, and baking-powder together.

Whisk the eggs and sugar till they are thick and creamy.

Stir in very lightly the almonds, flour, and water, and pour the mixture into the mould.

Bake the sponge in a moderate oven for from thirty to forty minutes.

Place it on a sieve to cool.

To ice the sponge mix the icing sugar, almond essence, and water in a saucepan and stir it over the gas for a few seconds.

Place it in an icing pump with a plain tube, and decorate the sponge with lines of icing.

If preferred, a few drops of almond essence can be used instead of the bitter almonds.

AMERICAN LAYER CAKE

INGREDIENTS.—1 breakfastcupful of castor sugar, ¼ lb. of butter or margarine, 3 level breakfastcupfuls of plain flour, ¾ cup of milk, 4 eggs, 2 teaspoonfuls of baking-powder.

FOR THE COFFEE NUT FILLING.—½ lb. of icing sugar, 3 oz. of walnuts (shelled), 4 oz. of butter, 1 tablespoonful of coffee essence.

FOR THE CREAM FILLING.—¼ lb. of icing sugar, ¼ gill of cream, a few drops of almond essence.

METHOD.—Grease and line a wide cake-tin.

Cream the butter and sugar till soft and add the yolks of the eggs.

Beat well and add small quantities of milk and flour alternately till all is added.

Beat the whites stiffly and stir them in very lightly.

Add the baking-powder, and put the mixture quickly into the tin and bake it at once for from fifty minutes to an hour in a moderately hot oven.

When the centre is spongy and elastic the cake is done.

Put it on a sieve to cool and remove the paper. When quite cold split into four.

This cake has three layers of filling. The top and lowest layers are filled with coffee butter icing and chopped walnuts and the middle layer is of cream and icing sugar.

Dredge castor sugar on the top of the cake when finished.

TO MAKE COFFEE AND NUT FILLING.—Cream the butter till soft and mix it with half a pound of icing sugar.

Add a tablespoonful of coffee or more if liked strong.

Chop the nuts and add them.

Spread the filling on two rounds of cake, making two sandwiches.

THE CREAM FILLING.—For the cream filling whip the cream stiffly. Rub the icing sugar through a hair sieve and mix it with the cream.

Add almond essence to taste and spread between the two sandwiches.

AMERICAN WHITE CAKE

INGREDIENTS.—10 oz. of plain flour, 2 oz. of cornflour, 1½ breakfastcupfuls of castor sugar, 3 oz. of margarine, 2 oz. of butter, ¾ cup of milk, 3 eggs, vanilla essence, 2 teaspoonfuls of baking-powder.

FOR THE ICING.—6 oz. of icing sugar, 1½ tablespoonfuls of tepid water.

METHOD.—Grease and line a wide cake-tin and light the gas in the oven.

Cream the butter and sugar, add the yolks of the eggs one at a time and beat well as each yolk is added.

Add the milk, flour, and cornflour alternately in small quantities. Beat the whites to a stiff froth and stir them in lightly with a few drops of essence.

Add the baking-powder.

Pour the mixture quickly into the tin and bake it at once in a moderately hot oven for about one hour. It is done when the centre feels firm and elastic.

Remove the paper and place the cake on a sieve to cool. When cold cut it into four.

Spread jam between the first two layers.

Use walnut filling for the bottom layer, and lemon curd for the middle one.

WALNUT FILLING

INGREDIENTS.—6 oz. of icing sugar, 3 oz. of butter, 1 tablespoonful of coffee essence, 2 oz. of chopped walnuts.

METHOD.—Cream the butter till soft. Rub the icing sugar through a hair sieve. Add it to the butter with the coffee essence and beat till smooth. Add the nuts.

LEMON CURD FILLING

INGREDIENTS.—2 oz. of butter, ½ lb. of granulated sugar, 3 eggs, rind of 1 lemon and the juice of 2 lemons.

METHOD.—Put the butter in a double saucepan and let it melt. Stir in the sugar.

Grate the lemon-rind thinly (yellow only) and add it to the sugar.

Beat the eggs.

Add eggs and lemon-juice to the mixture and stir till it is thick enough to coat the back of a wooden spoon.

Leave till quite cold and thick before using.

ANGEL CAKE

INGREDIENTS.—5 oz. of castor sugar, 5 egg-whites, 5 dessertspoonfuls of flour, ¼ teaspoonful of cream of tartar, orange or vanilla flavouring, a pinch of salt.

METHOD.—Add a pinch of salt to the egg-whites and whisk them to a very stiff froth. Sprinkle in the cream of tartar, and fold in the castor sugar gradually.

Lastly, fold in the flour, which should have been previously sieved, and add a few drops of flavouring as required.

Turn the mixture into a cake-tin— one with an adjustable base—and bake it in a very moderate oven for about forty minutes, until it feels spongy.

When the cake is cooked, turn it upside down on to a sieve and leave it to cool, when it should come out of the tin quite easily. The sides can be loosened with a knife if necessary.

If you have not a cake-tin with an adjustable base you may very lightly grease the bottom of the tin by rubbing it with a buttered paper, otherwise do not grease the tin at all.

ANGELICA RING CAKE

INGREDIENTS.—½ lb. of flour, 2½ teaspoonfuls of baking-powder, ½ level teaspoonful of salt, 2 oz. of margarine or butter, 2 oz. of castor sugar, ¼ pint of milk, rings of angelica, crystallised rose leaves.

FOR THE CHOCOLATE FILLING.— 6 oz. of icing sugar, 1½ oz. of grated chocolate, vanilla flavouring, water.

FOR THE VANILLA ICING.—6 oz. of icing sugar, egg-white, vanilla flavouring, colouring if desired, cold water.

METHOD.—Sift the flour with the baking-powder and salt. Rub in the butter lightly and add the sugar. Mix to a soft dough with milk.

Butter a pie-tin, turn the dough on to a lightly floured board, form it into a round and roll it out to the size of the tin. Put it in the tin and place it in a fairly hot oven to bake. It will take about half an hour to cook.

Cool it on a sieve and when cold turn it upside down. Split it in halves, spread it with chocolate filling and sandwich the two pieces together. Coat the top with icing and decorate it with rings of angelica and crushed rose leaves.

To Make the Filling.—Dissolve the chocolate in a saucepan with a spoonful of water, let it cool, then stir in the sifted sugar and flavour it with vanilla. If too thin leave the filling till it thickens, and if too thick add a few drops of water.

To Make the Icing.—Sift the icing sugar, add two teaspoonfuls of cold water and enough lightly beaten white of egg to make it of a coating consistency. Flavour with vanilla and beat the icing till smooth, and add a few drops of colouring as desired.

ANTLER CAKES

Ingredients.—1 egg, 2 yolks of eggs, 4 oz. of sugar, 2 oz. of butter, 2 oz. of cream or Ideal Milk, ½ level teaspoonful of ground cinnamon, ¼ level teaspoonful of soda, 4 oz. of cornflour, 8 oz. of flour, salt.

Method.—Beat the eggs and sugar, add the beaten butter, cream, also the cinnamon and soda, salt and flours, sifted together. Mix them well, and put the mixture aside until it is workable.

Roll the mixture out to about a quarter of an inch thick, and then cut it into pieces each about two inches by three inches. Make a crosswise cut in the centre of each. Take the ends of the slices and draw them under to form a curve, so that the cuts open a little. Bake the cakes in a moderate oven.

Sufficient for about twenty-four cakes.

APPLE FRUIT CAKE

Ingredients.—½ lb. of flour, ½ pint of apple pulp, 2 eggs, 2 oz. of shelled walnuts, 1 level teaspoonful of carbonate of soda, 1 level teaspoonful of powdered cinnamon, ½ level teaspoonful of ground ginger, ½ level teaspoonful of mixed spice, rind of ½ a lemon, 4 oz. of currants and sultanas (mixed), 4 oz. of seeded raisins, 2 oz. of glacé ginger, 2 oz. of candied peel, 5 oz. of margarine, 6 oz. Barbados sugar, castor sugar.

Method.—To obtain the apple pulp, peel and quarter some apples, remove the core and slice the fruit,

then stew it gently until tender, adding sugar to taste, and just a very little water to prevent burning. Rub the apple through a sieve and leave it to get cold.

Wash, pick over and dry the currants and sultanas.

Cut up the peel and ginger and separate the raisins.

Beat the sugar and fat to a cream, add gradually the flour (sifted with the soda and spices), also the prepared fruit, grated lemon-rind, and chopped walnuts, moistening the mixture with the well-whisked eggs and the apple pulp.

Beat the mixture well, turn it into a greased cake-tin, dredge castor sugar on the top and put it in a moderately hot oven to bake.

ARROWROOT CAKE

Ingredients.—½ lb. of margarine, 10 oz. of arrowroot, lemon or vanilla flavouring, 9 oz. of castor sugar, 2 oz. of flour, 3 eggs, 1 teaspoonful of baking-powder.

Method.—Beat the sugar and margarine to a cream. Sieve together the flour, baking-powder, and arrowroot. Grate the lemon-rind. Grease a round cake-tin and line it with greased paper.

Separate the yolks from the whites of eggs and whisk the latter to a very stiff froth. Beat up the yolks. When the sugar and margarine is well creamed, stir in quickly about half of the yolks.

When thoroughly mixed, add the remainder and beat for about ten minutes. Stir in the flour, etc., and lemon-rind, and just a little milk, if required ; then fold in lightly the whisked whites.

Turn into the prepared cake-tin and bake in a moderately hot oven for about one to one and a half hours, lessening the heat as required. When nicely browned, remove the browning-shelf and cover the top with a piece of white paper.

When cooked, turn carefully on to a sieve, remove the paper, and leave until cold. Keep it away from a draught.

BABA AU CREME

Ingredients.—6 oz. of flour, ¼ oz.

of solid yeast, 2 eggs, $\frac{1}{4}$ lb. of mar
garine, $\frac{1}{2}$ gill of milk, $\frac{1}{4}$ gill of water,
1 flat teaspoonful of castor sugar.

FOR THE SYRUP.—5 oz. of granulated sugar, 2 gills of water, 1 or 2
tablespoonfuls of sherry or rum.

METHOD.—Put the flour through a
sieve into a basin, make a hole in
the centre of it.

Mix together, in a small warm basin,
the yeast and sugar until they become liquid. Warm the milk and
water and add to the yeast.

Strain this all into the centre of
the flour, sprinkle a small quantity
of the latter over the surface of the
yeast and set the basin in a warm
place for about thirty minutes.

Then gradually begin to mix the
flour into the yeast, etc. At the same
time melt the margarine and mix in.
When this is well mixed, beat in
the eggs separately.

Beat all well together for a few
minutes.

Well grease some small baba moulds
or one large ring mould. Half fill
each mould with some of the mixture. Put them on a baking-sheet
in a warm place for about forty-five
minutes, or until they have risen to
twice their original size. Bake in a
moderately hot oven for about twenty
to thirty minutes.

TO MAKE THE SYRUP.—Boil together the sugar and water until
thick. It will take about six minutes.
Then stir in the sherry—just sufficient
to flavour the syrup.

Put the babas into a dish and soak
them well with the hot syrup. Serve
them either hot or cold and with
whipped cream.

If served cold, take them from the
syrup and put a small quantity of
whipped cream into the centre of
each. If served hot, leave them in
the syrup and hand the cream
separately.

BANANA CHERRY CAKES

INGREDIENTS.—$\frac{1}{2}$ lb. of flour, 2 oz.
of glacé cherries, 2 bananas, $\frac{1}{4}$ flat
teaspoonful of carbonate of soda,
$\frac{1}{4}$ lb. of margarine, $\frac{1}{4}$ lb. of sugar,
1 egg, milk, 1 lemon (rind only).

METHOD.—Peel the bananas and
mash them to a pulp.

Cut up the cherries.

Sieve the flour with the carbonate
of soda.

Rub in the margarine, and then
stir in the sugar, cherries, and the
grated lemon-rind.

Beat up the egg and mix it with
the dry ingredients, adding the banana
pulp, and some milk as required.

Beat well. Turn the mixture into
small greased tins, or baking cups,
and put them into a hot oven to
bake.

If liked, stick a small piece of cherry
on top of each.

This quantity makes about twenty
small cakes.

BANANA LAYER CAKE

INGREDIENTS.—$4\frac{1}{2}$ oz. of castor
sugar, 2 oz. of butter, 2 eggs, $\frac{1}{4}$ lb. of
flour, $2\frac{1}{2}$ level teaspoonfuls of baking-
powder, 2 bananas.

METHOD.—Cream the butter and
sugar. Add the flour, baking-powder,
and well-beaten eggs alternately, then
the mashed bananas. Mix them
thoroughly.

Divide the mixture between two
buttered sandwich-tins.

Bake it in a quick oven for twenty
minutes. When cold, put the halves
together with banana filling between
them. Dust the top with icing sugar.

BANANA FILLING

INGREDIENTS.—2 mashed bananas,
$\frac{1}{4}$ lb. of castor sugar, $\frac{1}{4}$ oz. of gelatine,
water, vanilla, $\frac{1}{2}$ gill of cream.

METHOD.—Mix the mashed bananas
with the sugar, and add the gelatine
dissolved in a little water.

Fold in the whipped cream, flavour
the filling with vanilla and leave it
until it begins to thicken.

BANANA MERINGUES

INGREDIENTS.—Whites of 2 fresh
eggs, one of them to be a duck's egg,
4 oz. of castor sugar, 2 bananas, 8d.
of double cream, 1 oz. of sugar for
cream.

FOR THE CHOCOLATE ICING.—4 oz.
of icing sugar, $1\frac{1}{2}$ oz. of chocolate (in
cake), vanilla essence, 3 tablespoonfuls
of tepid water.

METHOD.—Put the egg-whites in a
dry basin and whisk them (preferably
by an open window) until they form a

solid froth. When they are solid enough the basin can be turned upside down without the eggs moving.

Sprinkle the sugar over the egg-whites and stir it in *very* lightly. (If stirred too much the mixture will become too soft to shape nicely.)

Have ready a tin covered with two sheets of thick, white smooth paper.

To shape each meringue take a dessertspoonful of the white of egg and with a knife shape it like a meringue with a pointed ridge along the centre. Push it gently off the spoon on to the paper, using the knife to do so.

Dredge them thickly with fine castor sugar, and place them in a very moderate oven for two hours.

The meringues must not be cooked, only thoroughly dried. If the oven is at all hot leave the door ajar.

When the meringues are dry take them out of the oven and remove them from the paper. If they stick, moisten the back of the paper with water and they will come off easily.

Press in the underneath part and lay them upside down on the tin, putting them back in the oven for the inside to dry. If not wanted at once keep them in a tin.

Put about one-third of a banana in each meringue and place them ready for icing the tops.

To Ice the Meringues.—Put the chocolate in a double saucepan and let it melt. Stir in the water and mix well, but do not let the icing get hot or it will crack.

Rub the icing sugar through a hair sieve, and stir it in with a few drops of vanilla. Stir it over the gas for about ten seconds to make it liquid, then dip the top of each meringue into the icing.

When they are dry beat the cream till stiff and sweeten it with about one ounce of sugar. Stick two meringues together with a little cream.

Note.—When whipping cream always add the sugar afterwards. If added before whipping it sometimes makes the cream soft and oily.

BARBADOS CAKE

Ingredients.—¾ lb. of flour, ½ level teaspoonful of carbonate of soda, 9 oz. of Barbados sugar, ¼ lb. of margarine,

2 eggs, milk, 9 oz. of seeded raisins, 3 oz. of mixed peel, ¼ lb. of golden syrup, 1 level teaspoonful of mixed spice, 1 oz. of almonds.

Method.—Cut up the raisins and shred the peel.

Sift the flour with the spice.

Whisk the eggs, warm the golden syrup and add it to them, and whisk them together.

Beat the sugar and fat to a cream, then gradually stir in the egg mixture and flour alternately, adding also the prepared fruit and some milk as required.

When well mixed, stir in the soda dissolved in a spoonful of milk.

Turn the mixture into a greased square or oblong cake-tin, sprinkle blanched almonds (split in half) on the top and bake the cake in a moderate oven.

BARCELONA CAKE

Ingredients.—½ lb. of flour, 2 oz. of Barcelona nuts, 6 oz. of castor sugar, vanilla, 1 teaspoonful of baking-powder, ¼ lb. of butter or margarine, 1 egg, milk.

Method.—Grease a round cake-tin.

Sieve the flour. Mix the baking-powder with about one dessertspoonful of the flour and put aside. Rub the fat into the flour.

Chop up the nuts and add with the sugar, and mix together.

Beat up the egg and add to the dry ingredients, adding some milk as required.

Beat the mixture for a few minutes, then stir in the baking-powder.

Put into the greased tin and bake in a hot oven.

This can be made into little cakes if preferred.

"BASKET OF STRAWBER-RIES" CAKE

Ingredients.—¾ lb. of flour, ½ lb. of castor sugar, ½ lb. of margarine, 1 teaspoonful of baking-powder, 3 eggs.

For Strawberries and Handles.—½ lb. of ground almonds, ½ lb. of icing sugar, cochineal, 2 oz. of castor sugar, 1 egg.

For the Icing.—3 oz. of butter,

6 oz. of icing sugar, 1 dessertspoonful of orange-juice.

METHOD.—Grease and line an oblong two-pound tin. Cream the margarine and sugar.

Beat in the eggs, one at a time, and then sift in the flour and baking-powder.

Put the mixture in the tin and bake it in a moderate oven for about an hour and a quarter.

When it feels elastic in the centre, and a fine skewer stuck in comes out clean, take out the cake and remove the paper.

Stand the cake on a sieve to cool.

THE DECORATIONS

Before you begin the decorations, scoop out an oval piece from the top of the cake and cut a small triangular piece from the four corners at the bottom.

To MAKE THE ALMOND PASTE

Rub the icing sugar through a hair sieve on to the almonds.

Beat a small egg, leaving a very little of the white for further use, and add it to the almonds and sugar, mixing and kneading till smooth.

A third part of the almond paste is then shaped into two curved handles made so that they will rest *on* the edge of the cake as well as against the side.

Two-thirds of the almond paste is shaped to represent strawberries, which are painted with cochineal and dipped in castor sugar.

Wet with white of egg the parts of the handles that touch the cake and press them gently into place.

THE ICING

To make the icing, cream the butter and rub the icing sugar through a hair sieve.

Mix the butter and sugar with the orange-juice, half fill an icing bag with a rose-tube screwed on.

Force slanting lines three-quarters of an inch apart on to the cake to form a trellis work and decorate the handles and edge of the basket with roses.

NOTE.—It is better to make this cake one day and ice it the next.

BEE-HIVES

INGREDIENTS.—6 oz. cake-crumbs, about ⅓ gill of cooking sherry, 2 oz. of icing sugar, 1 oz. of ground almonds, egg, vanilla, jam.

METHOD.—To obtain the cake-crumbs, rub pieces of cake through a wire sieve. The bee-hives are made from about one part chocolate cake to three parts of madeira.

Turn the crumbs into a basin and add sufficient sherry to mix them to a paste.

Divide the paste into twelve portions and form them into fat shapes.

Sift the icing sugar and mix it with the ground almonds. Flavour them with vanilla and add sufficient egg to make a stiff paste.

Roll this out and cut it into rounds barely an inch and a half in diameter. Spread each with a very little jam or jelly and stand a portion of cake paste on top. Press your small finger into the top of each and complete the bee-hives with tiny balls of almond paste.

Sufficient to make twelve bee-hives.

A BIRTHDAY CAKE

INGREDIENTS.—1¼ lb. of self-raising flour, 1 gill of milk, ¾ lb. of butter or margarine, 1 lb. of sultanas (washed and dried), 4 oz. of mixed peel (chopped), 4 oz. of glacé cherries (cut in half), ½ lb. of raisins (stoned), 5 eggs, 1 teaspoonful of cinnamon, ¾ lb. of castor sugar.

FOR DECORATION (if desired).—Almond paste, (see below), mimosa flowers and a little angelica, royal icing (see below).

METHOD.—Line a very large tin with three thicknesses of greased paper. Cream the butter till soft.

Add the sugar and beat both together till they are white and creamy.

Add the eggs one at a time and beat the mixture well after adding each one.

Stir in the fruit, peel, flour, and spice, and moisten them with the milk.

Place the mixture in the tin and hollow out the centre.

Put the cake into a fairly hot oven, first laying a sheet of paper over the top. After twenty minutes, lower the gas and finish the cake in a moderate oven.

Bake it for about three hours.

NOTE.—The time for cooking depends on the thickness of the cake. Thick cakes are much more difficult to bake than thin ones, and take longer.

ALMOND PASTE

INGREDIENTS.—¾ lb. of ground almonds, 1 egg, ¾ lb. of icing sugar, 1 dessertspoonful of lemon-juice.

METHOD.—Rub the icing sugar through a hair sieve, add the almonds and mix them well together.

Beat the egg and pour it and the lemon-juice over the almonds and sugar, stirring all the time.

Mix them first with a wooden spoon and then with the hands, till the mixture is smooth.

Knead well. Turn the paste on to a board dusted with icing sugar, and roll it out to the same size round as the cake.

To put on the almond paste, turn the cake upside down on a soup-plate, also upside down, roll out the almond paste, and lay it on the cake. Press it firmly, and smooth the sides. Next day, spread it with two thin layers of royal icing, being sure to let the first one dry before putting on the second.

THE ROYAL ICING

INGREDIENTS.—1 lb. of icing sugar, 2 whites of eggs, 1 dessertspoonful of lemon-juice.

METHOD.—Sift the sugar. Beat the whites slightly. Stir the whites and lemon-juice into the sugar and beat them for fifteen minutes.

To decorate the cake, use an icing pump, with a plain tube screwed on it and fill it half full with royal icing. Make three or four long lines for the stalks of the mimosa.

For the dots press and withdraw quickly.

While the icing is wet press the strips of angelica and mimosa flowers in place.

BIRTHDAY ORANGE CAKE

INGREDIENTS.—5 oz. of flour, ¾ level teaspoonful of baking-powder, 2 oz. of desiccated coconut, 2 oz. of butter, 3 whole eggs and 1 yolk, 5 oz. of castor sugar, rind of 1 orange, juice of 1½ oranges, apricot jam.

FOR THE ALMOND PASTE.—½ lb. of ground almonds, ¾ lb. of icing sugar, 1 whole egg and 1 yolk, orange flavouring.

FOR THE ORANGE ICING.—1¼ lb. of icing sugar, 2 whites of eggs, juice of 1 orange, or more, as required, apricot yellow colouring, mixed coloured candlesticks and candleholders.

METHOD.—Grate the orange-rind finely. Squeeze out the juice and pour it over the coconut.

Put the eggs into a basin with the castor sugar and whisk them over hot water until thick and creamy and free from dark streaks, then remove the hot water and stir in gradually the flour, sifted with the baking powder, adding alternately the butter (melted but not hot). Stir in the coconut and orange-rind and juice. Bake the mixture either in one cake-tin or else in two sandwich-tins, until spongy. Leave it to get cold.

TO MAKE THE ALMOND PASTE.—Sift the icing sugar and mix it with the ground almonds. Beat up the eggs and stir them in and mix them to a stiff paste, adding sufficient orange essence to flavour.

TO COVER THE CAKE.—If baked in two tins, sandwich the two together with a layer of apricot jam between them. Form a piece of the paste into a long roll, then roll it out to a strip the same depth as the cake and long enough to reach round it. Brush the sides of the cake with the syrup part of some apricot jam, and mould the paste round it. Then brush the top and cover it also with a round of paste, making it quite level.

Put this aside for at least an hour or two before covering it with the second icing.

TO MAKE THE ORANGE ICING.—Sift the icing sugar, then take one pound of it and put it into a basin. Stir in the strained juice of an orange and the slightly frothed whites of the eggs, and mix them to a thick, smooth coating consistency. More sugar or orange-juice may be added if required. Colour the icing to a pale orange with apricot yellow colouring, then pour it over the cake, spreading it a little if necessary.

Let this set, then beat together any of the icing that is over, add some more sugar to make it of a stiffer consistency and colour it to a deeper orange than the coating icing. Force this through an icing pump and decorate the cake according to taste.

Finally, arrange the holders and candles round the edge.

BLONDE CAKES

INGREDIENTS.—½ lb. of flour, 3 whites of eggs, 6 oz. of castor sugar, 5 oz. of margarine, few almonds, ratafia or almond flavouring, 1 teaspoonful of baking-powder, milk.

METHOD.—Blanch a few almonds and split into quarters.

Sieve the flour and baking-powder.

Cream the fat and sugar.

Whisk the egg-whites to a stiff froth. Gradually stir the flour into the creamed fat and sugar, and a little milk as required.

Mix well, add a few drop of flavouring, then fold in the whisked whites.

Put into small, greased cake-tins, place quarter of an almond on each, and bake in a hot oven for about fifteen minutes.

Sufficient to make fourteen cakes.

BONNES BOUCHES

INGREDIENTS.—½ pint of water, 4 oz. of flour, 2 oz. of butter, 3 eggs, almond essence, pinch of salt, 6d. of whipped cream, sweetened to taste.

FOR THE LEMON WATER ICING.— 8 oz. of icing sugar (sifted), 2 tablespoonfuls of lemon-juice.

METHOD.—Put the water and butter in a saucepan on the gas. Sift the flour and salt and as soon as the water boils take the pan off the gas and pour the flour on to the liquid all at once.

Stir hard till smooth, replace on the gas and stir till the mixture leaves the sides of the pan quite clean (about three minutes). Turn out the gas and add a few drops of essence. Add the eggs one at a time, beating the mixture till smooth after each egg. Drop teaspoonfuls of the mixture on to a greased tin.

Bake for ten minutes in a quick oven. When cold fill with whipped cream.

To ice, mix lemon-juice and icing sugar in a pan, warm very slightly to soften it and pour a spoonful over each bonne bouche.

BOOK GATEAU

INGREDIENTS.—2 eggs, their weight in castor sugar, flour, and margarine, 1 flat teaspoonful of cream of tartar, ¼ flat teaspoonful of carbonate of soda.

FOR THE BUTTER ICING.—6 oz. of icing sugar, 3 oz. of butter, coffee essence.

FOR ALMOND PASTE ICING.—¼ lb. of ground almonds, ¼ lb. of castor sugar, ¼ lb. of icing sugar, 1 egg-white, vanilla flavouring, few drops of colouring as desired.

METHOD.—Sieve the flour with the cream of tartar and carbonate of soda.

Beat the sugar and fat to a cream.

Separate one of the eggs, and save the white for the almond paste. Add the whole egg to the creamed fat and sugar, stir it in quickly and beat well for a few minutes, then add the yolk and beat again.

Stir in the flour, etc., and a little milk as required. Mix all together lightly. Turn the mixture into a greased oblong cake-tin and bake it for about half an hour.

When cooked and cold, split the cake into halves and spread it with some of the butter icing. Put the halves together again, and if the cake has risen unevenly cut off a slice and level it.

Spread some butter icing round three edges (one long and two short) of the cake, and mark them with a fork to look like the leaves of a book.

Roll out the almond paste to an oblong shape, large enough to wrap round the cake, and cut it evenly so that it will just overlap the leaves.

Mould the trimmings of paste into a long roll and place it along the back edge (the one not covered with butter icing).

This will give the back of the book a rounded appearance when finished.

Now stand the cake on the rolled out paste and wrap the latter over it neatly. Write a suitable title on the book, using the remainder of the butter icing forced through a piping tube.

The Almond Paste Icing

Rub the icing sugar through a hair sieve, and mix it with the castor sugar and ground almonds.

Beat up the egg-white slightly and add it with a few drops of flavouring and colouring as desired. Mix to a stiff paste, then work it into a smooth lump. If there is not quite enough egg-white, add a little water to make up.

The Butter Icing.

Sieve the sugar, and add it to the butter. Beat both to a cream. Add some coffee essence—only enough to flavour the icing slightly and to make it a deep cream colour. Use as required.

BRAZIL NUT GATEAU

INGREDIENTS.—3 eggs, the weight of two eggs in flour and castor sugar, 1 oz. of ground Brazil nuts, 1 flat teaspoonful of cream of tartar, $\frac{1}{4}$ flat teaspoonful of carbonate of soda, Brazil nuts for decoration (whole and ground), a tablespoonful of water.

FOR THE COFFEE BUTTER ICING.— $\frac{1}{2}$ lb. of icing sugar, $\frac{1}{4}$ lb. of butter, coffee essence.

METHOD.—Sieve the flour with the cream of tartar and carbonate of soda.

Separate the eggs, whisk the yolks and sugar together until thick and creamy and free from dark streaks. Stir in the flour lightly, also the ground nuts, adding about a tablespoonful of water as required.

Whisk the egg-whites to a very stiff froth and fold them in last.

Turn the mixture into a greased tin and put it into a good, moderately hot oven to bake. It will take about half an hour to cook.

When cold, spread the sides with coffee butter icing, which should be coated with ground Brazil nuts. Decorate the top with lines of icing, forced through an icing tube. Sprinkle a few ground nuts over the top and put a ring of halved nuts round the edge.

Coffee Butter Icing

To make the coffee butter icing, roll the lumps out of the icing sugar and rub it through a hair sieve.

Beat the butter and sugar to a cream, then stir in sufficient coffee essence to flavour and colour.

BRIDGE BISCUITS

INGREDIENTS.—3 oz. of castor sugar, 4 oz. of margarine, 5 oz. of flour, $\frac{1}{4}$ level teaspoonful of baking-powder, large pinch of ground cinnamon, 1 egg-yolk.

METHOD.—Beat the sugar and fat to a cream, stir in the yolk of egg, and beat well. Add the flour, sifted, with baking-powder and cinnamon. Mix all together to a soft paste.

Roll the paste out thinly and stamp it into shapes with bridge cutters. Put the biscuits on a lightly buttered tin and bake them in a moderately hot oven for about ten minutes. Cool the biscuits on a sieve and dredge them with castor sugar.

BRIDGE CAKE

INGREDIENTS.—$\frac{1}{2}$ lb. of flour, 1 teaspoonful of baking-powder, 4 oz. of grated chocolate, 6 oz. of castor sugar, 4 oz. of butter or margarine, 2 eggs, vanilla, milk.

FOR THE ALMOND PASTE.—3 oz. of ground almonds, 6 oz. of icing sugar, vanilla, egg.

FOR THE ICING.—10 oz. of castor sugar, $2\frac{1}{2}$ tablespoonfuls of hot water, $1\frac{1}{2}$ oz. of butter, 6 oz. of marsh-mallows, vanilla.

METHOD.—Beat the sugar and fat to a cream, add each egg separately, stirring them in quickly and beating well, and when both are added stir in the chocolate, dissolved in a little milk, also the flour sifted with baking-powder. Mix all together lightly, adding a little more milk if required. Flavour it with vanilla and turn the mixture into a buttered cake-tin, pushing it a little from the centre so that it may rise evenly. Bake the cake in a moderately hot oven.

Cool the cake on a sieve and, when cold, split it into halves and place a layer of almond paste between the pieces. Sandwich the pieces together and pour the icing over the cake.

Decorate it with tiny shapes of almond paste, colouring the hearts and diamonds to a deep pink, and the spades and clubs to a dark chocolate colour.

To Make the Almond Paste.— Sift the icing sugar and mix it with the ground almonds. Add a few drops of vanilla and about half a beaten egg, or sufficient to make it into a stiff paste. Work it into a smooth lump, then roll it out and cut a round the same size as the cake.

Left-over almond paste can be utilised for the final decoration. Divide it into two portions and colour one to a deep pink with cochineal. Roll it out and cut it into shapes —hearts and diamonds. Colour the other portion with a little dissolved chocolate, roll it out, and cut it into spade and club shapes.

To Make the Icing.—Melt the butter in a saucepan, add the hot water and the sugar, and dissolve slowly. Bring the syrup to the boil, and boil it until a small quantity, when dropped into cold water and left for a few seconds, becomes a soft ball when taken out and rubbed between the fingers.

Have ready the marshmallows, dissolved in the top of a double boiler, and gradually stir the prepared syrup into them. Flavour the icing with vanilla and beat it until of a coating consistency. Pour it over the cake and coat it evenly.

When the icing is set, decorate it with the prepared shapes of paste, using a tiny dab of jam to make them adhere.

Note.—The marshmallows must be melted by the time the syrup is ready, so put them on to melt a few minutes before making the syrup.

Water Icing

If a simpler icing is preferred, sift three-quarters of a pound of icing sugar and mix it to a smooth coating consistency with two or three tablespoonfuls of warm water. Flavour it with vanilla and pour it over the cake.

BROWN AND WHITE CAKE

INGREDIENTS.—$2\frac{1}{2}$ oz. of chocolate, $\frac{1}{2}$ lb. of castor sugar, 9 oz. of flour, vanilla flavouring, chocolate butter icing, 3 oz. of butter or margarine, 3 eggs, 1 good tablespoonful of baking-powder, milk, vanilla butter icing (see below).

METHOD.—Cream the butter with half the sugar, then beat in the remainder of the sugar.

Whisk up the eggs and add them gradually, stirring in also the flour, sifted with the baking-powder. Add some milk as required. Flavour the mixture with vanilla.

Put half the mixture into a large, buttered sandwich-tin, and to the remainder add the chocolate, previously grated, and dissolved in a spoonful or two of milk. Turn the chocolate-flavoured mixture into another tin and bake both until spongy; then cool them on a sieve.

Spread a layer of chocolate butter icing on the white cake and a layer of vanilla butter icing on the chocolate cake, and sandwich the two pieces together. Decorate the cake with the two kinds of icing alternately, forcing them through a rose-patterned icing tube.

The Butter Icings

INGREDIENTS.—$\frac{1}{2}$ lb. of icing sugar, $\frac{1}{4}$ lb. of butter, vanilla, $1\frac{1}{2}$ oz. of grated chocolate, 1 or 2 dessert-spoonfuls of milk.

METHOD.—Sift the icing sugar, beat the butter and half the sugar to a cream, then beat in the remainder of the sugar and flavour it with vanilla. Divide the icing into two portions.

Mix the chocolate with a spoonful of milk and stir it until it is dissolved. Cool it and mix it with one portion of the icing.

BUTTERCUP CAKE

INGREDIENTS.—6 oz. of castor sugar, 6 oz. of margarine, 8 oz. of flour, yolk of 3 eggs, $\frac{1}{2}$ lb. of sultanas, 1 teaspoonful of cream of tartar, $\frac{1}{4}$ flat teaspoonful of carbonate of soda, milk.

METHOD.—Grease a cake-tin and line with greased paper to stand above the top. Wash, pick over, and dry the sultanas. Sieve the flour, cream of tartar, and carbonate of soda. Cream the fat and sugar.

Beat up the egg-yolks, stir in half of them and beat well, then add the remainder and beat again.

Gradually stir in the flour, etc., and sultanas, and mix together, lightly adding a little milk.

Turn into the cake-tin and bake in a moderately hot oven for about one to one hour and a half, lessening the heat as required.

BUTTERSCOTCH SANDWICH

INGREDIENTS.—2 oz. of butter or margarine, 4 oz. of castor sugar and flour, ½ teaspoonful of baking-powder, ¼ gill of milk, 1 egg, jam or red currant jelly, 1 teaspoonful of coconut, 2 oz. of ratafias.

FOR THE FILLING.—4 oz. of butter, ½ lb. of Demerara sugar, ½ lb. of golden syrup.

METHOD.—Grease an oval or round sandwich-tin.

Cream the butter till soft, add the sugar and beat till white and creamy.

Add the yolk of the egg and the milk and flour alternately, a little at a time.

Beat the white of egg stiffly and fold it in as lightly as possible, adding the baking-powder last.

Bake in a hot oven for about fifteen minutes.

When cold, split and spread with jam or jelly. Do not put the two halves together till the butterscotch filling is made.

Warm the golden syrup and slowly dissolve the butter and sugar in it.

Boil gently for fifteen minutes. It is done if a little hardens when dropped in water so that it will form a soft ball when rubbed between finger and thumb.

Let it cool till it is as thick as treacle, then pour half of it over the lower half of the cake.

Put on the top piece and pour the rest of the butterscotch over it.

To decorate, place ratafias round the edge and a dab of jelly and a spoonful of coconut in the centre.

CANDLESTICKS

INGREDIENTS.—A small Madeira cake, 2 oz. of ground almonds, 1 to 1¼ lb. of icing sugar, vanilla flavouring, colouring, water, egg-white, a few glacé cherries, some angelica or an orange.

METHOD.—Either make or buy a Madeira cake, and when cold cut it in thick slices.

Stamp out rounds with a plain cutter about four inches in diameter, then cut a small round from the centre of each. Coat the large rounds with soft icing, and when almost set stand a roll of almond paste in the centre of each to represent the candle. Place a glacé cherry on top and form a handle from either angelica or orange-rind and arrange it on one side.

To MAKE THE ALMOND PASTE FOR THE CANDLES.—Sift four ounces of the sugar and mix it with the ground almonds. Flavour them with vanilla and mix to a stiff paste with white of egg. Divide into portions and form each into a long sausage, working it until smooth. Leave to dry, otherwise they will not stand straight.

To MAKE THE SOFT ICING.—Sift three-quarters to one pound of icing sugar and mix to a smooth paste with warm water. Add colouring and flavouring as desired. This icing should be of a coating consistency.

Sufficient for four candlesticks.

NOTE.—The cake trimmings can be used up in a trifle, or made into crumbs and used in a Queen Pudding.

CARAMEL CAKES

INGREDIENTS.—½ lb. of flour, ¼ flat teaspoonful of carbonate of soda, 6 oz. of margarine, ½ lb. of castor sugar, 1 or 2 eggs, 3 tablespoonfuls of cold water.

METHOD.—Put a quarter of the sugar into a small, strong saucepan with half the water and dissolve it slowly. Then boil the syrup until it is a rich golden brown. Draw it aside for a minute or two, add the remainder of the water, and put the pan back over a very low burner to dissolve the caramel. Strain and leave until cold.

Beat the fat and the remainder of the sugar to a cream.

Add each egg separately, stirring it in quickly, and beating well before adding the second one.

When both are well beaten in, sieve the flour and carbonate of soda and add them to the egg and fat with the caramel as required.

Mix all together lightly. Turn the

mixture into small baking-cups, only half filling them, and put them into a hot oven to bake. They will take about fifteen minutes.

This quantity makes thirty cakes.

CARAMEL SANDWICH

INGREDIENTS.—7 oz. of flour, $\frac{1}{4}$ teaspoonful of salt, 2 good teaspoonfuls of baking-powder, $1\frac{1}{2}$ oz. of butter or margarine, 2 oz. of castor sugar, $\frac{3}{4}$ to 1 gill of milk, vanilla flavouring.

FOR THE FILLING.—$1\frac{1}{2}$ oz. of flour, 6 oz. of castor sugar, $\frac{1}{4}$ gill of water, $1\frac{3}{4}$ gills of milk, 1 yolk of egg.

METHOD.—Sift the flour with the salt and baking-powder. Rub in the fat and add the sugar, then stir in a few drops of vanilla and sufficient milk to make a soft dough.

Turn the mixture on to a lightly floured board and roll it out to a thick round the size of your sandwich-tin.

Butter the tin and put the mixture in it, brush the top with milk and place it in a fairly hot oven to bake. It will take from twenty to thirty minutes to cook.

When cold, split it in halves and spread it with caramel filling. Sandwich the two pieces together and dust the top with icing sugar.

TO MAKE THE FILLING.—Put half the sugar into a small strong saucepan with the water. Dissolve it slowly, then bring it to the boil and boil until deep golden brown. Take it off the heat and leave to grow cold. Mix the flour with the remainder of the sugar and mix them to a smooth paste with some of the milk, add the remainder of the milk to the caramel and dissolve it slowly, but do not let it boil. Stir it on to the flour, return them to the pan and bring the caramel mixture to the boil, keeping it well stirred. Cook it gently for a few minutes, take it off the heat, let it cool slightly and beat in the egg-yolk. Cook it again for a minute or two but do not let it boil. Use it as required.

CARAMEL SHORTBREAD

INGREDIENTS.—$\frac{1}{2}$ lb. of butter, $\frac{1}{4}$ lb. of castor sugar, $\frac{3}{4}$ lb. of flour, $\frac{1}{2}$ teaspoonful of baking-powder, $\frac{1}{2}$ teaspoonful of vanilla.

METHOD.—Heat the butter very carefully until it becomes a *light* brown colour, and let it cool. When it is cool, knead in the flour, baking-powder, sugar, and vanilla. Knead till smooth and make into small, round balls. Place the balls on a greased baking-sheet and flatten them by pressing with the hand. Bake in a slow oven.

This quantity makes about twelve shortbreads.

CAULIFLOWER CAKE

INGREDIENTS.—3 oz. of margarine, 2 oz. of sugar, 4 oz. of self-raising flour, 1 large egg, grated rind of a lemon, $\frac{1}{4}$ gill of milk, 9d. of double cream, 1 oz. of castor sugar.

FOR THE ALMOND PASTE.—$\frac{3}{4}$ lb. of ground almonds, 1 egg, $\frac{3}{4}$ lb. of icing sugar, 1 dessertspoonful of lemon-juice.

METHOD.—Cream the margarine and sugar and beat in the egg and lemon-rind. Stir in the flour and moisten it with a little milk.

Pour the mixture into a greased pudding-basin and bake it for about thirty minutes.

To make the almond paste, rub the icing sugar through a hair sieve, add the almonds and mix them well together.

Beat the egg, then pour it and the lemon-juice over the almonds and sugar, stirring all the time.

Mix them first with a wooden spoon and then with the hands till the mixture is smooth. Knead well.

When the cake is quite cold, divide the almond paste into three pieces and roll them out flat and round. Press these against the side of the cake letting the edges overlap.

Whip the cream and stir in the sugar.

Fill in the top with a teaspoonful of cream.

TO LINE THE CAKE-TIN.—Cut a double band of paper long enough to go round the tin.

Make a crease half an inch wide along one edge.

Snip the folded part here and there as far as the crease.

Grease the paper and line the tin smoothly with the crease at the bottom.

Cut a double round of greased paper to fit the inside.

CHELSEA BUNS

THESE sugary-topped yeast buns, with a few currants here and there, are specially spiced, but they may be made plain if preferred.

INGREDIENTS.—1 lb. of flour, pinch of salt, 1 egg, 2 level teaspoonfuls of ground cinnamon, ½ oz. of yeast, 3 oz. of margarine, ½ oz. of butter, 3 oz. of castor sugar, about 1½ gills of milk, ¼ lb. of currants.

FOR THE GLAZE.—1 tablespoonful of milk, 1 dessertspoonful of castor sugar.

METHOD.—Sift the flour, salt, and cinnamon into a basin. Mix in the sugar, keeping back one teaspoonful.

Make a well in the centre, heaping the ingredients to the sides of the basin.

Put the yeast into a small basin with the remaining teaspoonful of sugar and mix them together until they liquefy.

Turn the margarine into a saucepan and warm it sufficiently to melt it. Add the milk, and when they are *lukewarm*, stir them into the yeast. Add this mixture to the beaten egg; then strain them all into the centre of the flour.

Mix them to a soft dough, beating it well until it is smooth. A little more warm milk may be added if required.

Throw a cloth over the basin. Stand the dough in a warm place to rise for about one hour and a half, or until it has risen to double its bulk.

When the dough is ready, turn it on to a floured board, knead it lightly, and divide it into two portions. Roll each out to an oblong shape.

Melt the half ounce of butter and brush the rolled-out dough with it. Sprinkle the dough with currants— previously washed, picked over and dried—and dredge it with castor sugar.

Roll up the dough as you would a roly-poly pudding, cut each roll into about eight slices, and place them on a lightly greased and floured tin.

Stand them in a warm place again for about twenty to thirty minutes to rise before putting them into a hot oven to bake.

When the buns are cooked, brush them with sugar and milk, dredge them with sugar, and return them to the oven for a minute or two to dry the glaze; then put them on a sieve to cool.

To make the glaze, mix the milk and sugar together until they are dissolved.

CHERRY CAKE

INGREDIENTS.—½ lb. of flour, ¼ lb. of castor sugar, ¼ lb. of margarine or butter, ¼ lb. of glacé cherries, 1 teaspoonful of baking-powder, 1 oz. of candied peel (citron), 2 eggs, milk.

METHOD.—Grease a medium-sized round cake-tin and line it with greased paper. Cream the sugar and fat together. Sieve the flour and baking-powder together.

Cut the cherries each into four pieces. Cut up the peel. Mix the cherries and peel with the flour. Beat the eggs separately into the creamed sugar and fat; beat well for a few minutes.

Stir in lightly and gradually the flour and fruit, etc., adding a little milk if required. Mix all well together.

Put into prepared cake-tin and bake for about one hour in a moderately hot oven.

Cool on a sieve.

CHERRY DROPS

INGREDIENTS.—1 egg, 2 oz. of margarine, 2 oz. of flour, 1½ oz. of castor sugar, ½ teaspoonful of baking-powder, 1 dessertspoonful of lemon-juice, 1 oz. of glacé cherries.

METHOD.—Cream the margarine, add the sugar and beat till soft and white.

Beat in the egg and lemon-juice, add the flour and last of all stir in the baking-powder.

Half-fill four to six paper baking-cases and bake in a quick oven for about ten minutes.

NOTE.—The paper baking-cases are a great labour saver, as they need no greasing or washing.

CHERRY SANDWICH

INGREDIENTS.—2 oz. of sugar, 2 oz. of butter, 4 oz. of flour, ½ teaspoonful of baking-powder, ½ gill of cherry-juice, 1 egg, 1 small tin of cherries,

2 oz. of loaf sugar, apricot jam, 5d. of double cream.

METHOD.—Grease a small sandwich-tin. Cream the butter and sugar till soft and white.

Add the yolk of the egg and beat well. Sift the flour and baking-powder. Beat the white of egg stiffly.

Add the cherry-juice and flour lightly to the cake-mixture, and stir in the egg-white as lightly and carefully as possible.

Pour into the tin and bake in a hot oven for about fifteen minutes.

While it is cooking, boil the cherry-juice from the tin with the loaf sugar till it is a thick syrup (about ten minutes). Put the cherries in a basin and pour the syrup over them.

When the cake is cold, split it open and spread the lower half with jam. Cut the top half in two and stand nearly upright in the middle of the cake, keeping the pieces in place by pressing a few cherries against them.

Whip the cream with a fork and add a little castor sugar to sweeten.

Spread a little cream in the lower half of the cake and fill up with cherries.

Put a line of cherries between the two upright pieces of cake.

Put the rest of the cream into an icing pump in which a rose tube has been screwed, and decorate round the cherries with small roses. This quantity is enough for one small sandwich.

CHERRY SPONGE SAND-WICHES

INGREDIENTS.—1 egg, 3 oz. of castor sugar, ¼ lb. of flour, 1 oz. of margarine, 1 flat teaspoonful of baking-powder, 1 oz. of glacé cherries, milk or water, raspberry jam, icing sugar.

METHOD.—Cut the cherries into small pieces.

Whisk the egg and sugar together until they are thick and creamy and free from dark streaks.

Sieve the flour and baking-powder.

Warm the margarine just enough to melt it.

Gradually stir the flour and fruit into the egg and sugar, adding also the melted margarine and some milk or water as required. Mix lightly.

Turn the mixture on to a greased and lined baking-sheet (lined as for a swiss roll) and spread it over evenly.

Bake in a hot oven for a few minutes until the mixture feels spongy. Then turn it on to a sheet of paper sprinkled with icing sugar. Remove the greased paper from the sponge, and when cold spread it with jam and cut it into small sandwiches.

Stick a small piece of glacé cherry in the centre of each, extra to that given in the recipe.

CHERRY GATEAU

INGREDIENTS.—¾ lb. of flour, 2 teaspoonfuls of baking-powder, ¼ lb. of ground rice, 7 oz. of butter or margarine, 7 oz. of castor sugar, ½ lb. of glacé cherries, 1 oz. of citron peel, 3 eggs, milk.

FOR THE ICING.—½ a teacup of cold water, ½ lb. of lump sugar a small pinch of cream of tartar, 1 white of egg, a few cherries and angelica for decoration.

METHOD.—Grease a square cake-tin, and line with greased paper to stand above the side of the tin.

Cut up the cherries and peel.

Sieve the flour, ground rice, and baking-powder.

Beat the sugar and fat to a cream.

Add each egg separately, stir it in quickly, and beat the mixture for a few minutes before adding the next.

When all are added, stir in the flour, etc., and the prepared fruit, adding a little milk as required.

Mix all together lightly; do not make the mixture too moist or the fruit will sink to the bottom.

Put into the prepared tin and bake in a moderately hot oven for about one hour and a half.

When cooked, turn carefully on to a sieve and leave until cold.

If it has risen to a point, cut off a slice before icing it.

Make the icing as explained below.

Pour it on the top of the cake and let it run just to the edges—the sides are not to be iced.

Smooth the edge of the icing with a knife dipped in warm water—if necessary.

Halve some glacé cherries and decorate the cake by putting a line of cherries all round the edge.

Place one in the centre with some leaves of angelica round.

The Icing

Put the sugar and water into a saucepan and dissolve slowly.

Add a good pinch of cream of tartar, bring to the boil and keep boiling until a small quantity of the syrup, when dropped into cold water and left for about a second or so, can be lifted out and rolled into a soft ball between your finger and thumb.

(If you have a saccharometer, the syrup when ready should register 238° to 240°.)

Have ready the white of an egg, whisked slightly, stir the prepared syrup on to them and keep stirring quickly until the icing begins to thicken and set, then use at once.

CHESTNUT FINGERS

INGREDIENTS.—6 oz. of margarine, vanilla essence to taste, 4 oz. of sugar, 2 eggs, 6 oz. of flour, 8 oz. of peeled roast chestnuts.

METHOD.—Beat the margarine and sugar to a cream. Stir in one egg quickly and beat the mixture well. Add the vanilla, flour, and chopped chestnuts. Put the mixture aside until it is workable.

Roll it into small fingers and brush them with beaten egg. Sprinkle them with sugar, and brown them slightly in a fairly hot oven.

This quantity makes about thirty fingers.

CHESTNUT GATEAU

INGREDIENTS.—2 eggs, milk, 2 oz. of margarine, ½ lb. of flour, 1 teaspoonful of cream of tartar, ½ flat teaspoonful of carbonate of soda, 6 oz. of castor sugar, chocolate nonpareils.

FOR THE FILLING.—½ lb. of chestnuts 5 oz. of butter, ½ lb. of icing sugar, vanilla flavouring.

METHOD.—Whisk the eggs and sugar together until thick and creamy and free from dark streaks.

Sieve the flour with the carbonate of soda and cream of tartar and stir it into the eggs gradually with the margarine, melted but not hot. Mix all together lightly, adding a little milk as required. Turn into a prepared cake-tin and bake in a moderately hot oven.

When cold, split the cake into three portions, spread each layer with chestnut filling, put the pieces together again, then spread the outside with the same filling and coat it all over with chocolate nonpareils.

Put a dab of the chestnut filling in the centre.

The Chestnut Filling

To make the filling, put the chestnuts into boiling water and boil them for about ten or fifteen minutes. Shell and skin them, put them into fresh boiling water and boil till soft. Strain, then rub through a sieve.

Rub the icing sugar through a hair sieve and beat it to a cream with the butter. Stir in one quarter of a pound of the prepared chestnuts, add vanilla flavouring to taste and mix all together.

CHILDREN'S BIRTHDAY CAKE

INGREDIENTS.—1 lb. of flour, 2 oz. of angelica, 9 oz. of margarine, 4 eggs, ½ lb. of castor sugar, 2 teaspoonfuls of baking-powder, ½ lb. of glacé cherries, milk (½ gill), if required.

FOR THE ALMOND PASTE ICING.— 1¼ lb. of ground almonds, vanilla flavouring, 1¼ lb. of icing sugar, whites of 3 or 4 eggs.

For the Royal Icing

NOTE.—It is better to make your icing in two portions.

INGREDIENTS.—1½ lb. of sugar, whites of about 3 eggs, 1½ tablespoonfuls of lemon-juice, mauve or pink colouring, decoration, tiny candles.

Use about one pound of sugar with one tablespoonful of lemon-juice and the whites of about two eggs for the two layers. Then the remainder will do for the decoration and can be made the following day.

METHOD.—Grease a large round cake-tin and line with greased paper, reaching two inches above the tin.

Sieve the flour and baking-powder.

Cut the cherries and angelica into small pieces.

Beat the sugar and fat to a cream.

Stir in each egg separately, for five minutes. Then fold in the flour, ogether with the prepared fruit, and mix lightly.

Add a little milk, but remember not to make the cake too moist or he cherries will sink to the bottom.

Put the mixture into the tin, and bake in a moderately hot oven for about an hour and a half to two hours.

Lessen the heat after the first twenty minutes and cover with paper when sufficiently browned.

When cooked turn on to a sieve and leave until cold.

To make the almond paste, rub the icing sugar through a hair sieve, add the almonds and mix them well together.

Beat the egg and pour it and the lemon-juice over the almonds and sugar, stirring all the time.

Mix them first with a wooden spoon and then with the hands till the mixture is smooth. Knead well.

Turn the paste on to a board dusted with icing sugar, and roll it out quite thinly.

If the cake has risen in the centre cut off a slice and make it even.

Cover the sides with a thin layer of paste. Roll out the remainder of the paste to fit the top of the cake.

Fix it on, and make the top and sides perfectly even.

Turn a large dish upside down, and stand the cake on it.

Place in a *cool* oven to dry for about thirty minutes.

Leave for a day, then cover with Royal Icing.

To Make the Royal Icing

Sieve the sugar (use a finely meshed sieve).

Whisk the whites to a stiff froth, and add gradually to the sugar, together with the strained lemon-juice.

Mix together until quite smooth.

Beat well for about ten to fifteen minutes.

If the icing is of the correct thickness you can mark letters on it, and they will remain distinct.

So you must use your own judgment as to the exact amount of white of eggs, as they vary in size.

If you have the time to spare, you will get better results if the cake has two layers of icing, and then the decoration.

So it is better to make your icing in two batches as previously explained.

Icing the Cake

Keep the cake on the upturned dish and cover with a *thin* layer of icing. If you do not possess an icing knife, a flexible knife would serve the purpose.

Should the icing appear rough, smooth over with a knife dipped in hot water. But this must not be repeated too often, as it tends to crack the icing.

Leave to dry then well beat again the remainder of the icing and spread a *thick* layer all over the cake.

Smooth as previously directed and leave until the next day so that it will harden.

To Decorate the Cake

Lift the cake very carefully on to a cake-board, or a bread-board, covered with a paper doyley. Make the icing for the decoration and beat up well. Be sure you get the correct consistency.

You will require an icing bag and some icing tubes and a fixing-screw. The rose, shell, or ribbon patterns are the most useful tubes to buy.

Fix the screw on to one of the tubes, put it through the bottom of the bag, and tie with a piece of string to keep it in position.

Put some of the icing into the bag, twist the end of the latter down to the icing, then force some of it out. First test a little on a plate.

Decide on your scheme of decoration before you begin. Leave a space on the top of the cake for the greetings.

When you have finished with the first tube, fix on one with a different pattern and make another design. Colour the remainder of the icing a pretty pink or mauve.

Fix a fine piping tube on to another icing bag, and write the greetings in the centre of the cake.

Arrange the candles just inside the top edge of the cake, using a little icing to make them adhere.

Choose white and pink or mauve candles, according to the colour of the icing.

Leave until the decoration is quite hard.

CHILDREN'S CAKES

INGREDIENTS.—½ lb. of flour, 1 teaspoonful of baking-powder, 5 oz. of butter or margarine, 5 oz. of castor sugar, 1 egg, milk, glacé cherries.

METHOD.—Sieve the flour and baking-powder.

Beat the sugar and fat to a cream.

Add the egg, stir it in quickly and beat for about five minutes.

Gradually add the flour, together with a little milk as required.

Mix together lightly, put into small greased cake-tins and bake in a hot oven for about fifteen to twenty minutes.

Cut the cherries into halves, and place a piece on each cake lightly when they are just firm.

CHOCOLATE CAKE

INGREDIENTS.—4 oz. of butter, 4 oz. of castor sugar, 5 oz. of flour, 3 oz. of good cocoa, 2 eggs, vanilla essence, 1 teaspoonful of baking-powder, 1 oz. of almonds.

METHOD.—Grease and line a pound cake-tin or grease sixteen patty-pans.

Cream the butter and sugar till soft and white. Add the eggs and beat well. Mix in the cocoa and sifted flour and baking-powder, adding a little milk if necessary.

Bake in greased patty-pans for twenty minutes or in cake-tin for about forty-five minutes.

Ice with chocolate icing and decorate with blanched almonds.

THE CHOCOLATE ICING

INGREDIENTS.—8 oz. of icing sugar, 2½ oz. of chocolate (in cake), vanilla essence, 3 tablespoonfuls of tepid water.

METHOD.—The best way to soften the chocolate is to break the cake in two or three pieces and put it in a cup with the water. Stand it at the side of the fire or inside a double saucepan with boiling water underneath. A little warming in this way will soon make it soft ; it must not be made hot. Turn the pieces over when half dissolved.

If the icing sugar is hard, crush the lumps with a rolling-pin. Rub through a hair sieve and put in a saucepan with the vanilla essence and dissolved chocolate.

Mix to a smooth paste and stir ove a fairly high gas for twelve second till it dissolves and becomes mor liquid.

If it coats the back of a woode spoon it is ready, but if it seems to thick add a teaspoonful of wate Chocolate icing often needs a trifl more water than other kinds of icing

Place the cake on a small plat turned upside down in a large one Blanch the almonds with boiling wate and slip off the skins. Decorate a desired.

CHOCOLATE COCONUT CAKES

INGREDIENTS.—2 oz. of cocoa, ½ ll of flour, 1 teaspoonful of baking powder, 6 oz. of castor sugar, ¼ lb. c margarine, 2 oz. of desiccated coconu 1 egg, vanilla flavouring, milk.

METHOD.—Sieve the flour, cocoa and baking-powder.

Add the coconut and mix togethe

Beat the sugar and fat to a cream Add the egg, stir it in quickly an beat well for a few minutes. Sti in the dry ingredients with som milk as required, and mix all togethe

Add a few drops of vanilla.

Put into small greased cake-tins o baking-cups, and bake in a hot ove for fifteen to twenty minutes.

Sufficient to make about fiftee cakes.

CHOCOLATE CORNFLOUI BUNS

INGREDIENTS.—1½ oz. of cocoa ¼ lb. of flour, 1 teaspoonful of baking powder, 5 oz. of margarine, ½ lb. c castor sugar, ¼ lb. of cornflour, 2 eggs milk, vanilla essence.

METHOD.—Sieve the flour, cornflou cocoa, and baking-powder togethe

Separate the yolks from the white of eggs. Beat the sugar and fat to cream. Whisk the whites to a ver stiff froth. Beat up the yolks an stir quickly into the creamed fat an sugar, and beat well for a few minutes

Stir in the flour, etc., with a fev drops of vanilla, and milk if require Add the whites and mix in lightl Put into small greased cake-tins an bake in a hot oven for about fifteen to twenty minutes.

Cool on a sieve.

Sufficient to make fifteen buns.

CHOCOLATE FANCIES

INGREDIENTS.—2 eggs, 2 oz. of sugar, 3 oz. of flour, 1 oz. of butter (melted).

FOR THE ICING.—6 oz. of icing sugar, 3 oz. of butter, 6 oz. of cake chocolate, 2 tablespoonfuls of milk, 1 oz. of almonds (blanched), vanilla essence.

METHOD.—Grease twelve small round tins.

Whisk the eggs and sugar till white and thick. Stir in the flour and melted butter alternately and lightly.

Fill the tins half full and bake the cakes in a hot oven for fifteen minutes.

ICING THE CAKES.—Put two ounces of cake chocolate and the milk into a double saucepan. Turn the chocolate over when it begins to get soft. Beat the butter to a cream and stir in the sieved icing sugar, the softened chocolate, and a few drops of vanilla essence.

Mix all well together.

Split the cakes open and spread them with the icing. Put them together again and spread the outside also.

Soften the remainder of the chocolate by placing it in a saucer over hot water. When soft (but not liquid) rub it through a coarse sieve or strainer on to a plate. Dip the cakes in the chocolate vermicelli and stick an almond in top of each.

CHOCOLATE FANCY CAKES

INGREDIENTS.—¼ lb. of castor sugar, ¼ lb. of flour, ½ teaspoonful of baking-powder, 3 eggs, 1 oz. of shelled walnuts, milk (if required), chocolate icing (see below), shelled walnuts and crystallised violets (for decoration).

METHOD.—Grease a baking-sheet and line with greased paper to stand well above the sides.

Separate the yolks from the whites of two eggs. Chop up the walnuts.

Sieve the flour and baking-powder together and mix with the walnuts. Whisk the castor sugar, whole egg, and yolks of eggs together until thick and creamy and free from dark streaks of egg. Whisk the two whites to a very stiff froth. Stir the flour and whisked whites alternately into the castor sugar and egg mixture, and mix all together very lightly. Add a little milk if required. Put into a prepared tin and spread over evenly. Bake in a hot oven for about ten minutes or until it feels spongy, then leave on a sieve until cold. Cut the sponge into *small* fancy shapes—rounds, crescents, diamond shapes, etc.—put them on a cake-rack over a dish, and coat each with chocolate icing.

THE CHOCOLATE ICING

INGREDIENTS.—2 oz. of grated chocolate, 9 oz. of icing sugar, ½ gill of cold water, vanilla flavouring.

METHOD.—Put the chocolate into a saucepan with the water (half a gill) and dissolve, keeping it well stirred, then leave to cool. Add the sieved icing sugar and vanilla and mix together until smooth.

Stir over a very low burner until the base of the pan feels just warm.

The consistency should be so that it will coat the back of the spoon. If necessary, a little more water or sieved sugar may be added.

NOTE.—The icing must not get hot after the sugar is added or it will lose its gloss.

Decorate some of the cakes with walnuts and the remainder with crystallised violets.

Sufficient for about eight or more according to the size you cut the sponge.

CHOCOLATE GINGER CAKE

INGREDIENTS.—3 oz. of grated chocolate, 4 oz. of preserved ginger, 2 oz. of butter or margarine, 6 oz. of flour, 1 teaspoonful of baking-powder, 4 oz. of castor sugar, 2 eggs, 3 table-spoonfuls of milk, angelica, preserved ginger, chocolate hundreds and thousands.

FOR THE ICING.—¾ lb. of icing sugar, ginger syrup.

METHOD.—Dissolve the chocolate in a saucepan in about a tablespoonful of milk and let this cool. Beat the sugar and fat to a cream, then stir in the chocolate.

Cut the ginger into small pieces, and whisk up the eggs.

Sift the flour with the baking-powder and add it gradually to the creamed fat and sugar. Stir in the ginger and the eggs and milk as required.

Mix the ingredients lightly and turn the mixture into a greased and lined cake-tin. Bake the cake in a moderately hot oven. When it is cold, ice it with ginger icing, and decorate it with sliced ginger, leaves of angelica, and chocolate hundreds and thousands.

THE GINGER ICING

Rub the sugar through a hair sieve, and add sufficient ginger syrup to make a thick coating consistency. The syrup should be first warmed and, if it is not sufficient, it can be made up with warm water. About two or three tablespoonfuls of liquid will be required to mix the icing.

NOTE.—The icing may be tinted to a pale shade if liked.

CHOCOLATE GINGERBREAD

INGREDIENTS.—¾ lb. of golden syrup, 2 oz. of unsweetened chocolate, 9 oz. of flour, 1 level teaspoonful of carbonate of soda, 2 level teaspoonfuls of powdered cinnamon, 2 level teaspoonfuls of ground ginger, 1 egg, ¼ gill of milk, 1 oz. of almonds, ¼ lb. of margarine.

METHOD.—Grate the chocolate finely and mix it with the milk, then stir it over a low burner until dissolved.

Put the golden syrup and margarine into a saucepan, and warm them sufficiently to melt, then add them to the beaten egg and whisk well.

Sift the flour into a basin with the spices, stir in the egg and syrup, also the dissolved chocolate. Mix all together and beat the mixture. Add the soda mixed in a spoonful of milk.

Turn the gingerbread mixture into two greased tins, scatter the almonds (blanched and split in halves) on the top and put the cake into a moderately hot oven to bake.

CHOCOLATE LAYER CAKE

INGREDIENTS.—¾ lb. of plain flour, ½ lb. of granulated sugar, 3 oz. of butter, 2 oz. of margarine, 3 eggs, ½ cup of milk, 2 teaspoonfuls of baking-powder, vanilla essence, chocolate icing, 2 oz. of ground almonds, 2 oz. of icing sugar.

METHOD.—Grease and line a wide cake-tin.

Beat the butter and margarine to a cream.

Stir in the sugar and the yolks of the eggs, and beat till the mixture is thick and white.

Add the milk and flour alternately a little at a time.

Stir in the stiffly beaten egg-whites very lightly with a few drops of vanilla essence.

Add the baking-powder and pour the mixture quickly into the tin.

Bake it at once in a moderately hot oven for from fifty minutes to one hour.

The cake is done when the centre feels firm.

Leave it in the tin for five minutes, then remove the paper and place the cake on a sieve to cool.

When cold split it into three and spread it with a little chocolate icing (see below).

Fit the pieces together, stir the icing again over the gas for a few seconds until it is liquid, then pour it quickly over the cake. Mix the ground almonds and icing sugar with a little of the yolk of egg.

Roll it out and cut into fancy shapes.

THE CHOCOLATE ICING

INGREDIENTS.—¾ lb. of icing sugar, 4 oz. of chocolate (in cake), 4 tablespoonfuls of tepid water, vanilla essence.

METHOD.—Break up the chocolate and put it in a double saucepan with warm (not boiling) water in the lower pan.

Rub the icing sugar through a hair sieve.

Add the water to the softened chocolate, stir in the sugar and flavour it with vanilla.

Place the pan on the gas and stir till the chocolate is liquid (about twelve seconds). If it seems too thick add a trifle more water, as chocolate icing often needs more water than other kinds of icing. It is ready when it is liquid enough to coat the back of the spoon.

Place the cake on a small plate turned upside down on a large one and pour the icing quickly over.

Care should be taken not to make the icing hot as this will cause it to look dull instead of shiny.

Walnut Cakes

Dot Cakes

Iced Pyramids

PLATE 41

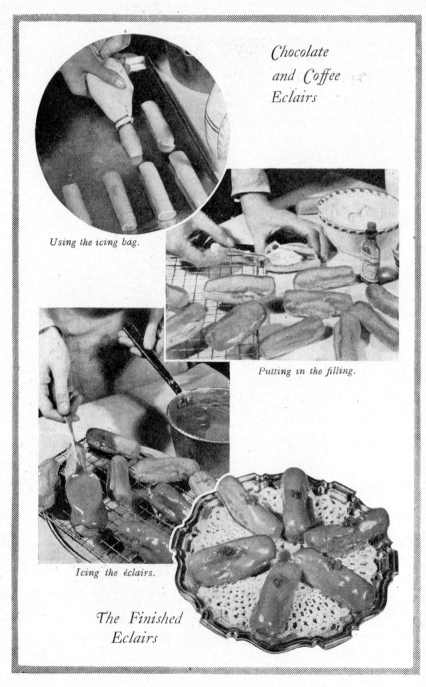

Chocolate and Coffee Eclairs

Using the icing bag.

Putting in the filling.

Icing the éclairs.

The Finished Eclairs

PLATE 42

CHOCOLATE LOG CAKE

INGREDIENTS.—2 eggs, 2 oz. of margarine or butter, ¼ lb. of castor sugar, 1 flat teaspoonful of baking-powder, ¼ lb. of flour, milk, jam.

FOR THE CHOCOLATE BUTTER ICING. —7 oz. of icing sugar, 3 oz. of butter, 1½ oz. of grated chocolate or cocoa, about 1½ tablespoonfuls of milk, vanilla.

METHOD.—Mix the flour and baking-powder together. Grease a baking-sheet and line with greased paper to stand above the sides. Beat the sugar and fat to a cream. Add each egg separately, stir it in quickly, and beat a few minutes before adding the second.

When both are well beaten in, stir in the flour and baking-powder and mix all together lightly, adding just a little milk if required. Put into the prepared tin and spread over evenly.

Bake in a *hot* oven for about seven to ten minutes, until it feels spongy.

Turn it on to a sheet of paper and spread over some jam (previously warmed).

Cut off the hard edge from each side of the sponge, then roll it up and leave on a sieve until cold. Cut a thin slice from each end to trim it.

THE CHOCOLATE BUTTER ICING

Roll the lumps out of the sugar, then rub it through a fine sieve.

Put the chocolate into a saucepan and mix with the milk, then stir until dissolved—a *little* more milk may be used if required.

Add the butter to the sieved icing sugar and beat both to a cream.

Add the prepared chocolate (when it has cooled slightly) and a few drops of vanilla, and mix all together, then leave, if necessary, until it becomes a little stiffer before using it.

Fix a rose or shell pattern tube in the bottom of an icing bag, put the icing into it and decorate the log in straight lines from end to end until completely covered.

CHOCOLATE LUNCH CAKES

INGREDIENTS.—½ lb. of flour, 1 good teaspoonful of baking-powder, 6 oz. of sugar, milk to mix, 1½ oz. of cocoa, 4 oz. of margarine, 1 egg, a few drops of vanilla flavouring.

METHOD.—Mix the flour and cocoa together. Rub in the margarine until like fine breadcrumbs. Add the sugar and baking-powder and mix.

Beat up the egg and add to the dry ingredients, with just a little milk and a few drops of vanilla. Mix all to rather a stiff consistency.

Put into small greased cake-tins and bake in a hot oven for about fifteen to twenty minutes.

Dust well with castor sugar.

Sufficient to make about twelve or fourteen cakes.

CHOCOLATE MACAROONS

INGREDIENTS.—6 oz. of ground almonds, 1 tablespoonful of chocolate powder, 9 oz. of castor sugar, whites of 1 or 2 eggs, vanilla flavouring, a few pistachio nuts.

METHOD.—Mix the ground almonds, chocolate powder, and castor sugar together. Whisk the whites to a stiff froth, and add sufficient to mix all to a stiff paste, together with a few drops of vanilla flavouring. Spread the prepared mixture on wafer paper, making small macaroons.

Brush them over with water, and place in a moderately hot oven. Bake for about twenty minutes. Blanch, skin, and split a few pistachio nuts, and place a piece on each macaroon directly they are cooked.

CHOCOLATE MOUNDS

INGREDIENTS.—4 oz. of castor sugar, 1½ oz. of cocoa, 2 oz. of Barcelona nuts, whites of about 1 or 1½ eggs.

METHOD.—Put the nuts through the mincer. Add the cocoa and sugar and mix all together.

Whisk the whites to a very stiff froth, and add sufficient to mix all to a stiff paste. Divide into portions and place on a buttered tin in small mounds, with a whole nut on the top of each (extra to that given in the recipe). Bake in a moderate oven for about ten to fifteen minutes. Dredge with castor sugar.

Sufficient to make eight cakes.

CHOCOLATE MUSHROOMS

INGREDIENTS.—½ lb. of flour, ¼ flat teaspoonful of carbonate of soda, ¼ lb. of margarine, 1 egg, 1 teaspoonful

P

of cream of tartar, 5 oz. of castor sugar, milk.

FOR THE CHOCOLATE BUTTER ICING.—9 oz. of icing sugar, ¼ lb. of butter, vanilla flavouring, 2 oz. of grated chocolate or cocoa, about 2 tablespoonfuls of milk.

FOR THE ALMOND PASTE.—¾ lb. of ground almonds, ¾ lb. of icing sugar, vanilla flavouring, about 2 whites of eggs (add more if required).

METHOD.—Sieve the flour, soda, and cream of tartar. Rub in the margarine finely. Add the sugar and mix the other ingredients. Beat up the egg and add with sufficient milk to mix all together. When well mixed, beat for a few minutes. Put into small greased cake-tins, putting only a small quantity into each one. Bake in a hot oven for about twelve to fifteen minutes, then put on to a sieve and leave until cold.

TO MAKE THE ALMOND PASTE.—Roll the lumps out of the sugar, then rub it through a fine sieve. Add the almonds and mix together. Whisk the whites slightly, and add sufficient, with a few drops of vanilla, to mix all to a stiff paste. Then work it until smooth. Cut off a piece and save for the stalks. Roll out the remainder thinly and cut into small rounds, and mould round the bottom of each, leaving the top of the cakes uncovered.

Fix a rose tube on to an icing bag, put some of the icing into it, and force on to the cakes, from the edge of the almond paste to the centre in straight lines, until the tops are completely covered.

Mould the remainder of the almond paste into stalks, and stick one in the centre of each mushroom.

NOTE.—If the cakes have risen much in the centre a small piece can be cut off before the butter icing is put on.

TO MAKE THE CHOCOLATE BUTTER ICING.—Put the chocolate into a saucepan and mix with the milk and stir until dissolved—a *little* more milk may be used if required—then cool slightly.

Sieve the icing sugar, add the butter and beat both to a cream.

Stir in the prepared chocolate and a few drops of vanilla and mix all together, then, if necessary, leave until it becomes a little stiffer before using.

Sufficient for about eighteen mushrooms.

CHOCOLATE PEPPERMINT CAKE

INGREDIENTS.—¼ lb. of castor sugar, 1½ oz. of butter or margarine, 1 whole egg and 1 yolk, 4½ oz. of flour, 1½ oz. of grated chocolate, 1¼ level teaspoonfuls of baking-powder, milk.

FOR THE PEPPERMINT ICING.—9 oz. of icing sugar, 3 dessertspoonfuls of warm water, ¼ teaspoonful of essence of peppermint, or to taste, peppermint balls.

METHOD.—Cream the butter, add the sugar and beat them together until they are soft. Then gradually stir in the beaten egg and yolk. Beat them well. Add the chocolate, dissolved in a little milk, and stir it into the flour, which should be sifted with the baking-powder. Mix all together lightly and add some milk as required. Turn the mixture into a buttered sandwich-tin and bake in a fairly hot oven until it is well risen and spongy. Turn it out and leave the cake to cool.

TO MAKE THE ICING.—Rub the sugar through a fine sieve and mix it to a smooth paste with the warm water, adding peppermint essence to taste.

Split the cake in half and spread each piece with some of the icing, then sandwich the two pieces together.

Add a few more drops of water to the remainder of the icing and coat the top of the cake with this. When this is nearly set, decorate the top of the cake with peppermint balls.

CHOCOLATE PETITS FOURS

INGREDIENTS.—1 oz. of cocoa, 3 oz. of ground almonds, 4 oz. of icing sugar, vanilla flavouring, about ¾ to 1 white of egg, a few glacé cherries, 1 oz. of shelled walnuts.

METHOD.—Chop the walnuts very finely. Roll the lumps out of the sugar, and rub it through a fine sieve. Add the cocoa, walnuts, and ground almonds and mix together.

Whisk the white of egg slightly and add to the dry ingredients as 'required, and mix all to a stiff paste, together with a few drops of vanilla.

When well mixed, work it until smooth, then divide into about sixteen portions. Roll each piece in the palm of your hand and make into a smooth round shape, then press your little finger in the centre, not through to the bottom, and make a small hole.

Place on a plate and brush the sides over with yolk of egg to glacé them, then stick half a cherry in the centre.

Put on top of the browning-shelf in a cool oven to dry for about fifteen minutes.

CHOCOLATE POTATO CAKE

INGREDIENTS.—6 oz. of flour, 2 eggs, $\frac{1}{4}$ nutmeg, $\frac{1}{2}$ lb. of castor sugar, $\frac{3}{4}$ level teaspoonful of ground cinnamon, $2\frac{1}{2}$ oz. of margarine or butter, a pinch of salt, 3 level teaspoonfuls of baking-powder, 5 oz. of hot mashed potatoes, about $\frac{1}{4}$ gill of hot milk, lemon cheese, $1\frac{1}{2}$ oz. of chocolate, chopped walnuts, soft icing (see p. 485).

METHOD.—Beat the butter and sugar to a cream. Add a little of the egg, well beaten. Stir in the potatoes.

Sift the flour, baking-powder, salt, cinnamon, and grated nutmeg together. Add them to the butter alternately with the hot milk in which the chocolate has been dissolved, and the remainder of the eggs.

Bake the mixture in two flat, round, buttered sandwich-tins for from twenty to thirty minutes.

When cold, spread each round with lemon cheese and chopped walnuts. Put the two halves together.

Ice the top of the cake with icing flavoured with vanilla.

Decorate the cake with cherries and silver balls.

CHOCOLATE RIBBON SAND-WICH

INGREDIENTS.—3 oz. of flour, $\frac{3}{4}$ level teaspoonfuls of baking-powder, 2 oz. of margarine, 2 oz. of castor sugar, 1 whole egg and one extra yolk, vanilla flavouring, milk, lemon-curd or apricot jam.

FOR THE CHOCOLATE ICING.—3 oz. of icing sugar, 1 oz. of chocolate, $1\frac{1}{2}$ oz. of butter, vanilla flavouring, milk.

METHOD.—Beat the sugar and fat to a cream, stir in the egg yolk and beat well, then add the whole egg and stir it in quickly.

Sift the flour with the baking-powder and mix them in lightly, adding a few drops of vanilla and about a spoonful of milk as required.

Turn the mixture into a small greased sandwich-tin and bake it in a hot oven until spongy. When cold split it in halves and spread it with lemon-curd or jam. Put the two halves together again and decorate the sandwich with chocolate icing forced through a shell-patterned tube in straight lines across both ways.

TO MAKE THE ICING.—Grate the chocolate finely and dissolve it in a little milk.

Sift the icing sugar.

Beat the butter to a cream with half the sugar, add the remainder, also the dissolved chocolate and a few drops of vanilla. Beat them all together until creamy.

CHOCOLATE ROCK CAKES

INGREDIENTS.—9 oz. of flour, 1 oz. of cocoa, 1 oz. of candied peel, $\frac{1}{4}$ lb. of sultanas, 5 oz. of sugar, 5 oz. of margarine, 1 teaspoonful of baking-powder, 1 egg, milk, a pinch of mixed spice.

METHOD.—Wash, pick over and dry the sultanas. Cut up the peel.

Mix the flour and cocoa together. Rub in the margarine finely. Add the spice, baking-powder, and sugar and mix in well. Add the peel and prepared fruit. Beat up the egg and add, with just a small quantity of milk if required, and mix to a *stiff* paste.

Put the mixture on to a greased baking-sheet in small rough heaps. Bake in a hot oven for about fifteen to twenty minutes. Cool on a sieve.

Sufficient to make from twelve to eighteen cakes.

CHOCOLATE ROLL

INGREDIENTS.—3 oz. of flour, 3 oz. of chocolate powder, $\frac{1}{2}$ gill of milk, 2 eggs, 3 oz. of castor sugar, $\frac{1}{2}$ teaspoonful baking-powder, vanilla flavouring, 2 oz. of margarine.

FOR THE FILLING.—4 oz. of icing sugar, 2 oz. of butter, vanilla.

METHOD.—Grease a baking-sheet and line with greased paper. Dissolve the chocolate in the milk, and mix to a smooth paste. Sieve the flour and baking-powder. Beat the sugar and margarine to a cream. Add one egg, stir it in briskly and beat well for about five minutes. Then add the other and beat again as before. Mix in the chocolate and milk, and flavour with vanilla. Last of all, fold in the flour and baking-powder, mix lightly and spread evenly over the prepared baking-sheet. Bake in a hot oven for about eight or ten minutes until it feels spongy. Turn over the chocolate sponge on to a tea-cloth and leave to cool. When cool, damp the paper to remove it, and cut off the outside rim all round the sponge. Spread the filling over, but not quite to the outside edges. Roll up evenly and stand on a sieve.

To PREPARE THE FILLING.—Sieve the icing sugar. Add the butter, and mix together to a cream, flavour with vanilla.

CHOCOLATE SLICES

INGREDIENTS.—¼ lb. of flour, 3 dessertspoonfuls of chocolate powder, ¼ lb. of castor sugar, 3 oz. of margarine or butter, 1 egg, ½ teaspoonful of baking-powder, vanilla, milk.

FOR THE ICING.—10 oz. of icing sugar, 2 tablespoonfuls of chocolate powder, vanilla, ½ gill of water, few pistachio nuts for decoration.

METHOD.—Grease a baking-sheet and line with greased paper, so that the latter stands just above the sides.

Sieve the flour, baking-powder, and chocolate powder. Beat the sugar and fat to a cream. Stir in the egg quickly and beat the mixture for about five minutes.

Add the flour, etc., also a few drops of vanilla, and one or two tablespoonfuls of milk.

Mix all together lightly, put into the prepared tin, and spread over evenly. Bake in a hot oven about eight to ten minutes. Turn it carefully out of the tin, remove the paper and leave until cold.

To MAKE THE ICING.—Rub the icing sugar through a sieve.

Put the chocolate powder into a small pan, and mix to a smooth paste with the water.

Cook slowly for a few minutes, keeping it stirred.

Leave until quite cool, then add the icing sugar and a few drops of vanilla. Mix all to a smooth paste and beat for a few minutes.

Stir over a very low burner until the base of the saucepan feels just warm. If necessary a little more cold water may be added, but the icing should be sufficiently thick to coat the back of the spoon.

Stand the chocolate sponge on a rack over a dish and pour over the icing, coating it evenly.

Have ready some finely chopped pistachio nuts and sprinkle on the top of the icing, leave until just set, then stand the cake on a flat surface, and cut it into oblong-shaped slices with a very sharp knife.

CHOCOLATE SODA CAKE

INGREDIENTS.—6 oz. of flour, 1 oz. of cocoa, ½ flat teaspoonful of carbonate of soda, 3 oz. of margarine, 5 oz. of castor sugar, 1 egg, milk, ½ teaspoonful of ground cinnamon.

METHOD.—Sieve the flour with the carbonate of soda, cinnamon, and cocoa.

Rub in the margarine. Add the sugar and mix together.

Whisk up the egg and add it to the dry ingredients with some milk as required.

Beat the mixture well for a few minutes, then turn into a greased cake-tin and put into a moderately hot oven to bake.

CHOCOLATE SPONGE

INGREDIENTS.—3 large eggs, ¾ cup of granulated sugar, 1¼ cups of self-raising flour, 1 dessertspoonful of cocoa, 1 teaspoonful of cinnamon, 1 teaspoonful of baking-powder, ½ cup of hot water.

METHOD.—Sift the flour, cocoa, cinnamon, and baking-powder through a sieve.

Grease two sandwich-tins.

Whisk the eggs and sugar together until they are thick, creamy and full of bubbles.

Add the flour and cocoa alternately

with the water, stirring them in as lightly as possible.

Pour the mixture into the tins and bake it for about fifteen minutes in a moderately hot oven. It is done when the centres feel spongy.

Remove the sponges from the tins and place them on a sieve to cool. When cold fill them with chocolate butter icing.

The Chocolate Butter Icing.

Ingredients.—6 oz. of icing sugar, 3 oz. of butter, 2 oz. of chocolate (in cake), 2 tablespoonfuls of milk.

Method.—Put the chocolate and milk in a saucer and stand it in a saucepan of hot water till the chocolate is soft.

Rub the icing sugar through a hair sieve.

Cream the butter till it is very soft, then stir in the sugar and chocolate and mix them till smooth.

CHOCOLATE SQUARES

Ingredients.—3 oz. of butter or margarine, 3 oz. of castor sugar, $\frac{1}{2}$ teaspoonful of baking-powder, $\frac{1}{2}$ oz. of cocoa, 3 oz. of flour, 2 eggs, milk, chocolate icing (see p. 485), 1 oz. of almonds (for decoration).

Method.—Mix the flour and baking-powder together.

Beat the butter and sugar to a cream.

Stir in the cocoa and beat together. Add each egg separately, stir it in quickly and beat well before adding the next.

When both are added, stir in the flour and baking-powder and mix together lightly.

Add about a tablespoonful of milk, if required. Have ready a small baking-sheet, lined with greased paper to stand just above the sides. Put the mixture on to it and spread over evenly.

Bake in a hot oven for from eight to ten minutes until it feels spongy.

When cooked, turn out and leave until cold.

To Ice the Cake.—Stand it on a cake-rack over a dish, with the flat side uppermost. Pour chocolate icing on it, and coat the top evenly. Sprinkle chopped almonds all over the icing. When the icing is set, cut into squares with a sharp knife.

Note.—Prepare the almonds before icing the cake ; just blanch, skin and chop them.

CHOCOLATE STRIPS

Ingredients.—1 oz. of chocolate, 2 oz. of flour, 1 oz. of shelled walnuts, 2 oz. of sultanas, 3 oz. of castor sugar, 1 egg, 1 oz. of margarine, milk, castor sugar for dredging.

Method.—Grate the chocolate finely and dissolve it in a spoonful or two of milk.

Wash, pick over and dry the sultanas, and chop the walnuts.

Whisk the castor sugar and egg together until thick and creamy and free from dark streaks.

Add the dissolved chocolate, then sift the flour and stir it in lightly with the margarine (warmed enough to melt it). Add also the prepared fruit and nuts.

Turn the mixture into a greased, shallow tin, dredge the top with castor sugar, and bake the cake in a fairly quick oven until spongy, then cut it into strips.

CHOCOLATE AND SULTANA CAKES

Ingredients.—10 oz. of flour, 2 oz. of ground rice, $1\frac{1}{2}$ teaspoonfuls of baking-powder, 3 tablespoonfuls of chocolate powder, 6 oz. of sultanas, 2 eggs, 6 oz. of margarine or butter, 6 oz. of castor sugar, milk.

Method.—Wash, pick over and dry the sultanas.

Sieve together the flour, ground rice, baking-powder, and chocolate powder.

Beat the sugar and fat to a cream.

Add each egg separately, stir it in quickly, and beat for a few minutes before adding the next.

When both are added stir in the flour, etc., and sultanas with a little milk as required.

Mix all together lightly.

Put into small greased cake-tins and bake in a hot oven for about twenty minutes.

CHOCOLATE VERMICELLI GATEAU

Ingredients.—4 oz. of margarine, 5 oz. of castor sugar, 5 oz. of flour,

1½ oz. of cocoa, ½ teaspoonful of baking-powder, 3 eggs.

FOR THE BUTTER ICING.— 8 oz. of icing sugar, 4 oz. of butter, vanilla flavouring.

FOR THE CHOCOLATE ICING.—¼ lb. of icing sugar, ¼ gill of water, 1 oz. of chocolate (grated) or cocoa, vanilla.

METHOD.—Sieve flour, cocoa, and baking-powder together.

Cream the fat and sugar.

Add each egg separately, stir it in quickly, and beat well before adding the next.

When all are added stir in the flour, cocoa, and baking-powder, and mix all together lightly.

Put into a greased cake-tin, and bake in a moderately hot oven for about thirty minutes. Put on to a sieve until cold.

TO MAKE THE BUTTER ICING.— Roll the lumps out of the sugar, then rub it through a fine sieve. Add the butter and beat both to a cream. Add vanilla to taste.

Split the cake into halves, spread some of the butter icing over it, then put together again.

TO MAKE THE CHOCOLATE ICING.— Put the chocolate into a saucepan with the water and dissolve, keeping it stirred, then leave to cool.

Add the sieved icing sugar and vanilla, and mix together until smooth.

Stir over a very low burner until the base of the pan feels warm.

TO ICE THE CAKE.—If the cake has risen in the centre, it is better to cut off a slice, and turn it upside down before icing it.

Pour the icing on the *top* and coat evenly.

Leave until set.

Spread the remainder of the butter icing round the side and sprinkle with chocolate vermicelli.

TO MAKE THE VERMICELLI.—Melt a sixpenny packet of Mexican chocolate in a double boiler, and when nearly set again rub it through a wire sieve. The chocolate will melt more readily if it is first broken up.

The consistency should be so that it will coat the back of the spoon. If necessary, a little more water or sieved sugar may be added.

NOTE.—The icing must not get hot after the sugar is added, or it will lose its gloss.

A CHRISTENING CAKE

INGREDIENTS.—6 oz. of butter or margarine, 6 oz. of soft brown sugar, ½ lb. of flour, ¼ flat teaspoonful of carbonate of soda, ½ lb. of peel, ½ lb. of small seedless raisins, ½ lb. of currants, 2 oz. of glacé cherries, nutmeg, 3 eggs, 1 oz. of ground almonds, orange essence, milk.

FOR THE ALMOND PASTE ICING.— 1 lb. of icing sugar, 10 oz. of ground almonds, 2 or 3 egg-whites, vanilla or orange essence.

FOR THE ROYAL ICING.—1¼ lb. of icing sugar, 1½ dessertspoonfuls of lemon-juice, 2 or 3 egg-whites, silver balls, silver cake band, and font or other suitable decoration.

METHOD.—Cut up the peel and cherries. Wash, pick over and dry the currants and raisins.

Sieve the flour with the soda, and add to it about half a small nutmeg (grated). Cream the fat and sugar.

Add each egg separately and stir them in quickly.

Beat the mixture well before adding each egg. When all three are well beaten in, gradually stir in the flour, ground almonds, and prepared fruit, with just a little milk if required, but be very careful not to make the mixture too moist, or the fruit will sink in the tin. Add orange essence to flavour.

If preferred, some sherry, rum, or brandy may be added.

When well mixed turn the cake into a greased and papered tin and put it into a moderate oven to bake. It will probably take from two and a half to three hours steady baking.

When cooked and cold, wrap the cake in greaseproof paper and keep it in an airtight tin until required.

NOTE.—The cake-tin should be lined with two or three thicknesses of greased paper.

ALMOND PASTE

To make the almond paste, roll the lumps out of the sugar and rub it through a fine sieve. Add the ground almonds, and then mix to a stiff paste with slightly beaten egg-whites. Add vanilla or orange flavouring to taste.

Work the paste until it is smooth, then roll it out and use as required.

To prepare the cake and ice it with almond paste, scrape it if necessary and knock off any loose crumbs. Brush it over with melted red currant jelly.

Put a strip of paste round the sides of the cake, then stand it on an upturned dish and cover the top with a round of paste, pressing it on firmly and making it quite level. If the cake has risen unevenly you can either cut off a slice before you begin, or else make it level with the almond paste.

Leave the cake for at least one day to allow the paste to dry before covering it with royal icing.

The Royal Icing

To make the royal icing, prepare the sugar as before. Add the lemon-juice, and enough *stiffly whisked* egg-white to make a fairly stiff paste, then beat it well until smooth. To test the consistency you should be able to mark letters on it and they will remain distinct.

To Ice and Decorate the Cake

Put some icing on top of the cake and spread it over evenly, using a knife occasionally dipped in hot water, to smooth it. Cover the sides in the same way, paying special attention to make the top edge neat.

Leave to dry, and meanwhile cover the remainder of the icing with a damp cloth to prevent it from getting too stiff.

Plan out a simple design before beginning to decorate.

Beat up the icing and put into an icing bag, pipe the top with straight lines across each way, and put a ring of rose patterns topped with silver balls round the edge.

Place a small font or other seasonable decoration in the centre, using a dab of icing to make it adhere.

When the icing is set put a silver cake band round the sides to give a finish to the cake.

Note.—Stand the cake on a cakeboard before beginning to pipe it. A revolving cake-stand is useful when doing this.

CHRISTMAS CAKE

Ingredients.—11 oz. of flour, $\frac{1}{2}$ flat teaspoonful of carbonate of soda,

$\frac{1}{4}$ flat teaspoonful each of ground mace, ginger, cloves, and cinnamon, grated rind and juice of 1 small orange 2 oz. of ground almonds, 1 oz. of shelled walnuts, 3 oz. of candied peel, 3 oz. of glacé cherries, 1 lb. of sultanas, 10 oz. of currants, 7 oz. of butter or margarine, 6 oz. of Barbados sugar, $\frac{1}{4}$ lb. of golden syrup, 4 eggs.

Method.—Wash, pick over and dry the currants and sultanas. Then cut up the cherries and peel, and chop the walnuts.

Sieve the flour with the soda and spices, and mix in the ground almonds. Whisk the eggs, then warm the golden syrup and mix it with the eggs.

Cream the fat and sugar, add the finely grated orange-rind, and gradually stir in the flour and the prepared fruit and nuts, alternately with the eggs and syrup. Lastly, add the orange-juice.

Mix and beat the ingredients well. Turn the mixture into a greased cake-tin lined with two or three thicknesses of greased paper, and put it in a moderate oven to bake. It will take from two hours and a half to three hours.

Turn the cake out carefully, and, when thoroughly cold wrap it in greaseproof paper, and store it in an airtight tin until it is going to be iced.

The Almond Paste

Ingredients.—1 lb. of ground almonds, $1\frac{1}{2}$ lb. of icing sugar, 1 egg-yolk and 4 or 5 egg-whites, $\frac{1}{4}$ teaspoonful of almond or ratafia flavouring essence, $\frac{1}{2}$ teaspoonful of vanilla flavouring essence, $\frac{1}{4}$ teaspoonful of pineapple flavouring essence, $\frac{1}{4}$ teaspoonful of orange flavouring essence, melted jelly or jam.

Method.—Rub the icing sugar through a sieve and mix it with the ground almonds. Beat up the yolk of egg and add it to the flavourings. Mix all the ingredients together with sufficient whites (slightly beaten) to make a stiff paste. If all these essences are not to hand, vanilla may be used alone.

To cover the cake, work the icing into a smooth lump and divide it into two portions. Roll out one to a long strip the same depth as the cake and long enough to go all round it.

Brush the sides of the cake with melted jelly or jam, and mould the paste on to it, making it stick securely.

Stand the cake on an upturned dish and cover the top in the same way, rolling the paste to a thick round. If the cake has risen in the centre, it must either be cut level or else an edge of paste must be put on to level it *before* it is covered. (If it is necessary to scrape the cake, remember to brush off the loose crumbs.)

Leave the cake until the next day, so that the paste may dry, then ice it with Royal Icing.

THE ROYAL ICING

INGREDIENTS.—2 lb. of icing sugar, 4 or 5 egg-whites, 1½ tablespoonfuls of lemon-juice.

METHOD.—Rub the icing sugar through a hair sieve and whisk the egg-whites to a stiff froth.

Stir the lemon-juice into the sugar and add sufficient whites to mix the icing to a thick consistency that will not run. Beat well for ten minutes, then use it as required.

If it has to stand by, keep a very damp cloth over it, otherwise it will harden.

To ice the cake, spread a layer of icing over the top and round the sides, then smooth it over with a knife dipped into hot water. A palette knife is the best kind to use, as it has a large flexible blade rounded at the top.

Let the icing dry ; then, if necessary, cover it with another layer, but this may be omitted, if liked.

Put the cake on to a cake-board, and lift it on to an upturned soup plate or a revolving stand. Beat up the remainder of the icing and use for piping, planning a simple design before beginning. Decorate with any seasonable decorations to give the cake the final touch.

CHRISTMAS LOG CAKE

INGREDIENTS.—3 eggs, 4 oz. of flour (light weight), 4 oz. of castor sugar, ½ teaspoonful of baking-powder, 1 tablespoonful of cold water, apricot jam (warmed).

FOR THE DECORATION.—3 blanched almonds, 3 strips of candied peel or angelica.

FOR THE CHOCOLATE BUTTER ICING. —½ lb. of icing sugar, ¼ lb. of butter, 4 oz. of cake chocolate, 2 tablespoonfuls of milk.

METHOD.—Line a large Swiss roll tin with greased paper, making it fit exactly into the corners.

Sift the flour and baking-powder on to a paper.

Light the gas in the oven.

Whisk the eggs and sugar together till they are thick, white and creamy, and full of bubbles.

Make sure that the oven is hot before adding the flour.

Stir in the flour lightly but quickly, add the water and pour into the lined tin.

Spread it evenly over the tin, and put it at once in the top of a quick oven under the browning-shelf.

Bake for seven minutes, and when it feels spongy, as it will if the oven is right, turn it out on to a sugared paper or cloth, spread on the jam and roll up.

MAKING THE ICING.

The best way to melt the chocolate is to break the cake in three or four pieces and put it in a saucer with the milk.

Stand it in a warm place at the side of the stove till the chocolate is soft, then turn it over. This way is simpler and easier than grating the chocolate and melting it in a saucepan.

Rub the icing sugar through a hair sieve. Cream the butter till soft, and add to it the chocolate and sugar.

Mix well. Half fill an icing pump with the icing, and screw on a large rose pattern tube.

Cut a slanting piece off the end of the cake and make circles of icing to represent the rings of wood in a log.

Ice the rest of the cake by forcing on straight lines, close together till it is covered.

Decorate with almonds and strips of peel or angelica to imitate mistletoe.

CINNAMON SLICES

INGREDIENTS.—½ lb. of flour, 4 level teaspoonfuls of baking-powder, a pinch of salt, 1 oz. of butter, 2 level tablespoonfuls of castor sugar, 1 egg-yolk, ¾ gill of milk, ground cinnamon and castor sugar.

METHOD.—Sift the flour into a

basin with the baking-powder, salt, and sugar.

Work in the butter with the tips of the fingers.

Add the beaten egg-yolk, mixed with a little milk.

Knead the dough for a few minutes on a well-floured board. Roll it out to an oblong, a good fourth-of-an-inch thick. Spread the rolled-out dough with a layer of soft butter (extra to that given in the ingredients). Sprinkle the butter with the cinnamon and castor sugar.

Roll up the dough like a Swiss roll. Cut the roll in thick slices.

Bake the slices in greased tins in a hot oven.

Serve the cinnamon slices hot either with tea or coffee at tea-time or breakfast-time.

Sufficient for about ten slices.

COCOA CUP CAKES

INGREDIENTS.—1 egg, ½ oz. of cocoa, 2 oz. of flour, ½ level teaspoonful of powdered cinnamon, 1 level teaspoonful of baking-powder, 1 oz. of margarine, 3 oz. of castor sugar, milk, some almond paste (see p. 486), jam.

METHOD.—Beat the sugar and fat to a cream, then soften it with just a little milk to make it of a more creamy consistency.

Sift the flour with the cinnamon, cocoa, and baking-powder and stir them into the creamed mixture gradually, adding the well-beaten egg and some milk as required.

Beat all together and turn the mixture into small baking-cases, only half filling them.

Stand them on a baking-sheet and bake in a quick oven for about ten minutes.

When cold, top each cake with a half moon of almond paste, using a spot of jam to make it adhere.

To cut half moons, stamp out tiny rounds with a small cutter, then stamp across the round again with the same cutter ; this makes a half moon, and an oval shape.

Sufficient for twelve small cakes.

COCONUT BISCUITS

INGREDIENTS.—4 oz. of desiccated coconut, 2 oz. of flour, 1 egg, 3 oz. of granulated or castor sugar, 1 oz. of cornflour.

METHOD.—Mix all the dry ingredients together.

Beat the egg and mix with dry ingredients.

Add a little milk, just sufficient to make a stiff paste.

Put the mixture on to a slightly floured board.

Roll it out to about a quarter of an inch to three-eighths of an inch in thickness.

Dust with sugar.

Cut into rounds about the size of a biscuit—use a sharp cutter for this.

Place on a greased baking-sheet and bake in a moderately hot oven for about fifteen to twenty minutes.

(These are better if baked the following day.)

COCONUT CAKES

INGREDIENTS.—½ lb. of flour, ¼ lb. of desiccated coconut, ¼ lb. of granulated sugar, 1 teaspoonful of baking-powder, 3 oz. of margarine, 1 egg, vanilla flavouring, ½ to 1 gill of milk.

METHOD.—Grease about twelve small cake-tins (fancy shapes).

Cream the fat and the sugar together.

Sieve the flour and baking-powder and mix with the coconut. Beat the egg into the creamed sugar and fat, beat well for a few minutes.

Stir in lightly the flour and coconut, etc., together with the milk and a few drops of vanilla flavouring. Mix all well together.

Put into the greased cake-tins.

Bake in a hot oven for about twenty minutes.

COCONUT CREAM SANDWICH

INGREDIENTS.—2 tablespoonfuls of desiccated coconut. ¼ lb. of flour, 1 flat teaspoonful of baking-powder, 1 egg and 1 yolk, 3 oz. of castor sugar, 1 oz. of margarine, milk, jam and coconut for the top of the sandwich.

FOR THE FILLING.—4 oz. of icing sugar, 2 oz. of butter, vanilla, 1 tablespoonful of desiccated coconut.

METHOD.—Sieve the flour with the baking-powder. Mix in the coconut. Whisk the eggs and sugar together until they are thick and creamy and free from dark streaks.

Warm the margarine just enough to melt it.

Gradually stir the flour and coconut into the egg and sugar, with the melted fat and some milk as required.

Mix all together lightly. Turn the mixture into a greased sandwich-tin and put it into a hot oven to bake ; it will take about ten or fifteen minutes to cook.

Cool the sandwich on a sieve, and when cold split it into halves, spread it with filling and put it together again. Spread the top with jam and sprinkle with coconut.

THE COCONUT FILLING

To make the filling, beat the butter and sugar to a cream, having first rolled the lumps out of the sugar and rubbed it through a fine sieve. Add the coconut and a few drops of vanilla essence and mix all together. Use as required.

COCONUT ALMOND DROPS

INGREDIENTS.—9 oz. of desiccated coconut, 6 oz. of castor sugar, 3 eggs, almond flavouring.

METHOD.—Whisk the sugar and eggs together for about twelve minutes, until the mixture becomes quite thick and free from dark streaks. Sprinkle in the coconut and beat thoroughly for a few minures. Mix in a few drops of almond flavouring.

Grease a baking-tin, take a dessert-spoonful of the mixture at a time, and drop on to the tin. Do not put them close together.

Cook in a moderately hot oven for about ten to fifteen minutes.

Cool on a sieve. Serve on a lace paper. Sprinkle with castor sugar.

Sufficient to make twenty-one cakes.

COCONUT DROP CAKES

INGREDIENTS.—6 oz. flour, $\frac{1}{4}$ flat teaspoonful of carbonate of soda, 1 orange (rind only), 1 lemon (rind only), 2 oz. of desiccated coconut, 3 oz. of castor sugar, 3 oz. of margarine, 1 egg.

METHOD.—Sieve the flour with the soda. Add the coconut.

Beat up the egg. Cream the fat and sugar. Add the grated lemon and orange-rinds. Then mix in the flour and coconut together with the egg.

Mix all to a stiff consistency.

Put the mixture on to a greased baking-sheet in small heaps.

Dredge them with castor sugar and sprinkle them with coconut.

Put the cakes into a hot oven to bake. They will take about fifteen minutes to cook.

This quantity makes about fifteen cakes.

COCONUT FAIRY CAKES

INGREDIENTS.—3 oz. of flour, 2 oz. of cornflour, 3 oz. of sugar, 2$\frac{1}{2}$ oz. of margarine or butter, $\frac{1}{2}$ teaspoonful of baking-powder, a few drops of essence of lemon, 2 eggs, about $\frac{1}{4}$ gill of milk, 2 oz. of desiccated coconut, jam, 2 oz. of almonds (blanched).

METHOD. — Grease twelve small round tins.

Cream the butter and sugar till soft and white, stir in the eggs, one at a time, and beat the mixture for five minutes.

Stir in the flour, cornflour, lemon-essence, and baking-powder, and moisten with a little milk.

Half fill the tins with the mixture. Bake the cakes in a moderately hot oven for twenty minutes.

Put the cakes on a sieve to cool.

To decorate the cakes warm two tablespoonfuls of jam till it is liquid, and if necessary add a tablespoonful of water.

Put the coconut on a paper and blanch the almonds. When the cakes are cold, brush them all over with jam and roll them in the coconut. Stick an almond on top with a little jam.

To blanch almonds, put them into a basin and pour boiling water over them to cover them.

Leave them for a minute and then slip off the skins. Put the almonds in cold water to whiten them. Dry them on a cloth.

COCONUT FRUIT CAKES

INGREDIENTS.—$\frac{1}{2}$ lb. of flour, $\frac{1}{4}$ flat teaspoonful of carbonate of soda, 1 teaspoonful of cream of tartar, 2 oz. of desiccated coconut, 4 oz. of sultanas, 3 oz. of margarine or butter, 3 oz. of sugar, 1 egg, milk and water.

METHOD.—Wash, pick over and dry the sultanas.

Sieve the flour, soda, and cream of tartar together.

Rub the fat into the flour.

Add the sugar, coconut, and prepared fruit, and mix all together.

Beat up the egg and add to the dry ingredients, with a little milk and water as required. Be careful not to make the mixture too moist. Mix together thoroughly and beat for a few minutes.

Put into small greased cake-tins and bake in a hot oven for about twenty minutes.

COCONUT GATEAU

INGREDIENTS. — 4 oz. of flour, 1 whole egg and 1 yolk, 4 oz. of castor sugar, 1½ oz. of desiccated coconut, 4 oz. of margarine, 1 flat teaspoonful of baking-powder, milk.

FOR THE COCONUT ICING.—½ gill of water, ½ lb. of white sugar, pinch of cream of tartar, 1 egg-white, 2 tablespoonfuls of desiccated coconut, angelica and shelled walnut for decoration.

METHOD. — Sieve the flour and baking-powder, and mix them with the coconut.

Cream the fat and sugar, beat in the yolks of the eggs, stir in the flour and coconut and just a little milk as required. Have the egg-white already whisked up stiffly, and fold it in lightly.

Turn the mixture into a greased pie-tin or cake-tin and bake it in a moderately hot oven.

When cooked and cold, pour the coconut icing on the top and decorate it with a shelled walnut and a few leaves of angelica.

THE COCONUT ICING.

To make the icing, put the sugar with the water into a saucepan and dissolve it slowly. Then bring it to the boil. Add a pinch of cream of tartar and boil until a small quantity of the syrup, when dropped into cold water and left for a few seconds, becomes a soft ball when taken out and rubbed between the fingers.

Have the egg-white ready—whisked to a stiff froth—and directly the syrup has boiled sufficiently, pour it on to it gradually, keeping it well stirred. Finally, add the coconut.

COCONUT LAYER CAKE

INGREDIENT.—¼ lb. of desiccated coconut, ½ lb. of castor sugar, ½ lb. of margarine, ¾ lb. of flour, 1½ teaspoonfuls of cream of tartar, ¼ flat teaspoonful of carbonate of soda, 3 eggs, milk.

FOR THE BUTTER ICING.—12 oz. of icing sugar, vanilla flavouring, 6 oz. of butter, desiccated coconut.

METHOD.—Grease a cake-tin and line with gerased paper in the usual way.

Sieve the flour with the cream of tartar and carbonate of soda. Whisk up the eggs. Cream the fat and sugar.

Gradually stir in the flour, etc., and coconut alternately with the eggs, and some milk as required.

Mix all together and beat well, put into the cake-tin and bake in a moderately hot oven for about one hour and a quarter, lessening the heat as the cake begins to brown.

When cooked, turn out carefully and leave on a sieve until cold.

TO MAKE THE ICING.—Roll the lumps out of the icing sugar and rub it through a fine sieve.

Add the butter and beat both to a cream.

Flavour with vanilla.

To ICE THE CAKE.—Split the cake into three and spread some of the icing between each layer, then sandwich together again.

Spread a layer of icing on the top and all round the sides of the cake, then coat with desiccated coconut.

COCONUT MACAROONS

INGREDIENTS.—¼ lb. of desiccated coconut, 2 oz. of ground almonds, 6 oz. of castor sugar, about 3 egg-whites, flavouring essence.

METHOD.—Mix all the dry ingredients together thoroughly. Whisk the egg-whites to a stiff froth and combine them lightly with the other ingredients, adding flavouring.

Place the mixture on rice paper in heaps, and bake in a moderate oven. If liked, this mixture may be used as a filling for little tarts.

COCONUT PYRAMIDS

INGREDIENTS.—½ lb. of desiccated coconut, ¼ lb. of granulated or castor sugar, 1 egg, vanilla flavouring, water (if required), cochineal.

METHOD.—Mix the coconut with the sugar.

Beat the egg and mix it with the sugar, etc. Add the vanilla and sufficient water to make the coconut and sugar adhere when pressed together.

Colour half of this mixture to a pale pink shade with the cochineal. Leave the remainder.

Take a small mould or egg-cup; rinse it with cold water.

Fill the mould with coconut mixture, press it well down with a teaspoon, then shake out on to a greased baking-sheet.

Proceed until all the mixture is utilised.

Bake in a moderately hot oven for fifteen to twenty minutes.

Serve on a lace paper; sprinkle with castor sugar.

(These are better baked the following day.)

COCONUT SAND CAKE

INGREDIENTS.—2 oz. of desiccated coconut, 6 oz. of cornflour, 1 teaspoonful of baking-powder, ¼ lb. of castor sugar, ¼ lb. of margarine, 2 eggs.

METHOD.—Sieve the cornflour with the baking-powder and mix it with the coconut.

Beat the sugar and fat to a cream, to which each egg should be added separately, stirring it in quickly and beating well before adding the second egg. When both are beaten in, stir in the cornflour and coconut and mix all together lightly.

Turn the mixture into a prepared cake-tin, dredge some castor sugar on top and put the cake into a moderately hot oven to bake. It will take about an hour to cook.

COCONUT SPONGE

INGREDIENTS.—A good short pastry made with 6 oz. of flour, 4 oz. of lard, margarine or butter, the yolk of 1 egg.

THE SPONGE FILLING.—2 eggs, 2 oz. of castor sugar and flour, 2 small tablespoonfuls of butter, 3 or 4 tablespoonfuls of apricot jam, 1 tablespoonful of desiccated coconut.

METHOD.—A flan-ring at least eight inches and a half in diameter should be placed in a baking-tin and lined with the pastry, which has been made by rubbing the fat into the flour and mixing it to a stiff dough with the yolk of egg and very little cold water.

An ordinary sandwich-tin may be lined instead of a flan-ring, but the pastry bakes more easily in a ring.

After lining the ring, the jam should be spread over the pastry. The sponge filling is then made.

THE SPONGE FILLING

To make this the eggs and sugar should be whisked until they are very thick, creamy, white and full of bubbles.

The butter should be melted but not made hot and the flour should be sifted. Half the flour, followed by half the butter, should be stirred in as lightly as possible and when it is smooth the rest of the flour and butter should be added.

The sponge mixture should at once be poured over the jam. It will fill the tart, and that is why care should be taken to make the pastry-case the right size.

The cake should be put into the top of a quick oven at once for the first ten minutes, when the heat should be lowered. The cake will be done when the underside of the pastry is a pale brown (about thirty minutes). When it comes out of the oven it should be brushed over with hot jam and sprinkled with coconut.

NOTE.—This recipe is delicious served cold as a cake, or if liked it may be served hot as a pudding.

COFFEE BUNS

INGREDIENTS.—7 oz. of flour, ¼ lb. of margarine, barely ¼ flat teaspoonful of carbonate of soda, 1 tablespoonful of coffee essence, 1 egg, 3 oz. of castor sugar, milk and water.

FOR THE COFFEE BUTTER ICING.—¼ lb. of icing sugar, 2 oz. of butter, coffee essence.

METHOD.—Sieve the flour with the carbonate of soda. Rub in the margarine. Add the sugar and mix well together.

Beat up the egg and stir it into the mixture with the coffee essence. Add sufficient milk and water to make a stiff paste.

Divide the paste into small portions. Mould them into smooth round shapes and mark a cross on each with the back of a knife.

Brush the tops with milk, stand them on a lightly greased baking-sheet (leaving a space between each), and put them in a hot oven to bake. They will take about fifteen minutes to cook.

When cold, decorate the buns with coffee butter icing.

COFFEE BUTTER ICING

To make the icing, rub the sugar through a hair sieve, add it to the butter, and beat both to a cream. Stir in enough coffee essence to flavour. Force the icing through an icing-bag on to the buns.

This quantity makes sixteen to eighteen buns.

COFFEE CAKE

INGREDIENTS.—1 lb. of flour, $\frac{1}{2}$ lb. of margarine, $\frac{1}{4}$ lb. of sugar, $\frac{1}{2}$ flat teaspoonful of carbonate of soda, 2 eggs, 4 tablespoonfuls of coffee essence, 2 tablespoonfuls of golden syrup, 1 tablespoonful of vinegar, 2 teaspoonfuls of mixed spice.

METHOD.—Grease and prepare a cake-tin. (Use an oblong-shaped cake-tin if available.)

Put the margarine, sugar, golden syrup, and vinegar into a saucepan and melt all together, but do not boil it.

Sieve the flour with the spice and mix well together.

Beat the eggs, and when the sugar and syrup, etc., have cooled, add them to the beaten eggs.

Mix together and add to the flour, etc.

Mix thoroughly together and beat well. Add the coffee essence, dissolve the soda in a teaspoonful of milk and add.

Mix all together, put into the prepared cake-tin and bake in a moderately hot oven for about an hour and a quarter.

Place on a sieve to cool.

ICED COFFEE CAKE

INGREDIENTS.—$\frac{1}{2}$ lb of castor sugar, $\frac{1}{4}$ lb. of butter, $\frac{1}{2}$ lb. of flour, $\frac{1}{2}$ cup of milk, 2 eggs, 1 teaspoonful of baking-powder, 1 tablespoonful of coffee essence.

FOR THE ICING.— 6 oz. of icing sugar, 3 oz. of butter, 1 tablespoonful of coffee essence.

METHOD.—Grease and line two sandwich-tins. Cream the butter till soft, add the yolks of the eggs and coffee, beat well and add the sugar. Cream till smooth, and add the milk and flour alternately, a little at a time.

Fold in the stiffly beaten egg-whites as lightly as possible and stir in the baking-powder last.

Bake the mixture in the two sandwich-tins for twenty or thirty minutes.

When cold decorate with coffee butter icing, using a large star tube screwed on to the icing pump.

The cake should stand on a revolving icing table or plate turned upside down while you are icing it.

THE COFFEE BUTTER ICING

To make the icing, rub the sugar through a hair sieve, add it to the butter and beat both to a cream. Stir in enough coffee essence to flavour.

COFFEE FRUIT CAKE

INGREDIENTS.—$\frac{3}{4}$ lb. of flour, 2 tablespoonfuls of coffee essence, $\frac{1}{3}$ flat teaspoonful of carbonate of soda, 2 oz. of glacé cherries, 2 oz. of citron peel, $\frac{1}{2}$ lb. of sultanas, 6 oz. of margarine, 5 oz. of sugar, $\frac{1}{4}$ teacup of golden syrup, 2 eggs, few almonds.

METHOD.—Wash, pick over and dry the sultanas. Cut up the peel and cherries. Sieve the flour with the carbonate of soda and then rub in the margarine. Add the sugar and fruit, and mix all the dry ingredients together.

Whisk up the eggs and stir in the golden syrup (warmed slightly) and coffee essence. Whisk these together and add them to the flour and other dry ingredients.

Beat the mixture well. Turn it into a greased cake-tin and strew some almonds, blanched and halved, on top.

Put the cake into a moderately hot oven to bake. It will take about one and a half to two hours to bake.

COFFEE CREAM SANDWICH

INGREDIENTS.—$\frac{1}{4}$ lb. of flour, $\frac{1}{4}$ lb. of castor sugar, 3 eggs, $\frac{1}{2}$ gill of milk (if required), 1 flat teaspoonful of baking-powder.

METHOD.—Grease and prepare a shallow, round cake-tin or sandwich-tin and line the sides with greased paper coming a few inches above the top of the tin.

Separate the yolks from the whites of eggs. Whisk the yolks of eggs with the sugar for fifteen minutes.

Mix the flour and baking-powder together and put through a sieve.

Add the flour to the eggs and sugar and mix well together.

Whisk the whites to a stiff froth and fold lightly into the other ingredients.

Add milk if required.

Put into a prepared tin and bake in a hot oven for about twenty minutes.

Turn carefully out and leave until cold.

THE BUTTER ICING

INGREDIENTS.—3 oz. of butter or margarine, 1 oz. of chopped walnuts, 7 oz. of icing sugar, coffee essence.

METHOD.—Beat butter and sugar to a cream.

Add sufficient coffee essence to taste.

Put about half of this icing aside, and to the other half add the chopped walnuts.

Split the cake into halves and spread the icing and walnuts over the lower half of the cake.

Place the top half on this icing and leave until firm.

THE OUTSIDE COATING

INGREDIENTS.—2 or 3 oz. of chopped walnuts, apricot jam as required.

METHOD.—Spread the outside with jam and coat with chopped walnuts. Decorate the top with remainder of butter icing.

To do this, get an icing tube, fix a screw on to it, and tie an icing bag round the screw. Put the icing into the bag and force on to the top of the sandwich, forming a pretty design.

COFFEE GATEAU

INGREDIENTS.—6 oz. of flour, ½ teaspoonful of baking-powder, 3 oz. of butter, 3 eggs, 4 oz. of castor sugar, 1 small tablespoonful of coffee essence.

FOR THE COFFEE BUTTER ICING.—6 oz. of icing sugar, 3 oz. of butter,

1 tablespoonful of coffee essence, 1 tablespoonful of desiccated coconut, 3 walnuts.

METHOD.—Grease a wide cake-tin. Beat the butter and sugar till creamy and thick, add the eggs one at a time and beat well.

Add the coffee and lightly mix in the sifted flour and baking-powder.

Bake in a moderate oven for from twenty-five to thirty minutes.

When cold make the icing by creaming the butter, adding the sifted sugar and mixing with coffee essence.

Spread over the cake and sprinkle the sides with coconut.

Decorate with the rest of the icing and the walnuts.

RICH COFFEE GATEAU

INGREDIENTS.—10 oz. of flour, 1 teaspoonful of cream of tartar, ½ flat teaspoonful of carbonate of soda, 2 whole eggs and 2 yolks, 2½ oz. of margarine, ½ lb. of castor sugar, coffee essence.

FOR THE COFFEE ICING.—¾ gill of water, ¾ lb. of lump sugar, pinch of cream of tartar, coffee essence, 1½ whites of eggs, crystallised violet (for decoration).

METHOD.—Grease and prepare a cake-tin in the usual way. Warm the margarine just sufficiently to melt it. Mix the flour with the cream of tartar and carbonate of soda and put through a sieve. Put the two whole eggs and yolks into a basin with the castor sugar and whisk together for fifteen minutes. Gradually stir in the flour, etc., and melted margarine, and mix lightly, adding also sufficient coffee essence to colour and flavour, and a little milk if required. Put into the prepared tin and bake in a moderately hot oven. Cool on a sieve.

TO MAKE THE COFFEE ICING.—Put the sugar and water into a saucepan and dissolve. Add a good pinch of cream of tartar and sufficient coffee essence to well flavour and colour. Bring to the boil and keep boiling until a small quantity of the syrup, when dropped into cold water and left for a few seconds, becomes a soft ball when lifted out and rubbed between the fingers.

Have ready the egg-whites, whisked

slightly, stir the prepared mixture on to them, and keep stirring until the icing begins to thicken and set, then pour it over the cake.

Place a crystallised violet in the centre.

NOTE.—If the cake has risen unevenly, either turn it upside down and ice it, or cut off a slice from the top. If baked in a fairly large tin, it will be flatter, and therefore better for icing. Stand it on a rack over a dish when coating it with the icing.

COFFEE ICED CAKES

INGREDIENTS.—2 eggs, milk, 6 oz. of flour, 4 oz. of castor sugar, 4 oz. of margarine, coffee essence, 1 flat teaspoonful of baking-powder, almond paste (see next column).

FOR THE COFFEE ICING.—10 oz. of icing sugar, coffee essence, 2 tablespoonfuls of cold water, crystallised violets.

METHOD.—Grease a medium-size baking-tin and line with greased paper. See that the paper reaches above the top of the tin.

Cream the fat and sugar.

Sieve the flour and baking-powder. Pour one of the eggs into the mixture and stir thoroughly for a few minutes.

Add the second egg and beat up again.

Stir in the flour and baking-powder lightly, together with sufficient coffee essence to flavour.

Add a little milk and mix all together. Put into the greased tin and spread evenly.

Bake in a hot oven for about twelve to fifteen minutes, until it is spongy and very lightly browned.

Place on a sieve, remove the greased paper and leave until cold.

Cut the sponge into small oblong-shaped cakes (use a sharp knife).

Mix the almond paste as explained below.

Make it into small sausage-shaped rolls, and place one on the top of each cake, using a little white of egg or jam to keep it in place.

Stand them on a cake-rack over a dish, ready for icing.

THE ICING

Sieve the sugar, and put into a saucepan. Add the water. Colour and flavour with coffee essence. Mix together until quite smooth.

Stir over the fire until the base of the pan is warm. It should be thick enough to coat the back of the spoon.

Take a tablespoonful of the icing and coat each cake.

Crush a few violets and sprinkle over the tops.

Leave until the icing is set.

Then remove carefully on to a cake-dish.

THE ALMOND PASTE

INGREDIENTS.—$\frac{1}{4}$ lb. of icing sugar, $\frac{1}{4}$ lb. of ground almonds, about $\frac{3}{4}$ of an egg-white, vanilla flavouring.

METHOD.—Roll the lumps out of the sugar and rub through a fine sieve.

Add to the ground almonds and mix together.

Beat the egg-white slightly, and add sufficient with a few drops of vanilla to mix to a stiff paste.

Put on to a board dusted with icing sugar, and work it until smooth.

COFFEE PETITS FOURS

INGREDIENTS.—3 dessertspoonfuls of ground rice, 6 oz. of icing sugar, about $1\frac{1}{2}$ egg-whites, $\frac{1}{4}$ lb. of ground almonds, coffee essence, angelica.

METHOD.—Roll the lumps out of the sugar and rub it through a fine sieve. Add the ground almonds and ground rice and mix together. Whisk the egg-whites to a stiff froth.

Add to the ground almonds, etc., sufficient coffee essence to flavour and as much whisked whites as required to mix all to a paste. The latter must not be too stiff, otherwise it will be difficult to put through the icing bag, and not too soft, or the petits fours will lose their shape when cooked.

Put the mixture into an icing bag with a shell or large rose-pattern tube fixed in the end, and force the mixture out in little scrolls.

Place on a baking-sheet and put into a moderately warm oven for twenty minutes.

Decorate each with tiny leaves of angelica. All sorts of shapes can be made with this mixture, and on some you can dab a tiny spot of icing, when cooked.

Sufficient to make about ten or twelve petits fours.

COFFEE ROLL

INGREDIENTS.—1 teacupful of flour, ½ teaspoonful of cream of tartar, a large pinch of carbonate of soda, 1½ oz. of butter or margarine, 2 eggs, 3 oz. of castor sugar, 1 tablespoonful of milk, coffee essence, apricot jam.

METHOD.—Grease a baking-tin and line it with greased paper, making it stand above the sides of the tin.

Sieve the flour, soda, and cream of tartar.

Whisk the eggs and sugar together until quite thick and creamy and free from dark streaks of egg.

Fold in the flour and milk, and add sufficient coffee essence to well flavour the mixture.

Melt the butter, but do not make it very hot, and stir in lastly.

Pour into the prepared tin and spread over evenly.

Bake in a hot oven for about eight to ten minutes. When cooked it will feel just firm and spongy.

Turn out on to a sheet of paper dredged with castor sugar.

Remove the greased paper and cut a strip of sponge off from each side—just the outside hard edge.

Have ready the jam, previously warmed, spread it over, then roll up the sponge.

Stand on a sieve and leave until cold.

NOTE.—Do not overcook the sponge or it will not roll.

COFFEE YULETIDE LOG

INGREDIENTS.—3 oz. of flour, 1½ oz. of butter or margarine, ½ teaspoonful of baking-powder, coffee essence, 3 eggs, the weight of 2 eggs in castor sugar.

FOR THE FILLING.—3 or 4 tablespoonfuls of apricot jam, 1 oz. of shelled walnuts.

FOR THE ALMOND PASTE.—1 oz. of ground almonds, 1 oz. of castor sugar, 1 oz. of icing sugar, ⅓ egg-white, coffee essence.

FOR THE BUTTER ICING.—¼ lb. of butter, ½ lb. of icing sugar, coffee essence.

METHOD.—Keep back enough egg-white to mix the almond paste, then put the remainder of the eggs into a basin with the castor sugar. Stand it over hot water and whisk the eggs until they are thick, creamy and free from dark streaks, being careful not to let them curdle.

When ready, remove the eggs from the hot water and stir in lightly the flour, sift it with the baking-powder, also the butter (warmed enough to melt it), and add a spoonful of coffee essence.

Turn the mixture into a baking-sheet lined with buttered paper, spread it evenly, and bake it in a quick oven for from seven to ten minutes until spongy. Turn the sponge on to a tea-cloth wrung out in hot water and sprinkled with castor sugar.

Cut off the hard outside edges, spread the sponge with filling and roll it up. Let it cool on a sieve. Stick a piece of almond paste on one side of the roll to form the stump—a little jam will make it stick—and trim off a slice from each end of the roll.

Put the butter icing into an icing pump with a shell pattern tube affixed, and force it on to the log in long lines from end to end, so as to cover the sponge completely. Spread a layer smoothly over each end, and finally, decorate the log with a sprig of mistletoe and holly.

To MAKE THE FILLING.—Warm the jam, chop the nuts and mix them with it. The filling must be ready by the time the roll is cooked.

To MAKE THE ALMOND PASTE.—Sift the icing sugar and mix it with the castor sugar and ground almonds. Flavour them with coffee essence, and mix them to a stiff paste with egg-white.

To MAKE THE BUTTER ICING.—Sift the icing sugar. Beat the butter to a cream with half the sugar, then add the remainder and beat them again until creamy, adding coffee essence to flavour and colour the icing.

CORNFLOUR CAKE

INGREDIENTS.—2 eggs, 8 oz. of sugar, 8 oz. of Ideal Milk (unsweetened), ½ level teaspoonful of soda, rind of 1 lemon, 8 oz. of flour, 4 oz. of cornflour.

METHOD.—Beat the eggs and half the sugar until creamy.

Add the rest of the sugar and beat the mixture again. Stir in the whipped Ideal Milk, grated lemon-rind, and flour, sifted with the soda.

Mix all together lightly and bake in a moderate oven.

CORNFLOUR NUT CAKES

INGREDIENTS.—2 oz. of cornflour, 2 oz. of shelled walnuts, 4 oz. of flour, ¾ teaspoonful of cream of tartar, ¼ flat teaspoonful of carbonate of soda, 5 oz. of castor sugar, 1 egg, milk, 4 oz. of margarine.

METHOD.—Chop up the walnuts with the exception of about half a dozen.

Sieve the flour with the cornflour, cream of tartar, and carbonate of soda.

Beat the sugar and fat to a cream. Stir the egg in quickly and beat the mixture well for a few minutes.

Gradually stir in the flour and cornflour, etc., also the chopped nuts. Add some milk as required, and mix all together lightly.

Stand some baking-cups on a baking-sheet about half filled with the prepared mixture, and stick a small piece of walnut on the top of each.

Put the cakes into a hot oven to bake. They will take about fifteen to twenty minutes.

This quantity makes eighteen or twenty cakes.

CORNFLOUR SHORTIES

INGREDIENTS.—4 oz. of cornflour, 3 oz. of flour, 5 oz. of margarine, 3 oz. of castor sugar, almond flavouring, few almonds.

METHOD.—Sieve the flour with the cornflour and mix thoroughly.

Beat the sugar and fat to a cream.

Stir in the flour and cornflour, also a few drops of flavouring, and mix all together.

Lightly grease some little cake-tins, put a small quantity of mixture into each, forming smooth, flat cakes.

Have a few almonds ready blanched, place one in the centre, and bake in a moderate oven for about twenty minutes.

They should only be a pale biscuit colour when cooked.

Sufficient to make about eight or ten shorties.

CORNISH ROCK CAKES

INGREDIENTS.—½ lb. of self-raising flour, ¼ lb. castor sugar, 1 egg, milk, 1 lemon-rind, ¼ lb. of butter or margarine, salt, 6 oz. of cleaned currants, 1 tablespoonful of mixed peel.

METHOD.—Rub the fat into the sifted flour.

Stir in the sugar, a pinch of salt, grated lemon-rind, currants, mixed peel, and beaten egg, and a little milk if required, but the mixture must be stiff.

Place the mixture on a buttered baking-sheet in little heaps an inch or two apart. Sift castor sugar on the top and bake the cakes for from fifteen to twenty minutes in a hot oven.

CORNISH CINNAMON CAKES

INGREDIENTS.—3 oz. of butter, milk, 9 oz. of flour, 1¼ teaspoonfuls of baking-powder, 1 teaspoonful of ground cinnamon, ¼ lb. of castor sugar, 1 tablespoonful of golden syrup, 1 egg, almonds.

METHOD.—Cream the butter and sugar.

Add the syrup and beat them well.

Sift the flour, baking-powder, and cinnamon together.

Add the beaten egg and milk as required to make a smooth and fairly thick batter.

Fill buttered patty-tins three-quarters full of the mixture, after putting a blanched almond in the bottom of each tin.

Bake the cakes in a quick oven for about twenty minutes, till they are firm and crisp.

CREAM BUNS

INGREDIENTS.—1 oz. of butter, a pinch of sugar, ½ gill of water, 1½ oz. of flour, 1 egg, vanilla or almond flavouring.

METHOD.—Melt the butter in the saucepan, add the water and sugar. Boil well. Add the flour, stir quickly over the fire for ten minutes. Remove to the side, and when cool beat in the egg ; add the flavouring. Drop this mixture in small round portions on to a greased baking-sheet (*use about one dessertspoonful for each*). Bake in a moderately hot oven for twenty minutes, being careful not to let them get too brown. Remove from tin and leave until cool. Cut a small hole in each and fill with whipped cream. If liked, coat each with coffee icing, leave until set. Serve on a lace paper.

COFFEE ICING

INGREDIENTS.—10 oz. of icing sugar, ½ gill of cold water (use as required), coffee essence.

METHOD.—Sieve the icing sugar.

Place in a saucepan, add water, and sufficient coffee essence to colour and flavour the icing. Mix well together until smooth. Slightly warm it.

Pour sufficient icing on each bun just to coat the top of it. If liked decorate with crystallised flowers. If the cream buns are not iced, serve with sprinkled icing sugar on the top of each.

WHIPPED CREAM

INGREDIENTS.—1 gill of cream, ½ teaspoonful of castor sugar, ¼ teaspoonful of vanilla.

METHOD.—Whisk the cream, then add sugar and flavouring.

CREAM PUFFS

(ICED ON TOP AND WITH CUSTARD FILLING)

INGREDIENTS.—½ pint of water, 3 oz. of butter, 4 oz. of flour, 3 eggs, vanilla essence.

FOR THE CUSTARD FILLING.—½ pint of milk, 2 eggs, 1 oz. of butter, 1 oz. of flour, vanilla essence, 2 oz. of sugar, ¾ gill of whipped cream (can be omitted).

FOR THE COFFEE ICING.—¾ lb. of icing sugar, 2 tablespoonfuls of tepid water, 1 tablespoonful of coffee essence.

METHOD.—Sift the flour, and grease a baking-sheet.

Heat the butter and water together in a small saucepan.

As soon as they boil take the pan off the gas and immediately put in the flour. Stir hard, and when the mixture is smooth, put the pan over a low gas and stir until the mixture leaves the sides of the pan quite clean (about three minutes).

Take the pan off the gas and stir in the vanilla and one egg (unbeaten). Beat for five minutes.

Add the other eggs, beating well between each one. Put dessertspoonfuls of the paste on the baking-sheet, leaving plenty of room for rising.

Bake the puffs in the top of a moderately hot oven for about half an hour.

If they are properly baked they should be crisp, light and hollow, and should rise to at least twice their size.

THE CUSTARD FILLING

Melt the butter and stir in the flour and sugar with the pan off the gas. Add the milk gradually and stir till boiling.

Beat the eggs well and pour the hot (but not boiling) mixture on to them. Pour it into a double saucepan and stir for five minutes over the gas. When cold add the whipped cream if desired.

NOTE.—For an economical filling use three-quarters of a pint of custard made from custard-powder.

FILLING AND ICING THE PUFFS

When the puffs are cold, open one side of each and put in a spoonful of custard.

To make the icing, rub the icing sugar through a hair sieve, put it into a saucepan with the water and coffee essence and mix well.

Place the icing on the gas and stir till it softens enough to pour (about ten seconds). Do not make it hot or it will crack.

Pour a spoonful of icing over the top of each puff.

This quantity will make about eight puffs.

CRINOLINE SANDWICH

INGREDIENTS.—1 egg, 2 oz. of margarine or butter, 3 oz. of castor sugar, 3 oz. of flour, 1 level teaspoonful of baking-powder, 1 oz. of desiccated coconut, rose-flavouring essence, milk.

FOR THE FILLING.—Jam or jelly, desiccated coconut.

FOR THE ICING.—½ lb. of icing sugar, ½ an egg-white, water, rose-flavouring essence, cochineal, small crinoline figure (for centre).

METHOD.—Beat the sugar and fat to a cream, then add the egg, stirring it in quickly and beating it well.

Sift the flour and baking-powder and stir them into the egg mixture lightly, adding the coconut and some milk as required.

Flavour the mixture with rose-flavouring essence. Turn it into a buttered sandwich-tin and bake it till spongy. Cool it on a sieve.

When cold, split the cake in half and spread each piece with a mixture of jelly or jam and coconut, adding about one dessertspoonful of coconut to two tablespoonfuls of jelly. (Crab-apple jelly makes a good filling.) Sandwich the two halves together and ice the top.

To MAKE THE ICING.—Sift the icing sugar and mix it to a thick paste with the lightly beaten egg-white and a little water as required. Flavour it with rose-flavouring essence.

Ice only the top of the cake, spreading it just to the edge.

Let this set lightly, then decorate the edge with the remainder of the icing stiffened with a little more icing sugar, and coloured to tone with the crinoline figure. The crinoline figure placed in the centre will complete the sandwich.

CUSTARD POWDER CAKES

INGREDIENTS.—6 oz. of flour, 2 tablespoonfuls of custard-powder, ¼ lb. of castor sugar, ¼ lb. of margarine, 1 egg, vanilla flavouring, milk, 1 teaspoonful of baking-powder.

METHOD.—Beat the sugar and fat to a cream.

Add the egg, stir it in quickly, and beat well for a few minutes.

Sieve the flour, custard-powder, and baking-powder, and stir in gradually, adding some milk as required.

Flavour with vanilla, and mix all together lightly.

Put into small, greased cake-tins and bake in a hot oven for about fifteen to twenty minutes.

Sufficient to make from ten to twelve cakes.

DAGO CAKES

INGREDIENTS.—2 oz. of butter or margarine, 3 oz. of castor sugar, 1 egg, 2 oz. of flour, 1 oz. of chocolate, ½ level teaspoonful of baking-powder, 1 oz. of shelled walnuts, 1 or 2 table-spoonfuls of cold strong coffee, a few whole walnuts for the top.

METHOD.—Sift the flour with the baking-powder and mix them with the finely grated chocolate.

Beat the sugar and fat to a cream, separate the egg and beat in the yolk. Then stir in the flour and chocolate, finely minced walnuts, and coffee, and when well mixed, fold in the stiffly whisked egg-white.

Arrange about twelve small baking-cups on a baking-sheet and turn sufficient mixture into each to fill not more than two-thirds of it.

Dredge the tops with castor sugar and bake the cakes for from ten to fifteen minutes.

When cold, place half a shelled walnut on top of each dago cake, using a little jam to make it adhere.

Sufficient for about twelve cakes.

DATE CAKES

INGREDIENTS.—10 oz. of flour, ½ lb. dates, ¼ flat teaspoonful of carbonate of soda, 5 oz. of margarine, 5 oz. of sugar, ½ or 1 egg, milk.

METHOD.—Stone and cut up the dates.

Sieve the flour and carbonate of soda.

Rub in the fat, add the sugar and dates and mix well.

Beat up the egg and add to the dry ingredients, with some milk as required.

Mix to rather a stiff consistency and beat well.

Put into small, greased, cake-tins, and bake in a hot oven for twenty minutes.

Sufficient to make about eighteen cakes.

DATE COMFITS

INGREDIENTS.—¼ lb. of dates (when stoned), 6 oz. of flour, ½ level teaspoonful of ground cloves, ¼ level teaspoonful of carbonate of soda, 1½ oz. of lard, 1½ oz. of margarine, 1½ oz. of castor sugar, 1½ oz. of Barbados sugar, 1 egg, few whole dates for the top, milk if required, soft icing (see below).

METHOD.—Sift the flour with the ground cloves and carbonate of soda. Stone and cut up the dates. Put both the sugars and fats into a basin and beat them until creamy. Gradually stir in the flour and prepared dates, and mix them together, adding also the beaten egg and a little milk if required. Beat the mixture well, then turn it into small greased cake-tins and bake the comfits in a hot oven.

They will take from fifteen to twenty minutes to cook. Cool them on a sieve.

Turn each comfit upside down and put a dab of soft icing on the top, and stand a stoned date in the centre of it.

To Make the Icing.—Mix six ounces of sieved icing sugar to a thick paste with a spoonful of warm water and add flavouring as desired.

Sufficient for twelve cakes.

DATE SANDWICH

Ingredients.—4 oz. of flour, ½ flat teaspoonful of mixed spice, ⅛ flat teaspoonful of carbonate of soda, 3 oz. of sugar, 3 oz. of margarine, 1 egg, milk.

For the Filling.—6 oz. of dates, 5 oz. of granulated sugar, 2 oz. of shelled walnuts, ½ gill of water.

Method.—Beat the sugar and fat to a cream. Add the egg, stirring quickly, and beat it well for a few minutes. Stir in the flour, soda, and spice (sieved together) and a little milk as required.

Turn the mixture into a large greased sandwich-tin and put it into a hot oven to bake.

When cooked and cold, split it into halves, spread it with the prepared filling and then sandwich together again.

The Date and Nut Filling

To make the filling, mince the walnuts. Stone and mince the dates.

Put the sugar and water into a saucepan and, when the sugar is dissolved, stir in the prepared dates and walnuts. Mix well together and leave it to cool. Use as required.

DIAMOND GATEAU

Ingredients.—½ lb. of flour, 6 oz. of butter or margarine, 1 teaspoonful of baking-powder, vanilla, 6 oz. of castor sugar, 3 eggs, milk.

For the Centre Icing (Almond Paste).—3 oz. of icing sugar, ½ white of an egg, vanilla, 3 oz. of ground almonds.

For the Soft Icing (for the Top).—10 oz. of icing sugar, ½ gill of cold water,

vanilla, mauve colouring, angelica (for decoration).

Method.—Grease a baking-tin and line with greased paper, to stand just above the sides of the tin. Sieve the flour and baking-powder.

Beat the sugar and fat to a cream.

Separate the yolks from the whites, and whisk the latter to a stiff froth.

Beat up the yolks and add gradually to the creamed fat and sugar, keeping it stirred quickly.

Beat the mixture well for a few minutes, then stir in the flour, etc., and a few drops of vanilla, and lastly the whites of eggs. Mix all together lightly, adding a little milk if required. Put into the prepared tin and bake in a moderately hot oven for about thirty minutes. Then put on to a sieve and leave until cold.

To Make the Almond Paste.—Sieve the icing sugar. Add the ground almonds and mix together. Whisk up the whites and add sufficient to mix it all to a stiff paste, adding some vanilla flavouring at the same time. Work it until smooth. Put it on to a board and roll it out rather thinly.

Take the prepared cake and cut out a large diamond-shaped piece.

Split it into halves. Cut a piece of almond paste, the same size as the cake, place it on one half, then fix on the top half.

Stand it on a rack, over a dish, ready for the icing.

To Make the Soft Icing.—Sieve the sugar. Put it into a saucepan and mix to a smooth paste with the cold water. Flavour with vanilla and colour with mauve colouring.

Put it over a low gas and stir until the bottom of the saucepan feels warm.

To test it, see if it will coat the back of the spoon, then pour it over the cake, and let it run over and coat it evenly. Cut a diamond-shaped piece of angelica and place in the centre.

Leave until the icing is set, then lift the cake carefully on to a lace paper.

DOMINO CAKES

Ingredients.—1 whole egg and 1 yolk, 3 oz. of castor sugar, 1½ oz. of butter or margarine, 3 oz. of flour, ½ teaspoonful of baking-powder, milk.

For the Almond Paste.—½ lb. of

icing sugar, ¼ lb. of ground almonds, vanilla, egg-white, water.

FOR THE CHOCOLATE ICING.—½ oz. of chocolate, 1 dessertspoonful of cold water, icing sugar, vanilla.

METHOD.—Beat the sugar and fat to a cream.

Add the egg, stir it in quickly and beat well, then beat in the yolk.

Sift the flour and baking-powder and stir them in lightly with a little milk as required.

Turn the mixture into a buttered baking-sheet lined with buttered paper and spread it over evenly. Bake it in a hot oven for a few minutes, then turn it out and leave it to get cold.

Cut the sponge into oblong shapes about two and a half by one and a half inches. Spread them with jam and place a piece of almond paste (cut to the same size as the sponge) on each.

Make the chocolate icing and put it into an icing pump with a piping tube affixed, force this on to the cakes, making a line across each, and dots, so that the cakes resemble dominoes.

To make the almond paste, sift the icing sugar and mix it with the ground almonds. Flavour the almonds with vanilla and mix them to a stiff paste with white of egg and a little water as required. Form the paste into a smooth lump and roll it out.

To make the chocolate icing, grate the chocolate finely and put it into a saucepan with the water. Stir it till dissolved, take it off the heat and let it cool, then add enough sifted icing sugar to make the icing of a thick consistency. Flavour it with vanilla and use as required.

DOT CAKES

INGREDIENTS.—3 oz. of flour, ½ level teaspoonful of cream of tartar, ¼ level teaspoonful of carbonate of soda, 1 large egg-white, 3 oz. of castor sugar, 1½ oz. of butter or margarine, milk, vanilla.

FOR THE ICING.—2 oz. of icing sugar, 1 oz. of butter, vanilla.

METHOD.—Sift the flour with the cream of tartar and carbonate of soda.

Beat the sugar and fat to a cream, then gradually stir in the flour, adding some milk as required.

Beat the mixture well, flavour it with vanilla, and fold in the white of the egg whisked to a stiff froth.

Turn the mixture into small baking-cases, only filling them to about half full, stand them on a baking-sheet and bake them in a hot oven.

When cold, dot the top of each cake with butter icing, forcing this through an icing pump with a piping tube affixed.

To MAKE THE ICING.—Beat the butter to a cream with half the sugar (previously sifted), then add the remainder and beat again until creamy. Flavour with vanilla.

Sufficient for about twelve small cakes.

RING DOUGHNUTS

INGREDIENTS.—½ lb. of flour, ½ level teaspoonful of mixed spice, 2 teaspoonfuls of baking-powder, 3 oz. of castor sugar, 1½ oz. of margarine, 1 egg, milk, deep hot lard for frying, castor sugar, and cinnamon.

METHOD.—Sift the flour with the baking-powder and spice, rub in the margarine and add the castor sugar.

Beat up the egg and stir it into the flour with enough milk to make a soft dough.

Roll this out to about one fourth of an inch thick and cut it into rounds, then cut a piece from the centre of each with a smaller cutter, leaving a ring a good half-inch in width.

Have ready a deep pan half full of hot lard and put in the rings a few at a time. They will sink at first and then rise to the top. Fry them gently until golden, turning them over when brown on one side.

Drain them on paper and roll them in castor sugar and powdered cinnamon mixed in the proportion of one tablespoonful of castor sugar to one level teaspoonful of cinnamon.

This quantity will make about three dozen doughnuts.

DRIPPING CAKE

INGREDIENTS.—¾ lb. of flour, 6 oz. of clarified beef dripping, 1 teaspoonful of baking-powder, 6 oz. of sugar, 4 oz. of sultanas, 2 oz. of candied peel, 2 eggs, 1 gill of milk, ¼ teaspoonful of salt.

METHOD.—Grease and line a two-pound tin. Wash, pick and dry the sultanas, and chop the peel.

Rub the dripping into the flour till there are no lumps.

Add the sultanas and peel, also the sugar, baking-powder, and salt. Beat the eggs and put three-quarters of the milk with them.

Add this to the dry ingredients, using the rest of the milk if the mixture seems too stiff.

Put into a greased tin, and bake in a moderate oven for about an hour.

The cake is done when the centre feels firm and elastic.

DUNDEE CAKE

INGREDIENTS.—¾ lb. of flour, 7 oz. of margarine, 6 oz. of sultanas, ½ lb. of currants, 2 oz. of mixed peel, 1½ oz. of ground almonds, 5 oz. of granulated sugar, 3 eggs, milk (if required), 1 oz. of almonds.

METHOD.—Grease a square or oblong cake-tin and line it with greased paper. The latter should reach about two inches above the top.

Sieve the flour.

Wash, dry and stalk the fruit.

Blanch the almonds.

Cut the peel into small pieces.

Mix the sugar and margarine to a cream.

Beat in each egg separately for about five minutes.

When they are thoroughly mixed, stir in the ground almonds and flour, together with prepared fruit. Mix together and beat for a few minutes.

Put into the prepared cake-tin. Decorate the top with the blanched almonds.

Bake in a moderately hot oven for about two hours.

Lessen the heat after the first twenty minutes, and when lightly browned cover the top with paper.

Turn on to a sieve when cooked and leave until cold.

CHOCOLATE AND COFFEE ECLAIRS

CHOUX PASTE is the foundation of éclairs and cream buns, and is quite simply prepared.

CHOUX PASTE

INGREDIENTS.—3 oz. of flour, a pinch of castor sugar, 2 eggs, 1½ gills of water, 1½ oz. of butter.

METHOD.—Sift the flour, with a pinch of sugar, on to a sheet of paper.

Put the butter into a saucepan with the water and when the butter is dissolved, bring it to the boil. When boiling, add the flour, stirring vigorously all the time, and continue to stir until the mixture forms a smooth paste and leaves the sides of the pan. Then draw the pan aside and cool slightly.

Add one egg, stir it in quickly and beat well, then add the second egg and beat again.

To shape and bake éclairs, take an icing bag and fix a round screw in the bottom of it.

Put the prepared mixture into the bag and force it on to a buttered baking sheet in sausage shapes of about three inches and a half in length, cutting the mixture with a knife dipped in hot water when the required length is obtained.

Place them in a moderate oven to bake. They will take about twenty-five to thirty minutes to cook, and should swell and become almost hollow inside. Cool them on a sieve. This amount will make about one dozen éclairs.

THE FILLING

Whipped cream, sweetened and flavoured to taste, is the favourite filling. This can be varied by adding chopped glacé fruits and different flavourings.

Other fillings, such as mock cream or custard, can also be used. If using pure cream you will need about one gill and a half for twelve éclairs. Whisk it until it hangs from the whisk, then add sugar and flavouring to taste.

To fill the éclairs, split them down one side and insert the filling.

THE ICING

A soft coating of icing is required for éclairs; it can be flavoured with coffee, chocolate, ginger, or as desired.

To make coffee icing, take three-quarters of a pound of icing sugar and rub it through a hair sieve. Mix it to a smooth paste with two tablespoonfuls of warm water, and add sufficient coffee essence to colour and flavour. The consistency should be so that it coats the back of the spoon. If necessary, a little more water may be added.

To ice the éclairs, place them on a rack over a dish, then take a spoonful of icing at a time and coat each of them. Decorate the éclairs with violets or other crystallised fruit, and when the icing is set arrange on a paper doyley.

CUSTARD FILLING

INGREDIENTS.—1 gill of milk, ½ oz. of flour, 1 or 2 yolks of egg, ¼ oz. of butter, flavouring as desired, 2 dessert-spoonfuls of castor sugar.

METHOD.—Mix the flour and sugar to a smooth paste with some of the milk. Heat the rest of the milk in the top of a double boiler and add it to the mixed flour and sugar. Return it to the pan and bring to the boil, keeping it stirred. Boil gently for a few minutes, then draw the pan aside and cool slightly.

Add the butter and beaten egg-yolks, stand the pan in another pan of hot water, and stir until the custard thickens, being careful not to let it curdle. Take it off the gas, add flavouring to taste, and leave it to get cold.

MOCK CREAM FILLING

INGREDIENTS.—1 oz. of flour, 1¼ gills of milk, 2 oz. of butter, 1 oz. of castor sugar, flavouring.

METHOD.—Mix the flour to a smooth paste with some of the milk, heat the rest of the milk and add it to the mixed flour. Return the mixture to the pan with half the butter and stir until it boils. Boil it gently for a few minutes, then take it off the gas and *stir* until the mixture is almost cold.

Have ready the remainder of the butter beaten to a cream with the sugar. Beat this gradually into the flour mixture and continue beating until creamy, then add flavouring as desired.

CHOCOLATE ICING

INGREDIENTS.—¾ lb. of icing sugar, 2 or 3 oz. of chocolate, warm water, vanilla.

METHOD.—Mix the chocolate to a smooth paste with a little warm water, stir till dissolved, then cool.

Sift the sugar, and mix it with the chocolate. Stir together to a smooth

coating consistency with more warm water if required. Add flavouring to taste.

ECONOMICAL CAKE

INGREDIENTS.—½ lb. of flour, 1 teaspoonful of mixed spice, 1 teaspoonful of cream of tartar, 4 oz. of sultanas, ¼ flat teaspoonful of carbonate of soda, 2 teaspoonfuls of vinegar, ¼ lb. of margarine, ¼ lb. of sugar, water (about 1 gill).

METHOD.—Grease a small round cake-tin and line with greased paper. The latter should reach about two inches above the top of the tin.

Wash and dry the sultanas. Remove the stalks.

Sieve together the flour, soda, spice, and cream of tartar.

Rub in the margarine until it is like fine breadcrumbs. Add the sugar and sultanas and mix all together.

Add the vinegar and sufficient water to form a paste, but be careful not to make the mixture too moist.

Beat up thoroughly for five minutes.

Place in the prepared cake-tin and bake in a moderately hot oven for about forty-five minutes.

Turn on to a sieve and leave until cold.

ESSEX CAKES

INGREDIENTS.—1 lb. of flour, 6 oz. of scraps, nutmeg, ¼ teaspoonful of carbonate of soda, ½ lb. of currants, 6 oz. of sugar, milk to mix.

METHOD.—Wash, pick over and dry the currants. Sieve the flour, then add a little grated nutmeg. Rub the scraps into the flour. Add the sugar and prepared fruit and mix well. Add sufficient milk to mix all the dry ingredients together.

Beat for a few minutes, then stir in the soda, mixed in about a tablespoonful of milk.

The mixture when finished should be rather a stiff consistency. Put it into small greased cake-tins and bake in a hot oven for about twenty minutes.

NOTE.—Scraps are the residue obtained after making lard. If they are very hard and all caked together, warm them slightly, but not sufficiently to melt them, and separate them before rubbing them into the flour.

FAMILY CAKE

INGREDIENTS.—¼ lb. of margarine, 5 oz. of castor sugar, ¼ lb. of seedless raisins, ¼ lb. of sultanas, 2 oz. of candied peel, 2 oz. of glacé cherries, 2 eggs, ½ lb. of flour, some grated nutmeg, 1 teaspoonful of baking-powder, milk.

METHOD.—Wash, pick over and dry the sultanas and raisins. Shred the peel and cut the cherries into small pieces.

Cream the fat and sugar, add each egg separately, stirring it in quickly and beating the mixture well.

When both eggs are added, gradually stir in the flour sifted with the baking-powder, adding also the prepared fruits, some grated nutmeg, and a little milk as required.

Mix all together lightly, turn the mixture into a greased cake-tin and bake it in a moderately hot oven.

Cool the cake on a sieve and dust it with icing sugar.

FAMILY CURRANT CAKE

WITHOUT ANY EGGS

INGREDIENTS.—¾ lb. of flour, ½ lb. of Demerara sugar, ¼ lb. of margarine, ½ lb. of currants (cleaned), 2 oz. of mixed candied peel, ½ teaspoonful of mixed spice, 1 teaspoonful of baking-powder, ½ teaspoonful of bicarbonate of soda, ½ wineglassful of vinegar, a pinch of salt, ½ gill of sour milk.

METHOD.—Mix the flour, baking-powder, salt, and spice. Rub the margarine into the flour and add the currants, peel, and sugar.

Dissolve the soda in the milk.

Stir the vinegar and milk and soda into the dry ingredients, making rather a stiff mixture. Place the cake in a greased tin and bake it for about one hour.

FANCY BASKETS

INGREDIENTS.—1 breakfastcupful of flour, 1 teacupful of sugar, 2 oz. of butter or margarine, 3 eggs, 1 teaspoonful of cream of tartar, ¼ of a flat teaspoonful of carbonate of soda.

FOR THE DECORATION AND FILLING. —1 gill of whipped cream, ¼ lb. of desiccated coconut, 4 oz. of raspberry jam, 1½ oz. chopped pistachio nuts, 4 oz. of apricot jam, few pieces of angelica.

METHOD.—Grease some round small cake-tins—about one dozen. Beat the eggs and sugar together for fifteen minutes.

Mix the cream of tartar with the flour and put through a sieve.

Fold the flour lightly into the eggs and sugar.

Melt the butter and add.

Lastly, mix the soda in one table-spoonful of water and add ; mix all lightly together.

Put into the prepared tins.

Bake in a hot oven for about ten to fifteen minutes.

Turn on to a sieve and leave until cold.

Cut a small, thin slice from the top of each cake in the form of a lid.

Spread half of the cakes with apricot jam all round the sides and the lids.

Spread the remainder with the raspberry jam.

Roll the cakes coated with raspberry jam in the coconut ; the latter will adhere to the jam.

Roll three of the cakes coated with apricot jam in the chopped pistachio nuts and the remainder in coconut. Place on a lace paper.

Fill each basket with whipped cream. Bend the lids in the centre and place on top of the filling.

Cut long, thin strips of angelica and fix a handle to each basket.

Pistachio nuts must be put into boiling water and blanched before they are chopped, and if moist they must be dried in a very cool oven for a few minutes before being used for coating the baskets.

FIG CAKE

INGREDIENTS.—1 lb. of flour, 1 flat teaspoonful of ground ginger, ¼ teaspoonful of carbonate of soda, ½ lb. of cooking figs, 3 oz. of candied peel, 6 oz. of golden syrup, 6 oz. of sugar, 9 oz. of margarine, 2 eggs.

METHOD.—Stalk, wash and dry the figs, and cut them into fairly small pieces. Cut up the peel.

Whisk up the eggs, add the golden syrup (this may be warmed *slightly* to make it more liquid) and whisk them again.

Cream the fat and sugar and stir in the figs and peel. Gradually add the flour, ginger, and soda (sieved together) alternately with the eggs and golden syrup.

Beat all together. Turn the mixture into a prepared cake-tin and put it into a moderately hot oven to bake.

It will take about an hour and a half or two hours.

CAKE FILLINGS

AMERICAN NUT FILLING

INGREDIENTS.—1 lb. of loaf sugar, 1 gill of water, 2 whites of eggs, ½ lb. of walnuts.

METHOD.—Boil the sugar and water till it forms a ball when a little is dropped in cold water, or till it spins a thread (about fifteen minutes). Pour it while boiling on to two stiffly beaten whites of eggs and beat all the time till nearly cold. Add the chopped walnuts and any flavouring desired, and use for filling the cake.

BUTTER FILLING

This is made by beating butter and sieved icing sugar to a cream. To each half pound of icing sugar allow half as much butter.

It can be flavoured in various ways, a few of which are :
1. Vanilla, orange, or pineapple essence.
2. Melted chocolate and vanilla essence.
3. Coffee essence or strong coffee.
4. Caramel.
5. Rum or sherry.
This filling may be used as an icing.

CHESTNUT FILLING

INGREDIENTS.—½ lb. of chestnuts, 5 oz. of butter, ½ lb. of icing sugar, vanilla flavouring.

METHOD.—Put the chestnuts into boiling water and boil them for about ten or fifteen minutes. Then shell and skin them, put them into fresh water, and boil them until soft. Strain them, then rub them through a sieve.

Rub the icing sugar through a hair sieve, beat the butter and sugar to a cream, stir in a quarter of a pound of the prepared chestnuts, add vanilla flavouring to taste and mix all well together.

NOTE.—Preserved ginger, chopped mixed nuts, and desiccated coconut can also be used for fillings.

COCONUT FILLING

INGREDIENTS.—4 oz. of icing sugar, 2 oz. of butter, vanilla, 1 tablespoonful of desiccated coconut.

METHOD.—To make the filling, beat the butter and sugar to a cream, having first rolled the lumps out of the sugar and rubbed it through a fine sieve. Add the coconut and a few drops of vanilla essence and mix all together. Use as required.

COFFEE FILLING

INGREDIENTS.—¼ lb. of butter, ½ lb. of icing sugar, 1 tablespoonful of coffee essence.

METHOD.—Cream the butter till soft, add coffee and stir in the icing sugar.

CORNFLOUR CUSTARD FILLING

INGREDIENTS.—1½ oz. of cornflour, 1½ gills of milk, ¾ oz. of butter, 1 egg, vanilla flavouring, 3 dessertspoonfuls of castor sugar.

METHOD.—Mix the cornflour to a smooth paste with a small quantity of the milk. Put the remainder of the milk into a saucepan with the butter and sugar, and when hot stir on to the cornflour. Return it to the pan and boil for a few minutes, then draw it aside and continue to stir until slightly cool. Add the egg and stir very quickly until well mixed in.

Stand the pan over a very low burner to cook the egg, stirring well all the time and being careful not to let it boil. If preferred, it may be finished off in a double boiler. Add vanilla to taste, and when cold, use as required.

NOTE.—This filling can be used in pastry, sponge sandwiches, éclairs, and cream buns, etc.

CREAM NUT FILLING

INGREDIENTS.—1 lb. of icing sugar, 2 oz. of chopped walnuts, 1 gill of double cream, a few drops of almond essence.

METHOD.—Rub the sugar through a hair sieve. Mix with the cream and nuts, and flavour to taste.

DATE AND NUT FILLING

INGREDIENTS.—6 oz. of dates, 5 oz. of granulated sugar, 2 oz. of shelled walnuts, ½ gill of water.

METHOD.—To make the filling, mince the walnuts. Stone and mince the dates.

Put the sugar and water into a saucepan, and when the sugar is dissolved stir in the prepared dates and walnuts. Mix well together and leave it to cool. Use as required.

ORANGE CURD FILLING

INGREDIENTS.—2 sweet oranges, 2 eggs, 2 oz. of butter, ¼ lb. of castor sugar.

METHOD.—Grate the yellow rind from the oranges and squeeze out the juice. Put the butter in a double saucepan and melt it, stir in the sugar and juice with the grated rind.

Separate the yolks of the eggs from the whites and beat the latter to a stiff froth. Add the yolks to the mixture and stir them in. Add the beaten whites and whisk or stir all the time till the mixture thickens.

PINEAPPLE AND WALNUT FILLING

INGREDIENTS.—¾ teacup of minced pineapple, 8 oz. of icing sugar, 4 oz. of butter, 1½ oz. of shelled walnuts.

METHOD.—To obtain minced pineapple, drain some tinned pineapple from the syrup, put it through the mincer and drain it again.

Roll the lumps out of the icing sugar and rub it through a hair sieve. Chop up the walnuts. Beat the butter and sugar to a cream, then stir in the minced pineapple and walnuts and mix all together.

This makes an excellent filling for a cake or sponge sandwich.

Sufficient filling for two sandwiches.

FIVE O'CLOCK FRUIT CAKE

INGREDIENTS.—6 oz. of flour, 1 oz. of cocoa, 4 oz. of butter or margarine, 4 oz. of castor sugar, 2 oz. of currants, 2 oz. of sultanas, 1 teaspoonful of baking-powder, 2 eggs, almond flavouring, milk.

METHOD.—Wash, pick over and dry the fruit. Sieve the flour, cocoa, and baking-powder together.

Grease a cake-tin and line with greased paper to stand above the sides.

Beat the sugar and fat to a cream.

Add the eggs separately, stir in each one quickly and beat the mixture well before adding the next.

When both are beaten in, stir in the flour, etc. and prepared fruit alternately, with some milk as required.

Add a few drops of almond flavouring and mix all together lightly.

Put into the prepared cake-tin, place it in a moderately hot oven, and bake for about forty-five minutes.

Turn on to a sieve and leave until cold.

FLORAL CAKES

INGREDIENTS.—2 eggs, 5 oz. of castor sugar, 4 oz. of margarine or butter, 5 oz. of flour, 1½ level teaspoonfuls of baking-powder, 1 oz. of ground rice, milk, vanilla flavouring, cochineal or apricot yellow, jam, few pistachio nuts, about ¼ lb. of almond paste (see below).

METHOD.—Beat the sugar and fat to a cream.

Add each egg separately, stirring it in quickly and beating well. Add the flour sifted with the ground rice and baking-powder, and mix all together lightly, adding a few drops of flavouring and a little milk as required.

Colour the mixture with cochineal or apricot yellow, and turn it into two buttered sandwich-tins. Bake it in a hot oven until spongy, and then cool it on a sieve.

Cut the cakes each into about five rounds, an inch and three-quarters in diameter, and sandwich pairs together with jam between.

Spread jam on top, and arrange rounds of almond paste, three-quarters of an inch in diameter on each cake. Heap a little jam in the centre, and sprinkle this with chopped pistachio nuts.

FOR THE ALMOND PASTE.—Use equal quantities of ground almonds and icing sugar, flavour them with vanilla and mix to a stiff paste with white of egg, adding also sufficient colouring to make a deep shade—darker than the cake mixture.

Work the paste until smooth, then roll it out and use as required.

FOUR O'CLOCK TEA BISCUITS

INGREDIENTS.—¼ lb. of flour, 1 yolk of egg, 2 oz. of margarine, 2½ dessertspoonfuls of castor sugar, ½ oz. of butter, ½ flat teaspoonful of ground cinnamon, 3 oz. of currants and sultanas (mixed), ½ small lemon (rind only).

METHOD.—Wash, dry and pick over the fruit, and put it through the mincer.

Work the butter until soft and creamy, add the finely grated lemon-rind, one dessertspoonful of sugar, the cinnamon, and prepared fruit, and mix all together.

Rub the margarine into the sifted flour, add the remainder of the sugar.

Beat the egg-yolk and mix it with a teaspoonful of water and add it, and mix all to a stiff paste, adding a little more water as required.

Roll it out and cut it into rounds.

Take half of them and put the prepared fruit mixture in the centre, damp the edge and cover each with another round, pressing it down lightly.

Make two cuts in the centre, brush the tops with water, sprinkle them thickly with castor sugar, then put them on a baking-sheet and bake them in a quick oven for from ten to fifteen minutes.

Sufficient for fourteen biscuits.

FRENCH BISCUITS

INGREDIENTS.—3 oz. of flour, 3 oz. of butter, 1 oz. of icing sugar, vanilla flavouring, few crystallised rose petals, a little jam.

METHOD.—Sift the icing sugar and add it to the butter. Beat them until very creamy, then sift the flour and stir it in, and beat the mixture again until soft and creamy. Add vanilla flavouring to taste.

Put the mixture into an icing bag with a rose patterned tube affixed, and force it on to a buttered baking-sheet, leaving a good space between each as they spread when cooked.

Leave them in a cool place to harden, then bake them in a quick oven for a few minutes.

Garnish each with a small piece of crystallised rose petal, using a spot of jam to make it adhere.

Sufficient for sixteen buscuits.

FRENCH BUNS

INGREDIENTS.—½ lb. of flour, 1 teaspoonful of cream of tartar, ¼ flat teaspoonful of carbonate of soda, 3 oz. of margarine, 3 oz. of sugar (white), 2 oz. of candied peel, milk to mix, 1 egg.

METHOD.—Grease some small cake-tins (fancy shapes).

Cream the fat and sugar together.

Sieve the flour with the cream of tartar and soda.

Cut the peel into small pieces and mix with the flour.

Beat the egg into the creamed sugar and fat, beat well for a few minutes.

Lightly mix in the flour and peel, adding a little milk as required.

Put into the greased tins.

Bake in a hot oven for twenty minutes.

A FRUIT CAKE

STEAMED BEFORE IT IS BAKED!

INGREDIENTS.—4 oz. of margarine, 2 oz. of castor sugar, 4 oz. of soft brown sugar, 1 orange (grated rind and juice), ½ lb. of flour, 2 eggs, some grated nutmeg, 1 flat teaspoonful of ground ginger, 1 flat teaspoonful of mixed spice, ½ flat teaspoonful of carbonate of soda, ¼ lb. of candied peel, 1 oz. of shelled walnuts, ¼ lb. of figs, ¾ lb. of currants, ¼ lb. of sultanas, milk.

METHOD.—Wash, pick over and dry the fruit—figs, currants, sultanas. Cut up the peel and stalk and cut up the figs.

Chop the walnuts.

Sieve the flour with the soda, ginger, and spice, and add a little grated nutmeg.

Put the margarine and sugars into a basin and beat them to a cream.

Add the grated orange-rind and gradually stir in the prepared fruit, nuts, and flour, alternately with the well-beaten eggs.

Mix all together, adding the strained orange-juice, and a little milk if required.

Turn the mixture into a well-greased cake-tin—it should only be two-thirds full—cover it securely with a greased paper, and steam it for an hour and three-quarters.

Then uncover the cake and put it into a very moderate oven and bake it gently for about another hour and three-quarters.

FRUIT GENOA CAKE

INGREDIENTS.—½ lb. of butter or margarine, 2 oz. of glacé cherries, 7 oz. of granulated sugar, 2 oz. of mixed peel, ¾ lb. of flour, 1 oz. of angelica, 1 lemon, 1 oz. of almonds, ¼ lb. of sultanas, 3 eggs, 2 oz. of currants, 1½ teaspoonfuls of baking-powder, milk (if required).

METHOD.—Wash the currants and sultanas in warm water, drain well, and rub in a cloth. Pick them over and dry in a warm place. Grease a cake-tin and line with greased paper, as previously explained.

Sieve the flour with the baking-powder. Grate the rind of the lemon. Blanch and chop the almonds; if very moist, dry them. Cut the angelica and cherries, then peel into small pieces. Beat the butter and sugar to a cream.

Add the eggs separately, and beat each one in well before adding the next; then, after incorporating the last, beat the mixture for five minutes. Mix together the fruits and half of the almonds. Fold in gradually the flour, fruit, etc., and mix well, stirring very lightly. Add a tiny drop of milk if required.

Put the mixture into the prepared tin, sprinkle the remainder of the chopped almonds on the top, and bake in a moderately hot oven for about an hour and a half to two hours. Lessen the heat after the first twenty minutes. When sufficiently brown, cover the top of the tin with paper. When cooked, put on to a sieve and leave till cold.

RICH FRUIT CAKE

INGREDIENTS.—1 lb. of flour, ¾ lb. of margarine, ¼ flat teaspoonful of carbonate of soda, ½ lb. of currants, ½ lb. of sultanas, ¼ lb. of candied peel, 2 oz. of glacé cherries, ¼ lb. of sugar (granulated), ¼ lb. of golden syrup,

3 eggs, 1 gill of milk, 1½ oz. of almonds (for top of cake).

METHOD.—Grease a large round cake-tin and line it with greased paper.

Wash the currants and sultanas, dry them well and remove stalks. Cut the peel and cherries into small pieces.

Blanch the almonds and put to dry.

Mix the flour and soda together and rub through a sieve.

Rub the fat into the flour until it is like fine breadcrumbs.

Add to the flour the sugar and all the prepared fruit, mix all well together.

Break the eggs in another basin and beat well.

Add to the eggs the golden syrup and milk.

Whisk these well together.

Add the wet ingredients to the dry and mix all thoroughly together. Beat well.

Put into prepared cake-tin. Cover the top of the cake with the blanched almonds.

Bake.

Bake in a moderately hot oven for from two hours and a half to three hours. Turn on to a sieve and leave until cold.

FRUIT GINGERBREAD

INGREDIENTS.—½ lb. of flour, ½ lb. of fine oatmeal, 6 oz. of lard or butter, 6 oz. of moist sugar, 4 oz. of crystallised ginger, 4 oz. of any crystallised fruits, 2 oz. of shelled walnuts, 1 dessert-spoonful of ground ginger, 1 teaspoonful of mace, ½ teaspoonful of bicarbonate of soda, 3 eggs, ⅓ cup of milk, 2 oz. of citron peel, 1 lb. of treacle or golden syrup.

METHOD.—Grease two oblong tins.

Sift the flour, oatmeal, and ground ginger into a basin, and rub in the butter.

Add the peel, cut in strips, the mace, and the fruit, left whole or cut in large pieces, and the walnuts.

Mix the soda with the milk and add it to the flour, making a hollow in the centre to receive it.

Pour in the treacle and mix while adding the beaten eggs. Pour into well-greased meat-tins and bake in a moderate oven for about an hour. Sufficient for two cakes.

FRUIT SANDWICH CAKE

INGREDIENTS.—5 oz. of flour, $\frac{2}{3}$ level teaspoonful of carbonate of soda, $1\frac{1}{3}$ level teaspoonfuls of cream of tartar, 3 whites of eggs, grated rind of $\frac{1}{2}$ a lemon and $\frac{1}{2}$ an orange, 3 oz. of margarine, $3\frac{1}{2}$ oz. of castor sugar, milk, about $\frac{1}{2}$ gill, a few almonds, 2 oz. of currants, 3 oz. of sultanas, 2 oz. of candied peel or angelica, 3 oz. of crystallised fruit—pine, apricot or ginger, lemon curd, castor sugar.

METHOD.—Wash, pick over, and dry the currants and sultanas.

Cut up the peel and crystallised fruit.

Sift the flour with the carbonate of soda and cream of tartar, and mix it with the prepared fruit.

Beat the sugar and fat to a cream, add the finely grated lemon and orange rind, then stir in the flour and fruit with the milk as required.

Beat the mixture well, then fold in the stiffly whisked egg-whites.

Turn the mixture into two buttered sandwich-tins, dredge *one* with castor-sugar and scatter a few blanched almonds (split in halves) on the top. Bake both in a moderately hot oven.

Cool the sponges on a sieve and sandwich them together with a good layer of lemon curd.

FRUIT SHORTBREAD

INGREDIENTS.—9 oz. of flour, 5 oz. fat, 3 oz. of castor sugar, $1\frac{1}{2}$ oz. of currants, 1 yolk of egg, 1 tablespoonful of water.

METHOD.—Wash the currants, pick them over and put to dry.

Sieve the flour.

Rub in the fat.

Add the currants and sugar and mix together well.

Beat up the yolk of egg and mix with the water.

Add to the dry ingredients and work all into a lump.

Knead it until smooth. Roll it out to about half an inch thick.

Cut into rounds—use a large size fancy cutter.

Place on a baking-sheet and bake in a moderate oven until lightly browned.

GATEAU FROMAGE

(So called because it has the appearance of a round cheese.)

INGREDIENTS.—6 oz. of flour, $\frac{1}{4}$ lb. of butter or margarine, $\frac{1}{2}$ teaspoonful of baking-powder, $\frac{1}{4}$ lb. of castor sugar, 1 egg and 1 extra yolk, milk (if required), apricot jam (for the outside coating).

FOR THE ICING.—$\frac{1}{2}$ lb. of ground almonds, $\frac{1}{2}$ lb. of icing sugar, 1 large white of egg, vanilla, water, colouring.

METHOD.—Grease a small, round cake-tin, about five inches and a half in diameter, and line it with greased paper.

Sieve the flour and baking-powder.

Beat the sugar and fat to a cream.

Add the egg, stir it in quickly and beat for a few minutes.

Add the extra yolk, and beat it in well.

Stir in the flour and baking-powder, adding a little milk if required.

Mix all together lightly, put into the prepared tin and bake in a moderately hot oven for about forty minutes.

When cooked, turn carefully on to a sieve and leave until cold.

TO MAKE THE ALMOND PASTE.—Rub the icing sugar through a fine sieve.

Add the ground almonds and mix together.

Add a few drops of vanilla.

Whisk up the white slightly and add to the sugar and almonds, and mix to a stiff paste, adding a little cold water if required.

Work in a few drops of yellow colouring to make the paste resemble the rind of a small Dutch cheese.

Cut off a slice from the top to give it a flat surface.

Remove the sharp lower edge by cutting off a small piece all round the rim.

Rub two or three tablespoonfuls of apricot jam through a sieve, then spread all over the cake. (If very stiff, warm the jam slightly.)

Roll the almond paste to a round shape and completely cover the cake, moulding it round evenly.

Stand it in a cool oven for about half an hour to dry the icing.

GENOA CAKE

INGREDIENTS.—$\frac{1}{2}$ lb. of butter or margarine, $\frac{1}{2}$ lb. of granulated sugar

1 lb. of currants or sultanas (or ½ lb. of each), ¼ lb. of mixed candied peel, 4 eggs, ¾ lb. of flour, 2 oz. of almonds.

METHOD.—Grease and line a cake-tin measuring seven inches across.

Wash and pick the fruit and dry it in a cloth or in a moderate oven. Chop the peel.

Put the almonds in boiling water and slip off the skins.

Mix the butter and sugar together with a wooden spoon till they are soft, light and creamy.

Stir in the eggs one at a time, and beat the mixture for five minutes after adding each one.

Add the fruit and peel and stir in the flour.

Place the mixture in the tin and hollow the centre slightly. Sprinkle the almonds over the top. Bake the cake for about one and a quarter hours in a moderately hot oven to start with. After twenty minutes lower the gas a little.

The cake is done when the centre feels firm.

Remove the paper when the cake has cooled slightly and leave it on a sieve till cold.

GENOESE CAKE

INGREDIENTS.—2 eggs, 3 oz. of castor sugar, 3 oz. of flour, ½ teaspoonful of baking-powder, 1½ oz. of butter or margarine, angelica, and almond paste (see p. 486).

FOR THE ICING.—¾ lb. of icing sugar, 2 or 3 tablespoonfuls of water, cochineal, flavouring essence as desired.

METHOD.—Put the eggs and castor sugar into a basin, stand it over a saucepan of hot water and whisk until the eggs and sugar are thick and creamy, and free from dark streaks, being careful not to let them curdle.

When ready, remove them from the hot water and gradually stir in the flour (sieved) with the baking-powder, also the butter, melted but not hot.

Mix all together lightly, turn the mixture into a greased cake-tin and bake it in a moderately hot oven for from twenty to thirty minutes, until spongy. Cool it on a sieve.

To MAKE THE ICING.—Rub the sugar through a hair sieve, then mix it to a smooth paste with water, add a few drops of flavouring and colouring

as desired. The icing should be thick enough to coat the spoon.

To ICE THE CAKE.—Stand it on a rack, place this on a dish and pour the icing over the cake. Coat it evenly, and when nearly set decorate it with flowers of almond paste cut with a small fancy cutter. Put a dab of icing in the centre of these and add stalks of angelica.

GINGER AND ALMOND BUNS

INGREDIENTS.—½ lb. of flour, 2 oz. of almonds, 1 teaspoonful of ground ginger, 2 oz. of sultanas, ¼ flat tea-spoonful of carbonate of soda, 3 oz. of margarine, 4 oz. of sugar, ½ an egg, milk.

METHOD.—Wash, pick over, and dry the sultanas. Sieve the flour, soda, and ginger. Rub in the fat. Add the sugar and sultanas. Blanch and skin the almonds. Take about three-quarters of them and chop coarsely, then add them to the flour, and mix all the dry ingredients together.

Beat up the egg and add it with sufficient milk to mix it all.

Beat the mixture for a few minutes, then put into small greased tins.

Split the remainder of the almonds into halves and place a piece on each cake. Bake in a hot oven for about fifteen to twenty minutes.

GINGER BUNS

INGREDIENTS.—¼ lb. of flour, 2 oz. of sugar, 2 oz. of golden syrup, 2 oz. of margarine or butter, 1 egg, ¼ tea-spoonful of bicarbonate of soda, ¼ teaspoonful of ground ginger, a little grated nutmeg.

METHOD.—Sift the flour, ginger, and soda together.

Put the butter, sugar, and treacle in a saucepan and melt them without making them very hot.

Pour in the beaten egg with the pan off the gas, and stir in the flour. Mix all well together. Pour into small well-greased tins.

Bake in a moderate oven for about twenty minutes.

To make twelve buns.

GINGERBREAD

WHEN making gingerbread, the soda should be added last, mixed in a spoonful of milk or water. Just crumble it in your fingers first to get rid of the lumps, or press them out with a spoon, then smooth it in the liquid. The lumps dissolve very readily if mixed with boiling milk or water, but if you do this, you must *add it immediately and bake at once* as the soda " acts " when mixed with a warm, moist ingredient.

INGREDIENTS.—½ lb. of flour, few almonds, ¼ flat teaspoonful of carbonate of soda, 1 teaspoonful of ground ginger, milk, 1 oz. of candied peel, 3 oz. of brown sugar, 3 oz. of margarine, 1 egg, ½ teacup of golden syrup.

METHOD.—Sieve the flour with the ginger. Cut up the peel and add it to the flour. Dissolve the sugar, syrup, and margarine in a saucepan, but do not boil it. Cool it a little, then add it to the beaten egg and turn it into the centre of the flour.

Mix all together and beat well, adding a little milk as required. Stir in the soda smoothed in a tablespoonful of milk or water.

Put the mixture into a greased tin, strew blanched almonds on the top. Bake the gingerbread in a moderate oven.

CARAWAY GINGERBREAD

INGREDIENTS.—1 lb. of flour, 2 teaspoonfuls of ground ginger, 1 teaspoonful of ground caraway seeds, 6 oz. of margarine, 2 eggs, ¼ flat teaspoonful of carbonate of soda, 1 teacupful of golden syrup (1 gill), ¼ lb. of Demerara sugar, 2 oz. of candied peel, milk, 1 oz. of almonds (if liked).

METHOD.—Mix the ground ginger and caraway seeds with the flour and sieve them together into a basin. Put the margarine, golden syrup, and sugar into a saucepan, heat slowly until the sugar is dissolved, but do not boil it.

When dissolved, let it cool slightly. Put the eggs into a basin and whisk them. Cut the peel into small pieces and add to the flour. Mix together and make a hole in the centre.

Add the golden syrup, etc., to the beaten eggs, whip together and add to the centre of the flour. Mix well, add a little milk if required, and beat for a few minutes.

Mix the soda in about one tablespoonful of milk, add to the gingerbread and mix it well in.

Pour the mixture into a greased tin (use a rather shallow oblong or square tin ; a baking-tin will do), and bake in a moderately hot oven for about forty minutes. Lessen the heat after the first fifteen minutes. If the almonds are used, blanch them, and place them on the gingerbread just before it is put into the oven.

NOTE.—Test the gingerbread with a warm iron skewer before taking it out of the oven. Put the skewer into the centre of the cake. If it comes out clean, it is sufficiently cooked. If the gingerbread browns too quickly, remove the browning-shelf.

GINGER BISCUITS

INGREDIENTS.—6 oz. of flour, ¼ flat teaspoonful of carbonate of soda, 1½ flat teaspoonfuls of ground ginger, few almonds, 1 oz. of Barbados sugar, 1½ oz. of margarine, 2 dessertspoonfuls of golden syrup (or more if required), 1 teaspoonful of treacle.

METHOD.—Sift the flour into a basin with the carbonate of soda and ground ginger.

Put the margarine in a saucepan with the treacle, golden syrup, and sugar, dissolve them slowly, but do not boil. Take the saucepan off the gas and cool the syrup before adding it to the flour.

Mix it to a stiff paste, adding a little syrup if required ; then work it into a smooth dough and roll it out. Stamp it into rounds and place them on a baking-sheet. Press half a blanched almond in the centre of each biscuit and bake them in a very moderate oven for from ten to twelve minutes.

ICED GINGER CAKE

INGREDIENTS.—2 oz. of crystallised ginger, 6 oz. of butter or margarine, 6 oz. of castor sugar, 10 oz. of flour, ½ teaspoonful of baking-powder, 3 eggs.

FOR THE ICING.—3 oz. of citron peel, 4 oz. of icing sugar, 1 tablespoonful of lemon-juice.

METHOD.—Grease and line a small cake-tin. Cut the ginger into thin slices.

Cream the butter and sugar till soft

and white, and beat in the eggs, one at a time.

When the mixture is light and creamy, stir in the flour and baking-powder.

Place the mixture in the tin, hollowing out the centre of the cake so that when it rises it will be nearly flat.

Bake in a moderate oven for about an hour.

Put the cake on a sieve to cool and remove the paper.

ICING THE CAKE.—When the cake is cold, cut the peel in fairly thick slices and lay them all over the top.

Warm the lemon-juice in a small saucepan and stir in the icing sugar. Warm the icing for a few seconds till it is liquid enough to coat the back of the spoon, then pour it over the peel.

GINGERBREAD LAYER CAKE

INGREDIENTS.—10 oz. of flour, 1 level teaspoonful of carbonate of soda, 10 oz. of golden syrup, 2 oz. of sugar, 5 oz. of margarine, 1 whole egg and 2 yolks, ½ level teaspoonful of ground cloves, 1½ level teaspoonfuls of ground ginger, milk.

FOR THE ICING AND FILLING.— 1 lb. of castor sugar, ¼ pint of water, pinch of cream of tartar, 2 egg-whites, 1 oz. of chocolate (grated), vanilla, glacé cherries, angelica, few chopped nuts.

METHOD.— Put the margarine, golden syrup, and sugar into a saucepan and warm them enough to melt. Let them cool, add this syrup to the well-beaten eggs and whisk all together.

Sift the flour, soda, and spices into a basin, stir in the wet ingredients and beat all well, adding a little milk as required.

Turn the mixture into three buttered sandwich-tins, put them in the oven to bake and, when cooked, cool the sponges on a sieve.

TO MAKE THE ICING.—Put the sugar into a saucepan, add the water (hot), and dissolve it slowly ; then bring this syrup to the boil. Add a pinch of cream of tartar, and continue boiling until a small quantity when dropped into cold water, becomes a soft ball. Draw the pan aside, add the chocolate and vanilla to taste and

when this is dissolved, pour it at once, but steadily, on to the whisked egg-whites, keeping the icing well stirred until it begins to set.

Spread a little between each layer, then sandwich the sponges together. Pour the remainder of the icing over the cake.

Decorate the cake with glacé cherries and leaves of angelica, and sprinkle a few chopped nuts on the top.

GINGER GATEAU

INGREDIENTS.—½ lb. of crystallised or glacé ginger, 1 lb. of flour, 2 teaspoonfuls of cream of tartar, ¼ teaspoonful of carbonate of soda, ½ lb. of castor sugar, 9 oz. of butter or margarine, 3 eggs, milk.

FOR THE ALMOND PASTE ICING.—¾ lb. of icing sugar, ¼ lb. of ground almonds, vanilla or almond flavouring, about 2 whites of eggs.

FOR THE WHITE ICING.—6 oz. of icing sugar, ½ white of egg, flavouring, water (about 1 tablespoonful as required), ginger (for decoration).

METHOD.—Cut the ginger into small pieces. Grease a large round cake-tin and line with greased paper to stand above the sides of the tin. Sieve the flour, cream of tartar, and carbonate of soda together. Whisk up the eggs.

Beat the sugar and fat to a cream. Stir in the flour, etc., and the ginger, also the eggs. Mix all together, adding a little milk if required, but do not make the mixture too moist or the fruit will sink.

Beat for a few minutes, put into the prepared tin and bake in a moderately hot oven for about one hour and a half to two hours.

Put on to a sieve and leave until cold.

TO MAKE THE ALMOND PASTE.— Roll the lumps out of the icing sugar and rub it through a fine sieve.

Add the ground almonds and mix together. Whisk the egg-whites slightly and add sufficient, with a few drops of flavouring, to mix it to a stiff paste ; then work it until smooth.

TO ICE THE CAKE.—Roll out the paste and place a strip of it all round the top to make it perfectly even. Roll out the remainder of the paste, cut out a round to completely fit the top

Simnel Cake

The Finished
Simnel Cake.

Turn the mixture
into a greased tin.

Make a border
of almond paste.

Pour soft icing
into the centre.

PLATE 43

Mushroom Cake

Layer Cake

Shortbread

PLATE 44

of the cake, and fix it on firmly. Now roll out the trimmings and place a small piece to stand up all round the top edge. Pinch it with your finger and thumb to make it look decorative. Put the cake into a cool oven for about half an hour to dry the icing, then leave for two or three hours.

To Make the White Icing.— Rub the icing sugar through a fine sieve. Whisk the white of egg until slightly frothy. Put the sugar into a saucepan, stir in the white of egg and a few drops of flavouring and mix all to a smooth, thick paste, adding some cold water *as required*.

Beat the icing for a few minutes, then stand the saucepan over a very low burner and stir until the base of the saucepan feels warm ; the icing, when finished, should coat the back of the spoon. Pour the icing on to the almond paste in the centre of the cake and let it run to the edge. Decorate the top with pieces of ginger.

PRESERVED GINGER CAKE

INGREDIENTS.—¾ lb. of flour, 6 oz. of butter or margarine, 6 oz. of castor sugar, 3 eggs, 5 oz. of preserved ginger (in syrup), ½ gill of milk, 2 teaspoonfuls of baking-powder.

METHOD.—Remove the ginger from the syrup and cut it into small squares.

Leave one ounce for the top of the cake, which should be cut rather larger.

Grease a cake-tin. (Use a square cake-tin if preferred.)

Cream the fat and sugar together.

Sieve the flour and baking-powder together.

Beat the eggs separately into the creamed fat and sugar, beat well.

Lightly stir in the flour, also the four ounces of ginger.

Add one tablespoonful of the ginger syrup and a little milk and mix all well together.

Put into prepared tin and bake for from one hour to one hour and a half in a moderately hot oven.

Place on a sieve until cold.

NOTE.—Place the few pieces of ginger, which were left out, carefully on top of cake when the latter has been cooked for twenty minutes.

GINGER SANDWICH CAKES

INGREDIENTS.—6 oz. of flour, 1½ flat teaspoonfuls of ground ginger, ¼ flat teaspoonful of carbonate of soda, 3 oz. of margarine, 2 oz. of sugar, 4 oz. of golden syrup, 2 eggs, few almonds, milk.

FOR THE FILLING.—2 dessertspoonfuls of honey, 5 oz. of icing sugar, 2 oz. of butter.

METHOD.—Sieve the flour with the ground ginger and put them into a basin. Blanch and chop up a few almonds.

Put the sugar, fat, and golden syrup into a saucepan to melt (*do not boil*), then cool the mixture a little and add it to the beaten eggs.

Pour this into the centre of the flour, mix together and beat well. Stir in the carbonate of soda mixed in a teaspoonful of milk.

Turn the mixture into small greased sandwich-tins, sprinkle the almonds on the top and bake in a hot oven.

Cool on a sieve and when cold split the cakes in halves and spread them with a layer of filling. Then sandwich them together again.

THE HONEY FILLING.—To make the filling, roll the lumps out of the icing sugar and rub it through a fine sieve. Add the butter and beat both to a cream. Stir in the honey.

GINGER RICE BUNS

INGREDIENTS.—9 oz. of flour, 3 oz. of ground rice, 4 oz. of crystallised ginger, 1½ tablespoonfuls of baking-powder, 5 oz. of castor sugar, 5 oz. of margarine, 1 egg, milk.

METHOD.—Sieve the flour, ground rice, and baking-powder.

Cut the ginger into very small pieces.

Cream the fat and sugar.

Add the egg, stir it in quickly, and beat well for a few minutes.

Gradually stir in the flour, ground rice, baking-powder, and ginger, with a little milk as required.

Mix all together lightly, put into small greased cake-tins, and bake in a hot oven for about fifteen to twenty minutes.

Sufficient to make about eighteen cakes.

GINGER SLAB CAKE

INGREDIENTS.—1 lb. of flour, 1 flat teaspoonful of carbonate of soda, 2 teaspoonfuls of cream of tartar, 1½ teaspoonfuls of ground ginger, 6 oz. of crystallised or glacé ginger, ⅛lb. of margarine, 6 oz. of golden syrup, 6 oz. of sugar, 2 eggs, about 1 gill of milk.

METHOD.—Sieve the flour with the cream of tartar, carbonate of soda, and ground ginger.

Rub in the margarine, add the sugar and the crystallised ginger, cut into fairly small pieces.

Whisk up the eggs. Warm the golden syrup *slightly* and add it to them.

Whisk well together.

Stir the egg and syrup into the dry ingredients and mix all together, adding some milk as required.

Beat the mixture well, turn it into a greased oblong cake-tin and bake it for about one and a half hours.

When cooked, turn the cake out carefully and cool it on a sieve.

NOTE.—This shaped cake is very convenient for cutting into slices.

GINGER NUTS

INGREDIENTS.—½ lb. of flour, 1½ teaspoonfuls of ground ginger, 3 oz. of margarine or butter, 3 oz. of castor sugar, golden syrup (about 3 table-spoonfuls), few almonds.

METHOD.—Sieve the flour and ginger. Rub in the fat. Add the sugar and mix together. Gradually add some golden syrup and mix all to a stiff paste. Work it until smooth, then roll it out. Cut into rounds and place on a very slightly greased baking-sheet. Blanch, skin, and split the almonds, and place one piece on each biscuit. Cook in a moderately warm oven for about twenty minutes.

GINGER SNAPS

INGREDIENTS.—4 oz. of golden syrup, 2 oz. of margarine, 4 oz. of plain flour, 4 oz. of Demerara sugar, 1 teaspoonful of ground ginger.

METHOD.—Melt the margarine, sugar, and golden syrup in a saucepan, but do not make them hot. Add the flour and ginger.

Place an asbestos mat under the saucepan and stir the mixture until it boils.

Simmer for three minutes. Take the pan off the gas and leave the mixture in it to get cold.

When cold it will be firm enough to cut. Roll it into balls the size of a walnut.

Roll these out very thinly, the size of a small plate.

Grease two baking-sheets and place four snaps on each. Bake them in a moderate oven for ten minutes.

Remove the tins from the oven and let the snaps cool for a minute or two before rolling them up.

To shape them, lay a clean, nicely-shaped carrot (or a cornucopia tin) at the side of each and roll it up quickly.

NOTE.—If they set before there is time to roll them up, warm them in the oven again.

GLACE FRUIT CAKES

INGREDIENTS.—10 oz. of flour, 2 oz. of glacé ginger, 2 oz. of glacé cherries, 6 oz. of margarine, 5 oz. of castor sugar, 1 teaspoonful of cream of tartar, ¼ flat teaspoonful of carbonate of soda, 1 egg, milk.

METHOD.—Cut the cherries and ginger into small pieces.

Sieve the flour, soda, and cream of tartar.

Beat the sugar and fat to a cream.

Whisk up the egg.

Gradually stir the flour, etc., and prepared fruit into the creamed fat and sugar alternately, with the egg and some milk as required.

Mix all together and beat well.

Put into small greased cake-tins and bake in a quick oven for about fifteen to twenty minutes. Cool on a sieve.

Sufficient to make about eighteen cakes.

GOLDEN CAKE

INGREDIENTS.—1 lb. of flour, ½ teaspoonful of carbonate of soda, ½ lb. of ground almonds, 7 oz. of margarine, 6 oz. of sugar, 1 teacupful of golden syrup, 2 eggs, milk (about 1 gill).

METHOD.—Grease a cake-tin and line with greased paper to stand well above the side of the tin.

Sieve the flour and soda.

Rub the fat into the flour.

Add the sugar and ground almonds, and mix together.

Beat up the eggs, add the golden syrup, and whisk well; if necessary, the latter may be warmed slightly.

Add these to the dry ingredients, with a little milk as required.

When well mixed, beat for a few minutes.

Put into the greased cake-tin and bake in a moderately hot oven for about one hour and a half.

GROUND RICE CAKE

INGREDIENTS.—6 oz. of ground rice, 6 oz. of flour, ½ lb. of butter or margarine, ½ lb. of castor sugar, 3 eggs, 1½ teaspoonfuls of baking-powder, vanilla flavouring, milk.

METHOD.—Grease a cake-tin and line with greased paper so that the latter stands well above the sides of the tin.

Sieve together the flour, ground rice, and baking-powder.

Beat the sugar and fat to a cream.

Stir in each egg very quickly, and get the first well beaten in before adding the next.

When all are added, fold in the ground rice, etc., together with a little milk as required.

Add a few drops of flavouring and mix all together lightly.

Put into the prepared tin and bake in a moderately hot oven for about one to one hour and a half.

Lessen the heat after the first twenty minutes and, when sufficiently brown, cover with a paper (not greased).

When cooked, turn carefully on to a sieve and leave until cold.

GROUND RICE CAKE

INGREDIENTS.—3 oz. of ground rice, 3 oz. of flour, 4 oz. of margarine, 4 oz. of castor sugar, 2 eggs, 1 teaspoonful of baking-powder, milk.

METHOD.—Whisk up the eggs. Beat the sugar and fat to a cream. Sieve the flour with the ground rice and baking-powder, and add them to the creamed fat and sugar, stirring in the eggs at the same time.

Mix together lightly, and add a little milk if required. Turn the mixture into a cake-tin and bake the cake in a moderately hot oven.

GROUND RICE FRUIT CAKE

INGREDIENTS.—¼ lb. of ground rice, ¼ lb. of small seedless raisins, 6 oz. of margarine, ¼ lb. of flour, 1 teaspoonful of cream of tartar, ½ flat teaspoonful of carbonate of soda, 4 oz. of castor sugar, 2 eggs, milk.

METHOD.—Grease a cake-tin and line it with greased paper.

Wash, pick over and dry the fruit. Cream the fat and sugar. Add each egg separately, and beat the mixture for a few minutes.

When both eggs are added, gradually stir in the flour, ground rice, cream of tartar, and carbonate of soda (all sieved together), also the prepared fruit, adding some milk, *if required*.

Turn the mixture into the cake-tin, dredge the top with castor sugar, and put it into a moderately hot oven to bake.

It will take about an hour or a little longer to cook.

NOTE.—The packet raisins do not require washing.

GROUND SEED CAKE

INGREDIENTS.—¾ lb. of flour, ½ oz. of ground caraway seeds, ¼ flat teaspoonful of carbonate of soda, 5 oz. of margarine or dripping, 5 oz. of sugar, 2 oz. of peel, 1 or 2 eggs, 3 tablespoonfuls of golden syrup, milk or milk and water.

METHOD.—Grease a cake-tin and line with greased paper to stand well above the sides of the tin.

Sieve the flour, soda, and ground caraway seeds together.

Cut up the peel and add to the flour.

Cream the fat and sugar.

Beat up the eggs, warm the golden syrup and add and whisk together.

Add some of the flour, etc., and some of the egg, etc., alternately to the creamed fat and sugar until it is all mixed together, adding a little milk as required.

Beat the mixture for a few minutes and put it into the prepared tin.

Bake in a moderately hot oven for about one hour and a quarter.

HAYLEIGH CAKES

INGREDIENTS.—6 oz. of flour, 2 oz. of ground rice, 4 oz. of castor sugar,

5 oz. of margarine, 1 teaspoonful of baking-powder, 1 egg, milk, almond flavouring.

METHOD.—Grease about ten small cake-tins. Cream the sugar and fat together. Sieve the flour, ground rice, and baking-powder together. Beat the egg into the creamed sugar and fat, beat well for a few minutes.

Lightly stir in the flour, rice, and baking-powder, together with a few drops of almond flavouring and a little milk. Beat all together. Place in the greased tins. Bake in a hot oven for twenty minutes.

Sufficient to make about ten cakes.

HOLLY GATEAU

INGREDIENTS.—9 oz. of flour, 3 oz. of cornflour, 1 teaspoonful of baking-powder, 3 eggs, ½ lb. of castor sugar, milk, ½ lb. of butter or margarine.

FOR THE ICING.—10 oz. of icing sugar, ½ gill of cold water, vanilla flavouring.

FOR THE ALMOND PASTE DECORATION.—3 oz. of icing sugar, 3 oz. of ground almonds, about ½ a white of egg, vanilla, green and red colouring, a piece of imitation holly can be used instead, if preferred.

METHOD.—Grease a cake-tin and line with greased paper to stand above the sides. Sieve the flour, cornflour, and baking-powder. Beat the sugar and fat to a cream.

Add each egg separately, stir in quickly, and beat well before adding the next. When all have been beaten in, stir in the flour, etc., adding a little milk, if required, and mix together lightly.

Put into the prepared tin and bake in a moderately hot oven for about one to one and a half hours. Turn on to a sieve and leave until quite cold.

TO MAKE THE ALMOND PASTE.— Rub the icing sugar through a fine sieve, then mix with the ground almonds.

Add a few drops of vanilla. Whisk up the white of egg and add sufficient to mix it all to a stiff paste. Work it until smooth, then colour some of it red and some bright green. Make the red paste into small balls to represent the holly berries.

Roll out the green and cut some leaves, mark veins on them, and shape them to look natural. Mould some stems, then make up a few sprays. Put these aside.

TO MAKE THE ICING.—Rub the icing sugar through a fine sieve. Add the cold water and mix to a smooth paste. Stir in the vanilla. Stir the icing over a very low burner, until the bottom of the saucepan feels warm.

TO ICE THE CAKE.—Stand it on a rack over a dish and pour the icing over, and coat it evenly. Leave for a minute or two, then arrange the holly sprays on the top.

When the icing is quite set, lift the cake carefully on to a lace paper.

HOLLY SANDWICH

INGREDIENTS.—4½ oz. of margarine, 6 oz. of castor sugar, 6 oz. of flour, 1 teaspoonful of baking-powder, 2 eggs, grated rind and juice of 1 orange, milk.

FOR THE FILLING.—Apricot jam.

FOR THE ICING.—¾ to 1 lb. of icing sugar, white of 1 egg, orange-juice.

METHOD.—Beat the sugar and fat to a cream. Add each egg separately. Stir the first in quickly and beat the mixture well before adding the next egg.

When both are well beaten in, add the grated orange-rind, and stir in the flour, sifted with the baking-powder, adding the orange-juice, and then some milk, if required.

Mix all together lightly, then turn the mixture into two buttered sandwich-tins, and bake it till spongy. Cool the two sponges on a sieve and, when cold, sandwich them together with apricot jam. Pour the icing over the cake and, when it is nearly set, sprinkle it with desiccated coconut and stick a sprig of holly in the centre.

TO MAKE THE ICING.—Sift the icing sugar and mix it to a thick coating consistency with the lightly beaten egg-white and some strained orange-juice as required.

HONEY BUNS

INGREDIENTS.—1 lb. of flour, 1 lemon (rind only), 1 egg, 2 teaspoonfuls of baking-powder, ½ lb. of butter or margarine, 4 tablespoonfuls of honey, milk, 4 oz. of sugar.

METHOD.—Sieve the flour.

Mix the baking-powder with about a tablespoonful of the flour and put aside.

Rub the fat into the flour.

Grate the lemon-rind, and add.

Add the sugar, and mix all the dry ingredients together.

Beat up the egg, and add with the honey, and some milk as required.

When well mixed, beat for five minutes, then stir in the baking-powder.

Put into small greased cake-tins and bake in a hot oven for about twenty minutes.

NOTE.—Do not make the mixture too moist.

HONEY CAKE

INGREDIENTS.—2 eggs, 4 oz. of sugar, 2 oz. of brown honey, ¼ level teaspoonful of ginger, ½ level teaspoonful of grated dried orange-peel, breadcrumbs, 4 oz. of flour, water.

METHOD.—Beat the egg-yolks well with half the sugar.

Warm the honey and the rest of the sugar. Beat them until they are cool, and add them to the sugar and eggs, Stir in the ginger and orange-peel. flour, and a spoonful or two of water, and lastly add the beaten egg-whites.

Pour the mixture into a greased cake-tin which has been sprinkled with breadcrumbs, and bake in a steady oven.

HONEY GINGERBREAD

INGREDIENTS.—6 oz. of honey, ½ lb. of flour, 3 oz. of margarine, 3 oz. of sugar, 1 teaspoonful of ground ginger, ¼ teaspoonful of mixed spice, ¼ flat teaspoonful of carbonate of soda, 1 egg, milk.

METHOD.—Sieve the flour with the ground ginger and spice, and put them into a basin, making a well in the centre.

Put the margarine, honey, and sugar into a saucepan to dissolve (but do not boil), then cool them slightly.

Whisk up the egg, and stir into it the honey, etc. Then pour the egg mixture into the centre of the flour and mix all together, adding a little milk as required.

Beat well for a few minutes, then stir in the soda mixed smoothly in a spoonful of milk.

Turn the mixture into a greased baking-tin, and put it into a moderately hot oven to bake. It will take about forty-five minutes to cook.

Put the cake on to a sieve to cool, and when it is cold cut it into even-sized pieces.

If preferred, the mixture may be baked in a cake-tin, but it will require more time.

NOTE.—Plain, everyday gingerbread can be made in the same way, using golden syrup instead of honey.

A few almonds or a little candied peel may be added to give variety. The spice may be omitted, if not liked.

ICINGS FOR CAKES

IN all kinds of icings which contain icing sugar the sugar should first be rubbed through a hair sieve. If it is very lumpy it should be crushed first with a rolling-pin.

SOFT ICING

THIS is made with sieved icing sugar and water. Put the sugar into a saucepan and mix it to a smooth, thick paste with water (either cold or warm). For each half a pound of sugar, about one and a half or two tablespoonfuls of water will be required. Stir the icing over a *very low* burner, until the base of the pan feels just warm, then pour over the cake.

If you make soft icing too warm it will lose its gloss.

It should be of a coating consistency. It can be flavoured with any suitable essence—vanilla, orange, etc., and coloured, if liked.

Pineapple syrup, ginger syrup, or caramel may be used to mix the icing sugar instead of water. Any of these give the icing a distinct flavour.

CHOCOLATE ICING

INGREDIENTS.—10 oz. of icing sugar, ½ gill of water, ¼ teaspoonful of vanilla flavouring, 2 oz. of chocolate (grated) or powder.

METHOD.—Rub the icing sugar through a hair sieve.

Place the grated chocolate in a

saucepan with the water and stir over the fire until dissolved.

Leave until cool.

Add the sieved icing sugar and stir all together over the fire until warm and smooth.

Flavour with vanilla.

The icing is of the right consistency if it coats the back of the spoon.

Be careful not to get it too hot after the sugar is added or it will lose its glossy appearance.

BOILED ICING

INGREDIENTS.—½ lb. of white sugar, ½ gill of water, a pinch of cream of tartar, 1 egg-white, vanilla or other suitable essence.

METHOD.—Put the sugar with the water into a saucepan, and dissolve it slowly.

Bring it to the boil, add a good pinch of cream of tartar, and boil (without stirring) until a small quantity, when dropped into cold water and left for a few seconds, becomes a soft ball when lifted out and rubbed between the fingers.

When ready, pour gradually the icing on to a stiffly whisked egg-white, keeping it well stirred, add a few drops of flavouring essence, then pour it over the cake.

NOTE.—When making boiled icing every grain of sugar must be dissolved before it comes to the boil.

ALMOND PASTE ICING

INGREDIENTS.—1½ lb. of icing sugar, 1½ lb. of ground almonds, whites of about 5 eggs, vanilla flavouring.

METHOD.—Roll the lumps out of the sugar and rub it through a hair sieve.

Add the ground almonds and mix together.

Whisk the whites slightly and add sufficient, with a few drops of vanilla flavouring, to mix it to a stiff paste.

Work it until smooth, then roll it out.

ICING A CAKE WITH ALMOND PASTE

Cover the sides of the cake with a wide strip of paste, then cut out a round and fix on to the top.

Be sure to make the sides and top perfectly level, paying special attention to the edge.

Place the cake on an upturned dish and put into a very *cool* oven to dry for about half an hour ; then leave for at least a day before icing it with the royal icing.

To MAKE MISTLETOE AND HOLLY FROM ALMOND PASTE

Mould some almond paste into small balls for the mistletoe berries. Colour some of the paste to a pale green, mould some stalks from this, roll out the remainder for the leaves. Cut them out and mark veins on them, then make up a spray of mistletoe.

Make also a spray of holly, colouring some of the paste to bright green for the leaves, and some red for the berries.

Fruit can be fashioned from moulded and coloured almond paste. The most realistic apples are achieved by using a clove pushed through a ball of the paste to represent the apple's core.

ROYAL ICING

INGREDIENTS.—1 lb. of best icing sugar, 2 whites of eggs, 1 dessertspoonful of lemon-juice, for piping add 1 more white of egg.

METHOD.—If the sugar is lumpy it must be put on a pastry-board and crushed with a rolling-pin. All icing sugar, whether lumpy or not, should be rubbed through a hair sieve. A wire sieve is not suitable, as the meshes are too coarse.

Having sieved the sugar, the whites of egg should be beaten to a light froth (not at all stiff, or the icing will be hard). The egg is only beaten stiffly when required for piping and elaborate ornamenting.

Add the egg and the strained lemon-juice to the icing sugar, making a hollow in the centre. Stir till mixed, and then beat well. The longer the icing is beaten the finer in texture and the whiter it will become.

It should be beaten for at least fifteen minutes.

NOTE.—The above recipe is for royal icing that is to be spread on the cake. For elaborate piping three eggs are better, as the icing will dry quicker and keep its shape.

Do not make large quantities of icing ; a pound is usually enough at a time. It hardens when exposed to the air for long, and should be covered in the basin with a piece of damp muslin.

Lemon-juice is added to the icing, not so much to flavour it as to render it more pliable and easier to work. It should never be omitted.

There are various ways of using this icing. One of the most simple is to cover the cake *roughly* with icing, giving the appearance of snow ; this is very suitable for a Christmas cake and most effective.

If a more elaborate method of icing is required, cover the cake smoothly all over with a layer of royal icing and when this has hardened decorate it by forcing icing through an icing bag.

Before beginning to do this, it is necessary first to decide on a suitable design.

In addition to the icing bag, a few icing tubes will be required. The Rose, Shell, and Plain or Piping tubes are the most useful, the latter being used chiefly for writing on cakes.

It is most important to get the icing to the correct consistency. It must not be *too* stiff or it is difficult to manipulate, but if it is too soft the pattern will " run."

It is not advisable to make more of this icing at one time than is required for immediate use, as it so soon hardens.

USING AN ICING BAG

THE icing bags can be bought for about a shilling, and the tubes cost about threepence each. Then you will also require a screw which you fix on to whatever tube you want to use. The tube is put through the bottom of the bag and fixed securely to the latter with a piece of string tied round the screw. After use, the bags and tubes, etc., must be washed and thoroughly rinsed and dried before being put away. New ones should also be washed before being used.

To Fill and Use the Icing Bag

Open the bag as much as possible by turning the top part half-way down on to the outside. Put in some icing, close up bag again, and twist it round and round, beginning at the top, until you get down to the icing, then force it out. Remember not to fill more than half the bag at a time.

Always decide on a design before starting, and force some of the icing on to a plate first to test it before forcing it on to the cake.

If icing a log cake, use a shell-pattern tube and force the icing in straight lines from end to end until it is completely covered.

Suggestions for Icing a Round Cake

Force about five or seven straight lines of icing across the top, all in the same direction, keeping one exactly in the centre and the others at equal distances apart. Then cross these with the same number of lines in the opposite direction.

Put also a line of icing all round the top edge.

Either a shell, rose, or ribbon pattern are most suitable for this.

Another pretty effect is obtained by using two colours in this way. Mark four lines across the top of the cake, dividing it into quarters, and force small rose patterns into each, completely filling them and using alternate colours for each quarter.

Simple decorations are usually more effective than elaborate ones.

Decorating Cakes

Icing can be made to look very attractive by the addition of a little colouring. Small bottles of mauve, pink, green, etc., can be obtained from the big stores at a cost of about $6\frac{1}{2}$d. per bottle.

Crystallised flowers and angelica together can be made into pretty sprays of flowers for decorating iced cakes.

Little Esquimaux figures, Father Christmas figures, bells and candle holders can all be obtained from a first-class confectioners.

They should be fixed in place with a dab of icing.

BUTTER ICING

BUTTER ICING is one of the most simple kinds of icing to make. It is used chiefly for cakes of a spongy or Madeira mixture.

There are many varieties of it—vanilla, coffee, chocolate—but the same foundation is used for all.

The most important point to remember when making this icing is that the butter must not be *oiled*.

Margarine can be used instead of butter, but the icing is much more creamy if butter is used.

Vanilla Butter Icing

INGREDIENTS.—½ lb. of icing sugar, ¼ lb. of butter, vanilla flavouring.

METHOD.—Roll the lumps out of the sugar, and rub it through a hair sieve. Beat the butter and sugar to a cream. Stir in a few drops of vanilla to flavour.

NOTE.—If very hard the butter may be warmed slightly, but be careful not to oil it. This icing can be coloured to any desired shade. It can also be varied by adding different flavourings—lemon, orange, etc.

Coffee Butter Icing

INGREDIENTS.—½ lb. of icing sugar, 3 oz. of butter, coffee essence—as required.

METHOD.—Make as in the previous recipe, adding sufficient coffee essence to colour and flavour.

Chocolate Butter Icing

INGREDIENTS.—9 oz. of icing sugar, 4 oz. of butter, 2 oz. of grated chocolate or cocoa, about 2 or 3 tablespoonfuls of milk, vanilla flavouring.

METHOD.—Put the chocolate into a saucepan and mix with milk. Let it dissolve slowly, keeping it well stirred, then cool slightly and add to the creamed butter and sugar.

Do not use any more milk than necessary to mix with the chocolate or the icing will be too moist.

Using Butter Icing

The simplest method to ice a cake is just to spread it over with a knife; it can then be coated with chopped nuts or desiccated coconut, etc.

Another way is to put the butter icing into an icing bag and force it on to the cake.

To ensure success when doing it in this way the icing must be just the correct consistency. If too soft the pattern will not remain distinct, and if too stiff it is very difficult to force through the bag.

If, when first made, it is a little soft, as is sometimes the case, leave for about ten minutes or until it becomes a little stiffer. Do not let it get too stiff, and always beat it up again just before putting it into the bag.

If liked, the sides of the cake can be iced by the first method and the top by the second.

PLAIN ICED CAKE

INGREDIENTS.—½ lb. of flour, ¼ lb. of castor sugar, 2 eggs and 1 extra yolk, ¼ lb. of margarine, 1½ teaspoonfuls of baking-powder, milk (if required).

METHOD.—Grease a round cake-tin and line the sides with greased paper, so that the paper comes a few inches above the top of the tin.

Mix the sugar and margarine together and beat well until it resembles thick cream.

Mix the flour and baking-powder together and put through a wire sieve.

Add the yolk of egg to the creamed sugar and fat; stir quickly. When well mixed in add the other eggs, stirring each in separately. Beat all well together.

Lightly fold the flour and baking-powder into the other ingredients.

Add a little milk if required.

Pour this mixture into the prepared cake-tin and bake in a moderately hot oven for three-quarters of an hour.

To Test if Cooked.—Put a warm iron skewer into the middle of the cake, then draw it out again. If the cake is cooked the skewer will be quite clean, but if the cake adheres to the skewer this proves the cake is not quite cooked.

When the cake is cooked turn it carefully on to a sieve and leave until cold.

The Icing

INGREDIENTS.—½ lb. of icing sugar, 1 white of an egg, 1 teaspoonful of vanilla flavouring, cold water to mix (about 1 tablespoonful), a few drops of cochineal, crystallised rose leaves.

METHOD.—Put the icing sugar through a sieve, then put it into a saucepan.

Slightly beat the white of egg and add the vanilla flavouring to it. Add these to the icing sugar, also sufficient cold water to make a smooth paste.

Stir over the fire until warm.

Colour with cochineal until it is pale pink.

The consistency of the icing should be just so that it will coat the back of the spoon.

Icing the Cake

Place the cake upside down on a cake-rack over a dish—if this is not obtainable use the rack of the grill-tin.

If the cake has risen much and will not stand well, cut a piece of the raised part off.

Pour the prepared icing carefully over the top of the cake, and it will gradually fall over the sides and coat the sides as well as the top.

Leave until the icing is set.

Place carefully on to a lace paper on a dish.

Decorate the top of the cake with the rose leaves.

ICED CHERRY CAKE

INGREDIENTS.—6 oz. of butter or margarine, $\frac{1}{2}$ lb. of flour, 6 oz. of castor sugar, 4 oz. of glacé cherries, 2 oz. of citron peel, 3 eggs, $\frac{1}{2}$ teaspoonful of baking-powder.

FOR THE ICING.—$\frac{1}{2}$ lb. of icing sugar, 2 tablespoonfuls of tepid water.

METHOD.—Grease and line a pound and a half cake tin.

Cut the cherries in half and the peel in short strips.

Sift the flour and baking-powder.

Cream the butter till it is soft, add the sugar and beat well.

Add the eggs unbeaten, one at a time, and beat the mixture after adding each one till it is light and creamy.

Stir in the flour, adding a very little milk if necessary.

Put the cake-mixture in the tin and bake it in a moderate oven for about an hour.

Remove the paper and put the cake on a sieve or grid to cool.

When it is quite cold rub the icing sugar through a hair sieve and put it in a thin saucepan with the water.

Put the cake ready on a plate turned upside down on a large plate or tin.

Stir the icing over a moderately high gas for a short time (about twelve seconds) till the icing softens sufficiently to coat the spoon.

Pour most of the icing over the cake, leaving a tablespoonful in the pan. Colour this icing pink with cochineal and place it in a small paper cornet.

Enclose it carefully at the wide end and cut a tiny piece off the pointed end.

At one side of the cake press out a zig-zag line, then a straight one next to it with a few dots alongside. Repeat this design at the other side.

No icing pump or tubes are required. Finish with a cherry in the centre.

ICED CHOCOLATE CAKE

INGREDIENTS.—6 oz. of butter or margarine, $\frac{1}{2}$ lb. of flour, 6 oz. of castor sugar, vanilla flavouring, 3 eggs, 6 oz. of grated chocolate or chocolate powder, $\frac{1}{2}$ gill of milk, 1 teaspoonful of baking-powder.

METHOD.—Grease a cake-tin and line it with paper.

Cream the sugar and fat together till they resemble thick cream.

Grate the chocolate and dissolve it in a saucepan with the milk.

Mix the flour with baking-powder and put through a sieve.

Beat each egg separately into the creamed sugar and fat.

Add the dissolved chocolate and mix well.

Lightly fold in the flour and baking-powder; add a little more milk if required.

Add the vanilla and mix all lightly together.

Put into the prepared tin and bake in a moderately hot oven for about one hour.

When cooked, turn carefully on to a sieve and leave until cold. Then ice with chocolate icing.

Chocolate Icing

INGREDIENTS.—9 oz. of icing sugar, $\frac{1}{2}$ a gill of water, vanilla flavouring, 2 oz. of chocolate (grated or powder), crystallised violets.

METHOD.—Place the grated chocolate in a saucepan with the water and stir over the fire until dissolved.

Leave until cool.

Add the sieved icing sugar and vanilla, and mix together until smooth.

Stir over a very low burner until the base of the pan feels warm.

The consistency should be just so that it will coat the back of the spoon ; if necessary, a little more cold water or sieved sugar may be added.

NOTE.—The icing must not get hot after the sugar is added or it will lose its gloss.

ICED CREAM SANDWICH

INGREDIENTS.—5 oz. of flour, 1 flat teaspoonful of baking-powder, 2 eggs, ¼ lb. of castor sugar, 3 oz. of butter or margarine, milk.

FOR THE FILLING.—Raspberry jam, 4 oz. of icing sugar, 2 oz. of butter, vanilla.

FOR THE TOP ICING.—A few chopped nuts, 10 oz. of icing sugar, ½ gill of water, cochineal, vanilla flavouring.

METHOD.—Grease a jam-sandwich tin and line with greased paper so that the latter stands about an inch above the top of the tin.

Sieve together the flour and baking-powder.

Whisk up the sugar and butter to a cream, add the eggs separately.

Stir each one in quickly and beat well for about ten minutes.

Fold in the flour and baking-powder, mix together lightly, adding a little milk if necessary.

Spread evenly over the prepared tin and bake in a hot oven for about ten to fifteen minutes.

Turn on to a sieve and leave until cold.

THE FILLING

Sieve the icing sugar, then cream the butter and sugar together and flavour with vanilla.

Split the sandwich into halves, spread with jam, then with a thick layer of the prepared filling.

THE ICING

Roll the lumps out of the sugar and rub through a fine sieve, put it into a saucepan, and mix to a smooth paste with the water.

Flavour with vanilla and colour with a few drops of cochineal.

Stir over a very low burner until the base of the pan feels just warm.

Pour the icing over the sandwich and coat it evenly.

Sprinkle the chopped nuts round the top edge on the icing. Serve on a lace paper.

NOTE.—If the icing is of the correct consistency it will coat the back of the spoon. Add more sieved sugar or water if required.

ICED CUP CAKES

INGREDIENTS.—½ lb. of flour, 6 oz. of margarine, 4 oz. of castor sugar, ½ flat teaspoonful of baking-powder, a little milk.

FOR THE ICING.—6 oz. of icing sugar, 1½ tablespoonfuls of cold water, cochineal, vanilla flavouring, hundreds and thousands.

METHOD.—Sieve the flour with the baking-powder.

Cream the fat and sugar. Stir in the flour and baking-powder and mix to a fairly *stiff* consistency, adding just a little milk as required.

Turn the mixture into baking-cups, only three parts full, and put them into a moderately hot oven. They should take about twenty minutes to cook.

When cold spread a little icing on top of each cake and sprinkle it with hundreds and thousands.

THE WATER ICING

To make the icing, rub the icing sugar through a hair sieve. Put it into a saucepan and mix it to a thick paste with cold water. Flavour it with vanilla and colour slightly with cochineal.

Stand the saucepan over a *low* burner and stir the icing until the base of the pan feels warm, then use as required. Sufficient for twenty cakes.

ICED DESSERT CAKES

INGREDIENTS.—6 oz. of flour, 2 oz. of coconut, ¼ lb. of margarine or butter, 1½ oz. of glacé cherries, 2 eggs, 1 teaspoonful of baking-powder, few drops of ratafia flavouring, milk (about ½ gill), 5 oz. of white sugar.

METHOD.—Grease some small, round, plain cake-tins.

Cream the sugar and fat together.

Sieve the flour with the baking-powder and mix with the coconut.

Cut the cherries into small pieces.

Beat the eggs separately into the

creamed sugar and fat; beat well for a few minutes.

Add the dry ingredients gradually together with the cherries and a little milk.

Mix all together, add the ratafia flavouring.

Put the mixture into greased tins and bake in a hot oven for twenty minutes. Place on a sieve until cold.

THE ICING

INGREDIENTS.—10 oz. of icing sugar, ½ gill of cold water, vanilla flavouring, cochineal.

METHOD.—Sieve the icing sugar.

Place in a saucepan, add the water, and mix well together until smooth.

Slightly warm it, add the vanilla essence, and colour pale pink with a few drops of cochineal. Pour sufficient icing on each cake just to coat the top of it. Decorate with glacé cherries.

ICED GENOESE SANDWICHES

INGREDIENTS.—4 oz. of castor sugar, 3 egg, 3½ oz. of flour, 2½ oz. of butter or margarine, raspberry jam.

FOR THE ICING.—10 oz. of icing sugar, ½ gill of cold water, mauve colouring, vanilla flavouring, crystallised violets and rose leaves.

METHOD.—Grease a small baking-sheet and line with greased paper so that it stands about an inch above the top of the sheet.

Place the eggs and sugar in a basin over a saucepan of warm water, and whisk over the fire until the mixture becomes thick and creamy and free from dark streaks.

It will take about fifteen to twenty minutes. Be careful not to overheat, or the eggs will curdle.

Remove the basin from the saucepan and cool slightly. Sieve the flour. Melt the butter.

Fold the flour lightly into the eggs and sugar, together with the melted butter. Mix all together lightly and spread evenly over the prepared baking-sheet. Bake in a hot oven for about eight or ten minutes, or until it feels spongy. It should only be lightly browned.

When cooked, turn over gently on to a sheet of paper and remove the greased paper from the sponge. Place on a sieve to cool.

TO MAKE THE SANDWICHES

Stand the sponge on a board and cut it into small, pretty shapes—half-moons, diamonds, rounds, etc. Split each into halves and spread with raspberry jam, then fit together again.

Stand them on a cake-rack over a dish, ready for icing. Leave a space between each.

THE ICING

Sieve the icing sugar. Use a fine-meshed sieve. Place in a saucepan, pour on the water, and mix until smooth.

Flavour with vanilla, and stir over a small burner until the icing is just warm. Do not make it hot or it will lose its gloss. The icing should be sufficiently thick to coat the back of the spoon.

Pour about one tablespoonful of the icing on each sandwich and coat it all over.

Coat half the number with the white icing, then add a few drops of colouring to the remainder of the icing and coat the rest of the sandwiches.

Place a small piece of crystallised rose-leaf in the centre of the white cakes and a piece of violet on the mauve cakes. Leave until the icing is set, then place carefully in small paper cases and serve on a lace paper.

ICED OPERA CAKES

INGREDIENTS.—½ lb. of ground rice, 3 eggs, 6 oz. of castor sugar, 1 lemon (grated rind) or ratafia flavouring.

METHOD.—Grease some very small cake-tins. Whisk the sugar and eggs together for fifteen minutes.

Add the ground rice and grated lemond-rind.

Mix all well together, pour into prepared tins.

Bake in a hot oven for about ten to fifteen minutes. Place on a sieve and leave until cold.

Dip each cake in glacé icing. (Use a skewer to do this.) Decorate with rose leaves, whole or crushed.

Serve in paper cases.

THE GLACE ICING

INGREDIENTS.—1 lb. of loaf sugar, water to cover (about ½ pint).

METHOD.—Place the sugar and water in a saucepan and dissolve.

Bring to the boil and boil until it

is reduced to a syrup (about fifteen minutes). Remove from fire and stir slowly until it is white and thick. Ice cakes quickly, before the icing sets.

ICED ORANGE LAYER CAKE

INGREDIENTS.—3 eggs, 7 oz. of margarine, ½ lb. of castor sugar, ¾ lb. of flour, 1 teaspoonful of baking-powder, milk, if required.

FOR THE FILLING.—2 or 3 oranges (according to size), 2 oz. of flour, 1 oz. of butter, whites of 2 eggs, ¼ lb. of castor sugar.

FOR THE ICING.—½ gill of orange-juice, 10 oz. of icing sugar.

METHOD.—Grease a round cake-tin, and line with greased paper to come above the tin.

Sieve the flour with the baking-powder.

Separate the yolks from the whites of eggs.

Beat the fat and sugar to a cream.

Whisk the whites to a very stiff froth.

Beat up the yolks, and briskly stir half into the creamed fat and sugar.

Beat well, then stir in the remainder.

Beat again for ten minutes.

Stir in the flour and a little milk as required.

Fold in the whisked whites (very lightly).

Place in the greased cake-tin, and bake in a moderately hot oven for about an hour, until it is lightly browned and spongy.

Turn carefully on to a sieve, and leave until cold.

THE FILLING

Wipe the oranges and finely grate the rinds. Squeeze, and strain the juice.

Mix the flour to a smooth paste with the orange-juice.

Turn into a saucepan and add the sugar, rinds, and butter.

Bring to the boil and boil gently for a few minutes, keeping it stirred. The mixture should now be like a thick sauce; if the oranges are not very juicy it may be necessary to add a little water.

Whisk the whites to a stiff froth.

Let the mixture cool, then stir the whites in lightly

Split the cake into three, spread the filling over each piece, then fit together again.

If the cake has risen much in the centre, cut off a slice and make it level.

Turn it upside down on a cake-rack over a dish, ready for icing.

THE ICING

Sieve the sugar. Squeeze the oranges and strain the juice. Put into a saucepan, and mix together until quite smooth.

Warm the mixture, keeping it well stirred all the time.

The icing should coat the back of the spoon.

Pour it over the cake and coat it all over.

Thinly slice a small round of orange-rind or place a slice of crystallised orange in the centre.

Leave until the icing is set, then move carefully on to a lace paper.

ANOTHER ORANGE FILLING

This filling can be used, if liked, instead of the above.

INGREDIENTS.—3 oz. of butter, 6 oz. of icing sugar, a few crystallised orange slices, orange flavouring.

METHOD.—Roll the lumps out of the icing sugar, and rub it through a fine sieve.

Add the butter and beat both to a cream.

Cut the crystallised orange slices into small pieces, and mix in with a few drops of orange flavouring.

ICED ORANGE SPONGE

INGREDIENTS.—3 eggs, their weight in butter, sugar, and flour, 1 teaspoonful of baking-powder, rind of orange (grated), juice of ½ orange (strained).

METHOD.—Grease a jam sandwich-tin and line with paper.

Cream the fat and sugar together.

Sieve the flour and baking-powder.

Add the grated lemon-rind to the flour.

Beat the eggs separately into the creamed fat and sugar; beat well for a few minutes.

Lightly fold in the flour, etc., and the juice of half the orange.

Put into the prepared tin.

Bake in a hot oven for ten to fifteen minutes.

Place on a sieve to cool.
Then ice with Orange Icing.

THE ORANGE ICING

INGREDIENTS.—10 oz. of icing sugar, ½ gill of orange-juice (strained).

METHOD.—Sieve the icing sugar. Mix well together with the juice until smooth. Place in a saucepan and make slightly warm ; stir well all the time.

Place sandwich on a cake - rack. Pour the icing over. Leave until set. Serve on a lace paper.

NOTE.—If the sandwich has risen very much, cut a small piece off the top and turn it upside down to ice it.

ICED PYRAMIDS

INGREDIENTS.—½ lb. of cake crumbs, 2 or 3 tablespoonfuls of sherry.

FOR THE ICING.—½ lb. of icing sugar, warm water, flavouring essence and colouring as desired, stalks of angelica.

METHOD.—To obtain the cake crumbs, rub some stale cake through a wire sieve, or crumble it finely.

A mixture of Madeira and chocolate cake crumbs makes a very good combination.

Put them into a basin and mix them to a stiff paste with the sherry. Divide this mixture into eight portions, and form each into a smooth pyramid.

To MAKE THE ICING.—Rub the sugar through a hair sieve and mix it to a smooth paste with one or two tablespoonfuls of warm water.

The icing may be flavoured with coffee essence, which will also colour it, or it may be coloured with cochineal and flavoured with vanilla.

The icing must be of a coating consistency, so add more water or sugar if required.

To ICE THE PYRAMIDS.—Put them on a cake - rack, leaving a space between each. Stand the rack on a meat dish, and cover each pyramid by pouring a spoonful of icing over it.

When the icing is set decorate the pyramids with trails of Royal Icing (see p. 486) in a contrasting colour. Decorate each pyramid with a stalk of angelica on top.

To make the trails, force the icing through a pump with a piping tube affixed.

ICED SHORTBREAD BISCUITS

INGREDIENTS.—5 oz. of flour, good pinch of mixed spice, 1 oz. of currants, 3 oz. of margarine, 2 oz. of castor sugar.

FOR THE ICING.—¼ lb. of icing sugar, about a tablespoonful of water, vanilla flavouring.

METHOD.—Cream the fat and sugar, stir in the flour, spice, and currants (previously cleaned), and work it all into a stiff paste.

Turn the paste on to a lightly floured board, roll it out thinly and cut it into rounds.

Place them on a lightly greased baking - sheet and bake in a very moderate oven for about twenty minutes.

When the biscuits are cold, make some thin white icing, pour a little in the centre of each biscuit and spread it to the edge. Leave the icing to set. The currants should show through the icing.

THE WATER ICING

To make the icing, rub the sugar through a hair sieve. Put it into a saucepan and mix it with the water. Add vanilla flavouring to taste and stir it over a *low* burner until the base of the pan feels warm.

The icing should not be quite thick enough to coat.

Sufficient to make about twelve biscuits.

ICED TEA BISCUITS

INGREDIENTS.—1 lb. of plain flour, 5 oz. of margarine, 4 oz. of castor sugar, 1 egg, ¼ teaspoonful of cinnamon, raspberry jam.

FOR THE ICING.—½ lb. of icing sugar, 1 tablespoonful of water, 1 tablespoonful of syrup from the jam, cochineal.

METHOD.—Cream the margarine and sugar together with a wooden spoon.

When they are soft and white, add the flour and cinnamon and mix them well.

Beat the egg and stir it into the dough ; then knead all together with the hands until it is of the same consistency throughout.

Turn it on to a floured board and roll it out to one-eighth of an inch thickness.

Cut it into small rounds and bake them in a moderate oven for about fifteen minutes.

When the biscuits are cold, stick two together with a little jam and ice their tops.

To Make the Icing.—Sift the sugar and put it into a saucepan with the water and syrup.

Stir it over the gas for ten seconds, or until it is liquid enough to coat the back of the spoon. Add two or three drops of cochineal.

Pour a teaspoonful of the icing over the top of each biscuit.

ICED TRIANGLES

Ingredients.—3 oz. of castor sugar, 3 oz. of margarine, 1 whole egg and 1 yolk, 3 oz. of flour, 1 level teaspoonful of baking-powder, milk.

For the Filling.—3 oz. of icing sugar, 1½ oz. of ground almonds, flavouring essence, green colouring, water, lemon-cheese.

For the Icing.—10 oz. of icing sugar, white of 1 egg, water, green colouring, flavouring essence.

Method.—Cream the fat and sugar. Beat in the yolk of egg, then add the whole egg, stirring them in quickly and beating the mixture well.

Sift the flour with the baking-powder and stir them in lightly, adding a little milk as required. Bake the mixture in a buttered sandwich tin.

To Make the Filling.—Sift the icing sugar and mix it with the ground almonds. Mix them to a stiff paste with the lightly beaten egg-white and water (using about one-fourth of the egg-white for the icing). Add flavouring to taste and colour the filling to a pretty green shade.

Form the filling into a smooth lump and roll it out to a round the size of your cake. Split the latter in half and spread each piece with a thin layer of lemon cheese. Cover one piece with the round of green almond paste. Sandwich the two halves together, then cut the cake into twelve triangles.

To Make the Icing.—Sift the icing sugar and mix it to a smooth thick paste with the lightly beaten egg-white and a little water as required.

Add flavouring essence to taste, and green colouring to tone with the filling.

This icing should be stiff enough just to hold its shape.

Force it through a shell-patterned icing tube and ice the top of each triangle, beginning at the pointed end, and working from side to side of the triangle.

Sufficient to make twelve triangles.

JACK-IN-THE-BOX CAKE

Ingredients.—1 lb. of flour, ¾ lb. of margarine, ¾ lb. of castor sugar, ⅓ lb. of sultanas, 2 oz. of candied peel, 4 eggs, 1 teaspoonful of baking-powder, a little milk, 4 oz. of glacé cherries.

For the Decoration.—A little jam, 2 oz. of desiccated coconut, ½ lb. of ground almonds and icing sugar, 1 small egg, 1 dessertspoonful of lemon-juice.

Method.—Grease a deep square cake (or biscuit) tin, and line it with greased paper to come just above the edge.

Clean the sultanas, chop the peel and cut the cherries in half.

Cream the margarine and sugar till soft.

Add the eggs (unbeaten) one at a time and beat the mixture for five minutes between each egg.

Stir in the fruit and add a very little milk.

Sift the flour and baking-powder and stir in lightly.

Turn the mixture into the lined tin and hollow out the centre to make the cake flat when it rises.

Bake for about two hours in a moderate oven.

When cold, brush over the cake with jam and sprinkle it with coconut.

Make a hole in the top and put in a napkin ring or cork covered with greaseproof paper. This will form the neck of the Jack-in-the-Box.

For the decorations, rub the icing sugar through a hair sieve and mix it with the ground almonds. Beat the egg and add it, also the lemon-juice. Mix and knead the paste till smooth. Use a little of it to cover the " neck " and make the rest into a ball for the head. Set it in place and make the eyes with bits of cherries or currants, and the mouth with a piece of peel.

A foolscap sheet of paper is used as a cap and the lid of the box is made of thick cardboard covered with white or silver paper.

JAM BUNS

INGREDIENTS.—½ lb. of flour, 1 level teaspoonful of baking-powder, ¼ lb. of margarine, ¼ lb. of castor sugar, 1 yolk of egg, milk, jam.

METHOD.—Sift the flour into a basin with the baking-powder.

Rub in the fat and add the sugar. When they are well mixed, moisten them with the beaten egg-yolk, and a little milk as required to make a fairly stiff paste.

Roll out the paste to about a good eighth of an inch thick, and stamp it into rounds four inches in diameter.

Turn these over on to the other side. Place a little jam in the centre of each.

Damp the edges and draw them together, pinching them securely.

The jam should now be completely covered and the shapes still round, although smaller.

Turn the buns over and shape them evenly. Mark a cross on each with the back of a knife. Place them on a baking-sheet, brush them with milk, and put them in a hot oven to bake.

JAM SANDWICH

INGREDIENTS.—½ lb. of flour, 6 oz. of castor sugar, 2 eggs, 2 oz. of margarine, 1 teaspoonful of cream of tartar, ¼ flat teaspoonful of carbonate of soda, 1 tablespoonful of milk, jam.

METHOD.—Grease two sandwich-tins.

Whisk the sugar and eggs together for fifteen minutes.

Sieve the flour and cream of tartar together.

Put the margarine in a saucepan to melt, but do not allow it to get very hot.

Lightly fold the flour into the eggs and sugar.

Add the melted margarine.

Mix the soda in one tablespoonful of milk and lightly mix into the other ingredients.

Pour half the mixture into each tin. Bake in a hot oven for ten to fifteen minutes.

Place on a sieve until cold. When cold split each sandwich and spread with jam.

Place top over jam.

Sprinkle with castor sugar and cut each sandwich into eight pieces and serve.

ANOTHER JAM SANDWICH

INGREDIENTS.—2 eggs, 4 oz. of self-raising flour, 1 oz. of butter, 3 oz. of sugar, ½ a teaspoonful of baking-powder, 1 dessertspoonful of water, jam.

METHOD.—Grease two medium sandwich-tins.

Whisk the eggs and sugar till they are light and frothy.

Melt the butter, but do not make it hot, and stir it in.

Add the flour and water lightly, and last of all the baking-powder.

Pour the mixture into the tins and bake it for fifteen or twenty minutes in a moderately hot oven.

Spread jam between the two sponges when cold.

ONE EGG JAM SANDWICH

INGREDIENTS.—1 large fresh egg, 2 oz. of butter, ½ teacupful of sugar, 1 teacupful of flour, 1 teaspoonful of baking-powder, 1 tablespoonful of milk or water.

METHOD.—Grease a sandwich-tin.

Beat the butter and sugar together till thick and creamy.

Add the yolk of the egg and beat them well together.

Beat the white of the egg to a stiff froth.

Stir in the flour and white of egg alternately, mixing as lightly as possible.

Lastly add the milk and baking-powder and pour the mixture into the tin.

Bake it for fifteen minutes—split it open when cold and spread with jam.

JAP CAKES

INGREDIENTS.—2 egg-whites, about 2 tablespoonfuls of castor sugar, light brown cake or biscuit crumbs.

FOR THE BUTTER ICING.—½ lb. of icing sugar, ¼ lb. of butter, vanilla flavouring.

METHOD.—Add a pinch of salt to the egg-whites, and whisk to a very stiff froth, then fold in the castor sugar lightly. The amount of sugar required varies with the size of the egg-whites, but the meringue mixture must be sufficiently stiff to remain in position.

Put the mixture on to a lightly buttered tin in flat rounds to resemble fairly small biscuits, and place in a cool oven to dry, but do not brown. When ready, remove carefully from the tin and leave until cold.

Sandwich two or three of these meringue rounds together with a layer of butter icing between each.

Spread a layer of icing all round the outside as evenly as possible, and coat with finely powdered crumbs.

When finished, these cakes should resemble the shape of a fish-cake.

If liked, place half a glacé cherry or a dab of soft icing in the centre.

The Butter Icing

Roll the lumps out of the sugar and rub through a fine sieve.

Add the butter and beat both to a cream.

Stir in a few drops of vanilla flavouring.

Sufficient to make about eight or more, according to the size they are made.

JAZZ LAYER CAKE

INGREDIENTS.—1 lb. of flour, $\frac{3}{4}$ cup of granulated sugar, 5 oz. of margarine, 3 eggs, 2 teaspoonfuls of baking-powder, grated rind of 1 lemon, $\frac{1}{2}$ cup of milk.

FOR THE DECORATIONS.—8 oz. of icing sugar, 4 oz. of butter, 1 table-spoonful of lemon-juice, 2 oz. of chopped walnuts, 2 oz. of desiccated coconut, 2 oz. of chopped angelica, 2 oz. of chopped cherries.

METHOD.—Grease and line a large cake-tin.

Beat the margarine and sugar together.

Stir in the yolks of the eggs and lemon-rind and beat all well together.

Add the flour and milk alternately a little at a time.

Whisk the whites of the eggs stiffly and stir them in lightly, also the baking-powder.

Place the mixture in the tin and

bake it in a moderately hot oven for one hour.

To decorate the cake, cream the butter, and stir in the icing sugar and lemon-juice.

Split the cake in three when cold and spread it with the icing.

Sprinkle one layer with coconut and one with some chopped angelica and cherries.

Put the cake together and spread the outside with icing.

Roll the sides in chopped walnuts, and put dabs of chopped cherries, angelica, and coconut here and there on the top.

LARD CAKES

INGREDIENTS.—$\frac{3}{4}$ lb. of flour, 4 oz. of lard, 6 oz. of raisins, 2 oz. of candied peel, $1\frac{1}{2}$ teaspoonfuls of baking-powder, 5 oz. of sugar, 1 egg, milk and water.

METHOD.—Wash and stone the raisins, then put into a warm place to dry.

Sieve the flour and baking-powder. Cut the peel into small pieces.

Beat the lard and sugar to a cream.

Add the egg, stir it in quickly and beat for five minutes.

Add the flour and prepared fruit alternately, with a little milk and water as required.

Mix all together lightly, put into small greased cake-tins and bake in a hot oven for about twenty minutes.

LAYER CAKE

INGREDIENTS.—3 eggs, $\frac{1}{2}$ lb. of castor sugar, 6 oz. of margarine, 9 oz. of flour, $1\frac{1}{2}$ teaspoonfuls of baking-powder, $\frac{3}{4}$ gill of milk, jam.

FOR THE ICING.—$1\frac{1}{4}$ lb. of icing sugar, warm water, colouring and flavouring as desired, crystallised knots or other suitable decoration.

METHOD.—Mix the fat and sugar together till they are soft and creamy. Add each egg separately, stirring it in quickly and beating it well.

When all three are added, gradually stir in lightly the flour and baking-powder sifted together, adding also the milk by degrees.

When it is thoroughly mixed, divide the mixture equally between three buttered sandwich-tins, measuring about seven inches in diameter. Spread it over the tins one inch in depth, evenly.

Bake the cakes in a hot oven till they are light and spongy. They will take from fifteen to twenty minutes.

Place them on a rack to cool. When they are cold, spread one cake with jam and sandwich another on top of it. Then spread this with jam and top it with the third cake.

Brush off the loose crumbs and place the cake again on the rack. It is then ready for icing.

NOTE.—The cake may be made with four eggs, if preferred, and a little less milk.

TO MAKE THE ICING.—Rub the sugar through a hair sieve. Put it into a basin and mix it to a smooth, thick coating consistency with warm water.

Three-fourths of a gill of water may be required, but it must be added gradually until the icing is of the correct consistency. This can be tested on the back of your spoon.

Add a few drops of flavouring essence and colouring, as desired, unless the icing is to be left white.

Then pour it on the top of the cake, when it should run over it gently and coat it evenly. A dish should be placed under the rack to catch the icing as it trickles off. Let the icing nearly set, then decorate the cake as desired. When it is quite set, lift the cake on to a plate.

The icing that runs into the dish may be picked up and mixed again until it is smooth, then used again for icing small cakes.

If you like the cake to have a distinctive flavour, some flavouring essence or grated lemon-rind may be added. But remember to let the flavour of the icing blend with the flavour of the cake mixture.

TO MAKE AN ORANGE CAKE.—Add orange-juice instead of milk.

TO MAKE A COFFEE CAKE.—Flavour the mixture with coffee-essence or cold strong coffee, and lessen the milk accordingly.

TO MAKE A CHOCOLATE CAKE.—Add a little dissolved chocolate and flavour the cake with vanilla essence.

SUITABLE FILLINGS

APRICOT NUT FILLING.—This is a favourite one, and is prepared by mixing chopped walnuts with apricot jam.

If whole fruit jam is to be used, it is advisable to rub it through a sieve.

If the filling is to be made with very stiff jam, warm it and add just a dash of water to make it more spreadable. Add about an ounce of chopped walnuts to two or three tablespoonfuls of prepared apricot jam.

BUTTER CREAM FILLING.—Beat the butter and icing sugar to a cream, then flavour the mixture to taste. Use four ounces of icing sugar to two ounces of butter. This mixture may also be used for piping the top of the cake.

The cake may be coated with Boiled Icing if preferred.

BOILED ICING

INGREDIENTS.—¾ lb. of lump sugar, ¾ gill of hot water, 2 egg-whites, vanilla flavouring, pinch of cream of tartar.

METHOD.—Put the sugar into a saucepan with the water and dissolve it slowly. Then bring it to the boil.

Add a good pinch of cream of tartar. Boil it from 238 degrees to 240 degrees F., or until a small quantity, when dropped into cold water and left for a few seconds, becomes a soft ball when taken out and rolled between the fingers.

Have the frothed egg-whites ready by the time the syrup has boiled sufficiently. Then pour the syrup slowly on to the whites, keeping them well stirred.

Flavour the icing with vanilla, and continue to stir it until the icing begins to set. Then pour it over the cake.

LEMON BASKETS

INGREDIENTS.—4 oz. of margarine, 6 oz. of castor sugar, 7 oz. of flour, 1 teaspoonful of baking-powder, 2 eggs, milk, lemon cheese as required, desiccated coconut, 2 oz. of baked almonds, angelica.

FOR THE ICING.—½ lb. of icing sugar, 1½ to 2 tablespoonfuls of water, cochineal, flavouring to taste.

METHOD.—Beat the sugar and fat to a cream.

Add the eggs separately, and when they are well beaten in, stir in the flour and baking-powder (sieved together) and a little milk as required.

Mix all lightly together. Turn the mixture into a greased cake-tin or a deep sandwich-tin lined with paper, and bake in a moderately hot oven.

The mixture should be nearly two inches in depth when baked.

Turn out when cooked, and leave on a sieve until cold.

To Make the Baskets

Take a plain round pastry cutter, almost two inches in diameter, and cut out as many rounds as possible, cutting through to the bottom. There should be above five.

Now take a smaller cutter—about three-quarters of an inch in diameter—and cut out a small piece from the centre of each round, but only half-way through.

Warm some lemon cheese and, if necessary, thin it down with a little water. Brush the rounds of sponge with this, and coat some of them with finely chopped baked almonds, and the remainder with coconut.

Fill the centres with lemon cheese, and affix a handle of angelica to each.

The Angelica Handles

Cut long strips of angelica. Put them into moderately hot water for a minute or two to make them more supple.

Make a hole with an iron skewer on either side of each basket, at the top, and fix the handles in position.

LEMON CAKES

INGREDIENTS.—½ lb. of flour, ¼ lb. of margarine, ¼ lb. of granulated sugar, 1 lemon (grated rind and juice), ¼ flat teaspoonful of carbonate of soda, ½ an egg, about ½ gill of milk.

METHOD.—Grease about ten small cake-tins. Sieve the flour and soda together. Add the sugar and grated lemon-rind, mix all the dry ingredients together.

Beat the egg and pour into the middle of the flour, etc.; mix with a small portion of the flour, etc.

Add the strained lemon-juice, and when the latter is mixed in add sufficient milk to mix in the remainder of the dry ingredients.

Beat all together for a few minutes.

Put into the prepared tins.

Bake in a hot oven for about twenty minutes.

LEMON CHEESE GATEAU

INGREDIENTS.—3 eggs, 5 oz. of castor sugar, 6 oz. of flour, ½ teaspoonful of baking-powder, lemon flavouring, milk (if required).

THE FILLING.—Lemon cheese.

THE ICING.—10 oz. of icing sugar, ½ gill of water and lemon-juice (mixed), yellow colouring, crystallised violet.

METHOD.—Grease a sandwich-tin and line the sides with greased paper to stand above the top.

Separate the yolks from the whites of two of the eggs.

Put the castor sugar, one whole egg, and the two yolks into a basin and whisk together until thick and creamy and free from dark steaks of egg.

Sieve the flour and baking-powder.

Add a pinch of salt to the whites of eggs, and whisk them to a stiff froth.

Stir the flour into the sugar and eggs, then fold in the whites lightly.

Flavour with lemon essence and add a little milk if required.

Put into the prepared tin and bake in a hot oven for about twenty minutes.

When cold, split open and spread with lemon cheese, then put together again.

Stand on a cake-rack, over a dish ready for icing.

To Make the Icing.—Roll the sugar to get rid of the lumps, then rub it through a fine sieve.

Put it into a saucepan, add the strained lemon-juice and water, and mix to a smooth paste.

Add a few drops of colouring.

Stand the pan of icing over a very low burner, and stir until the base of the saucepan feels just warm.

If the icing is of the correct consistency it will coat the back of a spoon.

Pour it over the cake and coat it evenly.

Arrange a crystallised violet in the centre.

Leave until the icing is set, then lift carefully on to a lace paper.

LEMON LAYER CAKE

INGREDIENTS.—2 eggs, 5 oz. of castor sugar, 6 oz. of margarine, $\frac{1}{2}$ lb. of flour, 1 teaspoonful of baking-powder, 1 lemon, milk.

FOR THE LEMON BUTTER ICING.—6 oz. of icing sugar, 1 lemon, 3 oz. of butter, yellow colouring.

METHOD.—Grease a cake-tin and line with greased paper to stand above the top.

Cream the fat and sugar.

Separate the eggs.

Grate the lemon-rind finely. Sieve the flour and baking-powder.

Whisk the egg-whites to a very stiff froth.

Beat the yolks into the creamed fat and sugar. When well beaten, gradually stir in the flour, lemon-rind, and a little milk, then fold in the whisked whites.

Put the mixture into the prepared tin and bake in a moderately hot oven for about an hour, lessening the heat as required.

Leave on a sieve until cold.

THE BUTTER ICING

Roll the lumps out of the sugar and rub through a fine sieve.

Add the butter and beat both to a cream.

Stir in the finely-grated rind of the lemon and sufficient colouring to make a lemon colour.

Split the cake into three, spread a layer of the prepared icing on two pieces, then sandwich together again.

LOG CAKE

INGREDIENTS.—3 eggs, 4 oz. of castor sugar, 3 oz. of flour, $\frac{1}{2}$ teaspoonful of baking-powder, $1\frac{1}{2}$ oz. of butter or margarine, angelica for decoration.

FOR THE FILLING.— $\frac{3}{4}$ lb. of apricot jam, 1 oz. of shelled walnuts.

METHOD.—Whisk the eggs and castor sugar in a basin over a saucepan of hot water until they are thick and creamy and free from dark streaks, taking care that the mixture does not curdle.

When it is ready, take it off the hot water and stir in the flour and baking-powder, sieved together, and the butter, melted.

Spread the mixture over a baking sheet, lined with buttered paper, and bake it in a hot oven until it feels spongy. Turn the sponge on to a sugared paper. Cut off the hard outside edges, spread it with filling and roll it up. Leave it on a sieve until it is cold.

Have the filling ready by the time the sponge is cooked. To prepare it, warm the jam and stir in the walnuts, chopped finely.

FOR THE ALMOND PASTE.—2 oz. of icing sugar, 1 oz. of ground almonds, $\frac{1}{3}$ egg white, coffee essence.

METHOD.—Sieve the sugar and mix it with the ground almonds. Beat the egg-white slightly and add a little coffee essence to it. Then mix all the ingredients to a stiff paste. Form this to resemble a stump at the side of the log, sticking it on to one side of the roll with a little jam.

FOR THE COFFEE ICING.—$\frac{1}{2}$ lb. of icing sugar, $\frac{1}{4}$ lb. of butter, coffee essence.

METHOD.—Beat the butter to a cream with half the sugar (previously sieved). Then beat in the remainder of the sugar and add sufficient coffee essence (or strong coffee) to flavour.

Put the icing into an icing tube with a shell-patterned tube affixed and force the icing through in straight lines, completely covering the roll. Cover the stump in the same way and decorate the cake with rings of angelica.

LUNCH CAKE

INGREDIENTS.—$\frac{3}{4}$ lb. of flour, $\frac{1}{2}$ teaspoonful of mixed spice, $\frac{1}{4}$ flat teaspoonful of carbonate of soda, 4 oz. of margarine, 4 oz. of seedless raisins, 6 oz. of sugar, 1 egg, milk and water.

METHOD.—Grease a cake-tin and line it with greased paper to stand well above the sides.

Sieve the flour, spice, and soda.

Rub in the fat.

Separate the raisins and add with the sugar, and mix all together.

Beat up the egg and add to the dry ingredients with some milk and water, as required.

Mix all together, then beat for a few minutes.

Put into the greased tin and bake

in a hot oven for about one to one hour and a half.

LUNCH DRIPPING CAKE

INGREDIENTS.—¾ lb. of flour, 3 oz. of margarine, 3 oz. of clarified beef dripping, 6 oz. of sugar, 6 oz. of sultanas, 2 oz. of mixed candied peel, 1 teaspoonful of baking-powder, ¼ teaspoonful of salt, nearly 1 gill of milk, 2 eggs.—

METHOD.—Sift the flour, salt, and baking-powder.

Grease and line a two-pound cake-tin.

Wash and pick the sultanas and dry them in a cloth.

Chop the peel coarsely.

Rub the dripping and margarine into the flour until there are no lumps. Add the fruit, sugar, and flour.

Beat the eggs and put three-quarters of the milk with them.

Stir this into the dry ingredients, using the rest of the milk if it seems too stiff. When cakes are made too liquid the fruit sinks to the bottom.

Put the mixture into the tin and bake it in a moderate oven for about one hour.

The cake is done when the centre feels firm and elastic.

NOTE.—In order to make a cake have a rocky appearance on top when baked, it should be mixed with very little milk.

MACAROONS

INGREDIENTS.—½ lb. of finely minced almonds, ¾ lb. of castor sugar, 3 egg-whites, rice paper, vanilla or almond flavouring essence, a few whole almonds or glacé cherries for decorating.

METHOD.—Blanch the almonds by putting them into cold water and bringing them up to boiling point. Then drain and skin them.

Put them through the mincer twice, then weigh them.

Add the castor sugar to the almonds and rub them together until they are thoroughly incorporated. Then add a few drops of flavouring essence and mix them to a paste with the egg-whites as required, the latter only slightly beaten.

Line some baking-sheets with rice paper and place the mixture on it in small heaps. One teaspoonful is enough for each macaroon, and leave a good space between them. Put a halved blanched almond, a few strips of almond, or a piece of a glacé cherry on the top of each biscuit and bake them in a moderate oven. They will probably take twenty minutes to cook.

When cooked, leave them to cool for a few minutes, then trim the rice paper neatly round them.

If liked, a few glacé cherries may be added to the mixture, these being added before the egg-whites. Three or four ounces should be sufficient for this quantity, which will make about thirty biscuits.

NOTE.—If preferred, ready prepared ground almonds may be used in place of the minced almonds.

Rice paper can be obtained from any of the big stores, usually in the confectionery department.

MACAROON TARTS

INGREDIENTS.—Some short or flaky pastry (see p. 252), raspberry jam, ½ lb. of castor sugar, 6 oz. of finely minced almonds, 1½ oz. of ground rice, 2 to 2½ egg-whites, flavouring essence.

METHOD.—Prepare the almonds as in the previous recipe, weighing them after they are minced. Mix them thoroughly with the sugar and ground rice.

Add a few drops of flavouring essence and mix the ingredients to a paste with the slightly beaten egg-whites.

Roll out the pastry fairly thinly, stamp it into rounds and line some small cake-tins. Then put a little jam in the base of each before adding the prepared macaroon mixture.

Place two tiny strips of pastry crosswise on top of each tart and put them into a hot oven to bake, lessening the heat as they begin to brown.

They will take about twenty minutes.

MADEIRA CAKE

INGREDIENTS.—5 oz. of castor sugar, 4 oz. of margarine, 7 oz. of flour, 2 eggs, 1 lemon, citron peel, 1 flat teaspoonful of baking-powder.

METHOD.—Grease a small round cake-tin and line it with greased paper so that the latter reaches about two inches above the top.

Sieve the flour, measure out about a tablespoonful of it and mix with the baking-powder, then set aside.

Grate the lemon-rind finely and mix with the remainder of the flour. Beat the sugar and fat together into a cream.

Pour in one egg, stir it in quickly, and beat well for a few minutes, then add the other one and beat again—this time for about ten minutes.

Fold in lightly the flour and lemon-rind, and if necessary add about a tablespoonful of milk.

Lastly, add the baking-powder. Stir lightly and pour the mixture into the prepared tin.

Bake in a moderately hot oven for about forty-five minutes.

Cut two thin slices of peel and place them very lightly on the cake when half cooked.

MADELINES

INGREDIENTS.—2 eggs, their weight in castor sugar, 4 oz. of flour, 2½ oz. of butter or margarine, ½ teaspoonful of baking-powder, milk (½ gill), raspberry jam (or any red jam), apricot jam, desiccated coconut, glacé cherries, angelica.

METHOD.—Grease some small plain tin moulds, similar in shape to small flowerpots.

Sieve the flour and baking-powder together.

Beat the sugar and fat to a cream.

Add the eggs separately, and stir each one in briskly, beating well for about ten minutes.

Fold in the flour and baking-powder, and a little milk if necessary. Stir lightly.

Put into greased moulds. They should not be more than three parts full.

Stand on a baking-sheet and bake in a hot oven for about twelve to fifteen minutes, until they are lightly browned and spongy to the touch.

Turn on to a sieve and leave until cold.

Heat separately about two tablespoonfuls of each kind of jam, and, if very thick, thin down with a little water.

Rub the jams through a sieve. Brush the sides and tops of some cakes with red jam and the others with the apricot, then coat with coconut.

Stand on a lace paper and decorate the top of each with a small piece of angelica and half a cherry.

MARBLED CAKE

INGREDIENTS.—5 oz. of margarine, 6 oz. of castor sugar, 6 oz. of flour, 1½ flat teaspoonfuls of cream of tartar, ⅓ flat teaspoonful of carbonate of soda, coffee essence, cochineal, almond flavouring or rum, 2 eggs, milk.

METHOD.—Sieve the flour with the cream of tartar and carbonate of soda. Beat the sugar and fat to a cream. Add each egg separately, stirring it in quickly and beating it well before adding the next one.

When both eggs are well beaten in, gradually stir in the sieved flour with a little milk as required.

Divide the mixture into three portions, colour one with a few drops of cochineal, flavour one with a little almond essence or, if preferred, with a little rum, and add some coffee essence to the remaining portion—enough to colour and flavour.

Put the mixture into a greased and prepared cake-tin in alternate spoonfuls. Dredge castor sugar on the top of the cake and bake it in a moderately hot oven. It will take about an hour to bake.

MARSHMALLOW BISCUITS

INGREDIENTS.—8 marshmallows. ½ lb. of flour, 2 oz. of Barbados sugar, 4 oz. of margarine, pinch of carbonate of soda, about 1 tablespoonful of milk.

METHOD.—Sift the flour with the soda.

Put the sugar and margarine into a saucepan to melt. Let them cool, then add them to the flour, and mix to a dough, adding some milk, if required.

Form the dough into a smooth lump and roll it out. Cut it into rounds, place them on a lightly buttered baking-sheet, and bake in a moderate oven for about fifteen minutes. Then put half a marshmallow on top of each, and return them to the oven to melt and brown a little. Sprinkle the biscuits with ground cinnamon if liked.

Sufficient for about sixteen biscuits.

MARY CAKES

INGREDIENTS.—2 oz. of flour, 1 oz. of ground almonds, 2 oz. of margarine, 1 oz. of castor sugar, 1 egg, ratafia flavouring.

FOR THE ICING.—6 oz. of icing sugar, 3 oz. of butter, pale green colouring, 2 oz. of chocolate in cake, 1 dessertspoonful of milk.

METHOD. — Grease about twelve boat-shaped tins (or any small tins will do).

Cream the margarine and sugar till soft. Stir in the egg. Beat them for five minutes, and add the flour, ground almonds, and three or four drops of ratafia flavouring. Half fill each tin with the mixture.

Bake the cakes in a hot oven for about fifteen minutes.

Place the cakes on a sieve to cool and when cold ice them.

TO MAKE THE ICING.—Cream the butter till quite soft, then stir in the sieved icing sugar and a little green colouring. Spread the tops of all the cakes smoothly with the pale green icing.

Put the chocolate in a saucer with a dessertspoonful of milk and stand it in a saucepan of hot water.

When the chocolate is soft, stir it into the remainder of the icing.

Put it in an icing pump with a rose forcer screwed on and decorate one side of each cake with roses.

MARZIPAN FLOWERPOTS

INGREDIENTS.—4 oz. of castor sugar, 6 oz. of flour, 1 small teaspoonful of baking-powder, 4 oz. of margarine, 1 egg, milk, jam.

FOR THE ALMOND PASTE.—½ lb. of ground almonds, ½ lb. of icing sugar, whites of about 1½ eggs, vanilla flavouring, saffron colouring and cochineal.

FOR THE CHOCOLATE BUTTER ICING.—¼ lb. of icing sugar, 1¾ oz. of butter, 1 oz. of grated chocolate, vanilla flavouring, milk.

METHOD.—Grease some small, plain castle moulds. Sieve the flour and baking-powder. Beat the sugar and fat to a cream. Add the egg, stir it in quickly and beat well for a few minutes. Stir in the flour and baking-powder and mix together lightly, adding some milk as required.

Put into the castle moulds sufficient to about two-thirds fill them. Place on a baking-sheet and bake in a fairly hot oven for about twenty minutes.

Cool on a sieve.

THE ALMOND PASTE

Roll the lumps out of the icing sugar and rub through a hair sieve. Add the ground almonds and mix together. Whisk the egg - white slightly and add sufficient, with a few drops of vanilla, to mix to a stiff paste. Work in also a few drops of cochineal and a few drops of saffron until it is evenly coloured to the shade of a flowerpot.

THE CHOCOLATE BUTTER ICING

Dissolve the chocolate in about two tablespoonfuls of milk, then cool slightly.

Roll the lumps out of the icing sugar and rub it through a fine sieve. Add the butter and beat to a cream. Stir in the chocolate and a few drops of vanilla and mix together.

TO ICE THE CAKE

Roll the almond paste out thinly and cut into rounds large enough to cover the sides and bottom of each cake. Spread a little sieved jam on the outward side of the cakes, then mould the almond paste round so that it stands above the top. Cut narrow strips of paste and put round the top to represent the rim of the pot. Then spread some chocolate icing roughly on top of the cake in each pot.

An artificial flower can then be inserted if liked.

MAYFAIR CAKE

INGREDIENTS.—14 oz. of flour, ½ lb. of butter or margarine, 11 oz. of castor sugar, 2 teaspoonfuls of baking-powder, 3 eggs, milk, pineapple essence.

METHOD.—Beat the sugar and fat to a cream.

Sift the flour with the baking-powder.

Separate the eggs and whisk the whites to a stiff froth.

Add the yolks one at a time to the creamed fat and sugar and beat well. When all are added, gradually stir in the flour and baking powder with some milk as required.

Flavour the mixture with a few drops of pineapple essence or other suitable flavouring. Lastly, add the stiffly whisked egg-whites, folding them in lightly.

Turn the mixture into a greased square cake - tin and put it into a moderately hot oven to bake. It will take about one hour and a half to cook.

NOTE.—This cake can be cut in dainty slices for afternoon tea.

MERINGUES

INGREDIENTS.—Whites of 4 eggs, ½ lb. of castor sugar, pinch of salt, cream, vanilla flavouring.

It is essential to use very fresh egg-whites, otherwise they will not whisk up well.

METHOD.—Add a pinch of salt to the egg-whites and whisk them to a very stiff froth. When sufficiently whisked the whites should stand upright on the whisk when this is lifted out sharply.

At this stage the sugar is added, and there are two different methods of adding it.

THE FIRST METHOD is to take a spoonful of sugar at a time and sprinkle it over the egg-white, then fold it in lightly, continuing in this way until it is all added. The action of folding in is to take up a spoonful of the mixture and turn it over, repeating this until the ingredients are thoroughly incorporated.

THE SECOND METHOD is to take three-fourths of the sugar and *whisk it in gradually*, continuing to whisk until the mixture will hold its shape and will stand upright on the whisk when this is lifted out. The remainder of the sugar is then folded in lightly.

TO SHAPE THE MIXTURE.—Take a spoonful at a time and shape it in the spoon to an oval shape, then slip this gently on to a strong baking-sheet lined with a thick sheet of paper, leaving a small space between each meringue

Sprinkle them lightly with castor sugar and put them into a cool oven to dry. They will probably take about an hour and a half or two hours, and they should be cream in colour when finished.

If you have an oven thermometer, the heat should register 225 deg. F. This may be lessened a little later if required. When ready, take the meringues from the tin. If liked, turn them over and press in the centres lightly on the flattened side, then put them back in the oven to dry for a short time ; but this is not really necessary so long as the meringues are thoroughly dried.

Let them get thoroughly cold, and when ready to serve them, sandwich them together in pairs with whipped cream between. The cream should be sweetened and flavoured to taste. Sometimes a little crushed crystallised rose leaves, or chopped pistachio nuts, may be sprinkled over the cream.

The meringues can be shaped either in a tablespoon or dessertspoon according to the size preferred. This quantity will make about twelve large ones.

NOTE.—When making meringues it is advisable to plan a use for the left-over egg-yolks. There are heaps of ways of using them, and they are especially good for making custards, and can be used for scrambling, etc. When using egg-yolks for a custard use four to one pint of milk.

MERINGUE TWIRLS.—These are shaped by forcing the mixture through an icing pump with a shell tube affixed. In this case, make the meringue mixture only by the second method. Made by the first method the meringue mixture will not take the impression of the tube. Meringue twirls require about three-quarters of an hour to dry, and are very dainty to serve for tea. They may also be sandwiched together in pairs with cream between, or they may be served with ice cream.

MERINGUE SHELLS make a very delightful sweet if each is upturned and filled with well-drained stewed or tinned fruit. They may be topped with whipped cream, sweetened and flavoured to taste, or served with ice cream. The shells should not be filled until they are required.

A Meringue Trifle is also a favourite dish. To prepare this, split some sponge cakes in half or quarter, then arrange them in a dish and soak them with rum. Do not use jam, as this would make the trifle too sweet.

Make half a pint of custard with one egg and half a pint of milk, flavour it with vanilla and sweeten it slightly, and when it is cool pour sufficient of it over the sponge cakes to moisten them. The custard should not swim round the dish.

Then arrange the meringue shells on the top and pipe whipped cream between them.

MERINGUE DROPS

INGREDIENTS. — 2 whites of eggs, 2 oz. of icing sugar, ¾ to 1 gill of cream, 1 tablespoonful of grated chocolate, sugar and vanilla, angelica, salt.

METHOD.—Add a pinch of salt to the egg-whites and whisk them to a stiff froth, then gradually whisk in the icing sugar (previously rubbed through a hair sieve), when the mixture should be quite stiff.

Drop it on to a buttered baking-sheet in small heaps, or force it through an icing pump, then put them into a cool oven to set.

Remove them carefully from the tin, and when cold sandwich them together in pairs with whipped cream and chocolate between.

Decorate the edge of the filling with small pieces of angelica.

To Prepare the Cream.—Whisk it until thick, then stir in the chocolate, and add vanilla flavouring and a little sugar to taste.

Sufficient for twenty drops or ten pairs.

MINT COOKIES

INGREDIENTS.—1 cup of currants, 1 tablespoonful of chopped mint, ½ oz. of butter, ½ oz. or sugar, 1 yolk of egg, ½ lb. of short of flaky pastry (see p. 252).

METHOD.—Wash and pick the currants and melt the butter. Mix currants, sugar, mint, and butter with the egg-yolk.

Roll the pastry out and cut it into fairly small rounds. Spread a dessert-spoonful of the mixture on each round and moisten the edge with water.

Press a round of pastry on the top.

Brush them with water, dredge them with sugar, and bake them in a hot oven for twenty minutes.

MOCHA CAKE

INGREDIENTS.—2 oz. of butter or margarine, ¼ lb. of flour, 1 teaspoonful of baking-powder, coffee essence, ½ gill of milk, 4 oz. of castor sugar, 1 egg.

FOR THE ICING.—½ lb. of icing sugar, coffee essence, warm water.

FOR THE BUTTER ICING.—3 oz. of icing sugar, 1½ oz. of butter, coffee essence.

METHOD.—Beat the butter and sugar to a cream, stir in the yolk of the egg and a little milk ; then add the flour (sifted with baking - powder), also the remainder of the milk, and coffee essence to flavour. Fold in the stiffly whisked egg-white. Turn the mixture into a well-buttered pie-tin and bake it in a fairly hot oven until spongy. Cool it on a sieve.

Stand the cake on a rack, place this on a dish and pour the icing over it. Let this set before decorating it with the butter icing. This should be tinted with coffee essence to a deeper shade than the coating icing, and forced through an icing pump. For this design the leaf patterned tube is required.

To Make the Coating Icing.— Sieve the sugar, and mix it to a smooth coating consistency with warm water and a little coffee essence.

To Make the Butter Icing.—Sieve the sugar. Beat the butter to a cream with half the sugar, then add the remainder and beat the icing again until creamy. Add coffee essence as required.

MOCHA FINGERS

INGREDIENTS.—¼ lb. of flour, 3 oz. of castor sugar, 2 eggs, 1 tablespoonful of milk (if required).

FOR THE ICING.—10 oz. of icing sugar, ⅓ gill of water, coffee essence, a few shelled walnuts.

METHOD.—Grease some sponge cake finger-tins.

Pass the flour through a sieve.

Break the eggs into a basin, add the sugar, and whisk well for about ten minutes, or until quite thick. Fold in the flour, adding a little milk if required.

Put a small quantity of the mixture into each finger-tin, but do not quite fill them.

Bake in a hot oven for about ten minutes—they should only be a very pale colour when cooked. Place on a sieve until cold.

To Make the Icing.—Rub the sugar through a fine sieve.

Put it into a saucepan with the water, mix well together until very smooth. Add a few drops of coffee essence—just enough to flavour and slightly colour the icing. Put over the fire and stir until warm. Be careful not to make it hot or the icing will lose its gloss.

When finished, it should be sufficiently thick to coat the back of the spoon. If too thin more sieved icing sugar must be added.

To Ice the Fingers.—Place them on a cake-rack, leaving a space between each, and stand the rack on a dish. Take a tablespoonful of the icing and carefully coat one finger.

Do all the others in the same way. If the icing in the saucepan gets too cool, it can be warmed again. Place a small piece of walnut in the centre of each.

MUSHROOM CAKE

INGREDIENTS.—2 eggs, their weight in flour, 1 level teaspoonful of baking-powder, 3 oz. of castor sugar, 2 oz. of margarine, jelly.

FOR THE ALMOND PASTE.—¼ lb. of icing sugar, ¼ lb. of castor sugar, 6 oz. of ground almonds, egg-white or whole egg to mix, flavouring.

FOR THE CHOCOLATE ICING.—2 oz. of butter, 2 oz. of plain chocolate, about 1 tablespoonful of water, ¼ lb. of icing sugar, ¼ teaspoonful of vanilla flavouring.

METHOD.—To make the cake mixture, beat the sugar and fat to a cream. Add the eggs separately, stirring each one in quickly and beating it well before adding the next one.

When both the eggs are well beaten in, stir in the flour sifted with the baking-powder. Mix these ingredients together lightly before turning the mixture into a buttered pie-tin

This is a round tin rather deeper than a sandwich-tin, with sloping sides.

Put the cake into a fairly hot oven to bake. It will take about twenty-five minutes. Place it on a sieve to cool.

To Make the Almond Paste.—Rub the icing sugar through a sieve. Then mix it with the castor sugar and ground almonds.

Make them into a stiff paste with lightly beaten egg-white or a beaten whole egg.

Flavour the paste with a few drops of vanilla. The white of egg will make a more real-looking mushroom, as the whole egg gives the paste a yellowish tinge.

One egg-white may not be quite sufficient to mix the paste, but to save breaking another egg just a little water may be added to make up the amount of moisture.

If liked a teaspoonful of orange flower water may be used to flavour the paste instead of vanilla.

Put a small piece of paste aside for the stalk and roll out the remainder to a round.

Brush the base and sides of the cake with melted jelly or jam. Then place it in the centre of the rolled-out paste and mould the paste round it. If the cake has risen in the centre it must be cut level before finally moulding the paste just over the top edge.

To Make the Chocolate Icing.—Break up the chocolate and dissolve it in a saucepan or basin, standing it over a pan of hot water. Stir in about a tablespoonful of water, then let the chocolate cool. Rub it through a hair sieve.

Beat the butter to a cream, then gradually beat the sugar into it. When it is soft and creamy, stir in the dissolved chocolate. Add the vanilla flavouring and mix the icing well.

If it seems too stiff, a little more water or milk may be added. Or the beaten yolk of the egg serves very well if it has not been used for the almond paste. If the icing is too soft, add a little more sifted sugar.

Put the icing into an icing pump with a shell-patterned tube attached, and force it on to the top of the cake. Work from the edge almost to the centre and fill it in completely. Finally, form the remaining piece of almond paste into a fat stalk and stick it in the centre of the mushroom.

MUSHROOM SHORTCAKES

INGREDIENTS.—9 oz. of flour, 1 egg, 6 oz. of margarine, 1 teaspoonful of baking - powder, 4 oz. of castor sugar, jam.

FOR THE BUTTER ICING.—4 oz. of icing sugar, 2 oz. of butter, vanilla flavouring.

METHOD.—Cream the sugar and margarine. Add the egg, stir it in quickly, and beat well for a few minutes. Sieve the flour and baking-powder and add and mix to rather a stiff consistency, with just a little milk as required.

Put into small baking-cups, but do not quite fill them. Stand on a baking-sheet and bake in a hot oven for about fifteen or twenty minutes.

When cold, take a small round pastry cutter, half or three-quarters of an inch in diameter, and cut out a piece from the centre of each cake, but not quite through to the bottom. This is to form the stalk of the mushroom. Level the top of it and dust with icing sugar. Put a little jam in the hole in each cake, then some butter icing. Replace the mushroom stalks so that they stand up well.

TO MAKE THE ICING.—Roll the lumps out of the sugar and rub through a fine sieve. Add the butter and beat both to a cream. Stir in a few drops of vanilla.

Sufficient to make about twelve cakes.

" MY LADY " CAKE

INGREDIENTS.—3 oz. of shelled walnuts, 2 oz. of desiccated coconut, 5 oz. of butter or margarine, 7 oz. of castor sugar, ¾ lb. of flour, 3 eggs, 1½ teaspoonfuls of baking-powder, milk, cochineal, rose water or rose essence to flavour.

FOR THE ALMOND PASTE DECORATION.—¾ lb. of ground almonds, 1 lb. of icing sugar, 2 or 3 whites of eggs, rose essence, cochineal, a china doll's head and bust, some crystallised rose leaves, a little jam.

METHOD.—Grease a round cake-tin five and a half inches in diameter, and line it with buttered paper to stand two or three inches above the sides.

Beat the butter and sugar to a cream, add each egg separately, stirring it in quickly, and beating the mixture well before adding the next. When all are beaten in, stir in gradually the flour and baking-powder (previously sifted), and a little milk as required; also the coconut and roughly chopped walnuts. Favour the mixture with a little rose water, or rose essence, and colour it with cochineal.

Turn it into the prepared cake-tin and bake it in a moderately hot oven. It will take about an hour or a little longer. When cooked, turn it out carefully and cool it on a sieve.

TO MAKE THE ALMOND PASTE ICING.—Sift the icing sugar and mix it with the ground almonds. Mix to a stiff paste with slightly beaten egg-whites—you will need two or three for this amount of icing—and flavour it with a few drops of rose essence.

Divide the icing into two portions, colour one with cochineal, and work each into a smooth lump.

TO ICE THE CAKE.—Place the china doll's head in the centre of the cake, using a little jam to make it adhere.

Take a small piece of the almond paste (either colour will do as it will not be seen), form into a long roll and place it round the bottom edge of the cake ; this will enable the lower layers of paste to stand out a little.

Now cover the cake with layers of paste in alternate colours, starting from the base and working towards the top and letting each one overlap the previous layer. The cake should first be brushed with jam to make the paste adhere.

Finally arrange a few crystallised rose petals at one side finished off with a loop and ends of almond paste.

NEAPOLITAN SANDWICH

INGREDIENTS.—3 oz. of flour, 2 oz. of margarine, ½ teaspoonful of baking-powder, cochineal, 3 oz. of castor sugar, 1 egg, milk, coffee essence.

FOR THE VANILLA CREAM FILLING.—½ gill of cream, 3 oz. of icing sugar, vanilla flavouring.

METHOD.—Beat the sugar and margarine to a cream. Stir in the egg quickly, and beat the mixture for a few minutes.

Sieve the flour and baking-powder and stir in lightly with a little milk as required. Colour half the mixture to a pale pink shade with a few drops of cochineal. Put this into a greased sandwich-tin and spread over evenly.

Add some coffee essence to the remainder and colour and flavour it to suit taste. Spread this over the pink mixture.

Place in a hot oven to bake for about ten or fifteen minutes or until it feels spongy.

Turn on to a sieve and leave until cold.

To MAKE THE FILLING.—Roll the lumps out of the sugar and rub it through a hair sieve.

Whisk the cream until it stiffens.

Gradually stir in the sugar and a few drops of vanilla and mix together lightly.

Split the sponge cake into halves, spread the filling over it, then sandwich it together again. Dust with icing sugar.

NEAPOLITAN SLICES

INGREDIENTS.—6 oz. of flour, 1 teaspoonful of baking-powder, 2 eggs, 6 oz. of castor sugar, 4 oz. of margarine or butter, milk.

FOR THE FILLING.—3 oz. of butter, 5 oz. of icing sugar, 1 egg-yolk, 3 dessertspoonfuls of desiccated coconut, vanilla, cochineal, coffee essence or melted chocolate.

METHOD.—Beat the sugar and fat to a cream, then beat in the yolks of the eggs one at a time.

Sift the flour and baking-powder and stir them in lightly with some milk, as required; then fold in the stiffly whisked egg-whites.

Have a large baking-sheet lined with buttered paper to stand well above the sides, turn the mixture into it and spread it evenly, then bake it in a hot oven until spongy.

Cool the sponge on a sieve and when cold cut it crosswise into halves, then into quarters.

Spread one piece with coffee or chocolate filling, sandwich another piece on top of this and spread this with cream filling, then cover this with a third piece and spread this with

pink filling. Top this with the remaining piece, press all together lightly and cut the cake in slices.

To MAKE THE FILLING.—Sift the sugar. Beat the butter with the sugar until creamy, then beat in the yolk of the egg and add the coconut.

Divide the filling into three portions, flavour one with vanilla, flavour a second portion with vanilla and colour it pink with cochineal. Tint and flavour the third portion with coffee essence, or flavour it with vanilla and add a little melted chocolate.

NEST CAKE

INGREDIENTS.—¼ lb. of flour, 2 oz. of butter, 1 large egg, 1 oz. of glacé cherries (cut in quarters), 1 oz. of citron peel (chopped), 2 oz. of sugar, ¼ gill of milk.

FOR DECORATING.—2 oz. of angelica, ¾ oz. of flour, 4 oz. of ground almonds, ¼ lb. of icing sugar, 2 large eggs or 3 small ones, 1 tablespoonful of lemon-juice, 4 drops of ratafia essence.

METHOD.—Grease a pudding-basin. Cream the butter and sugar, add the egg, and beat them well.

Stir in the fruit and flour and moisten it all with a little milk.

Pour the mixture into the basin and bake it in a moderate oven for about thirty minutes.

Leave the cake for ten minutes, then remove it carefully and place it on a sieve to cool.

To ice the cake next day, sieve the icing sugar and mix it with the almonds and flour and a few drops of essence. Beat the eggs and use them and the lemon-juice to bind the mixture into a paste. It should be sufficiently stiff to keep its shape, but not too stiff to put through the forcer.

Use a strong linen icing bag and a large rose forcer. Put in the paste, twist up the top of the bag, and force out lines of the paste till the cake is covered. Leave a hollow in the top.

Use a little of the mixture to make three small eggs.

Brush the cake with a little water, and bake it in a moderate oven to set the icing and slightly brown the edges.

Fill the hollow with chopped angelica and put in the eggs.

NEW YEAR CAKE

(A Rich Fruit Cake with Almond Paste and Royal Icing)

Ingredients.—13 oz. of flour, 4 oz. of castor sugar and 6 oz. of soft brown sugar, 10 oz. of butter or margarine, 4 eggs, 1 lemon (grated rind), ½ flat teaspoonful of grated nutmeg, ½ a flat teaspoonful of mixed spice, ¼ lb. of mixed peel, ½ lb. of sultanas, ¼ lb. of raisins, ¾ lb. of currants, ¼ lb. of crystallised or glacé apricots, ½ a flat teaspoonful of carbonate of soda, milk, if required, a little jelly preserve.

Method.—Wash, pick over and dry the fruit, and stone and cut up the raisins.

Shred the peel and slice the apricots in small pieces. Sieve the flour with the soda and spices, and grate the lemon-rind finely.

Beat the eggs with a quarter of a pound of castor sugar until thick and foamy.

Cream the fat with the brown sugar, then add gradually the flour, grated lemon-rind and prepared fruit, alternately with the eggs and sugar.

Beat the mixture well, stirring in a little milk if required. Turn it into a greased cake-tin lined with two or three thicknesses of greased paper and bake it in a very moderate oven for about three hours.

Cool the cake on a sieve, and when quite cold, wrap it in greaseproof paper and put it in a tin until you are ready to ice it.

The Almond Paste

Ingredients.—1¼ lb. of ground almonds, 1¼ lb. of icing sugar, ½ teaspoonful of vanilla flavouring, ½ teaspoonful of orange flavouring, ¼ teaspoonful of almond or ratafia flavouring, about 4 or 5 oz. of egg-whites and 2 yolks.

Method.—Rub the icing sugar through a hair sieve and mix it with the ground almonds.

Separate the eggs, beat the whites slightly, and beat the yolks with the flavouring essences. Add them to the dry ingredients, and also enough white of egg to make a stiff paste. Work it until smooth.

To Cover the Cake.—If it has risen unevenly, either cut it level or else make it level with piece of almond paste.

If you have been unlucky and have baked your cake too much, you may scrape it before beginning to cover it, but be sure to remember to brush off the loose crumbs.

Divide the paste into two portions, form one piece into a long roll, then roll it out with a rolling-pin, making it of the same depth as the side of the cake and long enough to reach round it.

Brush the sides first with a little melted jelly (preserve) and mould the paste round evenly, then stand the cake on an upturned dish, roll out the remainder of the paste to a round, and cover the top in the same way, making it adhere securely. When you have made it quite level, leave it to dry until the next day.

Note.—Put a small piece of almond paste aside before you begin. You will require this for the centre of the cake when finished.

The Royal Icing

Ingredients.—2 lb. of icing sugar, cochineal, 3 dessertspoonfuls of lemon-juice, about 4 or 5 egg-whites, some crystallised fruits, and bells for decorating.

Method.—Rub the icing sugar through a hair sieve, put it into a basin, pour the lemon-juice in the centre and add sufficient stiffly whisked egg-whites to make it of a thick consistency that will hold its shape.

Beat it well for about ten minutes then keep it covered with a very damp cloth, as it so soon hardens.

To ice the cake, spread a layer of icing on the top, using a palette knife, or, failing this, use a large knife with a flexible blade rounded at the top, then smooth the icing by dipping the knife in hot water. Do the sides in the same way. Leave the icing to dry, then, if you like, spread a second layer on the cake and when this is dry, pipe it.

The quantity of icing given only allows for one layer. If you put two on, you will require another pound of icing sugar, but it is not advisable to make more than the given quantity at one time.

Before beginning to pipe the cake lift it on to a cake-board, then on to a revolving cake-stand if you have one.

Plan out a simple design, colour the icing to a pale pink shade, beat well, then pipe it tastefully.

Colour the remaining piece of almond paste to a deeper shade, roll it out, cut a round and place this in the centre. Arrange some choice crystallised fruits round the edge of this, and bells or other seasonable decoration in the centre.

NOVELTY SHORTBREADS

INGREDIENTS.—6 oz. of margarine or butter, 4 oz. of castor sugar, 10 oz. of flour, 1½ oz. of cornflour, ¼ level teaspoonful of ground cloves, ¼ level teaspoonful of ground cinnamon, ¼ level teaspoonful of ground ginger, miniature bonbons.

METHOD.—Beat the sugar and fat to a cream.

Sift the flour with the cornflour and spices, repeating this process twice to get them well mixed.

Then add them to the creamed fat and sugar.

Mix them all together, forming the mixture into a smooth lump by working it with your hands.

Divide this into about eight portions. Work each portion into a smooth round cake. Flatten them with the palm of your hand and flute the edges with the thumb and two fingers.

Prick each shortbread with a skewer.

Place them on a baking-sheet and bake them in a slow oven. They will take about forty minutes.

Cool the shortbreads on a sieve and when they are cold place a miniature bonbon across the centre of each. Use a dab of icing to make it adhere.

Sufficient to make eight shortbreads.

NURSERY CAKE

INGREDIENTS.—1 lb. of flour, 3 oz. of lard or margarine, 4 oz. of sultanas, 6 oz. of sugar, 1 egg, 1½ gills of milk, 1 teaspoonful of baking-powder.

FOR THE ICING.—6 oz. of icing sugar, 1½ tablespoonfuls of tepid water, 1 oz. of glacé cherries.

METHOD.—Grease a large meat-tin. Sift the flour and baking-powder and rub in the lard.

Add the sugar and cleaned sultanas. Mix to a rather moist dough with the beaten egg and milk. Bake it for about forty-five minutes. When cold, ice with soft icing (see p. 485) and cut into fingers.

NURSERY FINGERS

INGREDIENTS.—7 sponge fingers, 5 oz. of Barbados sugar, 3 tablespoonfuls of milk, 2 oz. of butter, 2 oz. of almonds or shelled walnuts, 1 oz. of grated chocolate.

METHOD.—Put the milk, butter, and sugar into a saucepan and dissolve them slowly.

Bring them to the boil and boil them till the mixture thickens, keeping it well stirred. Take it off the heat and continue to stir it until it becomes quite cool.

Dissolve the chocolate in a saucepan with just one or two extra teaspoonfuls of milk.

Cool it and add it to the mixture with the chopped nuts.

Mix them all together. Then split the sponge fingers in halves and sandwich them together again with a thick layer of the prepared mixture in between.

NUT BISCUITS

INGREDIENTS.—3 oz. of flour, 1 flat teaspoonful of baking-powder 1 oz. of cornflour, 1 oz. of margarine, 1 yolk of egg, milk and water.

FOR THE FILLING.—1 tablespoonful of ground Brazil nuts, 2 dessertspoonfuls of castor sugar, ¾ oz. of butter, vanilla flavouring.

METHOD.—The filling should be made first.

Sieve the flour with the cornflour and baking-powder.

Rub in the margarine. Add the egg-yolk mixed with a spoonful of milk and water, and mix the ingredients to a dough, adding a little more milk and water as required.

Turn the dough on to a lightly floured board and roll it out thinly to rather an oblong shape.

Turn the dough over and spread it with the filling.

Roll it up like a roly-poly or Swiss roll and cut it into slices.

Stand the slices on a greased baking-sheet and put them into a fairly hot oven to bake. They should take about ten or fifteen minutes to cook.

THE BRAZIL NUT FILLING

To make the filling beat the butter and castor sugar to a cream. Stir in the ground nuts and a few drops of vanilla essence, and mix all together well.

Sufficient for fourteen biscuits.

NUT AND FRUIT SHORT-BREAD

INGREDIENTS.—½ lb. of flour, 1 oz. of ground rice, 6 oz. of margarine, 3 oz. of castor sugar, 1 oz. of glacé cherries, 1 oz. of angelica, 1½ oz. of almonds.

METHOD.—Blanch the almonds, and put some aside for the top of the shortbread. Chop the remainder roughly.

Cut the cherries and angelica into very small pieces.

Cream the fat and sugar, add the prepared nuts and fruit, and mix in the flour and ground rice sifted together.

Form the mixture into a smooth lump and roll it out to a square shape. Cut a square a shade smaller than your tin, neaten the edge, put the shortbread into the tin and press the almonds lightly on top of it.

Bake the shortbread in a very moderate oven for about half an hour, or longer as required.

NUT ROCKS

INGREDIENTS.—9 oz. of flour, 1½ oz. of walnuts (shelled), 5 oz. of castor sugar, 1 teaspoonful of cream of tartar, ¼ flat teaspoonful of carbonate of soda, 5 oz. of margarine, 1 egg.

METHOD.—Sieve the flour, cream of tartar, and carbonate of soda and put into a basin.

Rub in the margarine until like fine crumbs.

Chop up the walnuts and add with the sugar.

Beat up the egg and add and mix to a stiff paste, adding a little milk as required.

Place the mixture on a greased baking-sheet in rough heaps, and bake in a hot oven for about fifteen to twenty minutes.

Sufficient for about twelve or fourteen cakes.

OATCAKES

INGREDIENTS.—½ lb. of oatmeal, 2 oz. of flour, ½ egg, good pinch of salt, ¼ flat teaspoonful of carbonate of soda, 2 oz. of margarine, 1 teaspoonful of sugar, water.

METHOD.—Sieve together the flour, soda, and salt, and mix with the oatmeal.

Add the sugar and mix thoroughly.

Beat up the egg.

Melt the margarine.

Add the egg and mix with part of the flour, etc., then add the margarine and mix it in.

Add sufficient cold water to form a stiff paste, then divide into portions.

Roll each out to a round shape, thinly, then divide into four pieces.

Place on a baking-sheet and bake in a moderate oven.

Cool on a sieve.

OATMEAL CAKES

INGREDIENTS.—¾ lb. of fine oatmeal, ¼ lb. of flour, 4 oz. of margarine, ¼ lb. of granulated sugar, ½ lb. of golden syrup, ½ flat teaspoonful of carbonate of soda, 2 oz. of candied peel.

METHOD.—Grease some small cake-tins.

Sieve together the flour, soda, and oatmeal. Put the margarine, sugar, and golden syrup into a saucepan to heat.

Dissolve the sugar, but be careful not to boil the liquid.

Then set aside to cool.

Cut the peel into small pieces, and mix with the flour. Make a well in the centre of it and pour in the golden syrup, etc.

Mix to rather a stiff consistency.

Put into the prepared tins and bake in a moderately hot oven for about twenty minutes.

Cool on a sieve.

ORANGE BUNS

INGREDIENTS.—½ lb. of flour, 1 teaspoonful of baking-powder, 1 orange (large), 2 tablespoonfuls of orange marmalade, ¼ lb. of butter or margarine, ¼ lb. of castor sugar, 1 egg.

METHOD.—Grease some small cake-tins.

Sieve the flour and baking-powder. Grate the orange-rind.

Squeeze and strain the juice.

Beat the sugar and fat to a cream.

Add the egg, stir it in quickly, and beat for about five minutes.

Gradually add the flour and orange-rind, also the juice.

Stir in the marmalade and mix all together lightly.

Put into the prepared tins and bake in a hot oven for about twenty minutes.

ORANGE FRUIT CAKES

INGREDIENTS.—6 oz. of flour, 1 oz. of ground almonds, 1 large or 2 small oranges (rind and juice), ¼ flat tea-spoonful of carbonate of soda, 3 oz. of candied orange-peel, 2 oz. of seedless raisins, 2 oz. of sultanas, 2 oz. of currants, 3 oz. of castor sugar, 4 oz. of margarine, 2 eggs, few almonds.

METHOD.—Wash, pick over and dry the fruit. Cut up the peel.

Sieve the flour with the soda.

Beat the sugar and fat to a cream. Add the finely grated orange-rind. Gradually stir in the flour, ground almonds, and prepared fruit, together with the eggs (well beaten), and the strained juice of the orange. Mix well together.

Turn the mixture into greased sponge cake-tins. Sprinkle the top with castor sugar and add a few blanched almonds split into halves.

Bake for about twenty minutes.

This quantity makes sixteen cakes.

ORANGE GATEAU

INGREDIENTS.—3 oz. of butter, 4 oz. of castor sugar, 3 eggs, 6 oz. of flour, ½ teaspoonful of baking-powder, juice and grated-rind of an orange, 1 oz. of candied peel.

FOR THE DECORATION.—6 oz. of icing sugar, 3 oz. of butter, 1 table-spoonful of orange-juice, 1 orange.

METHOD.—Grease a sandwich-tin and line it with greased paper to come an inch above the top.

Cream the butter and sugar till soft and white.

Chop the candied peel, grate the rind and add both to the sugar and butter.

Beat in the eggs one at a time.

Sift the flour and baking-powder and add them lightly with the orange juice.

Put the mixture in a lined tin and bake it in a moderate oven for twenty-five or thirty minutes.

To make the icing, cream the butter till soft. Rub the sugar through a hair sieve on to the butter. Mix with the orange-juice and beat well.

When cold split the cake in half and spread it with half the icing.

Spread a thin layer of icing on top and put the remainder in an icing pump fitted with a rose or star tube.

Decorate with eight sections of a sweet orange, and force roses round them and round the edge.

ORANGE LAYER CAKE

INGREDIENTS.—3 eggs, 5 oz. of castor sugar, 1 orange (rind and juice), 4½ oz. of flour, ½ level teaspoonful of baking-powder, 2 oz. of butter or margarine.

FOR THE FILLING.—6 oz. of icing sugar, 3 oz. of butter, 2 oz. of crystal-lised orange quarters, orange flavouring essence.

FOR THE ORANGE ICING.—Juice of 1 orange, 4 to 6 oz. of icing sugar, crystallised orange quarters, and angelica.

METHOD.—Put the sugar and eggs into a basin with the finely grated orange-rind.

Whisk them over hot water until they are thick and creamy and free from dark streaks.

Then take them from the heat and whisk them again for a few minutes.

Gradually stir in the flour, sifted with baking-powder, adding it alter-nately with the butter. This should be warmed just sufficiently to melt it.

Add also the strained orange-juice.

This mixture must be mixed very lightly, but thoroughly, before being turned into three small buttered sand-wich-tins.

Bake the layers in a hot oven for a few minutes until they are spongy. Then cool them on a sieve.

To MAKE THE FILLING.—Sift the icing sugar. Beat the butter and half the sugar to a cream.

Then add the remainder of the sugar and beat the mixture again until it is creamy.

Cut the orange quarters in small pieces and stir them into the filling with a few drops of orange essence.

To Make the Orange Icing.—Squeeze out the juice from the orange and strain it.

Then stir into it sufficient icing sugar to make a thick smooth coating consistency.

To Ice the Cake.—Spread some filling on two of the rounds, and sandwich the three together.

Pour the orange icing on the top of the cake and decorate it with crystallised orange quarters and leaves of angelica.

ORANGE SANDWICH CAKE

INGREDIENTS.—1 orange (grated rind and juice), 2 eggs, their weight in castor sugar and margarine, 5 oz. of flour, $\frac{1}{2}$ teaspoonful of baking-powder.

METHOD.—Beat the sugar and fat to a cream. Add the eggs one at a time, stirring them in quickly and beating them well before adding the next one. When both are added, mix in the finely grated orange-rind and strained juice, then the flour and baking-powder sieved together.

Turn the mixture into a prepared sandwich-tin and bake it in a moderately hot oven.

When cold, split the cake open, spread it with orange marmalade or orange curd. Then sandwich the two halves together again.

ORANGE TWIRLS

INGREDIENTS.—9 oz. of flour, 3 oz. of margarine, 3 oz. of castor sugar, 2 yolks of eggs, 1 small orange (rind and juice), $1\frac{1}{2}$ oz. of candied orange peel.

METHOD.—Beat the sugar and fat to a cream, add the finely grated orange-rind, and beat in the yolks of the eggs one at a time.

Sift the flour and stir it in gradually, adding the finely minced candied orange peel, and the juice of the orange.

Mix to a pliable paste, adding a little water if more moisture is required.

Divide the paste into twelve portions, form each into a long sausage shape, then twist them into S shapes.

Lift them on to a lightly buttered baking-sheet, and bake them in a fairly quick oven.

Sufficient to make twelve twirls.

ORANGE AND GINGER CAKE

INGREDIENTS.—6 oz. of butter or margarine, 5 oz. of Barbados sugar, $\frac{1}{2}$ lb. of flour, $\frac{1}{2}$ level teaspoonful of carbonate of soda, 1 level teaspoonful of ground ginger, 6 oz. of preserved ginger, 2 oz. of ground almonds, $\frac{1}{4}$ lb. of candied orange peel, $\frac{1}{4}$ lb. of crystallised orange quarters, $\frac{1}{2}$ lb. of sultanas, $\frac{1}{4}$ lb. of dates, 3 eggs, rind of 1 orange, $\frac{1}{4}$ gill of ginger syrup, $\frac{1}{2}$ gill of golden syrup, a little jam or jelly for brushing the cake.

FOR THE ALMOND PASTE.—$\frac{1}{2}$ lb. of ground almonds, $\frac{3}{4}$ lb. of icing sugar, about 2 egg-whites, orange flavouring essence.

METHOD.—Wash, pick over and dry the sultanas.

Stone and cut up the dates.

Cut the ginger, candied peel, and crystallised orange slices into small pieces.

Sieve the flour with the soda and ground ginger and add the fine-grated orange-rind.

Whisk the eggs, warm the golden syrup and add it to them, then whisk them together.

Beat the sugar and fat to a cream, add gradually the flour, ground almonds, and prepared fruit, also the eggs and golden syrup. Mix and beat them well, and stir in the ginger syrup.

Turn the mixture into a greased cake-tin lined with two or three thicknesses of greased paper, and bake it for from two hours and a half to three hours in a very moderate oven. When cooked, take the cake up and leave it on a sieve until cold.

To Make the Almond Paste.—Sift the icing sugar and mix it with the ground almonds. Beat the whites slightly, and add sufficient with a few drops of orange essence to make a stiff paste.

Work this paste until smooth, then roll it out to a round and cover the top of the cake, brushing this first with a little jam or jelly.

If the cake is uneven, it is better to patch it up first with pieces of almond paste before putting on the top round, but you will find that if you heap the mixture a little to the sides before baking it, the cake will be level when cooked.

Christmas Cake

The Finished Christmas Cake.

Use a pallet knife to spread the icing.

Decorating the cake.

Smooth the icing round the sides of the cake.

PLATE 45

Almond Balls

Cornish Rock Cakes and Cinnamon Cakes

Nursery Fingers

PLATE 46

Soda
Biscuit
Rings

Almond
Biscuits

Ginger Biscuits

Bridge
Biscuits

PLATE 47

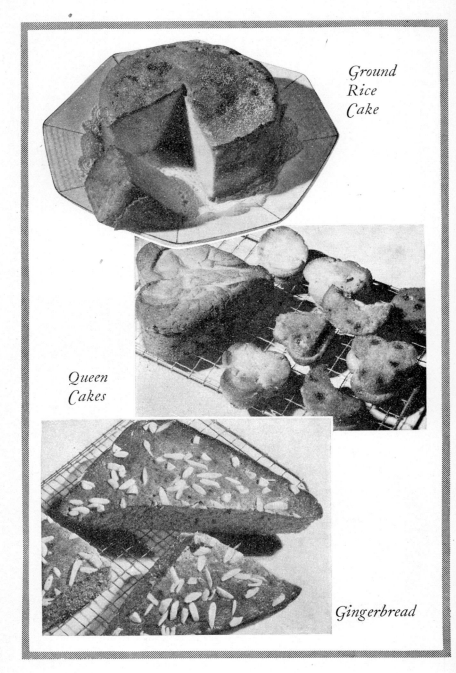

Ground
Rice
Cake

Queen
Cakes

Gingerbread

PLATE 48

Form the trimmings of paste into a thin long roll and place this round the top edge. Pinch it with thumb and finger. Finally, decorate the cake with crystallised orange quarters and put a cake frill round the sides.

OUR LITTLE HOUSE
(An Attraction for the Children's Party)

INGREDIENTS.—1¼ lb. of flour, 2 teaspoonfuls of cream of tartar, ¼ teaspoonful of carbonate of soda, 2 oz. of ground almonds, ¾ lb. of margarine, ¾ lb. of castor sugar, 10 oz. of glacé cherries, 2 oz. of mixed peel, 4 eggs, milk.

FOR THE ALMOND PASTE ICING.— 1 lb. of icing sugar, 1 lb. of ground almonds, whites of about 2½ eggs, vanilla flavouring, saffron colouring, cochineal.

METHOD.—Grease an oblong cake-tin, such as you would use for a tin loaf, and line with greased paper to stand above the top.

Cut the cherries and peel into small pieces.

Sieve the flour with the carbonate of soda and cream of tartar.

Beat the sugar and fat to a cream.

Add each egg separately, stir in quickly, and beat well before adding the next. If the mixture is inclined to curdle, stir in a little of the flour.

When all the eggs are beaten in, gradually stir in the flour, ground almonds, and fruit, and mix together lightly, adding some milk as required. Do not make too wet, or the fruit will sink.

Put into the cake-tin and bake in a moderately hot oven for about two hours, lessening the heat as the cake begins to brown. When cooked, put on a sieve and leave until cold.

To Make the Almond Paste

Roll the lumps out of the icing sugar and rub it through a hair sieve. Add the ground almonds and mix together.

Whisk the egg-whites slightly and add sufficient, with a few drops of vanilla, to mix to a stiff paste ; then work it until smooth.

To Shape the Cake

Cut the sides and ends quite straight, then cut the top of the cake to look like the slanting roof of a house. When finished, knock off all the loose crumbs.

To Ice the Cake

Take about one-third of the paste and roll out thinly, then cut eight strips not more than one inch wide, and just a little larger than the cake, and put aside for the roof. Shape also four pieces into small chimneys.

Colour the remaining two-thirds of the paste as near a brick colour as possible. (For this work in a few drops of saffron colouring, then add a few drops of cochineal until you get the desired colour.)

Roll this out to about one-eighth of an inch thick and cut pieces to cover the sides and ends of the cake, then mould them on to it.

Cut out two pieces of paste from either side of the cake for the windows, and replace with a thinner piece of uncoloured paste.

Cut out a piece from one side for the door, then replace one side of it and leave partly open. Fix a small handle of paste on it. If liked, a piece of the uncoloured paste can be made to a different colour for the door.

Mark lines across the paste all round the house to represent bricks.

Place the strips in position on top of the cake for the roof, so that each overlaps the previous one.

Mould a piece of brick-coloured paste into a small square shape for the chimney-stack.

Scoop out a piece from the lower part so that it will stand straight on the roof, place it in position, and stand the chimneys on it.

Brush the roof and chimneys with some egg-white (whisked until frothy), then dredge well with castor sugar to resemble snow.

Put the cake into a very *cool* oven for about twenty minutes or half an hour to set the white of egg and dry the almond paste.

If liked, when quite cold, mark lines of white icing across the windows and the outside to look like bricks and panes.

PARKIN

INGREDIENTS.—1¾ lb. of flour, 1 lb. of oatmeal, 1 lb. of butter or margarine, 1 lb. of sugar (moist).

R

1 oz. of ground ginger, ½ oz. of ground mace, 3 oz. of chopped candied peel, ½ of a nutmeg (grated), 1¾ lb. of treacle or golden syrup, ½ teaspoonful of carbonate of soda.

METHOD.—Rub the butter into the flour and add all the dry ingredients. Warm the treacle and add it to the mixture. Pour into two well-greased meat-tins and bake in a moderate oven for about forty-five minutes. Leave the cakes in the tin and while they are still warm cut them into square blocks.

When cold, put in tins and store till required. This cake improves by keeping, and is not supposed to be eaten at once.

Medium oatmeal may be used. Sufficient to fill two meat-tins.

YORKSHIRE PARKINS

INGREDIENTS.—½ lb. of flour, 1¾ lb. of medium oatmeal, 10 oz. of sugar, ¼ lb. of butter, ¼ lb. of lard, ½ lb. of treacle, 2 teaspoonfuls of ground ginger, 1 teaspoonful of cinnamon, ¼ nutmeg (grated), 1 teaspoonful of bicarbonate of soda, 2 oz. of almonds (blanched), ½ gill of milk.

METHOD.—Rub the butter and lard into the flour. Add the sugar, oatmeal, cinnamon, ginger, and nutmeg. Warm the treacle, pour it in and mix thoroughly. Add the soda mixed with the milk. Roll out the dough and cut it into large rounds. Place an almond on each round and bake them in a moderate oven for about twenty minutes.

Sufficient for eighteen to twenty-four parkins, according to size.

PARTY CAKES

INGREDIENTS.—1 teacupful of castor sugar, 2 eggs, ½ lb. of flour, 1 teaspoonful of cream of tartar, ¼ flat teaspoonful of carbonate of soda, 2½ oz. of butter or margarine, milk (if required).

FOR THE ICING.—9 oz. of icing sugar, 4 oz. of butter, coffee essence, 4 oz. of almonds (for coating).

METHOD.—Grease a baking-tin.

Sieve the flour, cream of tartar, and soda.

Whisk the eggs and sugar together until the mixture becomes thick and

creamy and free from the dark streaks of egg.

Melt the fat, but do not make it hot.

Stir the flour, etc., into the sugar and eggs, then add the melted fat.

Mix all together lightly, adding a little milk if required.

Put into the greased tin—it should only be half full.

Bake in a hot oven for about fifteen minutes.

Put on to a sieve and leave until cold.

TO PREPARE THE ALMONDS.—Blanch, skin and chop them up roughly.

Place on a tin—on a piece of paper—and put into the oven until lightly browned.

TO MAKE THE ICING.—Rub the icing sugar through a fine sieve.

Add the butter and beat both to a cream.

Add sufficient coffee essence to flavour.

Cut the prepared sponge into rounds about two inches in diameter.

Spread the icing round the sides and over the top of the cakes, then coat them with the baked nuts.

PEAR GATEAU

INGREDIENTS.—6 oz. of flour, 3 oz. of butter, 4 oz. of castor sugar, 3 eggs, ½ teaspoonful of baking-powder.

FOR THE DECORATION.—1/- of cream, 4 tinned pears, 2 oz. of chopped walnuts, ¾ lb. of icing sugar, 6 oz. of loaf sugar, ¾ gill of pear syrup.

METHOD.—Grease and line a cake-tin.

Cream the butter and sugar till soft and white, and beat in the eggs one at a time.

Add the flour and the baking-powder.

Place the mixture in the tin and bake it in a moderate oven for about half an hour.

Lay the pears on a plate. Boil the syrup and loaf sugar for ten minutes, without stirring.

Let the syrup cool and pour it over the pears. Whip the cream and mix half the icing sugar with it. When the cake is cold, split it open.

To decorate the cake, lay the pears

on the top half and decorate them with some of the cream (put in an icing pump with a rose-forcer screwed on).

Mix the chopped walnuts and the rest of the icing sugar with the cream that remains, and spread it over the lower half of the cake. Fit the two halves together again.

PETITS FOURS

INGREDIENTS.—3 oz. of ground almonds, 6 oz. of icing sugar, flavouring—orange, almond, or vanilla—one egg, chocolate nonpariels.

METHOD.—Roll the lumps out of the sugar and rub it through a fine sieve. Mix it with the ground almonds. Beat up the egg and add sufficient to the sugar and almonds to mix a very stiff paste, with flavouring as desired. Work it until smooth and then divide the paste into small portions and make them into fancy shapes. Small cottage loaves or acorn shapes look attractive.

To shape the former, make each portion into two smooth balls one larger than the other, put the smaller on top of the larger one and make a hole through the centre with a skewer.

To shape the latter, form some of the paste into small ovals and fix each into a cup-shaped piece.

Place the petits fours on a baking-tin, brush them over with egg, and bake them in a very moderate oven for about fifteen minutes. When cooked and cold, brush the cup-shaped piece of each acorn with white of egg and coat it with chocolate nonpariels.

Sufficient to make sixteen or eighteen petits fours.

PICNIC CAKE

INGREDIENTS.—1 lb. of flour, 1 level teaspoonful of carbonate of soda, ½ lb. of margarine, 1 tablespoonful of caraway seeds, ½ lb. of Barbados sugar, 2 teaspoonfuls of cream of tartar, 2 oz. of shelled walnuts, 2 oz. of candied peel, 2 oz. of sultanas, 2 eggs, milk, a little castor sugar.

METHOD.—Wash, pick over and dry the fruit, cut up the peel and chop the walnuts.

Sieve the flour with the soda and cream of tartar. Rub in the margarine and add the sugar, caraway seeds, prepared nuts, and fruit.

Whisk the eggs and add them, with some milk as required.

Beat the mixture well, and then turn it into a greased cake-tin. Sprinkle castor sugar and a few caraway seeds on top and put the mixture into a moderately hot oven to bake. It will take about one and a half hours.

PIE CAKE

INGREDIENTS.—6 oz. of self-raising flour, 4 oz. of butter or margarine, 4 oz. of castor sugar, ½ teaspoonful of baking-powder, grated rind of a lemon, 2 eggs, ¼ gill of milk.

FOR THE DECORATION.—6 oz. of icing sugar, 6 oz. of ground almonds, the yolk of an egg, 1 dessertspoonful of lemon-juice, jam.

METHOD.—Grease a pie-dish.

Rub the butter into the flour.

Add the sugar, lemon-rind, and baking-powder.

Beat the eggs with a little milk, and with them mix the dry ingredients to a fairly stiff paste.

Put this in the pie-dish.

Bake it in a moderately hot oven for forty-five minutes.

To ice the cake, rub the sugar through a hair sieve, and mix it with the almonds.

Bind them with the yolk of egg and lemon-juice and knead till smooth. Roll it out into an oval shape. Brush the top of the cake with jam and press the paste on it, cutting off any uneven edges.

Roll out the trimmings and cut them into diamond-shaped pieces to represent leaves. Lay these in a circle on top of the pie, sticking them on with a little jam.

PIERRETTES

INGREDIENTS.—Wafer cones or cornets (about 12 or 15), 1 gill of cream, castor sugar, vanilla flavouring, 2 oz. of preserved ginger.

FOR THE CHOCOLATE BUTTER ICING.—2 oz. of icing sugar, 1 oz. of butter, ½ oz. of grated chocolate, vanilla flavouring, milk.

METHOD.—Dissolve the chocolate

in about one tablespoonful of milk, then cool slightly.

Roll the lumps out of the icing sugar and rub it through a hair sieve.

Add the butter and beat both to a cream.

Stir in the chocolate and a few drops of vanilla and mix together. Whisk the cream until it stiffens, then sweeten and flavour it to suit taste.

Cut the ginger into small pieces and stir into it, then put into the cones.

Put the chocolate icing into an icing bag with a small rose tube fixed in it, and force three rose patterns at equal distances apart down each cone to look like a pierrette's hat.

PINEAPPLE BASKETS

INGREDIENTS.—5 oz. of flour, $\frac{1}{2}$ teaspoonful of baking-powder, 2 oz. of butter or margarine, 4 oz. of castor sugar, 2 eggs, milk and water—if required.

FOR THE FILLING.—7 oz. of icing sugar, 3 oz. of butter, few pineapple cubes (tinned pineapple), angelica.

METHOD.—Grease some small cake-tins. Sieve the flour and baking-powder. Whisk the eggs and sugar together until thick and creamy, and free from dark streaks of egg. Fold in the flour and baking-powder. Lastly, stir in the butter (melted). Mix all together lightly, put into the prepared tins, and bake in a hot oven for about fifteen minutes. Leave on a sieve until cold, then scoop out a round piece from the centre of each cake. (These pieces can be used in a trifle.)

TO MAKE THE FILLING.—Rub the icing sugar through a fine sieve. Beat the butter and sugar to a cream. Cut some cubes of pineapple into small pieces, and stir into the creamed butter and sugar. Fill the cavities, and completely cover the top of the cakes with the prepared filling, piling it on roughly. Cut some thin strips of angelica, dip them into warm water to remove the sugar, and make them pliable.

Fix a piece across each basket to form a handle—to do this make a small hole with a thin iron skewer on either side of the baskets.

Sufficient to make about nine baskets.

PINEAPPLE BUNS

INGREDIENTS.—1 lb. of flour, 9 oz. of margarine, 8 oz. of castor sugar, 2 eggs, 2 teaspoonfuls of baking-powder, $\frac{1}{2}$ lb. of glacé pineapple, milk (about $\frac{3}{4}$ gill).

METHOD.—Grease about two dozen small round cake-tins.

Sieve together the flour and baking-powder. Cut the pineapple into small pieces, and leave out a tiny piece to put on the top of each cake.

Cream the fat and sugar together, stir in each egg separately and quickly, beat the first one in well before adding the second.

Whisk up for about five minutes.

Add the glacé pineapple to the flour and stir in gradually to the other ingredients, together with a little milk.

When thoroughly mixed, put into the prepared tins, place a small piece of pineapple in the centre of each. Bake in a hot oven for about twenty minutes. Place on sieve to cool.

PINEAPPLE CREAM BUNS

INGREDIENTS.—2 oz. of flour, 1 egg or $1\frac{1}{2}$, according to size, 1 oz. of margarine or butter, $\frac{1}{4}$ pint of water, good pinch of castor sugar, $1\frac{1}{2}$ oz. of glacé pineapple, cornflour custard-filling (see p. 473).

METHOD.—Weigh the ingredients accurately and sieve the flour.

Put the water, sugar, and fat into a saucepan, and when the latter has melted and the water is boiling, sprinkle in the flour. Stir the mixture very quickly over a low burner until it forms a thick paste and afterwards leaves the sides of the pan. Draw the pan aside from the flame and cool the mixture slightly, then add the egg and stir quickly for a minute or two.

Drop the mixture on to a buttered baking-sheet in small round heaps (leaving a space between each), and put it into a fairly hot oven to bake. The heat can be reduced afterwards, as required. The buns will take about twenty minutes to cook and should only be very lightly browned.

When cold, split them open and fill them with custard filling (see p. 473), to which the pineapple has been cut up and added.

Sufficient to make eight or nine small, or five or six large buns.

PINEAPPLE GATEAU

INGREDIENTS.—5 oz. of butter or margarine, 6 oz. of castor sugar, 2 eggs, ¼ lb. of flour, ¼ flat teaspoonful of carbonate of soda, 1 teaspoonful of cream of tartar, milk, pineapple marmalade (for filling), use other jam if preferred.

FOR THE ICING.—10 oz. of icing sugar, 4½ oz. of butter, yellow colouring, pineapple-juice (about 2 teaspoonfuls), citron peel (for the stalk).

METHOD.—Grease a small, round cake-tin, about four inches in diameter, and line with greased paper to stand several inches above the sides.

Sieve the flour, soda, and cream of tartar.

Beat the sugar and fat to a cream.

Add each egg separately and stir in quickly, then beat for a few minutes before adding the second.

When both are added, stir in the flour, etc., and a little milk as required.

Mix all together lightly, put into the prepared tin, and bake in a moderately hot oven for about three-quarters of an hour ; then place on a sieve and leave until cold.

Split the cake into three and spread each layer with pineapple marmalade (or jam), then put together again neatly. The cake should stand about the height of a pineapple ; if too high, cut off a small piece before splitting it.

TO MAKE THE ICING

Rub the icing sugar through a fine sieve. Add the butter and beat both to a cream.

Stir in some pineapple-juice to flavour, and sufficient colouring to make the icing about the tint of the outside of a pineapple.

To ice the cake, fix an icing tube (large rose pattern) on to an icing bag.

Put some of the icing into it, and force it in little rose patterns on to the cake in straight lines, from top to bottom, completely covering the cake.

Cut the thick pieces of citron to represent the stalk, make a hole in the top, and put them into it.

NOTE.—If the icing is the correct consistency, each rose will be quite distinct. If too moist, leave for a few minutes until it becomes slightly stiffer.

If liked, the tip of each rose can be dabbed with a little chocolate icing.

Angelica is sometimes used instead of citron for making the stalk.

If, when serving the cake, you would prefer to slice it across, instead of down, in the usual way, do not split it into three and spread with jam, but cut it down into halves or quarters.

To make a variety, some crystalised pineapple can be cut up and added to the cake mixture. About one or two ounces would be sufficient, the latter should be added with the flour.

PINEAPPLE SHORTCAKE

INGREDIENTS.—½ lb. of flour, 4 oz. of margarine, 2½ teaspoonfuls of baking-powder, 3½ oz. of castor sugar, milk.

FOR THE FILLING.—¾ small tin of pineapple slices, ½ gill of cream, 2 oz. of icing sugar.

METHOD.—Grease a sandwich-tin.

Cream the fat and sugar.

Sieve the flour and baking-powder, stir in and mix to a fairly soft paste, adding some milk as required.

Turn on to a slightly floured board, make into a smooth ball and roll out to the shape of the tin. Put it into it, brush the top with milk, and bake in a good moderately hot oven for about half an hour. Cool on a sieve.

TO MAKE THE FILLING.—Strain the juice from the pineapple and cut the fruit into very small pieces, leaving out one or two larger pieces for decoration.

Whisk the cream until it stiffens, stir in the icing sugar and pineapple and mix all together.

Split the cake into halves, cover with the prepared filling and sandwich together again. Dust the top with icing sugar and put some pineapple in the centre.

Note.—The icing sugar must first be sieved.

PINEAPPLE TRIANGLE

INGREDIENTS.—2 eggs, 3½ oz. of castor sugar, 2 oz. of margarine, 4 oz. of flour, 1 level teaspoonful of baking powder, milk.

FOR THE FILLING.—1 oz. of flour, 1 gill of pineapple syrup, ½ to ¾ gill of minced pineapple (well drained), 1 oz. of desiccated coconut, 1 oz. of sugar, or to taste.

FOR THE ICING.—½ lb. of icing sugar, 1 white of egg, water or pineapple syrup, pineapple essence, green or apricot yellow colouring, some chocolate icing (see p. 485).

METHOD.—Beat the sugar and fat to a cream, add each egg separately, stirring it quickly, and beat well.

Stir in the flour sifted with baking-powder, and mix them lightly, adding a little milk as required.

Turn the mixture into a buttered tin—a square tin, seven by seven inches, and of about the depth of a sandwich-tin—and bake it in a hot oven until spongy. Cool it on a sieve.

Cut the sponge into two pieces cornerwise, spread the filling on one piece, then sandwich the two together.

Spread a thick layer of icing on top, and when this is set decorate it with dots of chocolate icing forced through an icing pump with a piping tube affixed.

To MAKE THE FILLING.—Mix the flour and sugar together and mix them to a smooth paste with some of the pineapple syrup.

Heat the remainder of the syrup and add this, then return all to the pan and bring it to the boil, keeping it well stirred.

Boil the filling gently for a few minutes, draw the pan aside, add the coconut, and stir in the pineapple gradually, and more sugar if required.

To MAKE THE ICING.—Sift the sugar into a basin. Beat the egg-white slightly and add it. Mix the icing to a thick, smooth consistency, adding a little water or pineapple syrup as required. Beat the icing well, flavour it with two or three drops of pineapple essence and tint it to a green or yellow colour, then spread a thick layer on top of the cake.

PLUM CAKE

INGREDIENTS.—1 lb. of flour, ½ lb. of margarine, ½ lb. of raisins, 2 oz. of angelica or candied peel, 6 oz. of granulated sugar, grated nutmeg, ½ flat teaspoonful of carbonate of soda, 2 eggs, milk to mix (about 1 gill).

METHOD.—Wash, stone, and dry the raisins. Sieve together the flour, soda, and a little grated nutmeg.

Grease a cake-tin and line with greased paper as before.

Rub the margarine into the flour until it is like breadcrumbs.

Cut the angelica and raisins into small pieces and add to the flour, together with the sugar. Mix all the dry ingredients together.

Whisk the eggs, then stir in about a gill of milk.

Pour on to the flour and mix thoroughly.

A little more milk may be added if required.

Be careful not to make the mixture too wet, or the fruit will sink to the bottom and the cake will be heavy. (This applies to all fruit cakes.)

Place in the greased cake-tin and bake in a moderately hot oven for about one hour and a half.

Cool on a sieve.

DARK PLUM CAKE

INGREDIENTS.—1 lb. of flour, ¼ lb. of butter, ¼ lb. of lard, ½ lb. of currants, ½ lb. of raisins, 1 teaspoonful of baking-powder, 2 oz. of mixed candied peel, ½ lb of moist sugar, 3 eggs, ½ teaspoonful of bicarbonate of soda, 1 tablespoonful of golden syrup, about ½ gill of milk, 1 teaspoonful of mixed spice or a little grated nutmeg.

METHOD.—Grease and line a large tin.

Wash and pick the currants and dry them in a cloth.

Stone the raisins and cut them in half.

Chop the peel.

Mix the flour, spice, and baking-powder.

Cream the butter, lard, and sugar, and beat in the eggs one at a time.

Warm the syrup without making it hot.

Dissolve the soda in the milk.

Add the flour and fruit to the creamed butter, sugar, and eggs, and mix them with the syrup and milk.

Place the mixture in the lined tin and flatten the centre slightly.

Bake the cake in a moderate oven about two hours.

Let the cake cool for ten minutes, then lift it out of the tin.

Remove the paper and put the cake on a sieve till cold.

STEAMED PLUM CAKE

INGREDIENTS.—10 oz. of flour, $\frac{1}{2}$ lb. of raisins (stoned), 1 lb. of currants (washed), $\frac{1}{2}$ lb. of butter, 4 eggs, 1 tablespoonful of golden syrup, 5 oz. of moist sugar, $\frac{1}{4}$ lb. of mixed peel (chopped), $\frac{1}{4}$ lb. of ground almonds, $\frac{1}{4}$ oz. of mixed spice, juice and grated rind of a lemon, $\frac{1}{2}$ gill of milk.

METHOD.—Grease a cake-tin, but do not line it with paper.

Cream the butter till soft, add the sugar and beat the mixture well till it is light and creamy.

Add the eggs (unbeaten) one at a time.

Beat the mixture for five minutes after adding each egg.

Stir in the fruit, ground almonds, spice, and the lemon-rind and juice.

Add the flour and moisten the mixture with a little milk and the golden syrup.

Put it in the tin, which should be about three-parts full. Cover it very carefully with two pieces of greased paper twisted over the top.

Put it in a steamer with boiling water in the lower pan and steam it steadily for five hours to make the cake a dark colour.

Remove the paper and bake the cake for half an hour.

POTATO FLOUR CAKES

INGREDIENTS.—3 oz. of potato flour, 5 oz. of flour, 1 teaspoonful of cream of tartar, $\frac{1}{2}$ flat teaspoonful of carbonate of soda, 6 oz. of castor sugar, 5 oz. of margarine, 2 eggs, milk, vanilla.

METHOD.—Sieve the flour with the potato flour, cream of tartar, and carbonate of soda.

Cream the fat and sugar. Separate the egg-yolks from the whites. Beat the yolks into the creamed fat and sugar.

Gradually stir in the flours with a little milk as required. Mix all together lightly and add half a teaspoonful of vanilla flavouring.

Whisk the egg-whites to a stiff froth and fold them into the mixture.

Stand some baking-cups on a baking-sheet. About half fill them with the mixture. Dredge the top of each with castor sugar.

Put the cakes into a hot oven to bake. They will take about fifteen or twenty minutes to cook.

Sufficient for thirty cakes.

POUND CAKE

INGREDIENTS.—$\frac{1}{4}$ lb. of flour, $\frac{1}{4}$ lb. of castor sugar, $\frac{1}{4}$ lb. of margarine, $\frac{1}{4}$ lb. of eggs (weighed with the shells), 1 orange (rind only), 1 lemon (rind only).

METHOD.—Grease a small cake-tin and line with greased paper to stand above the top.

Grate the orange and lemon-rinds finely.

Sieve the flour.

Beat the sugar and fat to a cream. Separate the eggs.

Whisk the egg-whites to a very stiff froth. Stir each yolk separately into the creamed fat and sugar and beat well for a few minutes.

When both are added, gradually stir in the flour and grated rinds, and mix together lightly with a little milk, then fold in the whisked whites.

Turn into the cake-tin and put into a moderately hot oven to bake, lessening the heat as required.

It will take about three-quarters of an hour.

PRALINE CAKE

INGREDIENTS.—6 oz. of short pastry (see p. 252), $\frac{1}{2}$ lb. of ground almonds, $\frac{1}{2}$ lb. of castor sugar, $\frac{1}{2}$ lb. of stale sultana cake, 2 oz. of crystallised cherries, 1 egg, juice of $\frac{1}{2}$ a lemon, strawberry jam, $\frac{1}{4}$ lb. of icing sugar.

METHOD.—Crumble the cake and put it in a mixing basin with the almonds and sugar. Add the cherries, cut in half. Beat the egg and add it to the mixture with the lemon-juice and one tablespoonful of jam. Leave it all night. Line a pie-dish with short pastry and trim the edges neatly.

Fill the centre with the cake mixture and make the pastry trimmings into crossway pieces. Bake for about half an hour.

When cold, ice the cake with the sifted icing sugar mixed with a tablespoonful of tepid water, heated for a few seconds in a saucepan (until the base of the pan feels warm) and poured over the top of cake.

PRINCESS CAKES

INGREDIENTS.—¼ lb. of margarine, ¼ lb. of castor sugar, 1 egg, 2 oz. of ground rice, 2½ oz. of flour, 1 teaspoonful of baking-powder, vanilla, jam, desiccated coconut.

METHOD.—Grease about a dozen small cake-tins. Sieve together the flour, ground rice, and baking-powder.

Beat the sugar and margarine to a cream.

Stir in the egg quickly and beat for five minutes. Fold in the flour, etc.

Flavour with a few drops of vanilla and mix thoroughly.

Place a small quantity into each tin and bake in a hot oven for about fifteen minutes.

Stand on a sieve to cool. Put a little jam in the centre of each and sprinkle with coconut.

NOTE.—Use red jam for half of them, and yellow for the remainder. Lift the cakes carefully out of the tins, as they are very liable to break.

PRUNE CAKE

INGREDIENTS.—½ lb. of flour, ¼ flat teaspoonful of carbonate of soda, ¼ lb. of margarine, ¼ lb. of prunes, 2 oz. of candied peel, 2 oz. of golden syrup, 1 egg, 3 oz. of granulated sugar, milk (½ gill).

METHOD.—Wash and dry the prunes. Prepare and line a cake-tin. Sieve the flour and soda. Rub the fat into the flour. Cut the peel into small pieces. Remove the stones and cut the prunes into small pieces. Add the sugar, peel, and prunes to the flour, etc.

Whisk the egg, add the golden syrup and milk to it, whisk all together. Add the wet ingredients to the dry and mix all together, and beat for a few minutes. Put into the prepared cake-tin and bake in a moderately hot oven for about one hour. Turn on to a sieve and leave until cold.

QUEEN CAKES

INGREDIENTS.—9 oz. of flour, 5 oz. of castor sugar, 5 oz. of margarine, 1 flat teaspoonful of baking-powder, 1 lemon, ¼ lb. of glacé cherries, 1½ oz. of candied peel, 2 eggs, milk (if required).

METHOD.—Grease some small fancy cake-tins — heart-shaped, diamond, half-moons, etc.

Beat the sugar and margarine together until they resemble thick cream.

Wipe the lemon and finely grate the rind.

Sieve together the flour and baking-powder, and mix with the grated rind.

Cut the cherries and peel into small pieces. Then stir them into the flour, etc.

Whisk one egg quickly into the creamed fat and sugar and beat well for a few minutes. Then add the other egg, and beat up again for about six minutes.

Fold in the flour and fruit, etc., and mix all together lightly.

Put into the prepared tins and bake in a hot oven for about twenty minutes.

Place on a sieve to cool.

SULTANA QUEEN CAKES

INGREDIENTS.—½ lb. of flour, 1 lemon (rind only), 1 oz. of almonds, 1 teaspoonful of cream of tartar, ½ flat teaspoonful of carbonate of soda, 5 oz. of castor sugar, 6 oz. of margarine, 2 oz. of glacé cherries, 1 oz. of citron peel, 6 oz. of sultanas, 2 eggs, milk.

METHOD.—Wash and pick over the sultanas.

Rub them in a cloth and dry them in a warm place.

Cut up the cherries and peel.

Blanch and chop the almonds and grate the lemon-rind finely.

Beat the sugar and fat to a cream, then gradually stir in the flour, sieved with the cream of tartar and the carbonate of soda, the prepared fruit, and the almonds.

Add the well-beaten eggs, and some milk as required.

Mix all together lightly.

Turn the mixture into a large cake-tin and bake the cake in a moderate oven.

If preferred, the mixture may be baked in small tins.

RAINBOW CAKE

INGREDIENTS.—¾ lb. of flour, ½ lb. of butter or margarine, ¼ gill of milk, ½ lb. of sugar, 3 eggs, ½ oz. of cocoa, cochineal, 4 good tablespoonfuls of jam, 2 tablespoonfuls of rum or lemon-juice, ½ teaspoonful of baking-powder, almond paste (see p. 486).

FOR THE ICING.—6 oz. of icing sugar, 1½ tablespoonfuls of tepid water, cochineal.

METHOD.—Grease three small square tins. Cream the butter and sugar till soft. Add the eggs one at a time and beat them well.

Stir in the flour, milk, and baking-powder. Put one-third of the mixture into one of the tins and put one-third into each of two basins.

Add the cocoa to the mixture in one basin and colour the other pink with cochineal. Place the cakes in the tins and bake them in a moderate oven for about thirty minutes.

Next day line an oblong tin with a strip of double greaseproof paper long enough for the ends to wrap over.

Cut the cakes into neat pieces of different shapes and sizes. Heat the jam and rum together.

Dip a white piece of cake in the jam and put it in the tin. Next dip in a pink piece and press it against the white. Continue with alternate colours till the tin is full.

Fold over the ends of the paper tightly and put a weight on top.

Next day turn it out of the tin, remove the paper and press a strip of almond paste firmly on the cake.

To ice the cake mix the icing sugar and water in a small saucepan and stir over the gas a few seconds till it melts. Pour half the icing on top of the cake and spread it quickly with a knife. Colour the rest of the icing

pink with cochineal and put it in a small pointed bag (made by twisting a double triangular piece of greaseproof paper into a cornet shape).

Cut off the end and while the white icing is still wet make straight lines *across* the cake about one inch apart. Before it dries take a skewer and very lightly mark straight lines *along* the cake. This will alter the shape of the pink lines and give them a pretty wavy appearance.

To make wavy lines of *three* colours, i.e., pink, green, and brown, colour three small portions of icing and put each in a separate bag.

After spreading white icing on the cake as described, very quickly make the lines across, putting three different coloured ones close together, then leaving a space of one inch.

A RAISIN CAKE

INGREDIENTS.—½ lb. of flour, ¼ flat teaspoonful of carbonate of soda, ½ lemon (rind only), ¼ lb. of margarine, 6 oz. of seedless raisins, ¼ lb. of sugar, 1 egg, milk.

METHOD.—Wash and dry the raisins if loose ones ; packet raisins are already cleaned. Sieve the flour with the carbonate of soda. Rub in the margarine. Grate the lemon-rind and add it with the sugar and raisins to the flour.

Whisk up the egg and stir it in with some milk as required.

Beat the mixture well, turn it into a greased cake-tin and put it in a moderately hot oven to bake.

PLAIN RAISIN CAKE

INGREDIENTS.—6 oz. of flour, 4 oz. of rice flour, 4 oz. of sugar, 5 oz. of clarified beef dripping or margarine, 2 eggs, 1 teaspoonful of baking-powder, ½ gill of milk, 6 oz. of raisins.

METHOD.—Grease an oblong cake-tin.

Stone the raisins and cut them in half.

Mix the flour and rice-flour. Rub in the dripping until there are no lumps.

Add the sugar, raisins, and baking-powder.

Beat the eggs well and add about half a gill of milk to them.

Mix the cake stiffly and place it in the tin.

Bake in a moderately hot oven for about fifty minutes.

If the centre feels firm and elastic when pressed the cake is done.

Leave it for five minutes to cool a little, then remove it from the tin and place it on a sieve for the steam to escape.

NOTE.—A hot cake should never be put on a plate as the steam cannot then escape, and the cake will be heavy.

RASPBERRY AND CURRANT SHORTCAKE

INGREDIENTS.—6 oz. of flour, 1 oz. of butter, $\frac{3}{4}$ gill of milk, 1 teaspoonful of baking-powder, $\frac{1}{2}$ teaspoonful of salt, $\frac{3}{4}$ lb. of raspberries, $\frac{1}{4}$ lb. of red currants, sugar to sweeten, 1 gill of cream.

FOR THE GLAZE.—1 dessertspoonful of castor sugar, 1 tablespoonful of milk.

METHOD.—Grease a baking-sheet and light the gas in the oven.

Rub the butter into the flour and add the salt and the baking-powder.

Mix quickly with the milk to a soft but not sticky dough, as for scones.

Press the dough into a flat round cake by kneading it and place it on the tin.

Bake for twenty minutes in the top of a quick oven. Five minutes before taking it from the oven glaze the cake with a dessertspoonful of castor sugar dissolved in a tablespoonful of milk.

While the cake is baking remove the stalks from the fruit.

Mash the fruit in a basin with enough sugar to sweeten to taste.

Whip the cream till it is stiff and sweeten it.

As soon as the cake is done, split it open, and while it is still hot fill with half the sweetened fruit.

Pour the rest of the fruit over the top and finish off with a good dab of cream.

RASPBERRY GATEAU

INGREDIENTS.—6 oz. of flour, $\frac{1}{4}$ lb. of margarine, 2 oz. of cornflour, castor sugar (about 1 tablespoonful), milk to mix (about $\frac{3}{4}$ gill), a pinch of salt, 3 teaspoonfuls of baking-powder, raspberry jam, as required, 2 whites of eggs, 4 dessertspoonfuls of castor sugar, cochineal, $\frac{1}{2}$ oz. of pistachio nuts.

METHOD.—Mix and sieve the cornflour, salt, baking-powder, and flour.

Rub in the margarine.

Stir in the tablespoonful of sugar and mix with the other ingredients.

Add milk as required and mix to a stiff paste, not sticky but just pliable.

Grease a deep sandwich-tin and roll out the pastry to a round shape about an inch thick.

Place in the tin and brush over with milk.

Bake in a hot oven for about twenty minutes.

Place on a sieve until cold.

Split into halves and spread with jam. Fit on the top.

Whisk the whites to a stiff froth, fold into them the castor sugar, with a few drops of cochineal.

Shake on to the top of the cake in little heaps.

Place in a warm oven for a few minutes to set the meringue.

Sprinkle the top with a few chopped pistachio nuts. Serve cold.

NOTE.—Blanch the nuts before chopping.

RATAFIA SANDWICH

INGREDIENTS.—1 oz. of crushed ratafia biscuits, 3 oz. of margarine, 2 eggs, their weight in flour and castor sugar, 1 level teaspoonful of baking-powder, ratafia flavouring essence, jam.

FOR THE ICING.—6 oz. of castor sugar, 1 white of egg, 5 dessertspoonfuls of water, cochineal, ratafia flavouring, ratafia biscuits, and hundreds and thousands.

METHOD.—Beat the margarine and sugar to a cream, add each egg separately. Stir them in quickly and beat well. Add the ratafia crumbs, also the flour and baking-powder (previously sifted), and mix all together lightly. Add a few drops of ratafia flavouring, turn the mixture into a greased sandwich-tin and bake it in a fairly quick oven until spongy. When cold, split it in halves and spread it with jam.

To Make the Icing.—Put the sugar into a saucepan with the water and white of egg, and whisk them together over hot water until thick and creamy, then add flavouring and colouring to taste.

Ice the top of the sandwich with this icing, sprinkle it with hundreds and thousands, and arrange ratafia biscuits round the edge.

RICE BUNS

Ingredients.—1½ oz. of ground rice, 2½ oz. of flour, ¼ level teaspoonful of baking-powder, 1 yolk of egg, vanilla flavouring, 2 oz. of margarine, 3 dessertspoonfuls of castor sugar, a few glacé cherries, soft icing.

Method.—Beat the sugar and fat to a cream, then beat in the egg-yolk.

Sift the flour with the ground rice and baking-powder and mix all the ingredients together into a paste, flavouring it with a few drops of vanilla.

Put the mixture aside until it becomes a little more solid and workable, then divide it into eight portions.

Form each one into a ball, flatten it slightly, and place the buns on a lightly greased baking-sheet. Bake them in a quick oven for about ten minutes.

When cold, put a dab of soft icing, flavoured with vanilla, in the centre of each and decorate it with a glacé cherry.

Sufficient for eight cakes.

RICE CAKES

Ingredients.—3 eggs, their weight in flour, butter, or margarine and sugar, ¼ lb. of ground rice, 1 teaspoonful of baking-powder, lemon essence, 3 oz. of currants, 2 oz. of candied peel, milk.

Method.—Wash the currants and put to dry.

Grease some small cake-tins (fancy shapes).

Cream the sugar and fat together.

Sieve the flour, ground rice, and baking-powder together.

Beat the eggs separately into the creamed sugar and fat.

Cut the peel into small pieces, pick over the currants, and add these to the flour, etc.

Add gradually the dry ingredients to the sugar, fat, and eggs, together with a little milk.

Add a few drops of essence of lemon and mix all well together. Put into the greased tins.

Bake in a hot oven for twenty minutes.

RICE FANCIES

Ingredients.—3 oz. of flour, 3 oz. of ground rice, 2 oz. of margarine, 2 oz. of castor sugar, 1 egg, ½ teaspoonful of baking-powder, a little raspberry jam, ½ gill of milk.

For the Pink Icing.—6 oz. of icing sugar (sifted), 3 oz. of butter, 1 teaspoonful of raspberry jam (syrup only), cochineal. Mix these ingredients well.

Method.—Grease twelve patty-pans. Cream the margarine and sugar till soft. Put in the egg and beat well ; add the dry ingredients.

Mix with the milk. Put quickly into the patty-pans and bake for about fifteen minutes. When cold cut in half and spread with jam, then decorate with icing, in a trellis pattern.

RICE GATEAU

Ingredients.—6 oz. of ground rice, ¼ lb. of margarine, 8 oz. of castor sugar, 6 oz. of flour, 3 eggs, milk, flavouring, 2 teaspoonfuls of baking-powder.

For the Icing.—1 lb. of castor sugar, a good pinch of cream of tartar, 1 gill of hot water, 2 egg-whites, cochineal, flavouring, rings of angelica (for decorating).

Method.—Beat the sugar and fat to a cream, add each egg separately. Stir each in quickly and beat it well before adding the next one.

When all are beaten in, gradually stir in the flour sifted with the ground rice and baking-powder and mix all together lightly, adding some milk as required, and a few drops of flavouring essence as desired.

Turn the mixture into a greased and lined cake-tin and bake it in a moderately hot oven.

When cold, coat it with icing and decorate it with rings of angelica.

To Make the Icing.—Put the sugar in a saucepan with the water, dissolve it, then bring it to the boil.

Add the cream of tartar and boil

the syrup until a small quantity, when put in cold water and left for a few seconds, becomes a soft ball when rolled between the fingers. Have the egg-whites whisked to a stiff froth by the time the syrup is ready, then pour the latter on to them gradually, stirring well all the time.

Colour the icing with cochineal and add a few drops of flavouring of the same kind as used in the cake, and when the icing begins to thicken and set, pour it over the gâteau.

RICE SPONGE SANDWICH

INGREDIENTS.—2 oz. of ground rice, 2 oz. of flour, ½ teaspoonful of baking-powder, 3 oz. of castor sugar, 3 oz. of margarine or butter, 1 egg, 1 table-spoonful of milk (if required), rasp-berry jam.

METHOD.—Sieve the flour, ground rice, and baking-powder together.

Beat the sugar and fat to a cream.

Stir the egg in quickly, then beat for about five minutes.

Lastly, fold in the ground rice and flour, etc., and the milk, if required.

Mix all together lightly, put into a greased sandwich-tin and bake in a hot oven for about ten to twelve minutes.

Put on to a sieve to cool, and when cold, split open and spread with jam, then put together again and dredge with castor sugar.

ROCK CAKES

INGREDIENTS.—½ lb. of flour, 3 oz. of margarine, 3 oz. of sugar, 4 oz. of currants, 1 egg, 1 teaspoonful of baking-powder, a spoonful of milk, if required.

METHOD.—Wash, pick over and dry the fruit. Sieve the flour with the baking-powder. Rub in the fat, then mix in the sugar and fruit.

Beat up the egg and add it to the dry ingredients and mix them to a stiff consistency.

Place the mixture on a greased baking-sheet in small heaps and put the cakes into a hot oven to bake.

They will take from fifteen to twenty minutes, and after the first few minutes the heat can be lessened as required.

NOTE.—Rock cakes so often lose their shape when they are baked.

There are two causes—making the mixture too moist, or else not having your oven quite hot enough when they are first put in to bake.

The consistency of the mixture for these cakes should be about as stiff as pastry is when mixed, and the mixture should be put on to the baking-sheet in small, rough heaps. If you keep these two details in mind you will have no further trouble.

ROLLED OATCAKES

INGREDIENTS.—1 egg, 4 oz. of sugar, 2 oz. of butter, ½ lb. of rolled oats, 2 or 3 bitter almonds, 1 oz. of flour.

METHOD.—Beat the sugar and the egg till thick and creamy. Add the melted butter, oats, chopped almonds, and flour. Form the dough into small balls, and brown them lightly on a baking-sheet in a good oven.

Sufficient to make eighteen cakes.

ROSE GATEAU

INGREDIENTS.—3 oz. of flour, 1 teaspoonful of baking-powder, ¼ lb. of margarine, ¼ lb. of castor sugar, 3 oz. of potato flour, 2 eggs, milk.

FOR THE BUTTER ICING.—6 oz. of icing sugar, 3 oz. of butter, vanilla flavouring, cochineal, biscuit or cake crumbs.

METHOD.—Grease a small cake-tin and line with greased paper to stand above the top. Sieve the flour, baking-powder, and potato flour together. Beat the sugar and fat to a cream. Add each egg separately, stir in quickly, and beat well for a few minutes before adding the second.

When both are beaten in, gradually stir in the flour, baking-powder, and potato flour, and mix all together lightly, adding a little milk as required.

Put into the prepared tin and bake in a moderately hot oven.

When cooked, place on a sieve until cold.

To Make the Butter Icing

Roll the lumps out of the sugar and rub it through a hair sieve.

Add the butter and beat both to a cream.

Flavour with a few drops of vanilla flavouring, and colour half the icing to a pale pink shade by adding a few drops of cochineal.

TO ICE THE CAKE

Split it into halves, and spread over a layer of the pink icing, then sandwich it together again.

If the top of the cake has risen unevenly cut off a slice. Spread a layer of white icing round the sides and coat it with some light-brown cakecrumbs (finely sieved).

Put the remainder of the pink-and-white icing into two icing bags with a rose tube fixed in the end of each.

Mark two lines across the top of the cake, dividing it into quarters. Force the icing on to it in small rose patterns, using alternate colours for each quarter.

SOME OTHER SUGGESTIONS FOR DECORATING THIS GATEAU

1. A circle of pink rose patterns can be forced round the top edge, placing them closely together, then a circle of white ones inside this, and so on, until the centre is reached.

2. With a fine piping tube, such as is used for writing on cakes, make a trellis-work of lines across the top in alternate colours, and decorate with crystallised rose leaves.

3. Instead of using an icing tube, just spread the icing over evenly and then mark lines across and across with the back of a knife. Place some whole crystallised roses round the edge and sprinkle the centre with crushed ones.

NOTE.—If the icing is a little too creamy when first made to use in the icing bag, leave it to stiffen slighly, otherwise the patterns will not remain distinct. But remember not to let it get too stiff, and to beat it up just before putting it into the icing bag.

ROUT BISCUITS

INGREDIENTS.—4 oz. of ground almonds, 5 oz. of icing sugar, 1 teaspoonful of lemon-juice, 1 teaspoonful of flour, 1 egg, 1 oz. of crystallised cherries.

FOR THE ICING.—2 oz. of icing sugar, 1 dessertspoonful of lemon-juice.

METHOD.—Rub the icing sugar and flour through a hair sieve and add the ground almonds.

Mix them together and bind them into a fairly stiff paste by stirring in a well-beaten egg and the lemon-juice.

Do not have the mixture either too stiff or too soft. If it is too stiff it will be very hard to force it through a bag, and if too soft the biscuits will not keep their shape.

For the shaping, a linen icing bag is needed and a very large pattern icing tube, the kind that is sometimes used for decorating dishes with mashed potato.

Put the paste into the bag, shake it well down and twist the top of the bag. As you do so the paste will be forced out.

Shape the mixture into rounds on a floured baking-sheet. If preferred they can be forced in straight lines or like the letter S. Bake in a moderate oven for twenty minutes.

Decorate the biscuits with half a teaspoonful of icing dropped into the centre of the round ones, and stick half a cherry on top.

TO MAKE THE ICING.—Sift the icing sugar, and put it in a small saucepan with the lemon-juice.

Mix them smoothly and stir the icing over the gas for about six seconds or till it is liquid enough to pour.

To make about sixteen biscuits.

TO MAKE FANCY BISCUITS WITHOUT A FORCER

Wet a small teaspoon and with it take a spoonful of the biscuit mixture, described above. Smooth it over with a wet knife, shaping it like a tiny meringue.

Push it gently on to a floured tin with the point of a knife.

Bake the biscuits in a moderate oven for fifteen or twenty minutes.

When cold spread the underside of each biscuit with jam and stick two biscuits together.

The ordinary metal icing pump can be used for this mixture if preferred, but without any icing tube. It will make plain round biscuits when forced out.

BISCUIT BAKING

After placing the biscuits on a greased tin it is best to leave them for twenty minutes before baking, as they will then keep a better shape and look more professional.

Biscuits should be baked in a moderate oven and not allowed to get brown, only lightly coloured.

They are cooked when the underside is a pale golden colour.

RUSSIAN SLICES

INGREDIENTS.—1 lb. of flour, ¾ lb. of margarine, ¾ lb. of sugar, 4 eggs, 1 teaspoonful of baking-powder, 1 oz. of cocoa, cochineal, 4 good tablespoonfuls of red jam, 2 tablespoonfuls of rum.

FOR THE ICING.—¾ lb. of icing sugar, 3 tablespoonfuls of tepid water, ½ a cake of chocolate, 1½ oz. of cochineal, green colouring, ½ lb. of almond paste (see p. 486).

METHOD.—Cream the margarine till soft, add the sugar and cream well together. Beat in the eggs, one at a time, and sieve and lightly stir in the flour. Add the baking-powder last.

Have ready three square cake-tins or small meat-tins, well-greased. Put one-third of the mixture into one of them and one-third into a small basin. The mixture is now divided into three. That in the tin is to be left as it is—it will form the white part of the cake. Of the other two parts one is coloured bright pink with cochineal, and to the other is added the cocoa. Spread the mixture over the tins and bake in a moderately hot oven for thirty minutes.

Next day cut the cake up into triangular, diamond, oblong and square pieces, some large and some small, and put them in a mixing-basin. Put the jam in a small pan with half a gill of water and bring it to the boil.

Add the rum to the jam.

Strain it quickly over the cake in the mixing-basin and stir enough to mix it, but not enough to break up the cake more than can be helped.

Line a deep, oblong bread-tin with greaseproof paper, leaving enough to fold over at the top. Line the bottom of the tin with half the almond paste.

Take the pieces of cake and fit them into the bottom of the tin, putting contrasting colours together and large and small pieces side by side. Fill in corners where necessary with crumbs, but do not have too many of these.

Fill the tin tightly and make the top level. Fold the ends of the greaseproof paper over the cake and press firmly to wedge all the pieces together. Leave till next day.

Unfold the paper and cover the cake with a strip of almond paste. Turn the whole cake out on to a board or tin, cut the ends straight, and if necessary trim the sides neatly.

The cake is now ready to be iced with water icing.

Three small paper bags of greaseproof paper will be needed.

Mix the sifted icing sugar with the tepid water in a small thin saucepan. Leave half in the pan and divide the rest into three small portions, putting each in a cup and colouring one with half a cake of softened chocolate. The others should be coloured pink and green. Fill the small paper bags one with each colour.

Put the pan containing the white icing on the gas till it melts. It must be well stirred and must not be made hot, only melted. Pour it on top of the cake and spread it quickly over. Now take the bag of chocolate icing and make straight lines across the cake; the lines should be one inch apart. Close to the chocolate line make another line of pink, and close to this still another of green.

Before the icing has time to set, take a skewer or pointed knife and draw it right through the icing in the opposite direction to the lines. This gives the wavy effect of the icing generally seen on Russian Slices.

To finish, cut the cake in slices.

RUSSIAN CAKE SQUARES

INGREDIENTS.—4 eggs, ½ lb. of flour, 9 oz. of castor sugar, ¼ lb. of margarine, 1 flat teaspoonful of baking-powder, milk (if required), cochineal, plum jam.

FOR THE ALMOND PASTE ICING.—1 lb. of ground almonds, 1 lb. of icing sugar, 3 whites of eggs, vanilla.

METHOD.—Grease two small baking-tins and line with greased paper. The latter should reach just above the sides of the tin. Whisk the eggs and sugar together for about fifteen minutes until the mixture becomes thick and creamy and free from dark streaks.

Melt the margarine, be careful not to more than warm it.

Sieve the flour and baking-powder. Fold the flour into the eggs, together with the melted margarine.

Mix lightly, and, if necessary, add a small quantity of milk.

Place half of this mixture into one of the greased tins and spread it over evenly. Colour the remainder with a few drops of cochineal and put into the other tin.

Bake in a hot oven for about ten minutes. Turn carefully on to a sieve, remove the greased paper and leave until cold.

Cut each cake into long strips, about one inch square.

Warm the jam, and, if very thick, thin it down with a little water. Rub through a sieve.

Now take two strips of the white cake and two of the pink.

Brush one side of each with jam and stick them together, arranging the colours afternately.

Make another block in the same way. Wrap each block tightly in grease-proof paper.

THE ICING

Sieve the icing sugar and mix with the ground almonds.

Beat the whites of eggs slightly and add sufficient with a few drops of vanilla to make a stiff paste.

Put the almond paste on to a board, dusted with icing sugar, and knead it for a few minutes until smooth.

Roll it out to a long, thin sheet. Carefully remove the greaseproof paper.

Brush the outside of the blocks with jam and cover the sides with the almond paste.

Join it neatly, and make it smooth.

Trim off a slice from each end, and the cake is ready.

SAFFRON CAKE

INGREDIENTS.—1 lb. of flour, ½ lb. of currants, 2 oz. of peel, ½ lb. of margarine, 2 eggs, saffron (one penny-worth), 6 oz. of sultanas, 6 oz. of sugar, ¼ flat teaspoonful of carbonate of soda, milk.

METHOD.—Put the saffron into a basin with a pinch of salt and half a gill of cold water, and leave soaking all night.

Wash, pick over, and dry the fruit. Grease a cake-tin and line with greased paper to stand above the top.

Sieve the flour and soda and rub in the fat. Cut up the peel and add with the sugar and prepared fruit. Whisk the eggs and stir in ; strain off the saffron water and add, and mix all together with some milk, as required.

Beat well, put into the greased cake-tin, and bake in a moderately hot oven for about one and a half to two hours, lessening the heat as required.

When cooked, turn out carefully and leave on a sieve to cool.

SAND CAKE

INGREDIENTS.—¾ lb. of cornflour, ½ lb. of castor sugar, 7 oz. of margarine, 1½ teaspoonfuls of baking-powder, lemon or vanilla flavouring, 3 eggs, milk (if required).

METHOD.—Grease an oblong or round cake-tin and line with greased paper. The latter should reach just above the top of the tin. Sieve the cornflour. Measure out about one tablespoonful and mix with the baking - powder. Then set aside. Separate the yolks from the whites of eggs. Whisk the sugar and fat to a cream. Beat up the yolks and stir half into the creamed fat and sugar. Beat for five minutes. Then add the remainder and beat again.

Fold the cornflour in lightly. Then add the whites (previously whisked to a stiff froth).

Flavour with lemon or vanilla and mix thoroughly.

Lastly, add the baking-powder and stir it in with the other ingredients.

Put into the greased cake-tin and bake in a moderately hot oven for about three-quarters of an hour.

When lightly browned cover with a paper.

Turn on to a sieve and leave until cold.

SANDWICH BISCUITS

INGREDIENTS.—6 oz. of flour, 3 oz. of butter or margarine, 1½ oz. of castor sugar, 1 lemon, 1 yolk of egg.

FOR THE FILLING.—2 oz. of icing

sugar, 1 dessertspoonful of lemon juice.

FOR THE ICING.—4 oz. of icing sugar, 1 oz. of chocolate (in cake), almond essence, 1 good tablespoonful of tepid water.

METHOD.—Cream the butter and sugar and grate the lemon-peel thinly.

Add the peel and yolk of egg to the mixture and beat well.

Add the flour and knead till smooth.

Roll out to an eighth of an inch thick and cut into small rounds. Place on greased tin and bake about fifteen minutes in a slow oven. The biscuits are done when they are brown underneath.

When cold, spread on the rounds the filling, made by mixing the sieved icing sugar to a stiff paste with lemon-juice. Press two biscuits together to make a sandwich and place them on a baking-sheet.

To make the icing, put the chocolate on a saucer with the water and stand it at the side of the stove in a warm place till the chocolate is soft, then turn it over. Rub the icing sugar through a hair sieve and put it in a small saucepan.

Mix the icing with the chocolate and water to a fairly stiff paste, adding a trifle more water if necessary.

Stir it over a fairly high gas for about twelve seconds or till it dissolves and softens. It must not be made hot.

Pour a small spoonful of icing over half of each biscuit.

Sufficient for about twelve to sixteen biscuits.

SCOTCH BUN

INGREDIENTS.—FOR THE PASTRY.— 10 oz. of flour, 6 oz. of margarine, 1 yolk of egg, water, salt, a little egg or milk for glazing.

FOR THE FILLING.—9 oz. of flour, 1 level teaspoonful of cream of tartar, ½ level teaspoonful of carbonate of soda, 1 level teaspoonful of ground ginger, ½ level teaspoonful of mixed spice, 2 level teaspoonfuls of ground cinnamon, 5 oz. of Barbados sugar, 1 oz. of almonds, 5 oz. of mixed peel, 4 oz. of sultanas, 6 oz. seeded raisins, 1¼ lb. of currants, milk, 1 egg.

METHOD.—To make the pastry, sift the flour with a pinch of salt and rub in the fat.

Beat the egg-yolk and mix it with a spoonful of water, then add it to the flour. Mix them to a stiff paste, adding a little more water as required.

TO MAKE THE FILLING.—Wash, pick over and dry the currants and sultanas.

Cut up the raisins and peel.

Sift the flour with the cream of tartar, soda, and spices, add the sugar and prepared fruits, also the almonds blanched and cut up. Mix all together and moisten with beaten egg and milk.

FILLING THE CASE

Butter a cake-tin about seven inches in diameter, roll out the pastry thinly and line the tin as evenly as possible.

Put in the prepared mixture, heaping it a little to the sides, then roll out the remainder of the pastry, damp the edge and cover the top.

Trim the edge and press it firmly on to the lining.

Brush the pastry with egg or milk, prick the top with a skewer, making two or three pricks through to the base. Bake the bun in a moderate oven. It will take about two hours to cook.

When cold, wrap the Scotch Bun in greaseproof paper and store it in an airtight tin for a week or two.

SEED CAKE

INGREDIENTS.—1 lb. of flour, ½ lb. of margarine (or 6 oz. of dripping), ¼ teaspoonful of carbonate of soda, 2 oz. of candied peel, 7 oz. of granulated sugar, 2 eggs, milk to mix (about 1½ gills), 1 oz. of caraway seeds.

METHOD.—Grease a cake-tin and line it with greased paper.

Sieve the flour with the carbonate of soda and put into a basin.

Rub the fat into the flour.

Cut the peel into small pieces.

Add the sugar, caraway seeds, and candied peel to the flour, etc.

Mix all the dry ingredients well together.

Beat the eggs well, mix with the milk.

Add the eggs and milk to the dry ingredients.

Mix well together and beat

thoroughly; add more milk if required.

Place the mixture in the prepared cake-tin and bake in a moderately hot oven for about an hour and a half.

SEED AND DATE CAKE

INGREDIENTS.—¾ lb. of self-raising flour, 6 oz. of castor sugar, 5 oz. of dripping, ¼ lb. of dates (when stoned), 1 good tablespoonful of caraway seeds, 1 teaspoonful of vinegar, 1 egg, milk.

METHOD.—Beat the sugar and dripping to a creamy consistency.

Stone and cut up the dates, whisk up the egg.

Gradually stir the flour, caraway seeds, and dates into the creamed fat and sugar, alternately with the egg, and some milk as required. Add the vinegar. Beat well. Turn the mixture into a greased cake-tin. Sprinkle a few caraway seeds on the top and put the cake into a moderately hot oven to bake.

It will take about one hour and a half to cook.

RICH SEED CAKE

INGREDIENTS.—10 oz. of flour, 2 oz. of almonds, ½ lb. of castor sugar, ¼ flat teaspoonful of carbonate of soda, 1½ dessertspoonfuls of caraway seeds, ½ lb. of margarine, 1 teaspoonful of cream of tartar, 2 eggs, milk.

METHOD.—Grease and prepare a cake-tin in the usual way.

Sieve the flour, cream of tartar, and carbonate of soda.

Blanch and chop up the almonds.

Whisk the eggs well.

Beat the sugar and fat to a cream.

Gradually stir the flour, etc., almonds and caraway seeds into the creamed fat and sugar, alternately with the eggs, and some milk as required.

Mix all together and beat well.

Turn into the cake-tin and put in a moderately hot oven to bake for about one to one hour and a half, lessening the heat as required.

SHELL CAKES

INGREDIENTS.—7 oz. of flour, 1 teaspoonful of baking-powder, ¼ lb. of citron peel, 1 lemon (rind only), grated nutmeg, ¼ flat teaspoonful of ground cinnamon, ¼ lb. of castor sugar, ¼ lb. of margarine, 1 egg.

METHOD.—Sieve the flour with the ground cinnamon and baking-powder, then add some grated nutmeg.

Beat the sugar and fat to a cream. Add to it the finely grated rind of the lemon. Stir in the egg quickly and beat well together.

Gradually stir in the flour and citron peel (cut in small pieces) and mix them together lightly, adding some milk as required.

Put the mixture into small greased cake-tins with a shell-patterned base and bake in a quick oven. They will take about fifteen minutes.

Turn the cakes over and cool them on a sieve.

This quantity makes about twenty cakes.

SHORTBREAD

INGREDIENTS.—6 oz. of flour, 2 oz. of ground rice, 1 oz. of glacé cherries, ½ oz. of shelled walnuts, 5 oz. of margarine or butter, 2½ oz. of castor sugar.

METHOD.—Sift the ground rice and flour into a basin. Rub in the butter. Add the sugar and rub them together.

Then add the minced walnuts and cherries, cut in small pieces. Work the mixture into a smooth lump with your hands. Turn it on to a board and form it into a round. Then press or roll it to a size a little smaller than your tin.

Decorate the edge and put the shortbread into the tin.

Prick the top and bake the cake in a moderate oven for about forty minutes.

When it is cold decorate it with artificial holly and dots of royal icing (see p. 486). The latter should be coloured pink and forced through a piping tube.

SHORTBREAD
(ANOTHER METHOD)

INGREDIENTS.—1½ lb. of flour, ¾ lb. of margarine, 7 oz. of castor sugar, candied peel.

METHOD.—Beat the sugar and margarine together until they resemble thick cream.

Sieve the flour and work it into the creamed fat and sugar.

Mix well together into a large lump. Divide into three equal portions, work each into a smooth ball and roll out to a round shape (on a slightly floured board) about three-quarters of an inch thick.

Pinch round the edge of each with the first finger and thumb.

Prick the tops with a fork and decorate the centres with thin pieces of candied peel.

Place on to a baking-sheet and bake in a moderate oven for about thirty to forty minutes.

They should be only very lightly coloured.

Cool on a sieve.

SHORTBREAD (WITH EGG)

INGREDIENTS.—10 oz. of flour, 5 oz. of margarine, 4 oz. of castor sugar, 1 egg, angelica, glacé cherries.

METHOD.—Cream the margarine and sugar together as in the previous recipe.

Stir in the egg quickly and beat well for a few minutes. Sieve the flour and work it into the creamed fat and sugar, etc. Mix into a smooth ball with the hand and roll out to about half an inch thick. Cut into small rounds with a fancy cutter. Place half a cherry in the centre of each and a small ring of angelica round the cherry. Place on a baking-sheet and cook in a moderate oven until very lightly browned. Cool on a sieve.

SHORTBREAD BISCUITS

INGREDIENTS.—½ lb. of flour, 4 oz. of butter, 2 oz. of castor sugar, 1 yolk of egg, grated rind of ½ a lemon.

METHOD.—Cream the butter and sugar till soft, add the egg and lemon-rind and mix well.

Add the flour and knead well till quite smooth.

Roll out on a floured board, about a fifth of an inch thick, and cut into rounds with a fluted cutter.

Place on a greased tin and bake for twenty minutes in a slow oven.

Sufficient for about sixteen biscuits.

SHORTBREAD SNIPPETS

INGREDIENTS.—¾ lb. of flour, 6 oz. of butter, 4 oz. of castor sugar.

METHOD.—Snippets are a favourite tea-time dainty and keep well in a tin if made in large quantities. Plain flour (not self-raising) should be used.

No milk or egg is required.

Cream the butter with a wooden spoon until it is soft and white.

Stir in a little sugar and then a little flour, adding them alternately till all is used up.

Knead the dough a little till it is quite smooth and evenly mixed. Turn it on to a floured board and roll it out square about half an inch thick.

Cut the dough into long strips half an inch wide and cut them across into squares.

Place them on a greased tin and leave them for twenty minutes before baking.

Bake the squares in a moderately hot oven for about twenty minutes.

While the snippets are still hot roll them in castor sugar.

SHORT CAKES

INGREDIENTS.—¾ lb. of flour, 7 oz. of margarine, ¼ flat teaspoonful of carbonate of soda, 3 oz. of currants, 3 oz. of sultanas, 1 oz. of candied peel, 5 oz. of sugar, 1 egg, a pinch of mixed spice, milk and water.

METHOD.—Wash, pick over and dry the fruit. Sieve the flour, spice, and soda. Rub in the fat. Cut the peel into small pieces and add to the flour, with the fruit and sugar. Mix all together.

Beat up the egg and add, together with just a little milk and water, and mix all to rather a stiff paste.

Place on a greased tin in small lumps, leaving a space between each. Bake in a hot oven for about ten to fifteen minutes.

SIMNEL CAKE

INGREDIENTS.—½ lb. of flour, 1 level teaspoonful of mixed spice, 1 level teaspoonful of ground cinnamon, ½ level teaspoonful of ground cloves, ¼ level teaspoonful of carbonate of soda, ¾ lb. of currants, 4 oz. of candied peel, 3 oz. of sultanas, 3 eggs, 4 oz. of Barbados sugar, 6 oz. of margarine, 2 oz. of golden syrup, milk.

FOR THE ALMOND PASTE.—½ lb. of ground almonds, ½ lb. of castor sugar, 2 oz. of icing sugar, orange or vanilla essence, about 1½ eggs.

For the Soft Icing.—¼ lb. of icing sugar, water, vanilla, colouring as desired, tiny chicken and eggs for decoration.

Method.—Wash, pick over and dry the fruit and shred the peel.

Whisk up the eggs, warm the golden syrup, add it and whisk together.

Sift the flour with the carbonate of soda and spices.

Beat the sugar and fat to a cream, then gradually add the flour and prepared fruit, adding them alternately with the egg mixture and some milk, as required.

Beat the cake mixture well, then turn half of it into a greased and lined cake-tin. Add a round of almond paste, then the remainder of the cake mixture. Bake the cake in a moderate oven for about two hours, testing it with a warm skewer before taking it out.

When cooked leave it till almost cold. Form the remainder of the paste into a roll and place it on top of the cake to make a border. Rough this with the point of a knife or a fork and return it to the oven to brown, covering the centre with a thick round of paper.

If liked, the almond paste may be glazed with a little beaten yolk of egg mixed with a spoonful of water or milk.

Cool the cake on a sieve, and when cold pour soft icing in the centre. When this is almost set decorate it with a tiny chicken and a few wee eggs. These may be made from almond paste and dotted with colouring, or they may be bought ready to use from a confectioner's store.

To Make the Almond Paste.—Sift the icing sugar and mix it with the ground almonds and castor sugar, then add a little flavouring essence to taste and mix all to a soft paste with beaten egg.

Take about one-third or a little more, form it into a smooth lump and roll it out to a round just a shade smaller than the cake-tin. This is baked in the centre of the cake mixture. Leave the remainder for the top of the cake.

To Make the Soft Icing.—Sift the icing sugar and mix it to a smooth thick paste with warm water, adding a few drops of colouring and flavouring as desired. This icing should be of a coating consistency.

The top decoration of almond paste may be varied by dividing the paste into small portions and shaping each one into a ball. Then press your little finger into the centre of each. These may be placed on top of the cake instead of the ring of paste.

Instead of baking the almond paste in the centre of the cake mixture, the cake may be split in half when it is cold ; each piece should be spread sparingly with jam and a layer of almond paste sandwiched between them.

If liked, the almond paste may be mixed with either the yolks or the whites of egg instead of with whole eggs, but the latter is more economical unless there is a special use for the remaining part of the egg.

For instance, if requiring to make a custard or scrambled eggs, mix the almond paste with the egg-whites and save the yolks. On the other hand, for making meringues save the whites and use the yolks for mixing the almond paste. In this case, add a little lemon-juice to make up the amount of liquid required.

MINIATURE SIMNELS

Ingredients.—3 oz. of castor sugar, 3 oz. of margarine, 1 egg, ¼ lb. of flour, ½ flat teaspoonful of mixed spice, ½ flat teaspoonful of ground ginger, ¼ flat teaspoonful of carbonate of soda, 2 oz. of currants, 2 oz. of seedless raisins, 2 oz. of candied peel, milk.

For the Almond Paste.—½ lb. of icing sugar, ¼ lb. of ground almonds, egg, vanilla flavouring.

Method.—Wash, pick over and dry the fruit. Cut up the peel.

Sieve the flour with the ground ginger, spice, and carbonate of soda.

Beat the sugar and fat to a cream.

Add the egg, stir in quickly and beat the mixture well.

Gradually stir the flour and spices and the prepared fruit into the creamed fat, with just a little milk as required.

Put the mixture into baking-cups or greased tartlet-tins, filling them about two-thirds full, and bake them for about twenty-five minutes in a moderately hot oven.

Cool the cakes on a sieve and when cold decorate them with almond paste.

To decorate the cakes, put a wide edge of paste on the top of each, mark it with a fork to give it a rough appearance, or prick it with a skewer.

Brush the paste with egg and brown it very lightly under the grill.

Fill the centre with tiny eggs of paste.

These may be tinted to a pale shade with a few drops of colouring, if desired.

ALMOND PASTE

To make the almond paste, roll the lumps out of the icing sugar and rub it through a hair sieve.

Add the ground almonds and mix well together.

Beat the egg well and add enough of it, with a few drops of vanilla, to mix the almonds and sugar to a stiff paste.

Work the mixture until smooth, then roll out and use as required.

Sufficient for twelve small cakes.

SNOW CHRISTMAS CAKE

INGREDIENTS.—7 oz. of flour, $\frac{1}{4}$ level teaspoonful of carbonate of soda, 1 level teaspoonful of ground cinnamon, $\frac{1}{2}$ level teaspoonful of mixed spice, 5 oz. of butter or margarine, 5 oz. of sugar, $\frac{1}{2}$ lb. of currants, $\frac{1}{4}$ lb. of sultanas, 2 oz. of candied peel, 1 tablespoonful of black treacle, 1 oz. of shelled walnuts, 2 eggs, 1 or 2 tablespoonfuls of milk or sherry.

METHOD.—Wash, pick over and dry the fruit. Chop the walnuts and cut up the peel. Whisk the eggs. Warm the treacle and add it to the eggs and whisk together.

Beat the butter and sugar to a cream, then gradually stir in the flour, sifted with the soda and spices. Add also the prepared fruit and the eggs, the treacle, and a little milk or cooking sherry.

Beat the mixture well, then turn it into a buttered and lined cake-tin barely six inches square.

Bake the cake in a very moderate oven. It will take about two hours, but test it with a skewer before taking it up. When cold cover the cake with a layer of almond paste and royal icing.

THE ALMOND PASTE

INGREDIENTS.—$\frac{3}{4}$ lb. of ground almonds, $1\frac{1}{4}$ lb. of icing sugar, 2 eggs, flavouring, red currant jelly.

METHOD.—Sift the icing sugar and mix it with the ground almonds. Flavour them with essence and mix then to a stiff paste with the beaten eggs.

If you find it is not quite moist enough, add a spoonful of water or a little more egg.

TO COVER THE CAKE.—Take about two-thirds of the almond paste and work it until it is smooth on a board dredged with icing sugar.

Then form it into a roll that will reach round the four sides of the cake. Next roll it out to the same depth as the sides of the cake.

Brush the cake with melted red currant jelly or other jelly preserve. Stand the cake on the paste and wrap the latter round it, pressing it on securely and keeping it a good square.

Cover the top with the remaining piece of paste, rolled to a square to fit it. Mould it on firmly and make it level. Leave the cake till the next day.

THE ROYAL ICING

INGREDIENTS.—$1\frac{1}{4}$ lb. of icing sugar, 1 small tablespoonful of lemon-juice, 2 or 3 egg-whites (as required), tiny bonbons, bells and mistletoe (for decorating).

METHOD.—Rub the icing sugar through a hair sieve. Add the strained lemon-juice and stiffly whisked whites of eggs to it, and beat them until they are smooth. Then spread the icing roughly over the cake.

Lift the cake on to a cake-board and spread a little icing also on the board—round the base of the cake.

Leave the icing to harden, then decorate the cake. Use a dab of icing to make the decorations adhere.

SNOW-HUT CAKE

INGREDIENTS.—$\frac{1}{2}$ lb. of butter, $\frac{1}{2}$ lb. of sugar, $\frac{1}{2}$ lb. of sultanas (cleaned), 3 oz. of glacé cherries, 3 oz. of almonds (blanched), 2 oz. of citron peel, $\frac{1}{2}$ lb. of flour, grated rind of 1 lemon, a little nutmeg, $\frac{1}{4}$ gill of milk, 4 eggs, $\frac{1}{2}$ teaspoonful of mixed spice, royal icing, almond paste (see p. 486).

METHOD.—Line a two-pound cake-tin with three thicknesses of greased paper.

Cut the peel in strips and the cherries in half.

Cream the butter and sugar till soft and white.

Add the eggs one at a time, beating the mixture well after adding each one.

Stir in the fruit, nutmeg, spice, and lemon-rind.

Stir in the flour and milk.

Place the mixture in the tin and hollow out the centre. Lay a paper on top and bake the cake for about one hour and a half or two hours. Have a moderately hot oven to start with and lower the heat gradually after the first twenty minutes.

Remove the paper carefully and place the cake on a sieve to cool. When cold, wrap it in greaseproof paper and keep it in a tin till required A cake as rich as this will keep well for six months or more.

To make the snow-hut, use almond paste consisting of one pound each of sugar and almonds. Shape like a hut and then spread the sides and top of it with royal icing.

Spread the cake with two thin layers of royal icing and rough it up with a fork. Put the hut on top with a few little china snowmen and dredge it with icing sugar to represent snow.

ROYAL ICING

INGREDIENTS.—1 lb. of icing sugar, 2 whites of eggs, 1 dessertspoonful of lemon-juice.

METHOD.—Sift the sugar.

Beat the whites slightly.

Stir the whites and lemon-juice into the sugar and beat them together for fifteen minutes.

For elaborate decoration use three whites instead of two.

Never omit the lemon-juice, as it makes the icing more pliable and easier to use for decorating. A large cake generally needs from three to four pounds of icing sugar, but it is best only to make one pound at a time as it soon hardens when exposed to the air. It is better to spread on two thin layers rather than one thick one, but be sure the first one is hard and dry.

SODA BISCUIT RINGS

INGREDIENTS.—2 oz. of butter or margarine, 2 oz. of sugar, 3 oz. of Ideal Milk (unsweetened), $\frac{1}{4}$ level teaspoonful of soda, 4 oz. of cornflour, 4 oz. of flour.

METHOD.—Beat the sugar and butter till creamy, and add the beaten Ideal Milk. Add gradually the cornflour, and flour sifted with the soda.

Roll out the mixture, prick it, and cut it into small round biscuits. Cut a small hole in the centre of each, using a thimble or small cutter.

Bake the biscuits in a moderate oven for from eight to ten minutes.

Sufficient for about twenty-four biscuits.

SODA CAKE

INGREDIENTS.—1 lb. of flour, 6 oz. of dripping or margarine, $\frac{1}{2}$ flat tea-spoonful of carbonate of soda, 10 oz. of currants, 2 oz. of candied peel, 7 oz. of sugar, 1 egg, milk and water to mix.

METHOD.—Grease an oblong or round cake-tin and line it with greased paper so that it reaches about two inches above the top.

Wash the currants in several warm waters. When well drained, rub in a cloth and pick them over. Put in a warm place to dry.

Sieve together the flour and soda, rub in the fat until it resembles fine breadcrumbs, and add the sugar.

Cut the peel into small pieces and add the flour, together with the currants. Well mix all the dry in-gredients. Whisk the egg and stir in about one gill and a half of milk and water, pour into the centre of the flour, and mix thoroughly, adding a little more milk if necessary.

Beat well for a few minutes, then put into the prepared cake-tin and bake in a moderately hot oven for about an hour and a half.

Lessen the heat after the first fifteen minutes. Turn to on a sieve, remove the paper and set aside to cool.

NOTE.—If the dripping is very hard, shred it finely in the flour before rubbing it in.

SPICE BUNS

INGREDIENTS.—$\frac{1}{2}$ lb of flour, $\frac{1}{4}$ lb. of margarine or dripping, 2 teaspoon-fuls of mixed spice, $\frac{1}{4}$ flat teaspoonful of carbonate of soda, $\frac{1}{4}$ lb. of granulated sugar, 2 oz. of candied peel, $\frac{1}{2}$ egg, 1 gill of milk.

METHOD.—Grease about ten small cake-tins.

Sieve the flour with the spice and soda.

Rub the fat into the flour.

Add the sugar and peel cut into small pieces.

Mix all the dry ingredients together.

Beat the egg and mix with the milk.

Add the egg and milk to the dry ingredients and mix, then beat well for a few minutes.

Place in the greased tins.

Bake in a hot oven for from fifteen to twenty minutes.

SOFT SPICE CAKE

INGREDIENTS.—2 eggs, 5 oz. of sugar, $\frac{1}{4}$ level tablespoonful of ground cardamon, 1 level teaspoonful of ground cinnamon, 1 level teaspoonful of ground ginger, 6 oz. of Ideal Milk, 3 oz. of melted butter, $\frac{1}{3}$ level teaspoonful of soda, 10 oz. of flour, 1 teaspoonful of grated orange-peel.

METHOD.—Beat the eggs and sugar until they are creamy.

Gradually add the flour, sifted with the spices. Stir in the melted butter and the whipped Ideal Milk, and lastly the soda mixed in a spoonful of the milk.

Turn the mixture into a buttered-tin and bake it in a moderate oven.

SPICED GINGER-CUP CAKES

INGREDIENTS.—6 oz. of flour, $\frac{1}{2}$ level teaspoonful of ground ginger, $\frac{1}{2}$ level teaspoonful of grated nutmeg, 3 oz. of castor sugar, 1 egg, $\frac{1}{4}$ lb. of treacle, $\frac{1}{2}$ level teaspoonful of baking-soda, $\frac{1}{2}$ level teaspoonful of ground cloves, $\frac{1}{2}$ level teaspoonful of ground cinnamon, $2\frac{1}{2}$ oz. of butter, pinch of salt, $\frac{3}{4}$ gill of hot water, baked almonds for decoration.

METHOD.—Sift together into a basin the flour, ginger, cloves, nutmeg, salt, and cinnamon.

Grease about eighteen small tins.

Beat the butter and sugar to a cream. Add the beaten egg, the treacle (warmed) and the flour to which the spices have been added. Lastly, stir in slowly the hot water and soda.

Beat the mixture well. Fill the tins half full.

Bake the cakes for about fifteen minutes in a moderately hot oven. When cool, stick a baked almond on each.

Sufficient for eighteen cakes.

SPICED SEED CAKE

INGREDIENTS.—$\frac{1}{2}$ lb. of flour, $\frac{1}{4}$ flat teaspoonful of carbonate of soda, $1\frac{1}{2}$ flat teaspoonfuls of ground cinnamon, 2 level tablespoonfuls of caraway seeds, $\frac{1}{4}$ lb. of butter or margarine, 5 oz. of Barbados sugar, 2 eggs, milk.

METHOD.—Sift the flour with the carbonate of soda and ground cinnamon.

Beat the sugar and fat to a cream, then gradually stir in the flour and caraway seeds, adding the well-whisked eggs and some milk as required.

Beat the mixture well, turn it into a greased cake-tin, and bake it in a moderately hot oven.

This cake looks well if baked in a toast-rack shaped tin. If using one of these, be very careful not to fill it more than two-thirds full, as it cannot be lined with paper.

SPONGE CAKES

INGREDIENTS.—3 eggs, 6 oz. of castor sugar, 4 oz. of flour, 2 teaspoonfuls of castor sugar, 2 teaspoonfuls of flour.

METHOD.—Grease some small sponge cake-tins. Mix the two teaspoonfuls of sugar and flour together and coat the greased tins with it, then shake out the loose sugar and flour. Break the eggs into a basin. Add to them the castor sugar, and whisk well together for fifteen minutes. Lightly fold in the sieved flour. Pour into the prepared tins. Shake a small quantity of castor sugar over each cake. Bake in a hot oven for about ten to fifteen minutes.

SPONGE FINGERS

INGREDIENTS.—2 eggs, $4\frac{1}{2}$ oz. of castor sugar, 4 oz of flour.

METHOD.—Mix together two teaspoonfuls of castor sugar with about one teaspoonful and a half of flour.

Grease some sponge finger tins and coat with this mixture, then turn them over and knock off the loose sugar and flour.

Whisk the eggs with the remainder of the sugar, until it becomes quite thick and free from streaks. It will take about ten to fifteen minutes.

Sieve the flour and fold lightly into the eggs and sugar.

Mix well together and put a very small quantity into each tin.

Bake in a hot oven for about six or eight minutes. Do not let them brown.

When hot clap them carefully together in pairs.

Place on a sieve to cool.

Sufficient to make about nine cakes.

STRAWBERRY BUNS

INGREDIENTS.—$\frac{1}{2}$ lb. of flour, 1 egg, $\frac{1}{4}$ lb. of castor sugar, $\frac{1}{4}$ lb. of margarine, $\frac{1}{2}$ teaspoonful of baking-powder, milk (if required), strawberry jam.

METHOD.—Sieve the flour with the baking-powder.

Rub the fat into the flour.

Add the sugar and mix well with the flour, etc. Make a well in the centre.

Beat the eggs and put into the centre of the flour, mix to rather a stiff paste, adding a little milk if required.

Slightly flour a board and roll out the paste until it is about an eighth of an inch in thickness.

Cut the paste into rounds about four inches in diameter.

Turn each round over so that the *floured* side is uppermost.

Place half a teaspoonful of strawberry jam in the centre and damp round the edge of each piece.

Then draw the edge to the centre and squeeze together over the jam.

Turn on to the other side, shape into a round again, using one hand and a knife.

With the back of the knife mark two lines, forming a cross over the surface.

Place on a greased baking-sheet.

Brush over buns with milk.

Bake in a quick oven for ten to fifteen minutes.

STRAWBERRY CAKES

INGREDIENTS.—1 egg, 3 oz. of margarine, 3 oz. of castor sugar, 1 teaspoonful of baking-powder, $2\frac{1}{2}$ oz. of flour, 2 small packets of strawberry blancmange powder (3 oz. in all), 3 tablespoonfuls of milk, cochineal, strawberry jam.

METHOD.—Grease some small fluted cake-tins.

Sieve the flour together with the baking and blancmange powders.

Cream the fat and sugar together.

Stir in the egg briskly, and beat well for ten minutes.

Fold in the flour, etc., lightly, together with the milk, as required.

When well mixed, colour with a few drops of cochineal.

Put into the prepared cake-tins and bake in a hot oven for about twelve to fifteen minutes.

Place on a sieve to cool.

Dab half a teaspoonful of jam on the top of each.

SUGAR CAKE

INGREDIENTS.—3 eggs, 3 tablespoonfuls of sugar, $1\frac{1}{2}$ tablespoonfuls of cornflour, 2 tablespoonfuls of flour, vanilla or almond essence, 1 or 2 tablespoonfuls of water.

METHOD.—Beat the yolks of the eggs and the sugar for about a quarter of an hour.

Add the flour, water, almond or vanilla essence, and lastly fold in the whites of eggs, which should have been beaten to a stiff froth. Pour the mixture into a greased cake-tin which has been sprinkled with breadcrumbs, and bake the cake in a steady oven.

SULTANA CAKE

INGREDIENTS.—1 lb. of flour, 6 oz. of sugar, $\frac{1}{2}$ lb. of margarine or butter, 3 eggs, 2 teaspoonfuls of baking-powder, milk to mix (about 1 gill), $\frac{1}{2}$ lb. of sultanas, 1 lemon (grated rind), 2 oz. of candied peel.

METHOD.—Wash and dry the sultanas.

Grease a cake-tin and line it with greased paper.

Cream the fat and sugar together.

Cut the peel into small pieces, remove the stalks from the sultanas.

Sieve the flour and baking-powder, add the grated lemon-rind to the flour.

Mix the flour, etc., with the sultanas and peel.

Beat the eggs separately into the creamed fat and sugar.

Beat well for a few minutes.

Stir in lightly the flour and fruit, etc.

Add a little milk as required.

Put into the prepared cake-tin and bake in a moderately hot oven for an hour and a half.

Turn on to a sieve to cool.

GOOD SULTANA CAKE

INGREDIENTS.—¾ lb. of self-raising flour, 6 oz. of granulated sugar, 1 lb. of sultanas (cleaned), ¼ lb. of butter and ¼ lb. of margarine, ¼ lb. of citron peel, 2 oz. of almonds, 3 eggs, ½ teaspoonful of bicarbonate of soda, ½ gill of milk, 2 teaspoonfuls of vinegar.

METHOD.—Grease and line a tin about eight inches across.

Pour boiling water on the almonds, slip off the skins. Chop the almonds coarsely and cut the citron peel into strips. Cream the butter, margarine, and sugar till they are soft and white.

Stir in the yolks of the eggs and beat the mixture for ten minutes.

Add the sultanas, peel, and almonds and stir in the flour.

Dissolve the soda in the milk and mix the cake.

Last of all, stir in the stiffly beaten whites of the eggs and the vinegar.

Place the mixture in the tin and bake it for about one hour and a quarter, starting with a hot oven and lowering the gas by degrees after the first twenty minutes.

The cake is done when the centre feels firm. Let it remain in the tin for about ten minutes, then lift it on to a sieve and remove the paper.

SULTANA ORANGE CAKE

INGREDIENTS.—7 oz. of flour, 6 oz. of sultanas, 1 oz. of angelica, 3 oz. of butter or margarine, 1 orange, 4 oz. of castor sugar, 2 eggs, 1 teaspoonful of baking-powder.

METHOD.—Wash, pick over and dry the sultanas, and cut the angelica into shreds.

Beat the sugar and fat to a cream, add the eggs one at a time, stirring them in quickly and beating the mixture well.

Add the finely grated orange-rind, and gradually stir in the flour, sifted with the baking-powder.

Add also the angelica, sultanas, and juice of the orange.

Turn the mixture into a large baking-case (the latter should be placed in a round cake-tin to fit the case). Bake the cake in a moderately hot oven for about an hour and a quarter or an hour and a half.

The case should only be filled to about three-fourths of its capacity.

SULTANA TEA-RING

INGREDIENTS.—2 cupfuls of flour, 2 oz. of butter, 5 level tablespoonfuls of golden syrup, 3 teaspoonfuls of baking-powder, ¼ lb. of sultanas (cleaned), 2 oz. of walnuts, 1 teaspoonful of salt, about ½ cup of milk or a little more. 2 oz. of loaf sugar, 1 egg (beaten).

METHOD.—Chop the walnuts and crush the sugar with a rolling-pin ; keep them both for decorating.

Sift the flour, baking-powder, and salt, and add the sultanas. Melt the butter and syrup without making them hot, and stir into them the milk and half the egg.

Before mixing make sure that a fairly hot oven is ready.

Stir the liquid ingredients into the flour and make a soft but not sticky dough.

Turn the dough on to a floured board and roll it into a long, narrow piece half an inch thick.

Cut this into two strips and twist them together. Shape them into a ring and pinch the ends together. Place it on a greased tin.

Brush the ring with egg and sprinkle it with chopped walnuts and sugar.

Leave it for five minutes to rise a little, then bake it for twenty or twenty-five minutes.

Serve the tea-ring hot. It should be eaten with butter.

SWISS ROLLS

LARGE AND SMALL

INGREDIENTS.—3 eggs, 4 oz. of flour (light weight), 4 oz. of castor sugar, ½ teaspoonful of baking-powder, 1 tablespoonful of cold water, 1 pot of stoneless jam.

METHOD.—To make an ordinary

Swiss roll, line a large Swiss roll tin smoothly with greased paper, making it fit well into the corners.

Light the gas in the oven.

Sift the flour and baking-powder on to a paper.

Beat the eggs and sugar together until they are creamy white, thick and full of bubbles. This should take about ten minutes if done with a good egg-whisk. If they are beaten only with a wooden spoon it will take from fifteen to twenty minutes.

Be sure that the oven is hot before adding the flour.

Stir in the flour and water lightly, and pour the mixture into the lined tin. Spread it evenly all over the tin.

Place the sponge at once in the top of a quick oven under the browning-shelf.

Bake it for seven minutes, and if it feels spongy in the centre, as it will if the oven is right, turn it on to a sugared paper.

Have some hot jam ready and spread it over the sponge, putting it thicker at the side you will start to roll up.

Cut off any hard edges.

The best way to roll up a sponge is to turn in a piece about an inch all along one side and press it nearly flat. Then roll up the rest of the cake by lifting the paper up and forward with both hands.

MINIATURE SWISS ROLLS

The same recipe is used for the small as for the large rolls, and the mixing is done in the same way, but the baking is different.

Line two tins instead of one, and spread the prepared mixture *thinly* over both of them.

Bake them in a hot oven for about five minutes.

If Swiss rolls are baked too long they will split when rolled up.

After baking, turn the sponges quickly on to a sugared paper.

Remove the baking-papers, spread the sponges with hot jam, and cut them in half lengthwise.

Roll each piece into a long, narrow roll.

When cold, cut each roll into three. This quantity makes twelve small Swiss rolls.

SWISS TARTS

INGREDIENTS.—6 oz. of flour, 4 oz. of margarine, 2 oz. of castor sugar, 1 tablespoonful of water, jam (about 1 teaspoonful of any red jam).

METHOD.—Sieve the flour into a basin.

Rub in the margarine until it is like breadcrumbs.

Add the sugar, and mix all the dry ingredients together.

Pour in the water and mix thoroughly into a lump with your hand.

Divide into six equal portions.

Round each into a smooth ball.

Grease six small cake-tins, put one ball into each, press your little finger in the centre of each ball, and make a hole almost to the bottom.

At the same time it will press the ball to the shape of the tin.

Drop a little jam into the hole and decorate the top with a knife, making sharp cuts from the centre all round the tart.

Bake in a moderately hot oven for about twenty minutes, until very light brown in colour.

Cool on a sieve.

Sprinkle a little sieved icing sugar over the top of each.

TENNIS CAKE

INGREDIENTS.—$\frac{1}{4}$ lb. of castor sugar, $\frac{1}{4}$ lb. of margarine, 2 eggs, 1 oz. of ground almonds, almond flavouring, $\frac{1}{4}$ lb. of flour, 1 flat teaspoonful of baking-powder, few glacé cherries, a few whole almonds.

FOR THE ALMOND ICING.—$\frac{1}{2}$ lb. of icing sugar, $\frac{1}{4}$ lb. of ground almonds, almond flavouring, egg.

METHOD.—Cream the fat and sugar, Add each egg separately, stirring it in quickly, and beat well.

When both eggs are added, stir in the ground almonds and a few drops of flavouring, then the flour and baking-powder (previously sieved), and mix together lightly.

Turn the mixture into a greased and lined square cake-tin, and bake it in a moderately hot oven for about forty-five minutes. Cool the cake on a sieve.

THE ALMOND PASTE

To make the almond paste, rub the sugar through a hair sieve and mix it with the ground almonds. Beat up the egg and add enough, with a few drops of flavouring, to make a stiff paste. Work it until smooth, then roll it out.

THE DECORATION

To decorate the cake, cut long strips of paste about three-quarters of an inch wide and cover the top and two sides of the cake. The cake may first be brushed with some white of egg or melted red currant jelly to make the paste adhere. Then cut shorter strips of the same width and cover the remaining two sides.

Mark the paste with the back of a knife so as to divide it into squares, then decorate it with glacé cherries and baked almonds.

TOFFEE SANDWICH

INGREDIENTS.—¼ lb. of flour, 3 oz. of castor sugar, 1 tablespoonful of golden syrup, ¼ lb. of margarine, ⅛ flat teaspoonful of carbonate of soda, 1 egg, milk (if required.)

FOR THE TOFFEE ICING.—¼ lb. of icing sugar, 1 tablespoonful of golden syrup, 1¾ oz. of butter, coffee essence.

METHOD.—Grease a sandwich-tin and line the side with greased paper to stand just above the top.

Cream the margarine and sugar.

Whisk up the egg.

Warm the golden syrup slightly and add to it, and whisk together well.

Sieve the flour and carbonate of soda and gradually stir into the creamed fat and sugar, with the egg and golden syrup.

Mix all together and beat well. Put into the prepared tin and bake in a quick oven for about fifteen minutes, or until spongy. Cool on a sieve.

TO MAKE THE ICING.—Roll the lumps out of the sugar and rub it through a hair sieve. Put the butter and golden syrup into a saucepan to melt, draw aside, then stir in the icing sugar.

Add sufficient coffee essence to colour and slightly flavour, mix until smooth, then leave to cool. Split the cake into halves, spread over some of the icing, then sandwich it together. Make the remainder of the icing warm again, then pour it on to the sandwich and coat the top.

TREACLE FRUIT CAKE

INGREDIENTS.—1 lb. of flour, 6 oz. of currants, ½ lb. of margarine, 6 oz. of sultanas, ¼ flat teaspoonful of carbonate of soda, 2 oz. of candied peel, ¼ lb. of sugar, 2 eggs, ¼ lb. of golden syrup or treacle, 1 gill of milk.

METHOD.—Wash the fruit, rub well and put to dry.

Grease a large, round cake-tin and line with greased paper.

Sieve the flour with the carbonate of soda. Rub the fat into the flour until it is like fine breadcrumbs. Cut the peel into small pieces. Remove the stalks from the currants and sultanas. Add the sugar and fruit to the flour, etc. Mix all well together. Break the eggs into a small basin, whisk them well.

Add the golden syrup to the eggs and whisk again.

Add the wet ingredients to the dry, with milk as required. Mix all well together, beat well for a few minutes, Put into the prepared cake-tin.

Bake in a moderately hot oven for one and a half to two hours ; after the first twenty minutes the gas should be lowered.

If the cake gets brown before it is cooked, cover the top with a paper not greased.

Test with a warm iron skewer to see if cooked.

Turn on to a sieve and leave until cool.

TREACLE PARKIN

INGREDIENTS.—1 lb. of medium oatmeal, 1¾ lb. of flour, 1 lb. of moist sugar, 1 lb. of butter or margarine, 1 oz. of ground ginger, ½ oz. of ground mace, 3 oz. of candied peel, ½ nutmeg (grated), 1¾ lb. of golden syrup, ½ teaspoonful of bicarbonate of soda.

METHOD.—Rub the butter or margarine into the flour until there are no lumps left and add the oatmeal, sugar, peel, spices, and bicarbonate of soda.

Stand the tin of syrup in the oven until it is sufficiently warmed to be liquid. Stir the syrup into the dry ingredients and mix well.

Grease two meat-tins, fill them with the mixture and bake it in a moderate oven for one hour and a quarter.

Do not turn out the cakes in the

ordinary way, but leave them in the tins till they are lukewarm. Before they are cold cut them into square blocks and when cold put them into tins and store till required.

This cake improves with keeping and is not supposed to be eaten at once. It is better if left at least a fortnight.

TURNOVER ROLLS

INGREDIENTS.—¾ lb. of flour, 2 good teaspoonfuls of baking-powder, ¼ level teaspoonful of salt, ½ oz. of margarine or butter, about 1½ to 2 gills of milk, 1 egg-yolk.

METHOD.—Sift the flour into a basin with salt and baking-powder. Rub in the fat.

Beat up the yolk of egg and mix it with one and a half gills of the milk, and add these to the flour.

Mix them to a soft dough, adding more milk as required. Roll out the dough until it is half an inch thick. Cut it into rounds three or four inches in diameter.

Fold each over lightly into half and put them on a greased and floured baking-sheet.

Then bake them in a hot oven from twenty to thirty minutes.

NOTE.—The rolls may be glazed with milk before baking, if liked.

UWANT-A-CAKE

INGREDIENTS.—1 breakfastcupful of sugar, 2 cupfuls of plain flour, 2 oz. of lard, 3 eggs, 1 cupful of milk, 2 teaspoonfuls of baking-powder, essence of lemon.

FOR THE ICING.—4 oz. of icing sugar, 2 oz. of butter, grated rind of a lemon, 1 dessertspoonful of lemon-juice.

METHOD.—Cream the lard and sugar and when they are soft beat in the yolks of the eggs. Add half the milk and half the flour, mix carefully, and add the rest of the milk and flour and a few drops of essence.

Beat the egg-whites to a stiff froth, add the baking-powder to the mixture and stir in the whites as lightly as possible.

Bake in a moderate oven for from fifty minutes to an hour. When cold cut the cake in half and fill it with lemon butter icing.

LEMON BUTTER ICING

Rub the icing sugar through a hair sieve.

Cream the butter till soft and add the lemon-rind and juice.

Add the sugar and mix all smoothly together.

VALENCIA LAYER CAKE

INGREDIENTS.—10 oz. of Barbados sugar, ½ lb. of margarine, ¾ lb. of flour, 2 teaspoonfuls of baking-powder, 1 level teaspoonful of powdered cinnamon, 3 eggs, milk, stoned raisins and blanched almonds for top of cake.

FOR THE FILLING.—6 oz. of icing sugar, 3 oz. of butter, 1 oz. of ground almonds, 1 oz. of shelled walnuts, 3 oz. of raisins (when stoned), 1 oz. of almonds, 1 dessertspoonful of rum.

FOR THE ICING.—1 egg-white, ½ lb. of white sugar, ⅛ gill of water, pinch of cream of tartar, colouring as desired.

METHOD.—Beat the sugar and fat to a cream.

Add each egg separately, stirring it in quickly and beating well. Stir in the flour sifted with the baking-powder and cinnamon, and mix all together lightly, adding some milk as required.

Turn the mixture into three buttered sandwich-tins and put them in a hot oven to bake. When cooked, cool them on a sieve.

Sandwich the three layers together with filling between them, then put icing on the top, and decorate the cake with a few blanched almonds and stoned raisins.

To MAKE THE FILLING.—Stone and chop the raisins, chop the shelled walnuts and almonds (blanched), and sift the icing sugar.

Beat the butter to a cream with half the sugar, then add the remainder and beat again until creamy.

Stir in the prepared raisins, almonds, and walnuts, also the ground almonds and rum, and mix well together.

To MAKE THE ICING.—Put the sugar into a saucepan with the water and let it dissolve, then bring it to the boil. Add a pinch of cream of tartar, and boil the syrup until a small quantity when dropped into cold water becomes a soft ball. Pour it steadily on to the stiffly whisked egg-white, keeping it well stirred until it begins to set. Add colouring if desired.

VALENTINE BISCUITS

INGREDIENTS.—3 oz. of flour, 1 yolk of egg, ¼ level teaspoonful of baking-powder, 1 lemon, 3 oz. of margarine, 1½ oz. of castor sugar.

METHOD.—Beat the sugar and fat to a cream, add the finely grated rind of half a small lemon, and beat in the egg-yolk. Sift the flour with the baking-powder and stir them in, mixing to a soft dough.

Roll the mixture out fairly thinly, cut it into shapes with a heart-cutter, put these on a very lightly buttered and floured tin, and bake them in a moderate oven for a few minutes until light brown.

Sufficient for about twenty biscuits.

VALENTINE CAKE

INGREDIENTS.—2 oz. of castor sugar, 2 oz. of margarine, 2 oz. of self-raising flour, 1 oz. of ground rice, ½ oz. of ground almonds, 1 whole egg and 1 yolk, vanilla or almond flavouring essence, apricot jam.

FOR THE ALMOND PASTE.—2 oz. of ground almonds, 4 oz. of icing sugar, ½ egg-white, flavouring essence, colouring as desired.

FOR THE ICING.—½ egg-white, 5 oz. of icing sugar, water, flavouring essence and colouring.

METHOD.—Beat the sugar and fat to a cream, stir in the egg-yolk and beat the mixture well.

Then add the whole egg and stir it quickly for a minute or two.

Add the ground almonds and sift the flour with the ground rice. Stir them in lightly, adding a spoonful of milk if required. Then flavour the mixture with vanilla or almond essence and turn it into a buttered heart-shaped tin.

It should take about twenty minutes to bake.

Cool the sponge on a sieve and when it is cold split it in half, spread each piece with apricot jam and add a layer of almond paste. Then sandwich the two pieces together.

Spread some icing on the top, and when it is just set decorate the cake with hearts of almond paste. These are made by colouring some almond paste to any desired shade. It is then rolled out to the required thickness and stamped into shapes with a small heart-shaped cutter.

It will look well if the top icing is tinted to a primrose shade and the small hearts are pale green.

To make the almond paste, sift the icing sugar and mix it with the ground almonds. Add the flavouring essence and mix it to a stiff paste with slightly beaten egg-white. Roll the paste out to the required thickness and from it cut a heart shape to fit the cake.

Colour the remainder of the paste and use it to make the heart decorations for the top of the cake. Stiffen it with a little more icing sugar if it is too moist.

To make the icing, sift the icing sugar and mix it to a thick, smooth paste with half a lightly beaten egg-white and a few drops of water. Add colouring and flavouring as desired.

VANILLA CREAM CAKE

INGREDIENTS.—¼ lb. of margarine, 5 oz. of flour, ¾ teaspoonful of cream of tartar, ⅓ flat teaspoonful of carbonate of soda, ¼ lb. of castor sugar, 2 eggs, 1 tablespoonful of cornflour, milk, vanilla.

FOR THE FILLING.—¼ lb. of icing sugar, 2 oz. of butter, vanilla.

METHOD.—Sieve the flour with the cornflour, cream of tartar, and carbonate of soda.

Cream the fat and sugar.

Separate the eggs and beat the yolks into the fat and sugar. When well-beaten, gradually stir in the sieved flour with a little milk as required.

Add a few drops of vanilla essence, then fold in the egg-whites, whisked stiffly.

Turn the mixture into a greased pie-tin or cake-tin and put into a moderately hot oven to bake.

When cold cut off a thick slice from the top of the cake and divide it into four.

Spread the cake with the filling, replace the four quarters, and dust the top with icing sugar.

THE VANILLA FILLING

To make the filling, rub the sugar through a fine sieve, beat the butter and icing sugar to a cream, and add vanilla to taste.

VANILLA ICED ROLL

INGREDIENTS.—2 eggs, their weight in castor sugar, 2 oz. of margarine, ¼ lb. of flour, 1 flat teaspoonful of cream of tartar, ⅛ flat teaspoonful of carbonate of soda, vanilla flavouring, jam.

FOR THE ICING.—10 oz. of icing sugar, cold water (about 2 tablespoonfuls), vanilla flavouring, crystallised rose leaves.

METHOD.—Grease a baking-sheet and line with greased paper to stand just above the sides. Cream the sugar and margarine, then beat in the eggs separately. When both are added, sieve the flour, cream of tartar, and carbonate of soda and stir in lightly. Flavour with vanilla and add a spoonful of milk, if required. Put into the prepared tin and spread over evenly. Bake in a hot oven for about eight or ten minutes, or until it feels spongy.

Turn on to a sugared paper, remove the greased paper and cut off the hard outside edge from each side of the sponge. Have ready some hot jam, spread it over, but not quite to the edge, then roll up and leave on a sieve until cold.

To make the icing, roll the lumps out of the sugar and rub through a hair sieve. Put into a saucepan and mix to a smooth paste with the cold water, add also a few drops of vanilla. Stand it over a low burner and stir the icing until the base of the pan feels just warm. The icing should coat the back of the spoon. Stand the roll on a rack above a dish. Pour the icing over and coat evenly. Crush a few rose leaves and sprinkle over the top.

VANILLA LAYER CAKE

INGREDIENTS.—6 oz. of castor sugar, 5 oz. of margarine or butter, ½ lb. of flour, 3 eggs, 3 oz. of chopped almonds or walnuts, 1 teaspoonful of baking-powder, milk, vanilla flavouring.

METHOD.—Grease and prepare a cake-tin.

Cream the sugar and fat.

Mix the flour and baking-powder and put through a sieve.

Mix flour with the chopped nuts.

Beat each egg separately into the creamed fat and sugar.

Fold in lightly the flour and nuts,

etc. Add the vanilla, and a little milk if required. Put into the prepared tin and bake in a moderately hot oven for about three-quarters to one hour. Turn on to a sieve and leave until cold.

THE FILLING

INGREDIENTS.—1 oz. of chopped nuts (same kind as used in the cake), ½ lb. of apricot jam.

METHOD.—Split the cake into three even pieces and spread each with the filling of jam and nuts. Place together again. Turn the cake upside down on a rack or a dish. Make the icing as given below. Pour it on the top of cake, and it will gradually coat the sides as well as the top. Decorate the top with crystallised violets. When the icing is set, place the cake on a lace paper.

THE ICING

INGREDIENTS.—¾ lb. of icing sugar, 1 egg-white, vanilla flavouring, cold water, crystallised violets (for decoration).

METHOD.—Roll the lumps out of the sugar and put through a fine sieve.

Slightly beat the egg-white and add to the icing sugar, with a few drops of vanilla and a little cold water, and mix to a smooth paste.

Stir over a low gas until the bottom of the pan feels just warm.

The consistency of the icing should be so that it will coat the back of the spoon.

WALNUT CAKE

INGREDIENTS.—½ lb. of flour, 1 teaspoonful of cream of tartar, ½ flat teaspoonful of carbonate of soda, 3 oz. of shelled walnuts, 7 oz. of castor sugar, 6 oz. of margarine, 2 eggs, milk.

METHOD.—Sieve the flour with the cream of tartar and carbonate of soda. Chop up the walnuts, leaving a few whole ones for the top of the cake.

Beat the sugar and fat to a cream. Separate the eggs and beat in the yolks. Stir in the flour and walnuts, adding a little milk as required. Fold in lightly the stiffly whisked whites of egg.

Turn the mixture into a cake-tin and bake it in a moderately hot oven

ICED WALNUT CAKE

INGREDIENTS.—6 oz. of shelled walnuts, ½ lb. of butter or margarine, 6 oz. of castor sugar, 10 oz. of flour, 1 teaspoonful of baking-powder, 3 eggs, 2 oz. of citron peel, a little jam.

FOR THE ALMOND PASTE.—6 oz. of ground almonds and icing sugar, 1 yolk of egg, 1 teaspoonful of lemon-juice.

FOR THE ICING.—4 oz. of icing sugar, about half the white of the egg.

METHOD.—Grease and line a pound and a half cake-tin. Chop the walnuts and peel coarsely. Cream the butter and sugar till soft, and beat in the eggs one at a time. Sift the flour and baking-powder and add them to the egg mixture. Add the peel and half the walnuts.

Put the mixture into the tin, hollowing out the centre so that it will be flat on top when it rises. Bake the cake in a moderate oven for an hour and a quarter. Remove the paper and place the cake on a wire sieve to cool.

THE ALMOND PASTE

Sift the icing sugar on to the almonds, mix them together and bind them with the egg-yolk and the lemon-juice. Knead the mixture till smooth, make it into a ball and flatten till it is the size of the cake. Put it on the top and press gently. Brush the sides of the cake with a little warm jam, stand it on a paper containing the rest of the walnuts and press them round the cake.

ICING THE CAKE

Rub the icing sugar through a hair sieve. Beat the white of egg slightly, and add about half of it to the sugar with a few drops of lemon-juice. Spread the icing over the top with a knife and put chopped walnuts round the edge of it, and a whole one in the middle.

SMALL WALNUT CAKES

INGREDIENTS.—3 oz. of shelled walnuts, 3 oz. of butter or margarine, 6 oz. of castor sugar, 7 oz. of flour, 2 eggs, 1 teaspoonful of baking-powder, milk.

FOR THE FILLING.—2 or 3 table-spoonfuls of apricot jam, 1½ oz. of shelled walnuts, jam and coconut, and a few chopped nuts for the top of the cakes.

METHOD.—Chop up the walnuts and sift the flour with the baking-powder. Cream the fat and sugar, then gradually stir in the flour and the well-beaten eggs. Add the chopped nuts and a little milk as required, mix together lightly and turn the mixture into a large, buttered baking-tin to cook.

Cut the cake into fancy shapes when cold.

Split the cakes in halves and spread them with the filling, then sandwich them together again. Spread a little jam on top, and sprinkle some with desiccated coconut and some with chopped walnuts.

FOR THE FILLING.—Warm the jam and mix it with the chopped nuts. If using whole fruit apricot jam, it is better to rub it through a sieve.

WALNUT SANDWICH

INGREDIENTS.—2 eggs, their weight in castor sugar and flour, 2 oz. of butter or margarine, 1 oz. of walnuts, ½ teaspoonful of baking-powder, milk.

FOR THE FILLING.—8 oz. of icing sugar, 4 oz. of butter, vanilla, a few walnuts for decoration.

METHOD.—Grease a sandwich-tin and line the sides with greased paper to stand just above the top.

Sieve the flour and baking-powder. Chop up the walnuts roughly.

Beat the sugar and fat to a cream. Add each egg separately. Stir one in quickly, and beat for a few minutes before adding the second.

When both are added stir in the flour and walnuts, and about a table-spoonful of milk.

Mix all together lightly and put into the prepared tin.

Bake in a hot oven for about ten minutes, then put on to a sieve and leave until cold.

TO MAKE THE FILLING.—Rub the sugar through a fine sieve, then cream it with the butter.

Flavour with vanilla.

Split the sandwich into halves and spread over some of the prepared filling, then put together again.

Fix a rose icing tube on to an icing bag, put the remainder of the filling into it, and decorate the top of the sandwich in straight lines, going across each way.

Place halves of walnuts all round the top edge.

WHITE CAKE

INGREDIENTS.—6 oz. of castor sugar, 1½ teaspoonfuls of baking-powder, 4 oz. of butter or margarine, 3 eggs, 1 teacupful of cornflour, lemon essence (one teaspoonful), 1 teacupful of flour, ½ gill of milk (if required).

METHOD.—Grease a cake-tin and line it with greased paper.

Cream the sugar and fat together.

Sieve the flour, cornflour, and baking-powder and mix well together.

Separate the whites from the yolks of the eggs.

Whisk the whites to a stiff froth and put aside.

Beat the yolks each separately into the creamed sugar and fat; beat well for a few minutes.

Lightly fold in the flour, etc.

Add milk, if required, and lemon flavouring.

Lastly, fold in very lightly the whisked whites of eggs.

Put the mixture into the prepared cake-tin.

Bake in a moderately hot oven for about one hour.

Turn on to a sieve and leave until cold.

WHITE FRUIT CAKES

INGREDIENTS.—2 oz. of margarine, 2½ oz. of castor sugar, 2 large whites of eggs, 3½ oz. of flour, ½ level teaspoonful of carbonate of soda, 1 level teaspoonful of cream of tartar, 2 oz. of glacé cherries, ¼ lb. of seedless raisins, 2 oz. of candied peel, milk, a little jam, few shelled walnuts.

METHOD.—Sift the flour with the carbonate of soda and cream of tartar.

Cut up the cherries and peel, add them to the flour with the raisins, and mix all together.

Beat the sugar and fat to a cream, then stir in the flour and prepared fruit with a little milk as required, and beat well. Fold in the stiffly whisked egg-whites.

Turn the mixture into small, greased cake-tins and put them in the oven to bake. Turn them upside down

and let them cool on a sieve. Stick a piece of shelled walnut on top of each, using a spot of jam to make it stick.

Sufficient to make about twelve cakes as shown.

WHITE GINGER ROCKS

INGREDIENTS.—¾ lb. of flour, 6 oz. of white sugar, 7 oz. of margarine, 1 teaspoonful of ground ginger, ¼ teaspoonful of powdered cinnamon, 1 flat teaspoonful of caraway seeds, ¼ flat teaspoonful of carbonate of soda, 1 egg, milk (if required), 1 oz. of almonds.

METHOD.—Sieve together the flour, ginger, cinnamon, and soda. Rub in the margarine until it resembles breadcrumbs. Add the sugar and caraway seeds. Mix all the dry ingredients together. Then add the egg (previously beaten up). Mix to a stiff paste. If necessary, add a little milk. Grease a baking-sheet and drop the mixture on to it in small, rough heaps, leaving a space between each. Blanch the almonds and stick one in the top of each cake. Bake in a hot oven for fifteen to twenty minutes. Cool on a sieve.

WINDSOR CAKES

INGREDIENTS.—3 oz. of arrowroot, 3 oz. of cornflour, 3 oz. of flour, 3 oz. of ground rice, 6 oz. of butter or margarine, 9 oz. of castor sugar, 2 lemons (rinds only), 2 eggs, milk (if required), 1½ teaspoonfuls of baking-powder.

METHOD.—Sieve together the arrowroot, cornflour, flour, ground rice, and baking-powder.

Grate the lemon-rinds.

Beat the sugar and fat to a cream. Add each egg separately, stir quickly, and beat for a few minutes before adding the next.

When both are added, beat again, then stir in the lemon-rind and flour, etc., very lightly.

Add a little milk if required.

Put a small quantity into each tin and bake in a hot oven for about fifteen minutes.

YELLOW COCONUT CAKES

INGREDIENTS.—4 yolks of eggs, 2 oz. of desiccated coconut, 7 oz. of flour, 1 teaspoonful of baking-powder, pineapple flavouring essence, 6 oz. of castor sugar, 4 oz. of margarine, milk.

METHOD.—Beat the sugar and fat to a cream, then beat in the egg-yolks one at a time.

Sift the flour with the baking-powder and stir it in with the coconut, adding some milk as required.

Flavour the mixture with a few drops of pineapple flavouring essence, and turn it into a greased cake-tin.

Dredge castor sugar and sprinkle coconut on top of the mixture, and put it in a moderately hot oven to bake.

YULETIDE CAKE

INGREDIENTS.—6 oz. of castor sugar, 6 oz. of butter or margarine, 3 or 4 eggs, ¼ lb. of glacé ginger, ¼ lb. of glacé pineapple, ¼ lb. of mixed peel, ¼ lb. of sultanas, ½ lb. of currants, 2 oz. of shelled walnuts, ½ lb. of flour, milk, 1 level teaspoonful of baking-powder, 1 level teaspoonful of ground cloves, 1 level teaspoonful of grated nutmeg, seasonable decorations.

FOR THE ALMOND PASTE.—½ lb. of ground almonds, 1 lb. of icing sugar, 2 yolks and 1 whole egg, flavouring essence.

FOR THE WHITE ICING.—1¼ lb. of icing sugar, 2 egg-whites, water, flavouring essence.

METHOD.—Wash, pick over and dry the fruit, shred the peel, chop the walnuts and cut the ginger and pineapple into small pieces.

Cream the fat and sugar, then add the eggs. Stir each one in separately and beat it well before adding the next. When all the eggs are well beaten in, gradually stir in the flour, sifted with the spices and baking-powder.

Add also the prepared fruit and a little milk as required.

Turn the mixture into a buttered and lined cake-tin and bake it in a moderate oven. It will take about two hours and a half to bake. Test it with a warmed skewer before taking it up, and leave it for a few minutes before turning it on to a sieve to cool.

To MAKE THE ALMOND PASTE.—Sift the icing sugar and mix it with the ground almonds.

Beat up the whole egg and yolks together, and add them to the mixture, with flavouring essence to taste.

Mix them to a stiff paste, adding a little more beaten egg, if required.

To cover the sides of the cake, turn the paste on to a board lightly sprinkled with icing sugar. Form it into a smooth lump and then into a fat sausage or roll long enough to reach round the sides of the cake.

Take a rolling-pin and roll the paste rather wider than the depths of the sides.

Brush the sides of the cake with melted jam or jelly.

Place the cake on the paste and roll it over until the sides are covered. Stand it on its base. Shape the paste evenly, and leave it for a few hours. Trim the top of the paste so that it stands a little higher than the cake.

To MAKE THE WHITE ICING.—Sift one pound of the icing sugar and mix it to a thick coating consistency with the lightly beaten egg-whites and a little water as required, and flavour it.

To ICE THE CAKE.—Stand the cake on a cake-board and pour some of the prepared icing on the top until it is up to the level of the edge of the almond paste. Let it set.

Meanwhile, sift the remainder of the sugar, and beat it into the rest of the icing. Add a little more egg-white, if required.

The icing must now be of a consistency that it will hold its shape.

Put some of it into an icing pump with a leaf-patterned tube affixed and decorate the cake with ladder shapes each having three rungs all round the edges. Continue the icing on to the board at the lower ends of the ladders, using a shell patterned tube, and then put a thin, rough layer of this stiffer icing on top of the smooth white icing. When the icing is almost set, decorate the cake tastefully with any seasonable decorations. Small balls of almond paste made from the trimmings with a little gnome figure on each one look well.

Honey
Gingerbread

Sugar
Cake

Cornflour
Cake

PLATE 49

Mocha Cake

Orange Layer Cake

Genoese Cake

PLATE 59

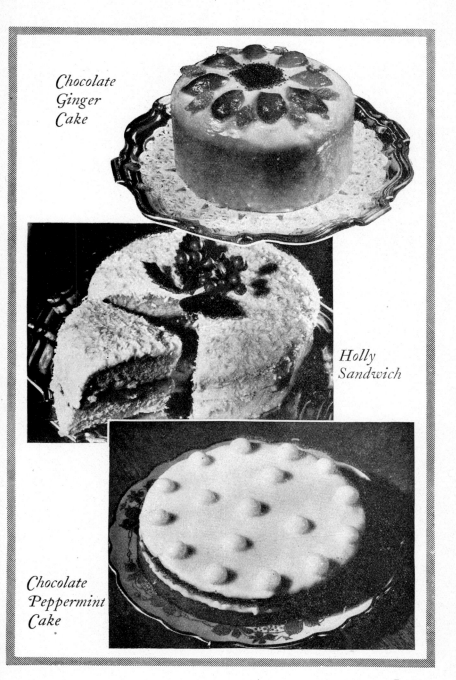

Chocolate
Ginger
Cake

Holly
Sandwich

Chocolate
Peppermint
Cake

PLATE 51

Fruit
Crescents

Tea-Cake

Turnover
Rolls

Plate 52

BREAD, BUNS AND SCONES

HOME-MADE BREAD

YEAST and flour are the two most important ingredients in bread-making. Yeast acts as a raising property in bread. Under certain conditions the yeast cells grow and multiply, giving off a gas which lightens the dough. In order to do this the yeast requires *warmth*.

Warm water should be used to mix the dough, and it should be put in a *warm* place to rise. In cold weather it is advisable to warm the basins before beginning.

Cold prevents the yeast's growth, and *heat* kills it ; so it is of the utmost importance that the water used is not too hot or the place where the dough is put to rise is not too warm. A little sugar is first mixed with the yeast to start its action.

Flour rich in gluten is the best to use for bread-making.

There are two kinds of yeast, liquid and compressed. The latter is more convenient and usually more satisfactory to use, and there should be no difficulty in obtaining it from a baker.

THE OBJECT OF KNEADING

Dough is kneaded to make it smooth and to distribute the yeast evenly through it. Large holes in bread are brought about by insufficient kneading. It should be done quickly, so that the dough does not become chilled.

RISING AND BAKING

The dough should rise to about double its bulk. If it rises too much it is liable to become sour ; so after it has " risen " and " proved " sufficiently it must be put into a hot oven to bake, as this will kill any further action of the yeast.

To test whether the bread is baked tap it underneath with the knuckles, and it should sound hollow.

WHITE YEAST BREAD

INGREDIENTS.—3½ lb. of flour, 1 teaspoonful of castor sugar, 1 oz. of yeast, 4 level teaspoonfuls of salt, 1¾ pints of water (lukewarm).

METHOD.—Sieve the flour and salt into a large basin and make a hole in the middle, heaping the flour round the sides of the basin.

Put the yeast into a small basin with the sugar, and mix them together until they become liquid. Then stir in the lukewarm water.

Strain this mixture into the middle of the flour and mix sufficient flour with it to make a stiff batter. Leave it in a warm place for from fifteen to twenty minutes, or until there are bubbles on the surface. This process is called " setting the sponge."

After this time work in the remainder of the flour and mix it to a pliable dough, adding a little more warm water or flour if required. Turn it on to a floured board and knead it for a few minutes.

Flour the basin, turn the dough into it again and throw a cloth over the top and put it to rise in a warm place from one and a half to two hours, or until it is twice the bulk. It may be put in a box in front of the fire or on the rack over the fire, or, if nowhere else is available, in a very cool oven.

When it is risen turn out the dough and knead it lightly, then divide it into portions and form it into loaves. If a tin loaf is required, form the dough into an oblong and put it into a greased and floured bread-tin, pressing it lightly to the shape of the tin. It should be only half full.

Stand it in a warm place to " prove " until it is risen again to double its size —this will probably take half an hour —then bake it in a hot oven, lessening the heat as required.

NOTE.—The quantity of ingredients given is sufficient for two half-quartern loaves. The average time required to cook each loaf is three-quarters of an hour.

S

Shaping Loaves

To make a cottage loaf, divide the dough into two parts, one part being about four times as large as the other. Form each part into a smooth, round shape, put the small one on top and make a hole in the centre.

To make a Coburg, form the dough into a smooth round. Flour a knife, cut the top of the dough across each way, dividing it into four, then raise each quarter a little at the centre.

Fancy Breads

Fancy breads can be made by the addition of a little fat, such as butter, lard, or margarine. This may be rubbed into the flour or melted and mixed with the liquid. Milk or milk and water can be used instead of water, and sometimes an egg is added. About one or two ounces of fat to a pound of flour is sufficient.

Fancy loaves may be glazed with a little beaten egg or some melted butter and warm milk before being baked.

If making sweet bread with the addition of fruit and sugar, the amount to use is, roughly, two ounces of each to one pound of flour.

Glaze sweet bread after it it is cooked and return it to the oven to dry.

AFTERNOON TEA SCONES

INGREDIENTS.—½ lb. of flour, 1½ oz. of butter, 1 teaspoonful of baking-powder, ¼ teaspoonful of salt, ¾ gill of milk.

METHOD.—Sift the flour, salt, and baking-powder.

Rub in the butter. Have a hot oven ready.

Stir in the milk, making a soft but not sticky dough.

Turn the dough on to a floured board and roll it out very lightly half an inch thick.

Cut the scones out quickly with a small floured cutter and place them on a greased baking-sheet. Brush the tops with a beaten egg. Bake them in a hot oven for twelve minutes.

BAKING-POWDER LOAVES

INGREDIENTS.—¾ lb. of flour, 3 teaspoonfuls of baking-powder, 1 level teaspoonful of salt, 1½ oz. of margarine, milk to mix.

METHOD.—Sift the flour, salt, and baking-powder into a basin.

Rub in the fat, then mix the ingredients to a soft dough with milk. Divide it into portions and shape them into small cottage loaves. Place them on a baking-sheet and bake them in a hot oven. They will take about fifteen minutes.

Baking-Powder Loaves should be eaten new, as they quickly become stale.

BAKING-POWDER ROLLS

INGREDIENTS.—1 lb. of flour, 1 flat teaspoonful of salt, 2 teaspoonfuls of baking-powder, 1½ gills of milk and water.

METHOD.—Sieve the flour, salt, and baking-powder and mix well together.

Add the milk and water and mix to a soft consistency.

Slightly flour a board and lightly knead the dough for a few minutes.

Divide into six portions and make into six small cottage loaves.

Brush over with milk.

Place on a slightly greased and floured baking-sheet.

Bake in a hot oven for from twenty to thirty minutes.

BAKING-TIN BREAD

INGREDIENTS.—1 oz. of yeast, 1 egg, 4 oz. of sugar, 1½ gills of lukewarm milk, 6 oz. of margarine (melted), 1 lb. of flour.

FOR THE ALMOND MIXTURE.—3 oz. of almonds, 3 oz. of brown sugar, 4 oz. of butter, 2 small tablespoonfuls of flour.

METHOD.—Sift the flour and add the sugar. Cream the yeast with one teaspoonful of sugar. Add the warm milk and the warm melted margarine, straining this into the flour. Mix them all together, add also the beaten egg.

Put the mixture aside to rise for about an hour and a half or two hours, then knead it lightly and put it into a greased and floured baking-tin.

Only half-fill the tin and leave the mixture to rise until the tin is full.

Chop the almonds and mix them with the sugar, flour, and melted butter. Place the mixture over the bread lightly and bake in a good oven.

BATH BUNS

INGREDIENTS.—1 lb. of flour, ½ lb. of butter, 3 eggs, 1 oz. of compressed yeast, 2 oz. of crushed loaf sugar, 6 oz. of granulated sugar, ½ cupful of milk (tepid), 2 oz. of citron peel, 2 oz. of currants (washed).

METHOD.—Mix the yeast with a teaspoonful of sugar, and when liquid stir in the milk.

Rub the butter into the flour, make a hollow in the centre and pour in the milk and yeast. Beat the eggs, pour in nearly all of them, keeping back a little to brush over the top of the buns.

Mix to a soft, smooth dough. Cover the basin with a cloth and stand it in a warm place for one hour for the dough to rise.

Then beat in the granulated sugar, currants, and chopped peel. Knead the dough with floured hands, form it into buns and place them on two greased tins, leaving room for them to rise.

Let them " prove " in a warm place for thirty minutes.

Brush the tops with egg and sprinkle with crushed sugar or carraway comfits and a few currants.

Bake in a quick oven for from twenty to thirty minutes.

Sufficient for ten or twelve buns.

BREAKFAST ROLLS

INGREDIENTS.—¾ lb. of flour, a pinch of salt, 2 teaspoonfuls of baking-powder, 2 oz. of margarine, milk and water to mix (about 1¼ gills).

METHOD.—Sieve together the flour, baking-powder, and salt.

Rub in the margarine until it is like fine crumbs. Then gradually pour in the milk and water to form a fairly soft paste—not sticky, but pliable.

Put on to a floured board and knead for a few minutes until quite smooth.

Divide into about eight equal portions.

Shape each into a fat roll about four inches long.

Work them to a point at either end. Make two or three sharp cuts across the top of each roll.

Grease and flour a baking-sheet.

Put the rolls on to it and brush over with milk.

Bake in a hot oven for about fifteen to twenty minutes.

Sufficient to make eight rolls.

BREAKFAST SCONES

INGREDIENTS.—¾ lb. of flour, 1½ oz. of margarine, ¼ level teaspoonful of salt, ½ level teaspoonful of carbonate of soda, sour milk.

METHOD.—Sift the flour with the salt and soda. Rub the fat into them and mix them to a soft dough with sour milk.

Turn the dough on to a lightly floured board and either roll it out thickly and cut it in small rounds, or roll it to about one-fourth of an inch thick and cut it into larger rounds.

Place the scones on lightly buttered tins and bake them in a quick oven, allowing a few minutes longer for the thick rounds.

SWEET BREAKFAST SCONES

INGREDIENTS. — ½ lb. of flour, a pinch of salt, ¼ flat teaspoonful of carbonate of soda, 1 oz. of lard, 1 dessertspoonful of castor sugar, sour milk.

METHOD.—Sieve the flour with the soda and salt.

Rub in the lard and add the sugar.

Stir in enough sour milk to make a soft dough.

Turn it on to a floured board and roll it out to about a quarter of an inch thick.

Cut it into rounds with a plain cutter (about three inches in diameter), put them on a greased and floured baking-sheet, and bake them in a quick oven for about ten minutes.

Sufficient for about seven scones.

BRIDGE SCONES

INGREDIENTS.—9 oz. of flour, a pinch of salt, 1 oz. of sugar, 1 level teaspoonful of carbonate of soda, 2 level teaspoonfuls of cream of tartar, 2 oz. of margarine, 1½ oz. of almonds, milk.

METHOD.—Blanch and mince the almonds.

Sift the flour with the salt, cream of tartar, and carbonate of soda. Rub in the fat, and add the sugar and almonds.

Mix them well, then stir in enough

milk to make a soft dough, and roll this out until it is barely half an inch thick.

Stamp it into shapes with bridge cutters.

Place the scones on a baking-sheet, brush them with milk and bake them in a quick oven.

Sufficient for twelve or more scones.

BRIOCHES

INGREDIENTS.—1 lb. of flour, 6 oz. of butter, 3 eggs, ¼ pint of tepid water, 1 small teaspoonful of salt, ½ teaspoonful of castor sugar, ½ oz. of compressed yeast.

METHOD.—Cream the yeast and sugar till liquid and mix in the water, which must only be tepid, not hot. Cover with a cloth and stand in a warm place for an hour.

Beat the eggs and melt the butter. Sift the flour and salt into a basin, and make a hollow in the centre into which pour the eggs and melted butter. Mix with a wooden spoon and work till smooth. Spread the dough out flat and pour in the sponge which has been rising. Mix thoroughly, cover the basin and set to rise in a warm place for an hour.

Flour some tartlet-tins. Knead the dough on a floured board and cut it into the required number of pieces.

These are made into small cottage loaves, one-fifth of each piece being used for the top. Both rounds should be kneaded till smooth, the lower one moistened and the smaller one placed on top and pressed into place.

Prove the brioches for fifteen minutes in a warm place, and brush them well all over with beaten egg. Bake in a moderately hot oven for about fifteen minutes.

This quantity of dough makes twelve to sixteen brioches.

RICH BRIOCHES

INGREDIENTS.—1 lb. of flour, 1 gill of milk (warm), ½ oz. of solid yeast, 10 oz. of butter or margarine, 6 eggs, ½ gill of water (warm), 2½ oz. of castor sugar, ¼ teaspoonful of salt.

METHOD.—Sieve a quarter of a pound of the flour into a basin.

Mix together the yeast and one teaspoonful of sugar in a small warm basin until they become liquid.

Add to this half a gill of water, previously warmed.

Strain this mixture into the centre of the flour, and stir all together into a smooth paste.

Put in a warm place to rise for about one hour.

Into another basin sieve the remainder of the flour, add to it the salt and remainder of sugar. Mix together and make a hole in the centre.

Melt the margarine in a saucepan, add the milk and just warm it.

Beat up the eggs.

Pour the warm milk and margarine into the centre of the flour, also the eggs.

Mix thoroughly.

Then when the dough in the first basin is ready, add it to the above ingredients and get all well kneaded together.

Stand in a cool place for about twelve hours.

Then form it into balls, crescents, or tiny loaves.

Place on a greased and floured baking-sheet.

Bake in a hot oven for about thirty minutes.

If desired, the loaves may be glazed.

Brush them over with a mixture of warm milk and melted butter—about two tablespoonfuls of milk and one ounce of butter.

Cool on a sieve.

Sufficient to make about a dozen.

BROWN BREAD

INGREDIENTS.—1¾ lb. of wholemeal flour, ½ oz. of yeast, 2 level teaspoonfuls of salt, 1 level teaspoonful of castor sugar, warm water to mix, about 3½ gills.

METHOD.—When making brown bread, always omit the process of "setting the sponge."

Mix the wholemeal and salt in a large basin.

Mix the yeast and sugar until they liquefy, add the warm water and strain the mixture into the wholemeal.

Mix to a pliable dough, adding more warm water as required.

Knead the dough lightly and then put it to rise for about three-quarters of an hour.

Knead it again, form it into a smooth

shape, and put it into a bread-tin, greased and floured.

Press it lightly to the shape of the tin and let it " prove " for from twenty to thirty minutes. Then bake it in a hot oven at first, lessening the heat as required.

The average time for cooking is about one hour.

BROWN SCONES

INGREDIENTS.—5 oz. of wholemeal, 3 oz. of flour, 2 oz. of margarine, a pinch of salt, 1½ teaspoonfuls of baking-powder, 1 dessertspoonful of castor sugar, milk to mix.

METHOD.—Sieve together the flour, wholemeal, salt, and baking-powder.

Rub in the margarine.

Add the sugar and mix all together. Pour the milk in gradually and mix to a paste, which should be just pliable.

Put it on a slightly floured board and knead it for a few minutes until smooth.

Roll into a thick, round shape.

Put into a greased sandwich-tin. Cut across twice.

Brush over with milk. Bake in a fairly hot oven for about twenty to thirty minutes.

Serve with butter.

BUN CAKE

INGREDIENTS.—¾ oz. of yeast, ¾ lb. of flour, 1½ gills of milk, ½ lb. of sultanas, 2 oz. of mixed peel, 3 oz. of margarine, 5 oz. of sugar, 1 egg, ¼ level teaspoonful of mixed spice.

METHOD.—Sift one-third of the flour into a basin. Cream the yeast with one teaspoonful of the sugar. Warm the milk and add it to the yeast; then strain this gradually into the centre of the flour and mix it to a smooth batter.

Cover the basin and put it in a warm place to rise for about an hour.

Meanwhile, wash, pick over and dry the sultanas and shred the peel.

Sift the remainder of the flour, with the spice, into another basin. Rub in the fat and add the prepared fruit and sugar. Mix them well together.

When the first mixture is ready, gradually work in the prepared dry ingredients, adding also the beaten egg and a little more warm milk, if required.

Beat the mixture well before turning it into a greased cake-tin. This should only be about half-filled. Let the mixture rise till it is nearly double its size, then put it into a hot oven to bake. Brush the top of the cake when it is cooked with milk and sugar glaze, and return it to the oven to dry for a minute or two.

FOR THE GLAZE : Mix one teaspoonful of castor sugar with one dessertspoonful of milk and stir them till dissolved.

BUN RING

INGREDIENTS.—1 lb. of flour, 2 oz. of castor sugar, a pinch of salt, ½ pint of milk (warm), cinnamon and sugar, ½ oz. of yeast, 1 yolk of egg, 2 oz. of margarine, a few currants, a few chopped walnuts.

METHOD.—Mix the yeast with half a teaspoonful of castor sugar (extra to that given) until it liquifies, then stir in half the milk, which should be just lukewarm.

Sift the flour with salt and put three-quarters of it aside ; the remainder put into a basin and gradually strain in the yeast and milk, mixing it all to a thick batter.

Beat this well and put it into a warm place for forty-five minutes.

Gradually stir in the remainder of the flour, mixed with the castor sugar (2 oz.), also the other half of the warm milk mixed with the beaten egg-yolk and melted margarine, which should also be lukewarm.

When well mixed, put the dough to rise until double its size, then knead it lightly and form it into a long roll.

Roll this out to an oblong shape, then brush it with melted butter.

Strew a few currants over the shape and sprinkle it with castor sugar and cinnamon in the proportion of two teaspoonfuls of castor sugar to one level teaspoonful of cinnamon.

Roll the shape up, twist it into a round ring and put it on a baking-sheet—lightly greased and floured.

Cut the ring with the scissors not quite to the centre and leaving about an inch of space between each cut, turn each cut piece over a little and pull it out slightly.

Put the ring in a warm place for twenty minutes.

Finally, put the bun ring into a hot oven to bake. It will take from twenty to thirty minutes to cook.

When ready, brush it with sugar and milk glaze, sprinkle it with a few chopped walnuts, and return it to the oven for a minute or two to dry the glaze.

NOTE.—To MAKE THE GLAZE : Mix one dessertspoonful of castor sugar with two dessertspoonfuls of milk, until dissolved.

BUTTERMILK SCONES

INGREDIENTS.—¾ lb. of flour, ½ teaspoonful of carbonate of soda, ½ teaspoonful of cream of tartar, ½ teaspoonful of salt, 1 teaspoonful of golden syrup, 1½ gills of buttermilk.

METHOD.—Sift the flour, soda, cream of tartar, and salt into a basin.

Add the syrup and buttermilk, and mix lightly with a wooden spoon.

The dough should be moist and light. *Do not knead it.*

Turn it on to a board and cut it in three.

Roll out into rounds about a quarter of an inch thick, and cut each round into four.

The girdle should be ready heated, and should be hot enough to brown a little flour lightly if sprinkled on it. (If the flour burns at once it is too hot.)

Place the scones on the girdle and turn them soon, allowing longer for the second side.

They should take about six minutes to cook.

CAKE SCONES

INGREDIENTS.—½ lb. of flour, a pinch of salt, 1½ teaspoonfuls of baking-powder, 2 oz. of margarine, 1½ oz. of castor sugar, 1 egg, milk.

METHOD.—Sieve the flour with the salt and baking-powder.

Cream the fat and sugar, then add the flour gradually, also the well-whisked egg and some milk as required.

Put the mixture into small greased cake-tins and bake it in a quick oven.

Sufficient for twelve scones.

CHEESE SCONES

INGREDIENTS.—1½ oz. of margarine, ¾ lb. of flour, 3 teaspoonfuls of baking-powder, ¼ teaspoonful of salt, cayenne to taste, 3 oz. of Cheddar cheese, 2 oz. of Parmesan cheese, about ½ pint of milk.

METHOD.—Sift the flour with the salt and baking-powder, and rub in the margarine.

Grate the cheeses finely, and add them to the flour, with a pinch of cayenne, then mix well and add enough milk to make a soft dough.

Turn the dough on to a floured board, and roll it out to about half or three-quarters of an inch thick. Stamp into rounds and place on a buttered baking-sheet. Bake the scones in a quick oven for about fifteen or twenty minutes.

Split them open and serve them hot, with butter.

This quantity makes fifteen scones.

CINNAMON TOAST

INGREDIENTS.—Several slices of stale bread, 1 level teaspoonful of cinnamon, butter, 2 dessertspoonfuls of castor sugar.

METHOD.—Cinnamon Toast, a great delicacy across the Atlantic, is a variation of buttered toast, equally popular with young and old.

Slice the bread to toast thickness. Toast it, and butter it while hot.

Mix together the cinnamon and sugar. Sprinkle them over the toast, then place this in the top of the oven or under the griller to melt the sugar slightly.

If liked, brown sugar may be used instead of castor.

CORNFLOUR SCONES

INGREDIENTS.—½ lb. of flour, 2 oz. of cornflour, 1 teaspoonful of baking-powder, 1 oz. of margarine or butter, 1 dessertspoonful of castor sugar, milk to mix.

METHOD.—Sieve the flour, cornflour, and baking-powder. Rub in the fat.

Add the sugar and mix all together.

Gradually add some milk and mix to a pliable dough.

Roll it out to about three-eighths of an inch thick and cut into small rounds.

Place on a slightly greased tin.

Brush the scones over with milk,

and bake in a hot oven for about ten to fifteen minutes.

Sufficient to make seven or eight scones.

CORNISH SAFFRON CAKE

INGREDIENTS.—1½ lb. of flour, 1 lb. of currants (cleaned), 1 lb. of butter or margarine, ½ lb. of peel (chopped), 2 oz. of yeast, 1 teaspoonful of sugar, ½ teaspoonful of saffron, ¾ pint of cold water, ½ teaspoonful of salt.

METHOD.—Grease and flour two oblong tins.

Put the saffron and water in a jug and stand it in a pan of boiling water. When the saffron water is tepid it is ready for mixing.

To set the sponge, mix the yeast and sugar for a minute, and when liquid pour the saffron water on to it. Stir it into the flour, cover with a cloth, and let it rise in a warm place till it is three times its original size. It will take about twenty-five minutes.

To mix the cake, melt the butter, add it by degrees and beat till smooth. Stir in the currants, peel, and salt. Cover the cake and let it rise for one hour. Turn it on to a floured board, and knead it very little till smooth.

Divide the dough into two. Place it in the tins and let them " prove " for twenty minutes.

Bake in a moderate oven for one hour and a quarter.

Sufficient for two oblong cakes.

CREAM SCONES

INGREDIENTS.—½ lb. of flour (light weight), 2 oz. of butter, ½ gill of cream, 1 teaspoonful of baking-powder, a little milk (about ⅛ gill), salt.

METHOD.—Sift the flour and baking-powder into a basin with a quarter of a teaspoonful of salt.

Rub in the butter, add the cream and enough milk to make a soft dough, but not enough to be sticky.

Scones must always be mixed and put in the oven as quickly as possible.

After mixing, roll the dough out quickly on a floured board from a quarter to half an inch thick.

Cut it into rounds with a small cutter, place them on a greased tin, and bake in a quick oven for about twelve minutes.

The scones will look very nice if the tops are quickly brushed with beaten egg before baking.

SOUR CREAM SCONES

INGREDIENTS.—10 oz. of flour, 1 teaspoonful of baking-powder, a pinch of salt, 1½ oz. of currants, 1½ oz. of sugar, 1½ oz. of margarine or butter, sour cream to mix.

METHOD.—Wash, pick over and dry the currants. Sieve the flour, salt, and baking-powder. Rub in the fat.

Add the sugar and prepared fruit, and mix all together.

Mix to a pliable dough with sour cream.

Roll out to just over half an inch thick.

Cut into small rounds with a very sharp cutter.

Place on a greased baking-sheet and bake in a hot oven for about fifteen to twenty minutes.

When cooked, brush over with sugar and milk glaze, and return to the oven for a few seconds to dry the glaze.

For the glaze, mix together half a gill of milk and one dessertspoonful of castor sugar.

Sufficient to make about eight or nine scones.

CRULLERS

INGREDIENTS.—9 oz. of flour, 1 level teaspoonful of carbonate of soda, 2 level teaspoonfuls of cream of tartar, 1 oz. of margarine or lard, 3 oz. of castor sugar, 1 egg, lemon-rind, about ¾ gill of milk.

METHOD.—Beat the sugar and fat to a cream, stir in two or three teaspoonfuls of milk, then beat in the egg, and a little grated lemon-rind.

Add the flour (sifted) with soda and cream of tartar, and mix all to a soft dough, stirring in the remainder of the milk as required.

Roll out the dough and cut it into shapes as desired. These should be rather flat, as they swell much when cooked. Put them into deep hot lard, and fry them gently until golden, turning them over when brown. Drain them and serve them with butter, for tea or breakfast.

Crullers may be flavoured with spice sometimes to make variety.

Sufficient for about twenty or more crullers, according to the size.

CURRANT BUNS

INGREDIENTS.—1 lb. of flour, 3 oz. of castor sugar, ½ oz. of solid yeast, 3 oz. of currants, 1 egg, 2 oz. of margarine, milk and water (1½ gills).

METHOD.—Sieve the flour. Then measure out four ounces into a basin, and make a hole in the centre.

Place the yeast in a small warm basin, and add a teaspoonful of castor sugar.

Mix well until it liquefies.

Warm the milk and water and stir into the yeast.

Then strain into the basin containing the flour.

Mix thoroughly.

Cover the basin and stand it in a warm place for about fifty minutes.

Wash the currants, pick them over and dry in a warm oven.

Now take the remaining flour and pour into a separate basin.

Rub the fat into it until it is like fine crumbs. Add the sugar and currants, and well mix.

When the yeast mixture is ready beat into it the prepared dry ingredients, add the egg, and beat well (with your hands) for about ten minutes.

Cover the basin, and stand in a warm place for about one hour and a quarter.

Divide the mixture into small, equal portions. Place on a floured board and shape each into a round.

Put the buns on a greased and slightly floured baking-sheet, and stand in a warm place for about twenty minutes.

The buns will swell, so allow room between each one.

Bake in a hot oven for about twenty to thirty minutes.

Just before they are quite cooked glaze the tops, then place in the oven again for a few minutes. Set aside on a sieve to cool.

To make the glaze, mix together one tablespoonful of milk and two teaspoonfuls of castor sugar.

DATE BREAD

INGREDIENTS.—6 oz. of flour, ½ gill of milk, 2 oz. of wholemeal, 3 oz. of dates (when stoned), 1 oz. of walnuts, ½ flat teaspoonful of bicarbonate of soda, 6 oz. of golden syrup.

METHOD.—Chop the walnuts. Stone and chop the dates.

Sieve the flour with the wholemeal and bicarbonate of soda.

Add the dates and walnuts and mix well together.

Put the golden syrup into a saucepan and warm it slightly, then mix it with the milk. Add it to the dry ingredients and mix all together.

Turn the mixture into a greased charlotte-tin or other suitable tin, filling it not more than three parts full.

Cover it securely with well-greased paper, and steam it for about two and a half or three hours.

To weigh golden syrup, weigh a small saucepan, add the weight of the pan to the weight of the syrup required, and pour sufficient syrup into the pan to balance the combined weights.

DEVONSHIRE SPLITS

INGREDIENTS.—2 lb. of flour, 1½ teaspoonfuls of salt, ¼ lb. of butter, 1 oz. of yeast, 1 pint of tepid milk and water, 2 teaspoonfuls of castor sugar.

METHOD.—Put the yeast and sugar in a pudding basin, and mix them for a minute. When they are liquid add the milk.

Rub the butter into the flour, and make a hollow in the centre. Pour in the yeast and milk, and sprinkle the salt round the edge of the flour. Let it rise in a warm place for ten minutes.

When the top of the sponge is covered with bubbles stir in the flour and knead the dough on a floured board till smooth.

Roll out the dough and cut it into small or medium-sized rounds.

Place the splits on a greased tin, and let them " prove " on the plate rack till they have risen to twice their original size.

Bake in a quick oven for about fifteen minutes.

The splits are eaten with strawberry jam and clotted cream, or sometimes with golden syrup and cream.

Sufficient for sixteen splits, or more, according to size.

DOUGH

INGREDIENTS.—1¾ lb. of flour, ½ oz. of yeast, ½ teaspoonful of castor sugar, ¾ to 1 pint of warm water, 1 teaspoonful of salt

METHOD.—Mix the flour and salt together, place in a warmed basin and leave in a warm place for a few minutes.

Place the yeast in a small, warmed basin, add the sugar ; mix these two ingredients together with a teaspoon until a liquid is formed.

Add three-quarters of a pint of warm water to the yeast and sugar and stir round.

Make a well in the centre of the flour and strain the prepared yeast, sugar, and water into the well.

Sprinkle a small portion of the flour from the side of the basin over the top of the yeast, etc.

Cover the basin with a cloth and stand in a warm place for about fifteen to twenty minutes, or until there are bubbles on the surface. This process is called " setting the sponge."

Now remove the basin and mix all the flour from the sides into the middle with the yeast and water, etc.

The dough now should be a pliable consistency ; if it is sticky more flour must be added, and if rather dry a little more warm water may be added.

When the dough is mixed, slightly flour the board and knead it for a few minutes.

Place the dough again into the basin, cover lightly, and put into a warm place to rise for one and a half to two hours.

This dough may be used for making cakes and buns when you bake at home.

DOUGH CAKE

INGREDIENTS.—½ a quartern of dough (see previous recipe), 3 oz. of margarine, 2 oz. of currants, 2 oz. of sultanas, 2 oz. of mixed peel, ¼ lb. of white sugar, 1 egg.

METHOD.—Wash the currants and sultanas, rub them in a cloth, remove the stalks and then dry the fruit.

Cut the peel into small pieces.

Beat the margarine to a cream, put the dough into a basin and work the fat into it. Then mix in the prepared fruit and sugar. Beat up the egg, and work it into the dough, knead it well (in the basin), and when it is thoroughly mixed, put it into a greased cake-tin.

Cover the tin lightly with a piece of paper or cloth, and stand in a warm place to rise for about thirty minutes.

Bake in a hot oven at first, then lessen the heat.

When cooked, put on to a sieve and leave until cold.

DOUGH NUTS

INGREDIENTS.—¾ lb. of flour, pinch of salt, 1 teaspoonful of castor sugar, 1 oz. of butter or margarine, 1 egg, 1½ gills of milk, ¾ oz. of yeast, jam, deep fat for frying.

METHOD.—Sift the flour and salt into a basin and make a well in the centre.

Put the yeast and sugar into a small basin, and mix them together until they liquefy.

Melt the butter or margarine in a saucepan, add the milk, and make it lukewarm, then stir it on to the yeast. Mix this with the beaten egg and strain it into the centre of the flour.

Mix them all together and beat the mixture well.

Throw a cloth over the basin and stand the dough in a warm place to rise for two hours, then turn it on to a lightly floured board, knead it lightly and divide it into eighteen portions.

Form each portion into a smooth ball, flatten it out, and drop a little jam in the centre, then form it into a ball again, covering the jam completely. Place the dough nuts on a lightly floured baking-sheet and let them stand in a warm place till they begin to rise.

TO FRY THE DOUGH NUTS.—Put a deep pan of fat on to heat. Lard, or a mixture of lard and dripping, can be used. When it is hot, drop in the balls, and fry them gently till golden, frying only a few at a time. They will take about ten minutes to cook.

When cooked, lift them on to a baking-sheet lined with paper, roll them in castor sugar, coating them thickly, and leave them to get cold.

Sometimes they may be rolled in a mixture of sugar and cinnamon, using one teaspoonful of powdered cinnamon to four teaspoonfuls of castor sugar.

NOTE.—The fat should be strained when finished with, and can be used again for frying.

Dough nuts must be eaten very new, so they should be made the day they are required.

EASTER LOAF

INGREDIENTS.—About ½ pint of milk, 1 lb. of flour, 1 oz. of yeast, 2 oz. of butter or margarine, 2 oz. of sugar, 2 oz. of raisins, almonds, 1 egg.

METHOD.—Cream the yeast with one teaspoonful of the sugar. Mix it with the warm milk and add it to the flour, mixing this to a dough.

Leave it to rise for three-quarters of an hour.

Mix in the creamed butter, raisins (keeping back a few to sprinkle on the top), and the egg beaten with the sugar.

Let the mixture rise again, then shape it into a big loaf tin, only half-filling it. Allow it to rise until the tin is full.

Put the loaf in a hot oven to bake and, when it is nearly cooked, brush the top with beaten egg and sprinkle it with sugar, chopped almonds, and raisins.

Return the loaf to the oven and finish baking it.

FIG TEA-BREAD

INGREDIENTS.—3 oz. of figs, 9 oz. of flour, pinch of salt, 3 oz. of castor sugar, 1 egg, 2 oz. of shelled walnuts, 1 oz. of margarine, about 1 gill of milk, 2 teaspoonfuls of baking-powder.

METHOD.—Chop the walnuts and cut the figs into small pieces.

Sift the flour with salt and baking-powder, and mix it with the fruit and nuts.

Whisk the egg and castor sugar until thick and creamy, and then gradually mix in the dry ingredients, adding also the margarine (melted) and the milk.

Beat well together, turn the mixture into a greased tin and bake it in a moderately hot oven. It will take about an hour to cook. When cooked, brush the top lightly with sugar and milk glaze, and return the

tea-bread to the oven for a minute or two to dry.

To MAKE THE GLAZE.—Mix one level teaspoonful of castor sugar with one teaspoonful of milk until dissolved.

FLANNEL CAKES

INGREDIENTS.—½ lb. of flour, ⅓ flat teaspoonful of carbonate of soda, ¼ teaspoonful of salt, 1 oz. of castor sugar, ¾ pint of milk, a walnut of butter or margarine, 2 eggs.

METHOD.—Sift the flour with the carbonate of soda and salt. Rub in the fat and add the sugar.

Separate the eggs, put the yolks in the centre of the flour, then gradually stir in about two-thirds of the milk and mix all to a smooth batter. Add the remainder.

Whisk the whites to a stiff froth, and stir them in lightly.

Grease a small frying-pan with lard and pour in sufficient batter to coat it thinly. Cook this until it bubbles and is brown underneath, then turn it over and brown the other side. Cook the remainder in the same way, and serve the cakes at once, heaped on a dish.

These are excellent served hot for tea with strawberry jam.

Sufficient to make about ten flannel cakes.

FRUIT CRESCENTS

INGREDIENTS.—½ lb. of flour, 2 level teaspoonfuls of cream of tartar, 1 level teaspoonful of carbonate of soda, 2 oz. of currants, 1½ oz. of margarine, 1½ oz. of castor sugar, 1 yolk of egg, milk.

METHOD.—Wash, pick over and dry the fruit.

Beat the sugar and fat to a cream, then stir in the yolk of the egg.

Sift the flour with cream of tartar and carbonate of soda and add them with the currants, stirring in enough milk to make a soft dough.

Divide this into five or more portions, according to the size required. Roll each piece out to a three-cornered shape, then roll it over from the base to the point and twist it round into a crescent shape.

Put the crescents on to a lightly buttered baking-sheet, brush them with milk or egg, and bake them in a quick oven.

Sufficient for five crescents.

FRUIT FINGER SCONES

INGREDIENTS.—9 oz. of flour, 2 oz. of lard, 2 level teaspoonfuls of cream of tartar, 1 level teaspoonful of carbonate of soda, good pinch of salt, 1½ oz. of peel (candied orange), 1½ oz. of castor sugar, about ¼ pint of milk.

METHOD.—Sift the flour into a basin with the salt, soda, and cream of tartar.

Rub in the lard, then add the peel, cut into fine shreds, and the sugar, and mix well.

Stir in enough milk to make a soft dough. Divide this into portions, shape, and bake them in greased sponge finger tins, or else shape them and put on a greased baking-sheet.

Cook the scones in a quick oven, and serve them with butter.

If liked, they may be brushed with milk before they are baked, to glaze them.

This quantity will make from eighteen to twenty-four scones, according to the size.

NOTE.—To make successful scones, remember that the dough must be soft, and they must be baked in a quick oven.

FRUIT SCONES

INGREDIENTS.—¾ lb. of flour, pinch of salt, 1 teaspoonful of cream of tartar, ¼ teaspoonful of carbonate of soda, 1 oz. of lard, 1 oz. of margarine, 2 oz. of granulated sugar, 3 oz. of currants, milk or milk-and-water to mix (about 1½ gills).

METHOD.—Wash the currants, rub them in a cloth, stalk them and put them in a warm place to dry.

Mix the flour with the salt, cream of tartar, and soda, and sieve them into a basin. Rub in the lard and margarine until the mixture is like fine crumbs.

Add the sugar and currants, and mix all the dry ingredients together.

Pour in the milk and mix to a stiff paste.

Put this on to a pastry board, and roll it out until it is about half an inch in thickness.

Cut into triangular-shaped pieces, and place on a greased baking-sheet.

Bake in a hot oven from fifteen to twenty minutes.

Just before they are quite cooked, brush them over with milk and sugar glaze.

Put them back into the oven for a few seconds to dry the glaze. Place on a sieve to cool.

NOTE.—These scones are excellent if split open, toasted, and buttered, and served hot, especially when stale.

MILK AND SUGAR GLAZE.—Ingredients : 1 tablespoonful of milk, 1 dessertspoonful of castor sugar.

Mix well together.

GAILETTES

(SMALL CURRANT BUNS WITH SUGARY TOPS)

INGREDIENTS.—1 lb. of dough (see below), 3 oz. of white sugar, ¼ lb. of sultanas or currants, 1 egg, 2 oz. of lard.

METHOD.—Wash the fruit, dry it and remove the stalks.

Knead the dough in the usual way until quite smooth.

Roll it out to a square shape about a quarter of an inch in thickness.

Turn it on to the other side.

Spread the lard in dabs all over the surface of the rolled-out dough.

Sprinkle on the fruit and the sugar.

Roll the whole thing up and knead again until these ingredients are all well mixed into the dough.

Divide it into equal portions about the size of very small buns, only, instead of making them round, make them into squares.

Grease a baking-sheet and slightly flour it.

Place the squares on the sheet, leaving a large space between each to allow them plenty of room to swell when set aside to rise.

Put into a warm place for about forty-five minutes, or until they are double their original size.

Brush them over with beaten egg and sprinkle with castor sugar.

Bake in a hot oven until nicely browned.

They will take about twenty to thirty minutes.

Place on a sieve to cool

THE DOUGH

INGREDIENTS.—¾ lb. of flour, ½ teaspoonful of castor sugar, ½ oz. of solid yeast, warm water to mix, pinch of salt.

METHOD.—Mix together the flour and salt, and pass through a wire sieve into a basin.

Put the yeast into a small warm basin, add to it the sugar, stir round until it forms a liquid.

Add to the yeast one gill and a half of warm water.

Make a hole in the centre of the flour and pour in the yeast.

Sprinkle a small quantity of the flour over the surface of the yeast.

Put the basin in a warm place for about fifteen minutes, or until the surface of the yeast is full of bubbles.

Then mix it all together with the flour to a stiff paste ; if necessary, more warm water may be added.

The dough should be of a soft consistency, not too dry and not sticky.

It is ready for making the gailettes.

GINGER SCONES

INGREDIENTS.— 1 teaspoonful of ground ginger, ½ lb. of flour, 1 oz. of margarine, 2½ flat teaspoonfuls of baking-powder, golden syrup, milk.

METHOD.—Sieve the flour with the ground ginger and baking-powder.

Rub in the margarine.

Warm some golden syrup enough to thin it down, then take two dessertspoonfuls of it and pour it into the centre of the flour.

Mix to a soft dough, adding some milk as required.

Roll it out and cut it into small rounds about a quarter of an inch thick.

Brush the top with milk or egg, and bake in a quick oven for about ten minutes.

Sufficient to make eighteen scones.

GRIDDLE CAKES

INGREDIENTS.—1 breakfastcupful of plain flour, 2 teaspoonfuls of baking-powder, ¼ teaspoonful of salt, 1 oz. of lard, 1 large egg, 1 breakfastcupful of milk, Canadian maple syrup, butter.

METHOD.—Sift the flour and salt into a basin. Rub in the lard.

Put the unbeaten egg in the centre of the flour with a little of the milk.

Stir a little in the centre only ; add more milk, and continue stirring till all the flour is worked in.

Beat till smooth, and add a teaspoonful of the syrup. Grease a large oval frying-pan and make it hot. Add the baking-powder just before starting to fry the griddle cakes.

When the pan is hot, drop on it four or five tablespoonfuls of the batter, and place the pan over an asbestos mat.

Cook slowly till the tops of the cakes are covered with bubbles, then turn them over with a knife and cook the other side. They should take about six minutes. Keep the first batch hot on a plate standing on boiling water, and cook the others in the same way.

This quantity makes about sixteen cakes.

Serve them very hot in a heap with butter between each griddle cake and a pat of butter on top. Pour maple syrup over. If this is not obtainable, use golden syrup.

HARVEST BUNS

INGREDIENTS.—1 lb. of wholemeal, ¼ teaspoonful of salt, 3 dessertspoonfuls of castor sugar, ½ oz. of yeast, 2 oz. of small seedless raisins, about 1¾ gills of milk, 1½ oz. of margarine.

METHOD.—Sieve the wholemeal and salt.

Put about one-third of it into a basin and make a well in the centre.

Put the yeast into a small basin with half a teaspoonful of the sugar and mix them until they liquefy.

Warm the milk, and margarine in a saucepan and add them to the yeast. Strain the liquid into the wholemeal, mix all together and beat well.

Cover the basin loosely and put it in a warm place for half an hour, then gradually stir in the remainder of the wholemeal mixed with the prepared fruit and remainder of castor sugar.

Knead the dough for a few minutes. Divide it into small portions and make it into smooth bun shapes.

Put them on a slightly greased and floured tin and stand them in a warm place for half an hour, then put them in a hot oven to bake. They will take about half an hour to cook.

Sufficient for fourteen or sixteen buns.

HOT CROSS BUNS

HOT CROSS BUNS are made with yeast, so similar rules apply to them as to bread (see p. 545). As the mixture requires warmth to make it rise, warm milk is used for mixing, and the dough is put in a warm place to rise. The buns must be baked in a hot oven to kill any further action of the yeast.

INGREDIENTS.—1 lb. of flour, pinch of salt, ¾ oz. of yeast, 2 tablespoonfuls of castor sugar, 1 level teaspoonful of powdered cinnamon, 1 level teaspoonful of mixed spice, 2 oz. of margarine, 2 oz. of mixed candied peel, 2 oz. of currants, 2 oz. of sultanas, 1 egg, ½ pint of milk.

METHOD.—Sift the flour with the salt and spices. Rub in the margarine and add the prepared fruit and sugar, keeping back half a teaspoonful to mix with the yeast.

Mix the yeast and sugar in a small basin until they liquefy, then stir in the warm milk. Strain this mixture into the centre of the dry ingredients and mix them to a soft dough, adding the beaten egg also.

Turn the mixture on to a lightly floured board, divide it in small portions, and form them into smooth bun shapes.

Put the buns on greased and floured tins, mark them with a cross, stand them to rise until double their size, and then put them in a hot oven to bake.

When cooked, brush the buns with sugar and milk, and return them for a minute or two to the oven to dry.

ICED BUNS

INGREDIENTS.—¾ lb. of flour, pinch of salt, ½ oz. of yeast, 1 teaspoonful of castor sugar, 3 oz. of margarine, milk, 1 yolk of egg, few glacé cherries.

FOR THE ICING.—10 oz. of icing sugar, 1 egg-white, water, colouring and flavouring to taste.

METHOD.—Sift the flour and salt into a basin. Cream the yeast and sugar until they liquefy. Melt the margarine in a saucepan, add one gill of milk, and make them lukewarm. Stir them into the yeast and add this to the beaten egg-yolk.

Strain the mixture into the flour and mix it to a soft dough, adding a little more warm milk if required.

Cover the mixture and put it to rise for about one hour and a quarter, or until it is risen to twice its bulk.

Turn the dough on to a lightly floured board and divide it into ten or twelve portions. Form each one into a smooth oblong shape and place the buns on a greased and floured tin, arranging them at short distances apart.

Leave them to rise again for about a quarter of an hour, and put them into a hot oven to bake.

Cool the buns on a sieve, pull them apart and, when cold, spread a little icing on top of them and decorate them with glacé cherries.

TO MAKE THE ICING.—Sift the icing sugar and mix it to a thick paste with lightly beaten egg-white and water; add colouring and flavouring to taste.

Sufficient for ten or twelve buns.

MILK LOAF

INGREDIENTS.—1 lb. of flour, 2 teaspoonfuls of cream of tartar, ½ flat teaspoonful of carbonate of soda, 1½ oz. of margarine, pinch of salt, milk to mix.

METHOD.—Sieve the flour with the cream of tartar, soda, and salt.

Rub in the fat. Add milk gradually and mix to a dough; the latter should be quite pliable.

Put on to a slightly floured board and knead until smooth.

Lightly grease and flour a small oblong tin, put the dough into it, brush the top with milk and place in a fairly hot oven to bake, lessening the heat as required.

It will take about an hour.

MILK ROLLS

INGREDIENTS.—1 lb. of flour, ¾ oz. of yeast, 1½ teaspoonfuls of castor sugar, 1 egg, 2 oz. of margarine or butter, ½ pint of milk (warm), 1 teaspoonful of salt.

METHOD.—Sieve the flour and salt together; place in a warmed basin.

Rub the fat into the flour until it is very fine.

Mix the yeast and sugar in a small, warmed basin.

Beat the egg and mix with the warmed milk.

Add the warm milk and egg to the yeast and sugar.

Pour this into the centre of the flour.

Mix all the flour with the wet ingredients, and beat well together.

Put this mixture in a warm place to rise for an hour and half to two hours ; cover as before.

After it has risen, slightly flour a board and make the dough into fancy rolls or into one large loaf.

For fancy rolls divide the dough into eight portions—make two plaits, two horseshoes, two rolls, and two tiny loaves with a plait across the top.

To Make a Plait divide the dough into three equal portions.

Roll out each portion with the hand until it is five or six inches in length.

Pinch the three rolls together at one end and plait as you would plait hair, then pinch the ends together at the bottom of plait.

To Make a Horseshoe roll out a piece of dough to the shape of a triangle.

Take the longest side and roll over to the point of the triangle.

Twist the roll round to the shape of a horseshoe.

Mark with finger three or four impressions on each side of the horseshoe.

To Make a Roll take a piece of dough and roll it to a fat roll about four or five inches long. Make two or three cuts across the top of the roll.

To Make a loaf with Plait divide the dough into two unequal portions. Make the large portion into an oblong shape. Take the small portion and make into a small plait as described above, and place the plait over the top of the oblong shape.

When the loaves are ready place them on a slightly greased and floured baking-sheet and put into warm place to rise for about twenty minutes.

Brush over with milk and place in a hot oven and bake for from twenty to thirty minutes.

SMALL MILK LOAVES

(Made with Baking-Powder)

Ingredients.—1 lb. of flour, 2 oz. of butter, 1 egg, 1 teaspoonful of salt, $\frac{1}{2}$ pint of milk, 2 teaspoonfuls of baking-powder.

Method.—Grease a baking-sheet and light the gas in the oven.

Sift the flour and salt and rub in the butter.

Add the baking-powder and mix well.

Beat the egg and add nearly all the milk to it, keeping back a little egg to use for glazing the loaves.

Mix very quickly and do not knead. Cut into sixteen pieces.

Cut one-third off each piece.

Shape all the pieces into rounds and moisten the top of the large ones with a little water.

Put a small round on each piece on the baking-sheet and press the small piece on to the other with the little finger. If liked, instead of making cottage loaves, simply shape into plain oval pieces.

The quicker the shaping is done the better.

Brush over with egg and bake in a quick oven for about twelve minutes.

These make nice breakfast rolls.

Sufficient for sixteen to twenty-four loaves, according to size.

OATMEAL NUT SCONES

Ingredients.—4 oz. of fine oatmeal, 9 oz. of flour, 2 teaspoonfuls of baking-powder, $1\frac{1}{2}$ oz. of shelled walnuts, 1 oz. of lard, $1\frac{1}{2}$ oz. of margarine, $1\frac{1}{2}$ oz. of castor sugar, milk.

Method.—Sift the flour, oatmeal, and baking-powder into a basin. Rub in the lard and margarine, then chop up the walnuts and add them with the sugar.

Mix all together, then stir in sufficient milk to make a soft dough.

Roll this out and stamp it into rounds about four and a half inches in diameter.

Cut these rounds across into halves.

Put them on a lightly greased baking-sheet and, if you prefer your scones glazed, brush their tops with milk before baking.

Sufficient for ten scones.

OATMEAL SCONES

INGREDIENTS.—3 oz. of fine oatmeal, 1 oz. of lard, 1 oz. of margarine, 2 teaspoonfuls of baking-powder, 7 oz. of flour, 1 tablespoonful of castor sugar, milk to mix (about 1 gill).

METHOD.—Sift the flour, oatmeal, and baking-powder into a basin.

Rub in the lard and margarine and add the sugar. Then stir in sufficient milk to make a soft dough.

Roll out the mixture until it is half an inch thick. Cut it into rounds.

Place them on a lightly greased baking-sheet and bake them in a quick oven.

They will take from ten to fifteen minutes.

NOTE.—If preferred, the scones may be brushed with milk before baking, to glaze them.

POTATO PANCAKE SCONES

INGREDIENTS.—2 lb. of potatoes, 1 oz. of butter, 1 oz. of flour, or more as required, salt.

METHOD.—Peel and wash the potatoes and put them on to cook, with water to cover and salt to flavour.

Boil them till tender, drain them well and rub them through a wire sieve.

Add the butter, and when cool stir in sufficient flour to make a soft dough, adding a little more salt if required.

Roll the dough out on a well-floured board, stamp it into rounds and cook the scones on a hot, buttered girdle, turning them over when brown on one side.

Serve them hot, with butter.

This quantity will make about twenty scones.

POTATO SCONES

INGREDIENTS.—½ lb. of freshly boiled, dry, floury potatoes, 4 oz. of butter or dripping, ½ lb. of flour, ½ teaspoonful of baking-powder, ½ teaspoonful of salt, about 1 gill of milk (warm).

METHOD.—Sift the flour, salt and baking-powder, and rub in the butter till it is quite fine.

Mash the hot potatoes and rub them through a wire sieve placed over the basin of flour.

Mix the flour and potatoes with the milk. Work together quickly with a wooden spoon till the mixture is smooth, then turn it on to a floured board.

Shape the dough into a round and roll it out lightly half an inch thick. Cut it in half, and then into about eight three-cornered pieces.

Place them on a greased tin and bake in a moderately hot oven for about twelve minutes.

When they have baked for about eight minutes turn them over with a knife. They are best split open, spread with plenty of butter, and served hot.

NOTE.—If the potatoes are cold they do not mix so well.

SAFFRON BUNS

INGREDIENTS.—One pennyworth of saffron, 1 gill of cold water, 1 gill of milk, pinch of salt, 1 lb. of flour, ½ teaspoonful of castor sugar, 3 oz. of margarine or butter, 3 oz. of currants, 1 oz. of candied peel, ½ oz. of yeast, 2 oz. of sugar.

METHOD.—Put the saffron into a small basin, add a pinch of salt and a gill of cold water, and leave in soak until the next day. Then strain off the saffron water.

Wash, pick over, and dry the currants. Cut up the peel.

Sieve the flour into a basin. Rub in the fat.

Add the sugar and prepared fruit and mix together.

Put the yeast into a small warmed basin with half a teaspoonful of castor sugar and mix until a liquid is formed.

Heat the milk and add to the saffron water, making the whole just lukewarm.

Add this to the yeast, strain it all into the centre of the flour and mix to a pliable dough.

Cover the basin loosely and put it into a warm place to rise for about one hour and a half.

Turn the dough on to a floured board and knead it for a few minutes, then divide into small equal portions.

Make each into a smooth bun shape and place on a greased baking-sheet, leaving a space between each to allow room for them to rise.

Stand in a warm place to rise for about twenty to thirty minutes.

Put into a hot oven and bake for about twenty-five minutes.

When cooked, brush them over with sugar and milk glaze, then return to the oven for a minute or two to dry the glaze.

Sufficient to make from a dozen to a dozen and a half cakes, according to the size they are made.

GLAZE.—Mix together 1½ tablespoonfuls of milk and 1½ dessertspoonfuls of castor sugar.

SAFFRON SCONES

INGREDIENTS.—½ lb. of flour, 1 teaspoonful of baking-powder, 1½ oz. of lard, 2 oz. of sultanas, 1½ oz. of sugar, saffron, pinch of salt, milk.

METHOD.—For these the saffron needs to be put to soak in cold water the night before making the scones.

Take just a small quantity of saffron —one halfpennyworth will be sufficient for this quantity—put it into a teacup, add a pinch of salt to it, and half a gill of cold water. Leave soaking all night.

Wash, pick over and dry the sultanas.

Sieve the flour and baking-powder. Rub in the lard.

Add the sugar and fruit and mix together.

Strain off the saffron water and add to the dry ingredients.

Mix to a stiff paste, adding a little milk as required.

Roll out to about three-eighths of an inch thick.

Cut into small triangular-shaped pieces.

Place on a slightly greased baking-sheet and bake in a hot oven for about ten to fifteen minutes.

When cooked, brush the scones with a little sugar and milk mixed together, then return to the oven for a few seconds to dry the glaze.

SCOTCH PANCAKES

INGREDIENTS.—½ lb. of flour, 1 small teaspoonful of bicarbonate of soda, 1 egg, 2 teaspoonfuls of soft sugar, ½ teaspoonful of tartaric acid, 1 breakfastcupful of milk, ¼ teaspoonful of salt.

METHOD.—Sift the flour, salt, soda, and tartaric acid into a basin and add the sugar. Put the egg in the centre. Stir in the milk gradually, keeping the batter smooth. Beat well.

Grease and heat a girdle or a thick oval frying-pan.

Drop on it the batter in tablespoonfuls.

Cook them slowly till the top is covered with bubbles, then turn them over with a knife and do the other side.

Time, about six minutes.

Sufficient for sixteen pancakes.

SCOTCH SCONES

INGREDIENTS.—½ lb. of flour, ½ gill of milk, ½ gill of cream, a pinch of salt, 1 teaspoonful of cream of tartar, ¼ flat teaspoonful of carbonate of soda, 1 oz. of sugar, 1½ oz. of sultanas.

METHOD.—Wash and dry the sultanas. Sieve the flour, cream of tartar, and soda together.

Add the sugar and prepared sultanas to the flour, etc.

Add the cream and milk to the dry ingredients and mix all together.

Flour a board, roll out the mixture until it is about half an inch in thickness.

Cut into triangular-shaped pieces. Place on a greased baking-sheet. Brush the scones over with milk. Bake in a hot oven from fifteen to twenty minutes.

SCOTTISH TEA CAKES

INGREDIENTS.—1 lb. of flour, 1 oz. of margarine, ½ oz. of yeast, 1 level teaspoonful of salt, 1 teaspoonful of castor sugar, milk and water (about ½ pint).

METHOD.—Sieve the flour and salt into a basin and rub in the margarine.

Put the sugar and yeast into a small, warmed basin, and mix them together until they liquefy.

Warm the milk and water and add it to the yeast. Strain the liquid into the centre of the flour and mix it to a soft dough.

Turn the dough on to a floured board, knead it for a few minutes, then return it to the basin and put it in a warm place to rise for about an hour and a half or two hours.

Finally, turn it out and knead it again.

Divide the dough into three portions, work each into a smooth, flat round, and put them into greased and floured sandwich-tins (only about half full).

Prick the top of each cake and put it to rise until the tins are full.

Then put them into a hot oven to bake.

They will take about twenty or thirty minutes.

Sufficient to make three cakes.

SODA SCONES

INGREDIENTS.—½ lb. of flour, 2 oz. of margarine, 1 gill of milk and water, 1 teaspoonful of cream of tartar, ¼ flat teaspoonful of carbonate of soda, 1 teaspoonful of granulated sugar.

METHOD.—Sieve the flour with the carbonate of soda and cream of tartar.

Rub the fat into the flour.

Add the sugar, mix all the dry ingredients together. Add the milk and mix to a dry paste.

Flour a board and slightly knead the mixture until smooth.

Grease a round jam sandwich-tin, place the mixture in the tin, press it lightly to the shape of the tin.

Cut it across each way so that it is in four portions.

Brush over with milk and bake in a hot oven for twenty to thirty minutes.

SPICED SCONES

INGREDIENTS.—½ lb. of flour, 1½ teaspoonfuls of baking-powder, 2 oz. of margarine, ½ level teaspoonful of powdered cinnamon, 1½ oz. of currants, 1½ oz. of castor sugar, milk.

METHOD.—Sift the flour, baking-powder, and cinnamon into a basin.

Rub in the fat, and add the sugar and fruit—which should have been previously cleansed and picked over.

Mix them well, then stir in sufficient milk to make a soft dough.

Roll the mixture to a large round, barely three-eighths of an inch thick.

Cut this evenly with the aid of a large plate. Then cut the round into quarters and then each quarter into three.

Place the scones on a lightly greased baking-sheet and brush them with milk.

Then bake them for about ten minutes in a quick oven.

SULTANA LOAF

INGREDIENTS.—1¾ lb. of flour, a pinch of salt, 3 oz. of sugar, 1 teaspoonful of castor sugar, ¾ to 1 pint of milk and water (warm), ¼ lb. of sultanas, ¼ lb. of margarine or butter, 1 oz. of yeast.

METHOD.—Wash, pick over and dry the sultanas.

Sieve the flour and salt.

Rub in the fat.

Put the yeast into a small warmed basin with a teaspoonful of castor sugar, and mix together until they liquefy.

Add the warm milk (three-quarters of a pint), and strain it all into the centre of the flour, etc.

Mix a small quantity of the latter with the yeast, etc., then cover the basin and stand it in a warm place for twenty minutes.

After this time, mix in all the flour, also the sugar and fruit, and mix all together, adding some more warm milk if required ; it should be a pliable consistency when finished.

Turn the dough on to a slightly floured board and knead it for a few minutes, then return it to the basin and place in a warm place to rise for about one hour and a half.

Turn it out and knead again for a few minutes, then put it into a greased and floured tin (oblong shape).

Put to rise in a warm place for twenty to thirty minutes.

Bake in a hot oven for about three-quarters of an hour.

When cooked, brush top with sugar and milk glaze, then return to the oven for a few minutes to dry the glaze.

SULTANA SCONES

INGREDIENTS.—2 level teaspoonfuls of cream of tartar, ½ level teaspoonful of carbonate of soda, 2 dessertspoonfuls of sultanas, 2 dessertspoonfuls of castor sugar, milk to mix, 1 oz. of margarine, 1 oz. of lard, 9 oz. of flour.

METHOD.—Wash, pick over and dry the fruit.

Sieve the flour with the cream of tartar and carbonate of soda.

Rub in the lard and margarine, add the sugar and fruit and mix these ingredients to a soft dough with the milk.

Divide the dough into two portions, make each into a smooth lump and roll it to a round the size of the sandwich-tins to be used.

Grease the tins and put one piece of dough into each. Brush them with egg, and put them in a fairly hot oven to bake. They will take about twenty minutes to cook.

Sufficient to make two large scones.

SYRUP SCONES

INGREDIENTS.—½ lb. of flour, pinch of salt, ¼ flat teaspoonful of carbonate of soda, 1 oz. of lard, 1 oz. of candied peel, 2 dessertspoonfuls of golden syrup, sour milk.

FOR THE GLAZE.—2 teaspoonfuls of castor sugar, 2 tablespoonfuls of milk.

METHOD.—Sieve the flour, salt, and soda. Rub in the lard.

Cut the peel into small pieces and add.

Mix all the dry ingredients together, put the golden syrup in the centre of them, and add sufficient sour milk to make a fairly soft dough.

Turn on to a slightly floured board and roll out thickly.

Cut into triangular shapes, place on a lightly greased tin, and bake in a hot oven for about fifteen minutes.

Brush over with sugar and milk glaze, and then return them to the oven to dry.

To MAKE THE GLAZE.—Mix the sugar and milk together until dissolved.

Sufficient for about six.

TEA CAKES

INGREDIENTS.—1 lb. of flour, ¼ level teaspoonful of salt, ½ oz. of yeast, 1 teaspoonful of castor sugar, 1 egg, 2 oz. of margarine, ½ pint of milk.

METHOD.—Put the yeast and sugar into a small basin and mix them until they liquefy.

Sift the flour into a large basin with the salt.

Melt the fat in a saucepan and to it add the milk and make them lukewarm. Then stir them on to the yeast.

Add this mixture to the beaten egg, strain them all into the flour and mix them together.

Beat the mixture well, then turn it on to a lightly floured board. Divide it into three portions and knead it till it is smooth.

Then put each portion into a small, round, buttered cake-tin.

Throw a cloth over the top and stand them in a warm place until they rise to double their size. Next put them in a hot oven to bake. They will take about fifteen minutes.

When they are cooked, brush the tops of the tea cakes with sugar and milk glaze.

Return them to the oven for a minute or two to dry. These are delicious toasted, buttered, and served hot for tea.

FOR THE GLAZE.—Mix one dessertspoonful of castor sugar with one tablespoonful of milk, and stir them until it is dissolved.

NOTE.—The tins must not be more than half full when the mixture is put to rise.

SMALL TEA CAKES

INGREDIENTS.—1 lb. of flour, 2 oz. of butter or lard, 1 egg, 1 teaspoonful of sugar, also 2 oz. of sugar, 1 level teaspoonful of salt, 1½ gills of warm milk, ¾ oz. of yeast, 1½ oz. of currants or sultanas.

METHOD.—Dissolve the butter or lard in the warm milk.

Beat the egg and add it also to the milk.

Beat the yeast to a cream in a small basin, adding the teaspoonful of sugar.

Stir in the milk and egg.

Put the flour and salt into a basin.

Make a well in the centre of the flour and stir in the dissolved yeast.

Mix in sufficient flour from the sides of the bowl to make a stiff batter.

Sprinkle some over the top and cover the basin with a clean cloth.

Stand it in a warm place to allow the batter to rise for about one hour.

Knead in about two ounces of sugar and the currants or sultanas.

Turn the dough on to a board and divide it into ten equal parts.

Roll them out into rounds and place them on a greased baking-tin.

Set them aside to rise for about fifteen minutes.

Bake the tea cakes in a quick oven for about twenty minutes or until they are brown.

When the cakes are done, rub a little butter over the tops to glaze them.

Sufficient for ten tea cakes.

TEA SCONES

INGREDIENTS.—½ lb. of flour, 2 oz. of sugar, 1 oz. of candied peel, milk to mix, 2 oz. of margarine or butter, nutmeg, 1 teaspoonful of cream of tartar, ¼ flat teaspoonful of carbonate of soda.

METHOD.—Sieve the flour, soda, and cream of tartar. Rub in the fat. Cut the peel into small pieces and add with the sugar. Add just a very little grated nutmeg and mix all together.

Add milk gradually and mix to a pliable dough.

Roll it out to about three-eighths of an inch thick.

Cut into rounds with a fancy cutter.

Place on a slightly greased baking-sheet. Brush over with milk.

Bake in a hot oven for about fifteen minutes.

Sufficient to make about seven or eight scones.

PLAIN TEA SCONES

INGREDIENTS.—½ lb. of flour, 1 teaspoonful of baking-powder, ½ an egg, milk to mix (about 1 gill), 1 oz. of margarine.

METHOD.—Sieve the flour with the baking-powder.

Rub the fat into the flour, mix all these ingredients together.

Beat the egg and add to the flour, etc.

Add sufficient milk to make a soft but not sticky consistency.

Flour the board, roll out mixture until it is about half an inch in thickness.

Cut scones into rounds with a plain round cutter.

Place on a greased baking-sheet.

Brush scones with milk.

Bake in a hot oven for about ten to fifteen minutes.

These tea scones are nice split open and spread with butter.

You can vary this recipe by adding a small quantity of sugar and fruit to make it into a sweet tea scone.

TREACLE SCONES

INGREDIENTS.—½ lb. of flour, ¼ lb. of treacle, ½ flat teaspoonful of carbonate of soda, 1½ oz. of margarine, pinch of salt, milk.

METHOD.—Sieve the flour, salt, and soda into a basin.

Put the treacle and margarine into a saucepan to warm, and when the latter is dissolved, let it cool a little and then pour into the flour.

Mix all to a soft dough with some milk as required.

Roll out the dough to about three-eighths of an inch thick, cut it in three-cornered shapes and put these on a lightly greased baking-sheet.

Bake the scones in a quick oven.

Sufficient for from six to eight scones.

TURNOVER ROLLS

INGREDIENTS.—¾ lb. of flour, 2 teaspoonfuls of baking-powder, ¼ teaspoonful of salt, ½ oz. of butter or margarine, about 1½ gills of milk, ½ or 1 small egg.

METHOD.—Sift the flour with the salt and baking-powder, rub in the butter and mix all to a soft dough, adding the egg, beaten, and some milk as required.

Roll the dough out thickly and cut it into rounds about four inches in diameter.

Turn them on to the other side and fold each round over lightly in half.

Smear a baking-sheet with butter or margarine, put the rolls on it, brush the tops with milk, and put them in a fairly hot oven to bake.

They will take about twenty-five minutes to cook.

Sufficient for nine or ten rolls.

WAFFLES

INGREDIENTS.—½ lb. of flour, ¼ teaspoonful of salt, 1½ teaspoonfuls of baking-powder, 2 eggs, 1¾ to 2 gills of milk, ½ oz. of margarine or butter.

METHOD.—Sift the flour with the salt and baking-powder and make a well in the centre.

Separate the eggs, beat up the yolks, and whisk the whites to a stiff froth.

Melt the fat and pour it into the flour; add also the yolks of eggs and milk and mix all to a smooth batter; then fold in the whisked whites.

Grease the waffle iron and heat it until a faint smoke rises, then pour a little batter into each of the two compartments and spread it over quickly.

Fold the top half of the waffle iron over this, and leave it for a minute, then open it again and if the waffle is golden brown place it on a hot dish.

Cook the remainder of the waffles in the same way and serve them at once with butter and honey.

This quantity makes ten waffles.

WALNUT BREAD

INGREDIENTS.—1¼ lb. of flour, ¾ oz. of yeast, 1½ oz. of lard, 1 teaspoonful of castor sugar, 1½ flat teaspoonfuls salt, 1 egg, about ½ a pint of milk and water, 2 oz. of walnuts.

METHOD.—Sieve the flour and salt into a large basin.

Chop up the walnuts and add them to the flour. Mix all together, and make a well in the centre.

Melt the lard, add the milk and water to it and make it lukewarm.

Put the yeast and sugar into a small warm basin and mix them until they liquefy. Add the lard, milk and water to the yeast, then pour them on to the egg (which should have been beaten).

Strain the liquid into the flour. Mix well together and beat for a few minutes. Put the mixture in a warm place to rise for about an hour and a half or two hours.

Turn the dough on to a floured board and knead it well. Divide it into portions and make it into loaves, large or small as required.

Put the loaves into greased and floured tins, only about half-filling them. Stand them in a warm place until full, then brush them with egg and put in a hot oven to bake.

This quantity makes one oval and one border loaf, also eleven small ones. The latter baked in tartlet-tins.

NOTE.—If a sweetened bread is preferred, add two or three ounces of castor sugar.

WHOLEMEAL BREAD

INGREDIENTS.—2 lb. of wholemeal, 1 lb. of flour, 1½ teaspoonfuls of salt, 1 oz. of compressed yeast, ½ teaspoonful of sugar, about ¼ of a pint of tepid water, 3 oz. of margarine, ½ a pint of tepid milk.

METHOD.—Put the flour and wholemeal in a warm basin.

Rub in the margarine.

Cream the yeast and sugar till liquid (a minute or two is enough).

Stir in the tepid water and milk.

Make a hollow in the flour, pour in the liquid and sprinkle the salt on the surrounding flour.

Stir with a wooden spoon and mix into a smooth dough.

Place a cloth over it and set it to rise in a warm place, but not *too* near the fire.

Grease and flour two oblong tins.

When the dough has risen to twice its original size (in about an hour), knead till smooth and not sticky, shape into loaves and put into the tins, which should be half-full.

Bake in a quick oven for the first fifteen minutes and finish cooking in a moderate oven for about forty-five minutes.

Bread is done when it sounds hollow on being tapped underneath.

WHOLEMEAL LOAF (2)

(MADE WITH BAKING-POWDER)

INGREDIENTS.—2 lb. of wholemeal flour, 6 teaspoonfuls of baking-powder, 2 teaspoonfuls of salt, 2 teaspoonfuls of golden syrup, about 1 pint of milk.

METHOD.—Put the flour, salt, and baking-powder into a basin and mix together.

Make a well in the centre, put in the golden syrup, and add sufficient milk to mix all to a pliable dough.

Form it into a smooth tin loaf, place in a lightly greased and floured tin, and put into a fairly hot oven to bake, lessening the heat as required.

It will take from one to one and a half hours to bake.

WHOLEMEAL ROLLS

INGREDIENTS.—5 oz. of wholemeal flour, 3 oz. of household flour, ½ teaspoonful of salt, 1 oz of butter, 1 teaspoonful of baking-powder, about ¼ gills of milk.

METHOD.—Grease a baking-sheet. Mix together the flour, salt, and baking-powder. Rub in the butter.

Mix quickly with the milk and shape into eight rolls.

Place on the baking-sheet and give each roll three slanting cuts.

Bake for about twelve or fifteen minutes in a quick oven.

WHOLEMEAL SCONES

INGREDIENTS.—½ lb. of wholemeal, one egg-yolk, ½ flat teaspoonful of carbonate of soda, ¼ lb. of flour, 1 oz. of lard, 1 tablespoonful of golden syrup, about ¾ gill of milk, 1 oz. of margarine.

METHOD.—Sieve the flour with the wholemeal and carbonate of soda.

Rub in the lard and margarine. Warm the golden syrup *slightly* so as to thin it down.

Beat up the egg-yolk and mix it with some of the milk.

Pour the golden syrup into the centre of the wholemeal, add also the egg and milk and mix to a soft dough, adding more milk as required.

Divide the dough into three portions and roll out each portion to a round shape about half an inch thick, and cut it into four.

Put the scones on a lightly greased baking-sheet and bake them in a quick oven for fifteen minutes.

Brush their tops with sugar and milk glaze, and return them to the oven for a minute to dry. To make the glaze, mix one dessertspoonful of castor sugar with one tablespoonful of milk until dissolved.

Sufficient to make twelve scones.

YEAST CREAM BUNS

INGREDIENTS.—1 lb. of flour, ½ oz. of yeast, ¼ lb. of castor sugar, ¼ lb. of margarine, 1 egg, milk and water (about 1¾ gills), 1 gill of cream, vanilla, icing sugar.

METHOD.—Put the yeast into a small warm basin, add half a teaspoonful of castor sugar, and mix to a liquid.

Warm the milk and water and add to the yeast.

Sieve the flour.

Measure out a quarter of a pound into a basin.

Make a hole in the centre. Pour in the yeast and milk, etc., and gradually mix in the flour.

When mixed thoroughly, beat for a few minutes.

Cover the basin and stand in a warm place for about three-quarters to an hour.

Put the remainder of the flour into another basin.

Rub in the margarine.

Add the sugar and mix together.

Work these dry ingredients into the yeast, etc., together with the beaten egg.

When well mixed, cover the basin and stand in a warm place for about one hour.

Divide into small buns.

Shape them and put on a greased baking-sheet, leaving a space between each.

Stand in a warm place to rise for from twenty to thirty minutes.

Bake in a hot oven for about twenty-five minutes.

Glaze the tops.

Return to the oven to dry the glaze.

Stand on a sieve to cool.

Whisk the cream until thick, then sweeten and flavour it.

Make a cut just underneath the top of the buns and insert some of the cream.

Sprinkle a little sieved icing sugar on the top of each.

To make the glaze, mix together one and a half tablespoonfuls of milk with one and a half dessertspoonfuls of castor sugar.

Sufficient to make from about a dozen to a dozen and a half cakes, according to the size they are made.

YELLOW CORN MEAL BREAD

INGREDIENTS.—6 oz. of yellow corn meal, 1½ lb. of flour, 2 level teaspoonfuls of salt, 1 level teaspoonful of castor sugar, ¾ oz. of yeast, almost 1 pint of warm water.

METHOD.—Sift the flour, corn meal, and salt into a basin.

Put the yeast and sugar into a small basin and mix them until they liquefy, then stir in three-quarters of a pint of warm water.

Strain this into the flour and mix all to a soft dough, adding more water as required.

Beat the dough well, then throw a cloth over the basin, and put it in a warm place to rise for about one hour and a half, or until it has doubled in size.

Turn the dough on to a floured board, knead it lightly until smooth.

Divide it into three portions, and shape it to your tins, which should be greased slightly and then floured, and the loose flour removed.

Only half fill the tins with dough, then stand them in a warm place until the tins are full, when they should be put into a hot oven to bake.

They will take about thirty-five minutes, or until they feel hollow when tapped underneath with the knuckles.

When nearly cooked, the bread may be turned out of the tins to allow the sides and bottom of the loaf to brown.

This quantity makes three small loaves.

YORKSHIRE TEA CAKES

INGREDIENTS.—2 lb. of flour, 1 oz. of yeast, 4 oz. of butter or lard, 4 oz. of currants or sultanas (cleaned), 4 oz. of sugar, 1½ teaspoonfuls of salt, 1 pint of milk and water.

METHOD.—Mix the yeast with a teaspoonful of sugar for a minute and when it is liquid add half the milk.

Rub the lard into the flour, make a hollow in the centre and pour in the milk.

Let it rise for ten minutes.

Sprinkle the salt, sugar, and currants round the edge, and stir till mixed to a smooth, soft dough, adding the rest of the milk gradually.

Cover the basin with a cloth and let the dough rise for one hour in a warm place.

Make the dough into smooth tea cakes on a floured board and put them on two greased tins or in small tea cake-tins sold for the purpose.

Let them rise for twenty minutes.

Bake them in a hot oven for fifteen minutes.

They may either be served straight out of the oven on baking day or split and each half toasted on both sides and buttered.

Sufficient for ten tea cakes.

INVALID COOKERY

Invalids take their meals alone, so some diversion, in place of table talk, must be discovered to amuse them.

Always choose colourful china for the tray. A bright little cruet, for instance, may divert thoughts from the beef-tea of which the patient is tired. A flower-head, floating in a tiny saucer, or anything unusual in the arrangement will stimulate the imagination.

The thing to remember is that your patient does not *want* to eat, and that you must arouse his appetite.

Remember to serve as much nourishment as possible in a small space. Serve only small portions, and make them look as tempting as possible.

A CUP OF ARROWROOT

Ingredients.—1 teaspoonful of arrowroot, 1 small breakfastcupful of milk, sugar to taste.

Method.—Mix the arrowroot to a smooth paste with a little milk.

Heat the remainder and stir on to it.

Return to the pan and bring to the boil, and boil gently for about six to ten minutes, keeping it well stirred all the time.

Add sugar to taste, pour into a cup, and serve.

ARROWROOT SHAPE

Ingredients.—1½ pints of milk, 3 tablespoonfuls of arrowroot, about 2 dessertspoonfuls of sugar (more if required), vanilla flavouring, 1½ oz. of butter.

Method.—Mix the arrowroot to a smooth paste with a small quantity of the milk.

Heat the remainder and stir on to it.

Return to the saucepan and bring to the boil, keeping it well stirred all the time.

Stir in the butter and sugar and simmer gently for about six minutes, then add a few drops of vanilla.

Pour into a wet border mould and leave until set.

BARLEY WATER

Ingredients.—2 dessertspoonfuls of pearl barley, ½ a lemon, sugar, 1½ pints of water.

Method.—Wash the barley, put it into a saucepan, cover with cold water and bring up to the boil. Strain off the water, rinse out the saucepan, return the barley to it, and add the one and a half pints of cold water.

Wipe the lemon and peel very thinly, and add to the barley.

Bring slowly to the boil, and simmer for about one to one and a half hours.

Strain and sweeten to taste.

Note.—Barley water should be freshly made each day. Make it in small quantities.

BEEF TEA

Ingredients.—1 lb. of shin of beef, 1 pint of cold water, salt.

Method 1 (*Not Cooked*)

Remove the fat, if any, then scrape the meat into shreds and put into a jar or basin. Add the water and a little salt, and leave to soak until the goodness is drawn out of the meat, then strain and serve.

Method 2 (*Quick Method*)

Prepare the meat as above and put into a basin with the water and salt. Leave to soak for about forty minutes, then turn into a saucepan and bring very slowly *almost* to boiling-point. Stir it up, then strain, and press the meat well to extract all the gravy.

Method 3 (*Slowly Made*)

Prepare the meat as above, or cut it into small pieces, and put into a jar with the water and salt.

Let it soak for a time, then stand the jar in a saucepan of water or in the oven, cover it securely and cook *slowly* for three hours, being careful not to let it boil.

Then strain and serve.

NOTE.—If there is any grease on the top, this must be removed before serving it.

BLACK CURRANT TEA

INGREDIENTS.—¾ pint of water, 1 good tablespoonful of black currant jam.

METHOD.—Put the jam into a jug, add the water (boiling), also a squeeze of lemon-juice, and mix together. Cover and let it stand for a few minutes, then strain.

A little sugar may be added, if required.

A TASTY BROTH

INGREDIENTS.—Take equal quantities of shin of beef, scrag end of neck of mutton and knuckle end of veal, salt, cold water to just cover.

METHOD.—Cut up the veal, mutton and beef. The two former require to be well chopped so that they may be divided into fairly small pieces. Remove the marrow from the scrag of mutton before cutting it up.

Put the prepared meats into a jar and add sufficient cold water just to cover, also a little salt.

Cover securely and put in the oven, or stand in a saucepan of water, and let it cook gently for three or four hours.

When ready stir it up, strain and skim off the fat.

REAL CALVES'-FOOT JELLY

INGREDIENTS.—2 calves' feet, 4 pints of cold water, 4 lemons, the whites and shells of 4 eggs, ½ lb. of lump sugar, ½ pint of sherry, ½ gill of brandy.

METHOD.—The calves' feet should be already scalded when you buy them. Wash them and cut up.

Put into a pan with the water, bring slowly to the boil, remove the scum, and simmer gently for several hours, until the liquor is reduced to about two pints.

Strain it and leave until cold, then remove the fat and any sediment there may be.

Put it into a pan, and add the sugar, sherry, and brandy.

Wipe the lemons and peel two of

them very thinly, and strain the juice from all of them.

Wash the egg-shells and remove the inner skins. Add the lemon-rinds and juice, and whites and shells of eggs to the above ingredients. Whisk well over a low gas until it comes *nearly* to boiling point. By this time there should be a good head on it.

Then stop whisking, and let it boil up.

Put the lid on the pan, and leave it to simmer gently for about fifteen minutes, then turn out the gas, and let it stand for thirty minutes.

Have ready a jelly bag, previously scalded, and strain the jelly through it. If not very clear, strain it again.

Put into wet moulds, and when set turn out.

NOTE.—If the jelly sets before it has all run through, stand a basin of hot water in the bag. The brandy can be omitted, but it is a great improvement to the flavour.

CHICKEN BROTH

INGREDIENTS.—Some chicken's feet, cold water to well cover, salt and pepper, ½ onion and carrot, To ½ pint of broth, allow 1 egg.

METHOD.—Scald and skin the chicken's feet, then put them into a saucepan with cold water to well cover them, and a little salt.

Bring slowly to the boil, then remove any scum there may be on the top.

Peel the onion, scrape and wash the carrot, and add both, not cut up, and simmer gently for three or four hours, then strain.

Measure the broth, allow the eggs in proportion, beat them well, and mix with it.

Turn into a jug, and cook in a saucepan of hot water until the broth thickens, being careful not to let it curdle.

Season to taste and serve.

CORNFLOUR CREAM

INGREDIENTS.—1 pint of milk, 1¼ oz. of cornflour, sugar to taste, 2 eggs, ¼ oz. of leaf gelatine, 2 tablespoonfuls of water, almond or vanilla flavouring.

METHOD.—Mix the cornflour to a smooth paste with some of the milk.

Heat the remainder and stir it on to the cornflour. Return it to the pan, bring it to the boil, and boil it gently for from six to ten minutes, keeping it well stirred all the time.

Draw the pan to the side, add the sugar, and cool the mixture slightly.

Separate the yolks from the whites of eggs.

Beat up the yolks and stir them into the cornflour, then stir the mixture over a low gas for a few minutes to cook the egg, but do not let it boil.

Add flavouring to taste, and cool it slightly.

Put the gelatine into a saucepan with the water and dissolve it slowly, then strain it into the other ingredients, and mix all together.

Whisk the egg-whites to a stiff froth, and fold them in lightly.

Pour the Cornflour Cream into a dish, and leave it until set, or, if liked, put it into a large or small wet mould, and turn it out when set.

BAKED CUSTARD

INGREDIENTS.—2 eggs, 1 pint of milk, 1 tablespoonful of sugar, vanilla flavouring.

METHOD.—Whisk up the eggs. Put the milk into a saucepan with the sugar, and when hot pour on to the eggs. Mix together and add a few drops of vanilla flavouring.

Turn into a pie-dish, and, if liked, grate a little nutmeg on the top.

Put into a moderately warm oven and bake gently for about thirty to forty-five minutes until set, being careful not to let it boil.

NOTE.—The milk should be just below boiling point when added to the eggs.

STEAMED CUTLET

PUT the cutlet on a buttered enamel plate. Season it with salt, and cover it with a buttered paper and another plate. Stand over a saucepan of boiling water and steam until tender. The time required depends on the thickness. Choose a lean cutlet.

EGG JELLIES

INGREDIENTS.—1 egg, water, rind and juice of 1 lemon, ½ oz. of leaf gelatine (take light weight), 18 lumps of sugar (medium size).

METHOD.—Wipe the lemon and peel it very thinly, being careful not to remove any of the white pith with the peel. Squeeze out the juice and measure it, then make it up to half a pint with water.

Put this into a white-lined saucepan with the gelatine, sugar, and lemon-rind.

Beat up the egg and add.

Whisk gently over a *very low gas* until the egg is cooked and the gelatine melted. Be careful not to make it too hot or the egg will curdle.

When ready, strain and pour into small, wet moulds and leave until set.

Dip in warm water. Turn out carefully on to a dish and serve.

EGG AND MILK

WHEN preparing an egg and milk for an invalid never omit to remove the little white " tread " before whisking the egg.

Whisk it well—then stir in hot or cold milk.

Add a little castor sugar, if liked. A dash of brandy is a great improvement, or a spoonful of port wine may be added.

POACHED EGG ON TOAST

TOAST a slice of bread, butter it, and keep it warm. Break the egg carefully into a cup, being very careful not to break the yolk.

Put some water into a frying-pan, add a little salt and lemon-juice, and boil, then draw aside.

Pour in the egg and cook gently over a low burner for a few minutes until the white is set, keeping the pan slightly tilted at first.

Lift up with a fish-slice and drain off the water, then serve on the toast.

GROUND RICE PUDDING

INGREDIENTS.—4 flat tablespoonfuls of ground rice, 1½ pints of milk, 2 oz. of sugar, flavouring, nutmeg.

METHOD.—Mix the ground rice with about half a gill of the milk.

Put the remainder of the milk to get hot with the sugar.

Pour the hot milk on to the ground rice.

Pour back into the saucepan and boil for five minutes, stirring all the time.

Add the flavouring.

Pour the pudding into a pie-dish, grate nutmeg on the top of it.

Bake in a moderately warm oven for thirty minutes.

Serve hot.

GRUEL

INGREDIENTS.—½ pint of milk, sugar to taste, 1½ teaspoonfuls of patent groats.

METHOD.—Mix the groats to a smooth paste with a small quantity of the milk.

Heat the remainder and stir on to it. Return to the pan, bring to the boil, and boil gently for ten minutes, keeping it well stirred.

Add sugar as required.

MILK JELLY

INGREDIENTS.—1 pint packet of vanilla jelly, ½ pint of hot water, ½ pint of milk.

METHOD.—Dissolve the jelly in the hot water, and when cold stir in the milk.

Turn into a wet mould, and when set turn on to a dish.

STEAMED FILLETS OF PLAICE

HAVE the plaice filleted and the fillets skinned.

Roll them up, place on an enamel plate, and stand over a saucepan of boiling water.

Cover the fish with a buttered paper and a basin, and steam.

When cooked, the flesh will be quite white.

Serve with plain white sauce, if liked.

A PLAIN OMELET

INGREDIENTS.—2 eggs, pepper and salt, ¾ oz. of butter.

METHOD.—Separate the yolks from the whites of the eggs. Beat up the yolks and season with pepper and salt.

Add a pinch of salt to the whites and whisk them to a very stiff froth, then fold lightly into the yolks.

Melt the butter in an omelet pan. When hot, pour in the egg mixture.

When it begins to set round the edge, fold the edge over and draw the omelet towards the handle of the pan, keeping the latter tilted that way. Continue to cook for a few seconds, then put under the hot grill and lightly brown the top.

Turn on to a hot dish and serve at once.

RATAFIA CUSTARD

INGREDIENTS.—3 eggs, 1½ pints of milk, 3 oz. of ratafia biscuits, ½ teaspoonful of ratafia flavouring, 2 dessertspoonfuls of sugar.

METHOD.—Put the milk into a saucepan to heat with the sugar.

Beat the eggs well and put into a pie-dish.

Add milk and sugar to the eggs and mix well together. (The milk must be added to the eggs just below boiling-point.)

Add flavouring.

Cover the surface of the custard with ratafia biscuits.

Bake in a moderately warm oven for about forty minutes, or until the custard is set.

NOTE.—This pudding should not be brown on top, so either cover it with a plate, or remove the browning shelf from the oven before putting in the pudding.

Also great care must be taken to prevent the pudding from boiling, as this would curdle the eggs. For the same reason the milk must not be actually boiling when added to the eggs.

BAKED SOLE

INGREDIENTS.—1 small sole, pepper and salt, 1½ oz. of butter, milk.

METHOD.—Fillet the sole, skin the fillets and wash them. Put them on to an enamel plate, with the butter and two or three tablespoonfuls of milk.

Sprinkle a little pepper and salt over, cover with a plate and cook in a moderately hot oven until the flesh becomes perfectly white.

When ready, put on to a hot dish with the butter and milk.

NOTE.—This is also an excellent

method of cooking fish for young children.

STEAMED SOLE

INGREDIENTS.—Fillets of sole as required, a squeeze of lemon-juice, seasoning, milk, butter.

METHOD.—Wash the fillets and dry them. Sprinkle a little lemon-juice over them and season them with salt and pepper.

Roll up the fillets and place them on an enamel plate with a little milk in the bottom.

Put a dab of butter on each fillet. Cover them with a buttered paper and then with the lid of a saucepan or with another deep plate.

Stand the fish over a saucepan of boiling water and steam till it is tender.

STEWED TRIPE

INGREDIENTS.—½ lb. of tripe, ½ pint of milk (or sufficient to cover), 1 onion, seasoning, ½ oz. of butter, cornflour (about 1 teaspoonful).

METHOD.—Put the tripe into a saucepan and cover it with water, bring it to the boil, then pour off the water.

Cut the tripe into square or oblong-shaped pieces, and put it into a pan with the milk and butter and seasoning to taste.

Peel the onion and cut it into small pieces, and add it to the tripe.

Bring the tripe to the boil and simmer it gently for about two hours.

Take out the tripe and thicken the milk with some cornflour mixed to a smooth paste with water.

Let this boil for a few minutes, keeping it well stirred, put in the tripe, make it thoroughly hot and serve.

A COLD SWEET

SEPARATE the yolk and white of an egg. Add one teaspoonful of castor sugar to the yolk and whisk until thick and creamy.

Dissolve one sheet of leaf gelatine in a tablespoonful of water and strain into the yolk, then, when beginning to set, whisk the egg-white to a stiff froth and fold in lightly. Add a few drops of vanilla or orange essence, then turn into a small glass dish to set.

VEAL BROTH

INGREDIENTS.—1½ lb. of knuckle of veal, 1 carrot and onion, salt, a few peppercorns, 3 pints of water, 1 oz. of pearl barley.

METHOD.—Have the knuckle of veal chopped into small pieces.

Wash it, and put into a pan with the water (cold).

Add a little salt and a few peppercorns and bring very slowly to the boil. Then remove the scum.

Peel the onion, scrape the carrot, and add, and simmer gently for about three to four hours, then strain and return the broth to a clean pan.

Put the pearl barley into a saucepan with some cold water, bring to the boil, then strain off the water and add the barley to the veal broth, and cook gently until tender.

Remove any grease from the top before serving.

STEAMED WHITING

INGREDIENTS.—1 whiting and white sauce (see p. 41).

METHOD.—The whiting must be thoroughly cleaned and skinned, the eyes removed, etc. Twist the fish into a round shape, keep it in position by fixing the tail in its mouth, or putting it through the hole from where the eyes were taken.

Put the whiting into a steamer, put on the lid and stand it over boiling water. Let it steam until quite cooked. It will take about ten minutes, according to the size.

Place it on a hot dish and serve plain white sauce with it, or any other suitable sauce. (For Fish Sauces, see pp. 41 to 43).

If you have no steamer you can stand the whiting on an enamel plate over a saucepan of boiling water and cover it with a basin.

It will take a little longer to cook in this way, or, if you could, suspend a colander in a large saucepan, with boiling water reaching to the bottom of the colander.

Stand the fish in this and cover it, and it will steam quite satisfactorily.

Remember you must have a well-fitting lid or cover in order to keep in the steam.

SWEETS AND CANDIES

SWEET-MAKING is a very fascinating occupation, and with careful attention to small details (which mean so much if success is to be attained) it is not difficult.

Follow with great care the various hints and directions given in these pages, and you will be certain of success.

Do not use enamel pans, as the high temperature to which many of the sweets have to be boiled would probably crack the enamel. Use metal pans.

Aluminium is quite good, also unlined copper and brass. (This must not be lined with tin, as the high temperature would boil the tin lining off.) Nickel pans are splendid.

It is best to use wooden spatulas and not spoons. They may be had in various sizes, according to the quantity of sweet one is making. They are flat, and do not have a bowl like a spoon, but are shaped wider at the end, while the handle is straight and narrower.

For making fondant and other sweets, you will need a piece of marble, or the top of an old marble table or washstand will do perfectly. One can often buy an odd piece of marble at a stonemason's.

You must have a sugar scraper made of tin or aluminium. This is wide and folded over at one end. This is where it is held while working.

Always use the best ingredients, best cane sugars, glucose, and butter when mentioned in recipes (not margarine), also fresh thick cream and milk, and good almonds, walnuts, etc.

We will begin by giving full and clear directions for making fondant, as this is the foundation of many sweets. Also we shall give full details of the boiling of sugar.

MAKING FONDANT

TAKE 2 lb. of the best granulated sugar and put it into a clean saucepan. Add ½ pint of cold water and 1 good dessertspoonful of glucose.

Put the pan over a low gas and thoroughly dissolve *every* grain of sugar before letting it come to the boil, taking care not to get grains of sugar on the side of the pan above the syrup. Keep the sides of the pan clean. (The glucose is put in to make and keep the fondant creamy, otherwise it would grain and return to sugar.) If you allow it to boil before all the sugar is dissolved the fondant will be gritty and grainy instead of smooth and creamy.

When the sugar is *all* dissolved, leave off stirring it, turn up the gas (never let the flames come up to the sides of the pan, but keep them well underneath), and allow the syrup to boil.

Put a lid on the pan for a few minutes. This condenses the steam and quite clears the sides of the pan. But the syrup must not be stirred again, or the pan shaken whilst it is boiling. Remove the lid and gently put in the sugar-boiling thermometer (which must have first been put into a jug of very hot water. For the safety of the thermometer it must not be put directly into the boiling syrup, but must always be warmed first). Leave the thermometer undisturbed until it reaches 240° exactly.

Then gently take the pan off the gas, remove the thermometer and place it in a jug of hot water. Let the syrup become perfectly still, and the air bubbles all die down, then gently pour it on to the marble, which should have been wetted all over with cold water, but do not leave superfluous water on it.

Leave the syrup until the edges crinkle up when touched with a finger ; in cold weather you will have to start creaming it almost at once ; in hot weather you must leave it for a few minutes.

Take the scraper and with it go all round the edge of the syrup, collecting it towards the centre. Then remove the scraper to the left hand (it would get very messy if allowed to fall on the slab), and with the spatula in your right hand, work the syrup evenly and gently with an up-and-down movement, collecting it together again with the scraper as it spreads. Continue to cream it with these movements until it has turned into a *firm* mass and you cannot work it any more.

If you want to use the fondant at once, knead it with your hands on the slab until it is a nice, smooth, creamy mass, quite free from lumps.

If it is not to be used until the next day, put it as it is into a large jar, cover the top of the jar with waxed paper, on top of that place a thickly folded towel, and a heavy plate on top of that to exclude all air. By the next day this will be creamed without the kneading.

Fondant made and treated thus, and put in a *cool*, dry place, will keep for months, but *not* if it is kept in a hot or damp place.

PEPPERMINT CREAMS

You will need some small plain peppermint rings which are wider at the top than the bottom. Place them on the slab, close together, narrow end downwards. If you have twenty-four, then you will need about ¾ lb. of cream fondant weighed into a small saucepan.

Stand this pan in another one containing some warm water and, using a small spatula, gently move and stir the fondant, adding a few drops of stock syrup, (given below), but remember as the fondant melts it becomes thinner, so *do not add too much syrup at first*. One cannot tell how much to add ; it all depends on the condition of the fondant. In hot weather it is more creamy than in cold, and you must keep it gently stirred all the time, or a skin will form on the top.

Add a few drops of essence or oil of peppermint (the latter is stronger, so use less than of essence), and mix it in well.

It should be of the consistency of thickish cream, and fairly hot, but not too hot.

You can let the water simmer in the pan underneath, but never let the fondant simmer. If it is too hot, the cream will become hard quickly, and look spotted. But the fondant must be fairly hot or the creams will not set. A little practice will soon show you how to make it.

Quickly pour the fondant into a warmed dropper, and with this fill the rings about one-third full, or if you have a small lipped pan, pour the fondant from this into the rings and leave the creams to become quite cold. When cold, turn each one upside down, and gently tap it and the cream will drop out cleanly.

The dropper is made of tin in the shape of a funnel, having a band of copper round the nozzle end and a stick to fit it, which one gently lifts to allow the fondant to drop into the ring, quickly replacing the stick when sufficient is in the ring.

Move quickly on to the next one until all are made. With a little practice one gets quite quick at this, and as fondant soon sets in the saucepan, or dropper, it is important to do this as quickly as possible.

STOCK SYRUP

THIS is used in many sweets as well as for thinning down fondant. Put 1 lb. of granulated sugar, a good ½ pint of cold water, ¼ teaspoonful of cream of tartar, and 1 teaspoonful of glucose into a saucepan. Boil them exactly as fully directed for sugar boiling in the fondant recipe (see p. 572) to 221°. Pour the syrup into a jar and keep it for use.

MOULDED FONDANTS

MANY delicious sweets are made from fondant mixture (see p. 572). If you care to invest in a rubber mat, you can make moulded fondants.

The rubber mats are made in various sizes and are in very pretty designs.

Fondants moulded in a rubber mat make very effective and popular sweets, and they can be made any colour and flavour desired. For instance, for Raspberry Fondants, use raspberry essence and a *very* few drops of carmine, or geranium-red colouring. If you put *one* drop of saffron yellow to about *three* drops of the red, you get a pretty soft shade of pink.

For Strawberry Fondants, you do likewise, using strawberry essence ; for Orange using orange essence, and yellow to colour. Lemon is used in the same way, or any selected flavour and colour.

The mats must be used absolutely clean and dry. If they are at all damp, or if any small remains of former fondants are left in the mat, the new fondants will not turn out.

To wash the mat, use warm water with no soda or soap of any kind. After washing it, shake it well, to enable it to dry more quickly, and then leave it to dry naturally, *not* by the fire or in the sun.

It is a good plan to put the mat in a plate-rack to dry, or out of doors if there is no sun or smuts to soil it whilst drying.

If care is taken with the details given and the fondant is melted to the right heat and consistency, you can refill the mat several times without washing it. But if, after once filling and emptying the mat, there should be one or two impressions which look damp, do not fill these when refilling.

If you do not make your fondant hot enough, or make it too thin in consistency, the sweets will not set in the mat. If this should happen, get the fondant out of the mat carefully, using the handle of a teaspoon. You can use this fondant again by adding more to it.

Do not try to wash the mat at once, but leave it in a large bowl of warm water, and let the fondant remaining in the mat soak out of the impressions.

Then rinse it in one or two clean waters, to remove all stickiness, shake it, and leave it to dry. Finally wash the mat, dry it well, and put it away from dust for future use.

When making Moulded Fondants, melt the fondant exactly as fully directed for Peppermint Creams (see p. 573), adding stock syrup (see p. 573), if necessary, also essence and colouring. Make it hot, stirring it gently all the time, pour it quickly into the warmed dropper, and with this just fill the impressions in the mat.

Be sure not to overfill them, or they will not look professional. *Never* over-flavour or over-colour the sweets.

When the fondants are moulded leave them in the mat until cold, when they should turn out quite easily by just bending the mat, and helping them out. They should be perfect impressions of the mat. The mat can be used without washing, providing it is quite dry.

CHERRY CREAM KISSES

INGREDIENTS.—½ lb. of fondant (see p. 572), 3 oz. of glacé cherries, cut into small pieces, vanilla to flavour.

METHOD.—Melt the fondant as before (standing the pan in another one containing water), and if necessary, add a few drops of stock syrup. (NOTE.—Do not add much, as the sweets must keep their shape when dropped on the slab.) Make the fondant fairly hot, then gently stir in the cherries and vanilla.

Remove the pan from the hot water and, using the ends of two teaspoons, drop small, round, high heaps on to your slab. Let these become perfectly set, then place each in a small crinkled-paper case.

Mixed with other bonbons, these look most attractive.

ALMOND CREAM BONBONS

ALMOND CREAM

INGREDIENTS.—1 lb. of fondant (see p. 572), ¼ lb. of ground almonds, vanilla or almond essence, as preferred.

METHOD.—Warm the fondant as before (standing the pan in another one of hot water). Add the flavouring and the ground almonds, but you will not need any stock syrup.

Turn the fondant mixture on to a slab, and work it well, till it is quite pliable. Divide it into portions, colouring each as desired, but do this quickly, as the colours mix in better and more evenly while the almond cream is warm. Leave one portion uncoloured.

NEAPOLITAN CREAMS

Have four portions of Almond Cream and make one a pretty soft pink, one a pale green, one a deep coffee colour, and leave one portion uncoloured.

Put a piece of waxed paper on a

board, and press and pat out a piece of the brown cream into a square or oblong. On top of this place the green cream, on that put some uncoloured, and the pink on top, having each colour the same thickness. Gently press them all together, and with a thin, sharp knife, cut the cream into strips with a sawing movement. Do not cut straight downwards. Then cut them into oblong bricks, or into squares as preferred. Leave them a little apart on wax paper to dry, before packing them away.

ALMOND CREAM WALNUTS

Make some equal-sized balls of Almond Cream by rolling them gently in the palms of the hands. Place each ball between two halves of shelled walnut, leaving them neat, and not showing any finger-marks on them. Leave them on wax paper to become dry and firm.

Another delicious bonbon is made by removing the stones from some French plums or some dates, and inserting a neat roll of almond cream. Press the fruit together and make it neat.

ALMOND CREAM POTATOES

Roll some Almond Cream into small rounds or ovals, and drop them, as you do them, into chocolate powder, covering them well all over with the powder, using a spoon for this and not your fingers. When several rounds are coated, lift them out with a fork, poking in two or three places with the fork to represent the eyes in potatoes. Leave them to dry. Put each potato into a small paper case.

If you should pack any of these potatoes with other bonbons for sending away, be sure to roll them in tinfoil, otherwise the powder will shake off on to the other sweets.

Almond cream makes delicious centres for stuffed fondants, also it is splendid for almond icing for cakes.

EDINBURGH ROCK

PULLED sweets are very interesting to make, and first we will give full instructions for making Edinburgh rock. This is not costly, and it is very popular. You can use many flavourings and colourings to correspond.

For raspberry rock, use raspberry essence, and colour it a pretty shade of pink. Strawberry, too, would be pale pink. For lemon, use lemon-essence, and colour the rock pale yellow. Orange should have a deeper shade of yellow and orange flavouring. Vanilla is left white.

Use the best granulated sugar.

INGREDIENTS.—1 lb. of sugar, 1 gill of cold water, a small level quarter-teaspoonful of cream of tartar, colouring and essence are added later.

METHOD.—Dissolve every grain of the sugar in the water before letting it come to the boil ; then add the cream of tartar and let that dissolve. Remove the spatula and put the lid on the saucepan, and let the sugar boil quickly for a few seconds.

This condenses the steam and washes down the sides of the pan, and so absolutely frees it from any granules of sugar.

Remove the lid and put your thermometer in gently.

This *must* be warmed first, by standing it in a jug of hot water, as it would not be wise to put the cold thermometer into the boiling syrup.

Let the syrup boil to 262° in cold weather and 264° in hot, but the flame should not be allowed to come up the sides of the pan.

You will want a marble slab (any old piece of marble will do), and while the syrup is boiling, grease this slab very well with butter. You will also want a palette knife, or one with a very broad blade. Grease this, too, with butter. A palette knife is very pliable, and is most useful in cooking. When the syrup has reached the required degree, take it off the gas *at once*, put the thermometer into a jug of hot water, and carefully pour the syrup on to the slab.

Now put in the centre a few drops of the selected flavouring and colouring. You must be guided by the strength of these as to how much to use, but make the colouring deeper than you want it to be, as the pulling makes it lighter.

With the greased knife gently *fold* over the cooled edges towards the centre of the batch. Gently raise it on to the knife, a little at a time, and fo d it towards the centre, working all round.

If the edges are again setting, repeat the process, but if it is too soft to fold over, wait a few seconds, until it gets a little firmer, as you must not stir it about carelessly. In winter it cools much more quickly than in summer, but a little practice will soon tell you. Continue to fold it gently, until firm enough to take in your fingers. This folding over keeps it all at an even temperature, otherwise the outside edges would get set too soon.

By this time it will not be very hot, but it is apt to stick to your fingers. To obviate this, either rub your fingers well on the greased slab, or dust them with sifted icing-sugar. Do not get the mass into the palms of your hands, but keep it in your fingers as much as possible.

When you can pick it up, pull it out into a roll, keeping it over the greased slab until it gets firmer, in case the roll has to be put down.

Do not let it fall into a ball, or it may turn sugary, when you would not be able to pull it. With care, you will be able to pull it evenly and gently. (If it should at any time turn sugary, put it back in a saucepan, add a good gill of water, and dissolve it again, as you did with the sugar at first, and nothing will be wasted. But this need not happen if you are careful.)

Pull the strip out, fold over the end in your right hand, and put it with that already in your left hand. Quickly take the folded end in your right hand, pull the strip evenly and gently, again put the end in your right hand into your left, without twisting the roll at all, fold it over evenly, and keep the strip as much as possible the same thickness all along.

Continue doing this until it is firm enough to hold its shape when cut up. It will by now be nicely ribbed. Try not to lose this ribbed effect in handling it. It will probably take from ten to fifteen minutes to pull. If the weather is very cold and the rock seems inclined to set too quickly, hold it over a gas ring, still pulling it.

When firm enough, dust a board with icing sugar, and pull out the strip to the thickness required. Cut it into equal-sized lengths, using a large pair of scissors, leaving each strip on the board, and not letting them touch one another.

If you wish to cut some into cushions, cut the strip right across, then quickly give the strip a half-turn right, which brings the point of the strip up, clip a cushion off, again give the strip a half-turn left, and cut off, each time reversing the way you turn the strip, so that it does not become twisted.

Leave the sticks and cushions on the board in a warm room to become powdery. Often it is ready by the next day, but it may take longer if not sufficiently pulled. When powdery, it is ready to eat, or to pack in boxes.

LINING A NOUGAT FRAME

WE are now going to make sweets in a nougat frame, which is really four strips of wood joined together, two long ones for the length and two short ones for the ends.

A convenient size is sixteen inches long by three inches across and three-quarters of an inch in depth, reckoning the measurements inside the frame, as wood varies in thickness. The frame is, of course, hollow. It is useful to have a small separate block of wood the same depth and width as the frame, so that if you are not making sufficient sweet to fill the frame, you can put this small block in to it, thus leaving part of the frame empty.

The frame must be lined with wax paper before beginning to make the sweet. Lay the frame on a piece of wax paper. (If you do not wish to fill it all, lay the small block across the frame to the size required.) Then, with a pencil, mark the wax paper all round exactly inside the frame.

Lift the frame off the paper, and fold it down at the pencil marks, creasing the paper well. Cut the short ends at the fold so that it exactly fits the frame, then place the neat lining of wax paper inside the frame ready to pour the sweet into when made. By lining the frame in this way the sweets turn out a perfect shape.

Neapolitan
Creams

Edinburgh
Rock

Caramels

Humbugs

PLATE 53

Coconut Ice and Fudge

Nougat

Truffles

Plate 54

French
Almond
Rock

Pulled
Cream
Toffee

Molasses Candy

PLATE 55

Moulded
Fondant

Cherry
Cream
Kisses

Peppermint
Creams

PLATE 56

FUDGE

INGREDIENTS.—1 lb. of granulated sugar, 1 good gill of milk, 1 oz. of butter, 1 large tablespoonful of glucose, 3 oz. of plain fondant (see p. 572), ¼ lb. cut-up nuts of any kind, or ¼ lb. cut-up glacé fruits, or both mixed if preferred, vanilla. If Chocolate Fudge is required, 2 oz. of dissolved, unsweetened chocolate.

METHOD.—Put the sugar, glucose, milk, and butter in the pan and dissolve them carefully, stirring all the time. When the sugar is all dissolved, bring it to the boil, put in a warmed thermometer, and stir carefully to 238°.

Then take out the thermometer and put it into a jug of hot water (this enables the thermometer to come down safely). Remove the pan to a table and let it stand for three or four minutes.

In the meantime, work the three ounces of fondant with the finger-tips to a thin, pliable sheet, and lay it in the syrup with the nuts or fruits (which ever you use) and a few drops of essence of vanilla.

Stir well with the spatula (this is like a wooden spoon, only flat at the end instead of a bowl) to mix the fondant and other ingredients in thoroughly, and rub the spatula against the side of the pan a few times. This grains the mixture slightly. Now quickly stir this grained portion into the rest of the syrup.

Grain it again slightly by rubbing the spatula against the side of pan with a quick backward-and-forward movement, stir again to mix all together, and quickly pour the mixture into the prepared frame. Make the batch about half an inch thick, helping it out of the saucepan with the spatula, and have a nice, smooth, level surface along the top.

Leave the sweet some hours until it is quite set, then cut it into bars with a thin, sharp knife, using a sawing movement, and wrap each bar in wax paper.

FOR CHOCOLATE FUDGE.—Instead of the nuts or fruit, stir in the two ounces of unsweetened block chocolate, first dissolving it by putting it in a cup or small basin, *without any liquid*, and, standing it in a pan of hot water. This will dissolve the chocolate. This must be ready to pour into the syrup with the fondant and vanilla. Mix it well in, grain and proceed as before. As this is a dry sweet, wrapping it is optional.

COCONUT ICE

This is a choice sweet, not like the ordinary rough kind. You will need to line the nougat frame with wax paper as before. The syrup is boiled in two portions, one being white, the other a pretty soft pink.

INGREDIENTS.—For each portion you will need 12 oz. of granulated sugar, small ¼-pint of cold water, 2½ oz. of plain fondant (see p. 572), ⅛ level teaspoonful of cream of tartar, 2½ tablespoonfuls of thick cream, and 2½ oz. of desiccated coconut.

METHOD.—Put all the cream into a small saucepan and bring it to the boil (this is to make it keep), stirring it all the time. Mix in all the coconut, divide it into two, cover the pan, and set it aside.

Now make the white portion of the ice.

In a pan put the sugar and water and dissolve every grain before letting it come to the boil. Then add the cream of tartar and dissolve that. Remove the spoon, put on the lid, and let it boil quickly for a minute or two just to wash down the sides of the pan. Remove the lid, put in the warmed thermometer, and boil the syrup, without stirring or shaking it, to 240°. Put the thermometer into a jug of hot water and stand the pan on the table for three or four minutes.

Work the two and a half ounces of fondant to a thick, pliable sheet with the finger-tips and lay it in the syrup, also half of the cream-soaked coconut, and stir all carefully in. Then grain and thicken it by rubbing the spatula against the sides of the pan.

Stir the sweet to keep it of equal consistency, repeat this movement, but before it gets too thick pour it quickly into the prepared frame. Make another batch in exactly the same way, using the second twelve ounces of sugar, etc.

T

When you have boiled it to 240° leave it for three or four minutes, lay in the other two and a half ounces of fondant, and the other half of the cream-soaked coconut, and a drop or two of carmine and saffron colour. By using these two colours you get a pretty soft shade, not a crude pink. Then stir all in and grain the mixture, and pour it into the frame on top of the white batch.

Leave the Coconut Ice for some hours to become perfectly set, then turn it out of the frame, remove the wax paper and cut it into bars with a thin, sharp knife, using a sawing movement.

Wrap each sweet neatly in wax paper, placing it so that it shows the two colours on top when wrapped.

CARAMELS

The sweet-maker who possesses a sugar thermometer will have no difficulty in making caramels. Before you begin, however, read over these very useful hints.

Do not use a small pan, as caramels and toffees boil up so much at first, and do not use enamel saucepans. Any metal ones will do that are unlined with tin, such as copper or brass.

Nickel or aluminium will do, but not the very thin light ones.

Have all you need ready to hand before you begin, and your tin, or tins, well buttered and within reach, as you have to pour the caramel out very quickly directly it is taken off the gas, as it continues to cook in the pan.

Let all the caramel drop out of the saucepan into the tin of its own accord, but never scrape any out, or you may grain the caramel and turn it sugary. The little that remains in the pan can be scraped on to a greased plate for tasting.

Put boiling water into the emptied pan. Cold water might crack it.

As the caramel cooks and begins to thicken, do not allow the flame of the gas to be strong under the pan and never let it come up the sides. This is important.

Be sure to stir thoroughly but carefully all over the base of the pan, or the caramel will stick and burn

there. Always add the vanilla essence or other flavouring just before pouring out the caramel, otherwise much of the flavouring will be lost.

When the caramel is set sufficiently in the tin, turn it out on to a board. This must be done before the caramel is too set, or you will not be able to mark the lines where it is to be cut. On the other hand, if it is not set enough, it will spread a little when marking and so spoil the shape. Practice will soon show you the right consistency.

When it is turned out on the board, mark the caramel with a caramel marker. These can be bought at any stores in various sizes to mark a small or large quantity, but the size of the caramel never varies. If preferred, the caramel can be marked in little squares with a knife.

Sometimes these markers are called caramel cutters, but you must not try to cut the caramel right through. It is only to mark it into the small, neat squares.

With a sharp, thin knife, using a sawing movement backwards and forwards (not cutting right down), remove the strips all round the slab of caramel first, as the outside edges always get firmer sooner than the centre. Then, still using the sawing movement, divide the caramel into the marked divisions, leaving the squares apart on the board, or they may stick together again.

It is best to have tins with straight sides, not slanting, like Yorkshire pudding tins. There will then be no waste in cutting up. A tinsmith will make these tins quite reasonably. It is important to use a tin the right size for the quantity of caramel you are making, so it is well to have two or three different sizes in stock. The caramel should be nearly half an inch in depth.

Cut some wax papers into the sizes you require for wrapping the caramels, and wrap them neatly so that all the edges come underneath. The best or top side of the caramel is where you marked it, which gives it a slightly shaped top.

Keep the caramels in a tin box with a tight-fitting lid in a cool, dry room. If they are kept in a hot place or exposed to the air, they are apt to get a sugary crust.

Always use butter for sweets, not margarine.

CHOCOLATE CARAMELS

INGREDIENTS.—4 oz. of glucose, 12 oz. of granulated or soft pale-brown cane sugar, 4 oz. of butter, 2 oz. of sweetened block chocolate, 1 gill of milk, 3 tablespoonfuls of thick cream, a few drops of vanilla essence added at the last.

METHOD.—Weigh the saucepan, then weigh into it the glucose. Add the sugar, milk, cream, one ounce of the butter, and the chocolate, cut up into small pieces.

Dissolve these over a gentle heat, and be sure every grain is dissolved before letting it come to the boil, or it may be sugary.

When it boils, put in the thermometer (previously warmed by putting it into hot water), then boil the mixture steadily, not letting the flame of the gas touch the base of the pan. Stir it carefully all the time to 230°, then add the remaining three ounces of butter cut in thin slices so that it quickly boils through the sugar, and continue to stir carefully all the time to 250° in winter. In hot weather it should be 252 or 253°. Take the mixture quickly off the gas and add the few drops of vanilla essence. Remove the thermometer, putting it into a jug of boiling water, and pour the caramel quickly into the buttered tin. Then proceed as already directed.

A slightly different flavour is obtained in the caramels by using *soft* pale-brown cane sugar.

Various caramels can be made by this recipe and method, such as vanilla, lemon, ginger, and raspberry. Colour and flavour each accordingly, adding the colour with the flavouring. Any of the alternatives should be boiled to 252° in winter and 254 or 256° in hot weather. The chocolate ones are boiled at a lower degree because, when the caramels are cold, the chocolate in them solidifies and so makes the caramels firmer.

BUTTERSCOTCH

INGREDIENTS.—8 oz. of castor sugar, 8 oz. of glucose, 5 or 6 oz. of butter (as preferred), 1 gill of milk, a few drops of vanilla added at the last.

METHOD.—Weigh the pan, then weigh into it the glucose. Add the sugar, milk, and butter. Dissolve every grain of sugar before letting it come to the boil. Put in the warmed thermometer and stir most carefully all the time to 252°, not letting the flame touch the base of the pan or you will scorch the toffee and spoil the flavour.

When 252° is reached, quickly add the vanilla. Remove the thermometer into a jug of boiling water, pour the mixture into a buttered tin and proceed as before.

A great improvement is made by using three tablespoonfuls of cream and three of milk instead of the gill of milk.

RUSSIAN TOFFEE

INGREDIENTS.—6 oz. of castor sugar, 3 oz. of soft brown cane sugar, 1 tablespoonful of honey, 1 dessertspoonful of glucose, 3 oz. of butter, 3 tablespoonfuls of thick cream, 3 tablespoonfuls of water, a few drops of vanilla added at the last.

METHOD.—Put into a saucepan the sugar, glucose, honey, cream and water, and dissolve them before letting the mixture come to the boil. Put in the warmed thermometer and boil toffee steadily, stirring it carefully all the time.

When 240° is reached, add the butter cut in thin slices to enable it to boil quickly through the sugar. Boil it, still stirring, until it reaches 256° in winter and 258° in hot weather.

Quickly add the vanilla, remove the thermometer into a jug of boiling water, and pour the caramel into the buttered tin and proceed as before.

ITALIAN CREAM

THIS is a delicious sweet. Do not use a small pan, as it boils up considerably. Line a nougat frame with wax paper (see p. 576), and as you must stir the sweet all the time until finished, you must make all your preparations, such as lining the frame, cutting up the walnuts, etc., before you begin to boil the sweet.

INGREDIENTS.—8 oz. of castor sugar, 2 oz. of soft brown cane sugar, 2 oz. of plain fondant, 4 oz. of dried walnuts cut up into small, even-sized pieces (not chopped), 4 oz. of glucose, ¼ pint of thick cream, 4 tablespoonfuls of warm water, a few drops of essence of vanilla.

METHOD.—Weigh the pan, then weigh a quarter of a pound of glucose into it, add the sugar, cream and water. Put the pan on a gas-ring and be sure every grain of sugar is dissolved before letting it come to the boil ; then put in the thermometer. This should be warmed by putting it into hot water for safety, before putting it into the boiling syrup.

Continue to stir carefully until 238° in winter, 239° in hot weather.

Remove the thermometer into fresh hot water, put the pan on the table, and let it stand for three or four minutes.

Meanwhile work the two ounces of fondant to a thin, pliable sheet with the finger-tips, and lay it in the syrup ; add the vanilla, and mix all well in, then quickly but gently rub the spatula against the side of the pan, with a quick to-and-fro movement, to grain the syrup.

Stir well to mix evenly. Do this two or three times, then quickly add the cut-up walnuts.

Mix all well together, and quickly pour into the prepared frame.

Leave for some hours to set, then turn out of the frame, remove the wax paper (it will come off easily) and cut the sweet into half-an-inch-wide bars, using a sharp knife with a sawing movement, and wrap each in wax paper. If you stir too much, you will grain it too strongly. It should cut smoothly, like cheese.

NOUGAT AND NOYEAU

FOR making nougat you will need a nougat frame, but instead of lining it with wax paper (as you do for Fudge and Coconut Ice), it is lined with wafer or rice paper. This is not removed when the sweet is finished, but is left on as it is edible.

To prepare the frame, lay a piece of greaseproof paper on a board, and then a piece of wafer paper a little wider than the frame over it. If the sheet of wafer paper is not long enough, another piece may be joined to it by damping the edges of the join very slightly with cold water. Very little water must be used as the wafer paper will melt if it is made too wet.

If the frame is not to be filled quite full, a little block of wood should be placed in the frame. In this case only the part of the frame to be used should be lined and one side of the little block. When the sweet is in the frame the little block can be pushed up to make the size required. It is important that the sweet should fill the frame exactly, as the nougat has to be pressed. If it is overfilled the sweet will be pressed out and be very messy, and if it is not full enough the sweet cannot be pressed.

Lay the frame on the wafer paper and then line the sides of it with narrow strips of wafer paper cut to fit the sides of the frame exactly. You will also need a wide strip of wafer to cover the top of the sweet when it is in the frame and a piece of grease-proof paper to go on top of the wafer.

Remember that the thermometer should always be taken out of a jug of very hot water before putting it into the boiling syrup, and it should be put back into the hot water immediately after use.

GOLDEN HONEY NOYEAU

INGREDIENTS.—2 oz. of glucose, 2 oz. of honey, 1 lb. of granulated sugar, 3 oz. of small almonds (blanched, split and well dried, but kept white), ¼ pint of water, vanilla, and 1 or 2 drops of yellow colouring.

METHOD.—Put the honey into a cup or small basin and stand it in a small pan of hot water till it becomes liquid and warm. Put the almonds where they will be warmed.

Weigh a saucepan and then weigh into it two ounces of glucose. Add the sugar and water.

Dissolve every grain of the sugar over a gentle heat before letting the syrup come to the boil.

When it is dissolved, put the lid on the pan and bring the syrup to boiling point ; boil it for a minute or so to clear the sides of the pan.

Remove the lid, put the warmed

thermometer into the syrup and boil it carefully, without shaking or stirring it, to 248°.

Care must be taken not to let the flame come up the sides of the pan. This is a very important point in boiling sugar.

As soon as 248° is reached, lift the pan off the gas carefully, take out the thermometer and place it in a jug of hot water. Pour the syrup gently on to a wetted slab. Into the centre of it pour the warm, melted honey, one or two drops of vanilla, and some yellow colouring.

Begin to cream it at once, using a spatula and scraper (as directed in the article on Fondant Making, see p. 572). Work it with the movement explained there until it is quite turned and formed into a lump and cannot be worked any more. Then work it until it is soft with the fingers, and work in the warmed almonds, taking care not to break them. Should the mixture be too stiff (this does not happen often), add a few drops of Stock Syrup (see p. 573). The mixture should now be a nice soft paste, but it must not be too soft.

Press it *level* into a frame, cover it with the wafer paper and then with the greaseproof paper. Lay a piece of board on top of this, and on this place the heavy weights to press the sweet.

Leave it for some hours until it becomes quite firm. Then cut it into bars, using a sharp knife with a sawing movement. Wrap each bar in wax paper.

RASPBERRY NOYEAU

This is made exactly like Honey Nougat (see p. 580), but instead of using honey use two ounces of sieved and warmed raspberry jam. This should be weighed after it has been sieved. Use Raspberry Essence and red colouring instead of vanilla and yellow colouring. Put these on top of the syrup, as soon as it has been poured on to the slab, and proceed to finish making the sweet as explained above.

NOUGAT MONTELIMART

INGREDIENTS.—9 oz. of granulated sugar, 3 oz. of honey, 2 oz. of glucose

small ¾ gill of water, 1 large egg-white, 4 oz. of almonds, ½ oz. or 1 oz. of pistachio nuts (as preferred).

METHOD.—The nuts should be blanched and split through once, the day before the nougat is made, to ensure that they are thoroughly dry. They should not be allowed to colour. Put the nuts where they will become warm. It spoils the nougat to add the nuts when they are cold.

Weigh a saucepan, then weigh into it the honey and glucose, and add the water and sugar.

Dissolve every grain of sugar over a gentle heat before letting it come to the boil. Stop stirring it, bring it to the boil, and put in the warmed thermometer.

Boil the syrup carefully to 277°, but keep the gas quite low or the syrup will become coloured (the honey is responsible for this).

When the syrup is boiling gently, add a tiny pinch of salt to the egg-white and whisk it up till it is very stiff. The bowl in which this is done should be made of metal; either copper, nickel, or aluminium is suitable, as the syrup is boiled to such a high degree that it would crack a china bowl. Try to have the egg-white very stiff by the time the syrup is boiling at 277°. Take out the thermometer and put it in hot water.

Trickle the syrup gently into the egg-white.

Arrange the bowl so that it will stand steadily. Beat the mixture well all the time with a spatula. Continue to beat it till it is very stiff, then quickly add the warmed nuts, mixing them in carefully.

Turn the mixture into a wafer-lined nougat frame. Dust your fingers with icing sugar when working with the mixture, as this will prevent it sticking to them. Level it in the frame. You must work quickly as the nougat sets in the bowl almost at once, and it is necessary to get as much of it as possible into the frame. Press it *quite level*, cover the top with the wafer paper and then with the greaseproof paper, place the board on top and the weights on it.

Leave the nougat to get quite firm before cutting it into bars. To do this, use a sharp knife and a sawing movement. Wrap each bar in wax paper and store the nougat in an airtight tin.

ITALIAN NOUGAT

THIS is a quickly made sweet and not at all costly when one has the fondant made.

INGREDIENTS.—1 lb. of fondant (see p. 572), 2 oz. of blanched and shredded almonds, 2 oz. of glacé cherries (cut into small pieces), 1½ oz. of angelica (with the sugar washed off and cut into tiny pieces), orange or other fruit flavouring, stock syrup, if necessary (see p. 573).

METHOD.—See that the fondant is free from small lumps. If there are any, work it till it is soft with the fingers. Put it in a pan and stand the pan in another one containing hot water. Stir it carefully over a gentle heat until it is melted, adding a few drops of Stock Syrup if necessary. It should be of a consistency of good cream, but remember that the fondant get thinner as you warm it.

Make it fairly hot. Add flavouring to taste and stir in the nuts and fruits. Then pour into the wafer-paper-lined nougat frame.

Proceed as in the other recipes, leaving the sweet being pressed for some hours—or, better still, till next day—to become firm.

Then cut into bars, using a sharp knife and a sawing movement. Wrap each bar in wax paper. If liked, this sweet may be cut into squares and each one placed in a paper case. They would make very effective bon-bons.

CHOCOLATE TRUFFLES

Chocolate truffles are not at all difficult to make. Rough truffles are those coated with granulated chocolate, and the smooth ones have a coating of chocolate powder.

You will need a coarse wire sieve when making the granulated chocolate.

TO MAKE THE GRANULATED CHOCOLATE.—Cut up half a pound of good sweetened block chocolate into small pieces and put them in a saucepan. It is not necessary to add water. Place the saucepan in another one containing hot water (never melt chocolate over a direct flame—always over hot water). Use a wooden spoon or a spatula to stir the chocolate until it is melted. Then gradually stir into this two tablespoonfuls of Stock Syrup (see page 573).

Take the pan with the chocolate out of the hot water and stand it in a pan of cold water and stir the mixture till it is thick and almost set.

Place a sieve on a sheet of greaseproof paper. Take a little of the chocolate and rub it through the wire sieve, using the wooden spatula, so that the granulated chocolate falls on to the paper. Do not put much mixture on to the sieve at one time. If the chocolate is of the right consistency the paper will be covered with little pieces of chocolate and these are used for covering the truffles. If the chocolate is too moist, beat it a little longer before rubbing it through the sieve, and if it is too dry it should be warmed *very slightly* again, and then rubbed through the sieve.

If the little granules cling together just as they come through the sieve, they will probably separate as they dry. This they will do quite quickly.

Should they be too powdery, then the mixture has become a little too cool. After putting the whole of the chocolate through the sieve, return it to the sieve again and shake it so that any powder there is will drop through. Do not rub it at all. The granulated chocolate is now emptied out on to the greaseproof paper, and is ready for coating the centres.

CENTRES FOR ROUGH TRUFFLES

INGREDIENTS.—6 oz. of sweetened block chocolate, 1 gill of thick cream, vanilla.

METHOD.—Melt the chocolate by standing the pan containing it in another pan of hot water, then add the cream gradually, stirring it in well, and the vanilla essence.

In hot weather the cream should be boiled before use. Put it in a pan, and bring it to the boil, stirring it all the time. Stand the pan in cold water for two or three minutes, and continue to stir it.

This will ensure that the truffles will

keep. In cold weather this is not necessary unless the truffles are to be kept for longer than a week.

Take the pan containing the chocolate mixture and stand it in one of cold water, then stir the chocolate till it is nearly set. It will now be much lighter in colour.

Do not try to form the centres if the mixture is too soft or they will lose their shape, but care must be taken that it is not too stiff, or the granules of chocolate will not adhere to the centres. If after beating the chocolate mixture seems to be too stiff, heat it again *very slightly* and beat it again.

When the mixture is of the right consistency, take two teaspoons and, using the handles, form the mixture into round balls. Drop each one as it is made into the granulated chocolate. Use a spoon to cover the truffles, and leave each one lying in the granulated chocolate until all the centres have been coated and the truffles are firm.

Use a fork to lift the truffles out of the granulated chocolate mixture and place them on a tin covered with a sheet of greaseproof paper, and leave them till they are thoroughly firm before packing them away.

The granulated chocolate which is left over can be put into an airtight tin and used for coating more truffles provided that these are made within a reasonable time.

If liked, it can be used for the centres. Half quantities of the ingredients given can be used for a first experiment.

SMOOTH TRUFFLES

SMOOTH truffles are coated with chocolate powder. Have some ready on a sheet of greaseproof paper before beginning to make the centres.

INGREDIENTS.—6 oz. of sweetened block chocolate, 2 full dessertspoonfuls of cream, 3 oz. of butter, 2 yolks of eggs, 3 dessertspoonfuls of icing sugar, vanilla.

METHOD.—In hot weather the cream should be boiled as explained in the previous recipe. The icing sugar should be sieved very finely and free from small lumps.

Melt the chocolate over hot water as before, add the cream and then the butter gradually. The butter should

be cut into small pieces and each piece should be stirred in well before the next one is added. Add the well-beaten yolks of eggs and cook the mixture over hot water for a minute or two, just enough to cook the eggs but not to curdle them.

Remove the pan from the hot water and stir in gradually the icing sugar and then add the vanilla. The amount of vanilla depends on the strength of the essence.

Now stand the saucepan in a pan of cold water and beat the mixture till it is light in colour and it increases in bulk. It should just be stiff enough to hold its shape when formed.

In winter the mixture will soon set to the right consistency, but in hot weather it will require more beating. Do not leave the pan standing in cold water, but beat the mixture constantly till it is ready, this will make it of a light consistency.

When it is firm and dry enough to hold its shape (it should not be too dry or the chocolate powder will not adhere) use two teaspoons to form the mixture into oval shapes. These should be much the shape and size of Brazil nuts.

As each truffle is shaped, drop it into the chocolate powder, covering the centre all over. Use a spoon to do this.

Leave the truffles lying in the powder until all the mixture for the centres has been used up. Then lift the truffles out with a fork and leave them to become perfectly dry and cold.

If either kind of chocolate truffle is to be packed in a box with other sweets they should be wrapped in tinfoil, as the granulated chocolate and the chocolate powder would rub off and spoil the look of the other sweets. If, however, they are to be packed alone, place each truffle in a crinkled paper case.

MOLASSES CANDY

INGREDIENTS.—½ lb. of light soft brown sugar, ¼ lb. of Fowler's treacle (golden syrup is not suitable for this purpose), 1 dessertspoonful of glucose, 3 oz. of butter, 4 tablespoonfuls of water.

METHOD.—Choose a large pan, as the treacle and brown sugar boil up considerably. Weigh the pan, then weigh in the treacle, and add the rest of the ingredients. Dissolve them in the usual way before letting them come to the boil. Put in the thermometer.

Boil the candy steadily to 254° in winter, and to 256° in summer, stirring most carefully all the time, but you must *not* let the flame be at all strong on the bottom of the pan, or you will spoil the flavour of the candy and make it harsh.

Put the thermometer in hot water, and gently pour the syrup on to the well-buttered slab, having a palette knife greased also (or one with a broad blade), and when the edges of the batch are setting slightly, carefully lift them with the knife and fold them towards the centre, doing this all round to make it cool evenly.

By the time you have been all round, if the edges are not sufficiently set to lift up, wait a minute or so and then proceed as before until the sweet is firm enough to pick up in your fingers.

As the mass is inclined to stick to your fingers more at first, either dust them with icing sugar or rub them on the greased slab, while pulling the sweet. Instructions for pulling sweets appear on p. 575, Edinburgh Rock recipe.

Pull it lightly and quickly for ten or fifteen minutes, keeping it even and not twisted. It will get lighter in colour and increase in bulk, but this sweet does not need any added colour or flavouring, as its own flavour is delicious.

Pull the candy until it is firm enough to hold its shape, then cut the stick into cushions with large scissors.

To do this, cut the stick right across, then quickly give it a half-turn right which brings the point of the stick up, clip a cushion off, again give the stick a half-turn left, and cut off a cushion, each time reversing the way you turn the stick so that it does not become twisted.

Let the cushions get cold. Cut some rather long pieces of waxed paper and put a piece of candy in the centre of each, folding it over the candy. Then twist the paper at each end, close to the sweets, and let the long ends of the paper spread out.

TOFFEES AND HUMBUGS

FULL directions for pulling sweets are given on p. 575, and the sweets now given are made in the same way.

When any weight of glucose is given in a recipe, always weigh the pan first, then weigh the glucose into the pan. This is far the best and easiest way, as then you add the rest of the ingredients to the glucose.

PULLED CREAM TOFFEE

PULLED cream toffee costs a little more to make, on account of the cream used, and you will find it most delicious.

INGREDIENTS.—1 lb. of granulated sugar, 2 oz. of glucose, 1 gill of cold water, selected flavouring and colouring, 1 gill of cream.

METHOD.—For raspberry flavour use a little pink colouring (remember that as you pull the sweet the colour becomes lighter) ; for lemon flavouring use yellow ; but vanilla-flavoured sweets are always left white.

Weigh the pan (use a large one, as cream boils up considerably), weigh in the glucose, and add the sugar and water. Dissolve every grain over a slow heat before letting it come to the boil (this is essential for all sugar boiling).

When the ingredients are dissolved and nearly ready to boil, take out the spoon, put the lid on the pan, and let it boil quickly for a few seconds. This condenses the steam and cleans down the sides of the pan, should there be any grains of sugar left there.

Remove the lid from the pan and put in the thermometer, warmed by putting it in a jug of hot water. (For the safety of the thermometer, it should never be put into the boiling syrup while it is cold.) Let the syrup boil to 255° without stirring, gently add the cream, and stir carefully till it reaches 265°. Take care that the flame is not strong under the pan or you will scorch the toffee.

Take the pan off the gas, remove the thermometer, and place it in a jug of fresh hot water. Very gently pour the contents of the pan on to a well-buttered marble slab. In the centre put a few drops of the flavouring and the colouring chosen.

Have a palette knife ready greased (or one with a broad blade), and when the edges of the batch are setting slightly, carefully lift it with the knife and fold them towards the centre, doing this all round to make it cool evenly.

By the time you have been all round, if the edges are not set sufficiently to lift up, wait a minute or so and then proceed as before until the sweet is firm enough to pick up in your fingers. As the mass is inclined to stick to the fingers more at first, either dust them with icing sugar or rub them on the greased slab as necessary while pulling (as directed in the recipe for Edinburgh Rock on p. 575).

Pull the sweet until it will hold its shape. This will take from ten to fifteen minutes, and care should be taken not to twist the sweet. Draw it out in strips to the thickness required, cut them into four-inch lengths with a pair of large scissors, and leave the strips on a board, dusted with icing sugar, in a warm room until the next day. They can be cut in cushions, if preferred.

HUMBUGS

THESE are a very popular sweet, but as they are boiled to a much higher degree—300°—they are much hotter to handle and harden very quickly.

It is necessary to work rapidly but carefully, taking care to grease your fingers well or dust them liberally with icing sugar.

Have the slab and knife ready greased. Never scrape the boiling out of the saucepan on to the slab, but always allow it to flow out or you will grain the whole of the sweet.

INGREDIENTS.—1 lb. of good, soft, pale sugar, 1 oz. of butter, ¼ pint of cold water, ¼ level teaspoonful of cream of tartar, 6 or 8 drops of oil of peppermint (a little more if essence of peppermint is used, because the oil is much stronger).

METHOD.—Dissolve the sugar and water in a large pan (the soft brown sugar boils up very much), and make sure that it is dissolved before allowing it to boil.

Then add the cream of tartar and butter, and dissolve these. Put in the warmed thermometer and stir the sweet very carefully all the time until it reaches the temperature of 300°.

Take care not to have the gas strong under the pan, keeping it low, especially after the temperature has reached 260° (or it may scorch the sweet).

Directly the temperature reaches 300° take the pan off the gas quickly, remove the thermometer, and place it in a jug of boiling water. (This is necessary when the thermometer is removed from syrup at a temperature of 300°.)

Pour the boiling quickly and gently on to the well-greased slab, and add the peppermint in the centre.

With the buttered knife, fold the outside edges towards the centre, as before, and pull the sweet straight and evenly for from three to five minutes.

Pull the sweet into strips quickly, as it soon hardens, and cut it into cushions with a pair of large scissors, giving a half-turn to the strip after each cut. (See the recipe for Edinburgh Rock on p. 575.)

Should the boiling become too set before it is all cut up, mark the remainder of the strip with a knife, and when it is cold it will break into pieces at the marks.

EVERTON TOFFEE

IT is better to have tins with vertical sides for toffee or caramels, as then there is no waste.

Have all the tins ready greased, because the toffee must be poured out directly it comes to the required degree. Never scrape any of the boiling toffee out of your saucepan, but let it flow out. Put the scrapings on to a greased plate for tasting.

INGREDIENTS.—1 lb. of granulated sugar, 1 gill of cold water, 3 or 4 oz. of butter, 1 large tablespoonful of golden syrup, ⅛ teaspoonful of cream of tartar, essence of lemon, if liked (some prefer its own flavour).

METHOD.—Put the sugar, water, syrup and one-third of the butter in a large pan, dissolve them, then add the cream of tartar and dissolve that.

Let it come to the boil, but in this case do not put the lid on the pan, as the syrup and butter are likely to boil over. Put in the warmed thermometer and boil the sweet, stirring gently all the time, to 260°.

Add the rest of the butter in small pieces (so that it boils quickly into the sugar), and continue to stir it carefully to the temperature of 300°. After the heat reaches 260°, lower the gas, as the flame must not be strong.

Directly it reaches 300° remove the pan from the fire, carefully stir in the essence, if you are using any, and pour the sweet quickly into the buttered tin, making it about half an inch deep. When cold, turn out the toffee and break it into pieces with a small hammer. This toffee is too firm to mark into squares.

FRENCH ALMOND ROCK

INGREDIENTS.—1 lb. of best granulated sugar, ¼ lb. of glucose, good ¼ pint of cold water, ½ lb. of almonds, blanched, cut through once, and well dried.

METHOD.—It is best to blanch the almonds the day before, so that they are perfectly dry.

To do this, put boiling water in a saucepan, drop the almonds in, and let them come to the boil.

Pour them into a strainer and run the cold-water tap on them at once. This makes the skins come off more easily than if they are left hot. Rub off the skins and split each almond.

Weigh the pan, then weigh the glucose into it; add the sugar and water, and dissolve every grain before letting it come to the boil. When it is all dissolved, take out the spoon, put the lid on the pan for a few seconds, and then remove the lid.

Put in the warmed thermometer and boil the sweet, without stirring, to the temperature of 300°, keeping the flame low under the pan. Take the pan off the fire and gently stir in the almonds.

Return the pan to the fire and let the toffee come to the boil again, stirring it most carefully. Directly it turns a pale golden colour pour it gently into a buttered tin, or into buttered rings.

When cold turn out the toffee

FRUIT DISHES

APPLE SNOWBALLS

INGREDIENTS.—4 apples, 2 teaspoonfuls of sugar, 4 cloves, whites of 3 eggs, 1½ dessertspoonfuls of castor sugar, angelica.

METHOD.—Peel the apples and with an apple-corer remove the core from the centre of each, being careful not to break them.

If a corer is not available, scoop out as much of the core as possible from each end of the apple.

Place them on to a baking-sheet, put half a teaspoonful of sugar and a clove into the centre of each apple.

Just cover the bottom of the baking-sheet with water and bake the apples until they are soft, but not broken ; they will take about thirty minutes.

Remove them carefully into a shallow dish and arrange them at equal distances apart.

Whisk the whites to a stiff froth and lightly fold the castor sugar into them.

Cover each apple all over with the white of egg and place in a warm oven for fifteen minutes to set the meringue.

Garnish with stalks of angelica.

Serve cold.

APRICOT BATTER

INGREDIENTS. — 1 small tin of apricots, a pinch of salt, 3 oz. of castor sugar, 1 gill of apricot syrup, ½ lb. of flour, 2 yolks and 2 whites of eggs, ½ pint of milk and water, 2 oz. of dripping.

METHOD.—Mix the flour and salt together and put through a wire sieve.

Make a well in the centre of the flour.

Separate the whites from the yolks of eggs.

Place the yolks in the well in the flour and mix just a sprinkling of flour with them. Gradually add the milk and water to the egg in the centre, and as the milk is added so more flour must be mixed in. Continue in this way until all the flour has been mixed in and all the milk and water added, An even consistency, about the thickness of custard, must be maintained all the time the batter is being mixed. When well mixed, beat for about ten minutes until the surface is covered with bubbles.

Strain the syrup from the apricots and lightly stir one gill of this into the batter and stand it aside for about one hour.

Cut the apricots into quarters ; use only about half of them, as too many would make the batter heavy.

Whisk the whites to a stiff froth.

When ready to cook the batter add the sugar and apricots and lightly fold in the whites of egg.

Melt the dripping in a pie-dish ; when hot pour the batter into it.

Bake in a moderately hot oven for about forty-five minutes.

Place carefully on to a hot dish, cut into six, and serve at once.

NOTE.—The remainder of the apricots can be heated and served with the batter if liked.

APRICOT AND TAPIOCA PUDDING

INGREDIENTS.—1 small tin of apricots, 1½ pints of milk, 3 oz. of sugar, 3 oz. of tapioca, lemon flavouring.

METHOD.—Well wash the tapioca, cover with cold water and soak for a few hours (all night, if possible). The next morning strain off the water (if any).

Place the tapioca in a saucepan with the milk and sugar,-and simmer carefully until it is quite soft and the milk is absorbed.

Flavour with a few drops of lemon essence.

Take two or three apricots from the syrup and cut each into seven or eight pieces, and stir into the tapioca.

Pour this into a wet mould and leave until quite set.

Turn on to a dish carefully ; just ease the tapioca from the sides of the mould and shake gently and it will easily turn out. Pile two or three apricots on the top of the pudding ; the remainder arrange in heaps at either end of the dish.

Pour the apricot syrup round the pudding and serve.

BAKED BANANA PUDDING

INGREDIENTS.—½ lb. of flour, ¼ lb. of margarine, 1 teaspoonful of cream of tartar, 1 orange (rind only), 3 bananas, ¼ lb. of castor sugar, ¼ flat teaspoonful of carbonate of soda, 1 egg, 1 gill of milk.

METHOD.—Sieve the flour with the cream of tartar and carbonate of soda. Beat the sugar and fat to a cream. Grate the orange-rind finely and add.

Add the egg, stir it in quickly and beat well for a few minutes.

Gradually add the flour, etc., alternately with the milk, and mix all together.

Then peel and slice the bananas and stir in.

Turn into a greased pie-dish and put into a moderately hot oven to bake, lessening the heat as required. It will take about one to one hour and a quarter.

BANANA BISCUIT SAND-WICHES

(FOR THE CHILDREN)

INGREDIENTS.—2 bananas, 2 oz. of icing sugar, 3 oz. of ground almonds, 1 oz. of ratafia biscuits, vanilla flavouring, ½ lb. of fancy arrowroot biscuits.

METHOD.—Peel the bananas and mash to a fine pulp. Crush the ratafia biscuits to a powder and add, with the ground almonds and icing sugar.

Mix all together to a paste and flavour with a few drops of vanilla, then spread on arrowroot biscuits and sandwich together in pairs.

BANANA BLANCMANGE

INGREDIENTS.—1¼ pints of milk, 1¾ oz. of cornflour, 1 lemon (rind only), 1 tablespoonful of sugar, 3 bananas.

METHOD.—Mix the cornflour to a smooth paste with some of the milk.

Put the remainder into a saucepan, add the grated lemon-rind and sugar.

When hot, stir on to the cornflour.

Return to the saucepan and bring to the boil, keeping it well-stirred, then boil gently for a few minutes.

Draw aside, stir in the bananas (sliced), and pour into a wet mould.

When set, turn out carefully.

BOILED BANANA PUDDING

INGREDIENTS.—4 bananas, ¾ lb. of flour, 1 teaspoonful of ground ginger, milk to mix—about 1½ gills, 6 oz. of suet, ¼ lb. of sugar, 1 lemon (rind and juice).

METHOD.—Chop the suet finely and mix with the flour and ginger.

Grate the lemon-rind and stir in with the sugar.

Peel and slice the bananas and add. Stir in the strained lemon-juice and then the milk, and mix all together.

Put into a greased pudding-basin, cover with a greased paper and floured pudding-cloth and tie securely.

Stand in a saucepan of boiling water and boil for about two hours and a half.

Turn on to a hot dish and dredge with castor sugar.

NOTE.—The basin must be full, or the water will get into the pudding. This pudding looks very attractive if it is spread with hot jam and coated with desiccated coconut when turned out.

BANANA BORDER

INGREDIENTS.—3 sponge cakes, ¾ pint packet of pineapple jelly, ¾ pint of hot water, 2 or 3 bananas, 1 oz. of almonds, cochineal, ¼ pint of cream, sugar, and vanilla flavouring.

METHOD.—Dissolve the jelly in the hot water and leave until cold.

Crumble the sponge cakes. Blanch and cut up the almonds. Add both these ingredients to the jelly and colour with a few drops of cochineal.

When it is almost beginning to set, stir it up and turn into a wet border mould.

When quite set, turn out carefully.

Peel and slice the bananas and arrange round the border ; put a few pieces also in the centre hole.

Whisk the cream until it stiffens, sweeten and flavour it to taste, and pile in the centre.

BANANA BULBS

INGREDIENTS.—1 round flat sponge cake, ½ pint packet of cherry jelly, 1 gill of hot water, bananas as required, 1 gill of milk, chocolate hundreds and thousands.

METHOD.—Put the sponge cake in a dish ; choose one only a little larger than the sponge. Cut small rounds out all over it, using a cutter about the same size as the bananas. Cut the ends off some bananas and arrange one in each hole, the point end upwards.

Dissolve the jelly in the hot water, and when cold stir in the milk and pour over the sponge.

Leave to set, then sprinkle the sponge with chocolate hundreds and thousands.

NOTE.—The middle part of the bananas can be used for another purpose.

BANANA BUTTER FILLING
(FOR SANDWICHES)

INGREDIENTS.—10 oz. of icing sugar, ¼ lb. of butter, 2 bananas, vanilla flavouring, 2 oz. of ground Brazil nuts.

METHOD.—Roll the lumps out of the sugar and rub through a hair sieve.

Add the butter and beat to a cream.

Peel the bananas and mash to a fine pulp. Add this to the creamed butter and sugar with the ground nuts and vanilla to taste, and mix all together.

BANANA CABINET PUDDING

INGREDIENTS.—3 bananas, 2 macaroon biscuits, 2 sponge fingers, 2 eggs, ¼ pint of milk, about 1 tablespoonful of rum, or a few drops of vanilla or almond flavouring, 1½ dessertspoonfuls of sugar, ½ oz. of leaf gelatine, ½ gill of water, crystallised rose, few silver balls.

METHOD.—To make the custard : Beat the eggs, heat the milk and stir on to them. Pour into a jug and stand in a saucepan of hot water and cook until the custard thickens, keeping it stirred occasionally. When ready, remove from the hot water and sugar to taste, cool slightly and stir in the rum.

Put the gelatine into a saucepan with the water and dissolve slowly, then strain into the other ingredients.

Rinse a mould with cold water, pour about half a gill of custard in the bottom, and leave to set.

Add a macaroon and some slices of banana, cover with custard, then add a crumbled sponge finger and slices of banana and cover with custard.

Repeat this until all the ingredients are used.

Leave to set, turn on to a dish and decorate with a crystallised rose and silver balls.

NOTE.—If preferred, the rum can be omitted, and a few drops of flavouring (vanilla or almond), added to the custard.

BANANA CHARLOTTE

INGREDIENTS.—1 gill of banana pulp, 1½ to 2 teaspoonfuls of castor sugar, vanilla or almond flavouring, ½ gill of cold water, ¼ lb. of Savoy biscuits (use as required), ¼ pint of hot water, 1 gill of cream, 3 tablespoonfuls of milk, ⅜ oz. of leaf gelatine, 2 bananas (sliced), ¼ pint packet of apricot jelly, few chopped pistachio nuts.

METHOD.—Dissolve the jelly in the hot water. To prepare the tin, rinse a small charlotte-tin with cold water, pour a quarter of an inch layer of jelly in the bottom and leave to set.

Cut a piece off each end of the Savoy biscuits so that they will stand quite firmly and just reach to the top of the tin. Place them flat on the board and straighten the sides, then stand them on the jelly and line the sides of the tin. If there are any small cracks between, cover them with a paste made of biscuit crumbs and jelly.

TO MAKE THE FILLING.—Whisk the cream until it stiffens, gradually stir in the banana pulp and milk and add sugar and flavouring to taste.

Put the gelatine in a saucepan with the water and dissolve slowly, then strain into the other ingredients and mix lightly.

When the mixture begins to thicken turn it into the prepared mould and leave to set.

Dip the bottom of it into warm water, turn on to a dish and decorate with sliced bananas and chopped pistachio nuts. The latter must be blanched before being chopped.

CHARTREUSE OF BANANAS

INGREDIENTS.—1½ pint packets of lemon or pineapple jelly, ½ gill of sherry, 5½ gills of hot water, 4 or 5 bananas.

METHOD.—Dissolve the jelly in the hot water; when cold, stir in the sherry. Rinse a plain mould with water, pour a little jelly in the bottom and leave until set, then decorate with pieces of bananas (dipped in jelly). When set, cover with jelly and set again.

Now add sliced bananas (also dipped in jelly), place them all over in rings and let each slice overlap the previous one. When set, cover with jelly to about a depth of half an inch, and when this is set, proceed in the same way until the mould is full.

When quite firm, dip in warm water, turn on to a dish and serve with cream.

NOTE.—Put a little of the jelly aside and use for dipping the bananas in.

BANANA CHEESE SALAD

INGREDIENTS.—4 bananas, 1 egg, 1 or 2 apples, 2 tomatoes, 2 oz. of cheese, lemon-juice.

METHOD.—Boil the egg for fifteen minutes until hard, then cut into slices. Peel and quarter the apple, remove the core, and cut into slices. Grate the cheese finely, slice the tomatoes, peel and slice the bananas. Arrange all these prepared slices tastefully in a dish, sprinkle with lemon-juice and a little grated cheese, pile the remainder of the cheese in the centre and serve with salad cream.

BANANA CHEESE CAKES

INGREDIENTS.—1 egg, its weight in castor sugar, 1½ oz. of margarine, 2 bananas, ½ lemon (rind only), 1 oz. of ground almonds, 2 oz. of flour, jam, about ½ to ¾ lb. of flaky pastry (see p. 252).

METHOD.—Roll out the pastry and line some patty-tins.

Peel the bananas and mash to a pulp.

Cream the fat and sugar.

Add the egg, stir it in quickly, and beat well for a few minutes.

Stir in the grated lemon-rind, flour, and ground almonds, then the banana pulp, and mix all together.

Put a little jam into each patty-tin, then cover with about a teaspoonful of the prepared mixture. Stand on a baking-sheet and bake in a hot oven for about fifteen minutes.

When cold, dredge with castor sugar.

BANANA AND CHOCOLATE MARSHMALLOW

INGREDIENTS.—4 bananas, ½ gill of water, ½ teacupful of tapioca, ¼ lb. of marshmallows, 6d. packet of Mexican chocolate, ½ pint of milk, desiccated coconut.

METHOD.—Wash the tapioca, cover with cold water and soak for an hour or so. Break up the chocolate and melt in a double boiler. Put the marshmallows in a saucepan with the water and dissolve, then stir into the melted chocolate and remove from the fire. Pour off the water (if not all absorbed) and put the tapioca in a saucepan with the milk. Cook gently until tender and the mixture thick, keeping it stirred frequently. Then mix with the chocolate and marshmallow.

Peel and slice two bananas and add.

Turn into a dish, place two halved bananas on the top, sprinkle with some desiccated coconut and serve cold.

BANANA CREAM

INGREDIENTS.—½ pint of banana pulp, ½ pint packet of lemon jelly, ½ teacupful of chopped pineapple, ¼ pint of cream, ⅝ oz. of leaf gelatine, 1¾ gills of hot water, ½ gill of pineapple syrup, 1 dessertspoonful of castor sugar, angelica—for decoration.

METHOD.—Dissolve the jelly in hot water; when cold, rinse a mould with cold water and pour a little jelly in the bottom of it. Leave this to set, then decorate the bottom with a slice of banana and pieces of angelica dipped in jelly. When the decoration is set, cover it with jelly and leave to set again. Peel some bananas and mash up sufficient to make half a pint of pulp. If a sieve is available, rub them through it.

Whisk the cream until it stiffens, then stir in the chopped pineapple, banana pulp, and sugar.

Put the gelatine into a saucepan with the pineapple syrup and dissolve slowly, then strain into the other ingredients.

Mix together lightly, and when it begins to thicken turn into the prepared mould.

When set, dip the mould into warm water, turn on to a dish and garnish with chopped jelly. For the latter use the remainder of the lemon jelly.

BANANA CREAM PIE

INGREDIENTS.—2 bananas, 1½ oz. of flour, 2 eggs, ½ lb. of pastry (see p. 252), rind of 1 lemon, ½ pint of milk, 2½ tablespoonfuls of castor sugar, 1 dessertspoonful of lemon-juice.

METHOD.—Roll out the pastry and line a fairly deep sandwich-tin. Trim the edges neatly, then line the pastry with a round of buttered paper, and put some uncooked rice in the bottom.

Bake in a hot oven for about fifteen to twenty minutes, then remove the paper and rice. Mix the flour to a smooth paste with a little milk, heat the remainder and stir on to it, then return to the saucepan and bring to the boil, keeping it stirred.

Cook for a few minutes, then cool slightly. Add the beaten egg-yolks, grated lemon-rind, and about one to one and a half dessertspoonfuls of the sugar. Cook again for a few minutes, keeping it stirred, but do not boil.

Draw off the fire, peel and slice the bananas, and add, then turn into the pastry-case.

Whisk the egg-whites to a very stiff froth and fold in the remainder of the castor sugar and the lemon-juice. Heap this on the top, dredge lightly with castor sugar and put into a cool oven to set.

BANANA CREAM SAND-WICHES

INGREDIENTS.—4 bananas, 12 slices of brown bread-and-butter (cut from small tin loaf), 12 slices of white bread-and-butter (cut from small tin loaf), 2 oz. of Devonshire cream, marmalade.

METHOD.—Peel the bananas and slice thinly. Spread half the slices of bread-and-butter with marmalade, then with Devonshire cream. Cover with sliced bananas, then with another piece of bread-and-butter. Press down.

trim the edges and cut the sandwiches into three-cornered shapes.

BANANA COLUMNS

INGREDIENTS.—3 bananas (choose straight ones), ½ pint packet of lemon jelly, 3 glacé cherries, a few cloves, 1 lemon (rind only), ½ pint of water, 3 apples, sugar, cochineal.

METHOD.—Peel and core the apples and place in a pie-dish with half a pint of water.

Grate the lemon-rind finely.

Put a clove, a little sugar, and some grated lemon-rind in the centre hole of each apple.

Bake them gently until tender, being careful to keep them whole. Then lift on to small plates.

Dissolve the jelly in the water in which the apples were cooked—if not sufficient, make up to half a pint with hot water—then strain it. If liked, the jelly can be flavoured with a tablespoonful of sherry.

Pour half the jelly into another basin and colour with a few drops of cochineal.

Put a little jelly in the centre hole of each apple, and when nearly set, peel the bananas, cut a piece off one end, and stand one in each apple.

Stick a cherry on the top, and when the remainder of the jelly is set, chop it up and serve some of each colour round the apples.

BANANA CORONET

INGREDIENTS.—Small sponge-ring, 1 pint packet of pineapple jelly, 1 pint of hot water, 1 oz. of almonds, 2 tablespoonfuls of jam, 7 or 8 bananas, few glacé cherries.

METHOD.—Dissolve the jelly in the hot water. Blanch and chop up the almonds. Split the sponge-ring into halves and spread with jam, then sprinkle with some of the nuts.

Put it in a dish and soak with a little jelly.

Peel the bananas and split five or six of them into halves, lengthways. Cut a small piece off one end, and make them all the same length. Make small incisions all round the middle of the border, and as you do so, stick half a banana into each, making them stand up in the form of a coronet.

Mash up the trimmings of bananas and mix with a little jam and a few nuts, and put in the centre hole. When the jelly is just beginning to set, baste the bananas carefully over with some of it, then place slices of bananas all round the edge of the dish, and cover these with jelly. When quite firm, place half a glacé cherry on top of each half-banana, and if there is still any jelly over, chop it up and put in the centre of the coronet with a few of the chopped nuts.

BANANA CRESCENTS

INGREDIENTS.—Bananas (as required), 4 or 5 slices of tinned pine-apple, few glacé cherries.

METHOD.—Peel the bananas and cut into slices. Cut the pineapple slices into halves, and place the two pieces together (one on top of the other).

Put these in rather a shallow dish, and arrange slices of banana on them in the form of a crescent, making each slice overlap the previous one.

Place a thick piece of banana in the centre hole of the pineapple, and stick a cherry on top of it. Pour a little syrup round and serve with cream.

BANANA FLAN

INGREDIENTS.—2 or 3 bananas, 7 oz. of flour, 1 flat teaspoonful of baking-powder, ¼ lb. of margarine, 1 egg-yolk, water, apricot jam.

METHOD.—Sieve the flour and baking-powder.

Rub in the margarine.

Break up the egg-yolk and mix with a spoonful of water, then add to the dry ingredients, with more water as required to make a very stiff paste.

Form it into a smooth lump, then roll it out to almost a quarter of an inch thick and cut out a round.

Grease a flan-ring, and place on a greased baking-sheet. Put the pastry inside this ring, and line it, pressing it a little thinner in the bottom.

Trim the edges, line the pastry with a round of buttered paper, and shake in some uncooked rice.

Place in a moderate oven and bake for about twenty-five or thirty minutes. Then lift up the flan-ring, remove the paper and rice and leave the pastry-case on a sieve until cold. It should only be *very lightly* browned.

Peel the bananas and cut into slices, and arrange (each slice overlapping the previous one) in the ring.

Heat about half a pound of apricot jam and rub through a wire sieve, then cover the bananas with it.

BANANA FOOL

INGREDIENTS.—Bananas as required, juice of 1 orange or lemon, 1 egg, 1½ gills of milk, ¼ pint of cream, orange or vanilla flavouring, sugar to taste, ½ pint packet of lemon or orange jelly, ½ pint of hot water.

METHOD.—Dissolve the jelly in hot water and leave to set.

To MAKE THE EGG CUSTARD.—Beat up the egg, heat the milk and stir on to it, pour into a jug, stand it in a saucepan of hot water and cook until it thickens. Be careful not to let it curdle, and keep it stirred occasionally.

When ready, remove from the hot water, add a few drops of flavouring and sugar to taste, then leave until cold. Peel and mash sufficient bananas to make half to three-quarters of a pint of pulp, add the strained orange or lemon-juice, and when well mixed stir in the custard. Add sugar as required. Whisk the cream until it stiffens, sweeten and flavour it to taste, and stir half of it into the banana pulp, etc. Turn into small glasses, chop up the jelly and sprinkle a little on the top, and heap the remainder of the cream in the centre.

BANANA FRITTERS

INGREDIENTS.—8 bananas, lemon-juice, ¼ lb. of flour, pinch of salt, 1 gill of water, 1 egg-white, deep fat for frying, castor sugar.

METHOD.—Sieve the flour and salt and mix to a smooth batter with the water. Whisk the egg-white until slightly frothy, and stir in.

Beat well for a few minutes, then leave the batter to stand for a few hours. Peel the bananas and cut each into two or three pieces. Sprinkle with lemon-juice and leave for a few minutes.

Dip some of them into the batter and coat well, then put into a deep pan of hot fat and fry until golden-brown. Drain on paper. Coat and fry the others in the same way. Serve on a lace paper, and sprinkle with castor sugar.

NOTE.—When the fat is hot a faint smoke will rise from it.

GINGER BANANAS

INGREDIENTS.—6 bananas, 1 gill of cream, 3 oz. of preserved ginger, apricot jam, a few almonds, castor sugar, vanilla.

METHOD.—Blanch and chop some almonds. Place them on a sheet of paper on a tin, and put into the oven until a golden-brown. Peel the bananas and split into halves, length-ways, then scoop out a little ridge down the centre.

Cut the ginger into tiny pieces and place along this centre hollow. Heat a little jam, and if it is stiff, thin down with just a very small quantity of water, then rub through a sieve.

Spread the edges of the halved bananas with this, then coat with the prepared almonds.

Whisk the cream until it stiffens, sweeten and flavour it to taste.

Put this into an icing bag and force a line of cream down the centre of each halved banana.

Decorate with pieces of ginger.

BANANA GLOBE

INGREDIENTS.—¼ lb. of rice, vanilla flavouring, 4 bananas, 1 tablespoonful of castor sugar, ¼ pint packet of lemon jelly, ¼ pint of hot water, 1 pint of milk, 1 oz. of butter, angelica.

METHOD.—Wash the rice, put it into a saucepan with the butter and milk, and cook very gently until tender and all the milk absorbed and the mixture very stiff, keeping it stirred frequently.

When ready, stir in the sugar and a few drops of vanilla. Turn the rice into a pudding-cloth and tie in a round ball, then hang up and leave until the next day, when it will be quite firm.

Dissolve the jelly in the hot water, and leave until almost beginning to set. Peel and slice the bananas thinly.

Remove the pudding-cloth and stand the rice in a shallow dish (if liked,

put an upturned saucer in the dish and stand it on that).

Baste it with jelly and dip the banana slices in jelly and arrange all over it. Then put the remainder of the slices and jelly round the dish.

When quite set, decorate with a few stalks of angelica.

Serve with jam.

BANANA GRAPE FRUIT

INGREDIENTS.—2 grape fruit, 4 bananas, desiccated coconut, castor sugar, glacé cherries.

METHOD.—Peel the bananas and mash to a fine pulp. Cut the grape fruit into halves (across the sections), remove the centre pith and pips. Then loosen the fruit from the rind and pith by cutting it all round the edge. Now cut between each section.

Turn all the grape fruit pulp and juice into a bowl (but not the skin), and mash up; then mix with the banana pulp and dredge with castor sugar.

Remove the remaining skin from inside the grape-fruit rinds, then serve the prepared pulp in the latter, and sprinkle with a little desiccated coconut.

Arrange a glacé cherry in the centre.

BANANA FRUIT SALAD

INGREDIENTS.—4½ bananas, ¼ lb. of grapes, 1 large or 2 small oranges, 2 slices of tinned pineapple, 1 round of lettuce.

METHOD.—Prepare and wash the lettuce, then drain thoroughly.

Peel the bananas, split into halves, then into three or four pieces.

Peel and quarter the oranges, remove pips and pith.

Cut up the pineapple.

Make a bed of lettuce leaves in a dish and arrange the prepared fruit and grapes on them.

Serve with mayonnaise sauce.

BANANA HEDGEHOGS

INGREDIENTS.—4 bananas, apricot jam, desiccated coconut, 2 oz. of almonds.

METHOD.—Heat some apricot jam, and if very stiff, thin down with just a little water, then rub through a sieve. Peel the bananas and spread with jam, then coat with desiccated coconut.

Blanch the almonds and split into pieces, and arrange all over the bananas.

BANANA HONEYCOMB

INGREDIENTS.—4 bananas, 1 pint of hot water, 1 pint packet of vanilla jelly, cochineal.

METHOD.—Dissolve the jelly in the hot water and leave until it is beginning to set. Peel the bananas and mash to a fine pulp, then add to the jelly and whisk all together for a few minutes. Stir in a few drops of cochineal. Turn into a wet mould and leave to set, then turn on to a dish.

HOT BANANA PUDDING

INGREDIENTS.—2 eggs, 3 oz. of margarine, 5 oz. of castor sugar, 4 oz. of flour, 4 oz. of cornflour, 1 tablespoonful of lemon-juice, grated rind of $\frac{1}{2}$ a lemon, 4 bananas, 1 teaspoonful of baking-powder, $\frac{3}{4}$ gill of milk, jam.

METHOD.—Separate the yolks from the whites of egg.

Mix the flour, cornflour, and baking-powder together, and put through a sieve.

Grate the lemon-rind and add to the flour, etc.

Peel the bananas and mash them and mix with the lemon-juice.

Whisk the whites to a stiff froth.

Beat the sugar and margarine together until they are like thick cream.

Beat the yolks of eggs in separately.

Add the flour and cornflour, etc., and mix in thoroughly, together with the milk and mashed bananas.

Lastly, fold in whisked whites of eggs.

Put into a greased pie-dish and bake in a moderately hot oven for about one and a quarter hours. Turn on to a hot dish, and serve with hot jam.

BANANA LAYER CAKE

INGREDIENTS.—$\frac{1}{2}$ lb. of castor sugar, $\frac{1}{2}$ lb. of margarine, 10 oz. of flour, $1\frac{1}{4}$ teaspoonfuls of cream of tartar, $\frac{1}{3}$ flat teaspoonful of carbonate of soda, 3 eggs, milk, 2 bananas, 1 oz. of shelled walnuts.

FOR THE ICING.—12 oz. of soft brown sugar, 1 gill of cold water (take light measure), a pinch of cream of tartar, 2 egg-whites.

METHOD.—Grease a cake-tin and line with greased paper to stand above the top. Sieve the flour with the cream of tartar and carbonate of soda.

Beat the sugar and fat to a cream.

Add each egg separately, stir in quickly, and beat well for a few minutes before adding the next.

When all are added, gradually stir in the flour, etc., with some milk as required.

Mix together lightly, turn into the prepared tin, and put into a moderately hot oven to bake, lessening the heat as required.

It will take about one hour and a quarter.

When cooked, put on a sieve and leave until cold, then split into three.

To MAKE THE ICING

Put the sugar and water into a saucepan and dissolve slowly. Add a good pinch of cream of tartar, bring to the boil and boil until a small quantity, when dropped into cold water and left for a few seconds, becomes a fairly soft ball if taken out and rubbed between your fingers.

When ready, pour it gradually on to the stiffly whisked egg-whites, stirring all the time.

Beat well, then spread a little over the first layer of cake, cover with sliced banana and a few chopped walnuts. Spread some icing on the underside of the next layer and place on firmly.

Repeat this, then add the top layer, and coat the cake with the remainder of the icing (just pour it over).

Decorate the centre with a slice of banana and leaves of angelica, and when the icing is set put a cake frill round.

NOTE.—It is advisable to make the icing in two lots, otherwise it becomes rather stiff and is difficult to coat the cake evenly.

BANANA LIQUEUR CAKE

INGREDIENTS.—1 round sponge cake, $\frac{1}{2}$ gill of maraschino, $\frac{3}{4}$ gill of cream, 2 oz. of almonds, about 1 gill of milk, 4 bananas, sugar and vanilla.

METHOD.—Put the sponge cake in a dish and soak it with hot milk and maraschino. Blanch and split the almonds and stick them all over it.

Peel the bananas, mash them to a pulp, and put this in the bottom of the dish round the base of the sponge instead of custard. If the sponge-cake has a hole in the centre, this can also be filled with banana pulp.

Whisk the cream until it stiffens, then sweeten and flavour it to taste. Put it into an icing bag with a rose tube fixed in the end and decorate the top of the sponge, then force the remainder round the dish on top of the banana pulp.

BANANA DE LUXE

INGREDIENTS.—5 bananas, 2½ gills of hot water, ¾ gill of cream, ¾ pint packet of cherry or orange jelly, 1½ tablespoonfuls of sherry, few dried walnuts, sugar and vanilla.

METHOD.—Dissolve the jelly in hot water and leave until cold, then stir in the sherry.

Pour this into five champagne or similar-shaped glasses, dividing it equally.

When nearly set, peel and slice two bananas and place a few pieces in the jelly in each glass, then leave until quite set.

Peel the remainder of the bananas and mash it to a pulp, then pile on top of the jelly.

Whisk the cream until it stiffens, and sweeten and flavour it to taste. Heap on top of the banana pulp and sprinkle some chopped walnuts over it.

MARZIPAN BANANAS

(FOR THE CHILDREN'S PARTY)

INGREDIENTS.—6 bananas, ½ lb. of icing sugar, 7 oz. of ground almonds, about 1 to 1½ egg-whites, vanilla flavouring, apricot-yellow colouring.

METHOD.—Roll the lumps out of the sugar and rub through a hair sieve.

Add the ground almonds and mix together.

Whisk the egg-whites stiffly and add sufficient to make a stiff paste, at the same time add a few drops of vanilla, and work in sufficient colouring to make the paste about the same tint as a banana skin.

Work the paste until smooth and evenly coloured, then divide into six portions.

Dust the board with icing sugar, roll out each piece to an oblong shape rather longer than the bananas and wide enough to go round them.

Peel the bananas and mould a piece of paste round each one, so that they resemble the fruit before being peeled.

Then, with a small brush and some browning (gravy browning) make little brown masks on them and make them look as natural as possible.

BANANA MERINGUE CUSTARD

INGREDIENTS.—6 bananas, 2 egg-yolks and 3 whites, ½ pint of milk, 1 teaspoonful of granulated sugar, juice of ½ grape fruit, 5 sponge cakes, 2 dessertspoonfuls of cornflour, ¼ lb. of castor sugar.

METHOD.—Mix the cornflour to a smooth paste with a little milk, heat the remainder and stir on to it. Then return to the saucepan and bring to the boil, keeping it stirred all the time.

Let this cook slowly for a few minutes, then draw aside. Add the granulated sugar and cool slightly.

Beat up the yolks and add, stir over a low burner for a few minutes to cook the eggs, but be careful not to let it boil. Add a few drops of vanilla flavouring.

Peel the bananas and mash to a pulp. Crumble up the sponge-cakes and add to the banana pulp with the strained juice of the grape fruit.

Mix these together, turn into a dish, add the cornflour custard, and leave until cold.

Whisk the egg-whites to a very stiff froth and fold in the castor sugar.

Heap this on the top, then put into a cool oven to set the meringue.

Serve cold.

BANANA MOULDS

INGREDIENTS.—2 sponge cakes, ¼ pint of milk, 5 or 6 bananas, ¼ pint of cream, ½ gill of sherry, ⅝ oz. of leaf gelatine, ½ gill of water, about 1 dessert-spoonful of castor sugar, few pistachio nuts.

METHOD.—Bring the milk to the boil, crumble the sponge cakes and add to it. Leave until cold and well soaked, then beat up with a fork.

Peel the bananas and mash to a pulp, whisk the cream until it stiffens, stir in the banana pulp, sugar, sherry, and sponge-cake and milk pulp.

Put the gelatine in a saucepan with the water and dissolve slowly, then strain into the other ingredients and mix all together lightly.

When it begins to thicken, turn into small wet moulds and leave until set.

Turn out and sprinkle with chopped pistachio nuts ; if liked, garnish the dish with chopped jelly.

To prepare the nuts, blanch, then chop finely.

BANANA PLUM PUDDING

INGREDIENTS.—4 bananas, ¼ lb. of flour, 6 oz. of raisins, ¼ lb. of peel, 7 oz. of suet, 1 oz. of almonds, 4 tea-spoonfuls of ground almonds, 1 tea-spoonful of ground ginger, ¼ lb. of sultanas, ¼ lb. of currants, ¼ lb. of sugar, 2 eggs, 1 gill of milk.

METHOD.—Wash, pick over and dry the fruit and stone the raisins.

Chop the suet finely and mix with the flour and ground ginger.

Cut up the peel, blanch and cut up the almonds and add to the flour with the prepared fruit, ground almonds, and sugar.

Mix well, then peel and slice the bananas and stir in.

Whisk up the eggs and add to the dry ingredients with the milk.

Mix together thoroughly, then put into a well-greased basin,. cover with a greased paper and floured pudding-cloth, and boil for about six hours.

BANANA ROLLS

INGREDIENTS.—About 1 lb. of flaky pastry (see p. 252), jam, 6 bananas.

METHOD.—Roll out the pastry fairly thinly and cut into pieces about four by four and a half inches, then turn on to the other side and spread a little jam over them.

Peel the bananas and cut across into halves.

Place a piece of banana on each piece of pastry, damp the edges and fold over like a sausage-roll.

Trim the edges, place the rolls on a baking-sheet, and brush over with milk.

Put into a *hot* oven to bake. They will take about fifteen to twenty minutes.

When cold, dredge with castor sugar.

BANANA SAVOURY

INGREDIENTS.—3 bananas, 6 finger slices of bread, 1 small cream cheese, seasoning, lemon-juice, 1 hard egg-yolk, fat for frying.

METHOD.—Split the bananas into halves and cut a small piece off the end of each half.

Cut slices of bread the same length as the prepared bananas and fry in deep fat until golden-brown. Then drain on paper.

Spread a thick layer of cream cheese on the fried bread and season with pepper.

Place a piece of banana on each, sprinkle with lemon-juice and pepper and garnish with powdered egg-yolk.

To powder the egg-yolk, just rub it through a wire sieve or strainer.

BANANA SCONES

INGREDIENTS.—¼ lb. of flour, pinch of salt, ¼ flat teaspoonful of bicarbonate of soda, 1 teaspoonful of cream of tartar, ¼ lb. of fine oatmeal, 1 oz. of sugar, 1 oz. of margarine, 2 bananas, milk.

METHOD.—Sieve the flour, salt, soda, cream of tartar, and oatmeal.

Rub in the margarine, then mix in the sugar.

Peel the bananas, mash finely, and add to the dry ingredients with just a very little milk as required.

Mix all to a fairly soft dough, then turn on to a pastry-board and roll out thickly.

Cut into rounds, then cut across into halves.

Place on a baking-sheet, brush with milk, and bake in a hot oven for about ten to fifteen minutes. Split open and spread with butter.

BANANA SEED CAKES

INGREDIENTS.—¾ lb of flour, 3 bananas, 5 oz. of margarine, 4 flat teaspoonfuls of caraway seeds, 2 teaspoonfuls of baking-powder, 1 oz. of candied lemon-peel, 6 oz. of sugar, 1 egg, milk.

METHOD.—Peel the bananas and mash finely. Sieve the flour and baking-powder. Cut up the peel and add to the flour with the caraway seeds. Cream the sugar and margarine. Add the egg, stir it in quickly and beat for a few minutes.

Stir in some of the flour, etc., add the mashed bananas, then the remainder of the flour and some milk as required.

Mix all together, put into small baking-cups (about half-fill them), stand on a baking-sheet, and put into a hot oven to bake.

They will take about twenty minutes.

BANANA SOUFFLE

INGREDIENTS.—1½ gills of banana pulp, 3 oz. of castor sugar, ⅜ oz. of leaf gelatine, ¼ pint packet of lemon jelly, few silver balls, 2 eggs, ½ lemon, ¼ gill of water, 1 gill of hot water, angelica, 6 small soufflé cases.

METHOD.—Pin a band of foolscap paper round the outside of each soufflé case so that it stands an inch above the top.

Separate the eggs. Put the yolks into a basin with the sugar, strained lemon-juice, and grated rind.

Whisk these ingredients over a saucepan of hot water until thick and creamy, cool slightly, then stir in the banana pulp.

Whisk the egg-whites to a very stiff froth and fold in.

Put the gelatine into a saucepan with the water and dissolve slowly, then strain into the other ingredients and mix together lightly.

Keep it stirred occasionally until it begins to thicken, turn into the prepared soufflé cases, filling them to about half an inch from the top of the paper, and leave to set.

Dissolve the jelly in the hot water, and when cold and beginning to set, pour a little on top of each soufflé.

When set, remove the foolscap paper and decorate with silver balls and leaves of angelica.

BANANA TOAD-IN-THE-HOLE

INGREDIENTS.—3 bananas, 2½ gills of milk, 1 egg, lemon-juice, 5 oz. of flour, castor sugar, pinch of salt, dripping.

METHOD.—Sieve the flour and salt. Make a well in the centre, pour in the egg, and mix with some of the flour.

Take one and a half gills of the milk and add gradually, working in the flour by degrees.

When it is all mixed to a smooth batter, beat well for a few minutes.

Then stir in the remainder of the milk and leave the batter to stand for an hour or so.

Peel the bananas and cut into halves crossways, sprinkle with castor sugar and lemon-juice.

Melt a lump of dripping in a pie-dish; when hot, pour in the batter and put in the bananas, covering them with some of the batter.

Put into a fairly hot oven to bake, lessening the heat as required.

It will take about three-quarters of an hour.

Serve with castor sugar and lemon-juice.

BANANA TOAST

INGREDIENTS.—¾ gill of banana pulp, 5 oz. of cheese, seasoning, 3 oz. of butter, 1 egg-yolk, 6 or 7 rounds of bread, chopped parsley.

METHOD.—Toast the bread, then spread with butter and keep hot. Grate the cheese finely. Peel and mash up sufficient bananas to make the pulp.

Melt one ounce of butter in a saucepan, add the grated cheese and banana pulp, and stir over a low burner until creamy. Draw aside, stir in the egg-yolk, and cook gently for a few minutes, then season with pepper, salt, and mixed mustard.

Spread on the prepared toast and garnish with finely chopped parsley.

BANANA TWISTS

INGREDIENTS.—2 bananas, 2 oz. of cornflour, 2 oz. of castor sugar, 3 oz.

of margarine, 7 oz. of flour, 1 egg-yolk, vanilla flavouring.

METHOD.—Sieve the flour and corn-flour.

Peel the bananas and mash to a fine pulp.

Cream the fat and sugar, then add the egg-yolk and stir the mixture quickly for a few minutes.

Stir in the mashed banana, flour, and cornflour, also a few drops of vanilla, and mix all together to a stiff paste.

Turn it on to a floured board and roll out. Cut into strips about six or seven inches long and three-eighths of an inch wide, twist each strip and cross the two ends.

Place on a slightly buttered tin, put into a moderate oven, and bake gently until biscuit colour. They will take about fifteen minutes, or perhaps a little longer.

BANANA PANCAKES

INGREDIENTS.—6 oz. of flour, pinch of salt, 1 egg and 1 extra yolk, 3 gills of milk, lard for frying (about 6 or 8 oz.). FOR THE FILLING.—2 bananas, 1 oz. of castor sugar, 1 oz. of butter, 1 orange, 1 lemon, 1 dessertspoonful of rum.

METHOD.—Add a pinch of salt to the flour and put through a sieve. Make a well in the centre, pour in the whole egg and yolk and mix with a small quantity of the flour.

Take half a pint of the milk and add it gradually until it is all mixed to a smooth batter, then beat well for a few minutes.

Stir in the remainder of the milk gradually, and leave the batter to stand for an hour or so.

TO MAKE THE FILLING.—Beat the sugar and butter to a cream. Peel the bananas and mash to a pulp and stir in. Add also the grated orange and lemon-rind and the rum, and mix all together.

TO FRY THE PANCAKES.—Melt a small piece of lard in a frying-pan. Let this get hot, then pour in sufficient batter just to cover the bottom of the pan. If using a small frying-pan, barely half a gill of batter is sufficient for each pancake.

Fry until golden brown, then toss or turn on to the other side.

When both sides are brown, turn it on to a baking-sheet lined with paper, spread some of the prepared filling over, then fold into halves, and add a squeeze of lemon-juice.

Fry the remainder of the pancakes in the same way.

Serve on a dish paper and dredge with castor sugar.

BANANA AND WALNUT SALAD

INGREDIENTS.—4 bananas, 1½ oz. of shelled walnuts, 1 round lettuce, mayonnaise.

METHOD.—Prepare and wash the lettuce in the usual way, then drain thoroughly.

Peel and slice the bananas.

Line a dish with lettuce leaves, arrange the banana slices, and walnuts on top of them, and pour a little mayonnaise in the centre.

BAKED BLACKBERRY AND APPLE PUDDING

INGREDIENTS.—1 lb. of apples, 1 lb. of blackberries, 3 tablespoonfuls of Demerara sugar, 1 tablespoonful of water, 6 oz. of breadcrumbs, ½ lb. of suet, 1 teaspoonful of baking-powder, water to mix, ½ lb. of flour.

METHOD.—Peel, core and slice the apples. Well wash and pick over the blackberries. Make the breadcrumbs (rub some stale bread on a bread grater or through a wire sieve). Chop the suet finely. Mix well together the flour, baking-powder, shredded suet, and breadcrumbs. Add sufficient water to make a stiff paste—not too dry, but not sticky. Grease a pie-dish, cut off one-third of the pastry and put aside, then roll out the large piece and line the bottom and sides of the pie-dish with it. Trim off any rough pieces. Put in the prepared fruit mixed together, also the sugar and water. Roll out the small piece of pastry, together with the trimmings, until it is large enough to cover the top of the pie-dish. Fix it on to the pastry that lines the dish by damping the edge with cold water ; make the edges look neat.

Brush over with milk and bake in a moderately hot oven for about one hour and a half. Sprinkle with castor sugar, serve hot in the pie-dish with either custard or cream.

NOTE.—The sugar should be put in the middle of the fruit, as it then gets well mixed with it. If it touches the crust it is apt to make it heavy. Cranberries may be used, if liked, instead of blackberries.

CHERRY CREAM

INGREDIENTS.—¾ lb. of cherries, 2 oz. of granulated sugar, 1 gill of water, ½ pint of custard (½ pint of milk, vanilla, 1½ oz. of sugar, custard-powder), 1 gill of cream, ½ oz. of French leaf gelatine, 1 pint packet of cherry jelly, ¾ pint of hot water, a few glacé cherries.

METHOD.—Dissolve the jelly in hot water and leave until cool. Stalk and wash the cherries. Put the granulated sugar and water in a saucepan and boil for five minutes. Add the cherries to the syrup and cook until quite tender. Scald a fancy mould and rinse with cold water, and mask with some of the jelly (as explained for Mixed Fruit Jelly on page 600). Decorate the bottom of the mould with glacé cherries (previously dipped in jelly; when set, cover with jelly and set again. Strain the syrup from the cherries and remove the stones from the latter. Make the custard according to directions given on the packet. Add sugar and leave until cold. Dissolve the gelatine in half a gill of cherry syrup. Whip the cream until it thickens, and lightly mix it with the custard. Add the stoned cherries, and, lastly, strain in the dissolved gelatine. Mix all together and stir over ice until it begins to thicken. Pour into the prepared mould. When set turn on to a dish and chop the remainder of the jelly and serve round it.

NOTE.—If liked, use a small tin of cherries instead of stewing fresh ones.

DRIED FRUIT PUDDING

INGREDIENTS.—2 oz. of dried apple rings, 2 oz. of dried pears, 2 oz. of dried peaches, 3 oz. of raisins, 3 oz. of Demerara sugar, 4 oz. of semolina, 2 pints of milk, grated rind of 1 small lemon, 1 gill of cream, 2 whites of eggs, 2 dessertspoonfuls of granulated sugar, angelica.

METHOD.—Thoroughly wash all the dried fruits, including the raisins. Cut the peaches and pears each into three or four pieces.

Put all the fruit into a basin and well cover with cold water, and soak for twenty-four hours. Put them into a saucepan with the water in which they have been soaking, add the Demerara sugar and cook well until they are quite soft. Take out the fruit and put into a dish and boil the syrup fast for about five minutes to thicken it. When cold pour over the fruit.

Put the milk on to boil, sprinkle in the semolina, add the grated rind and granulated sugar and cook until quite soft and creamy. Stir it well to keep it from burning. When slightly cool, pour over the fruit, but do not mix together. Whisk together to a stiff froth the cream and white of egg; fold into it about a teaspoonful of castor sugar. Shake on to the top of the semolina and decorate with strips of angelica.

If a plain pudding is required, this may be served without the addition of the cream and white of egg.

FRUIT COMPOTE

INGREDIENTS.—½ lb. of black currants, ½ lb. of red currants, ½ lb. of strawberries, ½ lb. of raspberries, 1 pint of gooseberries, ½ lb. of cherries, 3 to 4 tablespoonfuls of Demerara sugar, 3 gills of cold water.

METHOD.—Put the sugar and water on to boil for about five minutes, until a syrup is formed.

String the currants, top and tail the gooseberries, and pick over the cherries, strawberries, and raspberries.

Wash all the fruit well, being very careful with the raspberries.

Add the cherries to the syrup, and when they have cooked slowly for about ten to fifteen minutes, add the rest of the fruit and cook all slowly until tender. Do not get the fruit broken.

When cool pour into a china or glass bowl, and serve with thick cream.

MIXED FRUIT JELLY

INGREDIENTS.—1 small tin of fruit salad, 1 pint packet of cherry jelly, ¾ pint of hot water, cochineal.

METHOD.—Dissolve the jelly in the hot water, then put aside until cold, but not set.

Strain the juice from the fruit salad and add one gill of it to the dissolved jelly, and, if not a good colour, add a few drops of cochineal.

FRUIT SALAD

INGREDIENTS.—2 oranges, 2 apples, 3 bananas, a few black and white grapes, a small piece of melon, a few strawberries, raspberries, and white heart cherries, castor sugar, 4 gills of water, 8 oz. of granulated sugar, 3 tablespoonfuls of sherry, cochineal, 1½ gills of cream.

METHOD.—Prepare all the fruit. Peel and quarter the oranges, removing pith and pips. Peel, core, quarter and slice the apples, then cut across.

Peel and slice the bananas.

Cut the melon into small squares, having removed the skin and seeds.

Wash and pick over the other fruits. Mix them all together, sprinkle well with castor sugar, and leave them to soak for about an hour. (Leave out a few black grapes for decoration.)

Boil the granulated sugar and water together until a thick syrup is formed. Skim it well.

When cold, add three tablespoonfuls of sherry and sufficient cochineal to make a pale pink syrup.

Heap the raw fruit in fancy custard glasses; add a little syrup to each glass, but not sufficient to cover the fruit. Whisk the cream until it thickens. Shake a little on to each, and garnish with black grapes.

Rinse out a fancy mould and mask it with some of the jelly. To do this put two or three tablespoonfuls of jelly into the mould, turn it on to its side, and move the mould round on a piece of ice until a thin coating of jelly is formed all round the sides and bottom of the tin.

Set one or two pieces of fruit in the bottom of the mould, having previously dipped them in jelly.

When set cover with jelly and set again.

Proceed in this way until all the fruit and jelly are used.

When the whole jelly is firm, dip it into warm water and turn on to a dish.

GOOSEBERRY AND CHERRY CUSTARD

INGREDIENTS.—1½ pints of gooseberries, ½ lb. of cherries, 3 oz. of Demerara sugar, 1 gill of water, ½ pint packet of cherry jelly.

FOR THE CUSTARD.—1 pint of milk, 1 oz. of sugar, vanilla flavouring, custard-powder, ½ pint of hot water.

METHOD.—Dissolve the jelly in hot water and put in a cold place until set. Put the sugar and water in a saucepan to boil for five minutes to a syrup. Top and tail the gooseberries, stalk the cherries, and wash both well. Put the cherries into the syrup, and simmer for about ten minutes; then add the gooseberries and simmer all until tender.

Make the custard according to directions given on the packet, and set aside until cool. Put the stewed fruit into the bottom of a glass dish and very carefully cover with the custard, but do not mix with the fruit. Leave until quite cold.

When the cherry jelly is set put it on to a piece of wet kitchen paper and chop it slightly; do not chop it too much, otherwise it will look cloudy. Garnish the top of the custard with the jelly. Serve very cold.

NOTE.—Do not use an iron-lined saucepan for stewing the fruit, as this spoils the colour and flavour of it. Use either enamel, earthenware, or aluminium ware

MULBERRY SYRUP

INGREDIENTS.—3 lb. of mulberries, 2¼ lb. of loaf sugar, 3 tablespoonfuls of cold water.

(Loganberries may be treated in the same way.)

METHOD.—Well pick over the mulberries, and, if very dirty, carefully wash and well drain them.

Put into a jar with one pound of sugar and the water, and cover with a saucer.

Stand the jar in a saucepan of water

and cook slowly at the side of the fire for three or four hours.

Strain through a jelly-bag or tanny-cloth.

Put into a saucepan with the rest of the sugar and boil for twenty to thirty minutes to thicken the syrup. Skim it to keep it clean.

Bottle it and keep it airtight.

ORANGE SYRUP

INGREDIENTS.—12 oranges, ¾ lb. of lump sugar.

METHOD.—Squeeze the juice from the oranges and strain it. (There will be about three-quarters of a pint altogether.)

Boil with the sugar until thick, skim it and bottle.

PEAR SOUFFLE

INGREDIENTS.—2½ oz. of best white flour, 1½ gills of milk, 2 oz. of castor sugar, 2 oz. of margarine or butter, ½ gill of pear syrup, 3 eggs, 2 halves of pears (tinned or bottled fruit).

METHOD.—Take a soufflé tin, well grease it, and tie round the outside of it a greased paper so that it reaches about two or three inches above the top of the tin. Melt the margarine in a saucepan, add the flour, and mix to a smooth paste, add the milk and pear syrup, and stir well over the fire until it boils and thickens and does not stick to the saucepan. This is the foundation for the soufflé and must be well cooked before the other ingredients are added.

Separate the whites from the yolks of eggs, and beat each yolk separately into the foundation just made, having first slightly cooled it.

Add the sugar, cut the pears into small pieces and add.

Whisk the whites of eggs to a stiff froth, and lightly fold them into the other ingredients.

Pour all into the prepared soufflé tin, cover with a greased paper and steam for one and a half hours. Turn carefully on to a hot dish, and serve with pear sauce.

NOTE.—When cooked the soufflé should have risen well and feel spongy on the top.

Soufflés must be taken up directly they are cooked, or they lose their lightness.

If the soufflé is steamed in a saucepan of water the water must not reach more than one-third up the side of the soufflé tin.

It is also advisable to stand the tin on a thick piece of paper, or on a saucer turned upside down, so that it does not touch the bottom of the saucepan.

PEAR SAUCE

INGREDIENTS.—½ gill of pear syrup, 1½ oz. of castor sugar, 1 gill of water, 2 halves of pears.

METHOD.—Boil together for five minutes the pear syrup, sugar, and water. Cut the pears into small dice and add.

Pour hot sauce round soufflé.

PINEAPPLE SOUFFLE

INGREDIENTS.—1 large tin of sliced pineapple, 1½ gills of milk, 4 oz. of castor sugar, 2 eggs and 1 extra white, ½ to ¾ oz. of French leaf gelatine, crystallised roses.

METHOD.—Separate the yolks from the whites of eggs. Beat the yolks and add to them the milk. Pour this into a jug, stand the jug in a saucepan of cold water, and stir the custard over the fire until it thickens, being careful not to let it get too hot or it will curdle. When cooked stand aside to cool.

Rub the pineapple slices through a hair or wire sieve, then mix with the custard and castor sugar.

Dissolve the gelatine in about three-quarters of a gill of the pineapple syrup, but do not boil it. Add a pinch of salt to the whites of eggs and whisk them to a stiff froth, then lightly fold them into the pineapple, etc.

Lastly, strain in the dissolved gelatine and stir it all together. Rinse a fancy mould with cold water. Pour this mixture into it and leave in a cold place until set. Turn carefully on to a dish. Sprinkle the top with some crushed crystallised roses.

RHUBARB FLAN

INGREDIENTS.—6 oz. of flour, 4 oz. of margarine, ½ teaspoonful of baking-powder, a pinch of salt, 1 yolk of egg, ½ gill of water, 1 lb. of rhubarb,

3 oz. of castor sugar, 2 whites of eggs, 2 dessertspoonfuls of castor sugar.

METHOD.—Wipe the rhubarb and cut it into thin slices, place on a large dish and sprinkle the castor sugar over it and leave for one hour.

Sieve together the flour, salt, and baking-powder.

Rub the fat into the flour until it is like fine breadcrumbs.

Mix the yolk of egg with the half-gill of water.

Add the egg and water to the flour and mix to a stiff paste.

Take a flan-ring—if this is not available use a sandwich-tin—and well grease it. Grease a baking-sheet and stand the ring firmly on to it.

Roll out the pastry until it is about one quarter to three-eighths of an inch in thickness, and very carefully line the inside of the flan-ring and baking-sheet with the pastry ; cut the rough edges at the top.

Now line the pastry with greased paper, and fill it with rice. Place in a moderately hot oven and bake for about thirty minutes ; be careful to keep it only light brown.

After the rhubarb and sugar have well soaked, put into the oven and just cook slowly until it is tender, but it must not be broken. It can cook at the same time as the pastry. When the rhubarb is soft put it aside until cold.

Take the flan of pastry from the oven when ready, carefully remove the rice and paper together and gently lift the flan-ring from the pastry. Place on a sieve to cool ; when cold put on to a lace paper on a plate.

THE MERINGUE

Fill the flan with cooked rhubarb, leaving out one or two pieces for the top.

Add a pinch of salt to the whites of eggs, whisk them to a stiff froth, fold into them two dessertspoonfuls of castor sugar and cover the rhubarb with the same. Put back into a warm oven just to set the meringue.

Decorate with pieces of rhubarb and serve cold.

NOTE.—If a flan-ring is not available, line a sandwich-tin with the pastry. Great care must be taken when this is removed from the tin, as it is very liable to break.

STRAWBERRY CHARLOTTE

INGREDIENTS.—½ pint of strawberry purée (made by rubbing strawberries through a hair sieve), 3 oz. of castor sugar, 1 teaspoonful of lemon-juice, 1 gill of cream, ½ oz. of French leaf gelatine, ½ gill of strawberry syrup and water, a few sponge-finger biscuits, 1 pint of lemon jelly (packet), ¾ pint of hot water, a few pieces of angelica, a few fresh strawberries.

METHOD.—Dissolve the jelly in hot water and allow it to cool.

Scald and rinse with cold water, a plain round tin mould.

Just cover the bottom of the mould with lemon-jelly, and leave until set.

Remove the stalks from the strawberries, carefully wash and wipe them and dip each one in some of the melted jelly and place all round the bottom edge of the tin. For this use equal-sized strawberries—rather small ones.

In the centre of the bottom of the tin place a few pieces of angelica, cut into diamond-shaped pieces. These should also be first dipped in jelly.

Leave until set, then carefully cover the decoration with more jelly, and leave again until set.

Cut each sponge finger so that both sides are quite straight, and cut a small piece off one end so that they stand firmly.

This must be very carefully done, as the biscuits are brittle and easily break.

When the jelly in the tin is set, arrange the biscuits all round the sides of the tin, standing them on the jelly. The biscuits should just reach to the top of the tin ; if too long a piece more must be cut off each.

Now mix a few of the biscuit crumbs with two tablespoonfuls of melted jelly, and if there are any cracks between the biscuits through which the cream could run, just patch with this jelly and crumb paste.

Then set aside in a cool place.

The strawberry purée is made by rubbing strawberries through a hair sieve. Either fresh or tinned may be used. If tinned ones are used, strain the syrup from them first. If fresh ones, just stalk and wash them first.

Add the castor sugar and lemon-juice to the purée, and mix well together.

Put the gelatine into a saucepan to dissolve with half a gill of strawberry syrup.

If fresh strawberries have been used for this dish, the gelatine can be dissolved in half a gill of water.

Whisk the cream until it thickens.

Add the strawberry purée, etc., to it gradually, and mix together.

Lastly, strain in the dissolved gelatine and mix again.

Stir the mixture over ice until it begins to thicken.

Pour into the prepared mould and leave until set.

Dip the bottom of the mould in warm water, then turn on to a dish.

Chop the remainder of the jelly and serve round it, or use one or two strawberries for decoration.

NOTE.—If fresh strawberries are not in season, use only angelica for decoration, as tinned strawberries are not usually a very good colour.

ICES AND SUNDAES

THERE are many kinds of ices—custard, cream, and water ices—and each of these can be flavoured in endless ways.

One important point to remember is that mixtures to be frozen require extra sugar and flavouring, as they lose part of their sweetness and flavour during the freezing process ; but, on the other hand, if too much sugar is added, you will have difficulty in freezing the mixture.

The most convenient freezers are those with no handle to turn. The ice-cream mixture is put in at one end and the ice and salt at the other, and there is nothing to do except stir the mixture now and again, to make it freeze evenly. An ice pick is not a necessity, as the ice can be easily broken with a darning-needle tapped with a hammer.

You will find that a quart size freezer is the most useful for the average housewife.

The ice and freezing salt can be bought at the fishmonger's, and both are quite cheap.

For a small quantity of ice cream about six pounds of ice (in one block) are needed, and two pounds of freezing salt. The ice may not all be needed, but it is, of course, best to be on the safe side.

USEFUL HINTS

1. Be sure to prepare the ice cream mixture in plenty of time, preferably the day before, as it must be quite cold when it is put into the freezer.

2. When breaking up the ice put it in a large enamelled bowl and stick a long darning-needle in the ice near the edge. Tap the needle with a hammer and the ice will chip off easily. It should be broken into pieces the size of a walnut.

3. Use three cups of ice to each cup of freezing salt and pack the freezer as tightly as possible.

If too much salt is used the ice cream will freeze too quickly and will be coarse instead of smooth.

After freezing about fifteen minutes take off the lid and stir with a wooden spoon to mix it smoothly.

The mixtures that ices are made of vary greatly in richness. They may be made of :

1. Cornflour or custard-powder and milk sweetened and flavoured to taste.

2. Egg custard and fruit purée with or without cream.

3. Cream and fruit purée.

AN IMPROVISED FREEZER

A home-made freezer is only possible when making a small quantity.

When the custard has become cold and is ready to be frozen, put it into an aluminium saucepan and cover securely with the lid.

Stand it in rather a shallow enamel basin so that the handle of the pan is above the sides of the basin.

Pack it round with layers of ice and freezing salt, and turn the saucepan round and round in the basin of ice until the custard, etc., becomes sufficiently frozen.

During this process the lid of the pan must be removed occasionally and the custard stirred from the sides into the mass so that it all gets evenly frozen. Care must be taken when doing this not to get any of the freezing salt into the custard.

The ice must be replenished as required and the melted ice poured off.

ICE CREAM (VANILLA)

INGREDIENTS.—2 whole eggs or 4 yolks, 1 pint of milk, ¼ lb. of castor sugar, 10d. of cream, 1 teaspoonful of vanilla or other flavouring.

METHOD.—Put the milk and sugar into a saucepan and bring it almost to the boil. Add it to the beaten eggs, then pour it into the top of a double boiler and stir over hot water until the custard thickens. Remove it at once, strain into a basin and leave it 'o get thoroughly cold, stirring it occasionally.

Lastly, whisk the cream until it thickens, add the custard gradually and flavour it with vanilla. The mixture is then ready for the freezer.

To PREPARE THE FREEZER.—Scald out the ice cream container, together with the scraper and lid, dry them thoroughly and let them get quite cold, then fix them into the pail.

Pack the space between the container and pail with ice and freezing salt, using about one part of salt to three parts of ice. The ice should be chipped into rather small pieces.

Now remove the lid and pour in the prepared mixture, being careful not to get any salt into the container and remembering not to fill it more than two-thirds full, as the mixture expands in bulk when frozen.

Put the lid on, fix the handle in position and finish packing the freezer to the top of the pail with ice and freezing salt. Turn the freezer until the mixture becomes frozen ; this is easily ascertained, as the handle becomes difficult to turn. When ready, drain off the water, remove the handle and lid, again being careful not to get any salt into the mixture.

Take out the centre piece and scrape off the ice cream. Replace the lid, place a cork in the top, pack up again, then fold a piece of sacking over the pail and leave it in a cool place for an hour or two.

The hole in the side of the pail is to allow the water to run out as the ice melts.

To VARY THE ICE CREAM

The preceding recipe can be varied by adding chocolate or coffee to flavour, or the cream may be omitted entirely if only a custard ice is required.

Having made the ices, they can be served in different ways : just plain with wafer biscuits, in iced drinks, or in sundaes.

To MAKE FRUIT SUNDAES

Place a portion of ice cream in a stem glass, add two tablespoonfuls of chopped tinned fruit and a little of the syrup. You can buy tins of *grated* pineapple which are much used for sundaes. Then top the ice with a little whipped cream mixed with stiffly frothed egg-white and flavoured and sweetened to taste. Sprinkle chopped walnuts over the top and stick a glacé cherry in the centre of each one.

BANANA SUNDAE

INGREDIENTS.—1 pint of ice cream, 5 bananas, 6d. of cream, raspberry syrup, 5 glacé cherries.

METHOD.—Slice the bananas and lay two slices on each dish with syrup poured round.

Place ice cream on top with a little cream and cherry to decorate.

BUTTERFLY SUNDAE

INGREDIENTS.—Vanilla ice cream, 1 pint tin of sliced pineapple, whipped cream, raspberry syrup, any crystallised fruit.

METHOD.—Put the ice cream on a slice of pineapple and cover with cream. Pour the syrup round.

Decorate the top with a butterfly made as follows :

Cut two three-cornered pieces of pineapple to make each wing and a strip of crystallised fruit for the body.

Two pieces of fern stalk or three strips of angelica will make the antennæ.

CHERRY SUNDAE

INGREDIENTS.—1 pint of ice cream, 1 tin of cirio cherries, 2 oz. of ground nuts, pineapple syrup, 6d. of cream, ½ lb. of ripe cherries.

METHOD.—Chop the tinned cherries, removing the stones. Put the chopped cherries and nuts in a glass with a little pineapple syrup.

Put the ice cream in the middle with cream and fresh cherries on top.

CHOCOLATE ICE CREAM

INGREDIENTS.—1 pint of warm milk, 2 eggs, 1 gill of cream, 1 gill of unsweetened condensed milk, 3 tablespoonfuls of best cocoa, 2 teaspoonfuls of vanilla essence, a pinch of cinnamon, 4 to 6 oz. of sugar, according to taste, 4 bananas, 1 oz. of almonds (blanched).

METHOD.—Mix the cocoa, sugar, and cinnamon, and stir in half the milk gradually. Boil the rest of the milk and pour the mixed cocoa into it. Let it boil for one minute, then remove it from the fire.

Beat the eggs well, pour them into the cocoa and put it into a double saucepan.

Stir till it thickens enough to coat the back of a spoon. Add the condensed milk and more sugar if desired. When cold, add vanilla to taste and the cream.

Pack the freezer tightly with broken ice and freezing salt, and add a cup of cold water.

Pour the ice cream mixture in other end and freeze for one hour to one hour and a half, turning the freezer upside down. Every fifteen minutes open the freezer and stir well to make the chocolate ice smooth.

Heap the ice cream in a dish, lay banana round and sprinkle with sliced almonds.

ICED CHOCOLATE SHAPE

INGREDIENTS.—6 oz. of sugar, 3½ gills of hot milk, 2 teaspoonfuls of vanilla, 2 squares of unsweetened chocolate, 1½ oz. of cornflour, pinch of salt, 1½ gills of cream, cold milk.

METHOD.—Add sugar and salt to the hot milk and stir it on to the cornflour mixed with a little cold milk. Boil it for ten minutes, stirring it constantly.

Add the melted chocolate and leave it to cool.

Add the vanilla and fold in the stiffly whipped cream.

Pour the mixture into a mould and freeze it, taking three parts of ice to one part of salt, and let it stand for three or four hours.

Decorate the Iced Chocolate Shape with whipped cream and serve it with ice wafers.

COFFEE NUT SUNDAE

INGREDIENTS.—1 pint of ice cream flavoured with coffee, 2 oz. of shelled walnuts, 2 oz. of ratafia biscuits, 9d. of cream.

METHOD.—Chop the nuts and crush the ratafia biscuits, mix with the ice, and put in glasses with cream and a walnut on top.

CONDENSED MILK ICE CREAM

INGREDIENTS.—¾ pint of unsweetened condensed milk, 1 pint of warm milk, 2 eggs, 4 oz. of sugar, 2 teaspoonfuls of vanilla essence (or more, according to taste).

METHOD.—Beat the eggs and sugar together and pour on the milk. Place the custard in a double saucepan and stir till it is thick.

Add the unsweetened condensed milk and vanilla to taste. When cold freeze for one hour as explained on pp. 604 and 605.

CORNFLOUR ICE CREAM

INGREDIENTS.—1 quart of milk, 4 to 6 oz. of sugar, 1 oz. of cornflour (light weight), 2 sheets of gelatine, ½ gill of water, 1 tablespoonful of vanilla essence.

METHOD.—This plain ice cream is made from cornflour and milk, sweetened and flavoured to taste.

In order to be really good the cornflour should be well cooked.

Soak the gelatine in half a gill of water. Mix the sugar and cornflour with a gill of cold milk.

Boil the rest of the milk and pour it on the mixed cornflour, stirring all the time.

Stir till it boils, and simmer gently for five minutes, placing the pan on an asbestos mat to prevent it burning.

Add the essence and gelatine and taste to see if it is properly flavoured.

Leave it till it is quite cold, then strain into the freezer.

ECONOMICAL VANILLA ICE CREAM

WITHOUT EGGS OR CREAM

Plain ice creams can be made without eggs or cream, using either a packet of ice cream powder (sold in various flavours) or custard made from custard powder.

INGREDIENTS.—1 packet of ice cream powder, 1 pint of boiling milk.

METHOD.—Empty the packet of ice cream powder into a perfectly dry basin.

Boil the milk, and while it is still boiling pour it quickly on to the powder, stirring hard all the time.

Leave it to get quite cold. An hour and a half before the ice cream is required, chip the ice with a darning needle into pieces the size of a walnut. Put three cups of ice into the ice compartment and sprinkle on one cup of freezing salt (sometimes called rock salt).

Add three more cups of ice and one more cup of salt and shake it down, then press it with a piece of wood, as it must be made to fit tightly in the freezer.

Continue adding ice and freezing salt until the freezer cannot hold any more. Pour in a cup of cold water, put on the rubber ring and close down the lid.

Pour the cold ice cream mixture into the other end and put on the rubber ring and lid.

Turn the freezer upside down. In fifteen minutes open the cream compartment and scrape round the sides which will be partly frozen. Mix it all well together, put on the lid again, and turn the freezer upside down to go on freezing.

Do this every fifteen minutes in order to make the ice creamy and smooth. If the freezer has been well packed with ice and salt the ice cream will be frozen in about an hour.

Ice creams look well in paper cases or they can be served on small cardboard plates covered with greaseproof paper.

NOTE.—To make ice cream without a freezer use a two-pint fruit-bottling jar with a screw top and place it inside an icing sugar tin, packing it well with ice and salt, and covering the top with an old blanket.

For larger quantities use a larger jar and put it in an enamelled pail.

When no freezer is used be sure to have plenty of ice, and when it melts pour away all the water and pack the tin or pail again tightly with more broken ice and salt. In this way quite good ices can be made, but it takes rather longer than when a proper freezer is used. It is not necessary to turn the jar round. All that is needed is to stir the ice cream now and again, scraping the frozen part off the sides and bottom of the jar.

FAVOURITE ICE CREAM PUDDING

FLAVOURED WITH MARASCHINO AND CHOCOLATE

INGREDIENTS.—1 gill of cream, ½ pint of unsweetened condensed milk, 1 pint of warm milk, 2 eggs, 6 oz. of sugar.

FOR THE COLOURS AND FLAVOURS FOR THE TWO PARTS.—(1) Green colouring, 1 oz. of pistachio nuts, 1 tablespoonful of maraschino; (2) 2 oz. of chocolate, 1 teaspoonful of vanilla essence, ¾ gill of milk.

METHOD.—To make the foundation ice cream, beat the eggs and sugar together and pour on the warm milk.

Place the custard in a double saucepan and stir till it thickens. When cold, add the cream and unsweetened condensed milk.

Pack a freezer very tightly with ice and freezing salt in alternate layers, one cup of freezing salt to three cups of ice.

Pour the custard mixture in at the other end, and turn the freezer upside down.

Let it freeze for one hour, stirring it every fifteen minutes.

While it is freezing, melt the chocolate in the milk and add the vanilla. Blanch the pistachio nuts by pouring on boiling water and slipping off the skins. Have ready two basins, a large pail of broken ice, and a piece of wet sacking.

Take the frozen ice cream from the freezer and divide it between the two basins.

Into the first basin of ice cream stir the pistachio nuts and maraschino, and a very few drops of colouring to make it the palest green.

Into the second basin stir the paste of milk and dissolved chocolate, with vanilla to flavour.

Put some chocolate ice cream at each end of the mould and the pale-green ice cream in the centre.

Cover with greaseproof paper, put on the lid, and to be sure of keeping out the salt, smear a little butter round the edge.

Wrap greased paper all round it and bury it in the pail of ice.

Cover it with sacking and leave it for about three hours.

To serve it, stand a fancy dish on ice.

Remove the paper and dip the mould in water that is barely luke warm.

Wipe it carefully, remove the lid and turn the pudding on to the cold dish.

FRUIT PARFAIT

INGREDIENTS.—Ice cream or ice brick, some tinned fruit (plain or salad), 1 white of egg, 1½ dessertspoonfuls of castor sugar, few glacé cherries.

METHOD.—Whisk the white to a very stiff froth, then fold in the castor sugar lightly.

Put good-sized lumps of ice cream into some custard-glasses.

Cut up the fruit and add some to each, with just a spoonful of syrup.

Pile some of the meringue mixture over it and serve at once.

FRUIT SUNDAE

INGREDIENTS.—Ice cream or ice brick, crushed fruit (sweetened), 1 white of egg, finely ground nuts, 1½ dessertspoonfuls of castor sugar, 2 tablespoonfuls of cream, vanilla.

METHOD.—Whisk the cream until it stiffens. Whisk the white to a very stiff froth, fold in the castor sugar, then add the cream and a few drops of vanilla, and mix together lightly. Have ready some crushed fruit, any suitable kind can be used, tinned or fresh. Tinned pineapple is frequently used.

Put good-sized lumps of ice cream into about four or five custard glasses, then cover with crushed fruit.

Pile some of the white of egg and cream mixture on the top, sprinkle with the nuts and serve at once.

NOTE.—You can buy the nuts and get them ground at vegetarian shops, where they sell special nut foods. Failing this, just chop them finely. Barcelona nuts are generally used.

GINGER BOMBE

INGREDIENTS.—1 pint of milk, 4 yolks of eggs, 10d. of cream, ½ teaspoonful of vanilla, ¼ lb. of preserved ginger, 3 oz. of castor sugar, 2 tablespoonfuls of ginger syrup, extra ginger, leaves of angelica, and cream for decorating.

METHOD.—Make a custard with the egg-yolks, sugar, and milk, and when ready, strain it into a basin and leave it to get thoroughly cold.

Whisk the cream until it thickens, then stir it into the custard. Add the vanilla, and also the ginger syrup.

Half-pack the freezing pail (between the container and the pail) with ice and freezing salt, using about one part salt to three parts ice, then pour the prepared custard into the container.

Put on the lid and fix the handle in position, then finish packing the pail. Turn the handle until the mixture becomes frozen, but not hard.

Take off the handle, the lid of the container and the scraper, and stir in the ginger which should previously have been cut into small pieces.

Turn the mixture into an ice cream mould, filling it to the brim, cover it with a buttered paper, buttered side uppermost, fix the lid on firmly and pack the mould in a basin or pail with ice and freezing salt.

Leave it for three or four hours, then unmould the Ginger Bombe, and serve it on a chilled dish decorated with pieces of ginger, leaves of angelica, and whipped cream.

To unmould the Ginger Bombe, remove the lid and paper, and hold a damp cloth (wrung out of *cold* water) round the mould until it shows signs of loosening.

NOTE.—When making the ice cream, fill the container only two-thirds full, as the mixture expands a little as it freezes.

As the ice melts, pour off the water and replenish the freezer with fresh ice and freezing salt. The ice must be chipped into fairly small pieces.

Sufficient for eight persons.

GRAPE SUNDAE

INGREDIENTS.—1 tin of grape fruit, 1 lb. of grapes, strawberry syrup, 2 oz. of ground nuts, 1 pint of bought ice cream, 9d. of cream,

METHOD.—Squeeze the pulp from half the grapes and remove the pips.

Mix the grape fruit and grape pulp and put them into glasses with a little syrup and a few ground nuts.

Add the ice cream and put a dab of cream on top. Decorate with a few grapes.

Iced
Chocolate
Shape

Strawberry
Sundae

Pineapple
Ice Block

PLATE 57

Marshmallow
Sundae

How to
Serve
Ice Cream

Ginger
Bombe

PLATE 58

ICE BRICK FRUIT MOULDS

INGREDIENTS.—1 apple, 1 banana, 1 orange, lemon-juice, castor sugar, 1 large ice brick, a few glacé cherries.

METHOD.—Peel and quarter the apple, remove the core and cut into slices. Peel and slice the banana. Peel and quarter the orange.

Mix the prepared fruit together, and spread on a large plate, sprinkle with castor sugar, and just a squeeze of lemon-juice, and leave for a time.

Divide the ice brick into about four portions, and place on small plates (glass plates if available).

Heap some of the prepared fruit on top of each, stick a cherry in the centre, and pour round any juice that has come from the fruit. Serve at once.

ICE CREAM AND HOT CHOCOLATE SAUCE

INGREDIENTS.—1 ice cream brick, a 4-oz. cake of chocolate, 10 oz. of loaf sugar, 1 gill of milk, vanilla essence, ½ gill of cream.

METHOD.—Dissolve the chocolate in the milk over a very low gas. Add the sugar and boil, keeping it well stirred.

It has boiled enough when a very little dropped into a cup of cold water forms a soft ball.

Keep the ice cream brick in a basin with some ice till required.

Turn it out on to a fireproof dish, whip the cream and sweeten it to taste.

Let the sauce cool a little, stir it till it begins to thicken, then pour it over the ice cream.

Put the cream on top and serve at once.

ICE CREAM SODA

INGREDIENTS.—Vanilla ice cream, fruit syrup (strained), soda water.

METHOD.—Put a good-sized lump of ice cream into a tumbler, pour over some fruit syrup, then fill it up with soda water.

Stir round and serve at once. Add castor sugar if required.

ICE PUDDING

INGREDIENTS.—¾ pint of milk, 1 gill of cream, 2 eggs, 3 teaspoonfuls of maraschino, ½ oz. of pistachio nuts, ½ oz. of almonds, ¼ lb. of glacé fruits, vanilla flavouring, 3 oz. of castor sugar, ice wafers.

METHOD.—To make the custard, beat up the eggs, add the milk, strain into a jug and stand in a saucepan of cold water.

Stir over the fire until it thickens, being careful not to let it curdle.

When cooked, flavour it well with vanilla and add the castor sugar. Stir until thoroughly mixed.

Leave until quite cold.

Put into a freezing-pail, cover tightly.

Pack round well with freezing mixture and half freeze the custard.

Take an ice-pudding mould, decorate it with the best of the glacé fruits, cut the remainder into small pieces.

Put the almonds and pistachio nuts into a saucepan, cover with cold water, bring to the boil, then skin them and chop finely.

Whisk the cream until quite thick.

When the custard is ready, stir into it the chopped nuts, glacé fruits, maraschino, and whipped cream.

Stir all lightly together, and half-freeze as before.

Then put into the prepared mould, press down firmly, cover tightly, and pack in the freezing mixture.

When ready, take out the mould, wipe it, then carefully turn on to a dish. Serve with ice wafers.

NOTE.—Freezing mixture consists of ice and freezing salt—use about half pound of freezing salt to four pounds of ice. As this melts more must be added.

Sufficient for about eight persons.

LEMON WATER ICE

INGREDIENTS.—Lemons (as required), ½ lb. of loaf sugar, 1 pint of water, cream, or 2 whites of eggs.

METHOD.—About three or four lemons will be required, according to the amount of juice in them.

Wipe and grate the lemon-rind on to the lumps of sugar.

Put the sugar and water into a saucepan and dissolve slowly.

Bring to the boil and boil for about ten minutes, remove any scum, and leave the syrup until cold.

U

Squeeze sufficient lemons to make a quarter of a pint of juice, strain it into the cold syrup, and mix together.

Put into the freezer and partly freeze, then stir in lightly some whipped cream, or the stiffly whisked white of eggs.

When thoroughly mixed, finish freezing the mixture.

NOTE.—Orange or Tangerine Water Ices can be made in the same way.

MERINGUES GLACES

INGREDIENTS.—1¼ tablespoonfuls of custard-powder, 1½ pints of milk, 2 oz. of sugar, 12 bought meringue cases, 2 oz. of glacé cherries, 1s. of cream (may be omitted), 2 oz. of sugar.

METHOD.—Mix the custard-powder and sugar with one gill of the milk.

Boil the rest of the milk and pour it on to the mixed custard-powder, stirring all the time.

Simmer for five minutes and leave till cold.

Pack the freezer as tight as possible with ice and freezing salt.

Strain the custard into the other end and freeze for one hour, stirring the ice cream well together every fifteen minutes.

When ready to serve whip the cream, and when it is stiff stir in about two ounces of sugar.

To serve the meringues glacés place a lump of firmly frozen ice cream between two meringue cases and decorate with a few dabs of cream and cherries.

PEACH ICE CREAM AND CAKE

INGREDIENTS.—1 tin of peaches, 2 eggs, ½ pint of milk, ½ pint of cream, 1 gill of unsweetened condensed milk, 1 cupful of granulated sugar, juice of a lemon, a bought jam sandwich, 2 oz. of crystallised rose leaves.

METHOD.—Beat the eggs and sugar and put them in a double saucepan with the milk. Stir till the custard is thick.

When cold, strain the mixture into a basin and add the condensed milk and cream. Rub the peaches through a hair sieve and measure three-quarters of a pint of the purée.

Add the fruit purée and the lemon-juice to the cold custard and freeze

for about one hour and a half, stirring it well every fifteen minutes.

To serve fill the sandwich with half the ice cream and spread the rest on top.

Sprinkle with crystallised rose leaves and cut into three-cornered slices.

NOTE.—Fruit cream ices can be made with any kind of fruit purée, using one pound of fruit, three-quarters of a pint of custard and quarter of a pint of cream, or one pound of fruit, half a pint of custard and half a pint of cream, or for very good rich ones, one pound of fruit to one pint of cream.

PEACH WATER ICE

INGREDIENTS.—1 tin of peaches (¾ pint size), juice of ½ a lemon, ¾ pint of water, 6 oz. of castor sugar.

METHOD.—Dissolve the sugar in the water and leave it to get cold.

Rub the peaches through a hair sieve, stir in the peach syrup, and add the strained lemon-juice. Pour into the sugar and water, and turn the liquid into the freezer and freeze as directed for Vanilla Ice Cream (see p. 604).

Another variety can be made by adding a stiffly whisked egg-white to the mixture when it is half frozen, then finish freezing in the usual way.

PEAR MELBA

INGREDIENTS.—½ pint of Jersey or nursery milk, ½ pint of double cream, 1 gill of unsweetened condensed milk, 4 oz. of sugar, 1 teaspoonful of vanilla essence, 1 tin of pears, 1s. of cream, (whipped and sweetened).

FOR THE RASPBERRY SYRUP.—1 lb. of raspberries, ½ lb. of fresh currants, 1 lb. of loaf sugar.

METHOD.—Heat the sugar and milk, letting it come just to the boil. When cold, whisk the cream and add the milk to it gradually with the condensed milk.

Flavour with vanilla and freeze for one hour and a half, keeping the ice cream well stirred every fifteen minutes.

To serve, put the ice in a dish with pears round it and decorate with cream.

Pour raspberry syrup over the ice and decorate with cream.

Make the raspberry syrup two or three days beforehand.

To MAKE THE RASPBERRY SYRUP.— Pick the fruit, put it in a basin and mash it well with a wooden spoon. Next day strain it through a hair sieve. Measure the juice, and add the sugar. Stir till it boils and boil for ten minutes. Bottle and keep for use.

NOTE.—Peach Melba can be made in the same way, using peaches instead of pears.

PINEAPPLE ICE BLOCK

INGREDIENTS.—Large tin of sliced pineapple, ice and freezing salt (as required), cream, sugar.

METHOD.—Chip the ice up small and allow about half a pint of freezing salt to each quart of ice. If a freezing pail is not available, use an ordinary pail, or deep basin.

Pack the tin of pineapple in the ice and freezing salt, sprinkling each layer of ice with salt, and leave it for about four or five hours. The ice and salt must be replenished as it melts, and the melted ice poured off.

To UNMOULD THE PINEAPPLE. — Open the tin round the side instead of the top so as completely to remove the top, then turn the pineapple out on to a dish. If it does not unmould readily, hold a warm, damp cloth over it for a few seconds.

Decorate the ice block with whipped cream and serve it with castor sugar.

Sufficient for six persons.

PINEAPPLE MERINGUE ICE

INGREDIENTS.—1 pint of custard, $\frac{1}{4}$ pint of cream, $\frac{1}{4}$ pint of unsweetened condensed milk, 4 oz. of sugar, 1 tin of grated pineapple with $\frac{1}{2}$ gill of the syrup, 2 sheets of wafer gelatine, pineapple essence, 1 bought Swiss roll, 6 or 8 bought meringue cases.

FOR THE CHOCOLATE ICING.—4 oz. of icing sugar, 1 level dessertspoonful of cocoa, 2 tablespoonfuls of water.

METHOD.—Soak the gelatine in the syrup for five minutes and dissolve it over a low gas. Add it to the hot custard with the sugar and strain into a basin.

Just before freezing add the essence, cream, and condensed milk and the pineapple (strained free from juice).

Pour it into the freezer ready packed with ice and rock salt and freeze for about one hour and a half.

Every fifteen minutes stir the mixture.

Mix the cocoa and water smoothly and boil it for two seconds. Stir in the icing sugar.

If it is too thick add a few drops of hot water.

Dip the tip of each meringue in the chocolate icing. Place a spoonful of ice cream on a slice of Swiss roll with a meringue on top.

POIRE GELEE

INGREDIENTS.—$\frac{3}{4}$ pint size tin of pears, ice and freezing salt, strips of angelica, cream, sugar, and vanilla.

METHOD.—For this dish use the long, slender tin of pears, rather than the short, fat shape.

Pack it in a basin with ice and freezing salt, and leave it for three or four hours, pouring off the water as the ice melts and replenishing the basin with fresh ice and freezing salt.

When ready to serve, open the tin round the side just under the top rim, remove the top entirely, then unmould the shape by holding a damp cloth wrung out of *cold* water round the tin until the shapes show signs of loosening.

Cut the shape into slices and serve them on individual plates, decorating each one with whipped cream, sweetened and flavoured to taste, and stalks of angelica.

Sufficient for six or seven slices.

RASPBERRY SUNDAE

INGREDIENTS.—1 lb. of raspberries, 1 tin of crushed pineapple, 1 quart of vanilla ice cream, 1s., of double cream raspberry syrup.

METHOD.—Crush the raspberries, keeping back some of the largest ones.

Put the ice cream into ten or twelve glasses and pour the raspberries over and a little syrup.

Cover the raspberries with a little pineapple and put cream and whole raspberries on top of the ice.

STRAWBERRY BOMBE

INGREDIENTS.—1 pint of milk, 2 teaspoonfuls of flour, $\frac{1}{4}$ pint of cream,

¼ pint of unsweetened condensed milk, 4 oz. of sugar, 2 eggs, 1 teaspoonful of essence of vanilla.

FOR THE STRAWBERRY FILLING.— ⅓ lb. of strawberries, 4 oz. of sugar, juice of ½ a lemon, 1½ gills of cream.

METHOD.—For this delicious sweet, plain ice cream mixture should be first half frozen. The centre is then scooped out and filled with strawberry cream, when it is frozen again till solid and turned out whole.

To make the plain ice cream, boil half the milk and pour into it the rest of the milk mixed smoothly with the flour and sugar. Stir well and boil for three minutes. Cool slightly and stir in the beaten eggs.

When cold stir in the cream, condensed milk and vanilla.

To make the strawberry filling rub the ripe strawberries through a hair sieve and mix the purée with the sugar. Add the lemon-juice. When ready to freeze the ice, whip the cream and stir in the fruit purée.

Fill the freezer with chipped ice and freezing salt, using three cups of ice to each one of the salt. As it takes some hours to freeze care must be taken to pack the ice in very tightly.

Pour the plain mixture in the other end, close it up and turn it upside down.

In fifteen minutes scrape the frozen part from the sides, and mix it smoothly, then freeze again.

In about twenty minutes have ready an empty basin and the strawberry mixture.

Scoop out the centre of the ice cream, having it an inch thick round the sides. This is put in the basin.

Put the strawberry and cream mixture into the hole and heap the plain ice cream on top. Do this quickly, close it up and freeze till solid, say two and a half hours. The time depends a good deal on how closely the ice was packed.

When ready to serve empty out the ice and salt and in its place put a cupful of warm water. Open the other end and hold the freezer over a dish when the bombe will slide out easily.

On putting in the warm water, care must be taken that it is only lukewarm as if too hot it would melt the ice cream.

As the bombe has to be frozen hard it is best to dish it up about twenty minutes before it is required.

It will keep its shape perfectly well if put in a cool place.

To serve Strawberry Bombe cut it in slices half an inch thick.

Any other fruits such as raspberries, apricots, and pineapple can be used for the filling instead of strawberries.

STRAWBERRY ICES

INGREDIENTS.—1 lb. of strawberries, 5 or 6 oz. of castor sugar, juice of ½ a lemon, ½ pint of cream, few drops of cochineal (if required).

METHOD.—Stalk and pick over the strawberries. Lay out on a dish, and sprinkle with the castor sugar and lemon-juice.

Leave to soak for several hours, then mash it up, and rub it all through a fine sieve to a pulp.

Whisk the cream until it stiffens, and stir into the strawberry pulp ; add a few drops of cochineal.

Mix together well, and freeze.

NOTE.—When strawberries are not in season, strawberry jam can be used, in which case very little sugar is required.

Rub the jam through a fine sieve ; if rather stiff, first warm it slightly in a saucepan.

Stir in the lemon-juice, and when quite cold add the cream, then freeze the mixture.

If less expensive ices are required, use half custard and half cream, or all custard.

STRAWBERRY SUNDAE

INGREDIENTS.—1 pint of vanilla ice cream, lemon syrup, 1 lb. of strawberries, 9d. of cream.

METHOD.—Keep back five or six nice strawberries and mash the rest.

Put the ice cream into glass cups and pour the crushed strawberries over, and a little lemon syrup.

Place the cream and a nice strawberry on top.

WATER ICES

INGREDIENTS.—¾ lb. of loaf sugar, 1 pint of hot water, juice of 1 lemon.

METHOD.—Put the sugar and water in a saucepan. Stir till it boils and boil for six minutes. Add the lemon-juice and strain.

It is a good plan to make a large quantity of syrup and bottle it for use as required.

Any kind of water ice can then be made by adding different fruit juices such as strawberry, orange, loganberry.

The usual proportions are : Half a pint of fruit juice to one pint of syrup.

RASPBERRY WATER ICE

INGREDIENTS.—1 pint of cold syrup, juice of 1 lemon, 1½ lb. of raspberries, the white of an egg, carmine colouring.

METHOD.—Rub the raspberries through a hair sieve and add the lemon-juice to the purée.

Mix the syrup and fruit juice, colour with a few drops of carmine and freeze for twenty minutes.

Beat the white of egg to a stiff froth and stir it well in.

Freeze for about one hour and a half, or till firm enough.

A YULETIDE BOMBE

INGREDIENTS.—3 egg-yolks, or 1 whole egg and 1 yolk, ¾ pint of milk, 2 oz. of castor sugar, ½ teaspoonful of vanilla flavouring, 1 gill of cream, ¼ lb. of stoned raisins, ¼ lb. of glacé apricots, 2 oz. of glacé cherries, 1 oz. of angelica, ¼ gill of cooking rum, ice and freezing salt.

METHOD.—Beat up the yolks, or whole egg and yolk. Heat the milk and add it to them.

Turn them into the top of a double-boiler, add the sugar and stir the mixture over hot water until it thickens, being careful not to let it curdle. Then remove it and strain it into a basin. Leave it to get cold.

Meanwhile, prepare the fruit, which should all be cut into small pieces. Turn it into a dish, pour the rum over it, and leave it in a cool place until required.

Whisk the cream until it thickens and gradually stir the cold custard into it, and add the vanilla flavouring.

To PREPARE THE FREEZER.—Scald out the ice-cream container together with the dasher or scraper. Dry them thoroughly and let them get quite cold, before fitting them into the pail.

Pack the space between the container and pail with ice and freezing salt, not quite to the top, using about three parts of ice to one part of salt, and chipping the ice into very small pieces. Remove the lid and pour in the custard (the container should be only about half full). Cover the container, fix the handle in position, and finish packing.

Turn the handle until the mixture is only about half-frozen, then remove the lid and scraper, etc. (after wiping off any salt there may be on them) and stir in the prepared fruit. Turn this into the ice pudding mould and fill it to the brim. Cover the mixture with buttered paper, butter side uppermost, and fix on the lid securely, then immerse the container in a pail, and pack it with ice and freezing salt.

Leave the bombe for about four hours until it is frozen solidly, then dip it in cold water, and when loosened turn it on to a very cold plate, lined with a paper doyley.

Serve Yuletide Bombe immediately, with ice wafer biscuits.

NOTE.—The ice pudding mould should be chilled before the mixture is turned into it.

EMPIRE RECIPES

ALMOND AND RAISIN SPONGE

INGREDIENTS.—1 sixpenny sponge cake ring, ½ lb. of Empire raisins, 2 or 3 oz. of almonds, 1 tablespoonful of sherry, 3 eggs, 1½ pints of milk, 1 tablespoonful of sugar, almond flavouring.

METHOD.—Wash and stone the raisins and blanch the almonds. Leave out a few of each for decorating, then put the remainder through the mincer.

Split the sponge cake into halves and spread with the minced raisins and almonds (moistened with the sherry), then put together again.

Beat up the eggs. Boil the milk, and when just off the boil add to them.

Stir in the sugar, add a few drops of flavouring, then strain.

Put the sponge-ring in a pie-dish or Pyrex dish, pour in the custard, and decorate with the remainder of the almonds and raisins.

Bake in a moderately warm oven for about forty minutes or until set, and serve cold.

Do not let it boil.

Sufficient for eight persons.

APPLE CHARLOTTE

INGREDIENTS.—2 lb. of Empire apples, 1 lemon, 1 oz. of crystallised ginger, 9 oz. of breadcrumbs, 4 oz. of suet, 4 tablespoonfuls of sugar, ½ oz. of Empire butter.

METHOD.—Skin the suet, then grate or chop it finely. Make the breadcrumbs.

Grease a pie-dish and coat with some of them, then shake out the loose ones. Mix the remainder with the suet. Peel, quarter, and core the apples, and cut in slices.

Grate the lemon-rind finely and cut up the ginger; mix the latter with the suet and crumbs.

Put about a third of the breadcrumbs and suet in the bottom of the dish, then add half the apple sprinkled with half the sugar.

Add another third of the crumbs and suet, then the remainder of the apples and sugar. Cover with the remaining portion of crumbs, etc., and press down firmly.

Place two or three dabs of butter on the top. Put in a moderately hot oven to bake. It will take about one hour and a half.

Sufficient for six persons.

APPLE AND CRANBERRY FOLLY

INGREDIENTS.—1 lb. of cranberries, 6 sponge cakes, ½ gill of sherry, 1 lb. of Empire apples, water (about 1½ to 2 gills), 2 eggs, 1 pint of milk, flavouring, 3 or 4 tablespoonfuls of sugar.

METHOD.—Peel, core and slice the apples, wash and stalk the cranberries.

Stew these together until tender, adding a little water and about two or three tablespoonfuls of sugar, or sufficient to sweeten them.

When cooked, rub through a sieve, then crumble the sponge cakes and add. Mix all together, and when cool, stir in the sherry.

Beat up the eggs. Heat the milk and add to them. Then strain into a jug or double boiler. Add the sugar (one good tablespoonful) and cook in a saucepan of water until the custard thickens, keeping it stirred occasionally and being careful not to let it curdle.

Add flavouring to taste and leave until cold.

Turn the apple and cranberry mixture into a dish, pour the custard on top and, just before serving, decorate with a few glacé cherries.

Sufficient for about eight persons.

NOTE.—The sherry may be omitted if desired, and a little grated lemon-rind and some lemon-juice added to flavour.

APPLE DUMPLINGS

INGREDIENTS.—1¼ lb. of short or flaky pastry (when mixed) (see p. 252), 6 Empire apples of even size, 1½ flat teaspoonfuls of ground cinnamon, ½ flat teaspoonful of ground ginger, 6 teaspoonfuls of sugar, ¼ flat teaspoonful of ground cloves.

METHOD.—Peel the apples and remove the core, being careful to keep the fruit whole.

Roll out the pastry to one-eighth of an inch thick and cut out six large rounds—they must be large enough to wrap round the apple.

You can use the lid of a saucepan to cut the rounds.

Turn them on to the other side and stand an apple in the centre of each.

Mix the sugar and spices together and divide between the apples, putting it into the centre hole.

Damp the edge of pastry and draw to the top of the fruit, moulding it round smoothly, then turn on to the other end, shape evenly and stand on a baking-sheet.

Brush with milk and put into a hot oven to bake, lessening the heat when the pastry is cooked ; they will take about half an hour or until the apples are tender.

Dredge with castor sugar before serving.

APPLE MERINGUE PUDDING

INGREDIENTS.—2 lb. of Empire apples, 2 tablespoonfuls of granulated sugar, water (about 1 gill), 2 eggs, 1 lemon (grated rind), 2 tablespoonfuls of castor sugar, ½ oz. of Empire butter, 1 oz. of crystallised ginger—cut in small pieces.

METHOD.—Peel and quarter the apples, remove the cores and cut them in slices.

Stew in a saucepan, adding granulated sugar to taste and just a little water. When tender, rub through a sieve. Add the finely grated lemon-rind, the butter, ginger, and the beaten yolks of the eggs.

Turn into a pie-dish and bake gently in a moderate oven for about twenty minutes without letting it boil.

Cool slightly, then whisk the egg-whites to a stiff froth and fold in the castor sugar.

Put this into a forcing bag and force on to the pudding, dredge with castor sugar, and put in a slow oven to set and lightly colour the meringue. Serve cold.

Sufficient for six persons.

APPLE AND SULTANA TART

INGREDIENTS.—½ lb. of Empire apples, ¼ lb. of Empire sultanas, 1 lemon (rind only), 2½ gills of cold water, 2 teaspoonfuls of cornflour, 2 dessertspoonfuls of granulated sugar, 1 oz. of almonds, about ¾ to 1 lb. of flaky pastry (when mixed) (see p. 252).

METHOD.—Wash the sultanas and soak them in two gills of the water for about an hour. Then turn them into a saucepan, add the sugar and stew them gently for two or three minutes. Draw the pan aside from the flame.

Mix the cornflour to a smooth paste with the half gill of cold water. Stir the syrup from the sultanas on to the cornflour. Turn it into a pan and boil for a few minutes, keeping it stirred. Draw the pan aside, add the sultanas, grated lemon-rind, chopped almonds, and apples, peeled, cored, and either grated or chopped, but not cooked.

Mix all well together and leave until cold.

Roll out the pastry into two rounds, one rather thinner than the other. Line a sandwich-tin with the thinner piece, put in the prepared mixture, then damp the edge and cover the fruit with a thicker round of pastry.

Mark straight lines across the top (both ways), brush with milk, and put into a hot oven to bake.

It will take about twenty minutes.

Sufficient for six persons.

APRICOT BASKETS

INGREDIENTS.—4 oz. of Empire butter, 6 oz. of castor sugar, 8 oz. of flour, 1 teaspoonful of baking-powder, 2 eggs, milk, apricot jam as required, desiccated coconut, 2 oz. of baked almonds, angelica, a tin of Empire apricots.

METHOD.—Beat the sugar and fat to a cream Add the eggs separately, and when they are well beaten in stir in the flour and baking-powder (sieved together) and a little milk as required.

Mix all lightly together. Turn the mixture into a greased cake-tin or a deep sandwich-tin lined with paper, and bake in a moderately hot oven.

The mixture should be nearly two inches in depth when baked.

Turn out when cooked, and leave on a sieve until cold.

To Make the Baskets

Take a plain round pastry cutter, almost two inches in diameter, and cut out as many rounds as possible, cutting through to the bottom. There should be about five.

Now take a small cutter—about three-quarters of an inch in diameter—and cut out a small piece from the centre of each round, but only half-way through.

Warm some apricot jam, and, if necessary, thin it down with a little water, then rub it through a sieve. Brush the rounds of sponge with this, and coat some of them with finely chopped baked almonds and the remainder with coconut.

Fill the centres with apricots cut in dice, put one whole one on the top, and affix a handle of angelica to each.

The Angelica Handles

Cut long strips of angelica. Put them into moderately hot water for a minute or two to make them more supple.

Make a hole with an iron skewer on either side of each basket, at the top, and fix the handles in position.

APRICOT RAMEQUINS

INGREDIENTS.—1 tin of Empire apricots, 1 pint packet of lemon jelly, 1 egg, 1½ gills of milk, 2d. of cream, cochineal, 1 oz. of sugar.

METHOD.—Dissolve one-eighth of the jelly in half a gill of hot water. Rinse six or eight small moulds in cold water and pour a dessertspoonful of jelly into each.

Let it set while preparing some apricot purée and custard.

Put aside six apricots and rub the rest through a hair sieve.

Put half a pint of the purée in a saucepan and make it hot, then dissolve the jelly in it.

Leave it to cool.

To make the custard, beat the egg and put it in a double saucepan with the milk and sugar.

Stir till thick, remove from the fire, and leave it to cool.

When custard and purée are cold, mix them together and add the cream.

Fill the moulds and leave to set.

To serve, put one apricot into each of six ramequins or baking-cases and turn the creams out on to them.

NOTE.—If preferred, turn the creams on to a dish and put an apricot on the top of each.

BALMORAL PUDDING

INGREDIENTS.—¼ lb. of Empire butter, 3 oz. of Empire sultanas, 1 or 2 eggs, ¼ lb. of castor sugar, 5 oz. of flour, ¼ flat teaspoonful of carbonate of soda, ½ pint of custard, 1 lemon.

METHOD.—Wash, pick over and dry the fruit. Sieve the flour with the carbonate of soda. Grate the lemon-rind finely.

Beat the sugar and fat to a cream, add each egg separately, stir in quickly, and beat well before adding the second. When both are well beaten in, stir in the flour, lemon-rind, and sultanas, and a little milk as required. Mix together lightly, turn into a greased basin or mould, cover securely with a well-greased paper and steam for two hours.

Just before you are ready to dish up the pudding, make half a pint of custard (with custard-powder).

Turn the pudding on to a hot dish and pour the custard round it.

Sufficient for about six or seven persons.

BREAD-AND-BUTTER PUD-DING

INGREDIENTS.—Slices of brown or white bread-and-butter (about 3 to 4 oz.), 2 oz. Empire sultanas, 2 eggs, 1 pint of milk, ratafia flavouring, 1 to 1½ tablespoonfuls of sugar.

METHOD.—Stale bread-and-butter left over can be used, or freshly cut.

Wash, pick over and dry the sultanas. Divide the bread-and-butter into convenient sized pieces, put half of them into a pie-dish and sprinkle with sugar and sultanas.

Beat up the eggs, mix with the milk, and add a few drops of flavouring. Pour some over the bread-and-butter in the dish, then add the remainder of the slices and the egg and milk. Leave to soak for an hour or so, then bake in a moderately warm oven until set, being careful not to let the pudding boil.

Note.—If liked, this pudding may be browned lightly under the grill before being served, in which case it is better to have the sultanas mostly on the under slices.

CARAMEL FRUIT FOOL

Ingredients.—Tin of Empire pears, 2 dessertspoonfuls of sugar, 1 egg, 1½ gills of milk, 1 oz. of ground Brazil nuts, 1½ dessertspoonfuls of water.

Method.—Drain the syrup from the pears, then rub the fruit through a sieve.

Put the sugar in a small, strong saucepan with the water. Let it dissolve slowly, then boil into a rich golden-brown.

Draw aside and leave until cold. Add the milk and dissolve the caramel over a low burner.

Beat the egg, add the caramel milk, strain into a jug and cook in a saucepan of water until it thickens.

When cold, mix this with the pear pulp, add about three parts of the ground nuts and a little sugar if required.

Two or three tablespoonfuls of pear syrup may be added if liked, but take care not to make the mixture too thin.

Serve in custard glasses with the remainder of the ground nuts sprinkled on the top.

Sufficient for six persons.

YOUNG CARROTS AND CHEESE SAUCE

Ingredients.—½ bunch of young carrots, Empire butter, slices of bread as required.

For the Sauce.—1 oz. of flour, 1 oz. of Empire butter, ½ pint of milk or milk and water, 3 oz. of Empire cheese, salt and pepper.

Method.—Scrape the carrots and cook in boiling water with a little salt added. Drain and split into halves.

Cut as many oblong pieces of bread as you have carrots, toast and butter them, then arrange two halves of carrot on each piece.

Make a thick white sauce and when it boils, stir in the cheese, grated finely.

Season to taste and cook for a few minutes.

Then coat the carrots and toast with the cheese sauce, and serve them with some finely grated cheese sprinkled over.

CHEESE SOUFFLES

Ingredients.—2 oz. of Empire cheese, 1 yolk and 2 whites of eggs, salt, pepper, and mixed mustard, 1 gill of milk, ½ gill of water, 3 sheets of leaf gelatine.

Method.—Beat up the yolk of the egg, heat the milk, and add to it, and cook in a double boiler until it thickens, keeping it stirred.

Remove from the pan and leave until cold.

Grate the cheese very finely and add to the custard.

Season with salt, pepper, and mixed mustard.

Dissolve the gelatine in a saucepan with the water and strain into the cheese mixture. Leave until beginning to set.

Whisk the egg-whites to a very stiff froth, and fold in lightly. Put in small soufflé cases and, when quiet set, sprinkle a little finely grated cheese on top of each.

Sufficient to fill ten small soufflé cases.

CHRISTENING CAKE

Ingredients.—6 oz. of Empire butter, 6 oz. of soft brown sugar, ½ lb. of flour, ¼ flat teaspoonful of carbonate of soda, ¼ lb. of peel, ¾ lb. of Empire sultanas, ¼ lb. of Empire currants, 2 oz. of glacé cherries, nutmeg, 2 or 3 eggs, 1 oz. of ground almonds, orange essence, milk.

For the Almond Paste Icing.—1 lb. of icing sugar, 10 oz. of ground almonds, 2 or 3 egg-whites, vanilla or orange essence.

For the Royal Icing.—1½ lb. of icing sugar, 1½ dessertspoonfuls of lemon-juice, 2 or 3 egg-whites, silver balls, silver cake-band, and font or other suitable decoration.

Method.—Cut up the peel and cherries. Wash, pick over and dry the currants and sultanas.

Sieve the flour with the soda, and add to it about half a small nutmeg (grated).

Cream the fat and sugar.

Add each egg separately and stir them in quickly. Beat the mixture well before adding each egg.

When all three are well beaten in, gradually stir in the flour, ground almonds, and prepared fruit, with just a little milk if required, but be very careful not to make the mixture too moist or the fruit will sink in the tin. If preferred, some sherry, rum, or brandy may be added.

When well mixed, turn the cake into a greased and papered tin and put it into a moderate oven to bake. It will probably take about from two hours and a half to three hours' steady baking.

When cooked and cold, wrap the cake in greaseproof paper and keep it in an airtight tin until required.

Note.—The cake-tin should be lined with two or three thicknesses of greased paper.

The Almond Paste

To Make the Almond Paste.— Roll the lumps out of the sugar and rub it through a fine sieve. Add the ground almonds and then mix to a stiff paste with slightly beaten egg-whites. Add vanilla or orange flavouring to taste.

Work the paste until it is smooth, then roll it out and use as required.

To Prepare the Cake and Ice it with Almond Paste.—Scrape it if necessary and knock off any loose crumbs. Brush it over with melted red currant jelly.

Put a strip of paste round the sides of the cake, then stand it on an upturned dish and cover the top with a round of paste, pressing it on firmly and making it quite level. If the cake has risen unevenly, you can either cut off a slice before you begin or else make it level with the almond paste.

Leave the cake for at least one day to allow the paste to dry before covering it with royal icing.

The Royal Icing

To Make the Royal Icing.—Prepare the sugar as before. Add the lemon-juice and enough *stiffly whisked* egg-white to make a fairly stiff paste, then beat it well until smooth. To test the consistency you should be able to mark letters on it and they will remain distinct.

To Ice and Decorate the Cake.— Put some icing on top of the cake and spread it over evenly, using a knife occasionally, dipped in hot water, to smooth it. Cover the sides in the same way, paying special attention to make the top edge neat.

Leave to dry, and meanwhile cover the remainder of the icing with a damp cloth to prevent it getting too stiff.

Plan out a simple design before beginning to decorate.

Beat up the icing and put into an icing bag, pipe the top with straight lines across each way, and put a ring of rose patterns topped with silver balls round the edge.

Place a small font or other suitable decoration in the centre, using a dab of icing to make it adhere. When the icing is set, put a silver cake-band round the sides to give a finish to the cake.

Note.—Stand your cake on a cake-board before beginning to pipe it. A revolving cake-stand is useful when doing this.

CHRISTMAS PUDDING

(Made with Empire Fruits)

Ingredients.—1½ lb. of Empire currants, 1 lb. of Empire sultanas, ½ lb. of mixed peel, 2 lb. of Empire raisins, 1½ lb. of suet, ½ lb. of bread-crumbs, 1 lb. of flour, ¾ lb. of sugar, 1 large carrot, ¼ lb. of shelled walnuts, 1 orange and 1 lemon (rind and juice), 1 nutmeg, 1 large saltspoonful of ground ginger, 6 eggs, 1 lb. of black treacle, 1½ gills of milk, ¾ gill of rum, a little ratafia flavouring.

Method.—Wash the fruit, dry thoroughly, then remove the stalks. Cut up the peel and stone the raisins. Chop the suet finely and mix well with the flour and breadcrumbs; add also the ginger, grated nutmeg, and sugar, and mix together.

Scrape the carrot, then grate it finely, and add to the dry ingredients with the grated orange and lemon-rind, prepared fruit, and the walnuts (chopped up roughly).

When well mixed, stir in the beaten eggs, mixed with the treacle (this may be warmed slightly). Add also the milk.

Beat all together, then stir in the rum and ratafia flavouring.

Put into well-buttered basins, cover with buttered paper and floured pudding-cloths, and cook in boiling water for about six hours.

Sufficient to make three large puddings or four medium-sized ones.

NOTE.—The puddings may be served plain or stuck with baked almonds.

To PREPARE THE ALMONDS.—Blanch them and put them on a baking-sheet lined with a sheet of white paper, and bake slowly in the oven until golden-brown.

The rum may be omitted if desired.

COCONUT FRUIT DUFF

INGREDIENTS.—¼ lb. of desiccated coconut, 2 oz. of candied peel, 6 oz. of Empire raisins, 1 lemon (rind only), ¼ lb. of flour, 6 oz. of breadcrumbs, 5 oz. of sugar, 5 oz. of suet, 1 egg, milk and water to mix.

METHOD.—Wash the raisins, stone them and cut them in halves. Cut up the peel.

Chop the suet finely and mix with the flour. Add the breadcrumbs, coconut, grated lemon-rind, sugar, and prepared fruit, and mix together.

Beat up the egg and add with some milk and water as required. Turn into a greased basin or mould, cover securely with a well greased paper and steam for about two hours and a half to three hours, then turn on to a hot dish and serve.

Sufficient for eight or ten persons.

COFFEE FRUIT CAKE

INGREDIENTS.—¾ lb. of flour, 2 tablespoonfuls of coffee essence, ½ flat teaspoonful of carbonate of soda, 2 oz. of glacé cherries, 2 oz. of citron peel, ½ lb. of Empire sultanas, 6 oz. of Empire butter, 5 oz. of sugar, ⅓ teacupful of Empire honey, 2 eggs, a few almonds.

METHOD.—Wash, pick over and dry the sultanas. Cut up the peel and cherries. Sieve the flour with the carbonate of soda and then rub in the butter. Add the sugar and fruit and mix all the dry ingredients together.

Whisk up the eggs and stir in the honey (warmed slightly) and coffee essence. Whisk these together, add them to the flour and other dry ingredients.

Beat the mixture well. Turn it into a greased cake-tin and strew some almonds (blanched and halved) on top.

Put the cake into a moderately hot oven to bake. It will take about one and a half to two hours to bake.

CURRANT SCONES

INGREDIENTS.—½ lb. of flour, pinch of salt, ¼ flat teaspoonful of carbonate of soda, 1 oz. of Empire butter, 2 dessertspoonfuls of castor sugar, sour milk, 1½ oz. of Empire currants.

METHOD.—Wash, pick over and dry the currants. Sieve the flour with the soda and salt. Rub in the butter, and add the sugar and fruit.

Stir in enough sour milk to make a soft dough.

Turn it on to a floured board and roll it out to about a quarter of an inch thick.

Cut it into rounds with a plain cutter (about three inches in diameter), put them on a greased and floured baking-sheet and bake them in a quick oven for about ten minutes.

Sufficient for about seven scones.

CURRANT ROCK CAKES

INGREDIENTS.—6 oz. of flour, ¼ flat teaspoonful of carbonate of soda, 1 orange (rind only), 1 lemon (rind only), 2 oz. of desiccated coconut, 3 oz. of castor sugar, 3 oz. of Empire butter, 1 egg, 3 oz. of Empire currants.

METHOD.—Wash, pick over and dry the fruit. Sieve the flour with the soda.

Beat up the egg. Cream the fat and sugar. Add the grated lemon and orange rinds. Then mix in the flour, currants, and coconut together with the egg. Mix all to a *stiff* consistency. Put the mixture on to a greased baking-sheet in small heaps. Dredge them with castor sugar and sprinkle them with coconut. Put the cakes into a hot oven to bake. They will take about fifteen minutes to cook.

This quantity makes about fifteen cakes.

EMPIRE APPLE JELLIES

INGREDIENTS.—2 lb. of Empire apples, 1 gill of water, 5 oz. of sugar, juice and rind of a lemon, 1½ pint packets of pineapple jelly, cochineal, 8 strips of angelica, small carton of cream.

METHOD.—Peel, core and slice the apples and stew them with the water and sugar. When soft rub them through a hair sieve and add the lemon-juice and grated lemon-rind.

Put it in a saucepan with the jelly, stir over a low gas till dissolved and add a few drops of cochineal. Rinse fluted cake-tins in cold water and fill up with the jelly.

When cold put in handles made of strips of angelica and decorate with cream, using an icing pump fitted with a rose tube.

NOTE.—If the angelica is put into moderately hot water for a minute or two it will make it more supple.

EMPIRE CABINET PUDDING

INGREDIENTS.—5 sponge cakes, 2 eggs, 1 pint of milk, ¼ lb. of Empire raisins, 1½ dessertspoonfuls of castor sugar, a few drops of orange essence, 2 small macaroon biscuits.

METHOD.—Wash, pick over and dry the raisins, then stone them. Butter a plain mould or basin and decorate with some of the raisins, dipping the latter in a little melted butter.

Beat the eggs and mix with the milk and orange essence. Crumble the sponge cakes and macaroons. Put a layer of these in the bottom of the mould, then add a few raisins, a little sugar and some egg and milk.

Continue in this way until the ingredients are used and the mould full, when cover with a buttered paper.

Let it stand for an hour then, and steam gently for about one hour and a quarter or until set, being careful not to let it curdle.

Leave for a minute or two before turning out, and serve hot.

Sufficient for five persons.

EMPIRE RIBBON CAKE

INGREDIENTS.—3 oz. of Empire sultanas, 2 eggs, 1 oz. of Empire butter, 2 oz. of castor sugar, 4 oz. of flour, ½ tablespoonful of water, cochineal, 1 level teaspoonful of baking-powder.

METHOD.—Grease a shallow tin. Wash, dry and pick the sultanas. Rub the butter into the sieved flour and baking-powder, and add the sugar and sultanas.

Beat the eggs with the water and then mix with the dry ingredients.

Put in the tin and bake in a quick oven for about fifteen minutes.

RIBBON ICING

INGREDIENTS.—8 oz. of icing sugar, 3 to 4 dessertspoonfuls of tepid water, essence of lemon, cochineal, 2d. glass tube of silver balls.

METHOD.—Have ready a skewer and an icing pump with a plain icing tube screwed on.

Sieve the icing sugar and put it in a saucepan. Add the water and flavouring.

Stir over the gas for a few seconds till the base of the pan feels warm. Put a quarter of the icing in a cup and colour bright pink with cochineal, then put it in the icing pump, as both the white and pink icing must be ready at the same time.

Pour the white icing quickly on top of the cake, then with the pink icing press out *straight* lines across the cake. The lines should be about one inch apart.

If this is done quickly the pink icing will sink into the white.

To make the wavy lines mark straight, deep lines with a skewer across the pink lines. This must be done before the icing hardens. To finish, press silver balls round the edge.

EMPIRE FRUIT CAKE

INGREDIENTS.—4 oz. of Empire butter, 2 oz. of castor sugar, 4 oz. of soft brown sugar, 1 orange (grated rind and juice), ½ lb. of flour, 2 eggs, some grated nutmeg, 1 flat teaspoonful of ground ginger, 1 flat teaspoonful of mixed spice, ½ flat teaspoonful of carbonate of soda, ¼ lb. of candied peel, 1 oz. of shelled walnuts, ¼ lb. of figs, ¾ lb. of Empire currants, ¼ lb. of Empire sultanas, milk.

METHOD.—Wash, pick over and dry the fruit—figs, currants, sultanas. Cut up the peel. Stalk and cut up the figs. Chop the walnuts.

Sieve the flour with the soda, ginger, and spice, and add a little grated nutmeg.

Put the butter and sugars into a basin and beat them to a cream. Add the grated orange-rind and gradually stir in the prepared fruit, nuts, and flour alternately with the well-beaten eggs.

Mix all together, adding the strained orange-juice and a little milk if required.

Turn the mixture into a well-greased cake-tin—it should only be two-thirds full—cover it securely with a greased paper and steam it for an hour and three-quarters. Then uncover the cake and put it into a very moderate oven, and bake it gently for about another hour and three-quarters.

GINGER SANDWICH CAKE

INGREDIENTS.—6 oz. of flour, 1½ flat teaspoonfuls of ground ginger, ¼ flat teaspoonful of carbonate of soda, 3 oz. of Empire butter, 2 oz. of sugar, 4 oz. of Empire honey, 2 eggs, few almonds, milk.

FOR THE FILLING.—2 dessertspoonfuls of Empire honey, 5 oz. of icing sugar, 2 oz. of Empire butter.

METHOD.—Sieve the flour with the ground ginger and put them into a basin. Blanch and chop up a few almonds.

Put the sugar, fat, and honey into a saucepan to melt (do not boil), then cool the mixture a little and add it to the beaten eggs.

Pour this into the centre of the flour, mix together, and beat well.

Stir in the carbonate of soda mixed in a teaspoonful of milk.

Turn the mixture into small greased sandwich-tins, sprinkle the almonds on the top, and bake in a hot oven.

Cool on a sieve, and when cold split the cakes in halves and spread them with a layer of filling. Then sandwich them together again.

THE HONEY FILLING.—To make the filling, roll the lumps out of the icing sugar and rub it through a fine sieve.

Add the butter and beat both to a cream.

Stir in the honey.

GROUND RICE SULTANA CAKE

INGREDIENTS.—¼ lb. of ground rice, ¼ lb. of Empire sultanas, 5 oz. of Empire butter, ¼ lb. of flour, 1 teaspoonful of cream of tartar, ½ flat teaspoonful of carbonate of soda, 4 oz. of castor sugar, 2 eggs, milk.

METHOD.—Grease a cake-tin and line it with greased paper.

Wash, pick over and dry the fruit. Cream the fat and sugar. Add each egg separately and beat the mixture for a few minutes.

When both eggs are added, gradually stir in the flour, ground rice, cream of tartar, and carbonate of soda (all sieved together), also the prepared fruit, adding some milk, if required.

Turn the mixture into the cake-tin, dredge the top with castor sugar, and put it into a moderately hot oven to bake. It will take about an hour or a little longer to cook.

HONEY CAKES

INGREDIENTS.—4 oz. of Empire honey, ½ lb. of flour, 1 teaspoonful of ground cinnamon, ¼ flat teaspoonful of carbonate of soda, 4 oz. of Barbados sugar, 4 oz. of Empire butter, 1 egg, milk.

METHOD.—Sieve the flour with the ground cinnamon and carbonate of soda.

Cream the fat and sugar. Separate the egg-yolk from the white. Beat the yolk into the creamed fat and sugar, then add the honey gradually.

Stir in the flour with a little milk as required, and mix all together lightly.

Whisk the egg-white to a stiff froth and fold into the mixture.

Stand some baking-cups on a baking-sheet. About half fill them with the mixture. Dredge the top of each with castor sugar.

Put the cakes into a hot oven to bake. They will take about fifteen or twenty minutes to cook.

HONEY GINGERBREAD

INGREDIENTS.—6 oz. of Empire honey, ½ lb. of flour, 3 oz. of Empire butter, 3 oz. of sugar, 1 teaspoonful of ground ginger, ¼ teaspoonful of mixed spice, ¼ flat teaspoonful of carbonate of soda, 1 egg, milk.

METHOD.—Sieve the flour with the ground ginger and spice and put them into a basin, making a well in the centre.

Put the butter, honey, and sugar into a saucepan to dissolve (but do not boil), then cool them slightly.

Whisk up the egg, stir into it the honey, etc. Then pour the egg mixture into the centre of the flour and mix all together, adding a little milk as required.

Beat well for a few minutes, then stir in the soda mixed smoothly in a spoonful of milk.

Turn the mixture into a greased baking-tin and put it into a moderately hot oven to bake. It will take about forty-five minutes to cook.

Put the cake on to a sieve to cool, and when it is cold cut it into even-sized pieces.

If preferred, the mixture may be baked in a cake-tin, but it will require more time.

NOTE.—A few almonds or a little candied peel may be added to give variety. The spice may be omitted if not liked.

HONEY PUDDING

INGREDIENTS.—3 or 4 tablespoonfuls of Empire honey, 3 oz. of breadcrumbs, 3 oz. of flour, 3 oz. of Empire butter, 3 oz. of castor sugar, barely ¼ flat teaspoonful of carbonate of soda, 1 or 2 eggs, milk.

METHOD.—Grease a basin and put the honey in the bottom of it.

Sieve the flour with the carbonate of soda, then mix with the breadcrumbs. Cream the fat and sugar.

Separate the eggs. Beat the yolks into the creamed fat and sugar, then stir in the flour and breadcrumbs with some milk, as required.

Whisk the egg-whites to a stiff froth and fold in lightly.

Turn into the prepared basin, cover securely with a well-greased paper, and steam for about one hour and a half.

Sufficient for six persons.

HONEY ROLY-POLY

INGREDIENTS.—½ lb. of flour, ¼ lb. of suet, 1 flat teaspoonful of baking-powder, water to mix, 2 tablespoonfuls of Empire honey, 2 oz. of breadcrumbs, ½ flat teaspoonful of ground ginger, 1½ oz. of shelled Brazil nuts.

METHOD.—To make the filling, warm the honey in a saucepan, then stir in the breadcrumbs, mixed with the ground ginger, also the Brazils (previously put through a mincer). Mix all together, then leave to cool.

Chop the suet finely and mix with the flour and baking-powder, add water gradually, and mix to a dough. It must not be at all sticky. Turn on to a floured board and roll to an oblong shape (not too thin). Then turn on to the other side and spread over the prepared filling, leaving a good margin all round.

Damp the edges and roll up, pinching it well together at either end; then roll in a scalded and floured pudding-cloth and tie securely.

Put into boiling water and boil for about one and a half to two hours.

Sufficient for about six persons.

NOTE.—Some prefer to roll a roly-poly in a greased paper, in which case place the latter on the pudding-cloth (floured but not scalded) and roll the pudding in both at the same time. In this way the paper and cloth will unroll together.

HOT CROSS BUNS

INGREDIENTS.—½ oz. of yeast, 1 lb. of flour, pinch of salt, 2 oz. of Empire butter, ½ pint of milk, 1 flat teaspoonful of mixed spice, 1 flat teaspoonful of ground ginger, 3 dessertspoonfuls of castor sugar, 2 tablespoonfuls of Empire currants, 1 oz. of candied peel, 1 teaspoonful of castor sugar (for mixing yeast).

METHOD.—Put the yeast into a small basin with one teaspoonful of castor sugar and mix them together until they liquefy.

Warm the milk and add it to the yeast.

Take half the flour and sieve it with the salt. Stir in the yeast and milk and mix all together, then cover the basin loosely and put it into a warm place for about forty-five minutes to an hour.

Wash, pick over and dry the currants.

Sieve the remainder of the flour with the spice and ground ginger. Rub in the butter, and add the sugar, currants, and the peel, cut in small pieces. Mix all these ingredients together and, when the yeast mixture is ready, gradually beat them into it.

Turn the dough on to a floured board and knead it for a few minutes. Divide it into portions and make them into smooth bun shapes.

Put them on a lightly greased baking-sheet, mark each with a cross, using the back of a knife, and stand them in a warm place to rise for twenty minutes or half an hour, or until double their size. Then put them into a hot oven to bake. They will take about half an hour.

Brush the tops of the buns with milk and sugar glaze, and return them to the oven for a minute or so to dry.

THE GLAZE.—To make the glaze, mix one dessertspoonful of castor sugar with one tablespoonful of milk until dissolved.

Sufficient to make eighteen buns or more, according to size.

ICED SCOTTISH CAKES

INGREDIENTS.—½ lb. of flour, 6 oz. of Empire butter, 4 oz. of castor sugar, ½ flat teaspoonful of baking-powder, a little milk, 3 oz. of Empire sultanas.

FOR THE ICING.—4 oz. of icing sugar, about 1 tablespoonful of cold water, cochineal, vanilla flavouring, hundreds and thousands.

METHOD.—Sieve the flour with the baking-powder. Cream the fat and sugar. Stir in the sultanas, previously washed and dried, also the flour and baking-powder and mix to a fairly stiff consistency, adding just a little milk as required.

Turn the mixture into baking-cups, only three parts full, and put them into a moderately hot oven. They should take about twenty minutes to cook.

When cold spread a little icing on top of each cake and sprinkle it with hundreds and thousands.

WATER ICING.—To make the icing, rub the icing sugar through a hair sieve. Put it into a saucepan and mix it to a thick paste with cold water.

Flavour it with vanilla and colour slightly with cochineal.

Stand a saucepan over a low burner and stir the icing until the base of the pan feels warm, then use as required. Sufficient for twenty cakes.

ICED SHORTBREAD BISCUITS

INGREDIENTS.—5 oz. of flour, good pinch of mixed spice, 1 oz. of Empire currants, 3 oz. of Empire butter, 2 oz. of castor sugar.

FOR THE ICING.—¼ lb. of icing sugar, about a tablespoonful of water, vanilla flavouring.

METHOD.—Cream the fat and sugar, stir in the flour, spice, and currants (previously cleaned) and work it all into a stiff paste.

Turn the paste on to a lightly floured board, roll it out thinly and cut it into rounds.

Place the rounds on a lightly greased baking-sheet and bake in a very moderate oven for about twenty minutes.

When the biscuits are cold, make some thin white icing, pour a little in the centre of each biscuit and spread it to the edge. Leave the icing to set. The currants should show through the icing.

WATER ICING.—To make the icing, rub the sugar through a hair sieve. Put it into a saucepan and mix it with the water. Add vanilla flavouring to taste and a few drops of colouring, then stir over a low burner until the base of the pan feels warm.

The icing should not coat too thickly. Sufficient to make about twelve biscuits.

HONEY TART

INGREDIENTS. — ½ lb. of short pastry (when mixed), 4 tablespoonfuls of Empire honey, 5 tablespoonfuls of breadcrumbs, 1 lemon.

METHOD.—Roll out the pastry fairly

thinly and cut a round. Line a sandwich-tin with it, then trim and decorate the edge. Melt the honey in a saucepan, and stir in the breadcrumbs and finely grated rind of the lemon. Let this cool before turning it into the pastry-lined tin. Cut four strips of pastry out of the trimmings, twist them, and put across the tart. Then put into a hot oven to bake. It will take about fifteen to twenty minutes.

SHORT PASTRY

INGREDIENTS.—½ lb. of flour, pinch of salt, 5 oz. of Empire butter, ½ teaspoonful of baking-powder, water to mix.

METHOD.—Sieve the flour with the salt and baking-powder. Rub in the butter finely, then mix in sufficient cold water to make a stiff paste, when roll out and use as required.

JERSEY PUDDING

INGREDIENTS.—2 lb. of Empire apples, about 1 gill of water, 2 tablespoonfuls of granulated sugar, 1 or 2 eggs, their weight in castor sugar and Empire butter, 5 oz. of flour, 1 flat teaspoonful of baking-powder, milk.

METHOD.—Peel and quarter the apples, remove the cores and cut in slices. Cook in a saucepan with the water and granulated sugar, and when tender mash to a pulp.

More or less water may be used as required, and sugar to taste. Beat the castor sugar and fat to a cream. Add each egg separately, stir in quickly, and beat well before adding the second.

When both are added, sieve the flour and baking-powder and stir in. Mix together lightly, adding a little milk as required.

Grease a pie-dish or Pyrex dish, put the apple pulp in the bottom of it, and turn the prepared mixture on top of the apples. Put into a moderately hot oven to bake. It will take about one hour and a quarter.

Sufficient for six to eight persons.

MERINGUE PEACHES

INGREDIENTS.—A tin of Empire peaches, some shortbread biscuits (allow one for each peach), 1 egg-white, 1 tablespoonful of castor sugar, jam.

METHOD.—Drain the peaches from the syrup and place one on each biscuit—cup side downwards.

Whisk the egg-white to a stiff froth and then fold in the castor sugar.

Turn the meringue into an icing bag with a rose or shell tube fixed in the bottom of it, and force it out to form a border all round each peach.

Put in a cool oven to set the meringue, and when cold serve with a little jam on the top of the peach.

Allow one or two for each person.

NOTE.—For these use the round shortbread biscuits (with or without currants). If not home-made they can be obtained from almost any baker, and the cost is about seven for sixpence.

MINCEMEAT

INGREDIENTS.—¾ lb. of Empire sultanas, 1 lb. of Empire raisins, ½ lb. of peel, 1½ lb. of Empire currants, 1 lb. of Empire apples (when peeled and cored), 1 lb. of beef suet, 1 lb. of sugar, ¼ lb. of shelled Brazils, ½ teaspoonful of ground ginger, rind and juice of 2 lemons, ⅓ bottle of ratafia flavouring, ⅓ gill of rum (if liked).

METHOD.—Wash and dry the currants, raisins, and sultanas, then remove the stalks.

Stone and chop the raisins and cut up the peel.

Peel, core and mince the apples.

Chop the suet finely, add the sugar, ground ginger, grated lemon-rind, prepared fruit, and Brazil nuts, the latter put through the mincer.

Mix all the ingredients together very thoroughly, then moisten with the strained lemon-juice, and stir in the ratafia flavouring and rum.

Put into jars and press down well, cover with parchment covers, and make airtight.

NOTE.—If preferred, almonds may be used in place of Brazils; if using the former, blanch, skin and chop them roughly. The rum may be omitted if desired.

MINCE PIES

INGREDIENTS. — Mincemeat (made with Empire fruits and apples), ½ lb.

of flour, pinch of salt, ¼ lb. of lard, 3 oz. of Empire butter, water to mix.

METHOD.—TO MAKE THE FLAKY PASTRY.—Sieve the flour and salt into a basin, rub in the butter, then add cold water and mix to a stiff paste.

Put the lard on a well-flowered board and roll into thin pieces. Put this aside and roll out the pastry fairly thinly to a square or oblong shape, using only as little flour as possible.

Turn this on to the other side, put the lard all over it and press down lightly. Then fold sides to the centre both ways, then over in half—the pastry will then be folded into eight. This pastry improves if left a day before being baked, in which case leave in a cool place and cover with a buttered paper to prevent it getting dry on the outside.

To MAKE MINCE PIES.—Roll out the pastry to a quarter of an inch thick and cut rounds for the top of the pies. Put these aside, roll the remainder of the pastry out thinly and cut as many thin rounds as you have thick ones. Line patty-pans with the thin rounds, fill with mince-meat, and cover with a thick round. Stand them on a baking-sheet and put into a hot oven to bake ; they will take about twenty minutes.

To GLAZE THEM.—When cooked, brush the tops with frothed white of egg, dredge freely with castor sugar, and return to a cooler oven for a minute or two. Or, if you prefer, you may glaze them before cooking by brushing with milk.

MINIATURE SIMNELS

INGREDIENTS.—3 oz. of castor sugar, 3 oz. of Empire butter, 1 egg, ½ lb. of flour, ½ flat teaspoonful of mixed spice, ½ flat teaspoonful of ground ginger, ⅛ flat teaspoonful of carbonate of soda, 4 oz. of Empire currants, 2 oz. of Empire sultanas, 1 oz. of candied peel, milk.

FOR THE ALMOND PASTE.—½ lb. of icing sugar, ¼ lb. of ground almonds, egg, vanilla flavouring.

METHOD.—Wash, pick over and dry the fruit. Cut up the peel. Sieve the flour with the ground ginger, spice, and carbonate of soda. Beat the sugar and fat to a cream.

Add the egg, stir in quickly and beat the mixture well.

Gradually stir the flour and spices and the prepared fruit into the creamed fat, with just a little milk as required.

Put the mixture into baking-cups or greased tartlet-tins, filling them about two-thirds full, and bake them for about twenty-five minutes in a moderately hot oven. Cool the cakes on a sieve, and when cold decorate them with almond paste.

To decorate the cakes, put a wide edge of paste on the top of each, mark it with a fork to give it a rough appearance, or prick it with a skewer.

Brush the paste with yolk of egg mixed with a few drops of milk, and brown it very lightly under the grill. Fill the centre with tiny eggs of paste. These may be tinted to a pale shade with a few drops of colouring if desired.

ALMOND PASTE

To make the almond paste, roll the lumps out of the icing sugar and rub it through a hair sieve. Add the ground almonds and mix well together.

Beat the egg well and add enough of it, with a few drops of vanilla, to mix the almonds and sugar to a stiff paste. Work the mixture until smooth, then roll out and use as required.

Sufficient for twelve small cakes.

NEW YEAR PASTRIES

INGREDIENTS.—Some flaky pastry (as required) (see p. 252), 1 oz. of Empire butter, 2 oz. of castor sugar, 2 oz. of shelled walnuts, 2 oz. of Empire sultanas, 2 oz. of ground almonds, 1 egg, 1 tablespoonful of desiccated coconut.

METHOD.—Roll out some pastry thinly and line a small baking-sheet or the base of a baking-tin. Put the walnuts and sultanas (the latter previously washed and dried) through the mincer, and mix them with the coconut.

Beat the sugar and fat to a cream, then stir in the egg quickly and beat well. Add the ground almonds and prepared fruit and nuts and mix them all together. Cover the pastry with this mixture and bake in a quick oven.

When cooked, brush over the top with frothed egg-white, dredge with castor sugar and coconut. Return the pastry to the oven to dry and brown lightly.

As soon as it is cold, cut it into slices.

NUT FRUIT BATTER

INGREDIENTS.—4 oz. of Empire sultanas, 1 oz. of almonds, 2 eggs, ½ lb. of flour, 1 pint of milk, pinch of salt.

METHOD.—Sieve the flour and salt into a basin, make a well in the centre and pour in the eggs. Mix these with some of the flour, then take half the milk and add gradually, and mix to a smooth batter. Beat well, then stir in the remainder of the milk and leave the batter to stand for an hour or so.

When ready to bake, stir in the sultanas and the almonds, the latter blanched and cut up previously, and the former washed, picked and dried.

Turn into a greased pie-dish or Pyrex dish and bake for about an hour.

Serve with castor sugar.

Sufficient for six or eight persons.

ORANGE FRUIT CAKES

INGREDIENTS.—6 oz. of flour, 1 oz. of ground almonds, 1 large or 2 small oranges (rind and juice), ¼ flat tea-spoonful of carbonate of soda, 3 oz. of candied orange-peel, 4 oz. of Empire sultanas, 2 oz. of Empire currants, 3 oz. of Empire butter, 3 oz. of castor sugar, 1 egg, few almonds.

METHOD.—Wash, pick over and dry the fruit. Cut up the peel.

Sieve the flour with the soda.

Beat the sugar and fat to a cream. Add the finely grated orange-rind. Gradually stir in the flour, ground almonds, and prepared fruit, together with the egg (well beaten) and the strained juice of the orange. Mix well together and add a little milk if required.

Turn the mixture into greased sponge cake-tins. Sprinkle the top with castor sugar and add a few blanched almonds split into halves. Bake for about twenty minutes.

This quantity makes sixteen cakes.

PASTRY CAKE

INGREDIENTS.—About ½ lb. of short pastry—when mixed (see p. 252), 4 oz. of flour, 2 oz. of Empire butter, 2 oz. of sugar, 4 oz. of Empire sultanas, 2 oz. of candied peel, ½ flat tea-spoonful of ground ginger, ½ flat teaspoonful of ground cinnamon, ⅓ flat teaspoonful of carbonate of soda, 1 egg, milk.

METHOD.—Lightly grease a small round cake-tin. Roll out the pastry thinly and line the cake-tin evenly. Trim and decorate the edge.

Wash, pick over and dry the fruit. Cut up the peel.

Sieve the flour with the carbonate of soda, ground ginger, and cinnamon. Rub in the fat and add the sugar and fruit.

Mix all these dry ingredients together.

Whisk the egg, add it to the dry ingredients, and mix together to a fairly stiff cake consistency, adding only a very small quantity of milk.

Beat well. Turn the filling into the pastry-lined tin and bake it for about one hour and a half.

The oven must be rather hotter then usual at first on account of the pastry, but the heat should be lessened afterwards.

PEACH BLANCMANGE

INGREDIENTS.—A tin of Empire peaches, ½ lemon, ½ pint of milk, 3 oz. of castor sugar, ½ oz. of leaf gelatine.

METHOD.—Rub sufficient peaches through a sieve to give you about half a pint of pulp.

Dissolve the gelatine in a sauce-pan with half a gill of peach syrup, and strain into it, stir in the juice of the lemon, then add the milk and sugar to taste.

Leave until beginning to thicken, when stir up and pour into a wet border mould to set. Turn out, heap the remainder of the peaches in the centre and pour the syrup round.

Sufficient for about five persons.

PEACH GATEAU

INGREDIENTS.—A tin of Empire peaches, 2 eggs, 1 pint of milk, vanilla flavouring, 4 sponge cakes,

1 tablespoonful of sugar, 2 tablespoonfuls of desiccated coconut.

METHOD.—Beat up the eggs. Heat the milk and add to them with the sugar and coconut. Crumble the sponge cakes and stir in ; add also a few drops of vanilla flavouring.

Turn into a buttered mould, cover with a buttered paper and steam gently for about thirty to forty-five minutes, or until set, being careful not to let it curdle, or else bake gently until set.

When cold, turn out, pour peach syrup round, and heap some peaches on the top.

Sufficient for about five persons.

PEACH SOUFFLE PUDDING

INGREDIENTS.—1 pint of milk, 1 heaped tablespoonful of custard-powder. About 1 dozen almonds, 1 tin of Empire peaches, 1½ to 2 tablespoonfuls of sugar, 2 eggs, some flavouring essence.

METHOD.—Mix the custard-powder to a smooth paste with some of the milk. Boil the remainder and stir on to it, return to the pan, and boil for two or three minutes, keeping it well stirred, then draw aside and cool slightly.

Drain the syrup from the peaches and cut six of them into small pieces. You will also need a whole peach for the top of the pudding.

Blanch and cut up the almonds and add to the custard, with the sugar, peaches, and half a gill of the syrup. Separate the eggs, beat up the yolks and stir in. Flavour with a few drops of flavouring. Whisk the egg-whites to a stiff froth, and fold in lightly.

Turn into a pie-dish or Pyrex dish, dredge the top of the mixture with castor sugar, and bake slowly for about forty minutes, being careful not to let it boil.

Serve cold, with a peach in the centre.

Sufficient for six persons.

PEACH TRIFLE

INGREDIENTS.—A tin of Empire peaches, 1 sponge cake-ring, 1 oz. of almonds, 2 eggs and 1 extra white of egg, 1 pint of milk, 2 tablespoonfuls of castor sugar, vanilla flavouring, jam, angelica.

METHOD.—Blanch, skin and chop the almonds. Split the sponge-ring in halves, spread with jam and sprinkle with the nuts, then put half into a dish. Soak this with peach syrup and sandwich it together, and soak the top half. Heap peaches in the centre of the ring, the remainder cut up and put round the base.

Beat up the two eggs, heat the milk and add to them, then turn into a jug, stand in a saucepan of hot water, and cook until the custard thickens, keeping it stirred occasionally. Add sugar and flavouring to taste, and when cool pour round the outside of the ring.

Before serving, whisk the egg-white to a stiff froth, then fold in one tablespoonful of castor sugar. Cover the top of the sponge-ring with this, and decorate with rings of angelica.

NOTE.—If the sponge-ring is stale, it is advisable to heat the peach syrup.

Sufficient for six to eight persons.

PEAR MACAROONS

INGREDIENTS.—A tin of Empire pears, large macaroon biscuits—allow one for each pear, red jam and apricot jam, desiccated coconut, angelica.

METHOD.—Put the macaroons into a shallow serving dish and soak with pear syrup—previously heated.

Warm the jams and brush some of the pears with red jam and others with apricot, using only the syrup part of it. Then coat with coconut.

Put stalks of angelica into the pears, place one on each macaroon, and serve with cream, if liked.

PEAR MOULD

INGREDIENTS.—A tin of Empire pears, 1½ gills of milk, 2 eggs, ½ to ¾ oz. of leaf gelatine, sugar to taste, rind of ½ a lemon.

METHOD.—Separate the eggs and beat up the yolks. Heat the milk and mix with the latter, and finally grated lemon-rind, then cook in the top part of a double boiler until it thickens, keeping it well stirred, when remove and cool.

Rub the pears through a sieve and mix with the custard.

Dissolve the gelatine in a saucepan with one gill of the pear syrup, then strain it into the pulp and custard, and add the sugar. Leave until beginning to thicken before whisking the egg-whites to a stiff froth.

Stir these in lightly, turn into a wet mould, and when set unmould and serve with the remainder of the pear syrup and a little cream.

Sufficient for six persons.

RAISIN CAKE

INGREDIENTS.—½ lb. of flour, ¼ flat teaspoonful of carbonate of soda, ½ lemon (rind only), ¼ lb. of margarine, 6 oz. of Empire raisins, when stoned (or sultanas), ¼ lb. of sugar, 1 egg, milk.

METHOD.—Wash and dry the raisins. Stone them and cut in halves. Sieve the flour with the carbonate of soda. Rub in the margarine.

Grate the lemon-rind finely and add with the sugar and raisins.

Whisk up the egg and stir in with some milk as required. Beat the mixture well, turn into a greased cake-tin, and put it in a moderately hot oven to bake.

RAISIN WHOLEMEAL SCONES

INGREDIENTS.—¼ lb. of wholemeal, ¼ lb. of flour, ½ flat teaspoonful of carbonate of soda, 1½ oz. of Empire butter, 2 oz. of Empire raisins, 1 dessertspoonful of castor sugar, milk to mix.

METHOD.—Wash, pick over and dry the raisins, then stone them and cut them in halves. Sieve the flour and soda, rub in the butter, then add the wholemeal, sugar, and raisins, and mix well. Stir in sufficient milk to make a soft dough.

Turn on to a board, form into a smooth bun shape, and put into a greased sandwich-tin, pressing it lightly to the shape of the tin.

Flour a knife and cut the dough across each way into four, separating the top of each section slightly from the centre. Brush with milk and bake about half an hour.

SAGO AND CURRANT MOULD

INGREDIENTS.—3 oz. of Empire currants, 1 oz. of Empire butter, lemon flavouring, 2½ oz. of sago, 2 oz. of sugar, 1¼ pints of milk.

METHOD.—Wash and pick over the fruit. Boil the milk and sprinkle in the sago.

Simmer for five minutes, stirring now and then, then add the currants. Cook gently until the mixture is thick and the grains of sago quite transparent, add the butter, sugar, and flavouring, then pour into a wet mould. When cold shake gently on to a glass dish.

NOTE.—Pineapple or other suitable flavouring essence may be used sometimes in place of lemon.

SULTANA CAKE

INGREDIENTS.—1 lb. of flour, 2 teaspoonfuls of baking-powder, ¾ lb. of Empire sultanas, ½ lb. of Empire butter, ½ lb. of castor sugar, 2 eggs, lemon flavouring, milk, 2 oz. of candied peel.

METHOD.—Sieve the flour and baking-powder and cut up the peel. Beat the sugar and fat to a cream. Stir in the eggs quickly, adding each one separately, and beating the mixture for a few minutes between each addition.

Gradually mix in the flour, peel, and sultanas, the latter previously washed and dried, with some milk as required. Mix all together lightly and add half a teaspoonful of lemon flavouring.

Turn the mixture into a prepared cake-tin, dredge the top with castor sugar, and put it into a moderately hot oven to bake. It will take about one hour and a half to two hours.

SULTANA CHEESE CAKES

INGREDIENTS.—About ½ to ¾ lb. of flaky pastry (see p. 252), 1 oz. of Empire sultanas, 1 egg and its weight in ground rice, Empire butter, and castor sugar, ¼ flat teaspoonful of ground ginger, marmalade.

METHOD.—Roll out the pastry fairly thinly. Cut it into rounds and line about sixteen or eighteen patty-pans.

Put just a little marmalade in the bottom of each patty-pan.

Beat the sugar and fat to a cream. Add the egg, stir it in quickly, and beat well together.

Stir in the ground rice and ground ginger, sieved together, also the sultanas, previously washed and dried.

Mix all the ingredients lightly. Put about a teaspoonful of the mixture into each patty-pan.

Stand the cakes on a baking-sheet and put them into a hot oven to bake.

They will take about fifteen to twenty minutes to cook.

Cool them on a sieve and dredge finally with castor sugar.

Sufficient for sixteen or eighteen cheese cakes.

BAKED SULTANA PUDDING

INGREDIENTS.—½ lb. of self-raising flour, ½ lb. of Empire sultanas, 4 oz. of suet, 3 oz. of sugar, some grated nutmeg, ½ teaspoonful of ground cinnamon, milk to mix, 1 oz. of candied peel.

METHOD.—Wash, pick over and dry the sultanas. Cut up the peel.

Chop the suet finely and mix with the flour, add the ground cinnamon, some grated nutmeg, the sugar, and prepared fruit. When well mixed, stir in sufficient milk to make it about the consistency of a good fruit cake.

Beat well, turn into a greased pie-dish, and put into a moderately hot oven to bake.

It will require about one hour and a quarter to one hour and a half.

Sufficient for five or six persons.

SULTANA AND FIG PUDDING

INGREDIENTS.—¼ lb. of figs, 6 oz. of Empire sultanas, 7 oz. of breadcrumbs, ½ teaspoonful of ground ginger, ¼ teaspoonful of mixed spice, 4 oz. of Empire butter, 6 oz. of castor sugar, 2 eggs, milk.

METHOD.—Make the breadcrumbs and mix with the ground ginger and mixed spice. Wash and stalk the figs and sultanas, dry them, and cut the figs into fairly small pieces. Beat the sugar and fat to a cream, then gradually add the breadcrumbs and prepared fruit alternately with the well-beaten eggs, and some milk as required.

Beat together well, turn into a greased basin or mould, and cover securely with a well-greased paper. Steam for about two hours, and when cooked turn on to a hot dish, and if liked, serve a hot custard with it.

Sufficient for about six persons.

SULTANA NUT BREAD

INGREDIENTS.—1½ lb. of flour, 1½ oz. of Empire butter, 1½ flat teaspoonfuls of salt, ¾ oz. of yeast, 1½ oz. of shelled walnuts, 3 oz. of castor sugar, 4 oz. of Empire sultanas, milk and water (about 2½ to 3 gills).

METHOD.—Wash, pick over and dry the sultanas. Chop up the walnuts.

Sieve the flour and salt into a basin. Add the sugar with the exception of one teaspoonful, also the fruit and nuts. Mix together and make a well in the centre. Melt the butter in a saucepan, add the milk and water to it and make lukewarm. Put the yeast into a small, warm basin with one teaspoonful of sugar, mix them until they liquefy, then stir in the milk and butter.

Strain this into the flour and mix to a soft dough, throw a cloth over the basin and put in a warm place to rise for about an hour and a half, until double its size, then turn out and knead for a few minutes.

Divide into portions large or small, as required, and work until smooth. Put them into greased and floured tins, only about half filling them. Stand in a warm place until full, then brush the top of each with a little beaten egg-yolk mixed with a spoonful of milk, and put in a hot oven to bake.

When cooked they will sound hollow if tapped underneath with the knuckles.

If preferred, you may glaze the top of the loaves with sugar and milk after they are cooked, in which case return them to the oven for a minute or two to dry the glaze. Use one tablespoonful of milk to two teaspoonfuls of castor sugar, and mix until dissolved.

SULTANA SCONES

INGREDIENTS.—9 oz. of flour, 2 level teaspoonfuls of cream of tartar, ½ level teaspoonful of carbonate of soda, 1 oz. of lard, 2 dessertspoonfuls of castor sugar, 1 oz. of Empire butter, 2 dessert-spoonfuls of Empire sultanas, milk to mix.

METHOD.—Wash, pick over and dry the fruit. Sieve the flour with the cream of tartar and carbonate of soda.

Rub in the lard and butter, add the sugar and fruit, and mix these ingredients to a soft dough with milk.

Divide the dough into two portions, make each into a smooth lump, and roll it to a round the size of the sandwich-tins to be used.

Grease the tins and put one piece of dough into each. Brush them with egg and put them in a fairly hot oven to bake.

They will take about twenty minutes to cook.

Sufficient to make two large scones.

SULTANA SHELLS

INGREDIENTS.—9 oz. of flour, 1 teaspoonful of baking-powder, 2 oz. of citron peel, 1 lemon (rind only), grated nutmeg, $\frac{1}{2}$ flat teaspoonful of ground cinnamon, $\frac{1}{4}$ lb. of castor sugar, $\frac{1}{4}$ lb. of Empire butter, 1 egg, $\frac{1}{4}$ lb. of Empire sultanas.

METHOD.—Sieve the flour with the ground cinnamon and baking-powder ; then add some grated nutmeg.

Beat the sugar and fat to a cream. Add to it the finely grated rind of the lemon. Stir in the egg quickly and beat well together.

Gradually stir in the flour and citron peel cut in small pieces, also the sultanas, the latter previously washed and dried, and mix together lightly, adding some milk as required.

Put the mixture into small greased cake-tins with a shell-patterned base, and bake in a quick oven. They will take about fifteen minutes.

Turn the cakes over and cool them on a sieve.

This quantity makes about twenty cakes.

SUNFLOWER SWEET

INGREDIENTS.—7 sponge cakes, 2 bananas, a tin of Empire peaches, $1\frac{1}{2}$ pint packets of lemon jelly, $1\frac{1}{4}$ pints of hot water, apricot jam, a few chocolate nonpareils (hundreds and thousands), 5d. of cream, sugar, vanilla flavouring.

METHOD.—Peel and mash the bananas. Split the sponge cakes in halves and spread with jam and banana ; then sandwich together again. Arrange them on a dish in the form of a star, leaving a small space in the centre.

Dissolve the jelly in the hot water, and make up to one pint and a half with peach syrup. Soak the sponge cakes with just a small quantity of the jelly, and when they are set with the jelly, pour in the remainder (cold).

When lightly set, cut peaches to resemble the petals of a sunflower, and arrange on the jelly. Before serving, fill the centre with whipped cream, flavoured and sweetened to taste, and sprinkle it with chocolate nonpareils.

Sufficient for seven persons.

TAPIOCA AND SULTANA PUDDING

INGREDIENTS.—$2\frac{1}{2}$ oz. of tapioca, $1\frac{1}{2}$ pints of milk, $1\frac{1}{2}$ tablespoonfuls of sugar, nutmeg, or other flavouring, $\frac{1}{2}$ oz. of Empire butter, 6 oz. of Empire sultanas, $\frac{1}{2}$ pint of water.

METHOD.—Wash the tapioca and sultanas, pick over the latter and soak them both together in about half a pint of water for a few hours, or until the water is absorbed.

Put them in a pie-dish, add the sugar (one tablespoonful and a half), and stir in the milk.

Grate some nutmeg on the top, add the butter, cut in small pieces, and bake gently, allowing it about one hour after it comes to the boil.

Serve hot or cold.

TOFFEE PUDDING

INGREDIENTS.—$\frac{1}{2}$ lb. of flour, $\frac{1}{4}$ lb. of Empire butter, $\frac{1}{4}$ flat teaspoonful of carbonate of soda, 4 or 5 oz. of golden syrup, 1 good tablespoonful of coffee essence, 3 oz. of soft brown sugar, 1 egg, a few almonds, 4 oz. of Empire sultanas.

METHOD.—Wash, pick over and dry the sultanas, then mix them with the flour. Grease a basin and decorate it with a few blanched almonds.

Put the butter, golden syrup, sugar, and coffee essence in a saucepan to melt, but do not let them boil. When dissolved, cool a little.

Whisk the egg, then add the toffee mixture and whisk together. Pour into the centre of the flour and beat well. Lastly, stir in the soda mixed in a spoonful of milk. Put into the prepared basin, cover securely with a well-greased paper, and steam for about two hours.

Sufficient for eight persons.

VEGETABLE CURRY

INGREDIENTS.—1 lb. of carrots, ½ pint of cooked peas, ½ lb. of tomatoes, 1 or 2 pimentos, 1 good-sized onion, 1½ oz. of Empire butter, ¾ to 1 dessertspoonful of curry-powder, 1¼ dessertspoonfuls of flour, ½ pint of water, 1 or 2 dessertspoonfuls of chutney, 1 dessertspoonful of lemon-juice, ¼ lb. of Patna rice.

METHOD.—Scrape and wash the carrots and cut them into dice, and cook them in slightly salted boiling water until they are tender. Then drain them. Peel and mince the onion and fry it lightly in one ounce of the butter ; then add the remainder of the butter and stir in the curry-powder. Cook this for a minute over a low burner, then add the flour and a little more butter if required, and when the mixture is well blended, stir in the skinned and chopped tomatoes and the water.

Bring it to the boil and boil it gently for two or three minutes, then stir in the chutney, and add the carrots, peas, and chopped pimentos.

Season the curry to taste, and when the vegetables are thoroughly heated, add the lemon-juice.

Turn the curry into a dish, garnish it with boiled rice, and serve it accompanied with boiled rice.

TO BOIL THE RICE. — Cook it in slightly salted boiling water until it is tender, then drain it in a colander. Pour cold water through the rice to separate the grains, drain it again, and heat it and dry it in the oven before serving it.

Use Patna rice.

NOTE.—The pimentos may be omitted if liked. Sufficient for five persons.

PRESERVES AND PICKLES

JAMS

A TABLE OF QUANTITIES FOR JAMS.

The following table gives the average quantities of sugar and water to use for the various kinds of fruit :—

Fruit	Sugar	Water
Gooseberries ..	1 lb. to 1 lb. fruit	1 gill to 1 lb. fruit
Raspberries ..	¾ to 1 lb. to 1 lb. fruit	None
Plums	¾ to 1 lb. to 1 lb. fruit	None
Damsons	1 lb. to 1 lb. fruit (when stoned)	None
Apricots	1 lb. to 1 lb. fruit (when stoned)	1 gill to 1 lb. fruit
Cherries	1 lb. to 1 lb. fruit	1 gill to 1 lb. fruit
Rhubarb	1 lb. to 1 lb. fruit	None
Strawberries ..	¾ to 1 lb. to 1 lb. fruit	None
Loganberries ..	1 lb. to 1 lb. fruit	None
Black Currants ..	1 lb. to 1 lb. fruit	½ gill to 1 lb. fruit
Red Currants ..	1 lb. to 1 lb. fruit	None

SOME ESSENTIALS FOR GOOD JAM

1. The fruit must be *perfectly* fresh and never over-ripe. Never use bruised fruit or the jam will fail to keep.

2. Use a good-sized pan, allowing plenty of space for the jam to boil without any risk of it boiling over. A strong aluminium pan is the best.

3. The sugar must all be dissolved before the contents of the pan come to the boil. Otherwise the jam is liable to be sugary. Either granulated, lump, or preserving sugar may be used.

4. If whole-fruit jam is being made, a syrup must be made first and the fruit added afterwards.

5. Remember to skim the jam when it comes to the boil, and to keep it skimmed throughout the boiling as required. This ensures the jam being clear when it is cold.

6. Stir the jam occasionally to prevent sticking to the pan.

7. Always test the jam before taking it off the stove by putting a small quantity on a saucer and leaving it to get cold. It should form a jelly. During this time turn out the gas so that the jam does not continue to boil.

If it should not set stiff enough, light the gas again and boil the jam a little longer.

8. The pots must be perfectly dry and clean.

9. Be sure to made the jam air-tight. It may be potted either hot or warm. If hot, pour it at once into *hot* jam pots, cover them immediately and make them airtight. (The pots must be heated or the hot jam will crack them. The best method is to put them into a cool oven—this will warm them gradually.) Otherwise, let the jam cool for a while, then turn it into pots, and when thoroughly cold make them airtight.

10. Store jam in a cool, dry place, labelling it with name and date.

SEALING THE POTS

Particular care must be given to the sealing of the pots as, if they are not airtight, the jam will not keep.

Parchment or adhesive covers can be used. The latter are not quite so good as parchment, for when the jam is ready to be used it means the breaking of the cover ; whereas string may be untied from the parchment covers and re-tied after use.

Choose thick parchment covers, immerse them in cold water, dry them lightly on a tea-cloth. Place them when damp on the jars and tie them securely. When dry they should be quite taut.

Some fruits combine well in making mixed jams. For instance—raspberries and cherries, gooseberries and strawberries, rhubarb and strawberries, red currants and raspberries.

Rhubarb jam is improved by the additional flavourings of lemon-rind and juice, also ginger. If using lump ginger, bruise it and tie it in muslin, and add it with the sugar ; if preserved ginger, cut it up and mix it into the jam when it has nearly finished boiling.

Half an ounce of lump ginger and the rind of half a lemon are sufficient for one pound of rhubarb, which should, like all other fruit, be weighed after being prepared.

APPLE JAM

INGREDIENTS.—4 lb. of apples (peeled and cored), rind and juice of 1 lemon, 1½ oz. of lump ginger, few cloves, 1 pint of water, allow ¾ lb. of sugar to every pint of pulp.

METHOD.—Wipe the apples, peel them thinly cut into quarters and take out the core.

Cut the lemon-rind thinly and tie in a bag with a few cloves.

Bruise the ginger and tie in muslin.

Put the apples into a pan with the water and flavourings, and cook gently until soft.

Take out the ginger and clove-bag. Rub the apples through a sieve.

Measure the pulp and allow the sugar in proportion.

Return to the pan with the flavouring bags, add the lemon-juice and sugar, cook slowly until the sugar is dissolved, then boil until it will jelly when cold.

Take out the bags before potting the jam.

Remember to use good flavoured cooking apples. If liked, this jam may be coloured pink with a few drops of cochineal. This should be added when the jam is boiling. It looks very attractive if potted in small glass potted-meat jars.

APPLE AND ONION KETCHUP

INGREDIENTS.—12 tart apples, 2 minced onions, 1 level teaspoonful of mustard, 1 level teaspoonful of ground cloves, 2 level teaspoonfuls of ground cinnamon, 1 small level tablespoonful of salt, 1 pint of pure malt vinegar, 6 oz. of castor sugar.

METHOD.—Pare, quarter and core the apples. Place them in a saucepan with water to cover. Simmer them till soft when all the water should be evaporated. Rub the apple pulp through a sieve. Add to each quart the other ingredients given. Should the apples not be large enough to yield a quart, it is better to cook a few more than to alter the quantities of the other ingredients. Simmer the ketchup gently for one hour.

APRICOT CHUTNEY

INGREDIENTS.—1½ lb. of apricots, 1 pint of vinegar, ¾ lb. of Barbados sugar, 1 oz. of mustard seeds, 1 level teaspoonful of salt, 1 lb. of onions, 10 oz. of sultanas, 4 level teaspoonfuls of ground ginger.

METHOD.—Wipe the apricots, stalk and stone them and chop them roughly. Wash, pick over and dry the sultanas and put them through the mincer with the onions.

Put the prepared ingredients into a pan with the salt, ginger, and sugar, add also the vinegar and mustard seeds, the latter tied in a piece of muslin. Cook them slowly until the sugar is dissolved, then bring them to the boil and boil them gently for about three-quarters to an hour until of a good consistency.

Cook the chutney, then squeeze out the mustard bag, and pot the chutney.

Makes about four pounds of chutney.

APRICOT JAM

INGREDIENTS.—1 lb. of apricots (after being stoned), 1 lb. of sugar, 1 gill of water.

METHOD.—Wipe, stalk and pick over the apricots.

Remove the stones and weigh the fruit.

Put into a preserving-pan with the sugar and water.

Cook slowly until the sugar is

dissolved, then bring to the boil, and boil until it will form a jelly when cold, keeping it skimmed and stirred as required.

Pot when cool.

NOTE.—The stones can be cracked, and the kernels blanched and added to the jam just before it has finished boiling.

DRIED APRICOT JAM

INGREDIENTS.—2 lb. of dried apricots, 5 pints of water, 2 or 3 oz. of almonds, 6 lb. of sugar.

METHOD.—Cut the apricots in quarters and wash them thoroughly.

Put them into a basin and cover them with cold water in the proportion given, and soak them for forty-eight hours.

After that time, turn them into a preserving-pan and add the sugar.

Cook the jam slowly until the sugar is dissolved, then bring the jam to the boil, and continue boiling until it will jelly when cold.

Blanch, skin and cut up the almonds and add them to the jam a few minutes before it has finished boiling.

NOTE.—Peach jam from dried peaches can be made in exactly the same way.

APPLE CHUTNEY

INGREDIENTS.—6 lb. of apples (after being peeled and cored), 2½ pints of vinegar, ¾ lb. of onions, 1 lb. of raisins, 1 lb. of brown sugar, 3 table-spoonfuls of salt, 2 teaspoonfuls of ground ginger, 6 chillies.

METHOD.—Peel and core the apples, and weigh them.

Chop them up, or grate finely.

Wash, dry and stone the raisins, chop them, or put through a mincer.

Peel and grate the onions.

Put all the prepared ingredients into a pan, add the sugar, vinegar and chillies, ginger and salt.

Stir them all together.

Bring to the boil, and boil the chutney gently for about twenty minutes.

NOTE.—Choose sour, unripe apples for this chutney.

BANANA CHUTNEY

INGREDIENTS.—1 lb. of bananas (without skins), ½ pint of white vinegar, ¾ pint of brown vinegar, ½ lb. of soft brown sugar, 1 oz. of mustard seeds, ¾ lb. of marrow (without peel and seeds, etc.), ¾ lb. of apples (after peeled and cored), 6 oz. of currants or raisins, ¼ flat teaspoonful of cayenne, salt, 1 lb. of onions.

METHOD.—Wash, pick over and dry the currants or raisins. If using the latter, stone and put through the mincer.

Peel and mash the bananas. Peel and grate or chop the onions. Peel the marrow, remove the seeds, etc., then grate it. Peel, core and grate the apples. Put all these prepared ingredients into a pan with the vinegar and sugar.

Add also the mustard seeds tied in muslin, the cayenne and salt to taste. Mix all together, bring to the boil, and boil gently for about half an hour.

NOTE.—Remove the bag of mustard seeds before potting the chutney.

BANANA AND MARROW JAM

INGREDIENTS.—1 lb. of bananas (without skins), 1¼ lb. of sugar, juice and rind of 1 orange, juice and rind of 2 lemons, ½ gill of water, 1 lb. of marrow—when cut up.

METHOD.—Peel the marrow and remove the seeds, etc., then cut it into cubes, and weigh. Put it into a basin and sprinkle with the sugar, then leave until the next day. Turn it into a pan (with the liquid it has made) and cook slowly until the sugar is dissolved. Bring to the boil, remove the scum and boil for thirty minutes. Peel and weigh the bananas, cut into cubes and add to the jam with the grated rinds and strained juice of the orange and lemons, also the water. Bring to the boil again, and continue boiling until the jam is sufficiently thick.

NOTE.—Use a preserving marrow—a hard one.

BANANA MINCEMENT

INGREDIENTS.—½ lb. of bananas (without skins), ¼ lb. of soft brown sugar, ¼ lb. of beef suet, ¼ lb. of small seedless raisins, ¼ lb. of candied peel,

1 oz. of almonds, ½ lemon (rind and juice), ¼ of a nutmeg, ¼ lb. of sultanas, ¼ lb. of currants, a few drops of almond essence, 1 tablespoonful of rum, ¼ lb. of apples (after peeled and cored).

METHOD.—Wash, pick over and dry the fruit, then put the raisins through the mincer.

Cut the candied peel into small pieces, or mince it.

Blanch and chop the almonds, peel, core and chop the apples, chop the suet finely.

Mix all these prepared ingredients together, add also the sugar, grated nutmeg, and lemon-rind and bananas, the latter mashed to a pulp.

Now stir in the strained lemon-juice, a few drops of almond essence, and the rum.

When well mixed put into pots, pressing it down well. Tie down with parchment covers and make airtight.

PICKLED BEETROOT

INGREDIENTS.—3 beetroots (well cooked), 3 onions, vinegar to cover. To every pint of vinegar allow 20 peppercorns, 20 allspice.

METHOD.—Peel the onions and cut into very thin slices.

Peel the beetroot and slice very thinly.

Place these prepared slices in jars in alternate layers, covering each layer with vinegar until the jars are full.

Add the peppercorns and allspice to each jar in proportion to the vinegar.

Tie down with bladders.

NOTE.—If preferred, the onion may be omitted.

BLACKBERRY JAM

INGREDIENTS.—4 lb. of blackberries, ½ pint of water, ½ lb. of sugar. Allow to every pint of juice ¾ lb. of sugar.

METHOD.—Pick over the blackberries, remove the stalks, and very carefully wash the fruit.

Put them into a large jar with half a pound of sugar and the water. Cover with a saucer, and stand in a large pan of water at the side of the fire.

Cook slowly for several hours until the fruit is quite soft.

Turn it all into a jelly bag, or on to a fine sieve, and strain off all the juice.

You may press the fruit to extract the juice, but do not rub it through.

Measure the juice, and allow the sugar in proportion.

Put the juice and sugar into a preserving pan and boil for about forty minutes. Pot in small glass jars.

BLACKBERRY AND APPLE JAM

INGREDIENTS.—4 lb. of blackberries, 1 pint of water, 2 lb. of apples (after they are cut up), 4½ lb. of lump sugar.

METHOD.—Remove the stalks from the blackberries.

Put the sugar and water into a preserving-pan, and let it slowly dissolve.

Wipe the apples, peel them, cut into quarters, remove the core, cut into slices.

Put the apples and blackberries into the pan with the dissolved sugar and water.

Bring to the boil, and boil for about one hour.

BLACK CURRANT JAM

INGREDIENTS.—2 lb. of black currants, 1¾ lb. of sugar, 1 gill of water.

METHOD.—String the black currants, and pick them over.

Put them into a pan with the water and sugar, and heat slowly until the sugar dissolves.

Bring to the boil, and boil for three-quarters to one hour.

HOW TO BOTTLE FRUIT

CHOICE OF FRUIT

ALMOST any kind of fruit can be bottled. The fruit should always be gathered on a dry day, so that it is free from moisture. It should be not quite ripe, and free from bruises, etc.

The success of bottling fruit depends largely on the condition of the fruit used for that purpose.

PREPARATION OF THE FRUIT

Whenever possible the fruit should be wiped only, but in some cases it is necessary to wash it. If it is washed, it must be treated very carefully and well drained.

When removing the stalks be careful to do this without bruising or tearing the fruit. When preparing apples, these should be wiped, peeled thinly, cut into quarters and cored.

Pears should be peeled and cored, and cut in halves.

Both apples and pears will discolour very quickly, so they should be peeled with a silver knife and dropped at once into water to which a little lemon-juice has been added (about one teaspoonful to a pint of water is sufficient). Then when they are all finished they can be drained and used immediately.

Hard pears must be cooked before they are bottled, as they take so long to soften.

Put them into a saucepan, cover with cold water, add a few cloves and a little lemon-rind, and cook gently until almost tender. They will take two or three hours.

Gooseberries should be topped and tailed. Use either a knife or a pair of scissors for doing this.

Remove the green leaf of rhubarb, wipe the sticks and cut them into even-sized pieces.

The Bottles

The proper screw-top bottles, such as the Kilner jar, are excellent for bottling fruit, and, of course, they last for years.

Otherwise, use wide-mouthed bottles or jam jars. Whichever kind is used, remember that they must be perfectly sound, clean and dry.

Filling the Bottles

Pack the fruit firmly into the bottles, getting in as much as possible without injuring it in any way.

Choose, as far as possible, even-sized fruit in each jar—in this way it gets evenly sterilised and the appearance is better.

The fruit should only reach to the neck of the bottle, it can then be well-covered with water without touching the lid of the bottle.

Syrup or Water

Either syrup or water may be used for filling the bottles. Syrup is preferable but more expensive. The sugar in the syrup helps to preserve the fruit, and it is a better flavour than if bottled in plain water and sweetened afterwards.

To Make the Syrup

Put some lump sugar and cold water into a pan in the proportion of about eight ounces of sugar to a pint of water.

Dissolve slowly, bring to the boil, and boil quickly for about six minutes.

Remove any scum that rises, and leave the syrup until cold.

Cover the fruit in the bottles with cold water or cold syrup.

Sterilising the Fruit

The bottles can be covered or left uncovered when put into the boiler, but if covered do not make them airtight, as the air must escape as the temperature rises, otherwise the bottles will burst.

Stand the bottles in a large boiler or fish-kettle, lined at the sides and bottom with hay, or newspaper thickly folded.

They must not touch the sides or the bottom of the boiler, or one another, or they will be liable to crack.

Hay should also be loosely packed between them.

Fill the boiler with cold water to reach up to the necks of the bottles. By this you will see that it is necessary that all the bottles should be the same height.

Bring the water slowly to 185° to 190° F., and leave for twenty-five to thirty minutes.

Use an ordinary cooking thermometer to ascertain the degree of heat required. When sufficiently sterilised turn out the gas, and leave the bottles in the water for about ten minutes.

The above degree of heat is sufficient for most kinds of fruit, but for cherries heat the water to 190° to 195° F., and leave for twenty-five to thirty minutes.

The fruit must be sufficiently cooked or it will not keep, but do not overcook it or the skins will burst. It is advisable to do only one kind of fruit at a time in the same boiler.

Before Storing

After the bottles have stood in the water for ten minutes, take them out, remove the covers, and if the liquid has evaporated add a little more boiling water at once and cover the fruit.

Then pour in sufficient melted mutton fat to form a layer on the top—this should reach to the top of the bottle, and will exclude all air.

Leave until cold, then tie down with parchment covers or bladders. When taking the bottles from the boiler, stand them in a warm place and let them cool slowly, as if put directly into a cool place the bottles are liable to crack.

If screw-top bottles are used, these should only partially be screwed down when put into the boiler, then tightly screwed down when they are removed from it.

When the bottles are quite cold, store them in a cool, dry, dark place. They should be stood upright.

Darkness helps to preserve the colour of the fruit.

ANOTHER METHOD

Pack the fruit into bottles or jars. Stand them on a backing sheet, leaving a space between each bottle. Place in a warm oven, and leave until the fruit changes colour, but do not let the skins burst. Have ready some boiling water.

Remove the hot jars from the oven, and just cover the fruit with the boiling liquid.

Pour in melted fat as before, leave until cold, then tie down.

CARE OF THE BOTTLES

Many people take little care of preserving jars once the contents are taken from them, and the following season when they want to use them they are surprised that they are not in good condition. Remember to wash the jars (including all the small parts) well and dry them thoroughly after use. Then store them in a dry place. If you find the rubbers have perished in any way be sure to replace these with new ones, or the bottling will not be successful.

PICKLED CABBAGE

INGREDIENTS.—2 red cabbages, salt and vinegar. To every 1½ pints of vinegar allow 1 or 2 small pieces of ginger (bruised), ½ oz. of peppercorns, 5 or 6 allspice, a few cloves.

METHOD.—Prepare the cabbages—cut away the stump and outside leaves ; then cut them into quarters.

Cut each quarter into very thin slices.

Lay it out on large dishes and sprinkle freely with salt.

Leave for about twenty-four hours, then put a little of it at a time into a colander and drain it well, and dab lightly with a dry cloth.

When well drained put it into dry jars—large glass jars are the best to use. Fill up each with vinegar, adding sufficient to cover the cabbage.

Measure the vinegar as you put it in ; then add the ginger, allspice, cloves, and peppercorns in proportion.

Make the jars airtight, and leave for two or three weeks before using it.

NOTE.—The cabbages are best for pickling after a frost.

ANOTHER METHOD is to measure roughly the amount of vinegar that will be required, and to boil the flavourings in the vinegar for about eight minutes before adding it to the cabbage. But remember that the vinegar must be *cold* when poured over the cabbage.

CHERRY JAM

INGREDIENTS.—1 lb. of cherries (after they have been stoned), ¾ gill of water, 1 lb. of sugar.

METHOD.—Stalk and wipe the cherries, and remove the stones ; then weigh the fruit.

Put them into a pan with the sugar and water.

Cook slowly until the sugar has dissolved.

Bring to the boil and boil for about three-quarters to one hour.

CHERRY AND APRICOT JAM

INGREDIENTS.—2 lb. of cherries (when stoned), 4 lb. of sugar, 2 lb. of apricots (when stoned), ¾ pint of water.

METHOD.—Stalk and pick over the fruit. Stone the cherries and stone and quarter the apricots, then weigh them.

Put the prepared fruits into a preserving-pan, sprinkle each layer with sugar, and leave for about twelve hours, after which time add the water.

Stand the pan over a low burner, and when the sugar is dissolved boil the jam until it will jelly when cold, keeping it skimmed and stirred, as required.

The stones from the apricots can be cracked, the kernels blanched and added to the jam when boiling.

Sufficient to make about six pounds of jam.

CHERRY AND GOOSEBERRY JAM

INGREDIENTS.—Cherries and gooseberries as required, sugar, water.

METHOD.— Stalk and wash the cherries then drain and stone them. Top and tail and wash the gooseberries.

Allow an equal amount of sugar, and put it into a preserving pan with the fruit, adding half a pint of water to four pounds of mixed fruit. Cook them slowly until the sugar is dissolved, then bring the jam to the boil and boil it till it will jelly when cold, keeping it skimmed and stirred as required.

NOTE.—Weigh the cherries and gooseberries after they are prepared, and then allow an equal amount of each.

CHERRY AND NUT PRESERVE

INGREDIENTS.—1½ lb. of cherries (when stoned), 2 oz. of shelled walnuts, 1 orange, 4 oz. of stoned raisins, ½ a lemon, 1½ lb. of sugar, water.

METHOD.—Stalk, stone and weigh the cherries, and put them into a preserving pan with the sugar, sprinkling it over in layers.

Squeeze out the juice from the orange and lemon and make it up to one gill and a half with water. Add this to the cherries, cook them slowly at first until the sugar is dissolved. Then bring it to the boil and remove the scum.

Cut up the raisins and chop the walnuts and add and boil all together until it will set when tested on a plate.

CRANBERRY AND APPLE CHEESE

INGREDIENTS.—2 lb. of cooking apples, 2 lb. of cranberries, ¾ to 1 pint of water, 3 lb. of sugar.

METHOD.—Pick over and stalk the cranberries, peel and quarter the apples.

Remove the core and cut the apples in thick slices.

Put both into a pan with the water and cook slowly until tender, stirring frequently.

Rub through a sieve, then return to the pan.

Add the sugar and when dissolved boil until it will set when cold, keeping it skimmed and stirred as required.

Sufficient to make about five or six pounds of cheese.

CRANBERRY JELLY

INGREDIENTS.—Cranberries as required. To each pound allow about ¾ pint of water. To each pint of juice obtained allow 1 lb. of sugar.

METHOD.—Pick over and stalk the cranberries and put them into a saucepan with the water. Then cook them very gently until the fruit is tender, or if preferred, cook in a jar in the oven.

Strain through a jelly bag or fine hair sieve, and squeeze out all the juice but do not press the fruit through.

Turn the juice into a preserving-pan, bring to the boil, and add sugar in proportion.

Cook slowly until the sugar is dissolved, then boil until it will jelly when cold, keeping it skimmed as required.

Turn into warm pots and make airtight.

DAMSON CHEESE

INGREDIENTS.—6 lb. of damsons, to every pint of pulp allow 1 lb. of sugar.

METHOD.—Pick over the damsons and wash them. Put them into a jar, cover with a saucer, and stand in a saucepan of water.

Cook over the fire until the fruit in quite soft, then rub it through a sieve to a pulp, together with the juice.

Measure it and allow the sugar in proportion. Pour into a pan, cook slowly until the sugar has dissolved, then bring to the boil, and boil until it will set when cold.

Keep it well stirred and skimmed all the time.

Pot it when slightly cool.

When cold, tie down and exclude all air.

DAMSON JAM

INGREDIENTS.—1 lb. of damsons, 1 lb. of sugar.

METHOD.—Stalk and wipe the damsons. Put them into a preserving pan with the sugar.

Heat slowly until the sugar dissolves. Bring to the boil.

Boil for about one hour.

NOTE.—Remove the stones as they boil out of the damsons.

DAMSON JELLY

INGREDIENTS.—Damsons (as required), allow ¾ lb. of sugar to each pint of damson-juice.

METHOD.—Stalk and wipe the damsons, put them into a jar and cover the jar with a saucer.

Stand it in a saucepan of water, and cook gently until all the juice is extracted from the fruit ; it will take several hours.

Then strain it through a jelly bag or fine hair sieve, and press out all the juice, but do not press any of the fruit through.

Measure the juice, and add the sugar in proportion.

Put into a preserving-pan, cook slowly until the sugar is dissolved, then bring to the boil, and boil until it will form a jelly when cold, keeping it skimmed as required.

Pot in small jars.

NOTE.—When the fruit is cooking, the water in the saucepan should reach about half-way up the jar.

PICKLED DAMSONS

INGREDIENTS.—Damsons, vinegar to cover, allow 6 oz. of white sugar to ¼ pint of vinegar.

METHOD.—Pick over the damsons, stalk and wipe them. Put them into a bowl and cover them with vinegar.

Leave for a day, then pour off the vinegar and measure it.

Add the sugar to the vinegar in the given proportion.

Pour into the saucepan, bring to the boil, skim it, and let it boil for from eight to ten minutes.

Add the damsons and boil gently for two or three minutes, but do not let them burst. Leave until cold, then bottle and tie down.

NOTE.—There should be sufficient vinegar to cover the damsons when bottled.

FIG JAM

INGREDIENTS.—2 lb. of figs, 2 pints of cold water, 4 lemons (rind and juice), 3 lb. of sugar.

METHOD.—Wash the figs, then remove the stalks and cut the fruit into about six pieces. Put them into a basin with the water and leave soaking for about twenty-four hours.

Turn into a preserving-pan, add the sugar, and cook slowly until dissolved. Then bring to the boil and remove the scum.

Wipe the lemons and grate the rinds finely ; squeeze out the juice and strain it. Add both these to the figs, and boil all together until it will jelly when cold, keeping it stirred and skimmed as required.

Cool, then turn into pots. When cold, tie down and make airtight.

Sufficient to make about five or six pounds of jam.

PICKLED GHERKINS

INGREDIENTS.—Gherkins, vinegar, salt and water, allow to every quart of vinegar ¾ oz. of allspice, ½ oz. of peppercorns, ½ oz. of lump ginger (bruised).

METHOD.—Wipe the gherkins. Put them into a bowl and cover them with salted water. (The latter should be strong enough to float an egg.)

Leave in soak for four or five days.

Pour off the salted water and dry the gherkins in a cloth. Put them into a dry jar. Estimate roughly the quantity of vinegar required to cover them well.

Add to it the allspice, peppercorns, and lump ginger in proportion, and boil together for about eight minutes.

Pour it over the gherkins, cover with a saucer and stand at the side of the fire until the next day.

Then pour off the vinegar, boil it again and pour it over the gherkins. Cover with a saucer and leave until cold.

If the gherkins are not a good colour, pour off the vinegar, boil it again and pour over them.

When cold, tie down and exclude all air.

NOTE.—Leave for about five or six weeks before using.

GOOSEBERRY CHEESE

INGREDIENTS.—Gooseberries, water; to 1 lb. of pulp allow 1 lb. of sugar.

METHOD.—Top and tail and wash the gooseberries. Put them into a jar with just a little water (*allow about half a gill to six pounds of fruit*), cover with a saucer, and stand in a saucepan of water and cook until tender. Then rub through a fine sieve, together with the juice.

Weigh the pulp and add the sugar to it in proportion.

Put into a pan and cook slowly at first until the sugar is dissolved, then bring to the boil and boil until it will set, keeping it stirred and skimmed.

Pot as usual.

GOOSEBERRY CHUTNEY

INGREDIENTS.—2¼ lb. of gooseberries (3½ pints), ¾ lb. of onions, ¾ pint of vinegar, 10 oz. of soft brown sugar, 6 oz. of seedless raisins, 1 flat teaspoonful of ground ginger, 1 oz. of mustard seeds, 2 flat teaspoonfuls of salt, ½ flat teaspoonful of cayenne.

METHOD.—Top and tail the gooseberries. Peel and grate the onions. The raisins may be left whole or put through a mincer as preferred.

Put all the prepared ingredients into a pan with the sugar, ginger, vinegar, salt, and cayenne. Add the mustard seeds tied in a piece of muslin.

Cook gently, keeping it well stirred until the sugar is dissolved, then bring to the boil and boil gently for forty-five minutes.

Cool slightly, then remove the bag of mustard seeds and pot the chutney. Tie down securely when cold and make airtight.

Sufficient to make five pounds.

GOOSEBERRY JAM

INGREDIENTS.—Gooseberries as required, to each 1 lb. of fruit allow 1 lb. of sugar, 1 gill of water.

METHOD.—Top and tail the gooseberries.

Weigh them.

Put the water into the pan, add the prepared fruit, sprinkling each layer with sugar.

Cook the jam slowly until the sugar

is dissolved, then bring it to the boil and continue boiling it until it will jelly when cold, keeping it skimmed and stirred as required.

GOOSEBERRY AND ORANGE JAM

INGREDIENTS.—1 lb. of gooseberries, rind and juice of one orange, 1 lb. of sugar.

METHOD.—Top and tail the gooseberries and wash and drain them. Put them into a preserving pan, and add the finely grated orange-rind and the juice of the orange. Add also the sugar.

Cook the jam slowly till the sugar is dissolved, then bring it to the boil, and boil it until it will jelly when cold.

GOOSEBERRY AND RED CURRANT JAM

INGREDIENTS.—Gooseberries and red currants as required, sugar, water.

METHOD.—Top and tail the gooseberries and string the currants. Wash and drain them carefully, put an equal amount of each prepared fruit into a preserving-pan, adding a quarter of a pint of water and four pounds of sugar to four pounds of the combined fruits.

Cook the jam slowly until the sugar is dissolved, then bring it to the boil, and boil it until it will jelly when cold, keeping it skimmed and stirred as required.

GRAPE JAM

INGREDIENTS.—2 lb. of grapes, 1¾ lb. of sugar, 1 gill of water.

METHOD.—Use very small unripe grapes. Pick them off the stalks. Put them into a pan with the water and sugar, and cook slowly until the sugar has dissolved.

Bring to the boil, and boil for about three-quarters of an hour.

GRAPE FRUIT MARMALADE

INGREDIENTS.—Grape fruit as required, to each pound allow 1½ pints of water and 1½ lb. of sugar.

METHOD.—Wipe and weigh the grape fruit and put it into a preserving-pan with the water.

Cover with plates so as to keep them

Marmalade

Put the oranges in
a preserving pan
with the water.

Use scissors when
shredding peel finely.

The finished
marmalade.

Slice the fruit
thinly.

PLATE 59

Chutney

Mincemeat

Plum Jelly

PLATE 60

under the water, bring to the boil and boil gently for about one and a quarter to one and a half hours, until the rinds are tender.

Then leave until the next day.

Unless using an enamel lined pan, it is advisable to turn the fruit and water into a basin when cool, as if left in an aluminium pan for any length of time it will discolour it.

Take out the fruit and drain it, then cut into quarters and scrape out the pulp and soft pith.

Rub this through a sieve, it will nearly all rub through with the exception of the pips.

Measure the water in which the fruit was boiled, and if it has reduced to less than half, make up to half with water.

Return it to the pan with the pulp and sugar, also the peel, sliced thinly.

Boil the pips in just a little water for about half an hour, then strain and add.

Cook slowly until the sugar has dissolved, then bring to the boil and boil until it will jelly when cold, keeping it stirred and skimmed as required.

It will probably take about one and a half hours.

GREENGAGE JAM

INGREDIENTS.—Greengages (as required), allow ¾ lb. of sugar to 1 lb. of fruit.

METHOD.—Stalk, pick over, and wipe the greengages.

Put into a preserving-pan with the sugar, and cook very slowly until some of the juice is drawn from the fruit.

When the sugar has dissolved, bring all to the boil, and boil until it will form a jelly when cold, keeping it skimmed and stirred as required.

NOTE.—Remove the stones as they boil out of the greengages, crack them, blanch the kernels, and put into the jam before it has finished boiling.

GREEN TOMATO CHUTNEY

INGREDIENTS.—2½ lb. of apples, 2 lb. of tomatoes, 1 lb. of raisins, 2 lb. of onions, 3 pints of vinegar, 1 lb. 6 oz. of soft brown sugar, 1 tablespoonful of salt, ½ flat teaspoonful of cayenne, 1½ oz. of mustard seeds, 2 oz. of lump ginger.

METHOD.—Peel the apples, cut into quarters, remove the core and either chop or grate them.

Wipe and slice the tomatoes, and put them into a pan with half of the vinegar.

Cook slowly until quite soft, then rub them through a sieve (with the vinegar).

Wash and dry the raisins; then stone and chop them.

Peel and grate the onions finely.

Put the sieved tomato and vinegar into a pan.

Add the apples, raisins, onions, sugar, and the remainder of the vinegar.

Bruise the ginger, and tie in muslin. Tie the mustard seeds in another piece.

Add these to the other ingredients, and season well with the salt and cayenne.

Bring to the boil, and boil for about half an hour.

Squeeze out the flavouring bags before potting the chutney.

PICKLED HORSERADISH

INGREDIENTS.—1 thick stick of horseradish, vinegar.

METHOD.—Put the stick of horseradish into a bowl of water and scrub off all the earth, etc.

Peel it, and grate it finely by rubbing it on a bread-grater.

Put it into a jar in layers, covering each layer with vinegar before the next is added. In this way it will all get thoroughly moistened with vinegar. Cover, and make it quite airtight.

This can be used at once, but is improved if kept for a few weeks before using.

If the vinegar evaporates, more should be added.

NOTE.—Choose a thick stick of horseradish. It is easier to grate, and not so wasteful as a thin one.

LEMON CHEESE

INGREDIENTS.—2 lemons, 2 eggs, 8 oz. of sugar, 5 oz. of margarine.

METHOD.—Peel the lemons as thinly as possible and squeeze out the juice.

Put both these ingredients into a saucepan with the sugar and margarine, and dissolve very slowly.

Beat up the eggs; stir the lemon,

X

etc., on to them, then strain, return to the pan, and stir over a low burner until the mixture comes to the boil and is thick and creamy.

LOGANBERRY JAM

INGREDIENTS.—Loganberries (as required), allow ¾ lb. of sugar to each pound of fruit.

METHOD.—Pick over the fruit and put into the preserving-pan with the sugar.

Cook very slowly at first until some of the juice is extracted.

When the sugar has dissolved, bring it all to the boil, and boil until it will form a jelly when cold, keeping it skimmed and stirred as required.

Leave to cool slightly, then pot it. Tie down when quite cold and exclude the air.

Store in a cool, dry place.

MARMALADE

SOME people prefer sweet and others a bitter marmalade, but if a smaller amount of sugar than that given in the recipe is added, less water must be used in proportion, or the marmalade will not jelly.

HINTS ON MAKING MARMALADE

1. The oranges are boiled first without the sugar to soften them, and then with the sugar to make the marmalade jelly.

2. Quantities should be weighed and measured very accurately.

3. The sugar must dissolve before the marmalade boils.

4. The marmalade should be skimmed occasionally to keep it clear, and stirred now and again to prevent it burning. Towards the end, when it begins to thicken, the marmalade should be stirred more carefully.

5. If sweet oranges are used, it is better to discard the white pith, as this gives the marmalade a rather cloudy appearance.

6. When the marmalade seems to have boiled sufficiently the gas should be turned out and a little of the marmalade tested on a plate to see if it jellies. If not, it must be boiled a little longer.

7. The pots should be made perfectly airtight, and should be labelled before they are put on the store shelf.

USE THE MARMALADE SKIMMINGS

When skimming marmalade it is difficult to prevent some of the marmalade being removed with the scum, but this need not be wasted. Leave it to settle, then remove just the top part carefully. Utilise the remainder in a tart, or in a steamed or baked pudding.

Jam skimmings may be used in the same way.

SEVILLE ORANGE MARMA-LADE (1)

INGREDIENTS.—Seville oranges, as required, allow 1 lemon to 9 oranges, allow 2 pints of water to 1 lb. of fruit.

METHOD.—Remove the peel from the oranges and lemons and cut it in fine shreds. Slice the fruit thinly, removing the pips. Cut the slices into four and put them into a basin with the peel and water to soak overnight.

Next day, turn the fruit into a preserving-pan and boil it until it is tender. Leave it until it is cold, then weigh it and allow an equal quantity of sugar.

Let the sugar dissolve slowly, then bring the marmalade to the boil and boil it until it jellies.

NOTE.—If the preserving-pan is weighed before any cooking is done the weight of the cooked fruit and water can be obtained quite easily.

SEVILLE ORANGE MARMA-LADE (2)

INGREDIENTS.—1 lb. of Seville oranges, 1¾ pints of water, 1¼ lb. of sugar.

METHOD.—Wipe and weigh the oranges and put them into a preserving-pan with the water. Cover the oranges with plates to prevent them floating, and boil them gently for one hour and a half, or until the fruit is tender. Let the fruit get cold, then drain it in a colander, saving the water in which it has been cooked.

Cut the oranges in quarters and scrape out the pulp. Rub the pulp through a sieve and return it to the water in which the oranges were cooked. Cut the peel as finely as possible, and add it to the pulp and water. Stir in the sugar, dissolve it, then bring the marmalade to the boil and boil it until it will jelly.

SEVILLE, SWEET ORANGE AND LEMON MARMALADE

INGREDIENTS.—12 Seville oranges, 4 lemons, 4 sweet oranges ; weigh them and allow 2 lb. of sugar and 2 pints of water to 1 lb. of fruit.

METHOD.—Wipe the oranges and lemons, and weigh them. Cut them into quarters and remove the pips.

Put the pips into a basin with a pint of cold water, and leave them to soak for a few hours ; then strain off the water, and add it to the oranges and lemons.

Slice the orange and lemon quarters very thinly, cutting pulp and rind together. Put them into a large pan and add the water in proportion, less the pint that was added from the pips.

Leave the fruit to soak for about twenty-four hours, then boil it gently until the rinds are quite tender.

Leave it soaking again until the next day, then add the sugar in proportion.

Bring the marmalade slowly to the boil, and boil for about one hour and a half, or until it will jelly.

FINELY SHRED MARMALADE

(MADE FROM SWEET ORANGES)

INGREDIENTS.—2 lb. of sweet oranges, 4 pints of water ; allow 1 lb. of sugar to 1 lb. of cooked fruit and water.

METHOD.—Wipe the oranges and peel the rind very thinly. Cut it in fine strips, either with a knife or a pair of scissors. Put it into a pan with half the water to soak for a few hours, then let it boil gently until tender.

Meanwhile, peel off the white pith from the oranges, being careful not to waste any of the juice. Slice the fruit and cook it until tender with the remaining half of the water.

Rub the cooked fruit through a

sieve and return it to the pan with the peel and its liquor. Weigh all together and allow an equal amount of sugar. Cook it slowly until the sugar is dissolved, then bring the marmalade to the boil and boil it until it will jelly when cold.

GINGER MARMALADE

INGREDIENTS.—1 lb. of Seville oranges, 1¾ lb. of sugar, 2 pints of water, 6 oz. of glacé ginger.

METHOD.—Wipe the oranges, put them into a saucepan with the water, and bring them to the boil. Boil them gently for about one hour and a quarter. Leave them until they are cold, then drain them.

Cut them into quarters, scrape out the pulp and soft pith and rub them through a sieve.

Return the pulp to the water in which the oranges were boiled, add the sugar, cook slowly until it is dissolved, then bring the marmalade to the boil.

Cut the ginger into small cubes and add them. Boil all together until it will jelly when cold.

NOTE.—If the water in which the oranges are boiled has reduced to less than half, add a little more to make it up before adding the sugar.

GRAPE FRUIT MARMALADE

(See p. 640).

LEMON MARMALADE

INGREDIENTS.—12 lemons (3 lb. in weight), 7½ pints of water, allow 1 lb. of sugar to 1 lb. of pulp.

METHOD.—Wipe the lemons and cut them into quarters. Take out the pips and put them into the basin with one pint of the water, and leave in soak for a few hours. Slice the lemon quarters very thinly. Put them into a preserving pan with the remainder of the water. Add also the strained water from the pips. Let this stand for about twenty-four hours. Then boil it gently for about one to one hour and a half until the rinds are quite tender. Leave it to stand until the next day, then weigh it and add the sugar in proportion. Bring to the boil, and boil for about one hour, or until it will jelly.

ORANGE GINGER MARMA-LADE

INGREDIENTS.—6 lb. of sweet oranges, 6 pints of water, 6 lb. of sugar, ¼ lb. of lump ginger.

METHOD.—Wipe the oranges, peel them, and divide them into quarters, removing the pips as you do so.

Put the peel through the mincer, then put it into a preserving-pan with the water and orange quarters. Bruise the ginger, tie it in muslin and add it.

Bring it to the boil, add the sugar and, when dissolved, boil the marmalade until it will jelly when cold, keeping it stirred and skimmed as required

Sufficient to make about eleven pounds.

ORANGE AND RHUBARB MARMALADE

INGREDIENTS.—4 lb. of rhubarb (when cut up) 2 lb. of sweet oranges, 1 lemon, 5 lb. of sugar, 1 pint of water.

METHOD.—Wipe the oranges and peel them. Put the peel into a pan with sufficient water to cover it well, and boil it gently until it is tender, adding more water if it is required.

When the peel is ready, drain off the water and save it. Shred the peel finely.

Remove the green leaves from the rhubarb, wipe the sticks and cut them into even-sized pieces.

Cut up the oranges and remove the pips. Put the orange-pulp into a preserving-pan with the prepared rhubarb, the shredded peel, sugar, lemon-juice, and grated lemon-rind, and a pint of the water in which the orange-peel was boiled.

Cook the marmalade slowly until the sugar is dissolved, then bring it to the boil and boil it till it will " jelly " when cold.

ORANGE AND TANGERINE MARMALADE

INGREDIENTS.—Allow 6 tangerines to 12 Seville oranges. Weigh the fruits together and allow 2 lb. of sugar and 2 pints of water to 1 lb. of fruit.

METHOD.—Make the Tangerine Orange Marmalade in the same way as the second recipe for Seville Orange Marmalade (see p. 642).

The tangerines will not take quite so long to boil as the oranges, so they can be taken out when they are sufficiently cooked.

TANGERINE MARMALADE

INGREDIENTS.—Allow 2 tangerines to 1 Seville orange. Allow 2 pints of water to 1 lb. of fruit when cut up. Weigh when cooked and cold, and allow 15 oz. of sugar to 1 lb. of fruit and water.

METHOD.—Wipe the oranges and tangerines, cut them into quarters and slice them finely, removing all the pips.

Add the water to the prepared fruit, and let it soak for twenty-four hours, then boil it gently till tender, adding the pips tied in muslin.

Weigh them when cooked and cold, and add the sugar in proportion, let this dissolve slowly, then boil it until the marmalade will jelly when cold.

Remove the pips before adding the sugar.

MARROW CHEESE

INGREDIENTS.—1 marrow. Allow to each pint of cooked marrow pulp ¾ lb. of sugar, 1 lemon.

METHOD.—Peel the marrow, cut it into quarters and remove all the seeds. Weigh the marrow, and steam it until quite soft. Put it into a colander to drain, then mash it up in a basin, or rub it through a sieve to a pulp.

Put it into a preserving-pan. Add the sugar. Grate the lemon-rind. Squeeze the lemons and strain the juice.

Add these also to the marrow, etc. Bring to the boil. Boil for half an hour keeping it well stirred.

MARROW PICKLE

INGREDIENTS.—2¼ lb. of marrow (when prepared), 1½ pints of vinegar, ¾ oz. of lump ginger, salt and pepper, 4 or 5 chillies, ¾ lb. of apples, ¾ lb. of onions, 10 oz. of sugar, 3 teaspoonfuls of cornflour, 1½ teaspoonfuls of turmeric.

METHOD.—Peel the marrow and remove the seeds, etc., then cut it into small cubes and weigh it.

Put it into a basin, sprinkle each

layer with salt and leave for about twelve hours. Then drain well.

Peel, core and either chop or grate the apples.

Peel and grate the onions.

Put all these prepared ingredients into a pan, with the vinegar and sugar and a little pepper.

Bruise the ginger and tie in a piece of muslin with the chillies, and add.

Bring to the boil and boil for about half an hour, then draw aside. Mix the cornflour with the turmeric and mix to a smooth paste with a little cold vinegar—extra to that given—and stir in. Bring up to the boil again, keeping it stirred, and boil for about five minutes to cook the cornflour.

When cool remove the ginger-bag and pot the chutney.

Tie down when cold and make airtight.

MARROW AND PINEAPPLE MARMALADE

INGREDIENTS.—4 lb. of marrow (when prepared), 1 large tin of pine-apple, 4½ lb. of sugar, 2 lemons (rind and juice).

METHOD.—Peel the marrow, cut it across into halves, then split them lengthwise and remove the seeds.

Weigh the prepared marrow and put through a mincer.

Turn into a basin, sprinkle with sugar and leave overnight.

The next morning, mince the pine-apple and add it with the syrup.

Put it all into a preserving-pan, cook slowly until the sugar is dissolved, then bring to the boil and remove the scum.

Add the finely grated lemon-rind and strained juice and boil together until it will jelly when cold, keeping it skimmed and stirred, as required.

Sufficient to make about eight pounds.

MARROW PRESERVE

INGREDIENTS.—Allow (to every pound of marrow after it is cut up) 1 lb. of sugar, 1 lemon, and ¾ oz. of lump ginger.

METHOD.—Peel the marrow, cut it open and remove all the seeds.

Cut the marrow into small, square pieces.

Weigh it, and allow the sugar in proportion.

Put the marrow and sugar into a preserving-pan, and let it stand for twenty-four hours.

Grate the lemon-rind.

Squeeze the lemons and strain the juice.

Bruise the ginger and tie it in a piece of muslin.

After the marrow and sugar have stood for twenty-four hours add the ginger-bag and lemon-juice.

Put the pan over the fire and cook slowly until the sugar is dissolved, then bring the contents to the boil.

Take off the first scum, then add the lemon-rind.

Boil altogether for about one hour and a quarter or until it will form a jelly when cold.

Take out the ginger-bag, squeezing it as you do so, before potting the jam.

NOTE.—Marrows used for preserves should be quite hard. They are usually ready about the end of September or October.

MEDLAR CHEESE

INGREDIENTS.—6 lb. of medlars. To every lb. of medlar pulp allow 1½ lb. of lump sugar, 1 flat teaspoonful of allspice.

METHOD.—Put the medlars into a jar, cover with a saucer and stand in a saucepan of water.

Cook until the fruit is tender, then rub it all through a very fine sieve.

Weigh the pulp and put it into the pan with the sugar and allspice, in the proportions given.

Cook slowly at first, until the sugar has dissolved, then bring to the boil, and boil steadily until it will set.

Be very careful not to let it burn, and keep it frequently skimmed and stirred.

When ready, pot as before.

MINCEMEAT

INGREDIENTS.—½ lb. of cooking apples, ½ lb. of beef suet, rind and juice of ¼ lemon, ½ lb. of sugar, 2 oz. of almonds, ratafia flavouring essence, 3 oz. of candied orange-peel, 3 oz. of candied citron-peel, 2 oz. of candied lemon-peel, ½ lb. of stoned raisins.

½ lb. of currants, ½ lb. of sultanas, grated nutmeg, a little rum.

METHOD.—Peel, core and chop the apples. Wash, pick over, and dry the fruit, then stone and chop the raisins, taking their weight after they are stoned.

Blanch, skin and chop the almonds, shred the peel, and skin and chop the suet.

Mix all the prepared ingredients together, adding the sugar, the finely grated lemon-rind, and some grated nutmeg.

Flavour with ratafia essence and moisten the mincemeat with lemon-juice and a little rum, as required.

Press the mincemeat into jars, cover it and make it airtight.

MINCEMEAT
MADE WITH FIGS AND DATES

INGREDIENTS.—¾ lb. of dates (when stoned), 1 lb. of figs, ½ lb. of peel, 1½ lb. of currants, 1 lb. of apples (when peeled and cored), 1 lb. of beef suet, ½ lb. of sugar, ¼ lb. of shelled Brazils, ½ teaspoonful of ground ginger, rind and juice of 1 lemon, ⅓ bottle of ratafia flavouring, ⅛ gill of rum.

METHOD.—Wash, pick over and dry the currants, also the figs, then remove the stalks and put the figs through the mincer.

Stone and mince the dates and cut up the peel.

Peel, core and mince the apples. Chop the suet finely, add the sugar, ground ginger, grated lemon-rind, and prepared fruit and Brazil nuts, the latter also put through the mincer.

Mix all the ingredients together very thoroughly, then moisten with the strained lemon-juice and stir in the ratafia flavouring and rum.

Put into jars and press down well, cover with parchment covers and make airtight.

Sufficient to fill about seven one pound jars.

A GOOD MIXED JAM

INGREDIENTS.—1 lb. of cherries (when stoned), 1 lb. of strawberries, 1 lb. of gooseberries, 1 lb. of red currants, 1 lb. of black currants, 1 lb. of raspberries, 2 gills of water, 5 lb. of sugar.

METHOD.—Prepare all the fruit and put into a preserving-pan with the water and sugar.

Cook slowly until the sugar is dissolved, then bring to the boil and boil until it will jelly when cold, keeping it skimmed and stirred as required.

PICKLED MUSHROOMS

INGREDIENTS.—Button mushrooms, vinegar to cover, salt, pepper and mace.

METHOD.—Peel the mushrooms and remove the stalks.

Wash them thoroughly in cold water, and dry them carefully in a cloth. Take each mushroom and rub it with salt.

Put them into a pan at the side of the fire, and cook them slowly in the liquid which the salt draws out of them. Leave cooking until this liquid has soaked into them again.

Season with pepper and mace to taste.

Cover with vinegar, bring to the boil and boil slowly for a few minutes. Cool slightly, then pour into bottles or jars.

When cold tie down and make them airtight.

PICKLED NASTURTIUM SEEDS

INGREDIENTS.—Nasturtium seeds, vinegar. To each quart of vinegar allow : ¾ oz. of lump ginger (bruised), ¾ oz. of allspice.

METHOD.—Gather the seeds in dry weather, so that they are free from moisture.

Choose green, unripe seeds.

Wipe each one, and put them into clean jars (about three-parts fill the jars).

Put the ginger and allspice into the vinegar in the above proportions.

Bring to the boil, and boil for about six minutes, then cool slightly.

Pour it over the seeds and fill up the jars.

Tie down when quite cold.

NOTE.—These are useful to take the place of capers. They should be left for about ten weeks before being used.

PICKLED ONIONS

INGREDIENTS.—Small round onions

or shallots, vinegar to cover. Allow to every 1½ pints of vinegar 20 allspice, 20 peppercorns, 1 or 2 small pieces of lump ginger (bruised).

METHOD.—Peel the onions and put them into glass jars.

Cover them with vinegar at the same time, measure the quantity of vinegar put into each jar, and add the allspice, peppercorns, and ginger in proportion.

Make the jars airtight.

Keep for two or three weeks before using.

NOTE.—September is the time for pickling onions.

ORANGE CONSERVE

INGREDIENTS. — 2 lb. of sweet oranges, 3 pints of cold water. To each pint of pulp allow 1 lb. of sugar, 2 oz. of raisins, 1 oz. of shelled walnuts.

METHOD.—Wipe the oranges, grate the rinds finely and put them aside, then slice the oranges and put them into the pan with the cold water. Simmer them gently until tender, then rub them through sieve. Measure the pulp and put it into a preserving pan with the finely grated rinds and the sugar in proportion as given. Cook it slowly until dissolved, bring it to the boil, and boil it for about twenty minutes. Add the raisins, previously washed, stoned and cut up, also the walnuts chopped roughly, and boil all together until the conserve will set when cold.

ORANGE RHUBARB JAM

INGREDIENTS.—1¼ lb. of oranges, 4 lb. of rhubarb (when cut up), 4 lb. of sugar, 1 gill of water.

METHOD.—Wipe the rhubarb, remove the green leaves, etc., and cut the fruit into short lengths. Then weigh it and put it into a preserving-pan with the sugar and water.

Wipe the oranges, grate the rinds finely and add.

Cut the oranges into halves, remove the pips, then squeeze out the juice, and add it with the soft pulp.

Cook slowly until the sugar is dissolved, then bring to the boil, and boil until it will jelly when cold, keeping it stirred and skimmed as required.

This will make about seven pounds.

PEACH JAM

INGREDIENTS.—1 tin of peach pulp, 1 oz. of almonds, ¾ lb. of sugar to each pound of pulp.

METHOD.—Weigh the tin of pulp, then put the contents into a preserving-pan. Weigh the empty tin, then the weight of the pulp can be ascertained.

Add the sugar to it in the above proportions.

Bring to the boil, and boil for about one hour to one hour and a half.

Blanch and cut up the almonds. Add them to the jam about ten minutes before it has finished boiling.

NOTE.—This jam needs to be well stirred, as it is very liable to burn. Apricot jam from apricot pulp can be made by the same method.

PICCALILLI

INGREDIENTS.— Marrow, button onions, cauliflower, beans (vegetables suitable for piccalilli), salt, vinegar.

To every 1½ pints of vinegar allow ½ oz. of curry-powder, ¾ oz. of mustard, ¾ oz. of flour, ½ oz. of lump ginger, 1½ teaspoonfuls of turmeric, 1½ oz. of sugar, few peppercorns.

METHOD.—Any of the above vegetables can be used for piccalilli.

Prepare them in the usual way, and thoroughly cleanse.

Cut the marrow into thick, chunky pieces, and divide the flower of the cauliflower into small branches.

Do not slice the beans, only string them, and choose small ones. Leave the onions whole.

Spread the vegetables on dishes and sprinkle with salt, and leave for twenty-four hours.

Then drain and leave to dry. Estimate the amount of vinegar required to cover them, and put into a pan with the sugar, peppercorns, and ginger, the latter bruised and tied in muslin with the peppercorns.

Mix the curry-powder, turmeric, mustard, and flour to a smooth paste with some of the cold vinegar, and add to the bulk.

Stir until it boils ; then add the vegetables and boil gently for about six minutes.

When cool, remove the bag of ginger and peppercorns and bottle the piccalilli. Tie down when cold and make airtight.

PICKLES WHICH HAVE BEEN OPENED

When a jar of pickles or chutney has been opened, and only part of the contents used, remember to tie it down again tightly.

A good plan is to fit the jar with a cork covered underneath with a piece of linen or chamois leather.

Draw the ends of the linen over the top of the cork, and sew them together so that the bottle can be easily opened when required and at once tightly closed again.

Use a wooden spoon for stirring pickles, and keep it for that purpose.

PINEAPPLE AND MARROW JAM

INGREDIENTS.—5 lb. of marrow (after it is cut up), 2 tins of pineapple (large), 1 lb. of sugar to each pound of cut marrow, 1 lemon to each pound of cooked marrow (if liked), ½ oz. of lump ginger to each pound of cut marrow (if liked).

METHOD.—Peel the marrow and remove the seeds. Cut it into small squares and weigh it. Put it into a preserving-pan with the sugar and leave it to stand for twenty-four hours.

Strain the juice from the pineapple, and cut the pineapple into small square pieces—about the same size as the marrow squares after they have stood for twenty-four hours.

Grate the lemon-rind. Squeeze the lemons and strain the juice. Bruise the ginger and tie it in muslin. Add the pineapple, lemon-juice, ginger-bag and the strained juice of one tin of pine-apple to the marrow. Bring to the boil and remove the scum.

Add the lemon-rind. Boil the jam for about an hour and a quarter.

NOTE.—The pineapple syrup is not all used in the jam, but it need not be wasted. It can be used for flavour-ing trifles or blancmanges, etc. Prunes are very delicious if stewed in pine-apple syrup.

If preferred this jam can be made without the addition of the ginger and lemon.

PLUM JAM

INGREDIENTS.—1 lb. of plums, ¾ lb. of sugar.

METHOD.—Wipe the plums and stalk them. Put the fruit and sugar into a preserving-pan and cook slowly until the sugar has dissolved, keeping it frequently stirred.

The heat must be very gentle at first, so that the sugar melts and the juice comes out of the plums and the mixture does not burn.

Bring to the boil, and boil for three-quarters to one hour. While the jam is boiling, most of the stones will boil out of the plums. These can be cracked and the kernels blanched and put into the jam.

NOTE.—The green egg plums are very inexpensive, and excellent for jam.

PLUM JELLY

INGREDIENTS.—Victoria Plums as required. To each pound allow 1 pint of water. To each pint of juice allow 1 lb. of sugar.

METHOD.—Stalk and wipe the plums and put them into a preserving-pan with the water. Simmer them gently until the plums are quite soft, then strain the liquid through a jelly bag and squeeze out all the moisture, but do not press the fruit through.

Measure the juice and turn it into a clean pan, add sugar in proportion and cook it slowly until dissolved, then bring the jelly to the boil and boil it until it will jelly when cold, keeping it skimmed as required.

QUINCE JAM

INGREDIENTS.—Quince, as required, water. To each pint of quince pulp allow ¾ lb. of sugar.

METHOD.—Peel and quarter the quince and remove the core. Put the fruit into a pan and boil gently until tender, adding sufficient water to cook it.

It will take rather a long time, and, being very dry, will require more water than other fruits.

When cooked, rub the fruit and juice through a sieve and make into a pulp. Measure this and add the sugar in proportion.

Turn into a preserving - pan and cook slowly until dissolved ; then bring to the boil and boil until it will set when cold, keeping it stirred and skimmed as required.

RASPBERRY JAM

INGREDIENTS.—1 lb. of raspberries, $\frac{3}{4}$ lb. of sugar.

METHOD.—Pick over the raspberries, and put them into a preserving-pan with the sugar.

Cook very slowly, and keep well stirred until the sugar has dissolved.

Bring to the boil.

Boil for about one hour.

RASPBERRY AND CHERRY JAM

INGREDIENTS.—2 lb. of raspberries, 2 lb. of cherries (when stoned), 4 lb. of sugar, 1 gill of water.

METHOD.—Pick over the raspberries. Stalk and stone the cherries.

Weigh the prepared fruits and put into a preserving-pan with the water and sugar.

Cook slowly until the sugar is dissolved, then bring to the boil and boil the jam until it will jelly when cold, keeping it skimmed and stirred as required.

This will make about six pounds.

RASPBERRY AND GOOSE-BERRY JAM

INGREDIENTS.—2 lb. of raspberries, 2 lb. of gooseberries, 4 lb. of sugar, 1½ gills of water.

METHOD.—Stalk and pick over the raspberries, top and tail the goose-berries and weigh them. Put the fruit and water into a pan, add the sugar and cook slowly until dissolved. Then bring to the boil.

Boil the jam until it will jelly when cold, keeping it skimmed and stirred as required.

This will make about six pounds.

RED CURRANT JELLY

INGREDIENTS,—4 lb. of red currants, 1 gill of water, ½ lb. of sugar. To every pint of juice allow ¾ lb. of sugar.

METHOD.—String the currants, and pick them over. Put them into a jar, and sprinkle with half a pound of sugar and one gill of water.

Cover the jar with a saucer, and stand in a large pan of water, so that the latter comes half-way up the side of the jar. Cook slowly at the side of the fire until the fruit is quite soft, and the juice is extracted.

Turn it all on to a fine sieve, or into a jelly-bag, and strain off the juice.

Do not rub the fruit, but press it, to extract all the juice.

Measure it, and allow the sugar in proportion.

Put both into a preserving-pan and when the sugar is dissolved, boil until it will form a jelly when cold.

RED CURRANT AND CHERRY JAM

INGREDIENTS.—Red currants and cherries as required, sugar, water.

METHOD.—Stalk, wash and stone the cherries, string and wash the currants, then drain them well. Take an equal amount of each of these fruits when prepared, put them into a preserving-pan with their combined weight of sugar, adding one gill of water to four pounds of mixed fruit,

Dissolve the sugar slowly, then bring all to the boil, and boil the jam till it will jelly when cold, keeping it skimmed and stirred as required.

RED CURRANT AND RASP-BERRY JAM

INGREDIENTS.—To 1 lb. of rasp-berries and 1 lb. of red currants, add 1½ lb. of sugar.

METHOD.—Pick over the fruit care-fully and put into a pan with the sugar.

Cook slowly at first until some of the juice is drawn from the fruit.

When the sugar is dissolved, bring to the boil and boil it until it will jelly when cold, keeping it skimmed and stirred as required.

RHUBARB JAM

INGREDIENTS.—1 lb. of rhubarb (after it is cut up), 1 lb. of sugar, ½ oz. of lump ginger, ½ lemon (rind).

METHOD.—Wipe the sticks and cut away the green leaf.

Cut the rhubarb into pieces about three-quarters of an inch square, weigh it, and allow the sugar in proportion.

Put both into a preserving-pan and heat slowly until the sugar has dissolved.

Bruise the ginger and tie in muslin.

Peel the lemon-rind very thinly, and tie in another bag.

Add these to the rhubarb and sugar, bring to the boil and boil for about one hour and a quarter.

Remove the ginger and lemon-bags before potting the jam.

RHUBARB AND FIG JAM

INGREDIENTS.—4 lb. of rhubarb, 4 lb. of sugar, 1 lb. of cooking figs, 2 lemons, 1 orange, ¾ pint of water.

METHOD.—Stalk and wash the figs, cut them into small pieces, and put them into a basin with the water and soak them overnight.

Wipe the rhubarb sticks with a damp cloth, trim them and remove green leaves, etc., then cut the rhubarb into short lengths and weigh it.

Put it into a preserving-pan, add the water from the figs and the sugar, dissolve this slowly, then boil the jam up and remove the scum.

Add the finely-grated rind and juice of the orange and lemons, also the figs, and boil all together until it will jelly when cold, keeping it skimmed and stirred, as required.

If potting the jam hot, heat the pots first.

Tie them down when cold and make them airtight.

Makes about nine pounds of jam.

STRAWBERRY JAM

INGREDIENTS.—1 lb. of strawberries, ¾ lb. of sugar.

METHOD.—Stalk the strawberries, and pick them over. Put them into a preserving-pan and start slowly to cook them.

When some of the juice has come from the fruit add the sugar, and heat slowly until the latter has dissolved. Bring to the boil and boil for about one hour.

STRAWBERRY AND GOOSE-BERRY JAM

INGREDIENTS.—1 lb. of strawberries, 1 lb. of gooseberries, 1¼ lb. of sugar, 1 gill of water.

METHOD.—Top and tail and wipe the gooseberries.

Pick over the strawberries.

Put the sugar and water into a preserving-pan and dissolve the sugar slowly.

Add the fruit.

Bring the jam to the boil, and boil for about one hour.

STRAWBERRY AND RHU-BARB JAM

INGREDIENTS.—1 lb. of rhubarb (after it is cut up), 1 lb. of strawberries, 1¾ lb. of sugar.

METHOD.—Wipe the rhubarb sticks and cut away the green, then weigh it.

Cut the sticks into pieces, about the same size as the strawberries.

Remove the stalks from the strawberries, and pick them over.

Put the fruit and sugar into a preserving-pan and heat slowly until the sugar has dissolved.

Bring to the boil, and boil for about one hour.

TANGERINE CHEESE

INGREDIENTS.—2 lb. of tangerines, 3 pints of water, juice of 2 lemons, 3 lb. of sugar.

METHOD.—Wipe the tangerines and grate the rinds lightly, then put the tangerines into a pan with the water and boil them gently until tender.

Drain them and cut them up in quarters and scrape out the pulp.

Mince the pith in a meat-mincer, then rub it through a sieve with the pulp.

Boil the pips in about half a pint of water until it is reduced to a quarter of a pint.

Strain this water into the water in which the tangerines were boiled, adding also the sieved pulp and pith, grated rinds, sugar, and lemon-juice.

Cook the mixture slowly until the sugar is dissolved, then bring it to the boil and boil it till it will jelly when cold.

To make about four pounds.

RIPE TOMATO CHUTNEY

INGREDIENTS.—1½ pints of vinegar, 10 lb. of tomatoes, ¾ lb. of soft brown sugar, 1 lb. of onions, pepper, salt (about 2 tablespoonfuls), ½ oz. of cloves, ½ oz. of allspice.

METHOD.—Wipe the tomatoes and cut them into slices. Peel the onions and grate them. Put the prepared tomatoes and onions into a pan with the vinegar and cook gently until soft.

then rub them all through a sieve with the vinegar.

Tie the cloves and the allspice in a piece of muslin.

Rinse out the pan and return the tomato and onion pulp to it.

Add the sugar and the flavouring bag.

Season with pepper and salt to taste. Bring to the boil and boil for about half an hour, to thicken it.

Leave until cool, squeeze out the flavouring bag and pot the chutney.

TOMATO PICKLE

INGREDIENTS.—1½ lb. of green tomatoes, ½ pint of vinegar, 1 oz. of salt, a few cloves, allspice and peppercorns, ½ oz. of lump ginger, ¼ lb. of golden syrup, 3 level dessertspoonfuls of brown sugar, ½ lb. of onions, ¼ flat teaspoonful of cayenne.

METHOD.—Wipe the tomatoes and cut them in slices, spread them on dishes and sprinkle them with salt and leave them till the next day.

Then pour off the salt liquor and put the tomatoes into a saucepan.

Bruise the ginger and tie it in muslin with the other spices, add these, also the golden syrup, sugar, vinegar, and onions, the latter peeled and sliced. Boil the pickle very gently for about one hour and a half, season it with cayenne, and when cool remove the spices and pot the pickle. Cover it and make it airtight.

This quantity will make only about two or three pounds.

PICKLED GREEN TOMATOES

INGREDIENTS.—½ peck of green tomatoes, ½ teacupful of salt, 1 level tablespoonful of allspice, 1 quart of water, 1 level tablespoonful of ground ginger, 2 oz. of mustard seed, 3 large onions, 2 quarts of pure malt vinegar, 1 lb. of brown sugar, 1 level tablespoonful of ground cloves, 1 level tablespoonful of ground cinnamon, ½ level tablespoonful of paprika.

METHOD.—Slice the tomatoes into a large crock. Add the sliced and peeled onions. Cover them with salt,

stirring it well into both the tomatoes and the onions. Leave it to stand overnight. Next morning drain off the liquor and throw it away.

Mix together one quart of the vinegar and the water and pour it over the tomatoes and the onions. Turn it all into a preserving-pan. Boil it for twenty minutes. Drain off the liquor and throw it away.

Now place the cooked tomatoes and onions back in the preserving-pan and pour the remainder of the vinegar over them. Add the sugar, allspice, cloves, cinnamon, ginger, paprika, and mustard seed. Mix all together. Simmer the mixture for one hour or until the tomatoes and onions are tender and the pickle well flavoured. Serve it with cold meats.

PICKLED WALNUTS

INGREDIENTS.—Green walnuts, salt, and water. Vinegar to cover. Allow to every 1½ pints of vinegar 1 oz. of black peppercorns, ¾ oz. of allspice, ½ oz. of lump ginger (bruised).

METHOD.—Walnuts must be pickled before they get woody.

The end of June or early in July is the time to do them.

Wipe the walnuts and prick them well with a darning-needle.

Put them into a bowl, and cover with salted water (use three ounces of salt to one pint of water).

Soak for about six days, changing the brine after about half the time. Take them out of the brine, and drain them well.

Lay them on dishes and place in the sun to dry, keeping them turned occasionally. Leave until they are quite dry and black all over, then put them into jars.

Tie the allspice, peppercorns, and lump ginger in muslin.

Put into the vinegar and boil for about eight minutes.

Take out the spices when the vinegar has cooled, and cover the walnuts with it.

Tie down when cold.

NOTE.—Keep for five or six weeks before using them.

SANDWICHES

Sandwiches can be varied in all kinds of ways, brown as well as white bread can be used, and bridge rolls should sometimes be included. Ready-sliced sandwich loaves can now be bought, which is a saving of much time and labour.

Liver sausage makes an excellent filling ; it should be sliced thinly and the skin removed.

Minced ham flavoured with a few chopped chives makes another good filling, as does also cold scrambled egg, well seasoned and flavoured with a little chopped pimento.

Sandwiches should not be made long before they are required, as they so soon get dry.

For picnics, they are best wrapped in greaseproof paper, then put in an airtight tin ; failing this, wrap them in a cloth.

BANANA AND JAM SANDWICHES

Ingredients.—12 thin slices of bread, butter, apricot jam, 3 bananas.
Method.—Spread the slices of bread with butter, then with the apricot jam.

Peel the bananas and cut them into thin slices (use a fruit-knife for this).

Take six slices of the bread-and-butter, etc., and cover with the banana.

Place a slice of bread, butter and jam over each, put them on top of one another and press well together.

Cut off the crust and cut the sandwiches into diamond shapes, cutting each into four.

Place on a lace paper.
Note.—Use a stale sandwich loaf.

BEEF AND DRIPPING SANDWICHES

Ingredients.—4 oz. of cold beef, 8 slices of thin brown or white bread, beef dripping, mustard, pepper and salt, horseradish cream.

Method.—Put the beef through the mincer, mix it with a little horseradish cream, and season it with salt, pepper and mustard.

Spread the bread with dripping, season it with salt.

Place the prepared meat on four of the slices and cover it with the remaining slices.

Press the two halves together firmly, remove the crusts if liked, and cut each sandwich across cornerwise into two.

Sufficient for eight sandwiches.

CHEESE SANDWICHES

Ingredients.—3 oz. of grated cheese, 1 oz. of butter, mixed mustard, pepper and salt, thin slices of bread or bread-and-butter.

Method.—Grate the cheese very finely. You can use up any little scraps of stale cheese for this.

Mix well with the butter and season with pepper (and salt, if required) and just a very little mixed mustard.

Spread on slices of bread or bread-and-butter and make into sandwiches.

CHEESE AND CELERY SANDWICHES

Ingredients.—2 oz. of butter, 2 oz. of cheese, 1 cupful of finely chopped celery, pepper, salt and mustard, slices of bread-and-butter.

Method.—Beat the butter to a cream, then grate the cheese finely and mix it with it.

Add the celery and season well with salt, pepper and mixed mustard.

Spread on thin slices of lightly buttered bread and make into neat sandwiches.

CREAM CHEESE AND WATERCRESS SANDWICHES
IN THREE LAYERS
Ingredients.—A small cream cheese, watercress, salt, white bread-and-butter as required.

METHOD.—Pick over and wash the cress, drain it well and chop finely.

Cut thin slices of bread-and-butter and spread them with cream cheese beaten to a creamy consistency, then add a layer of chopped watercress, seasoning each layer with salt.

Add another thin slice of bread, buttered both sides, spread it with cheese and cress, then cover it with a third layer of bread-and-butter, and cut into neat shapes.

CUCUMBER SANDWICHES

INGREDIENTS.—Brown or white bread-and-butter (thin slices), cucumber (as required), pepper and salt.

METHOD.—Peel the cucumber and cut it into very thin slices.

Arrange neatly on half of the bread-and-butter. Season well with pepper and salt.

Place a slice of bread-and-butter on the top of each one. Stack the sandwiches on top of one another and press them well.

(Invert a large china plate or dish over them and press the plate.)

Cut off the crust and cut the sandwiches into shape with a very sharp knife.

EGG AND ANCHOVY SAND-WICHES

INGREDIENTS.—3 eggs, pepper, $1\frac{1}{2}$ teaspoonfuls of anchovy essence, $1\frac{1}{2}$ oz. of butter, about 10 thin slices of bread-and-butter.

METHOD.—Put the eggs into a saucepan of cold water, bring to the boil, and boil for fifteen minutes. Crack the shells, stand the eggs in cold water.

Remove the shells, cut the eggs into halves, take out the yolks and press them through a sieve. Chop up the whites finely.

Mix the yolks and butter together until quite soft and creamy, season with pepper, stir in the anchovy essence and chopped whites.

Mix all together.

Spread on to the bread-and-butter and make into sandwiches.

Serve on a lace paper.

NOTE.—Salt is not required, as the anchovy essence is sufficiently salt.

EGG AND SALAD SAND-WICHES

INGREDIENTS.—4 eggs, 10 or 12 slices of thin bread-and-butter, pepper and salt, few lettuce leaves, small basket of mustard and cress.

METHOD.—Boil the eggs for fifteen minutes, as in previous recipe.

Remove the shells and cut the eggs into very thin slices, yolk and white together.

Leave until quite cold.

Wash the salad and leave to soak until quite clean.

Drain well and dry in a cloth, then shred into small pieces. (Leave a small quantity for garnishing.)

Take half the slices of bread-and-butter, first cover them with a layer of salad, then one of egg, and lastly salad again.

Clap on the other slices of bread-and-butter, press together and cut into small sandwiches.

Serve on a lace paper. Garnish with a few small bunches of uncut cress or parsley.

HAM ROLLS

INGREDIENTS.—12 small finger rolls, 6 oz. of cooked ham, mixed mustard, butter, mustard and cress.

METHOD.—Split open the rolls, well butter them. Put a slice of cooked ham into each, season with mustard. Fit on the other half roll.

Serve on a lace paper. Garnish with mustard and cress (previously washed).

NOTE.—If you prefer, chop in a little mustard and cress with the ham.

HARE AND CRANBERRY JELLY SANDWICHES

INGREDIENTS.—2 or 3 joints of cooked hare, some cranberry jelly, seasoning, bread-and-butter.

METHOD.—Remove the flesh from the joints of hare and put it through the mincer.

Mix it to a paste with cranberry jelly, and add seasoning to taste. Spread on lightly buttered slices of bread, and make up into sandwiches.

HONEY AND WALNUT SAND-WICHES

INGREDIENTS.—Brown bread-and-butter, shelled walnuts, honey.

METHOD.—Chop the walnuts finely and mix them with the honey (warmed slightly, if it is stiff).

To three or four ounces of honey allow one ounce of walnuts.

Cut thin slices of brown bread-and-butter, and spread them with the prepared mixture, then make them into sandwiches and cut them into three-cornered shapes.

HOT TOAST SANDWICHES

INGREDIENTS.—Slices of bread (as required), butter, Cheddar cheese, salt, mustard and pepper, mayonnaise, tomatoes.

METHOD.—Cut slices of bread about one-eighth of an inch thick and spread them with butter.

Cover half the slices with very thin slices of cheese, add also a little chopped tomato previously freed from skin.

Season them with mustard, pepper and salt, and add a few drops of mayonnaise, then cover them with the remaining slices of bread-and-butter.

Sandwich the halves together firmly, put them under the hot grill and toast them on both sides, turning them over carefully, then cut them into small squares or triangles and serve hot.

PASTE SANDWICHES

INGREDIENTS.—Thin slices of bread-and-butter, fish or meat paste, 2 oz. of butter, 2 eggs, seasoning.

METHOD.—Put the eggs in a saucepan of cold water, bring to the boil, and boil for twelve to fifteen minutes.

Shell the eggs, cut into halves, take out the yolks, and rub through a sieve.

Cream the yolks and butter together, add sufficient paste to well flavour.

Stir it in well and add seasoning. Spread on to bread-and-butter, and make into sandwiches as before. Place on lace paper and garnish with cress.

NOTE.—The whites can be saved and used for a salad.

PINEAPPLE SANDWICHES

CREAM some butter and stir into it some minced pineapple. If liked, a few chopped nuts can be added as well.

Spread on bread-and-butter and make into sandwiches.

SARDINE SANDWICHES

INGREDIENTS.—1 small tin of sardines, 12 thin slices of bread, pepper, butter, parsley.

METHOD.—Spread the slices of bread with butter. Cut the tails from the sardines, open them and take out the backbone.

Flake the flesh into very small pieces, and well mash it. Season it with pepper, mix in a little of the oil and, if liked, just a tiny drop of vinegar.

Spread this over six of the slices, put another slice over each.

Place them on top of one another, press together, cut off the crust, and cut each into four.

Arrange on a lace paper. Garnish with parsley.

TOMATO AND CHEESE SANDWICHES

INGREDIENTS.—12 slices of thin bread-and-butter, 3 or 4 tomatoes (according to size), 3 oz. of cheese, 1 tablespoonful of salad cream, pepper and salt, parsley.

METHOD.—Skin the tomatoes, and mash them up well with a fork. Grate the cheese and add to the tomato pulp.

Season well, and mix together with the salad cream.

Spread on to the bread-and-butter, and make up the sandwiches as previously explained.

Heap on a lace paper and garnish with parsley.

NOTE.—If the tomatoes are difficult to skin, put them into boiling water for two or three minutes. The skin can then be easily removed.

TONGUE SANDWICHES

INGREDIENTS.—Thin slices of white bread - and - butter, cooked tongue, mixed mustard, parsley.

METHOD.—Cut thin slices of cooked

tongue and place on the bread-and-butter.

Season with mustard.

Make up the sandwiches and arrange them in a stack and press them well. Remove the crusts, then cut them into small diamond or square shapes.

Arrange them on a lace paper and garnish with parsley.

TONGUE AND HAM SAND-WICHES

INGREDIENTS.—2 eggs, 2 oz. of tongue (cooked), 2 oz. of ham (cooked), pepper, salt, and mustard, 1 oz. of butter, 2d. of mustard and cress, thin slices of bread-and-butter.

METHOD.—Boil the eggs for twelve minutes.

Remove the shells, cut the eggs into halves. Rub the yolks through a sieve, chop up the whites.

Put the tongue and ham through a mincer.

Well wash the mustard and cress, drain it, dry in a cloth, and chop finely.

Cream the butter and yolks together, add the chopped whites and minced meat. Season well.

Spread this over half the slices of bread-and-butter, then a layer of prepared cress.

Arrange the sandwiches in a stack, press them well. Remove the crusts, cut into fancy shapes, and serve.

A LITTLE DINNER

FOR EVERY MONTH OF THE YEAR

JANUARY

TABLE DECORATIONS

Lilies of the valley and violets in a bowl of green glass—a ring of violets surrounding the centre piece—a charming flower picture and so fragrant.

MENU

Brussels Sprouts Purée
Sole Maître d'Hotel
Braised Fillet of Beef
Boiled Potatoes
Carrots and Cream Sauce
Turban Cups

FOR SIX PEOPLE

A dinner for six on New Year's Eve. It must be beautifully appointed to set an example through the months that follow.

BRUSSELS SPROUTS PUREE

INGREDIENTS.—2½ lb. of brussels sprouts, boiling water, 2¼ pints of milk, salt and pepper, 1 onion.

METHOD.—Prepare the sprouts in the usual way, removing the base of the stalks and the outer discoloured leaves. Wash thoroughly in salted, cold water. Drain them, and put them to cook in boiling water, with salt and a tiny piece of soda. Boil the sprouts (with the lid off the pan) until they are tender, then turn them into a colander and drain them well. Rub the sprouts through a sieve, return them to a clean pan and add the onion, peeled and cut in half. Stir in the milk, bring the purée slowly to the boil, and add seasoning to taste. Remove the onion before serving the soup. If liked, one or two whole sprouts may be used to garnish each cup of soup.

SOLE MAITRE D'HOTEL

INGREDIENTS.—2 lemon soles (about 1 lb. each), ¾ oz. of butter, 1 teaspoonful of lemon-juice, ½ flat teaspoonful of chopped parsley, salt and pepper, brown breadcrumbs.

FOR THE SAUCE.—1 oz. of flour, 1¼ oz. of butter or margarine, 1 egg-yolk, 1½ dessertspoonfuls of lemon-juice, salt and pepper, ½ pint of milk, ½ gill of water.

METHOD.—Have the soles filleted and skinned on both sides. Wash the fillets, dry them, season them with salt and pepper, and roll them up neatly.

Arrange them in a buttered pie-dish, cover them with a buttered paper and cook them in the oven for about fifteen minutes, or until they become quite white and a milky liquid runs from them.

Meanwhile, break up the butter (three-quarters of an ounce) with a fork and work the finely chopped parsley and the lemon-juice into it, and season it well. Form it into a block and put it into a cold place to harden.

When the fillets are cooked, roll them in brown crumbs and put them into a serving dish with a cube of the prepared butter placed on each, and the sauce poured round.

To Make the Sauce.—Melt the butter, add the flour and when they are blended stir in the milk and water and bring the sauce to the boil. Let it simmer gently for a few minutes, then draw it aside and cool it a little.

Beat the yolk of egg and stir it into the sauce, with seasoning to taste, and cook it for a minute or so without letting it boil. Then take it off and stir in the lemon-juice very gradually.

To Make Brown Crumbs.—Bake some stale pieces of bread until light brown and hard, then crush them with a rolling-pin and rub them through a sieve.

This is a good way of using up stale pieces of bread. The crumbs may be stored for future use and will keep well in an airtight jar.

BRAISED FILLET OF BEEF

INGREDIENTS.—4 lb. of fillet of beef, 2 carrots, 2 onions, dripping, flour, browning, about ½ pint of stock or water, sprig of marjoram, thyme and parsley, salt and pepper.

METHOD.—Scrape and wash the carrots and cut them in thick, chunky pieces.

Peel and quarter the onions.

Melt a little dripping in a stew-pan and brown the meat lightly on all sides, then take it out and add the vegetables to brown them a little.

Pour off the fat, arrange the vegetables to form a bed, place the meat on them and cover it with a buttered paper. Then add the stock or water, and the herbs.

Cover the pan and put it into a moderately hot oven and cook it for about one and a quarter hours. Serve the beef on a hot dish, garnished with slices of cooked carrot.

Thicken the liquor in the stewpan with a little flour, brown and season it, then strain it and serve it with the beef.

If the gravy is too greasy, skim off some of the fat.

NOTE.—This joint appears to be rather small, but it is entirely free from bone.

VEGETABLES

Allow about two pounds of potatoes. Peel them thinly, wash them, and cut them in halves if they are large. Boil them in the usual way, and drain and dry them well before serving.

About two pounds of carrots will be sufficient. Choose even-sized carrots rather than large ones.

Scrape and wash them well, put them into boiling water, with a little salt added, and boil until they are tender. They will take about one hour and a half. Drain them in a colander and serve them with the following sauce :

Melt one and a half ounces of butter in a saucepan. Add one and a quarter ounces of flour, and when well mixed add three-quarters of a pint of milk, and continue to stir until the sauce boils.

Boil gently for a few minutes, then season well and stir in one or two tablespoonfuls of cream.

TURBAN CUPS

INGREDIENTS.—¼ lb. of crystallised apricots, ¾ lb. of Turban dates, 6 oz. of dessert figs, ¾ pint of water, 1 oz. of almonds, 1 oz. of shelled walnuts, 3 tablespoonfuls of rum, ¼ pint of cream (or more if liked), 1 egg-white, sugar and vanilla.

METHOD.—Stone and cut up the dates. Cut the apricots in small pieces and cut up the figs after removing the stalks. Put these prepared fruits into a saucepan with the water and stew them till they are " mushy." Then leave them to get cold. Blanch, skin, and chop the almonds, and chop the walnuts roughly. Mix these with the fruit, stir in the rum and then divide the mixture between six glasses.

Whisk the egg-white to a stiff froth and whisk the cream until thick. Mix these together, add a few drops of vanilla and sugar to taste, then heap it on top of the fruit.

Serve each glass with half a shelled walnut in the centre. This is a delicious cold sweet.

FEBRUARY

TABLE DECORATIONS

Anemones—crimson, purple and every shade of mauve, arranged loosely in a cut-glass bowl.

N.B.—These flowers look lovely used in conjunction with vivid Chinese table-mats.

MENU

Halibut and Cheese Sauce
Crown Roast of Lamb
Potatoes
Turnip Tops
Peach Cream
Prune Toast

FOR SIX PEOPLE

A dinner for six in February—the last short month of winter.

HALIBUT AND CHEESE SAUCE

INGREDIENTS.—2 to 2½ lb. of halibut, lemon-juice, a small piece of butter, salt and pepper, seasoning.

FOR THE SAUCE.—1 oz. of flour, 3 oz. of cheese, ¼ pint of milk, 1 egg-yolk, 1½ oz. of butter or margarine, salt and pepper.

METHOD.—Choose a small halibut weighing from two to two and a half pounds, and have it filleted, then rinse and dry the fillets. Put them in a well-buttered fireproof dish or pie-dish, season them with salt and pepper, squeeze some lemon-juice over them, and add a few dabs of butter.

Cover them with a buttered paper and cook them in the oven for about ten minutes, or till they are tender.

Take the fillets up, arrange them on a dish, or, if preferred, serve in the dish in which they are cooked, and garnish them with lemon, and serve them with the following sauce.

To MAKE THE SAUCE.—Melt the butter or margarine, stir in the flour, and when they are well blended add the milk and keep stirring until the sauce boils.

Let it cook gently for a few minutes. Draw the pan aside and add the finely grated cheese, beaten yolk of egg, and salt and pepper to taste. Cook it for a few minutes without letting it boil, then turn it into a sauce-boat.

CROWN ROAST OF LAMB AND CHESTNUT STUFFING

INGREDIENTS.—2 necks of lamb (best end), small pieces of fat bacon, parsley for garnish.

FOR THE STUFFING.—¾ lb. of chestnuts, 3 oz. of breadcrumbs, 1 onion, 1½ oz. of butter or margarine, 1 tablespoonful of finely chopped parsley, 1 egg, stock or water, milk, if required, salt and pepper, egg and breadcrumbs (for coating).

METHOD.—The two necks of lamb will weigh about four and a half pounds. Have the chine bone removed and scrape the meat from the end of the bones to the depth of about an inch.

Form each neck into a half circle, arranging the bone side outwards, and sew them together with string to keep them in position. Wrap a piece of bacon fat round the top of each bone (these should be a uniform length). Stand the prepared joint in a baking-tin and bake it for about an hour and a half.

Remove the bacon fat and put a cutlet frill on each bone, fill the centre with balls of stuffing, garnish the crown with parsley, and serve it with slightly thickened gravy.

A little of the stuffing may be cooked in the centre of the lamb, but this must not be pressed in tightly or the fat on the inner side of the meat will not be well cooked.

To prepare the stuffing, put the chestnuts in water. Boil them for a few minutes, then remove the outer and inner skin. Put them into fresh water or some white stock, and boil them gently until tender.

Drain them and rub them through a sieve. Add the onion (peeled and minced), the parsley, breadcrumbs, and seasoning to taste. Stir in the fat (melted) and bind the mixture with the egg. If any more moisture is required, a little milk may be added.

Divide the stuffing into small portions, making them into balls. Brush them with egg and coat them with breadcrumbs. Fry them until golden.

TURNIP TOPS

Allow about four pounds of turnip tops. Pick them over and remove the outside leaves. Soak the tops in cold water with salt to cleanse them. These greens require to be very well washed, as they usually contain much grit.

Put them into boiling water to cook, with salt and a tiny piece of soda added, and boil them until tender. They will take about twenty minutes to cook.

Allow about two pounds of potatoes, and boil them in the usual way.

PEACH CREAM

INGREDIENTS.—1 large tin of peaches, 2 egg-yolks, ½ pint of milk, ½ lemon, 1½ gills of cream, ¾ oz. of gelatine, ¼ pint of peach syrup, 3 oz. of castor sugar, a few glacé cherries and angelica for decorating the mould, ½ pint packet of lemon-jelly, 1½ gills of hot water.

METHOD.—Dissolve the jelly in the hot water, and when cold pour a thin layer of it in the bottom of a plain mould and leave it to set.

Decorate the mould with cherries, angelica, and pieces of peach, first dipping each in some jelly. When these decorations are set, cover them with jelly and leave them to set again. Meanwhile, beat the yolks of the eggs, heat the milk, and add it to them, then cook the custard in a jug in a saucepan of hot water, or in the top of a double boiler until it thickens. Be careful not to let it curdle, and to keep it well stirred. When ready, turn it into a basin to cool.

Rub the peaches through a sieve, add the castor sugar and strained lemon-juice.

Whip the cream until thick, stir in the peach pulp and the custard. Strain in the gelatine dissolved in the peach syrup, leave it until it begins to thicken, then turn the mixture into the prepared mould. When set, unmould and serve chopped jelly round the cream.

PRUNE TOAST

INGREDIENTS.—12 prunes, 12 almonds, 6 thin streaky rashers, salt and pepper, a small cream cheese, 6 oblongs of buttered toast.

METHOD.—Choose even-sized prunes. Wash and soak them overnight, then cook them gently until tender, but do not add sugar. (If preferred you may cook them in a little cider or white wine.) Let them cool, then drain them, split them down one side and remove the stones.

Blanch the almonds, season the inside of the prunes and insert a piece of cream cheese and an almond in each.

Remove the rind from the rashers, cut them in halves and wrap them round the prunes.

Run a skewer through them to keep the bacon in position, put them on a tin and bake them until the bacon is cooked and the whole heated thoroughly.

Arrange two together on oblongs of buttered toast.

MARCH

TABLE DECORATIONS

Have you realised the loveliness of mauve tulips with yellow jonquils as a contrast ? The yellow flowers against the lovely translucent green of the tulip leaves are delightful.

MENU

Clear Soup à la Royale
Fried Sole and Tartar Sauce
Vienna Steaks
Potatoes   Cauliflower
Baked Pancakes

FOR SIX PEOPLE

At last we are able to have spring flowers to deck our table, but winter winds blow chill outside, and a little homely dinner-party is still one of the jolliest entertainments.

CLEAR SOUP A LA ROYALE

INGREDIENTS.—3 pints of brown stock, a few peppercorns, 1 small onion and carrot, $\frac{1}{2}$ a turnip, 4 to 6 oz. of lean, uncooked beef, tiny sprig of parsley and thyme, 1 egg-white and egg-shell.

FOR THE CUSTARD.—1 egg, $\frac{1}{4}$ pint of white stock, seasoning.

METHOD.—Remove every particle of fat from the stock and put it into a pan with the vegetables, prepared and washed, but not cut up, also the herbs and peppercorns.

Scrape the beef and add it. Remove the inner skin from the shell of the egg, and then wash and crush the shell. Add the egg-white and the crushed shell to the stock.

Whisk these all together over the fire until almost boiling and there is a head of frothy scum on it, then let it barely simmer for from twenty to thirty minutes.

Strain the soup through a scalded jelly-bag or clean cloth, putting the scum first into the bag and pouring the soup through it slowly.

TO MAKE THE SAVOURY CUSTARD.— Whisk the egg, heat the white stock and add it, season it to taste, and strain it into a small buttered basin or plain mould.

Cover it with a buttered paper, and bake it gently until it is set, being careful not to let it boil.

Cool it a little, then turn it out, cut it into slices, and then stamp out tiny rounds and use them as a garnish for the soup.

TO SERVE THE SOUP.—Put a few rounds of custard into six soup plates, heat the consommé, but do not quite boil it, and then pour it into the plates. Allow about one and a half gills for each person.

FRIED SOLE AND TARTAR SAUCE

INGREDIENTS.—6 small Dover or lemon soles, egg and breadcrumbs, fat for frying, parsley and lemon for garnish, 2 or 3 lemon baskets.

FOR THE SAUCE.—2 egg-yolks,

½ pint of salad oil, about a tablespoonful of vinegar, 1 teaspoonful of onion-juice, a few capers, seasoning.

METHOD.—The soles should be about half a pound in weight. They should be cleaned and skinned, but not filleted.

Wash and dry them in a cloth, then coat them with egg and breadcrumbs and fry them in hot fat, turning them over when brown. Drain them on paper and serve them garnished with parsley and lemon and accompanied by tartar sauce.

To MAKE THE SAUCE.—Mix the yolks of eggs in a basin, using a wooden spoon ; then stir in the oil drop by drop, adding seasoning to taste, and also onion-juice.

As the sauce thickens, stir in a little vinegar. When ready to use it should be of a thick, creamy consistency. The oil has a thickening effect, while the vinegar thins it, so add more vinegar as required. A little Tarragon vinegar improves the flavour of this sauce.

Finally, stir in a few roughly chopped capers, and serve the sauce in lemon baskets. It is essential to add the oil very gradually, especially at first, otherwise the sauce will curdle.

LEMON BASKETS

Cut the lemons almost in halves lengthwise, cutting from each end towards, but not quite to, the centre. Remove the two quarters of lemon by cutting down on either side of the centre-piece, which will then form the handle.

Scoop out the pulp from the basket and from under the handle. It can then be filled with sauce.

VIENNA STEAKS

INGREDIENTS.—2 lb. of lean buttock steak, 1 onion, 1 egg, 2½ oz. of bread-crumbs, salt and pepper, 6 tomatoes, a few sprigs of cauliflower.

METHOD.—Put the steak through the mincer, and peel and mince a good medium-sized onion. Mix these together, add the breadcrumbs, season the mixture with pepper and salt, and stir in the beaten egg.

Divide the mixture into twelve portions and form each into a flat, round cake. Dredge them with flour

and then gently fry them in a small quantity of either butter or dripping, turning them over when brown.

Serve them on halved tomatoes, which have been baked lightly in the oven, and garnish them with a small sprig of boiled cauliflower, dusted with red pepper.

Serve the steaks with thick gravy, made by browning a little flour in some of the fat in which the steaks were fried, then adding stock and seasoning. This gravy should then be boiled up and strained.

Prepare and cook the potatoes and cauliflower in the usual way.

BAKED PANCAKES

INGREDIENTS.—6 oz. of flour, 4 eggs, rind of 1 small lemon, rind of 1 small orange, ¾ pint of milk, 1 teaspoonful of baking-powder, 4 oz. of castor sugar, 3 oz. of butter or margarine.

METHOD.—Beat the butter and sugar to a cream, and add the finely grated rind of the orange and lemon. Sift the flour with the baking-powder and stir it in gradually, adding also the well-whisked eggs and then the milk.

Butter some old, strong saucers, and pour a little of the mixture into each. Bake them in a fairly hot oven for about twenty minutes.

Serve them as soon as possible after baking, heaped on a dish and sprinkled with castor sugar. This quantity will make about one dozen pancakes.

APRIL

TABLE DECORATIONS

Spring on its way—and we use the first bluebells with daffodils to give our table a festive air. With mats of Normandy lace—a pretty scheme.

MENU
Corn Soup
Leg of English Lamb and Mint Sauce
New Potatoes   Spring Cabbage
Pineapple Pie
Anchovy Fingers
FOR SIX PEOPLE

Easter is a joyful season. Surely a fitting time to introduce fresh dishes into our menu.

The little dinner given this month contains one or two variations from the ordinary run of recipes.

CORN SOUP

INGREDIENTS.—1 pint tin of sweet corn, 1¼ pints of water or white stock, 1 oz. of butter or margarine, 1 onion, ¾ oz. of flour, seasoning, 1¾ pints of milk.

METHOD.—Turn the sweet corn into a saucepan, add the onion, cut in slices, and the water, and let it simmer gently for about half an hour, or until the corn and onion are tender. Rub them all through a sieve. Return this pulp to the pan and add the butter or margarine and nearly all the milk.

Mix the flour to a smooth paste with the remainder of the milk and stir it into the saucepan. Bring the soup to the boil and let it boil gently for a few minutes, stirring well. Add seasoning to taste and serve the soup in soup cups.

LEG OF ENGLISH LAMB AND MINT SAUCE

CHOOSE a leg of lamb about five pounds in weight and bake it for about one hour and a half.

For the first few minutes the oven should be very hot, to seal in the meat juices. Lessen the heat as required and cook the meat till tender.

Serve the lamb with thin brown gravy, which is made by adding stock to the brown particles which are left in the meat-tin after the dripping has been poured off. The gravy is boiled up, seasoned to taste and strained. A few drops of browning may be added if required.

MINT SAUCE

Pick the mint from the stalks. Wash it, drain it, and *chop very finely*.

To 2 flat tablespoonfuls of chopped mint allow 1½ tablespoonfuls of sugar and ¼ pint of vinegar.

Mix the mint with the sugar. Add about two tablespoonfuls of boiling water or two tablespoonfuls of the water in which the cabbage is cooking. Stir the sauce until the sugar is dissolved, then add the vinegar.

Prepare and cook the potatoes and cabbage in the usual way.

PINEAPPLE PIE

INGREDIENTS.—1 pint tin of grated pineapple, 3 dessertspoonfuls of cornflour, 1 dessertspoonful of sugar, ½ oz.

of butter, ½ gill of water, 2 egg-yolks, 3 egg-whites, 3 tablespoonfuls of castor sugar, a few glacé cherries, 6 oz. of flour, 4 oz. of margarine, a pinch of salt, water to mix.

METHOD.—Sift the flour and salt into a basin. Rub the margarine into the flour and mix them to a stiff paste with cold water.

Roll the paste out thinly and cut out a round a little larger than a Pyrex plate. Line the plate and fold the top edge of the pastry in towards the rim. This makes a double edge, which should now be fluted with your finger and thumb.

Prick the pastry in the base of the plate and line the whole of it with a round of buttered paper. Sprinkle in some rice to keep the paper in place and put the pastry in a hot oven to bake. The paper and rice should be removed about five minutes before the pastry is ready.

Turn the grated pineapple and its syrup into a saucepan. Mix the cornflour to a smooth paste with water and stir it into the saucepan. Bring them all to the boil and boil for a few minutes, stirring them well. Then draw the pan aside and add to it the butter, about one dessertspoonful of sugar—or sufficient to taste—and the beaten yolks of the eggs.

Cook this mixture for a few minutes, but do not let it boil again. When cool turn it into the prepared pastry-case.

Whisk the whites of eggs to a stiff froth. Fold the three tablespoonfuls of castor sugar into them.

Cover the pineapple filling with some of this meringue, spreading it over evenly. Force the remainder through an icing-bag. Dredge the meringue with castor sugar and put in a cool oven to set and brown lightly. Decorate the pie with glacé cherries and serve it cold with cream, if liked.

ANCHOVY FINGERS

INGREDIENTS. — 10 anchovies, 12 bread fingers, 1½ oz. of butter, pepper, 3 hard-boiled eggs, parsley, butter for toast.

METHOD.—Mash up the anchovies and mix them with the butter. Boned anchovies bottled in oil can be used for this dish.

To hard-boil the eggs put them into boiling water and boil them gently for twelve to fifteen minutes. Shell them and remove the yolks.

Add the yolks to the butter and anchovy mixture. When they are well mixed together rub them through a sieve and season them to taste with pepper. Salt is not usually required as the anchovies are already rather salt.

Cut twelve fingers of bread, cutting them to a point at one end. Either toast and butter them, or fry them in butter until they are golden-brown in colour.

Put the prepared anchovy mixture on to the fingers of toast or fried bread, decorate them with small pieces of white of egg, and serve them either hot or cold. Garnish them with parsley.

Note.—Anchovy paste can be used for these fingers.

MAY

Table Decorations

Four old pewter drinking-cups holding daffodils and narcissi are chosen for this month's table. Linen place mats, with orange or yellow hems, will look well with them.

Menu

Sole and White Wine Sauce
Roast Veal with Stuffing
and Bacon Rolls
Potatoes   Spinach
Rhubarb   Meringue Jelly
Cheese Sticks

For Six People

Here are four delicious recipes, not difficult to prepare, but daintily garnished and very appetising.

SOLE AND WHITE WINE SAUCE

Ingredients.—2 or 3 lemon soles, bottle of French mushrooms, ½ gill of white wine, salt and pepper, lemon-juice, ½ oz. of butter, 1 oz. of margarine or butter, 1 oz of flour, ¼ pint of milk, ¼ pint of fish stock.

Method.—You will require either two soles, each weighing about one pound, or three rather smaller ones.

Have them filleted, and the fillets skinned on both sides. Season them with pepper and salt, and sprinkle them with lemon-juice.

Fold the fillets into shawl shapes and put them into a buttered dish. Add the white wine and the butter, cut into small dabs. Cover them with a buttered paper and put them into a moderate oven for about twelve minutes or until the flesh is quite white.

Arrange the fillets on a serving-dish and garnish them with the mushrooms (previously heated), and serve them with the following sauce.

To Make the Sauce.—Melt the margarine, add the flour, and when well blended stir in the milk and fish stock. Bring this liquid to the boil, then gradually stir in the wine in which the fish was cooked. Simmer the sauce for a few minutes and add the seasoning to taste, and pour it into a sauce-boat. If the sauce seems too thick, thin it down a little.

Note.—Make the fish stock for the sauce from the fish bones.

ROAST STUFFED VEAL WITH BACON ROLLS

Ingredients.—Chump end of loin of veal (about 4 to 4½ lb.), dripping, 4 oz. of breadcrumbs, 2 oz. of suet, 4 level dessertspoonfuls of chopped parsley, ½ teaspoonful of mixed herbs, ½ lemon, salt and pepper, 1 egg, rashers of bacon.

Method.—To make the stuffing, chop the suet finely and mix it with the breadcrumbs. Add the parsley, herbs, seasoning and grated lemon-rind. Mix them together well and stir in the lemon-juice. Bind the mixture with the egg and, if the stuffing seems too dry, add a little milk.

Have the cup bone removed from the veal. Put in the stuffing, keeping it in position with a skewer.

Put the veal into a baking-tin with the dripping. Cover it with a thickly greased paper or a piece of thin caul and bake for about an hour and three-quarters. Baste it occasionally.

Serve the meat with slightly thickened gravy and garnish it with bacon rolls.

To Make the Gravy.—Prepare

some stock from the veal bone, flavouring it with a few herbs, an onion, and a little powdered mace. Brown some flour in the baking-tin after pouring off most of the dripping. Then gradually add the stock and boil it up.

Allow two or three bacon rolls for each person. These can be prepared from back or streaky rashers, preferably the latter. The rashers must be cut very thinly. After removing the rind, cut them in halves, making two rolls from each rasher. Stick them on a skewer and either bake them in the oven or cook them under the grill.

Sausages and bread sauce can also accompany this dish. Allow one pound of sausages (these can be cooked in the veal-tin or else fried separately) and three-quarters to one pint of bread sauce.

If you prefer it, a piece of boiled bacon may be served instead of the bacon rolls.

THE POTATOES.—Allow about two pounds of potatoes and boil them in the usual way. Floury potatoes are preferable to the waxy variety, but they require to be carefully cooked as they crumble so easily.

THE SPINACH.—Allow five pounds of spinach. To prepare it, remove the discoloured leaves and pull out the stalk that runs through each leaf.

Wash the spinach well in several waters and leave it to soak for a time. When it is clean, lift into a colander to drain.

Spinach is a very gritty vegetable and needs to be washed very thoroughly.

Cook the spinach in only a *small* amount of boiling water, stirring it occasionally at first until more water is drawn from it. Add salt to flavour it, and a *tiny* pinch of soda.

Boil it till tender. It will take about twenty-five minutes.

Strain the spinach through a colander. Drain it well, then turn it on to a board and chop it finely or rub it through a sieve.

Return the vegetable to the pan, and re-heat it. Add a lump of butter and some pepper to taste.

RHUBARB MERINGUE JELLY

INGREDIENTS.—1½ pint packets of lemon jelly, 1 pint of water (hot), 3 egg-whites, 1 lb. of rhubarb (when cut up), 3 tablespoonfuls of sugar.

METHOD.—Dissolve the jellies in the hot water. Cut up the rhubarb and cook it in the top of a double boiler. Add the sugar to it, but no water.

When the rhubarb is tender strain off the syrup (there will be almost half a pint of it), and add it to the jelly.

Leave the jelly until it begins to set, then whisk the whites of eggs to a stiff froth. Add these also to the jelly and whisk them together for a few minutes.

Turn the rhubarb into a serving-dish, keeping back a few pieces for the top. Pour in the prepared jelly and when set, decorate it with cooked rhubarb. If there is any jelly over, break it up roughly and heap it into the centre.

Half a gill of sherry may be added to the jelly after adding the rhubarb juice. In this case, use rather less water to dissolve the jelly.

CHEESE STICKS

INGREDIENTS.—½ lb. of flaky pastry, 2 oz. of Parmesan cheese, 1 oz. of stale Cheddar cheese, salt and cayenne, 1 egg-yolk, a little milk.

METHOD.—Grate the cheeses finely and mix them together. Then divide them into four or six portions.

Roll out the pastry to a thin, oblong shape. Turn it on to the other side. Damp one half of it and sprinkle it with one portion of cheese seasoned with salt and cayenne. Fold the other half over it and press the edges together.

Roll out the pastry again to an oblong. Repeat this process three or five more times until all the cheese is used. Be careful to fold and roll it evenly.

Finally, roll the pastry to about a quarter of an inch thick. Cut it into strips half an inch wide and five and a half inches long, and put it on a baking-sheet.

Brush the tops of the sticks with beaten yolk of egg, mixed with a little milk. Bake them in a hot oven for about ten minutes until they are well risen and golden-brown.

This quantity is sufficient to make about twenty-four sticks.

JUNE
TABLE DECORATIONS
Roses—and they will look their proudest and their best if they are in a bowl of cut crystal. (Choose thick-stemmed roses, and scrape the ends.) It is best to buy them the day before, so that they have time to open a little.

MENU
Asparagus
Milannaise Cutlets
Potato Chips
Caramel Trifle
Eggs en Cocottes

FOR SIX PEOPLE
Asparagus is the perfect beginning for a little dinner in June. Here you will find it, the first of our four delightful dishes in a menu arranged for six people.

BOILED ASPARAGUS WITH OILED BUTTER
INGREDIENTS.—About 6 doz. heads of asparagus, boiling water, salt, 1 or 2 slices of toast, butter, pimento or tomato for garnish.

METHOD.—Trim off the ends of the asparagus, cutting them into equal lengths. Scrape the stalks, scraping downwards.

Put them into cold water with a little salt added to cleanse them. When they are ready to cook, drain them and tie them in bundles, arranging the heads all one way.

Put the asparagus into slightly salted boiling water. Bring it to the boil quickly, and then remove the lid from the pan and boil the asparagus gently until tender. It will take roughly about twenty-five minutes.

When cooked, drain the asparagus and untie it, and serve the heads on a slice of toast.

Garnish them with a strip of pimento or tomato, and serve the oiled butter in a small sauce-boat.

To OIL THE BUTTER.—Just melt it and remove the scum, then pour it into a sauce-boat, leaving the sediment in the pan.

NOTE.—Tinned asparagus may be used when fresh asparagus is not in season. This only requires heating through. Two tins will be sufficient.

MILANNAISE CUTLETS
INGREDIENTS.—12 bones of best neck of lamb, egg and breadcrumbs, butter or dripping.

FOR THE SAUCE.—½ pint of milk, 1 oz. of flour, 1½ oz. of margarine or butter, seasoning, 1 dessertspoonful of onion-juice, 2 oz. of cooked ham, 2 oz. of mushrooms, 2 oz. of spaghetti.

FOR THE GRAVY.—1 dessertspoonful of flour, ¾ pint of stock, seasoning.

METHOD.—Have the chine bone removed from the lamb, then cut it into cutlets, shaping the fat to a point at the end of each bone, and leaving only a thin rim of fat round each cutlet.

Brush the cutlets with eggs and coat them with breadcrumbs. Fry them gently in a little heated butter or dripping, turning them over when they are browned on one side.

Serve the cutlets in a hot entrée dish, placing a cutlet frill on the end of each, and arranging them to form a circle.

Pour thick gravy round them. Heap the white sauce mixed with the spaghetti and strips of ham and mushrooms in the centre.

To MAKE THE GRAVY.—Pour off nearly all the dripping from the pan, leaving only sufficient to mix with one dessertspoonful of flour. Add the latter and let it brown slowly. Draw the pan aside and stir in three-quarters of a pint of stock, then boil it up, season it, and strain it.

To PREPARE THE WHITE SAUCE.—Melt the margarine and add the flour. When these are well blended, stir in the milk and bring the sauce to the boil.

Boil it gently for a few minutes Add the seasoning and the onion-juice, also the ham and mushrooms, both cut into strips, and the spaghetti, which should have first been broken in pieces and boiled in slightly salted water until tender.

Make the sauce thoroughly hot and heap it in the centre of the cutlets.

To prepare the mushrooms, peel and stalk them, and cleanse them in salted water. Drain them and fry them gently in a little butter, then cut them into strips.

Prepare and serve potato chips in the usual way.

CARAMEL TRIFLE

INGREDIENTS.—1 tower-shaped sponge cake, 2 eggs, 1 pint of milk, cooking sherry or rum, apricot jam, 1 small dessertspoonful of castor sugar, 2 oz. of lump sugar, ½ gill of water, cream, a few shelled walnuts.

METHOD.—Put the lump sugar into a small, strong saucepan with the water. Let it dissolve slowly, then bring it to the boil and boil it till golden-brown. Then draw it aside and leave it to get cold.

Add the milk and put the pan over a low burner to dissolve the caramel.

Beat the eggs and mix them with the caramel milk. Strain it into the top of a double boiler and stir it over hot water until the custard thickens.

Add the castor sugar and leave the custard to cool.

Cut the sponge cake into about four slices. Spread these with jam and put them together again, soaking each piece with sherry or rum, and a little milk, if required.

Pour the custard round them and, when thoroughly cold, decorate the trifle with whipped cream (sweetened and flavoured), and shelled walnuts.

EGGS EN COCOTTES

INGREDIENTS.—6 eggs, ½ pint of milk, ¾ oz. of flour, 1 oz. of margarine, sale and pepper, 2 oz. of Parmesan cheese, gherkin and chopped tomato for garnish.

METHOD.—Melt the fat in a saucepan and add the flour. When these are well blended, stir in the milk and bring it to the boil.

Boil the sauce gently for a few minutes. Add seasoning to taste, and the finely grated cheese and stir till it is melted.

Cover the bottom of six buttered cocotte dishes with sauce. Break an egg into each and cover it with sauce. Put the eggs into the oven and bake them gently until they are set.

Garnish them with slices of gherkin and a little chopped tomato.

JULY

TABLE DECORATIONS

Sweet peas—shall they be pink or the spiritual mauve ? Shades of one colour with a little fairy-like greenery make a gracious summer centre-piece.

MENU

Salmon Mayonnaise
Roast Lion of Lamb
New Potatoes, Peas and Carrots
Gooseberry Pie and Cream
Tomato Toast

FOR SIX PEOPLE

Appetites in July often need tempting, for summer days are not conducive to eating. But few could resist the little menu which is given above.

SALMON MAYONNAISE

INGREDIENTS.—2 lb. of salmon, 1 round of lettuce, endive, 1 hard-boiled egg, a few capers, 1 cucumber, oil mayonnaise, salt.

METHOD.—Scrape the skin of the salmon to remove the scales. Rinse it with cold water and put it into boiling water just to cover it, with a little salt added.

Cook it very gently until it is tender. It will take from fifteen to twenty minutes, according to its thickness. Then lift it out and drain off the water.

Remove the skin and bones from the fish and cut the flesh into as even-shaped chunks as possible. Moisten these thoroughly with oil mayonnaise. Serve them surrounded with lettuce leaves and a little endive (both well washed and drained).

Garnish the salmon with slices of hard-boiled egg and a few capers, and serve it with a dish of sliced cucumber.

PROPORTIONS FOR OIL MAYONNAISE. —To one yolk of egg add about a quarter of a pint of salad oil and one dessertspoonful of vinegar.

Break up the yolk of the egg and season it with pepper, salt, and a little dry mustard. Then add fhe oil *very gradually*. As the sauce thickens, thin it down with a little of the vinegar, and continue mixing until all the oil and vinegar are added.

The sauce should be of a thick, creamy consistency when finished. If available, use Tarragon vinegar, or half Tarragon and half plain.

ROAST LOIN OF LAMB

CHOOSE a loin of lamb about four to five pounds in weight, and put it into a hot oven to bake. Lessen the heat later, as required. It will take about one hour and three-quarters to cook.

Serve the roast with thin, brown gravy, the foundation of which should be stock. Boil the stock in the baking-tin after pouring off the dripping. Add seasoning, and a little browning, if required, and strain the gravy.

Mint sauce should also accompany the joint. Turn to p. 661 for directions for making this.

VEGETABLES

Allow two pounds of new potatoes. Scrape and wash them and put them in boiling water to cook with a sprig of mint and salt. Strain off the water when they are tender.

Add a lump of butter to the potatoes and toss them in it. Serve them sprinkled with finely chopped parsley.

PEAS AND CARROTS

Allow about one pint of cooked green peas, and the same amount of cooked carrot, cut in dice.

Scrape a few carrots and cut them into slices, and then in small dice. Cook them in boiling water until they are tender, adding salt to flavour.

Melt a lump of butter in a saucepan. Add the carrots and peas (both drained from their liquor), and toss them in the butter for a few minutes.

Season them with pepper and turn them into a hot vegetable dish.

If fresh peas are used, cook them in a separate pan of boiling water.

GOOSEBERRY PIE

INGREDIENTS.—3 pints of goose-berries, about 4 tablespoonfuls of sugar, ½ gill of water, ¼ lb. of flour, a pinch of salt, 1 level teaspoonful of baking-pow-der, 6 oz. of margarine, 1 egg, water.

METHOD.—Top, tail, and wash the gooseberries. Put a pie-funnel in the centre of a pie-dish, then add the prepared fruit, water, and sugar.

The sugar should be put between the gooseberries, not on top of them.

Sift the flour with salt and baking-powder. Rub in the margarine. Sepa-rate the egg. Beat the yolk and mix

it with a spoonful of water, and add it to the flour, etc. Mix it to a stiff paste, adding a little water as required. Roll out the pastry and cover the pie-dish, putting a strip of pastry first round the rim of the dish.

Trim and decorate the edge and put the pie in a hot oven to bake.

It will take from twenty to thirty minutes. When it is cooked, brush the pastry with the white of egg, slightly frothed and dredge it with castor sugar. Then return the pie to the oven for a minute or two.

Serve it cold, with cream.

TOMATO TOAST

INGREDIENTS.—6 slices of tomato, 2 oz. of cheese, salt and pepper, 6 rounds of bread, 2 oz. of streaky bacon, butter, parsley.

METHOD.—Cut six thick slices of tomato of even size, and put them in the oven to heat through.

Cut also six rounds of bread (toast thickness) the same size as the tomato slices. Toast these on one side, and then butter the untoasted side.

Remove the rind from the rashers, cut them into small dice, and fry the bacon until it is crisp.

Place a slice of tomato on each round of toast, and season it with salt and pepper. Add a little chopped, cooked bacon. Sprinkle grated cheese on top.

Put them under the hot grill for a few minutes to melt the cheese and brown it lightly. Serve them garnished with parsley.

AUGUST

TABLE DECORATIONS

Something quite fresh in colour schemes — marigolds and love-in-a-mist! Consider each flower separately if you would arrange a bowl with charm.

MENU
Prawns
Veal-and-Ham Pie and Salad
Iced Pineapple
Cheese Soufflés

FOR SIX PEOPLE

Although perhaps it is not con-sidered ideal menu-making to serve all the courses cold, yet after a hot summer's day this is often the only type of meal we feel we can enjoy.

On such a night the little menu chosen this month would be very welcome.

PRAWNS

Allow half a dozen prawns for each person and arrange them on a lemon, from which a slice has been cut at the top and base.

Tiny slices of thin brown bread-and-butter may also accompany the prawns.

VEAL-AND-HAM PIE

INGREDIENTS.—1 lb. of veal (when prepared), ¾ lb. of bacon, ½ lb. of pork sausages, rind of ½ a lemon, 1 teaspoonful of chopped parsley, pepper and salt, powdered mace, ½ to ¾ gill of water, 2 hard-boiled eggs, gelatine, some flaky pastry (see p. 252) (about 1½ to 2 lb. when prepared), 1 egg-yolk and a little milk.

METHOD.—Use either neck or middle of the shoulder of veal, and remove the bone and skin.

Then put the meat through the mincer. There should be a good pound of veal when it has been prepared.

Cut the bacon in small dice after removing the rind, and skin the sausages.

Season the veal with the parsley, finely grated lemon-rind, salt, pepper, and mace. Season the bacon also with pepper and mace.

Put about one-third of the veal into a pie-dish, then add half the bacon, half the sausage, and one egg (sliced).

Put in two or three sheets of leaf gelatine, then another layer of veal, and the remainder of the bacon, sausage, and egg.

Pour in a little water—just sufficient to moisten the meat—and then add the remainder of the veal, which should fill the pie-dish.

Roll out the pastry about three-eighths of an inch thick, and cut a piece of it to cover the pie. Cut also small shapes of pastry for decorating it—either leaves or half-moons, etc.

Damp the rim of the dish and line it with a strip of pastry. Damp this and then cover the pie. Trim and decorate the edge of the pie and

make a hole in the centre—this is important—so that the steam may escape. Decorate the top of the pie with the small fancy shapes of pastry.

Brush over the pastry with beaten yolk of egg mixed with a little milk, and put the pie into a hot oven to bake.

When it is well risen and lightly browned, reduce the heat and finish cooking the pie. It will take from one and a quarter to one and a half hours altogether. If it is necessary, cover the crust with a sheet of paper to prevent it getting too brown.

When the pie is cooked, fill it up with veal stock that will jelly when cold. Serve the pie with a salad.

NOTE.—Make the stock from the veal bones, flavouring it slightly with onion and herbs and mace to taste. If necessary, dissolve a little gelatine in the stock before adding it to the pie.

ICED PINEAPPLE

INGREDIENTS.—Large tin of sliced pineapple, whipped cream, sugar and vanilla, glacé cherries, ice and freezing salt.

METHOD.—Take a tin of pineapple and pack it in your freezing pail in a mixture of ice and freezing salt.

The ice should be chipped into rather small pieces, and each layer sprinkled with salt. Use half a pint of freezing salt to every quart of chipped ice.

If a freezing pail is not available, a deep enamel basin or pail will answer the purpose.

The ice and salt must be replenished as the ice melts and the melted ice poured off at intervals.

Leave the pineapple for about four or five hours. Then open the tin. It should be opened round the side, just below the edge. The top can then be completely removed.

Turn out the pineapple on to a chilled dish and decorate it with whipped cream, sweetened and flavoured to taste, and glacé cherries. It should be served at once with sugar.

Other kinds of tinned fruit, such as pears, peaches, and apricots, can be served in this delicious way. The shape can be cut into slices and it may then be served on individual plates.

CHEESE SOUFFLES

INGREDIENTS.—1 oz. of Parmesan cheese, 2 oz. of Cheddar cheese, ½ pint of milk, 2 egg-yolks, salt and pepper, mixed mustard, ⅜ oz. of leaf gelatine, ¼ gill of water, 2 dessertspoonfuls of cream, 3 egg-whites, paprika pepper.

METHOD.—Pin a band of foolscap paper round each of six small soufflé cases so that it stands well above the top.

Bring the milk almost to the boil, then add it to the beaten yolks of eggs. Turn the custard into the top of a double boiler and stir it over hot water until it thickens, keeping it well stirred. Then remove it and leave it to get cold.

Grate the cheeses finely and stir them into the custard with the cream and seasoning to taste.

Dissolve the gelatine in a saucepan with the water, and strain it into the mixture. When it begins to set, fold in the stiffly whisked whites of egg. Turn the mixture into the prepared case. When it is set, remove the bands of foolscap paper very carefully, and decorate each soufflé with a cross of paprika pepper.

SEPTEMBER

TABLE DECORATIONS

What can equal the prim, old-fashioned charm of zinnias in mixed colours ? Their bright hues are enhanced by the soft delicacy of a Chinese bowl.

MENU

Cauliflower Cream Soup
Roast Chicken   Bread Sauce
Potatoes   Beans
Plum Jelly Creams
Mushroom Toast

FOR SIX PEOPLE

Here is a delightful menu for the betwixt-and-between season when the days of fresh fruit are behind us, and the time for the heat-giving foods of winter is not yet come.

CAULIFLOWER CREAM SOUP

INGREDIENTS.—1 cauliflower, 1½ pints of white stock, 1 pint of milk, 1½ oz. of butter or margarine, 1 oz. of flour, seasoning, 1 onion, paprika, few celery seeds.

METHOD.—Trim the cauliflower and cleanse it in cold, salted water. Put it into boiling water with salt to flavour it and boil it till tender. Then drain it well.

Remove the green part from the cauliflower, keep back a few white sprigs, and rub the remainder of the white flower through a sieve.

Peel and mince finely the onion and cook it in the butter for a few moments without browning it. Stir in the flour and, when they are well blended, add the stock and stir till it boils.

Tie a few celery seeds in muslin and add them with the sieved cauliflower and the milk to the pan.

Boil the soup up again and add seasoning to taste. Let it simmer for about five minutes, then remove the celery seeds. Serve the soup in cups.

Sprinkle the cups with paprika pepper, and garnish the soup with a tiny sprig of cooked cauliflower.

ROAST CHICKEN

INGREDIENTS.—A pair of chickens, dripping.

FOR THE STUFFING.—4 oz. of bread-crumbs, 1 tablespoonful of chopped onion, 3 level tablespoonfuls of chopped parsley, 1 egg, salt and pepper, 2 oz. of butter, the livers from the chickens.

FOR THE GRAVY.—Pinch of herbs, 1 onion.

METHOD.—Have the chickens drawn and trussed.

Wash the giblets in cold, salted water. Drain the livers and put them aside for the stuffing.

Put the remainder of the giblets on the gas to make stock for the gravy, adding an onion and a pinch of herbs, and water to cover.

To make the stuffing, mix the breadcrumbs with the chopped onion and parsley.

Chop up the two livers and add them, with seasoning to taste, to the breadcrumbs. Then moisten the mixture with the butter (melted) and bind it with the egg.

If liked, the stuffing can be flavoured with lemon or herbs.

Stuff the birds and put them into a baking-tin with some dripping. Cover the breast of each chicken with a thickly greased paper or a thin piece of caul.

Place the birds in a hot oven at first, then lessen the heat later as required. They will take from one to one and a half hours to cook, according to their size.

Keep the chickens well basted and remove the caul or paper fifteen minutes before dishing up, so that they may brown.

Serve them with slightly thickened brown gravy and bread sauce.

A piece of boiled bacon or a few bacon rolls should also accompany them, and sausages, too, if liked.

BREAD SAUCE

INGREDIENTS.—3 oz. of breadcrumbs, 1 oz. of butter, 3 or 4 cloves, 1 pint of milk, 1 onion, seasoning.

METHOD.—Put the milk into a saucepan with the butter. Peel the onion, stick the cloves into it, and add it to the milk.

Leave the pan at the side of the fire until the milk is well flavoured.

Bring it to the boil, and add the breadcrumbs. Lift the pan to the side again until the sauce is thick.

Then season it to taste. Re-heat it, and then remove the onion. Serve the sauce in a tureen.

If the sauce is thick, add a little more milk or some cream.

VEGETABLES

POTATOES.—Allow from two to three pounds, and boil them in the usual way.

BEANS.—String the beans and slice them thinly, then wash them well.

Put them into boiling water to cook with salt to flavour, and a tiny piece of soda. They will take about twenty minutes to cook.

When they are tender, drain them well. Return them to a clean pan with a good lump of butter and toss them lightly in it for a few minutes. Season them with pepper before turning them into a hot vegetable dish.

Allow about two pounds of beans.

PLUM JELLY CREAMS

INGREDIENTS.—1½ lb. of plums, 1½ pint packets of lemon jelly, 1½ oz. of almonds, ¾ pint of hot water, ¾ gill of cold water, 3 tablespoonfuls of sugar, 9d. of cream, few glacé cherries.

METHOD.—Stalk and wash the plums and stew them till tender, adding the sugar and cold water. Then rub them through a sieve.

Dissolve the jelly in the hot water, and when it is cold stir in the plum purée, making it up to one and a half pints together. If there is more than three-quarters of a pint of plum purée, use less water to dissolve the jelly.

Blanch, skin, and chop the almonds and add them to the jelly. Leave it till it begins to thicken. Whip the cream and stir it in lightly, and add more sugar if required.

Turn the plum jelly cream into small, wet moulds. When they are set, dip them in warm water, unmould them, and decorate each with half a glacé cherry.

This quantity will fill about ten small moulds.

MUSHROOM TOAST

INGREDIENTS.—6 good medium-sized mushrooms, 6 rounds of bread, salt and pepper, butter.

METHOD.—Peel the mushrooms, remove their stalks, and trim them. Cleanse them for a few minutes in cold water to which a little salt has been added. Then drain them.

Cut a tiny round from the centre of each mushroom. Season the mushrooms with pepper and salt, and fry them in some butter till they are tender. Fry the stalks also.

Cut rounds of bread of toast thickness. Toast them on one side. Butter the untoasted side with the mushroom butter.

Place a mushroom on each round of toast. Replace the stalks, and serve the mushrooms.

OCTOBER

TABLE DECORATIONS

The last roses—deep red and heavy-scented. Arrange them loosely in a silver bowl and your table will look hospitable—and quite perfect.

MENU

Cream of Tomato Soup
Saddle of Mutton and Red Currant Jelly
Potatoes   Spinach
Apple Meringue
Soft Roes on Toast
FOR SIX PEOPLE.

A little four-course dinner such as

we give here will suffice for most occasions, but this may be lessened or added to as required.

The quantities are for six people with the exception of the joint, which must be of good average size.

CREAM OF TOMATO SOUP

INGREDIENTS.—1½ lb. of tomatoes, 1 or 2 shallots, ½ small clove of garlic, few celery seeds, ⅓ level teaspoonful of carbonate of soda, 1 oz. of flour, 1 oz. of margarine or butter, salt and pepper, 1¼ pints of milk, ¼ pint of water.

METHOD.—Slice the tomatoes, and cook them gently in a pan until they are tender, with just a tablespoonful of water, adding a few celery seeds (tied in muslin), the shallots, and garlic.

When ready, remove the last three ingredients and rub the tomatoes through a sieve. Stir in the soda.

Melt the fat in another saucepan, stir in the flour, and when it is mixed smoothly add the milk and water. Stir the sauce until it boils and thickens. Then let it cook gently for a few minutes.

(If preferred, *all* milk may be used for the sauce.)

Add the tomato pulp, stirring it in gradually. Season it to taste, and when hot serve the soup with fried croûtons. These are dice of fried bread.

CROUTONS

To prepare the croûtons, cut slices of bread about a quarter of an inch thick. Cut these in fingers, then into dice, and put them into hot fat to fry until golden. Drain them on paper and serve them on a paper doyley.

A frying basket is the best to use for these croûtons, as they can all be taken out at the same moment, and this ensures their being evenly browned.

Put the diced bread into the basket. Shake off the loose crumbs, then stand the basket in a fairly deep pan containing enough fat to float them.

A faint smoke should rise from the fat when it is hot enough for the bread to be added.

SADDLE OF MUTTON

THIS, as you may already know, consists of two loins joined together.

Choose a saddle of small Scotch mutton or, if preferred, buy the best Canterbury lamb.

Heat your oven first. Then put the joint on one of the racks, or else hang it on a hook in the oven, letting the fat drip into a tin at the bottom.

The oven should be fairly hot for the first fifteen minutes, then the heat should be reduced. A saddle weighing six pounds will take about one and three-quarter hours to cook.

Serve this joint with thin brown gravy and red currant jelly.

Make the gravy from some good plain stock, pouring this round the meat tin after draining off the dripping and leaving just the brown particles.

Boil up the stock, add a little browning, seasoning to taste, and then strain the gravy.

Garnish the meat with balls of carrot and turnip cut out with a vegetable ball-cutter before boiling.

POTATOES

Allow two pounds of potatoes for six persons.

Choose floury potatoes and boil them carefully, so that they are still whole when served. If you remember to pour off the water before they are quite cooked and let them finish cooking in the steam, there will be no difficulty in keeping them whole.

SPINACH

Allow five pounds of spinach for six persons.

Spinach is a very gritty vegetable, and it needs to be thoroughly washed in at least three or four waters and then left to soak for a time between each washing.

Before washing, prepare the spinach by throwing out old and discoloured leaves and pulling out the stalk that runs through each leaf. When clean, lift the leaves out of the water into a colander and drain them well.

To cook the vegetable, put about a cupful of water into a large saucepan, or enough to cover the bottom of the pan. When the water is boiling, add the spinach, sprinkling each layer of the leaves with salt.

Boil the spinach until it is tender, keeping the spinach well stirred at first until it has mashed down considerably and the water has increased in bulk.

It will take from twenty-five to thirty minutes to cook. When tender, strain it through a colander and press out the water. Turn the spinach on to a board and chop it finely.

Return it to the pan with a lump of butter, re-heat it, and season it with pepper, and serve it.

APPLE MERINGUE

INGREDIENTS.—3 lb. of cooking apples, 3 eggs, 3 tablespoonfuls of castor sugar, 1½ gills of water, 3 tablespoonfuls of granulated sugar (or enough to sweeten), rind of 1 lemon, few glacé cherries and stalks of angelica, 2 oz. of glacé ginger, 1 oz. of butter, cream.

METHOD.—Peel and quarter the apples and remove the core. Cut them into slices.

Put them into a saucepan with the water and granulated sugar, and cook them until tender. Then rub them through a sieve.

Grate the lemon-rind finely and add it, with the ginger cut in small pieces, and the butter, to the apples.

Separate the eggs, beat the yolks, and mix them into the apple pulp. Turn the mixture into a buttered Pyrex dish and cook it gently for from twenty to thirty minutes without letting it boil. Remove the apples from the heat and cool them slightly.

Whisk the whites of eggs to a stiff froth, then gradually whisk in the castor sugar. Put this mixture into an icing-bag and force it on to the top of the apple, covering it completely. Return the Apple Meringue to a cool oven to set, and brown it lightly on the top.

Serve Apple Meringue cold, decorated with glacé cherries and stalks of angelica, accompanied by cream.

SOFT ROES ON TOAST

INGREDIENTS.—½ lb. of soft herring roes, rounds of buttered toast, salt and pepper, lemon, cooking butter.

METHOD.—Wipe the roes carefully. Season them with salt and pepper. Fry them gently in a small quantity of butter. Meanwhile, cut rounds of bread, toast and butter them. Arrange the roes on the toast and garnish them with lemon.

NOVEMBER

TABLE DECORATIONS

Mauve Michaelmas daisies with bronze chrysanthemums make a glad array, glowing with the wonderful rich tones of an autumn day—and giving a suggestion of the cosiness within.

MENU
Oysters
Beef Olives
Mashed Potatoes   Peas
Ginger Trifle
Savoury Aigrettes
FOR SIX PEOPLE

Allow six oysters for each person and serve in the deep halves of the shells, arranging them on a plate with chipped ice and garnished with lemon.

They should be accompanied by brown bread-and-butter, cut as thin as a wafer and formed into rolls.

BEEF OLIVES

INGREDIENTS.—1½ lb. of buttock steak (cut thinly), ½ gill of tomato purée, butter or dripping, 1¼ pints of stock, salt and pepper, 2½ flat tablespoonfuls of flour.

FOR THE STUFFING.—1 level teaspoonful of mixed herbs, 2½ level dessertspoonfuls of chopped parsley, 3 oz. of breadcrumbs, 1 egg, 1½ oz. of suet, ½ lemon, seasoning.

METHOD.—TO MAKE THE STUFFING.—Chop the suet finely and mix it with the breadcrumbs. Add the herbs and finely chopped parsley, also the finely grated lemon-rind and salt and pepper to taste. Strain in the juice of the lemon and bind the mixture with the egg.

TO PREPARE THE OLIVES.—Cut the steak into pieces about four inches by three and beat them flat with a cutlet bat or a large knife.

Spread them with stuffing and roll them up, tying them securely but not too tightly with string.

Roll them in flour and fry them in hot fat, just enough to seal the outside. Take them out and put them into a saucepan or casserole.

Pour off some of the fat, all but about one or two tablespoonfuls. Add the flour to the remainder and stir this gravy over a low burner until it is brown. Draw the pan aside, cool the gravy for a minute and stir in the stock.

Bring it to the boil, add the tomato purée and seasoning to taste. The gravy should be thick and brown; a few drops of browning may be added if required. Strain this over the olives, cover it with a lid and simmer it gently for about an hour.

When cooked, untie the olives and arrange them on a line of mashed potato. Pour the gravy round and garnish the olives with tiny force-meat balls, made from the remainder of the stuffing. These should be either floured or egged and crumbed, and then fried.

The tomato purée can be bought ready prepared. It is sold in small tins and can be obtained from any big store. Or you can make some purée by baking one or two tomatoes until tender, then rubbing them through a sieve.

MASHED POTATOES

Prepare two pounds of potatoes in the usual way. Use some of the mashed potato to dish the olives on, and serve the remainder separately.

PEAS

Allow two tins of peas.

The directions for use are usually given on the tin. Some kinds can be heated in their liquor, others require to be drained off and heated in a double saucepan with a lump of butter. Season them with pepper and salt.

GINGER TRIFLE

INGREDIENTS.—2 sponge rings, 1¼ pints of milk, 3 eggs, ½ small pot of preserved ginger in syrup, sugar to taste, ½ gill of ginger wine, ¼ pint of cream, sugar and vanilla, angelica.

METHOD.—For this dish one whole sponge ring (sixpenny size) will be required, and half of another.

Split them in half and put the three halves into a dish, one piece on top of the other, covering each with ginger cut in small pieces.

Soak the sponge with ginger wine and syrup. Separate one of the eggs and beat the two whole eggs and the odd yolk together.

Bring the milk almost to the boil

and pour it on to them. Turn this custard into the top of a double boiler or into a jug, stand it in a pan of hot water, and cook it until the custard thickens, keeping it well stirred.

Take it off the gas, add sugar to taste, and a few drops of vanilla.

Cool it a little, then pour it over the sponge. Decorate it with pieces of ginger and angelica.

Before serving, whisk the remaining white of egg to a stiff froth, and the cream until it is thick. Mix these together, add sugar and vanilla to taste and heap it in the centre. If the pieces of ginger required for decoration are cut first, the trimmings can be used for the inside of the trifle.

SAVOURY AIGRETTES

INGREDIENTS.—2½ oz. of cheese, ½ oz. of margarine or butter, 1½ gills of water, seasoning (pepper, salt, mixed mustard), 3 oz. of flour, 2 eggs, deep fat for frying.

METHOD.—Put the water and butter or margarine into a saucepan, and bring it to the boil. Stir in the flour, sieved and weighed accurately, and continue to stir until the mixture becomes a smooth, thick paste which easily leaves the sides of the pan and does not stick to the fingers. When ready, draw the pan aside and cool the mixture a little, then gradually beat in the eggs. Add nearly all the cheese, finely grated, and seasoning to taste. Spread the mixture on a plate and leave it until thoroughly cold.

Have a deep pan of hot fat ready, dip a teaspoon into it, then fill it with cheese mixture and drop this carefully into the fat, with the aid of another teaspoon also dipped in fat.

Fry the aigrettes gently, a few at a time, until golden brown. Then drain them on paper and serve them sprinkled with some finely grated cheese.

DECEMBER

TABLE DECORATIONS

What shall we have for Christmas ? Mistletoe with gay orange and scarlet winter fruits cleverly arranged in a bowl, and scarlet candles in green glass holders.

MENU

Grape fruit or Jaffa Oranges
Roast Turkey and Bread Sauce
Potato Balls
Brussels Sprouts
Christmas Pudding
Hard Sauce
Cheese Eggs

FOR SIX PEOPLE

Allow half a grape fruit for each person or, if you prefer it, serve half a large Jaffa orange prepared in the same way as the grape fruit.

Cut the fruit in halves, crosswise, remove the centre pith and pips, then divide each section by cutting along each side of the dividing membranes.

Cut round the edge of the fruit to loosen it from the pith and rind, sprinkle with castor sugar and serve with a crystallised cherry in the middle,

Special grape fruit knives may be obtained for preparing the fruit ; these are quite inexpensive and have stainless steel blades.

ROAST TURKEY

WITH STUFFING, BREAD SAUCE, AND BROWN CRUMBS

INGREDIENTS.—Turkey, 1 lb. of sausage meat, 6 oz. of breadcrumbs, 4 oz. of suet, dripping, 3 level tablespoonfuls of chopped parsley, $\frac{1}{2}$ teaspoonful of mixed herbs, salt and pepper, 1 or 2 eggs, milk, $\frac{1}{2}$ lemon.

METHOD.—Choose a turkey weighing about eight to ten pounds, and have it drawn and trussed.

TO MAKE THE STUFFING.—Chop the suet and mix it with the breadcrumbs parsley, and herbs. Add the finely grated lemon-rind and seasoning. Then moisten them with lemon-juice, egg, and some milk, as required.

Put the sausage meat in the body of the bird and the prepared stuffing in the neck, and then draw the skin over it on to the back and skewer it.

Lay the turkey in a baking-tin with plenty of dripping. Cover the breast with a thickly greased paper and cook for from two to two and a half hours, keeping it well basted.

Serve with slightly thickened gravy, bread sauce, and brown crumbs. A piece of boiled bacon or rolls of bacon should also accompany the bird.

TO PREPARE THE ROLLS OF BACON.—Remove the rind, roll up the rashers and stick them on to a skewer. Cook them for a few minutes either in the oven or under the grill. Thin rashers are required for this purpose.

THE GRAVY.—The stock used for this should be made from the giblets. Wash them thoroughly in cold water with salt, and cook them gently for two or three hours, adding a flavouring of onion, herbs, and one or two cloves. Thicken this gravy with a little flour and boil it up in the tin in which the turkey was cooked, after pouring off the dripping. Add browning and seasoning to taste and strain the gravy before serving it.

BREAD SAUCE

INGREDIENTS.—1 pint of milk, 1 small onion, 3 or 4 cloves, 1 oz. of butter or margarine, seasoning, $\frac{1}{2}$ pint of breadcrumbs (pressed down).

METHOD.—Put the milk into a saucepan with the onion and cloves, and leave it at the side of the fire for an hour or so. Then bring it to the boil. Add the breadcrumbs, butter, and seasoning to taste.

Stand the pan aside for a few minutes to allow the crumbs to swell, then remove the flavourings, re-heat the sauce and serve it in a sauce-boat.

TO PREPARE THE BROWN CRUMBS.—Make half a pint of breadcrumbs and fry them gently until brown in a very small quantity of butter. Serve these on a lace paper.

BRUSSELS SPROUTS

Allow two pounds of sprouts.

Prepare them in the usual way, wash them thoroughly and cook them in boiling water with salt and a tiny piece of soda added. They will take about twenty minutes.

POTATO BALLS

INGREDIENTS.—2 lb. of potatoes, 2 eggs, salt and pepper, a lump of butter or margarine, 1 level teaspoonful of chopped parsley, breadcrumbs, deep fat.

METHOD.—Peel the potatoes and boil them in salted water until tender. Drain them and rub them through a sieve

Y

Separate the eggs, beat up the yolks and add them to the potatoes with the butter, parsley, and seasoning. Leave the potato to cool. Divide it into small portions and shape it into balls. Brush them with the whites of egg, and coat them with breadcrumbs. Put them into a frying-basket and fry in deep fat until golden-brown.

Drain them and serve.

CHRISTMAS PUDDING

INGREDIENTS.—10 oz. of raisins, 5 oz. of suet, 3 oz. of breadcrumbs, 2 oz. of flour, 3 oz. of candied peel, 3 oz. of currants, 2 oz. of sultanas, 5 oz. of sugar, 1 oz. of almonds, some grated nutmeg, $\frac{1}{2}$ grated lemon-rind, $\frac{1}{4}$ flat teaspoonful of ground cinnamon, $\frac{1}{4}$ flat teaspoonful of ground cloves, 2 eggs, $\frac{1}{2}$ gill of rum, some milk.

METHOD.—Wash, pick over and dry the fruit, and stone the raisins. Cut up the peel, blanch and shred the almonds.

Chop the suet finely and mix it with the breadcrumbs, flour, grated lemon-rind, and spices. Add the sugar, almonds, and prepared fruit, and mix all together.

Moisten the mixture with the well-beaten eggs, the rum, and some milk as required. Beat well, turn it into a well-buttered mould, and cover it securely with buttered paper and a floured pudding-cloth.

Stand the pudding in a pan of boiling water, and cook it for about six hours, adding more boiling water as required.

It is a good plan to leave the pudding mixture to stand for twelve hours before turning it into the mould to cook, when it may require a little more moisture.

When cooked, unmould the pudding, and serve it with hard sauce.

HARD SAUCE

INGREDIENTS.—$\frac{1}{2}$ lb. of icing sugar, $\frac{1}{4}$ lb. of butter, flavouring,

METHOD.—Rub the icing sugar through a fine sieve. Beat the butter with half the sugar to a cream, then add the remainder, and beat it again. Flavour it with vanilla or a little rum or brandy.

CHEESE EGGS

INGREDIENTS.—3 eggs, 6 slices of tomato, 2 oz. of cheese, salt and pepper, 1 oz. of butter, about 1 tablespoonful of milk.

METHOD.—Hard-boil the eggs, cut them in halves crosswise, and remove the yolks. Melt the butter, add the finely grated cheese, and stir them over a very low burner until the cheese is melted and the mixture creamy. Then add it to the pounded yolks.

Season it to taste and stir in the milk. Rub it through a sieve.

Heap the mixture in the half-whites, cutting a small piece from the base of the whites so that they stand firmly. The egg-mixture can be forced through an icing bag if preferred.

Stand each half-egg on a slice of tomato, and garnish with a little mustard and cress.

BEVERAGES

CHERRY BRANDY

INGREDIENTS.—1 lb. of Morella cherries, 6 oz. of castor sugar, brandy to cover.

METHOD.—Stalk the cherries and wipe them; they must be fresh and not over ripe.

Take rather a wide-mouthed bottle or jar, be sure that it is quite dry and clean.

Put the cherries and castor sugar in the bottle in layers until the bottle is three parts full. Then add sufficient brandy just to cover.

Cork it very securely and leave for about fourteen weeks in a cool, dry place.

It may then be strained and bottled.

CIDER CUP

INGREDIENTS.—1 lemon, 1 tablespoonful of castor sugar, sliced cucumber (about 1 inch), ½ wineglass of sherry, ice, soda-water, 1 pint of cider.

METHOD.—To make cider cup, put the juice of the lemon and the castor sugar into a jug with about an inch of sliced cucumber.

Add half a wineglass of sherry and a pint bottle of cider, and stir them together.

Let the liquid stand for an hour in a cool place or on ice. Strain it and add the soda-water to it, and also some chipped ice, then it is ready to serve.

CLARET CUP

INGREDIENTS.—1 bottle of claret, 1 wineglassful of brandy, 2 pint bottles of soda-water, 1 lemon, a piece of cucumber (about 2 or 3 inches), ice, 2 sprigs of borage, ¼ lb. of lump sugar.

METHOD.—Cut the lemon into four. Slice the cucumber. Put both into a large jug, add the sugar, soda-water, claret, and brandy.

Stir it round until the sugar is dissolved.

Add the borage.

Cover the jug and stand on ice for about one hour, then strain it.

Break up about a pound of ice into small pieces, wash it well and add to the claret cup.

Serve at once.

NOTE.—Claret Cup should only be made for immediate use.

COCOA

ALLOW a teaspoonful of cocoa to one teacup.

Mix the cocoa to a smooth paste with a little milk.

Then stir on to it boiling water, milk and water, or all milk.

Pour into a saucepan, bring to the boil and boil for a minute or two.

Add sugar to taste.

COFFEE

INGREDIENTS.—3 tablespoonfuls of coffee, a pinch of salt, 2 pints of boiling water, milk and sugar.

METHOD.—Heat the coffee-pot with boiling water, then empty.

Place the coffee in the heated pot and immediately pour on freshly boiling water.

Add a pinch of salt.

Stir well. Then let it stand at the side of the fire for a few minutes.

Lastly, clear it.

To clear coffee, pour out a cupful of the liquid, then return it to the pot.

Repeat this several times, then let it stand again for a few minutes.

When serving, pour it through a coffee-strainer.

Serve it black or with hot milk.

Add sugar to taste.

DAMSON GIN

INGREDIENTS.—4 pints of gin (unsweetened), 3 lb. of damsons, 4 doz. cloves, ¾ lb. of lump sugar, cinnamon, if liked (about 10 inches).

METHOD.—Wipe the damsons, pick them over, remove the stalks and prick them with a needle. Put them into a large stone jar.

Add the gin, sugar, cloves, and cinnamon.

Cork it very securely and shake it well.

Continue to shake it every day for two or three months ; then leave for a few days. It can then be strained and bottled.

NOTE.—The damsons must be very fresh and ripe, but not over ripe. If the flavour of cinnamon is not liked it may be omitted.

GINGER BEER

INGREDIENTS.—1 gallon of boiling water, 14 oz. of loaf sugar, 1 lemon, ¾ oz. of lump ginger (bruised), ½ oz. of solid yeast, 2 teaspoonfuls of castor sugar, 1 teaspoonful of cream of tartar.

METHOD.—Wipe the lemon and peel very thinly. Put the rind into a large jar or pan, and add the lump sugar, ginger, and cream of tartar.

Pour the boiling water over these ingredients, and stir together. Leave until lukewarm.

Mix the yeast and castor sugar together until they become liquid, then stir into the other ingredients with the lemon-juice.

Partly cover.

Leave in a warm place for twelve hours.

Remove the scum, strain the ginger-beer and bottle it.

Cork the bottles very securely, and tie the corks with wire.

Leave for about four or five days.

LEMONADE

INGREDIENTS.—1 lemon, ¾ lb. of sugar (lump or granulated), 1½ pints of boiling water, 1 dessertspoonful of citric acid.

METHOD.—Peel the lemon thinly, squeeze out the juice.

Put into a jug, add the sugar and citric acid.

Pour on boiling water, stir well.

Leave for about twelve hours.

Then strain.

Use about one tablespoonful of lemonade to a tumbler of water.

LEMON WHEY

INGREDIENTS.—3 gills of milk, juice of ½ a lemon, 1 teaspoonful of castor sugar.

METHOD.—Make the milk warm.

Add the strained lemon-juice and mix together.

When well curdled, strain through muslin or a fine strainer. The whey will go through and the curds remain in the strainer.

Add the castor sugar to the whey.

MILK WITH A DASH OF COFFEE

PUT two tablespoonfuls of coffee into a tumbler and fill up with milk. Turn into a saucepan and heat almost to boiling-point.

Add sugar to taste.

ORANGEADE

INGREDIENTS.—2 oranges, ¼ lb. of sugar, 1½ pints of boiling water.

METHOD.—Peel the oranges thinly and squeeze out the juice.

Put into a jug with the sugar.

Add the water, stir round, and leave until cold. Strain. Use undiluted.

ORANGE LIQUEUR

INGREDIENTS.—1 1½ pint size bottle of whisky, 7 oz. of lump sugar, or granulated, 2 lemons (small), 2 Seville oranges (medium size).

METHOD.—Wipe the oranges and lemons and peel them thinly.

Put the peel into a jar, and add the whisky and sugar.

Cork tightly, and leave for five or six days ; during this time keep it well shaken each day.

Leave until the next day, then strain through muslin or a very fine strainer, then bottle it.

SUMMER PUNCH

INGREDIENTS.—3 oz. of castor sugar, 2 or 3 tablespoonfuls of water, ½ pint of mint leaves, 1½ lemons, 1 pint of ginger ale, ice.

METHOD.—Put the castor sugar and water into a saucepan and heat them sufficiently to dissolve the sugar. Leave them to cool.

Pick over the mint leaves, wash them thoroughly and drain them. Put the mint into a jug with the juice of the lemons. Add the dissolved sugar and water, mix them together and leave the liquid to stand in a cool place for about forty - five minutes, giving it an occasional stir.

Strain it into a bowl and add a pint bottle of ginger ale and about one pint of chipped ice.

Serve Summer Punch garnished with slices of lemon, and some small sprigs of mint.

SLOE GIN

INGREDIENTS.—3 lb. of sloes, $\frac{1}{2}$ gallon of gin (unsweetened), $1\frac{1}{2}$ lb. of Demerara sugar, $\frac{1}{2}$ oz. of bitter almonds.

METHOD.—Wipe the sloes and pick off the stalks, then prick them well with a needle in several places.

Put them into a large jar, a stone gallon jar is the best to use.

Add the gin and sugar.

Blanch and skin the almonds, and add.

Remember to buy bitter, not sweet, almonds.

Cork the jar very tightly and shake well.

Continue to shake it well once every day for about fourteen weeks, when it will be ready for use.

It can then be strained and bottled. Remember to cork it securely.

TO MAKE TEA

HEAT the teapot, put in the tea (allowing one teaspoonful for each person and one for the pot), pour in freshly boiling water, put the lid on the teapot and leave to stand for about three minutes. Then serve with milk and sugar to taste.

HOME-MADE WINES

THE cask should be full when the wine is put to ferment, unless very strong wine is required, and there should be sufficient liquid to fill up the cask as the wine ferments.

Always leave the cask open at the bunghole until the fermentation has finished, then close it and make a hole for the vent-peg; this should be loosened occasionally for about a week, so that there is no danger of the cask bursting. It can then be left tightened.

Keep a vessel under the cask to take the scum as the wine ferments.

Stand the cask in a warm place during the fermentation.

If necessary, a little cream of tartar can be added to help the fermentation. This should be added after the sugar has dissolved.

Use one ounce to four gallons of liquid.

CLOUDY WINE

WHEN bottling wines be very careful not to shake the cask ; if so, you will disturb any sediment there may be, and so make the wine cloudy.

Cloudy wine can be cleared by the addition of isinglass or whites and shells of eggs.

If isinglass is used, about a quarter of an ounce is required for ten gallons of wine.

If eggs are used, three whites and shells will be sufficient for ten gallons.

Whichever are used should be added to the cask and left for about eight or twelve days, then the wine should be strained.

Isinglass must first be dissolved in a small quantity of the wine or water, then added to the cask and mixed with the whole amount.

If whites and shells are added, the whites must be beaten slightly, the shells washed and the inner skins removed, and then the shells broken.

BLACK CURRANT WINE

INGREDIENTS.—Black c u r r a n t s. Allow $1\frac{1}{4}$ gallons of water to 1 gallon of fruit-juice. Allow $3\frac{1}{2}$ to 4 lb. of white sugar (according to taste) to each gallon of fruit-juice and water mixed.

METHOD.—Choose ripe fruit, not over-ripe, and be sure it is quite fresh.

Pick over the fruit thoroughly and remove the stalks.

Squeeze out all the juice from the fruit—to do this it can be put into a piece of muslin and pressed well to extract the juice.

Or, if preferred, it can be put into a saucepan with just a little water in the bottom to prevent it from sticking.

Bring it slowly to the boil, then strain the fruit through a fine hair sieve or strainer, or through a piece of fine muslin, and press all the juice out of it.

Measure the juice and put it into a large vessel with the water in proportion.

Add the sugar and stir it at intervals until dissolved.

Let it stand for one or two days; during this time throw a cover over the vessel.

Now pour it into a cask and leave it in a warm place to ferment.

It will take about two weeks.

When the fermentation has quite finished, close the cask and leave it in a cool place.

It can be bottled after about six or eight months.

NOTE.—Brandy may be added if liked. For this, see Note in Orange Wine recipe.

GOOSEBERRY WINE

INGREDIENTS.—6 lb. of gooseberries, 1 gallon of water, 3¼ lb. of sugar to 1 gallon of fruit-juice and water.

METHOD.—Wipe the gooseberries, pick them over carefully and top and tail them. Put into a large vessel and bruise them well. They must be well pressed in order to get the juice and pulp out of them, but do not crush the seeds.

Add the cold water. Mix the mashed fruit well with it and squeeze the fruit. Leave it to stand for about one day with a cloth thrown over.

Then strain it and measure the liquid. Put it into another large vessel, add the sugar in proportion, and stir occasionally until dissolved.

Leave for two days, then pour into a cask, and leave in a warm place until the fermentation has finished. It will take about two or three weeks. The bunghole can now be corked and the vent-peg slightly loosened for a few days, then tightened, as explained before. Store the cask in a cool place for about eight months.

It can then be bottled.

MIXED FRUIT WINE

INGREDIENTS.—1 lb. of raspberries, 1 lb. of strawberries, 1 lb. of black heart cherries, 1 lb. of gooseberries, 2 lb. of black currants, 1½ lb. of red currants, 1½ lb. of white currants,

1½ gallons of water. Allow to each gallon of fruit-juice and water 3½ lb. of white sugar.

METHOD.—Pick over all the different fruits and stalk them.

Bruise the gooseberries as explained in the Gooseberry Wine recipe, add about one quart of the water to them, and squeeze them well in the water. Leave to stand for two days.

Squeeze all the juice from the currants, as explained in the Black Currant Wine recipe.

Mash the strawberries and raspberries to extract the juice. Stone the cherries and press out the juice. Put these mashed fruits and juices together, and add the remainder of the water to them, and leave in soak for two days.

Then strain them through a fine hair sieve or strainer or muslin.

Strain also the water and juice from the gooseberries and press them well to extract all moisture. Put all this liquor together and measure it.

Add the sugar in proportion, stir it occasionally until dissolved.

Leave for about twenty-four hours, then pour into a cask and put into a warm place to ferment. It will take about fifteen days.

If desired, brandy may be added (see Note in Orange Wine).

When the fermentation has finished, close the cask as before explained.

Store in a cool place for about eight months, then bottle it.

ORANGE WINE

INGREDIENTS.—50 Seville oranges, 4 gallons of water, 16 lb. of white sugar.

METHOD.—Wipe six of the oranges and peel them thinly. Put the peel into a pan and add a quart of boiling water to it.

Let it stand for one day, then strain off the water, and put it into a large vessel with the remainder of the water (cold) to make up the four gallons.

Squeeze the juice from all the oranges, strain it and add it to the water.

Add the sugar and stir it occasionally until dissolved.

Pour into a cask and leave in a warm place to ferment. When fermentation has finished, close up the cask and leave it in a cool place. It can be bottled after about ten months.

NOTE.—If liked, brandy may be added in the proportion of three-quarters of a gill to one gallon of wine. This should be put into the cask just before the wine has finished fermenting. If a sweeter wine is preferred, do not use any of the orange rinds.

PARSNIP WINE

INGREDIENTS.—3½ lb. of parsnips (after they are peeled), 1 gallon of water, 3 lb. of white sugar to 1 gallon of liquor.

METHOD.—Wash the parsnips and peel them thinly. Cut them into thick slices, then weigh them, and put into a pan with the water in proportion.

Boil them until they are quite soft, then strain the liquor through a sieve, measure it, and allow the sugar in proportion.

Boil these together for forty-five minutes.

Pour into a large vessel and leave until lukewarm, then add a little yeast spread on a slice of toast.

Leave this liquor to stand for ten days, and during this time it must be well stirred each day. Then pour it into a cask.

The wine will be ready to bottle in about eight or nine months.

NOTE.—When straining the parsnips, squeeze out as much liquor as possible from them, but do not press them through a sieve.

The yeast is added to help the fermentation and need only be left in a day or two.

RHUBARB WINE

INGREDIENTS.—5½ lb. of rhubarb (after it is cut up), 1 gallon of water, 3½ lb. of white sugar to 1 gallon of fruit-juice and water, 2 lemons to 1½ gallons of fruit-juice and water.

METHOD.—June is the best month for making this wine. Wipe the sticks, cut off the green, but do not skin the rhubarb.

Cut it into small pieces, put it into a large vessel and mash the fruit to extract the juice.

Pour the cold water over it, and leave for about eight days, keeping it stirred occasionally.

Then strain and measure it.

Add the sugar in proportion, also the strained juice of the lemons.

Stir at intervals until the sugar has dissolved, then pour into a cask and leave in a warm place to ferment.

When the fermentation has finished, cork up the bunghole and leave the wine for about five months in a cool place, then bottle it.

MILK DISHES

ARROWROOT WHIP

INGREDIENTS.—¾ pint of milk, 3 eggs, 1½ dessertspoonfuls of arrowroot, 3 tablespoonfuls of castor sugar, 1 oz. of pignolia nuts (these are quite inexpensive and can be obtained from any nut shop), 2 tablespoonfuls of cream, if liked, ¾ oz. of leaf gelatine, ¾ gill of water, vanilla flavouring, angelica.

METHOD.—Mix the arrowroot to a smooth paste with a little of the milk. Heat the remainder and stir on to it, then return to the pan and bring to the boil, keeping it well stirred.

Cook gently for a few minutes. Then draw aside and cool slightly.

Separate the eggs. Beat up the yolks and add. Stir over a low burner to cook the eggs, but do not let it boil. When ready remove from the fire, add the sugar and leave until cold.

Whisk the cream until it thickens. Stir in the arrowroot and add the pignolias.

Dissolve the gelatine in a saucepan with the water and strain in.

Leave until the mixture begins to thicken. Fold in the egg-whites, whisked to a very stiff froth.

Mix together lightly and flavour with vanilla. Heap in individual glasses and, when set, decorate with angelica.

This quantity will fill five or six glasses.

ARTICHOKE PUREE

INGREDIENTS.—1 lb. of artichokes, ½ pint of milk, 1¼ pints of white stock, few celery seeds, pepper and salt, lemon-juice.

METHOD.—Scrub and peel the artichokes. When peeling dip them frequently into a basin of cold water to which a little lemon-juice has been added. Put the stock into a saucepan and bring to the boil. Cut the artichokes into halves or thick slices and add. A few celery seeds tied in a piece of muslin should also be added. Boil gently until the artichokes are tender, then remove the celery seeds and rub the soup through a sieve.

Return it to the pan, add the milk, season well, and make hot.

Serve with dice of fried bread.

BATTER CAKES

INGREDIENTS.—½ lb. of flour, pinch of salt, 1 teaspoonful of cream of tartar, ¼ level dessertspoonful of carbonate of soda, 2 dessertspoonfuls of castor sugar, 1¾ gills of milk, lard, jam, 2 eggs.

METHOD.—Sieve together the flour, salt, soda, and cream of tartar and add the sugar. Whisk up the eggs, pour into the centre, and mix to a smooth thick batter, adding the milk gradually. Beat well for a few minutes, then leave it to stand for about an hour or so.

Melt some lard in a frying-pan and, when hot, put the batter into it, allowing a small tablespoonful for each cake; about four of these can be fried at a time. Fry until golden-brown, keeping them well basted with fat, and then turn over.

When both sides are brown lift out and drain on paper.

Spread with hot jam, sandwich two together, and dredge with castor sugar. This quantity will make about fourteen pairs.

BROWNIE PUDDING

INGREDIENTS.—¾ pint of milk, ¼ lb. of brown bread, about 3 dessertspoonfuls of sugar, 2 eggs, ¼ lb. of preserved ginger, 1 dessertspoonful of ginger syrup (if liked, glacé or crystallised ginger from a confectioner's can be used, in which case, of course, there will be no syrup).

METHOD.—Beat up the eggs and mix with the milk. Cut the ginger into small pieces. Cut the bread into slices as for toast, then into small square pieces, and add to the egg and milk with the ginger, sugar, and ginger syrup.

Mix all together and leave soaking for about half an hour. Turn into a buttered basin, cover securely with a buttered paper and steam for about one hour and a half.

When cooked, remove from the hot water and leave the pudding for a few seconds so that it may shrink from the sides of the basin, then turn it out carefully. If preferred, this pudding may be served cold, in which case decorate the top with a stiffly beaten egg-white mixed with a little castor sugar.

CAFE ROYAL

INGREDIENTS.—½ pint of milk, coffee essence, ½ teacup of chopped walnuts, ¾ gill of cream, 1 egg and 1 extra yolk, ½ oz. of leaf gelatine, ½ gill of water, 2½ dessertspoonfuls of castor sugar.

METHOD.—Make a nice thick custard with the eggs and milk and let it get cold. Whisk the cream until it stiffens, then stir in the custard, walnuts, and sugar, and add sufficient coffee essence to flavour. Dissolve the gelatine in a saucepan with the water and strain in.

Mix all together and, when it begins to thicken, turn into a mould and leave to set.

Turn out and decorate with whipped cream—forced through an icing bag—and walnuts, extra to those given in the recipe.

CARAMEL CREAM

INGREDIENTS.—18 lumps of sugar, 2 gills of milk, about 1 dessertspoonful of sugar, 4 tablespoonfuls of cold water, ¾ to 1 gill of cream, ½ oz. of leaf gelatine, 1 egg.

METHOD.—Put the lump sugar and one tablespoonful of the water into a small, strong saucepan and dissolve slowly. Boil until it becomes brown. Draw aside and leave to cool slightly, then add the milk, and stand it over a low burner until the caramel is dissolved.

Beat up the egg and add the hot caramel milk. Strain into a jug and cook the custard (in a saucepan of hot water) until it thickens.

Whisk the cream until it stiffens and, when the custard is cold, stir it into it. Add also the sugar.

Dissolve the gelatine in the remainder of the water. Strain in and mix all together lightly.

Pour into a wet mould to set, then turn on to a dish.

CHEESE CUSTARD

INGREDIENTS.—3 oz. of cheese, ¾ pint of milk, 2 eggs, salt and cayenne, 1 fairly thin slice of bread-and-butter, sippets of toast.

METHOD.—Grate the cheese finely—odd pieces of hard cheese can be utilised for this, and are more easily grated than new cheese.

Beat up the eggs, mix with two-thirds of the cheese, and season with salt and cayenne. Heat the milk and stir on to it. Place the bread-and-butter on the top. Put into the oven and bake gently until set.

Let it cool slightly, then sprinkle the top with the remainder of the cheese and brown under the grill.

Garnish the dish with sippets of toast and serve. To prepare the sippets, cut a slice of bread (not too thickly) and toast it. Cut it into squares, and then across into three-cornered shapes.

CHEESE PASTRIES

INGREDIENTS.—1½ gills of milk, 2 eggs, salt and pepper, 3 oz. of margarine or butter, 3¼ oz. of flour.

FOR THE FILLING.—2 gills of milk, 2 small teaspoonfuls of cornflour, 5 oz. of cheese, salt and cayenne, 1 oz. of margarine or butter.

METHOD.—Melt the margarine or butter and boil the milk in a saucepan. Sieve the flour and add to the boiling milk, etc., keeping it well stirred.

Continue to stir over a low burner for a few minutes until the mixture leaves the sides of the pan. Then draw aside and cool slightly.

Add each egg separately, and beat vigorously for a minute or two before adding the next. When both are added, season with salt and pepper and force the mixture through an icing bag on to a buttered baking-sheet in little sausage shapes. For this you will require just a round screw tied in the end of the icing bag, such as is used for screwing on to the icing tubes.

Put into a moderate oven and bake for about twenty minutes until golden-brown When cold, split the pastries open down one side and fill with the prepared filling. Serve with finely grated cheese sprinkled over.

To Make the Filling

Grate the cheese finely. Mix the cornflour to a smooth paste with some of the milk. Heat the remainder with the butter and add to it. Return to the pan and bring to the boil, keeping it well stirred.

Add the grated cheese, leaving out just a little for the top, stir for a few minutes over a low burner to cook the sauce. Then season well.

Leave to cool, then put into the pastry-cases.

This quantity will make about eighteen or twenty pastries.

COCONUT CUSTARD PIE

INGREDIENTS.—About 10 oz. of short pastry (see p. 252), 3 eggs, 2½ gills of milk, 3½ tablespoonfuls of castor sugar, vanilla or ratafia flavouring, 1 table-spoonful of desiccated coconut.

METHOD.—Roll out the pastry, cut out a round, and line a deep sandwich-tin (slightly greased), pressing the pastry a little thinner at the bottom than at the sides.

Trim and decorate the edges, being careful not to stretch the pastry.

Line it with a round of buttered paper and put some raw rice in the bottom. Put into the oven and bake very lightly, then remove the paper and rice and any soft underneath pastry there may be.

Pour in the hot custard. Return to a cooler oven and bake slowly until set.

Remove carefully from the tin and leave until cold.

Whisk the egg-whites to a very stiff froth and fold in three tablespoonfuls of castor sugar.

Heap this on top of the custard, sprinkle with coconut (extra to that given in the recipe), put into a cool oven to set, and lightly brown the meringue. Serve cold.

To Make the Custard

Separate the eggs. Beat up the yolks and mix with the coconut and sugar (½ tablespoonful). Heat the milk and add. Mix together and add a few drops of flavouring.

COCONUT TRIFLE

INGREDIENTS.—5 gills of milk, 8 sponge cakes, apricot jam, vanilla flavouring, angelica, 2 eggs, 2 or 3 tablespoonfuls of sherry or rum, if liked, 3 tablespoonfuls of desiccated coconut, 1½ tablespoonfuls of castor sugar, ½ gill of cream, 1 oz. of almonds.

METHOD.—Split the sponge cakes into halves and spread with jam, then arrange in a dish and soak with hot milk and either a little sherry or rum, if liked. For this about a gill of milk will be required, but more may be used if necessary.

Beat up the eggs. Heat four gills of milk and add to them, then pour into a jug and stand in a saucepan of hot water, and cook until the custard thickens.

Stir it occasionally and, when ready, remove from the hot water and add the sugar, coconut, and a few drops of vanilla.

Blanch and split the almonds and stick into the sponge cakes. When the custard is cool, pour it over.

Before serving, sprinkle with coconut, and decorate with angelica and whipped cream, the latter sweetened and flavoured with vanilla.

CUSTARD SOUFFLE

INGREDIENTS.—½ pint of milk, 2 eggs and 1 extra white, ¾ teacup of sponge cake crumbs, 1 lemon (rind only), 2 tablespoonfuls of castor sugar ½ oz. of leaf gelatine, ½ gill of water.

FOR THE DECORATION.—½ gill of cream, few glacé cherries, angelica.

METHOD.—Separate the eggs. Beat up the yolks. Heat the milk and add to them and cook in a double sauce-pan, or in a jug in a saucepan of water until the custard thickens. Keep it stirred occasionally. When ready, turn into a basin and leave to cool. Grate the lemon-rind finely and add with the sponge crumbs and sugar. Put the gelatine into a saucepan with the water and dissolve slowly, then strain it in and mix together lightly.

When it begins to set, fold in the stiffly whisked egg-whites.

Turn into a large soufflé case with a band of foolscap paper tied round it so that it stands above the top.

When set, remove the paper and decorate the soufflé with glacé cherries, angelica, and whipped cream —the latter sweetened and flavoured to taste.

If the custard is cooked in a double saucepan it will cook more quickly than if cooked in a jug in a saucepan of water, and so will require frequent stirring.

If a soufflé case is not available, a glass tongue jar makes a very good substitute.

When the soufflé is set and the foolscap paper removed, the jar can be hidden by tying a piece of ribbon round or a fold of fancy paper.

CUTLETS WITH CHAUD-FROID SAUCE

INGREDIENTS.—Best end of neck of mutton (about 5 cutlets), lettuce, tomato, few potherbs, stock, pepper and salt, sprig of parsley and marjoram or thyme, $\frac{1}{4}$ oz. leaf gelatine, $\frac{1}{2}$ pint of thick savoury white sauce, $\frac{1}{4}$ pint of savoury calf's-foot jelly.

METHOD.—When buying the mutton have the chine-bone removed. Prepare the potherbs and cut into quarters or thick, chunky pieces. Place them in a casserole and put the meat on top of them. Pour in sufficient stock to cover the vegetables. Add the herbs and seasoning and cover the meat with a greased paper.

Put the lid on the casserole and cook gently for about one hour and a half, keeping it basted occasionally.

When cooked, cut carefully into cutlets and press between dishes with weights on top.

When thoroughly cold, trim the cutlets and scrape off the meat round the ends of the bone.

Place them on a rack over a dish. (The rack of the grill tin will do.)

They are now ready for coating.

Make the savoury white sauce, let it cool slightly, keeping it well stirred.

Dissolve the gelatine in the jelly and add gradually to the sauce.

Strain, then leave until it begins to thicken, stirring it occasionally.

Coat each cutlet with some of the prepared sauce. These can be decorated with small pieces of truffle or tomato.

When the sauce is quite set, put a cutlet frill on each and serve on a bed of lettuce. Add also a few pieces of tomato.

NOTE.—The method of making a savoury white sauce is explained on p. 693.

EMPRESS PUDDING

INGREDIENTS.—2 gills of milk, 5 dessertspoonfuls of castor sugar, 3 eggs, 4 oz. of margarine, 4 oz. of flour, 1 orange, marmalade.

METHOD.—Beat the sugar and fat to a cream. Separate the eggs. Add the yolks to the creamed fat and sugar, stir them in quickly, and beat well for a few minutes. Grate the orange-rind finely and add.

Stir in the flour, then gradually add the milk.

Lastly, fold in the egg-whites whisked to a very stiff froth.

Turn into a greased dish and bake in a moderately hot oven for about an hour.

If liked, some hot marmalade can be served with it.

NOTE.—When adding yolk of egg to creamed butter and sugar, if it curdles add one dessertspoonful of flour.

FISH AU GRATIN

INGREDIENTS.—1 lemon sole or plaice (about $\frac{3}{4}$ lb.), 4 oz. of cheese, $\frac{1}{2}$ pint of milk, 1 oz. of margarine, salt and pepper.

METHOD.—Clean and skin the sole and put into a fireproof dish. Season it with salt and pepper.

Grate the cheese finely.

Melt the fat in a saucepan, add the flour, and mix together.

Stir in the milk and bring to the boil, keeping it well stirred.

Season to taste and add three parts of the cheese. When the latter is melted pour the sauce over the fish and put into a moderately hot oven to cook—it will require about twenty minutes.

Sprinkle the remainder of the cheese on the top and brown under the grill.

FLAKED RICE BLANCMANGE

INGREDIENTS.—$1\frac{1}{2}$ pints of milk, $3\frac{1}{2}$ teacupfuls of flaked rice, 2 good tablespoonfuls of sugar, 1 oz. of butter or margarine, vanilla flavouring.

METHOD.—Put the flaked rice and milk into a saucepan and bring to the boil, keeping it well stirred. Let it cook gently until the mixture is quite stiff and the rice cooked.

Add the butter and sugar and stir until dissolved, then flavour with vanilla. Turn into a wet mould and leave to set. Turn out when ready and serve with fruit or jam.

FRUIT IMPERIAL

INGREDIENTS.—1 large tin of fruit—pineapple or peaches, $1\frac{1}{4}$ oz. of leaf gelatine, $\frac{3}{4}$ pint of milk, 4 or 5 dessert-spoonfuls of castor sugar, a few pistachio nuts for decoration. A cherry could be used instead, if liked.

METHOD.—Strain the syrup from the fruit, and put the latter through the mincer. Put the minced fruit into a basin, and gradually stir in the milk.

Add also the sugar and fruit syrup, with the exception of about one gill of it. In this dissolve the gelatine and strain it into the other ingredients.

Mix all together, leave until it begins to thicken, then stir it up and mould.

When set, unmould and decorate with pistachio nuts.

NOTE.—Pistachio nuts are blanched in the same way as almonds.

GINGER JUNKET

INGREDIENTS.—1 pint of milk, 2 oz. of preserved ginger (sold in jars in syrup), 4 teaspoonfuls of ginger syrup, (if preferred, glacé or crystallised ginger, bought from a confectioner's, can be used, in which case, of course, there is no syrup), 3 teaspoonfuls of castor sugar, essence of rennet, vanilla.

FOR THE DECORATION.—$\frac{1}{2}$ gill of cream, ginger.

METHOD.—Cut the ginger into small pieces and put into individual glasses. Add also one teaspoonful of ginger syrup to each glass. Put the milk into a saucepan, add the sugar, and make just lukewarm.

Draw aside. Stir in a few drops of vanilla and from one to two teaspoon-fuls of essence of rennet, according to the direction given on the bottle. Pour at once into the glasses and leave undisturbed until set.

Whisk the cream until it stiffens, sweeten and flavour to taste.

Decorate each glass with ginger and the prepared cream.

This quantity will fill four glasses.

If the ginger which has no syrup is used, flavour the milk with a few drops of vanilla.

HADDOCK MAITRE D'HOTEL

INGREDIENTS.—1 dried haddock (about 1 lb.), $1\frac{1}{2}$ gills of milk, 1 oz. of butter, seasoning, a squeeze of lemon-juice, 1 level teaspoonful of chopped parsley.

METHOD.—Trim and wash the haddock and put into a pie-dish or fireproof dish with the milk.

Season with pepper and cover with a plate, then cook in a moderate oven until the flesh moves easily from the bone ; it will be cooked almost as soon as the milk boils.

When ready, garnish the centre of the haddock with cubes of maître d'hôtel butter.

If cooked in a fireproof dish, serve it in the same dish.

TO PREPARE THE BUTTER.—Beat it until pliable, then work in the chopped parsley, and add seasoning and lemon-juice.

Mix all well together, make into a block, and leave to harden. Then cut into cubes.

HOLLANDAISE SOUP

INGREDIENTS.—$\frac{1}{2}$ pint of milk, 2 pints of white stock, 2 oz. of margarine, 2 egg-yolks, 2 oz. of flour, $\frac{1}{2}$ gill of cream or milk.

FOR THE SEASONING.—2 or 3 table-spoonfuls of dice of carrot, 2 or 3 tablespoonfuls of green peas, 2 or 3 tablespoonfuls of dice of cucumber.

METHOD.—Scrape and wash the carrot and cut into small dice. Peel and cut up a small piece of cucumber. Boil these two vegetables, and also the peas, each in separate pans until tender. Then strain. Melt the fat in a saucepan, add the flour and mix together. Stir in the stock (strained) and the milk, and continue to stir until it boils. Boil gently for a few minutes, then cool slightly.

Beat up the egg-yolks, and mix with the cream. Strain the soup, then return it to the pan and stir in the prepared vegetables, the eggs, and the cream.

Season to taste and stir over a low burner to cook the eggs, but do not let it boil. When ready the soup should thinly coat the spoon.

ITALIAN EGGS

INGREDIENTS.—1¼ pints of milk, 3 oz. of macaroni, pepper and salt, ¼ pint of good white stock, ¼ lb. of ham, parsley, 4 eggs.

METHOD.—Break up the macaroni and wash it. Put it into a saucepan with the milk and stock, add a little salt, and cook gently until the macaroni is tender and the mixture thick and creamy, keeping it stirred occasionally.

Cut the ham into strips and add.

Season with pepper and, when the ham is heated sufficiently, turn it all into a dish.

Poach the eggs and serve on it, and garnish with chopped parsley.

LENTIL MILK SOUP

INGREDIENTS.—1 lb. of lentils, 6½ pints of stock (white), 2d. of potherbs, a piece of celery, 1½ oz. of margarine, a few mixed herbs, salt and pepper, 1½ pints of milk.

METHOD.—Wash the lentils, prepare the potherbs and cut into slices.

Melt the fat, add the prepared vegetables, and stir over a low burner for a few minutes until the fat is absorbed, then draw aside. Wash the celery and add with the stock and herbs the latter tied in muslin.

Bring the soup to the boil and let it cook gently until all the vegetables are tender.

Rub it through a sieve, return to the pan, add the milk and seasoning, then re-heat and it is ready.

LIVER CUTLETS

INGREDIENTS.—6 oz. of liver, about ½ to ¾ gill of thick savoury white sauce, pepper, salt, and mixed mustard, 1½ oz. of vermicelli, breadcrumbs, 4 oz. of ham, 1 onion, ½ pint of milk, 1 egg, deep fat for frying.

METHOD.—Peel and slice the onion. Cut the liver into slices and fry until lightly cooked, frying the onion at the same time. Drain and put through the mincer with the ham. Break the vermicelli into small pieces and cook in the milk until the mixture is quite stiff. Keep it stirred occasionally. Stir the white sauce into the prepared liver and ham, etc., then add the vermicelli. Season with pepper, salt, and mixed mustard. Mix all together and spread on a plate.

Leave until cold and firm, then divide into about ten or twelve portions.

Make into cutlet shapes and place some of them in a frying-basket.

Put into a deep pan about half full of hot fat and fry until golden-brown, then drain. Fry the others in the same way. Stick a small piece of spaghetti in the end of each cutlet. Serve on a paper and garnish with parsley.

NOTE.—The making of savoury white sauce is explained on p. 693.

MACARONI PUDDING

(SPAGHETTI OR VERMICELLI CAN BE USED IN THE SAME WAY)

INGREDIENTS.—1½ oz. of macaroni, 1 pint of milk, 1 oz. of sugar, 1 egg, flavouring—as desired.

METHOD.—Break the macaroni into convenient-sized pieces and wash it. Put the milk into a saucepan and bring to the boil. Add the macaroni and cook gently until tender. It will take about half an hour.

Stir in the sugar, then draw aside and cool slightly.

Beat up the egg and add.

Turn into a pie-dish and bake gently for about half an hour, or until set, being careful not to let it boil.

NOTE.—Spaghetti and vermicelli take less time to cook than macaroni.

Another method is to cook the macaroni partly in boiling water, then to finish cooking it in milk, in which case use two ounces to a pint.

MILK FRUIT JELLIES

INGREDIENTS.—¾ pint of milk, 1 pint packet of apricot jelly, ¼ pint of hot water, vanilla, sugar, a few chipped nuts for decoration, 1 small tin of

apricots, cream (if liked). If this is
not used turn the apricots the other
way up for decoration.

METHOD.—Cut the jelly into small
pieces and dissolve in the hot water,
then leave until cold. Cut up some of
the apricots, and put into individual
glasses. Stir the milk into the cold
jelly, mix together, and pour some into
each glass. Leave until set, then
place an apricot, cup side upwards,
in the centre. Whisk up a little cream,
sweeten and flavour it to taste, and
put a dab in each apricot cup. Blanch
and finely chop a few nuts and sprinkle
round the edge. A little grated
nutmeg can take the place of the nuts
if preferred. This quantity will fill
five glasses.

PLAIN MILK JELLY

INGREDIENTS.—1 pint packet of
jelly, ½ pint of hot water, ½ pint of
milk.

METHOD.—Dissolve the jelly in
the hot water and, when cold, stir in
the milk. Turn into a wet mould
and leave until set, then turn out
carefully. If liked, it can be decorated
with small pieces of crystallised roses
or violets.

MILK JELLY GATEAU

INGREDIENTS.—1 pint of milk, 1
sponge cake ring, 2 oz. of almonds,
1 pint packet of pineapple jelly, 1 gill
of hot water, 2 oz. of glacé pineapple,
2 or 3 tablespoonfuls of rum or sherry
(if liked), cream, sugar, vanilla,
cochineal.

METHOD.—Cut up the jelly and
dissolve in the hot water. Put the
sponge ring into a dish and partially
soak with a little rum, sherry, or a little
milk. Cut up the glacé pineapple
and put round the base of it.

When the jelly is cold stir in the
milk, add a few drops of cochineal,
and colour to a pale pink shade.
Pour over the sponge, but do not
quite cover the top of it.

Blanch and split the almonds and
stick some round the top of the sponge.

Sprinkle the remainder on the milk
jelly when the latter is set.

Before serving decorate the centre
with whipped cream sweetened and
flavoured with vanilla.

MILK LOAVES

INGREDIENTS.—1½ lb. of flour, 1
teaspoonful of salt, ½ oz. of yeast,
1 small teaspoonful of castor sugar,
2 oz. of margarine, about 3 gills of
milk.

METHOD.—Sieve the flour and salt.
Put the yeast into a small warmed
basin, add the sugar, and mix together
until they liquefy. Melt the margarine, warm the milk in a saucepan,
and add to the yeast.

Strain this all into the centre of the
flour and mix to a soft dough. Beat
well for a few minutes, then cover the
basin lightly and stand it in a warm
place for about one hour and three-
quarters. When risen, turn on to a
floured board and knead for a few
minutes. Then divide into about
twelve or fourteen portions, and make
into cottage loaves.

To do this, divide each portion into
two, about one-third in one piece and
two-thirds in the other. Work each
piece until smooth, then place the
small one on top of the larger and put
your little finger partly through the
centre.

Put the loaves on a slightly greased
and floured baking-sheet and stand in
a warm place for twenty to thirty
minutes.

Brush over with egg to glaze them
and bake for almost twenty-five to
thirty minutes. The oven must be
very hot at first, but the heat should
be lessened afterwards.

MILK MOULD

INGREDIENTS.—1¼ pints of milk,
¾ gill of water, 1 oz. of leaf gelatine,
2 tablespoonfuls of rum, if liked (if it is
not used, flavour with lemon or vanilla),
2 tablespoonfuls of desiccated coconut,
2 good tablespoonfuls of castor sugar,
½ pint packet of lemon jelly, ½ pint
of hot water, few glacé cherries.

METHOD—Dissolve the jelly in the
hot water and, when cold, set a thin
layer in the bottom of a mould—the
latter previously rinsed with cold
water. Decorate it with a few glacé
cherries halved and dipped in jelly.
When these are set, cover with some
more jelly and set again.

Put the gelatine into a saucepan with
the water, and dissolve slowly.

Warm the milk, then strain in the gelatine, stirring well all the time. Turn into a basin, add the sugar and rum, and, when the mixture begins to set, add the coconut. Mix all together, turn into the prepared mould and, when set, dip into warm water and unmould carefully.

Decorate the dish with the remainder of the jelly chopped up roughly.

MILK MERINGUE JELLY

INGREDIENTS.—½ pint of milk, 2 egg-whites, 2 tablespoonfuls of sherry (if liked), ½ pint of hot water, 1 pint packet of cherry jelly, angelica, and a few glacé cherries.

METHOD.—Dissolve the jelly in the hot water and, when cold, stir in the milk and sherry. Leave until beginning to set, then whisk the egg-whites to a very stiff froth and fold in lightly.

Turn into a dish and, when quite set, decorate with glacé cherries and leaves of angelica.

MILK SOLID

INGREDIENTS.—1½ pints of milk, ½ lb. of granulated sugar, 2 lemons, 1 gill of water, 1¼ oz. of gelatine.

METHOD.—Put the milk and sugar into a saucepan. Add the finely grated rind of the lemons, and when the sugar is dissolved draw aside.

Dissolve the gelatine in the water and strain in, stirring all the time.

Squeeze the lemons and strain the juice, and add.

Mix all together, and turn into a wet mould and leave to set. Then turn out carefully or, if liked, put into a basin and when set, break into rough pieces and serve.

MEAT BATTER

INGREDIENTS.—6 oz. of flour, 1 teaspoonful of baking-powder, 1 small onion, 2 eggs, pinch of salt, ¼ lb. of cooked meat, pepper and salt, 2½ gills of milk, dripping.

METHOD.—Sieve the flour and salt. Separate the eggs and turn the yolks into the centre of the flour. Add half a pint of the milk gradually and mix it to a smooth batter. Beat well for a few minutes, then stir in the remainder of the milk, and leave the batter to stand for about an hour or so.

Peel and finely mince the onion and fry in a little dripping until tender, then drain off the fat.

Put the meat through the mincer, season it well, and mix with the prepared onion.

When ready to cook the batter, add the meat and baking-powder and lightly fold in the stiffly whisked egg-whites.

Have ready a baking-tin with a little melted dripping in it, pour in the prepared batter and bake for about three-quarters of an hour.

When cooked, cut into slices and serve with thick gravy.

MOCK CREAM

INGREDIENTS.—2½ gills of milk, 4 oz. of butter or margarine, 2 oz. of cornflour, 3 dessertspoonfuls of castor sugar, vanilla flavouring.

METHOD.—Beat the sugar and fat to a cream. Mix the cornflour to a smooth paste with a little milk. Heat the remainder and stir on to it, then return to the pan and bring to the boil.

Cook gently for a few minutes, keeping it well stirred all the time.

Draw aside and continue to stir until slightly cool. Then gradually mix in the creamed fat and sugar.

Flavour with vanilla and beat all together until creamy.

Served with stewed fruit.

NEAPOLITAN SHAPE

INGREDIENTS.—1½ pints of milk, 1 oz. of almonds, 2 tablespoonfuls of sugar, 1 tablespoonful of custard-powder, 1 tablespoonful of cornflour, 1 oz. of butter or margarine, vanilla flavouring, cochineal, few silver balls.

METHOD.—Blanch the almonds and chop up roughly. Mix the cornflour and custard-powder together and mix to a smooth paste with a little milk. Put the remainder into a saucepan with the sugar and butter and, when hot, stir on to the custard-powder. Return to the saucepan and bring to the boil, keeping it well stirred all the time.

Cook gently for a few minutes, then add the almonds, flavour with vanilla and colour with a few drops of cochineal.

Turn into a wet mould and, when set, turn on to a dish and decorate with a few silver balls.

ONION SOUP

INGREDIENTS.—¾ lb. of onions, 1½ pints of milk, salt and pepper, 2 or 3 very thin slices of bread, 1½ pints of white stock, 1 oz. of margarine or butter, 2 oz. of cheese, cornflour.

METHOD.—Peel and finely mince the onions. Melt the fat and cook them in it for a few minutes without browning. Draw aside, add the stock, and cook gently until the onions are quite tender. Add the milk and slightly thicken the soup with cornflour previously mixed to a smooth paste with water.

Season to taste and boil for a few minutes.

Cut the thin slices of bread into small rounds and put into the oven until quite crisp and a very pale biscuit colour. They must be baked slowly.

Grate the cheese finely, sprinkle each round of toast with cheese, and brown under the grill. Then serve in the soup.

ORANGE CUSTARD

INGREDIENTS.—2 oranges, 1 egg, ½ pint of milk, 1 dessertspoonful of sugar, flavouring.

METHOD.—Peel the oranges and remove the white pith, then cut them into slices, cutting them across the sections. Remove the pips, arrange the slices in a dish and sprinkle with a few drops of lemon-juice and a little castor sugar.

Beat up the egg. Heat the milk and add to it with the sugar.

Strain into a jug and stand in a saucepan of hot water. Cook gently until it thickens, keeping it stirred occasionally.

When ready, add vanilla flavouring to taste, leave until cold, and pour over the oranges.

PEACH BASKETS

INGREDIENTS.—½ pint of milk, large tin of peaches, 1½ oz. of crushed tapioca, sugar, vanilla, small piece of apple and banana, one or two glacé cherries and almonds, angelica.

METHOD.—Strain the syrup from the peaches—there will be about half a pint—put it into a saucepan with the milk. Sprinkle in the tapioca and cook until tender and the mixture thick and creamy. Keep it stirred occasionally. When ready, draw aside and add sugar and vanilla to taste.

Turn into a dish and leave until cold. Then arrange some of the peaches—cup side uppermost—on the tapioca mixture.

Cut up half of one of the remaining peaches and mix with a few pieces of apple, banana, almonds, and glacé cherries. Fill the cups with this prepared fruit and fix a handle of angelica over each.

For the handles, cut the angelica into long strips and dip into warm water to make them more pliable.

PEAR CREAMS

INGREDIENTS.—½ pint of milk, 1 teaspoonful of cornflour, ½ gill of pear syrup, 1½ dessertspoonfuls of castor sugar, crystallised violets and cream (for decoration), small tin of pears, ½ gill of cream, ½ oz. of leaf gelatine.

METHOD.—Mix the cornflour to a smooth paste with a small quantity of the milk. Heat the remainder and stir on to it. Then return to the pan and bring to the boil, keeping it well stirred. Let it simmer gently for a few minutes. Then leave to cool.

Strain the syrup from the pears and rub them through a sieve.

Whisk the cream, stir in the prepared cornflour and pear pulp, and add the sugar to taste.

Dissolve the gelatine in some of the pear syrup and strain into the other ingredients.

Pour into small wet moulds and, when set, turn out and decorate the top of each with a dab of whipped cream and add a piece of crystallised violet.

This quantity will fill six small moulds.

FRICASSEE OF PLAICE

INGREDIENTS.—2 plaice (about 1½ lb. together), ½ pint of milk, 1 oz. of margarine, 1 oz. of flour, salt and pepper, sprig of parsley and marjoram or thyme, chopped parsley for decoration.

METHOD.—Put the milk into a saucepan, add also the parsley and marjoram or thyme. Bring almost to the boil, leave at the side of the fire until the milk is quite cool and well flavoured. Then strain.

Mix the flour to a smooth paste with a small quantity of the milk, put the remainder back into the pan with the margarine, and, when hot, stir on to the flour.

Return to the pan and bring to the boil, keeping it well stirred.

Have the fish ready prepared and add.

Simmer gently for about twelve minutes or until cooked.

Take out the fillets, untie the string, then place on a dish and coat with the sauce.

Garnish with the chopped parsley.

To prepare the fish have the plaice filleted and the fillets skinned on both sides. Wash them, roll up each one separately, and tie with string.

NOTE.—If preferred, one large plaice can be used.

PRIMROSE CREAM

INGREDIENTS.—1 pint of milk, 2 egg-yolks, ¾ oz. of leaf gelatine, vanilla flavouring, 1 dessertspoonful of custard-powder, ¾ gill of cream, ½ gill of water, about 3 dessertspoonfuls of sugar, crystallised flower—for decoration.

METHOD.—Put the custard-powder into a jug and mix to a smooth paste with a small quantity of the milk. Boil the remainder and stir on to it. Let it cool slightly, and add the egg-yolks (beaten). Stand it in a saucepan of hot water and cook until it thickens, keeping it stirred occasionally.

When ready, remove from the hot water and leave until cold. Whisk the cream until it stiffens, gradually stir in the custard, and add sugar and vanilla. Dissolve the gelatine in a saucepan with the water, strain it in, and mix together lightly. Turn into a wet mould, and when set, unmould carefully and serve.

Decorate the centre with a piece of crystallised lilac or violet.

FLAKED RICE PUDDING

INGREDIENTS.—1½ to 1¾ teacupfuls of flaked rice, 1 pint of milk, 1 tablespoonful of sugar, nutmeg.

METHOD.—Put the flaked rice into a pie-dish with the sugar. Stir in the milk and grate some nutmeg on the top. Put into the oven and bring slowly to the boil, then bake gently for about half an hour.

NOTE.—This is delicious served cold with jam or stewed fruit.

GROUND-RICE PUDDING

(ARROWROOT OR CORNFLOUR CAN BE USED IN THE SAME WAY)

INGREDIENTS.—1½ oz. of ground rice, 1 pint of milk, 1 oz. of sugar, lemon-rind or other flavouring.

METHOD.—Mix the ground rice to a smooth paste with a small quantity of the milk.

Peel some lemon-rind thinly and add to the remainder of the milk. Heat slowly, then strain it on to the rice, stirring well. Return to the pan and bring to the boil, keeping it stirred ; then let it boil gently for about eight or ten minutes.

Turn into a pie-dish and bake slowly for half an hour.

NOTE.—If liked, this pudding can be put under the hot grill for a few minutes and browned lightly on the top before it is served. If a richer pudding is desired, add an egg to the mixture just before turning it into the pie-dish.

A PLAIN RICE PUDDING

INGREDIENTS.—3 oz. of rice, 2 pints of milk, 2 oz. of sugar, nutmeg.

METHOD.—Wash the rice and put into a pie-dish. Add the sugar and mix together. Stir in the milk, then grate a little nutmeg on the top.

Put into a warm oven and bring slowly to the boil. Then let it simmer gently for about one and a half to two hours.

A rice pudding must be cooked slowly.—This is very important, otherwise the milk boils away before the rice grains have time to soften and absorb it.

RICE SALAD

INGREDIENTS.—1 pint of milk, salt and pepper, 1 small cucumber, 1 hard-boiled egg, lettuce, 3 oz. of rice, salad cream, 2 oz. of cheese, tomatoes, mustard and cress.

METHOD.—Wash the rice and put into a saucepan with the milk. Bring to the boil and cook gently until the rice is soft and the mixture quite stiff, keeping it stirred occasionally. Then leave until cold.

Peel the cucumber and cut into small squares. Grate the cheese finely.

Make some of the rice into tiny balls, and leave aside for garnishing.

Mix the remainder of it with some salad cream. Add the grated cheese, cucumber, chopped egg-white, and just a little chopped mustard and cress.

Season well with pepper and salt and serve on a bed of lettuce. Garnish with cucumber, quarters of tomato, rice balls, and powdered egg-yolk.

To powder the egg-yolk, rub it through a sieve or strainer.

SAGO FRUIT PUDDING

INGREDIENTS.—1½ pints of milk, ¼ lb. of suet, grated nutmeg, ¼ lb. of currants, 2 eggs and an extra yolk, ¼ lb. of sago, 4 dessertspoonfuls of sugar, 1 oz. of glacé cherries, 1 oz. of citron peel.

METHOD.—Put the milk into a saucepan to boil. Sprinkle in the sago, and cook until it is tender and the mixture quite stiff, keeping it stirred occasionally. When ready, turn it into a basin, add the sugar and some grated nutmeg, clean and pick over the currants, cut up the peel and cherries. Chop the suet finely.

Add all these prepared ingredients to the sago, and then whisk up the eggs and stir in. Mix all together, put into a well-greased basin, cover securely with a greased paper, and steam for about three hours.

SALAD DRESSING

INGREDIENTS.—1 pint of milk, ¼ pint of salad oil, ¼ lb. of flour, ¾ pint of white vinegar, ¼ lb. of margarine or butter, 2 teaspoonfuls of salt, 2 teaspoonfuls of castor sugar, 6 teaspoonfuls of mustard, ½ flat teaspoonful of pepper.

METHOD.—Mix the flour to a smooth paste with some of the milk. Put the remainder into a saucepan with the margarine, and when hot (but not boiling) stir it on to the flour. Return to the pan and bring to the boil,

keeping it well stirred all the time. Let it boil gently for a few minutes to cook the flour.

When ready, turn it into a large basin and cover the sauce with cold water. Leave until cold, then pour off the water. Whisk the sauce well, then gradually whisk in the oil and vinegar alternately.

Mix the mustard to a smooth paste with vinegar—extra to that given in the recipe—and add with the sugar, salt, and pepper.

When all the ingredients are well whisked and blended together, put into bottles and cork securely.

SEMOLINA PUDDING

(A SAGO OR CRUSHED TAPIOCA PUDDING CAN BE MADE IN THE SAME WAY.)

INGREDIENTS.—1½ oz. of semolina, 1 pint of milk, 1 egg, 1 oz. of sugar, grated nutmeg.

METHOD.—Put the milk into a saucepan and bring to the boil. Sprinkle in the semolina and cook gently until the mixture becomes thick and creamy, keeping it stirred. Add the sugar and cool slightly. Beat up the egg and add, then turn into a pie-dish.

Sprinkle a little grated nutmeg on the top and bake slowly for about half an hour, being careful not to let it boil.

NOTE.—If a cheaper pudding is required, the egg may be omitted.

SEMOLINA SUNFLOWERS

INGREDIENTS.—4 oz. of semolina, ½ oz. of butter, vanilla flavouring, 1½ pints of milk, about 2 good tablespoonfuls of sugar, some chocolate hundreds and thousands, tin of sliced peaches.

METHOD.—Bring the milk to the boil, sprinkle in the semolina and cook until it is tender and the mixture quite stiff, keeping it stirred frequently.

Draw aside, add the butter and sugar, and vanilla to taste, and stir until dissolved.

Turn into two small sandwich-tins—the latter rinsed with cold water—and leave until set. Then turn out and arrange sliced peaches on each, to resemble sunflowers.

Put some chopped-up peaches in

the centre and sprinkle it with chocolate hundreds and thousands.

Serve with some of the peach syrup and some cream if liked.

STEAMED SPAGHETTI PUDDING

INGREDIENTS.—1¼ pints of milk, 2 eggs, 1 small lemon (rind only), 2 oz. of sugar, 3 oz. of spaghetti, ½ oz. of butter or margarine, jam or stewed fruit.

METHOD.—Break the spaghetti into very small pieces and wash it. Put it into a saucepan with the milk and cook gently until soft and the mixture quite thick, keeping it stirred occasionally.

Draw aside, add the grated lemon-rind, butter, and sugar.

Separate one of the eggs. Beat the whole egg and yolk together and stir into the mixture when slightly cool.

Whisk the egg-white to a stiff froth and fold in lightly.

Turn into a greased basin, cover securely with a well-greased paper, and steam for one hour and a half.

Turn out and serve with jam or stewed fruit.

TAPIOCA AND COCONUT PUDDING

INGREDIENTS.—3 oz. of tapioca, 2 pints of milk, 3 oz. of sugar, 3 tablespoonfuls of desiccated coconut, vanilla flavouring, ½ pint of water (to soak tapioca).

METHOD.—Wash the tapioca, put into a pie-dish, well cover with the water, and leave to soak for a few hours or all night.

When soaked, pour off the water (if any left), add the sugar and coconut, also the milk and a few drops of flavouring, and mix all together.

Put into a moderately warm oven and bring slowly to the boil, then bake gently for about an hour.

Serve hot or cold.

NOTE.—If a plain tapioca pudding is required, omit the coconut.

TAPIOCA FLAN

INGREDIENTS.—FOR THE FILLING : 2½ gills of milk, 1 oz. of crushed tapioca, 1 tablespoonful of sugar, 2 oz. of figs, 1 oz. of candied lemon-peel, 1 egg-yolk, ½ oz. of margarine.

FOR THE PASTRY.—6 oz. of flour, 4 oz. of margarine, water, 1 flat teaspoonful of baking-powder.

FOR THE MERINGUE.—1 egg-white, 1 tablespoonful of castor sugar.

METHOD.—Wash the figs and soak for an hour or so. Put the milk into a saucepan and bring to the boil. Add the tapioca and cook until tender and the mixture thick and creamy, keeping it stirred occasionally.

Stalk and cut up the figs and the peel and cook in with the tapioca. When ready draw aside and cool slightly, add the margarine, sugar, and egg-yolk. Stir over a low burner for a few minutes to cook the egg, but do not boil. Then leave until cold.

Grease a flan-ring and stand on a greased baking-sheet.

Sieve the flour and baking-powder. Rub in the fat, then add just a little cold water and mix to a *stiff* paste.

Roll it out to nearly a quarter of an inch thick and cut to a round. Line the flan-ring with the pastry, pressing it thinner in the bottom.

Line the pastry with a round of buttered paper and put some uncooked rice in the bottom.

Trim the edge and bake for about twenty-five to thirty minutes.

When ready remove the paper and rice and lift up the flan-ring.

Leave the pastry to cool on a sieve, then fill with the prepared tapioca.

Whisk the egg-white to a very stiff froth and fold in the castor sugar.

Put this meringue into an icing bag with a rose or shell tube fixed in the end of it and decorate the flan in straight lines across both ways.

Bake in a very cool oven to set the meringue and serve cold.

TEA MADE WITH MILK

INGREDIENTS.—Allow 1 good teaspoonful of tea to ½ pint of milk.

METHOD 1.—Heat the teapot, bring the milk to the boil, put the tea in the teapot and pour in the boiling milk.

Leave for two or three minutes to draw before serving.

METHOD 2.—Tie the tea in a piece of muslin, allowing space for it to swell. Bring the milk just to the boil.

then add the tea and simmer for one minute.

Turn into a hot teapot and serve.

STEWED TRIPE

INGREDIENTS.—1½ lb. of tripe, 1 lb. of onions, milk, salt and pepper, arrowroot.

METHOD.—Cover the tripe with cold water, bring to the boil, then strain off the water. Cut the tripe into portions and put into a pan with the onions, the latter peeled and cut into small pieces. Add sufficient milk just to cover and a little salt. Bring to the boil and simmer gently for about two hours.

Remove the tripe and thicken the milk with arrowroot, etc., mixed to a smooth paste with cold milk. Boil for a few minutes, season to taste, then add the tripe and re-heat and serve.

UNIVERSITY PUDDING

INGREDIENTS.—¾ pint of milk, 10 oz. of flour, 6 oz. of suet, ½ small teaspoonful of carbonate of soda, 1 lemon (rind only), 4 oz. of sugar, 10 oz. of golden syrup.

METHOD.—Well grease a basin or mould and put the golden syrup in the bottom. Sieve the flour and soda. Chop the suet finely and add with the sugar and finely grated lemon-rind and mix all together. Add the milk gradually and mix to rather a wet consistency. Then beat well. Turn into the prepared basin.

Cover with a greased paper and floured pudding-cloth. Stand in a saucepan of boiling water and steam for about four hours. Turn out carefully. The golden syrup will form a sauce round the pudding.

VANILLA PYRAMID

INGREDIENTS.—2½ gills of milk, ¾ gill of cream, vanilla flavouring, ½ oz. of leaf gelatine, ½ gill of cold water, ¼ pint packet of vanilla jelly, 1 gill of hot water, about 2½ dessertspoonfuls of castor sugar.

METHOD.—Dissolve the jelly in the hot water and leave until cold. Then stir in the milk. Put the gelatine into a saucepan with the cold water and dissolve slowly. Strain into the jelly and milk.

Whisk the cream until it stiffens.

When the above mixture begins to thicken gradually stir it into the cream and add sugar and vanilla to taste.

Mix together lightly, put into a wet mould, and when set turn on to a dish.

CREAMED VEAL AND HAM

INGREDIENTS.—About ½ lb. of cooked veal, 1 egg (hard-boiled), ¼ lb. of ham (if less ham is available, use a little more veal), 2 oz. of mushrooms, if liked, 1½ gills of thick savoury white sauce, ½ gill of savoury aspic or calf's foot-jelly, 2 sheets of leaf gelatine pepper, salt, and powdered mace, few cooked green peas.

METHOD.—The remains of cold boiled or stewed veal is the best to use for this dish. Remove all the skin and gristle and put the meat through the mincer. Mince the ham also and mix with it. Prepare the mushrooms and stew in a little stock until tender, then chop finely and add to the ham and veal.

Make the white sauce, then draw aside and stir in the prepared veal, etc. Season with pepper, salt, and mace.

Dissolve the gelatine in the jelly, then strain in and mix all together.

Turn into a dish and, when cold, garnish with a few peas and a hard-boiled egg—the white chopped and the yolk powdered by rubbing it through a sieve.

Serve cold.

NOTE.—Savoury calf's-foot or aspic jelly can be bought ready prepared. The method of making savoury white sauce is explained on p. 693.

VEGETABLE SOUP

INGREDIENTS.—2 carrots, 2 onions, 1 pint of milk, 1½ oz. of margarine, 3 dessertspoonfuls of flour, 1 turnip, ½ a small stick of celery, a few mixed herbs, pepper and salt, 2⅓ pints of white stock or water.

METHOD.—Prepare the vegetables in the usual way and wash them. Mince the onions and cut the other vegetables into fine strips. Melt the fat in a saucepan, add the prepared vegetables, and cook them in it for a few minutes without browning.

Draw aside, add the stock, a few herbs tied in muslin, and seasoning to taste.

Cook gently until the vegetables are tender—do not leave the herbs in too long or they will discolour the soup—then add the milk, and thicken with the flour mixed to a smooth paste with water.

VERMICELLI PUDDING

INGREDIENTS.—1 pint of milk, 2 tablespoonfuls of sugar, vanilla flavouring, 2 eggs, 3 oz. of vermicelli, 2 tablespoonfuls of breadcrumbs, 2 oz. of figs, 1½ oz. of margarine.

METHOD.—Wash the figs and soak for an hour or so. Break up the vermicelli, put it into a saucepan of boiling water, and boil gently for about five or six minutes. Then strain and put into a saucepan with the milk. Cook gently until the vermicelli is quite tender and the mixture fairly creamy, then draw aside.

Add the margarine, sugar, and breadcrumbs, also the figs, having cut them into fairly small pieces and removed the stalks. Separate the eggs, beat up the yolks, and stir in the vermicelli when it has cooled slightly.

Whisk the egg-whites to a very stiff froth and fold in lightly. Add a few drops of vanilla, then turn into a pie-dish and bake for about forty-five minutes, being careful not to let it boil. Serve hot or cold.

TO MAKE A SAVOURY WHITE SAUCE

MAKE a thick white sauce in the usual way, using 2 oz. of margarine and 3 oz. of flour to one pint of milk, only flavour the milk before using it.

To do this, put it into a saucepan, add to it an onion, a piece of carrot, and a sprig of parsley and thyme. Slowly bring the milk almost to the boil and leave until cool and well flavoured. It can then be strained and used as required.

PARTY DISHES

ALMOND JELLY

INGREDIENTS.—1 pint packet of vanilla jelly, 3½ gills of hot water, ½ gill of marsala, 1 oz. of almonds.

METHOD.—To blanch the almonds—put them into a saucepan, cover with cold water and bring to the boil, strain off the water and remove the skins.

Chop the almonds into rough pieces.

Dissolve the jelly in the hot water; there is no occasion to cut up the jelly, just stir it frequently in the water until dissolved. The water should be just below boiling-point.

When dissolved and cool, add the marsala to it and stir together.

Put into small custard glasses, and sprinkle the tops with chopped almonds.

Set aside to cool, and serve in the glasses.

APRICOT MERINGUE

INGREDIENTS.—A large tin of apricots, 1 oz. of cornflour, 2 eggs, 2 tablespoonfuls of castor sugar, ½ oz. of butter, ½ oz. of sugar.

METHOD.—Rub the apricots through a sieve. Keep back just a little of the syrup to mix to a smooth paste with the cornflour.

Turn the apricot pulp into a saucepan. Stir in the cornflour mixture and bring it to the boil. Let it boil gently for a few minutes, then cool it a little.

Separate the eggs. Beat up the yolks and stir into them the half-ounce of butter, and sugar to taste. Turn the mixture into a buttered pie-dish and cook it gently in a moderately warm oven for from fifteen to twenty minutes, without letting it boil.

Whisk the whites of the eggs to a stiff froth and gradually fold in the two tablespoonfuls of castor sugar.

Put this on top of the pudding and put it in a cool oven until the meringue is set and lightly browned. Decorate it tastefully and serve cold.

BLACKBERRY MOULD

INGREDIENTS.—1½ pints of milk, 3½ flat tablespoonfuls of cornflour, cochineal, 1 oz. of butter or margarine, 3 tablespoonfuls of blackberry jelly, 1 tablespoonful of cream.

METHOD.—Mix the cornflour to a smooth paste with a small quantity of milk.

Heat the remainder, and pour on to the cornflour, return to the saucepan, and bring to the boil, keeping it well stirred.

Add the butter and jelly, mix well. Simmer for about eight minutes.

Draw off the fire, add the cream and a few drops of cochineal.

Pour into a wet border-mould and leave until set. Turn on to a dish.

CHARLOTTE RUSSE

A CHARLOTTE RUSSE is a favourite cold sweet which one finds almost certainly on every wedding menu.

Many readers will love to know the whys and wherefores of making this exquisite dish, which consists chiefly of a cream filling set in a charlotte-tin, which has been first decorated with jelly and the sides lined with finger biscuits.

The cream filling is set lightly with gelatine, and care must be taken not to make it too stiff, otherwise the Charlotte Russe entirely loses its delicacy. In very hot weather it may be necessary to add just a little more gelatine than the quantity given in the recipe. If you follow these directions carefully, you cannot fail to be successful.

INGREDIENTS.—½ pint packet of lemon jelly, 1½ gills of hot water, few glacé cherries and pieces of angelica, 2 oz. of Savoy biscuits, 1½ gills of cream, ½ gill of milk, ¼ gill of water, ¼ oz. of gelatine, 1 white of egg, 3 level dessertspoonfuls of castor sugar, ½ teaspoonful of vanilla flavouring.

METHOD.—Dissolve the jelly in the hot water, and when cold pour about one tablespoonful of it into the bottom of a charlotte-tin, or sufficient just to coat the bottom of the tin. The latter should be first rinsed with cold water, and for this quantity of ingredients you will need a charlotte-tin to hold about a pint and a quarter. A charlotte-tin is just a plain tin with slightly sloping sides.

When the jelly in the tin is set, halve some glacé cherries and dip them in a little of the remaining jelly, then arrange them in the bottom of the tin to form a decoration. A few leaves, cut from the angelica and dipped in jelly, may be used with them. Let the decoration get firm, then cover it with jelly and leave it to set again.

Meanwhile, you can prepare the biscuits. First split them in halves. As they are usually very brittle, this must be done carefully, then straighten the sides of each half and cut a piece off one end, so that they may stand firmly on the jelly, and be about the same height as the tin.

Now arrange them round the tin, filling up any cracks with a paste made from biscuit-crumbs and jelly, so as to prevent the cream mixture oozing through the cracks.

To PREPARE THE CREAM MIXTURE.—Whisk the cream until it hangs from the whisk, stir in the castor sugar and vanilla, and gradually add the milk. Dissolve the gelatine in a saucepan with the water, and strain it in, when of a moderate heat, keeping the mixture stirred lightly.

Lastly, whisk the egg-white to a stiff froth and fold it in. Leave till the mixture begins to thicken, then turn it into the prepared tin and let it set.

To UNMOULD.—Dip the bottom of the mould in warm water, then turn it over and shake it sharply, keeping one hand firmly on each end of the mould. When you can feel it loosened, slip the Charlotte Russe carefully on to a dish.

Chop up the remainder of the jelly on a piece of wet paper and serve a little of it round the base of the charlotte.

The filling can be varied in numerous ways, and sometimes when making this sweet, half a pint of cream may be used and the white of egg omitted.

To MAKE A CHOCOLATE FILLING.—Dissolve a little grated chocolate in the milk and add it.

To MAKE A COFFEE FILLING.—Flavour the cream with coffee essence and omit the vanilla.

Sufficient for six persons.

CHERRY JELLY

INGREDIENTS.—1 pint packet of cherry jelly, 3 gills of hot water, 1 small tin of red cherries in syrup, 1 gill of cream, vanilla (few drops), good pinch of castor sugar, angelica.

METHOD.—Dissolve the jelly in the hot water.

Strain the juice from the cherries, and measure out a gill, then mix with the jelly.

Stir in the cherries and pour all into a glass dish ; the cherries will come to the top.

Leave in a cool place to set.

Add the sugar and vanilla to the cream, whisk it until it thickens.

Shake on to the jelly in a rough heap.

Cut a few small stalks of angelica, and stick into the cream.

CHERRY MERINGUE JELLIES

INGREDIENTS.—1 pint packet of cherry jelly, 1 tin of cherries (¾ pint size), 2 whites of eggs, ¾ pint of hot water, cream.

METHOD.—Dissolve the jelly in hot water and make it up to a pint with cherry syrup.

Leave it till almost beginning to set, add the stiffly whisked whites of eggs, and whisk all together for a few minutes.

Put a few cherries in individual glasses and fill them up with the frothed jelly. When set, decorate taste-fully and serve with cream.

The jelly may be flavoured with a little cooking sherry or rum, if liked.

CHESTNUT MOULD

INGREDIENTS.—¾ lb. of chestnuts, 1 pint packet of lemon jelly, ¾ pint of hot water, 1 oz. of pistachio nuts, 1 pint of milk, vanilla flavouring, 1 egg, 3 or 4 dessertspoonfuls of castor sugar, ½ oz. of gelatine, ½ gill of water, 1 gill of cream.

METHOD.—Dissolve the jelly in the hot water, and when cool set about a tablespoonful of it in the bottom of a wet mould.

Scald and skin the pistachio nuts, cut them into thin slices, dip in melted jelly, and decorate the bottom of the mould with them.

When cold just cover with a little more jelly, and leave to set.

Put the chestnuts in a saucepan, cover with water, and boil for about ten minutes; remove the shells and skins.

If the skins are difficult to remove, boil them again for a few minutes.

When skinned, put them into a saucepan with the milk, and cook slowly until tender. They will take an hour or more.

When quite soft, rub them through a sieve.

Measure one gill and a half of the milk in which the chestnuts were cooked, and add this to the egg (previously beaten up).

Strain the mixture into a jug and stand in a saucepan of water.

Stir over the fire until the custard thickens, being careful not to let it curdle.

When cooked, remove at once from the saucepan, and set aside to cool.

Mix the custard with the chestnut purée, add the sugar, and sufficient vanilla to well flavour it.

Whisk the cream until it thickens, fold it into the other ingredients.

Dissolve the gelatine in the water, strain it in, and mix thoroughly. Pour into the prepared mould, and leave until set.

Dip in warm water, then turn on to a dish.

Chop the remainder of the jelly and serve round.

CLARET CUP

INGREDIENTS.—1 bottle of claret, 1 wineglassful of brandy, 2 pint bottles of soda-water, 1 lemon, a piece of cucumber (about 2 or 3 inches), ice, 2 sprigs of borage, ¼ lb. of lump sugar.

METHOD.—Cut the lemon into four.

Slice the cucumber.

Put both into a large jug, add the sugar, soda-water, claret, and brandy.

Stir it round until the sugar is dissolved.

Add the borage.

Cover the jug, and stand on ice for about one hour, then strain it.

Break up about a pound of ice into small pieces, wash it well, and add to the Claret Cup.

Serve at once.

NOTE.—Claret Cup should only be made for immediate use.

COCONUT CREAM

INGREDIENTS.—2 pints of milk, 1½ oz. of margarine or butter, 2 oz. of white sugar, vanilla or almond flavouring, 2 oz. of coconut (desic-cated), 3 oz. of ground rice (take light weight), 2 oz. of glacé cherries, ½ gill of cream (if liked).

METHOD.—Cut the cherries into quarters.

Mix the ground rice to a smooth paste with half a gill of the milk.

Put the remainder into a saucepan, with the butter and sugar.

When hot, pour on to the rice, return to the saucepan and bring to the boil, keeping it well stirred.

Add the coconut, and cook slowly for about eight or ten minutes.

Draw away from the fire. Add the flavouring, cream, and about half of the cherries.

Mix together, pour into a bowl, and leave until quite cold.

Decorate the top with the remainder of the cherries.

CORNFLOUR MOUSSE

INGREDIENTS.—1 oz. of cornflour, 1 pint of milk, 2 eggs, 2 dessertspoon-fuls of castor sugar, vanilla flavouring,

¼ oz. of leaf gelatine, ½ gill of water, 1 oz. of butter.

METHOD.—Mix the cornflour to a smooth paste with a little of the milk.

Put the remainder in a saucepan with the butter. When hot, pour it on to the cornflour, return to the saucepan, and bring to the boil, keeping it well stirred all the time.

Simmer for six minutes, add the sugar, then draw off the fire, and cool slightly.

Separate the yolks from the whites of eggs.

Beat up the yolks and stir them quickly into the cornflour, cook slowly at the side of the fire for a few minutes, but do not make it too hot, or the eggs will curdle.

Cool again slightly.

Dissolve the gelatine. Be careful not to boil it, or it will not readily dissolve.

Whisk the whites to a very stiff froth.

Fold them into the cornflour, etc., add a few drops of vanilla. Finally strain in the gelatine.

Stir all lightly together. Pour into a wet mould and leave until set.

Turn into a glass dish.

CUCUMBER SANDWICHES

INGREDIENTS.—Brown or white bread-and-butter (thin slices), cucumber (as required), pepper and salt.

METHOD.—Peel the cucumber, and cut it into very thin slices.

Arrange neatly on half of the bread-and-butter. Season well with pepper and salt.

Place a slice of bread-and-butter on the top of each one.

Stack the sandwiches on top of one another and press them well.

(Invert a large china plate or dish over them and press the plate.)

Cut off the crust and cut the sandwiches into shape with a very sharp knife.

EGG-AND-SALAD SAND-WICHES

INGREDIENTS.—4 eggs, 10 or 12 slices of thin bread-and-butter, pepper and salt, few lettuce leaves, small basket of mustard and cress.

METHOD.—Boil the eggs for fifteen minutes,

Remove the shells and cut the eggs into very thin slices, yolk and white together. Leave until quite cold.

Wash the salad and leave to soak until quite clean.

Drain well and dry in a cloth, then shred into small pieces. (Leave a small quantity for garnishing.)

Take half the slices of bread-and-butter, first cover them with a layer of salad, then one of egg, and lastly salad again.

Clap on the other slices of bread-and-butter, press together and cut into small sandwiches.

Serve on a lace paper. Garnish with a few small bunches of uncut cress or parsley.

FRUIT CUP

INGREDIENTS.—1 pint of cider, 1 small wineglass of curaçao, 6 lumps of sugar, juice of 1 lemon, sliced banana, grated pineapple, sliced orange and apple, grapes (peeled and stoned).

METHOD.—Rub the sugar on the lemon-rind, then crush it and mix with the cider, also the curaçao and lemon-juice. Ice the cider and also the fruit by surrounding them with crushed ice.

When ready to serve, place some mixed fruit in a glass goblet and pour cider over.

HAM ROLLS

INGREDIENTS.—12 small finger rolls, ¼ lb. of cooked ham, mixed mustard, butter, 1d. of mustard and cress.

METHOD.—Split open the rolls, well butter them.

Put a slice of cooked ham into each, season with mustard.

Fit on the other half roll.

Serve on a lace paper.

Garnish with mustard and cress (previously washed).

NOTE.—If you prefer, chop in a little mustard and cress with the ham.

ICED PEACHES

INGREDIENTS.—1 large tin of peaches, 2 whites of eggs, 1 gill of cream, ½ lemon, ¼ lb. of granulated sugar, ¾ gill of peach syrup.

METHOD.—Take half the peaches and rub them through a wire sieve. Then add the strained juice of a lemon to the peach pulp. Strain the peach syrup into a saucepan, add the sugar, and boil it to a thread (216° F.).

While it is boiling whisk the whites to a very stiff froth.

When the syrup is ready, pour it gradually over the whisked whites, and whisk until it is cool. Beat up the cream until thick.

Fold the peach pulp and cream lightly into the whites, etc.

Put into a freezing pot, cover closely, pack it well round with freezing mixture.

Fix on the handle and turn, beginning slowly, and gradually increasing the speed. When sufficiently frozen, cover the pail with a damp cloth (an old piece of blanket is best to use), and leave until ready to serve.

Take the remainder of the peaches, put each into a fancy custard glass, and serve the iced peach mixture round or under the peaches.

Serve with ice wafers.

KINFAUNS DELIGHT

INGREDIENTS.—1 pint packet of cherry jelly, 1 pint of hot water, 2 yolks of eggs, 1½ gills of milk, vanilla flavouring, 2 oz. of white grapes, 1 oz. of almonds, 1 large or 2 small bananas, 1 oz. of castor sugar.

METHOD.—Dissolve the jelly in the water, and leave until cool.

Wash the grapes, peel and slice the bananas, and add to the jelly.

Leave until set.

Blanch the almonds and chop them roughly.

Beat up the yolks, add the milk.

Pour into a jug, stand in a saucepan of water, and stir over the fire until the custard thickens. Do not let it boil or it will curdle.

Remove from the saucepan, stir in the vanilla and sugar, leave until cold.

Break up the jelly into rough pieces, pile it up in the centre of a glass dish.

Sprinkle the top with chopped almonds, and pour round the custard.

LEMONADE

INGREDIENTS.—1 lemon, 1 pint of cold water, 2½ tablespoonfuls of castor sugar.

METHOD.—Peel the lemon thinly, squeeze out the juice. Put both into a jug, add the sugar and water. Stir well until dissolved. Stand for a few hours. Strain.

Use equal quantities of water and lemonade.

LEMONADE
(ANOTHER METHOD)

INGREDIENTS.—1 lemon, ¾ lb. of sugar (lump or granulated), 1½ pints of boiling water, 1 dessertspoonful of citric acid.

METHOD.—Peel the lemon thinly, squeeze out the juice,

Put into a jug, add the sugar and citric acid.

Pour on boiling water, stir well.

Leave for about twelve hours.

Then strain.

Use about one tablespoonful of lemonade to a tumbler of water.

LEMON JELLIES

INGREDIENTS.—The whites and shells of 2 eggs, 1½ gills of lemon-juice, 5 gills of water, 2 or 3 cloves, the rind of 3 lemons, ¼ lb. of lump sugar, 1¾ oz. of leaf gelatine.

METHOD.—Wipe the lemons and thinly peel the rind. Squeeze out the juice from the lemons and measure out one gill and a half. Wash the egg-shells and remove the inner skin.

Put these prepared ingredients into a saucepan, add the whites of eggs, water, cloves, sugar, and gelatine.

Whisk well over the fire until just below boiling-point, then let it boil up with a good head on it. Draw off the fire, let it stand for a few minutes, then bring up to the boil again. Strain through a jelly bag into a basin.

Put the top scum first into the bag, and pour through the jelly. It should be quite clear, so if necessary repeat the straining.

Should it set before it has all run through, place a basin of boiling water inside the jelly bag. When it is quite clear pour it into small, wet, fluted moulds and leave until set. Dip each in warm water and turn on to a dish.

NOTE—Before straining the jelly, pour boiling water through the bag.

LEMON SQUASH

INGREDIENTS.—1 lemon, cold water, soda-water, glacé cherry, ½ oz. of castor sugar.

METHOD.—Dilute the strained juice of the lemon with an equal quantity of water. Sprinkle in the sugar, and fill up the glass with soda-water. Stir together, add the cherry, serve at once while effervescing.

LOBSTER PATTIES

INGREDIENTS.—1 tin of lobster, 1 oz. of butter, ¾ oz. of flour, ½ pint of milk, salt and pepper, 2 oz. of mushrooms, butter for frying, patty-cases (see p. 253).

METHOD.—Make a sauce with the flour, butter, and milk. Season it well and boil it for a few minutes. Then add the lobster cut in dice, also the mushrooms, previously peeled and cleansed and fried in butter and cut into convenient-sized pieces.

Make the mixture hot, and heap it into the hot patty-cases.

NOTE.—There should be a good half-pint of diced lobster for this amount of sauce.

MINCE PIES

INGREDIENTS.—½ lb. of flour, ¼ lb. of lard, ¼ lb. of margarine, a pinch of salt, water to mix, mincemeat.

METHOD.—Add a pinch of salt to the flour and sieve it.

Rub in the margarine until quite fine.

Gradually add cold water and mix to a stiff paste. It should be just pliable.

Well flour the pastry-board and rolling-pin, and press out the lard into thin pieces.

Roll out the pastry to a thin, oblong shape, then turn it over.

Divide the lard into three equal portions.

Spread one portion over the surface of the rolled-out pastry.

Fold into three, and roll out again the same way as before.

Turn it over and spread on it another portion of lard, fold into three.

Repeat this once again, when all the lard will be used.

Cut off a third of the pastry, and roll it out quite thinly. Shape into rounds to fit the patty-tins; about ten or twelve will be sufficient.

Line the tins with the rounds of pastry, and put about a dessertspoonful of mincemeat into each.

Now roll out the large piece of pastry until about a quarter of an inch in thickness. Cut into rounds, and place one on each tin, and slightly press the edges together.

Stand on a baking-sheet and glaze the tops with milk.

Place in a hot oven and bake for about twenty minutes.

When cooked they should be well risen and golden-brown.

Place on a sieve until cool.

Dredge well with castor sugar and serve.

OEUF A LA NEIGE

INGREDIENTS.—6 large macaroon biscuits, 6 tinned apricots, 1 white of egg, 1 dessertspoonful of castor sugar, 1 pint packet of lemon jelly, 1 pint of hot water.

METHOD.—Dissolve the jelly in hot water.

Take six soup plates, pour a little jelly in them, and then place a macaroon biscuit in the well of each plate.

Dip the apricots in jelly, and place one in the centre of each biscuit.

Leave until set, then cover the biscuits and the base of the apricots with jelly, and set again.

Whisk the white to a stiff froth, and fold in the castor sugar.

Stand the soup plates in warm water, and slip each round of jelly, etc., on to a dish.

Spread the meringue mixture round the apricots, to give the appearance of the white of the egg.

Chop the remainder of the jelly and serve round.

PASTE SANDWICHES

INGREDIENTS.—Thin slices of bread-and-butter, fish or meat paste, 2 oz. of butter, 2 eggs, seasoning

METHOD.—Put the eggs in a saucepan of cold water, bring to the boil, and boil for twelve to fifteen minutes. Shell the eggs, cut into halves, take out the yolks, and rub through a sieve. Cream the yolks and butter together, add sufficient paste to well flavour. Stir it in well and add seasoning.

Spread on to bread-and-butter, and make into sandwiches as before.

Place on a lace paper and garnish with cress.

NOTE.—The whites can be saved and used for a salad.

PINEAPPLE MOULD

INGREDIENTS.—1 large tin of crushed pineapple, 1 oz. of gelatine, ¾ pint of milk, 3 to 4 oz. of castor sugar, 1 tablespoonful of lemon-juice, 1 gill of water.

METHOD.—Dissolve the gelatine in a saucepan with the water.

Turn the pineapple into a basin, strain in the gelatine, then mix in the sugar and lemon-juice, and lastly the milk.

When beginning to thicken turn the mixture into a wet mould to set. When ready, unmould and serve with cream. Decorate it with finely chopped pistachio nuts (blanched and skinned).

PRUNES A LA CREME

INGREDIENTS.—3 dessertspoonfuls of white sugar, ¾ lb. of prunes, cold water to cover (not more than 1 pint), ½ oz. of almonds, 1 lemon, ½ gill of sherry, 1 oz. of candied peel, ½ packet of lemon jelly, 2 gills of hot water, ½ oz. of leaf gelatine, cochineal, 1 gill of cream, vanilla flavouring, large pinch of castor sugar, 1 oz. of pistachio nuts.

METHOD.—Wash the prunes, cover with cold water and soak for twelve hours.

Dissolve the jelly in hot water, and leave until cool.

Blanch the almonds and pistachio nuts. Cut up the almonds roughly and chop the pistachio nuts.

Rinse a mould with cold water, and set about two tablespoonfuls of jelly in the bottom of it.

Mix half the pistachios with a little jelly, and cover the bottom of the mould with them, set aside to cool, then cover with jelly, and leave until set.

Put the prunes, together with their liquor, in a saucepan, and add the white sugar, candied peel (previously cut into small pieces), and grated lemon-rind.

Cook gently until tender.

Remove the prunes, and boil the syrup for a few minutes to thicken it, then set aside to cool.

Stone the prunes.

Dissolve the gelatine in about half a gill of the prune syrup.

Add the prunes to the remainder of the syrup, together with the strained lemon-juice, almonds, and sherry, and the remainder of the jelly.

Strain in the gelatine, mix all together, and stir until it thickens. Colour with a few drops of cochineal.

Pour into the prepared mould and leave until set.

Stand the mould in warm water and turn on to a dish.

Add the flavouring and sugar to the cream, whisk until thick, put it into an icing bag and force round the base of the mould.

Sprinkle the cream with the remainder of the chopped nuts.

SAUSAGE ROLLS

INGREDIENTS.—1 lb. of sausages, about 1½ lb. of flaky pastry (see p. 252), egg-yolk and milk to glaze pastry.

METHOD.—Use either pork sausages or sausage meat. To remove the skins from the sausages, place them in cold water for a few seconds, then split down the skins, when the sausage can be removed cleanly.

One pound of sausages will make about fifteen rolls, so divide the sausages into the number of portions required, and form each piece into a roll.

Roll out the pastry fairly thinly, cut it into wide strips, then cut each strip into pieces not quite square. Turn them over and place a piece of sausage on each piece. Damp the edge and fold the paste over, mark two lines (with the back of a knife) on top of the rolls and along the other three sides. Trim up the edges, place the rolls on a baking-sheet, and brush them with beaten yolk of egg mixed with a little milk. Put the rolls in a hot oven to bake. They will take about twenty minutes to cook.

SUPREME DE FRUITS GLACES

INGREDIENTS.—1 large sponge cake (toast-rack shape), 1 small box of glacé fruits, 5½ gills of milk, ½ gill of sherry, 1 oz. of sugar, 1 tablespoonful of custard-powder, 1 gill of cream, vanilla flavouring, large pinch of castor sugar.

METHOD.—Pour one gill and a half of the milk into a saucepan, and bring to the boil.

Split the sponge cake into halves. Place the lower half into a glass dish, soak it with some of the hot milk and sherry.

Thinly slice some of the glacé fruits and cover the soaked portion with them.

Put on the top half, and soak with the remainder of the hot milk and sherry.

Cover the top of the sponge cake with whole glacé fruits.

To make the custard—mix the custard-powder with a little milk.

Boil the remainder with the sugar, and pour on to the powder, keeping it well stirred. This prevents the mixture from becoming lumpy. Flavour with vanilla.

When cool, pour it round the sponge cake, but do not cover the fruit decoration.

Leave until quite cold.

Add the castor sugar and vanilla to the cream, whisk until it thickens, shake on to the custard.

PLAIN TRIFLE

INGREDIENTS.—6 small sponge cakes, strawberry jam, 1½ pints of milk, 1 tablespoonful of custard-powder, 1 oz. of white sugar, vanilla flavouring, 1½ oz. of glacé cherries.

METHOD.—Split the sponge cakes open and spread them with jam.

Arrange the lower halves in a dish with the cut side uppermost.

Boil half a pint of milk, and soak the cakes with some of it.

Put on the top halves, and soak with the remainder of the hot milk.

To MAKE THE CUSTARD.—Mix the custard-powder to a smooth paste with a little of the milk.

Boil the remainder with the sugar, pour on to the mixed powder, keeping it well stirred. Add vanilla flavouring to taste.

When half cold, pour the custard over the sponge cakes, and set aside until quite cold.

Decorate with glacé cherries.

ORANGE TRIFLE

INGREDIENTS.—6 sponge cakes, 2 oranges (large), 1 oz. of pistachio nuts, orange marmalade, 1¼ pints of milk, ½ gill of orange wine, 3 eggs, crystallised violets, 3½ dessertspoonfuls of castor sugar.

METHOD.—Split the sponge cakes and spread them with marmalade. Arrange the lower halves in a glass dish.

Boil one gill of the milk, and soak them with some of the hot milk. Then pour over half of the wine.

Wipe the oranges, grate the rind of one of them, squeeze and strain the juice.

Sprinkle the grated rind on to the soaked portions. Fit on the top halves and soak with the remainder of the hot milk and wine. Sprinkle the orange-juice over the sponge cakes.

Thinly peel the remaining oranges, and cut some of them into fancy shapes. This is used later for decorations.

Scrape off the pith, divide the orange into quarters. Remove the pips and arrange the quarters between the sponge cakes. Take two eggs and separate the yolks from the whites.

Then beat up the remaining egg with the other two yolks. Add the pint of milk, together with one and a half dessertspoonfuls of sugar, and flavour with a few pieces of orange-rind.

Pour into a jug, stand in a saucepan of cold water, stir over the fire until it thickens. Be careful not to make it too hot, or it will curdle.

When cooked lift from saucepan, remove the rind, and leave the custard until cool.

Blanch and split the pistachio nuts, then stick them into the sponge cakes.

When cold pour the custard over the sponge cakes, etc.

Whisk the whites to a stiff froth, fold in the castor sugar (two dessert-spoonfuls), and cover trifle with it.

Decorate with violets and orange-peel.

A RICH TRIFLE

INGREDIENTS.—1 large sponge cake (tower-shaped), apricot jam, ¾ gill of sherry, 1½ pints of milk, 3 eggs, 2 dessertspoonfuls of white sugar, vanilla flavouring, 2 oz. of almonds, angelica, 1½ gills of cream, ¼ teaspoonful of castor sugar.

METHOD.—Split the sponge cake into three portions, spread each with jam and soak with hot milk, then with sherry. (Use about one gill of the milk.)

When well soaked, build it up into its original shape.

Beat up the eggs and stir in one and a quarter pints of milk, together with the white sugar.

Pour into a jug, stand in a saucepan of water, and stir until the custard thickens.

When cooked, lift it out of the saucepan, add the flavouring, and set aside to cool.

Blanch the almonds, and split each into three or four pieces.

Stick them all over the sponge cake, but especially on the top.

Pour over the custard, then leave until cold.

Sweeten and flavour the cream, whisk it until it thickens.

Decorate the trifle with the whipped cream and a few stalks of angelica.

NOTE.—The custard should be thick enough to coat the sponge.

AN A.B.C. OF CLEANING AND REMOVING STAINS

ALCOHOL STAINS on a woolly material can be removed by washing with plenty of cool dissolved soap containing a little ammonia. Brush this into the material and then rinse thoroughly in tepid water.

ANTELOPE SKIN BAGS can be cleaned by brushing with some non-inflammable liquid dry cleaner, using a small brush that will not scratch the leather. After cleaning wipe with a dry cloth.

BLOOD STAINS can be removed by soaking the stain in cold water containing a teaspoonful of ammonia.

Leave it for five minutes, and then brush lightly.

If the stain is still obstinate, lay it in a saucer of methylated spirit, and finally wash away in a cold, thick solution of soap.

CANDLE-GREASE SPOTS can be moved by ironing with a moderately warm iron over a good thick sheet of clean blotting paper.

CHOCOLATE STAINS can be removed by soaking in a saucer of methylated spirit for two minutes. Then lay flat and very gently rub in enough cold dissolved soap to make a lather. Finish by washing in lukewarm water and rinsing well.

COFFEE STAINS on materials can be removed, so long as they have not been boiled, with glycerine. Soak each stain well with the glycerine, brushing it into the material, and then leave it for two or three hours. After this pour on a little dissolved soap and brush out the stains. Afterwards, wash, rinse and iron as usual.

A *polished table* which has had coffee spilt on it can be polished again by rubbing the stains extremely lightly with methylated spirit, polishing immediately afterwards with linseed oil.

This method needs great care as it would not do to use too much methylated spirit or to be too long using it before polishing.

CREOSOTE can be removed from *cotton material* with methylated spirit. The methylated spirit will dissolve the creosote. The best thing to do is to soak the stain in methylated spirit and then wash with a cool thick solution of dissolved soap.

Creosote can be removed from *tweed* in the same way, but the stain should be brushed out afterwards, and then rinsed in tepid water. If the stain is still obstinate, wash in tepid soapy water.

CRETONNE is best when washed in bran water. The advantage of this is that it preserves the colours to a great extent.

Half a pound of bran is required for each gallon of water. Put the bran in a large bag of butter muslin and fill this not more than half full, then tie it securely. Place the bag of bran in the copper with the required amount of cold water. Bring slowly to the boil and boil for half an hour. Then draw off the water and add cold water to make it tepid. Squeeze the bag of bran well in this and before adding dissolved soap to make a lather, keep some of the bran water for rinsing.

Wash the cretonnes quickly and use the water tepid, or even cold, if the colours run. Rinse them in tepid water and finally bran water. When partly dry, iron on the wrong side.

CUSTARD STAINS can be removed by first soaking in methylated spirit and then washing in a thick solution of soap.

DYE STAINS on *white materials* can be removed by bleaching out the stains with peroxide of hydrogen (20 vols.). Dab on the peroxide and let it dry in the sun. Two or three treatments may be needed.

Another remedy is to soak the stain in methylated spirit and then wash out.

Dye stains *on a coloured silk* can very often be removed by first soaking in cold water and then in hot water containing one-third as much methylated spirit.

EIDERDOWNS can be washed quite well, using a good lather of tepid, soapy water, squeezing and pressing it as for woollies.

Very thorough rinsing in tepid water is needed to remove all the soap. You should put a cup of vinegar in the last rinse to brighten the colour.

The eiderdown should be dried out of doors and aired in front of the fire.

FINGERMARKS ON BOOKS can be removed by leaving French chalk on the soiled spots for some hours. Cover with blotting-paper and iron carefully.

FLANNEL that is very harsh can be softened by soaking for ten minutes in a bath of tepid water containing one ounce of borax dissolved in a cup of boiling water. Afterwards rinse well in vinegar and water.

Vinegar helps to make wool soft and silky.

FRUIT STAINS can be removed by soaking the marks in a saucer of methylated spirit for three minutes, and then washing with a thick, cool solution of soap. Spread the material on a plate and pour a little dissolved soap over it. If the colour is fast, a few drops of ammonia should be added. Gently rub the soap into the material and leave it till the stain goes. Then dip it in the methylated spirit again and wash in a mixture of soap and methylated spirit.

When the material is clean, rinse well and iron when nearly dry.

FUR can, as a rule, be cleaned with bran. This should be used as hot as the hands can bear it. Have two basins of bran and heat one in the oven whilst using the other. Lay the fur on a newspaper, heap the bran over, and rub it into the fur with the fingers.

After it is clean, hang it in the sun and beat with a cane. Finish by combing carefully with a steel comb.

FUR THAT IS NOT VERY DIRTY can be cleaned by first rubbing cedar dust and naphthalene well into the roots with the fingers, then shake and comb the fur. Afterwards lay it on a table and brush it well.

Finally clean the surface by wiping it well with non-inflammable liquid dry-cleaner, using this according to the directions on the bottle.

WHITE FUR can be cleaned by rubbing some calcined magnesia well into the roots of the hairs. Leave this all night, and the next day shake and brush well.

GINGER WINE STAINS can be removed by soaking the marks in warm vinegar and water (half a cupful of vinegar to three cupfuls of water) and squeezing gently. This will improve the marks even if it does not remove the stain. Afterwards lay the material on a folded cloth, wrong side up, and rub very gently with another cloth till partly dry.

Be careful to rub across the grain of the material.

GLOVES.—Chamois Leather Gloves should be squeezed in tepid water containing one tablespoonful of olive oil. Use a good oil soap for preference. When clean, rinse them by squeezing again in soapy water as the soap keeps them pliable. Do not wring them, but hang them up wet out of doors on a glove-stretcher, and let them dry as slowly as possible.

SUEDE GLOVES can be cleaned, if they are only slightly soiled, with suede powder. This should be mixed with turpentine. Rub this into the leather with a rag and brush it off when dry.

You will be able to get at the dirty places more easily if you put the handle of a wooden spoon up the fingers.

NAPPA GLOVES can be cleaned by sponging them with soap and water. Besides that they should be sponged with clean tepid water and afterwards put on the hands and rubbed dry, or nearly dry, with a cloth. Be careful not to leave any soap on the gloves or this will cause them to dry in streaks.

Some cleaners put a tablespoonful of olive oil in the washing water, which is quite a good plan.

GRASS STAINS can be removed from woolly materials with acetic acid and warm water, or vinegar and water. After using these you should wash the material with an olive oil soap.

If acetic acid is used the proper strength would be one tablespoonful of the acid to two quarts of water. Vinegar can be used stronger—two tablespoonfuls to about one pint of water. The stain should be soaked in this, and then brushed with a nail-brush.

GREASE on a light woollen material can be removed with the following :

FRENCH CLEANING SOAP.
Ac. Oleic	..	..	..	$1\frac{1}{2}$ *oz.*
S.V.M.	..	..	..	$1\frac{1}{2}$ *oz.*
Liq. ammonia	..	..		$\frac{1}{2}$ *oz.*
Aq. ad.	..	..	..	5 *oz.*

The material must first be well brushed to remove all dust. Lay the stained part on a dish and rub the mixture into the fibres of the material, leaving it all night. Next day rub some more of the mixture on the stain and wipe off with a rag. Afterwards remove all the soap and dirt with non-inflammable liquid dry cleaner, wipe with a dry cloth and repeat. Finally, lay the costume on a folded cloth and wipe perfectly dry with a clean cloth.

HATS.—Panama Hats can be cleaned again and again in tepid soapy water containing a little ammonia. Brush the hat with a nail-brush and, when clean, rinse it by immersing it well in a deep bath of water containing a teaspoonful of glycerine.

Press out some of the moisture with a towel, and then dry the hat slowly out-of-doors, as this will keep it stiff.

FELT HATS can be cleaned very quickly with an ordinary ink eraser. Lay the hat on the table, slipping a basin inside when rubbing the crown to give resistance to the pressure. Be sure to rub the hat all over with the eraser.

ICE CREAM STAINS on silk materials can easily be washed. First soak the stained part in a plate of methylated spirit. After this, pour on some cold melted soap and rub it in gently. Add some more soap and a little tepid water, and then wash out the stain. There must be enough soap to make a lather. Rinse in tepid water, and when partly dry, iron on the wrong side first and then on the right.

Take care to use cool water all the time, and also a fairly cool iron.

IRONMOULD.—Stains can often be removed with the juice from a stick of stewed rhubarb. Do not put any sugar with it and use while hot. Leave the stain in the juice for some minutes until it fades.

If a stronger remedy is required a teaspoonful each of cream of tartar and citric acid mixed with a table-spoonful of hot water will remove the stains. The effect of this should always be tested on a scrap of material before on the stains themselves.

INK STAINS can be removed by dipping them in a cup containing one teaspoonful of oxalic acid crystals dissolved in two egg-cups of boiling water. *THIS IS POISON.* The greater part of the ink will come out almost immediately. Remove the material and soak for ten minutes in a second cup of acid of the same strength to remove the rest of the stains. Finish by rinsing thoroughly.

If a very faint mark still remains it can be bleached out on colours that are fast to light with peroxide of hydrogen.

RED INK STAINS can be removed by soaking them in methylated spirit containing a few drops of ammonia. After five minutes, wash slowly in a cold, thick solution of soap, and finish by rinsing in tepid water.

z

MARKING INK STAINS can be removed from white material by moistening the stains with strong iodine. Then, after waiting a minute or two, rinse and apply a solution of sodium hyposulphite (a chemist will mix this for you), rinse once more.

IVORY.—Yellow Piano Keys can be improved by wiping them with methylated spirits, but for really whitening ivory there is nothing so good as gentle heat.

KNIFE HANDLES can be cleaned by rubbing them with a slice of lemon.

JAM STAINS can be removed by dipping the marks in one pint of hot water containing two tablespoonfuls of vinegar. If the colour of the material is not fast use tepid or cold water. Afterwards lay a folded cloth underneath the stain and dab with another cloth, especially round the edges of the mark.

JEWELLERY.—Precious stones in a ring or brooch can be cleaned with spirit of wine, or better still, a little eau-de-Cologne. After using the spirit, polish the stone with a leather.

LACE. — Coloured Lace can be cleaned with french chalk. Rub the material all over with this and then leave it for a few hours. After you have done this the chalk should be shaken out. Remember that the french chalk should be rubbed well into the lace.

WHITE LACE which has gone yellow can be whitened by soaking it in tepid water and then putting it into some cold, soapy water containing a tea-spoonful of dissolved borax, and gently heating it. Stewing like this will bring out the disfiguring " yellow." The lace will need thorough rinsing afterwards.

A NET VEIL can be cleaned by putting it in a pillow-case with plenty of dry flour and calcined magnesia. Roll this up. Leave the pillow-case like this for two days, rolling and shaking it from time to time. Shake out the flour and the veil should be nearly as clean as if it had been washed.

LEATHER.—A Smooth Leather Coat can be cleaned with soft soap and lukewarm water. After rinsing off and drying, polish with a good wax or white boot polish.

THE INSIDE OF A GRUBBY LEATHER BAG, if lined with smooth leather, could be painted with leather stain to get rid of the marks. If the lining is of material it could either be washed or a new lining put in.

INK STAIN ON LEATHER can be removed with either tomato-juice, followed by washing, or else with salt of lemon. *THIS IS POISON.*

SEA WATER STAINS ON LEATHER can be removed by cleaning a small part at a time with cool water containing a little powdered soap. Rinse and wipe off the soap and, when dry, clean with a good wax shoe polish.

A black leather handbag can be renovated by rubbing it with a dry cloth to remove any loose dust, then dip a piece of flannel in ammonia and rub the leather all over. Next put on a coat of American ink with a paint brush, and when dry, polish with a wax furniture polish.

LEATHER STAINS ON TWEED can be removed by soaking in methylated spirit and then brushing in enough cold soap to make a lather. Continue until the stain disappears.

MACKINTOSHES.—Mud on Silk Mackintoshes can be removed by warm water to which a little ammonia has been added. One teaspoonful of ammonia to one pint of fairly hot water is the correct amount.

GREASE STAINS ON MACKINTOSHES can be removed with eucalyptus oil. Simply rub the marks with a rag soaked in eucalyptus and finish with a clean rag. If the oil shows afterwards the marks can be removed with a non-inflammable liquid dry cleaner.

A Rubber Mackintosh can be cleaned by laying it on a table and using cold soap and water and a very soft brush that will not scratch the surface. Tepid water will not hurt for the soiled parts, but do *not* use soda or hot water. It is very important that the mackintosh should be thoroughly rinsed. If any soap is left it will dry in white patches. Avoid making any creases during the cleaning process, and hang it up dripping wet on a coat hanger. It will take about two days to dry.

MARBLE.—The marks on a fireplace, etc., or in the crevices can be removed with the following cleaning paste : Four ounces each of shredded soap and whiting in a jug with one ounce each of powdered pumice stone and soda. Pour on one pint of boiling water. Stand the jug in a saucepan of boiling water for twenty minutes, stirring now and again. Spread the paste, while still hot, over the soiled part of the marble, using a pointed sink brush for crevices which are hard to reach. Leave for twenty-four hours, and wash off. Brush over again with warm soapy water. Then rinse and dry.

MILDEW ON A WOOL MATERIAL, such as gabardine or a blanket, can be removed by thoroughly drying the material, and then laying it on a hard surface and brush with a stiff brush.

MILK STAINS can, as a general rule, be removed from satin by soaking it in a saucer containing equal parts of glycerine and warm water. Brush it a little, and then wash it.

MILK STAINS ON ARTIFICIAL SILK can be removed by soaking the stain in a saucer containing five teaspoonfuls of water, and a drop or two of ammonia (this if the colour is fast). Leave it for three minutes, and then wash in tepid water.

MOSS STAINS can be removed by soaking in cold water containing half a cup of vinegar. Next brush in some methylated spirit and leave it for five minutes. Finally brush with a thick solution of soap and finish off by washing and rinsing thoroughly.

MUD STAINS ON VELVETEEN can be removed by washing, using tepid soapy water, pressing and kneading the material.

Velveteen (not velvet) washes beautifully, but the material must not be twisted. Rinse in tepid water and hang over a pole to dry. To hang it over a clothes line would only make creases.

When partly dry place it near a fire. Iron it very gently on the wrong side, and brush with a velvet pad.

MUD STAINS ON SILK can be removed by washing it in tepid water with soap flakes.

NET DANCE DRESSES will usually wash quite well in tepid soapy water, though it is wise to cut off a tiny piece and wash it first to see whether it will shrink.

After washing, let it drain a little, and then roll it up in a bath towel, leaving it for a couple of hours before doing the ironing.

Net is very difficult to iron. It must always be ironed across the width, as if it is ironed along the direction of the selvedge, it will stretch greatly, and become stringy in appearance. Unless you are expert at getting up dresses of this sort you will find it very difficult to get a smart effect.

Net that seems limp after washing, can be starched in fairly thick boiling water starch, after which it should be dried and damped again before ironing. Always iron net on the wrong side.

OIL PAINTINGS can be cleaned with a large Spanish onion. This should be peeled and cut in half. Rub the cut surface on a very small portion of the painting, using a circular motion. As soon as one piece is clean move on to the next. As the onion becomes soiled simply cut off a slice.

OIL STAINS can be removed by soaking the stain in eucalyptus oil and then squeezing till clean. Two applications of this may be needed before the stain is quite gone. After you have removed the stain, place blotting paper under the spot and dab with cottonwool soaked in non-inflammable liquid dry cleaner. This is done to remove the eucalyptus.

OXYDISED DOOR HANDLES, etc., can be cleaned by mixing a soft paste of olive oil and whiting. When clean they can be polished with liquid veneer which will help to protect the metal from damp. No chemical should be used as it may remove the oxydised surface.

PAINT STAINS can be removed with ammonia and turpentine. First soak the stain with turpentine to soften the paint, and then add some ammonia. Brush this now and again, and wait about half an hour. After this wash in very cool, soapy water containing ammonia, and the stain will go after persevering a little.

PARAFFIN STAINS can be removed by rubbing gently in plenty of cold dissolved soap until a lather comes. This lather will come when the paraffin is gone. After this you should rinse the marks in tepid water and then a little water and methylated spirit to brighten the silk.

Do not use hot water in case the colour of the material should run.

PERSPIRATION STAINS can be removed, if the colour of the material is fast to light, and if the material itself is not the kind that rots, by dabbing them with peroxide of hydrogen (20 vols.), and drying in the sun. Two or three applications may be needed. Before using peroxide it is necessary to test the effect on a cutting of the material.

If the material is not fast to light the stains can be removed by moistening them with warm water, covering with borax, and then pouring hot water through. After this soak and squeeze a little. Then soak the stains for a few minutes in cold water containing one tablespoonful each of salt and vinegar.

PORT WINE STAINS.—If the stains do not take the dye out of the material they can be removed with a solution of cold, soft soap and methylated spirit. First soak the stained part in a saucer of methylated, and then wash slowly with the soap. Rinse this, and when it is nearly dry, iron carefully.

RAINSPOTS ON VELVET can be removed by steaming. It would probably be best to have this done at a professional cleaners, but you can do it at home with care and perseverance. Pass the material quickly to and fro close to the spout of a fast-boiling kettle, and then dry it in front of the fire. When dry, brush in one direction only. Two or three treatments will probably be needed to get it right again.

RAINSPOTS ON SATIN can be removed by first brushing off any traces of mud left by the rain. Pour one and a half pints of boiling water on to a teaspoonful of seccotine, and when tepid, add a dessertspoonful of methylated spirit. Damp the material evenly with this, and lay over it a muslin cloth, wrung out in the same water. Iron over the muslin, using a moderately hot iron.

RAINSPOTS ON VELOUR OR ANY HEAVY MATERIAL can be removed by steaming. First, shake the material and dry it thoroughly, even if it seems dry already. Get two pieces of muslin, one dry and the other squeezed out in water. Lay the dry one on the right side of the coat, and place the damp cloth on top of this. Iron on the damp cloth. This will send the steam through the dry muslin on to the coat. On no account have the iron too hot. After you have finished ironing, dry the material, shake, and brush it. The marks should by now have quite disappeared.

REPP can be washed quite easily in nearly cold, soapy water, and then rinsed in tepid water. Iron it on the wrong side.

SATIN.—Satin which is only slightly soiled can very easily be cleaned with calcined magnesia. Lay the magnesia over the surface and rub it very gently into the material with the flat of the hand. Leave it like this for twenty-four hours, and next day shake it all out and brush with a stiff brush.

SCORCHES can generally be removed with peroxide of hydrogen (20 vols.). This can only be used on colours that are fast to light, and should be tested on a small piece of the material first.

Scorch marks on crêpe-de-Chine can be removed in the same way with a little ammonia added to the peroxide. Moisten the silk with this, and place in the sun to dry. Several applications will be needed according to the depth of the scorch.

SCORCH marks on silk stockings can be bleached, if the colour is fast to light, with peroxide of hydrogen (20 vols.). Give it time to act, and lay the stockings in the sun. If the stockings are not fast to light it will bleach the stockings, too, and the only remedy is re-dyeing.

SEA WATER STAINS can generally be removed with brushing. If they do not come out in this way washing may be needed. Often sea water destroys the colour, and if this has happened, the only remedy is re-dyeing.

SEA WATER ON COLOURED STOCKIN ETTE MATERIAL will sometimes change the colour, and this can be remedied by soaking the marks in acetic acid and water, or vinegar and water. This should restore the colour, but if it does not do so, re-dyeing is the only remedy.

SHINE can be removed by brushing lightly with half a pint of water containing one tablespoonful of ammonia and half a pint of methylated spirit. Lay a piece of damp muslin over the surface and iron lightly.

Steaming by a shop would also be effective for a time. There is, however, no really permanent way of removing shine.

SHOES.—GREASE ON BROWN LEATH-ER SHOES is rather difficult to remove unless tackled at once before it has time to sink in. The best thing to do is to rub the stain with eucalyptus oil, and then clean with non-inflammable liquid dry cleaner. If this is not sufficient the shoes could be re-stained with an ordinary leather stain after scrubbing them first with soda water.

LIZARD SHOES that have rain marks on them can be cleaned by rubbing the dark stains with a little lemon-juice. This will remove the stain, but should be wiped off immediately as it is bad for the leather.

BROWN LEATHER SHOES that have been stained can be cleaned by scrubbing them with warm water and plenty of saddle soap to make a lather. It is also a good plan to add a little turpentine to the water. After scrubbing the shoes you should let them dry, and then polish as usual.

SHOES THAT HAVE GONE TOO DARK IN COLOUR can be remedied by rubbing the shoes with warm water containing a little turpentine, scrub them with a nail brush, and then dry with a cloth.

TO SOFTEN THE LEATHER rub well with the inside of a banana skin and leave overnight. Next day, polish as usual, when the shoes will look like new.

SOOT can be removed by brushing lightly with dry salt. Follow this treatment by rubbing with a cloth rung out in soda and water.

STIFFENING. — Gum-water is very good for stiffening soft silk. It should be made fairly thin—say, one good teaspoonful of Seccotine to one and a half pints of water. Put the Seccotine in a jug and pour on half a pint of boiling water. Stir this until the Seccotine dissolves. Then add the cold water and put in the dress.

Let this drain a little, and then lay it flat on a bath towel, and roll it up fairly tightly. Leave this for two hours before ironing.

STOCKINETTE.—Silk stockinette can be washed in tepid soapy water. It should not be hung up to dry, but laid flat to drain a little, and then rolled up in a towel for two hours before ironing with a fairly cool iron.

SUEDE COATS can be freshened up by using a piece of art-gum. This can be obtained from all large chemists.

Rub the dirty place with the art-gum. After this clean it with a very fine wire brush or coarse sandpaper. Take care not to rub too hard as it is only the surface that has to be freshened.

TARNISH on gold lace or slippers can sometimes be removed with methylated spirit containing a little ammonia.

Another method on a thick lace or strong material is to use a mixture of methylated spirit and a very little rouge. In *very bad* cases ether and rouge can be used.

TAPESTRY.—A tapestry chair can be cleaned by beating and then rubbing into the material plenty of dry bicarbonate of soda. Leave it for a few hours and then brush hard with a very stiff brush, and, if possible, clean with a vacuum cleaner.

TAR STAINS can be removed by dipping them in a saucer containing some eucalyptus oil. Then squeeze well till the tar goes, as it will do in a few minutes. When clean, remove the oil with non-inflammable liquid dry-cleaner. This is dabbed on with cottonwool, putting a piece of blotting paper under the stain.

TEA STAINS ON MAHOGANY can be removed by gently rubbing the marks with spirit of camphor. Finish off with a gentle rubbing with ordinary furniture polish. Tea stains *on material* can be removed with glycerine. Mix five teaspoonfuls of glycerine and five teaspoonfuls of water in a saucer. Lay the stained part in the mixture, rubbing it gently with the tips of the fingers. Afterwards moisten well with methylated spirit, and wash slowly with thick dissolved soap.

TRANSFER MARKS can usually be removed quite easily, by laying the material in a plate containing some methylated spirit, and brushing with a soft brush.

The spirit will loosen the marks almost at once, and when they have been brushed off the material can be rinsed and wiped.

If the marks are more difficult they can be bleached out with peroxide of hydrogen. *This is only if the material is fast to light.* Dab on the peroxide and then dry in the sun. Continue this treatment until the stain goes. Wash out the peroxide afterwards.

TWEED can be washed quite well in tepid soapy water.

The only other way of cleaning it would be to brush it well with fig dust and cedar dust and naphthalene. Use a very stiff brush.

Fig dust is sold by most corn-chandlers, and tins of cedar dust and naphthalene are sold by most chemists.

UMBRELLAS can be cleaned with a soft brush and a nice soapy lather. The lather must be tepid. Open out the umbrella and protect the silk from the frame with rolls of paper. Moisten the soiled part with methylated spirit, and then brush gently with soap and water. Rinse well, and dry in the open air in a good wind.

VERDIGRIS on woollens can be removed with an acid such as vinegar. First rub in plenty of salt, then pour on enough vinegar to cover, and squeeze till clean. Afterwards wash in soapy water.

VELVET.—Marks on white velvet can be cleaned by rubbing in some dry calcined magnesia, leaving overnight and brushing out next day.

VINEGAR STAINS on white linen should be soaked in water immediately. If this is impossible the article should be put in a clean aluminium boiler or large pan with a cake of shredded soap and a dessert-spoonful of borax. Stew this very gently until the stain goes.

WATER STAINS on artificial silk can be removed by soaking them in methylated spirit, and then washing slowly in tepid, soapy water. If, however, the water stains were made by very hot water it will sometimes affect the nature of the silk and leave a permanent mark, especially if it has been ironed.

WINDOW BLINDS can be cleaned by laying them flat on a table and giving them a brush to remove all dust.

To clean any embroidery on the blinds you should use cold, soapy water containing a little borax. This should be brushed in. To rinse it off use a cloth wrung out in warm water. Dab well with a dry towel, and then pull it into shape. When it is dry enough iron on the wrong side over a soft cloth.

If the blind is rubberised do not iron the rubber part, but wipe with cold, soapy water.

WOOD.—A Hot Iron mark is worse than the usual hot plate marks on polished wood. A very good remedy for marks that are not too bad is to rub the surface quickly and lightly with methylated spirit and then polish it immediately with linseed oil.

In the case of very bad marks, especially if there are bits of fluff sticking to the table, you could leave the linseed oil lying thickly on the table until next day, and then wipe it off, and, when dry, polish.

HOT WATER STAINS on wood can be removed by rubbing gently with spirits of camphor; finish off with a gentle rubbing with ordinary furniture polish.

PREPARING FOR A WEDDING

THE BRIDE'S KITCHEN

It has so often been said that anyone can be a housekeeper, but that
seldom one finds a true home-maker ;
and in the new world we are all striving
to build out of the old, we shall
surely prove through actual living
rather than words that the home-
maker is amongst us, and every bride
has made it her own joyous study,
to be wrought out with her chosen
mate in the home they build together.

There is much to say on every phase
of home life, but this article is confined
to the kitchen.

That the home may run smoothly
it is necessary that the kitchen, which
is the workshop, should be in order.

"Order is heaven's first law,"
and what more agreeable task is set
the bride than to make her home a
little heaven on earth. Saucepans,
baking-tins, grocery jars, pots and
pie-dishes, should have their own
place and be kept in it sweet and clean,
and ready for action.

THE WORKSHOP

The kitchen needs to be a pleasant
room to work in. Painted walls of
a light ivory colour and bright blue
paint for the door, dresser and windows, makes a cheery appearance,
with white casement curtains at the
windows in summer time, or orange
curtains in winter, a gay tablecloth,
either of plain colour or of coloured
plaid, which blends itself with the
colour of the paint, and a few bright
pictures round the room.

Chairs to be durable, and simple
in shape—a movable rack for airing
clothes, which may be drawn up to
the ceiling and either in the kitchen
or the adjoining scullery, a gas or oil
stove and a sink.

Over the sink a plate-drainer to
help in the washing-up, and a few
shelves on which to stow the saucepans out of the way when not in
use.

Then comes the selection of the
best pans, and the ones most easily
cleaned, for no doubt the washing-
up not only of the dainty tea set,
but the collection of saucepans which
have been used to prepare the meal
may fall to the bride's share.

The house where it becomes irk-
some to wash up the saucepan is not
exactly reflecting heaven, and, after
all, the old iron saucepan was a thing
most people felt like dismissing by
" leaving in soak," and in itself not
a reflection of heaven, either ; so why
not choose aluminium pans instead,
which would certainly introduce a
better sense of harmony and are
easily cleaned. Although soda must
not be used in cleaning aluminium
pans, yet a weak solution of vinegar
and water boiled in the pan will
remove any tarnish. Frying-pans,
preserving-pans, saucepans of aluminium and a casserole which makes
excellent stews should form part of
the kitchen equipment.

GROCERY JARS MAY BE INTERESTING

Interesting sets of grocery jars
can be bought complete, to be hung
on shelves on the wall near, if not
over, the kitchen table so that the
cooking ingredients may be within
easy reach.

BRIGHT COLOURS WILL HELP

Another interesting and useful
asset is a set of wooden spoons and
mashers, a rolling-pin in a wooden
frame of plain white wood, also made
to hang on the wall. As the walls
are of ivory colour, a touch of life may
be added by painting the wooden
frame in a bright blue to match the
other paint, or orange to go with the
tablecloth and curtains.

A pretty brass toasting-fork with

a long handle could hang on a nail near the stove, if it is an open range, and a hearth-brush with a wooden handle painted in some bright colour at the other side of the stove.

The knives and forks, etc., used in the kitchen, can be kept in a wooden knife-box, with two compartments, and put away in the table-drawer. In one of the dresser-drawers have the teacloths and tablecloths, and in another the dusters and oven cloths, and a bag of old rag, so useful in cleaning and polishing.

There should also be a flour-bin, a pastry-board, and a mincing machine, and a useful adjustable cloth-dryer can be obtained to fasten on the wall, made of an iron fixture in which wooden sticks are either hanging loosely on the wall or extend one by one as the need requires, to support the cloths.

The floor should have suitable covering, and linoleum seems the most practical, as it can be washed over every day, and with one rug near the fireplace, the whole room gains a homely, cosy appearance.

Either hanging on the wall or inside the cupboard door, should be a small writing-pad where the housewife can jot down her menu for the week, or any orders she may want each day, at the baker's, the fishmonger's, the butcher's, etc. This helps the daily work of the kitchen to be well organised, and so the whole home runs more smoothly with the greatest possible harmony in the meeting of everyday needs.

A set of trays in wood, and pottery in pretty bright colours, also adds a touch of life to the kitchen, and here, the more individual the pottery, the more interesting the home.

MARKING THE LINEN

WHAT an exciting time it is buying a trousseau! How lovely to peep into the cupboard and see the new clothes all ready to be worn, but perhaps it is nicer still to be able to look with eyes of pride on the piles of snowy sheets and pillowcases and the neat dusters and teacloths.

You realise then that you are soon to become the mistress of your own establishment

Linen-marking is not a boring job. There are so many different ways of doing the marking that it need not be monotonous.

Some are superstitious about marking their linen too soon before the wedding, but really the sooner you start marking it the better. There are so many things to be done at the last minute that you are often unable to give as much time to it as you would like, and the linen is spoilt by careless marking. It takes time if it is to be done properly, and is well worth the trouble spent on it.

It is usual to mark the table and bed linen with your future husband's name, and your personal linen with your future name.

WHICH INITIALS?

To start with the sheets, pillowcases and tablecloths, some people mark them with marking-ink, but it is very difficult to do this neatly. It so often looks untidy, that by far the better way is to have some *woven names* done at the draper's. These can be had in blue or red, script or block lettering, and they are so easy to sew on, and always look neat.

While we are on the subject of bedclothes, a hint on marking blankets may be useful. Cut out a small piece of fairly coarse canvas (the size varies according to the length of your name), and tack it on to the corner of the blanket, then in blue or red cotton, work your name in cross-stitch in the squares of the canvas. This is quite simple to do. When you have finished, the threads of the canvas can be easily pulled out.

Huckaback towels look very nice with large embroidered initials on them. You can buy transfers of these large initials to stamp on the towels, and they look very effective worked in a thick outline stitch in white embroidery cotton with French knots in the centre.

Table-napkins, too, have a much handsomer appearance if you can spare the time to embroider an initial on them.

It is a good plan to mark all the odd cloths, such as cloths for the slops, or lavatory cloths, to prevent them getting mixed. With a sharp-pointed pencil write in the corner of the cloth, B for bath, or L for lavatory as the case may be, and work in cross-stitch with bright coloured cotton.

It is not necessary to put your name on the dusters and teacloths, as these are usually washed at home.

PERSONAL LINEN

Now a word about the marking of personal linen. The neatest way of marking it is to sew on woven names. Many girls, however, like to embroider their initials on their underclothes. Many lovely sets have the initials beautifully worked, and intertwined with true lovers' knots, but the woven names will do quite well for ordinary everyday clothes.

Handkerchiefs need daintily working in very fine cotton. If you send your handkerchiefs to a Society for Distressed Gentlewomen, or to any shops where they specialise in linen goods, you can have them most beautifully embroidered very inexpensively.

THE WEDDING CAKE

To make a wedding-cake is not the difficult task many folk imagine it to be. So long as you are a good cook and have plenty of patience, the crowning glory of the wedding-table may easily be the work of amateur fingers.

Of course, you must have an unusually rich and delicious recipe. The one we are giving has been tried with excellent results.

Fancy twirls and trimmings are all a matter of practice, and the finishing touches of silver leaves and plaster flower vases can be bought or borrowed from a confectioner.

In Three Tiers

For a three-tier wedding-cake you must choose three cake-tins of different sizes, which, standing on the top of one another, look nicely in proportion.

The diameter of the centre cake-tin should be about nine inches ; one of the others slightly smaller and the other larger.

The mixture for a wedding-cake is always rich, so it should be made at least a month before required, to give

it time to ripen. Otherwise, the cakes will be too moist in the centre.

The Centre Cake

INGREDIENTS.—$\frac{3}{4}$ lb. of soft brown sugar, 1 lb. of butter, 1$\frac{1}{4}$ lb. of flour, 2$\frac{1}{2}$ lb. of currants, $\frac{1}{2}$ lb. of mixed peel, 2 oz. of almonds, 5 or 6 eggs (according to size), 2 teaspoonfuls of mixed spice, $\frac{1}{2}$ gill of brandy.

METHOD.—Well grease a cake-tin and line it with two or three thicknesses of greased paper, so that it stands well above the sides of the tin.

Wash the currants in several warm waters, rub them in a cloth, pick off the stalks and put the fruit to dry.

Cut the peel into small pieces, having first removed the sugar from it.

Blanch the almonds and cut them into small pieces.

Sieve the flour and spice together. Whisk up the eggs.

Beat the butter and sugar together until they resemble thick cream. Gradually add a little of the flour, fruit, almonds, and eggs in turn until they are all well mixed.

When all the egg has been added, mix in the brandy.

The mixture can now be beaten with the hands if you find it easier.

Put the mixture into the prepared tin and bake it in a moderately hot oven for about four or five hours.

As the cake begins to cook, gradually decrease the heat. If it gets too brown before it is cooked, cover it with a sheet of paper (not greased).

Test the cake with a warm iron skewer before taking it out of the oven—stick it through the centre of it. If the cake is cooked it will come out quite clean and free from any of the cake mixture. If ready, take the cake out and stand it on a sieve until cold.

When thoroughly cold, wrap it in greaseproof paper and store it in an airtight tin for at least a week, until it is to be iced.

NOTE.—Remember that the sugar and fat must be well creamed before the other ingredients are added to it.

If the butter is very hard you may warm it slightly, but do not " oil " it, or you will spoil the cake.

The fruit must be quite dry before

it is added, so it is advisable to wash it the day previous to making the cake.

THE TOP CAKE

INGREDIENTS.—6 oz. of soft brown sugar, ½ lb. of butter, 10 oz. of flour, 1¼ lb. of currants, ¼ lb. of mixed peel, 1 oz. of almonds, 3 eggs, 1 teaspoonful of mixed spice, ¼ gill of brandy.

Make the mixture in the same way and bake it slowly in a small tin (prepared as before explained), for about three to three hours and a half.

THE LOWEST CAKE

INGREDIENTS.—2¼ lb. of soft brown sugar, 3 lb. of butter, 3¾ lb. of flour, 7½ lb. of currants, 6 oz. of almonds, 1½ lb. of peel, 15 or 18 eggs (according to size), 6 teaspoonfuls of mixed spice, 1½ gills of brandy.

METHOD.—Bake this in the largest tin for about six or seven hours.

If you have a bowl sufficiently large for the mixing it is advisable to make the mixture for the three cakes all together.

This is a great saving of time and labour. In any case the cakes can all be baked at one time.

(SUFFICIENT FOR THREE TIERS MIXED TOGETHER)

Here we are giving the total ingredients for the three tiers together for those who prefer to make them all at once.

INGREDIENTS.—5 lb. 10 oz. of flour, 3 lb. 6 oz. of soft brown sugar, 4½ lb. of butter, 11¼ lb. of currants, 2¼ lb. of mixed peel, 9 oz. of almonds, 23 eggs, 9 teaspoonfuls of mixed spice, 1½ gills of brandy.

METHOD.—Make the mixture as explained before, divide out the mixture, putting about one-ninth of it into the small tin, about twice as much into the medium-sized tin, and the remainder into the large tin.

TO PREPARE THE CAKES FOR ICING.

Cut off any burnt fruit, etc., and, if necessary, scrape the cake and knock off the loose crumbs.

The almond paste can be prepared and put on the cakes two or three weeks before the wedding.

Then the whole wedding cake can be absolutely finished and out of the way at least a week before the great occasion.

ALMOND PASTE

(SUFFICIENT FOR THE THREE CAKES)

INGREDIENTS.—7 lb. of icing sugar, 7 lb. of ground almonds, the whites of about 18 eggs, vanilla flavouring.

METHOD.—Rub the icing sugar through a very fine sieve. Mix it with the ground almonds.

Whisk the whites to a froth and add them with a few drops of vanilla.

Mix to a stiff paste. (If necessary, more whites can be added.)

Divide the paste into portions, using about one-ninth part for the top cake, about double this quantity for the centre one and the remainder for the bottom cake.

ICING THE CAKES

Take the large portion of almond paste and put it on to a board dusted with a little sieved icing sugar.

Roll it out (with a rolling-pin) to a round shape to fit the top of the large cake.

Place it on the cake and make it perfectly smooth and level.

If necessary roll a rolling-pin across the top, or smooth it with a knife dipped in hot water.

Be sure that the top edge is quite level, or the finished appearance of the cake will be spoiled.

Stand the cake on an upturned dish and place it in a cool oven to dry for about half an hour, then leave it until the next day.

Ice the two small cakes in the same way.

NOTE.—If preferred, a layer of almond paste can be put round the sides as well as on the top of the cakes.

In this case a thinner layer is put on the top.

ROYAL ICING

(SUFFICIENT FOR THE FIRST LAYER OF THE THREE CAKES)

INGREDIENTS.—4½ lb. of icing sugar, juice of 4 lemons (medium size), whites of about 10 or 12 eggs.

METHOD.—Rub the icing sugar through a very fine sieve.

Squeeze the lemons and strain the

juice. Whisk the whites to a very stiff froth.

Add the lemon-juice to the sugar and sufficient white of egg to form a very thick, smooth paste.

Mix well with a wooden spoon, then for about ten to fifteen minutes. To test the consistency of the icing, mark letters on the icing with the spoon. They will remain quite clear if the icing is of the right consistency.

Another method of testing it is to lift the spoon from the centre of it. If of the correct consistency, the icing should not run or sink, but remain in position. If the icing is too thin, add more sieved icing sugar. If too thick, add more white of egg.

Icing the Cakes

First of all, as before, divide the icing into proportions for each cake.

Take the large cake and spread some of the icing evenly all round the sides of it.

It should only be quite a thin layer.

Smooth it with a knife dipped in hot water, but do not use this more than necessary as it is liable to crack the icing.

When the sides are finished, cover the top in the same way.

Keep the top edge very level.

Use either a palette knife or a large knife with a round, flexible blade.

Ice the other two cakes in the same way, and leave them to dry until the next day.

Note.—Beat each amount of icing again just before using it.

TO MAKE THE ROYAL ICING
(For the Second Layer)

Ingredients.—9 lb. of icing sugar, the juice of 8 lemons (medium size), whites of about 20 to 24 eggs.

Method.—Make as before explained and spread a second layer over each cake.

This should be quite a thick layer.

Be sure that it is perfectly smooth and that the top edges are quite level. Leave it to dry for a day or two until it is quite hard.

Now make the Royal Icing for the Decoration. For this use: Three pounds of icing sugar, juice of about three lemons, whites of about seven eggs.

Make as before and beat the icing well.

To Decorate the Cakes

For this you will require an icing bag or pump and some icing tubes.

There are many different patterns of tubes, but if you have two or three different ones, this is quite sufficient.

The tubes are fixed on with a screw, then put through the bottom of the bag and kept in position with string.

Before beginning to decorate, decide roughly on a design.

Remember that a large space must be left free from decoration in the centre of the two large cakes so that the cakes will stand firmly one upon another. So before beginning, mark out a circle to show where the decoration can begin from.

On the small cake at the top leave a space for a white vase of flowers.

These can be hired or bought from a big store or confectioner, and make a nice finish to the cake.

Decorate each cake separately.

Put some icing in the bag, twist the end of the bag until you get to the icing, then force some on to a plate first to be sure it is working correctly, before touching the cake.

When you have finished with one tube fix on a different pattern and refill the bag with icing.

Stand the large cake on a cakeboard to decorate it, and put a line of decoration round the edge of the board as well. It then need not be moved again.

When all the cakes are decorated, leave them for a day or two until the icing has thoroughly hardened, then stand them on top of one another on a paper doyley, with a round of greaseproof paper under the doyley and the white vase on top.

Silver balls and silver horseshoes, leaves or bells, are also required for decoration. These can be bought in various sizes.

Stick the balls on the tips of the decorations of the icing before it sets.

It would be better to leave spaces for the horseshoes and then to stick them on to the cakes with a little icing after the other decorations have set.

Note.—Remember if the icing gets

too stiff before you have finished decorating it must be beaten again. In fact, it is advisable to beat it well each time before the bag is filled.

WEDDING REFRESHMENTS

When doing home catering it is always necessary to plan your work, so that there is not too much left until the last.

The big cakes for the wedding reception could quite well be made a few days in advance. They will keep moist if wrapped in greaseproof paper and put in an airtight tin.

The lemonade could also be made one or two days beforehand. It will be better if not airtight, so leave it uncovered.

The pastries, cream buns and sweets should only be made the day previous to the wedding, on account of the cream in them.

If the weather is very hot, it would be better not to fill such things as meringues and cream buns until the day they are required.

The sandwiches should only be made the day required, but if desired the eggs can be prepared beforehand.

For the claret cup have all the ingredients to hand, but make it only about one hour before it is to be served.

The coffee could quite well be made early and strained, then reheated as required.

At a summer wedding ices are usually served. There is always so much to do at these times that it were wiser not to add the making of ice cream to your tasks. Order it from a reliable confectioner and you will be saved much trouble.

MENU
(FOR TWENTY-FIVE PEOPLE)
Sandwiches
Ham   Eggs and Cress

CAKES AND PASTRIES
Almond Cake   Cherry Cake
Cream Buns
Meringues   Iced Genoese Sandwiches

SWEETS
Charlotte Russe
Small Peach Moulds
Orange Soufflés

Lemonade   Claret Cup
Tea and Coffee

FOR THE SANDWICHES
(Including both kinds)

Allow about six or eight small sandwiches for each person. Four thin slices of bread from a sandwich loaf will be sufficient to make eight small sandwiches. So you will require, roughly :

FOR HAM SANDWICHES

One and a half to two half-quartern sandwich loaves, one pound of butter, one pound and a half of ham, mustard.

FOR THE EGG AND CRESS SANDWICHES

One and a half to two half-quartern sandwich loaves, one pound of butter, twelve eggs, two small baskets of mustard and cress, pepper and salt.

THE CAKES

Make a cherry cake according to the recipe given in this book.

Use one pound of flour and other ingredients in proportion.

Make an almond cake about the same size as the cherry cake.

These two cakes will cut up into quite a good number of small portions.

We would advise their being baked in square or oblong tins, as it will be easier to cut them into even-sized pieces.

THE PASTRIES

About four dozen and a half will be sufficient altogether. These can be made at home, but if time will not allow they may be bought ready-made.

If you are making them yourself, see that they are very small, as they will be so much daintier, and the mixture will go further.

FOR THE CREAM BUNS

Make three times the quantity given in this book. For the filling, half a pint of cream will be sufficient for all ; a little less cream in each will not matter at all. It is not necessary to make icing for the top. Just dust a little icing sugar over them.

FOR THE MERINGUES

Make about twice or two and a half times the amount given in this book.

To make them smaller, shape them in a dessertspoon instead of a table-spoon.

FOR THE ICED GENOESE SANDWICHES

Make about one and a half times the quantity given and cut the sponge into very small shapes.

THE SWEETS

You must have three moulds of Charlotte Russe, each to be about the same size as the recipe in this book. When doing this you can make two packets of jelly sufficient for the three, and use five instead of six gills of cream altogether.

Make three times the amount of orange soufflés as given in this book. Also three times the amount of peach moulds.

LEMONADE

Allow twice the quantity suggested for the lemonade—the kind which is made with citric acid. This kind goes farther.

CLARET CUP

Make twice the amount given in this book.

FOR TEA AND COFFEE

Allow about a quarter of a pound of each. About three or four pints of milk, and a pound of lump sugar (small lumps).

NOTE.—If preferred, a fruit salad can be substituted in the place of the Charlotte Russe. This is always a favourite dish and very suitable for the occasion.

THE WEDDING ARRANGE-MENTS

THE CHURCH SERVICE

In arranging the details of the service the first essential is to give the vicar concerned plenty of notice. This will save much vexation of spirit, for however obliging a clergyman naturally is, he is only human, and has to run his parish with the same care as a doctor shows in his practice.

The happy couple should talk the matter over several weeks ahead and decide precisely what they want. If they wish for a choral service, the following directions will be useful.

CALL ON THE VICAR

First of all one or other should call on the vicar of the church where they are to be married. The most convenient times for the average clergyman are before 10.30 a.m. or between 5 and 7 p.m.

"How much will it cost?" Put this question to the verger, who is usually to be found on duty in the church. The charges are usually scheduled, and the experienced verger will arrange as splendid a service as you wish. The musical details can be arranged with the vicar, and unless you have any decided taste in the matter you will be quite safe in leaving it to him to suggest suitable choices.

The custom varies in different parishes, but as a rule you will be wiser to ask the vicar to convey your musical wishes to the organist and choirmaster. The latter officials are always busy men, so are the clergy for that matter, but in every well-run parish one clergyman is always on duty. Those who are to be married in a "fashionable" church will naturally expect the cost to be in proportion. Most of these churches provide even a red carpet.

THE FLORAL DECORATIONS

Wherever you are married you are naturally expected to provide whatever you want in the way of floral decoration. Choose your own florist, but tell the verger that he will be sending along what you have ordered. The verger, fortified by experience and inspired with hopes of favours to come, will do the rest. A good verger will never let you down. He takes pride in the way "my church" does things. These are general hints, but a few suggestions as to the music may be helpful.

You can be married in the suburbs for 7s. 6d., but if you want music, etc., the charges will be roughly as follows:—

Organist	.. ..	2 guineas
Choir boys	..	2s. 6d. each
Organ blower	..	5s. gratuity
Verger	.. ..	10s. gratuity
Bells	.. ..	2 guineas

Flowers, etc., for decorations are supplied by the bride's people. Red carpets are needless luxuries, but the verger will tell you where you can hire one if you wish for one. You must pay the cost direct to the shop.

A Question of Cards (Invitation)

Wedding invitations are now very plain. Black lettering is more used now than the silver lettering which used to be considered indispensable. The invitations may be printed on sheets of notepaper, which form a kind of combination of a notepaper sheet and envelope, having a flap at the upper end, which is folded over and so posted. Or they may be issued on a simple card with envelope to match. It is really a question of individual taste.

The wording should be as follows :

Mr. and Mrs. Jones request the honour (or pleasure) of Mr. and Mrs. Brown's company at the marriage of their daughter, Hilda, with Mr. Reginald White, at St. Stephen's, Knightsbridge, on Monday, June 17th, at 2 p.m., and afterwards at 4, Ranelagh Square.

R.S.V.P. to (private address of bride's parents).

The invitations should be issued within a fortnight of the wedding day.

Acceptances and Refusals

Formal invitations sent in the third person should be answered in the same manner if the answer is an acceptance.

In sending a refusal, however, it is always more courteous to give some explanation, and this should run as follows :

Mr. and Mrs. Brown regret that absence from town prevents them from accepting Mrs. Black's kind invitation for the 4th of March.

When the Bride is a Widow

When the bride is a widow she should not wear a veil or orange blossoms. Brides who have been married before often wear their travelling clothes for the ceremony.

A widow is not attended by bridesmaids at her wedding, but an intimate friend may hold her gloves and flowers.

There is no obligation for her to be given away by her father or other male relations, though it is nicer for someone to perform this office on her behalf.

The Best Man

The responsibilities of the best man, who should always be a bachelor, are many and varied. He is the right-hand man of the bridegroom. He should accompany the bridegroom to the church and see that he does not leave the wedding ring behind, or leave the church without his hat. Bridegrooms seem to have a large-sized weakness in this direction !

He must see to the arrangements of the carriages, both from the house to the church and back again, and also from the house to the station, when the " happy couple " leave for their honeymoon.

Pay all fees on behalf of the bridegroom and relieve him of all the little incidental worries in his power.

Dress of Bridegroom and Best Man

The usual dress of the bridegroom and best man is a morning coat, light striped (very fine stripes) trousers, light waistcoat, light gloves and a buttonhole.

The Bridesmaids' Dresses

Strictly speaking the bride has a right to enforce her wishes on this subject, but as a matter of fact she never does ; she prefers to have a little consultation and come to an arrangement. One thing, of course, must always be avoided, and that is a " mixture." A colour scheme must be planned and carried out rigorously, otherwise the " picture " will be ruined.

Expenses of the Bride's Parents

First and foremost among the expenses of the bride's parents comes the trousseau. And this should be prepared with due regard to the position the bride is to occupy after she is married.

Then there are various At-homes and parties given before the marriage to celebrate the engagement.

On the wedding-day the bride's parents give the reception and pay for all the floral decorations in the church.

If the service is a choral one they must also bear the expenses of the choir.

The bride's parents also pay for the carriages used by themselves and their household.

They do not pay for the carriages used by the guests invited to the wedding.

Tips are expected by all the chauffeurs on the wedding-day and these usually run to five shillings in each case.

When wedding favours are given, these are also provided by the bride's parents, but they are not nearly so popular as they were at one time.

The wedding announcement is also paid for by the bride's father.

THE QUESTION OF PRESENTS

The bride usually gives a present to the bridegroom on the wedding-day. The bridegroom provides the wedding-ring and the bride's bouquet and also a present.

The bouquets of the bridesmaids are the gift of the bridegroom, and should be sent to them on the morning of the wedding. He is also expected to make a present to each bridesmaid —either a brooch, or a bracelet, or something of this kind—which should be sent either the day before the wedding, or on the morning of the wedding with the bouquet.

The bridegroom should provide the carriage to take the bride and himself from the church to the wedding breakfast, and again from the house to the railway station.

The bridal carriage is the only one the bridegroom is expected to provide.

Everyone who is invited to a wedding invariably makes the bride and bridegroom a present. Many send presents as soon as the engagement is known. There is no rule as to the time before the wedding that presents should be sent.

Presents are displayed on various tables. In each case care should be taken to see that the card of the giver is attached to each gift. This is most important.

GOING TO THE CHURCH

The bridesmaids should arrive at the church a short time before the bride.

If the bride's sisters are acting as bridesmaids they should drive in the carriage with their mother, the carriage afterwards returning for the bride and her father.

The bridegroom and best man should arrive at the church well before the bride and stand below the chancel steps. It is one of the best man's duties to see that the bridegroom arrives in good time.

The date and time of the wedding should be arranged with the vicar concerned. On his arrival the bridegroom should go to the vestry and hand the clerk the necessary particulars for entry. This saves time and confusion afterwards. Particulars in writing are best. Full name and age of bride, spinster, or widow, residence, names of father and whether alive, occupation of father. The best man should pay the fees to the clerk before the service ; there is not time afterwards ; there are too many duties awaiting him.

IN THE CHURCH

The bridesmaids assemble in the church porch waiting for the arrival of the bride.

The bridegroom's relations and friends should seat themselves at the right of the nave of the church, the bride's relations seating themselves on the left.

The bride enters the church on the right arm of her father or guardian to the chancel steps, the bridesmaids, two by two, following her. If there are pages they would, naturally, precede the bridesmaids.

The bridegroom takes his place at her right side, with the best man standing immediately behind him. He simply bows to the bride. The father stands at the bride's left hand. Her mother sits in the front seat with the nearest relatives.

At the question, " Who giveth this woman ? " the father bows to the clergyman, signifies that he is the giver, and then steps back to his place, and then takes his seat by the bride's mother. The bride hands her gloves and bouquet to the chief bridesmaid, who holds them until the end of the service.

The bridegroom should unglove directly the service begins and have the ring handy. It is so embarrassing to have to wait while he fumbles about desperately for the ring.

After the first blessing, the bride and bridegroom alone follow the priest to the altar, the others remaining in their places.

When the ceremony is over the bride, taking her husband's left arm, and followed by her bridesmaids, father and mother, and the principal relations and friends, go to the vestry to sign the register.

Afterwards, on going slowly from the church, the bride takes her husband's left arm, unless he is in uniform, in which case she takes his right arm, to avoid the sword, both recognising their friends with smiles and bows. The bridesmaids follow two and two, and then the bride's mother with the bridegroom's father, and the bridegroom's mother with the bride's father.

The best man waits until the very last to see everybody into their carriages.

THE RECEPTION

ON arriving at the house where the wedding reception or luncheon is to be held, the gentlemen should leave their hats in the hall. Ladies should not remove their hats, neither should the bridesmaids do so.

On entering the drawing-room where the company is assembled, the guests at once offer their congratulations and shake hands with the bride's parents, afterwards making their way to do likewise to the happy couple.

When the refreshments have been handed round, the bride should then cut the wedding cake. Usually she only makes an incision with a knife, the icing is so hard; it is afterwards removed to a side table and cut up into small pieces and handed to the guests. Cakes are now supplied with a wedge cut out at the confectioner's. A tab of ribbon is arranged under the piece that is cut, and the bride has only to pull the ribbon.

TOASTS

The health of the bride and bridegroom should then be proposed by the most distinguished guest present, or most intimate friend of the family. To this the bridegroom should return thanks on behalf of himself and his bride. He should then propose the health of the bridesmaids, for which the best man should return thanks.

Formal speeches are no longer the order of the day. At one time, the " speechifying " was a very real terror, a long drawn-out agony under which bride and groom and guests writhed. Now, only a few words are spoken, the main things being brevity and brightness.

DEPARTURE OF THE NEWLY-MARRIED COUPLE

As soon as the bride has cut the cake and the healths have been drunk, she retires to change her dress for the wedding journey, accompanied by the chief bridesmaid, if she is a relative or very intimate friend. And the company adjourns to the drawing-room to view the presents. When the bride comes downstairs the farewells are made, and the bridegroom leads her to the carriage.

The leave-takings should be as brief as possible.

The guests should not linger after the bride and bridegroom have left, but should immediately say good-bye to the host and hostess, at the same time offering a little congratulatory speech.

WHAT THE HUSBAND BUYS TOWARDS THE HOME

From basement to garret the husband is expected to provide the essentials for the home—the tables, chairs, beds, carpets, curtains, blankets (though sometimes the bride provides these as well as the linen), even down to the buckets and brooms for the kitchen.

Unless they are given as wedding presents, such things as plate and china are also included in the bridegroom's contribution.

But neither bride nor bridegroom nowadays are expected to make such formidable preparations in the "home" line as they used to be.

What the Bride Provides

The household linen—even if it is cotton—is the bride's affair. Very often it is the wedding gift of the bride's mother. Sheets, pillow-cases, bed-room towels, toilet covers, table-cloths, table napkins, kitchen towels of all kinds she is responsible for.

She is not expected to provide furniture or china other than her own personal possessions.

A nice thing to do is for friends to join together and buy a dinner or tea service—one buying plates, another dishes, and so on, all the same pattern —a much greater help to the young couple than three brass toasting forks, two sugar shakers, or a couple of cruets, and so on!

TRAINING A MAID

When visitors are paying an after-noon call, explain that the maid must open the door wide to them. Nothing looks worse than merely opening the crack of the door and peeping through. If they have umbrellas, she should take them and put them in the stand, and then, throwing open the drawing-room door, announce the visitors in a clear voice.

If it is a formal At-Home day the maid should assist with the tea, bring-ing the cups of tea in on a tray, together with the milk and sugar and handing the tea round to the visitors.

This leaves the mistress free to talk to them, and as each visitor is ready to go the hostess rings the drawing-room bell, and the maid must be ready to open the front door and hand out the umbrellas.

When guests arrive for a dinner-party she asks the gentlemen to remove their hats and coats in the hall and escorts the ladies to the bed-room and be ready to assist them if desired. She then takes them down and an-nounces them to their host and hostess. When dinner is ready, she either rings the gong or, coming to the door, says: " Dinner is served, madam."

When giving a little dinner party, have a rehearsal beforehand with imaginary visitors at the table, and you will find that your maid will be far less nervous on the evening.

Waiting at Table

It is in the matter of waiting at table that a maid so often becomes nervous and blunders, but show her that it is a much simpler thing than she imagines.

If her master is carving she takes her place immediately behind him. She does not wait for him to hand each plate to her as it is ready to be served, but removes it from the stack in front of him.

When handing round the plates of fish or meat she serves the lady on the right of the host, and then goes right round the table, serving each lady in turn and then each gentleman. In her left hand she should hold the salver with the fish sauce-boat on it, or if meat is being served, one of the vegetable dishes with the cover re-moved. After placing the plate before the guest she then offers the sauce or vegetable. This saves a lot of time, and by then the carver has the next plate ready.

Immediately she has served the meat the maid should take the other vegetable dish from the dinner wagon or side table, remove the cover, and offer it in her right hand to the guests. She should keep a folded table napkin for holding hot dishes, and always hand them on the left side of the person to be served. The gravy or sauce boats for the meat dishes are then handed round on a salver.

Then she must ask each visitor what he or she will take to drink.

The maid should keep an eye on the glasses and see that they are never empty. She should also watch that the visitors are kept supplied with bread.

After making certain that no second helping is required, each empty plate is removed, the host's plate being removed last. The meat is then taken away.

A pudding plate is then placed before each guest and the maid hands round the sweets. If sugar and cream are to be taken with the sweets they should be handed on a salver. As the maid removes each empty pudding plate with her left hand, she puts a small plate in its place with her right hand for the cheese or savoury. Bread plates are not used at a dinner-party.

Before placing the dessert on the

table she must clear the table of glass and unused silver, and sweep the crumbs off, leaving only the port glasses. Each dessert plate should have a doyley and finger-bowl on it, with a knife and fork each side of the finger-bowl. The finger-bowl should be half full of water. She places the port on the table for the host to pass round.

Coffee is usually served to the ladies in the drawing-room, and the men in the dining-room. The maid should bring in the coffee cups on a tray with the milk and sugar.

Teach your maid to be dainty in small things. Point out that if the traycloths and doyleys are free from stains it makes the meals so much more appetising. If she has to do the dishing up, the dishes and sauce-boats should be wiped round the edges with a cloth before serving.

The salt in the salt-cellars should be tidied and the mustard-pots also cleaned round the edges.

Last thing at night a well-trained maid will take the quilt off the bed, turn it down, remove the night attire from its case, and arrange it on the turned-down sheet. She will put a hot-water bottle in the bed if required.

EARLY MORNING DUTIES

In the morning one of the maid's duties is to knock at the bed-room door and then walk in with the tea, which is arranged on a tray with a biscuit and a piece of bread-and-butter.

She pulls up the blinds and inquires if her mistress would like a bath, and if so, fills it and puts the bath mat on the floor. She knocks at the door when the bath is quite ready.

When the maid has change to give to her mistress, or when letters, parcels, and newspapers arrive, they must be brought in on a salver, which is kept in the hall for that purpose.

THE CLEVER HOSTESS

MANY hostesses serve salad inside the peel of half a scooped-out lemon or orange or grape fruit. All the inside is scraped or cut away, leaving the firm skin, and the base is cut quite flat so that the skin does not wobble about on its salad plate.

The filling consists of various vegetables, cut into dice, and some fruit, provided it is not of the "squashy" kind. The mixture, whatever it may be, is moistened with mayonnaise, and sprinkled with paprika, or crushed walnuts, or both, after it has been piled up inside the fruit skins.

For instance, chopped beetroot, celery, and apple is a good mixture. So is cooked carrot, turnip, and celery, with some chopped nuts mixed with the vegetables. Dates, celery, and apples will be found very good, too. When the scooped-out half lemon or orange is put on a plate, filled with salad, all ready to serve, decorate it with watercress or mustard and cress.

Others serve salad inside half a pimento, which is that nice soft kind of red pepper which you can buy anywhere in tins.

The same sort of mixtures mentioned above are excellent in pimento, and the case itself can be eaten, which is more than one can say for a casing of orange or lemon-peel.

A salad that is particularly delicious is of crisp lettuce, spread on a plate without any dressing, and decorated with six stewed prunes, stoned, and filled with cream cheese. One lettuce leaf, at the side of the plate, should be filled with mayonnaise.

Cherries, tinned or fresh, make a lovely salad served with lettuce and French dressing; a complete dish for lunch is a salad of this sort, with crisp toast, according to present-day standards. When serving Lettuce and Cherry Salad, always have the stones taken out of the cherries, and the centres filled with cream cheese or half a salted almond.

A COCKTAIL SAUCE

ANYONE who knows what a real Cocktail Sauce can be cherishes the recipe. You taste it, and you say, "How is that made?" It is quite simple, really, though its final perfection has only been reached after considerable experimenting.

It requires cream, tomato ketchup, and mayonnaise, in exactly equal quantities. These ingredients are beaten well together to taste. Then a teaspoonful—or less— of Worcester Sauce is added. Add a very little of this to the sauce and taste carefully, because the Cocktail Sauce must not be fiery.

To this sauce, when it is as cold as possible, add shrimps, prawns, shredded crab or lobster (tinned or fresh), or hard-boiled eggs, cut into rough dice. There should be plenty of sauce; and this dish should be served in glasses and eaten with a spoon.

Smoked haddock or kipper, cooked, boned, skinned, and broken up into fine pieces, mixes admirably with this sauce, and is far less expensive than the shell fish for which the sauce was originally designed. Remember to serve it as cold as possible.

As a first course, a Fruit Cocktail is always good. Grape fruit, orange, and pineapple is a good mixture; melon, cut with a circular scoop into small rounds, goes well with orange or grape fruit.

A mixture of syrup of granadine and lemon-juice gives an unusual pink look and a very attractive flavour to the most simple fruit cocktail. These cocktails are served in tall glasses, if possible, and should have a small sprig of fresh mint stuck at the top. If mint is not available, use watercress instead.

At every party you should meet new

sandwiches. One of the nicest mixtures is cream cheese, red currant jelly, and lettuce, served between brown bread. Butter two slices of brown bread, spread one with cream cheese and one with red currant jelly. Put a large lettuce leaf on the side with the jelly and cover it with the cheese side.

Pineapple and red currant jelly is another good mixture, also with a lettuce leaf separating these two ingredients. Use tinned pineapple, and crush or mash it so that it can be spread on bread easily. Cover one buttered slice of bread with it, and another with jelly ; put a lettuce leaf on one or other slice, and press both together.

Cream cheese, marmalade, and brown bread is delicious. Others can be made of minced olives and Bovril spread on rather thick white bread.

ROLLED SANDWICHES

ASPARAGUS, too, of the tinned variety, can be unusually delicious if it is rolled in a slice of thin brown bread, and baked in a medium oven for about ten minutes. See that each stalk of asparagus is cut the same length as the bread, which must be cut quite thin, and sprinkled with salt.

Put a piece of asparagus at the edge of a slice of bread, and start rolling it carefully till it is covered by the bread. Use a board as it is so much easier to roll on a flat surface.

Keep a box of small wooden toothpicks in the kitchen, and secure each asparagus-roll with a little wooden stick driven through it, leaving some wood sticking out each side. The stick is left in when it is served, and can be used to hold the rolled sandwich while it is being eaten. The bread should be quite crisp, and slightly brown, like toast, before these rolls are taken from the oven.

The asparagus must be thoroughly drained before it is used, and should be put on a dish and slightly warmed in an oven before it is rolled in the bread.

Another kind of rolled sandwich is tomato-cheese. Take some cream cheese and mash it up in a bowl with tomato ketchup and a little Worcestershire sauce. It should be of the consistency of soft butter and should taste of tomato.

Cut some *thin* slices of white or brown sandwich bread, and take off the crusts. Spread rather thickly with the cheese mixture ; roll up, and fasten with a wooden stick. Bake in the oven till the bread is crisp, and slightly toasted. Eat while hot.

AN EXCELLENT HOT SAVOURY

AN excellent hot savoury is made with stuffed olives rolled in very thin streaky bacon. Choose bacon that is as lean as possible, and quite narrow, and not too long ; and have it cut in size 5, which makes it really thin.

Trim each slice ; then put a large stuffed olive at the end of a slice, and roll it up. Put it on a long skewer, and go on adding as many as are wanted till the skewer is full. Take care to leave a space between each roll, or they will not get properly brown.

Put the skewer across a shallow baking-tin, and bake in a hot oven, ten to fifteen minutes, turning the rolls on the skewer so that every side becomes brown. Pull them off the skewer, and serve on a hot dish if they are to be used as hors d'œuvres, or put two or three rolls on hot buttered toast if they are to be a savoury.

When making this dish choose stuffed olives of as large a size as you can get. The stuffing is made of pimento (red pepper) and they are bought almost anywhere. But the small ones are not much use ; the only thing to do with them would be to use two inside each roll of bacon.

TWO HORS D'ŒUVRES

HERE are two delicious dishes of the savoury or hors d'œuvres variety. The first consists of small, very crisp, round biscuits, buttered and spread thickly with cream cheese to which some vinegar or lemon-juice had been added.

This cheese should be arranged to form a sort of mound ; a slice of pickled walnut is put on the top and paprika shaken lightly over. This sweet pepper is a very useful addition to any kitchen for decorating salads and all kinds of savoury dishes.

Another dish consists of small squares that appear to be Welsh Rarebit. But when one starts to bite through the hot cheese, one discovers something quite cold and very delicious underneath. This is one large slice, or several small slices, of pickled gherkin or cucumber. The mixture of hot cheese and cold hidden pickle and the blend of flavours is excellent.

A delicious sweetmeat can be made from marshmallows. Cut a small slit in the underside of each one, and through the slit insert a lump of preserved ginger or of crystallised pineapple. This is really a delicious mixture and proves a big surprise to one's guests.

A FEW HINTS ON SERVING MEALS

At dinner, soup is generally put on the table, in each person's place, before dinner is announced. So each table napkin, folded in some pretty design, with a piece of bread partially concealed in it, should stand on the small bread plate at the left-hand side.

The soup-plates, when finished with, should be removed by the maid from the right-hand side.

A clean plate is laid before each person (from the left) and the maid then hands round the fish course. She stands on the left, and holds the dish at a height convenient for the guest to help herself.

For smelts and oysters she then hands round a small salver on which is a plate of very thin slices of brown bread-and-butter, rolled.

A fruit tart should have one portion cut from the pastry (it is laid upon the other crust) when it comes into the dining-room, to make serving easier.

When the savoury is finished, the plates are cleared. Also salts, etc., unless nuts are included in the dessert, in which case the salts only remain, all glasses, except port, and all cutlery.

The maid should then go round to the left of each person, and with a soft cloth and small salver, remove crumbs. A fruit plate with fruit knife and fork already in position on it, is then put before each guest. If finger-bowls are to be used, these should have a little water in them and stand on a doyley on the fruit plate. Sometimes a tiny leaf of verbena is put in each bowl, which lends a touch of fragrance.

Dessert is handed round on a fruit dish, the maid standing, as usual, on the left of the guest. If there are nuts they are placed in a dish on the table, with nut-crackers also on the dish, and are passed around the company by the guests themselves.

The maid retires from the dining-room when the dessert has been served and prepares the coffee-tray. This she takes to the drawing-room on hearing the party leave the dining-room. It should have on it coffee-pot, milk jug, and sugar, and the required number of coffee cups. The maid holds the tray before each person in turn, and each helps himself.

She should return in about a quarter of an hour and remove the cups and tray.

When your dining-room has a polished floor, it is a wise precaution to provide your maid with rubber heels to her shoes.

Tea is usually brought into the drawing-room on a tray. The plates remain stacked on the tea-table, the knives being placed beside them, each person taking a plate and knife as required. If it is dining-room tea, though, each plate and knife is laid separately.

The kettle boiling on the tea-table adds to the charm of its appearance. Have your spirit-kettle filled with almost boiling water before it is brought to the table, though, and save a long wait. If you make tea in this way you must have a pretty tea caddy with its spoon of some quaint design placed on the tea-tray.

If rolled bread-and-butter and dainty sandwiches, sweet and savoury, are served, there will be no necessity for tea-knives to be provided.

MISCELLANEOUS

TO COOK RASHERS OF BACON

REMOVE the rind and either grill or fry the bacon (the first method is preferable). It will only take a few minutes, the exact time depending on the thickness of the rashers ; but when the fat is semi-transparent they are ready. If frying them, warm the pan and put in the rashers. No fat is required.

Fried apples with bacon make a pleasant change for breakfast.

TO FRY APPLES.—Peel and core, cut into rings, then fry until lightly browned and tender.

BAKING HINTS

ONE of the most important points to remember is to have the oven the correct temperature *when the food is put into it.*

To do this, the oven must be looked to beforehand, as some mixtures will spoil if not baked immediately they are mixed. For example, cakes and puddings containing baking-powder are ruined if they are not cooked immediately.

Oven thermometers can be obtained, and by them the exact degree of heat required can be ascertained. The use of one of these is quite good for the inexperienced, as it gives them confidence ; but at the same time the oven should be tested with the hand, so that one is soon able to distinguish roughly the different temperatures without a thermometer.

THE TOP OF THE OVEN.—This is the hottest part, as the hot air rises.

THE BOTTOM TIN.—This should be put in the bottom of the oven as soon as the gas is lighted.

THE USE OF THE BROWNING-SHELF

If food is required to brown quickly, it should be put just underneath the browning-shelf, leaving sufficient space for the food to rise.

Puddings, pies and cakes, etc., requiring rather a long time to cook, often get sufficiently brown before they are cooked through, in which case the browning-shelf can be removed and the food covered with a sheet of paper—not greased—to prevent further browning.

TESTING AN OVEN

The following tests are useful though they are a little slow.

Place a little flour on a paper on the oven sheet. If, after *one minute* in the oven the flour is

Dark Brown, then the oven is Very Quick.

Light Brown, then the oven is Quick.

Dark Yellow, then the oven is Moderate.

Light Yellow, then the oven is Moderately Slow.

For Very Slow, the flour should only be of a Pale Biscuit tint after five minutes in the oven. After one or two uses of this test you will find yourself automatically knowing the right heat of your oven by putting in your hand, wide open, and feeling the heat.

BATH SALTS

WEIGH out several pounds of carbonate of soda crystals, spread them out on an enamel tray, and spray them over with a little very strong, cold tea.

NOTE.—Take care not to use too much. When uniformly coloured, stir in a little perfumed oil, e.g., lavender. Allow a teaspoonful of oil to every two pounds of crystals.

TO LINE A CAKE-TIN

CUT from a sheet of greaseproof paper a long doubled strip. This strip should be two inches deeper than the tin you intend to use, and should be long enough to overlap by an inch when in the tin.

Crease up an inch at the base of the strip (at the fold), and uncrease it again, and with the scissors cut sloping snips at intervals of about an inch from the fold to the crease.

Place the tin on the remaining (doubled) paper and draw with a pencil a circle round the outside of the tin. Cut out the double circle *inside* the pencilled ring so that the circles of paper will fit inside the cake-tin quite snugly.

Have ready a little melted lard and with a pastry-brush brush over one circle of paper and the doubled strip evenly with the lard. Remember to grease the inner side of the strip so that the snipped portion will fall easily into position. The outer side of the strip needs no grease. Place only a dab of lard on the second circle and fit this into the bottom of the tin.

Arrange the notched strip carefully and evenly with the cut part to the centre of the tin and then put in the remaining circle. There will not be a wrinkle or any unevenness if this description is properly followed.

There should be an inch of paper showing at the top of the tin, but not more, as a taller edge would char and deposit burnt paper on the cake.

When the cake is cooked strip off the lower circle and, if liked, the side paper, but leave the greased circle on till the cake is served, as this helps to keep it moist.

Always line your tin the first thing. A mixture that has to wait while the tin is lined will be a certain failure.

CODDLED EGGS

PLACE the egg in boiling water and then put the saucepan to the side of the stove where the water will keep warm but not boiling. Leave the egg in for six to eight minutes.

When this is done you will find that the white of the egg is quite set and looks like a clear jelly.

FRIED EGGS

HEAT sufficient fat just to cover the pan, but do not make it too hot or the white of egg will bubble and get brown underneath.

Fry the eggs gently.

Eggs used for frying or poaching should be opened into a cup first, being careful not to break the yolk.

EGGS POACHED

WELL cover the bottom of a frying-pan with water, bring it to the boil, add a little salt and lemon-juice, then lower the gas and pour in the egg.

Cook gently for a few minutes until the white is set, keeping the pan slightly tilted towards the egg at first and basting with the hot water while it is cooking.

When ready, lift up with a slice, drain, and serve on hot buttered toast.

FROSTING A WINDOW

ORDINARY Epsom-salt dissolved in warm beer is a very effective way of frosting a window. Paint on the mixture while still warm. The beer will evaporate as the mixture dries, and the result will be a frosted effect.

A HOME-MADE FURNITURE POLISH

MIX up a gill of linseed oil, a gill of turpentine, and a gill of vinegar. This can be kept in a bottle and used in the usual way.

PORRIDGE

INGREDIENTS.—3 oz. of oatmeal, 2 pints of water, 1 flat teaspoonful of salt.

METHOD.—Put the water in the top part of a double boiler, bring to the boil, add the salt, then sprinkle in the oatmeal, stirring well.

Boil for a few minutes, then stand it in the bottom of the boiler, the latter containing hot water.

Cook gently for three hours, keeping it stirred occasionally.

Serve with hot milk and sugar.

This can be prepared overnight and reheated in the morning. Medium or coarse oatmeal may be used.

POTTED MEAT

SERVE THIS FOR BREAKFAST

INGREDIENTS.—½ lb. of cooked beef, about 2 oz. of butter, ½ flat teaspoonful of powdered mace, cayenne, salt, nutmeg.

METHOD.—The beef should be well cooked, but not dry, and freed from fat, skin, and gristle. Fresh meat, roasted or baked, can be used, or boiled salt beef. Put it through a mincer once or twice, then rub it through a fine wire sieve

Beat the butter to a cream and gradually mix into it the prepared meat, with seasoning to taste. Only a very little nutmeg is required and, if using salt beef, very little or no salt. When very smooth and of a good consistency for spreading, press it into pots and cover with clarified butter (extra to that given in the recipe).

To CLARIFY BUTTER.—Melt it, remove the scum and let it cool, then pour a good thick layer over the top of the meat.

POT POURRI

INGREDIENTS.—Dried rose leaves in any quantity desired. A handful each of dried bay leaves and dried lavender flowers, ½ lb. of bay salt, ¼ lb. of saltpetre, 2 oz. of common salt, 1 oz. of powdered storax, 6 grains of musk, ¼ oz. cloves (crushed).

METHOD.—Pick the flowers on a hot, dry morning before the sun has taken off the scent.

Lay the petals on sieves, through which the air can penetrate, and dry the flower petals well in the sun.

When the petals are quite dry rub them with the common salt. Mix together the bay salt, saltpetre, storax, musk, and cloves, and bruise well (a rolling-pin can be used for this purpose).

Put layers of dried flowers and the salt mixture into a covered jar, keeping it covered for some weeks and stirring each day.

Be sure to keep the jar in a dry place.

PRESERVING LEAVES

PICK the sprays of beech leaves or autumn foliage as fresh as possible and put them into a deep vase of water mixed with a 1s. 6d. bottle of glycerine.

Leave them standing in the mixture for about ten days, and then put them into an empty vase, and they will last all through the winter.

It is essential that the vase filled with glycerine and water should be tall so that the stems are well steeped in the mixture.

PRESERVING AND DECORATING POPPY HEADS

THE poppies should dry as long as possible in the garden, and only be finished indoors. If they are picked too soon, they will not dry so well.

When they are perfectly dry, the heads and stalks are coated entirely with clear varnish, to preserve them.

The heads can afterwards be decorated in any way you like. They may be done with bronze, silver or gold paint, or with a frosted silver paint, which may be obtained at most ironmongers.

Another way is to do them with coloured sealing wax, dissolved in methylated spirit. A jazz effect can be obtained by using dabs of contrasting colours, and letting them run into one another slightly.

After choosing the colours you want, break up the sealing wax and put it in a jam jar, adding enough methylated spirit to cover it well. Stir now and again until it has all dissolved, and, if necessary, thin down with a little more spirit. The solution should be of the consistency of cream.

SPINACH CUSTARD

To SERVE WITH SOUP

INGREDIENTS : 1 lb. of spinach, 1 large egg, salt and pepper.

METHOD : Remove any large stalks from the spinach. Wash the spinach in three or four waters. Put it in a saucepan with half a teaspoonful of salt. No water is needed. Cook slowly for ten minutes, with the lid on. Stir well, and let the spinach finish cooking in its own juice, with the lid off, till tender, about twenty-five minutes in all.

Turn it on to a wire sieve and let the juice run through. Use this for soup ; it has excellent food values. Rub the dry spinach through the sieve, and mix it in a small basin with a beaten egg and pepper and salt to taste.

Grease an enamel plate, pour in the custard and bake in a moderate oven for about forty minutes, or till set firm.

Let it get cold, put a knife round the edge and turn it out on to a board. Cut into strips and then into diamonds, or else cut into fancy shapes with small vegetable cutters sold for the purpose.

Before putting the custard shapes

in the tureen warm them in the plate placed over the saucepan of consommé for about ten minutes.

One pound of spinach cooked dry will make a large plateful of custard.

CHESTNUT STUFFING

INGREDIENTS.—¾ lb. of chestnuts, 3 oz. of breadcrumbs, 1 good-sized onion, 1 tablespoonful of chopped parsley, 1½ oz. of butter, salt, pepper, 1 egg, milk stock or water.

METHOD.—Put the chestnuts in water and boil. Remove the outer and inner skins. Put them into a saucepan with either stock or water, and boil until tender. Strain off the stock, rub the chestnuts through a sieve and mix them with the breadcrumbs, parsley, and onion, peeled and minced finely. Stir in the butter (melted), add seasoning to taste, and bind the stuffing with egg and moisten it with milk.

SAGE AND ONION STUFFING

INGREDIENTS.—1½ oz. of breadcrumbs, 1 level teaspoonful of powdered sage, ¼ lb. of minced onions, 1 oz. of butter, seasoning.

METHOD.—Mix the breadcrumbs with the minced onions and the powdered sage. Add seasoning to taste, and moisten with butter—the latter warmed sufficiently to melt it.

Use the stuffing as required.

FORCEMEAT BALLS

TAKE a good cupful of breadcrumbs and mix them with two ounces of chopped suet, add one tablespoonful of chopped parsley, half a teaspoonful of herbs, and the grated rind of half a lemon. Season them with pepper and salt, moisten with the juice of half a lemon, and a beaten egg. Form the mixture into small balls, flour and fry them till brown in a little hot fat, then take them up and add them to the bird, allowing them about half an hour to cook.

INDEX

M